Handbook of School Violence and School Safety

D0911550

The *Handbook of School Violence and School Safety: International Research and Practice* has become the premier resource for educational and mental health professionals and policymakers seeking to implement effective prevention and intervention programs that reduce school violence and promote safe and effective schools. Its 44 chapters cover the full range of school violence and safety topics from harassment and bullying to promoting safe, secure, and peaceful schools. It also examines existing school safety programs and includes the multidisciplinary research and theories that guide them. Examinations of current issues and projections of future research and practice are embedded within each chapter. This volume maps the boundaries of this rapidly growing and multidisciplinary field of study. Key features include:

Comprehensive Coverage—The 44 chapters are divided into three parts: Foundations (chapters 1–18); Assessment and Measurement (chapters 19–24); Prevention and Intervention Programs (chapters 25–44). Together they provide a comprehensive review of what is known about the types, causes, and effects of school violence and the most effective intervention programs that have been developed to prevent violence and promote safe and thriving school climates.

Evidence-based Practice—Avoiding a one-size-fits-all approach to prevention and intervention, the focus throughout is on the application of evidence-based practice to address factors most commonly associated with school violence and safety.

Implications for Practice—Each chapter bridges the research-to-practice gap, with a section delineating implications for practice of the foregoing research.

Chapter Structure—To ensure continuity and coherence across the book, each chapter begins with a brief abstract and ends with a table showing the implications for practice.

International Focus—Acknowledging the fact that school violence and safety is a global concern, this edition has increased its focus on insights learned from cross-national research and practice outside the USA.

Expertise—The editors and authors are experienced researchers, teachers, practitioners, and leaders in the school violence field. Their expertise includes their breadth and depth of knowledge and experience, bridging research, policy, and practice and representing a variety of international organizations studying school violence around the world.

Shane R. Jimerson, Ph.D., is a Professor at the University of California, Santa Barbara.

Amanda B. Nickerson, Ph.D., is an Associate Professor at the University at Buffalo.

Matthew J. Mayer, Ph.D., is an Associate Professor at the State University of New Jersey.

Michael J. Furlong, Ph.D., is a Professor at the University of California, Santa Barbara.

Handbook of School Violence and School Safety

International Research and Practice

Second Edition

Edited by
Shane R. Jimerson
Amanda B. Nickerson
Matthew J. Mayer
Michael J. Furlong

NEW YORK AND LONDON

Second edition published 2012
by Routledge
711 Third Avenue, New York, NY 10017

Simultaneously published in the UK
by Routledge
2 Park Square, Milton Park, Abingdon, Oxon OX14 4RN

Routledge is an imprint of the Taylor & Francis Group, an informa business

First edition published by Routledge 2006

Library of Congress Cataloging in Publication Data
Handbook of school violence and school safety : international research and practice / edited by Shane R. Jimerson ... [et al.]. — 2nd ed.
p. cm.
    Includes bibliographical references and index.
    1. School improvement programs—Handbooks, manuals, etc. I. Jimerson, Shane R.
    LB3013.3.H346 2012
    371.7'82—dc23
    2011018194

ISBN: 978-0-415-88461-7 (hbk)
ISBN: 978-0-415-88462-4 (pbk)
ISBN: 978-0-203-84137-2 (ebk)

Typeset in Bembo and Stone Sans
by EvS Communication Networx, Inc.

Printed and bound in the United States of America on acid-free paper
by Edwards Brothers, Inc.

Dedicated to

our families, who remind us of the importance of our efforts and inspire us everyday:
Gavin & Taite Jimerson
Kathryn O'Brien

Brian, Ethan, and Alex Nishiyama

Solanger Frota-Mayer
(Matthew's loving, patient, and understanding wife)

The Furlong family four score strong

and to all the those who are victims of violence at school, the dedicated professionals who promote school safety through efforts to prevent acts of violence and provide support for victims of violence, and the scholars who inform our understanding of important facets of school violence and school safety. Through bringing the best of science to professional practice, it is hoped that the information presented in this handbook serves as an impetus to prevent school violence and promote safe and effective schools around the world.

Contents

Contents

Contents

Preface

The *Handbook of School Violence and School Safety: International Research and Practice* offers an international analysis of school violence and school safety, which provides a foundation (conceptually, empirically, and practically) for implementing and examining prevention and intervention programs to reduce school violence. The *Handbook of School Violence and School Safety: International Research and Practice* shares insights from scholarship around the world, to advance our collective understanding of (a) theoretical and empirical foundations for understanding school violence, (b) relevant assessment and measurement, and (c) research-based prevention and intervention for school violence. Leading scholars and practitioners from numerous countries provide information about their attempts to prevent school violence, which in many cases includes innovative approaches to theory, assessment, and intervention. The information included in the chapters provides fundamental information of interest to scholars, practitioners, and other professionals.

The following provides a brief description of the information that is included in each section of the handbook:

Theoretical and empirical foundations for understanding school violence. Chapters in this first section of the handbook provide important information regarding conceptual foundations related to specific issues, reviews relevant scholarship, and also identify areas where future research is needed. This information is essential in establishing a solid foundation for engaging in research as well as implementing school violence prevention and intervention programs around the world.

Assessment and measurement of school violence. Chapters in this section identify and discuss important aspects related to assessing and measuring school violence and school safety. Reviewing previous research, including measures used, and identifying convergence and discrepancies as well as related implications are each invaluable in advancing both the science and practice regarding school violence.

Research-based prevention and intervention for school violence. Chapters in the third section provide an overview of numerous efforts around the globe to implement prevention and intervention programs to address school violence. Authors detail the conceptual foundations underlying the particular programs, delineate the specific strategies incorporated in the programs, report results of research related to the effectiveness of the strategies, and identify limitations and areas of need for further scholarship.

Editors' Biographies

Shane R. Jimerson, Ph.D., is a Professor at the University of California, Santa Barbara. His international appointments have included: The University of Hong Kong; Tallinn University, Estonia; Sri Venkateswara University, Tirupati, India; Massey University, New Zealand; Bahria University, Islamabad, Pakistan; The University of Manchester, England; and The University of Athens, Greece. Dr. Jimerson is the co-founder of the International Institute of School Psychology (http://education.ucsb.edu/jimerson/IISP). His scholarly publications and presentations have provided insights regarding school violence and school safety, school crisis prevention and intervention, developmental pathways of school success and failure, the efficacy of early prevention and intervention programs, school psychology internationally, and developmental psychopathology. Among numerous publications, he is the lead-editor of *The Handbook of Bullying in Schools: An International Perspective* (2010, Routledge), he is also the lead-editor of the *Handbook of School Violence and School Safety: From Research to Practice* (2006, Erlbaum), a co-editor of *Best Practices in School Crisis Prevention and Intervention* (2002, National Association of School Psychologists), the lead-editor of *The Handbook of International School Psychology* (2007, Sage), and the lead editor of *The Handbook of Response to Intervention: The Science and Practice of Assessment and Intervention* (2007, Springer Science). He is also co-author of *School Crisis Prevention and Intervention: The PREPaRE Model* (2009, National Association of School Psychologists), a co-author of a five-book grief support group curriculum series *The Mourning Child Grief Support Group Curriculum* (2001, Taylor and Francis), co-author of *Identifying, Assessing, and Treating Autism at School* (2006, Springer Science), co-author of *Identifying, Assessing, and Treating Conduct Disorder at School* (2008, Springer Science), co-author of *Identifying, Assessing, and Treating PTSD at School* (2008, Springer Science), co-author of *Identifying, Assessing, and Treating ADHD at School* (2009, Springer Science), and co-author of the *Promoting Positive Peer Relationships (P3R): Bullying Prevention Program* (2008, Stories of Us). He has also served as the Editor of *The California School Psychologist* journal, Associate Editor of *School Psychology Review*, and on the editorial boards of numerous journals, including the *Journal of School Psychology* and *School Psychology Quarterly*. Dr. Jimerson has chaired and served on numerous boards and advisory committees at the state, national, and international levels, including President-Elect of Division 16 (School Psychology) American Psychological Association, Vice President for Convention Affairs and Public Relations of Division 16 (School Psychology) American Psychological Association, Chair of the Research Committee of the International School Psychology Association, Chair of the Division 16 (School Psychology) conference proceedings for the American Psychological Association conference, and Chair of the School Psychology Research Collaboration Conference. The quality and contributions of his scholarship are reflected in the numerous awards and recognition that he has received, including the Best Research Article of the year award from the Society for the Study of School Psychology, the Outstanding Article of the Year Award from the National Association of School Psychologists, appearing in *School Psychology Review*, the American Educational Research Association Early Career Award in Human Development, the Outstanding Research Award from the California Association of School Psychologists, membership in the Society for the

Study of School Psychology, the Lightner Witmer Early Career Contributions Award from Division 16 (School Psychology) of the American Psychological Association, and Fellow of the American Psychological Association, Division 16 (School Psychology). His scholarship continues to highlight the importance of early experiences on subsequent development and emphasize the importance of research informing professional practice to promote the social and cognitive competence of children.

Amanda B. Nickerson, Ph.D., is an Associate Professor and Director of the Jean M. Alberti Center for the Prevention of Bullying Abuse and School Violence in the Department of Educational and Counseling Psychology at the University at Buffalo, the State University of New York (SUNY). She was previously at the University at Albany, SUNY, where her research focused on school crisis prevention and intervention, with an emphasis on violence and bullying prevention. She has also written on the critical role of schools, parents, and peers in promoting social-emotional strengths and competencies of children and adolescents. Dr. Nickerson is the lead author of *Assessing, Identifying, and Treating Posttraumatic Stress Disorder at School* (2009, Springer) and co-author of *School Crisis Prevention and Intervention: The PREPaRE Model* (2009, National Association of School Psychologists). She reviews for several major journals and is on the editorial board of *School Psychology Quarterly, Psychology in the Schools,* and the *Journal of School Violence.*

Matthew J. Mayer, Ph.D., is an Associate Professor in the Department of Educational Psychology in the Graduate School of Education at Rutgers, the State University of New Jersey. Dr. Mayer's research includes analyzing national level data and modeling processes associated with school violence and disruption and related prevention programming. He also has written on cognitive-behavioral interventions and methodological issues in structural equation modeling and evidence-based standards in education and the allied professions. He reviews for several major journals and is an editorial board member of the journals *Behavioral Disorders* and *Journal of School Violence.* Dr. Mayer currently serves as President of the Consortium to Prevent School Violence, a national group dedicated to disseminating evidence-based violence prevention best practices to schools and allied youth agencies.

Michael J. Furlong, Ph.D., is a Professor in the Department of Counseling, Clinical, and School Psychology, Gevirtz Graduate School of Education, University of California, Santa Barbara. He is a member of the Society for the Study of School Psychology and a fellow of the American Psychological Association (Division 16) and the American Education Research Association. He is the Editor of the *Journal of School Violence* and the Director of the Center for School-Based Youth Development.

Contributors

Handbook of School Violence and School Safety:

International Research and Practice

(Second Edition)

Edited by

Shane R. Jimerson, Amanda B. Nickerson, Matthew J. Mayer, & Michael J. Furlong

The following provides information about the contributors to the *Handbook of School Violence and School Safety: International Research and Practice.* For each chapter, the information includes author's name, degree, affiliation.

Author Biographical and Contact Information

I. Foundations of School Violence and Safety

1 Conceptual Foundations for Understanding Youth Engaged in Antisocial and Aggressive Behaviors
   Shane R. Jimerson, Ph.D., is a Professor of Counseling, Clinical, and School Psychology at the University of California, Santa Barbara.
   Shelley R. Hart, Ph.D., the University of California, Santa Barbara.
   Tyler L. Renshaw, Ph.D., is School Psychologist, Alpine School District, American Fork, UT.

2 Making the Case for an International Perspective on School Violence: Implications for Theory, Research, Policy, and Assessment
   Rami Benbenishty, Ph.D., is a Professor of Social Work, at Bar Ilan University, Israel.
   Ron Avi Astor, Ph.D., is Richard M. and Ann L. Thor Professor in Urban Social Development at University of Southern California, Los Angeles.

3 Developing Safe, Supportive, and Effective Schools: Facilitating Student Success to Reduce School Violence
   David Osher, Ph.D., is Vice President at American Institutes for Research, Washington, DC.
   Kevin P. Dwyer, M.A., is a School Psychologist and Education and Mental Health Consultant affiliated with the American Institutes for Research, Washington, DC.
   Shane R. Jimerson, Ph.D., is a Professor of Counseling, Clinical, and School Psychology at the University of California, Santa Barbara.

Jacqueline A. Brown, M.A., is a doctoral student at the University of California, Santa Barbara.

4 A Problem-Solving Approach to School Violence Prevention
Jim Larson, Ph.D., is a Professor of Psychology in the School Psychology Program at the University of Wisconsin-Whitewater.
R. T. Busse, Ph.D., is an Associate Professor in the Counseling and School Psychology Program at Chapman University, Orange, California.

5 Social Support in the Lives of Students Involved in Aggressive and Bullying Behaviors
Michelle Kilpatrick Demaray, Ph.D., is an Associate Professor in the Department of Psychology at Northern Illinois University, DeKalb.
Christine Kerres Malecki, Ph.D., is an Associate Professor in the Department of Psychology at Northern Illinois University, DeKalb.
Lyndsay N. Jenkins, M.A., is a doctoral student in the Department of Psychology at Northern Illinois University, DeKalb.
Lauren D. Westermann is a School Psychologist in the Indian Prairie School District, Aurora, Illinois.

6 Coercion and Contagion in Family and School Environments: Implications for Educating and Socializing Youth
Gregory M. Fosco, Ph.D., is a Assistant Professor, Department of Human Development and Faculty Studies, Pensylvania State University, University Park.
Jennifer L. Frank, Ph.D., is a Research Associate, Prevention Research Center for the Promotion of Human Development, Pennsylvania State University.
Thomas J. Dishion, Ph.D., is a Professor of Clinical Psychology and School Psychology, University of Oregon, Eugene.

7 On the Personality Mechanisms Leading to Violence
Guido Alessandri, Ph.D., is a Research Assistant at the Sapienza University of Rome, Italy.
Michele Vecchione, Ph.D., is an Assistant Professor at the Sapienza University of Rome, Italy.
Gian Vittorio Caprara, is a Professor of Personality Psychology at the Sapienza University of Rome, Italy.

8 Cyberbullying and Cyber Aggression
Peter K. Smith, Ph.D., is Professor of Psychology and Head of the Unit for School and Family Studies, Goldsmiths College, University of London, England.

9 Addressing the Needs of Marginalized Youth at School
Tracey G. Scherr, Ph.D., is an Associate Professor of Psychology at the University of Wisconsin-Whitewater.

16 Monitoring School Violence in Israel, National Studies and Beyond: Implications for Theory, Practice, and Policy
Rami Benbenishty, Ph.D., is a professor of Social Work, at Bar Ilan University, Israel.
Ron Avi Astor, Ph.D., is Richard M. and Ann L. Thor Professor in Urban Social Development at University of Southern California, Los Angeles.

17 Youth Suicidal Behavior in the Context of School Violence
David N. Miller, Ph.D., is an Associate Professor of School Psychology at the University at Albany, State University of New York.

18 World Report on Violence and Health: International Insights
Shane R. Jimerson, Ph.D., is a Professor of Counseling, Clinical, and School Psychology at the University of California, Santa Barbara.
Jacqueline A. Brown, M.A., is a doctoral student at the University of California, Santa Barbara.
Skye Stifel, M.A., is a doctoral student at the University of California, Santa Barbara.
Matthew A. Ruderman is a doctoral student at the University of California, Santa Barbara.

II. Assessment and Measurement

19 Evidence-Based Standards and Methodological Issues in School Violence and Related Prevention Research in Education and the Allied Disciplines
Matthew J. Mayer, Ph.D., is an Associate Professor in the Department of Educational Psychology at Rutgers, the State University of New Jersey, New Brunswick.

20 An Overview of Measurement Issues in School Violence and School Safety Research
Jill D. Sharkey, Ph.D., is an Academic Coordinator in the Department of Counseling, Clinical, and School Psychology at the University of California, Santa Barbara.
Erin Dowdy, Ph.D., is an Assistant Professor in the Department of Counseling, Clinical, and School Psychology at the University of California, Santa Barbara.
Jennifer Twyford, Ed.S., is a Doctoral Candidate in the Department of Counseling, Clinical, and School Psychology at the University of California, Santa Barbara.
Michael J. Furlong, Ph.D., is a Professor in the Department of Counseling, Clinical, and School Psychology at the University of California, Santa Barbara.

21 Using Self-Report Anger Assessments in School Settings
Douglas C. Smith, Ph.D., is an Associate Professor in the Department of Psychology, Southern Oregon University, Ashland, Oregon.
Michael J. Furlong, Ph.D., is a Professor in the Department of Counseling, Clinical, and School Psychology at the University of California, Santa Barbara.
Peter Boman, Ph.D., is a Senior Lecturer in Education at the Queensland University of Technology, Brisbane, Australia

Victoria Gonzalez, M.Ed., is a Doctoral Candidate in the Department of Counseling, Clinical, and School Psychology at the University of California, Santa Barbara.

22 Assessment of Bullying
Dewey Cornell, Ph.D. is a Professor of Education in the Programs in Clinical and School Psychology, Curry School of Education, University of Virginia, Charlottesville.
Joanna C. M. Cole, Ph.D., is an Assistant Professor in the Department of Psychiatry at Boston University School of Medicine, Boston, Massachusetts.

23 Using Office Discipline Referrals and School Exclusion Data to Assess School Discipline
Kent McIntosh, Ph.D., is an Associate Professor, Faculty of Education at the University of British Columbia, Vancouver, Canada.
Emily S. Fisher, Ph.D., is an Assistant Professor in the School of Education at Loyola Marymount University, Los Angeles, California.
Kelly S. Kennedy, Ph.D., is an Assistant Professor in the College of Educational Studies at Chapman University, Orange, California.
Calli B. Craft is a graduate student, Faculty of Education at the University of British Columbia, Vancouver, Canada.
Gale M. Morrison, Ph.D., is the Dean of the Graduate Division and a Professor in the School of Education at the University of California, Santa Barbara.

24 Gauging the System: Trends in School Climate Measurement and Intervention
Meagan O'Malley, Ph.D., is a Research Associate in the Department of Health and Human Development, WestEd.
Kristin Katz, Ph.D., is School Psychologist, Santa Barbara County Office of Education.
Tyler L. Renshaw, Ph.D., is School Psychologist, Alpine School District, American Fork, UT.
Michael J. Furlong, Ph.D., is a Professor in the Department of Counseling, Clinical, and School Psychology at the University of California, Santa Barbara.

III. Research-Based Prevention and Intervention Programs

25 A Socio-Ecological Model for Bullying Prevention and Intervention in Early Adolescence
Susan M. Swearer, Ph.D., is a Professor of School Psychology, University of Nebraska-Lincoln.
Dorothy L. Espelage, Ph.D., is a Professor of Educational Psychology, University of Illinois, Urbana-Champaign.
Brian Koenig, M.A., is a K12 Associates, Madison, Wisconsin.
Brandi Berry, M.A., is a doctoral student in the School Psychology Program at the University of Nebraska-Lincoln.
Adam Collins, M.A., is a doctoral student in the School Psychology Program at the University of Nebraska-Lincoln.
Paige Lembeck, M.A., is a doctoral student in the School Psychology Program at the University of Nebraska-Lincoln.

Mark T. Greenberg, Ph.D., holds the Bennett Chair in Prevention Science in Human Development and Family Studies at Pennsylvania State University, University Park. He is the Director of the Prevention Research Center for the Promotion of Human Development.

33 School-Wide Positive Behavioral Supports
Jeffrey R. Sprague, Ph.D., is a Professor of Special Education and Co-Director of the University of Oregon Institute on Violence and Destructive Behavior, Eugene.
Robert H. Horner, Ph.D., is a Professor of Special Education and Director of the University of Oregon Institute on Educational and Community Supports, Eugene.

34 Preventing, Preparing for, and Responding to School Violence with the PREPaRE Model
Stephen E. Brock, Ph.D., is a Professor of School Psychology at California State University, Sacramento.
Shane R. Jimerson, Ph.D., is a Professor of Counseling, Clinical, and School Psychology at the University of California, Santa Barbara.
Shelley R. Hart, Ph.D., the University of California, Santa Barbara.
Amanda B. Nickerson, Ph.D., is an Associate Professor of School Psychology at the University at Albany, State University of New York.

35 Enhancing School Connectedness to Prevent Violence and Promote Well-being
Ian M. Shochet, Ph.D., is a Professor, School of Psychology and Counselling at the Queensland University of Technology, Brisbane, Australia.
Coral L. Smith, MClinPsyc, is a Senior Research Officer, the School of Psychology and Counseling at the Queensland University of Technology, Brisbane, Australia.

36 The United States Safe Schools/Healthy Students Initiative: Turning a National Initiative into Local Action
Jill D. Sharkey, Ph.D., is the School Psychology Coordinator in the Department of Counseling, Clinical, and School Psychology at the University of California, Santa Barbara.
Michael J. Furlong, Ph.D., is a Professor in the Department of Counseling, Clinical, and School Psychology at the University of California, Santa Barbara.
Erin Dowdy, Ph.D., is an Assistant Professor in the Department of Counseling, Clinical, and School Psychology at the University of California, Santa Barbara.
Erika D. Felix, Ph.D., is an Assistant Researcher in the Department of Counseling, Clinical, and School Psychology at the University of California, Santa Barbara.
Lindsey Grimm, M.A., is a doctoral candidate in the Department of Counseling, Clinical, and School Psychology at the University of California, Santa Barbara.
Kristin Ritchey, M.Ed., is a doctoral candidate in the Department of Counseling, Clinical, and School Psychology at the University of California, Santa Barbara.

37 Student Threat Assessment as a Strategy to Reduce School Violence
Dewey Cornell, Ph.D., is a Professor of Education, the Programs in Clinical and School Psychology, Curry School of Education, University of Virginia, Charlottesville. **Farah Williams, Ph.D.,** is a Licensed Clinical Psychologist and Director of Child and Adolescent Services at Scott County Behavioral Health Services, Scott County, Virginia.

38 Reforming School Discipline and Reducing Disproportionality in Suspension and Expulsion
Russell J. Skiba, Ph.D., is a Professor of Counseling and Educational Psychology and Director of the Equity Project at Indiana University-Bloomington.
Lauren A. Shure, Ph.D., is a Research Associate at the Equity Project at Indiana University-Bloomington.
Laura V. Middelberg is a Graduate Research Assistant at the Equity Project at Indiana University and a doctoral student in the School Psychology Program at Indiana University-Bloomington.
Timberly L. Baker is a Graduate Research Assistant with the Equity Project at Indiana University and a doctoral student in the Educational Leadership and Policy Studies Program at Indiana University-Bloomington.

39 The Impact of Safe Schools/Healthy Students Funding on Student Well-Being: A California Consortium Cross-Site Analysis
Thomas L. Hanson, Ph.D., is a Senior Research Associate in the Health and Human Development Program at WestEd and Co-Director of Research of the Regional Educational Laboratory-Western Region, San Francisco, California.
Amy Jane Griffiths, Ph.D., is the Assistant Director at The Help Group's Residential Treatment Facility for Adolescents with Social, Emotional, and Behavioral Challenges, Sherman Oaks, California.
Michael J. Furlong, Ph.D., is a professor in the Counseling, Clinical, and School Psychology Department at the University of California, Santa Barbara.

40 School Violence in South Korea: An Overview of School Violence and Intervention Efforts
Seung-yeon Lee, Ph.D., is an Assistant Professor of Department of Psychology at Ewha Womans University, Seoul, Korea.
Insoo Oh, Ph.D., is an Assistant Professor of Department of Education at Ewha Womans University, Seoul, Korea.

41 Preventive Programme of Tolerance Against Violence at Schools in Slovakia
Eva Gajdošova, is a Professor of School Psychology at the Comenius University, Bratislava, Slovakia.
Zita Rijakova, is a Professor of Educational and Social Psychology at the Comenius University, Bratislava, Slovakia.

42 Preventing Youth Gang Involvement with G.R.E.A.T.
Dana Peterson, Ph.D., is an Associate Professor in the School of Criminal Justice at the University at Albany, State University of New York.

Finn-Aage Esbensen, Ph.D., is the E. Desmond Lee Professor of Youth Violence, Department of Criminology and Criminal Justice, at the University of Missouri–St. Louis.

43 Cognitive-Behavioral Intervention for Anger and Aggression: The Coping Power Program

John E. Lochman, Ph.D., ABPP, is Professor and Doddridge Saxon Chairholder in Clinical Psychology, and Director of the Center for Prevention of Youth Behavior Problems at The University of Alabama, Tuscaloosa.

Caroline L. Boxmeyer, Ph.D., is a Research Scientist in the Center for Prevention of Youth Behavior Problems at The University of Alabama, Tuscaloosa.

Nicole P. Powell, Ph.D., is a Research Scientist in the Center for Prevention of Youth Behavior Problems at The University of Alabama, Tuscaloosa.

44 Meta-Analysis and Systematic Review of the Effectiveness of School-Based Programs to Reduce Multiple Violent and Antisocial Behavioral Outcomes

Aaron A. Alford, Ph.D.,M.Ph., is a Research Scientist at the Battelle Centers for Public Health Research and Evaluation, Arlington, Virginia.

James Derzon, Ph.D., is a Research Teacher at the Battelle Centers for Public Health Research and Evaluation, Arlington, Virginia.

Section I

Foundations of School Violence and Safety

Conceptual Foundations for Understanding Youth Engaged in Antisocial and Aggressive Behaviors

Shane R. Jimerson and Shelley R. Hart

THE UNIVERSITY OF CALIFORNIA, SANTA BARBARA

Tyler L. Renshaw

ALPINE SCHOOL DISTRICT, AMERICAN FORK, UT

Abstract

In efforts to address violence that occurs at school, it is important to consider the conceptual foundations informing our understanding of youth who engage in antisocial and aggressive behaviors. Careful consideration of the developmental trajectories, characteristics, and contexts associated with antisocial behaviors reveals that there is no single profile associated with aggressive behavior. This chapter emphasizes developmental, contextual, and mental health factors that inform our understanding of youth who engage in antisocial and aggressive behaviors, with an emphasis on research-derived models describing how antisocial and aggressive behaviors emerge from the developmental process. A central tenet of this chapter is that youth engaged in antisocial and aggressive behaviors have many needs that community and school-based professionals may address. A summary table highlights practical implications derived from the conceptual and theoretical literature.

Although news media often popularize high-profile incidences of school violence, evidence indicates that schools are among the safest places for youth. Over the past two decades, the safeness of schools has been corroborated by two major, national studies—the Indicators of School Crime and Safety (e.g., Dinkes, Kemp, & Baum, 2009) and the Youth Risk Behavior Surveillance System (YRBSS; e.g., Eaton et al., 2009)—which reveal favorable trends regarding crime, safety, and harm indicators related to youth in the United States. These studies indicate that severe forms of youth victimization (e.g., assault with a deadly weapon) have declined at school, while use of school-based safety and security measures have increased. Nevertheless, concurrent with these favorable trends, two unfavorable trends have surfaced. First, the prevalence of youth possessing weapons at school persists at a high and stable rate, as 27% of males and 7% of females in grades 9–12 reported carrying a weapon on campus within the last 30 days (Eaton et al., 2009). Second, mild forms of youth victimization (e.g., bullying) are becoming increasingly prevalent at school. For example, during the 2007–2008 school year alone, 1.5 million nonfatal, school-based crimes of violence or theft were reported among 12- to 18-year-old students, while 32% of secondary students and 43% of sixth-grade students reported experiencing bullying at school (Dinkes et al., 2009). Taken together, these emerging trends suggest that, despite much positive headway, there is still ample reason to be concerned about school violence.

The sporadic occurrence of high-profile incidences of school violence, paired with the increasing prevalence of milder forms of violence on campus, has resulted in magnified attention from educators on the origins of antisocial and aggressive behaviors among youth. Educators are primarily concerned about the nature of such behaviors given that any form of violence—and even the potential for it—is antithetical to the nurturing and educational mission of schools and, by extension, the positive development of students. Moreover, educators desire to understand the origins of such behaviors so they can utilize empirical knowledge to enhance the effectiveness and efficiency of intervention efforts—aiming to reduce the prevalence and curb the severity of current cases, while preempting the genesis of new cases. These aims, reduction and prevention, are especially important in light of developmental scholarship suggesting that the majority of severe violent behaviors exhibited in adulthood are the fruits of antisocial and aggressive behaviors engendered throughout childhood or adolescence (van Domburgh, Loeber, Bezemer, Stallings, & Stouthamer-Loeber, 2009). Such violence can have far-reaching effects, harming both perpetrators and innocent victims, as well as exacting costs on society as a whole. For example, the monetary costs to society for youth criminal behaviors are especially great, as longitudinal findings estimate that some youth can cost up to $177,000 to $542,000 in public funds over a decade (Welsh et al., 2008). These and other ominous costs have rocketed professional interest in school violence to new heights during the past two decades, making it a global concern (e.g., Jimerson, Swearer, & Espelage, 2010).

The first step toward addressing school violence and ameliorating its menacing effects is to carefully consider the characteristics and contexts of youth who engage in antisocial and aggressive behavior. This chapter addresses these vital considerations, with an emphasis on developmental, contextual, and mental health factors. Specifically, the first section provides an overview of aggressive conduct patterns as delineated in the *Diagnostic and Statistical Manual of Mental Disorders* (American Psychiatric Association [APA], *DSM-IV-TR*, 2000); the subsequent sections explore research-derived models regarding the emergence of antisocial and aggressive behaviors from human developmental processes; and the final section explores the interface of such behaviors within school contexts.

Diagnosis of Antisocial and Aggressive Behaviors

Aggressive behaviors are one of the most common reasons for referral of children and adolescents to mental health professionals (Sugden, Kile, & Hendren, 2006). Such behaviors may have different origins (e.g., impulsivity, affective instability, predatory) and be linked with several different mental health diagnoses (e.g., bipolar disorder, anxiety, autism; Sugden et al., 2006). The disorder of particular interest to the development of antisocial and aggressive behaviors, and thus to school violence, is conduct disorder (CD). Oppositional defiant disorder (ODD) is often a precursor to CD; however, ODD also predicts mood and anxiety disorders. The following section reviews the nature of CD, its subtypes, and related aggressive and antisocial behaviors.

Conduct Disorder: Diagnosis, Prevalence, and Comorbidity

Conduct disorder encompasses a pervasive and persistent pattern of aggressive, deceptive, and destructive behaviors (APA, 2000). Youth who meet diagnostic criteria for this disorder (see Table 1.1) usually present challenges in school environments, and are likely to have poor academic performance and exhibit other negative life outcomes (e.g., school dropout, early pregnancy, substance abuse). Recent scholarship estimates the lifetime prevalence of CD at 9.5%, with a significantly higher rate in males than females (12% and 7%, respectively) and a median age-of-onset of between 11- and 12-years-old. Furthermore, recent scholarship suggests that having a diagnosis of CD is a significant risk factor for a plethora of other psychiatric diagnoses—suggesting high comorbidity with mood, anxiety, impulse control, and substance abuse disorders (Nock, Kazdin, Hiripi, & Kessler, 2006)—as well as speech and language disorders and learning disabilities (Benner, Mattison, & Nelson, 2009). Overall, such findings indicate that there can be many shared characteristics among youth with CD diagnoses (Achenbach, 1998).

Subtypes of Conduct Disorder and Related Aggressive and Antisocial Behaviors

Whereas there appear to be similarities among individuals diagnosed with CD, current diagnostic criteria (see Table 1.1) promote identification of a variety of aggressive and antisocial youth. As only three of fifteen criterions are required within the last year, with one symptom endorsed in the last six months—the result is a plethora of possible symptom constellations. Furthermore, given different developmental trajectories have been shown to lead to aggressive and antisocial behavior, much attention has been focused on identifying subtypes of CD and their associated developmental pathways (e.g., Loeber, Pardini, Stouthamer-Loeber, & Raine, 2007). Specifically, one way of identifying subtypes via the current diagnostic system is by using the age criterion (i.e., 10 years old) as the specifier for distinguishing between childhood- and adolescent-onset types (APA, 2000). Although this age-based distinction may seem arbitrary, it has been supported by growth mixture models from longitudinal studies and has demonstrated clinical utility, as childhood-onset cases have developed substantially poorer outcomes than adolescent-onset cases (Moffitt et al., 2008).

Several additional subtypes of CD have been proposed, yet the distinctions between *overt* (e.g., public fighting) versus *covert* (e.g., vandalism) and *reactive* (e.g., defensive responses) versus *proactive*

Table 1.1 DSM-IV-TR Criteria for Conduct Disorder

A repetitive and persistent pattern in which the rights or societal norms or rules are violated as manifested by the presence of at least three of the following criteria in the past 12 months (with at least one criterion present in the past 6 months).

Aggression to people and animals, for example, bullying, threatening, or intimidating others, initiating physical fights, using a weapon that can cause serious physical harm to others (e.g., a bat, brick, broken bottle, knife, gun), being physically cruel to people or animals, or has stolen while confronting a victim (e.g., mugging, purse snatching, extortion, armed robbery), or has forced someone into sexual activity.

Destruction of property, such as having deliberately engaged in fire setting with the intention of causing serious damage, or has deliberately destroyed others' property (other than by fire setting).

Deceitfulness or theft, for instance, has broken into someone else's house, building or car, having often lied to obtain goods or favors or to avoid obligations (i.e., "cons" others) or has stolen items of nontrivial value without confronting a victim (e.g., shoplifting, but without breaking and entering; forgery).

Serious violation of rules such as, staying out at night despite parental prohibitions (beginning before age 13 years), running away from home overnight (at least twice while living in parental or parental surrogate home or once without returning for a lengthy period), or is often truant from school (beginning before age 13 years).

(e.g., goal-directed acts) subtypes appear to have the strongest internal and external validation (Connor, 2002). However, Nock and colleagues (2006) recently used latent class analysis to identify five subtypes of CD present in their nationally representative sample (i.e., Rule Violation, Deceit/Theft, Aggressive, Severe Covert, and Pervasive), providing more differentiation than preexisting dichotomous subtypes—allowing for distinctions between both type and severity of symptoms. Despite these and similar scholarly advances regarding subtypes, relatively few changes have been proposed for the new CD diagnostic criteria in the fifth edition of the *DSM* (see http://www.dsm5.org). One consideration is the addition of a callous and unemotional specifier, suggesting the presence or lack of psychopathy underlying the CD (Lynam et al., 2009). Ultimately, such variance among existing, tentative, and proposed subtypes suggests that youth diagnosed with CD can exhibit a variety of problematic aggressive and antisocial behaviors, have varying levels of genetic and biological risk, and possess differing neurocognitive profiles (Moffitt et al., 2008).

Pathways to Antisocial and Aggressive Behaviors

A review of the relevant research literature and theories indicates there is no singular developmental trajectory leading to long-term antisocial and aggressive behavior, but that such behavior evolves through periods of quiescence and dynamic growth (Patterson & Yoerger, 2002). Developmental and ecological models of antisocial and aggressive behavior focus on family, peer, and school contexts as the primary settings in which these behaviors evolve. The following section briefly overviews the major perspectives accounting for the development of harmful behaviors among youth.

Social Learning Theory Models

Social learning theory posits that (a) learning is a social as well as internal process, (b) behavior is goal directed and eventually becomes self-regulated, and (c) reinforcement and punishment have direct (i.e., behavioral) and indirect (i.e., cognitive) effects (Bandura, 1986). The *social learning model* emphasizes the importance of antecedents and consequences of behaviors occurring in daily social exchanges between children and others in their social milieus (e.g., parents, siblings, and school staff; Patterson & Yoerger, 2002). For example, if children's home environments are characterized by parenting styles that include inconsistent discipline and coercion (i.e., positive and negative reinforcement, paired with physical or verbal aggression), such patterns of interaction are likely to become cyclical and reinforced, resulting in parents modeling inappropriate problem-solving methods and inadvertently teaching aggressive behaviors. The *social development model* integrates social learning theory, control theory, and differential association theory, focusing on how both prosocial and antisocial developmental pathways—influenced by biological and environmental risk and protective factors—underlie all social behavior (Catalano & Hawkins, 1996). This model emphasizes transitional periods (i.e., preschool, elementary, middle, and high school), acknowledging that certain factors have stronger or weaker influence on social development during sensitive periods (e.g., the family is primary during preschool), and that outcomes from these periods are influential in shaping subsequent developmental manifestations.

Social Information-Processing Model

Rather than placing primary influence on external modeling and reinforcement, the social information-processing model focuses on the role of social cognitions in shaping various antisocial behaviors (Crick & Dodge, 1994). This model hypothesizes that flaws in processing social information (i.e., encoding, interpretation, generation of possible responses, selection of a response, and enaction of behavior) lead to antisocial and aggressive behaviors. Such information process-ing flaws have been identified in habitually aggressive children, who tend to concentrate more on hostile or aversive social cues, have memory difficulties that interfere with their processing of social information, and interpret cues from their preexisting aggressive schema (Zelli et al., 1999). As a result, these youth often seek only self-interested goals, retaliate against persons presenting obstacles to obtaining such goals, generate few prosocial solutions for accomplishing their goals, and tend to appraise their aggressive solutions as more effective than prosocial solu-tions (Calkins & Keane, 2009; Carlson & Cornell, 2008).

Persistence/Desistence Models of Aggression

Another way of conceptualizing the origins of youth's antisocial and aggressive behaviors is by distinguishing between *life-course persistent* (i.e., aggressive behaviors exhibited from child-hood through adulthood) and *adolescent-limited* trajectories (i.e., aggressive behaviors exhibited between ages 14 and 17; Moffitt, 1993). Youth within these categories have been shown to have distinct differences in etiology, developmental course, prognosis, and severity of harm-ful behaviors. Specifically, *life-course persistent* aggression is believed to begin with neurological impairment—caused by genetics, maternal drug exposure, or traumatic brain injury, among other things (Moffitt, 1993)—that has detrimental effects on language-based verbal skills and executive functioning (Moffitt, 1990). Deficiencies in these areas often lead to a host of deleteri-ous outcomes, including poor academic performance, impaired social-information processing, and impulsive behavior, which, in turn, place the child at risk for more negative outcomes, such as substance abuse, school dropout, and gang membership. On the other hand, *adolescent-limited aggression* involves those youth who engage in antisocial behaviors between early adolescence and young adulthood, primarily as the result of social influences grounded in reinforcement and punishment contingencies. This perspective also hypothesizes that such harmful behaviors exhibited by youth may be part of a natural quest for obtaining maturity and autonomy—seeking a pathway into adulthood (Moffitt, 1993). Overall, contemporary longitudinal research contin-ues to support the distinction between life-course persistent and adolescent-limited aggression, showing that childhood-onset leads to significant impairment in educational, social, behavioral, and vocational domains (Bradshaw, Schaeffer, Petras, & Ialongo, 2010; Odgers et al., 2008); however, even adolescent-limited aggression patterns tend to indicate poorer outcomes (e.g., lower graduation rates, higher unemployment, more incarcerations; Loeber et al., 2007).

Transactional-Ecological Developmental Model

Similar to the previously described models, the *transactional-ecological developmental model* is a framework for understanding the dynamic processes by which children and contexts shape each other (Sameroff, 2009). Specifically, this model posits that all human development is an adaption that is shaped at three primary levels: the (a) *genotype* (i.e., genetic and biochemical makeup), (b) *phenotype* (i.e., phenomenological experience and current developmental expressions), and (c) *environtype* (i.e., multilevel nested environments; Sameroff, 2000). These three levels interface via transactions—or multilevel interactions throughout time—continuously taking place among them. To take a simplified example, a child's biological makeup (genotype) may predispose him to poor decision-making skills, while the family environment (environtype) may be characterized by chaotic or volatile interactions, and thus the child may behave (phenotype) in a manner that further elicits negative responses from within the given context. As a result, over time, this dynamic interplay may serve as a pathway for developing antisocial or aggressive behaviors. However, this perspective allows for different developmental pathways—or combinations of risk and protective factors—to lead to similar developmental expressions (i.e., *equifinality*), while allowing that initially similar developmental pathways may lead to divergent developmental expressions (i.e., *multifinality*; Gutman, Sameroff, & Cole, 2003). In this way, no particular constellation of personal or environmental variables determines antisocial or aggressive behaviors among youth; rather, children and contexts both influence each other, forming interactive feedback loops throughout time that fuel human development and ultimately manifest in such harmful behaviors (Sameroff, 2009).

Antisocial and Aggressive Behaviors and the School Context

The boundaries between antisocial or aggressive behaviors and typical behaviors are often first met within educational contexts when youth's behavior exceeds acceptable norms. As a result, schools are also the most likely setting for providing intervention to remediate such behaviors. To facilitate the best interventions possible, it is imperative for school personnel to be equipped with an accurate understanding of how harmful behaviors develop, as described above, and how such behaviors interface with various elements in school systems. The following section focuses on the latter, describing how schools react to antisocial and aggressive behaviors and how these reactions influence such behaviors—and vice versa.

Common Educational Practices Associated with Antisocial and Aggressive Behaviors

Common educational practices utilized by schools may have unfavorable influences on the development of students' antisocial or aggressive behaviors. Specifically, methods employed by schools to identify students with disabilities impact how school personnel address the needs of youth manifesting antisocial and aggressive behaviors. For example, given that students classified with emotional disturbance (ED) are reported by teachers to have higher rates of substantive threats and fighting at school (e.g., Bradley, Doolittle, & Bartolotta, 2008; Kaplan & Cornell, 2005), students exhibiting antisocial or aggressive behaviors may be hastily classified with ED, without full consideration of their constellation of presenting problems. Students exhibiting such behaviors may also, sometimes, be excluded from disability consideration altogether, because they are deemed to be "socially maladjusted," despite no diagnostic or legal definition for this term (Olympia, Farley, Christiansen, Pettersson, & Clark, 2004). Moreover, students identified with both learning disabilities (LD) and antisocial or aggressive behaviors are disproportionately more likely to be served under the LD category only, unless the behaviors become a primary focus for intervention, in which case they are also at risk for exclusion from services (Morrison & D'Incau, 2000). These discouraging trends suggest that many students manifesting antisocial or aggressive behaviors may be inappropriately classified for special education services, resulting in missed opportunities for appropriate intervention. To remedy this situation, school professionals must diligently attend to the nuances of the identification process, making sure to link all assessment information—despite the resulting classification status—to appropriate prevention and intervention services.

Once a youth engages in antisocial or aggressive behaviors, the disciplinary reactions of school officials, teachers, parents, and others may facilitate more or less favorable outcomes (Caspi, Elder, & Bem, 1988). Because school disciplinary systems address only rule-violating behaviors, and because zero-tolerance policies are common, school personnel may often ignore extenuating circumstances surrounding youth exhibiting harmful behaviors (Krezmien, Leone, & Achilles, 2006), resulting in high rates of school exclusion (i.e., suspension and expulsion) for such students. School exclusion, although a popular and modern practice, has been shown to have negative effects on many students exhibiting antisocial and aggressive behaviors, resulting in increased perpetration of offending behaviors (Hemphill, Toumbourou, Herrenkohl,

McMorris, & Catalano, 2006). While protected by additional safeguards, students in special education who exhibit antisocial and aggressive behaviors may be disproportionately subject to exclusionary practices, given suspension and expulsion rates of students classified with ED (i.e., 64%) are three times higher than those of students in other disability categories (Bradley et al., 2008). Thus, the discipline trends of particular schools, as well as the disciplinary zeitgeist of school systems in general, may unintentionally serve as a contextual risk factor contributing to continued misbehavior. However, given the transactional nature of human development, common educational practices are not the only forces shaping students' behavior; individual protective and risk factors also play a key role in shaping how students interface with school contexts (Masten, Best, & Garmezy, 1990).

Individual Characteristics Associated with Antisocial and Aggressive Behaviors

Students exhibiting antisocial and other harmful behaviors at school often show early signs of aggression, defiance, victimization, academic failure, and peer rejection (White & Loeber, 2008). Such youth may also show deficits in (a) social behaviors, (b) cognitive and affective empathy, (c) self-regulation, (d) generation of prosocial solutions, (e) conflict resolution, and (e) work habits (Calkins & Keane, 2009; Campbell et al., 2010; Dodge, Coie, & Lynam, 2006; Walker, Ramsey, & Gresham, 2004). Moreover, such children typically do not often engage in teacher-pleasing behaviors (e.g., working neatly and quietly; Bradley et al., 2008), and they tend to disproportionately endorse aggressive behaviors as a means to positive social outcomes (Carlson & Cornell, 2008). Recognition of these and other risk factors is imperative, given the recent developmental scholarship indicating the predictive power of certain personal characteristics with particular future-life outcomes. For example, personal risk factors such as hyperactivity, fearlessness, and low prosocial behaviors in Kindergarten have been shown to predict deviant peer group affiliation twelve years later (Lacourse et al., 2006).

In contrast, protective—or resilience—factors may counterbalance some of the aforementioned risk factors, facilitating more prosocial outcomes for such students. For instance, personal characteristics such as sociability, problem-solving ability, planning ability, and internal locus of control are likely to help children establish better relationships with parents, teachers, and other critical adults. In turn, such relationships are likely to result in students making increased positive life-course decisions and having more positive perceptions of their self-control, cooperation, self-efficacy, cognitive abilities, and social problem-solving ability (Clarke & Clarke, 1994; Elias & Branden, 1988; Jessor, Van Den Bos, Vanderryn, Costa, & Turbin, 1995; Rutter, 1979). Thus, when working with children exhibiting antisocial and aggressive behaviors, the challenge for school systems and professionals is to minimize the effect of personal risk factors by maximizing and emphasizing the development of personal protective factors. But beyond personal factors, schools may also shape students' behavior through both group and schoolwide influences.

Group Influences Associated with Antisocial and Aggressive Behaviors

The influence of social or peer affiliations in students' development of antisocial and aggressive behaviors is pivotal (Dodge et al., 2006). Specifically, peer social clusters are highly influential given that they create and maintain group behavioral norms that may be transmitted into adulthood, even following group affiliation changes. Thus, research has found that peer social networks, and even brief experiences that facilitate a similar in-group sentiment, can profoundly influence negative behaviors such as aggression, bullying, and ostracism (Nipedal, Nesdale, & Killen, 2010). However, the opposite is also true, as group influences have been demonstrated to shape positive student behaviors in both academic and social realms (Farmer et al., 2010). Within the school context, classrooms serve as quintessential group settings, where students and teachers create and negotiate a climate that influences academic, behavioral, and social adjustment of all students within the group. For this reason, teachers' skills and personal characteristics can serve as settings events—or risk and protective factors—for students' development of antisocial and aggressive behaviors (Farmer et al., 2010).

Some common risk factors for students struggling with such behaviors include teachers lacking strategies for addressing students' developmental delays (La Paro, Pianta, & Cox, 2000), as well as an increase of negative teacher-attention that hampers the development of positive student-teacher relationships (Blankemeyer, Flannery, & Vazsonyi, 2002; Reinke & Herman, 2002). In contrast, some common protective factors for such students include teachers employing effective instructional techniques (e.g., classwide and peer tutoring), reinforcement of student strengths and behaviors, early intervention for learning problems, and positive regard for students and student-teacher relationships (Farmer et al., 2010; Scott, Nelson, & Liaupsin, 2001). Thus, such findings indicate that teachers can play a significant role as classroom architects who shape an environment that can, in turn, exacerbate or curb students' development of antisocial and aggressive behaviors.

Schoolwide Influences Associated with Antisocial and Aggressive Behaviors

Schoolwide influences can also help to exacerbate or curb students' development of antisocial and aggressive behaviors. A disorderly school environment—characterized by vague rules and expectations, low academic achievement, and high antisocial behaviors—is likely to be an especially potent risk factor for students who need clear expectations and structure (Gottfredson, 1989; McEvoy & Welker, 2000), resulting in high suspension and expulsion rates for such students (Civil Rights Project, 2000). Furthermore, school environments characterized by ambiguous sanctions, punitive teacher attitudes, poor teacher-administrator cooperation, and use of physical safety restrictions (e.g., metal detectors, high fencing, etc.) are associated with problem behaviors and alienation among students (Mayer & Leone, 1999). Also, schools with higher rates of suspension, as discussed above, often have higher student-teacher ratios, more negative teacher attitudes and lower expectations of students, and poorer academic performance (Ostroff, 1992; Wu, Pink, Crain, & Moles, 1982). In such schools, school personnel spend more time on discipline-related matters and therefore pay significantly less attention to issues of school climate (Bickel & Qualls, 1980), which affect all students' development. A reciprocal cycle is thus established, in which schools with poorer climates and environments serve as contextual risk factors for developing antisocial and aggressive behaviors, while students exhibiting such behaviors shape even poorer school climates and environments, and so on. Considering this situation, recent scholarship suggests that schools combine elements of social emotional learning with schoolwide positive behavioral support programming, to better support students with interrelated needs in both social-emotional, behavioral, and academic domains (Osher, Bear, Sprague, & Doyle, 2010).

Concluding Comments Regarding Youth Exhibiting Antisocial and Aggressive Behaviors

Youths engaged in antisocial and aggressive behaviors represent a heterogeneous group of students. Given that both the presence and potential for school violence hampers the educational environment, it is imperative that educators and scholars are equipped with current empirical information that will help them better understand, intervene with, and prevent antisocial and aggressive behaviors among youth (implications for practice are delineated in Table 1.2). This chapter provided a brief overview of such timely information, focusing on (a) the relation of

Table 1.2 Implications for Practice: Towards an Understanding of Youth Engaging in Antisocial and Aggressive Behaviors

1. Youth engaged in antisocial and aggressive behaviors represent a diverse group; there is no single profile, thus, education professionals should aim to identify risk factors and facilitate healthy adjustment among all students.

2. Many youth engaged in antisocial and aggressive behaviors face numerous challenges in multiple settings (e.g., at home, with peers, at school), and thus, have many needs to be addressed.

3. Each of the theories recognizes the importance of early identification and intervention to address the needs of youth engaged in antisocial and aggressive behaviors; thus, early antisocial and aggressive behaviors warrant serious attention to provide appropriate early interventions to address both behavioral and underlying emotional problems.

4. There is no single theory to explain the patterns of antisocial and aggressive behaviors among youth; thus, education professionals are encouraged to consider the transactional-ecological developmental perspective, which better models the complex interplay among factors influencing antisocial and aggressive trajectories.

5. Applied research focusing on the interface of antisocial developmental patterns and the schooling process has the potential support screening, prevention, and intervention efforts.

6. School policies, practices, and relationships have important influences on the well-being of youth engaged in antisocial and aggressive behaviors; thus, it is essential to carefully consider school factors in efforts to address problem behaviors.

7. Intervention plans emphasizing skills students need in order to behave in a more appropriate manner, or plans providing motivation to conform to required standards, are generally most effective.

8. The school is a premier social setting which affords the opportunity to systematically screen for youth with antisocial behavioral patterns.

9. Schools are generally among the safest places for youth and provide an important context to promote their well-being and address their needs (e.g., academic, cognitive, social, emotional, and mental health).

antisocial and aggressive behaviors to the psychiatric diagnosis of conduct disorders and its subtypes, (b) the various and interrelated pathways for conceptualizing the origins of students' antisocial and aggressive behaviors, and (c) the multiple factors influencing the development of such behaviors as they interface with school contexts. With such information, it is imperative to recognize that youth exhibiting antisocial and aggressive behaviors have significant needs, and that the most efficient and effective approach toward helping such students is early identification and intervention services. Moreover, universal-level prevention programs aimed at enhancing the social and cognitive competence of *all* youth are especially warranted—to promote schoolwide well-being and academic success, while simultaneously reducing the potential for school violence. Ultimately, such efforts will facilitate the development of healthier children, families, schools, and communities.

Note

Portions of this chapter were adapted from Jimerson, S. R., Morrison, G. M., Pletcher, S. W., & Furlong, M. J. (2006). Youth engaged in antisocial and aggressive behaviors: Who are they? In S. R. Jimerson & M. J. Furlong (Eds.), *Handbook of school violence and school safety: From research to practice* (pp. 3–19). Mahwah, NJ: Erlbaum.

References

Achenbach, T. (1998). Diagnosis, assessment, taxonomy, and case formulations. In T. Ollendick & M. Hersen (Eds.), *Handbook of child psychopathology* (3rd ed., pp. 63–87). New York, NY: Plenum Press.

American Psychiatric Association. (2000). *The diagnostic and statistical manual of mental disorders* (4th ed., text revision). Washington, DC: Author.

Bandura, A. (1986). *Social foundations of thought and action*. Englewood Cliffs, NJ: Prentice Hall.

Benner, G. J., Mattison, R. E., & Nelson, J. R. (2009). Types of language disorders in students classified as ED: Prevalence and association with learning disabilities and psychopathology. *Education and Treatment of Children, 32*, 631–653. doi: 10.1353/etc.0.0077

Bickel, F., & Qualls, R. (1980). The impact of school climate on suspension rates in the Jefferson County Public Schools. *The Urban Review, 12*, 79–86.

Blankemeyer, M., Flannery, D. J., & Vazsonyi, A. T. (2002). The role of aggression and social competence in children's perceptions of the child–teacher relationship. *Psychology in the Schools, 39*, 293–304.

Bradley, R., Doolittle, J., & Bartolotta, R. (2008). Building on the data and adding to the discussion: The experiences and outcomes of students with emotional disturbance. *Journal of Behavioral Education, 17*, 4–23. doi: 10.1007/s10864-007-9058-6

Bradshaw, C. P., Schaeffer, C. M., Petras, H., & Ialongo, N. (2010). Predicting negative life outcomes from early aggressive-disruptive behavior trajectories: Gender differences in maladaptation across life domains. *Journal of Youth and Adolescence, 39*, 953–966. doi: 10.1007/s10964-009-9442-8

Calkins, S. D., & Keane, S. P. (2009). Developmental origins of early antisocial behavior. *Development and Psychopathology, 21*, 1095–1109. doi: 10.1017/S095457940999006X

Campbell, S. B., Spieker, S., Vandergrift, N., Belsky, J., Burchinal, M., & The NICHD Early Child Care Research Network. (2010). Predictors and sequelae of trajectories of physical aggression in school-age boys and girls. *Development and Psychopathology, 22*, 133–150. doi: 10.1017/S0954579409990319

Carlson, L. W., & Cornell, D. G. (2008). Differences between persistent and desistent middle school bullies. *School Psychology International, 29*, 442–451. doi: 10.1177/0143034308096433

Caspi, A., Elder, G. H., & Bem, D. (1988). Moving against the world: Life course patterns of explosive children. *Developmental Psychopathology, 24*, 824–831.

Catalano, R. F., & Hawkins, J. D. (1996). The social development model: A theory of antisocial behavior. In J. D. Hawkins (Ed.), *Delinquency and crime: Current theories. Cambridge criminology series* (pp. 149–197). New York, NY: Cambridge University Press.

Civil Rights Project. (2000). *Opportunities suspended: The devastating consequences of zero tolerance and school discipline policies*. Cambridge, MA: Harvard University.

Clarke, A. M., & Clarke, A. D. B. (1994). Individual differences as risk factors: Development, birth weight, and chronic illness. In W. B. Carey & S. C. McDevitt (Eds.), *Prevention and early intervention: Individual differences as risk factors for the mental health of children* (pp. 83–91). New York, NY: Brunner/Mazel.

Connor, D. F. (2002). *Aggression & antisocial behavior in children and adolescents: Research and treatment*. New York, NY: Guilford.

Crick, N. R., & Dodge, K. A. (1994). A review and reformulation of social information-processing mechanisms in children's social adjustment. *Psychological Bulletin, 115*, 74–101.

Dinkes, R., Kemp, J., & Baum, K. (2009). *Indicators of school crime and safety: 2009*. Washington, DC: National Center for Education Statistics, Institute of Education Sciences, U.S. Department of Education, and Bureau of Justice Statistics. Available from http://nces.ed.gov or http://www.ojp.usdoj.gov/bjs

Dodge, K. A., Coie, J. D., & Lynam, D. (2006). Aggression and antisocial behavior in youth. In W. Damon (Series Ed.) and N. Eisenberg (Vol. Ed.), *Handbook of child psychology: Vol. 3. Social, emotional, and personality development* (6th ed., pp. 719–788). New York, NY: Wiley.

Eaton, D. K., Kann, L., Kinchen, S., Shanklin, S., Ross, J., Hawkins, J., … Wechsler, H. (2002). Youth Risk Behavior Surveillance—United States, 2009: Surveillance summaries. *Morbidity and Mortality Weekly Report, 59* (SS05), 1–142.

Elias, M. J., & Branden, L. R. (1988). Primary prevention of behavioral and emotional problems in school-aged populations. *School Psychology Review, 17*, 581–592.

Farmer, T. W., Hamm, J. V., Petrin, R. A., Robertson, D., Murray, R. A., Meece, J. L., & Brooks, D. S. (2010). Supporting early adolescent learning and social strengths: Promoting productive contexts for students at-risk for EBD during the transition to middle school. *Exceptionality, 18*, 94–106. doi: 10.1080/0936283100367192

Gottfredson, D. G. (1989). *Reducing disorderly behavior in middle schools*. Baltimore, MD: Center for Research on Elementary and Middle Schools.

Gutman, L. M., Sameroff, A. J., & Cole, R. C. (2003). Academic growth curve trajectories from 1st grade to 12th grade: Effects of multiple social risk factors and preschool child factors. *Developmental Psychology, 39*, 77–790.

Hemphill, S. A., Toumbourou, J. W., Herrenkohl, T. I., McMorris, B. J., & Catalano, R. F. (2006). The effect of school suspensions and arrests on subsequent adolescent antisocial behavior in Australia and the United States. *Journal of Adolescent Health, 39*, 736–744.

Jessor, R., Van Den Bos, J., Vanderryn, J., Costa, F. M., & Turbin, M. S. (1995). Protective factors in adolescent problem behavior: Moderator effects and developmental change. *Developmental Psychology, 31*, 923–933.

Jimerson, S. R., Swearer, S. M., & Espelage, D. L. (Eds.). (2010). *Handbook of bullying in schools: An international perspective.* New York, NY: Routledge.

Kaplan, S. G., & Cornell, D. G. (2005). Threats of violence by students in special education. *Behavioral Disorders, 31*, 107–119.

Krezmien, M. P., Leone, P. E., & Achilles, G. M. (2006). Suspension, race, and disability: Analysis of statewide practices and reporting. *Journal of Emotional and Behavioral Disorders, 14*, 217–226. doi: 10.1177/10634266060140040501

La Paro, K. M., Pianta, R. C., & Cox, M. (2000). Teachers' reported transition practices for children transitioning into kindergarten and first grade. *Exceptional Children, 67*, 7–20.

Lacourse, E., Nagin, D. S., Vitaro, F., Côté, S., Arsenault, L., & Tremblay, R. E. (2006). Prediction of early-onset deviant peer group affiliation: A 12-year longitudinal study. *Archives of General Psychiatry, 63*, 562–568.

Loeber, R., Pardini, D. A., Stouthamer-Loeber, M., & Raine, A. (2007). Do cognitive, physiological, and psychosocial risk and promotive factors predict desistance from delinquency in males? *Development and Psychopathology, 19*, 867–887. doi: 10.1017/S0954579407000429

Lynam, D. R., Charnigo, R., Moffitt, T. E., Raine, A., Loeber, R., & Stouthamer-Loeber, M. (2009). The stability of psychopathy across adolescence. *Development and Psychopathology, 21*, 1133–1153. doi: 10.1017/S0954579409990083

Masten, A. S., Best, K. M., & Garmezy, N. (1990). Resilience and development: Contributions from the study of children who overcome adversity. *Development and Psychopathology, 2*, 425–444.

Mayer, M. J., & Leone, P. E. (1999). A structural analysis of school violence and disruption: Implications for creating safer schools. *Education and Treatment of Children, 22*, 333–356.

McEvoy, A., & Welker, R. (2000). Antisocial behavior, academic failure, and school climate: A critical review. *Journal of Emotional and Behavioral Disorders, 8*, 130–140.

Moffitt, T. E. (1990). The neuropsychology of juvenile delinquency: A critical review. In M. Tonry & N. Morris (Eds.), *Crime and justice: A review of research* (vol. 12, pp. 99–169). Chicago, IL: University of Chicago Press.

Moffitt, T. E. (1993). Adolescence-limited and life-course persistent antisocial behavior: A developmental taxonomy. *Psychological Review, 100*, 674–701.

Moffitt, T. E., Arseneault, L., Jaffee, S. R., Kim-Cohen, J., Koenen, K. C., Odgers, C. L., … Viding, E. (2008). Research review: DSM-V conduct disorder research needs for an evidence base. *Journal of Child Psychology and Psychiatry, 49*, 3–33. doi: 10.1111/j.1469-7610.2007.01823.x

Morrison, G. M., & D'Incau, B. (2000). Developmental and service trajectories of students with disabilities recommended for expulsion from school. *Exceptional Children, 66*, 257–272.

Nipedal, C., Nesdale, D., & Killen, M. (2010). Social group norms, school norms, and children's aggressive intentions. *Aggressive Behavior, 36*, 195–204. doi: 10.1002/ab.20342

Nock, M. K., Kazdin, A. E., Hiripi, E., & Kessler, R. C. (2006). Prevalence, subtypes, and correlates of DSM-IV conduct disorder in the National Comorbidity Survey Replication. *Psychological Medicine, 36*, 699–710. doi: 10.1017/S0033291706007082

Odgers, C. L., Moffitt, T. E., Broadbent, J. M., Dickson, N., Hancox, R. J., Harrington, H., … Caspi, A. (2008). Female and male antisocial trajectories: From childhood origins to adult outcomes. *Development and Psychopathology, 20*, 673–716. doi: 10.1017/S0954579408000333

Olympia, D., Farley, M., Christiansen, E., Pettersson, W. J., & Clark, E. (2004). Social maladjustment and students with behavioral and emotional disorders: Revisiting basic assumptions and assessment issues. *Psychology in the Schools, 41*, 835–846.

Osher, D., Bear, G. G., Sprague, J. R., & Doyle, W. (2010). How can we improve school discipline? *Educational Researcher, 39*, 48–58. doi: 10.3102/ 0013189X09357618

Ostroff, C. (1992). The relationship between satisfaction, attitudes and performance: An organizational level analysis. *Journal of Applied Psychology, 77*, 963–974.

Patterson, G. R., & Yoerger, K. (2002). A developmental model for early- and late-onset delinquency. In J. B. Reid, G. R. Patterson, & J. Snyder (Eds.), *Antisocial behavior in children and adolescents: A development analysis and model for intervention* (pp. 147–172). Washington, DC: American Psychological Association.

Reinke, W. M., & Herman, K. C. (2002). Creating school environments that deter antisocial behaviors in youth. *Psychology in the Schools, 39*, 549–560.

Rutter, M. (Ed.). (1979). *Protective factors in children's responses to stress and disadvantage.* Hanover, NH: University Press of New England.

Sameroff, A. J. (2000). Dialectical processes in developmental psychopathology. In A. J. Sameroff, M. Lewis, & S. M. Miller (Eds.), *Handbook of developmental psychopathology* (2nd ed., pp. 23–40). New York, NY: Kluwer Academic/ Plenum.

Sameroff, A. J. (Ed.). (2009). *The transactional model of development: How children and contexts shape each other.* Washington, DC: American Psychological Association.

Scott, T., Nelson, C. M., & Liaupsin, C. J. (2001). Effective instruction: The forgotten component in preventing school violence. *Education and Treatment of Children, 24*, 309–322.

Sugden, S. G., Kile, S. J., & Hendren, R. L. (2006). Neurodevelopmental pathways to aggression: A model to understand and target treatment in youth. *Journal of Neuropsychiatry and Clinical Neuroscience, 18*, 302–317.

van Domburgh, L., Loeber, R., Bezemer, D., Stallings, R., & Stouthamer-Loeber, M. (2009). Childhood predictors of desistance and level of persistence in offending in early onset offenders. *Journal of Abnormal Child Psychology, 37*, 967–980. doi: 10.1007/s10802-009-9329-x

Walker, H. M., Ramsey, E., & Gresham, F. (2004). *Antisocial behavior in school: Evidence-based practices* (2nd ed.). Pacific Grove, CA: Brooks/Cole.

Welsh, B. C., Loeber, R., Stevens, B. R., Stouthamer-Loeber, M., Cohen, M. A., & Farrington, D. P. (2008). Costs of juvenile crime in urban areas: A longitudinal perspective. *Youth Violence and Juvenile Justice, 6*, 3–27. doi: 10.1177/1541204007308427

White, N. A., & Loeber, R. (2008). Bullying and special education as predictors of serious delinquency. *Journal of Research in Crime and Delinquency, 45*, 380–397. doi: 10.1177/0022427808322612

Wu, S. C., Pink, W. T., Crain, R. L., & Moles, O. (1982). Student suspension: A critical reappraisal. *The Urban Review, 14*, 245–303.

Zelli, A., Dodge, K. A., Lochman, J. E., Laird, R. D., & Conduct Problems Prevention Research Group. (1999). The distinction between beliefs legitimizing aggression and deviant processing of social cues: Testing measurement validity and the hypothesis that biased processing mediates the effects of beliefs on aggression. *Journal of Personality and Social Psychology, 77*, 150–166.

Making the Case for an International Perspective on School Violence

Implications for Theory, Research, Policy, and Assessment

Rami Benbenishty

BAR ILAN UNIVERSITY, ISRAEL

Ron Avi Astor

UNIVERSITY OF SOUTHERN CALIFORNIA, LOS ANGELES

Abstract

Based on review of empirical data on school violence internationally, the present chapter proposes a global perspective. Cross-country comparisons could help gain a perspective on how extreme the school safety situation is in a given country. Further, a cross-cultural perspective of school violence provides a rich source of insights about effective policies and interventions. Theories advanced to explain school violence in one culture can inform and stimulate comparative research in other countries to examine theoretical issues such as the relative influence of student characteristics and school context on victimization and perpetration of school violence. Finally, the chapter proposes an international study on school violence, discusses conceptual and methodological challenges in such a global collaboration, and suggests ways to overcome these challenges.

Concerns about school violence are shared around the world. Although lethal shootings in the United States have attracted most of the international media coverage (Herda-Rapp, 2003), reports from other parts of the world reveal that school violence is a serious global problem (Due et al., 2005; Due, Merlo, Harel-Fisch, & Damsgaard, 2009). Time and again the public in countries with cultures as diverse as Japan, Jordan, Brazil, Norway, Israel, Malaysia, the United States, and Ethiopia are alarmed by acts of senseless violence in their schools. Data suggest that an array of violent acts occur across all segments of U.S. society and in many countries across the globe, including decapitations in Japan, hangings in Norway, and group stabbings in Israel (Kachur et al., 1996; Smith et al., 1999).

Akiba, LeTendre, Baker, and Goesling (2002) also put forth a global perspective stating: "… school violence is a global phenomenon that affects one of the core institutions of modern society to some degree in virtually all nation-states" (p. 830). Based on the current review of empirical data on school violence internationally, we strongly support a global perspective on these phenomena.

This chapter is based on a review of numerous empirical studies and publications that examine school violence in a wide range of countries (e.g., Akiba et al., 2002; Akiba, 2008; Chen & Astor, 2009a; Currie et al., 2004; Eslea et al., 2003; Farrington & Ttofi, 2009; Obeidat, 1997; Ohsako, 1997; Smith, 2003; Smith, Cowie, Olafsson, & Liefooghe, 2002; Smith et al., 1999). The chapter discusses the potential contributions of international and cross-cultural perspectives and presents a range of questions and challenges that should be addressed by international studies. Finally, this chapter includes recommendations for a conceptual and methodological framework to design an international monitoring system for school violence.

Why an International and Cross-Cultural Perspective?

There are many reasons for advocating a perspective on school violence that incorporates the examination and comparison of multiple national and cultural contexts.

Raising National Awareness and Providing International Context

One important function of examining school violence in different countries is to develop cross-country comparisons. Such comparative data could be used to gain a perspective on how extreme the school safety situation is in a given country. Such international comparisons have a strong impact on the public within countries and greatly facilitate policy creation surrounding school violence in specific counties.

For instance, Menesini and Modiano (2003) report that comparative research showed that school violence in Italy was reported at a higher level than in other European and Western countries (being about as twice as high as in England and almost three times higher than in Norway). The authors claim that there was a major response by newspapers and television programs to these data that brought about awareness of the problem in Italian schools. These cross country comparisons prompted school principals and staff to become more interested in Italian-based interventions and to study school safety issues in-depth. This type of narrative has been repeated in other countries across the globe when the media has reported high rates of school violence compared with other countries (Astor, Benbenishty, Vinokur, & Zeira, 2006).

From a different perspective, in the United States, Akiba and associates (2002) examined the data of an international study (TIMSS) and made the argument that many other countries are experiencing either similar or higher levels of school violence than the United States. This kind of global contextualization helps countries situate their standings independent of media stories associated with school violence.

Creating a Global Inventory of Interventions and Policies

A cross-cultural perspective of school violence provides a rich source of insights about policies and interventions. In a recent special issue of *Educational Researcher* on school safety (Mayer & Cornell, 2010), Astor, Guerra, and Van Acker (2010) provided examples as to how learning from empirical approaches developed around the world could improve school violence research.

Countries across the globe could learn from each other's experience in terms of the effectiveness of policies and interventions (United Nations Educational, Scientific and Cultural Organization, 2007). To illustrate, the United States has invested billions of dollars in recent decades to address school violence. In fact, rates of serious school violence are on a steady decline for more than a decade (Dinkes, Kemp, & Baum, 2009). During this period many interventions were created and evaluated, and major policy guidelines were put in place in order to prevent school violence. Similar progress has been made in other countries (e.g., Australia; Slee, 2006). Further, international collaborations were created to develop training programs to build capacity in schools to prevent school violence (for instance, VISTOP, http://vistop.org/). The wealth of knowledge accumulated in these countries can help inform other countries which are facing similar issues.

To illustrate, the awareness to school violence in France has increased significantly in recent years. Dissatisfaction with current levels of violence, existing policies, and interventions has led to a new national initiative to address this social problem, headed by a school violence scholar, the president of the International Observatory of School Violence, Eric Debarbieux. As an important step in this national effort, an international scientific advisory board was assembled. The aim is to tap into the lessons learned in other countries and to examine their relevance to the French context.

The deliberations in this international advisory board highlight the complexity of transporting interventions and policies from one context to another. As the recent burgeoning literature on translational science amply demonstrates, interventions and policies developed and proved effective in one context may not translate well to other contexts (Brekke, Ell, & Palinkas, 2007; Glasgow & Emmons, 2007). For instance, evidence-based interventions that were developed in the United States to address school violence in urban schools with a large number of minority African American and Latino/a students may not be successful when implemented in French urban schools with a large number of Muslim North African students or with a significant proportion of Roma children. This challenge requires international collaboration to identify the factors that promote transporting school safety interventions and policy from country to country.

Understanding why certain cultures endorse or reject specific interventions may provide insights as to the likelihood of success of programs transported from another context. For example, mediation programs are mentioned in almost every U.S. national school safety report. By contrast, Olweus and Smith's anti-bullying programs are common in Europe, the United States, and Australia. Programs of restorative justice are common in Australia and New Zealand. Zero-tolerance policies and the use of electronic security (i.e., video cameras, sensors, metal detectors, and professional guards) are more common in the United States and England (e.g., Taylor, 2010).

An important step toward clarifying some of these issues would be systematic reviews that would compare the relative success of specific school violence programs across contexts. Thus, for instance, Farrington and Ttoti (2009) reviewed the literature on the effectiveness of anti-bullying programs across many countries. The findings indicate a wide variability in the outcomes of these programs. For instance, of ten U.S studies included in the analysis only half had strong effect sizes and close to half were more marginal. It is helpful to have these outcomes seen from a comparative interventional perspective. How is the cultural and social context of the country associated with the relative success of the program? The review suggests that programs implemented in Norway seem to work best. This could be related to the long Norwegian tradition of bullying research. It could also be associated with the fact that Scandinavian schools are of high quality, with small classes and well-trained teachers, and there is a Scandinavian tradition of state intervention in matters of social welfare.

Theoretical Issues Amenable to a Global Perspective

An international perspective can contribute significantly to theories of school violence. On the most basic level, theories advanced to explain school violence in one culture can inform and stimulate comparative research in other countries. For instance, Yoneyama and Naito (2003) advanced the theory on factors contributing to bullying by examining Japanese literature on school factors that contribute to *ijime* (bullying). Their analysis connects aspects of the role and structure of the Japanese educational system and characteristics of bullying behavior. They identified a relationship between class in Japan as a social group and the fact that most bullying behavior is carried out by a group of classmates against individual students. Also, they analyzed role expectations of Japanese teachers and showed how teacher-student interactions contribute to both teacher and student bullying behaviors. Such hypotheses and theoretical propositions advanced in the Japanese context should inform and enrich theory development in other countries that may differ in specific characteristics of their educational systems. For instance, one might expect to find different patterns of bullying (i.e., more individuals bullying other individuals) in educational systems that emphasize more individualistic ethos rather than the collectivistic ethos of the Japanese system.

The following sections present examples of how an international perspective can contribute to exploration of important theoretical issues.

The Relative Influence of Student Characteristics on Victimization and Perpetration of School Violence

An international perspective is needed in order to determine whether student characteristics are universally associated with school violence, or the nature of the relationships is sensitive to social contexts. To illustrate this issue the following sections will examine briefly two basic characteristics: gender and age. Smith, Madsen, and Moody (1999) reviewed the literature on bullying and demonstrated a clear decline in victimization as students grow older. These findings were replicated in several studies conducted in Western countries (Craig & Harel, 2004) and in Asian cultures (Chen & Astor, 2009a, 2009b). Still, the question remains whether this pattern is true in other parts of the world. The volume edited by Ohsako (1997) provides indications based on research in countries such as Ethiopia and Malaysia this age pattern may not hold in non-Western cultures.

Age may be connected to cultural norms surrounding bullying. For example, where the culture emphasizes the importance of seniority and age, older students may be more involved in bullying their younger peers. According to the accounts of Terefe and Mengistu (1997), school authorities view this form of bullying as normative and accept this kind of behavior. However, readers are cautioned not to make national or cultural interpretations without a convergence of data that is representative, qualitative, and otherwise empirically sound. Hypotheses about different national norms in non-European and Anglo/English-speaking cultures should be tested in future international research.

International studies may also shed new light on the relationships between gender and school violence. Currently, there is broad consensus that males are both perpetrators and victims of physical violence in school to a greater degree than females. Findings from several European countries regarding gender differences related to relational and indirect violence seem to be less consistent (see recent reviews and studies by Currie et al., 2004; Salmivalli & Kaukiainen, 2004; Tapper & Boulton, 2004). For instance, Craig and Harel (2004) noted that whereas males tend to bully others more than females in most counties surveyed in the Health Behaviors in School-aged Children study (HBSC; Currie et al., 2004), patterns of gender differences in bully victimization are far less consistent. The picture is even more complicated with regard to the interaction between age and gender. Benbenishty and Astor (2005) reported that the gap between victimization rates of males and females *grows* with age. In contrast, Craig and Harel (2004) concluded that in most of the 24 countries surveyed in the HBSC study, the trend was in the opposite direction and gender gaps were smaller among older students.

The Relative Influences of Multiple Contexts on School Violence

The questions as to similarities of effects across countries and cultures are not limited to student personal characteristics. In recent years, there have been calls urging scholars to move from a focus on individual characteristics of victims and bullies, such as age and gender, to an understanding of how contexts, both within and outside of school impact school violence (Akiba et al., 2002; Benbenishty & Astor, 2005; Chen & Astor, 2009a,b; Furlong & Morrison, 2000; Yoneyama & Naito, 2003). These approaches help examine how external contexts in which a school is embedded interact with internal school and student characteristics to influence levels of victimization in schools. These layered and nested contexts include the *school* (e.g., structural characteristics, social climate and policies against violence), the *neighborhood* (e.g., poverty, social organization, crime), students' *families* (e.g., education, family structure), *cultural* aspects of student and teacher population (e.g., religion, ethnic affiliation), and the *economic*, social, and political makeup of the country as a whole. An international system of research will help clarify both theoretically and practically the role of these nested contexts.

As an example, Akiba and colleagues (2002) utilized international survey data (TIMSS) on student victimization in 37 countries to test theoretical assumptions about the nature of school violence in different countries. They tested two sets of national-level variables: (a) known predictors of crime (both general and juvenile) and (b) factors related to the educational system itself. Their investigation demonstrated that factors inherent in the educational system (e.g., academic achievement, school climate, teacher-child relationships) are more strongly correlated with school violence than general crime, basic national economic conditions, and demographic characteristics. Additionally, secondary analyses by Akiba (2008) revealed that the same variables (witnessing a friend victimized and being the victim of theft) predict fear of being victimized in eighth graders in all participating countries. The author notes that whereas individual predictors of student fear (e.g., gender) were relatively consistent, school predictors varied more across the countries studied. Somewhat in contrast, recent research (Due et al., 2009; Elgar, Craig, Boyce, Morgan, & Vella-Zarb, 2009) suggests that between-countries differences in prevalence rates of school violence may be connected to levels of income inequality in the country.

Such conflicting international findings may help refine a theory on the "spill over" of political and community violence into schools (Benbenishty & Astor, 2005). For instance, Akiba and associates (2002) noted variable levels of association of different types of school victimization (e.g., sexual assaults) to community crime. This pattern was also found in a study in Israel (Khoury-Kassabri, Benbenishty, Astor, & Zeira, 2004) in which more severe types of school victimization were related to poor neighborhoods, compared with mild/moderate types of victimization.

A Proposal for a World Wide Study of School Violence

Based on a review of reports on school violence from across the world and the above analysis, Benbenishty and Astor (2008) recommended a proactive research agenda for an international perspective on school violence and suggested a worldwide study to monitor school violence. Such a study would follow examples of international studies on academic achievements (e.g., TIMSS) and health behaviors (HBSC) and would utilize standardized measures and methods to serve as a platform for global learning and monitoring of school violence over time.

The proposed study would address the multiple perspectives of students, teachers, princi-pals, and whenever possible, parents. Each of these constituents should be asked questions about aspects of school victimization and climate that are relevant to their specific roles and manifesta-tions of problems in the school community in addition to a set of questions that will be identical for all participating schools. This ecologically sensitive approach could help illuminate multiple perspectives, as well as facilitate analyses addressing nested systems.

The suggested international study would provide a detailed picture for each participating country. Due to the use of standardized and highly congruent instruments across participating countries, meaningful comparisons would be facilitated. These comparisons could include preva-lence rates for a wide array of school violence behaviors and school climate measures, as well as comparisons across sub-groups of students, staff, and parents. Furthermore, the interrelationships between the different perspectives of the various members of the school community would be compared across countries, to identify settings in which significant congruence or discord is more pronounced.

Such an international collaboration would provide an excellent opportunity to address theo-retical questions presented in earlier sections, such as the role of multiple contexts in determin-ing school violence. In order to be able to test these hypotheses, sampling and analysis could be conducted from both student- and school-level perspectives. This design would enable the measurement of school and neighborhood level variables, facilitating tests of hypotheses on the role of contexts in explaining levels of school violence. Further, this approach could also create a foundation for examining how different countries vary in homogeneity of levels of violence in their schools. Thus, among other advantages, such a design would allow examination of what is similar and different in schools high or low on school violence across the world (Astor, Benben-ishty, & Estrada, 2009).

Conceptual Considerations and Challenges in an International Study on School Violence Definitions, Connotations, Interpretations, and Meanings

When cross-cultural comparisons are made, very often, different forms of violence are inappro-priately compared. The two most used terms in the English literature are "bullying" and "school violence." In many publications, they are often used interchangeably, even though they are not conceptually or theoretically the same. There is a pressing need to either distinguish between what is school violence and bullying, or better explain the relationship between the two terms. As Devine and Lawson (2003) noted, bullying is more often used in European countries whereas school violence is a term used more often in the United States. School violence is a general term that may include many different aspects of victimization. It is practically impossible to com-pare reports that use "school violence" as a generic term without providing the kinds of specific behaviors that are included under this term. Bullying, on the other hand, has had a quite precise theoretical definition (e.g., Olweus, 1991), to the point that it could allow direct international comparisons. Hence, the World Health Organization conducted a cross-national study of Health Behaviors in School-Aged Children (HBSC) that uses and defines the term "bully" (e.g., Currie et al., 2004). Nevertheless, most current, large-scale international research does not strictly use commonly agreed upon definitions of bullying (e.g., that the bully have asymmetrical power over the victim, that the bullying event be part of a large repeating pattern of events, etc.). Yet, infer-ences are made about bullying. Benbenishty and Astor (2005) argued that bullying is a specific subset of school violence that could overlap with a wide array of school violence behaviors (e.g., sexual harassment, weapon use, school fights). However, those behaviors may not be considered bullying if they do not conform to the formal definition of bullying. Furlong and colleagues also make this similar and important point (Furlong, Morrison, & Greif, 2003; Greif, Furlong, & Morrison, 2003).

Review of the literature suggests that most international studies employ diverse meanings, measures, and understanding of which behaviors should be included in the term bully (Benbenishty & Astor, 2003). This could have a dramatic impact on the interpretation of cross-national comparisons. For example, Harel, Kenny, and Rahav (1997) asked Israeli students whether they were "bullied." The questions (in Hebrew) stated that they were being asked about *hatrada* (harassment), *hatzaka* (teasing), and *biryonoot* (mainly physical bullying). Each of these words in Hebrew has quite a specific meaning. The direct word for bullying in Hebrew strongly implies physical force exerted by a strong, well-built student (an antisocial "thug"). The overall term "bullying" in Japan has a strong connotation of social isolation, impurity, and shame. To a large extent, the set of behaviors, connotations and cultural interpretations the Japanese associate with "ijime" seem distant from the Israeli term "biryonoot" for bully. How might data on students in different cultures with different connotations for the word bullying be synthesized and integrated in order to respond to questions about bullying?

Indeed, Smith Cowie, Olafsson, and Liefooghe (2002) studied school children (ages 8–14) from 14 countries and found significant differences in the ways the term "bullying" was understood in the different countries. Similarly, a study among parents of school-aged children in five countries (Italy, Spain, Portugal, England, and Japan) found clear differences in the ways the term was understood by parents. Cultures also varied on the extent to which the term "bullying" used in everyday language resembled the scientific definition of the term (Smorti, Menesini, & Smith, 2003; Smith & Monks, 2008). In a recent review, Swearer Espelage, Vaillancourt, and Hymel (2010) analyzed how such differences in definitions and conceptualizations negatively affect efforts to learn from research on how to implement bullying interventions in schools.

One potential solution is to use the same scientific definition, and agreed upon instruments, across many countries. The World Health Organization uses the Health Behavior in School-aged Children (HBSC) instruments that provide the definition of bullying to the respondents. This effort could be coupled with smaller qualitative studies that aim towards understanding the social and cultural meanings of the term bullying in each of the participating countries. It should be noted, however, that policy makers and the public in different countries are likely to have diverse understandings and interpretations of the same concept, regardless of formal scientific definitions. Hence, Israeli policy makers presented with findings on high levels of bullying would probably have a different image of the problem compared with South African, Brazilian, Canadian, or Japanese policy makers considering similar findings.

An Operational Solution: Using Self-Reports of a Wide Range of Specific and Concrete School Violence Behaviors

Based on the above analysis, the authors propose using self reports as the primary source of information on victimization, perpetration, and school climate (see a discussion of the merits of self-report on school victimization in the report from the Surgeon General, Department of Health and Human Services, 2001). Further, in order to reduce variability in cultural definitions and interpretations, these self reports should focus on specific behaviors and refrain as much as possible from using loosely defined abstract labels (such as bully) that may have different meanings and connotations in different countries. Hence, asking students whether larger or stronger students pushed them is probably understood more similarly across cultures than the question of whether or not they were bullied.

The work by Furlong and associates (e.g., Furlong, Chung, Bates, & Morrison, 1995; Furlong, Greif, Bates, Whipple, Jimenez, & Morrison, 2005) provides a good example of the suggested approach. The California School Climate & Safety Survey contains questions about victimization linked to an extensive list of concrete and specific victimization types. The merits of this approach were clear when the instrument was utilized in the first National Study of

School Violence in Israel. Translation of the specific and concrete behaviors in the instrument and the comparisons with available U.S. data were relatively straightforward, especially when compared to parallel attempts to translate terms such as "bully" (Benbenishty & Astor, 2005).

Further, the analyses of the findings showed the advantages of using this wide range of victimization types. The detail-rich instrument yielded a complex and nuanced picture and highlighted the multifaceted nature of school victimization. It enabled analysis and description of which forms of victimization are more frequent in Israeli schools and which behaviors are relatively rare. The findings in Israel were comparable with data in Furlong and colleagues' studies in Southern California (Benbenishty & Astor, 2005) that examined differences in prevalence rates and structure of victimization.

Furthermore, the findings that included a wide range of behaviors showed that various aspects of victimization have different patterns of association with student characteristics, such as gender and age, and with school context variables, such as poverty in the school neighborhood. Without the large number of behaviors examined, it would not have been possible to ascertain how forms of school violence were related to each other and to other social phenomena in the Israeli context. These patterns may or may not be similar across cultures. Thus, school violence studies should examine the prevalence of a wide range of victimization types.

Psychometric Challenges in Comparing across Contexts

Using the same instrument across different contexts is not without challenges. In order to interpret differences across contexts in a valid manner, it is important to examine scale comparability across contexts. It is common to examine several aspects of such comparability: (a) to what extent the *structure* of the instrument is similar (e.g., to what extent the same items create similar factors across the different settings); (b) to what extent each of the individual items in the scale have the same relationship to the full scale score, across settings (scalar equivalence, van de Vijver and Poortinga, 2005; Waller, Compas, Hollon, & Beckjord, 2005); and (c) to what extent the scores generated by a measure have similar precursors, consequents, and correlates across the various settings (functional equivalence, Knight, Little, Losoya, & Mulvey, 2004).

Establishing scale comparability is a complex process and a discussion of the psychometric issues is beyond the scope of this chapter. Nevertheless, the authors caution against over-reliance on methodological considerations, at the expense of understanding the real complexities involved in comparing across nations and cultures. To illustrate, factor analyses of self reports of victimization in schools in two countries may reveal two different structures—in one country items are grouped into two factors pertaining to severe and moderate victimization, and in the other country they align with two other factors—direct vs. indirect types of victimization. From a strictly methodological point of view, these findings may be interpreted as reflecting low structural equivalence that reduces the value of the comparison. From a more conceptual and theoretical point of view, these findings may tell an important story on two cultures that have different ways of experiencing and interpreting interpersonal behaviors in school.

Including a Focus on Staff-Initiated Victimization

Studies of school violence across the world differ in whether they include staff victimization of students. Studies on prevalence of school violence in the U.S. rarely address victimization by staff. Although there have been state and federal mandates to survey school staff, few if any have asked about staff maltreatment of students. The extensive work by Hyman and associates (e.g., Hyman, 1990; Hyman & Perone, 1998) on the role of staff in inducing trauma among students is the exception rather than the norm. Similarly, a review of reports from 24 European countries

Table 2.1   Summary of Implications for Practice and Policy

- Cross country comparisons are important because they could provide:
  - Context and perspective to understand local data on school violence
  - A rich source of insights about policies and interventions proven effective
- Evidence-based programs and interventions do not always translate across country contexts, and transferability should be examined carefully
- Global perspective could contribute to theory and help identify the role of individual characteristics and school contexts which influence school violence
- A world wide study of school violence should be designed. This collaborative study should:
  - Address the multiple perspectives of students, teachers, principals, and whenever possible, parents
  - Design sampling and analysis from both student- and school-level perspectives
  - Use self-report of a wide range of specific and concrete violent behaviors and perceptions of school cli mate and policies
  - Include a focus on staff-initiated victimization

reveals minimal reference to staff victimizing students (Smith, 2003). In contrast, reports from other parts of the world address the role of staff vis-à-vis school violence. Staff may play direct and indirect roles in victimizing students. The international literature reveals how teachers' behaviors may actually promote bullying of certain students by their peers (Yoneyama & Naito, 2003). Other studies, mainly from developing countries, present teachers as one of the main sources of victimization of students. Hence, in places like Malaysia, Ethiopia, Brazil, and other countries in Latin America, teachers may use physically and verbally aversive discipline measures (e.g., Salas, 1997).

The potential contribution of including staff-initiated violence in studies of school violence has been clearly demonstrated in Israel. As described in Chapter 16 of this volume and in a series of papers (Benbenishty, Zeira, & Astor, 2002; Benbenishty, Zeira, Astor, & Khoury-Kassabri, 2002; Khoury-Kassabri, Astor, & Benbenishty, 2008), representative findings on staff violence contribute to better theoretical understanding of the phenomenon and to efforts to address this problem that affect so many students, especially students in more vulnerable groups in society. In conclusion, given that staff may play such an important role in victimizing, as well as protecting students, reference to staff-initiated violence and more protective behaviors of staff should be included in international comparisons of school violence.

Concluding Comments

School violence is a global phenomenon. A review of the literature from across the world shows both the similarities across diverse cultures and many different patterns that reflect the unique characteristics of cultural and national contexts. This richness provides unique opportunities for comparisons and mutual learning that can facilitate examination and development of theories of school violence, and can help expand the repertoire of effective interventions. In the present chapter the authors propose a collaborative study that will bring together researchers and policy makers from across the world and employ methods and instruments that will help further theory and global efforts to reduce school violence. The authors' call for an international study of school violence was accepted by the International Observatory of School Violence in its annual meeting in Lisbon (2008). Since then, however, the first steps toward realizing this mission revealed major practical obstacles. Language barriers in combination with major discrepancies between developing and developed countries in access to resources are formidable challenges. There is a clear need to form a global collaboration, perhaps through the United Nations or World Bank, in order to address this significant global social problem of school violence.

References

Akiba, M. (2008). Predictors of student fear of school violence: A comparative study of eighth graders in 33 countries. *School Effectiveness and School Improvement, 19*, 51–72. doi:10.1080/09243450801936878

Akiba, M., Letendre, G. K., Baker, D. P., & Goesling, B. (2002). Student victimization: National and school systems effects on school violence in 37 nations. *American Educational Research Journal, 39*, 829–853. doi:10.3102/00028312039004829

Astor, R. A., Benbenishty, R., & Estrada, J. (2009). School violence and theoretically atypical schools: The principal's centrality in orchestrating safe schools. *American Educational Research Journal, 46*, 423–461. doi:10.3102/0002831208329598

Astor, R. A., Benbenishty, R., Vinokur, A., & Zeira, A. (2006). Arab and Jewish elementary school students' perception of fear and school violence: Understanding the influence of school context. *British Journal of Educational Psychology, 76*, 91–118. doi:10.1348/000709905X37307

Astor, R. A., Guerra, N., & Van Acker, R. (2010). How can we improve school safety research? *Educational Researcher, 39*, 69–78. doi:10.3102/0013189X09357619

Benbenishty, R., & Astor, R. A. (2003). Cultural specific and cross-cultural bully/ victim patterns: The response from Israel. In P. K. Smith, (Ed) *Violence in schools: The response in Europe* (pp. 317–331). New York: RoutledgeFalmer.

Benbenishty, R., & Astor, R. A. (2005). *School violence in context: Culture, neighborhood, family, school, and gender.* New York: Oxford University Press.

Benbenishty, R., & Astor, R. A. (2008). School violence in an international context : A call for global collaboration in research and prevention. *International Journal of School Violence, 7*, 59–80.

Benbenishty, R., Zeira, A., Astor, R. A., & Khoury-Kassabri, M. (2002). Maltreatment of primary school students by educational staff in Israel. *Child Abuse and Neglect, 26*, 1291-1309. doi:10.1016/S0145-2134(02)00416-7

Benbenishty, R., Zeira, A., & Astor, R. A. (2002). Children's reports of emotional, physical and sexual maltreatment by educational staff in Israel. *Child Abuse & Neglect. 26*, 763–782. doi:10.1016/S0145-2134(02)00350-2

Brekke, J. S., Ell, K., & Palinkas, L. A. (2007). Translational science at the National Institute of Mental Health: Can social work take its rightful place? *Research on Social Work Practice, 27,* 123–133.doi:10.1177/1049731506293693

Chen, J. K., & Astor, R. A. (2009a). Students' reports of violence against teachers in Taiwanese schools. *Journal of School Violence, 8*, 2–17. doi:10.1080/15388220802067680

Chen, J. K., & Astor, R. A. (2009b). The perpetration of school violence in Taiwan: An analysis of gender, grade level, school type. *School Psychology International, 30*, 568–584. doi:10.1177/0143034309107076

Craig, W. M., & Harel, Y. (2004). Bullying, physical fighting and victimization. In C. Currie, C. Roberts, A. Morgan, R. Smith, W. Settertobulte, O. Samdal, & V. B. Rasmussen (Eds.), *Young people's health in context: Health Behavior in school-aged children (HBSC) study: International report from the 2001/2002 survey* (pp. 133–144). Health Policy for Children and Adolescents, No. 4. Copenhagen, Sweden: World Health Organization.

Currie, C., Roberts, C., Morgan, A., Smith, R., Settertobulte, W., Samdal, O., & Rasmussen, V. B. (Eds.). (2004). *Young people's health in context: Health behavior in school-aged children (HBSC) study: International report from the 2001/2002 survey.* Health Policy for Children and Adolescents, No. 4. Copenhagen, Sweden: World Health Organization.

Department of Health and Human Services (DHHS). (2001) Youth violence: A report from the Surgeon General. Retrieved July 1, 2004, from http://www.surgeongeneral.gov/library/youthviolence/report.html#foreward

Devine, J., & Lawson, H. A. (2003). The complexity of school violence: Commentary from the US. In P. K. Smith (Ed.), *Violence in schools* (pp. 332–350). London: RoutledgeFalmer.

Dinkes, R., Kemp, J., & Baum, K. (2009). *Indicators of School Crime and Safety: 2009* (NCES 2010–012/NCJ 228478). National Center for Education Statistics, Institute of Education Sciences, U.S. Department of Education, and Bureau of Justice Statistics, Office of Justice Programs, U.S. Department of Justice. Washington, DC: U.S. Government Prnting Office.

Due, P., Holstein, B. E., Lynch, J., Diderichsen, F., Gabhain, S. N., Scheidt, P., et al. (2005). Bullying and symptoms among school-aged children: international comparative cross sectional study in 28 countries. *The European Journal of Public Health, 15*, 128–132. doi:10.1093/eurpub/cki105

Due, P., Merlo, J., Harel-Fisch, Y., & Damsgaard, M. T. (2009). Socioeconomic inequality in exposure to bullying during adolescence: A comparative, cross-sectional, multilevel study in 35 countries. *American Journal of Public Health, 99*, 907–914. doi:10.2105/AJPH.2008.139303

Elgar, F. J., Craig, W., Boyce, W., Morgan, A., & Vella-Zarb, R. (2009). Income inequality and school bullying: Multilevel study of adolescents in 37 countries. *Journal of Adolescent Health, 45*, 351–359. doi:10.1016/j.jadohealth.2009.04.004

Eslea, M., Menesini, E., Morita, Y., O'Moore, M., Mora-Merchan, J. A., Pereira, B., & Smith, P. K. (2003). Friendship and loneliness among bullies and victims: Data from seven countries. *Aggressive Behavior, 30*, 71–83. doi:10.1002/ab.20006

Farrington, D. P., & Ttofi, M. M. (2009). School-based programs to reduce bullying and victimization [Special issue]. *Campbell Systematic Reviews, 6.*

Furlong, M. J., Chung, A., Bates, M., & Morrison, R. L. (1995). Profiles of non-victims and multiple-victims of school violence. *Education and Treatment of Children, 18*, 282–298.

Furlong, M. J., Greif, J. L., Bates, M. P., Whipple, A. D., Jimenez, T. C., & Morrison, R. (2005). Development of the California School Climate and Safety Survey–Short Form. *Psychology in the Schools, 42*, 137–149. doi:10.1002/pits.20053

Furlong, M., & Morrison, G. (2000). The school in school violence: Definitions and facts. *Journal of Emotional and Behavioral Disorders, 8*, 71–82. doi:10.1177/106342660000800203

Furlong, M. J., Morrison, G. M., & Greif, J. (2003). Reaching an American coherence on bullying prevention: Reactions to the School Psychology Review special issue on school bullying. *School Psychology Review, 32*, 456–470.

Glasgow, R. E., & Emmons, K. M. (2007). How can we Increase translation of research into practice? Types of evidence needed. *Annual Review of Public Health, 28*, 413–433. doi:10.1146/annurev.publhealth.28.021406.144145

Greif, J. L, Furlong, M. J., Morrison, G. (2003, November). Operationally defining "bullying" [Letter to the editor]. *Archives of Pediatrics and Adolescent Medicine, 157*, 1134–1135. doi:10.1001/archpedi.157.11.1134-b

Harel, Y., Kenny, D., & Rahav, G. (1997). *Youth in Israel: Social welfare, health and risk behaviors from international perspectives.* Jerusalem: Joint Distribution Committee. [Hebrew]

Herda-Rapp, H. (2003). The social construction of local school violence threats by the news media and professional organizations. *Sociological Enquiry, 73*, 545–574. doi:10.1111/1475-682X.00071

Hyman, I. A. (1990). *Reading, writing, and the hickory stick.* Lexington, MA: Lexington Books.

Hyman I. A., & Perone, D. C. (1998). The other side of school violence: Educator policies and practices that may contribute to student misbehavior. *Journal of School Psychology, 36*, 7–27. doi:10.1016/S0022-4405(97)87007-0

Kachur, P., Stennies, G., Powell, K., Modzeleski, W., Stephens, R., Murphy, R., … Lowry, R. (1996). School-associated violent deaths in the United States, 1992 to 1994. *Journal of the American Medical Association, 275*, 1729–1733.

Khoury-Kassabri, M., Astor, R. A., & Benbenishty, R. (2008). Student victimization by school staff in the context of an Israeli national school safety campaign. *Aggressive Behavior, 34*, 1–8. doi:10.1002/ab.20180

Khoury-Kassabri, M. Benbenishty, R. Astor, R. A., & Zeira, A. (2004). The contributions of community, family, and school variables on student victimization. *American Journal of Community Psychology, 34*, 187–204. doi:10.1007/s10464-004-7414-4

Knight, G. P., Little, M., Losoya, S. H., & Mulvey, E. P. (2004). The self-report of offending among serious juvenile offenders: Cross-gender, cross-ethnic/race measurement equivalence. *Youth Violence and Juvenile Justice, 2*, 273–295. doi:10.1177/1541204004265878

Mayer, M. J., & Cornell, D. G. (2010). New perspectives on school safety and volence prevention: Guest editors' preface. *Educational Researcher, 39*(5), 5–6. doi:10.3102/0013189X09356778

Menesini, E., & Modiano, R. (2003). A multifaceted reality: A report from Italy. In P. K. Smith (Ed.), *Violence in schools: The response in Europe* (pp. 153–168). London: RoutledgeFalmer.

Obeidat, Z. (1997). Bullying and violence in the Jordanian school. In T. Ohsako (Ed.), *Violence at school: Global issues and interventions* (pp. 20–33). Paris: UNESCO.

Ohsako, T. (Ed.). (1997). *Violence at school: Global issues and interventions.* Paris: UNESCO.

Olweus, D. (1991). Bully/victim problems among school children: Some basic facts and effects of a school-based intervention program. In D. Pepler & K. Rubin (Eds.), *The development and treatment of childhood aggression* (pp. 411–448). Hillsdale, NJ: Erlbaum.

Salas, L. M. (1997). Violence and aggression in the schools of Columbia, El Salvador, Guatemala, Nicaragua and Peru. In T. Ohsako (Ed.), *Violence at school: Global issues and interventions* (pp. 110–127). Paris: UNESCO.

Salmivalli, C., & Kaukiainen, A. (2004). "Female aggression" revisited: Variable and person-centered approaches to studying gender differences in different types of aggression. *Aggressive Behavior, 30*, 158–163. doi:10.1002/ab.20012

Slee, P. T. (2006). The P.E.A.C.E. Pack: A whole-school program for reducing school bullying. In H. McGrath and T. Nobel (Eds.), *Bullying solutions: Evidence-based approaches to bullying in Australian schools* (pp. 85–101). Sydney, Australia: Pearson Longman:.

Smith, P. K. (Ed.). (2003). *Violence in schools: The response in Europe.* London: RoutledgeFalmer.

Smith, P. K., Cowie, H., Olafsson, R. F., & Liefooghe, A. P. (2002). Definitions of bullying: A comparison of terms used, and age and gender differences, in a fourteen-country international comparison. *Child Development, 73*, 1119–1133. doi:10.1111/1467-8624.00461

Smith, P. K., Madsen K. C., & Moody J. C. (1999). What causes the age decline in reports of being bullied at school? Towards a developmental analysis of risks of being bullied. *Educational Researcher, 41*, 267–285.

Smith, P. K., & Monks, C. P. (2008). Concepts of bullying: Developmental and cultural aspects. *International Journal of Adolescent Medicine and Health, 20*, 101–112.

Smith, P. K., Morita, Y., Junger-Tas, J., Olweus, D., Catalano, R., & Slee, P. (1999). *The nature of school bullying: A cross-national perspective.* New York: Routledge.

Smorti, A., Menesini, E., & Smith, P. K. (2003). Parents' definitions of children's bullying in a five-country comparison. *Journal of Cross-Cultural Psychology, 34*, 417–432. doi:10.1177/0022022103034004003

Swearer, S. M., Espelage, D. L., Vaillancourt, T., & Hymel, S. (2010). What can be done about school bullying? Linking research to educational practice. *Educational Researcher, 39*, 38–47. doi:10.3102/0013189X09357622

Tapper, K., & Boulton, M. (2004). Sex differences in levels of physical, verbal and indirect aggression amongst primary school children and their associations with beliefs about aggression. *Aggressive Behavior, 30*, 123–145. doi:10.1002/ab.20010

Taylor, E. (2010). I spy with my little eye: The use of CCTV in school and the impact on privacy. *The Sociological Review, 58*, 381–405. doi:10.1111/j.1467-954X.2010.01930.x

Terefe, D., & Mengistu, D. (1997). Violence in Ethiopian schools: A study of some school in Addis-Ababa. In T. Ohsako (Ed.), *Violence at school: Global issues and interventions* (pp. 34–56). Paris: UNESCO.

United Nations Educational, Scientific and Cultural Organization (UNESCO). (2007, June). Expert meeting *"Stopping violence in schools: What works?"* UNESCO Headquarters, Paris. Downloaded September 29, 2010, from http://unesdoc.unesco.org/images/0015/001557/155767e.pdf

van de Vijver, F. J. R., & Poortinga, Y. H. (2005). Conceptual and methodological issues in adapting tests. In R. K. Hambleton, P. F. Merenda, & C. D. Spielberger (Eds.), *Adapting educational and psychological tests for cross-cultural assessment* (pp. 39–63). Mahwah, NJ: Erlbaum.

Waller, N. G., Compas, B. E., Hollon, S. D., & Beckjord, E. (2005). Measurement of depressive symptoms in women with breast cancer and women with clinical depression: A differential item functioning analysis. *Journal of Clinical Psychology in Medical Settings, 12*, 127–141. doi:10.1007/s10880-005-3273-x

Yoneyama, S., & Naito, A. (2003). Problems with the paradigm: The school as a factor in understanding bullying (with special reference to Japan). *British Journal of Sociology of Education, 24*, 315–330. doi:10.1080/01425690301894

Developing Safe, Supportive, and Effective Schools

Facilitating Student Success to Reduce School Violence

David Osher and Kevin P. Dwyer

AMERICAN INSTITUTES FOR RESEARCH, WASHINGTON, DC

Shane R. Jimerson and Jacqueline A. Brown

UNIVERSITY OF CALIFORNIA, SANTA BARBARA

Abstract

A safe and effective school framework aligns school safety, student support, and academic achievement across individual, classroom, school, and ideally, community levels. The risk and protective factors for academic, social, and behavioral problems are often intertwined; thus, interventions that target one domain frequently impact other domains. This chapter describes a comprehensive three-level approach to align student support, school safety, and academic achievement. The first section provides an overview of the connections between and among student support, school safety, and academic achievement. The second section provides the conceptual underpinnings for implementing and a comprehensive approach. The final section provides a brief description of how to apply this model to students and schools that have different needs and strengths. Creating safe, supportive, and effective schools will reduce school violence.

Aligning Safety, Support, and Achievement

Although student support, school safety, and academic achievement are often discussed independently, they are interactive and often interdependent. For example, school safety is one correlate of attendance and academic achievement (Barton, 2003; Bryk, Sebring, Allensworth, Luppescu, & Easton, 2009; Osher & Kendziora, 2010) and the school environment plays an important role in preventing childhood depression (Herman, Reinke, Parkin, Traylor, & Agarwal, 2009). Analyses of data from the National Longitudinal Study of Adolescent Health (Add Health) suggest that youth who are failing, skipping, and doing poorly in school or feel disconnected from school, are at higher risk of early health risk behavior (Blum, 2001). The Add Health data also show that teenagers report substantially stronger feelings of connectedness when they get along with each other, pay attention, and hand in assignments on time (Blum, 2001).

While some school safety approaches focus on threat assessment or physical safety, a comprehensive approach emphasizes and addresses the social and emotional as well as the physical aspects of safety. For example, students may miss school due to fears for their physical safety and of emotional ridicule or threat (Garbarino & deLara, 2002), including being bullied or harassed by students and staff for their gender, sexual orientation, appearance, and/or disability. Social and emotional threats appear to be far more common than physical attacks (Bear, Webster-Stratton, Furlong, & Rhee, 2000). Feeling emotionally safe, which often depends on whether students ask for help and acknowledge mistakes (Lee, Smith, Perry, & Smylie, 1999), is critical to learning (Osher & Kendziora, 2010; Osher et al., 2008). This climate of safety can contribute to students seeking help for themselves and others, and in doing so, reducing the risk of violence (Osher & Dwyer, 2005).

Effective schools foster and support high academic and behavioral standards making achievement within these schools both a collective and individual phenomena. Collective components of achievement involve the characteristics of the school community, including its culture, structure, human resources, and student members. These factors vary considerably across schools. Individual components comprise both student and adult characteristics. Adult characteristics include the knowledge, skills, beliefs, attitudes, and behaviors of school-based staff. Beliefs and attitudes include adults' sense of their role (e.g., Does a teacher view student support as part of their role), as well as teacher beliefs and attitudes towards students and each other (Bryk & Schneider, 2002; Osher et al., 2008). Capacity to meet the many challenges that adults face requires ongoing training and support of skills and practices. Training should be focused, support skill mastery and necessary attitudinal change, and be delivered in a manner that develops or enhances the capacity of school staff and families to collaborate and employ effective strategies and approaches. Adults should be prepared to be both interpersonally and culturally competent. Administrative support is vital, including the moral, logistical, and technical support needed to implement these approaches effectively (e.g., principal leadership, monitoring, and coaching).

Student characteristics consist of academic and social-emotional skills as well as behavioral and psychological characteristics. Behavioral characteristics include preparedness, attendance, attentiveness, and school engagement (e.g., time on task; Connell, Spencer, & Aber, 1994). Psychological characteristics include motivation, psychological engagement, and perseverance, the absence of which has been related to dropping out (Fredricks, Blumenfeld, Friedel, & Paris, 2005). Bryk and Thum's (1989) analysis of the effects of high school organization on dropping out found that absenteeism was higher in schools with more discipline problems and where principals reported teacher problems. In addition, the number of students dropping out is lower when they feel safe, academic emphasis is greater, faculty are interested in and engaged with students, students feel that discipline policies are fair, and there is less internal differentiation among students.

These adult and student factors both contribute to s,chool climate, which contributes to behavioral and academic outcomes. For example, research examining the effects of high school organization on dropping out has shown that school dropout rates are lower when students perceive themselves as having more positive relationships with their teachers (Lee & Burkam, 2003).

Because students need appropriate support to facilitate learning and address the barriers to learning, successful schools often have high levels of academic emphasis in combination with student support (Adelman & Taylor, 2000). This may be true in schools that serve students challenged by multiple risk factors (Ancess, 2003; Pianta & Walsh, 1996; Shouse, 1996). Academic emphasis includes instructional leadership, effective pedagogy, well-trained teachers, and an explicit focus on teaching and learning. Student support includes (a) connecting positively with adults, (b) supporting prosocial student interactions in an inclusive school community, (c) teaching and supporting the development and use of social emotional learning (SEL) skills, (d) employing positive behavioral supports, and (e) providing students with effective opportunities to learn. Successful schools provide students and staff with the support necessary to promote high achievement and the intensity of support is varied to address student and school needs. Connecting resources maximizes the chances for success by aligning school and community student support resources.

Conceptual Basis for a Three-Level Approach to Align Safety, Support, and Achievement

The conceptual roots of a comprehensive approach are grounded in a variety of disciplines, frameworks, and fields related to children's learning and behavior, which are described in Table 3.1. Although the models that come out of the described knowledge areas are distinct, the models and empirical data that ground them can be aligned (e.g., Dryfoos, 1990). For example, school-related transactions take place in nested environments (e.g., home, community, school, and classroom), and change over the life span as does the importance of social fields. Developmental epidemiological approaches can study the impact of interventions among populations over time (Kellam, Rebok, Wilson, & Mayer, 1994). Similarly, a public health model can integrate both promotion of positive youth development and prevention of problems (Davis, 2002).

Research suggests that risk and protective factors underlying problem behavior predict positive youth development, suggesting that an approach that reduces risk and enhances protection is likely to enhance youth wellness, while reducing future problem behaviors (Catalano, Berglund, Ryan, Lonczak, & Hawkins, 2004; Catalano, Hawkins, Berglund, Pollard, & Arthur, 2002). Further, although the intellectual foundations of work in positive youth development is not necessarily based in behavioral theory, the behavioral principles of reinforcement and social learning can be aligned with youth development approaches (Bandura, 1995). This does not mean that a hodgepodge approach be taken; the nuances and specifics of each framework must be addressed. For example, a focus on risk factors alone does not produce high quality outcomes (Pittman, 1991), but research on risk and protection suggests that an exclusive focus on developmental assets will not eliminate the impact of risk factors (Pollard, Hawkins, & Arthur, 1999). Further syntheses of research from different paradigms will help coordinate problem solving and help schools better predict and prevent individual and system failures.

In addition to the above considerations, there are a number of relevant fields of inquiry. They include research on school effectiveness, which examines school effects, improvement, reform, and size (Teddlie & Reynolds, 2000); school safety, discipline, and violence prevention (Gottfredson et al., 2000; Osher, Bear, Sprague, & Doyle, 2010; U.S. Public Health Service, 2000); and research on instruction, curriculum, and assessment, identifying effective approaches to working with students (Marzano, 2003). Other fields include research on consultation and team problem solving, where interventions are implemented through training, modeling, and ongoing coaching (Kratochwill & Bergan, 1990), as well as research on cultural competence, culturally responsive teaching, and multicultural education. This latter research examines the nature of disparities among youth of diverse cultural backgrounds and identifies what works in the education of children of color (Osher, Cartledge, Oswald, Artiles, & Coutinho, 2004; U.S. Public Health Service, 2001). There is a good deal of convergence across these areas on five matters:

Table 3.1 Disciplines, Frameworks, and Fields Related to Children's Learning and Behavior

Field	Description	Research
Public Health	Focus on population-based approaches to problems, prevention, and includes early and intensive interventions.	Davis, 2002; World Health Organization, 2002
Prevention and Developmental Science	Identifies risks and protective factors, including those that mediate and moderate outcomes.	Kendziora & Osher, 2004
Positive Youth Development and Social Emotional Learning	Includes research on social competence, and highlights the importance of promoting resilience, social and emotional learning, and developmental assets.	Catalano et al., 2004; Cicchetti, Rappaport, Sandler, & Weissberg, 2000; Greenberg et al., 2003
Behavioral Research in Special Education and Psychology	Contributes to the development of positive behavior supports, functional behavior analysis, and classroom management techniques.	Walker, Colvin, & Ramsey, 1995
Mental Health Services and Treatment Research	Identifies effective approaches and therapeutic interventions for mental health disorders.	Burns & Hoagwood, 2002
Life Course/Social Field Theory	Highlights the key role of social fields, natural raters, and how each of these changes throughout people's life course.	Kellam & Rebok, 1992
Ecological Theory	Emphasizes the importance of focusing on multiple-person systems of interactions, which may include an immediate setting (e.g., school), interrelations among major settings (e.g., home-school), other social structures that influence what goes on in these settings (e.g., presence of a system of care), and overarching institutional patterns (e.g., community resources).	Brofenbrenner, 1977
Transactional Analysis	Indicates that developmental outcomes are the result of ongoing dynamic interplay among child behavior, adult responses, and environmental variables that may influence both the child and those who interact with him.	Sutherland, 2000; Sutherland, Wehby & Yoder, 2002

1. Numerous school factors matter, which include the following: (a) teacher beliefs and expectations, (b) relationships with students, (c) leadership; (d) collaboration and coordination, (e) academic press, and (f) a commitment to doing what is necessary to help students succeed (e.g., Ancess, 2003; Osher, Woodruff, & Sims, 2002).
2. Students benefit from and need high-quality teaching and effective social support that engages them in the learning process. Effective instruction includes the ability to connect with students, manage the classroom, engage students at the zone of proximal development, and help them regulate their behavior (Ancess, 2003; Osher, Sandler, & Nelson, 2001; Osher et al., 2010).
3. Rigid and inflexible approaches to discipline do not work and disproportionately harm students of color and students with disabilities, and positive and relational approaches to discipline do the opposite (APA, 2006, 2008; Osher et al., 2001; Sugai et al., 2000; U.S. Public Health Service, 2000).
4. Culture matters and must and can be addressed (Allen & Boykin, 1992; U.S. Public Health Service, 2001).

5. Change is hard, takes time, and requires facilitation, trust, and support (Bryk & Schneider, 2002).

This convergence of literature supports the comprehensive framework, which is presented in the next section.

Student support is key for a comprehensive approach of student safety and achievement. This support can be understood from both a risk and asset-based perspective. From a risk perspective, student support addresses barriers to learning as well as factors that set the stage for or reinforce behavioral problems (e.g., alienating environments, bullying, punitive discipline, and inappropriate pedagogy). From an asset-based perspective, student support provides youth with the personal resources and social capital needed to help them succeed in school, handle problematic situations, meet the schools' behavioral expectations, and learn. Some interventions focus on risk and protection and aim at decreasing problem behaviors, and others focus on development of assets that provide building blocks for health development; however, they can be aligned. Prevention efforts that target risks are most successful when they are coordinated with explicit attempts to enhance children's competence, connection to others, and ability to contribute to their community (Greenwood, Terry, Utley, Montagna, & Walker 1993; Pittman, Irby, Tolman, Yohalem, & Ferber, 2001). For example, Durlak and Wells' (1997) meta-analysis of 177 primary behavioral and social prevention programs among youth under age 18 showed improved assertiveness, communication skills, self-confidence, and academic performance as well as reduced internalizing and externalizing problems. Moreover, Durlak, Weissberg, Dymnicki, Taylor, and Schellinger's (2011) analysis of 207 SEL programs found positive effects on SEL skills, behaviors, attitudes, and academic achievement.

A Comprehensive Framework for Student Support, Safety, and Achievement

Supportive schools as conceptualized in this chapter provide students with social, behavioral, and mental health support that facilitate achievement and address barriers to learning (Osher, Dwyer, & Jackson, 2004). Student support can be conceptualized as having four dimensions, each of which involves a cluster of attributes: (a) connection within caring schools, (b) social-emotional learning, (c) positive behavioral supports, and (d) engaging and appropriate learning opportunities (Osher et al., 2004, 2008). These four dimensions are interactive and interdependent.

There is some overlap between and among dimensions, both in terms of what each dimension includes, as well as the impact of some interventions across multiple dimensions. For example, there is a connection between helping students regulate their behavior (dimension 2) and teaching them the skills necessary to meet the schools' behavioral demands (dimension 3); however, there are differences. The second dimension explicitly targets SEL and focuses on internalization, application, and generalization of SEL skills. Skill instruction under the positive behavioral supports dimension, on the other hand, focuses on meeting the schools' behavioral demands. SEL, when taught and reinforced at school and home, is far more likely to be generalized and internalized than behavior modifications requiring token reinforcements (Greenwood et al., 1993; McConnell, Missall, Silberglitt, & McEvoy, 2002). Effective interventions may cross multiple dimensions or combine interventions that cross multiple dimension. For example, the Child Development Project involves the first, second, and fourth dimensions (Solomon, Battistich, Watson, Schaps, & Lewis, 2000), and BEST combines Second Step (second dimension) with EBS (Effective Behavioral Support; third dimension; Sprague et al., 2001).

This section explores the four dimensions, illustrating how they can be addressed for all students, some students who are at a greater level of risk, and for a smaller number of students who are at an even greater level of need.

The Four Dimensions of Violence Prevention–Intervention

Dimension 1: Belonging, Connection, and Care

The first dimension involves feelings of belonging at school, connection to students and adults, and caring school environments. Resnick and his colleagues (1997) called this phenomenon "connectedness," and included within it an adolescent's perception of safety, belonging, respect, and feeling cared for at school. Other researchers have pointed to the importance of bonding to the school (Hawkins & Weis, 1985), sense of community (Battistich & Horn, 1997), and school membership (Wehlage, Rutter, Smith, Lesko, & Fernandez, 1989) and linked them both to positive as well as negative academic and behavioral outcomes (McNeely & Falci, 2004; McNeely, Nonnemaker, & Blum, 2002; Metz, 2003; Valenzuela, 1999).

Schools, particularly large ones, can be alienating places, which students, particularly those who are socially disadvantaged or are not doing well, experience as uncaring (e.g., Page, 1991). Successful schools are often places of connection and engagement for all students (e.g., Bensman, 2000; Jimerson, Campos, & Greif, 2003; Maeroff, 1999; National Research Council, 2004). Osterman's (2000) review of research on student belongingness found that it influences achievement through its effects on engagement. Resnick, Harris, and Blum's (1993) multivariate analyses of data on 36,000 seventh to twelfth graders found that school connectedness was the most salient protective factor for both boys and girls against the acting out behaviors and was second in importance after family connectedness for internalizing behaviors (e.g., withdrawal, despondence, and panic, that are frequently associated with depression and anxiety disorders). Further analyses of the Add Health data (Blum, 2001) suggest that adolescents who feel connected to adults at school are less likely to use alcohol or other substances, experience less emotional distress, attempt suicide less, and engage in less deviant and violent behaviors. School connectedness was the only school-related variable that was protective for every single outcome measured (Resnick et al., 1993).

Research suggests that students who believe that they are cared for put more effort into their schooling, which, in turn, positively affects their learning (Smerdon, 1999). In a meta-analysis of over 100 studies Waters, Marzano, and McNulty (2003), found that the quality of teacher-student relationships drove other aspects of classroom management. Teachers who had high quality relationships with their students had 31% fewer discipline problems, rule violations, and related problems over a year's time than did teachers who lacked high quality relationships with their students. This finding is supported by a set of studies that range from preschool through high school. They suggest that supportive relationships between teachers and students promote student engagement, positive attitudes, and a sense of belonging toward school, motivation, and academic achievement (Birch & Ladd, 1997; Connell, Halpern-Felsher, Clifford, Crichlow, & Usinger, 1995; Hamre & Pianta, 2001; National Research Council, 2004; Sinclair, Christenson, Lehr, & Anderson, 2003; Wentzel, 1997, 1998; Wentzel & Wigfield, 1998).

Dimension 2: Social Emotional Learning (SEL)

The second dimension involves support for students' ability to regulate their emotions, as well as their social and academic behavior by developing their social and emotional skills. Effective SEL programming helps students develop skills that enable them to recognize and manage their emotions, understand and appreciate others' perspectives, establish positive goals, make responsible decisions, and handle interpersonal situations effectively (Collaborative for Academic, Social, and Emotional Learning, 2003; Lemerise & Arsenio, 2000). Wilson, Gottfredson, and Najaka's (2001) meta-analysis of 165 studies of school-based prevention found that self-control or social competency programming that employed cognitive-behavioral and behavioral instructional methods consistently was effective in reducing dropout, nonattendance, conduct problems, and substance use. Analyses by Zins, Weissberg, Wang, and Walberg (2004) suggest that that SEL positively contributes to school related attitudes, behavior, and performance:

1. attitudes include: (a) stronger sense of community (bonding), (b) more academic motivation and higher aspirations, and (c) positive attitudes toward school;
2. behavior includes: (a) understanding the consequences of behavior, (b) coping effectively with middle school stressors, (c) more prosocial behavior, (d) fewer or reduced absences, (e) more classroom participation, (f) greater effort to achieve, (g) reduction in aggression and disruptions, (h) lower rate of conduct problems, (i) fewer hostile negotiations and better conflict resolution skills, (j) fewer suspensions, (k) better transition to middle school, and (l) increased student engagement at school; and
3. performance includes: (a) increased grades and achievement, (b) more students on track to graduate, and (c) fewer dropouts.

These relations are supported by Durlak et al.'s (2011) meta-analysis, which found modest effect sizes on academic related attitudes, prosocial behavior (and reduction of antisocial behavior), and academic achievement.

Dimension 3: Positive Behavioral Approaches

The third dimension involves reducing inappropriate use of punitive responses and the use of positive behavioral supports. Schools sometimes emphasize punitive measures to manage student behavior, and teachers may use disapproval more frequently than approval as a consequence for student behavior (Mayer & Sulzer-Azaroff, 1991). Educators may respond to student behavioral problems in a reactive, negative, and harsh manner, which includes hostile adult responses, disciplinary referrals, punishment, segregation, and removal from the school environments (Mayer, 2001; Noguera, 2003). These responses are often disproportionately applied to students of color and students with emotional and behavioral disabilities (Skiba, Michael, Nardo, & Peterson, 2000). These negative responses can also affect the learning process; students with behavioral problems are provided with lower levels of instruction, praised less, and called upon less frequently than other students (Gunter & Denny, 1998; Sutherland, Wehby, & Yoder, 2002; Van Acker, Grant, & Henry, 1996).

In fact, what Gunter and his colleagues have conceptualized as a negative-reinforcement cycle (Gunter, Denny, Jack, Shores, & Nelson, 1993) reduces a student's opportunity to learn (Gunter & Coutinho, 1997; Osher, Morrison, & Bailey, 2003), which is dependent on instructional time and task engagement (Greenwood, Seals, & Kamps, 2010). These ongoing transactions contribute to a self-sustaining cycle of classroom disruption and negative consequences (Dumas, Prinz, Smith, & Laughlin, 1999; Farmer, Quinn, Hussey, & Holohan, 2001; Osher et al., 2002) that includes academic failure and forced segregation with antisocial peers, which may reinforce problem behavior (Dishion, McCord, & Poullin, 1999; Maag, 2001; Murphy, Beck, Crawford, Hodges, & McGaughy, 2002; Powell, Farrar, & Cohen, 1985).

Positive Behavioral Supports (PBS) can be employed at a schoolwide level. For instance, PBS as a universal intervention may include: clearly identifying a limited number of schoolwide behavioral rules, stating them positively, displaying them visibly, and structuring the school environment so that students meet behavioral expectations. PBS as a more intensive intervention may be in the form of functional behavioral assessment or school-based wraparound services. Positive supports also include the physical structure of the school (e.g., its size, layout, and lighting), as well as administrative practices.

This dimension is based upon research grounded in applied behavioral analysis and environmental design that demonstrates: (a) how teacher and schools can proactively reduce the incidence of problem behavior and respond in a proactive manner, (b) the ineffectiveness of punishment as an intervention, (c) the impact of environment, and (d) how schools can successfully use alternatives to punishment. For example, results of a study by Sutherland, Alder, and Gunter (2003), which examined the impact of an intervention aimed at increasing the opportunity to respond (OTR) for fourth graders with EBD, suggest that increased rates of OTR contributed to increased rates of students' correct responses, increased task engagement, and decreased disruptive behavior. This research has demonstrated inefficiencies of inconsistent and punitive school and classroom management systems including: (a) punitive and inconsistent school and classroom behavior management practices, unclear, invisible, or unachievable rules and expectations regarding appropriate behavior; (b) lack of adequate supervision and monitoring of student behavior; (c) failure to effectively correct rule violations and reward adherence to them; and (d) failure to individualize consequences (Colvin, Kameenui, & Sugai, 1993; Hawkins, Catalano, Kosterman, Abbott, & Hill, 1999; Mayer & Sulzer-Azaroff, 1991; Osher et al., 2010; Walker et al., 1996).

Dimension 4: Academic Engagement and Support

The fourth dimension includes what schools do academically to ensure that every child succeeds. This dimension can be conceptualized as having technical, cultural-structural, student-specific, and contextual dimensions. These dimensions interact with each other as well as with the other three dimensions. For example, in schools that lack community and positive behavioral supports, it is more likely that the enacted curriculum will be a curriculum of control (Knitzer, Steinberg, & Fleisch, 1990) or teaching for order (what some call defensive teaching), where teachers lower the academic press and accept disengagement as long as it is not disruptive (Murphy et al., 2002).

Three Additional Factors to Promoting Student Success

Technical Factors

Some students may learn regardless of the quality of the academic opportunities, whereas others require effective instruction or additional academic supports. Technical issues consist of the quality of organization, sequencing, presentation, and pacing of the curriculum as well as the manner in which learning is regularly assessed and feedback is provided. This includes the management of instructional time (Greenwood et al., 2010), and the extent to which students are actively involved in learning (Murphy et al., 2002; Osher et al., 2010). Technical issues also include the efficient and appropriate use of effective instructional strategies such as advance organizers, mastery learning approaches, homework and practice, direct instruction, peer tutoring, curriculum based assessment, and cooperative learning.

School Cultural and Structural Factors

Successful schools are ones in which: (a) there is a teacher community that focuses on learning, (b) individual teachers have high expectations for all students and believe that all students can learn and that they as teachers can teach them, and (c) teachers as a group believe that they are collectively accountable for student success (Lee, Smith, & Croninger, 1995; Murphy et al., 2002; Stewart, 2008). Teachers in these schools do not blame students or their families, for student failure. To facilitate student success, educational professionals must provide a supportive context and there needs to be a culture of problem solving rather than blame or avoidance, and principal leadership that supports a supportive school culture (Murphy et al., 2002; Quinn, Osher, Hoffman, & Hanley, 1998). For example, it is harder for teachers to maintain high standards for every student, have community among themselves, and feel collective responsibility for learning in large schools and in schools that track students (Metz, 1997). Structural factors also include efficient school and community systems that connect students and families to prevention and treatment resources (Blechman, Fishman, Fishman, & Lewis, 2004; Osher, 2002; Rappaport et al., 2002).

Student-Specific Factors

For learning to take place, teachers must engage and connect with students (National Research Council, 2004). Students learn best when learning is active, aligns with their experiences and goals, and builds upon their strengths. This includes using multiple modalities for learning, and scaffolding the learning process so that there is an appropriate balance between challenge and support (Moll & Greenberg, 1990). Effective instruction and assessment requires cultural competency, both in content and delivery, to successfully address student epistemology, student language proficiency, cultural world views, cultural communication and socialization styles, and student life context and values (Solano-Flores & Nelson-Barber, 2001).

Addressing Different Levels of Student Needs

Effective intervention should address the nature and intensity of student needs, and a three-level public health approach provides a way for organizing supportive resources. Because student needs are related to environmental factors that place them at risk, as well as the presence of protective factors and assets in the community, the percent of students in a school who require early or intensive interventions will vary (Scales & Leffert, 1999). The three levels of intervention are interactive. Universal approaches and interventions create a schoolwide foundation. When a strong foundation is in place, it is easier to identify students who require early intervention, making it more likely that these interventions will be effective. Similarly, universal interventions reduce the incidence of problem behavior in the school population. This means that fewer students will be available to tease or harass other students, induce their participation in problematic activities, or reinforce students who act in an antisocial manner (Espelage & Swearer, 2004; Patterson, Reid, & Dishion, 1992). Further, a reduction in problematic behaviors at a universal level will free adults to teach and connect with students, while reducing the likelihood that they will respond to students in a counter-aggressive manner, which would reinforce inappropriate behaviors.

All children require connection, need self-regulation, and benefit from effective, engaging instruction and positive behavioral support. However, what is done to support individual students—both the intensity and type of intervention—differs as a function of student strengths, assets, and needs. The following paragraphs illustrate how these supports can be implemented.

There are some common characteristics of interventions at each level. Universal interventions include both promotion efforts that build assets and protective factors (e.g., connection to adults in the school) and risk targeted interventions that address risk factors (e.g., behavioral problems in the classroom). As in the case of adding fluoride to water to prevent tooth decay, universal interventions or primary prevention efforts, are provided to everyone in a population whether it is a grade or the school—even though everyone may not require them. This is important because no matter how effective screening for risk factors is, there will always be false negatives (Derzon, 2001), and the purpose of primary prevention is to reduce the incidence of a problem (e.g., tooth decay) in a population. However, universal interventions will be insufficient to protect all children, hence the need for early and intensive intervention.

Early interventions include both selective and indicated interventions. Selective interventions are for individuals who, although they are not displaying early warning signs, are members of a population that research suggests are at higher risk for a particular problem (e.g., a child who was exposed to violence). Indicated interventions address the needs of students whose behavior indicates that they are at higher risk than other children (e.g., a child who exhibits early warning signs). Early interventions are often provided within group contexts, focusing on one ecological domain (e.g., the school) or one dimension (e.g., reading). Compared to intensive interventions, early interventions are less time consuming. Because early interventions should take place before an intensive problem manifests itself, it important to intervene in a nonstigmatizing manner, build upon strengths, and avoid self-fulfilling prophecies, where teachers, staff, students, or parents confound information about a risk of a bad outcome happening (or a label) with a belief in its inevitability, and act on that belief (Weinstein, 2002). This is particularly the case for selective interventions, where there are no or insufficient data to definitively support conclusion that a youth may develop a serious problem.

Intensive interventions should be individualized and focus on multiple ecological domains (e.g., family and school) as well as dimensions (e.g., academics, self-regulation, and behavior). To be effective, they must be strength-based, capacity building, address multiple risk factors, linguistically and culturally competent, child and family driven, monitored in an ongoing manner, and intensive and sustained.

Caring and Connection

While social connection is a universal need, some students may find it harder to connect with others due to temperament, learning or behavioral disabilities that affect their thought processing, cultural differences, and prior attachment issues. Some students are also more vulnerable to teasing or harassment due to such individual characteristics. Small classes where teachers have more opportunity to connect with individual students and small schools where every adult is expected to connect with and follow some of the students provide a platform to support social connections. Programs like the Child Development Program, which intentionally builds a school community, extend this connection at a classroom level. However, some students could still require more intensive efforts at connection; for example, to help their transition into high school or to prevent their dropping out of school (Felner, Ginter, & Primavera, 1982; Osher et al., 2003). The more students experience risks in their lives, the more it is important to engage families in a family-driven, respectful, and culturally competent manner (Osher, 2000; Osher & Osher 2002; Osher et al., 2004). Families and Schools Together (FAST) exemplifies such an approach for families (McDonald & Sayger, 1998).

Self-Regulation and SEL Skills

All students require self-regulation and SEL skills, but some students require additional support in developing these skills. Just as most students need to learn how to read in school, they must also learn how to interact appropriately with peers and adults and how to address academic challenges (e.g., frustration) and interpersonal conflicts (e.g., teasing). Effective SEL programs are developmentally appropriate and cover all age ranges. They aim at developing five core competencies: self-awareness, interpersonal and social awareness, self-regulation and management, relationship skills, and responsible decision making. There are many good programs that address universal needs in a developmentally appropriate way and they can be found in *Safe and Sound:*

An Educators Guide to Social and Emotional Learning Programs (Collaborative for Academic, Social, and Emotional Learning, 2003). However, some students require more intensive interventions; for example, those who have experienced trauma or struggle with depression or ADHD. In other instances, students may have an inability to control anger when provoked, cannot express their feelings, or have particularly tough times handling failure or group pressure. A good example of an early intervention is Aggression Replacement Therapy, which is provided in a group context and includes skill streaming, anger control training, and moral reasoning training (Feindler & Gerber, this volume; Goldstein & Glick, 2010). Some students, such as those experiencing an anxiety disorder or depression, may need more support than group counseling can provide. Some may benefit from cognitive-behavioral treatments where they learn to deal with fears by modifying the way they think and behave, others may require medication, and some may require both types of treatment (Substance Abuse and Mental Health Services Administration, 2005). Schools are rarely solely involved with medication management, hence, cross-agency collaboration and coordination is very important.

Positive Behavioral Supports

All students can benefit from schoolwide systems and school–community members that support a positive and proactive approach to discipline. This strategy is likely to include the articulation of positive behavioral expectations, teaching students desired behaviors, and providing procedures to encourage appropriate behavior and discourage inappropriate behaviors. Positive Behavioral Interventions and Supports (PBIS), Effective Behavioral Support (EBS), and Achieve are models that provide schoolwide strategies (Knoff & Batsche, 1995; Lewis & Sugai, 1999; Quinn et al., 1998; Sugai et al., 2000). However, some students (sometimes estimated as less than 15 to 20%; Sugai et al., 2000) require more intensive support, which is provided in small groups (e.g., a planning center) or individually (e.g., functional assessment) (Quinn et al., 1998; Scott & Eber, 2003). Like universal approaches, these approaches are useful because adults use data to identify and respond to what they may be doing to create or reinforce student behavior problems, as well as what supports can be put in place to address problems (Gable, Quinn, Rutherford, & Howell, 1998; Osher et al., 2004). An even smaller number of students require very intensive support, such as school-based wraparound, which might include a classroom aide (Scott & Eber, 2003). Wraparound and other effective intensive behavioral interventions must be youth and family driven, implemented in a culturally competent manner, and when school-based, address the concerns and training needs of school staff (Poduska, Kendziora, & Osher, 2008; Quinn & Lee, 2007; Woodruff et al., 1999).

Providing Effective Academic Support

All students require opportunities to learn. They learn best when schools provide them with effective, well-designed learning tasks that are presented in a meaningful manner and actively engage them. Effective teachers commonly draw upon the following technique to enhance their instruction: (a) set and communicate explicit learning goals; (b) connect learning to student experiences; (c) present new content multiple times and through a variety of modalities; (d) provide opportunities for practice, and additional challenges after students master content; (e) employ a quick pace; monitor student progress; (f) provide ongoing feedback to students; and (g) recognize efforts and celebrate progress (Howell & Nolet, 2000; McTighe & O'Connor, 2005). Effective interventions that facilitate this process include Class-wide Peer Tutoring (Greenwood et al., 1993) and Success For All (Slavin & Madden, 2001), which enable children to practice new skills and experience meaningful academic success. Although all students can benefit from effective instruction, some students will require group support that targets their linguistic background, and others may require individualized supports that address their specific learning disabilities or problems. Interventions will be most effective when they leverage student strengths and assets (e.g., interests and parental support) and align with the student's experiences and goals. Traditional approaches to addressing the needs of students (and teachers) involve tracking, pullout, and separate classes. Research (Brunello & Checchi, 2007; Oakes & Lipton, 1994) suggests that such approaches are counterproductive, and techniques that bring needed support into the classroom include: teaming special and regular educators, employing assistive technology, and leveraging service learning to scaffold learning and engage students (Muscott, 2000; Quinn et al., 1998).

Given the numerous demands on educators, it is important to recognize that challenges are likely in aligning, safety, support, and achievement. Among the most salient is the disproportionate emphasis of school evaluation on test scores. Within the context of high-stakes testing, too often, resources are only invested in those programs that purport to directly impact student achievement. Thus, many factors related to school safety and student support are ignored. Limited resources must be invested wisely. As discussed previously in this chapter, safety and student support are essential features in facilitating student achievement. Table 3.2 briefly delineates important implications for implementing comprehensive plans to promote student safety, support, and achievement.

Each school and community has unique values, needs, and strengths, which will affect how schools move forward. For some schools the starting point may be universal youth development,

Table 3.2 Implications for Practice: Comprehensive Plans to Promote Student Safety, Support, and Achievement

1.	Understand that student safety and student support are essential features in facilitating student achievement.
2.	Implement strategies and programs that promote student support.
3.	Utilize efficient and appropriate use of effective instructional strategies such as advance organizers, mastery learning approaches, homework and practice, direct instruction, peer tutoring, and cooperative learning.
4.	Carefully consider the quality of organization, sequencing, presentation, and pacing of the curriculum as well as the manner in which learning is regularly assessed and feedback is provided.
5.	Promote a school community that has high expectations for all students and is collectively accountable for student success.
6.	Develop a school context where learning is active, aligns with student experiences and goals, and builds upon their strengths.
7.	Implement effective intervention to address the nature and intensity of student needs.
8.	Establish a school culture that reflects caring and connectedness to promote school engagement and active participation among students.
9.	Provide programs that help students learn how to interact appropriately with peers and adults and how to solve academic problems and interpersonal conflicts, including: self-awareness, interpersonal and social awareness, self-regulation and management, relationship skills, and responsible decision making.
10.	Organize schoolwide systems and school-community members that support a positive and proactive approach to discipline.
11.	Apply effective, well-designed learning tasks that are presented in a meaningful manner and actively engage students.
12.	Recognize that some students will require group support that targets their linguistic background, and others may require individualized supports that address their specific learning needs.

for others, comprehensive behavioral approaches, and still for others intensive mental health support. Thus, no single strategy or program can be systematically implemented in all schools. This presents challenges for administrators and school personnel in determining appropriate strategies that align appropriately. Selection criteria can be found in *Safe, Supportive, and Successful Schools Step by Step* (Osher et al., 2004). This chapter provides a conceptual foundation for educators to build upon in promoting safety, support, and achievement at school.

References

Adelman, H. S., & Taylor, L. (2000). Moving prevention from the fringes into the fabric of school improvement. *Journal of Educational and Psychological Consultation, 11*, 7–36. doi:10.1207/S1532768XJEPC1101_3

Allen, B. A., & Boykin, A. W. (1992). African American children and the educational process: Alleviating cultural discontinuity through prescriptive pedagogy. *School Psychology Review, 21*, 586–596. Retrieved from http://www.nasponline.org/publications/spr/sprissues.aspx#21

American Psychological Association. (2006). *APA Zero Tolerance Task Force report.* Retrieved from http://www.apa.org/pubs/info/reports/zero-tolerance.aspx

American Psychological Association Zero Tolerance Task Force. (2008). Are zero tolerance policies effective in the schools? An evidentiary review and recommendations. *American Psychologist, 63*, 852–862. doi:10.1037/0003-066X.63.9.852

Ancess, J. (2003). *Beating the odds: High schools as communities of commitment.* New York, NY: Teachers College Press.

Bandura, A. (1995). *Self-efficacy in changing societies.* Melbourne, Australia: Cambridge University Press.

Barton, P. (2003). *Parsing the achievement gap: Baselines for tracking progress.* Princeton, NJ: Educational Testing Service.

Battistich, V., & Horn, A. (1997). The relationship between students' sense of their school as a community and their involvement in problem behaviors. *American Journal of Public Health, 87*, 1997–2001. doi:10.2105/AJPH.87.12.1997

Bear, G., Webster-Stratton, C., Furlong, M., & Rhee, S. (2000). Preventing aggression and violence. In G. Bear & K. Minke (Eds.), *Preventing school problems: Strategies and programs that work* (pp. 1–70). Bethesda, MD: National Association of School Psychologists.

Bensman, D. (2000). *Central Park East and its graduates: Learning by heart.* New York, NY: Teachers College Press.

Birch, S. H., & Ladd, G. W. (1997). The teacher-child relationship and children's early school adjustment. *Journal of School Psychology, 35*, 61–79. doi:10.1016/S0022-4405(96)00029-5

Blechman, E. A., Fishman, D. B., Fishman, C. A., & Lewis, J. E. (2004). *Caregiver alliances for at-risk and dangerous youth: Establishing school and agency coordination and accountability.* Champaign, IL: Research Press.

Blum, R. (2001). Early transitions: Risk and protective factors. *The Center,* 38-41.

Brunello, G., & Checchi, D. (2007). Does school tracking affect equality of opportunity? New international evidence. *Economic Policy, 22*, 781–861. doi:10.1111/j.1468-0327.2007.00189.x

Bryk, A. S., & Schneider, B. (2002). *Trust in schools: A core resource for improvement.* New York, NY: Russell Sage Foundation.

Bryk, A. S., Sebring, P. B., Allensworth, E., Luppescu, S., & Easton, J. Q. (2009). *Schools for improvement: Lessons from Chicago.* Chicago, IL: University of Chicago Press.

Bryk, A. S., & Thum, Y. M. (1989). The effects of high school organization on dropping out: An exploratory investigation. *American Educational Research Journal, 26*, 353–383. doi:10.2307/1162978

Catalano, R. F., Berglund, M. L., Ryan, J. A. M., Lonczak, H. S., & Hawkins, J. D. (2004). Positive youth development in the United States: Research findings on evaluations of positive youth development programs. *The Annals of the American Academy of Political and Social Science, 591*, 98–124. doi:10.1177/0002716203260102

Catalano, R. F., Hawkins, J. D., Berglund, L., Pollard, J., & Arthur, M. (2002). Prevention science and positive youth development: Competitive or cooperative frameworks? *Journal of Adolescent Health, 31*, 230–239. doi:10.1016/S1054-139X(02)00496-2

Collaborative for Academic, Social, and Emotional Learning. (2003). *Safe and sound: An educational leader's guide to evidence-based social and emotional learning (SEL) programs.* Chicago, IL: Author.

Colvin, G., Kameenui, E. J., & Sugai, G. (1993). Reconceptualizing behavior management and schoolwide discipline in general education. *Education and Treatment of Children, 16*, 361–381. Retrieved from http://www.education-andtreatmentofchildren.net/

Connell, J. P., Halpern-Felsher, B. L., Clifford, E., Crichlow, W., & Usinger, P. (1995). Hanging in there: Behavioral, psychological, and contextual factors affecting whether African American adolescents stay in high school. *Journal of Adolescent Research, 10*, 41–63. doi:10.1177/0743554895101004

Connell, J. P., Spencer, M. B., & Aber, J. L. (1994). Educational risk and resilience in African American youth: Context, self, actions, and outcomes in school. *Child Development, 65*, 493–506. doi:10.2307/1131398

Davis, N. J. (2002). The promotion of mental health and the prevention of mental and behavioral disorders: Surely the time is right. *International Journal of Emergency Mental Health, 4,* 3–29. Retrieved from http://www.researchgate.net/journal/1522-4821_International_journal_of_emergency_mental_health

Derzon, J. H. (2001). Antisocial behavior and the prediction of violence: A meta-analysis. *Psychology in the Schools, 38,* 93–106. doi:10.1002/pits.1002

Dishion, T. J., McCord, J., & Poulin, F. (1999). When interventions harm: Peer groups and problem behavior. *American Psychologist, 54,* 755–764. doi:10.1037//0003066X.54.9.755

Dryfoos, J. G. (1990). *Adolescents at risk: Prevalence and prevention.* New York, NY: Oxford University Press.

Dumas, J. E., Prinz, R. J., Smith, E. P., & Laughlin, J. (1999). The EARLY ALLIANCE prevention trial: An integrated set of interventions to promote competence and reduce risk for conduct disorder, substance abuse, and school failure. *Clinical Child and Family Psychology Review, 2,* 37–53. doi:10.1023/A:1021815408272

Durlak, J. A., Weissberg, R. P., Dymnicki, A. B., Taylor, R. D., & Schellinger, K. B. (2011). The impact of enhancing students' social and emotional learning: A meta-analysis of school-based universal interventions. *Child Development, 82,* 405–432. doi:10.1111/j.1467-8624.2010.01564.x

Durlak, J. A., & Wells, A. M. (1997). Primary prevention programs for children and adolescents: A meta-analytic review. *American Journal of Community Psychology, 25,* 115–152. doi:10.1023/A:1024654026646

Espelage, D. L., & Swearer, S. M. (Eds.). (2004). *Bullying in American schools: A social-ecological perspective on prevention and intervention.* Mahwah, NJ: Erlbaum.

Farmer, T. W., Quinn, M. M., Hussey, W., & Holohan, T. (2001). The development of disruptive behavior disorders and correlated constraints: Implications for intervention. *Behavioral Disorders, 26,* 117–130. Retrieved from http://www.ccbd.net/behavioraldisorders/index.cfm

Felner, R. D., Ginter, M., & Primavera, J. (1982). Primary prevention during school transition: Social support and environmental structure. *American Journal of Community Psychology, 10,* 277–290. doi:10.1007/BF00896495

Fredricks, J., Blumenfeld, P., Friedel, J., & Paris, A. (2005). School engagement. In K. A. Moore & L. Lippman (Eds.), *Conceptualizing and measuring indicators of positive development: What do children need to flourish?* (pp. 305–321). New York, NY: Kluwer Academic.

Gable, R. A., Quinn, M. M., Rutherford, R. B., & Howell, K. (1998). Addressing problem behaviors in schools: Use of functional assessments and behavior intervention plans. *Preventing School Failure, 42,* 106–119. doi:10.1080/10459889809603178

Garbarino, J., & deLara, E. (2002). *And words can hurt forever: How to protect adolescents from bullying, harassment, and emotional violence.* New York, NY: The Free Press.

Goldstein, A. P., & Glick, B. (2010). *Aggression replacement training: A comprehensive intervention for aggressive youth.* Champaign, IL: Research Press.

Gottfredson, G. D., Gottfredson, D. C., Czeh, E. R., Cantor, D., Crosse, S. B., & Hantman, I. (2000). *National study of delinquency prevention in schools.* Ellicott City, MD: Gottfredson Associates. Retrieved from http://www.gottfredson.com/national.htm

Greenberg, M. T., Weissberg, R. P., O'Brien, M. U., Zins, J. E., Fredericks, L., Resnik, H., & Elias, M. J. (2003). Enhancing school-based prevention and youth development through coordinated social, emotional, and academic learning. *American Psychologist, 58,* 466–474. doi:10.1037/0003-066X.58.6-7.466

Greenwood, C. R., Seals, K., & Kamps, D. (2010). Peer teaching interventions for multiple levels of support. In M. R. Shinn & H. M. Walker (Eds.), *Interventions for achievement and behavior problems in a three-tier model* (pp. 633–676). Silver Spring, MD: National Association of School Psychologists.

Greenwood, C. R., Terry, B., Utley, C. A., Montagna, D., & Walker, D. (1993). Achievement, placement, and services: Middle school benefits of classwide peer tutoring used at the elementary school. *School Psychology Review, 22,* 497–516. Retrieved from http://www.nasponline.org/publications/spr/sprissues.aspx

Gunter, P. L., & Coutinho, M. J. (1997). Negative reinforcement in classrooms: What we're beginning to learn. *Teacher Education and Special Education, 20,* 249–264. doi:10.1177/088840649702000306

Gunter, P. L., & Denny, R. K. (1998). Trends and issues in research regarding academic instruction of students with emotional and behavioral disorders. *Behavioral Disorders, 24,* 44–50. Retrieved from http://www.ccbd.net/behavioraldisorders/index.cfm

Gunter, P. L., Denny, K., Jack, S. L., Shores, R. E., & Nelson, C. M. (1993). Aversive stimuli in academic interactions between students with serious emotional disturbance and their teachers. *Behavioral Disorders, 18,* 265–274. Retrieved from http://www.ccbd.net/behavioraldisorders/index.cfm

Hamre, B. K., & Pianta, R. C. (2001). Early teacher-child relationships and the trajectory of children's school outcomes through eighth grade. *Child Development, 72,* 625–638. doi:10.1111/1467-8624.00301

Hawkins, J. D., Catalano, R. F., Kosterman, R., Abbott, R., & Hill, K. G. (1999). Preventing adolescent health-risk behaviors by strengthening protection during childhood. *Archives of Pediatrics and Adolescent Medicine, 153,* 226–234. Retrieved from http://archpedi.ama-assn.org/

Hawkins, J. D., & Weis, J. G. (1985). The social development model: An integrated approach to delinquency prevention. *Journal of Primary Prevention, 6,* 73–97. doi:10.1007/BF01325432

Herman, K. C., Reinke, W. M., Parkin, J., Traylor, K. B., & Agarwal, G. (2009). Childhood depression: Rethinking the role of the school. *Psychology in the Schools, 46,* 433–446. doi:10.1002/pits.20388

Howell, K. W., & Nolet, V. (2000). *Curriculum-based evaluation: Teaching and decision making* (3rd ed.). Belmont, CA: Wadsworth.

Jimerson, S. R., Campos, E., & Greif, J. (2003). Toward an understanding of definitions and measures of school engagement and related terms. *The California School Psychologist, 8,* 7–27. Retrieved from http://education.ucsb.edu/school-psychology/CSP-Journal/index.html

Kellam, S. G., Rebok, G. W., Wilson, R., & Mayer, L. S. (1994). The social field of the classroom: Context for the developmental epidemiological study of aggressive behavior. In R. K. Silbereisen & E. Todt (Eds.), *Adolescence in context: The interplay of family, school, peers and work in adjustment* (pp. 390–408). New York, NY: Springer-Verlag.

Knitzer, J., Steinberg, Z., & Fleisch, B. (1990). *At the schoolhouse door: An examination of programs and policies for children with behavioral and emotional problems.* New York, NY: Bank Street College of Education.

Knoff, H. M., & Batsche, G. M. (1995). Project ACHIEVE: Analyzing a school reform process for at-risk and underachieving students. *School Psychology Review, 24,* 579–608. Retrieved from http://www.nasponline.org/publications/spr/sprissues.aspx

Kratochwill, T. R., & Bergan, J. R. (1990). *Behavioral consultation in applied settings: An individual guide.* New York, NY: Plenum Press.

Lee, V. E., & Burkam, D. T. (2003). Dropping out of high school: The role of school organization and structure. *American Education Research Journal, 40,* 353–393. doi:10.3102/00028312040002353

Lee, V. E., Smith, J. B., & Croninger, R. G. (1995). Another look at high school restructuring: More evidence that it improves student achievement, and more insight into why. *Issues in Restructuring Schools* (Number 9). Madison: WI: Center on Organization and Restructuring of School, University of Wisconsin-Madison.

Lee, V. E., Smith, J. B., Perry, T. E., & Smylie, M. A. (1999). Social support, academic press, and student achievement: A view from the middle grades in Chicago. Chicago, IL: Consortium on Chicago School Research.

Lemerise, E., & Arsenio, W. (2000). An integrated model of emotion processes and cognition in social information processing. *Child Development, 71,* 107–118. doi:10.1111/1467-8624.00124

Lewis, T. J., & Sugai, G. (1999). Effective behavior support: A systems approach to proactive school-wide management. *Focus on Exceptional Children, 31,* 1–24. Retrieved from http://www.lovepublishing.com/catalog/focus_on_exceptional_children_31.html

Maag, J. W. (2001) Rewarded by punishment: Reflections on the disuse of positive reinforcement in schools. *Exceptional Children, 67,* 173–186. Retrieved from http://www.cec.sped.org/content/NavigationMenu/Publications2/exceptionalchildren/

Maeroff, G. I. (1999). *Altered destinies: Making life better for schoolchildren in need.* New York, NY: St. Martin's Griffin.

Marzano, R. (2003). *What works in schools: Translating research into action.* Alexandria, VA: Association for Supervision and Curriculum Development.

Mayer, G. R. (2001). Antisocial behavior: Its causes and prevention within our schools. *Education and Treatment of Children, 24,* 414–429. Retrieved from http://www.educationandtreatmentofchildren.net/

Mayer, G. R., & Sulzer-Azaroff, B. (1991). Interventions for vandalism. In G. Stoner, M. R. Shinn, & H. M. Walker (Eds.), *Interventions for achievement and behavior problems* (pp. 559–580). Bethesda, MD: National Association of School Psychologists.

McConnell, S. R., Missall, K. N., Silberglitt, B., & McEvoy, M. A. (2002). Promoting social development in preschool classrooms. In M. Shinn, G. Stoner, & H. M. Walker (Eds.), *Interventions for academic and behavior problems II: Preventive and remedial approaches* (pp. 501–536). Bethesda, MD: National Association of School Psychologists.

McDonald, L., & Sayger, T. (1998). Impact of a family and school based prevention program on protective factors for high-risk youth. *Drugs and Society, 12,* 61–86. doi:10.1300/J023v12n01_06

McNeely, C. A., & Falci, C. (2004). School connectedness and the transition into and out of health risk behavior among adolescents: A comparison of social belonging and teacher support. *Journal of School Health 74,* 284–292. doi:10.1111/j.1746-1561.2004.tb08285.x

McNeely, C. A., Nonnemaker, J. M., & Blum, R. W. (2002). Promoting student connectedness to school: Evidence from the National Longitudinal Study of Adolescent Health. *Journal of School Health 72,* 138–146. doi:10.1111/j.1746-1561.2002.tb06533.x

McTighe, J., & O'Connor, K. (2005). Seven practices for effective learning. *Educational Leadership, 63,* 10–17. Retrieved from http://www.ascd.org/publications/educational-leadership.aspx

Metz, M. H. (1997). *Keeping students in, gangs out, scores up, alienation down, and the copy machine in working order: Pressures that make urban schools in poverty different.* Paper presented at the Annual Meeting of the American Educational Research Association, Chicago, IL.

Metz, M. H. (2003). *Different by design: The context and character of three magnet schools*: New York, NY: Teachers College Press.

Moll, L. C., & Greenberg, J. B. (1990). Creating zones of possibilities: Creating social contexts for instruction. In L. C. Moll (Ed.), *Vygotsky and education: Instruction implications and applications of sociohistorical psychology* (pp. 319–348). New York, NY: Cambridge University Press.

Murphy, J., Beck, L., Crawford, M., Hodges, A., & McGaughy, C. (2002). *The productive high school: Creating personalized academic communities*. Thousand Oaks, CA: Corwin.

Muscott, H. (2000). A review and analysis of service-learning programs involving students with emotional/behavioral disorders. *Education and Treatment of Children, 23,* 346–368. Retrieved from http://www.educationandtreatmentofchildren.net/

National Research Council. (2004). *Engaging schools: Fostering high school students' motivation to learn*. Washington, DC: National Academy Press.

Noguera, P. (2003). *City schools and the American dream: Reclaiming the promise of public education*. New York, NY: Teachers College Press.

Oakes, J., & Lipton, M. (1994) Tracking and ability grouping. In G. Keating (Ed.), *Access to knowledge* (pp. 43–58). New York, NY: College Board.

Osher, D. (2000). Breaking the cultural disconnect: Working with families to improve outcomes for students placed at risk of school failure. In I. Goldenberg (Ed.), *Urban education: Possibilities and challenges confronting colleges of education* (pp. 4–11). Miami: Florida International University.

Osher, D. (2002). Creating comprehensive and collaborative systems. *Journal of Child and Family Studies, 11,* 91–101. doi:10.1023/A:1014771612802

Osher, D., Bear, G., Sprague, J., & Doyle, W. (2010). How we can improve school discipline. *Educational Researcher, 39,* 48–58. doi:10.3102/0013189X09357618

Osher, D., Cartledge, G., Oswald, D., Artiles, A. J., & Coutinho, M. (2004). Issues of cultural and linguistic competency and disproportionate representation. In R. Rutherford, M. Quinn, & S. Mather (Eds.), *Handbook of research in behavioral disorders* (pp. 54–77). New York, NY: Guilford.

Osher, D., & Dwyer, K. (2005). *Safeguarding our children: An action guide revised and expanded*. Longmont, CO: Sopris West.

Osher, D., Dwyer, K., & Jackson, S. (2004). *Safe, supportive, and successful schools step by step*. Longmont, CO: Sopris West.

Osher, D., & Kendziora, K. (2010). Building conditions for learning and healthy adolescent development: Strategic approaches. In B. Doll, W. Pfohl, & J. Yoon (Eds.), *Handbook of youth prevention science* (pp. 121–140). New York, NY: Routledge.

Osher, D., Morrison, G., & Bailey, W. (2003). Exploring the relationship between students: mobility and dropout among students with emotional and behavioral disorders. *Journal of Negro Education, 72,* 79–96. doi:10.2307/3211292

Osher, D., Sandler, S., & Nelson, C. (2001). The best approach to safety is to fix schools and support children and staff, *New Directions in Youth Development, 92,* 127–154. Retrieved from http://onlinelibrary.wiley.com/journal/10.1002/%28ISSN%291537-5781

Osher, D., Sprague, J., Weissberg, R. P., Axelrod, J., Keenan, S., Kendziora, K., & Zins, J. E. (2008). A comprehensive approach to promoting social, emotional, and academic growth in contemporary schools. In A. Thomas & J. Grimes (Eds.), *Best practices in school psychology V* (Vol. 4, pp. 1263–1278). Bethesda, MD: National Association of School Psychologists.

Osher, D., VanAker, R., Morrison, G., Gable, R., Dwyer, K., & Quinn, M. (2004). Warning signs of problems in schools: Ecological perspectives and effective practices for combating school aggression and violence. In M. J. Furlong, G. M. Morrison, D. Cornell, & R. Skiba (Eds.), *Issues in school violence research* (pp. 13–37). Binghamton, NY: Haworth.

Osher, D., Woodruff, D., & Sims, A. (2002). Schools make a difference: The relationship between education services for African American children and youth and their overrepresentation in the juvenile justice system. In D. Losen (Ed.), *Minority issues in special education* (pp. 93–116). Cambridge, MA: Harvard University, The Civil Rights Project.

Osher, T. W., & Osher, D. (2002). The paradigm shift to true collaboration with families. *Journal of Child and Family Studies, 11,* 47–60. doi:10.1023/A:1014715527823

Osterman, K. F. (2000). Students' need for belonging in the school community. *Review of Educational Research, 70,* 323–367. doi:10.2307/1170786

Page, R. N. (1991). *Lower track classrooms: A curricular and cultural perspective*. New York, NY: Teachers College Press.

Patterson, G. R., Reid, J. B., & Dishion, T. J. (1992). *Antisocial boys: A social interactional approach*. Eugene, OR: Castalia.

Pianta, R. C., & Walsh, D. J. (1996). *High-risk children in the schools: Constructing sustaining relationships*. New York, NY: Routledge.

Pittman, K. (1991). *Promoting youth development strengthening the role of youth serving and community organizations.* Washington DC: Academy for Educational Development.

Pittman, K., Irby, M., Tolman, J., Yohalem, N., & Ferber, T. (2001). *Preventing problems, promoting development, encouraging engagement: Competing priorities or inseparable goals?* Washington, DC: The Forum for Youth Investment.

Poduska, J., Kendziora, K., & Osher, D. (2008). *Coordinated and individualized services within systems of care.* Washington, DC: Center for Effective Collaboration and Practice, American Institutes for Research.

Pollard, J. A., Hawkins, J. D., & Arthur, M. W. (1999). Risk and protection: Are both necessary to understand diverse behavioral outcomes in adolescence? *Social Work Research, 23,* 145–158. Retrieved from http://www.naswpress.org/publications/journals/swr.html

Powell, A. G., Farrar, E., & Cohen, D. K. (1985). *The shopping mall high school.* Boston, MA: Houghton Mifflin.

Quinn, K. P., & Lee, V. (2007). The wraparound approach for students with emotional and behavioral disorders: Opportunities for school psychologists. *Psychology in the Schools, 44,* 101–111. doi:10.1002/pits.20209

Quinn, M. M., Osher, D., Hoffman, C. C., & Hanley, T. V. (1998). *Safe, drug-free, and effective schools for all students: What works!* Washington, DC: American Institutes for Research.

Rappaport, N., Osher, D., Dwyer, K., Garrison, E., Hare, I., Ladd, J., & Anderson-Ketchmark, C. (2002). Enhancing collaborations within and across disciplines to advance mental health programs in schools. In M. D. Weist, S. Evans, & N. Tashman (Eds.), *School mental health handbook* (pp. 107–118). New York, NY: Kluwer Academic.

Resnick, M. D., Harris, L. J., & Blum, R. W. (1993). The impact of caring and connectedness on adolescent health and well-being. *Journal of Child and Pediatric Health, 29,* 3–9. doi:10.1111/j.1440-1754.1993.tb02257.x

Resnick, M. D., Bearman, P. S., Blum, R. W., Bauman, K. E., Harris, K. M., Jones, J., et al. (1997). Protecting adolescents from harm: Findings from the National Longitudinal Study of Adolescent Health. *The Journal of the American Medical Association, 278,* 795–878. doi:10.1001/jama.278.10.823

Scales, P. C., & Leffert, N. (1999). *Developmental assets: A synthesis of the scientific research on adolescent development.* Minneapolis, MN: Search Institute.

Scott, T. M., & Eber, L. (2003). Functional assessment and wraparound as systemic school processes: Primary, secondary, and tertiary systems examples. *Journal of Positive Behavior Interventions, 5,* 131–143. doi:10.1177/10983007030 050030201

Shouse, R. (1996). Academic press and sense of community: Conflict and congruence in American high schools. *Research in Sociology of Education and Socialization, 11,* 173–202. doi:10.1007/BF02333405

Sinclair, M. F., Christenson, S. L., Lehr, C. A., & Anderson, A. R. (2003). Facilitating student engagement: Lessons learned from Check & Connect longitudinal studies. *The California School Psychologist, 8,* 29–42. Retrieved from http://education.ucsb.edu/school-psychology/CSP-Journal/index.html

Skiba, R. J., Michael R., Nardo, A., & Peterson, R. (2000). *The color of discipline: Gender and racial disparities in school punishment.* Bloomington: Indiana Education Policy Center.

Slavin, R. E., & Madden, N. A. (2001). *One million children: Success for all.* Newbury Park, CA: Corwin.

Smerdon, B. A. (1999). *How perceptions of school membership influence high school students' academic development: Implications for adolescents at risk of educational failure.* Dissertation, University of Michigan, Ann Arbor, MI.

Solano-Flores, G., & Nelson-Barber, S. (2001). On the cultural validity of science assessments. *Journal of Research in Science Teaching. 38,* 553–573. doi:10.1002/tea.1018

Solomon, D., Battistich, V., Watson, M., Schaps, E., & Lewis, C. (2000). A six-district study of educational change: Direct and mediated effects of the Child Development Project. *Social Psychology of Education, 4,* 3–51. doi:10.1023/A:1009609606692

Sprague, J., Walker, H., Golly, A., White, K., Myers, D. R., & Shannon, T. (2001). Translating research into effective practice: The effects of a universal staff and student intervention on indicators of discipline and school safety. *Education and Treatment of Children, 24,* 495–511. Retrieved from http://www.educationandtreatmentofchildren.net/

Stewart, E. B. (2008). School structural characteristics, student effort, peer associations, and parent involvement: The influence of school- and individual-level factors on academic achievement. *Education and Urban Society, 40,* 179–204. doi:10.1177/0013124507304167

Substance Abuse and Mental Health Services Administration. (2005). *Children and adolescents with anxiety disorders.* Retrieved from http://www.mentalhealth.samhsa.gov/publications/allpubs/CA-0007/default.asp

Sugai, G., Horner, R. H., Dunlap, G., Hieneman, M., Lewis, T. J., Nelson, C. M., et al. (2000). Applying positive behavioral support and functional behavioral assessment in schools. *Journal of Positive Behavioral Interventions, 2,* 131–143. doi:10.1177/109830070000200302

Sutherland, K. S., Alder, N., & Gunter, P. L. (2003). The effect of varying rates of OTR on the classroom behavior of students with EBD. *Journal of Emotional and Behavioral Disorders, 11,* 239–248. doi:10.1177/10634266030110040501

Sutherland, K. S., Wehby, J. H., & Yoder, P. J. (2002). Examination of the relationship between teacher praise and opportunities for students with EBD to respond to academic requests. *Journal of Emotional and Behavioral Disorders, 10,* 5–13. doi:10.1177/106342660201000102

Teddlie, C., & Reynolds, D. (2000). School effectiveness research and the social and behavioral sciences. In C. Teddlie & D. Reynolds (Eds.), *The international handbook of school effectiveness research* (pp. 301–321). London, England: Falmer.

U.S. Public Health Service. (2000). *Youth violence: A report of the surgeon general.* Washington, DC: Author.

U.S. Public Health Service. (2001). *Mental health: Culture, race, ethnicity: A supplement to the Surgeon General's Report on Mental Health.* Washington, DC: Author.

Valenzuela, A. (1999). *Subtractive schooling: U.S. – Mexican youth and the politics of caring.* Albany, NY: State University of New York Press.

Van Acker, R., Grant, S., & Henry, D. (1996). Teacher and student behavior as a function of risk for aggression. *Education and Treatment of Children, 19,* 316–334. Retrieved from http://www.educationandtreatmentofchildren.net/

Walker, H. M., Horner, R. H., Sugai, G., Bullis, M., Sprague, J. R., Bricker, D., & Kaufman, M. J. (1996). Integrated approaches to preventing antisocial behavior patterns among school-age children and youth. *Journal of Emotional & Behavioral Disorders, 4,* 194–209. doi:10.1177/106342669600400401

Waters, T., Marzano, B., & McNulty, B. (2003). Balanced leadership: *What 30 years of research tells us about the effect of leadership on student achievement.* Aurora, CO: Mid-continent Research for Education and Learning. Available online, from http://www.mcrel.org/

Wehlage, G. G., Rutter, R. A., Smith, G. A., Lesko, N., & Fernandez, R. R. (1989). *Reducing the risk: Schools as communities of support.* Philadelphia, PA: Falmer.

Weinstein, R. S. (2002). Overcoming inequality in schooling: A call to action for community psychology. *American Journal of Community Psychology, 30,* 21–42. doi:10.1023/A:1014311816571

Wentzel, K. R. (1997). Student motivation in middle school: The role of perceived pedagogical caring. *Journal of Educational Psychology, 89,* 411–419. doi:10.1037//0022-0663.89.3.411

Wentzel, K. R. (1998). Social relationships and motivation in middle school: The role of parents, teachers, and peers. *Journal of Educational Psychology, 90,* 202–209. doi:10.1037//0022-0663.90.2.202

Wentzel, K. R., & Wigfield, A. (1998). Academic and social motivational influences on students' academic performance. *Educational Psychology Review, 10,* 155–175. doi:10.1023/A:1022137619834

Wilson, D. B., Gottfredson, D. C., & Najaka, S. S. (2001). School-based prevention of problem behaviors: A meta-analysis. *Journal of Quantitative Criminology, 17,* 247–272. doi:10.1023/A:1011050217296

Woodruff, D. W., Osher, D., Hoffman, C. C., Gruner, A., King, M., Snow, S., & McIntire, J. C. (1999). *The role of education in a system of care: Effectively serving children with emotional or behavioral disorders.* Washington, DC: Center for Effective Collaboration and Practice, American Institutes for Research.

Zins, J. E., Weissberg, R. P., Wang, M. C., & Walberg, H. J. (2004). *Building academic success on social and emotional learning: What does the research say?* New York, NY: Teachers College Press.

4

A Problem-Solving Approach to School Violence Prevention

Jim Larson

THE UNIVERSITY OF WISCONSIN – WHITEWATER

R. T. Busse

CHAPMAN UNIVERSITY, ORANGE, CA

Abstract

This chapter describes how a problem-solving process can be employed effectively in the context of team decision making to design, implement, and evaluate a comprehensive school violence prevention program. Problem solving is conceptualized as the systematic effort to reduce the discrepancy between a current undesirable situation, such as frequent bully behavior, and that of a more preferred circumstance. A five-step process is identified: (a) problem identification, (b) problem analysis, (c) problem response proposals, (d) response implementation, and (e) evaluation of prevention strategies. The model places heavy reliance on data-gathering and analysis at the building level to define the problem accurately, and then to monitor effectively the progress of subsequent prevention programs and procedures.

A Problem-Solving Approach to School Violence Prevention

Virtually all plans to prevent the expression of aggressive or violent behavior in and around any school building arise out of some form of problem-solving process. Because violence is anathema to the educational process, the actuality or even the potential for it creates a problem in the school setting.

> A problem is a situation which is experienced by an agent as different from the situation which the agent ideally would like to be in. A problem is solved by a sequence of actions that reduce the difference between the initial situation and the goal.
>
> *(Heylighen, 1998)*

Simply stated and using Heylighen's definition, educators will become aware of situations in the school that are different from the way they desire them to be in the course of normal activities. Related to problems of school violence, this may be a new awareness of escalating incidences of bullying, finding a gun in a locker, or as was the case following the Columbine and other high profile school shootings, parental and media calls to hyper-protect children in school. Action will then be taken to reach a goal that reduces the difference between the way things are (e.g., too much bullying, too much parental concern) and the way the educators want them to be.

The elegance of the problem-solving process lies in its heuristic simplicity; the complexity lies in its execution. In this chapter, we examine how educators concerned with violence prevention can proceed most effectively from the first recognition of a need to act to the final goal attainment using a structured problem-solving methodology.

Conceptual Basis

The conceptual origins of problem solving as a process for service delivery in a system such as a school can be traced within modern psychology to theory and research in cognitive psychology, and more specifically, information processing psychology. In their seminal work, *Human Problem Solving*, Newell and Simon (1972) postulated that human beings are information processing organisms who, when presented with a stimulus, engage in a sequence of sensory reception, data transformation, memory integration, and behavioral output. When applied specifically to the process of cognitive problem solving, Newell and Simon theorized that the information must be further organized into a sequence of four tasks:

1. Identification of the problem space, which is the boundary between what is known and what the eventual goal is to be;
2. Identification of the intermediate states or sub-goals that must be attained to reach the final goal state;
3. Identification of the moves or action that must be enacted by the problem solver to move from one goal state to the next;
4. Identification of the resources necessary (e.g., time, knowledge, skills, people) to move from one goal state to the next.

These theoretical constructs have served as the foundation for applied work in clinical social problem solving, including therapy with adults (e.g., D'Zurrilla & Nezu, 1999), understanding aggressive children (e.g., Crick & Dodge, 1994; Dodge, 1986), and social skills training with children (e.g., Spivack, Platt, & Shure, 1976).

Problem solving as a model for service delivery in general and special education has expanded in recent years (Allen & Graden, 2002; Cantor, 2004; Deno, 2002). In the mid-1990s, the Heartland Area Education Agency in Iowa spearheaded a state-wide reformation of special education service delivery that systematized a problem-solving model to address learning and behavioral needs of students (Ikeda et al., 2003; Ikeda, Tilly III, Stumme, Volmer, & Allison, 1996). Subsequently, this model has been adopted by other school districts around the country, including the Milwaukee Public Schools (Haubner, Staum, & Potter, 2002) and the Minneapolis Public Schools (Marston, Cantor, Lau, & Muyskens, 2002). More recently, the emergence of Response to Intervention (RtI) and the three-tiered model of academic and social-emotional service delivery has helped to integrate the problem-solving model into the day-to-day decision-making process of an increasing number of schools (Cantor, 2006; Gresham, 2006).

Problem Solving and School Violence Prevention

In the period after the tragic school shootings between 1997–2000, and in the aftermath of the September 11, 2001, attacks on the World Trading Center and the Pentagon, the professional literature offered numerous organizational structures for educators to use as they approach the issue of school violence prevention (e.g., Dwyer & Jimerson, 2002; Dwyer & Osher, 2000; Dwyer, Osher, & Warger, 1998; Larson, Smith, & Furlong, 2003). More recently, the National Association of School Psychologists has developed an incident command system crisis prevention and response model, PREPaRE, based on the Department of Homeland Security's National Incident Management System (Brock et al., 2009). Central to each of these structures is the employment of a broadly representative, school-based team to initiate and oversee the effort. When constructing a school safety team, building representation should be secured from among diverse segments of the faculty as well as administration, pupil services, and unclassified staff. At the middle and high school levels, student representatives should be selected. This core team should subsequently identify which community and parent candidates will have the interest, expertise, and time to be a part of the team. A diverse team structure such as this can facilitate (a) topic-focused, data-based decision making; (b) enhanced buy-in and shared responsibility among stakeholders; (c) perspective sharing among stakeholders; and (d) centralized coordination of multiple services and programs. By its nature, problem solving thrives in a framework wherein ideas may be freely exchanged and fully analyzed from multiple perspectives, and a team format offers such a context. Readers should consult Dwyer and Jimerson (2002) and Brock et al. (2009) for comprehensive and practical guides to the design and organization of teams for school safety decision making.

The application of a problem-solving process to school violence prevention has been put forward (Larson, 2008; Larson et al., 2003). These authors identified a five-step process: (a) problem identification, (b) problem analysis, (c) problem response proposals, (d) response implementation, and (e) evaluation of prevention strategies. In the remainder of this chapter, we further articulate and expand this format with a special emphasis on procedures to acquire and analyze local school-based data to assist in decision making at each step. As a vehicle to enhance understanding at a practical level, we frame this discussion in part along the efforts of a hypothetical school safety team working at a school we will call Kennedy Elementary. Kennedy is a K–5 school of 600 students located in an ethnically diverse, major metropolitan area. Forty percent of its students qualify for free or reduced lunch.

Step 1: Problem Identification

Effective problem identification involves two essential processes: (a) understanding through assessment and (b) reframing for action. The school safety team must first gather enough reliable information to be able to frame the problems that the school is experiencing in language that lends itself to action plans. To accomplish this goal, the team needs to know the extent and nature of the gap that exists between the current reality and the desired reality. The current reality can be defined as an interaction between the nature and extent of existing violence-related behaviors in the school and the effectiveness of existing programs and procedures to prevent them. The essential questions are:

1. What are the personal experiences of school violence from the perspective of students, staff, and parents? What are the nature, frequency, and other pertinent characteristics of interpersonal aggression in the school?

2. What is the context of school violence (e.g., in the classroom, non-instructional areas, exterior grounds)? In what way does the context increase or decrease the likelihood of aggressive behavior?
3. What has been the impact of current prevention measures? Are there efficacy data on current approaches?

Archival Data

An appropriate starting place is with data already in archival form within school records. Disciplinary office referrals can be a useful index of day-to-day student behaviors that contribute to an unsafe learning environment (Morrison, Peterson, O'Farrell, & Redding, 2004). The team should examine the records for information regarding incident frequency within a defined time period, at a minimum within the most recently completed school year and continuing up to the present date. The team should graph the frequency of behavior problems such as fistfights, bully perpetration (including relational aggression and cyberbullying), gang-related behaviors, "hate crime" behaviors that target specific groups, weapon possession, vandalism, inappropriate sexual conduct, and drug possession. This exercise can also serve as an impetus to improve the incident reporting system if necessary.

Morrison et al. (2004) recommended that a disciplinary reporting system contain the following information: (a) demographic data on the referred student, such as academic status, special education status, ethnicity, and gender; (b) a full description of the nature of the problem behavior; (c) the location of the problem behavior; (d) the identity of the referring person; (e) date and time of the incident, and; (f) the effectiveness of the consequences. Software and Internet support are available to assist schools in collecting, maintaining, and analyzing discipline data. For example, *School Safety Software: SSP* (GBA Systems; http://www.glbsoft.com/docs/slicks/School%20Safety.pdf) is a sophisticated data collection and analysis program for schools that "meets or exceeds most of the recommendations by the National Forum on Educational Statistics with its ability to collect, report, and analyze incidents of crime and violence at school" (Minogue, Kingery, & Murphy, 1999, p.11). Additionally, the School-Wide Information System (SWIS; http://www.swis.org) is an Internet-based system that allows for secure storage and report generation of disciplinary data to monitor trends and to aid in the development of student interventions.

The team also should gather available data on existing programs and procedures of a preventative nature that function both in the school and in the community through a resource mapping exercise (e.g., Adelman & Taylor, 2006). This examination must differentiate those resources that are genuine and active from those that may be only "paper programs;" that is, those programs that are carried on the books but seldom accessed (Dwyer & Jimerson, 2002).

A comprehensive examination of existing prevention programs can help direct needed resources toward demonstrably effective efforts as well as identify needed improvements for promising programs. In addition, a wide-ranging examination of all of the prevention programs in the schools can provide the necessary documentation to eliminate those programs that fail to demonstrate a positive effect and may be usurping valuable resources that could be reallocated elsewhere.

Needs Assessment Surveys

Personal experience and context data can be most efficiently obtained through carefully considered needs assessment surveys and self-reports. Peterson and Skiba (n.d.a,b) designed a set of assessment tools for use within a school safety team that allow members to self-assess their own understanding of current prevention procedures in the school, and to organize their thoughts about what their colleagues outside of the committee believe about the problems. These tools are a useful starting point as the team prepares to assemble a wider needs assessment survey; they are available for download at http://www.unl.edu/srs/tools.html. Students also are an essential source of information; their input into the problem definition undertaking can provide the school safety team with substantial clarification and direction. *The California School Climate and Safety Survey – Short Form* (Furlong et al., 2005) is a 52-item revision of an original 102-item form. The scale yields self-report information from students in three principal areas: School Danger, School Climate, and School Victimization. This measure is available for download at http://web.me.com/michaelfurlong.

Our hypothetical school safety team at Kennedy Elementary School used these assessments methods to gather survey data from all staff members and all students in the fourth and fifth grades. They also examined office disciplinary forms that helped them identify "hot spots" in the school for problem behavior, including fighting. These data also illuminated periods in the week and school year that occasioned the most aggressive behavior and the referral rates of individual teachers. The team now needs to convert the accumulated data into practical information that can be useful for prevention planning.

Step 2: Problem Analysis and Hypothesis Development

This phase of the problem-solving process necessitates that the school safety team organize the data in a manner such that converging trends become evident. The main foci of the problem analysis phase are validation of the problem definition(s) and subsequent generation of hypotheses for responding to the problem. Care must be taken to avoid over- or under-interpretation, which can be accomplished by using a systematic process of data analysis. We suggest that the school safety team adopt a gating procedure to validate the problems that are identified through the first gate (i.e., the initial data collection). In the second gate, the problem is validated within a test-retest method. The retest can be accomplished by a second administration of the assessment methods to the initial sample, or randomly selecting a subset of respondents for follow-up validation surveys or interviews. Although a second assessment is time consuming, the gating method allows for more systematic identification of those areas in need of intervention by compensating for temporal or transient variables, and validating perceptions of problems as identified in the initial assessment data. The use of a gating procedure also provides for more focused problem response proposals, thereby offsetting potential wasted time and resources. Once the data are gathered, a simple component or item analysis can be conducted to identify and prioritize problem areas.

With analyzed data in front of them, the team next must convert the data to behaviorally worded action hypotheses. Hypothesis development involves translating what the data indicate into workable propositions about environmental or individual variables that mediate the problem. For example, data that showed high frequencies of lunchroom fights may be hypothesized to be a function of overcrowding, inadequate supervision, poor environmental design of the facility, student anger management deficits, lousy food, or some combination of any or all of these variables. Each action hypothesis should contain implications for intervention that are practical and testable.

A useful method for creating testable action hypotheses is through the use of Goal Attainment Scaling (Kirusek, Smith, & Cardillo, 1994; Roach & Elliott, 2005). Goal Attainment Scaling (GAS) is a criterion-referenced approach to operationalizing problem definitions that also can be used to document intervention effectiveness. The basic methodology can be used at either an individual or group level and involves operationally defining successive levels of program

Table 4.1 Goal Attainment Scale for Survey Item "I have stayed at home to avoid being bullied"

Level of Expected Outcome	Goal Attainment Criteria
Review date:	
Goal Attained (+2)	Less than 1% of students stayed home to avoid being bullied
Expected improvement (+1)	No more than10% of students stayed home to avoid being bullied
Current status (0)	18% of students stayed home to avoid being bullied
Less than expected outcome (–1)	19–25% of students stayed home to avoid being bullied
Much less than expected (–2)	More than 25% of students stayed home to avoid being bullied

progress on a 5-point or 6-point scale, i.e., –2 to +2, wherein a rating of 0 indicates baseline, –2 indicates that a problem is much worse and +2 indicates a program goal is attained. For example, consider the survey item "I have stayed at home to avoid being bullied." If baseline data indicate that 18% of fourth- and fifth-grade students responded to the item, then 18% is given a GAS rating 0. The school safety team then defines the level of goal attainment necessary for each rating. For example, the team may agree that a decrease to a rate of at least 10% would indicate progress toward the program goal (GAS = 1), a decrease to less than 1% would indicate the program goal was attained (GAS = 2), an increase up to 25% indicates a moderately worse problem (GAS = –1), and an increase to above 25% indicates the problem has significantly worsened. As shown in Table 4.1, the GAS method is simple to use, provides a format for writing testable hypotheses, is readily understandable, and it can be used to gather outcome data on a number of different action hypotheses. Finally, the GAS method reflects the criterion-based nature of data that can be most useful in individual school settings.

The school safety team at Kennedy Elementary found multiple sources of assessment data that converged on three major areas of concern: (a) bullying in the fourth and fifth grades; (b) fighting across all grade levels; and (c) staff desire to re-invigorate the building code of conduct.

Step 3: Problem Response Proposals

With the data now organized into focused student, staff, and environmental needs, school safety team members must consider options regarding how the building should address the identified needs. In recent years, a three-tiered public health schema for classifying prevention outcomes has been applied to the schools (Walker, Ramsey, & Gresham, 2004; see also Furlong, Morrison, Austin, Huh-Kim, & Skager, 2001; Larson, 2008). Using this model, prevention planners apply a *primary, secondary,* and *tertiary* needs hierarchy to the school population. At the primary level, *universal* interventions are designed and implemented to prevent the development and occurrences of antisocial, aggressive behavior. Universal interventions are considered necessary for all children in the school population, regardless of individual risk status. Universal procedures may take the form of schoolwide initiatives, such as a building code of conduct or a peer mediation program, classroom level instruction in anger management or conflict resolution, and heightened staff supervision of identified problem physical spaces (see Sprague & Walker, 2005).

Secondary prevention employs *selected* measures such as small group skills training to target a subset of students who because of individual exposure to risk factors already are exhibiting behaviors considered precursor or marker behaviors for more serious problems in the school. The goal of these interventions is to prevent these less serious problems from evolving into more serious aggressive or violent behaviors in later grades.

At the tertiary level of the prevention hierarchy, indicated programs target the smallest group of students whose high level of risk involvement may be manifested in severe emotional-behavioral disabilities, mental illness, or some form of volatile or aggressive behavior. Indicated prevention measures are best conceptualized as a structure of interacting supports under the direction of a collaborative team that figuratively "wrap" services around the student and often the family (see http://www.pbis.org/school/tertiary_level/wraparound.aspx and Eber, Sugai, Smith, & Scott, 2002).

At this juncture in the problem-solving process, the school safety team must align appropriate universal, selected, and indicated prevention measures with the action hypotheses developed from the assessment data. The focus of the programs and procedures that will comprise a comprehensive schoolwide violence prevention program will be guided by the assessment data from Steps 1 and 2 in the problem-solving process. Effective decisions about which particular program or procedure will be used to successfully address the action hypothesis demand that school safety team members become informed consumers of the research. Internet sites such as What Works Clearinghouse (http://ies.ed.gov/ncee/wwc/), the Hamilton Fish Institute (http://www.hamfish.org/), and the Center for the Prevention and Study of Violence (http://www.colorado.edu/cspv/index.html) can provide helpful research foundations. Additional discussion on the topic of evidenced-based interventions in schools can be found in Kratochwill (2002), Kratochwill and Shernoff (2004), and in this volume.

Our hypothetical school safety team at Kennedy Elementary School consulted with experts from a local university, visited a neighboring school district to observe a number of intervention programs in action, conducted an Internet search for exemplar codes of conduct, and examined the literature for bullying prevention programs and anger management interventions. They subsequently aligned the primary, secondary, and tertiary needs of all their students in the areas identified in their action hypotheses. This process allowed them to establish reasonable timelines so that they could meet budgetary and staff development imperatives.

Step 4: Response Implementation

This phase of the problem-solving process is a critical step because the success or failure of the best planned violence prevention program rests squarely on the quality of its implementation. Fundamental to successful implementation are issues of *social acceptability* and *intervention integrity*. Social acceptability refers to "judgments by laypersons, clients, and others of whether treatment procedures are appropriate, fair, and reasonable" (Kazdin, 2001, p. 401). The school safety team needs to consider the impact that the proposed intervention will have on the students, the staff directly involved in the implementation, and the larger body of additional stakeholders in and out of the building.

Intervention programs that students find embarrassing, demeaning, or excessively harsh may be met with resistance (Elliott, Witt, Kratochwill, & Stoiber, 2002). In a hypothetical example, a middle school may find that although the hallway behavior of the sixth-grade students was positively influenced by the staff distribution of "Positive Behavior Lottery" tickets during passing time, the eighth-grade students found the intervention childish and tore up the tickets. The management of aggressive behavior in the school setting can entail the use of out of the ordinary or controversial procedures such as exclusionary time-out (e.g., Kazdin, 2001), pull-out anger management skills training (e.g., Larson & Lochman, 2010), or even physical restraint (e.g., Klotz, 2010). Consequently, schools may find that the use of a district-level oversight body to review proposed interventions for possible legal, ethical, or student and staff acceptability concerns will help avoid potential problems.

When a teacher or pupil services professional put into practice an evidence-supported intervention, there is a presumption that the procedures will be implemented in the same or very similar manner as was done in the supporting research. When this happens, the intervention is said to have high treatment integrity (Gresham, 1989; Power et al., 2005). Integrity problems may arise if teachers or other personnel are asked to engage in intervention practices that they perceive as ineffective, overly complex, or poorly related to their own understanding of the problem. It is not enough for the school safety team alone to understand and be convinced of the merits of a school violence prevention plan; effective implementation demands that the personnel charged with carrying out that plan also share that understanding and conviction. The integrity of a prevention plan can be enhanced with thorough staff development training, assessment of training competencies, ongoing support and follow-through, and ongoing evaluation of adherence to the intervention program. Evaluating whether the intervention steps were followed can be accomplished through direct observations and through self-report and behavior rating scale methods that delineate each specific component of the intervention protocol (for examples, see Gresham, 1989).

School personnel also need to be cognizant of the impact that any new program will have on parents and on the greater community outside of the school. For instance, do all parents understand why instruction time is being taken away from traditional subjects in order to implement a new bully prevention curriculum? Is the prevention program targeting a specific group of students such that it could be perceived from the outside as racist, sexist, or otherwise discriminatory, in spite of benign, data-supported intentions? Are there significant budget issues to which taxpayers may object? Additionally, the age-old question "How will this play in the press?" is one worth asking. For example, a well-designed intervention that allows high risk youth to earn fast food coupons for identified positive behaviors may turn up in the newspaper as "Desperate School Now Paying Delinquents to Behave."

These issues underscore the importance of effective communication, training, and team-building throughout the problem-solving process. The broadly representative school safety team structure stressed earlier gives voice to the various constituencies affected by the plan and helps ensure that potential problems are proactively addressed.

The school safety team at Kennedy Elementary presented their comprehensive school violence prevention plan to the school board, providing opportunities to begin the budget request process and to receive citizen input. They sent a press release to the local media outlets that described the rationale for their plan and the anticipated benefits for the school community. An informational parent meeting was held at the school, and additional flyers were sent home with all the children. In consultation with the faculty and pupil services staff, the team constructed a phased implementation plan over a two year span that allowed for (a) the most critical needs to be addressed first, (b) adequate funding from grants and the regular budget to be accumulated, and (c) sufficient opportunities for staff development.

Step 5: Evaluation of Prevention Strategies

The final phase of the problem-solving model involves both formative and summative evaluations of the response programs. A formative evaluation component is important for monitoring *ongoing* progress toward program goals and allows for changes to be made in the response implementation as dictated by the outcome assessment methods. For example, it may be that intervention integrity data (e.g., direct observations, self-report, or behavior rating scales of each specific component of the intervention protocol) indicate that the response protocol is too difficult to consistently implement. One then must analyze the reasons for this difficulty (e.g., insufficient training, insufficient program support) and perhaps recycle to an earlier problem-solving phase. Ongoing assessment also will help with decisions about program goal attainment and subsequent implementation to address the next problem as prioritized by the team.

At the primary prevention level, we suggest that a sub-sample of staff and students complete ongoing, formative assessments at least once per month to evaluate progress toward the outcome goals. The GAS method can be readily applied to formative evaluations in a time-efficient manner by assessing only those variables that have been identified as problems. At the secondary and tertiary levels, progress monitoring should occur more frequently, perhaps weekly or even daily depending on the target behaviors. The GAS method and time-series graphing are well suited for use with small groups or individuals.

A summative evaluation can be achieved by evaluating the level of convergence of the outcome goals. At the primary prevention level, a simple method is to average the GAS ratings for each problem variable to provide an overall convergent evidence rating. To evaluate time-series data at the secondary and tertiary levels, useful methods include GAS ratings, single-case effect sizes, percentage of non-overlapping data (PND), and trend analysis. If rating scales are used to monitor progress in a pre-post fashion, the reliable change index (RCI) may be useful. (For applications of these methods within problem-solving models, see Busse, Kratochwill, & Elliott, 1995, and Riley-Tillman & Burns, 2009.)

Traditional statistical methods also may be used to evaluate change, however, we believe that a criterion-referenced approach is most useful in applied school settings. A statistically significant change from pre- to post-intervention may not reflect the desired *magnitude* of change and, as such, may not demonstrate social or educational significance. Regardless of the evaluation method, several aspects of the prevention program will be continuously implemented; therefore, the assessment will be an ongoing enterprise to ensure that the program goals have been maintained.

After four months of the phased implementation, the school safety team at Kennedy School collected evaluation data using average GAS ratings and authentic disciplinary data. They found that schoolwide bullying continued at near baseline rates with a GAS rating of 0, but was beginning to demonstrate a positive trend, and fighting was less of a problem but still below program goals with a GAS rating of 1. Intervention integrity data were gathered through self-report ratings of adherence to each intervention step, which indicated that the staff was only adhering to an average of 60% of intervention steps, although supervision of problem areas had been followed through with 90% adherence. Following a staff development inservice conducted by a team from the local university, staff satisfaction with crisis response obligations showed significant improvement (GAS = 2). The Work Team for the revised code of conduct had been productive, and the initial draft was distributed to the faculty. Formative evaluation is ongoing to identify and strengthen those areas in need of enhanced intervention adherence, and to identify individual student progress at the secondary and tertiary levels of intervention.

Advantages and Disadvantages of the Problem-Solving Model

The major advantage of applying the problem-solving model to school safety concerns is the team-based approach toward systematic assessment and intervention (Table 4.2 delineates how the problem-solving model can be applied to practice). The model provides focus that can maximize resources and enhance intervention outcomes. That focus, however, has initial cost due to the significant amount of time, effort, and resources required to engage in a complete problem-solving process. Among these costs are the potential difficulties with buy-in from the staff and community when solutions are not immediately evident. Educators, however, must systematically approach school safety and violence prevention. School professionals often set up themselves and their constituents for failure in problem solving when specificity is lacking. If the data are too general, the intervention vague, and follow-through lacking, the likelihood is high that the prevention efforts will be ineffective.

Table 4.2 Implications for Practice: Using a Problem-Solving Approach to Prevent School Violence

Develop a school safety team to enhance buy-in and shared responsibilities among stakeholders. Use the 5-step problem-solving approach:

1. Problem Identification
   - Collect systematic data using archival data, surveys, observations, and interviews to enhance specificity
2. Problem Analysis and Hypothesis Development
   - Use a gating assessment procedure to validate the problem(s)
   - Generate testable hypotheses
3. Problem Response Protocols
   - Employ data based response protocols for primary, secondary, and tertiary prevention
4. Response Implementation
   - Collect systematic data with the measures used in problem identification
   - Ensure intervention integrity
5. Evaluation of Prevention Strategies
   - Engage in frequent formative evaluations
   - Use a criterion-based approach to evaluation

References

Adelman, H., & Taylor, L. (2006). Mapping a school's resources to improve their use in preventing and ameliorating problems. In C. Franklin, M. B. Harris, & P. Allen-Meares (Eds.), *The school services sourcebook: A guide for social workers, counselors, and mental health professionals* (pp. 977–990). Retrieved from http://smhp.psych.ucla.edu/publications/53%20mapping%20a%20schools%20resources%20to%20improve1.pdf

Allen, S., & Graden, J. (2002). Best practices in collaborative problem solving for intervention design. In A. Thomas & J. Grimes (Eds.), *Best practices in school psychology IV* (pp. 565–582). Bethesda, MD: National Association of School Psychologists.

Brock, S. E., Nickerson, A. B., Reeves, M. A., Jimerson, S. R., Lieberman, R., & Feinberg, T. (2009). *School crisis prevention and intervention: The PREPaRE Model.* Bethesda, MD: National Association of School Psychologists.

Busse, R. T., Kratochwill, T. R., & Elliott, S. N. (1995). Meta-analysis for single-case consultation outcomes: Applications to research and practice. *Journal of School Psychology, 33,* 269–285. doi:10.1016/0022-4405(95)00014-D

Cantor, A. (2004). A problem-solving model for improving student achievement. *Principal Leadership Magazine, 34,* 5. Retrieved from http://www.nasponline.org/resources/principals/nassp_probsolve.aspx

Cantor, A. (2006). Problem-solving and RTI: New roles for school psychologists. *Communiqué'34,* 5. doi:10.1521/scpq.20.1.89.64192

Crick, N. R., & Dodge, K. A. (1994). A review and reformulation of social information-processing mechanisms in children's social adjustment. *Psychological Bulletin, 115,* 74–101. doi: 10.1037/0033-2909.115.1.74

Deno, S. L. (2002). Problem solving as "best practice." In A. Thomas & J. Grimes (Eds.), *Best practices in school psychology IV* (pp. 37–56). Bethesda, MD: National Association of School Psychologists.

Dodge, K. A. (1986). A social information processing model of social competence in children. In M. Perlmutter (Ed.), *Cognitive perspectives on children's social and behavioral development: The Minnesota symposium on child psychology* (Vol. 18; pp. 77–125). Hillsdale, NJ: Erlbaum.

Dwyer, K. P., & Jimerson, S. R. (2002). Enabling prevention through planning. In S. E. Brock, P. J. Lazarus, & S. R. Jimerson (Eds.), *Best practices in school crisis prevention and intervention* (pp. 23–46). Bethesda, MD: National Association of School Psychologists.

Dwyer, K., & Osher, D. (2000). *Safeguarding our children: An action guide.* Washington, DC: U. S. Departments of Education and Justice, American Institutes for Research. Retrieved from http://www2.ed.gov/admins/lead/safety/actguide/action_guide.pdf

Dwyer, K., Osher, D., & Warger, C. (1998). *Early warning, timely response: A guide to safe schools.* Washington, DC: U. S. Department of Education. Retrieved from http://cecp.air.org/guide/guide.pdf

D'Zurrilla, T. J., & Nezu, A. M. (1999). *Problem-solving therapy: A social competence approach to clinical intervention* (2nd ed.). New York: Springer.

Eber, L., Sugai, G., Smith, C., & Scott, T. M. (2002). Wraparound and positive behavioral Interventions and supports in the schools. *Journal of Emotional and Behavioral Disorders, 10,* 136–173. doi: 10.1177/10634266020100030501

Elliott, S. N., Witt, J. C., Kratochwill, T. R., & Stoiber, K. C. (2002). Selecting and evaluating classroom interventions. In M. R. Shinn, H. M. Walker, & G. Stoner (Eds.), *Interventions for academic and behavioral problems II: Preventive and remedial approaches* (pp. 243–294). Bethesda, MD: National Association of School Psychologists.

Furlong, M. J., Greif, J. L., Bates, M. P., Whipple, A. D., Jimenez, T. C., & Morrison, R (2005). Development of the California School Climate and Safety Survey–Short Form. *Psychology in the Schools, 42,* 137–149. doi: 10.1002/pits.20053

Furlong, M., Morrison, G. M., Austin, G., Huh-Kim, J., Skager, R. (2001). Using student risk factors in school violence surveillance reports: Illustrative examples for enhanced policy formation, implementation, and evaluation. *Law & Policy, 23,* 271–296. doi: 10.1111/1467-9930.00114

Gresham, F. M. (1989). Assessment of treatment integrity in school consultation and prereferral intervention. *School Psychology Review, 18,* 37–50.

Gresham, F. M. (2006). Response to intervention. In G. G. Bear & K. M. Minke (Eds.), *Children's needs III: Development, prevention, and intervention* (pp. 525–540). Bethesda, MD: National Association of School Psychologists.

Haubner, C., Staum, M., & Potter, A. (2002, June). Optimizing success through problem solving: School reform in Milwaukee Public Schools. *Communiqué, 30*(8), 31.

Heylighen, F. (1998). *Problem solving.* Retrieved from http://pespmc1.vub.ac.be/PROBSOLV.html

Ikeda, M., Grimes, J., Tilly III, W. D., Allison, R., Kurns, S., & Stumme, J. (2003). Implementing an intervention-based approach to service delivery: A case example. In M. Shinn, H. M. Walker, & G. Stoner (Eds.), *Interventions for academic and behavior problems II: Preventive and remedial approaches* (pp. 53–70). Bethesda, MD: National Association of School Psychologists.

Ikeda, M., Tilly III, W. D., Stumme, J., Volmer, L., & Allison, R. (1996). Agency-wide implementation of problem-solving consultation. *School Psychology Quarterly, 11,* 228–243. doi: 10.1037/h0088931

Kazdin, A. E. (2001). *Behavior modification in applied settings* (6th ed.). Belmont, CA: Wadsworth/Thomson Learning.

Kirusek, T. J., Smith, A., & Cardillo, J. E. (Eds.). (1994). *Goal attainment scaling: Application, theory, and measurement.* Hillsdale, NJ: Erlbaum.

Klotz, M. B. (2010, March-April). IDEA in practice. *Communiqué, 38*(6). Retrieved from: http://www.nasponline.org/publications/cq/mocq386idea.aspx

Kratochwill, T. R. (2002). Evidence-based interventions in school psychology: Thoughts on thoughtful commentary. *School Psychology Quarterly, 17,* 518–532. doi: 10.1521/scpq.17.4.518.20861

Kratochwill, T. R., & Shernoff, E. S. (2004). Evidence-based practice: Promoting evidence-based interventions in school psychology. *School Psychology Quarterly, 18,* 1–21. doi: 10.1521/scpq.18.4.389.27000

Larson, J. (2008). Best practices in school violence prevention. In A. Thomas & J. Grimes (Eds.), *Best practices in school psychology V* (pp. 1291–1307). Bethesda, MD: National Association of School Psychologists.

Larson, J., & Lochman, J. E. (2010). *Helping schoolchildren cope with anger: A cognitive-behavioral intervention* (2nd ed.). New York: Guilford.

Larson, J., Smith, D. C., & Furlong, M. J. (2003). Best practices in school violence prevention. In A. Thomas & J. Grimes (Eds.), *Best practices in school psychology IV* (pp. 1081–1098). Bethesda, MD: National Association of School Psychologists.

Marston, D., Cantor, A., Lau, M., & Muyskens, P. (2002, June). Problem-solving: Implementation and evaluation in Minneapolis schools. *Communiqué, (30)*8, 15–16, 18–19.

Minogue, N., Kingery, P., & Murphy, L. (1999). *Approaches to assessing violence among youth.* Rosslyn, VA: Hamilton Fish Institute on School and Community Violence.

Morrison, G. M., Peterson, R., O'Farrell, S., & Redding, M. (2004). Using office referrals records in school violence research: Possibilities and limitation. In M. Furlong, G. Morrison, R. Skiba, & D. Cornell (Eds.), *Issues in school violence research* (pp. 39–61). Binghamton, NY: Haworth Press.

Newell, A., & Simon, H. A. (1972). *Human problem solving.* Englewood Cliffs, CA: Prentice-Hall.

Peterson, R. L., & Skiba, R. J. (n.d.a). *Needs assessment questionnaire.* Retrieved from http://www.unl.edu/srs/index.html

Peterson, R. L., & Skiba, R. J. (n.d.b). *Practices and program inventory.* Retrieved from http://www.unl.edu/srs/index.html

Power, T. J., Blom-Hoffman, J., Clarke, A. T., Riley-Tillman, T. C., Kellerher, C., & Manz, P. (2005). Reconceptualizing intervention integrity: A partnership-based framework for linking research with practice. *Psychology in the Schools, 42,* 495–507. doi: 10.1002/pits.20087

Roach, A. T., & Elliott, S. N. (2005). Goal attainment scaling: An efficient and effective approach to monitoring student progress. *Teaching Exceptional Children, 37,* 8–17.

Riley-Tillman, T. C., & Burns, M. K. (2009). *Evaluating educational interventions: Single-case design for measuring response to intervention.* New York: Guilford.

Spivack, G., Platt, J. J., & Shure, M. B. (1976). *The problem-solving approach to adjustment*. San Francisco, CA: Jossey-Bass.

Sprague, J. R., & Walker, H. M. (2005). *Safe and healthy schools: Practical prevention strategies*. New York: Guilford.

Walker, H. M., Ramsey, E., & Gresham, F. M. (2004). *Antisocial behavior in school: Evidence-based practices* (2nd ed.). Belmont, CA: Wadsworth/Thomson Learning.

5

Social Support in the Lives of Students Involved in Aggressive and Bullying Behaviors

Michelle Kilpatrick Demaray, Christine Kerres Malecki, and Lyndsay N. Jenkins

NORTHERN ILLINOIS UNIVERSITY, DEKALB

Lauren D. Westermann

THE INDIAN PRAIRIE SCHOOL DISTRICT, AURORA, IL

Abstract

Engaging in bullying and other violent behavior is influenced by characteristics of the individual, family, peers, school, and community; thus, researchers have focused on understanding the many ecological and contextual variables surrounding bullying and school violence. This chapter focuses on one such contextual factor: perceptions of social support from peers, parents, and teachers. Current research about social support and school violence is discussed and the chapter concludes with a discussion of how this research can be translated into practice.

Violence in American schools has been identified as a concern to educators across the country. For example, in 2007, 32% of 12- to 18-year-old students reported being bullied at school during the previous year (Dinkes, Kemp, & Baum, 2009). Being bullied at school or engaging in bullying behaviors has been identified as a risk factor for other violent behaviors, such as carrying weapons, fighting, and incurring injuries from fighting (Nansel, Overpeck, Haynie, Ruan, & Scheidt, 2003). Engaging in bullying and other violent behavior is influenced by characteristics of the individual, family, peers, school, and community; therefore, researchers have focused on understanding the many ecological and contextual variables surrounding bullying and school violence (Espelage & Swearer, 2004). This chapter discusses perceptions of social support from peers, parents, and teachers. Current research regarding social support and school violence is described and the chapter concludes with a discussion of how this research can be translated into practice.

Social Support

Tardy (1985) described a conceptual model that includes five aspects of social support. First, *direction* describes whether the support is being given or received. Second, *disposition* describes whether the supportive behaviors are just *available* or if they are actually being *enacted* or used. *Description/evaluation* refers to whether a person *describes* the support they receive or *evaluates* that support. Fourth, Tardy describes one's *network* or the source(s) of an individual's support network (parents, teachers, friends, etc.). Finally, Tardy describes the *content* or type of support, which includes *emotional, instrumental, informational*, and/or *appraisal* support. Emotional support refers to caring support (e.g., providing empathy, hugs, and care). Instrumental support refers to spending time with someone or providing necessary resources. For example, a parent spending time with their child to work on math homework or practice soccer would be instrumental support. Providing the necessary resources, such as a calculator for a math class or a soccer ball to practice soccer, is also instrumental support. Informational support involves providing someone with valuable information or advice. Finally, people we care about provide appraisal support when they give feedback or evaluation that is beneficial. For perpetrators and/or their victims, various types of social support from different sources may play a role in the aggressive dynamic or in the aftermath of violent school behavior.

Social support may play a role in school violence in several ways. Two theoretical models generally describe how social support may function. First, the main effect model (Cohen, Gottlieb, & Underwood, 2000) suggests that positive social support is beneficial for all people. This theory posits that if we have adequate levels of social support, we will function more effectively and be healthier in general. The stress-buffering theory (Cohen et al., 2000) suggests that when we are under stress, social support plays a protective role resulting in more positive outcomes than if we did not have adequate social support. For victims of school violence and bullying, the stress-buffering model of support seems most salient. Students who are victims of violence or bullying may be under more stress and social support may buffer them from more negative outcomes.

Social Support and School Violence

Many researchers believe that social support may be a salient factor in preventing school violence. For instance, one focus of the National School Safety Center (NSSC) has been to expand the role of student support services in schools (Stephens, 2002). Creating supportive student environments includes establishing a sense of student ownership and pride in the school and offering services for troubled youth. The NSSC strategy for increasing school safety not only includes providing social support for students, but also for teachers, parents, and community members (Stephens, 2002). The creation and implementation of these programs rely on an understanding of various social support systems (i.e., family, peer group, and school) that may affect students' behavior (Espelage & Swearer, 2003). For example, Furlong, Pavelski, and Saxton (2002) suggest that the examination of supportive connections of students to their school is a useful way to identify the level of violence prevention program needed. Therefore, an understanding of the relationship among social support and school violence is one that must be understood if efforts to decrease violence are to be successful.

Despite the fact that policies meant to address violent behavior in schools often focus on creating meaningful relationships among students and supportive peers and adults (Austin, 2003), the research on social support and violent or aggressive behaviors remains scarce. Although some previous investigations have included students' significant others as a factor in the lives of victims (Furlong, Chung, Bates, & Morrison, 1995; Morrison, Furlong, & Smith, 1994), only a handful have investigated social support as a primary construct related to aggressive and violent behaviors in schools (Cowie & Olafsson, 2000; Davidson & Demaray, 2007; Demaray & Malecki,

2003; Holt & Espelage, 2007; Malecki & Demaray, 2003; Naylor & Cowie, 1999; Rigby, 2000). The use of socially supportive behaviors is often suggested as a method to decrease and prevent violence (Reinke & Herman, 2002; Scott, Nelson, & Liaupsin, 2001; Stephens, 1994), yet these suggestions are based on assumptions rather than scientific data.

However, some recent work by researchers Cowie and Jennifer (2007, 2008) has focused on programs that use peer social support to improve school safety and reduce instances of bullying and school violence. Their framework creates peer support systems in schools by training certain students to offer emotional and social support to peers who are in distress (Cowie & Smith, 2010). They propose three key aspects of their peer support programs: (a) selected peers are trained to be peer supporters, (b) certain peers will enact upon the peer support, and (c) longer-term training of peer supporters will reduce the rates of conflict and bullying in a school. Evaluation of the effectiveness of this framework has been evaluated by a range of means (e.g., case studies, testimonials, independent reviews), but Cowie and Smith (2010) report that the overall consensus is that the peer supporters as well as the support recipients have benefited from the program. Additionally, teachers report improvements in the safety of the school and more caring being demonstrated among students.

Though the term "school violence" may bring to mind extreme behaviors, such as school shootings, violence in schools encompasses a much wider range of behaviors including bullying, teasing, harassment, and assault (Furlong et al., 2002). These low-level forms of violence have been largely overlooked in previous decades of research, despite their potential to greatly influence the school environment (Dupper & Meyer-Adams, 2002). This oversight is troubling given that seemingly benign behaviors, like teasing or bullying, can lead to more serious, violent ones (Spivak & Prothrow-Smith, 2001).

An emerging area of school violence involves the use of technology to engage in peer aggression. This type of youth violence has been termed cyberbullying or electronic bullying. Raskauskas and Stolz (2007) found that among their sample of adolescents, involvement in traditional bullying predicted involvement in electronic bullying. Being a victim of electronic bullying was related to being a bully at school, but victims of traditional bullying were not found to be electronic bullies. Because the study of electronic bullying is relatively new, only one study was found that examined relations among internet bullying and verbal and physical traditional bullying with peer social support. Williams and Guerra (2007) found that when youth viewed their friends as caring, helpful, and trustworthy, they also reported significantly lower levels of involvement in all three types of bullying (i.e., verbal, physical, and Internet bullying). Future studies are needed to further understand the amount and type of social support that is perceived among participants of cyberbullying.

Victims' and Bully/Victims' Levels of Support

When attempting to understand why certain students are victimized, it is helpful to identify risk factors that may make them vulnerable to attack. One risk factor appears to be the lack of support, as previous research indicates that victims typically have poor support from adults and peers in their lives. Furlong et al. (1995) compared fifth- through twelfth-grade students who were victims of multiple incidents of school violence to those who were not victimized. Victims sought teacher and peer support significantly less than non-victimized students. Additionally, victims reported feeling less connected to their schools than non-victims. Similarly, using a sample of over 18,000 parents and students, Schreck, Miller, and Gibson (2003) found that students who felt alienated from school were more likely to be victims of violent and nonviolent crimes. Victims of school bullying exhibit similar patterns of low support as victims of violence. For instance, in a sample of 12- to 16-year-old students, status as a victim of peer bullying was related to low levels of support from best friends and classmates. For females, victimization was also related to low teacher support (Rigby, 2000). In their investigation of bullying and social support in sixth- through eighth-grade students, Demaray and Malecki (2003) found that students classified as victims had low support from their classmates, whereas students that exhibited characteristics of both bullies and victims (i.e., bully/victims) also had low support from the people in their lives. Bully/victims reported low support from their parents, classmates, and people in their schools, suggesting that students who are both the perpetrators and victims of such behaviors are at the greatest risk for negative outcomes (Demaray & Malecki, 2003). Holt and Espelage (2007) also examined perceptions of social support among middle and high school students and found that students who were victims and bully-victims reported significantly lower levels of social support compared to students uninvolved in bullying. In this study, however, victims did not significantly differ from bullies in levels of perceived social support. The overlap of the bully and victim categories and the great risk for students who are both bullies and victims creates concerns that some victims may become violent in an attempt to protect themselves. Kingery, Pruitt, and Heuberger (1996) reported that adolescents who brought guns to school were much more likely than non-gun-carriers to have been the victim of violent behavior in the previous year. These bully/victims appear to be especially vulnerable to negative outcomes, as they report lower levels of support than nonaggressive victims (Brockenbrough, Cornell, & Loper, 2002).

Perpetrators' Levels of Support

It is not only students who are at the receiving end of violent and bully behaviors that present a concern for schools; perpetrators of these behaviors have similarly low levels of support (Boulton & Smith, 1994; Duncan, 2004; Hanish, Kochenderfer-Ladd, Fabes, Martin, & Denning, 2004). This could indicate that violent and aggressive students may be disengaged from the very individuals that can help decrease their problem behaviors. In an investigation of the determinants of violent behavior in inner-city youth, Powell (1997) found that support from adults outside the family was able to protect against student involvement in violent behavior. Behaviors that could potentially lead to violent incidents, such as weapon carrying, also appear to be related to low support. Malecki and Demaray (2003) investigated the social support of early adolescents who self-reported bringing a weapon to school and found that low support from parents, teachers, and peers was predictive of weapon carrying. Similarly, McNabb, Farley, Powell, Rolka, and Horan (1996) reported that adolescent gun-carrying was correlated with the lack of an employed male role model in the home. Other low-level forms of aggressive behavior, such as bullying, have been linked to low support. Demaray and Malecki (2003) found that students who were classified as bullies had low amounts of support from parents, classmates, and people in their schools.

Bystanders Level of Social Support

An expanding area of research is to investigate social support in the lives of student that are classified as neither perpetrators nor victims of bullying and school violence. Researchers seek to understand the factors that lead these peers to either help or hinder perpetrators or victims. Salmivalli, Lagerspetz, Bjorkqvist, Osterman, and Kaukiainen (1996) and Salmivalli, Huttunen, and Lagerspetz (1997) have developed several categories for these groups, such as assistant to the bully, reinforcer of the bully, defender of the victim, and outsiders. A recent study by Summers and Demaray (2010) investigated perceptions of social support among various participants (i.e., Bully, Victim, Defender, Outsider, and Comparison) in the bullying situation. With regard to parent support, the Comparison, Bully, Defender, and Outsider groups all perceived more social support than the Bully/Victim group. For teacher support, the Comparison, Defender, and Outsider groups all perceived more social support than the Bully/Victim group and the Defender group perceived more social support than the Bully group. With respect to classmate support, the Comparison, Bully, and Defender groups all perceived more social support than the Victim group. In addition, the Defender group perceived more social support than the Victim/Defender and Outsider group. For close friend support, the Defender group perceived more support than the Victim group. Lastly, for school support, the Comparison and Defender groups perceived more support than Bully/Victims; in addition, the Defender Group perceived more support than Victims and Outsiders. In sum, victims and bully-victims often perceived lower levels of social support while the Comparison and Defender groups often perceived higher levels of support. This has important implications for understanding why some kids defend victims, suggesting that perhaps higher perceptions of social support allow them to stand up to bullies in bullying situations.

More work is needed on the role of social support for all of the bystanders in bullying, but in terms of intervention to benefit victims, the group of particular interest may be the defender group. Cowie and Smith (2010) describe defenders as groups of peers that are "usually friends of a victim who help them by intervening on their behalf, comforting them, confronting bullies, or seeking adult help, thus making future attacks less likely" (p. 177). Cowie and her colleagues have developed a peer support framework that seeks to train peers to intervene and comfort victims of bullying. The core of their work is centered on employing more peers as defenders in order to increase school safety.

One of the few studies that have examined factors related to the likelihood that peers will support victims during bullying situations was conducted by Rigby and Johnson (2006). The study produced some findings that can help inform intervention ideas for using social support to benefit victims of school violence. First, they found that elementary students are more willing to support victims than middle school students, and that elementary girls were more willing to intervene than elementary boys. Students in both elementary and middle school reported that they were more likely to support a victim of verbal bullying than in a physical bullying situation. Overall, even though most students reported a positive attitude towards the victim, the majority of students did not indicate that they would provide support to the victim. Though the researcher only assessed readiness to support (not why they would choose not to support) several implications can be inferred from this study.

The Protective Effects of Social Support after Victimization

One very promising direction in intervention for students involved in bullying may involve social support. The stress buffering model of social support (Cohen & Wills, 1985) has been a guiding theory in many recent studies that investigated how the provision of support may be a valuable tool in helping students cope with and recover from incidents of school violence and bullying. Davidson and Demaray (2007) found that for middle school girls, parent support played a buffering role between being victimized and distress from bullying. They also found that for middle school boys, teacher, classmate, and school support played this buffering role. Similarly, Stadler, Feifel, Rohrmann, Vermeiren, and Poustka (2010) found that for middle school students, parent support buffered victims against maladjustment and, for high school students, support from the school buffered victims against maladjustment.

Some researchers have examined the more complex patterns in this possible buffering relationship. In one study, the combination of both teacher and peer support showed the strongest buffering effects against victimization on more negative quality of life (Flaspohler, Elfstrom, Vanderzee, Sink, & Birchmeier, 2009). Finally, some interesting patterns of this buffering effect were found when examining victims, bullies, bully-victims, and non-involved students (Conners-Burrow, Johnson, Whiteside-Mansell, McKelvey, & Gargus, 2009). It was found that parent support buffered against depression especially well for bully-victims, but also for non-involved students, victims, and bullies. Furthermore, they found that when parent support was low, teacher support played a buffering role for non-involved students, bullies, and bully-victims against depression.

In sum, a number of researchers, studying a variety of outcomes, are finding promising results suggesting that social support from parents in particular, but also from teachers, peers, and other people in the school may buffer students involved in bullying from adverse outcomes such as maladjustment, negative quality of life, depression, and distress from bullying. This promising line of research should continue to help inform school staff specifically how they might utilize social support as an effective intervention.

Social Support from Negative Sources and Peer Groups

One factor that sometimes is overlooked when examining the relationship among social support and violent or aggressive behaviors is the impact of potential negative sources of social support. Just as social support from positive sources such as teachers, parents, and school staff can keep students from becoming involved in violent behaviors (McNabb et al., 1996; Schreck et al., 2003) and protect against the negative impact of victimization (Rigby, 2000), support from negative sources can have a harmful impact on students' lives. The influence of delinquent peers or family members has been related to a variety of aggressive and violent behaviors. While peers reject some aggressive children, others are popular and may gain support for engaging in violent or aggressive behavior (Estell, Cairns, Farmer, & Cairns, 2002; Perren & Hornung, 2005; Robertson et al., 2010; Rodkin, Farmer, Pearl, & Van Acker, 2000). In fact, some aggressive children receive support not only from other aggressive peers within deviant peer groups, but from nonaggressive peers as well (Rodkin, Farmer, Pearl, & Van Acker, 2006). Recent research has identified subsets of aggressive, antisocial, or delinquent students who are well liked by classmates and are considered leaders by both their teachers and peers (Estell, Farmer, Pearl, Van Acker, & Rodkin, 2008; Robertson et al., 2010; Rodkin et al., 2000). The presence of these well liked yet aggressive students in the classroom impacts the group social dynamic (Rodkin et al., 2000) and may promote the use of aggressive behaviors for social advancement (Robertson et al., 2010; Rodkin et al., 2000).

The influence of delinquent family and community members has also been related to children and adolescents' involvement in maladaptive behaviors. Powell (1997) reported that family member involvement in gangs was a risk factor for inner-city students' involvement in violent behavior. Parental incarceration also places children at a high risk of engaging in delinquent behavior (Murray & Farrington, 2006). Research investigating the impact of community settings on adolescent behavior indicates that adolescents are at a higher risk of engaging in delinquent activity when they are exposed to repeated violence within their communities (Zinzow et al., 2009). This community violence is likely to include relatives and family members as the perpetrators (Zinzow et al., 2009).

Similar to the potential for negative types of social support to increase children's involvement in violent behavior, certain types of social support may have the undesired effect of perpetuating low-level aggressive behavior, such as bullying. For example, some of the groups identified by Salmivalli et al. (1996), such as assistants to the bully and reinforcers of the bully, may be providing social support for the bullies and may perpetuate such behavior. In addition, investigations of the social dynamics of classroom bullies and victims have found that bullies are well liked by classmates and successful within their peer groups (Perren and Hornung, 2005; Witvliet et al., 2010). Witvliet et al. (2010) concluded that *bullies associate with each other to maintain their popular status among their peers.*

Summary and Implications of Social Support Research for School Violence Victimization

This chapter has examined the literature on the association between social support and school violence. Implications of this research can be summarized into four main points. First, it is well established that both perpetrators and victims of school violence tend to perceive lower amounts of positive social support from significant adults and peers in their lives compared to students who are uninvolved in school violence (Demaray & Malecki, 2003; Furlong et al., 1995; Holt & Espelage, 2007; Rigby, 2000; Schreck et al., 2003). Parents, teachers, peers, and students' school environments all seem to play a role in the complex set of factors that surround school violence, and each individual can impact outcomes for improved school safety. For example, teachers could be trained to create and maintain socially supportive classrooms and classmates could be trained how to intervene in a socially supportive manner if they witness violence or bullying. Recent work by Cowie and Jennifer (2007, 2008) suggests that directly intervening by providing victims of bullying and school violence with peer support can benefit both the victim as well as the peer providing the support.

Second, recently, there has been an increase in research regarding the role and the function of students that are classified as neither perpetrators nor victims of school violence. Several studies have identified roles such as assistant to the bullying, reinforcer of the bully, defender of the victim, and outsiders (Salmivalli et al., 1996, 1997). Some research has documented that perceptions of social support vary across these participant roles (Rigby & Johnson; 2006; Summers & Demaray, 2010). Specifically, defenders have been found to report perceived higher levels of social support (Summers & Demaray, 2010). It may be important to engage defenders of victims at an early age, which may increase their likelihood of defending victims in secondary school, which was when students reported that they were less likely to support victims. Giving students tools to comfort victims, confront bullies, and modes of contacting adults may boost their confidence in defending victims, particularly in the case of physical violence. Students reported they were more likely to support the victim of verbal bullying, so training students on what to do in both verbal and physical bullying is important. Cowie and Jennifer's (2007, 2008) framework for peer support is based upon the suggestion that peers in the defender role can play a crucial role in providing social support to victims of bullying and other school violence. As a first step, peers can approach a victim and let them know they are sorry for what happened and can help that peer get to the appropriate adult support. Peers should also be trained to inform adults in the school whenever they witness physical or verbal bullying.

Third, several recent studies have found that social support serves as a buffer against negative outcomes that are associated with school violence victimization (Conners-Burrow et al., 2009; Davidson & Demaray, 2007; Flaspohler et al., 2009; Stadler et al., 2010). Among these studies, parent support in particular emerged as a significant protective variable, but also social support from teachers, peers, and other people in the school. Therefore, one could argue that involving parents is particularly important for victims of school violence. Proactively, schools may want to provide information to parents about how to recognize warning signs that their child may be victim of school violence and how to handle these situations. If a school finds that a child is a victim of school violence, then involving the parent is an essential component for improving mental health outcomes for that child.

Fourth, though there is scarce research regarding the link between types of social support and school violence, many potential implications and interventions could be inferred. Youth look to their parents, classmates, and close friends for both emotional and information support (Malecki & Demaray, 2003). Thus, schools could provide information to parents about how to recognize signs in their children that they may be experiencing violence or may be perpetrating violence

Michelle Kilpatrick Demaray et al.

at school as well as ways to help their child emotionally. This information could be provided during a Parent Night hosted by the school or through literature sent to the home, for example. Information support from classmates and close friends could be enhanced if the school provided all students with information about what to do if they are the victim of school violence or rec-

Table 5.1   Implications for Practice: Social Support and School Violence

Source of Support	Implications for Practice
Parents	Provide parents with informational support about recognizing signs in their children of being either perpetrators or victims of violence in the schools.
	Provide parents with supportive contacts if they suspect their child is either a perpetrator or victim of school violence. These contacts should be people in the school they can contact for emotional and informational support.
	Have trained staff at the school conduct support groups for parents whose children have been involved in school violence to obtain emotional support from other parents.
	Encourage parents to take an active, supportive role in the lives of their children. Provide training to teach parents all the ways they can provide support including by providing accurate information, emotional/caring support, and being available (instrumental support) to their children to talk about bullying.
Teachers	Provide teachers with informational support about recognizing signs in their students of being either perpetrators or victims of violence in the schools.
	Train teachers in how to provide informational support, emotional support, instrumental support, and appraisal support to students who are bullies or victims of bullying.
	Train teachers to respond in supportive ways to an observance of school violence or bullying (e.g. along with implementing appropriate consequences for the bully, praise any students who intervened and immediately show caring for the student who was victimized and direct that student to resources, follow-up with the victim to ensure they had received the support and information they need).
	Train teachers how to, in general, encourage and create socially supportive classrooms, being sure to talk about all types of support and what those supportive behaviors look like. For example, teachers could model and expect respectful behavior and reward supportive behaviors exhibited by peers.
Other People in the School	Assess the perceptions of students with regards to levels of social support in schools or school climate.
	Train entire school staff in ways to be socially supportive to students in general (e.g. using students' names, noticing and rewarding positive social behaviors, and supporting victims of bullying or school violence (e.g. directing them to sources of support, communicating concern and care to the victims).
	Have a system in place so that victims of violence get services from supportive staff in the school to increase the connectedness victims of violence feel to the school.
	Have trained staff at the school conduct support groups with students who have been victims of violence to gain emotional, informational, instrumental, and appraisal support from other students
Classmates/ Friends	Train students how to intervene in a socially supportive manner when they witness violence or bullying acts (e.g. communicate caring and concern to the victim, direct the victim to adult sources of support, report the incident to adults in the school).
	Train students to communicate their *lack* of support for violent or aggressive behavior in the school. Students need to understand that silence may be interpreted as being supportive of negative acts.

ognize signs that someone may be a perpetrator of school violence. Peer support groups may also provide emotional support for victimized students (Cowie & Smith, 2010). Students report that teachers are a source of informational support most frequently, but Malecki and Demaray found that emotional support from teachers was significantly related to positive social skills and academic competence. Thus, school may need to provide training to teachers about how to increase the availability of emotional support for their students.

Conclusion

Many ecological and contextual variables surrounding bullying and school violence (Espelage & Swearer, 2004) are important to understanding bullying behavior and to preventing and intervening with participants in the bullying dynamic. This chapter summarized one important contextual factor, social support from parents, peers, teachers, and the school. However, this chapter also emphasizes that more research is needed. Further study is needed to understand the mechanisms of the many roles of social support in the bullying dynamic. Most importantly, more intervention research is needed to inform families and schools what types of socially supportive behaviors are effective to prevent, interrupt, and aid recovery in bullying situations.

References

Austin, V. L. (2003). Fear and loathing in the classroom: A candid look at school violence and the policies and practices that address it. *Journal of Disability Policy Studies, 14,* 17–22. doi:10.1177/10442073030140010301

Boulton, M. J., & Smith, P. K. (1994). Bully/victim problems in middle-school children: Stability, self-perceived competence, peer perceptions and peer acceptance. *British Journal of Developmental Psychology, 12,* 315–329.

Brockenbrough, K. K., Cornell, D. G., & Loper, A. B. (2002). Aggressive attitudes among victims of violence at school. *Education and Treatment of Children, 25,* 273–287.

Cohen, S., Gottlieb, B. H., & Underwood, L. G. (2000). Social relationships and health. In S. Cohen, L. G. Underwood, & B. H. Gottlieb (Eds.), *Social support measurement and intervention: A guide for health and social scientists* (pp. 3–25). New York: Oxford University Press.

Cohen, S., & Wills, T. A. (1985). Stress, social support, and the buffering hypothesis. *Psychological Bulletin, 98,* 310–357. doi:10.1037//0033-2909.98.2.310

Conners-Burrow, N. A., Johnson, D. L., Whiteside-Mansell, L., McKelvey, L., & Gargus, R. A. (2009). Adults matter: Protecting children from the negative impacts of bullying. *Psychology in the Schools, 46,* 593–604. doi:10.1002/pits.20400

Cowie, H., & Jennifer, D. (2008). *New perspectives on bullying.* Maidenhead, UK: Open University Press.

Cowie, H., & Jennifer, D. (2007). *Managing school violence: A whole school approach to good practice.* London: Paul Chapman.

Cowie, H., & Olafsson, R. (2000). The role of peer support in helping the victims of bullying in a school with high levels of aggression. *School Psychology International, 21,* 79–95. doi:10.1177/0143034300211006

Cowie, H. & Smith, P. K. (2010). Peer support as a means of improving school safety and reducing bullying and violence. In B. Doll, W. Pfohl, & J. S. Yoon (Eds.) *Handbook of youth prevention science* (pp. 177–193). Mahwah, NJ: Erlbaum.

Davidson, L. M., & Demaray, M. K. (2007). Social support as a moderator between victimization and internalizing-externalizing distress from bullying. *School Psychology Review, 36,* 383–405.

Demaray, M. K., & Malecki, C. K. (2003). Perceptions of the frequency and importance of social support by students classified as victims, bullies, and bully/victims in an urban middle school. *School Psychology Review, 32,* 471–489.

Dinkes, R., Kemp, J., & Baum, K. (2009). *Indicators of School Crime and Safety: 2009* (NCES 2010–012/NCJ 228478). Washington, DC: National Center for Education Statistics and Bureau of Justice Statistics.

Duncan, R. D. (2004). The impact of family relationships on school bullies and victims. In D. L. Espelage & S. M. Swearer (Eds.), *Bullying in American schools: A social-ecological perspective on prevention and intervention* (pp. 227–244). Mahwah, NJ: Erlbaum.

Dupper, D. R., & Meyer-Adams, N. (2002). Low-level violence: A neglected aspect of school culture. *Urban Education, 37,* 350–364. doi:10.1177/00485902037003003

Espelage, D. L., & Swearer, S. M. (2003). Research on school bullying and victimization: What have we learned and where do we go from here? *School Psychology Review, 32,* 365–383.

Espelage, D. L., & Swearer, S. M. (Eds.). (2004). *Bullying in American schools: A social-ecological perspective on prevention and intervention*. Mahwah, NJ: Erlbaum.

Estell, D. B., Cairns, R. B., Farmer, T. W., & Cairns, B. D. (2002). Aggression and inner-city early elementary classrooms: Individual and peer-group configurations. *Merrill-Palmer Quarterly, 48*, 52–76. doi:10.1353/mpq.2002.0002

Estell, D. B., Farmer, T. W., Pearl, R., Van Acker, R., & Rodkin, P. C. (2008). Social status and aggressive and disruptive behavior in girls: Individual, group, and classroom influences. *Journal of School Psychology, 46*, 193–212. doi:10.1016/j.jsp.2007.03.004

Flaspohler, P. D., Elfstrom, J. L., Vanderzee, K. L., Sink, H. E., & Birchmeier, Z. (2009). Stand by me: The effects of peer and teacher support in mitigating the impact of bullying on quality of life. *Psychology in the Schools, 46*, 636–649. doi:10.1002/pits.20404

Furlong, M. J., Chung, A., Bates, M., & Morrison, R. L. (1995). Who are the victims of school violence? A comparison of student non-victims and multi-victims. *Education and Treatment of Children, 18*, 282–298.

Furlong, M. J., Pavelski, R., & Saxton, J. (2002). The prevention of school violence. In S. E. Brock, P. J. Lazarus, & S. R. Jimerson (Eds.), *Best practices in school crisis prevention and intervention* (pp. 131–149). Bethesda, MD: National Association of School Psychologists.

Hanish, L. D., Kochenderfer-Ladd, B., Fabes, R. A., Martin, C. L., & Denning, D. (2004). Bullying among young children: The influence of peers and teachers. In D. L. Espelage & S. M. Swearer (Eds.), *Bullying in American schools: A social-ecological perspective on prevention and intervention* (pp. 141–159). Mahwah, NJ: Erlbaum.

Holt, M. K., & Espelage, D. L. (2007). Perceived social support among bullies, victims, and bully-victims. *Journal of Youth and Adolescence, 36*, 984–994. doi:10.1007/s10964-006-9153-3

Kingery, P. M., Pruitt, B. E., & Heuberger, G. (1996). A profile of rural Texas adolescents who carry handguns. *Journal of School Health, 66*, 18–22. doi:10.1111/j.1746-1561.1996.tb06252.x

Malecki, C. K., & Demaray, M. K. (2003). Carrying a weapon to school and perceptions of social support in an urban middle school. *Journal of Emotional and Behavioral Disorders, 11*, 169–178. doi:10.1177/10634266030110030401

McNabb, S. J. N., Farley, T. A., Powell, K. E., Rolka, H. R., & Horan, J. M. (1996). Correlates of gun-carrying among adolescents in south Louisiana. *American Journal of Preventive Medicine, 12*, 96–102.

Morrison, G. M., Furlong, M. J., & Smith, G. (1994). Factors associated with the experience of school violence among general education, leadership class, opportunity class, and special day class pupils. *Education and Treatment of Children, 17*, 356–369.

Murray, J., & Farrington, D. P. (2006). Parental imprisonment: Effects on boys' antisocial behaviour and delinquency through the life-course. *Journal of Child Psychology and Psychiatry, 46*, 1269–1278. doi:10.1111/j.1469-7610.2005.01433.x

Nansel, T. R., Overpeck, M. D., Haynie, D. L., Ruan, J., & Scheidt, P. C. (2003). Relationships between bullying and violence among US youth. *Archives of Pediatrics and Adolescent Medicine, 157*, 348–353. doi:10.1001/archpedi.157.4.348

Naylor, P., & Cowie, H. (1999). The effectiveness of peer support systems in challenging school bullying: The perspectives and experiences of teachers and pupils. *Journal of Adolescence, 22*, 467–479. doi:10.1006/jado.1999.0241

Perren, S., & Hornung, R. (2005). Bullying and delinquency in adolescence: Victims' and perpetrators' family and peer relations. *Swiss Journal of Psychology, 64*, 51–64. doi:10.1024/1421-0185.64.1.51

Powell, K. B. (1997). Correlates of violent and nonviolent behavior among vulnerable inner-city youths. *Family and Community Health, 20*, 38–47.

Reinke, W. M., & Herman, K. C. (2002). Creating school environments that deter antisocial behaviors in youth. *Psychology in the Schools, 39*, 549–559. doi:10.1002/pits.10048

Raskauskas, J., & Stoltz, A. D. (2007). Involvement in traditional and electronic bullying among adolescents. *Developmental Psychology, 43*(3), 564–575. doi:10.1037/0012-1649.43.3.564

Rigby, K. (2000). Effects of peer victimization in schools and perceived social support on adolescent well-being. *Journal of Adolescence, 23*, 57–68. doi:10.1006/jado.1999.0289

Rigby, K., & Johnson, B. (2006). Expressed readiness of Australian school children to act as bystanders in support of children who are being bullied. *Educational Psychology, 26*, 425–440.

Robertson, D. L., Farmer, T.W., Fraser, M. W., Day, S. H., Duncan, T., Crowther, A., & Dadisman, K. A. (2010). Interpersonal competence configurations and peer relations in early elementary classrooms: Perceived popular and unpopular aggressive subtypes. *International Journal of Behavioral Development, 34*, 73–87. doi:10.1177/0165025409345074

Rodkin, P. C., Farmer, T. W., Pearl, R., & Van Acker, R. (2000). Heterogeneity of popular boys: Antisocial and prosocial configurations. *Developmental Psychology, 36*, 14–24. doi:10.1037//0012-1649.36.1.14

Rodkin, P. C., Farmer, T. W., Pearl, R., & Van Acker, R. (2006). They're cool: Social status and peer group supports for aggressive boys and girls. *Social Development, 15*, 175–204. doi:10.1111/j.1467-9507.2006.00336.x

Salmivalli, C., Huttunen, A., & Lagerspetz, K. M. J. (1997). Peer networks and bullying in schools. *Scandinavian Journal of Psychology, 38*, 305–312. doi:10.1111/1467-9450.00040

Salmivalli, C., Lagerspetz, K., Bjorkqvist, K., Osterman, K., & Kaukiainen, A. (1996). Bullying as a group process: Participant roles and their relations to social status within the group. *Aggressive Behavior, 22,* 1–15. doi:10.1002/(SICI)1098-2337(1996)22:1<1::AID-AB1>3.0.CO;2-T

Schreck, C. J., Miller, J. M., & Gibson, C. L. (2003). Trouble in the school yard: A study of the risk factors of victimization at school. *Crime and Delinquency, 49,* 460–484. doi:10.1177/0011128703049003006

Scott, T. M., Nelson, C. M., & Liaupsin, C. J. (2001). Effective instruction: The forgotten component in preventing school violence. *Education and Treatment of Children, 24,* 309–322.

Spivak, H., & Prothrow-Smith, D. (2001). The need to address bullying: An important component of violence prevention. *Journal of the American Medical Association, 285,* 2131–2132. doi:10.1001/jama.285.16.2131

Stadler, C., Feifel, J., Rohrmann, S., Vermeiren, R., & Poustka, F. (2010). Peer-victimization and mental health problems in adolescents: Are parental and school supports protective? *Child Psychiatry and Human Development, 41,* 371–386. doi:10.1007/s10578-010-0174-5

Stephens, R. D. (1994). Planning for safer and better schools: School violence prevention and intervention strategies. *School Psychology Review, 23,* 204–216.

Stephens, R. D. (2002). Promoting school safety. In S. E. Brock, P. J. Lazarus, & S. R. Jimerson (Eds.), *Best practices in school crisis prevention and intervention* (pp. 47–65). Bethesda, MD: National Association of School Psychologists.

Summers, K., & Demaray, M. K. (2010). *Defending victims of bullying: The role of social support and school climate.* Manuscript submitted for publication.

Tardy, C. H. (1985). Social support measurement. *American Journal of Community Psychology, 13,* 187–202. doi:10.1007/BF00905728

Williams, K. R., & Guerra, N. G. (2007). Prevalence and predictors of internet bullying. *Journal of Adolescent Health, 41,* S14–S21. doi:10.1016/j.jadohealth.2007.08.018

Witvliet, M., Olthof, T., Hoeksma, J. B., Goossens, F. A., Smits, M. S. I., & Koot, H. M. (2010). Peer group affiliation of children: The role of perceived popularity, likeability, and behavioral similarity in bullying. *Social Development, 19,* 285–303. doi:10.1111/j.1467-9507.2009.00544.x

Zinzow, H. M., Ruggiero, K. J., Hanson, R. F., Smith, D. W., Saunders, B. E., & Kilpatrick, D. G. (2009). Witnessed community and parental violence in relation to substance use and delinquency in a national sample of adolescents. *Journal of Traumatic Stress, 22,* 525–533. doi:10.1002/jts.20469

6

Coercion and Contagion in Family and School Environments

Implications for Educating and Socializing Youth

Gregory M. Fosco and Jennifer L. Frank

PENNSYLVANIA STATE UNIVERSITY

Thomas J. Dishion

UNIVERSITY OF OREGON, EUGENE

Abstract

This chapter discusses the peer processes of coercion and contagion and their implications for public school efforts to educate and socialize youth. The systemic link between coercion in the family and in the classroom and deviant peer contagion is considered developmentally in terms of an ecological framework. Research has shown that in elementary school, aggressive behavior, normative peer rejection, and academic failure lead to formation of self-organized deviant peer groups by secondary school. Such peer groups provide a basis for the development of premature autonomy, which in turn can present a serious challenge to parents and teachers to recover or influence educational and social outcomes. These processes are described in respect to school settings, with a focus on application of a coercion model to the classroom and on contagion processes that emerge from aggregating problem youth. Preventive implications for family–school partnership are then discussed.

When one considers that by early childhood time spent with peers exceeds time spent with parents (Ellis, Rogoff, & Cromer, 1981), it is not surprising that peers are a core influence on social–emotional development and learning in the school environment (Hill, Bromell, Tyson, & Flint, 2007). Even in kindergarten, children's imitation of deviant behavior with their playmates predicts later antisocial behavior (Snyder et al., 2005). Peer rejection by fourth grade is prognostic of adult lifestyles characterized by antisocial behavior, even after controlling for adolescent antisocial behavior and academic achievement (Nelson & Dishion, 2004). Research on peer influence has commonly focused on externalizing behaviors, such as aggression, antisocial behavior, and substance use, yet deviant peers present risk for depression (Stevens & Prinstein,

2005), self-inflicted injurious behavior (Heilbron & Prinstein, 2008), poor academic achievement (DeBaryshe, Patterson, & Capaldi, 1993), and disordered eating (Crandall, 1988).

Focus has shifted from the links between deviant peer relationships and negative outcomes to the processes by which deviant peers affect child and adolescent developmental trajectories. Two processes have a consistent, yet distinct, impact on problem behavior: coercion and contagion. *Coercion* is an interpersonal, dynamic exchange during which aggressive behavior is used to escape, reduce, or avoid an aversive experience by means of escape conditioning or reinforcement (e.g., Patterson 1982). Common examples of coercion include tantrums, contesting sanctions with anger or aggression, and threats, posturing, or physical aggression. When a parent rescinds a sanction or directive, the child's aggressive behavior is reinforced, making it more likely to reoccur. Likewise, when the child terminates the aggressive behavior, it is reinforcing to parents, and they are more likely to acquiesce in the future and even cooperate before aversive behavior begins. These routine coercive interactions can shape children's aggressive behavior into a core strategy for getting their way.

Contagion generally describes a mutually influential peer process in which shared behavior or emotional patterns are amplified through aggregation and mutual reinforcement. A core mechanism is *deviancy training,* which is an interpersonal dynamic of reinforcing deviant talk and behavior (Dishion, Spracklen, Andrews, & Patterson, 1996). It involves sharing stories of deviant acts, encouraging peers to engage in deviant acts, and participating in storytelling about deviant acts.

To understand the peer dynamics underlying externalizing trajectories, one must move beyond simple univariate models of risk and protection to consider child risk factors and contextual influence on development. This complex interplay is captured in ecologically based theories (e.g., Bronfenbrenner, 1979; Dodge & Pettit, 2003) that recognize that (a) child and context influence development in direct and interactive ways, and (b) multiple complex environments and relationships that form within these contexts affect children's development. In this chapter we discuss developmental processes in deviant peer relationships, as well as key family and school contextual influences that promote or amplify problem behavior.

Deviant Peer Processes

Recent findings by Snyder and colleagues (2008) provide observational evidence that coercive behavior and deviancy training coexist as distinct processes that begin as early as age 5. Both processes guide youth in the same direction: escalating antisocial behavior.

Childhood coercion includes teasing, threats or verbal attacks, and shoving or hitting as a means of getting one's way (Snyder et al., 2008). Getting one's way through aversive means can socialize aggressive behavior over time. Snyder and colleagues (2008) found that kindergarteners who engaged in coercive behavior with their peers showed increased overt aggression by age 8. This pattern is exacerbated because coercive youth are commonly rejected by prosocial peers, which can lead the rejected children to affiliate with other aggressive children (Vitaro, Pedersen, & Brendgen, 2007) and eventually form deviant friendships that further escalate problem behavior into forms of serious violence (see Figure 6.1) (Dishion, Véronneau, & Myers, 2010). In spite of the repellant nature of aversive behavior, it appears that contagion processes function as a core foundation for deviant friendships. Deviant talk among problem youth is an organizing feature of the friendship, and the duration of deviant talk episodes in such friendships predicts uniquely the amplification of problem behavior in adolescence (Granic & Dishion, 2003). Although the friendships are not of high quality, the common ground of violating norms explains why deviancy training is such a powerful predictor of problems, and thus serves as a strategy to form and maintain significant relationships in their lives.

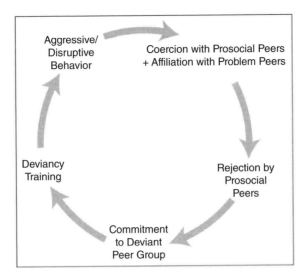

Figure 6.1 Coercion and contagion in the peer context.

Family Contributions to Deviant Peer Influences

A more complete picture of deviant peer influence emerges when one considers how the family context shapes early involvement with problem peer groups and contributes to the maintenance of deviant friendships and peer contagion. Two key family processes are understood to reinforce deviant peer processes: coercive family processes and premature autonomy. Family processes are the product of a bidirectional interaction over time: parenting shapes child behavior, and child behavior has a significant impact on the quality and effectiveness of parenting. Parenting practices and parental well-being are contextualized within a constellation of factors, including economic hardship (Conger et al., 1992), single parenting (Dodge et al., 2009), interparental conflict (Shelton, Harold, Goeke-Morey, & Cummings, 2007), and parent depression (Conger, Patterson, & Ge, 1995), all of which compromise one's ability to parent effectively.

Coercion

Coercive processes in family relationships are typically characterized by aversive, aggressive child behaviors in response to harsh and inconsistent parenting and density of punishment rather than praise or positive parenting (Dishion, Patterson, & Kavanagh, 1992). Coercive parenting is likely to include sudden and "explosive" discipline (Patterson, 1986), noncontingent negativity regardless of child behavior (Dishion et al., 1992), and physically attacking one's child (Dishion et al., 1999). Patterson, DeBaryshe, and Ramsey (1989) have referred to family coercion as "basic training," meaning that coercive parent–child exchanges can directly train children to engage in coercive and antisocial behaviors outside the home as well, such as with peers and teachers (Dishion et al., 1992). Using aggressive means to get one's way with peers is a coercive strategy that is linked with increases in problem behaviors in later development (Snyder et al., 2008). Youth from coercive homes are typically drawn to aggressive peers and are at greater risk for rejection from normative peers (e.g., Dishion et al., 2010), making them particularly vulnerable to the influences of other problem youth. Ultimately, all these processes increase a child's risk for a wide range of enduring problems with aggression, violence, substance use, and risky sexual behavior (Dishion & Patterson, 2006; Dishion et al., 2010).

Premature Autonomy

The pace at which adolescents are given freedom and successfully engage in self-monitoring without assistance from their parents is critical for their well-being. Consistent supervision, guidance, and connectedness with caregivers facilitate positive youth development and minimize the likelihood of deviant peer influences (Dishion, Nelson, & Bullock, 2004; Fosco, Stormshak, Dishion, & Winter, in press). When supervision remits too early and too quickly, youths can become disengaged from their families and experience freedom and unsupervised time in excess of what is developmentally appropriate, a process called *premature autonomy* (Dishion et al., 2004). When parents use monitoring and supervision to stay informed about their youth's activities and behavior, they also provide structure to his or her environment (Dishion & McMahon, 1998; Hoeve et al., 2009) and decrease the likelihood of deviant peer affiliation and outcomes, such as substance use and delinquent behavior (Hoeve et al., 2009; Laird, Criss, Pettit, Dodge, & Bates, 2008). Recent findings suggest that, after accounting for parental monitoring, parent–adolescent connectedness is a unique protective factor for youth (Fosco et al., in press) that provides an context in which adolescents to value their parents' opinions and seek guidance for difficult situations (Ackard, Neumark-Sztainer, Story, & Perry, 2006). Parents can then help their adolescent cope with pressures to conform to peers and instead make good decisions about relationships with peers. It is not surprising, then, that disengagement from parental monitoring and family relationships is a significant risk factor for a wide range of problems, including early-onset substance use, disrupted education, delinquency, depression, bullying, and suicide attempts (Ackard et al., 2006; Dishion et al., 2004; Flouri & Buchanan, 2003).

Integrating Family and Peer Developmental Processes

Dodge and colleagues (2009) proposed a broad developmental framework in which mutually influential and transactional dynamics across individual, peer, and family domains account for developmental processes that progress toward substance use initiation by the end of high school. Family contexts characterized by sociocultural risk, such as low socioeconomic status and single or teenage motherhood, were associated with family risk factors such as conflict, low father involvement and support, harsh parenting, and exposure to family and neighborhood violence. In turn, high-risk family environments in early childhood predicted child behavior problems in kindergarten, which were followed by peer difficulties in third grade. Problem peer relationships and deviant peer association were associated with less parental monitoring and supervision by age 11, as were early family risk factors. Problematic peer relationships in sixth and seventh grades were predicted by early peer rejection and by low levels of parental monitoring. In turn, adolescent deviant peer relationships mediated the effects of behavior and parenting problems on substance use initiation by 12th grade. Clearly, family and peer contexts are inseparably linked in the progression of problem behavior and peer deviance.

School Contributions to Deviant Peer Influences

Like families, schools represent an important natural setting for development. Most research has focused on how peer-group affiliation affects school functioning; far less is known about the specific ways in which the school environment affects the formation and function of student peer groups. Although concepts such as coercion and contagion are useful constructs for understanding the mechanism of prevention and intervention effects, few have considered how these processes operate within the context of school-based interventions (Reinke & Herman, 2002; Reinke & Walker, 2006). Broadly speaking, school environmental factors consist of schoolwide, classroom, and individual student systems. Following is a review of existing literature about each of these levels and an overview of the ways in which the application of these concepts may prove useful.

Schoolwide Factors

Schoolwide systems typically affect student behavior and peer group activity indirectly by establishing behavioral norms and structures within which individual students and peer networks evolve. Schoolwide programming that couples clear rules and expectations with predictable student reward structures sets prosocial norms and helps reduce problem behavior in schools (Lewis, Sugai, & Colvin, 1998). This programming is a key component of a variety of schoolwide prevention programs, including Unified Discipline (White, Algozzine, Audette, Marr, & Ellis, 2001) and Positive Behavior Intervention and Supports (PBIS) models; in two randomized, controlled trials (Bradshaw, Koth, Thornton, & Leaf, 2009; Horner et al., 2009), both programs were found to be effective. For implementation to be effective, rules and expectations must be observable, measurable, and developmentally appropriate (Mayer, 1995). It is helpful to link explicit rules to common procedures and routines (e.g., transitions) and specific areas (e.g., hallways, bathrooms) in which problematic student behavior or peer interactions arise (Colvin, Sugai, Good, & Lee, 1997; Lewis, Sugai, & Colvin, 2000). Schoolwide rules and expectations also shape teacher behavior so that it is consistent and predictable in response to student misbehavior (Nelson, Martella, & Galand, 1998). Although it has yet to be empirically established, this approach may also prove to promote and reinforce positive peer networks.

A common approach to addressing problem behaviors in schools is to create special classroom environments or groups for problem students. Although such practices may be efficient, research has clearly documented that the aggregation of students with behavior problems is linked with enduring increases in aggression and problem behavior over time (Kellam, Ling, Merisca, Brown, & Ialongo, 1998; Warren, Schoppelrey, Moberg, & McDonald, 2005). Likewise, group-format interventions for high-risk middle school youth have been found to lead to increases in delinquent behavior and substance use three years later (Dishion, McCord, & Poulin, 1999).

Classroom-Level Factors

At the classroom level, microenvironment practices related to student grouping, instruction, classroom management, and the dynamics involved in reciprocal teacher–student interactions have been demonstrated to shape student behavior and peer networks (Van Acker, Grant, & Henry, 1996; Walker, Colvin, & Ramsey, 1995). Research consistently points to the role of effective instruction and classroom management in the prevention of problematic behavior, student disengagement, and formation of disruptive student cliques (Caprara, Barbaranelli, Pastorelli, Bandura, & Zimbardo, 2000). Clearly, student disengagement promotes off-task behavior. Students who are off-task are inclined to recruit others to do the same, thus cycles of coercion and contagion develop during instructional tasks. By differentiating instruction and evenly distributing opportunities for students of varying abilities to respond to instruction, teachers promote task engagement and reduce the occurrence of problem behaviors (Gunter & Sutherland, 2005).

Coercion may prove to be a useful framework for examining the mechanisms through which troublesome classroom behavior and problematic teacher–student interactions arise and are maintained. The model illustrated by Figure 6.2 posits that the coercive cycle begins when teachers respond in a negative, coercive manner to student noncompliance or off-task behavior. Students respond by intensifying their behavior. Teachers may escape the situation by withdrawing their initial request or reducing task demands. Consistent with an escape conditioning model, disruptive students receive less academic instruction and fewer task demands (Walker

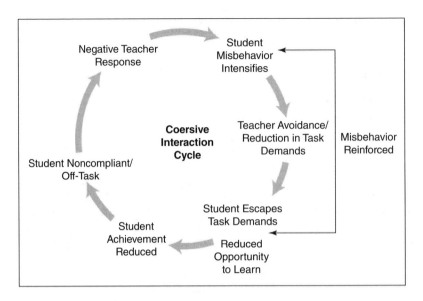

Figure 6.2 Coercion in the classroom.

et al., 1995). When students escape task demands in this fashion, the effects on learning and behavior are twofold: first, the student's misbehavior is reinforced and thus is likely to persist and strengthen over time. Second, the student's opportunities to learn are reduced and potential for achievement is compromised. Reductions in students' rate of learning and achievement, in turn, primes students to engage in noncompliant and off-task behaviors during instructional activities, thus perpetuating the cycle.

Only a handful of investigators have applied this particular theoretical model to the study of teacher–student interactions, but the effects of coercion have been documented across a number of common instructional settings (Gunter & Coutinho, 1997; Gunter et al., 1994). Shores and colleagues (1993) found that aggressive behaviors of children with emotional–behavioral disabilities can have a negative effect on the extent to which teachers interact with children. Nelson and Roberts (2000) extended this work by studying patterns of teacher–student interactions during problematic classroom behavior in general education settings. Their work revealed that interactions between students and teachers regarding problem behavior remained fairly stable over time and were not significantly influenced by contextual factors, such as time of day, academic content, or teacher proximity. As is the case with parent–child interactions, this stable dyadic process is self-sustaining and often resistant to change. Coercive processes affect not only the quality of teacher–student relationships, but may compromise the quality of instruction and academic achievement over time. Research examining the effects of student behavior on instruction have consistently found that students who exhibited more problem behavior were less involved in academic interactions with teachers and were typically provided less, and less effective, instruction than were students who did not exhibit problem behavior (Carr, Taylor, & Robinson, 1991).

Understanding and disrupting maladaptive coercive cycles in the classroom is important for the well-being of students and teachers. Teachers under stress may less effectively respond to student misbehavior in a noncoercive manner, are generally less tolerant of challenging student behavior (Kokkinos, Panayiotou, & Davazoglou, 2005), and are significantly more likely to report having negative relationships with their students (Yoon, 2008). A continuing cycle of coercive exchanges may also prevent students from accessing the protective benefits of positive teacher–student relations, which are a consistent predictor of school and overall behavioral adjustment (Pianta,

Steinberg, & Rollins, 1995). Teachers who "provide emotional support, reward competence, and promote self-esteem" help decrease the vulnerability of high-risk students when they are responding to stressful life events (Werner, 1990). Conversely, conflict and dependency in teacher–student relationships are associated with unfavorable outcomes, such as a negative school attitude, school avoidance (Birch & Ladd, 1997), and hostile aggression (Howes, Hamilton, & Matheson, 1994). Thus helping students at risk establish and maintain positive relationships with adults at school is key to risk reduction and to promoting a positive learning environment.

The Good Behavior Game (Barrish, Saunders, & Wolf, 1969; Medland & Stachnik, 1972) is a good example of a relatively simple behavior management program. When a behavior in the classroom is identified as a problem, for example, the entire group has an opportunity to be rewarded if the behavior terminates. This program was found to have substantial long-term prevention effects (Poduska et al., 2008) when it was used as a universal intervention in public school classrooms in high-risk communities. The game can also be used by families: days when a problem behavior is absent represent opportunities for reward (Dishion & Patterson, 2006). Schools and families can cooperate on structuring tasks and settings to optimize student success, teach self-regulation skills, and reinforce successful coping and avoidance of coercive exchanges. These classroom-management intervention programs that systematically alter "business as usual" in regular classroom settings hold promise for reducing the conditions that give rise to coercive exchanges and peer contagion.

Individual Student-Level Factors

School personnel may disrupt deviant peer processes indirectly by implementing prevention programs or curricula, embedding social–emotional learning (SEL) content into school practices, and defining the nature of extracurricular and after-school activities. Although most prevention programs target individual outcomes, many also are used to shape the formation and function of student peer groups. For example, the Botvin Life Skills training program (Botvin, 2000) has been shown to reduce problem behavior and the popularity of middle school students with deviant behavior (Osgood, Feinberg, Gest, Moody, & Bierman, 2010). Other programs that use risk awareness or resistance skills training strategies (e.g., Gang Resistance Education and Training [GREAT] or Drug Abuse Resistance Education [DARE]) have had mixed results (Flay, 2009; Pan & Bai, 2009).

Other comprehensive approaches, such as SEL, promote core social competency skills by helping students learn to recognize and manage emotions, develop caring and concern for others, make responsible decisions, establish positive relationships, and handle challenging situations effectively (CASEL, 2010; Payton et al., 2000). SEL is a broad approach to promoting mental health and resilience that uses curricular planning to teach social, emotional, and life skills and prevent negative life outcomes (Payton et al., 2000). These broadly applied SEL curricula help students develop skills and internal cognitive and affective processes necessary to achieve specific social behaviors and positive peer interactions across a range of contexts (McCombs, 2004). SEL has been shown to be effective for decreasing conduct problems, substance use, emotional distress, school dropout, and attendance problems (Benson et al., 2000; Wilson, Gottfredson, & Najaka, 2001; Zins, Bloodworth, Weissberg, & Walberg, 2004), and in one study, prompted an 11% increase in standardized test scores (Durlak, Weissberg, Dymnicki, Taylor, & Schellinger, 2011). Not surprisingly, cost analyses have revealed that universal SEL implementation results in a substantial return on investment (Aos, Lieb, Mayfield, Miller, Pennucci, 2004). As such, these comprehensive approaches provide a promising framework for delivering consistent and sustained messages and shaping a school culture that discourages formation of maladaptive peer networks.

Bridging Home and School Contexts: School–Family Connections

Coercion and contagion are parallel processes that have similar implications for intervention across home and school contexts. Both require effective behavioral management so that youth are not placed at risk for deviant peer influences, and so unsupervised interactions do not place youth at risk because of disengagement from parental supervision or aggregation of problem youth. The question is, how does one intervene after deviant peer cliques are established? Currently, the best approach to reducing deviant peer influences is to target risk factors that may lead at-risk youth to aggressive behavior, social rejection, and academic disengagement. At school and at home, effective and consistent response to disruptive behavior is critical for reducing youth aggression that precipitates social rejection and involvement in deviant peer relationships. Key strategies to reduce contagion effects are to structure unsupervised time and bolster parental monitoring (Laird et al., 2008).

From an ecological perspective, there is little question that home and school settings are interdependent contexts of development (e.g., Bronfenbrenner, 1979). Consistent with this view, evidence suggests that when youth perceive good coordination between home and school, they are less likely to engage in high-risk behaviors, including violence, substance use, and suicidality (Resnick et al., 1997). In two randomized, controlled trials we found that implementing the Family Check-Up model in schools as a family-centered intervention to target behavior management and monitoring was more effective than "school as usual" for decreasing problem behavior (Connell, Dishion, Yasui, & Kavanagh, 2007), increasing school attendance, and improving grades (Stormshak, Connell, & Dishion, 2009). From this perspective, we offer five recommendations for bridging home and school contexts to effectively reduce risk for deviant peer processes (Table 6.1).

First, we recommend creating consistent rules at home and in school that clearly define acceptable behavior. In both settings, strong communication and consistent expectations for student attendance, behavior, and academic performance are critical to ensuring that children's best interests do not get lost in the process (Dishion & Kavanagh, 2003). Youth perceptions of consistency across these contexts are linked with lower risk (Resnick et al., 1997).

Second, consistent and predictable positive reinforcement for good behavior must follow in order to eliminate coercive processes. Moreover, communication between home and school about a student's positive behavior facilitates additional positive reinforcement (e.g., parents rewarding student success at school) and also informs parents and teachers about which positive behaviors to watch for.

Third, it is important that teachers and parents become aware of youths' coercive processes at school and at home and learn how to disrupt the cycle to reduce youth risk. Coercion is likely getting started when teachers and parents (a) hesitate to give sanctions, (b) yell or threaten punishment in an attempt to make a child listen to directives, (c) tend to focus on negative behavior,

Table 6.1 Implications for Practice: Preventive Approaches to Reducing Risk for Deviant Peer Influences by Connecting Home and School

1.	Common rules at home and school that are clearly stated in both settings.
2.	Consistent, predictable positive reinforcement for good behavior.
3.	Awareness of the power of coercion, use of effective behavior management strategies at home and school.
4.	Structure, monitoring, and supervision at home and school.
5.	Communication and coordination among parents in the community, facilitated through schools.
6.	Structuring of peer social networks to reduce coercive peer grouping.

and (d) feel intimidated by the child. Coordination between school and home about how to effectively short circuit this dynamic by using effective requests and reinforcement of positive behavior can be key to reducing coercive processes in both settings.

Fourth, home and school communication must be used to bolster monitoring and supervision so that exposure to contagion effects is reduced. A collaborative effort must be made to increase structured time at school, increase communication so that parents are better aware of who their student is spending time with and when they are likely to be unsupervised, and help parents create plans for engaging students in supervised activities or for structuring after-school time until parents are home and able to supervise.

Fifth, school personnel can facilitate parental monitoring by helping establish parenting networks. To promote a network of parents who work effectively together to supervise their youth, school personnel can provide a venue for parents to share contact information, establish parent meetings about how to track adolescents' whereabouts, and promote parent networking in respect to after-school events (e.g., sporting events, school dances). Parent networking can be a critical strategy for learning information that adolescents may withhold, for ensuring that youth activities are appropriate, and for sharing family rules about issues such as curfew, "checking in," and unsupervised time.

Sixth, school personnel could more actively "design" peer environments that reduce rejection and self-organization into deviant peer clusters, bearing in mind that schools are a key influence in the formation of peer social networks. Rejection by the normative peer group and self-organization into deviant peer clusters together contribute to amplification of problem behavior throughout adolescence (Dishion et al., 2010). Research on social networks reveals that some schools are more strongly characterized by peer contagion dynamics than are others (Light & Dishion, 2007), suggesting that some schools are better than others at managing the peer learning environment. For example, the classic study by Feldman revealed that systematically integrating prosocial and antisocial boys reduced the effects of peer contagion (Feldman, Wodarski, Goodman, & Flax, 1973). The field would benefit from a data based (i.e., social network data) approach to assigning youth to classrooms, learning activities, lunch periods, and extracurricular activities, with a goal of reducing peer contagion and improving education and social outcomes.

References

Ackard, D. M., Neumark-Sztainer, D., Story, M., & Perry, C. (2006). Parent–child connectedness and behavioral and emotional health among adolescents. *American Journal of Preventive Medicine, 30*(1), 59–66.

Aos, S., Lieb, R., Mayfield, J., Miller, M., & Pennucci, A. (2004). *Benefits and costs of prevention and early intervention programs for youth*. Olympia, WA: Washington State Institute for Public Policy. Retrieved September 1, 2008, from http://www.wsipp.wa.gov/pub.asp?docid=04-07-3901

Barrish, H. H., Saunders, M., & Wolf, M. M. (1969). Good behavior game: Effects of individual contingencies for group consequences on disruptive behavior in a classroom. *Journal of Applied Behavior Analysis, 2*(2), 119–124.

Benson, H., Wilcher, M., Greenberg, B., Huggins, E., Ennis, M., Zuttermeister, P.C., … Friedman, R. (2000). Academic performance among middle school students after exposure to a relaxation response curriculum. *Journal of Research and Development in Education, 33*(3), 156–165.

Birch, S. H., & Ladd, G. W. (1997). The teacher–child relationship and children's early school adjustment. *Journal of School Psychology, 35*(1), 61–79.

Botvin, G. J. (2000). Preventing drug use in schools: Social and competence enhancement approaches targeting individual-level etiological factors. *Addictive Behaviors, 25*, 887–897.

Bradshaw, C. P., Koth, C. W., Thornton, L. A., & Leaf, P. J. (2009). Altering school climate through school-wide Positive Behavioral Interventions and Supports: Findings from a group-randomized effectiveness trial. *Prevention Science, 10*(2), 100–115.

Bronfenbrenner, U. (1979). *The ecology of human development: Experiments by nature and design*. Cambridge, MA: Harvard University Press.

Caprara, G. V., Barbaranelli, C., Pastorelli, C., Bandura, A., & Zimbardo, P. G. (2000). Prosocial foundations of children's academic achievement. *Psychological Science, 11*(4), 302–306.

Carr, E. G., Taylor, J. C., & Robinson, S. (1991). The effects of severe behavior problems in children on the teaching behavior of adults. *Journal of Applied Behavior Analysis, 24*(3), 523–535.

Collaborative for Academic, Social, and Emotional Learning, CASEL (2010, July). The benefits of school-based social and emotional learning programs: Highlights from a major new report. *SEL Research Group,* 1–3. Retrieved from http://www.casel.org/sel/meta.php

Colvin, G., Sugai, G., Good, R., & Lee, Y. (1997). Using active supervision and precorrection to improve transition behaviors in an elementary school. *School Psychology Quarterly, 12,* 344–363.

Conger, R. D., Conger, K. J., Elder, G. H. Jr., Lorenz, F. O., Simons, R. L., & Whitbeck, L. B. (1992). A family process model of economic hardship and adjustment of early adolescent boys. *Child Development, 63,* 526–541.

Conger, R. D., Patterson, G. R., & Ge, X. (1995). It takes two to replicate: A mediational model for the impact of parents' stress on adolescent adjustment. *Child Development, 66,* 80–97.

Connell, A., Dishion, T. J., Yasui, M., & Kavanagh, K. (2007). An adaptive approach to family intervention: Linking engagement in family-centered intervention to reductions in adolescent problem behavior. *Journal of Consulting and Clinical Psychology, 75,* 568–579.

Crandall, C. S. (1988). Social contagion of binge eating. *Journal of Personality and Social Psychology, 55,* 588–598.

DeBaryshe, B. D., Patterson, G. R., & Capaldi, D. M. (1993). A performance model for academic achievement in early adolescent boys. *Developmental Psychology, 29,* 795–804.

Dishion, T. J., & Kavanagh, K. (2003). *Intervening with adolescent problem behavior: A family-centered approach.* New York: Guilford.

Dishion, T. J., McCord, J., & Poulin, F. (1999). When interventions harm: Peer groups and problem behavior. *American Psychologist, 54,* 755–764.

Dishion, T. J., & McMahon, R. J. (1998). Parental monitoring and the prevention of child and adolescent problem behavior: A conceptual and empirical formulation. *Clinical Child and Family Psychology Review, 1,* 61–75.

Dishion, T. J., Nelson, S. E., & Bullock, B. M. (2004). Premature adolescent autonomy: Parent disengagement and deviant peer process in the amplification of problem behavior. *Journal of Adolescence, 27,* 515–530.

Dishion, T. J., & Patterson, G. R. (2006). The development and ecology of antisocial behavior. In D. Cicchetti & D. J. Cohen (Eds.), *Developmental psychopathology: Vol. 3. Risk, disorder, and adaptation* (2nd ed., pp. 503–541). Hoboken, NJ: Wiley.

Dishion, T. J., Patterson, G. R., & Kavanagh, K. (1992). An experimental test of the coercion model: Linking theory, measurement, and intervention. In J. McCord & R. Trembley (Eds.), *The interaction of theory and practice: Experimental studies of interventions* (pp. 253–282). New York, NY: Guilford.

Dishion, T. J., Spracklen, K. M., Andrews, D. W., & Patterson, G. R. (1996). Deviancy training in male adolescent friendships. *Behavior Therapy, 27,* 373–390.

Dishion, T. J., Véronneau, M.-H., & Myers, M. W. (2010). Cascading peer dynamics underlying the progression from problem behavior to violence in early to late adolescence. *Development and Psychopathology, 22,* 603–619.

Dodge, K. A., Malone, P. S., Lansford, J. E., Miller, S., Pettit, G. S., & Bates, J. E. (2009). A dynamic cascade model of the development of substance-use onset: Early peer relations problem factors. *Monographs of the Society for Research in Child Development, 74*(3), 51–54.

Dodge, K. A., & Pettit, G. S. (2003). A biopsychosocial model of the development of chronic conduct problems in adolescence. *Developmental Psychology, 39,* 349–371.

Durlak, J. A., Weissberg. R. P., Dymnicki, A. B., Taylor, R. D., & Schellinger, K. B. (2011). The impact of enhancing students' social and emotional learning: A meta-analysis of school-based universal interventions. *Child Development, 82,* 405–432. doi: 10.1111/j.1467-8624.2010.01564.x

Ellis, S., Rogoff, B., & Cromer, C. (1981). Age segregation in children's interactions. *Developmental Psychology, 17,* 399–407.

Feldman, R. A., Wodarski, J. S., Goodman, M., & Flax, N. (1973). Prosocial and antisocial boys together. *Social Work, 18*(5), 26–37.

Flay, B. R. (2009). The promise of long-term effectiveness of school-based smoking prevention programs: A critical review of reviews. *Tobacco Induced Diseases, 5*(1), 7–29.

Flouri, E., & Buchanan, A. (2003). The role of father involvement and mother involvement in adolescents' psychological well-being. *British Journal of Social Work, 33*(3), 399–406.

Fosco, G. M., Stormshak, E. A., Dishion, T. J., & Winter, C. (in press). Family relationships and parental monitoring during middle school as predictors of early adolescent problem behavior. *Journal of Clinical Child and Adolescent Psychology.*

Granic, I., & Dishion, T. J. (2003). Deviant talk in adolescent friendships: A step toward measuring a pathogenic attractor process. *Social Development, 12*(3), 314–334.

Gunter, P. L., & Coutinho, M. J. (1997). Negative reinforcement in classrooms. *Teacher Education and Special Education, 20*(3), 249–64.

Gunter, P. L., Kenton Denny, R., Shores, R. E., Reed, T. M., Jack, S. L., & Nelson, M. (1994). Teacher escape, avoidance, and counter control behaviors: Potential responses to disruptive and aggressive behaviors of students with severe behavior disorders. *Journal of Child and Family Studies, 3*(2), 211–223.

Gunter, P., & Sutherland, K. (2005). Opportunity to respond. In G. Sugai & R. Horner (Eds.), *Encyclopedia of behavior modification and cognitive behavior therapy* (Vol. 3, pp. 1403–1406). Thousand Oaks, CA: Sage.

Heilbron, N., & Prinstein, M. J. (2008). Peer influence and adolescent nonsuicidal self-injury: A theoretical review of mechanisms and moderators. *Applied and Preventive Psychology, 12,* 169–177.

Hill, N. E., Bromell, L., Tyson, D. F., & Flint, R. (2007). Developmental commentary: Ecological perspectives on parental influences during adolescence. *Journal of Clinical Child and Adolescent Psychology, 36*(3), 367–377.

Hoeve, M., Dubas, J. S., Eichelsheim, V. I., van der Laan, P. H., Smeenk, W., & Gerris, J. R. M. (2009). The relationship between parenting and delinquency: A meta-analysis. *Journal of Abnormal Child Psychology, 37,* 479–775.

Horner, R. H., Sugai, G., Smolkowski, K., Eber, L., Nakasato, J., Todd, A. W., … Esperanza, J. (2009). A randomized, wait-list controlled effectiveness trial assessing school-wide positive behavior support in elementary schools. *Journal of Positive Behavior Interventions, 11*(3), 133–144. doi:10.1177/1098300709332067

Howes, C., Hamilton, C. E., & Matheson, C. C. (1994). Children's relationships with peers: Differential associations with aspects of the teacher–child relationship. *Child Development, 65*(1), 253–263.

Kellam, S. G., Ling, X., Merisca, R., Brown, C. H., & Ialongo, N. (1998). The effect of the level of aggression in the first grade classroom on the course and malleability of aggressive behavior into middle school. *Development and Psychopathology, 10,* 165–185.

Kokkinos, C. M., Panayiotou, G., & Davazoglou, A. M. (2005). Correlates of teacher appraisals of student behaviors. *Psychology in the Schools, 42*(1), 79–89.

Laird, R. D., Criss, M. M., Pettit, G. S., Dodge, K. A., & Bates, J. E. (2008). Parents' monitoring knowledge attenuates the link between antisocial friends and adolescent delinquent behavior. *Journal of Abnormal Child Psychology, 36,* 299–310.

Lewis, T., Sugai, G., & Colvin, G. (1998). Reducing problem behavior through a school-wide system of effective behavioral support: Investigation of a school-wide social skills training program and contextual interventions. *School Psychology Review, 27*(3), 446–459.

Lewis, T., Sugai, G., & Colvin, G. (2000). The effects of pre-corrective and active supervision on the recess behavior or elementary students. *Education and Treatment of Children, 23*(2), 109–121.

Light, J. M., & Dishion, T. J. (2007). Early adolescent antisocial behavior and peer rejection: A dynamic test of a developmental process. In P. C. Rodkin & L. D. Hanish (Eds.), *Social network analysis and children's peer relationships* (pp. 77–89). San Francisco, CA: Jossey–Bass.

Mayer, G. (1995). Preventing antisocial behavior in the schools. *Journal of Applied Behavior Analysis, 28,* 467–478.

McCombs, B. L. (2004). The Learner-centered psychological principles: A framework for balancing academic achievement and social–emotional learning outcomes. In J. E. Zins, R. P. Weissberg, M. C. Wang, & H. J. Walberg (Eds.), *Building academic success on social and emotional learning: What does the research say?* (pp. 23–39). New York, NY: Teachers College Press.

Medland, M. B., & Stachnik, T. J. (1972). Good-behavior game: A replication and systematic analysis. *Journal of Applied Behavior Analysis, 51*(1), 45–51.

Nelson, J. R., Martella, R., & Galand, B. (1998). The effects of teaching school expectations and establishing a consistent consequence on formal office disciplinary actions. *Journal of Emotional and Behavioral Disorders, 6*(3), 153–161. doi:10.1177/106342669800600303

Nelson, J. R., & Roberts, M. L. (2000). Ongoing reciprocal teacher–student interactions involving disruptive behaviors in general education classrooms. *Journal of Emotional and Behavioral Disorders, 8,* 27–37.

Nelson, S. E., & Dishion, T. J. (2004). From boys to men: Predicting adult adaptation from middle childhood sociometric status. *Development and Psychopathology, 16,* 441–459.

Osgood, D., Feinberg, M., Gest, S. D., Moody, J., & Bierman, K. (2010, June). *Prevention and adolescents' friendship networks: Impact of an evidence-based program on the social status of antisocial versus prosocial youth.* Presentation at the Society for Prevention Research 18th Annual Meeting, Denver, CO.

Pan, W., & Bai, H. (2009). A multivariate approach to a meta-analytic review of the effectiveness of the DARE program. *International Journal of Environmental Research and Public Health, 6*(1), 267.

Patterson, G. R. (1982). *A social learning approach: III. Coercive family process.* Eugene, OR: Castalia.

Patterson, G. R. (1986). Performance models for antisocial boys. *American Psychologist, 41,* 432–444.

Patterson, G. R., DeBaryshe, B., & Ramsey, E. (1989). A developmental perspective on antisocial behavior. *American Psychologist, 44,* 329–335.

Payton, J. W., Wardlaw, D. M., Graczyk, P. A., Bloodworth, M. R., Tompsett, C. J., & Weissberg, R. P. (2000). Social and emotional learning: A framework for promoting mental health and reducing risk behavior in children and youth. *Journal of School Health, 70*(5), 179–185.

Pianta, R. C., Steinberg, M. S., & Rollins, K. B. (1995). The first two years of school: Teacher–child relationships and deflections in children's classroom adjustment. *Development and Psychopathology, 7*(02), 295–312.

Poduska, J. M., Kellam, S. G., Wang, W., Brown, C. H., Ialongo, N. S., & Toyinbo, P. (2008). Impact of the Good Behavior Game, a universal classroom-based behavior intervention, on young adult service use for problems with emotions, behavior, or drugs or alcohol. *Drug & Alcohol Dependence, 95*, 29–44.

Reinke, W. M., & Herman, K. C. (2002). Creating school environments that deter antisocial behaviors in youth. *Psychology in the Schools, 39*(5), 549–559. doi:10.1002/pits.10048

Reinke, W. M., & Walker, H. M. (2006). Deviant peer effects in education. In K. A. Dodge, T. J. Dishion, & J. E. Lansford (Eds.), *Deviant peer influences in programs for youth* (pp. 122–140). New York, NY: Guilford.

Resnick, M. D., Bearman, P. S., Blum, R. W., Bauman, K. E., Harris, K. M., Jones, J., ... Udry, J. R. (1997). Protecting adolescents from harm: Findings from the National Longitudinal Study on Adolescent Health. *Journal of the American Medical Association, 278*(10), 823–832.

Shelton, K. H., Harold, G. T., Goeke-Morey, M. C., & Cummings, E. M. (2007). Children's coping with marital conflict: The role of conflict expression and gender. *Social Development, 15*(2), 232–247.

Shores, R. E., Jack, S.L., Gunter, P. L., Ellis, D. N., DeBriere, T. J., & Wehby, J. H. (1993). Classroom interactions of children with behavior disorders. *Journal of Emotional and Behavioral Disorders, 1*, 27–39.

Snyder, J. Schrepferman, L., McEachern, A., Barner, S., Johnson, K., & Provines, J. (2008). Peer deviancy training and peer coercion: Dual processes associated with early-onset conduct problems. *Child Development, 79*, 252–268.

Snyder, J., Schrepferman, L., Oeser, J., Patterson, G., Stoolmiller, M., Johnson, K., ... Snyder, J. (2005). Deviancy training and association with deviant peers in young children: Occurrence and contribution to early-onset conduct problems. *Development & Psychopathology, 17*(2), 397–413.

Stevens, E. A., & Prinstein, M. J. (2005). Peer contagion of depressogenic attributional styles among adolescents: A longitudinal study. *Journal of Abnormal Child Psychology, 33*(1), 25–37.

Stormshak, E. A., Connell, A. M., & Dishion, T. J. (2009). An adaptive approach to family-centered intervention in schools: Linking intervention engagement to academic outcomes in middle and high school. *Prevention Science, 10*, 221–235.

Van Acker, R., Grant, S. B., & Henry, D. (1996) Teacher and student behavior as a function of risk for aggression. *Education and Treatment of Children, 19*, 316–334.

Vitaro, F., Pedersen, S., & Brendgen, M. (2007). Children's disruptiveness, peer rejection, friends' deviancy, and delinquent behaviors: A process-oriented approach. *Development and Psychopathology, 19*(2), 433–453.

Walker, H. M., Colvin, G., & Ramsey, E. (1995). *Antisocial behavior in school: Strategies and best practices.* Pacific Grove, CA: Brooks Cole.

Warren, L, Schoppelrey, S., Moberg, P., & McDonald, M. (2005). A model of contagion through competition in the aggressive behaviors of elementary school students. *Journal of Abnormal Child Psychology, 33*, 283–292.

Werner, E. (1990). Protective factors and individual resilience. In S. Meisels & J. Shonkoff (Eds), *Handbook of early childhood intervention* (pp. 97–116). New York, NY: Cambridge University Press.

White, R., Algozzine, B., Audette, R., Marr, M. B., & Ellis, E. D. (2001). Unified discipline. *Intervention in School and Clinic, 37*(1), 3–8. doi:10.1177/105345120103700101

Wilson, D. B., Gottfredson, D. C., & Najaka, S. S. (2001). School-based prevention of problem behaviors: A meta-analysis. *Journal of Quantitative Criminology, 17*(3), 247–272.

Yoon, J. S. (2008). Teacher characteristics as predictors of teacher–student relationships: Stress, negative affect, and self-efficacy. *Social Behavior and Personality, 30*, 485–494.

Zins, J. E., Bloodworth, M. R., Weissberg, R. P., & Walberg, H. J. (2004). The scientific base linking social and emotional learning to school success. In J. E. Zins, R. P. Weissberg, M. C. Wang, & H. J. Walberg (Eds.), *Building academic success on social and emotional learning What does the research say?* (pp. 3–22). New York, NY: Teachers College Press.

7

On the Personality Mechanisms Leading to Violence

*Guido Alessandri, Michele Vecchione,
and Gian Vittorio Caprara*

SAPIENZA UNIVERSITY OF ROME

Abstract

This chapter presents a theoretical framework that aims to reconnect basic individual differences in personality with cognitive mechanisms of disengagement of moral cognition within an integrative model of youth aggression. In particular, we extend previous research regarding the relations between basic traits from the Five Factor Model and individual differences in irritability, hostile rumination, and moral disengagement, trying to clarify the pathways through which each of the above constructs may contribute to violence. We theorized that basic traits, namely agreeableness and emotional instability, set the basis for specific tendencies like irritability and hostile rumination. Moral disengagement was posited as the gatekeeper, able to turn the influences of basic traits, irritability, and hostile rumination into aggression and violent behavior.

On the Personality Mechanisms Leading to Violence

Overview of the Issue

Among contemporary theorists, personality is viewed as a complex self-regulatory system including habitual behaviors, knowledge structures, and coping mechanisms (Caprara, 1996). Personality as a complex self-regulatory system includes the entire architecture of surface behavioral tendencies, and the underlying basic traits, as well as social cognitive mechanisms assigning meaningful behavior in the service of self-interest (Caprara & Cervone, 2000). A number of researchers have theorized about the importance of assessing individual differences in personality as an approach to understanding aggressive conduct (Anderson & Bushman, 2002; Anderson & Huesmann, 2003; Bettencourt, Talley, Benjamin, & Valentine, 2006). Across the past two decades, indeed, personality variables have been proved to be instrumental in clarifying various mechanisms conducive to aggression. For instance, offenders, in comparison to their non–offending peers, are likely to exhibit more impulsive behavior (Farrington, Ttofi, & Coid, 2009), have low self-control (Simons, Simons, Chen, Brody, & Lin, 2007), and suffer more from depressive symptoms (Wiesner & Kim, 2006), all of which are characteristics related to personality.

A triad of personality variables that are predictors of aggression in the laboratory as well as in natural settings—irritability, hostile rumination, and moral disengagement—has emerged as particularly crucial. Whereas both irritability and hostile rumination are anchored to the frustration-aggression hypothesis (Berkowitz, 1989; Dollard, Doob, Miller, Mowrer, & Sears, 1939), moral disengagement developed out of Bandura's social cognitive theory and his contributions to moral agency (1986, 1991). In this chapter, we focus on how these variables may act in concert in the development of youth antisocial behavior at school and with peers. Recent longitudinal studies demonstrated how these variables interact in the development of chronic conduct problems (Caprara, Alessandri, et al., 2010; Caprara, Fontaine, et al., 2010; Paciello, Fida, Tramontano, Lupinetti, & Caprara, 2008). Drawing upon results from empirical studies, we developed a conceptual model in which irritability, hostile rumination, and moral disengagement act as mediators in turning basic individual differences into aggressive and delinquent behaviors. The implications of this model for predicting violence in the school and for implementing preventive intervention programs are discussed.

Conceptual Basis

Irritability, Hostile Rumination, and Moral Disengagement

Irritability is defined as the "tendency to react impulsively, controversially or rudely at the slightest provocation or disagreement" (Caprara et al., 1985, p. 667); hostile rumination is defined as the tendency to "harbor and even to enhance, with the passing of time, feelings and desires of vengeance" (Caprara, 1986, p. 765); moral disengagement is defined as the process of convincing the self that ethical standards do not apply to oneself in a particular context, by separating moral reactions from inhumane conduct by disabling the mechanism of self-condemnation (Bandura, 1990; Fiske, 2010). Irritability, hostile rumination, and moral disengagement have all been shown to account for a notable portion of variability in aggression and violence across a variety of conditions and over the course of development, from early adolescence to young adulthood (Caprara, 1987, 1996; Caprara, Paciello, Gerbino, & Cugini, 2007; Paciello et al., 2008). Moreover, both irritability and hostile rumination accounted for a significant portion of aggression in experiments designed to study aggression in response to frustration and provocation contingently (Bandura, Barbaranelli, Caprara, & Pastorelli, 1996; Bandura, Caprara, Barbaranelli, Pastorelli, & Regalia, 2001; Caprara et al., 1985).

Irritability is related to one's capacity to dominate one's emotional reactions in either real or apparent situations of danger, offense, or attack (Caprara et al., 1985). Irritability highlights the role that defective control over negative emotions play in amplifying the effects of situations that may promote reactive aggression (responding to an aggressive provocation). A characteristic of irritability is the influence of excitatory processes in fostering aggressive reactions to instigator situations. During crucial ages of development, empirical studies (Caprara et al., 2007) demonstrated that different trajectories may be distinguished for irritability. Whereas most of the participants demonstrated stable mean levels of irritability, half of the youth either increased or decreased in their level of hostile rumination over time. In addition, high irritability trajectories were associated with high physical and verbal aggression.

Hostile rumination pertains to one's tendency to exhibit ill feelings, carrying desires and expectations of vengeance following self-threatening provocations (Caprara et al., 1985). It concerns the enduring influence of negative affect in distorting cognition in the pursuit of revenge. Self-concerns, attributions, and social attitudes play a role in transforming derogatory experiences into retaliatory reactions for purposes of revenge (see Caprara, 1987, for a review). Upon a thorough review of the literature on personality and aggressive behavior under both provocation and neutral conditions, Bettencourt and colleagues (2006) described irritability as a major expression of aggression proneness across situations, and hostile rumination as a major expression of provocation sensitivity, or the tendency to react aggressively to provocation (see also Collins & Bell, 1997). As for irritability, four developmental trajectories were distinguished for hostile rumination, half decreasing or increasing over time. Interestingly, hostile rumination trajectories were associated with high levels of violent behavior.

Moral disengagement represents one of the major contributions of Bandura's social cognitive theory. It pertains to the psychosocial processes that provide the cognitive framework within which aggression and violence appear appropriate reactions and acquire legitimacy in the pursuit of self-interest (Bandura, 1986, 1991; Caprara, 1996). Moral disengagement involves psychological schemes by which moral self-sanctions can be selectively disengaged from detrimental aggressive conduct by converting harmful acts to acceptable ones and by giving free reign to a variety of misbehaviors without carrying any moral sanctions. There are four points at which self-sanction can be disengaged from detrimental conduct: (a) the behavior itself, (b) the locus of responsibility (associated with the behavior causing detrimental effects), (c) the harmful consequences, and the (d) recipient (or victim). Additionally, there are eight mechanisms (e.g., moral justification, euphemistic labeling, advantageous comparison, displacement of responsibility, diffusion of responsibility, distortion of consequences, dehumanization, and attribution of blame), which operate at these four points. These mechanisms allow individuals to engage in self-serving behavior that is in contrast with their moral principles, while continuing to advocate those principles without incurring self-evaluative emotional reactions, such as guilt.

Ultimately, moral disengagement points either to mechanisms that promote detrimental behaviors through selective deactivation of moral standards, or to the influence that social cognition exerts upon internalization of norms and values conducive to detrimental conducts through various forms of self-deception in the pursuit of self-interest. Several factors may contribute to interpretations of situations that are conducive to detrimental behaviors in the pursuit of self-interest (see Gibbs, 2003). For instance, one may be biased in his or her social judgment and decision making due to social cognitive underdevelopment (e.g., the inability to identify and evaluate a range of social values and behavioral options) or because he or she has become inclined to rationalize immoral or aggressive conduct by removing the moral content by which it may otherwise be deterred or inhibited. As cognitive distortions may reflect either the lack or circumvention of moral standards, one may question whether moral disengagement is fully appropriate to convey the nature of self-serving cognitive distortions that may be due to causes other than selective deactivation of established moral principles. This may be particularly true in earlier stages of development, when children have not yet achieved moral standards from which to disengage, or in social and cultural environments in which norms and values justify intentions and actions that elsewhere would serve as a source of blame, remorse, and guilt. Nevertheless, whatever may be the source of the tendency to activate processes that are captured by moral disengagement, such a tendency has repeatedly been associated with aggression and violence (Bandura, Barbaranelli, Caprara, & Pastorelli, 1996; Bandura, Caprara, Barbaranelli, Pastorelli, & Regalia, 2001; Dodge, 1991; Dodge & Coie, 1987).

A number of findings have shown that above mechanisms can be traced to the common latent variable of moral disengagement (Bandura et al., 1996, 2001; Pelton, Gound, Forehand, & Brody, 2004). Developmental studies (Paciello et al., 2008) identified four developmental trajectories: (a) non-disengaged group that started with initially low levels of moral disengagement followed by an important decline, (b) normative group that started with initially moderate levels followed by a decline, (c) later desister group that started with initially high–medium levels followed by an increase from 14 to 16 years and an even steeper decline from 16 to 20 years, and (d) chronic group that started with and maintained medium–high levels. Results from this study (Paciello et al., 2008) demonstrated that adolescents who maintained higher levels of moral disengagement were more likely to show frequent aggressive and violent acts in late adolescence. In reality, a large body of research has demonstrated the disinhibitory power of moral disengagement in fostering aggressive behavior (Andrus, 1969; Bandura, 1990; Kelman & Hamilton, 1989; Rapoport & Alexander, 1989). Other research has also demonstrated its strong associations with various manifestations of aggression and violence, as well as other forms of antisocial conduct (Bandura et al., 1996; Bandura, Caprara, & Zsolnai, 2000; Gini, 2006; Menesini et al., 2003).

Agreeableness and Emotional Stability

Earlier studies (Caprara, Perugini, & Barbaranelli, 1994) have attempted to map individual differences in irritability, hostile rumination, and moral disengagement within the realm of a comprehensive model of personality, such as the Five Factor Model, the reference model to describe personality advocated by most researchers in the field. Using this model McCrae and Costa (1999) demonstrated that major dispositional tendencies can be described by five dimensions including: energy/extraversion (e.g., I like to meet with other people), agreeableness (e.g., I understand when others need my help), conscientiousness (e.g., I engage myself in the things I do), emotional stability (e.g., I easily get angry), and intellect/openness (e.g., I like to know and to learn new things).

Most relevant to aggression and violence are agreeableness and emotional stability. *Agreeableness* is the dimension that pertains to interpersonal relations (Jensen-Campbell & Graziano, 2001), in which the goal is to maintain positive relationships with other individuals (Graziano & Eisenberg. 1997; Jensen-Campbell et al., 2002). Agreeableness refers to concern and sensitivity toward other individuals, as well as kindness, civility, docility, and trust (Barbaranelli, & Caprara, 2000). Agreeableness has been negatively related to conflict and anger (Jensen-Campbell et al., 2002), impulsivity, manipulative, and confrontational behaviors (Robins, John, Caspi, Moffitt, & Stouthamer-Loeber, 1996), as well as delinquent or aggressive behaviors (Jensen-Campbell et al., 2002). *Emotional stability* refers to personality characteristics pertaining to the capabilities to cope adequately with one's own anxiety and emotionality, and to control irritation, discontent, and anger (Barbaranelli & Caprara, 2000). The opposite pole of emotional stability (neuroticism) is defined as the propensity to experience feelings of helplessness, discomfort, vulnerability, and inadequacy (Caprara, Barbaranelli, & Comrey, 1992). Caprara et al. (1992) demonstrated that emotional stability is linked to the emotional component of aggression. This finding is consistent with the research of Robins et al. (996), showing that emotional stability is negatively related to antisocial patterns, including manipulative, impulsive, and confrontational behaviors.

Description of the Specific Issues

Interrelatedness Among the Variables

Recent studies have focused on the developmental trajectories of irritability, hostile rumination, and moral disengagement, and on how they may influence each other over the course of development (Caprara, Fontaine, et al., 2010). Findings have shown that individual differences in irritability, hostile rumination, and moral disengagement are correlated over the entire course of adolescence. Moreover, their correlations increase with age, attesting to the gradual crystallization of a "mindset" in which proneness to irritation, revenge, and moral disengagement converge to foster and sustain aggressive and violent behaviors over the course of time. Whereas the higher stability of irritability attests to its temperamental roots, the increasing stability of hostile rumination and moral disengagement with the passing of time implies their social cognitive bases (Caprara et al., 2010).

As shown above, findings have revealed similar developmental trajectories from early adolescence to young adulthood, but slightly different outcomes (Caprara et al., 2007; Paciello et al., 2008). Whereas the contribution of irritability to aggression and violence declines with the passing of time, the contribution of hostile rumination and moral disengagement increases over the course of adolescence and becomes crucial at the onset of adulthood. Drawing upon these findings, one may theorize that defective capacities in dealing with anger and hostile feelings are conducive to aggression earlier in adolescence. Moral disengagement is mainly what allows one to indulge into aggression and violence later in adolescence.

Likewise, the influence that irritability, hostile rumination, and moral disengagement exert on each other is different over the entire course of adolescence. Irritability contributes to earlier hostile rumination, which in turns bridges the relationship between irritability and moral disengagement (Caprara et al., 2010). Hostile rumination contributes, in part, to maintaining irritability, but there is no direct link between irritability and moral disengagement, nor does moral disengagement contribute to hostile rumination (Caprara et al., 2010). It is likely that individual differences in irritability are mostly temperamental, whereas these differences in hostile rumination and moral disengagement attest to the influence that social experience exerts over mechanisms of affect regulation (Dodge, 1991; Fontaine, 2007). Careful examination of the mediational role of hostile rumination provides support for the conceptualization of the development of dispositional aggression during which emotional processes (associated with irritability) contribute through hostile ruminative cognitions to social cognitive mechanisms (moral disengagement), that leads one to value aggression and violence as instrumental means by which to achieve a variety of goals.

Empirical findings have shown that irritability, hostile rumination, and moral disengagement are located in the quadrant defined by the opposite pole of agreeableness and emotional stability. Whereas irritability is located close to the opposite pole of emotional stability, moral disengagement lies along the opposite pole of agreeableness, and hostile rumination at about 45 degrees between the opposite poles of emotional stability and agreeableness (Caprara, Perugini, & Barbaranelli, 1994). These findings are congruent with other results (Butler & Nolen-Hoeksema, 1994; Collins & Bell, 1997; Costa & McCrae, 1992; Halverson et al., 2003; Kochanska, Friesenborg, Lange & Martel, 2004; Nolen-Hoeksema, Parker, & Larson, 1994; Thayer, Rossy, Ruiz-Padial, & Johnsen, 2003). Together, these data point to individual differences in irritability, hostile rumination, and moral disengagement as expressions of different intrapersonal systems associated with emotion regulation and to management of self in relation with others. Irritability and moral disengagement are both intrapersonal systems, yet irritability predisposes one to aggression that is typically impulsive and reactive, whereas moral disengagement predisposes one to aggression that is typically instrumental to the pursuit of one's own interest. Hostile rumination is a social cognitive process associated with attributions and expectations capable of turning negative affect due to self-threatening provocation into feelings and thoughts legitimizing the pursuit of vengeance.

A Theoretical Model

Relying upon earlier cross-sectional and longitudinal research designed to map individual differences in irritability, hostile rumination, and moral disengagement, a theoretical model was developed with the aim to clarify the different contributions of the agreeableness and emotional stability personality traits to violent conduct (Bettencourt et al., 2006; Caprara, Alessandri, et al., 2010; Caprara, Fontaine, et al., 2010; Paciello et al., 2008; Gleason, Jensen-

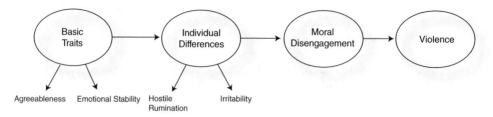

Figure 7.1 Conceptual mediation model for aggreeableness, emotional stability, hostile rumination, irritability, moral disengagement, and violence.

Campbell, & Richardson, 2004; Graziano, Jensen-Campbell, & Hair, 1996; Suls, Martin, & David, 1998).

This theoretical model (Figure 7.1) assigns primacy to emotional stability and agreeableness in the posited set of pathways, in accordance with a vast literature demonstrating the significant biological component of basic traits as well as in accordance with alternative views of traits as habitual responses resulting from chronic person-situations interactions that, once crystallized, operate as automatic behavioral tendencies (Cervone, & Shoda, 1999; Higgings, 1999; Jang, Livesley, & Vemon, 1996; Jang, McCrae, Angleitner, Rienmann, & Livesley, 1998; Johnson, & Krueger, 2004; Lohelin, 1982; Lohelin, McCrae, Costa, & John, 1998; Rienman, Angleitner, & Strelau, 1997). As agreeableness and emotional stability are early-appearing features of personality that mostly reflect their temperamental roots (Caspi & Shiner, 2006; Eisenberg, Fabes, & Spinrad, 2006; Rothbart & Bates, 1998), this model proposes that these traits operate as primary spontaneous behavioral tendencies, setting the basis for experiences fostering the crystallization of specific affective and cognitive intrapersonal organizations conducive to aggression and violence. In particular, *irritability* is considered as mainly associated with the opposite pole of *emotional stability*, which among basic traits is chiefly concerned with the management of emotions. In contrast, *moral disengagement* is deemed as predominantly associated with the opposite pole of *agreeableness*, which is concerned with the management of interpersonal relations and whose opposite has been associated with callousness, cynicism, and other forms of insensitivity to others' well being (DeYoung et al., 2010), similar to moral disengagement. Finally, hostile rumination is associated with both emotional stability and agreeableness, and as a tendency that reflects the regulation of both affect and interpersonal relations.

In line with previous findings demonstrating high intercorrelations among irritability, hostile rumination, and moral disengagement, we point to irritability as a predecessor of hostile rumination. While not disregarding the contribution of the latter to the former over the course of development, previous findings highlight the mediating role of hostile rumination between irritability and moral disengagement as well as the crucial role of the latter in fostering aggression and violence (Bandura et al., 1996; Bushman, Bonacci, Pedersen, Vasquez, & Miller, 2005; Caprara et al., 2007). In this model, irritability is considered as a temperament feature making people sensitive to angry feelings when under stressful situations, whereas hostile rumination is viewed as a tendency to nurture hostile feelings after provocations as a result of the inability to work effectively through dissipation of negative affect. Finally, moral disengagement is considered a mechanism that enables the turning of hostile feelings into thoughts and desires of revenge and, ultimately, into detrimental actions without feeling guilty or blameable.

Application and Relevant Research

A longitudinal study corroborated this mediational model, and confirmed the fruitfulness of bringing together the contributions of two major traditions of research on aggressive behavior through the systematic use of individual differences (Caprara, Alessandri, et al., 2010). Indeed, both the tradition of research that has focused on the role of negative emotions and affect regulation (Berkowitz, 1989; Dollard et al., 1939) and the tradition of research which has emphasized social cognition (Bandura, 1986, 1991) have been influential in exploring how individual differences in irritability, hostile rumination, and moral disengagement can be traced to basic traits like agreeableness and emotional instability. This integrative theoretical framework extends previous research regarding the relations between basic traits from the Five Factor Model and individual differences in irritability, hostile rumination, and moral disengagement and clarifies the pathways through which the former and the latter may contribute to violence. For example, it posits that the opposite poles of emotional stability and agreeableness were most associated with irritability, hostile rumination, and moral disengagement in accordance with earlier studies (Caprara et al., 1994). Yet the contribution of basic traits to violence was conceptualized as entirely mediated by individual differences in irritability and hostile rumination. It is likely that basic traits, namely lack of agreeableness and emotional instability, set the basis for specific tendencies like irritability and hostile rumination that in turn foster violent behavior, given proper conditions. However, it is most likely that irritability and hostile rumination do not turn into violence unless the mechanisms that allow one to hurt other people without incurring into blame or guilt get activated. Thus, it is not surprising that individual differences in moral disengagement are the gatekeepers to most of violence.

Emotional stability and agreeableness do not directly affect violent outcomes, despite their (moderate) associations (Caprara, Alessandri, et al., 2010). It is possible that opposite poles of emotional stability and agreeableness reflect intrapersonal systems associated with emotion regulation and management of self in relation with others. This sets a frame of mind that makes people prone to irritation and predisposes them to value revenge and act in self-exonerative ways that contribute to ongoing violent behavior. Clearly, the more people engage in violence, the more they need self-serving cognitive distortions that allow them to take distance from the detrimental effects of their actions (Gibbs, 2003; McCrady et al., 2008). The strong impact that moral disengagement exerts on engagement in violent episodes calls attention to social models and discourses that provide the cognitive framework within which violence appears appropriate and acquires legitimacy. Likewise, attention is needed to identify the major occasions and situations that, over the course of development, embed self-exonerative actions into a system of beliefs about the self and others, ultimately leading to the use of moral disengagement as a coping strategy, and the perception that aggression and violence are appropriate means to pursue one's own goals (Arsenio & Gold, 2006; Arsenio & Lemerise, 2004; Tisak, Lewis, & Jankowski, 1997; Turiel, 2006).

Ultimately, this chain leads to value violence as an instrumental means by which to achieve a variety of goals. Also it seems plausible that "hot" processes (mostly associated with both irritability) turn into "cold" processes (mostly associated with hostile rumination) that, to have access to action, need proper mechanism enabling individuals to distance themselves from the blameable consequences of their actions. In this developmental process, hostile rumination represents an important connection between emotional processes related to anger reactivity and cognitive mechanisms related to instrumental motivations (Dodge, 1991; Fontaine, 2007; Geen, 1998; Vitiello & Stoff, 1997). The distinctive influence that hostile rumination exerts on moral disengagement calls attention to how individual factors, such as attitudes, values, and attributional processes, can provide the cognitive framework in which retaliation and revenge appear appropriate. Social norms and experiences, in fact, can dictate why, when, and how it is appropriate to invest much of one's own resources in the pursuit of retaliation (Crane-Ross, Tisak, & Tisak, 1998; Huesmann & Guerra, 1997; Tisak & Tisak, 1996).

Implications

The proposed framework points to the importance of a systematic use of individual differences in personality to understand affective and cognitive processes conducive to aggression and violence. Indeed, they are postulated to operate in concert through self-regulatory mechanisms and behavioral tendencies that crystallize over time. Empirical studies that examined the longitudinal and mediational relations among emotional stability, agreeableness, irritability, hostile rumination, and moral disengagement (Caprara, 1987, 1996; Caprara et al., 2007; Paciello et al., 2008) have proved their usefulness in understanding commonalities, diversities, and reciprocities regarding the primacy and degree of influence that each dimension exerts over the others.

Moreover, the above model has practical value in view of prevention and interventions aimed to prevent school violence. In Table 7.1 we offer a systematic presentation of the ways in which this framework may be applied in the school. In reality, school represents an ideal setting for the promotion of interpersonal relationships and for the prevention of deviant development. Schools can be conceived of not only as developing learning and educational processes, but also as "positive institutions" for facilitating human and social development (Seligman & Csikszentmihalyi, 2000). The model presented above may be particularly important in order to understand more in depth episodes of violent behaviors and bullying in high schools. According to our proposal, aggression and violence are rooted not only in basic individual predisposition (i.e., agreeableness and emotional stability) and in lower order personality constituents (e.g., irritability and hostile rumination), but also in the individual's cognitive evaluations of the consequences of his own conduct that open the way to violent behavioral outcomes. Although it is not still clear if basic traits may be changed or not, the youths' ability to refrain from engaging in deviant conduct may be evaluated and modified through specific behavioral interventions (Bandura, 1997). Thus, the assessment of moral disengagement, along with personality disposition, may allow a deeper understanding of determinants of youth violent behavior and to its prevention. In this regard, our model offers a direction where effective strategies of prevention, control, and change should be implemented.

Table 7.1 Implications for Practice: On the Social Cognitive Mechanisms Leading to Violence

1.	Assessing individual differences in personality represents a basic approach to understanding aggressive conduct.
2.	A triad of personality variables that are predictors of aggression in the laboratory, as well as in natural settings—irritability, hostile rumination, and moral disengagement—has emerged as particularly crucial.
3.	Findings have shown that individual differences in irritability, hostile rumination, and moral disengagement are correlated over the entire course of adolescence.
4.	In school settings, a mental health professional working with an aggressive child may also want to assess for individual differences in personality such as irritability, hostile rumination, and moral disengagement.
5.	Several easy-to-use measures are available for the assessment of irritability and rumination (Caprara et al., 1985), as well as moral disengagement (Bandura et al., 1996).
6.	Youth profiles on these measures may be used to plan specific interventions aimed to enhance emotion regulation (with higher scores on irritability or hostile rumination) and to foster adherence to social norm and values.
7.	The youth habit to blame mates, to disregard school properties, or the inability to respect school properties should be regarded as warning signs of moral disengagement.

References

Anderson, C. A., & Bushman, B. J. (2002). Human aggression. *Annual Review of Psychology, 53,* 27–51. doi: 10.1146/annurev.psych.53.100901.135231

Anderson, C. A., & Huesmann, L. R. (2003). Human aggression: A social-cognitive view. In M. A. Hogg & J. Cooper (Eds.), *Handbook of social psychology* (pp. 296–323). London: Sage.

Andrus, B. C. (1969). *The infamous of Nuremberg.* London: Fravin.

Arsenio, W. F., & Gold, J. (2006). The effects of social injustice and inequality on children's moral judgments and behavior: Towards a theoretical model. *Cognitive Development, 21,* 388–400. doi: 10.1016/j.cogdev.2006.06.005

Arsenio, W. F., & Lemerise, E. (2004). Aggression and moral development: Integrating the social information processing and moral domain models. *Child Development, 75,* 987–1002. doi: 10.1111/j.1467-8624.2004.00720.x

Bandura, A. (1986). *Social foundation of thought and action: A social cognitive theory.* Englewood Cliffs, NJ: Prentice Hall.

Bandura, A. (1990). Mechanism of moral disengagement. In W. Reich (Ed.), *Origin of terrorism: Psychologies, ideologies, theologies, states of mind* (pp. 161–191). Cambridge, England: Cambridge University Press.

Bandura, A. (1991). Social cognitive theory of moral thought and action: In W. M. Kurtines & J. L. Gewirtz (Eds.), *Handbook of moral behaviour and development* (Vol. I, pp. 45–103). Hillsdale, NJ: Erlbaum.

Bandura, A. (1997). *Self-efficacy: The exercise of control.* New York: Freeman.

Bandura, A., Barbaranelli, C., Caprara, G. V., & Pastorelli, C. (1996). Mechanisms of moral disengagement in the exercise of moral agency. *Journal of Personality and Social Psychology, 71,* 364–374. doi: 10.1037/0022-3514.71.2.364

Bandura, A., Caprara, G. V., Barbaranelli, C., Pastorelli, C., & Regalia, C. (2001). Sociocognitive self-regulatory mechanisms governing transgressive behavior. *Journal of Personality and Social Psychology, 80,* 125–135. doi: 10.1037/0022-3514.80.1.125

Bandura, A., Caprara, G.V., & Zsolnai, L. (2000). Corporate transgressions through moral disengagement. *Journal of Human Values, 6,* 57–64.

Barbaranelli, C., & Caprara, G.V. (2000). Measuring the Big Five in self-report and other rating: A multitrait-multimethod study. *European Journal of Psychological Assessment, 16,* 29–41. doi: 10.1027//1015-5759.16.1.31

Berkowitz, L. (1989). Frustration–aggression hypothesis: Examination and reformulation. *Psychological Bulletin, 106,* 59–73. doi: 10.1037/0033-2909.106.1.59

Bettencourt, B. A., Talley, A., Benjamin, A. J., & Valentine, J. (2006). Personality and aggressive behavior under provoking and neutral conditions: A meta-analytic review. *Psychological Bulletin, 132*(5), 751–777. doi: 10.1037/0033-2909.132.5.751

Bushman, B. J., Bonacci, A. M., Pedersen, W. C., Vasquez, E. A., & Miller, N. (2005). Chewing on it can chew you up: Effects of rumination on triggered displaced aggression. *Journal of Personality and Social Psychology, 6,* 969–983. doi: 10.1037/0022-3514.88.6.969

Butler, L. D., & Nolen-Hoeksema, S. (1994). Gender differences in responses to depressed mood in a college sample. *Sex Roles, 30,* 331–346. doi: 10.1007/BF01420597

Caprara, G. V. (1986). Indicators of aggression: The dissipation-rumination scale. *Personality and Individual Differences, 7,* 763–769. doi: 10.1016/0191-8869(86)90074-7

Caprara, G. V. (1987). The disposition-situation debate and research on aggression. *European Journal of Personality, 1,* 1–16. doi: 10.1002/per.2410010103

Caprara, G. V. (1996). Structures and processes in personality psychology. *European Psychologist, 1,* 14–26. doi: 10.1027/1016-9040.1.1.14

Caprara, G. V., Alessandri, G., Tisak., M., Paciello, M., Gerbino, M. & Fontaine, R. G. (2010). *Individual differences in personality conducive to violence among adolescents.* Unpublished manuscript.

Caprara, G. V., Barbaranelli, C., & Comrey, A. L. (1992). A personological approach to the study of aggression. *Personality Individual Differences, 13,* 77–84. doi: 10.1016/0191-8869(92)90222-B

Caprara, G. V., & Cervone, D. (2000). *Personality: Determinants, dynamics, and potentials.* New York: Cambridge University Press.

Caprara, G. V., Cinanni, V., D'Imperio, G., Passerini, S., Renzi, P., & Travaglia, G. (1985). Indicators of impulsive aggression: Present status of research on irritability and emotional susceptibility scales. *Personality and Individual Differences, 6,* 665–674. doi: 10.1016/0191-8869(85)90077-7

Caprara, G. V., Fontaine, R., Fida, R. Paciello, M., Tisak, M. S., & Dodge, K. (2010). *The contributions and reciprocal influences of irritability, hostile rumination, and moral disengagement to aggression and violence in adolescence.* Manuscript under review.

Caprara, G.., Paciello, M., Gerbino, M., & Cugini, C. (2007). Individual differences conducive to aggression and violence: Trajectories and correlates of irritability and hostile rumination through adolescence. *Aggressive Behavior, 33,* 359–374. doi: 10.1002/ab.20192

Caprara, G. V., Perugini, M., & Barbaranelli, C. (1994). Studies of individual differences in aggression. In M. Potegal & J. F. Knutson (Eds.), *The dynamics of aggression: Biological and social processes in dyads and groups* (pp. 123–153). Hillsdale, NJ: Erlbaum.

Caspi, A., & Shiner, R. (2006). Personality development. In N. Eisenberg (Vol. Ed) and W. Damon & R. M. Lerner (Series Eds.), *Handbook of child psychology: Vol. 3. Social, emotional, and personality development* (6th ed., pp. 300–365). New York: Wiley.

Cervone, D., & Shoda, Y. (1999). Social-cognitive theories and the coherence of personality. In D. Cervone & Y. Shoda (Eds.), *The coherence of personality: Social-cognitive bases of personality consistency, variability, and organization* (pp. 3–33). New York: Guilford.

Collins, K., & Bell, R. (1997). Personality and aggression: The dissipation–rumination scale. *Personality and Individual Differences, 22,* 751–755. doi: 10.1016/S0191-8869(96)00248-6

Costa, P. T., & McCrae, R. R. (1992). *Revised NEO-Personality Inventory (NEO-PI-R) and NEO Five-Factor Inventory (FFI) manual.* Odessa, FL: Psychological Assessment Resources.

Crane-Ross, D., Tisak, M. S., & Tisak, J. (1998). Aggression and conventional rule violation among adolescents: Social-reasoning predictors of social behavior. *Aggressive Behavior, 24,* 347–365. doi: 10.1002/(SICI)1098-2337(1998)24:5<347::AID-AB2>3.0.CO;2-E

DeYoung, C. G., Hirsh, J. B., Shane, M. S., Papademetris, X., Rajeevan, N., & Gray, G. R. (2010). Testing predictions from personality neuroscience: Brain structure and the Big Five. *Psychological Science, 21,* 820–828. doi: 2010-13268-013

Dodge, K. A. (1991). The structure and function of reactive and proactive aggression. In D. Pepler & K. Rubin (Eds.), *The development and treatment of childhood aggression* (pp. 201–218). Hillsdale, NJ: Erlbaum.

Dodge, K. A., & Coie, J. D. (1987). Social-information-processing factors in reactive and proactive aggression in children's peer groups. *Journal of Personality and Social Psychology, 53,* 1146–1158. doi: 10.1037/0022-3514.53.6.1146

Dollard, J., Doob, C. W, Miller, N. E., Mowrer, O. H., & Sears, R. R. (1939). *Frustration and aggression.* New Haven, CT: Yale University Press.

Eisenberg, N., Fabes, R. A., & Spinrad, T. L. (2006). *Prosocial development.* Hoboken, NJ: Wiley.

Farrington, D., Ttofi, M., & Coid, J. (2009). Development of adolescence-limited, late-onset, and persistent offenders from age 8 to age 48. *Aggressive Behavior, 35,* 150–163. doi: 10.1002/ab.20296

Fiske, S. T. (2010). *Social beings: Core motives in social psychology.* New York: Wiley.

Fontaine, R. G. (2007). Disentangling the psychology and law of instrumental and reactive subtypes of aggression. *Psychology, Public Policy, and Law, 13,* 143–165. doi: 10.1037/1076-8971.13.2.143

Geen, R. G. (1998). Processes and personal variables in affective aggression. In R. G. Geen, & E. Donnerstein (Eds), *Human aggression.* (pp. 1–21). San Diego, CA: Academic Press.

Gibbs, J. C. (2003). *Moral development and reality: Beyond the theories of Kohlberg and Hoffman.* Thousand Oaks, CA: Sage.

Gini, G. (2006). Social cognition and moral cognition in bullying: What's wrong? *Aggressive Behavior, 32,* 528–539. doi: 10.1002/ab.20153

Gleason, K. A., Jensen-Campbell, L. A., & Richardson, D. S. (2004). Agreeableness as a predictor of aggression in adolescence. *Aggressive Behavior, 30,* 43–61. doi: 10.1111/j.1745-6924.2008.00084.x

Graziano, W. G., & Eisenberg, N. (1997). Agreeableness: A dimension of personality. In R. Hogan, J., Johnson, & S. Briggs (Eds.), *Handbook of personality psychology* (pp. 795–824). San Diego, CA: Academic Press.

Graziano, W. G., Jensen-Campbell, L. A., & Hair, E. C. (1996). Perceiving interpersonal conflict and reacting to it: The case for agreeableness. *Journal of Personality and Social Psychology, 70,* 820–835. doi: 10.1037/0022-3514.70.4.820

Halverson, C. F., Havill, V. L., Deal, J., Baker, S. R., Victor, J. B., Pavlopoulos, V., Besevegis, E., & Wen, L. (2003). Personality structure as derived from parental ratings of free descriptions of children: the inventory of child individual differences. *Journal of Personality, 71,* 995–1026. doi: 10.1111/1467-6494.7106005

Higgings, E. T. (1999). Persons and situations: Unique explanatory principles or variability in general principles? In D. Cervone & Y. Shoda (Eds.) *The coherence of personality: Social-cognitive bases of consistency, variability, and organization* (pp. 61–93). New York: Guilford.

Huesmann, L. R., & Guerra, N. G. (1997). Children's normative beliefs about aggression and aggressive behavior. *Journal of Personality and Social Psychology, 72,* 408–419. doi: 10.1037/0022-3514.72.2.408

Jang, K. L., Livesley, W. J., & Vemon, P. A. (1996). Heritability of the Big Five personality dimensions and their facets: A twin study. *Journal of Personality, 6,* 577–592. doi: 10.1111/j.1467-6494.1996.tb00522.x

Jang, K. L., McCrae, R. R., Angleitner, A., Rienmann, R., & Livesley, W. J. (1998). Heritability of facet-level traits in a cross cultural-twin sample: support for a hierarchical model of personality. *Journal of Personality and Social Psychology, 74,* 1556–1565. doi: 10.1037/0022-3514.74.6.1556

Jensen-Campbell, L. A., Adams, R., Perry, D. G., Workman, K. A., Furdella, J. Q., & Egan, S. K. (2002). Agreeableness, extraversion, and peer relations in early adolescence: Winning friends and deflecting aggression. *Journal of Research in Personality, 36,* 224–251. doi: 10.1006/jrpe.2002.2348

Jensen-Campbell, L. A., & Graziano, W. G. (2001). Agreeableness as a moderator of interpersonal conflict. *Journal of Personality, 69,* 323–362.

Johnson, W., & Krueger, R. F. (2004). Genetic and environmental structure of adjectives describing the domain of the Big Five Model of Personality: A national US twin study. *Journal of Research in Personality, 38,* 448–472. doi: 10.1016/j.jrp.2003.11.001

Kelman, H. C., & Hamilton, V. L. (1989). *Crimes of obedience: Toward a social psychology of authority and responsibility.* New Haven, CT: Yale University Press.

Kochanska, G., Friesenborg, A. E., Lange, L. A., & Martel, M. M. (2004). Parents' personality and infants' temperament as contributors to their emerging relationship. *Journal of Personality and Social Psychology, 5,* 744–759. doi: 10.1037/0022-3514.86.5.744

Lohelin, J. C. (1982). Are personality traits differentially heritable? *Behavior Genetics, 12,* 417–428. doi: 10.1007/BF01065633

Lohelin, J. C., McCrae, R.R., Costa, P. T., & John, O. P. (1998). Heritabilities of common and measure-specific components of the Big Five Personality Factors. *Journal of Research in Personality, 32,* 431–453. doi: 10.1006/jrpe.1998.2225

McCrady, F., Kaufman, K., Vasey, M. W., Barriga, A. Q., Devlin, R. S., & Gibbs, J. C. (2008). It's all about me: A brief report of incarcerated adolescent sex offenders' generic and sex-specific cognitive distortions. *Sexual Abuse: A Journal of Research and Treatment, 20,* 261–271. doi: 10.1177/1079063208320249

McCrae, R. R., & Costa, P. T. (1999). A five factor theory of personality. In L. A. Pervin, & O. P. John (Eds.), *Handbook of personality: Theory and research* (2nd ed.; pp.139–153). New York: Guilford.

Menesini, E., Sanchez, V., Fonzi, A., Ortega, R., Costabile, A., & Lo Feudo, G. (2003). Moral emotions and bullying: A cross-national comparison of differences between bullies, victims and outsiders. *Aggressive Behavior, 29,* 515–530. doi: 10.1002/ab.10060.

Nolen-Hoeksema, S., Parker, L., & Larson, J. (1994). Ruminative coping with depressive mood following loss. *Journal of Personality and Social Psychology, 67,* 92–104. doi: 10.1037/0022-3514.67.1.92

Paciello, M., Fida, R., Tramontano, C., Lupinetti, C., & Caprara, G. V. (2008). Stability and change of moral disengagement and its impact on aggression and violence in late adolescence. *Child Development 79,* 1289–1310. doi: 10.1111/j.1467-8624.2008.01189.x

Pelton, J., Gound, M., Forehand, R., & Brody, G. (2004). The moral disengagement scale: extension with an American minority sample. *Journal of Psychopathology and Behavioral Assessment, 26,* 31–39. doi: 10.1023/B:JOBA.0000007454.34707.a5

Rapoport, D., & Alexander, Y. (1989). *The morality of terrorism . Religious and secular justifications.* New York: Columbia University Press.

Rienman, R., Angleitner, A., & Strelau, J. (1997). Genetic and environmental influences on personality: A study of twins reared together using the self- and peer report NEO_FFI scales. *Journal of Personality, 65,* 449–475.. doi: 10.1111/j.1467-6494.1997.tb00324.x

Robins, R. W., John, O. P., Caspi, A., Moffitt, T. E., & Stouthamer-Loeber, M. (1996). Resilient, overcontrolled, and undercontrolled boys: Three replicable personality types. *Journal of Personality and Social Psychology, 70,* 157–171. doi: 10.1037/0022-3514.70.1.157

Rothbart, M. K., & Bates, J. (1998). Temperament. In W. Damon (Series Ed.) & N. Eisenberg (Vol. Ed.), *Handbook of child psychology: Vol. 3. Social, emotional and personality development* (5th ed., pp. 105–176). New York: Wiley.

Seligman, M., & Csikszentmihalyi, M. (2000). Positive psychology: An introduction. *American Psychologist, 55,* 5–14.

Simons, R., Simons, L., Chen, Y., Brody, G., & Lin, K. (2007). Identifying the psychological factors that mediate the association between parenting practices and delinquency. *Criminology: An Interdisciplinary Journal, 45,* 481–517. doi: 10.1111/j.1745-9125.2007.00086.x

Suls, J., Martin, R., & David, J. P. (1998). Person-environment fit and its limits: Agreeableness, neuroticism, and emotional reactivity to interpersonal conflict. *Personality and Social Psychology Bulletin, 24,* 88–98. doi: 10.1177/0146167298241007

Thayer, J. F., Rossy, L. A., Ruiz-Padial, E., & Johnsen, B. H. (2003). Gender differences in the relationship between emotional regulation and depressive symptoms. *Cognitive Therapy and Research, 27,* 349–364. doi: 10.1023/A:1023922618287

Tisak, M. S., Lewis, T., & Jankowski, A. M. (1997). Expectations and prescriptions for responding to peer aggression: The adolescent offenders' perspective. *Aggressive Behavior, 23,* 149–160. doi: 10.1002/(SICI)1098-2337(1997)23:3<149::AID-AB1>3.0.CO;2-H

Tisak, M. S., & Tisak, J. (1996). Expectations and judgments regarding bystanders' and victims' responses to peer aggression among early adolescents. *Journal of Adolescence, 19,* 383–392. doi: 10.1006/jado.1996.0036

Turiel, E. (2006). Thought, emotions, and social interactional processes in moral development. In M. Killen & J. G. Smetana (Eds.), *Handbook of moral development* (pp. 7–35). Mahwah, NJ: Erlbaum.

Guido Alessandri, Michele Vecchione, and Gian Vittorio Caprara

Vitiello, B., & Stoff, D. M. (1997). Subtypes of aggression and their relevance to child psychiatry. *Journal of the American Academy of Child and Adolescent Psychiatry, 36,* 307–315. doi: 10.1097/00004583-199703000-00008

Wiesner, M., & Kim, H. (2006). Co-occurring delinquency and depressive symptoms of adolescent boys and girls: A dual trajectory modelling approach. *Developmental Psychology, 42,* 1220–1235. doi: 10.1037/0012-1649.42.6.1220

Cyberbullying and Cyber Aggression

Peter K. Smith

GOLDSMITHS COLLEGE, UNIVERSITY OF LONDON, ENGLAND

Abstract

This chapter outlines the history of research in cyberbullying and cyber aggression, and some major publications. The chapter then discusses types of cyber aggression and cyberbullying, and features that tend to make it distinctive from "traditional" (noncyber) forms; and considers definitional issues that arise. This is followed by an overview of some main findings: incidence, who does it and where it happens, age and gender differences, other predictors of involvement in cyberbullying, the impact of cyberbullying, coping strategies, prevention and intervention procedures, and concluding with implications for research and practice.

Aggression refers to intentional behavior that hurts or harms another person. Bullying refers to aggression, where there is also an imbalance of power, and repetition of the act (Olweus, 1999); or a "systematic abuse of power" (Smith & Sharp, 1994). Cyber aggression and cyberbullying correspondingly refer to aggression and bullying carried out via electronic media—mobile phones and the Internet. As such, they are mainly phenomena of the 21st century. They have emerged with the rapid diffusion of mobile phones, and use of the Internet, internationally; most rapidly and thoroughly in the industrialized countries, and most notably in middle childhood and adolescence, with young people being the "digital natives," growing up with these new communication technologies.

For example, Rideout, Foehr, and Roberts (2010) studied representative U.S. samples of 8- to 18-year-olds in 1999, 2004, and 2009. The average number of hours spent in a typical day on a computer was 0.27 in 1999, 1.02 in 2004, and 1.29 in 2009. Time spent talking on mobile phones was 0.33 hours in 2009, and time spent texting on mobile phones was 1.33 hours (in 1999 there was no question on mobile phones at all, and in 2004 only one about talking on mobile *or* landline phones).

In this chapter, I will set the scene by outlining the history of research in this area, and some major publications so far. Next, I will mention some main types and forms of cyber aggression and cyberbullying, and discuss features that tend to make it distinctive from "traditional" (noncyber) forms. This leads to a consideration of definitional issues that arise. I then overview some main findings: incidence, who does it and where it happens, age and gender differences, other predictors of involvement in cyberbullying, the impact of cyberbullying, coping strategies, and prevention and intervention procedures. The chapter concludes with implications for research and practice.

History of Research on Bullying

As a research endeavor, the study of cyberbullying is a rapidly developing research program that has, in part, developed from the previous research program on "traditional" bullying. Bullying can occur in many contexts, in childhood and adult life (Monks et al., 2009). However, the earliest sustained work, and the largest volume of work, has concerned school bullying. Research on school bullying can be thought of as having gone through four waves, of which cyberbullying is the fourth (Smith, 2010). The *first wave: Origins 1970 –1988* saw the origins of systematic study, mainly in Scandinavia; notably Olweus' book *Forskning om skolmobbning* (*Aggression in Schools: Bullies and Whipping Boys,* 1973/1978). Through the 1980s, Olweus developed a self-report questionnaire to assess bullying, and, in parallel with the first Norwegian National Anti-Bullying campaign in 1983, a school-based intervention program, the original Olweus Bullying Prevention Program (1983–1985). Reports of reductions in bullying of around 50% encouraged researchers and inspired the next wave of research. The *second wave: Establishing a research program: 1989–mid-1990s* saw many books and journal articles appearing, and surveys in other countries beyond Scandinavia. Besides self-report surveys, some studies started to use peer nominations methodology. Some intervention campaigns took place. There was a broadening of researcher's definition of aggression (and thus bullying), to include indirect and relational bullying (such as rumor spreading, social exclusion). Also, work on bullying was becoming international; contacts were taking place between researchers in Europe, North America, and Australasia, and in Japan (where studies on *ijime*—the Japanese term closest to *bullying*—dated back in a previously separate tradition to the 1980s). The *third wave: An established international research program mid-1990–2004* saw research on traditional bullying becoming an important international research program. Surveys and interventions took place in many countries (see 21 country reports in Smith et al., 1999; and 11 country reports on interventions in Smith, Pepler, and Rigby, 2004). A notable methodological step was the introduction of participant roles in bullying, from Salmivalli's work in Finland (Salmivalli, Lagerspetz, Bjorkqvist, Osterman, & Kaukiainen, 1996). The *fourth wave: Cyberbullying 2004–on,* followed on from increasing awareness of cyberbullying, and press reports, mainly dating from around 2000–2001.

Academic publications in the cyberbullying area have increased very rapidly in the last five years. Notable publications are the book by Willard (2006), a special issue of the *Journal of Adolescent Health* (2007), the books by Shariff (2008), Kowalski, Limber, and Agatston (2008), and Hinduja and Patchin (2008a), a special issue of the *Zeitschrift fur Psychologie/Journal of Psychology* (2009), and books by Bauman (2010), Mora-Merchan and Jäger (2010), and Li, Cross, and Smith (2012). Further special journal issues are in press (*Australian Journal of Guidance and Counselling*), or in progress (in *European Journal of Developmental Psychology; Journal of Community & Applied Social Psychology; Journal of Educational Computing Research; Emotional & Behavioural Difficulties*). Previous reviews include Dooley, Cross, Hearn, and Treyvaud (2009), Smith and Slonje (2010), and Tokunaga (2010). Collaborative research networks include a COST Action IS0801 on Cyberbullying (Smith & Sittichai, 2009; Cyberbullying, n.d.), and an International Cyber Bullying Think Tank (University of Arizona, n.d.) funded by National Science Foudnation.

There are other strands to research in this area, apart from the origins in bullying research. These include researchers studying the effects of ICT and the Internet on human behavior, and specifically safety issues around Internet use; see for example Ybarra and Mitchell (2004). In Europe, the EUKidsOnline projects (I and II; Livingstone & Haddon, 2009) are providing cross-national information on opportunities and risks in children using the Internet, and cyberbullying features within this. Another source of input is from legal experts, who are examining rights and responsibilities of ICT users and monitoring the outcomes of legal cases (e.g., regarding defamation, privacy, harassment, etc.) in this relatively new domain (Gillespie, 2006; Shariff, 2009).

Types and Forms of Cyberbullying and Cyber Aggression

There are various methods of cyberbullying and cyber aggression or harassment. Starting with text messages and e-mails (Rivers & Noret, 2010), these have proliferated. Li (2007) distinguished e-mail, chatroom, and mobile phone bullying. Smith et al. (2008) used seven main media described by secondary school pupils: bullying by mobile phone calls, text messages, picture/video clip bullying, e-mails; chatroom, instant messaging, and websites.

Hinduja and Patchin (2010) used a 9-item cyber victimization scale, covering similar media. In South Korea, cyberbullying in Internet game contexts has been found to be a very common form (Tippett & Kwak, 2012).

Looking at the types of action, Willard (2006) described seven categories: flaming, online harassment; cyberstalking, denigration (put-downs), masquerade, outing, and exclusion. These are to some extent independent of the media used. Rivers and Noret (2010) have described the content of abusive text messages and e-mails, in an English sample. Their 10 main categories are: threat of physical violence, abusive or hate-related, name calling (including homophobia), death threats, ending of platonic relationship(s), sexual acts, demands/instructions, threats to damage existing relationships, threats to home/family, and menacing chain messages.

These lists of types of cyberbullying and aggression are not exhaustive, and as technology develops, new forms of cyberbullying emerge. The advent of smart phones that can access the Internet is making the earlier distinction between mobile phone and Internet bullying, less obvious. These bullying contexts are not restricted to young people, any more than is traditional bullying and aggression, and some forms have been mainly described in adults; for example, cyberbullying or "griefing" in virtual worlds (Coyne, Chesney, Logan, & Madden, 2009).

Distinctive Features of Cyberbullying and Cyber Aggression

Although there are many similarities between traditional bullying and cyberbullying, the latter clearly tends to have some particular distinguishing characteristics. These can be important in considering the likely impact of cyberbullying and the coping strategies that will be most effective. A number of commentators have discussed such distinctive features of cyberbullying, as compared to traditional forms of bullying (Dooley, Pyzalski, & Cross, 2009; Smith et al., 2008; Tokunaga, 2010; Vandebosch & van Cleemput, 2008). These include the following seven features of cyberbullying:

1. It depends on some degree of technological expertise. Although it is easy enough to send e-mails and text messages, more sophisticated attacks such as masquerading (pretending to be someone else posting denigrating material on a website) require more skill.
2. It is primarily indirect rather than face-to-face. Thus there is some "invisibility" of those doing the bullying. A perpetrator may try to withhold identification in text or Internet postings, to maintain anonymity.
3. Relatedly, the perpetrator does not usually see the victim's reaction, at least in the short term. On the one hand, this can enhance moral disengagement from the victim's plight

(Hymel, Rocke-Henderson, & Bonanno, 2005) and thus might make cyberbullying easier; without such direct feedback there may be fewer opportunities for empathy or remorse. On the other hand, many perpetrators enjoy the feedback of seeing the suffering of the victim, and would not get this satisfaction so readily by cyberbullying.

4. The variety of bystander roles in cyberbullying is more complex than in most traditional bullying. There can be three main bystander roles rather than one: the bystander is with the perpetrator when an act is sent or posted; the bystander is with the victim when it is received; or the bystander is with neither, but receives the message or visits the relevant Internet site.

5. Relatedly, one motive for bullying is thought to be the status gained by showing (abusive) power over others in front of witnesses (Salmivalli et al., 1996). The perpetrator will often lack this in cyberbullying, unless steps are taken to tell others what has happened or publicly share the material.

6. The breadth of the potential audience is increased. Over time, cyberbullying can reach particularly large audiences in a peer group compared with the small groups that are the usual audience in traditional bullying. For example, when nasty comments are posted on a website, the audience that may see these comments is potentially very large.

7. It is difficult to escape from cyberbullying—there is "no place to hide." Unlike traditional forms of bullying, where once the victim gets home they are away from the bullying until the next day, cyberbullying is more difficult to escape from; the victim may continue to receive text messages or e-mails, or view nasty postings on a website, wherever they are.

These are important distinctions that may impact particularly on both the motives for (cyber) bullying, and the impact such acts have on the (cyber) victim. However, they should not be overstated; some forms of traditional bullying (e.g., rumor spreading) are not face-to-face, for example. A case can be made that these are differences in degree rather than differences in kind (Pyzalski, 2011).

Definitions of Cyberbullying and Cyber Aggression

An early definition of cyberbullying (Belsey, 2004) is "the use of information and communication technologies ... to support deliberate, repeated and hostile behavior by an individual or group that is intended to harm others" (p. 3). Of the two distinguishing criteria for traditional bullying, this definition includes the criterion of repetition, but not imbalance of power. A similar definition in this respect was used by Sourander et al. (2010). Another definition that follows the Olweus approach in traditional bullying (Smith et al., 2008) is that cyberbullying is "An aggressive, intentional act carried out by a group or individual, *using electronic forms of contact*, repeatedly and over time against a victim who cannot easily defend him or herself" (p. 376). Li (2007) used a similar definition. Tokunaga (2010) lists these and other definitions, which vary as to whether repetition and imbalance of power are included, and also in other respects (e.g., types of bullying mentioned).

There are problems with defining cyberbullying as analogous to traditional bullying (Dooley, Pyzalski, & Cross, 2009; Vandebosch & van Cleemput, 2008). Regarding repetition, in traditional bullying, the acts or behaviors of the bully should be of a repetitive nature (more than just once). But due to the nature of cyberbullying, the act or behavior may repeat itself without the contribution of the cyberbully. For example, taking an abusive picture or video clip on a mobile phone may have occurred only once; but if the person receiving the image forwards it to anyone else, it could be argued that this falls under the category of repetition. Or, if something abusive is uploaded onto a webpage, every hit on that page could count as a repetition. Consequently, the use of repetition as a criterion for serious bullying may be less reliable for cyberbullying.

There are also problems with the imbalance of power criterion. In traditional bullying, this is usually taken as being in terms of physical strength or psychological confidence in a face-to-face confrontation, or in terms of a number of perpetrators against one victim. These are not so clear in cyberbullying, which is not face-to-face. There may, nevertheless, be an imbalance of power either through the anonymity of the perpetrator(s), if present; or if the perpetrators are known, then relative (physical, psychological, or numerical) strength offline may still be a factor in the victim's perception of the situation. In some cases, greater technological expertise could also contribute to an imbalance of power.

Nevertheless, a number of studies are on cyber aggression or harassment; that is to say, they focus on negative acts through ICT, irrespective of repetition or imbalance of power. For example, Law, Shapka, and Olson (2010) explicitly used an "online aggression" scale with 16 items. Some studies are on cyberbullying and employ similar items of mobile phone or Internet aggression, together with a repetition scale; for example, Calvete, Orue, Estévez, Villardón, and Padilla (2010) used a Cyberbullying Questionnaire (CBQ) with 16 items (*never/sometime/often*), and Cassidy, Jackson, and Brown (2009) used an 18-item scale (*never/occasionally/often*). But, in these and similar studies, analysis often focuses on those "involved;" that is, not replying *never*, which may of course mean just once or twice. Hinduja and Patchin (2010, p. 211) noted that their 10 cyber bullying and victimization items "might better be characterized as 'online harassment'" but restricted analysis to repeated incidents. Conversely, Wang, Iannotti, and Nansel (2009) explicitly examined only *once or twice or more* because "it is not uncommon in the literature of cyber bullying to count a single incident as an experience of cyber bullying" (p. 370); although this study did include imbalance of power in the definition.

There is thus some diversity and perhaps confusion in the literature on defining cyber bullying and cyber aggression. It is also an issue as to whether children/young people themselves use or recognize the term cyberbullying, or indeed what terms they do use (Grigg, 2010).

Incidence of Cyberbullying

Given the diversity in definition and measurement, it is not surprising that the reported incidence of cyberbullying varies quite widely. In general, studies have used anonymous self-report questionnaires assessing incidence of being a victim and/or perpetrator of different types of cyberbullying. A few examples from more recently published studies are considered here. Marsh, McGee, Nada-Raja, and Williams (2009), in New Zealand secondary school students aged 15 years, found that 7.9% of boys and 13.8% of girls received nasty text messages *sometimes or more this year at school*; and 6.9% of boys and 7.0% of girls did this to others (these figures being generally lower than for four types of traditional bullying that were also assessed). Calvete et al. (2010) surveyed 12- to 17-year-old Spanish adolescents. From 16 items, the most frequently perpetrated were deliberately excluding someone from an online group (18.1% *sometimes*, 2.1% *often*) and writing embarrassing jokes, rumors, gossip, or comments about a classmate on the Internet (18.3% *sometimes*, 1.8% *often*). Hinduja and Patchin (2010) asked about experiences of online harassment (cyberbullying and victimization) in U.S. middle school students (Grades 6 to 8) over the last 30 days. Some 22% *had cyberbullied* in some way two or more times, and some 29% *had been cyberbullied* two or more times (corresponding figures for traditional bullying were bullied others 34% and victimized 44%).

A cross-national study of 12- to 15-year-olds in Italy, Spain, and England, compared mobile and Internet cyberbullying over the last two months, using an Olweus-type definition (Genta et al., 2012). Percentages for severe (two or three times a month or more) mobile bullying ranged (across the three countries) from 0.9% to 2.7%, and Internet bullying from 1.0% to 1.6%; for mobile victim from 0.5% to 2.2%, and Internet victim from 1.3% to 2.6%. Generally, figures were somewhat larger in Italy and least in Spain.

There is clearly a very wide range of incidence figures reported. Many factors may be responsible for this. One is the definition of cyberbullying or cyber aggression used—does it include repetition, and/or imbalance of power? Rates of cyber aggression can be expected to exceed cyberbullying, more strictly defined. Second, what behaviors are sampled? Marsh et al. (2009) only assessed text message bullying, and Rivers and Noret (2010) only text message and e-mail bullying. Others have used a much broader range. Third, studies have varied in the time period used as a reference; for example, the period can be the last month or last couple of months (e.g., Hinduja & Patchin, 2010), or the entire year (Marsh et al., 2009), or if it ever happened (Calvete et al., 2010). Fourth, the nature of the sample is obviously an important factor. This may vary by country or culture, age, gender, and other demographic characteristics. Most studies have had samples from a number of schools, but some studies have investigated only Internet-using participants (Hinduja & Patchin, 2008b; Ybarra & Mitchell, 2004). Finally, the date of a survey is important in such a fast developing and changing area. Rivers and Noret (2010) have documented some increase (especially in girls), then a leveling off, of text and e-mail bullying in English 11- to 13-year-olds between 2002 and 2006. There is some evidence that bullying through websites, and specifically through social networking sites, has recently become a common form as social networking escalates in popularity in the adolescent years (Patchin & Hinduja, 2010).

Who Does It and Where It Happen?

Sometimes victims of cyberbullying do not know who the perpetrator is. For example, Vandebosch and van Cleemput (2008) found that half of victims did not know who the bully was. Smith et al. (2008) reported that about 1 in 5 of victims did not know who the bully was; when victims did know, for 58% the perpetrators were from the same school. Furthermore, whereas traditional bullying was mainly reported as being initiated in school, for cyberbullying most was initiated outside school. Many schools place restrictions on mobile phone and Internet use within the school premises. But even though cyberbullying may escape school boundaries, it will often be fellow pupils who are involved in the bullying.

Age and Gender Differences

We know little about when children start cyberbullying, and most studies have focused on the middle or secondary/high school age ranges. There have been some variations in reports, but the review by Tokunaga (2010) argued that there is a curvilinear relationship, with the greatest incidence at seventh and eighth grades (around 13 to 15 years). This appears to be consistent with much of the literature, and suggests a slightly later age peak than is found for traditional bullying.

The area of gender differences is more complex, and has been accurately described as "fraught with inconsistent findings" (Tokunaga, 2010, p. 280). Examples can be found of boys being more involved than girls (e.g., Calvete et al., 2010); few or no significant differences (e.g., Smith et al., 2008); and girls being more involved than boys (e.g., Rivers & Noret, 2010). Overall, there may be relatively greater involvement of girls in cyberbullying, just as there is in relational bullying, when compared to traditional physical (mainly boys) or verbal bullying; consistent with seeing cyberbullying as more similar to relational bullying.

Both age and gender differences may vary by different media of cyberbullying, cultural background, and historical time; for example, in recent years girls in some countries, including the U.K., are particularly involved in social networking sites such as Facebook, and thus more at risk of cyberbullying involvement in that medium (National Family Week Survey, 2010).

Other Predictors of Involvement in Cyberbullying

Who gets involved in being a cyber bully or cyber victim? One well-established predictor is involvement in traditional bullying. Many studies have found substantial overlap between involvement in traditional bullying and cyberbullying, for example, Hinduja and Patchin (2008b), Li (2007), Vandebosch and van Cleemput (2008), Smith et al. (2008), Marsh et al. (2009), and Rivers and Noret (2010). A related predictor is involvement in other antisocial behaviours; Ybarra and Mitchell (2004) reported that youth with problem behaviors were almost four times more likely to say they were an Internet aggressor or aggressor/target versus those who reported victimization only or not involved.

Ybarra and Mitchell (2004) suggested that some cyberbullies may be traditional victims who, being unable to retaliate face-to-face, may do so by electronic means as a form of compensation. This was not confirmed by Vandebosch and van Cleemput (2008), but partially supported by Smith et al. (2008) who found a trend for traditional bully victims to also be cyberbullies. The hypothesis that traditional victims and perhaps especially bully victims are at risk of moving into the world of cyber bullying deserves further study.

Another predictor of cyberbullying involvement is time spent with ICT, and relevant skills. Both Hinduja and Patchin (2008b) and Smith et al. (2008) found that more time spent on the Internet was a correlate of being a cyber victim. Vandebosch and van Cleemput (2008) found that pupils with more advanced Internet skills were more likely to have experience with deviant Internet and mobile phone activities.

Some studies have examined family and parental factors. Ybarra and Mitchell (2007) related Internet harassment to greater caregiver-child conflict, and Wang et al. (2009) found that lower parental support of adolescents predicted greater involvement in all kinds of bullying, including cyber. Law et al. (2010) linked adolescent online aggression to lack of communication with parents, but it was unrelated to attempts to limit time on the Internet, or sites visited.

The Impact of Cyberbullying

Although some of the distinctive features of cyberbullying (such as breadth of audience, and difficulty of escape) might suggest a greater negative impact of cyberbullying, this needs to be counterbalanced by the fact that it is, ultimately, a virtual world. Smith et al. (2008) investigated whether pupils in general perceived cyberbullying to have less, equal, or more of a negative impact compared to traditional bullying. This varied across media, with picture/video clip bullying especially perceived as having a greater negative impact than traditional bullying; but generally there was a range of opinion, with some pupils replying that cyberbullying has the same effect on the victim ("I think they are equally as bad"; "they both can hurt"), could be worse ("loads of people can see it if it's on the Internet"; "it's constant all the time, really hard to escape"), or could be less harmful ("you can be more damaged by face-to-face bullying than cyber bullying, that's just words"; "a text is easier to ignore than something that happened in a specific place").

Whatever the relative impact of cyberbullying compared to traditional bullying, it is certainly hurtful. For example Ybarra, Mitchell, Wolak, and Finkelhor (2006) found that 65% of the victims of cyberbullying felt worried or threatened by the incident, whilst 38% felt distressed. In a study of Austrian adolescents, Gradinger, Strohmeier, and Spiel (2009) found that being a cyber victim was significantly associated with both depressive and somatic symptoms. The association was about the same strength as for traditional victims; but combined victims (both traditional and cyber) were especially at risk. Hinduja and Patchin (2010) found that being a victim of cyberbullying was significantly associated with suicidal thoughts; although again at a comparable level to the association with traditional bullying.

Coping Strategies and Prevention and Intervention Procedures

Victims often need to seek help in order to deal with bullying, and we know from studies of traditional bullying that many victims are reluctant to do this. This also appears true of cyberbullying. When victims of cyberbullying do tell someone, it appears to be most often friends, followed by parents, with teachers told rather infrequently (Smith et al., 2008). Given the generational gap in use and awareness of new technologies, young people may feel that teachers and parents are less aware of the issues involved.

There are now many sources of advice, for children and young people, parents, and schools. These include actions young people can take themselves (such as reporting abuse, keeping evidence), information on legal rights and recourse, and information on websites and on schemes such as cybermentors. Many countries are now developing guidance on cyberbullying specifically, and/or Internet safety more generally. Curriculum materials and interventions are being developed. These are at an early stage, and a review of three short-term classroom-based interventions by Mishna, Cook, Saini, Wu, and MacFadden (2009) found rather little evidence of effectiveness. However, intervention programs to reduce traditional bullying have been found to reduce bullying by around 20%–23% and victimization by around 17%–20% (Ttofi & Farrington, 2011), and we can hope for similar success as cyberbullying interventions are developed and assessed. An EU-funded project has provided a training manual on cyberbullying, for trainers dealing with different target groups such as pupils, parents, teachers or whole schools, and these are available online as a user-friendly eBook in English, German, Spanish, Bulgarian, and Portuguese versions (Jäger, 2009).

Implications for Research

It is clearly important to include cyberbullying in current questionnaire and nomination instruments. While some surveys just assess cyberbullying as a global entity, different kinds of cyberbullying have some different characteristics, so for many purposes it will be important to distinguish different types of cyberbullying.

An interesting aspect is the importance of historical factors in work on cyberbullying. Awareness of cyberbullying in the media and in research studies is only some 10 years old, and yet even this period has seen shifts in popular ICT use from text messages and e-mails, to instant messaging, chatrooms, and most recently social networking sites. Further developments are inevitable. Thus, it is particularly important to know the dates of studies and surveys—something that is not routinely done, and absent in many published studies. This needs to change.

Historical changes provide a challenge for researchers, especially those doing longitudinal studies. Rivers and Noret (2010) provided longitudinal data on cyberbullying from 2002 to 2005, but asked, "How often have you received any nasty or threatening text messages or emails?"; this is now only a fraction of all cyberbullying. The shift from older mobile phones to smart phones having access to the Internet also blurs the distinction between mobile and Internet-based cyberbullying that many earlier studies have made.

There are also some opportunities for researchers in this area. The wide disciplinary base (including psychology, sociology, technology and media studies, legal studies) may prove helpful in using a range of both quantitative and qualitative methodologies, and broadening the context of study across settings (most cyberbullying by children is not in school but in many other outside settings), and developmentally (cyberbullying may have more age permeability than traditional bullying). It may also give a needed boost to theory development (Tokunaga, 2010). The use of young people as researchers might be considered (Jennifer & Cowie, 2009). Traditionally children/young people give their opinions via questionnaires, interviews, focus groups; but they could be involved further, helping gather data in a project, being involved in the planning and implementation of a project, or even designing a project. Such approaches may be especially useful for cyberbullying, where young people are the "digital natives."

Conclusion

While the challenges posed by cyberbullying are rather new, both researchers and practitioners are now becoming alerted to the issue, and based on the previous experience of general antibullying work gathered over the last 20 to 25 years, it can be hoped that the response to cyberbullying will have positive effects. Suggestions for young people, parents, and school personnel are offered in Table 8.1.

Table 8.1   Summary Table of Implications for Practice

For young people

1. Be aware of your rights and your responsibilities when using mobile phones and the Internet.
2. Behave responsibly and do not give out personal details unnecessarily.
3. Make use of advice and support through parents, teachers, websites, and helplines.

For parents

1. Discuss both general rights and responsibility issues, but also specifically those around use of ICTs, with your children.
2. Good communication about issues, and a good relationship generally, is likely to be preferable to instituting many controls and restrictions, which may get resented or circumvented.

For schools and other institutions hosting children

1. Cyberbullying should be included explicitly in antibullying policies (perhaps linked to a separate policy or policy section regarding appropriate use of mobile phones, and computers, within school). Personnel need up-to-date awareness raising and training on the nature and forms that cyber bullying and aggression can take; and in the legal issues around these actions. Teacher training materials for antibullying work should cover these aspects.
2. Antibullying materials used in the classroom need to embody examples of cyberbullying as well as traditional bullying. Some traditional methods for reducing bullying will be useful for cyberbullying, including general relationships education, embodying respect for others, rights of others, asserting one's own rights in nonaggressive ways, conflict management skills. But, some more specific interventions will be helpful for cyberbullying, including guidance on liaison with mobile phone companies, and Internet service providers; and the legal rights and responsibilities of all concerned.
3. Schools can also provide information and guidance for parents; the parent generation is generally less knowledgeable about new technological communication methods than young people; in that respect, it is young people who are the "experts."

References

Bauman, S. (2010). *Cyberbullying: What counselors need to know*. Alexandria, VA: American Counseling Association.

Belsey, B. (2004). *Cyberbullying: An emerging threat to the "Always On" generation*. Retrieved January 4, 2011, from http://www.cyberbullying.ca/pdf/Cyberbullying_Article_by_Bill_Belsey.pdf

Calvete, E., Orue, I., Estévez, A., Villardón, L., & Padilla, P. (2010). Cyberbullying in adolescents: Modalities and aggressors' profile. *Computers in Human Behavior, 26*, 1128–1135. doi:10.1016/j.chb.2010.03.017

Cassidy, W., Jackson, M., & Brown, K. N. (2009). Sticks and stones can break my bones, but how can pixels hurt me? *School Psychology International, 30*, 383–402. doi:10.1177/0143034309106948

Coyne, I., Chesney, T., Logan, B., & Madden, N. (2009). Griefing in a virtual community: An exploratory study of second life residents [Special issue]. *Zeitschrift für Psychologie/Journal of Psychology, 217*, 214–221.

Cyberbullying (n.d.). COST ACTION IS0801Cyberbullying: coping with negative and enhancing positive uses of new technologies, in relationships in educational settings. Retrieved from http://sites.google.com/site/costis0801/

Dooley, J. J., Cross, D., Hearn, L., & Treyvaud, R. (2009). *Review of existing Australian and international cyber-safety research*. Perth, Australia: Child Health Promotion Research Centre, Edith Cowan University.

Dooley, J. J., Pyżalski, J., & Cross, D. (2009). Cyberbullying versus face-to-face bullying: A theoretical and conceptual review [Special issue]. *Zeitschrift für Psychologie/Journal of Psychology, 217*, 182–188.

Genta, M. L., Smith, P. K., Ortega, R., Brighi, A., Giasrini, A., Thompson, … Calmaestra, J. (2012). Comparative aspects of cyberbullying in Italy, England and Spain: Findings from a DAPHNE project. In Q. Li, D. Cross, & P. K. Smith (Eds.), *Bullying goes to the global village: Research on cyberbullying from an international perspective*. Chichester, England: Wiley-Blackwell.

Gillespie, A. A. (2006). Cyber-bullying and harassment of teenagers: The legal response. *Journal of Social Welfare and Family Law, 28*, 123–136. doi:10.1080/09649060600973772

Gradinger, P., Strohmeier, D., & Spiel, C. (2009). Traditional bullying and cyberbullying: Identification of risk groups for adjustment problems [Special issue]. *Zeitschrift für Psychologie/Journal of Psychology, 217*, 205–213.

Grigg, D. (2010). Cyber-aggression: Definition and concept of cyberbullying. *Australian Journal of Guidance and Counselling, 20*, 143–156.

Hinduja, S., & Patchin, J. W. (2008a). *Bullying beyond the schoolyard: Preventing and responding to cyberbullying*. Thousand Oaks, CA: Sage.

Hinduja, S., & Patchin, J.W. (2008b). Cyberbullying: An exploratory analysis of factors related to offending and victimization. *Deviant Behavior, 29*, 1–29.

Hinduja, S., & Patchin, J. W. (2010). Bullying, cyberbullying, and suicide. *Archives of Suicide Research, 14*, 206–221. doi:10.1080/13811118.2010.494133 PMid:20658375

Hymel, S., Rocke-Henderson, N., & Bonanno, R. A. (2005). Moral disengagement: A framework for understanding bullying among adolescents. *Journal of Social Sciences, 8*, 1–11.

Jäger, T. (2009). CyberTraining: A research-based European training manual on cyberbullying [Special issue]. *Zeitschrift für Psychologie/Journal of Psychology, 217*, 234. See http://cybertraining-project.org/book/

Jennifer, D., & Cowie, H. (2009). Engaging children and young people actively in research. In K. Bryan (Ed.), *Communication in healthcare* (pp. 135–163). Oxford, England: Peter Lang.

Kowalski, R. M., Limber, S. P., & Agatston, P. W. (2008). *Cyber bullying*. Malden, MA: Blackwell. doi:10.1002/9780470694176

Law, D. M., Shapka, J. D., & Olson, B. F. (2010). To control or not to control? Parenting behaviours and adolescent online aggression. *Computers in Human Behavior, 26*, 1651–1656.

Li, Q. (2007). Bullying in the new playground: Research into cyberbullying and cyber victimisation. *Australasian Journal of Educational Technology, 23*, 435–454.

Li, Q., Cross, D., & Smith, P. K. (2012). *Bullying goes to the global village: Research on cyberbullying from an international perspective*. Chichester, England: Wiley-Blackwell.

Livingstone, S., & Haddon, L. (2009). EU Kids Online [Special issue]. *Zeitschrift für Psychologie/Journal of Psychology, 217*, 236–239.

Marsh, L., McGee, R., Nada-Raja, S., & Williams, S. (2009). Brief report: Text bullying and traditional bullying among New Zealand secondary school students. *Journal of Adolescence, 33*, 237–240. doi:10.1016/j.adolescence.2009.06.001 PMid:19573903

Mishna, F., Cook, C., Saini, M., Wu, M-J., & MacFadden, R. (2009). *Interventions for children, youth and parents to prevent and reduce cyber abuse*. Oslo, Norway: Campbell Systematic Reviews.

Monks, C. P., Smith, P. K., Naylor, P., Barter, C., Ireland, J. L. & Coyne, I. (2009). Bullying in different contexts: commonalities, differences and the role of theory. *Aggression and Violent Behavior, 14*, 146–156.

Mora-Merchan, J., & Jäger,T. (Eds.). (2010). *Cyberbullying: A cross-national comparison*. Landau, Germany: Verlag Empirische Pädagogik.

National Family Week Survey. (2010). *Facebook is a major influence on girls, says survey*. Retrieved May 19, 2010, from http://news.bbc.co.uk/1/hi/education/10121931.stm

Olweus, D. (1973/1978). *Forskning om skolmobbning.* Stockholm, Sweden: Almqvist & Wiksell (English translation, *Aggression in Schools: Bullies and Whipping Boys.* Washington DC: Hemisphere).

Olweus, D. (1999). Sweden. In P. K. Smith, Y. Morita, J., Junger-Tas, D. Olweus, R. Catalano, & P. Slee (Eds.), *The nature of school bullying: A cross-national perspective* (pp. 7–27). London, England: Routledge.

Patchin, J. W., & Hinduja, S. (2010). Trends in online social networking: adolescent use of MySpace over time. *New Media and Society, 12,* 197–216. doi:10.1177/1461444809341857

Pyzalski, J. (2011). Electronic aggression among adolescents: An old house with a new facade (or even a number of houses). In C. Hällgren, E. Dunkels, & G-M. Frånberg (Eds.), *Youth culture and net culture: Online social practices* (pp. 278–295). Hershey, PA: IGI Global.

Rideout, V. J., Foehr, U. G., & Roberts, D. F. (2010). *Generation M2. Media in the lives of 8- to 18-year-olds.* Washington, DC: Henry J. Kaiser Foundation. Available online, from http://www.kff.org

Rivers, I., & Noret, N. (2010). 'I h8 u': findings from a five-year study of text and email bullying. *British Educational Research Journal, 36,* 643–671. doi:10.1080/01411920903071918

Salmivalli, C., Lagerspetz, K. M. J., Bjorkqvist, K., Osterman, K., & Kaukiainen, A. (1996). Bullying as a group process: Participant roles and their relations to social status within the group. *Aggressive Behavior, 22,* 1–15. doi:10.1002/(SICI)1098-2337(1996)22:1<1::AID-AB1>3.0.CO;2-T

Shariff, S. (2008). *Cyber-bullying: Issues and solutions for the school, the classroom and the home.* London, England: Routledge.

Shariff, S. (2009). *Confronting cyber-bullying: What schools need to know to control misconduct and avoid legal consequences.* New York, NY: Cambridge University Press. doi:10.1017/CBO9780511551260

Smith, P. K. (2010). Cyberbullying: the European perspective. In J. Mora-Merchan & T. Jäger (Eds.), *Cyberbullying: A cross-national comparison* (pp. 7–19). Landau, Germany: Verlag Empirische Pädagogik.

Smith, P. K., Mahdavi, J., Carvalho, M., Fisher, S., Russell, S., & Tippett, N. (2008). Cyberbullying, its forms and impact in secondary school pupils. *Journal of Child Psychology and Psychiatry, 49,* 376–385. doi:10.1111/j.1469-7610.2007.01846.x PMid:18363945

Smith, P. K., Morita, Y., Junger-Tas, J., Olweus, D., Catalano, R., & Slee, P. (Eds.). (1999). *The nature of school bullying: A cross-national perspective.* London, England: Routledge.

Smith, P. K., Pepler, D. J., & Rigby, K. (Eds.). (2004). *Bullying in schools: How successful can interventions be?* Cambridge, England: Cambridge University Press.

Smith, P. K., & Sharp, S. (Eds.). (1994). *School bullying: Insights and perspectives.* London, England: Routledge.

Smith, P. K., & Sittichai, R. (2009). COST action IS0801 on cyberbullying [Special issue]. *Zeitschrift für Psychologie/Journal of Psychology, 217,* 235–236.

Smith, P. K., & Slonje, R. (2010). Cyberbullying: The nature and extent of a new kind of bullying, in and out of school. In S. R. Jimerson, S. M. Swearer, & D. L. Espelage (Eds.), *Handbook of bullying in schools: An international perspective* (pp. 249–262). New York, NY: Routledge.

Sourander, A., Klomek, A. B., Ikonen, M., Lindroos, J., Luntamo, T., Koskelainen, M., ... Helenius, H. (2010). Psychosocial risk factors associated with cyberbullying among adolescents: A population-based study. *Archives of General Psychiatry, 67,* 720–728. doi:10.1001/archgenpsychiatry.2010.79 PMid:20603453

Tippett, N., & Kwak, K. (2012). In Q. Li, D. Cross, & P. K., Smith (Eds.). *Bullying goes to the global village: Research on cyberbullying from an international perspective.* Chichester, England: Wiley-Blackwell.

Tokunaga, R. S. (2010). Following you home from school: A critical review and synthesis of research on cyberbullying victimization. *Computers in Human Behavior, 26,* 277–287. doi:10.1016/j.chb.2009.11.014

Ttofi, M. M., & Farrington, D. P. (2011). Effectiveness of school-based programs to reduce bullying: a systematic and meta-analytic review. *Journal of Experimental Criminology, 7,* 27–56. doi:10.1007/s11292-010-9109-1

University of Arizona (n.d.). International Cyber Bullying Think Tank. Retrieved from http://www.icbtt.arizona.edu

Vandebosch, H., & van Cleemput, K. (2008). Defining cyberbullying: A qualitative research into the perceptions of youngsters. *CyberPsychology & Behavior, 11,* 499–503. doi:10.1089/cpb.2007.0042

Wang, J., Iannotti, R. J., & Nansel, T. R. (2009). School bullying among adolescents in the United States: Physical, verbal, relational, and cyber. *Journal of Adolescent Health, 45,* 368–375. doi:10.1016/j.jadohealth.2009.03.021 PMid:19766941 PMCid:2751860

Willard, N. E. (2006). *Cyberbullying and cyberthreats.* Eugene, OR: Center for Safe and Responsible Internet Use.

Ybarra, M. L., & Mitchell, K. J. (2004). Online aggressor/targets, aggressors, and targets: A comparison of associated youth characteristics. *Journal of Child Psychology and Psychiatry, 45,* 1308–1316. doi:10.1111/j.1469-7610.2004.00328.x PMid:15335350

Ybarra, M. L., & Mitchell, K. J. (2007). Prevalence and frequency of Internet harassment instigation: Implications for adolescent health. *Journal of Adolescent Health, 41,* 189–195. doi:10.1016/j.jadohealth.2007.03.005 PMid:17659224

Ybarra, M. L., Mitchell, K. J., Wolak, J., & Finkelhor, D. (2006). Examining characteristics and associated distress related to Internet harassment: Findings from the second Youth Internet safety survey. *Pediatrics, 118,* 1169–1171. doi:10.1542/peds.2006-0815PMid:17015505

9

Addressing the Needs of Marginalized Youth at School

Tracey G. Scherr

THE UNIVERSITY OF WISCONSIN-WHITEWATER

Abstract

This chapter focuses on promoting the safety of marginalized youth in schools, with particular focus on Lesbian, Gay, Bisexual, Transgender, and Questioning (LGBTQ) students, especially those who are racial or ethnic minorities. These students are at elevated risk of victimization and, therefore, diminished access to educational opportunities and compromised mental health. This chapter addresses what is known about LGBTQ students in terms of school-based victimization, additional risk factors, and how to intervene to make their years in school safer and more enriching.

Some students are at elevated risk for victimization at school related to their membership in groups that are marginalized in the larger community or within their school buildings. Among them, this chapter addresses Lesbian, Gay, Bisexual, Transgender, and Questioning (LGBTQ) students, especially those who are racial or ethnic minorities. Membership in one of these minority groups puts a student at significant risk of victimization as well as poorer mental health and academic outcomes. Membership in more than one of these groups can mean additive risk.

Although these students are frequently underserved in schools, they have not evaded the attention of researchers and practitioners concerned about their well-being. Professional organizations of pupil service personnel and educators have developed publications calling for equitable treatment of LGBTQ students (e.g., Just the Facts Coalition, 2008; National Association of School Psychologists, 2006; National Education Association, 2006). Not only are school psychologists and other educators ethically obligated to meet the needs of all students in schools, including LGBTQ students, but they are also legally required to do so in the United States (McFarland, 2001). This chapter addresses the challenges faced by LGBTQ students, related research, and best practice implications.

Who Are LGBTQ Students?

People who are sexual minorities are referred to in the academic literature in multiple ways. LGBTQ references Lesbian, Gay, Bisexual, Transgender, Queer, and Questioning people. At least one group of researchers has included those who are intersex in their abbreviation as well (Varjas et al., 2008). These abbreviations include those whose sexual orientations involve some degree of same-sex attraction (i.e., gay, lesbian, and bisexual), and those whose gender identities and/or expression are unconventional or do not match sex assignment at birth (i.e., transgender). Queer and questioning generally refer to sexual orientation that does not conform to hetero-sexual norms, but may include gender identity and expression also. Those who are intersex share genitalia simultaneously resembling both females and males. Although individuals in these groups share similar experiences because of their minority status, they are also different despite the artificial melding of sexual orientation and gender identity inherent in LGBTQ abbrevia-tions. Estimates of percentages of LGBTQ youth vary anywhere from less than 1% to nearly 8% (Espelage, Aragon, Birkett, & Koenig, 2008; Russell, Seif, & Truong, 2001; Saewyc, Poon, Homma, & Skay, 2008).

Risk Factors for LGBTQ Youth

Victimization

Sexual minority students are victimized at alarming rates in their homes and communities, and schools offer no exception. The majority (65%) of the 230,000 LGBT students in the California Safe Schools Coalition and 4-H Center for Youth Development (CSSC & 4-HCYD, 2004) study reported being bullied based on their sexual orientation, and 27% had been bullied for their gender expression. Similarly, 65% of over 1,100 LGBTQ students in Britain experienced homophobic bullying including verbal taunts, relational aggression, cyber bullying, physical violence, property damage, death threats, sexual assault, threats of weapon use, and others (Hunt & Jensen, 2007).

The Gay, Lesbian and Straight Education Network (GLSEN) conducts large-scale, biennial school climate surveys across the United States. The latest, in 2007, included perspectives of more than 6,000 LGBT secondary school students. The largest percentage (60.8%) felt unsafe at school due to their sexual orientation, followed by their gender expression (38.4%), religion, (18.1%), race/ethnicity (8.9%), gender (8.7%), and disability (5.0%). The GLSEN study revealed 86.2% of LGBT students experienced verbal harassment, 44.1% physical harassment, and 22.1% physical assault at school because of their sexual orientation. Regarding gender expression, 66.5% experienced verbal harassment, 30.4% physical harassment, and 14.3% physical assault. These incidences have remained relatively stable since the survey conducted in 2001. Further, middle school students seem to fare worse than high school students (Kosciw, Diaz, & Greytak, 2008).

When transgender students were considered separately in the 2007 GLSEN survey, their school experiences seemed even bleaker than those of their LGB peers regarding victimization (Greytak, Kosciw, & Diaz, 2009). LGB youth in another, smaller study of older teens in the United States, Canada, and New Zealand also experienced slightly more victimization in middle school than high school, and an array of violence, including forms mentioned previously plus threats to dis-close sexual orientation and having objects thrown at them. In this study, as in most others sum-marized previously, males were victimized more often than females and greater gender atypicality was related to greater victimization (D'Augelli, Pilkington, & Hershberger, 2002).

Sexual minority students are a diverse group in terms of sexual orientation, gender identity and expression, race, ethnicity, and a number of other variables. Regarding LGBT students of color in the 2007 GLSEN study ($N = 2,130$), Diaz and Kosciw (2009) found nearly half of stu-dents reported being bullied based on a combination of sexual orientation, race/ethnicity, and/or gender. Native American students reported lower levels of bullying due to their race or ethnicity than other LGBT students of color, but elevated levels of bullying for their perceived religion. Further, they were more likely than other LGBT students of color to be physically assaulted due to their sexual orientation. There may be an additive risk of victimization for LGBT students of a variety of ethnicities and from otherwise diverse backgrounds.

Scherr and Larson (2010) identified that minority status within the school building exceeds importance of membership in majority or minority groups in the larger community in terms of vulnerability to victimization at school. Diaz and Kosciw (2009) drew a similar conclusion regarding LGBT students of color. They found that being a racial/ethnic minority within one's school building was associated with lower levels of perceived safety and higher levels of verbal bullying with racial themes. As for influence of the larger community, schools in the southern United States and schools in small towns or rural communities were most hostile in terms of verbal bullying regarding sexual orientation, race/ethnicity, and perceived religion. As the exception, Native American students in suburban areas received more verbal bullying based on their sexual orientation (Diaz & Kosciw). Hence, the ethnoracial constitution of the school building and characteristics of surrounding communities seem to interact to influence the experiences of sexual and ethnoracial minority youth at school.

Additional Risk Factors and Relevant Research

Academics

School engagement declines when students are bullied regarding their perceived sexual orientation or gender expression. Researchers found that being bullied by being called gay prompted boys to rate their school engagement lower than their male peers who were bullied for other reasons (Swearer, Turner, Givens, & Pollack, 2008). The same sort of bullying resulted in lowered school engagement ratings for all students in another investigation, but particularly for questioning youth (Espelage et al., 2008). In addition, researchers have found transgender students report lower school engagement than their LGB peers (Greytak et al., 2009).

When LGBT students are engaged with their schools, they may feel more connected to teachers than to other students, despite being out to more students than teachers. This may be because revealing sexual orientation or gender identity increases likelihood of bullying victimization. Also, being out to students and staff relates to greater willingness to address LGBT issues in school and, thus, improved student engagement (Kosciw et al., 2008).

Many LGBTQ students skip school out of fear for their safety. Sexual minority students report missing school because of safety concerns at rates between three to five times higher than their heterosexual peers. Prior victimization at school relates to more absenteeism (CSSC & 4-HCYD, 2004; Hunt & Jensen, 2007; Kosciw et al., 2008). In the GLSEN study, the majority of LGBT teens who were verbally bullied about their race/ethnicity and either their sexual orientation or their gender expression reported missing school within the month (Diaz & Kosciw, 2009). Presumably, many LGBTQ youth eventually drop out of school, although no reliable dropout statistics have been calculated for this group of students.

With so much missed school, it follows that GPA may suffer for LGBT students, particularly those who are bullied because of sexual orientation or gender expression (CSSC & 4-HCYD, 2004; Kosciw et al., 2008). In particular, bisexual boys have been found to have lower GPAs than other students (Russell et al., 2001). Transgender students who have been verbally bullied because of gender, gender expression, or sexual orientation tend to have lower GPAs (Greytak et al., 2009). In addition, LGBT students of color who are bullied about sexual orientation and race/ethnicity, as well as those who are bullied about race/ethnicity alone, have lower GPAs (Diaz & Kosciw, 2009).

In addition, LGBTQ students' long-term educational goals are often compromised. Twice as many LGBT students (12.4%) as heterosexual students lacked plans for postsecondary education in the GLSEN study. When bullying due to gender expression was considered, the percentage rose to 41.5% not planning to attend college (Kosciw et al., 2008). Almost half of transgender youth in the GLSEN study who experienced verbal bullying related to their gender, gender expression, or sexual orientation indicated they did not plan to pursue postsecondary education (Greytak et al., 2009). Further, gay students who were also ethnic minorities reported lower educational aspirations, regardless of bullying history, than their White, gay peers in a study of British youth (Hunt & Jensen, 2007). Nearly half of GLBT students show interest in postgraduate degrees, though, a higher percentage than the national average (Kosciw et al., 2008).

Substance Abuse

Sexual minority youth are at elevated risk of substance use and abuse. Twenty-three percent of LGB youth in a multinational study reported drinking at least weekly. Of the 39% who reported marijuana use, 11% used it at least weekly (D'Augelli et al., 2002). Sexual minority students in another large multidistrict study reported more alcohol and marijuana use than their heterosexual peers. Use by questioning teens was most pronounced (Espelage et al., 2008). Although they were more likely to drink alone, youth attracted to same-sex peers used drugs at a level comparable to heterosexual matched peers in a relatively small sample of young teens in northern England (Rivers & Noret, 2008). As with other risk factors, bullying history relates to substance abuse for LGBTQ youth. In the Espelage et al. study, all groups who had endured bullying for being gay, regardless of actual sexuality, reported more substance use, with the most use reported among questioning youth who had been bullied. In the CSSC and 4-HCYD (2004) study, students bullied because of sexual orientation were three times as likely as peers to use methamphetamines or inhalants. They were also more likely to smoke cigarettes, drink alcohol, and/or use other drugs.

Risky Sexual Activity

Despite declining rates of youth pregnancy overall in recent years, LGBTQ students remain at elevated risk of pregnancy. LGB youth in a large scale longitudinal study of teens in British Columbia were two to seven times more likely than their heterosexual peers to have become pregnant or impregnated someone (Saewyc et al., 2008). This may seem counterintuitive. However, LGB teens in this study reported elevated risk factors related to teen pregnancy and potential for contraction of sexually transmitted diseases. These included frequent sexual activity, early sexual activity, sexual abuse, multiple sexual partners, substance use prior to sexual intercourse, and infrequent contraceptive use. Those who experienced pregnancy were also more likely than peers to have been victimized due to their sexual orientation. An imbalance of risk and protective factors has been cited as explanation of these findings in this and other studies. In addition, variables such as survival sex during homelessness following coming out to family, lack of appropriate sexual education for sexual minority youth, and denying sexual orientation or attempting to prove gender status have been referenced (Saewyc et al., 2008).

Mental Health and Suicide

The mental health of LGBTQ youth is at risk. In a study of young English teens, Rivers and Noret (2008) found students attracted to same-sex peers were more likely to report feelings of loneliness and hostility than matched heterosexual peers. Additionally, victimization compromises the mental health of all students, but especially that of LGBTQ students. Victimization has been linked to posttraumatic stress for LGB youth and for gender atypical youth (D'Augelli et al., 2002; D'Augelli, Grossman, & Starks, 2006). Depressive symptoms are also more common among LGBTQ students who have been bullied than among their peers (CSSC & 4-HCYD, 2004; Espelage et al., 2008). Mental health decline, especially depression, contributes to suicidality among LGBTQ students.

Researchers disagree about the extent of suicidal risk faced by LGBTQ youth. Most contend sexual minority youth are at much greater risk for suicide than their heterosexual peers. Others argue that estimates of suicidality are inflated due to methodological flaws in related investigations.

In D'Augelli, Hershberger, and Pilkington's (2001) multinational study of 350 LGB teens, 42% reported thinking about suicide with some frequency at some point in their lives. Of those, 48% claimed suicidal ideation related to their sexual orientation. As for actual attempts, 35% acknowledged this behavior, and 57% of them indicated attempts related to their sexual orientation. Regarding lethality, 34% needed emergency medical treatment because of the attempts. The average age for attempts was 15.7 years, with significantly increased risk beginning at 16 years of age. Some gender differences were noted as well. Males attempted suicide earlier than females and were more likely to indicate their attempts were highly related to their sexual orientation. Grossman and D'Augelli (2007) found similar percentages of suicidal ideation in a sample of older transgender teens. Fewer transgender youth in their study attempted suicide, but all related attempts to their gender identity, and most (57%) attempts were considered serious by the researchers. Bisexual/homosexual males and females reported more suicide attempts (28.1% and 20.5%, respectively) than their heterosexual peers (14.5% of females, 4.2% of males) in a comparison study of teenage students. Further, bisexual/homosexual orientation predicted increased risk for suicidal intent and attempts (Remafedi, French, Story, Resnick, & Blum, 1998).

Conversely, Savin-Williams (2001) has cautioned against pathologizing LGBT youth by artificially inflating estimates of their suicidality. Savin-Williams acknowledges that sexual minority youth report more suicide attempts than do their heterosexual peers. However, according to Savin-Williams, many of their claims are false and reflect suicidal ideation rather than actual suicide attempts. In addition, Savin-Williams claims most attempts are not life-threatening. Instead, Savin-Williams and Ream (2003) assert, stressors in general and related to being a sexual minority youth contribute to suicidality among some at-risk subpopulations of LGBT youth.

Rather than focus on demographic variables such as sexual orientation, Rutter and Soucar (2002) suggested examining social support and feelings of isolation and hopelessness because they were related to suicide risk in sexual minority and heterosexual teens in their investigation. Similarly, although most LGBT youth in their study did not suffer from suicidal ideation or attempts, Russell and Joyner (2001) noted a comparison of more than 12,000 U.S. students revealed those with same-sex orientations were more than twice as likely as their peers to experience suicidal ideation and to attempt suicide. However, this was explained by elevated victimization among these youth. Those who experienced suicidal ideation and/or attempted suicide were also more likely to feel hopeless and depressed, abuse alcohol, and have family histories of suicide attempts. Bullying was related to suicidal ideation among youth in the CSSC and 4-HCYD (2004) study as well. In addition, Grossman and D'Augelli (2007) found histories of abuse from parents among transgender youth who attempted suicide.

Coming Out

Coming out, or sharing one's sexual or gender identity with others, appears to put LGBTQ students at further risk. It might seem that coming out would allow one to be true to their identities and thus promote psychological health. However, the earlier a young person identifies as LGBQ and/or transgender, and the earlier one reveals that identity to others, the worse that individual seems to fare.

Although they and others often suspect so earlier, LGB youth identify themselves as such between 15 to 16 years of age, on average, and share that identity with another person around 17 years of age (D'Augelli et al., 2002). Most transgender youth identify younger, presumably because this identity relates to gender versus sexual orientation, around 13 years of age, and reveal this identity at an average age of 14 years (Grossman, D'Augelli, & Salter, 2006). When youth do come out, they seem to share their identity with peers primarily, followed by teachers. Less share their identities with family members (Grossman & D'Augelli, 2007), although 61.3% of LGBT students in the 2007 GLSEN study were out to at least one parent (Kosciw et al., 2008). Also, transgender students may be more likely than their LGB peers to be out to school staff, perhaps because of the greater visibility of gender expression for some transgender students (Greytak et al., 2009).

The younger transgender youth self-identify, share their identity, or are noticed as gender atypical by others, the more likely they are to be victimized by parents or others (Grossman et al., 2006). Similarly, being out to peers regarding gender or sexual orientation has been associated with increased victimization at school for transgender students (Greytak et al., 2009). Openness about sexual orientation has been related to the amount of victimization for LGB youth as well (D'Augelli et al., 2002).

Coming out has been linked to increased suicide risk. The link may not be as direct as it seems, though. Within their multinational sample of LGB teens, D'Augelli et al. (2001) discovered about half of those youth who acknowledged at least one prior suicide attempt indicated the attempt occurred prior to coming out about their sexual orientation. However, 27% did attempt within the same year as they came out. Further, 19% attempted suicide more than one year following coming out. Family histories of both attempted and completed suicides were noted. Parents' negative responses to their children coming out were related to their suicide attempts. Educators should be aware that a number of LGBTQ students become homeless or enter foster care following coming out because of conflict with family. Maintaining confidentiality regarding students' sexual orientation and gender identity is essential.

Although being out increases risk for sexual minority students, there is a positive side also. Being out to school staff and students increases LGBT students' comfort with raising LGBT issues at school and, in turn, increases student engagement. Further, being out to school staff increases the likelihood that LGBT students will report victimization at school (Kosciw et al., 2008).

Jamie Nabozny's Example

Jamie Nabozny endured perhaps the most notable example of the difficulties faced by LGBTQ youth in schools. Jamie's peers in a small, midwestern school district bullied him verbally, physically, and sexually from seventh through eleventh grades due to his sexual orientation. The bullying resulted in surgery to repair damage caused to Jamie's body. Jamie attempted suicide multiple times and required emergency medical treatment as a result. He dropped out of school and ran away to a large, metropolitan area to escape the bullying at school. Jamie and his parents had reported the abuse to school officials repeatedly. They did not intervene and even blamed Jamie for being openly gay. Ultimately, Jamie and his parents sued the school district and its principals, claiming he was denied equal protection under the Fourteenth Amendment of the U.S. Constitution. The district did have a nondiscrimination policy that referenced sexual orientation, and a jury did not find the district liable. However, the jury found district administrators culpable, and they settled the suit for nearly $1,000,000. Now Jamie speaks publicly about his experiences to help others in similar situations (McFarland, 2001; Southern Poverty Law Center, 2010).

Although Jamie Nabozny's case was filed in the mid-1990s, these forms of egregious abuse against sexual minority students continue to occur. The websites of the American Civil Liberties Union, Lambda Legal, and other organizations working on behalf of oppressed peoples highlight many ongoing legal cases regarding offenses against LGBTQ students. The content ranges from verbal and physical abuse, death threats, and corresponding suicide attempts to freedom of expression cases. Schools have prohibited students from wearing t-shirts with gay pride slogans, wearing gender atypical dress, attending proms with same-sex dates, displaying affection towards same-sex girlfriends and boyfriends, and developing Gay Straight Alliances.

Interventions and Relevant Research

Supportive School Staff

As Jamie Nabozny's situation illustrated, staff can either help or perpetuate school problems for sexual minority students. A majority of respondents in the 2007 GLSEN survey indicated school staff made homophobic remarks, negative remarks about students' gender expression, or sexist remarks. A little over one third overheard staff make racist comments (Kosciw et al., 2008). Nearly half of students in the CSSC and 4-HCYD (2004) study, and in Hunt and Jensen's (2007) study of British youth, also heard teachers make homophobic comments. In fact, 30% of British youth claimed school staff had perpetrated homophobic bullying, and the majority of LGBTQ youth could not identify a supportive adult at school or home. Feelings about teachers predicted school problems (attention, homework completion, and student relationships) for bisexual males and females in another large U.S. study (Russell et al., 2001).

However, most (approx. 80%) LGBT students in the 2007 GLSEN study could identify a school staff member who was supportive of sexual minority students. When students could identify at least a half dozen school staff who were supportive, they were less likely to miss school, reported greater school engagement, and had higher GPAs and post-secondary goals (Kosciw et al., 2008). Students in the CSSC and 4-HCYD (2004) study who knew of supportive staff were less likely to be bullied, felt safer at school, and knew of other supportive adults outside of school.

The majority of LGBTQ students do not report bullying to school staff (Hunt & Jensen, 2007; Kosciw et al., 2008). When students do report bullying, adult responses are essential. However, when they tell, many students report nothing is done or that what is done is ineffective (Hunt & Jensen, 2007; Kosciw et al., 2008). Most teachers agree that they are obligated to ensure safety and be supportive of LGBTQ students (Guasp, 2009; Harris Interactive & GLSEN, 2005), yet many ignore homophobic language (Guasp, 2009; Hunt & Jensen, 2007). Three fourths of secondary school principals in one investigation claimed to discipline perpetrators of bullying, yet a similar proportion indicated that LGBTQ students probably would not feel safe in their schools. Perhaps this is because only 20% have taken specific action to ensure a safe, supportive school for sexual minority students (GLSEN & Harris Interactive, 2008). When staff intervene regarding homophobic comments, students report less related bullying, feeling safer at school, and having stronger support networks that include adults (CSSC & 4-HCYD, 2004; Hunt & Jensen, 2007).

Comprehensive Antidiscrimination Policies

Diversity education and bully prevention programs may help prevent bullying against LGBTQ youth, but they alone are insufficient. Students in schools with generic bullying policies report similar levels of victimization as those with no safety policy (Kosciw et al., 2008). Bullying policies must prohibit discrimination based on sexual orientation and gender expression explicitly, and many do not (Harris Interactive & GLSEN, 2005; Hunt & Jensen, 2007; Kosciw et al., 2008). Although gender may appear in some statements, gender identity and expression may not be identified specifically (Greytak et al., 2009). Students in schools with specific statements report less victimization, feeling safer at school, increased likelihood of reporting bullying to school staff, more intervention from school staff, and knowing supportive teachers (CSSC & 4-HCYD, 2004; Hunt & Jensen, 2007; Kosciw et al., 2008). The benefits of inclusive policies extend to sexual majority students as well (Harris Interactive & GLSEN, 2005). Further, methods for reporting and intervening with bullying should be clear and publicized to staff and students. Inclusive, respectful language should be used on school forms and in all communication.

Gay Straight Alliances (GSAs)

GSAs serve a variety of purposes. Some offer social opportunities and support for members, and others more actively advocate for the safety of LGBTQ youth in their schools through education and/or policy advocacy. Estimates of the prevalence of GSAs vary from only 6% of British students in the Hunt and Jensen (2007) study reporting a GSA at their school to about one third of students reporting one in the 2007 GLSEN study (Kosciw et al., 2008). Students in schools with a GSA hear fewer homophobic comments, experience less bullying focused on their gender expression and sexual orientation, are less likely to be absent from school because of safety concerns, feel more engaged with their school communities, and are more likely to report bullying problems to school staff, presumably because they are also more likely to have identified a supportive staff member or other adult (CSSC & 4-HCYD, 2004; Kosciw et al., 2008). On the other hand, membership in a GSA may require some degree of being out, especially if parental permission is required.

Inclusive Curricula

Most students (70%–90%) report no exposure to LGBTQ topics or people in their school curriculum or among their educational resources such as libraries, accessible Internet sites, etc. (Hunt & Jensen, 2007; Kosciw et al., 2008). When inclusive curricula and materials are present, some of the positive outcomes associated with comprehensive safety statements and GSAs are enhanced (CSSC & 4-HCYD, 2004; Hunt & Jensen, 2007; Kosciw et al., 2008). Even so, method of presentation is important. English youth reported low, but increased, coverage of LGB topics in school, but also identified problems with the coverage in one investigation. Problems included compartmentalizing the topic, pathologizing it, and shrouding it in morality judgments and power struggles (Ellis & High, 2004). Additionally, sex education that focuses only on heterosexual youth ignores the needs of sexual minority youth, putting them at increased risk for unplanned pregnancies and sexually transmitted diseases.

Staff and Student Training

School staff should be trained regarding the challenges encountered by LGBTQ students and how to intervene with related bullying. Similarly, students should be instructed about how to respond to bullying specific to sexual orientation and gender expression. Staff and students should be taught to recognize and respond to signs of suicide in all students as well. Staff trainings about LGBTQ issues are not occurring as much as they are needed. Although 69% of secondary principals believed staff training would be effective to reduce bullying of LGBTQ stu-

Table 9.1   Practice Implications for Working with LGBTQ Students

1.	Assess school climate with GLSEN's (2006) local climate survey available at www.glsen.org or another tool
2.	Consider climate specific to needs of transgender students (e.g., bathroom and locker room options, dress codes, gender segregated activities; Transgender Law Center, 2009)
3.	Ensure antidiscrimination policies explicitly prohibit bullying on the basis of sexual orientation and gender expression; sample policies are located at www.coloradosafeschools.org/climate/Samplepolicies.htm
4.	Identify safe, supportive school staff and administration
5.	Establish a Gay Straight Alliance according to guidelines provided by http://www.glsen.org, http://gsanetwork.org, and http://safeschoolscoalition.org
6.	Provide curricula and other educational resources inclusive of LGBTQ people and topics
7.	Provide staff training about gender and sexual development, LGBTQ youth, intervening with bullying specific to sexual orientation and gender expression, and recognizing suicidality and intervening appropriately
8.	Provide student training about intervening with bullying specific to sexual orientation and gender expression and about recognizing and reporting signs of suicide
9.	Provide parent education about gender and sexual development, responding to bullying, recognizing and responding to suicidality, the importance of supportive families, and negative outcomes of abuse
10.	Improve university training for preservice educators, administrators, and pupil service personnel regarding LGBTQ concerns
11.	Develop knowledge of community agencies that serve LGBTQ youth and their families
12.	Assess individual risk and protective factors of LGBTQ students by considering the variables presented in this chapter and by providing follow-up care for students identified at-risk during schoolwide mental health screenings, especially for depression and suicide
13.	Assess and intervene with suicidal students as necessary

Note. The Trevor Project has a crisis and suicide prevention helpline for LGBTQ youth.

dents, only 4% devoted staff training to LGBTQ concerns in the GLSEN and Harris Interactive (2008) study. Similarly, 90% of school staff in an extensive study of educators in Great Britain had not received training specific to addressing homophobic bullying (Guasp, 2009). Outreach to parents regarding gender and sexual development, responding to bullying, recognizing and responding to suicidality, the importance of supportive families, and negative outcomes of abuse may be necessary as well.

Ideally, school psychologists would provide these services. Yet, their university training is typically inadequate in this realm, so further professional development is usually needed. A survey of school psychologists revealed 85% had no graduate training specific to gay and lesbian topics (Savage, Prout, & Chard, 2004). Although training about LGBTQ students' challenges and needs is necessary, it may not be sufficient. Personal beliefs and perceptions about school norms must be worked through as well (McCabe & Rubinson, 2008). In the absence of appropriately trained staff, school districts may opt to seek support from districts that have hired LGBTQ liaison personnel or from advocacy organizations that offer related materials and trainings (e.g., GLSEN, Safe Schools Coalition, The Trevor Project, Transgender Law Center).

Relative Advantages/Disadvantages

School psychologists and other educators must consider risks facing LGBTQ youth in order to improve their school experiences. Those presented in this chapter are not exhaustive. Of those presented, some require further investigation. For example, more work is needed to understand how race, ethnicity, culture, immigration status, and language proficiency interact with sexual orientation and gender identity to influence students' experiences. Whenever practitioners assess risk, they should also assess resiliency. For example, supportive parents and positive school climate have been demonstrated to protect LGB and questioning youth against depression and drug use (Espelage et al., 2008). For the proportions of LGBTQ youth struggling regarding particular variables, there are percentages of youth who do not struggle or else have overcome the same things. We should not perpetuate negative stereotypes by ignoring positive psychology. We need to find out how these students are able to rise above the multitude of challenges they confront. Many LGBTQ students navigate childhood challenges and lead happy, fulfilling lives.

Change tends to be uncomfortable. Educators who have considered and/or implemented some of the strategies identified in this chapter have cited numerous obstacles. Fear of being perceived as gay or lesbian, fear of actually being outed or discriminated against, administrative resistance, and community resistance comprise some challenges. Some professionals reference personal conflict about the topic. Yet, educators are legally mandated and professionally obligated to protect and serve LGBTQ youth. Children's lives depend on this work.

References

California Safe Schools Coalition & 4-H Center for Youth Development, University of CA, Davis. (2004). *Safe Place to Learn: Consequences of harassment based on actual or perceived sexual orientation and gender non-conformity and steps for making schools safer.* Retrieved from http://www.casafeschools.org/20040112.html

D'Augelli, A. R., Grossman, A. H., & Starks, M. T. (2006). Childhood gender atypicality, victimization, and PTSD among lesbian, gay, and bisexual youth. *Journal of Interpersonal Violence, 21,* 1462–1482. doi:10.1177/0886260506293482

D'Augelli, A. R., Hershberger, S. L., & Pilkington, N. W. (2001). Suicidality patterns and sexual orientation-related factors among lesbian, gay, and bisexual youths. *Suicide and Life-Threatening Behavior, 31,* 250–264. doi:10.1521/suli.31.3.250.24246

D'Augelli, A. R., Pilkington, N. W., & Hershberger, S. L. (2002). Incidence and mental health impact of sexual orientation victimization of lesbian, gay, and bisexual youths in high school. *School Psychology Quarterly, 17,* 148–167. doi:10.1521/scpq.17.2.148.20854

Diaz, E. M., & Kosciw, J. G. (2009). *Shared differences: The experiences of lesbian, gay, bisexual, and transgender students of color in our nation's schools.* Retrieved, from Gay, Lesbian and Straight Education Network website, http://www.glsen.org/cgi-bin/iowa/all/research/index.html

Ellis, V., & High, S. (2004). Something more to tell you: Gay, lesbian or bisexual young people's experiences of secondary schooling. *British Educational Research Journal, 30,* 213–225. doi:10.1080/0141192042000195281

Espelage, D. L., Aragon, S. R., Birkett, M., & Koenig, B. W. (2008). Homophobic teasing, psychological outcomes, and sexual orientation among high school students: What influence do parents and schools have? *School Psychology Review, 37,* 202–216. Retrieved, from http://www.nasponline.org/publications/spr/sprmain.aspx

Gay, Lesbian, and Straight Education Network. (2006). *Local School Climate Survey.* Retrieved from http://www.glsen.org/cgi-bin/iowa/all/research/index.html

Gay, Lesbian and Straight Education Network & Harris Interactive. (2008). *The principal's perspective: School safety, bullying, and harassment.* Retrieved from http://www.glsen.org/cgi-bin/iowa/all/research/index.html

Greytak, E. A., Kosciw, J. G., & Diaz, E. M. (2009). *Harsh realities: The experiences of transgender youth in our nation's schools.* Retrieved, from Gay, Lesbian and Straight Education Network website, http://www.glsen.org/cgi-bin/iowa/all/research/index.html

Grossman, A. H., & D'Augelli, A. R. (2007). Transgender youth and life-threatening behaviors. *Suicide and Life-Threatening Behavior, 37,* 527–537. doi:10.1521/suli.2007.37.5.527

Grossman, A. H., D'Augelli, A. R., & Salter, N. P. (2006). Male-to-female transgender youth: Gender expression milestones, gender atypicality, victimization, and parents' responses. *Journal of GLBT Family Studies, 2,* 71–92. doi:10.1300/J461v02n01_04

Guasp, A. (2009). *Homophobic bullying in Britain's schools: The teacher's report.* Retrieved, from Stonewall website: www.stonewall.org.uk/old_at_school/resources/default.asp

Harris Interactive & Gay, Lesbian and Straight Education Network. (2005). *From teasing to torment: School climate in America.* Retrieved from GLSEN website. http://www.glsen.org/cgi-bin/iowa/all/research/index.html

Hunt, R., & Jensen. J. (2007). *The experiences of young gay people in Britain's schools*. Retrieved, from Stonewall website, http://www.stonewall.org.uk/old_at_school/resources/default.asp

Just the Facts Coalition. (2008). *Just the facts about sexual orientation and youth: A primer for principals, educators, and school personnel*. Retrieved from American Psychological Association website, http://www.apa.org/pi/lgbc/publications/justthefacts.html

Kosciw, J. G., Diaz, E. M., & Greytak, E. A. (2008). *2007 national school climate survey: The experiences of lesbian, gay, bisexual, and transgender youth in our nation's schools*. Retrieved, from Gay, Lesbian and Straight Education Network website, http://www.glsen.org/cgi-bin/iowa/all/research/index.html

McCabe, P. C., & Rubinson, F. (2008). Committing to social justice: The behavioral intention of school psychology and education trainees to advocate for lesbian, gay, bisexual, and transgendered youth. *School Psychology Review, 37*, 469–486. Retrieved from http://www.nasponline.org/publications/spr/sprmain.aspx

McFarland, W. P. (2001). The legal duty to protect gay and lesbian students from violence in school. *Professional School Counseling, 4*, 171–179. Retrieved from http://www.schoolcounselor.org/content.asp?contentid=235

National Association of School Psychologists. (2006). *Position statement: Gay, lesbian, bisexual, transgender, and questioning youth*. Retrieved from http://www.nasponline.org/about_nasp/positionpapers/GLBQYouth.pdf

National Education Association. (2006). *Strengthening the learning environment: A school employee's guide to gay, lesbian, bisexual, & transgender issues* (2nd ed.). Retrieved from http://www.nea.org/tools/30431.htm

Remafedi, G., French, S., Story, M., Resnick, M. D., & Blum, R. (1998). The relationship between suicide risk and sexual orientation: Results of a population-based study. *American Journal of Public Health, 88*, 57–60. doi:10.2105/AJPH.88.1.57

Rivers, I., & Noret, N. (2008). Well-being among same-sex and opposite-sex-attracted youth at school. *School Psychology Review, 37*, 174–187. Retrieved from http://www.nasponline.org/publications/spr/sprmain.aspx

Russell, S. T., & Joyner, K. (2001). Adolescent sexual orientation and suicide risk: Evidence from a national study. *American Journal of Public Health, 91*, 1276–1281. doi:10.2105/AJPH.91.8.1276

Russell, S. T., Seif, H., & Truong, N. L. (2001). School outcomes of sexual minority youth in the United States: Evidence from a national study. *Journal of Adolescence, 24*, 111–127. doi:10.1006/jado.2000.0365

Rutter, P. A., & Soucar, E. (2002). Youth suicide risk and sexual orientation. *Adolescence, 37*(146), 289–299. Retrieved from http://www.vjf.cnrs.fr/clt/php/va/Page_revue.php?ValCodeRev=ADO

Saewyc, E. M., Poon, C. S., Homma, Y., & Skay, C. L. (2008). Stigma management? The links between enacted stigma and teen pregnancy trends among gay, lesbian, and bisexual students in British Colombia. *The Canadian Journal of Human Sexuality, 17*, 123–139. Retrieved from http://www.sieccan.org/cjhs.html

Savage, T. A., Prout, H. T., & Chard, K. M. (2004). School psychology and issues of sexual orientation: Attitudes, beliefs, and knowledge. *Psychology in the Schools, 41*, 201–210. doi:10.1002/pits.10122

Savin-Williams, R. C. (2001). Suicide attempts among sexual-minority youths: Population and measurement issues. *Journal of Consulting and Clinical Psychology, 69*, 983–991. doi:10.1037//0022-006X.69.6.983

Savin-Williams, R. C., & Ream, G. L. (2003). Suicide attempts among sexual-minority male youth. *Journal of Clinical Child and Adolescent Psychology, 32*, 509–522.

Scherr, T. G., & Larson, J. (2010). Bullying dynamics associated with race, ethnicity, and immigration status. In S. R. Jimerson, S. M. Swearer, & D. L. Espelage (Eds.), *The handbook of bullying in schools: An international perspective* (pp. 168–182). New York, NY: Routledge.

Southern Poverty Law Center. (2010). *Bullied* [DVD]. (Available from Teaching Tolerance, http://www.tolerance.org)

Swearer, S. M., Turner, R. K., Givens, J. E., & Pollack, W. S. (2008). "You're so gay!": Do different forms of bullying matter for adolescent males? *School Psychology Review, 37*, 160–173. Retrieved from http://www.nasponline.org/publications/spr/sprmain.aspx

Transgender Law Center. (2009). *Student safety workshop tools*. Retrieved from http://transgenderlawcenter.org/cms/content/schools

Varjas, K., Dew, B., Marshall, M., Graybill, E., Singh, A., Meyers, J., & Birckbichler, L. (2008). Bullying in schools towards sexual minority youth. *Journal of School Violence, 7*, 59–86. doi:10.1300/J202v07n02_05

10

Toward an Understanding of Youth Gang Involvement

Implications for Schools

Dana Peterson and Kirstin A. Morgan

UNIVERSITY AT ALBANY, STATE UNIVERSITY OF NEW YORK

Abstract

This chapter provides an overview of research findings about youth gangs and young gang members, with a discussion of implications of this knowledge for school violence and school safety. This review of gangs and gang member characteristics, risk factors for gang joining, and desistance from the gang debunks common misperceptions. Attention is given to factors of particular import in the school context, such as school-related risk factors for gang involvement, the role of gangs/gang members in violence and victimization, and other implications for school safety, including zero tolerance policies and the role of the Internet.

Overview

Approximately 6% of public school students are gang involved (Esbensen, Peterson, Taylor, & Freng, 2010; Peterson, in press), approximately 20% of students age 12–18 report the presence of gangs in or around their schools, and 20% of public school administrators report some gang activity at their schools in the past year (Dinkes, Kemp, Baum, & Snyder, 2009). Because of their disproportionate involvement in delinquency, gangs contribute to negative school climate and victimization. It is therefore important that school personnel understand youth gang involvement to better address the issues faced by at-risk or gang-involved youths. This chapter debunks some myths about young gang members and provides schools with prevention and intervention guidance, as well as approaches to avoid, by drawing from research on risk factors for gang joining and reasons for desistance from gangs.

Gang Member Characteristics

The stereotypical image of a youth gang member in the United States is a young, minority, inner-city male. Data from multiple sources, however, reveal that youth gangs and their members are found not just in inner-city areas, but in large and small urban, suburban, and rural communities

117

throughout the United States (Esbensen & Peterson Lynskey, 2001; National Youth Gang Center [NYGC], 2007). The picture of who is a gang member, however, varies by data source.

Law enforcement agency surveys estimate that Blacks (nearly 50%) and Hispanics (approximately 35%) comprise the greatest proportion of gang members, while Whites and other races each make up 10% or less (NYGC, 2007). By contrast, youths' self-report surveys indicate that although Black and Hispanic youths are still over-represented given their proportions in the general youth population, White youths make up a larger proportion of gang members than shown in law enforcement data. In an 11-city study of youth in public middle schools, for example, Whites comprised 25% of the gang member sample (Esbensen & Winfree, 1998). Additionally, cross-site comparisons reveal that, contrary to many media portrayals and public perceptions, gang members are not solely inner-city, minority males; rather, they reflect the demographic make-up of the communities in which they live (Esbensen & Peterson Lynskey, 2001). These authors found that in Kansas City, Milwaukee, and Philadelphia, for example, the majority of gang members were African American; in Las Cruces, New Mexico, and Phoenix, Arizona, Hispanics made up the largest proportion of gang members; but in Will County, Illinois, and Pocatello, Idaho, the majority of gang members were White.

Similar disparities across data sources are seen in regard to the sex composition of gang members. In law enforcement data, females are less than 10% of gang members (NYGC, 2007), but studies using youths' self-reports reveal females' prevalence in gangs from 20% to nearly 50% (Esbensen & Huizinga, 1993; Esbensen & Peterson Lynskey, 2001; Thornberry, Krohn, Lizotte, Smith, & Tobin, 2003). Further, girls are not just girlfriends or associates; many are core members and have decision-making roles within the gang (Miller, 2001; Peterson, Miller, & Esbensen, 2001). As with race/ethnicity, the proportion of gang members that is female varies by location. In the 11-city study reported above, for example, females made up 25% of gang members in Philadelphia, but over 40% of gang members in six other study sites: Las Cruces, Orlando, Phoenix, Pocatello, Torrance, and Will County (Esbensen & Peterson Lynskey, 2001). The inconsistencies across data sources do not mean that one source of information is correct and others are invalid; they simply offer different parts of the same picture, with law enforcement data capturing older males and self-report surveys (particularly those that are school-based) capturing younger, more diverse samples.

Risk Factors for Gang Joining

Understanding the factors that lead youths to gangs can guide schools' and communities' prevention and intervention efforts. Research over the past 15 years has identified a number of risk factors associated with youths' gang involvement. These factors fall into five general domains: community, individual, family, peer, and school. Studies have also shown that the harmful effects of these factors are cumulative and exponential; the greater the number of factors within and across domains, the greater the risk of gang involvement, with dramatic increases in odds as factors accumulate (Esbensen et al., 2010; Thornberry et al., 2003).

In the community domain, a number of studies have shown that social disorganization characterized by poverty, unemployment, the absence of meaningful jobs, and presence of crime, firearms, and drugs contributes to gang formation and gang-joining (Gottfredson & Gottfredson, 2001; Hill, Howell, Hawkins, & Battin-Pearson, 1999; Howell, 2008; Maxson, Whitlock, & Klein, 1998; Vigil, 1988). Importantly, the majority of youth who live in disorganized communities do not join gangs. Factors from the other risk domains can therefore help to explain why some youth join gangs, whereas others who experience the same community conditions do not.

Most risk factor research has been conducted on the individual, peer, and family domains. The individual domain includes youths' constitutional characteristics, attitudes, and behaviors.

Various studies have found that engaging in prior problem behaviors and delinquency, having low involvement in conventional activities (e.g., school or community athletics, scouts, religious activities), and holding non-conventional attitudes puts youths at greater risk for gang involvement (Esbensen & Huizinga, 1993; Esbensen et al., 2010; Gottfredson & Gottfredson, 2001; Hill et al., 1999; Maxson et al., 1998). Also consistently supported is an individual's experience of "negative life events," such as serious illnesses, suspensions from school, or loss of or disruption in important affective relationships (Klein & Maxson, 2006).

Research within the family domain has produced inconsistent results, but some studies have noted the role of poor parental management practices or skills (e.g., inconsistent and/or harsh discipline, permissiveness, poor supervision) in engendering gang affiliation (Esbensen, Huizinga, & Weiher, 1993; Hill et al., 1999; Klein & Maxson, 2006; Maxson et al., 1998). It is thought that the more proximal risk factors for gang joining come from the peer and school domains, which begin to figure more prominently in early adolescence (the peak age of gang-joining), while the role of the family becomes relatively less important.

The role of peers has been well-established in the literature as one of the strongest predictors of an adolescent's own delinquency (Howell, 2008). Simply associating with delinquent peers and having few associations with prosocial peers leads youth to gang membership (Battin, Hill, Abbott, Catalano, & Hawkins, 1998). Further, affective ties or commitment to deviant peers are strongly and consistently linked with youth gang involvement (Esbensen et al., 1993, 2010; Klein & Maxson, 2006; Maxson et al., 1998; Thornberry et al., 2003).

As with family risk factors, findings about the role of school factors are also mixed. There is evidence, however, supporting the influence of some school variables on youth gang joining. Youths, especially girls, who experience academic failure or poor school performance, are suspended or expelled from school, exhibit a lack of commitment or low bonding to school, or drop out of school before age 15 are more likely to join a gang than their counterparts (Bjerregaard & Smith, 1993; Esbensen & Deschenes, 1998; Hill et al., 1999; Howell, 2008; Maxson et al., 1998). Similarly, negative school climate and perceptions of school disorder/crime have been linked to gang membership in some studies (Esbensen et al., 2010; Gottfredson & Gottfredson, 2001).

Despite some inconsistencies, the risk factor research to date suggests that if some risk can be alleviated, particularly the accumulation of risk, youths may avoid gang involvement. Examples of potential steps schools and communities might take in helping alleviate risk will be discussed in a later section. As the next section demonstrates, preventing youths from becoming involved with gang life also has potential for reducing crime and victimization in neighborhoods and schools.

Role of Youth Gang Membership in Violence and Victimization

Contrary to common perceptions and portrayals of gang life, the majority of gang members' time is spent in activities common to most adolescents: hanging out, playing video games, cruising in cars, and cavorting with the opposite sex (Klein, 1995). But, it is also the case that disproportionate rates of delinquency, violence, and victimization are found among gang members, according to multiple sources of data. Across various self-report studies, for example, gang members comprised 9% to 31% of the samples, but were responsible for 54% to 79% of all violent offenses committed (Battin et al., 1998; Esbensen et al., 2010; Huizinga, 1997; Thornberry et al., 2003). The high level of delinquency among gang members has prompted research on the question of whether gangs attract or recruit youths who are already delinquent (a "selection" explanation) or whether the gang provides a context in which youths are socialized into delinquency (a "social facilitation" explanation). Research to date supports an "enhancement" explanation that encompasses both of these: youths who are already delinquent or have delinquent tendencies are likely to join gangs and their delinquency increases while in the gang (e.g., Esbensen & Huizinga, 1993; Gatti, Tremblay, Vitaro, & McDuff, 2005; Gordon et al., 2004; Thornberry et al., 2003).

Group Processes

Understanding why gangs enhance delinquency and violence requires an understanding of the role of group processes (Klein, 1971; Papachristos, 2009; Short & Strodtbeck, 1963). Psychological processes of "de-individuation" mean that youths are able to abdicate individual responsibility for crime to the group, as "group esteem" supplants individual self-esteem (Vigil, 1988). Individuals' engagement in crime is rewarded by the group, increasing youths' commitment to anti-social ideals and to the group (Vigil, 1988). As more recent empirical work suggests, threats of and actual violence thus serve important uniting functions in the gang and result in increased violence in the forms of, for example, retaliation, "face-saving," and punishment for rule or norm violations (Anderson, 1999; Decker, 1996; Hughes & Short, 2005; Papachristos, 2009). In addition, external forces acting upon the group serve to reinforce group cohesion, as members view themselves as victims or unfair targets who are disrespected, oppressed, and justified in acting out (Decker, 1996; Klein & Maxson, 2006). These increases in cohesiveness are directly related to increases in delinquency and create a cycle of violence (Klein, 1971). Breaking this cycle requires recognizing youths as individuals (rather than members of a gang), holding them individually responsible for their actions, and avoiding strategies that reinforce gang loyalties. In addition, given gangs' enhancement of delinquency, it would be advantageous, as the risk factor literature also suggests, to address youths' anti-social attitudes and behaviors in an effort to reduce likelihood of gang joining and, therefore, escalation of delinquency.

Negative Consequences of Gang Involvement

Preventing gang membership may reduce not only crime associated with gang involvement, but also the negative consequences youths experience as gang members. Compared to non-gang youths, gang members have higher likelihood and levels of victimization before, during, and after their membership; gangs therefore also "enhance" victimization (Peterson, Taylor, & Esbensen, 2004). Furthermore, despite the fact that about half of gang youths reported joining their gangs for protection, there were no differences in victimization levels for these youths compared to youths who joined for other reasons. That is, gang membership appears to offer no additional protection. Membership in gangs also has long-term consequences, even for those who leave gang life behind. Having been gang-involved significantly increases the odds of dropping out of school, early pregnancy, teen parenthood, unstable employment, and adult arrests (Decker & Lauritsen, 1996; Hagedorn, 1998; Thornberry et al., 2003).

Gang Violence and the Internet

More recently the Internet has also come to play an important role in the perpetration of gang violence (Associated Press, 2006; Ferrell, 2008; Friedman, 2010; Gavin, 2009a,b; Van Hellemont, 2010). Gang members in many cities have taken to posting videos and information about their activities on Facebook, MySpace, or YouTube. Such postings often glamorize gang violence and allow gangs to recruit by touting their endeavors (Ferrell, 2008; Van Hellemont, 2010). Newspapers and some studies provide examples of gangs using the Internet to promote criminal acts, including violence. In 1999, for example, the first New York City Internet drug sales ring was uncovered, and 13 members of a gang were arrested (Blair, 1999). More recently, police in upstate New York connected three gang members to a high profile attempted robbery and subsequent shooting death of a university student after they had posted videos on YouTube touting their violent gang lifestyle and bragging of their involvement in the murder (Gavin, 2009a). In Brussels, Belgium, Black African youth gangs use Internet blogs to promote their gangs and taunt rival gang members (Van Hellemont, 2010). What often starts as an insult or threat posted on a blog, such as a photograph of one gang posing in disrespecting ways in another gang's territory, can easily turn into a violent encounter on the streets or in schools.

There is no empirical evidence as yet to suggest that gang members' use of the Internet has increased gang joining or violence, but police and other practitioners have noticed an increased use of the Internet by gang members (Ferrell, 2008). Extant research clearly shows that gang membership increases involvement in both violent and non-violent delinquency. Because gangs' use of the Internet can increase violence as rival members threaten and taunt each other online, monitoring Internet interactions can identify avenues to intervene with violence and victimization, as discussed later.

Desistance from the Gang

Intervention cues may also be gleaned from research on youths' desistance from gang life. Whereas the gang serves a variety of purposes for adolescents at particular points in their lives, for most, it is a temporary solution. Many have mixed thoughts and feelings about their gang membership, appreciating the benefits they received, but lamenting costs such as victimization and reduced educational and employment opportunities (Decker & Van Winkle, 1996; Hagedorn, 1998, Miller, 2001). Desistance has been relatively under-examined in the gang literature, however, and "gang myths" abound. It is commonly assumed, for example, that it is very difficult, if not impossible, for youths to leave gangs, that if they are able to do so, they must engage in some dire act such as crime commission or submit to a beating, and that there are negative consequences such as harm to self or family. The scant extant research reveals that gang membership is generally not forever. Although some individuals maintain involvement for extended periods or for life (Decker & Van Winkle, 1996; Hagedorn, 1998), gang membership is a transitory status for most. The peak age of gang-joining is 14 (e.g., Esbensen & Huizinga, 1993; Hill et al., 1999; Thornberry et al., 2003), and longitudinal self-report studies indicate that most (50%–69%) youths are gang-involved for just one year or less; about a quarter (22%–28%) are members for two years, and few remain in the gang longer than four years (Peterson et al., 2004; Thornberry et al., 2003). That youths do leave gangs, contrary to conventional wisdom (Klein & Maxson, 2006), allows research on why, how, and with what consequences they leave, uncovering the extent to which other gang myths are upheld.

Reasons for Leaving the Gang

Just as there are pushes and pulls into gangs, there are pushes and pulls out of gangs (Pyrooz & Decker, in press). While violence plays an important role within the gang, it may also serve as the impetus for leaving the gang. In a sample of adult ex-gang members in St. Louis, Missouri, two-thirds stated that threat of or actual violence to themselves or family was the key reason for them to make the move out of the gang (Decker & Lauritsen, 1996). Others left their gangs because they had moved or due to family reasons. In a younger (approximately 13 years old) sample of former gang members, violence was the second-most common reason for desistance (Peterson, in press). Asked to "circle all that apply," respondents reported leaving because a friend (30%) or family member (17%) had been hurt or killed or they themselves had been hurt (21%). The most common reason given by this sample was that they "just felt like it" (34%). This may represent either a push or a pull, but another response indicates some disillusionment with gang life: 19%

reported leaving because "it wasn't what I thought it would be." Parents or other authority figures also serve as both pushes and pulls; some youths desisted because they got in trouble with police (18%) or their parents made them leave (9%), while 22% left because an adult encouraged them to get out. Normal adolescent experiences are also at work: 15% moved to a new home or school, and 20% made new friends. This multitude of reasons is supported in other studies (e.g., Decker & Lauritsen, 1996; Harris, 1994; Pyrooz & Decker, in press).

Consequences for Leaving

While some former gang members report having been beaten out of their gangs or committed a crime, the majority of both females and males "just leave" (Decker & Lauritsen, 1996; Harris, 1994; Peterson, in press; Pyrooz & Decker, in press; Vigil, 1988). And, for most, their exits are without major consequences. In one recent study, for example, 55% of youths reported no consequences when they left their gangs (Peterson, in press). Ever-present in gang life, however, violence is associated with desistance for some. Approximately 15%–19% reported being beaten up by members of their former gangs or rival gangs, or having a friend hurt or killed. Between 9% and 13% said that family, friends, or themselves had been threatened or that a family member had been hurt or killed.

These findings point to at least three conclusions. First, youths do leave gangs. Second, many just decide that they do not want to continue and leave without consequences. Third, despite the more mundane experiences of most, violence and victimization associated with both gang membership and desistance means that we should not just "let nature take its course." Gang life poses additional risk for young people, and if knowledge about risk factors and desistance can be used to encourage youths to choose alternatives, some of these risks may be averted or alleviated.

School Responses

Research on gang joining, violence, and leaving can guide school personnel in developing appropriate responses to gangs in and around schools (see Table 10.1). It can also help them avoid responses that can either further alienate some youths (increasing their risk of gang involvement or continuation) or heighten gang loyalty and cohesion (potentially increasing delinquency and violence).

Strategies to Avoid

One method employed by U.S. school administrations to deal with violence, victimization, and other misbehavior on school grounds is zero tolerance (American Psychological Association [APA], 2008). This term refers to a loosely related group of policies and practices that mandate the use of predetermined consequences for student misbehavior, and the application of said consequences to all situations and students regardless of mitigating factors or extenuating circumstances (APA, 2008). Examples of zero tolerance in action include the expulsion of a 10-year-old girl whose mother had placed a knife in the student's lunchbox to cut an apple; locker checks, security guards, and metal detectors; and use of legal consequences for relatively minor delinquency, such as expelling and/or arresting students for fighting (APA, 2008). These policies became popular in the early 1990s as part of an approach to drug enforcement (APA, 2008; Verdugo, 2002), and the No Child Left Behind act created further incentives for schools to use them to exclude misbehaving students as a method to increase test scores and school safety (Payne, 2010).

School administrators argue that zero tolerance policies will deter students from disruptive behavior by removing students who cause trouble and reminding remaining students of

Table 10.1 Implications for Practice: Toward an Understanding of Youth Gang Involvement

1.	Avoid making assumptions about which students may be gang-involved based on sex or race/ethnicity. Research shows that gang members reflect the demographics of the general population.
2.	Take into account risk factors for gang joining and reasons for desistance when designing or adopting gang prevention and intervention services.
3.	Refrain from implementing policies that isolate and alienate students and instead focus on ways to encourage student bonding to school and involvement with pro-social peers.
4.	Beware of grouping gang members together and separate from the main student population, as group processes can increase isolation and cohesion of the group against authorities.
5.	Zero tolerance policies and practices are not the most effective way to increase school safety and are likely to diminish opportunities for students to form the bonds with prosocial peers and adults necessary for healthy adolescent development.
6.	To improve school climate and reduce bullying and victimization, schools can utilize strategies and programs known to be effective in addressing some of the multitude of risk factors faced by at-risk and gang youth.
7.	The internet, particularly social networking sites, can be a powerful tool for school administrators to learn about gang members and gangs in and around school and about gang violence and victimization among students.

the serious consequences of misbehavior (APA, 2008). This might therefore seem like an ideal approach to dealing with gang violence and victimization problems in school: expel gang members, and rates of violence and victimization will decrease, allowing remaining students to thrive in a safe and productive learning environment. This approach may also seem to be supported by research showing that gang presence at a school, school disorder, and lack of school commitment significantly increase students' risk for victimization and gang joining (Esbensen et al., 2010; Klein & Maxson, 2006; Schreck, Miller, & Gibson, 2003). Findings from research on zero tolerance, however, often contradict these claims, instead providing evidence of harm and unintended consequences (APA, 2008; Payne, 2010; Thompkins, 2000; Vigil, 2000). Punishment is widely inconsistent across schools, for example, particularly in respect to the disproportionate sanctioning of minority students; the performance and school bonding of remaining students does not improve; and, in many instances, such measures produce an increased culture of fear (APA, 2008; Schreck et al., 2003; Thompkins, 2000; Verdugo, 2002; Vigil, 2000).

Studies have also found that exclusionary discipline has negative consequences for students punished in this manner (APA, 2008; Payne, 2010). Research on adolescent development shows that adolescents' brains are not as developed as adults in the areas of decision making, risk assessment, and long-term planning (APA, 2008; Scott & Steinberg, 2008). Adolescents require strong bonds to prosocial adults and institutions to formulate decision making abilities that allow them to successfully function in society (APA, 2008). Excluding misbehaving students increases their alienation and feelings of rejection and decreases their chance of forming strong bonds to school or prosocial others. This can not only affect development (APA, 2008; Scott & Steinberg, 2008), but also close avenues for gang prevention and intervention (Peterson, in press; Thompkins, 2000).

Inclusionary Strategies

As opposed to using exclusionary measures such as zero tolerance, schools can increase at-risk or gang-involved youths' chances of avoiding or disengaging from gang life by integrating them into the school, rather than street, culture. In recognition of group processes, schools should avoid grouping such youths together in, for example, in-class group work or in-school suspension. Doing so can reinforce social isolation and cohesion of the group against authorities and/or provide an opportunity for gang rivalry to ignite. Further, the more unstructured environments in alternative or continuation schools may not be advantageous for youth who have received much of their socialization on the streets (Vigil, 2000). Therefore, schools should use interventions based on "respect and social expectations" (Vigil, 2000, p. 279) that recognize that at-risk or gang youths can contribute positively to the school environment if given the right opportunity. Gang members are often talented and personable young people coping with a multitude of risk factors through what appeared to their young minds to be a reasonable option: joining a gang. Providing an alternative may give them an avenue away from the gang. Vigil (2000) describes schools in gang-infested Los Angeles neighborhoods that have been successful in engaging gang members by identifying youths who appear to have leadership roles. Keeping in mind the cumulative disadvantage the youths have experienced and approaching them with respect, teachers gently encouraged the students to participate in class and gave them some responsibility for class activities. Similarly, administrators invited them to participate in school decision-making processes and/or student governing bodies. While such processes took time, eventually the targeted youths were more enmeshed in school culture and this effect fanned out: because those youths were respected within their gangs, some other gang members followed suit (see also, Klein, 1971).

Prevention and Intervention Programs

The extant literature also points to a continuum of prevention and intervention efforts to target different risk factors associated with gang membership. Specific to gang joining or activity, there are unfortunately few school-based programs that have been deemed "exemplary" or "effective" (see, e.g., the Office of Juvenile Justice and Delinquency Prevention's *Model Programs Guide*, 2010). One primary prevention program that may hold promise is G.R.E.A.T. (Gang Resistance Education and Training). Preliminary findings from an on-going evaluation indicate that G.R.E.A.T. improves students' skills in a variety of areas to help them better resist gang involvement (Peterson & Esbensen, this volume). Despite the lack of research evidence about gang-specific programs, there are other avenues by which schools can address many of the risk factors for gang joining and increase school performance and safety. Promising or effective early intervention programs such as the Perry Preschool Project (now High/Scope Curriculum; Parks, 2000), the Preventive Treatment Program for kindergartners (Tremblay, Masse, Pagani, & Vitaro, 1996), and Promoting Alternative Thinking Strategies (PATHS; Greenberg, Kusché, & Mihalic, 1998) for elementary school children can alleviate various community, family, and school risk factors to increase academic performance and decrease antisocial behavior, aggression/violence, and delinquency. In addition, programs that address school climate and student culture by focusing on a variety of school, individual, and peer risk factors have been found to improve perceptions about school and decrease bullying, fighting, and victimization; such programs include, but are not limited to, the Bullying Prevention Program (Olweus, Limber, & Mihalic, 1999), Responding in Peaceful and Positive Ways (RIPP; Meyer, Farrell, Northrup, Kung, & Plybon, 2000), and the School Transitional Environmental Program (STEP; Felner et al., 1993).

Monitoring the Internet

School personnel can also attempt to control gang violence and victimization by monitoring Internet postings of local gangs and gang members. By setting up accounts or profiles on MySpace and Facebook and being "friended" by gang youths, police personnel in cities from New York to Los Angeles have found that many gang members cannot refrain from bragging about their criminal exploits on such sites as Facebook, MySpace, and YouTube (Associated Press, 2006; Gavin, 2009a,b). Law enforcement considers any information posted on a social networking site as existing in the public domain, and "it has become a matter of routine (for police), to just automatically check (these websites)" (Friedman, 2010). MySpace has even formed an Anti-Gang Task Force, which includes law enforcement investigators and prosecutors, to examine gang members' use of MySpace, and the company has been extremely supportive of efforts to decrease gang involvement and violence (Ferrell, 2008).

School personnel can similarly use the Internet, particularly social networking sites, to gather information pertinent to school safety. By regularly monitoring postings to such sites, schools may learn which students might be gang-involved, whether there are problems between rival gangs that might spill over onto school grounds, and who might be responsible for recent crimes at the school. This would allow schools an opportunity to provide anti-gang services to at-risk or gang-involved students, possibly preventing campus violence and victimization.

Summary

Although they make up a small proportion of the student body, young gang members can pose a number of difficulties, including fear and victimization, within and around schools. The first step in addressing these problems is an understanding of gang myths and stereotypes, cumulative disadvantages faced by these youth, and the group processes that increase cohesion and crime. Schools can then use this knowledge adopt strategies and programs to decrease risk of gang-joining, increase opportunities for youths to leave their gangs, and improve overall school safety to create a more positive learning environment for all.

References

Anderson, E. (1999). *Code of the street: Decency, violence, and the moral life of the inner city.* New York, NY: Norton.

American Psychological Association Zero Tolerance Task Force. (2008). Are zero tolerance policies effective in the schools? An evidentiary review and recommendations. *American Psychologist, 63*(9), 852–862. doi: 10.1037/0003-066X.63.9.852

Associated Press. (2006, July 9). Gangs grow active online so the authorities home in. *New York Times.* Retrieved from http://www.nytimes.com/2006/07/09/us/09gangs.html?_r=1

Battin, S. R., Hill, K. G., Abbott, R. D., Catalano, R. F., & Hawkins, J. D. (1998). The contribution of gang membership to delinquency beyond delinquent friends. *Criminology, 36,* 93–115. doi: 10.1111/j.1745-9125.1998.tb01241.x

Bjerregaard, B., & Smith, C. (1993). Gender differences in gang participation, delinquency, and substance use. *Journal of Quantitative Criminology, 4,* 329–355. doi:10.1007/BF01064108

Blair, J. (1999, November 17). 13 on Staten Island accused in internet sales of illicit drugs. *New York Times.* Retrieved from http://www.nytimes.com/1999/11/17/nyregion/13-on-staten-island-accused-in-internet-sales-of-illicit-drugs.html

Decker, S. H. (1996). Collective and normative features of gang violence. *Justice Quarterly, 13,* 243–264. doi:10.1080/07418829600092931

Decker, S. H., & Lauritsen, J. L. (1996). Breaking the bonds of membership: Leaving the gang. In C. R. Huff (Ed.), *Gangs in America* (2nd ed., pp. 103–122). Thousand Oaks, CA: Sage.

Decker, S. H., & Van Winkle, B. (1996). *Life in the gang: Family, friends, and violence.* New York, NY: Cambridge University Press.

Dinkes, R., Kemp, J., Baum, K., & Snyder, T. D. (2009). *Indicators of school crime and safety, 2009.* Washington, DC: US Departments of Education and Justice.

Esbensen, F.-A., & Deschenes, E. P. (1998). A multisite examination of youth gang membership: Does gender matter? *Criminology, 36,* 799–828. doi:10.1111/j.1745-9125.1998.tb01266.x

Esbensen, F.-A., & Huizinga, D. (1993). Gangs, drugs, and delinquency in a survey of urban youth. *Criminology, 31,* 565–589. doi:10.1111/j.1745-9125.1993.tb01142.x

Esbensen, F.-A., Huizinga, D., & Weiher, A. (1993). Gang and non-gang youth: Differences in explanatory factors. *Journal of Contemporary Criminal Justice, 9*, 94–116. doi:10.1177/104398629300900203

Esbensen, F. A., & Peterson Lynskey, D. (2001). Young gang members in a school survey. In M. W. Klein, H.-J. Kerner, C. L. Maxson, & E. G. M. Weitekamp (Eds.), *The Eurogang paradox: Street gangs and youth groups in the U.S. and Europe* (pp. 93–114). Amsterdam, The Netherlands: Kluwer.

Esbensen, F.-A., Peterson, D., Taylor, T. J., & Freng, A. (2010). *Youth violence: Sex and race differences in offending, victimization, and gang membership.* Philadelphia, PA: Temple University Press.

Esbensen, F.-A., & Winfree, L.T., Jr. (1998). Race and gender differences between gang and nongang youths: Results from a multisite survey. *Justice Quarterly, 15*, 505–526. doi:10.1080/07418829800093861

Felner, R. D., Brand, S., Adan, A. M, Mulhall, P. F., Flowers, N., Sartain, B., & DuBois, D. L. (1993). Restructuring the ecology of the school as an approach to prevention during school transitions: Longitudinal follow-ups and extensions of the School Transitional Environment Project. *Prevention in Human Services, 10*, 103–136.

Ferrell, B. (2008). Gangs and the internet. *United States Attorneys Bulletin. 56*, 30–32.

Friedman, D. (2010, March 27). The latest tool in Greenwich police's toolbelt: Social media. *Albany Times Union.* Retrieved from http://www.timesunion.com/default/article/The-latest-tool-in-Greenwich-police-s-toolbelt-425162.php

Gatti, U., Tremblay, R. E., Vitaro, F., & McDuff, P. (2005). Youth gangs, delinquency, and drug use: A test of the selection, facilitation, and enhancement hypotheses. *Journal of Child Psychology and Psychiatry, 46*, 1178–1190. doi:10.1111/j.1469-7610.2005.00423.x

Gavin, R. (2009a, September 23). They paid homage to guns, gangs. *Albany Times Union.* Retrieved from http://www.timesunion.com/default/article/They-paid-homage-to-guns-gangs-554420.php

Gavin, R. (2009b, October 30). South End gang busted. *Albany Times Union.* Retrieved from http://www.timesunion.com/default/article/South-End-gang-busted-559549.php

Gordon, R. A., Lahey, B. B., Kawai, E., Loeber, R., Stouthamer-Loeber, M., & Farrington, D. P. (2004). Anti-social behavior and youth gang membership: Selection and socialization. *Criminology 42*, 55–87. doi:10.1111/j.1745-9125.2004.tb00513.x

Gottfredson, G. D., & Gottfredson, D. C. (2001). *Gang problems and gang programs in a national sample of schools.* Ellicott City, MD: Gottfredson Associates.

Greenberg, M. T., Kusché, C. A., & Mihalic, S. F. (1998). *Blueprints for violence prevention, book 10: Promoting Alternative Thinking Strategies.* Boulder, CO: Center for the Study and Prevention of Violence.

Hagedorn, J. M. (1998). *People and folks: Gangs, crime, and the underclass in a rustbelt city* (2nd ed.). Chicago, IL: Lakeview Press.

Harris, M. G. (1994). Cholas, Mexican-American girls, and gangs. *Sex Roles, 30*, 289–301. doi:10.1007/BF01420995

Hill, K. G., Howell, J. C., Hawkins, J. D., & Battin-Pearson, B. (1999). Childhood risk factors for adolescent gang membership: Results from the Seattle Social Development Project. *Journal of Research in Crime and Delinquency, 36*, 300–322. doi:10.1177/0022427899036003003

Howell, J. C. (2008). *Preventing and reducing juvenile delinquency* (2nd ed.). Thousand Oaks, CA: Sage.

Hughes, L. A., & Short, J. F., Jr. (2005). Disputes involving youth street gang members: Micro-social contexts. *Criminology, 43*, 43-76. doi:10.1111/j.0011-1348.2005.00002.x

Huizinga, D. (1997, February). *Gangs and the volume of crime.* Paper presented at the Annual Meeting of the Western Society of Criminology. Honolulu, HI.

Klein, M. W. (1971). *Street gangs and street workers.* Englewood Cliffs, NJ: Prentice-Hall.

Klein, M. W. (1995). *The American street gang: Its nature, prevalence, and control.* New York, NY: Oxford University Press.

Klein, M. W., & Maxson, C. L. (2006). *Street gang patterns and policies.* New York, NY: Oxford University Press.

Maxson, C. L., Whitlock, M. L., & Klein, M. W. (1998). Vulnerability to street gang membership: Implications for practice. *Social Service Review* (March), 70–91. doi:10.1086/515746

Meyer, A. L., Farrell, A. D., Northrup, W. B., Kung, E. M., & Plybon, L. (2000). *Promoting nonviolence in early adolescence: Responding in Peaceful and Positive ways.* New York, NY: Kluwer Academic/Plenum.

Miller, J. (2001). *One of the guys: Girls, gangs and gender.* New York, NY: Oxford University Press.

National Youth Gang Center (2007). *National Youth Gang Survey Analysis.* Retrieved from http://www.iir.com/nygc/nygsa/

Office of Juvenile Justice and Delinquency Prevention. (2010). *Model Programs Guide.* Retrieved from http://www.ojjdp.gov/mpg/Default.aspx

Olweus, D., Limber, S., & Mihalic, S. (1999). *Blueprints for violence prevention, book 9: Bullying Prevention Program.* Boulder, CO: Center for the Study and Prevention of Violence.

Papachristos, A. V. (2009). Murder by structure: Dominance relations and the social structure of gang homicide. *American Journal of Sociology, 115*, 74–128. doi:10.1086/597791

Parks, G. (2000). The High/Scope Perry Preschool Project. *Juvenile Justice Bulletin.* Washington, DC: U.S. Department of Justice, Office of Juvenile Justice and Delinquency Prevention.

Payne, A. A. (2010, September/October). Crime and education: Moving school discipline from exclusion and criminal justice to restoration and social justice. *The Criminologist, 35*(5), 1–4.

Peterson, D. (in press). Girlfriends, gun-holders, and ghetto-rats? Moving beyond narrow views of girls in gangs. In S. Miller, L. D. Leve, & P. K. Kerig (Eds.), *Delinquent girls: Contexts, relationships, and adaptation*. New York, NY: Springer.

Peterson, D., Miller, J., & Esbensen, F.-A. (2001). The impact of sex composition on gangs and gang member delinquency. *Criminology, 39*(2), 411–440. doi:10.1111/j.1745-9125.2001.tb00928.x

Peterson, D., Taylor, T. J., & Esbensen, F.-A. (2004). Gang membership and violent victimization. *Justice Quarterly, 21*(4), 793–815. doi:10.1080/07418820400095991

Pyrooz, D. C., & Decker, S. H. (2011). Motives and methods for leaving the gang: Understanding the process of gang desistance. *Journal of Criminal Justice*. doi:10.1016/j.jcrimjus.2011.07.001.

Scott, E. S., & Steinberg, L. (2008). *Rethinking juvenile justice*. Cambridge, MA: Harvard University Press.

Short, J. F., & Strodtbeck, F. L. (1963). The response of gang leaders to status threats: An observation on group process and delinquent behavior. *American Journal of Sociology, 68*(5), 571–579. doi:10.1086/223429

Schreck, C. J., Miller J. M., & Gibson C. L. (2003). Trouble in the school yard: A study of the risk factors of victimization at school. *Crime & Delinquency, 49*(3), 460–484. doi:10.1177/0011128703049003006

Thompkins, D. E. (2000). School violence: Gangs and a culture of fear. *Annals of the American Academy of Political and Social Science, 567*, 54–71. doi:10.1177/0002716200567001005

Thornberry, T. P., Krohn, M. D., Lizotte, A. J., Smith, C. A., & Tobin, K. (2003). *Gangs and delinquency in developmental perspective*. New York, NY: Cambridge University Press.

Tremblay, R. E., Masse, L., Pagani, L., & Vitaro, F. (1996). From childhood physical aggression to adolescent maladjustment: The Montreal Prevention Experiment. In R. D. Peters & R. J. McMahon (Eds.), *Preventing childhood disorders, substance abuse, and delinquency* (pp. 268–298). Thousand Oaks, CA: Sage.

Van Hellemont, E. (2010, June). *Gangland online: Living in the real imaginary world of gangstas and ghettos in Brussels*. Presented at the 10th workshop of the Eurogang Research Program, Neustadt an der Weinstrasse, Germany.

Verdugo, R. R. (2002). Race-ethnicity, social class, and zero-tolerance policies: The cultural and structural wars. *Education and Urban Society, 35*, 50–75.

Vigil, J. D. (1988). *Barrio gangs: Street life and identity in Southern California*. Austin: University of Texas Press.

Vigil, J. D. (2000). Streets and schools. *Harvard Educational Review, 69*, 270–288.

11

Juvenile Delinquency in Cyprus
The Role of Gender, Ethnicity, and Family Status

Ernestina Sismani Papacosta

THE MINISTRY OF EDUCATION AND CULTURE, CYPRUS

Abstract

This chapter provides an overview of the phenomenon of female juvenile delinquency in the secondary school system in Cyprus together with recommendations for effective preventive school-based interventions. A contextual–developmental model, emphasizing the importance of the dynamic environment, is used as a conceptual framework to facilitate understanding of the complex phenomenon of school violence, and in particular the role of gender, ethnicity and family status. Research from the International Self-Reported Delinquency Study–2 (ISRD-II: European Project in the context of Daphne) is discussed to examine the extent of the phenomenon of female delinquency in secondary schools in Cyprus. A description of the implementation and evaluation of a preventive community program is provided, and recommendations for effective psycho–educational interventions within the secondary school are described.

The role of schools in the generation and prevention of delinquent behavior is of primary importance (Gottfredson & Hirschi, 1990; Wilkstrom, 2006), as they have the potential to influence delinquency and act as a control agent for child and adolescent behavior. School environments can provide adequate support and be structured in a way that facilitates learning and minimizes opportunities for antisocial behavior inside or even outside of schools (Farrington, 2003).

In this chapter delinquent behavior is defined as behavior committed by a minor (under the age of 18) that violates the penal code of the governing jurisdiction in which the act is committed (Bartollas, 2000). To conceptualize the origins of delinquency adequately, antisocial behavior that is outside the realm of the law and illegal acts that do not always result in prosecution (due to age of criminal responsibility or other reasons), is also considered delinquent behavior.

Variables Associated with Delinquent Behavior

The extent to which individuals exhibit this broad range of behaviors varies greatly. Most individuals might exhibit antisocial and delinquent behavior during their life to some extent or degree. Distinguishing between delinquent and non-delinquent students can be a very difficult task. Thus, any study that deals with the phenomenon of delinquency needs to take into account the severity as well as the frequency of delinquent activities in respect to the broader range of antisocial features. Numerous studies have indicated that individuals who exhibit frequent delinquent behavior tend to differ from other members of the general population in a number of ways (Farrington, 1996, 2000).

Traditionally, adolescence is a period of development that has been perceived as transitional, or as a time marking the end of childhood and the beginning of adulthood. Many psychological theories have suggested that personality and developmental milestones in the early years of the developing child are achieved either positively or negatively in stages, and ultimately comprise the personality and cognitive processes of the individual (Blos, 1979; Erickson, 1959). Since the 1970s, a number of theorists (Bronfenbrenner, 1979; Elder, 1998; Lerner, 1995) have proposed theoretical frameworks to explain development through the reciprocal relationship of the individual and the social contextual systems within which one functions. These frameworks suggest that individual and contextual variables be included in any research study. Developmental contextualism (Lerner, 1995) is a systems approach that perceives behavior from a bio–psychosocial perspective, taking into account influences from genetic predispositions, psychological traits, and social environments. This theory adopts a holistic view of a phenomenon and tries to explain its different parameters.

A separate but closely related theory is social constructivism, which emphasizes the importance of culture and context in understanding what occurs in society and constructing knowledge based on this understanding. It is closely associated with the work of Vygotksy (1963), Bandura (1972), Piaget (1973), and cognitive theory. According to this theory, knowledge is a human product, socially constructed and developed.

Gender

One of the earliest recognized factors correlated with adolescent delinquent behavior is gender. The greater male involvement in delinquency and violent crime is a universal phenomenon that applies across cultures (Agnew, 2001; Heimer, 2000). Girls usually exhibit less violent behavior, drug use, and delinquent behavior across cultures (Heirtmeyer & Hagan, 2003; Junger-Tas, Marshal, & Ribeaud, 2003). Official statistics (Snyder & Sickmund, 2006) show a clear imbalance in offending by young men and young women, with women accounting for a far smaller proportion of recorded offenses and more often being involved in less serious offenses.

Traditional theories of juvenile delinquency have been criticized for the fact that they have been male oriented and thus fail to explain the delinquent behavior of females (Chesney-Lind & Shelden, 1998; Smith & Paternoster, 1987). Early theories on delinquency and crime either failed to include females or theorized about them in a stereotypical way (Burman, Batchelor, & Brown, 2001). Therefore, it is often argued that existing theories on delinquency do not reflect the reality of female antisocial behavior and its different parameters (Daly & Chesney-Lind, 1988). Feminist researchers (e.g., Chesney-Lind, 1998; Daly, 1994) have criticized existing explanations of crime and delinquency as theories conceived by male criminologists to explain male criminality. They claim that these theories are then perceived as universal and general, ignoring the different realities and experiences that are unique and specific to gender. Historically, literature has tended to be either gender-specific (Chesney-Lind, 1998; Daly, 1994) or gender neutral (Agnew, 2001; Gottfredson & Hirschi, 1990), and therefore for many years failed to adequately describe the importance of gender differences in delinquency.

As a result, a number of criminological as well as sociological and psychological theories have tried to examine the role of gender in delinquency and provide explanations. One theory that examines the gender issue is Gottfredson and Hirschi's (1990) general theory of crime. The main concept of their theory, self-control, provides an explanation in relation to impulsivity and delinquent behavior. Girls have higher levels of self-control (due to parental discipline and different parental style), thus exhibit less antisocial behavior, and commit fewer crimes than boys commit. A power control theory (Hagan, Simpson, & Gillis, 1979) provides a sociological framework for explaining differences in delinquency rates between males and females. According to this theory, differences in parental styles towards male and female children result in differences in readiness among boys and girls to take chances, accept risks, and, finally, to behave in a delinquent way. Daughters are the objects of parental control, and ideological schemas mediate these differences in parental styles.

Recent studies (e.g., Heirtmeyer & Hagan, 2003) support evidence of power control theory in different cultures. Boys are encouraged and allowed to take risks and experience less parental monitoring than girls, which may lead to the gender gap in delinquency. One of the strongest predictors of persistent offending is low constraint/negative emotionality, which is measured by an inability to defer gratification and anger (Moffitt, Caspi, Rutter, & Silva, 2001). These authors consider low constraint/negative emotionality to be a personality construct similar to the concept of "self-control."

Ethnicity

The issue of ethnicity and delinquent behavior is a matter still under investigation. There is a large and sometimes prejudiced literature on the supposed racial differences in crime and offending. Literature can sometimes be prejudiced, ignoring other parameters and emphasizing solely racial differences as predictors of delinquent behavior and criminal involvement. There are substantial differences in the rates of crime among ethnic groups. These differences are exaggerated by biases in the social judicial system and societies in general. For example, studies of the American juvenile justice process suggest that ethnicity is associated with crime, with African Americans more likely to be recommended for formal processing than white offenders (Junger-Tas et al., 2003; Sampson & Lauritsen, 1997). In England and Wales, young Black males are five to six times more likely than Whites to be in prison (Graham & Bowling, 1995). In the Netherlands, both Moroccans and Antilleans are overrepresented in the crime statistics (Junger-Tas et al., 2003). In Australia, Aboriginals and Torres Strait islanders are overrepresented in the youth justice system (Acoca, 1999). In Canada, those who are native born, leave the country, and then return to Canada are admitted to prison eight times more frequently than are non-natives (Tonry, 1994). In both France and Germany, foreigners have higher rates of crime (Smith, 1995).

Although there is evidence for racial differences in rates of adolescent delinquent behavior, these differences have been hypothesized to be a function of community context rather than individual differences, per se (Shaw & Mckay, 1995). Contributing factors of these underlying differences might be living conditions, joblessness, family risk factors, or other risk factors together with prejudice and bias from society (Farrington, 2003). Recent literature has found consistent evidence that exposure to violence and victimization in the community, family and school is a consistent variable for aggressive, delinquent behavior (Farrington 2003; Herrera & McCloskey, 2001).

Family

The role of family as a protective factor in delinquency has also been explored. Research indicates that consistent parental support and care can act as a protective factor for delinquent and antisocial behavior of adolescents (Cohen, 1995; Duncan, 1996; Farrington, 2003).

Hirschi's (1969) social bonding theory described four elements that act as protective factors of delinquency: attachment to conventional others, commitment to conventional objectives, involvement in conventional activities, and belief in the acceptance of a conventional value system. Attachment to parents is one of the most important factors in social bonding theory (Farrington, 2003; Hirschi, 1969). Positive modeling of conflict resolution in the household is vital for teaching conflict resolution without violence and aggression in any setting (Bartollas, 2000).

Purpose and Importance of Study

There were two major parts of the study. The first part used an analysis of the second International Self-Reported Delinquency Study (ISRD-II) to examine: (a) the prevalence of delinquency in secondary schools in Cyprus using a contextual framework, with a specific focus on female delinquency; and (b) the relation of female delinquency to student ethnic background. The second part was a case study of an intervention program ("Communities that Care") that targeted at-risk female youths, based on the information obtained from the survey- ISRD-II data, in a secondary school in Cyprus. Impact evaluation was conducted at the end of the intervention program using questionnaires completed by teachers, students, and parents.

In Cyprus, media coverage suggests that delinquency in general, and school violence, in particular, is increasing dramatically. The school system is facing the challenge of dealing with the problem and providing adequate mechanisms for prevention and early interventions. It is not possible, however, to ascertain whether the increase is real or due to increased reportability and changes in recording practices by the police and school authorities. Little research has been conducted in Cyprus that identifies the motivating and contextual variables that influence antisocial, delinquent behavior for female offenders (Hadjivasilis, 2003; Kapardis, 1986; Nicolaides, 2003). However, some recent studies in Cyprus regarding bullying (Georgiou, 2008, 2009; Georgiou & Stavrinides, 2008; Kokkinos & Panayiotou, 2004; Kyriakides, Kalogirou, & Lindsay, 2006) support the role of context (school and family) in the development of violent behavior.

These few existing studies refer mainly to male adolescent delinquent behavior; therefore, female delinquency is an understudied area. There is also a significant lack of research in Cyprus conducted in the school system, and thus, a consequent lack of adequate research-based intervention programs (preventive or therapeutic in nature) within the schools.

Second International Self-Reported Delinquency Study (ISRD-II)

The first International Study on self-reported delinquency was undertaken in 10 European countries and the United States (Junger-Tas et al., 2003). The study was launched in 1990 and included a sample of 10,371 youths between the ages of 14 to 21. The organization of the second ISRD study was considerably tightened, and the study has been undertaken in 33 countries. Most of the countries involved were mainly European, but non–European Union member states were also included in this international study. In an attempt to merge the databases of all countries and compare the findings, a common core questionnaire was used and common sampling methods, survey administration, data cleaning, data entry, and data analysis were employed. The long-term objective is to develop databases that will be systematic and will provide comparative surveys. The design of these systematic studies will allow for comparisons among countries and thus offer possibilities for policy development and changes regarding youth antisocial behaviour worldwide. In Cyprus the ISRD-II was coordinated by the University of Cyprus, Department of Law, starting in 2006.

The study explored the role of gender, family status, and ethnicity in the development of delinquent behavior in secondary schools. A part of the survey was analyzed to explore the extent of the problem of delinquency, as well as female delinquent behavior in particular, in secondary schools in Cyprus. The survey was conducted in all major cities of the free areas of the Republic of Cyprus. Drawing on similar studies internationally, a self-reported delinquency questionnaire was used in a school survey to provide information regarding the extent and nature of the problem.

Population and Sampling

The ISRD-II study was carried out with a representative stratified sample of both male as well as female students in secondary schools in Cyprus. Schools from all major cities in Cyprus (Nicosia, Limasol, Larnaca, Pafos, & Famagusta) were included in the sample. The age of students in the sample was 13 to 15 (first, second, and third grade of secondary school). The reason for choosing this particular age-range has to do with compulsory education policy in Cyprus. Education is compulsory until 15 years of age, and most of the students with severe antisocial behavior (delinquents) leave the school system after that age.

A representative stratified sample of 2,500 students (oversampling 5%) was drawn for the survey. Mainly due to a small number of students being absent on the day the survey was administered at a particular school, the survey sample actually included was 2,360 (i.e., 94.3%). The final sample of 2,360 included 1,174 males (49.2%) and 1,186 females (49.7%).

Development of the ISRD-II

The standardized, self-report ISRD-II that was used for all countries was also used in Cyprus. The questionnaire was translated into Greek with the intention of staying as close as possible to the original (English) version of the instrument, although some degree of adaptation to Greek conditions was necessary. Minor adjustments to the phrasing of certain questions were made after pilot testing the questionnaire with 25 secondary school students. The Greek version included an additional question at the beginning of the questionnaire regarding the number of cars a family owns. The paper and pencil administered questionnaire was anonymous.

The questionnaire included a large number of questions on different aspects of the adolescent's life situation, attitudes, and thoughts. The analyses are based in part on responses on individual items, but also on a number of scales constructed by combining responses to different items. A negative life events scale was formed with the response alternative being dichotomous (no = 0, yes = 1). This 8-item scale includes questions about different negative life events that the students might have experienced, such as a close relative having died or suffered a serious illness, parental alcohol problems, or serious distress and conflict between parents (questionnaire battery number 22).

The 6-item, family bond scale, focuses on the quality of the student's relations with his or her parents (Cronbach's alpha = 0.62). To measure involvement with delinquent peers, the questionnaire also included 5 items examining the extent to which students have peers who have committed different types of offenses and delinquent acts (a dichotomous answer: no = 0, yes = 1; Cronbach's alpha = 0.74).

Another 5-item scale, focuses on adolescents' attitudes and opinions towards violence with statements such as "One needs to make use of force to be respected" and "Without violence everything would be much more boring" (Cronbach's alpha = 0.72). Finally, another 12-item scale is employed as a measure of self-control (battery no. 39) (Cronbach's alpha = 0.86).

"Communities that Care" Case Study

The second phase of this study included a case study of an intervention program that targeted at-risk females, based on the information obtained from the survey–ISRD-II data in a secondary school in Cyprus. Educators, parents, and students were involved in this intervention. The aim of the intervention was to prevent delinquency and antisocial behavior in the school by using the Communities that Care Planning System, first developed by professors J. David Hawkins and Richard M. Catalano of the University of Washington in Seattle. The intervention included providing basic theoretical information to parents and students about problematic behavior and by providing guidance and support through the promotion of healthy activities and good practice (Hawkins, Catalano, & Miller, 2000: Hawkins et al., 2008).

One municipality in Cyprus, in collaboration with Doves Olympic Movements, implemented a sport and education initiative as part of the Communities that Care intervention. In this context, children and youths were taught to set goals, increase problem-solving skills, increase creativity, identify social goals and develop healthy habits. Every day, more than 160 participants met after school hours to practice sports (basketball, football, volleyball, handball), to enjoy dance (Greek dances, salsa, tango), and to practice theater, music, and painting. During the weekends, participants practiced non-traditional sports and activities (e.g., skiing, rock-climbing, canoeing). The program also had an educational component that included emotional education and conflict management discussions during daily meetings between psychologists, counselors, parents, and adolescents, and weekend lectures from experts about issues that interest adolescents (e.g., sports and violence, eating disorders, road safety). Parent workshops were developed during the afternoons and different topics of interest were discussed and analyzed with the help of school psychologists and counselors.

Female students were referred to the program by the secondary school counselor. Communities that Care made it possible to identify those risk factors in the lives of local youths that were making them vulnerable to violence and antisocial behavior. The community worked in close collaboration with schools to identify those students at risk (based on the ISRD-II findings and focus groups) for developing delinquent behavior and provided the aforementioned support through systematic psychological counseling and through creative activities.

Findings

The analysis presented is based primarily on the results of the female respondents, as this was the focus of this study. The results of the epidemiological study are presented in a descriptive way in an attempt to understand the extent of the problem of female antisocial behaviour in the secondary school system in Cyprus and its diverse parameters.

Of the total 1,186 females in the sample, 308 (26%) were 12 years old, 392 (33%) were 13 years old, 409 (34.5%) were 14 years old, and 75 (6.3%) were 15 years old or older. All of the respondents were students of first, second, and third grade of the Gymnasium (secondary school). The great majority of them (90.4 %) were of Cypriot Nationality and only 9.6% were of a different ethnic background. Most of the students (90.2 %) lived in intact families, while the other 10% lived in single families or with others (relatives, foster families, institutions).

Most of the students' fathers had permanent jobs (92.8%), and 71.9% of the students' mothers had permanent jobs. The great majority of students had their own rooms, a computer, and a mobile telephone; in addition, most reported that their family had its own car. More detailed demographic information about the sample is presented in Table 11.1.

Table 11.1 Demographic Characteristics of the Sample

	Frequency	Percentage (%)
Age		
12	308	26.0
13	392	33.1
14	409	34.5
15+	75	6.3
Place of birth		
Cyprus	1069	90.4
Other country	113	9.6
Language spoken at home		
Greek	1111	94.4
Other language	66	5.6
Mother's place of birth		
Cyprus	1003	85.9
Other country	165	14.1
Father's place of birth		
Cyprus	1049	89.9
Other country	118	10.1
Live with both parents		
Yes	1064	90.2
No	116	9.8
Discrimination		
Never	1100	93.2
Once	30	2.5
Sometimes	35	3.0
Often	15	1.3
Father's work status		
Permanent job	1088	92.8
Not a permanent job	84	7.2
Mother's work status		
Permanent job	844	71.9
Not a permanent job	72	6.1
Household	258	22.0
Child has own room		
Yes	879	74.2
No	305	25.8
Computer in the house		
Yes	1073	90.8
No	109	9.2
Child has own mobile		
Yes	1088	92.0
No	94	8.0
Family has a car		
Yes	1134	96.0
No	47	4.0

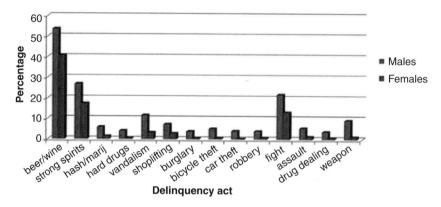

Figure 11.1   Delinquency by gender

Gender

Male adolescents were involved in delinquent behaviors more often than female adolescents. As shown in Figure 11.1, there is a significant difference between males and females in the frequencies of antisocial behaviors. An independent samples t-test was conducted to compare delinquency reported by males and delinquency reported by females. There was a significant difference between the scores of males and females regarding all classifications of delinquent behavior $t(2109) = 5.34$, $p < 0.001$, with males reporting significantly higher involvement in all delinquent behavior than females.

Ethnicity

A second purpose of the study was to explore ethnic differences in delinquent behaviour. As shown in Figure 11.2, female adolescents from different ethnic backgrounds reported significantly higher levels of delinquent behavior than Cypriot female adolescents. An independent

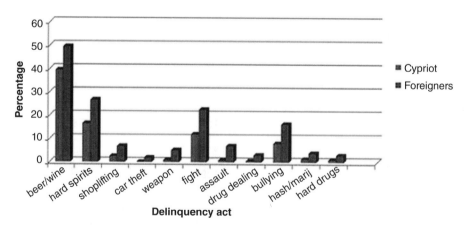

Figure 11.2   Delinquency among female Cypriot adolescents and foreigners

samples t–test confirmed that there were significant differences between the scores of foreigners and Cypriot females regarding classifications of delinquent behavior $t(1164) = 5.49$ $p < 0.01$, with Cypriots reporting less involvement in antisocial, delinquent acts.

Family

Females who lived with one parent or with others (relatives, foster families, and institutions) reported higher prevalence of delinquent behaviour than those who lived in intact families. More specifically, they reported higher frequency of alcohol use (83.7%) and drug use (13.3%) than female adolescents who lived with both parents (55.3% alcohol use and 1.6% drug use). Of the female respondents who lived with one parent or with others, 37.4% reported that they have engaged in some form of delinquent behavior. However, of the female adolescents who lived with both parents, only 7.3% reported being involved in delinquent acts. Female adolescents who lived with one parent or with others reported that they had been involved in shoplifting (10.5%), vandalism (9.4%), use of a weapon (5.0%), and assault (4%). Females from intact families reported that they had engaged in vandalism (2.8%), shoplifting (2.1%), use of a weapon (0.9%), and assault (1.1%). A statistically significant relationship was found between alcohol use, drug use, involvement in vandalism, shoplifting, burglary, bicycle theft, use of weapon and assault in relation to family structure $r(55) = .52$, $p < .01$.

An independent samples t-test was conducted to compare delinquency reported by females whose fathers had a permanent job and by females, whose fathers did not have a permanent job. There was significant difference $t(115) = 19.3$, $p < 0.01$ in classifications regarding burglary, car theft, and assault. Females whose fathers had a permanent job reported less involvement in delinquent acts. An independent samples t-test was also conducted to compare delinquency reported by females whose mothers had a permanent job and those whose mothers worked in the household. There was a significant difference between the scores of those whose mothers did not have a permanent job and those whose mothers worked in the household $t(324) = 2.92$, $p < 0.01$. Females whose mothers worked in household reported less involvement in delinquent acts than females whose mothers had a permanent job or no job. The results are depicted in Table 11.3.

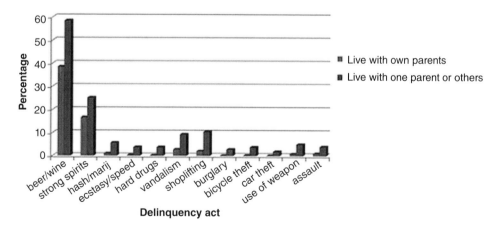

Figure 11.3   Delinquency and family structure

Communities that Care Evaluation

The impact evaluation of the program included educators, students, and parents. The evaluation data revealed that the program had positive effects on female students' behavior and achieved its anticipated targets. Students who participated in the Communities that Care program were less aggressive, more self confident, less anxious and more empathetic according to self-, parent, and educator reports. A paired sample t- test (pre- and post-data evaluation on the ISRD II) revealed significant differences in the overall delinquency index regarding females that participated in the program $t(55) = 5.45 \ p < 0.001$.

Students were satisfied with the content of the program and enjoyed its activities. They claimed that the program helped them become less aggressive and provided alternative healthy activities during afternoons. Parents of adolescents expressed the same opinion and claimed that the program was successful in keeping their youngsters away from trouble and interested in more healthy activities.

Critique and Implications of the Study

This study aimed to provide efficient suggestions and recommendations based on research findings on female delinquency for changes to be made in the traditional functioning and policy of the organization the Educational Psychological Services of the Ministry of Education and Culture and the school system in Cyprus. A strength of this research is its access to a very large data set ($N = 2,360$). The first stage of the study was an epidemiological research regarding delinquency. The questionnaire used was a valid instrument used in an International study (ISRD-II). In addition, the study provides a database for future comparisons between students from Cyprus as well as comparisons between students from Cyprus and students from different countries.

Limitations of the Study

Despite the large sample, there are limitations to the current study. Using self-reported adolescent delinquent behavior as the measure of delinquency is a limitation of this study. A few studies that examined differences between self-reported and observable adolescent behavior have reported differences (Elliot & Ageton, 1980; Farrington & Coid, 2003), suggesting that adolescents may forget, exaggerate, or under-report their behavior.

The use of a case study for the application of the program might also include some limitations. Case studies are not easily open to crosschecking and, therefore, they might be biased, selective, or subjective. It is thus not easy to understand whether the observed change was due to the program or to other parameters. In addition, there are no data to differentiate the most effective parts of the program.

In summary, the factors leading to participation in adolescent delinquent behavior are multifaceted. The problem of youth delinquency and school violence is a serious mental health problem. As shown in Table 11.2, interventions and preventive programs need to be developed and implemented in every school. These interventions must be coordinated and systematically evaluated by a committee of experts from different departments of the Ministry of Education and Culture and by other experts from different Ministries (e.g., Ministry of Health, Ministry of Labor). The research findings suggest that there is a problem with delinquent and antisocial behavior in the schools and that females are starting to engage in antisocial and violent behavior, especially school fighting and bullying. Although the problem of delinquency is less than in other European countries, Cyprus needs to develop the necessary prevention techniques and strategies to tackle the problem efficiently. Gendered specific interventions might have positive influence and targeted delinquent behavior most often displayed by females. The Ministry of

Table 11.2 Summary Table of Implications for Practice

1.	Delinquency among female adolescents is increasing and a policy regarding school violence and delinquency should be developed in the Ministry of Education and Culture.
2.	Research-based interventions should be incorporated into the school curriculum and constantly evaluated for their success in attaining their goals and objectives.
3.	Educators should have the necessary skills for early identification of at-risk students.
4.	At risk population (those older than 13 years old, students who live with one parent or with strangers, students from other countries who experience discrimination) should be included in preventive programs and provided support and help in developing their social skills and in managing their emotions and feelings.
5.	Programs should be implemented in schools that address racism and issues regarding acceptance of difference. These programs should become part of the academic curriculum.
6.	In the practice setting, educational psychologists can collaborate with professionals in planning, developing and implementing programs that strengthen protective factors and eliminate risk factors in the school setting.

Education and Culture needs to re-organize and re-structure its policy regarding preventive interventions and program implementations in the schools.

References

Acoca, L. (1999). Investing in girls. A 21st century strategy. *Juvenile Justice, 6*, 1–35.

Agnew, R. (2001). *Juvenile delinquency: Causes and control.* Los Angeles: Roxbury.

Bandura, A. (1972). *Aggression.* New York, NY: Prentice Hall.

Bartollas, C. (2000). *Juvenile delinquency* (5th ed.). Boston, MA: Allyn and Bacon.

Blos, P. (1979). *The adolescent passage.* New York, NY: International Universities Press.

Bronfenbrenner, U. (1979). *The ecology of human development.* Cambridge, MA: Harvard University Press.

Burman, M. J., Batchelor, S. A., & Brown, J. A. (2001). Researching girls and violence. *British Journal of Criminology, 41*, 443–459. doi: 10.1093/bjc/41.3.443

Chesney-Lind, M. (1998). Girls, violence and delinquency: Popular myths and persistent problems. In S. O. White (Ed.), *Handbook of youth and violence* (pp. 135–158). New York, NY: Plenum.

Chesney–Lind, M., & Shelden, R. G. (1998). *Girls delinquency and juvenile justice*: Belmont, CA: Wadsworth.

Cohen, A. K. (1995). *Delinquent boys: The culture of the gang.* New York, NY: Free Press.

Daly, K. (1994). *Gender, crime and punishment.* New Haven, CT: Yale University Press.

Daly, K., & Chesney-Lind, M. (1988). Feminism and criminology. *Justice Quarterly, 5,* 497–538. doi: 10.1080/07418828800089871

Duncan, D. F. (1996). Growing up under the gun. Children and adolescents coping with violent neighborhoods. *Journal of Primary Prevention, 16,* 343–356. doi:10.1007/BF02411740

Elder, G. H. (1998). The life course as developmental theory: *Child Development, 69,* 1–12. doi: 10.1111/j.1467-8624.1998.tb06128.x

Elliot, D. C., & Ageton, S. S. (1980). Reconciling race and class differences in self-reported and official estimates of delinquency. *American Sociological Review, 45,* 96–110. doi: 10.2307/2095245

Erickson, E. (1959). *Psychological issues.* New York, NY: International Universities Press.

Farrington, D. P. (1996). *Understanding and preventing youth crime: Social policy research.* New York, NY: Joseph Rowntree Foundation.

Farrington, D. P. (2000). Explaining and preventing crime: The globalization of knowledge. *The American Society of Criminology, 38*(1), 1–24. doi:10.1111/j.1745-9125.2000.tb00881.x

Farrington, D.P. (2003). Comparing delinquency careers in court records and self reports. *Criminology, 41*, 249–263. doi:10.1111/j.1745-9125.2003.tb01009.x

Farrington, D. P., & Coid, W. (2003). *Early prevention of adult antisocial behavior.* Cambridge, UK: Cambridge University Press. doi:10.1017/CB09780511489259

Georgiou, St. (2008). Bullying and victimization at school: The role of mothers. *British Journal of Educational Psychology, 78,* 109–125. doi: 10.1348/000709907X204363

Georgiou St. (2009). Parental style and child bullying and victimization experiences at school. *Social Psychology of Education, 11*, 213–227. doi:10.1007/511218-007-9048-5

Georgiou, St., & Stavrinides, P. (2008). Bullies, victims and bully-victims: Psycho-social profiles and attribution styles. *School Psychology International, 29*, 574–589. doi: 10.1177/0143034308099202

Gottfredson, M. R., & Hirschi, T. (1990). *A general theory of crime.* Stanford, CA: Stanford University Press.

Graham, J., & Bowling, B. (1995). *Young people and crime* (Home Office Research Study No. 45). London: Home Office Research Study.

Hadjivasilis, V. (2003). *Greek-Cypriot adolescents: Delinquency and psychological problems.* Limassol, Cyprus: Ten on Eleven Comp Services.

Hagan, J. Simpson, J. H., & Gillis, A. R. (1979). The sexual stratification of social control: A gender-based perspective on crime and delinquency. *British Journal of Sociology, 30*, 25–38. doi: 10.2307/589499

Hawkins, J. D., Brown, E. C., Oestrele, S., Arthur, M. W., Abot, R. D., & Catalano, R. F. (2008). Early effects of Communities that Care on targeted risks and initiation of delinquent behavior and substance use. *Journal of Adolescent Health, 43*, 15–22. doi: 10-1016/j.jadohealth.2008.01.22

Hawkins, J. D. Catalano, R. F., & Miller, J. L. (2000). Risk and protective factors for alcohol and other drug problems in early adulthood: Implications for substance abuse prevention. *Psychological Bulletin, 112*, 64–105. doi: 10.1037/0033-2909.112.1.64

Heimer, K. (2000). The nature of crime: Continuity and change. Changes in the gender gap in crime and women's economic marginalization. *Criminal Justice, 1*, 427–483. doi: 10.1007/s10940-008-9041-y

Heirtmeyer, W., & Hagan, J. (2003). *International handbook of violence research.* Dordrecht, The Netherlands: Kluwer Academic.

Herrera, V. P., & McCloskey, L. A. (2001). Gender differences in risk: Delinquency in children from violent homes. *Child Abuse and Neglect, 25*, 1037–1051. doi:10.1016/S0145-2134(01)00255-1

Hirschi, T. (1969). *Causes of delinquency.* Berkeley: University of California Press.

Junger-Tas, J., Marshal I., & Ribeaud, D. (2003). *Delinquency in an international perspective: The international self-reported delinquency study (ISRD).* New York, NY: Criminal Justice Press.

Kapardis, A. (1986). Juvenile delinquency and delinquents in Cyprus. *Cyprus Law Review, 4*, 2371–2379.

Kokkinos, C. M., & Panayiotou, G. (2004). Predicting bullying and victimization among young adolescents: Associations with disruptive behavior disorders. *Aggressive Behavior, 30*, 520–530.doi:10.1002/ab.20055 r 2004

Kyriakides, L., Kalogirou, C., & Lindsay, G. (2006). An analysis of the revised Olweus bully/victim questionnaire using the Rash measurement model. *British Journal of Educational Psychology, 76*, 781–780. doi: 10.1348/000709905X53499

Lerner, R. M. (1995). The place of learning within the human developmental system: A developmental contextual perspective. *Human Development, 38*, 361–366. doi:10.1159/000278342

Moffitt, T. E., Caspi, A., Rutter, M., & Silva, P. A. (2001). *Sex differences in antisocial behavior.* Cambridge, UK: Cambridge University Press.

Nicolaides, P. (2003). *Women, society and crime in Cyprus.* Unpublished doctoral dissertation, University of Cyprus-Nicosia.

Piaget, J. (1973). *To understand is to invent: The future of education.* New York, NY: Grossman.

Sampson, R. J., & Lauritsen, J. L. (1997). Racial and ethnic disparities in crime and criminal justice in the United States. In M. Tonry (Ed.), *Crime and Justice, 21* (pp. 311–374). Chicago, IL: University of Chicago Press. doi:10.1086/449253

Shaw, C. R., & McKay, H. D. (1995). *Juvenile delinquency and urban areas.* Chicago, IL: Univerity of Chicago Press.

Smith, D. J. (1995). Youth crime and conduct disorders: Trends patterns and causal explanations. In M. Rutter & D. J Smith (Eds.), *Psychosocial disorders in young people: Time trends and their causes* (pp. 389–489). Chichester, UK: Wiley.

Smith, A. D., & Paternoster, R. (1987). The gender gap in theories of deviance: Issues and evidence. *Journal of Research in Crime and Delinquency, 24*, 140–172. doi: 10.1177/0022427887024002004

Snyder, H. N., & Sickmund, M. (2006). *Juvenile offenders and victims: National report.* Washington, DC: U.S. Department of Justice, Office of Justice Programs, Office of Juvenile Justice and Delinquency Prevention.

Tonry, M. (1994). Racial disproportion in U.S prisons. *British Journal of Criminology, 34*, 97–105.

Vygotsky, L. S. (1963). *Thought and language.* Cambridge, UK: The MIT Press.

Wilkstrom, P. O. (2006). Linking individual, setting and acts of crime. Situational mechanisms and the explanation of crime. In P. O. Wilkstrom & R. J. Sampson (Eds.), *The explanation of crime: Contexts, mechanisms and development* (pp. 61–107). Cambridge, UK: Cambridge University Press.

12

A Synthetic Approach for the Study of Aggression and Violence in Greek Schools

Chryse Hatzichristou, Fotini Polychroni,
Philia Issari, and Theodora Yfanti

UNIVERSITY OF ATHENS, GREECE

Abstract

School violence has attracted a great deal of attention around the world leading to a significant increase in the number of empirical studies, as well as a variety of public responses, initiatives, and programs directed to tackle and prevent the problem of violence in schools. This chapter aims to contribute to the existing knowledge, both theoretically and empirically, concerning current definitional and conceptual issues arising in the international, European, and Greek literature on aspects of school violence. Following a concise review of relevant literature, this chapter presents results from four empirical studies conducted in the Greek educational context. The importance of the individual and system levels in the research on school violence and the implications for practice regarding the prevention of school violence in Greek schools are also discussed. The chapter also presents a synthetic framework proposed to be applied to Greek schools.

Drawing on the positive psychology perspective, the conceptual basis of the present chapter is the promotion of children's well-being and the holistic approach to assessment and intervention applied at an individual, system, and context level (Hatzichristou, Lykitsakou, Lampropoulou, & Dimitropoulou, 2010). Using a strength-based approach, for example incorporating prosocial variables along with antisocial variables, may be particularly helpful in the study of school violence.

Aggression, bullying, antisocial behavior and peer victimization are terms used to describe disruptive behaviors in school but, for the most part, they are not yet adequately defined. Generally, the two most commonly used terms in the English literature are bullying and school violence. In some publications, they are often used interchangeably, even though they are not conceptually or theoretically the same. There is a pressing need to either distinguish between what is school violence or bullying, or better explain the relationship between the two terms (Astor, Benbenishty, & Marachi, 2006). It is practically impossible to compare reports that use school violence as a generic term without providing the kinds of specific behaviors that are included under these terms.

Moreover, school violence could be a catch-all concept to refer to disorder and disruption in schools, as well as the unruliness of contemporary youth, juvenile delinquency, and other antisocial behaviors (Brown & Munn, 2008). School violence refers to a wide range of violent behaviors among students and between students and their teachers (Khoury-Kassabri, Astor, & Benbenishty, 2009) as well as students and school property (vandalism) (Ting, Sanders, & Smith, 2002). Forms of school violence are described through direct acts of violence (Ting et al., 2002), physical or verbal assaults, robbery, homicide (Brown & Munn, 2008), and harassment (Gumpel, 2008).

Aggression in school is another term used in the literature, and it is not clear if it is used as synonymous or similar with school violence. In addition to physical and overt forms of aggression, research has also recognized other forms such as relational aggression (Crick & Grotpeter, 1995; Kawabata, Crick, & Hamaguchi, 2010) and sexual aggression (Gumbel, 2008).

Regarding bullying, many researchers worldwide use Olweus' (1999) definition which uses three criteria for bullying (i.e., intentional harm, repetition, and power imbalance between the bully and the victim). Bullying can be verbal, physical, or relational. Despite the fact that the empirical differentiation between bullying, school violence and aggressive behavior is at times unclear, a large body of research has conceptualized bullying as a subset of general youth aggression (Ananiadou & Smith, 2002; Olweus, 1999; Smith, Cowie, Olafsson, & Liefooghe, 2002) or as a specific subset of school violence that could overlap with a wide array of school violence behaviors (sexual harassment, weapon use, school fights; Astor et al., 2006). In cross-cultural studies it appears that the term "bullying" is used mostly in European countries, whereas, the U.S. literature is focused on more dramatic forms of aggression, such as gang activity and violent assaults (Hilton, Angela-Cole, & Wakita, 2010).

Recently, research has also focused on cyberbullying. Many of the cyberbullying definitions are derived from definitions of traditional bullying. Each definition of cyberbullying contains some aggressive, hostile, or harmful act that is perpetrated by a bully through an unspecified type of electronic device (Tokunaga, 2010).

School Violence in Greece

School violence in Greece was initially examined within a legal context focusing on young offenders and juvenile delinquents. More recently, interest has shifted to the school context following a more sociological perspective (Artinopoulou, 2001; Beze, 1998). Overall, it seems that there are relatively few school violence incidents in the Greek schools, as compared to other European countries, and what violence there is, takes mainly the form of vandalism (e.g., school equipment), verbal attacks (insults, threats), peer conflicts, or social exclusion (Petropoulos & Papastylianou, 2001).

School violence has not been the focus of special interest among politicians and policy makers. In addition, media coverage of school violence incidents are sporadic and isolated. Greece's interest in school violence is related to the overall global concern and international interest on the subject, and a growing recognition of the problem within the context of the European Union and collaborative European initiatives (e.g., CONNECT, the European Observatory of Violence).

During the last 10 years in Greece, there has been a growing body of empirical research addressing behavior problems (internalizing and externalizing) as well as peer aggression and bullying. The majority of studies focus on bullying as a subtype of aggression and describe disruptions and problem behavior (Pateraki & Houndoumadi, 2001; Psalti & Konstantinou, 2007; Sapouna, 2008). An extensive study on bullying among Greek pupils showed that, overall, 15%

of students identify themselves as victims, 6% as bullies and 5% as bullies/victims (Pateraki & Houndoumadi, 2001). The most common forms of bullying were name calling and hitting and kicking. In a study involving secondary schools, it was found that more than 10% of male and female students have experienced some form of verbal bullying (Psalti & Konstantinou, 2007). In another extensive study in Greece, frequencies of antisocial behavior according to students and the perspectives of principals were really low, less than "rare" (2) on a Likert scale (Petropoulos, 2001).

Bullying as a term was first used in Scandinavian countries to describe certain aspects of aggression, however, different countries may be actually conceptualizing bullying in a number of different ways. Different definitions or methodological instruments used to study bullying make it complicated and difficult for multinational comparisons (Jimerson, Swearer, & Espelage, 2010; Kalliotis, 2000; Smith et al., 2002). Along these lines, Greece has participated in a number of cross-cultural studies regarding bullying or violence in schools (Akiba, LeTendre, Baker, & Goesling, 2002; Kalliotis, 2000; Rescorla et al., 2007; Smith et al., 2002).

Recent Studies Examining Aggression and Violence in Greek Schools

Four relevant recent studies conducted by the authors of this chapter, provide Greek data on different aspects of school violence in elementary and secondary school level. The studies used quantitative and qualitative methodology and different sources of data (teacher ratings, teachers' perceptions, and children self-ratings) to assess peer aggression, peer conflict, bullying and peer victimisation, and prosocial behavior as perceived at the individual level and at the contextual (class) level. The findings presented in this section are a synthesis of findings of relevant studies that investigated children's psychosocial adjustment, student engagement, and several aspects of school violence.

Study 1: Psychosocial and School Adjustments for Preschool and Elementary Children

The first study is part of a large scale research project funded by the European Union and the Greek Ministry of Education with the aim of developing and standardizing a Test for Psychosocial and School Adjustment for preschool and elementary school children (Hatzichristou, Polychroni, Besevegis, & Mylonas, 2008). The test assesses both strength and deficits, and is a teacher rating scale. It incorporates four main domains: social competence, emotional competence, school competence (strengths), and problem behavior (deficits) and includes 14 dimensions within these domains. Teachers rate children's behavior using a 5-point Likert scale ranging from 1 = never to 5 = always.

Using a stratified-quota sampling (age, gender, place of residence) data was collected for 432 kindergarten children, 189 (45%) girls and 231 (55%) boys, and 800 elementary school children, 393 girls (50%) and 400 boys (50%), rated by 97 preschool teachers and 184 elementary school teachers respectively. Table 12.1 presents the findings of psychosocial and school adjustment dimensions in terms of age and gender for elementary school students (Hatzichristou, Polychroni, & Mylonas, 2011). Regarding age, younger children (6–8 years old) received higher ratings in several psychosocial adjustment variables (e.g., school and social competence) indicating higher adjustment whilst their ratings were lower for externalising behavior problems such as aggression. The 8–10 year old age group had the highest scores in externalising behavior (e.g., aggression) and the 10–12 year old age group had the highest internalising scores (e.g., withdrawal, anxiety, fear etc). These age effects occur after controlling for teachers' demographic variables (e.g., teacher's experience) and teacher ratings of children's cognitive ability and academic performance. In terms of gender, girls scored higher in almost all dimensions of psychosocial

Table 12.1 Dimensions of Psychosocial Adjustment in Terms of Age and Gender for Elementary School Children

	Gender		Age group		
	Boys *M (SD)*	*Girls* *M (SD)*	*6 – 8* *M (SD)*	*8 – 10* *M (SD)*	*10 – 12* *M (SD)*
Subscales					
Social competency	95.7 (18.50)	96.6 (17.6)	97.7 (1.5)	95.4 (1.4)	95.4 (1.1)
School competence	97.0 (29.3)	103.9*** (29.8)	102.6 (30.1)	99.9 (28.5)	98.8* (30.22)
Emotional competence	85.1 (14.2)	89.3*** (15.4)	88.1 (14.5)	86.3 (14.89)	87.3***
Behavior problems[1]	89.1 (21.9)	98.4*** (21.6)	96.6 (21.5)	91.4 (22.4)	93.25*** (21.1)
Dimensions					
Interpersonal adjustment	20.1 (9.1)	15.8*** (9.1)	16.9 (8.3)	19.0 (9.5)	17. 9*** (9.3)
Intrapersonal adjustment	19.2 (6.3)	20.0 (6.6)	19.2 (6.7)	19.5 (6.1)	20.6*** (6.9)
Hyperactivity/attention problems	33.2 (11.9)	27.80*** (11.92)	29.27 (11.72)	32.0 (12.6)	30.2*** (11.5)

*** $p < .001$, ** $p < .05$, * $p < .01$
1. High scores on this dimension indicate more behavior problems.

adjustment. Boys had higher ratings for aggressive behavior (this finding was also repeated for preschool children) (Hatzichristou et al., in press). Results also showed that there was a higher proportion of boys than girls at risk of psychosocial difficulties both at preschool [$\chi^2(66) = 19,65$, $df = 1$, $p < .001$] and at elementary school [$\chi^2(131) = 7,34$, $df = 1$, $p < .01$]. Similar psychosocial and school adjustment profiles were observed for all age groups. Behavior problems (externalizing and interalizing) were rated higher than the strength-based psychosocial variables for the at-risk groups. Finally, a group of elementary school children with learning disabilities (N = 34) was rated higher on aggressive behavior as compared with a control group.

Study 2: Classroom Climate: Goals and Interpersonal Relationships

The second study examined individual and contextual variables related to social relationships in the classroom (both positive, i.e., support and negative, i.e., aggression). In particular, this study investigated goal orientation (personal goals) and students' perceptions of their classroom climate (classroom goals) including relational aspects such as student-teacher relationship, student-student relationship, peer conflict, and peer aggression (Polychroni, Hatzichristou, & Sideridis, 2011).

Participants were 1,493 fifth- and sixth-grade elementary school students, aged from 10 to 12 years, attending public schools in different areas of Greece. There were 721 (48% of the sample) boys and 762 girls (52% of the sample). Students completed questionnaires measuring goal orientation and school climate (Doll et al., 2009; Sideridis, 2005) on a 4-point Likert scale ranging from 1 = never to 4 = almost always. Table 12.2 and Table 12.3 present frequencies for the Peer Aggression and Peer Conflict Scale of the ClassMaps Scale (Doll et al., 2009) as perceived in the classroom. In this study, the subscale "I Worry That," where students describe their worries about peer aggression, is seen as an index of peer bullying, indicating the degree to which students worry about peers' becoming aggressive towards them (Doll et al., 2009). The

Table 12.2 Frequencies of the Subscale "I Worry That" of the CMS

Peer Aggression	F (%)			
	Never	Sometimes	Often	Almost always
1. I worry that other kids will do mean things to me.	525 (48%)	274 (25%)	162 (15%)	133 (12%)
2. I worry that other kids will tell lies about me.	393 (36%)	370 (34%)	172 (16%)	156 (14%)
3. I worry that other kids will hurt me on purpose.	645 (59%)	198 (18%)	141 (13%)	104 (9%)
4. I worry that other kids will say mean things about me.	28.3 (39%)	23.4 (32%)	11.7 (16%)	9.3 (13%)
5. I worry that other kids will leave me out on purpose.	548 (50%)	281 (25%)	157 (14%)	157 (11%)
6. I worry that other kids will try to make my friends stop liking me.	570 (52%)	241 (22%)	152 (14%)	133 (12%)
7. I worry that other kids will make me do things I don't want to do.	607 (56%)	234 (21%)	141 (13%)	110 (10%)
8. I worry that other kids will take things away from me.	684 (62%)	210 (19%)	122 (11%)	84 (8%)

"Kids In This Class" subscale evaluates the presence of peer conflict within the classroom. As observed in Table 12.2, a very small percentage (ranging from 9% to 14%) "almost always" worried about any aggression of their peers in their class. Regarding types of aggression that they worried most about in the classroom, the most frequently reported were other kids telling lies (14% worried "almost always"), saying mean things (13% worried "almost always"), doing mean things (12% worried "almost always"). Next in terms of frequency came worries about social exclusion ("other kids will leave me out on purpose," 26%, and "other kids will try to make my friends stop liking me," 25%,). Children were least likely to worry about other kids taking things away from them (62% responded "never") and about other kids hurting them on purpose (59% responded "never").

Regarding peer conflict in the classroom, "teasing and calling names" was reported as the most frequently experienced type of peer conflict (34% of children responded "almost always"). Physical aggression such as hitting or pushing was reported next in frequency (22% responded "almost always"). There were no significant differences between boys and girls in terms of peer aggression and peer conflict.

Table 12.3 Frequencies of the Subscale "Kids in this Class" of the CMS

Peer Conflict	F (%)			
	Never	Sometimes	Often	Almost always
1. Kids in this class pick on or make fun of each other.	204 (19%)	497 (46%)	211 (19%)	176 (16%)
2. Kids in this class tease each other or call each other names.	69 (6%)	262 (24%)	385 (35%)	372 (34%)
3. Kids in this class hit or push each other.	203 (18%)	388 (35%)	269 (24%)	244 (22%)
4. Kids in this class say bad things about each other.	248 (22%)	445 (40%)	226 (20%)	184 (17%)

In terms of how personal and classroom goals affect peer aggression and peer conflict in the classroom, it was found that students' perceptions of classroom goals and students' personal goals are significant predictors of these variables (Polychroni et al., 2011). This finding suggests that the type of classroom motivational discourse creates an "aura" that partly explains the dynamic and complex sphere of classroom relationships. It was found that positive interactions with teachers, peer friendships, and management of conflicts that occur between classmates are being shaped by the goal context that defines the classroom and the school in general. More specifically, classrooms adopting performance goals thus placing emphasis on relative ability and social comparison in learning situations are related to school relationships such as peer conflict and aggression) and can lead to feelings of disengagement from school. On the other hand, a classroom based on the principles of mastery, where teachers use varied and meaningful tasks and provide opportunities for students to make choices, is linked to adaptive types of classroom relationships and reduced conflict and aggression.

Study 3: Student Engagement Among Junior High Students

The data of the third study (Hatzichristou & Polychroni, 2011) were part of a multi-country project of ISPA initiated by professors Shui-Fong Lam and Shane Jimerson (Lam et al., 2009; Lam et al., in press). The purpose of this international collaborative project was to investigate both the personal and contextual antecedents of student engagement in schools across different countries. This was a large-scale project that involved many variables and themes of investigation.

For Greece, the sample consisted of 844 high school students (N = 319 first graders, N = 275 second graders, N = 243 third graders). This included 416 boys (49%) and 418 girls (50%). Table 12.4 and Table 12.5 present the frequencies of students' reports on the survey for the variables "peer aggression" and "peer victimisation." These variables are part of the social-relatedness contextual factors that affect student engagement and also include relationships with teachers and parents. The subscales include behaviors such as physical aggression (hitting, fighting, destruc-

Table 12.4 Frequencies of the Subscale "Peer Aggression" of the Student Engagement Survey

Items	F(%)				
	Never	At least 3 times a month	At least once a month	At least once a week	At least once everyday
1. You excluded someone you didn't like from group activities.	623 (74%)	10 (12%)	54 (6%)	26 (3%)	34 (4%)
2. You started a fist fight or shoving match.	563 (67%)	148 (2%)	50 (6%)	31 (4%)	46 (5%)
3. You ignored someone or stopped talking to someone.	293 (35%)	259 (31%)	116 (14%)	92 (11%)	74 (9%)
4. You spread rumors about someone you didn't like.	638 (76%)	97 (12%)	40 (7%)	23 (4%)	38 (7%)
5. You hit someone.	531 (64%)	156 (19%)	57 (7%)	34 (4%)	56 (7%)
6. You insulted someone or made fun of someone.	348 (42%)	250 (30%)	78 (9%)	73 (9%)	79 (9%)
7. You damaged or destroyed someone's property.	747 (89%)	40 (5%)	26 (3%)	11 (1.3%)	14 (1.7%)

Table 12.5 Frequencies of the Subscale "Peer Victimisation" of the Student Engagement Survey

Items	F(%)				
	Never	At least 3 times a month	At least once a month	At least once a week	At least once everyday
1. Someone who didn't like you excluded you from group activities.	635 (76%)	106 (13%)	42 (5%)	27 (3%)	30 (4%)
2. Someone started a fist fight or shoving match with you.	553 (66%)	158 (19%)	65 (8%)	29 (3%)	35 (4%)
3. Someone ignored you or stop talking to you.	371 (45%)	266 (32%)	90 (11%)	50 (6%)	53 (6%)
4. Someone who didn't like you spread rumors about you.	422 (51%)	193 (23%)	98 (12%)	64 (8%)	57 (7%)
5. Someone who didn't like you hit you.	343 (42%)	252 (31%)	101 (12%)	72 (9%)	55 (7%)
6. Someone insulted you or made fun of you.	577 (77%)	100 (13%)	28 (4%)	19 (2%)	26 (3%)
7. Someone damaged or destroyed your property	647 (78%)	77 (9%)	43 (5%)	35 (4.2%)	31 (4%)

tion of property) and social exclusion (stop talking, insults). Students responded on a 5-point Likert scale ranging from 1 = never to 5 = at least once every day regarding to the occurrence of certain behaviors.

Results showed that the vast majority of students (12–15 years old) responded that they never used any type of aggression towards others (the highest frequency for "never" was 89% for damaging someone's property and the lowest frequency was 35% for ignoring someone or stopped talking to someone). On the other end of the distribution, just 2% of the students reported that they damaged or destroyed someone's property frequently (i.e., "at least once a week" and "at least once everyday") and percentages increased to 9% for ignoring someone and to 10% for insulting or making fun of someone.

In terms of peer victimisation behavior, the majority of the students responded that they never experienced any type of aggressive behavior. The highest frequency for "never" was 78% for someone damaging their property and the lowest frequency was 45% for someone reporting that they were hit. Frequent behaviors that students report being the victims of, are physical aggression (15%), rumors (15%), and being ignored (12%). However, ratings both for peer aggression and peer victimisation were rather low as compared with the results of other studies. There were gender differences in terms of peer aggression and peer victimisation. Girls reported using significantly more frequently aggressive behavior, while boys reported more frequent experiences as victims.

Study 4: Qualitative Study on Teachers' Perceptions

A pilot qualitative study was conducted to explore Greek educators' views and perceptions on school violence and aggression. This pilot study is part of an ongoing wider project on *Violence in Schools from a Narrative Perspective* (Issari, 2011). While the majority of studies have focused on the student population, it is also important to consider teachers' perspectives, given their role as primary stakeholders in education and the school context. The study employed focus-group interviews with primary and secondary school teachers working in the wider Athens metropolitan area. Focus groups capitalize on communication between research participants to generate data and are especially suited for exploring views and experiences regarding complex and versatile constructs (Strauss, 1987), such as violence in schools.

The data elicited from the focus group discussions was analyzed using a thematic content analysis (Braun & Clarke, 2006). Narratives generated from the participants showed that the terms "violence" and "aggression" were used for the most part interchangeably. A number of teachers, however, attempted to differentiate somewhat between the two terms. For instance violence was conceptualized as a more serious form of aggression, associated mainly with physical acts and intentionality to cause pain. The term "aggression" was used within the context of low severity physical acts and verbal attacks. The teachers focused on interpersonal forms of violence involving mainly the student-student dyad; there were a few examples regarding student-teacher aggressive incidents. Student-student encounters included mainly direct verbal attacks (e.g., insults, threats, teasing within the context of play and sports), rough and tumble play, peer conflicts, and physical fights. Many incidents discussed fit the term "microviolence" or "incivilities" (Debarbieux, Blayer, & Vidal, 2003), namely, relatively minor impoliteness, rudeness, infringement of rules, classroom and school order disruption, and so on. Victimization (e.g., name calling, social exclusion) of children with special needs was an important concern. Bullying was recognized as a particular form of violence but did not seem to be of special concern. Overall, participants emphasized the rarity of extreme incidents of violence, serious injuries, or fatal events in Greek schools (i.e., gang activities, violent assaults, robbery, homicide, etc.).

Finally, teachers' perspectives attributed school violence and aggression to a variety of issues including behavior related to childhood and adolescent aspects of development (e.g., forms of aggression within the context of play and sports, ways of impressing the peer group), dysfunctional ways of communication, contextual and structural factors such as family and school environment, problems of the educational system, school disciplinary practices, and lack of clear school policies regarding violence and aggression in schools.

Discussion of the Results of These Four Studies in Greek Schools

Overall, the empirical data suggest that a very small percentage of students either use aggressive behaviors towards their classmates or are the victims of aggressive behavior. In terms of types of behaviors, spreading rumors, social exclusion, making fun of someone, and hitting were the most frequently reported. Rather high frequencies were observed for certain behaviors within the classroom environment (e.g., teasing each other, name calling, and saying mean things). These results are probably related to children interpretations of the specific questionnaire items and the extent to which they consider these as negative and disturbing and/or inappropriate behaviors among peers. Moreover, our studies found age and gender differences in behavior problems and psychosocial competence that have to be taken into consideration when studying school violence and aggression.

An issue emerging in these studies, which is also supported in the relevant literature, has to do with difficulties in identifying and classifying specific behaviors as school violence or bullying. Methodological variations have to be taken into account. Different samples of individuals (young children vs. older children) are likely to define violence differently and the same individuals may use the term "teasing" to refer to different behaviors in different contexts. These issues have hampered the study of school aggression and anti-social behavior, and researchers have struggled to find testable research models across cultural contexts and methods. The overlap in the definitions of teasing is considerable. Almost all investigators agree that teasing involves aggression (Smith et al., 2002). For some scholars, teasing is a type of bullying, whereas others argue that teasing incorporates also more prosocial behaviors such as, humor or play, depending on the target's interpretations (Crozier & Dimmock, 1999). An ideal definition of teasing would account for how teasing can lead to both to antisocial and prosocial outcomes (Keltner, Capps, Kring, Young, & Heerey, 2001).

Teasing and name calling were the most experienced behaviors, according to children aged 12–17 and parents of children aged 5–11 and 12–17 in a recent survey carried out by the United Kingdom Department for Children, Schools, and Families (DCSF, 2010). An interesting finding that adds to the growing literature on the methodological issues arising from the study of school bullying is that while bullying is one of the main concerns of parents in relation to their children's safety, and of children in relation to their own safety, after prompting (i.e., when participants are directly asked about bullying behavior), the level of concern greatly increases among parents and more than doubles for children. In a study in the United States, the majority of students reported that they sometimes or always struggled with classmates teasing them or arguing with them, although reported rates of physical aggression were much lower (Doll, Zucker, & Brehm, 2004).

In terms of contextual variables, the results corroborate that the social and affective characteristics of classrooms may exert a significant influence on student relationships. This provides a strong basis for applying interventions for violence at the system level. Schools can provide a setting where students can become connected with caring, competent adults and develop effective peer relationships (Osher, Dwyer, & Jimerson, 2006).

The qualitative data generated from teachers' accounts raises definitional issues in relation to violence and aggression in schools. Participants related both common and different understandings regarding those conceptualizations. Teachers' narratives adopted mainly a systemic-contextual perspective in making meaning of violence, and the language used did not include legal or clinical terms. There seemed to be consensus, that violence and aggression incidents are of low intensity and severity in Greeks schools, and that extreme events and serious injuries are rare. In their view, this may somewhat reflect the image of youth violence in the wider community (e.g., gang activities and youth violent acts seem less common in Greece than in other countries). Along these lines, participants expressed concerns that things related to violence might be in the process of changing, in the Greek context due to multicultural and economic issues. It should be noted that the findings were part of broader research projects with the primary focus on psychosocial adjustment and not on school violence.

Towards a Synthetic Conceptual Framework of Aggression and Violence in Schools

The development of a synthetic conceptual framework regarding violence in schools could contribute to a deeper understanding of the issue in theory and research. We adopt an ecologic/systemic/contextual approach which takes into account views, experiences, and understandings of different stakeholders involved in education and the school context (e.g. students, teachers, school staff, family, community leaders, policy makers, and the wider community; Hatzichristou, Lampropoulou, & Lykitsakou, 2006). The proposed synthetic conceptual framework regarding aggression and/or violence in schools includes the following dimensions: (a) clarification of *definitional issues* and assessment of particular aspects of *antisocial* (i.e., peer aggression, peer conflict, bullying, peer victimization) and *prosocial* behaviors (i.e., social and emotional competence); (b) combined research methodology (qualitative and quantitative); (c) *different sources of data* (teachers, students, school administrators, parents); (d) *individual* (i.e., teacher, students), *system* (i.e., class-classroom climate-classroom goals, school), *context* (i.e., education, culture) levels;

(e) taking into consideration interpretations and meanings within and across context/culture towards a *global perspective*.

Moreover, drawing on the positive psychology perspective, the conceptual basis of our work includes the promotion of children's well-being and the holistic approach to assessment and intervention applied at an individual and system level (see Table 12.6) (Hatzichristou et al., 2010). Using a strength-based approach, for example incorporating prosocial, emotional skills, promoting competence at both individual and system levels, encourages contextual changes that contribute to schools functioning as psychologically healthy environments.

A safe and effective school framework aligns school safety, student support, and academic achievement at an individual, classroom, school, and, ideally, community level (Osher et al., 2006). Social skills and social competence training programs promoting prosocial behavior, as well as professional development for teachers and administrators, can contribute to supportive educational environments. A primary prevention Program for the Promotion of Mental Health and Learning (PPMHL) was conceptualized, implemented and evaluated in the Greek educational system (Hatzichristou et al., 2010). The program links current relevant theory and research with practice, adjusting to the needs of students in Greek educational setting aiming at the enhancement of children's social and emotional skills within a network of caring schools.

School violence is a complex and multifaceted construct that can take many forms and can be conceptualized as a continuum and varies both cross-nationally and cross-culturally. A classification based solely on diagnostic clinical criteria does not reflect this complexity. Our view is that there are not violent or nonviolent behaviors in school. What actually happens is a wide range of externalizing and internalizing behaviors that occur in a continuum and are expressed according to the school and cultural context. Along these lines, it is preferable to use the term "aggression" and/or "violence" in schools, avoiding the term "school violence," which gives *hypostasis* to the phenomenon in question.

Table 12. 6 Implications for Research and Practice Considering the Greek Context

Carefully consider definitional issues within the particular socio-cultural context.

Consider thinking aggression and/or violence in schools rather than using specific terms such as school violence.

Use a combination of research methodology (quantitative and qualitative) and different sources of data (teachers, students, schools administrators) at individual, system, context levels.

Take into consideration interpretations and meanings within and across context/culture towards a global perspective.

Clarify the contributions of age, gender, context, and culture.

Adopt a strength-based approach. Need to move away from negative terms to more positive ones such as safety at school, positive school climate, supportive school, etc.

Examine to what extent aggression and violence in school constitutes a problem in a particular context / country. Use of valid culture specific tools.

Research needs to take into consideration the perspectives of key stakeholders involved in education and the school context, including people from different cultural backgrounds (e.g., students, teachers, school staff, parents, policymakers, community leaders).

Implementation of evidence-based interventions that fit the individual, the school, and the cultural context, promoting prosocial behavior, social skills, social competence, and resilience.

References

Akiba, M., LeTendre, G. K., Baker, D. P., & Goesling, B. (2002). Student victimization: national and school system effects on school violence in 37 Nations. *American Educational Research Journal, 39,* 829–853. doi: 10.3102/00028312039004829

Ananiadou, K., & Smith, P. K. (2002). Legal requirements and nationally circulated materials against school bullying in European countries. *Criminology and Criminal Justice, 2,* 471– 491. doi: 10.1177/17488958020020040501

Artinopoulou, V. (2001). *Via sta sxoleia. Erevna kai politikes stin Europi* [Violence in schools. Research and policies in Europe]. Athens: Metaixmio.

Astor, R. A., Benbenishty, R., & Marachi, R. (2006). Making the case for an International perspective on school violence. In S. R. Jimerson & M. J. Furlong (Eds.), *Handbook of school violence and school safety. From research to practice* (pp. 103–121). Mahwah, NJ: Erlbaum.

Beze, L. (1998). *Via sto sxoleio I via tou sxoliou* [Violence in school or violence of school]. Athens: Ellinika Grammata.

Braun, V., & Clarke, V. (2006). Using thematic analysis in psychology. *Qualitative Research in Psychology, 3*(2), 77–101. doi: 10.1191/1478088706qp063oa

Brown, J., & Munn, P. (2008). 'School violence' as a social problem: Charting the rise of the problem and emerging specialist field. *International Studies in Sociology of Education, 18*(3-4), 217–228. doi: 10.1007/s00267-010-9435-0

Crick, N. R., & Grotpeter, J. K. (1995). Relational aggression, gender, and social-psychological adjustment. *Child Development, 66*(7), 10–22. doi: 10.1111/j.1467-8624.1995.tb00900.x

Crozier, W. R., & Dimmock, P. S. (1999). Name-calling and nicknames in a sample of primary school children. *British Journal of Educational Psychology, 69*(4), 505–516.

Department for Children, Schools & Families (DCSF). (2010). *Staying Safe Survey: Young people and parents' attitudes around accidents, bullying and safety.* London, UK: Synovate (UK) Ltd, Research Report.

Debarbieux, E., Blayer, C., & Vidal D. (2003). Tackling violence in schools: A report from France. In P. K. Smith (Ed.), *Violence in schools: The response in Europe* (pp. 17–32). London: Routledge Falmer.

Doll, B., Zucker, S., & Brehm, K. (2004). *Resilient classrooms, Creating healthy environments for learning.* New York: Guilford.

Doll, B., Kurien, S., Leclair, C., Spies, R., Champion, A., & Osborn, A. (2009). The ClassMaps Survey. A framework for promoting positive classroom environments. In R. Gilman, E. S. Huebner, & M. J. Furlong (Eds.), *Handbook of positive classroom in the schools* (pp. 213–227). New York: Routledge.

Gumpel, T. P. (2008). Behavioral disorders in the school participant roles and sub-roles in three types of school violence. *Journal of Emotional and Behavioral Disorders, 16*(3), 145–162. doi: 10.1177/1063426607310846

Hatzichristou, C., Lykitsakou, K., Lampropoulou, A., & Dimitropoulou, P. (2010). Promoting the well-being of school communities: A systemic approach. In B. Doll, W. Phohl, & J. Yoon (Eds.), *Handbook of prevention science* (pp. 255–274). New York: Routledge.

Hatzichristou, C., Polychroni, F., & Mylonas, K. (in press). Investigation of developmental characteristics of school and psychosocial adjustment of preschool and elementary school children [in Greek]. *Journal of the Hellenic Psychological Society.*

Hatzichristou, C., Polychroni, F., Besevegis, E., & Mylonas, K. (2008). *Test of psychosocial adjustment for preschool and elementary school students* [in Greek]. Athens: Ministry of Education, OP Project.

Hatzichristou, C., Lampropoulou, A., & Lykitsakou, K. (2006). Adressing cultural factors in development of system interventions. *Journal of Applied School Psychology, 22,* 103–126. doi: 10.1300/J370v22n02_06

Hatzichristou, C., & Polychroni, F. (2011). *Exploring student engagement in Greek schools: A collaborative international study yields further insights.* Manuscript submitted for publication.

Hilton, J. M., Angela-Cole, L., & Wakita, J. (2010). A cross-cultural comparison of factors associated with school bullying in Japan and the United States. *The Family Journal, 18*(4), 413–422. doi: 10.1177/1066480710372919

Issari, P. (2011). *Violence in schools: A narrative perspective.* Manuscript in preparation.

Jimerson, S. R., Swearer, S. M., & Espelage, D. L. (2010). International scholarship advances science and practice addressing bullying in schools. In S. R. Jimerson, S. M. Swearer, & D. L. Espelage (Eds.), *The handbook of bullying in schools: An international perspective* (pp. 1–7). New York: Routledge.

Kalliotis, P. (2000). Bullying as a special case of aggression : Procedures for cross-cultural assessment. *School Psychology International, 21,* 47–64. doi: 10.1177/0143034300211004

Kawabata, Y., Crick, N. R., & Hamaguchi, Y. (2010). The role of culture in relational aggression: Associations with social-psychological adjustment problems in Japanese and US school-aged children. *International Journal of Behavioral Development, 34*(4), 354–362. doi: 10.1177/0165025409339151

Keltner, D., Capps, L., Kring, A. M., Young, R. C., & Heerey, E. A. (2001). Just teasing: A conceptual analysis and empirical review. *Psychological Bulletin, 127*(2), 229–248. doi: 10.1037//0033-2909.127.2.229

Khoury-Kassabri M., Astor Ron A., & Benbenishty R. (2009). Middle Eastern adolescents' perpetration of school violence against peers and teachers: A cross-cultural and ecological analysis. *Journal of Interpersonal Violence, 24*(1), 159–182. doi: 10.1177/0886260508315777

Lam, S.-f., Jimerson, S., Basnett, J., Cefai, C., Duck, R., Farrell, P. ... Zollneritsch, J. (2009 July). *Exploring Student Engagement in Schools Internationally: A Collaborative International Study Yields Further Insights.* A symposium at the 31st Annual International School Psychology Association Colloquium, Malta.

Lam, S.-f., Jimerson, S., Kikas, E., Cefai, C., Veiga, F. H., Nelson, B., ... Zollneritsch, J. (in press). Do girls and boys perceive themselves as equally engaged in school? The results of an international study from 12 countries. *Journal of School Psychology.*

Olweus, D. (1999). Sweden. In P. K. Smith, Y. Morita, J. Junger-Tas, D. Olweus, R. Catalano, & P. Slee (Eds.), *The nature of school bullying: A cross-national perspective* (pp. 7–27). London: Routledge.

Osher D., Dwyer K., & Jimerson, S. R. (2006). Safe, supportive & effective schools: Promoting school success to reduce school violence. In S. R. Jimerson & M. J. Furlong (Eds.), *Handbook of school violence and school safety. From research to practice* (pp. 51–73) Mahwah, NJ: Erlbaum.

Pateraki, L., & Houndoumadi, H. (2001). Bullying among primary school children in Athens, Greece. *Educational Psychology, 21*(2), 167–175. doi: 10.1080/01443410020043869

Petropoulos, N. (2001). Via kai diamartyria sta sxoleia tis protovathmias kai deuterovathmias ekpaideusis [Violence and protests in primary and secondary education]. In N. Petropoulos & A. Papastylianou (Eds.), *Proklisis sti sxoliki koinotita, erevna kai paremvasi* [Challenges to the school community, research and intervention] (pp. 31–74). Athens: Hellenic Pedagogical Institute.

Petropoulos, N., & Papastylianou, A. (2001). *Morfes epithetikotitas, vias kai diamartyrias sto sxoleio* [Types of aggression, violence and protest in school]. Athens: Hellenic Pedagogical Institute.

Polychroni, F., Hatzichristou, C., & Sideridis, G. (2011). The role of goal orientations and goal structures in explaining classroom social and affective characteristics. Manuscript submitted for publication.

Psalti, A., & Konstantinou, K. (2007). To phenomeno tou ekfovismou sta sxoleia tis deuterovathmias ekpaideusis. I epidrasi tou fylou kai tis ethnopolitismikis ekpaideusis. [Bullying in secondary schools. The effect of gender and culture]. *Journal of the Hellenic Psychological Society, 14*(4), 329–345.

Rescorla, L., Achenbach, T., Ginzburg, S., Ivanova, M., Dumenci, L., Almqvist, F., & Bathiche, M. (2007). Consistency of teacher-reported problems for students in 21 countries. *School Psychology Review, 36*(1), 91–110.

Sapouna, M. (2008). Bullying in Greek primary and secondary schools. *School Psychology International, 29*, 199–213. doi: 10.1177/0143034308090060

Sideridis, G. D. (2005). Goal orientations, academic achievement, and depression: Evidence in favor of revised goal theory. *Journal of Educational Psychology, 97*, 366–375.

Smith, P. K., Cowie, H., Olafsson, R. F., & Liefooghe, P. D. (2002). Definitions of bullying: A comparison of terms used, and age and gender differences, in a fourteen-country international comparison. *Child Development, 73*(4), 1119–1133. doi: 10.1111/1467-8624.00461

Strauss, A. (1987). *Qualitative research for social scientists.* Cambridge, UK: Cambridge University Press.

Ting, L., Sanders, S., & Smith, P. (2002). The teacher's reaction to school violence scale: Psychometric properties and scale development. *Educational and Psychological Measurement, 62*(6), 1006–1019. doi: 10.1177/0013164402238087

Tokunaga, R. S. (2010). Following you home from school: A critical review and synthesis of research on cyberbullying victimization. *Computers in Human Behavior, 26*, 277–287. doi:10.1016/j.chb.2009.11.014

13

Bullying in Perú
A Code of Silence?

César Merino Soto

UNIVERSIDAD DE SAN MARTIN DE PORRES, LIMA, PERÚ

Julio Carozzo Campos

THE OBSERVATORY ON VIOLENCE AND COEXISTENCE IN SCHOOLS, LIMA, PERÚ

Luis Benites Morales

UNIVERSIDAD DE SAN MARTIN DE PORRES, LIMA, PERÚ

Abstract

School violence in Perú consists of acts of confrontation that occur between students, and has been found to have three primary characteristics: (a) it is physical and psychological; (b) it is mostly perpetrated by males; and (c) it is typically committed by adolescent ages 11 to 16 years, not younger children. These three criteria in combination with prevailing Peruvian views of school violence have neglected the identification of hidden forms of school violence such as bullying. Given these conditions, bullying research in Perú is limited. Generally, antibullying prevention and intervention initiatives come from personal initiatives or private institutions without public sector participation. In addition, antibullying programs are located mostly in urban area of Lima. Among the works considered in this chapter are those of the Observatorio sobre la Violencia y Convivencia en la Escuela (OVCE) [Observatory on Violence and Coexistence in Schools] and other formal initiatives in Perú. It has been found that psychological bullying is more frequent than physical bullying in Peruvian schools and that harassment is present in all schools, without exception. Teachers were found to have an attitude of inaction on the issue of bullying, because they consider it normal behavior among students. Among the few interventions being used with bully victims is peer mediation. Thus far, a few private schools have implemented a comprehensive intervention protocol against bullying. It is concluded that the violence in the Peruvian schools is still unacknowledged and is affected by a code of silence.

Overview of the Peruvian Social Context

Cultural Diversity

In Perú there are different ethnic groups that mainly reside in regions outside the capital city and they comprise 17% of the Peruvian population (Mejía & Moncada, 2000). The migration of these rural people to the capital of Perú (Lima) has declined in recent years because of the promotion of decentralized social and economic development in the regions (Manrique, 2004). In rural Andean regions, the magnitude of poverty and inequality is much higher compared with the coastal region (Manrique, 2004), and the government has failed to effectively reduce the social justice needs sustainably. Due to recent economic growth and the increased availability of educational and social service resources in Lima, attention being given to bullying is more likely because of media influence. In this context, information on bullying research is beginning to emerge in Lima. Recently, empirical investigations of bullying in Lima have been published (Landázuri, 2007, Oliveros & Barrientos, 2007; Quintana, Montgomery, & Malaver, 2009). In addition, some data show its prevalence in regions outside Lima (Amemiya, Oliveros, & Barrientos, 2009; Oliveros et al., 2008). It is possible that the bullying prevalence reported in studies of European and American schools is not comparable to the prevalence of bullying in rural areas outside Lima. However, this is an issue not yet widely discussed between researchers and professional psychologists in Perú. Hence, this chapter summarizes initial investigations of the prevalence of bullying in Peruvian communities and factors that influence its occurrence.

Special Conditions in Perú

Since 1995, Perú has experienced the consequences of subversive violence. It has been hypothesized that this political subversive violence has an impact on bullying in school life (Centro de Desarrollo y Asesoría Psicosocial [CEDAPP], 1995), but research has not directly linked to these two phenomena, with the exception of one analysis (Universidad Nacional Mayor de San Marcos, 2009).

Bullying in the Peruvian News

In Perú, the impact of bullying is occasionally reported in the media (e.g., Noriega, 2010). There are also brief international references on the status of bullying in Perú (e.g., in Bolivia; *El Diario*, 2009), emphasizing information on the prevalence and superficial intervention suggestions. Furthermore, the need to understand how bullying occurs, the characteristics of its participants, and recommendations on how to prevent bullying, has recently attracted the interest of the Peruvian media (*El Comercio*, 2010). This interest in bullying has risen since the report of homicides and suicides related to bullying (Observatory on Violence and Coexistence in School and the Association Living in Peace, 2010).

Peruvian Bullying Research

Peruvian bullying studies have contributed to international Hispanic research (e.g., García, Paredes, Arenas, & Quintana, 2010), in national research meetings (Carozzo, 2008, 2009, 2010a; Landázuri, 2007, 2008), and in intramural events (e.g., Universidad Nacional Mayor de San Marcos, 2009). Publications about bullying have appeared in medical Peruvian journals (Amemiya et al., 2009; Oliveros & Barrientos, 2007; Oliveros et al., 2008) and in psychology journals

(García, 2008; Landázuri, 2007; Quintana, 2009). The primary foci of these presentations and empirical papers were, first, to report the prevalence and correlates of bullying in Lima and in other regions of the country, and to propose criteria for identifying the severity of bullying in a screening assessment in the context of a medical evaluation (e.g., Amemiya et al., 2009). These efforts provided preliminary descriptive and diagnostic information of bullying in Peru, not just centralized in Lima. Second, another contribution of this research has been to convey to the academic and nonacademic community the existence of bullying as a pattern of behavior that deserves serious academic and professional attention because it occurs frequently, and ignoring acts of bullying can lead to an increased frequency of bullying (Oliver & Barrientos, 2007, Oliveros et al., 2008).

Since 2005, professional and academic attention to bullying in Perú has increased, which provides the first quantitative data that can be (a) integrated in international comparative studies and (b) examined for correlates between bullying and other contextual and individual differences. However, the findings of these investigations require replication for generalization, concrete reports of quantitative results, and sensitivity to within-country cultural contexts that influence the strategies used by students to avoid or cope with bullying. Something that stands out in several Peruvian investigations is the term "law of silence" or "code of silence," which explains the results of prevalence studies in Lima and other Peruvian regions (Oliver & Barrientos, 2007; Oliveros et al., 2008). This code of silence is a way to hide or discount the acts seen or experienced by direct or indirect actors of bullying, and in this situation it involves all school participants, involved students, teachers, and principals.

This law of silence appears when survey participants show reluctance to disclose the true prevalence of bullying and its impacts on victims and bystanders (Landázuri, 2007). Finally, two influences on bullying could be the effects of the Peruvian government's war against terrorism, especially in families that migrated to Lima, and the effects of natural disasters on the violent behavior of children and adolescents; but it is clear this is a consequence of possible responses of post-traumatic stress.

In general, bullying research conducted to date in Perú has the following characteristics: (a) descriptive and epidemiological, and most of the studies were conducted in Lima; (b) poor conceptualization of the theoretical frameworks needed to generate explanatory hypotheses; (c) methodological approaches frequently use univariate instead of multivariate analyses; (d) construction and adaptation of instruments is questionable and not supported by appropriate practices from measurement theory; (e) no clear difference between frequent and sporadic bullying; and (f) moderating variables are not included in the design of these investigations.

Intervention Against Bullying

An evaluation of antibullying intervention efforts in Perú suggest that they are not completely supported by school personnel, even when their schools experience and report harassment. In Perú, bullying has not attracted public concern of teachers, principals, and other school staff, and this lack of concern inhibits the implementation of systematic intervention. This perception that ignores bullying in schools is reflected in the position of the Ministry of Education, which expressed in recent statements by the deputy minister that there are no specific antibullying strategies or programs being implemented in Perú (Noriega, 2010).

A recent approach to the understanding of bullying in Perú has emerged within a broader program to provide comprehensive care to victims of political violence. This approach was prepared by a public university (Oliveros et al., 2008; Universidad Nacional Mayor de San Marcos, 2009) and by a team of doctors and psychologists to research and intervene in communities outside of

Lima, which were affected by political terrorism. With the epidemiological data obtained in the studies, the team tried to link the occurrence of acts of bullying to the effects of terrorism, but they did not show direct evidence of this, and relevant covariate variables were not controlled (e.g., previous parenting practices, communication skills). Although the effects of subversive political violence on children have been confirmed (Rojas & Brondi, 1987), its connection to bullying is unclear. In addition, there were no reports on the specific strategies and outcomes of the psychological interventions attempted.

In summary, we conclude that, in Perú, intervention efforts in schools do not have government support to develop regulations, documents, or policies against bullying. Fieldwork experiences lead us to conclude that it is unlikely that schools have institutional plans on general intervention and prevention of bullying security practices. The bullying interventions being attempted are occasional individual school efforts, focused on solving immediate problems without a long-term plan that integrates all school staff. On the other hand, the apparent priority among bullying prevention professionals in Perú is to have publicly available school prevention plans that address male bullying (Landázuri, 2007; OVCE, 2010).

Importance of the Bullying Problem

We propose some essential criteria to characterize the importance of bullying in Perú. These criteria are discussed in the following section.

Varied Expressions of Bullying

It is fair to say that the occurrence of bullying is higher in urban areas and less in rural areas outside Lima, although there are no comparative studies in this regard. This observation emerges from reports made at psychology conferences and national academic forums held in 2008, 2009, and 2010. Sources for these observations come from public schools mainly in the cities of Huacho, Chimbote, Lima, and Trujillo (cities in the coastal region of Perú). As in other countries, it is reported that insults and name calling are the most common form of aggression (Benites & Carozzo, 2003). Another tendency is cyberbullying. Although specific research as yet to done on cyberbullying in Perú, it seems to be an increasing practice among high school students with less frequency among students ages 11 to 13 years. However, there is no reliable information about the prevalence of this new problem in Lima, and there are only a few reports on this issue (e.g., Carozzo, 2010c).

In addition, a recent report from public schools outside of Lima identified a bully who collected money from students just to let them enter the school toilet. This is an indication that a wide range of bullying behaviors are emerging in a context that has yet to develop preventive interventions in Peruvian schools.

Bullying Participation in Perú

The actors directly involved in bullying and witnesses are between 47% and 67% of the school population in elementary and high school, respectively (Amemiya et al., 2009; Oliveros & Barrientos, 2007; Oliveros et al., 2008), without establishing a distinction between offenders, victims, and witnesses. Some authors (Garcia, 2008) state that between 7% and 10% of students are bullies or victims, while others found a lower frequency rate in high school students (La Comisión Nacional para el Desarrollo y Vida sin Drogas [DEVIDA], 2007). In relation to gender, due to the nature and limitations of these studies, it has been only superficially examined, and the information is unclear.

Common Experience with Bullying

Many students have participated as actors or witnesses in bullying; therefore, it seems that bullying is a part of the common experience in most educational institutions in Perú. This observation suggests that bullying could be perceived as "natural" behavior at school and related to the impulsiveness of teenagers. Such an erroneous belief may explain how this problem is falls under the code of silence, which is characteristic of schools in Perú.

Generalized Impact of Bullying

School life is negatively affected by the presence and intensity of bullying at least in two aspects. First, at the *individual level* the experience of bullying in its various forms impacts the quality of student's life, and adversely alters learning and interpersonal and social relations (Cava, Musitu, & Murgui, 2007; Observatory on Violence and Coexistence in School, and the Association Living in Peace, 2010). Second, at the *institutional level* bullying (a) makes school an unsafe place that does not provide welfare to its members, (b) facilitates the insensitivity of teachers and assistants to violence, and (c) creates a culture of tolerance and passive participation (Monks et al., 2009). Moreover, it is known that there are long-term effects of bullying on the offender (Cava, Burlga, Musitu, & Murgui, 2010; OVCE, 2010), which means that offenders are prone to develop antisocial behaviors and to initiate early use of alcohol, cigarettes, and drugs. Victims of bullying are at increased risk to experience academic difficulties, unhappiness, school dropout, and suicide. The authors of this chapter also conducted extensive interviews with students who were bullied—who suffered severe and frequent acts of bullying, such as insults, beatings, forced request of objects and/or money, and threats of physical harm. In many of these cases, they report symptoms of anxiety, depression, and suicidal thoughts; they also show an intense desire to drop out of school. Currently, there are no published reports on the psychological impacts of bullying in Perú, but only a report published about its association with self-esteem (Landázuri, 2007). In this report, social and academic self-esteem (as measured with the Self-Esteem Inventory of Coopersmith, 1967) explains a significant amount of variance of the victim and bully roles among high school students.

Manifestation and Extreme Consequences of Bullying

The effects of bullying on social health and quality of life of victims, and the violence path of the bully perpetrator, are factors that could increase violence in institutional and cultural environments in which effective supports for students are not provided. Under these conditions, poor school climate would be a risk factor. Without making visible the problem of bullying, and breaking the code of silence, we could expect more severe levels of damage because of this situation.

Conceptual Basis for Prevention of Bullying in Perú

The Peruvian school curriculum emphasizes learning academic skills and promotes the knowledge of interpersonal values for the development of student wellbeing. However, it does not prioritize interpersonal relationship skills and good practices for civility and coexistence. Teachers are trained in university instruction with a wide didactic repertoire for teaching academic content, but not to teach content on good interpersonal relations that impact students' behavior. Therefore, changing the educational curriculum from kindergarten to high school level is essential to convey the knowledge and skills needed for positive living. It must be strongly associated with teacher training and supported by research.

The framework of using interpersonal relationships in school as a way to prevent, reduce, and minimize the effects of bullying allows considering prevention in a comprehensive, integrated schoolwide manner. However, individual differences provide a unique variance that cannot be ignored. This means that communication skills, management of anger expression, and stable attributes of personality and temperament may also be moderating factors in the strategies to promote positive interactions among students.

Communication and emotional expression are the main supports of the interpersonal relationships involved with school life. There are also beliefs and ideas in the school that can give rationality and justification for many events that occur in it. One of these situations seems to help define what happens with the invisibility of bullying, due to a common perception that it is natural and normal and which may partially explain the tolerance of the victim and witnesses (bystanders) that is observed in Perú. In analogy to Sartre (1943/1947), the school, parents, teachers, and even students themselves, repeat "hell is other people" (*el infierno son los otros*); i.e., it means that schools do not have any responsibility for the presence of bullying in the institution, and its causes are mainly the lack of control of parents, internal and subtle traits of the student, and family characteristics of moral and ethical behavior. It also reflects a common Peruvian cultural sentiment that one is either an aggressor or a victim, and that given the two options, it is better to be an aggressor. It is not enough to increase the awareness of bullying among school staff, it must be complemented by an awareness and education about the rights of individuals and how they should be protected and defended. An integrated bully intervention program that involves the entire school system is not frequently implemented in Perú. However, the limited intervention that does occur usually involves the administration of disciplinary measures, including harsh penalties such as expulsion from school.

We consider that the contributions of Bandura (1982) and his theory of social learning, attribution processes (Myers, 2000), psychological reactance (Brehm & Brehm, 1981), and locus of control (Rotter, 1966) as providing a meaningful framework for moving forward with anti-bullying programs in Perú. We propose that providing bully prevention training to popular students can have clear effects on the behavior of positive interactions among all students on campus. These popular students could receive training in conflict resolution, assertive and effective communication, positive expression of anger and hostility, and constructive strategies for coping with stress. It is expected that this group could learn vicariously to recognize patterns of bullying, identifying bullies, and discussed the protection needs of the school with the school staff.

Description of Specific Antibullying Approaches in Perú

Making Bullying Visible

It is necessary to develop a strong campaign on sensitization and education of bullying in schools and communities, because the problem of bullying is still largely invisible in Perú (Carozzo, 2008, 2009). Currently, one initiative aims to mobilize public opinion, media, and school staff via the publication of a *Pronouncement on Bullying* and the participation of important academic, political and educational institutions, and Peruvian professionals. The pronouncement is a statement about the problem of bullying, which emphasizes the need for an active and explicit plan to address the conditions that facilitate and maintain bullying in schools. The *Pronouncement* was written by the Observatory on Violence and Coexistence in School, and the Association Living in Peace (2010), both are Peruvian institutions.

Thematic Training and Preprofessional Education

There are university subjects that could integrate the issue of bullying as content to create intervention practices in the community, develop exploratory studies to adaptation of assessment in bullying research tests, or prepare monographs and reviews on the issue of bullying in Perú. These proposals would facilitate collaboration between university and community, create opportunities for applied research, and develop interventions using scientific methodology to measuring of effectiveness. Finally, adaptation and/or construction of psychometricaly sound psychological instruments sensitive to change in the Peruvian context could be emphasized during university training.

Programs of Professional Training and Research Methodology

In Perú, there is an effort to develop a second degree specializing in antibullying interventions, organized by the OVCE. This is an initiative that aims to empower the capacity of school psychologists, teachers, and other school staff to create effective interventions. Information relevant to this training program can be found at the OVCE website (http://www.observatorioperu.com).

Altruism and Prosocial Behavior Promotion in School Curricula

The existence of a greater number of spectators present when school violence occurs must be considered in prevention interventions used in Perú (Carozzo, 2010b). Knowledge about bullying may be increased and the frequency of its occurrence may be reduced via content-against-bullying arts activities (Haner, Pepler, Cummings, & Rubin-Vaughan, 2010). This means the curriculum should include assertive behavior skills, effective solving of social problems, empathic response, and educational organization consistent with prevention plans (Finnessy, 2009).

Relevant Research and Evidence of Effectiveness

Until the introduction of the *Pronouncement on Bullying* document (OVCE, and the Association Living in Peace, 2010), there were no reports of the effectiveness of interventions against bullying in Peruvian schools, in scientific or professional journals. Currently, interventions are mainly individual efforts or poor sustainability initiatives by specific school system or by isolated school guidance departments. In addition, there is no evidence of the degree of involvement of school psychologists in the organization, implementation, or evaluation of these interventions.

Within this emerging research, the formal intervention against bullying, Peruvian psychologists' participation in these two activities (research and intervention) occur unsystematically, without coordination between them and lack of organized actions based on common strategic principles. Also, this growing interest is being expressed to seek more information about the origin and characteristics of the bullying and for effective interventions that produce verifiable results that are consistent over time. Although more insight is needed to recognize research-based practices, educators and teachers are demanding more proactive school psychologists. Meanwhile, school psychologists are involved with individual efforts and seek information on the workshops held for the national association of Peruvian psychologist (Colegio de Psicólogos del Perú). To date, no known published documents describe in sufficient detail the strategies school psychologists, their effectiveness and sustainability of interventions.

Since its establishment in 2008, the OVCE has consistently promoted and demanded action against bullying. This nonprofit association aims to study, research, advice, and guide antibullying efforts in Perú. It is an agency for (a) receipt of conflicts and complaints about bullying; (b) supervision of research and thesis; (c) organization and implementation of training for educational, professional, and academic institutions; and (d) consulting, prevention, and intervention programs of bullying. The OVCE is planning to implement a National Survey on Bullying in 2011.

An Ongoing Experience of Intervention

In this section, we describe a bulling prevention intervention implemented at a private school in Lima. This intervention strategy provides a model to evaluate current efforts underway in Perú to implement systematic and synergic bullying prevention programs.

1. The program began in February (about the beginning of the annual school activities) with 40 hours of training of teachers and administrative management of the school.

2. In March, classes began, and we administered a survey to teachers and students to obtain their perceptions of school life. Altogether, the survey involved 40 teachers and 300 students of both genders from the last two grades of primary and two secondary grades. The administration of the survey was voluntary, approved for parents and school staff, and anonymous; the reaction of the student was involved and positive. The survey contains questions that directly asked about bullying behaviors, and perceptions of the school and teachers when they tried to cope. These questions were used to obtain information on prevalence of bullying.

3. The results of the survey found that 76% of students admitted that there were acts of harassment in school, 58% indicated that males were the main agents and victims of violence and violence receptors, 38% knew what bullying was, 52% reported that the use of nicknames and insults were the most common types of aggression, and 7% reported that they had been bullied. In addition, 3% admitted to being "leader" when it comes to harassing students; that is, verbal and physical intimidating, hitting, chasing, stealing, or spoiling personal school materials. Eight percent of students reported that they had been harassed and not helped by the tutors. On the other hand, 73% of students indicated that school officials call attention to the aggressor and the victim and do not establish differences between them. This discourages students' efforts to denounce violence against them or other students. Forty-two percent reported that the institutional environment is not safe.

4. In April, we proceeded with new training and bullying awareness activities. At this school, we included students and parents, in separate sessions. The content of the training focused on strategies of coexistence, conflict resolution, social skills, self-esteem, social learning, cognitive processing of social events and violence, and tolerance.

5. The first two strategies were proposed intervention protocols to monitor the areas where bullying tends to occur (e.g., when students are in transition between classes), and to assist bystanders via a network of "surveillance," and intervention in areas where bullying was known to occur. Because the most episodes of bullying occurred during the transition between classes (in this period, students are without supervision and monitoring of teachers), the team decided that teachers would stay in their classrooms until the next teacher arrived so that students are not left unattended. As a result, qualitative reports on incidents of harassment from teachers and students decreased. On the other hand, the intervention team made efforts to sensitize and educate the student population who were bystanders during the bullying. Awareness and education was based on the importance of solidarity and companionship, empathy, and zero tolerance of bullying. One consequence of this plan is that there was a greater positive involvement of bystanders in bullying situations. Although no written report is available, we note a decrease in bullying events in various places in school;

it is estimated that less than half the rate previously reported. This decrement was perceived for students and teachers. These two actions (monitoring and network) were considered successful and apparently helped to achieved better security for students and give them greater confidence in their social interaction.

The bullies were aided professionally without the use of aversive strategies, and their parents were involved in psychological counseling. Something similar was done with the victims and spectators. In all cases, parents were invited to report on progress of work with the school psychologist. Specifically, bullies and victims were attended in the department of psychology in the school, coordinating activities with their teachers and parents, to monitor progress toward goals. The main activity was a social skills program for life and resilience (self-esteem, empathy, autonomy, and creativity). Parents and teachers submitted reports related to changes in emotional behavior and affective (tolerance, conflict management and peaceful conflict resolution, ability to communicate in situations of tension and confrontation, attitudes of cooperation and assistance partner, and respect for differences).

Critiques and Limitations of Peruvian Efforts to Address Bullying

The main obstacle to the full implementation of bullying prevention strategies in Perú is that no government-led priorities have been established for research on bullying or for intervention plans. For example, there is no explicit plan for a national prevalence survey of bullying, except for the one developed by OVCE. This lack of proper preparation in methodology of research may be one of the fundamental barriers to developing research projects.

Because Perú is a multicultural country, this diversity in schools may contribute to the bullying of students across different ethnic groups. In the current status of reliable information and published reports, the frequency of bullying and its characteristics, processes, and cultural influences require additional research. In addition, thus far, the prevalence of cultural bullying in Perú is based on data of unknown reliability. This issue of cultural diversity as a basis for one type of bullying is largely unrecognized by school authorities. Successful bullying prevention and intervention in Perú will need to emphasize social inclusion issues. However, it is still difficult to make an effective intervention that involves an entire school system to promote the bullying prevention. This may indicate, perhaps, a reluctance to accept changes of a systemic nature within the school environment, which may manifest a reluctance to accept bullying as a problem that is serious. To this is added that in the annual plan of educational and administrative activities, school principals generally do not include activities of primary or secondary prevention, or an antibullying policy. This work plan is approved at the beginning of every year and can be a great opportunity to prepare members of the school community to give antibullying answers, and begin research on the correlates of bullying. On the other hand, usually, the teachers feel they are burdened by demands in return for poor compensation. There is also a belief among some educators that the way to combat bullying is to implement severe disciplinary measures and punitive actions at home and at school.

School psychologists need to be prepared to deal with bullying, but also how to address barriers to the implementation and sustainability of school system initiatives. The knowledge and strategies must be appropriate for changes in communication systems in the functional structure and intergroup cooperation. Although the Peruvian Ministry of Education has not taken a role in leading antibullying intervention, private institutions are providing training and consultation to schools and school psychologists. Moreover, the research in school psychology in Perú is still emerging in this area. However, the biggest challenge of Peruvian research psychologists is to publish their results, generate knowledge that impacts professional practice, and help to change educational policies of peaceful coexistence. And, to the psychologists in professional practice, the greatest challenge is to be good consumers of research and to use their judgment to design interventions on research-based evidence.

References

Amemiya, I., Oliveros, M., & Barrientos, A. (2009). Factores de riesgo de violencia escolar (bullying) severa en colegios privados de tres zonas de la sierra del Perú [Risk factors for school violence (bullying) severe in private schools in three areas in the mountains of Perú]. *Anales de la Facultad de Medicina, 70,* 255–258. Retrieved from http://redalyc.uaemex.mx/pdf/379/37912407005.pdf

Bandura, A. (1982). *Teoría del aprendizaje social* [Social learning theroy]. Madrid, Spain: Espasa-Calpe.

Benites, L., & Carozzo, J. (2003) *Habilidades sociales y violencia entre iguales: Estudio en niños de 8-10 años de edad del Colegio Fe y Alegría de Villa El Salvador* [Social skills and violence between peers: Research in children of 8–10 years old, of the Fe y Alegria School in Villa Salvador district]. Lima, Perú: Cámara de Comercio de Lima y USAID.

Brehm, S. S., & Brehm, J. W. (1981). *Psychological reactance: A theory of freedom and control.* New York, NY: Academic Press.

Carozzo, J. (2008, August). *El acoso entre iguales y su invisibilización en la escuela* [Bullying between peers and the invisibilization in the school]. Speech presented in the XV International Seminar on New Advances in the Psychological Intervention, Faculty of Psychology, Universidad de San Martín de Porres, Lima, Perú.

Carozzo, J. (2009, July). *La conspiración del silencio: El bullying y la convivencia escolar* [The conspiracy of silence: The bullying and school coexistence]. Speech presented in the XIV National Congress of Psychology, Chiclayo, Perú.

Carozzo, J. (2010a, August) *Habilidades para la vida y bullying* [Life skills and bullying]. Speech presented in the International Conference of School Life Skills in the XXI Century, Friends Private Schools Association, Lima, Peru.

Carozzo, J. (2010b). *¿Psicopatologizar el bullying?* [Psychopathologying to the bullying?]. Retrieved from http://www.observatorioperu.com/art_jcarozzo_psicopatologizar_el_bullying1.htm

Carozzo, J. (2010c). El bullying en la escuela [Bullying in school]. *Revista de Psicología, 12,* 329–345. Retrieved from http://sisbib.unmsm.edu.pe/BVRevistas/rev_psicologia_cv/v12_2010/pdf/a13.pdf

Cava, M., Buelga, S., Musitu, G., & Murgui, S. (2010). Violencia escolar entre adolescentes y sus implicaciones en el ajuste psicosocial: Un estudio longitudinal [School violence between adolescents and their implications in the psychosocial adjustment: A longitudinal study]. *Revista de Psicodidáctica, 15*(1), 21–34. Retrieved from http://www.ehu.es/ojs/index.php/psicodidactica/article/view/732/607

Cava, M., Musitu, G., & Murgui, S. (2007). Individual and social risk factors related to overt victimization in a sample of Spanish adolescents. *Psychological Reports, 101,* 275–290. Centro de Desarrollo y Asesoría Psicosocial. (1995) *Infancia y violencia 2: Experiencias y reflexiones sobre los niños y la violencia política en el Perú.* [Childhood and violence 2: Experiences and reflections about children and political violence in Peru]. Lima, Perú: Author. Retrieved, from http://www.cedapp.org.pe/principal.htm

Coopersmith, S. (1967). *The antecedents of self-esteem.* San Francisco, CA: W. H. Freeman.

El Comercio. (2010, Mayo 23). El agresor y la víctima: Por lo general el acosador tiene profundas necesidades afectivas, en tanto la víctima es muy sensible [The agresor and victim: Generally, the bullyers has deep emotional needs, and the victim is sensitive] [Suplemento Mi Hogar]. *El Comercio,* p. 15. Retrieved from http://elcomercio.pe/impresa/notas/agresor-victima/20100523/483533

El Diario. (2009, December 14). Mitad de los estudiantes sufre violencia escolar [Half of students suffers school violence]. *El Diario,* p. 1. Retrieved from www.eldiario.net/noticias/2009/2009_12/nt091214/prima.pdf

Finnessy, P. (2009). Ending the silence: Bullying in the curriculum. *The School Administrator, 66*(11), 34–35. Retrieved from http://findarticles.com/p/articles/mi_m0JSD/is_11_66/ai_n45182860/?tag=content;col1

García, L. (2008, October). *Estudio de la violencia en la escuela* [Study of the violence in the school]. Speech presented in the VIII International Conference of School Psychology: Development, achievement and motivation in the current educational scenario, Pontificia Universidad Católica del Perú.

García, L., Paredes, M., Arenas, C., & Quintana, A. (2010, February) *Problemáticas psicosociales en el Perú* [Psychosocial problems in Perú]. Speech presented in the Week of Social Psychology, Perspectivas actuales de la Psicología Social, Department of Sociology, Universidad Autónoma Metropolitana Unidad Iztapalapa, México.

Haner, D., Pepler, D., Cummings, J., & Rubin-Vaughan, A. (2010). The role of arts-based curricula in bullying prevention: Elijah's Kite — A children's opera. *Canadian Journal of School Psychology, 25,* 55–69. doi.org/10.1177/0829573509349031

La Comisión Nacional para el Desarrollo y Vida sin Drogas (DEVIDA). (2007) *Segundo Estudio Nacional: Prevención y Consumo de Drogas en Estudiantes de Secundaria* [2nd National Study: Prevention and Drugs Use in High School Students]. Lima, Perú: Author. Retrieved from http://www.devida.gob.pe/Documentacion/documentosdisponibles/II_Estudio_Regional_EscolaresSec_2007.pdf

Landázuri, V. (2007) Asociación entre el rol de agresor y el rol de víctima de intimidación escolar, con la autoestima y las habilidades sociales de adolescentes de un colegio particular mixto de Lima [Association between the role of aggressor and victim of intimidation, and self-esteem and social skills in adolescents from a mixed private school in Lima]. *Revista Herediana de Psicología, 2*(2), 71–80. Retrieved from http://www.buenastareas.com/ensayos/Bullying/479642.html

Landázuri, V. (2007, January). *Bullying-maltrato entre compañeros: Todos tienen una historia que contar* [Bullying-maltreatment between peers: Everyone has a story to tell]. Speech presented in the Second Congress of the Peruvian Association of Psychoanalytic Psychotherapy of Children and Adolescents, Lima, Perú.

Landázuri, V. (2008, October). *Bullying: Estrategias de intervención* [Bullying: Intervention strategies]. Speech presented in the VIII International Conference of School Psychology: Development, achievement and motivation in the current educational scenario, Pontificia Universidad Católica del Perú.

Manrique, N. (2004) *Sociedad: Enciclopedia temática del Perú* [Society: Thematic encyclopedia of Peru] (Vol. VII). Lima, Perú: El Comercio.

Mejía, J., & Moncada, G. (2000, November). *Las variables de etnia y raza en las encuestas de hogares en América Latina y Caribe* [The variables of ethnicity and race in household surveys in Latin America and Caribbean]. Paper presented in the First International Meeting "Todos Contamos: Los Grupos Étnicos en los Censos," in Cartagena City, Colombia.

Monks, C. P., Smith, P. K., Naylor, P., Barter, C., Ireland, J. L., & Coyne, I. (2009). Bullying in different contexts: Commonalities, differences and the role of theory. *Aggression and Violent Behavior, 14*, 146–156. doi:10.1016/j.avb.2009.01.004

Myers, D. G. (2000). *Psicología social* [Social psychology]. Bogotá, Columbia: McGraw-Hill.

Noriega, M. (2010, Mayo 23). Peligroso "bullying" [Dangerus "bullying"] [Suplemento Mi Hogar]. *El Comercio*, pp. 12–13.

Observatory on Violence and Coexistence in School, and the Association Living in Peace. (2010). Un fantasma recorre las escuelas, es el fantasma del bullying [A ghost run in schools: the bullying]. Retrieved, from http://www.observatorioperu.com/imagenes/Pronunciamiento del Observatorio setiembre 2010.pdf

Oliveros, M., & Barrientos, A. (2007). Incidencia y factores de riesgo de la intimidación (bullying) en un colegio particular de Lima-Perú [Incidence and risk factor of intimidation (bullying) in a private school of Lima-Perú]. *Revista Peruana de Pediatría, 60*, 150–155. Retrieved from http://sisbib.unmsm.edu.pe/bvrevistas/rpp/v60n3/pdf/a03v60n3.pdf

Oliveros, M., Figueroa, L., Mayorga, G., Cano, B., Quispe, Y., & Barrientos, A. (2008). Violencia escolar (bullying) en colegios estatales de primaria en el Perú [School violence (bullying) in public elementary schools in Perú]. *Revista Peruana de Pediatría, 61*, 215–220. Retrieved from http://revistas.concytec.gob.pe/pdf/rpp/v61n4/a04v61n4.pdf

Quintana, A., Montgomery, W., & Malaver, C. (2009). Modos de afrontamiento y conducta resiliente en adolescentes espectadores de violencia entre pares [Ways of coping and resilient behavior in bystander of violence between peers]. *Revista del Instituto de Investigación de Psicología, 12*, 153–171. Retrieved from http://www.scielo.org.pe/pdf/rip/v12n1/a11v12n1.pdf

Rojas, B., & Brondi, M. (1987). Los efectos físicos y psicológicos de la violencia en los niños [The physical and psychological effects of violence in childrens]. In R. Pérez Liu (Ed.), *Los niños de la guerra. Seminario: Violencia, familia y niño* (pp. 123–140). Ayacucho, Perú: IER.

Rotter, J. B. (1966). Generalized expectancies for internal versus external control of reinforcement. *Psychological Monographs, 80*(1), 1–28.

Sartre, J. P. (1943/1947). *No exit* (S. Gilbert, Translator). New York, NY: Knopf.

Universidad Nacional Mayor de San Marcos. (2009, April). Resúmenes del primer taller sobre investigación en violencia en la Universidad Nacional Mayor de San Marcos [Abstracts from the first workshop on research in violence, in the Universidad Nacional Mayor de San Marcos], Lima, pp. 21–22.

14

Exploring School Violence in the Context of Turkish Culture and Schools

Sefa Bulut and Samettin Gündüz

ABANT İZZET BAYSAL ÜNIVERSITY, BOLU, TURKEY

Abstract

In recent years, school violence has been extensively discussed in the media and has become a very popular topic in Turkey and many other countries around the world. In fact, it is possible to read and see news every day about school violence in newspapers and television in developing countries. Thus, the purpose of this chapter is to discuss the research advancing understanding of school violence and bullying in the Turkish school system. The chapter includes studies and reviews focused on school violence, including the prevalence and reasons of the violent actions in the context of Turkish culture. Contemporary studies are mostly focused on student violence and bullying behaviors. However, there is also teacher induced violence that has not been acknowledged due to its sensitive nature in previous studies. Therefore, this chapter also includes a discussion of violent actions instigated by teachers. Additionally, in recent years cyberbullying/violence have become very common among youngsters. Cyberbullying is also discussed as is the depiction of school violence in the media. Findings are examined in light of previous literature and data from other developing countries. Finally, effective intervention and prevention methods are also reviewed.

Bully/victim behaviors could be witnessed at all levels of schools in Turkey. Until recently, researchers in Turkey have regarded bully/victim behaviors in schools as a natural part of growing up (Güvenir, 2005). Although research studies about bully/victim behaviors in schools were initiated in other countries during the 1970s, it has not attracted attention in Turkey until the 1990s after becoming a major issue in schools. Related articles in Turkish literature appeared first in 1995, and many studies have been carried out pointing out the various aspects of bully/victim behaviors (Pişkin, 2002; Kapcı, 2004).

Primary reasons for the delay of research about bully/victim behaviors in Turkey include the following. Turkish culture has traditionally:

1. denied the existence of bullying,
2. ignored bullying,
3. made efforts to cover up bullying in schools,
4. attributed a sacred meaning to school,
5. regarded bullying as a natural part of growing up.

Efforts to cover up previous and ongoing bullying activities in Turkish society stem from the fact that there is a dominant conception that outsiders should not be informed about domestic issues. This approach could be summarized by a Turkish proverb that has a rough translation the "arm is broken but stays inside the sleeves" and meaning that only the person knows that the arm is broken and outsiders cannot see it. Such a cultural context enables bully/victim behaviors in schools to be covered up easily.

Most recently, Bulut (2008b) conducted archival research and reviewed violent events among students as it appeared in the Turkish media and press. The results revealed that all forms of bullying and maltreatment, including verbal, physical, social, emotional, and sexual, are commonly observed in Turkish educational systems, which is similar with other Western and industrialized nations..

In one of the early and leading study, Dölek (2002) reported that the degree of prevalence of being a victim in fifth, seventh, and ninth grades is 8.2%, of which 2.6% are female and 6.4% are male. The results of Pişkin's (2006) research examining fourth-, fifth-, sixth-, seventh-, and eighth-grade students in Ankara clearly demonstrates the extent of the bullying occurring in schools. According to study results, it was determined that 35% of the students suffered bullying on a regular basis and 6% of the students bullied others. Kepenekçi and Çınkır (2006) provide information about the different kinds of bullying and their distribution percentages in their research at the high school level. Among the students participating in the high school study, 33% reported that they were exposed to verbal bullying, 36% of them were exposed to physical bullying, 28% of them were exposed to emotional bullying and 16% of them were exposed to sexual bullying. The distribution of the typical bullying behaviors victims reported were pushing (58% in females and 64% in males) and nicknaming (44% in females and 62% in males. Özder (2005) discovered in a study titled "Violence and Harassment in Primary Schools" that among students in the age group of 13 to 16, 43% of participants were exposed to verbal harassment, 24% of them were exposed to physical harassment, and 25% of them were exposed to sexual harassment.

It could be said that the proportion for sexual bullying, 16%, among above bullying figures in schools is not accurate and does not show the actual extent of the sexual harassment in schools. Evaluation of sexual harassment in Turkish culture with regards to conception of "honor affair" leads these incidents to be kept secret. Hence, both the perpetrators and the victims of sexual harassment try to keep it secret because, if not, there is a large risk that it could lead to violence or even death. Thus, the fact that there are certainly many attempts to cover up sexual harassment incidents in schools confirms that these figures do not precisely reflect the reality. The reported low level of sexual harassment also strengthens the view that there might be discrepancies in other figures as well. This result was supported by the results of the Kartal and Bilgin (2007) study. The proportion of those victims who do not tell anything about the fact that they were bullied to one of their friends, an adult in the school, or their parents is very high. It was determined that the proportion of those victims, who do not report anything about the bullying to their friends or an adult, is 43%. The main reason victims reported that they do not tell anything about the bullying incident is their belief that telling it to others will both amplify and worsen the issue and create an unfavorable image for them.

According to the results of Totan's (2008) investigation of peer bullying in schools, it was determined that 41% of bullying is verbal, 29% of bullying is social, 18% of bullying is physical, and 12% of bullying is other behaviors. Totan investigated the predictive power of peer relationships about bullying behaviors in adolescents and found that the proportions of bullying behaviors are as follows: it was found out that 11% of participants were bullies, 13% of participants were victims, 8% of participants reported being both bullies and victims, and 68% of participants reported being neither bullies nor victims. The same study examined whether bullying in school shows any differences with respect to students' genders. It was found that bullying shows similarities with respect to the gender. The study found out that the proportion of female and male bullies was 11%. It also determined the proportion of female victims to be 14% and the proportion of male victims to be 11%. It is quite normal that the proportion of female victims is higher than male victims. One could link this result to the fact that we live in a patriarchic or androcentric, male-dominant, society. However, one should not try to justify the proportion of female victims and regard it as natural. On the contrary, this points to the fact that necessary measures have to be taken in schools to protect female students.

As one investigates the gender distribution of the participants who regard certain behaviors in schools as sexual harassment, Özönder's (2005) study, "Bullying and Harassment in Schools," found out that 67% of the students stated males, 29% of the students stated females, and 54% of the students stated both males and females committed shameful behaviors in schools.

According to the results of the study made by Ögel, Tarı, and Eke (2006) to determine the extent of the bullying in schools in 2004 in the district of Istanbul, it was found out that the proportion of the students involved in a dispute was around 50%, the proportion of the students having a physical fight was 15%, and the proportion of the students participated in at least an incident inflicting others any injuries was 26%.

In a study about in which surroundings bullying occurred in schools, Kepenekçi and Çınkır (2006) found out that 29% of the incidents occurred in classes, 24% of the incidents occurred outside the school, 17% of the incidents occurred in the school corridors, 14% of the incidents occurred in the playgrounds, and 16% of the incidents occurred in other areas such as sport centers, school canteens or refectories. These figures confirm the fact that there is much work to be done to create safe school environments in Turkey.

Many research studies have been carried out so far about bully/victim behaviors. The analysis of the research results reveal both the types and the proportions of intensity of bully/victim behaviors. However, there is no mention of brand-bullying that is needed to be cited among bully/victim behaviors. The ignoring of brand-bullying does not necessarily mean that it does not exist. One also needs to mention about the practice of brand-bullying among students in schools. The current practice of brand-bullying can be defined as follows: The set of complex relations emerging by the brands of tools and equipments one use in the schools in order for him/her to be regarded acceptable by his/her environment, to gain him/her a certain advantageous status, to acquire him/her a psychological superiority, or to attract others' attentions to him/her is referred to as brand-bullying. For example, wearing a famous and expensive brand of perfume, watch, or jeans can be considered "brand violence." In fact, it is very common in school settings for students to use clothes, note pads, pencils, backpacks, and other items that have a special name or logo, which is artfully designed, engraved, and embroidered to get the attention of other students. These eye-catching brands and logos get the attention of youngsters and preoccupy their ruminations about them. This poses a post-modern dilemma for parents as well as educators to deal with effectively and necessarily.

Students' tendencies to express themselves by the brands or the products they use and not by their own identities and personalities increase the level of brand-bullying in schools. Tendency to use branded items is very popular among students, e.g., clothing, sports equipments, school supplies, make-up, and accessories are widely used and become a conversation topic among children and adolescents. It is necessary not to ignore the cultural aspects, besides the psychological aspects, of this trend. It is observed that those students who use branded products in schools acquire an undeserved and unjustified superiority over others and not attaching any penalty to their unfavorable behaviors helps brand-bullying to be regarded natural in schools.

It is misleading to assess or justify the students' desires to use branded products with respect to their levels of economic income. This is a way to normalize the use of branded products in schools by those students who have good financial backings to regard the brand-bullying as innocent. Hence, the normalization of the brand-bullying creates an unfavorable psychological environment for those students who could not afford to buy those products, and these justification initiatives do not lead to concrete results in favor of students. One solution might be to have students wear standard school uniforms.. However, this is not a reasonable practice to prevent brand-bullying in schools in any way. As exemplified above, brand-bullying and brand-violence cover such a wide range of items that it is diffiuclt to minimize the brand-bullying in schools. Parents need to talk to their children and explain the cultural aspects of the use of branded products. The importance of using quality supplies, clothing, and other items should be promoted rather than trying to establish superiority of specific brands. It should be stressed in the best possible way that usage of branded products is quite normal within a certain cultural environment. Thus, one could ensure that students are less affected by brand-bullying.

Furthermore, even when such use of brands is applied to a bad habit (e.g., smoking cigarettes, drinking beer or other alcoholic beverages), young people still imitate their fellow students; they prefer to chose the expensive brand, the one with a special brand name, and the one that looks superior regardless of affordability. In some cases, youngsters spend their money only on miscellaneous items rather than on transportation or other necessities.

Teacher Induced Violence

Traditionally research has focused on more violence emerged from students or bullying behaviors among students. However, in recent years there are a few studies touched the issue of teacher induced violence. Gökütok (2008) conducted a study and investigated teacher violence in Turkish school systems, and later on she repeated the same study in Ankara schools and found out similar results. More recently, Bulut (2008a) conducted archival research looking at teachers' violent and bullying behaviors in school settings that appeared in printed media.

Being a "bully" is culturally considered as a "macho or masculine" character, and it is widely accepted and socially sanctioned by both male and females in Turkish society. Bulut named this cultural phenomenon "soft violence."

Mauer (1984) described corporal punishment as an old fashioned and ineffective disciplinary tool and mentioned that it was banned in many counties. Even though corporal punishment is officially banned in home and school settings in many countries, it is still widely used in many part of the worlds. Similarly, in Turkey a new form of government was established in 1923, and physical punishment "*falaka*" was outlawed and banned in schools. In 1930, a new law took effect that banned corporal punishment in schools. According to this law, a teacher who uses corporal punishment was to be given salary cuts for a month and appointment holds for a set amount of time. The same law was renewed again in 1948. However, even though corporal punishment was forbidden formally, it has not very successfully eradicated this problem, and corporal punishment just changed its form and still continuing today. According to the United Nations reports (Pinheiro, 2006), violent behaviors and physical punishments against children are very common and used to discipline children and youngsters. This report also mentioned that children are exposed to more serious form of punishments and violence at their home rather than schools. Pelendecioğlu and Bulut (2009) argued that this is also the context for Turkish parents. Pelendecioğlu and Bulut (2009) mentioned corporal punishment as a very common an socially accepted disciplinary vehicles in the home life of children in same part of Turkey; in particularly, in people from lower socioeconomically classes and lower educational levels. As a reflection of this problem, the same form of aggressive and violent behaviors is commonly observed in school systems.

Some authors also speculated that minors are being subjected to physical punishments in schools, social welfare institutions, and other places, but this goes unreported due to the nature of this action and the shame and stigma attached to the victims. This phenomenon is also commonly observed in domestic abuse cases in Turkey. Especially in school settings, victims are being teased or name called by their peers but they do not want to report this to the authorities or their parents (Arıcak et al., 2008; Bulut, 2008b).

Traditionally, the Turkish educational system is based on an authoritarian and discipline-oriented approach, which fits with the cultural norms in which the elderly, teachers, and parents have an undisputable and unquestionable power over children and adolescence and even on adult children. As a matter of fact, the Turkish language has many common sayings, phrases, and idioms about the unconditional respect and obedience of teachers (Gözütok, 2008, pp. 35–38). This is rooted in the history of the country that citizens are expected to obey the rulers and government authorities unconditionally. Against all of the forbidding rules, corporal punishment is still being informally used in many schools. And generally, the victims are being accused for making a mistakes and are ashamed to make a formal complains to the authorities. Therefore, this goes on and on without necessary changes being made. Thus, due to the aforementioned reasons, corporal punishment must be investigated. Only recently have officials started to realize the importance of this issue in schools.

In their seminal research, Gözütok, Er, and Karacaoğlu (2006) conducted a survey in 1992 and again in 2006 in four different schools in Ankara. Their results showed that the usage of corporal punishment by teachers is still very common and has not dropped down since the initial research. More surprisingly, the comparison of the 1992 and 2006 surveys shows that even after 14 years, teachers tend to develop more favorable attitudes toward the use of corporal punishment. Some of the teachers believed that students deserve corporal punishment and that it is for the well-being of the students.

Özpolat and Bayındır (2007) wrote about common usage of corporal punishment by teachers and other school personals in Turkish schools. Supporting their findings, Bulut (2008a) also found that children are still frequently exposed to teacher's aggressive and violent behaviors. Bulut (2008a) reviewed visual and printed media for the last five years and identified 172 teacher induced violent events towards students. Of course, this is less than actual events as most events are unreported or underreported. The reasons for teacher induced violence included 38 incidences of student behavior of a sexual nature, i.e., harassing or making sexual jokes with each other, 24 incidences of destroying school building or property, 22 cases of talking in class or causing disruptions, 15 cases of fighting with fellow students, 10 cases of students who did not do their homework, 9 cases of students who did not listen in class, 6 cases of students being dressed inappropriately, 6 cases of students with inappropriate hair styles, 5 cases of students who damaged teachers' goods, and 5 cases of students who smoked. It appears that adolescents have a natural interest in sexual topics and sexuality. Thus, schools need to operate sex education classes and seminars so that children and adolescents can have real information and be informed about sexual topics. In Turkish culture, sex is a taboo subject; it is not easy to talk about these matters openly and publicly. Therefore, it is imperative to offer sex education classes in schools as well as to integrate them into counseling and guidance programs. Among the violent actions, 49 cases took place in classrooms, 49 cases in the assistant principal's room, 28 cases in the school principal's room, 24 in hallways, and 22 in teachers' rooms.

In most incidences male students were the target of the violent actions; mostly male teachers preferred to use corporal punishment for male students. Results show that male teachers used corporal punishment 6.5 times more than did female teachers. It seems that teachers frequently attempt to use corporal punishment in schools. This is can be explained by the cultural attitudes toward machismo. Soft violence is somehow accepted or tolerated in daily life. It is interesting that student punishments and beatings have taken place in presidents', vice presidents', or teachers' rooms. In order to correct this problem of teachers using their authoritarian power, teacher education curriculum needs to include anti-corporal punishment and anti-bullying programs. Pre-service teachers and working teachers need to develop awareness, rationale, and consequences of teacher induced violent actions in school settings. In fact, the Turkish Minister of Education called for an emergent conference, and experts discussed the issues and suggested implementation of prevention programs in 2006. Later, Bulut (2008a) also suggested the inclusion of parents in decision making process of intervention programs. Furthermore, teachers who frequently and regularly use corporal punishment need to seek professional help and take care their own well-being (Bulut, 2008a).

Hyman and Wise's (1979) study on teachers' mental health reported that 9% of teachers had some form of adjustment problems. However, no data and research has been found regarding the mental health of Turkish teachers. This can be a new area for researchers to investigate and explore. On the other hand, Turkish scholars Şahin and Beyazova (2001) listed factors associated with leading teachers to corporal punishment; personality disorders, crowded classrooms, and social pressures. Additionally, Yıldız (1992) believes that teachers who are not well equipped with educational techniques and methods tend to use corporal punishment more often.

Twemlow (2005) defined "bully teachers" as those who use disciplinary methods beyond the acceptable methods for punishing students, manipulating students, and insulting them by using their power unjustly.

Sometimes teachers ignore the students who have been subjected to bullying, cooperate with bullies, or do not intervene thereby indirectly supporting the bullies (Turkel, 2007). In the same way, Twemlow (2005) believed that teachers' indifferences and encouraging attitudes towards the bully and aggressive children supports behavioral problems of students. Furthermore, students who have been targeted by teachers are also chosen as victim by their peers.

According to Gözütok and colleagues (2006), students believed that teachers who had personal problems and teachers who are not well equipped in teaching methods felt a sense of inadequacy and used more corporal punishment. In 1992, 31% of teachers used corporal punishment, whereas in 2006 the rate increased in 55%. Also surprisingly, the researchers have found out that well-educated and well-equipped teachers are also attempting to use corporal punishment quite often.

Cyberbullying is a new phenomenon since the Internet entered in our daily life as well as educational systems. Cyberbullying is basically described by Strom and Strom (2005) as "an electronic form of peer harassment" In Turkey, there are a few studies examining students bullying via computers or cell phones in different age levels. It seems that students tend to use more technology-oriented bullying behaviors as their get older.

Arıcak et al. (2008) found cyberbullying a new and emerging type of bullying and draws attention to this phenomenon in Turkey. In their study, 36% of students demonstrated bullying, 24% bully-victim, and 6% become victims. Male students were always higher in all three categories. As the demand increased for communication and technologies became more accessible, more children and adolescents have computers and cellular phones. As a mater of fact, amazingly 74% of students had a personal computer, 82% of them have cell phones, and 63% had both of them. It appears that computers and cell phones are very popular in Turkey to the extent that some people have more than one. In another study, Kaplan (2006) reported that 94% of Turkish adolescents have cell phones.

Regardless of a person's age, sex, educational level, ethnicity, and country of origin, he or she can be exposed to cyberbullying anywhere in the world (Arıcak et al., 2008). Research by

Arıcak and colleagues revealed that there is also a repeated cycling trend in cyberbullying; adolescents who have been bullied tend to bully others. For example, students whose pictures have been displayed on the Net or who received nasty emails as a form of bullying tend to strongly bully others in the same or similar manner. Second, as time spent by adolescents on the Internet increases, the possibility of being bullied and/or receiving a number of unwanted or harassing messages increases.

Arıcak et al. (2008) found a positive correlation between those who have been cyber victims and those who have also received threatening cell calls. Results show that the students bully via varied telecommunication devices. In fact, 36% reported being a victim of cyberbullying, 24% via cell phones. In terms of gender differences, 13% of boys and 10% of girls identified themselves cyber-bully victims. Additionally, 19% of boys and 17% of girls were cyberbullies, 3% of boys and 3% of girls were found to be cyber victims. A relatively, small percentage of bullied–victim students informed their families, only 25% of them told their parents, and only 1% told their teachers. The data suggested that the victims preferred to seek help and exchange information with their peers as they are perceived to be more technology savvy and can provide more technological help for their problems (Arıcak et al., 2008).

In a recent study with Turkish university students, Arıcak (2009) reported the rates as 2% of bully, 18% bully-victims, 37% victims, and 44% never engaged in neither bullying nor victim status. There was no gender difference in the victim status, but there were significantly more male students engaged in cyberbullying activities. In this study, results revealed that that hostility significantly predicted the cyberbullying actions and tendencies. On the other hand, the non-engaged group reported significantly less psychopathology. In addition to these findings, "interpersonally sensitive" students were less likely to be victims, likely due to the fact that sensitive people tend to be suspicious and avoid interactions with those they do not know very well. Similarly. Ybarra and Mitchell (2007) also believed cyberbullying is a complex behavioral and psychological problem that includes anger, aggression, and antisocial behaviors.

David-Ferdon and Hertz (2007) considered cyberbullying as a mental health and public health problem. Similarly, Arıcak et al. (2008) pointed out the mental health outcomes associated with

Table 14.1 Implications for Practice

"Brand Violence" and "Brand Bullying" is a new phenomenon that came out in the context of developing countries, which is also considered a form of violence and directly or indirectly affects a large number of children.
"Soft Violence" also stems from masculine and macho culture in which male hierarchy dominated the female; this can be in the form of accepted and culturally sanctioned forms, but eventually it has detrimental effect on women's life and development.
It appears that school bullying, violence, and cyberbullying are a universal problem and have been observed in every part of the world. Thus, the prevention and intervention programs should be global in nature. Universal institutions also can be part of the solutions.
Generally, all forms of violence and bullying actions are considered culturally shameful. Thus, it is considered to be a threat to someone's honor and social fame, so it is covered up by the individuals or the institutions.
All forms of bullying is gradually increasing, this shows a very similar profile to other countries and cultures.
Brand violence is a form of indirect violence and has not been addressed or researched in the literature. This is a new concept, and it merits attention to be in-depth investigated.
"Soft Violence" is also a new phenomenon which is very common in developing countries and Turkey. Women are oppressed by the use of this socially acceptable form of oppression. But this is not only limited to female gender, due to the nature of soft violence it is a form of expression that females can also use as a form of violence against their partners.

bullies and victims. They also draw attention to the use of the Internet and that it is not only a school's, a region's, or a country's problem but it is an international problem that is becoming increasingly more threatening to youngsters. Cyberbulling presents problems for parents and educators as well as for Internet space providers, web page designers, legal authorities, and governments. Finally, cyberbullied children may also develop psychopathology and stress symptoms, which may be content specific; thus a new counseling, therapy, and guidance approach may be needed for effective intervention and treatment of cyber victims.

The perception of anonymity in using technology appears to make some students more comfortable and less self-aware, to act impulsively and aggressively, and bully others (McKenna & Bargh, 2000). Thus, they are able to say things that they cannot or would not say face to face, lie, or pretend to be someone else.

Even though Turkish people retain strong ties to tradition and customs, the Turkish educational system is very much Western oriented and uses Western ideology and philosophy in the schools. Therefore, Turkish children demonstrate very similar violent and bullying behaviors as do their counterparts in Western countries.

More recently, media and government officials have paid more attention to violence, including bullying, in students and citizens lives; various conferences and seminars have been organized to address the issues. The Turkish Ministry of Education, for example, ordered immediate violence prevention programs be instituted for all public schools, and this issue is also required to be discussed in school guidance classes.

References

Arıcak, T. (2009). Psychiatric symptomatology as a predictor of cyberbullying among university students. *Eurasian Journal of Educational Research, 34,* 167–184

Arıcak, T., Siyahhan, S., Uzunhasanoğlu, A., Sarıbeyoğlu, S., Çıplak, S., Yılmaz, N., & Memmedow, C (2008). Cyberbullying among Turkish Adolescent. *CyberPsychology & Behavior, 11*(3), 253–261.

Bulut, S. (2008a). Öğretmenden öğrenciye yönelik olan fiziksel şiddet: Nicel bir araştırma [Violence that emerges from teachers to students: A quantitative investigation]. *Abant Izzet Baysal University Journal of Faculty of Education, 1*(8), 105–118.

Bulut, S. (2008b). Okullarda görülen öğrenciden öğrenciye yönelik şiddet olaylarının bazı değişkenler açısından arşiv araştırması yöntemiyle incelenmesi [An archival research study on the violent events between students at school]. *Abant Izzet Baysal University Journal of Faculty of Education, 2*(8), 23–38.

Çınkır, Ş. (2006, March). Okullarda Kabagüç. Türleri, etkileri ve önlem stratejileri [School bullying: types, effects and prevention strategie]. Paper presented at the Violence and school symposium, Istanbul, Turkey.

David-Ferdon, C., & Hertz, M. F. (2007). Electronic media, violence, and adolescents: An emerging public health problem. *Journal of Adolescent Health, 41,* 1–5.

Dölek, N. (2002). Öğrencilerde Zorbaca Davranışların Araştırılması ve Önleyici Bir Program Modeli [Research on bullying among students and a model prevention programme]. Unpublished Doctoral Dissertation. Marmara University Institute of Educational Sciences Istanbul, Turkey

Hyman, I. A., & Wise, J. H. (1979). *Corporal punishment in American Education.* Philadelphia: Temple University Press.

Gözütok, F. D., Er, O., & Karacaoğlu, C. (2006). Okulda Dayak: 1992 ve 2006 Yılları Karşılaştırması [Corporal punishment in school: The corporation of 1992 and 2006]. *Bilim ve Aklın Aydınlığında Eğitim, 7*(75), 29–33.

Gözütok, D. (2008). *Education and violence.* Ankara, Turkey: Gazi Kitapevi.

Güvenir, T. (2005). *Okulda Akran İstismarı* [Peer abuse in school]. Ankara, Turkey: Kok Publishing.

Kapcı, E. G. (2004). İlköğretim öğrencilerinin zorbalığa maruz kalma türünün ve sıklığının depresyon, kaygı ve benlik saygısıyla ilişkisi [Bullying type and severity among elementary school students and its relationship with depression, anxiety and self esteem]. *Ankara University Journal of Educational Sciences, 37*(1), 1–13.

Kaplan, P. (2006). Evde gençler Interneti chat için kullanıyor [Youngsters use the internet for chat at home]. Retrieved March 6, 2010, from http://arsiv.sabah.com.tr/ 2006/10/28/gun130.html#

Kartal, H., & Bilgin, A. (2007). İlköğretim Öğrencilerine Yönelik Bir Zorbalık Karşıtı Program uygulaması: Okulu Zorbalıktan Arındırma Programı [An implementation of an Anti-bullying program for elementary school students: Bully proofing your school]. *Journal of Theory and Practice in Education, 3*(2), 207–227.

Kepenekçi, Y., & Çınkır, Ş.(2006). Bullying among Turkish high school students.*Child Abuse & Neglect, 17*(17), 1–12.

Mauer, A. (1984). 1001 Alternatives to corporal punishment. A practical handbook of outrageous, original and sometimes useful ideas. Berkeley, CA: Generation Books.

McKenna, K. Y. A., & Bargh, J. A. (2000). Plan 9 from cyberspace: The implications of the Internet for personality and social psychology. *Personality and Social Psychology a Review, 4*(1), 57–75.

Ögel, K., Tarı, I., & Eke,Y. C. (2006). *Okullarda Suç ve Şiddeti Önleme* [Prevention of school crime and violence]. Istanbul, Turkey: Yeniden Publications.

Özönder, C. (2005). İlköğretim 7 ve 8. Sınıflarında Okuyan Öğrencilerin "Okulda Şiddet ve Taciz" kavramlarına ilişkin kavramsallaştırmaları [Conceptualization of the concepts of "School Violence and Abuse" by 7th and 8th grade students]. Ankara, Turkey: Türk Eğitim-Sen Press.

Özpolat, V., & Bayındır, N. (2007). Vaka Sorgulama Tekniği ile Okulda Fiziksel Ceza ve Çocuk Saldırganlığı [Corporal punishment and child agression with case questioning technique]. In A. Solak (Ed.), *Okullarda Şiddet ve Çocuk Suçluluğu* [School violence and child crimes] (pp. 37–54). Ankara, Turkey: Hegem Publications.

Pelendecioğlu, B., & Bulut, S. (2009). Physical abuse of children in their families. *Abant Izzet Baysal University Journal of Faculty of Education, 9*(1), 49–62.

Pinheiro, P. S. (2006). World report on violence against children. United Nations Reports. Geneva, Switzerland: United Nations. Retrieved from http://www.ncjrs.gov/App/Publications/abstract.aspx?ID=239950

Pişkin, M. (2002). Okul Zorbalığı: Tanımı, Türleri, İlişkili Olduğu Faktörler ve Alınabilecek Önlemler [School bullying: Definition, types, related factors and prevention]. *Journal of Theory and Practice in Education, 2*, 531–562.

Pişkin, M. (2006, March). *Akran zorbalığı olgusunun ilköğretim öğrencileri arasındaki yaygınlığın incelenmesi* [Prevalence among elementary school students study the phenomenon of peer bullying]. Paper presented at the school violence against children symposium, Istanbul, Turkey.

Strom, P. S., & Strom, R. D. (2005). Cyber bullying by adolescence: A preliminary assessment. *The Educational Form, 70*(1), 21–36.

Şahin, F. & Beyazova, U. (2001). Çocuğun şiddetten korunma hakkı [Child's right to be protected from violence]. *Milli Eğitim Dergisi* [*Journal of National Education*] (151). Retrieved December 12, 2010, from http://www.meb.gov.tr

Totan, T. (2008). Ergenlerde Zorbalığın Anne,Baba ve Akran İlişkileri Açısından İncelenmesi [Investigation of bullying among adolescents concerning parent and peer relations]. Unpublished Master's Thesis. Abant Izzet Baysal University Institute of Social Sciences, Bolu, Türkey.

Turkel, A. R. (2007). Sugar and spice and puppy dogs' tails: The psychodynamics of bullying. *Journal of American Academy of Psychoanalysis and Dynamic Psychiatry, 35,* 243–258.

Twemlow, S. (2005). The prevalence of teachers who bully students with differing levels of behavioral problems. *American Journal Psychiatry, 162,* 2387–2389.

Ybarra, M. L., & Mitchell, K. J. (2007). Prevalence and frequency of internet harassment instigation: Implications for adolescent health. *Journal of Adolescent Health*, *41*, 189–195.

Yıldız, M. (1992). Eğitimde dayak aczin ifadesidir [Corporal punishment in education is a sign of helplessness]. *Modern Education ,177*, 46–49.

15

The Association of Perceived Parental Understanding with Bullying Among Adolescents in Ghana, West-Africa

Andrew Owusu

MIDDLE TENNESSEE STATE UNIVERSITY

Aleesha Hoag

RUTHERFORD COUNTY SCHOOLS SYSTEM, TENNESSEE

Norman L. Weatherby and Minsoo Kang

MIDDLE TENNESSEE STATE UNIVERSITY

Abstract

This study explores the relationship between perceived parental understanding and bullying victimization among junior high school students in Ghana, West-Africa, using the 2007 Ghana Global School-based Student Health survey (GSHS). The sample included 2,795 students who were selected using a two-stage cluster sampling approach. A logistic regression analysis, controlling for grade level and being taught how to avoid bullying in school, found that boys and girls who perceive their parents to *sometimes* understand their worries and problems were more likely to be physically or nonphysically bullied than those who perceive that their parents *always* understand their worries and problems. Results for bullying victimization among students who perceived that they were never understood by their parents compared to always being understood were inconsistent. The Nagelkerke R^2 for the boys and girls models, respectively, was low at .072 and .084. Given the paucity of literature on bullying victimization in Ghana, additional studies are needed to better understand the problem.

Forms of violence in schools include sexual and gender-based violence, fighting, gang violence, assault weapons, and bullying, with bullying as the most prevalent (Pinheiro, 2006). Bullying includes verbal, physical, and psychological behaviors (Furrer, 2006; Pinheiro, 2006). The consensus in the literature is that bullying involves repeated behavior (verbal or nonverbal) over time in a relationship characterized by a power imbalance (Craig, 1998; Olweus, 1994; Pinheiro, 2006; Roland & Munthe, 1989; Smith & Sharp, 1994; Whitney & Smith, 1993).

There is an accumulation of evidence on the negative effects of bullying on children's well-being since the 1970s. The majority of past bullying research focuses on school dynamics, causes, long-term impact, and control (Dussich & Maekoya, 2007). Recent bullying research examines social and school environments, and family dynamics (Espelage & Swearer, 2003; Furrer, 2006). Although individual characteristics are often the focus of bullying research, there is evidence that family dynamics as they relate to child temperament and parenting practices are important factors (Veenstra, Lindenberg, Oldehinkel, De Winter, & Ormel, 2006). Positive relations between aspects of parenting and a decreased likelihood of peer aggression are documented in research conducted in Western, industrial countries (Chang, Lansford, Schwartz, & Farver, 2004). Although, bullying is considered a worldwide phenomenon (Pinheiro, 2006), there is limited research on bullying among school children in developing countries. To help bridge this gap, this study examines the relation between perceived parental understanding and bullying among junior high school students in Ghana, West-Africa.

Identifying Roles in the Bully/Victim Phenomenon

Olweus' (1993) definition of bullying, the most commonly used, includes three components: repeated negative action, intention to cause harm, and an imbalance of power. A bullying victim is a person exposed repeatedly over time to negative actions on the part of one or more persons (Olweus, 1993). A bully or aggressor is a person who repeatedly inflicts injury or discomfort, be it physical or nonphysical on another individual. Bullying roles are not fixed and can vary over time and situations. It is possible for children or adolescents to be both a bully and a victim at some point in their lives (Liang, Flisher, & Lombard, 2007).

Adolescence and Bullying

Adolescence is marked by major physical and psychological change, as well as great changes in social interactions and relationships (World Health Organization, 2008). Health and development, as it relates to physical, psychological, and social factors, are closely intertwined in adolescents. Much of what is experienced during adolescence can have lifelong consequences (World Health Organization, 2008). If health and social development are hindered during adolescence, consequences may occur throughout the remainder of a person's life (Parault, Davis, & Pellegrini, 2007). The adverse effects of bullying experienced by adolescents, both perpetrators and victims, may be manifested during adolescence or much later in life (Ando, Asakura, & Simons-Morton, 2005). Physical effects include headache, stomachache, backache, and dizziness, while psychological consequences include bad temper, nervousness, depression, and helplessness (Due et al., 2005). In addition, both bullies and victims report lower social, emotional, and physical health compared to their peers (Nansel, Craig, Overpeck, Saluja, & Ruan, 2004). This association between bullying and adverse psychosocial adjustment transcends culture and national borders (Nansel et al., 2004). In terms of long-term effect, victims during adolescence are more likely to be victims as adults in the workplace (Smith, Singer, Hoel, & Cooper, 2003). There is also an increased likelihood of perpetrators becoming law offenders (Glew, Rivera, & Feudtner, 2000; Olweus, 1993), having increased problems in interpersonal relationships (Hugh-Jones & Smith, 1999), and having substance abuse problems later in life (Kaltiala-Heino, Rimpela, & Rimpela, 2000). According to the WHO's Department of Child and Adolescent Health and Development, in the year 2000 alone, unintentional injuries and violence claimed the lives of over 350,000 young men ages 10 to 19 years (World Health Organization, 2003).

Bullying in Schools: Africa

School bullying is a perennial global problem with adverse consequences for a significant number of affected students (Baldry & Farrington, 2004). Global bullying prevalence within schools varies significantly between countries (Nansel et al., 2004). Students are bullied in school for a variety of reasons including appearance, how they talk, ethnicity, behavior, dressing, and socio-economic status (Frisen, Jonsson, & Persson, 2007).

Although there is extensive literature on school bullying in developed countries, there is a limited research on the phenomenon in developing countries (Liang et al., 2007). The finding of the number of relatively few bullying related studies in developing countries have varied significantly, even on the same continent. For example, in Africa, more literature is available for South Africa (Dussich & Maekoya, 2007; Liang et al., 2007; Neser, Ovens, van der Merwe, Morodi, & Ladikos, 2003; Reddy et al., 2003; Taiwo & Goldstein, 2006; Townsend, Flisher, Chikobvu, Lombard, & King, 2008; Wild, Flisher, Bhana, & Lombard, 2004) compared to countries such as Nigeria (Egbochuku, 2007) and Ghana (Amedahe & Owusu-Banahene, 2007). Among the African countries for which data are available on school bullying (Baldry & Farrington, 2000), there is significant variation in prevalence. The prevalence of bullying in South Africa ranges from 61% among high school students in Tshwane (Neser et al., 2003), 41% in a national sample of high school students (Reddy et al., 2003), 36% among eighth through eleventh graders in Cape Town (Liang et al., 2007), and 12% among students in rural high schools in Mpumalanga (Taiwo & Goldstein, 2006). In Nigeria, there is a documented bullying prevalence of 78% among junior secondary school students (Egbochuku, 2007). The divergent rates reflect varying methodology including sampling, scope and timeframe of measurement. Despite the relative lack of research on the determinants, effects, and interventions relating to the bullying phenomenon in Africa, there is an increasing amount of data available from the Global School-based Student Health Survey (GSHS). Published GSHS prevalence rates among 13- to 15-year-old students highlight the pervasiveness of bullying among African adolescents. Reported prevalence rates (22% to 65%) for African countries are as follows: Zambia 65%, Ghana 59%, Kenya 57%, Botswana 52%, Namibia 52%, Uganda 46%, Mauritius 40%, and Tanzania 28% (World Health Organization, 2009). As these data show, the incidence of bullying is common across various regions of Africa.

Parents and the Bullying Phenomenon

A number of external factors influence children's cognitive and behavioral disposition. This includes the dynamic relationship they have with friends, parents, and teachers. During adolescence, the values and behavior of friends are important, however, parents and other family members continue to influence adolescents in significant ways (World Health Organization, 2001). Parents influence the way adolescents feel about themselves and the subsequent choices they make. Parenting and family problems such as inconsistent supervision of children, harsh physical punishment, parental conflict in their child's early childhood, lax or inconsistent discipline, low level of family cohesion, and low parental involvement contribute to youth violence including bullying (Barboza et al., 2009; Bowers, Smith, & Binney, 1994; Centers for Disease Control and Prevention, 2007; Moore, 2009; World Health Organization, 2001). In addition, family structure, specifically single-parent households, is associated with a higher risk for adverse child behavior (Bjarnason et al., 2003; Griffin, Botvin, Scheier, Diaz, & Miller,

2000). Bowers and colleagues (1994) found that children involved in bullying were significantly more likely to have no father at home than children who were not involved in bullying. For bullying victims, an over protective parent (especially the mother) and over-involvement by the parent to control behavior increased the likelihood of the child being bullied (Ladd & Ladd, 1998). However, a positive parent-child relationship involving meaningful conversations and appropriate parental monitoring can negatively impact violent behavior (Pinheiro, 2006). Although the influence of parents diminishes during adolescence (U.S. Department of Health and Human Services, 2001), parents still play an important role, especially in the lives of younger adolescents.

From a conceptual perspective, attachment theory provides a useful framework for examining child-parent relationship and its connection to bullying (Eliot & Cornell, 2009). It states that healthy parent-child relationships serve as a secure base from which children can explore their environment (Bowlby, 1988). Extrapolating from attachment theory, children with sensitive and responsive parents develop a secure attachment with positive working models of themselves and others (Eliot & Cornell, 2009). *Securely* attached children have the ability to detach with confidence and elicit help and comfort when they feel threatened (Eliot & Cornell, 2009). *Insecure* children are more likely to be aggressive with peers because of perceive hostility to neutral peer interactions (Dodge, Bates, & Petit, 1990).

Purpose of this Study

Following up on the role of parents in the bullying phenomenon, this study seeks to examine the association between perceived parental understanding and the likelihood of being bullied among junior high school students in Ghana, West-Africa. The research question examined in this study is: When controlling for being taught how to avoid bullying in school, what is the relation between students' perceived parental understanding of their problems and worries and the extent to which they are bullied in school? It is hypothesized that when controlling for being taught how to avoid bullying in school, students who perceive that their parents understand their worries and problems are less likely to be bullied than those who perceive that their parents do not understand their worries and problems.

Method

Sampling Plan

This study was conducted using data from a national representative sample of all junior secondary school students in Ghana, West-Africa. The sampling frame consisted of all senior high schools (SHS) in Ghana. A two-stage cluster sampling approach was utilized to draw the sample. In the first stage, 75 schools representing all 10 geographic regions in Ghana were selected. Schools were selected with a probability proportional to enrollment size (World Health Organization & U.S. Centers for Disease Control and Prevention, 2006). In the second stage, intact, eligible classes from selected schools were randomly chosen. All students in a selected school had an equal probability of selection. Every student in selected classrooms was eligible to participate. Due to complex sampling, a numerical weight was assigned to each record to allow generalization of results to the eligible population.

Participants

Among participants in the 2007 GSHA, the school, student, and overall response rates were 97%, 86%, and 83%, respectively. Of the 3,813 participants, 49% and 51% were male and female students, respectively. Twenty-three percent (877) were 13 years of age, 33% (1,252) were age 14 years of age, and 44% (1,684) were 15 years of age. For regional comparison, the country was divided into three zones (south, central, and north) representing all 10 geographic regions.

Measures

The 2007 Ghana GSHS is a modified version of the generic World Health Organization (WHO) GSHS. The generic GSHS is a self-administered, school-based survey developed by WHO in collaboration with the United Nations Children's Fund, the United Nations Educational, Scientific and Cultural Organization, and the Joint United Nations Programme on HIV/AIDS, and with technical and financial assistance from the U.S. Centers for Disease Control and Prevention in Atlanta, Georgia. During development of the generic GSHS, focus groups were conducted in several countries representing each WHO region to ensure content validity. These focus groups provided important qualitative feedback on how the questions function in different cultures. Acculturated versions of the GSHS have been administered in 56 WHO member countries (World Health Organization, 2010).

The generic GSHS was modified into the 2007 Ghana GSHS by replacing all general examples of behavior, items, and issues with culturally appropriate ones. The included modules on the 2007 Ghana GSHS from the core modules in the generic GSHS were diet, physical activity, sexual behavior, mental health, hygiene, and drugs and alcohol use. Additional, information regarding development of the Ghana GSHS, design, testing and rational for survey content and, administration process is described elsewhere (World Health Organization & U.S. Centers for Disease Control and Prevention, 2006). This study is a secondary analysis of the 2007 Ghana GSHS data set focusing on bullying.

Bullying

The bullying section on the 2007 Ghana GSHS was introduced with a description of bullying. It describes bullying victimization as experiencing a negative behavior (physical, verbal, or relational) in an imbalanced relationship especially, physical power. The bulling victimization question used in the present study was: "During the past 30 days, how were you bullied most often?" The response options were: (a) I was not bullied during the past 30 days; (b) I was hit, kicked, pushed, shoved around, or locked indoors; (c) I was made fun of because of my race or color; (d) I was made fun of because of my religion; (e) I was made fun of with sexual jokes, comments, or gestures; (f) I was left out of activities on purpose or completely ignored; (g) I was made fun of because of how my body or face looks; and (h) I was bullied in some other way. The response options were recoded into three categories: not bullied, physical bullying, and nonphysical bullying. Physical forms of bullying included being hit, kicked, pushed or shoved, and forcefully being locked indoors. The nonphysical bullying category included verbal and relational bullying. Verbal bullying options included being made fun of because of skin color, religion, or physical appearance. Relational bullying refers to being left out of activities on purpose or completely ignored.

Parental Understanding

The item selected as independent variable was: during the past 12 months, how often did your parents or guardians understand your problems and worries? The five response options ranged from *never* to *always*. Of the GSHS items on parental involvement, this item best captures constructs of the parent child dynamic most relevant to bullying. It reflects communication (Desforges & Abouchaar, 2003) and emotional support (Zimmerman, Glew, Christakis, & Katon, 2005).

Control Variables

Gender, age, grade, and whether or not the students were taught in school about how to avoid bullying served as control variables. The *age* item had six options: (a) 11 years old or younger, (b) 12 years old, (c) 13 years old, (d) 14 years old, (e) 15 years old, and (f) 16 years old or older. Response options for the *grade* level item were (a) junior secondary school 1, (b) junior secondary school 2, and (c) junior secondary school 3. For the *being taught in school about how to avoid bullying* item, the response choices were (a) yes, (b) no, and (c) I do not know.

Analysis Plan

Descriptive statistics were produced with the complex samples procedure using SPSS 17.0. To produce results that conform to the actual sample size, the values of the sample's weight variable were reduced in magnitude by multiplying the original weight variable by the ratio of the actual sample size to the population estimate that was produced when the original weight was utilized (World Health Organization & U.S. Centers for Disease Control and Prevention, 2006). Multinomial logistic regression for complex samples was used to estimate the effects of parental understanding on physical bullying and nonphysical bullying with the reference category being students who did not report any form of bullying. Gender, age, grade, and whether or not the students were taught in school about how to avoid bullying served as statistical controls. Age was not a significant predictor of being bullied, so it was dropped from the analysis. Initial logistic regression models also included the interaction of gender with the other independent variables under the assumption that the effects of these variables on bullying were different for boys and girls. The significant interaction of gender and parental understanding remained in the final parsimonious model. To eliminate the interaction of gender and parental understanding, the logistic regression results are presented in this paper separately for boys and girls.

Results

Preliminary Results

Analyses using complex sampling techniques were conducted for the three categories of types of bullying experienced by students in Junior Secondary Schools (JSS) in Ghana. As shown in Table 15.1, 41.0% of children reported *not* being bullied. Physical bullying was experienced by 15.5% of the students; 43.6% of the children experienced nonphysical bullying.

Bivariate Pearson chi-square results for the cross tabulations between types of bullying experienced by students and the independent variables in this analysis indicate that there were no significant associations between gender and bullying type, $\psi^2 = 4.90$, $F = 1.89$ ($df\,1 = 1.96$, $df\,2 = 74.50$), $p = .159$, as well as age and types of bullying, $\psi^2 = 9.23$, $F = 1.35$ ($df\,1 = 3.108$, $df\,2 = 118.11$), $p = .262$. There were significant associations between bullying victimization and grade, $\psi^2 = 74.92$, $F = 9.98$ ($df\,1 = 3.48$, $df\,2\,132.05$), $p < .001$, being taught about how to avoid bullying in school, $\psi^2 = 53.44$, $F = 8.85$ ($df\,1 = 2.89$, $df\,2 = 109.85$), $p < .001$, and perceived parental understanding and types of bullying, $\psi^2 = 69.36$, $F = 14.56$ ($df\,1 = 3.36$, $df\,2 = 127.57$), $p < .001$.

Logistic Regression

Initial logistic regression analyses using complex sampling techniques were conducted for the three categories of types of bullying. Age was thought to be related to bullying, however, it was eliminated because of insignificant effect.

Table 15.1 Participant Characteristics

Characteristic	n	%
Ways children are bullied at school		
Not bullied	1,238	41.0
Kicked, pushed, shoved	467	15.5
Made fun of, etc.	1,317	43.6
Parents understood troubles, last 30 days		
Never	744	20.2
Sometimes	2,008	54.5
Always	931	25.3
Taught about how to avoid bullying		
No	1,267	34.5
Do not know	424	11.5
Yes	1,980	53.9
Junior secondary school grade		
First	1,444	38.1
Second	1,424	37.6
Third	923	24.3
Gender		
Boys	1,933	51.3
Girls	1,835	48.7
Age		
13 years	954	25.0
14 years	1,281	33.6
15 years	1,578	41.4

Note. Sample was weighted to represent the population (613,369), then unweighted by 3,813/613,369 to conform to actual sample size. Missing values are excluded for each characteristic.

The final parsimonious logistic regression model included gender, grade, parental understanding of problems or worries, and the extent to which children were taught about how to avoid bullying in school. There was a significant interaction between gender and parental understanding, Adjusted Wald $F = 3.27$ (3.37, 128.18), $p = .019$. Final results are presented in Tables 15.3 and 15.4 separately by gender.

The Nagelkerke R^2 for the boys and girls models, respectively, was .072 and .084. Classification tables comparing observed bullying behavior with the predicted behavior indicated that, overall, 50.7% for boys and 52.2% for girls were correctly predicted. These values are low. The hope was for correct predictions of at least 70%. No boy or girl was predicted to be physically bullied. At best, for boys the percent correctly predicted was 66.3% for those who were made fun of, left out of activities, or bullied in some other nonphysical way. For girls, 69.6% of those who were not bullied at school were correctly predicted to be in this category.

Physical Forms of Bullying

As shown in Table 15.2, boys whose parents or guardians never understood their problems and worries during the past 30 days were equally likely to be physically bullied as boys whose parents always understood their problems and worries (OR = 1.28, p = .311). Boys whose parents sometimes understood their problems were more likely to be physically bullied (OR = 1.81, $p < .001$) than boys whose parents always understood their problems.

As shown in Table 15.3, girls whose parents never understood their problems and worries (OR = 2.72, p = .001) and girls whose parents sometimes understood them (OR = 2.47, $p < .001$) were also more likely to be physically bullied than girls whose parents always understood their problems and worries.

Boys in the first year of junior secondary school (JSS-1) were more likely (OR = 2.37, p = .004) to be physically bullied than were boys in the third year. Boys in the second year were equally likely to be physically bullied than boys in the third year (OR = 1.60, p = .052). Girls in both the first (OR = 1.64, p = .046) and second (OR = 1.66, p = .026) JSS years were more likely to be physically bullied than girls in the third grade.

Table 15.2 Multinominal Logistic Regression Coefficients and Odds Ratios for the Ways Children Are Bullied at Junior Secondary Schools in Ghana — Boys (n = 1,390)

Ways children are bullied at school	β	OR	95% CI	π
Physical bullying				
Intercept	−1.676	0.187	0.115–0.304	.000
Parental understanding				
Never	0.243	1.275	0.789–2.060	.311
Sometimes	0.591	1.806	1.337–2.441	.000
Always	reference	1.000	—	—
Junior secondary school grade				
First	0.863	2.370	1.338–4.198	.004
Second	0.473	1.604	0.996–2.585	.052
Third	reference	1.000	—	—
Taught how to avoid bullying				
Not taught	−0.231	0.794	0.574–1.098	.158
Do not know	0.447	1.563	0.984–2.484	.058
Taught	reference	1.000	—	—
Nonphysical bullying				
Intercept	−0.936	0.392	0.247–0.623	.000
Parental understanding				
Never	0.635	1.887	1.156–3.081	.012
Sometimes	0.699	2.011	1.317–3.071	.002
Always	reference	1.000	—	—
Junior secondary school grade				
First	0.781	2.184	1.464–3.258	.000
Second	0.735	2.086	1.404–3.100	.001
Third	.000[a]	1.000	—	—
Taught how to avoid bullying				
Not taught	−0.339	0.712	0.495–1.025	.067
Do not know	0.500	1.649	0.988–2.752	.055
Taught	reference	1.000	—	—

Note. β logistic regression coefficient, OR = odds ratio, CI = confidence interval.

Table 15.3 Multinomial Logistic Regression Coefficients and Odds Ratios for the Ways Children Are Bullied at Junior Secondary Schools in Ghana — Girls (n = 1,405)

Ways children are bullied at school	β	OR	95% CI	π
Hit, kicked, pushed, shoved				
Intercept	-2.056	0.128	0.078–0.211	.000
Parental understanding				
Never	1.000	2.717	1.587–4.650	.001
Sometimes	0.904	2.468	1.670–3.648	.000
Always	reference	1.000	—	—
Junior secondary school grade				
First	0.495	1.641	1.009–2.670	.046
Second	0.504	1.655	1.065–2.573	.026
Third	reference	1.000	—	—
Taught how to avoid bullying				
Not taught	-0.663	0.515	0.291–0.911	.024
Do not know	0.526	1.693	0.957–2.993	.069
Taught	reference	1.000	—	—
Made fun of, left out, etc.				
Intercept	-0.827	0.437	0.314–0.610	.000
Parental understanding				
Never	0.208	1.231	0.910–1.665	.171
Sometimes	0.742	2.100	1.638–2.692	.000
Always	reference	1.000	—	—
Junior secondary school grade				
First	0.666	1.946	1.319–2.871	001
Second	0.469	1.599	1.164–2.196	
Third	reference	1.000	—	—
Taught how to avoid bullying				
Not taught	-0.417	0.659	0.445–0.977	039
Do not know	0.563	1.756	1.076–2.865	
Taught	reference	1.000	—	—

Note. β = logistic regression coefficient, OR = odds ratio, CI = confidence interval.

Girls who were not taught about avoiding bullying in school classes were less likely to be physically bullied (OR = .52, p = .024) than girls who were taught about bullying. Boys who were not taught about avoiding bullying were equally likely to be physically bullied (OR = 0.79, p = .159), as were boys and girls who reported that they did not know if they were taught about bullying.

Nonphysical Bullying

Forty-six percent of students reported nonphysical bullying or bullied in some other way. Boys whose parents or guardians never understood (OR = 1.89, p = .012) or sometimes understood (OR = 2.01, p = .002) their problems and worries were more likely to be bullied in nonphysical ways than boys whose parents always understood their problems and worries.

Girls whose parents never understood their problems and worries were equally likely to experience nonphysical bullying than girls whose parents always understood them (OR = 1.23, p = .171). Girls whose parents sometimes understood their problems and worries were more likely (OR = 2.10, p < .001) to be nonphysically bullied than girls whose parents always understood their problems and worries.

Boys and girls in the first and second years of JSS were more likely to experience nonphysical bullying than those in the third grade (boys: OR = 2.18, p < .001; OR = 2.09, p = .001, respectively; girls: OR = 1.95, p = .001; OR = 1.60, p = .005, respectively).

Taught How to Avoid Bullying

Boys who were not taught about how to avoid bullying in school, and boys who did not know if they had been taught, were equally likely to be nonphysically bullied as boys who were taught about this topic (OR = 0.71, p = .067) and (OR = 1.6, p = .055), respectively. Girls who were not taught about how to avoid bullying in classes were less likely to be physically bullied (OR = .66, p = .039) than girls who were taught about bullying. Girls who did not know if they had been taught about bullying were more likely (OR = 1.76, p = .025) to be bullied in nonphysical ways than girls who remembered being taught about bullying in school.

Discussion

This is the first study to document the bullying phenomenon at the national level in Ghana among junior high school students. The primary aim was to examine the association between perceived parental understanding of child worries and problems, and the likelihood of reporting being bullied among junior high school students' ages 13 to 15 years. The findings confirm that bullying is a substantial problem in Ghana with 59% of junior high students reporting being bullied one or more times in the 30 days preceding the survey. The latter figure exceeds published rates for other international studies that report rates of 9% to 54% (Nansel et al., 2004), although various measures and timeframes for bullying were used. For a more exact comparison among students ages 13 to 15 years, Ghana's published rate of 59% is the second highest among the 12 countries in Africa who have administered the Global School-Based Student Health Survey (World Health Organization, 2009). In general, these findings indicate that children's perceptions that their parent(s) always understand their problems and worries is associated with a reduction in likelihood of being victimized at school compared to students who perceive that their parents sometimes understand their worries and problems. This finding is consistent with existing literature indicating social support from parents as a significant mitigating factor in the bullying phenomenon (Demaray & Malecki, 2003; Pinheiro, 2006; Kaltiala-Heino, Rimpela, Marttunen, Rimpela, & Rantanen, 1999). Although parental influence decreases with age during adolescence (U.S. Department of Health and Human Services, 2001), this study demonstrates that there is still a significant association between perceived parental input and adolescent behavior, at least from the perspective of these Ghana students. Specifically, when considering nonphysical forms of bullying, children who always perceive that their parents understand their problems and worries are less likely to be bullied compared to those whose parents sometimes or never understand their problems. For physical forms of bullying, children who always perceive that their parents understand their problems and worries are less likely to be bullied compared to those whose parents sometimes understand their problems.

The lack of a significant difference in report of bullying victimization between the *always* and *never* groups might be explained using the attachment theory. For this explanation, we use parental understanding of a child's worries and problems as a proxy measure for parental attachment.

Extrapolating from the theory, *securely* attached children have the ability to detach with confidence and elicit help and comfort when they feel threatened (Eliot & Cornell, 2009). In contrast, *insecurely* attached adolescents can be aggressive, hostile, and antisocial (Erickson, Sroufe, & Egeland, 1985; LaFreniere & Sroufe, 1985; Renken, Egeland, Marvinney, Mangelsdorf, & Sroufe, 1989). *Insecure* children are more likely to be aggressive with peers because of perceive hostility to neutral peer interactions (Dodge et al., 1990). Using attachment theory as reference, the *always* group might be *securely* attached to parents whereas the *never* group may be insecurely attached. This leads to greater likelihood of positively dealing with bullying and as a result being less likely to report being bullied. Although individuals in the *never* group may be *insecurely* attached to parents, they are more likely to be perpetrators. Insecure attachment increases the potential for aggression towards peers. The 2007 Ghana GSHS did not contain any items to assess aggression towards peers. Therefore, we recommend additional research to examine the relationship between aggression towards peers, bullying victimization and, parental attachment.

Previous studies (Baldry & Farrington, 2000; Centers for Disease Control and Prevention, 2003, 2007; Frisen et al., 2007; Rigby, 2005) indicate that boys are somewhat more likely to report being bullied than girls. Our results did not confirm this finding for this population. In addition, the same (previous) studies indicate that boys are more likely to be physically bullied. Again, our results do not confirm this for our population; both genders are equally likely to report being bullied physically. Although this finding deviates from the other research, there is supporting evidence that in the early teen years, girls have a tendency to be more ready to use violence (Borg, 1999; Nansel et al., 2001; Rivers & Smith, 1994).

Gender differences were observed in the pattern of bullying when examining its association with perceived parental understanding on bullying. For both genders, when focusing on physical forms of bullying, *always* perceiving parental understanding is associated with a decreased likelihood of being bullied compared to the *sometimes* being understood. However, this does not hold true when comparing the *always* and *never* groups. Among boys, there was no difference in reported bullying between the *never* understood group and the *always* understood group. For girls, the *never* understood group was more likely to report experiencing physical forms of bullying compared to the *always* understood group. Additional gender-based differences in the pattern of bullying were observed when focusing on nonphysical forms. Boys in the *always* understood group are significantly less likely to report being bullied compared to the *sometimes* and *never* groups. For girls though, students whose parents sometimes understand their worries and problems consistently fair worse on reports of being bullied compared to the *always* and *never* understood groups. These findings suggest that when considering physical forms of bullying among JHS students in Ghana, parents may have less of an influence on boys compared to girls. For nonphysical forms of bullying and its association with parental understanding, the results are inconclusive for girls. Thus, we believe there is a need for further inquiry using a longitudinal design to better understand gender-based victimization patterns and its relation to parental understanding. Such a design would help address the issue of causality. That is, does parental understanding dictate bullying pattern within gender or does type of bullying experienced precede perceived parental understanding when controlling for gender?

The association between being taught how to avoid bullying in school and incidence of bullying was not significant for boys. The lack of significance is not surprising. This is consistent with existing literature that suggests antibullying programs lead to little observable effect on youth participants if not targeted specifically at at-risk youth (Ferguson, San Miguel, Kilburn, & Sanchez, 2007). Within the latter context, it is also possible that any expected reduction in reports of victimization did not materialize because of greater awareness about bullying. Existing literature suggests a corresponding increase in bullying reporting as bullying education increases (Creighton, 2004). Since GSHS items on bullying do not allow us to discern between general

Table 15.4 Implications for Practice: Tips for Educators, Administrators, Policy Makers, and Researchers

1.	Include antibullying programs as part of larger initiative to address school-based violence.
2.	Recognize and incorporate data on varying patterns of bullying victimization between subgroups when designing interventions.
3.	Develop comprehensive antibullying programs that focus beyond students to include teachers and parents.
4.	Initiate preservice and inservice training to help teachers proactively deal with school-based bullying.
5.	Include additional bullying related items on the Ghana GSHS questionnaire to allow for better insight on bullying roles.
6.	Encourage other West-African countries to adopt the GSHS as means of collecting valuable data on school-based violence including bullying.
7.	Base policy and curricula decisions about school violence in West-Africa on data from assessment instruments such as the GSHS where available.

in-school bullying programs and those that target at at-risk youth, we are unable to examine difference in victimization patterns between the latter groups. We recommend further studies designed to explore bullying and victimization in the context of general versus targeted interventions. Targeted bullying interventions should be grounded in theory and must consider the effect of relevant constructs on peer aggression.

For girls, the association between being taught how to avoid bullying in school and incidence of bullying was significant, although in an unexpected way. Girls who reported not knowing if they had been taught how to avoid bullying in school were less likely to experience nonphysical forms of bullying compared to the "taught' and "not taught" groups. We are a not sure why this is the case, thus, we recommend further inquiry using a more robust study design to re-examine the observed association.

Study Limitations

Although the study focused on school-based bullying, none of the questions used in analysis assessed the source of bullying. That is, there were no items to differentiate between intergroup and intragroup perpetration of bullying. There were also no items to help assess cross-gender bullying (perpetration) patterns. Thus, we were unable to examine whether victimization patterns across gender and grade level differ when considering bullying source. Furthermore, because of the cross sectional nature of the study, we cannot infer and or compare bullying pattern trajectory to expected developmental changes during adolescence.

Conclusion

This study contributes to the scant literature on bullying among school-age students in Africa and in Ghana specifically, the results confirm that bullying is a nationwide problem. Although several individual characteristics such as ethnicity, grade, anger, depression, and normative belief's influence bullying, familial dynamics also plays a crucial role. In Ghana, there is a strong association between student-perceived parental understanding, a protective factor, and the likelihood of being bullied. We recommend that future studies examine a more comprehensive set of independent variables grounded in theory to better understand the bullying phenomenon in Ghana. It is also suggested that policy makers take into account GSHS data when making or revising policies and or curricula to address school-based violence. On a broader scale we recommend basing policy and curricula decisions about school violence in sub-Saharan Africa on data from assessment instruments such as the GSHS.

References

Amedahe, F. K., & Owusu-Banahene, N. O. (2007). Sex differences in the forms of aggression among adolescent students in Ghana. *Research in Education 78*, 54–64.

Ando, M., Asakura, T., & Simons-Morton, B. (2005). Psychosocial influences on physical, verbal, and indirect bullying among Japanese early adolescents. *Journal of Early Adolescence, 25*, 268–297. doi:10.1177/0272431605276933

Baldry, A. C., & Farrington, D. P. (2000). Bullies and delinquents: Personal characteristics and parenting styles. *Journal of Community & Applied Social Psychology, 22*, 423–426.

Baldry, A., & Farrington, D. (2004). Evaluation of an intervention program for the reduction of bullying and victimization in schools. *Aggressive Behavior, 30*, 1–15. doi:10.1002/ab.20000

Barboza, G., Schiamberg, L., Oehmke, J., Korzeniewski, S., Post, L., & Heraux, C. (2009). Individual characteristics and the multiple contexts of adolescent bullying: An ecological perspective. *Journal of Youth and Adolescence, 38*, 101–121. doi:10.1007/s10964-008-9271-1

Bjarnason, T., Andersson, B., Choquet, M., Elekes, Z., Morgan, M., & Rapinett, G. (2003). Alcohol culture, family structure and adolescent alcohol use: Multilevel modeling of frequency of heavy drinking among 5–16 year old students in 11 European countries. *Journal of Studies on Alcohol, 64*, 200–208.

Bowers, L., Smith, P., & Binney, V. (1994). Perceived family relationships of bullies, victims and bully/victims in middle childhood. *Journal of Social and Personal Relationships, 11*, 215–232. doi:10.1177/0265407594112004

Bowlby, J. (1988). *A secure base: Parent-child attachment and healthy human development.* London, England: Basic Books.

Centers for Disease Control and Prevention. (2003). *Youth violence: Fact sheet.* Retrieved March 10, 2008, from http://www.cdc.gov/ncipc/factsheets/yvfacts.htm

Centers for Disease Control and Prevention. (2007). *Youth violence: Facts at a glance.* Retrieved March 1, 2008, from http://www.cdc.gov/injury

Chang, L., Lansford, J., Schwartz, D., & Farver, J. (2004). Marital quality, maternal depressed affect, harsh parenting, and child externalising in Hong Kong Chinese families. *The International Society for the Study of Behavioral Development, 28*, 311–318. doi:10.1080/01650250344000523

Craig, W. (1998). The relationship among bullying, victimization, depression, anxiety and aggression in elementary school children. *Personality and Individual Differences, 24*, 123–130. doi:10.1016/S0191-8869(97)00145-1

Creighton, S. J. (2004). Prevalence and incidence of child abuse: International comparisions. *NSPCC Information Briefing,* Retrieved December 5, 2009, from http://www.nspcc.org.uk/Inform/research/Briefings/prevalenceandincidenceofchildabuse_wda48217.html

Demaray, M. K., & Malecki, C. K. (2003). Perceptions of the frequency and importance of social support by students classified as victims, bullies, and bully/victims in an urban middle school. *School Psychology Review, 32*, 471–489.

Desforges, C., & Abouchaar, A. (2003). *The impact of parental involvement, parental support and family education on pupil achievements and adjustment: A literature review.* Research Report 443. London, England: Department for Education and Skills.

Dodge, K. A., Bates, J. E., & Petit, G. S. (1990). Mechanisms in the cycle of violence. *Science, 250*, 1678–1683. doi:10.1126/science.2270481

Due, P., Holstein, B. E., Lynch, J., Diderichsen, F., Gabhain, S. N., Scheidt, P., & Currie, C. (2005). Bullying and symptoms among school-aged children: International comparative cross-sectional study in 28 countries. *The European Journal of Public Health, 15*, 128–132. doi:10.1093/eurpub/cki105

Dussich, J., & Maekoya, C. (2007). Physical child harm and bullying-related behaviors: A comparitive study in Japan, South Africa, and the United States. *International Journal of offender Therapy and Comparative Criminology, 51*, 495–509. doi:10.1177/0306624X0 6298463

Egbochuku, E. O. (2007). Bullying in Nigerian schools: Prevalence study and implications for counselling. *Journal of Social Science, 14*, 65–71.

Eliot, M., & Cornell, D. G. (2009). Bullying in middle school as a function of insecure attachment and aggressive attitudes. *School Psychology International, 30*, 201–214. doi:10.1177/0143034309104148

Erickson, M. F., Sroufe, L. A., & Egeland, B. (1985). The relationship between quality of attachment and behavior problems in preschool in a high-risk sample. *Monographs of the Society for Research in Child Development, 50*, 147–166.

Espelage, D., & Swearer, S. (2003). Research on school bullying and victimization: What have we learned and where do we go from here? *School Psychology Review, 32*, 365–383.

Ferguson, C., San Miguel, C., Kilburn, J., & Sanchez, P. (2007). The effectiveness of school-based anti-bullying programs: A meta-analytic review. *Criminal Justice Review, 32*, 401–414. doi:10.1177/0734016807311712

Frisen, A., Jonsson, A., & Persson, C. (2007). Adolescents' perception of bullying: Who is the victim? Who is the bully? What can be done to stop bullying? *Adolescence, 42,* 749–761.

Furrer, M. (2006). *United Nations Secretary-General's Study on Violence Against Children.* Retrieved from http://www.violencestudy.org/r27

Glew, G., Rivera, F., & Feudtner, C. (2000). Bullying: Children hurting children. *Pediatrics in Review, 21,* 183–190. doi:10.1542/pir.21-6-183

Griffin, K. W., Botvin, G. J., Scheier, L. M., Diaz, T. L., & Miller, N. L. (2000). Parenting practices as predictors of substance use, delinquency, and aggression among urban minority youth: Moderating effects of family structure and gender. *Psychology of Addictive Behaviors, 14,* 174–184.

Hugh-Jones, S., & Smith, P. K. (1999). Self-reports of short- and long-term effects of bullying on children who stammer. *British Journal of Educational Psychology, 69,* 141–158. doi:10.1348/000709999157626

Kaltiala-Heino, R., Rimpela, M., Marttunen, M., Rimpela, A., & Rantanen, P. (1999). Bullying, depression, and suicidal ideation in Finnish adolescents: school survey. *British Medical Journal, 319,* 348–351.

Kaltiala-Heino, R., Rimpela, M., Rantanen, P., & Rimpela, A. (2000). Bullying at school: An indicator of adolescents at risk for mental disorders. *Journal of Adolescence, 23,* 661–674. doi:10.1006/jado.2000.0351

Ladd, G. W., & Ladd, B. K. (1998). Parenting behaviors and parent-child relationships: Correlates of peer victimization in kindergarten. *Developmental Psychology, 34,* 1450–1458.

LaFreniere, P., & Sroufe, L. A. (1985). Profiles of peer competence in the preschool: Interrelations between measures, influence of social ecology, and relation to attachment history. *Developmental Psychology, 21,* 56–69. doi:10.1037/0012-1649.21.1.56

Liang, H., Flisher, A., & Lombard, C. (2007). Bullying, violence, and risk behavior in South African school students. *Child Abuse & Neglect, 31,* 161–171. doi:10.1016/j.chiabu.2006.08.007

Moore, K. S. (2009). Children and bullying: How parents and educators can reduce bullying at school. *Family Journal, 17,* 91–93. doi: 10.1111/j.1475-3588.2009.00530_3.x

Nansel, T. R., Overpeck, M.D., Pilla, M., Ruan, W., Simmons-Morton, B., & Schmidt, P. (2001). Bullying behaviors among US youth. *Journal of American Medical Association, 285,* 2094–2100. doi:10.1001/jama.285.16.2094

Nansel, T. R., Craig, W., Overpeck, M. D., Saluja, G., & Ruan, W. (2004). Cross-national consistency in the relationship between bullying behaviors and psychosocial adjustment. *Archives of Pediatric Adolescent Medicine, 158,* 730–736. doi:10.1001/archpedi.158.8.730.

Neser, J. J., Ovens, M., van der Merwe, E., Morodi, R., & Ladikos, A. (2003). *Peer victimisation in schools: The victims.* Retrieved December June, 2010, from http://www.crisa.org.za /victimsp.pdf

Olweus, D. (1993). *Bullying at school: What we know and what we can do.* Malden, MA: Wiley-Blackwell.

Olweus, D. (1994). Bullying at school: Long-term outcomes for the victims and an effective school-based intervention program. In L. R. Huesmann (Ed.), *Aggressive behavior: Current perspectives* (pp. 97–130). New York, NY: Plenum.

Parault, S., Davis, H., & Pellegrini, A. (2007). The social contexts of bullying and vicitimization. *Journal of Early Adolescence, 27,* 145–174. doi:10.1177/0272431606294831

Pinheiro, S. P. (2006). *United Nations study on violence against children* (pp. 111–157). Geneva, Switzerland: United Nations.

Reddy, S. P., Panday, S., Swart, D., Jinabhai, C. C., Amosun, S. L., James, S., et al. (2003). *Umthenthe uhlaba usamila: The South African youth risk behaviour survey 2002.* Cape Town, South Africa: Medical Research Council.

Renken, B., Egeland, B., Marvinney, D., Mangelsdorf, S., & Sroufe, L. A. (1989). Early childhood antecedents of aggression and passive-withdrawal in early elementary school. *Journal of Personality, 57,* 257–281. doi:10.1111/j.1467-6494.1989.tb00483.x

Rigby, K. (2005). Why do some children bully at school? *School Psychology International, 26,* 147–161. doi:10.1177/0143034305052910

Rivers, I., & Smith, P. (1994). Types of bullying behaviour and their correlates. *Aggressive Behavior, 20,* 359–368. doi:10.1002/1098-2337(1994)20:5<359::aid-ab2480200503>3.0.co;2-j

Roland, E., & Munthe, E. (1989). A system oriented strategy against bullying. In B. Webber (Ed.), *Bullying: An international perspective* (pp. 143–151). Mahwah, NJ: Erlbaum.

Smith, P. K., & Sharp, S. (1994). *School bullying: Insights and perspectives.* London, England: Routledge.

Smith, P. K., Singer, M., Hoel, H., & Cooper, C. L. (2003). Victimization in the school and workplace: Are there any links? *British Journal of Psychology, 94,* 175–188. doi:10.1348/000712603321661868

Taiwo, T., & Goldstein, S. (2006). Drug use and its association with deviant behaviour among rural adolescent students in South Africa. *East African Medical Journal, 83,* 500–506.

Townsend, L., Flisher, A., Chikobvu, P., Lombard, C., & King, G. (2008). The relationship between bullying behaviours and high school dropout in Cape Town, South Africa. *South African Journal of Psychology, 38,* 21–32.

U.S. Department of Health and Human Services. (2001). *Youth violence: A report of the Surgeon General*. Rockville, MD: U.S. Department of Health and Human Services, Centers for Disease Control and Prevention, National Center for Injury Prevention and Control, Substance Abuse and Mental Health Services Administration, Center for Mental Health Services, National Institutes of Health, National Institute of Mental Health.

Veenstra, R., Lindenberg, S., Oldehinkel, A. J., De Winter, A. F., & Ormel, J. (2006). Temperament, environment, and antisocial behavior in a population sample of preadolescent boys and girls. *International Journal of Behavioral Development, 30*, 422–432. doi:10.1177/0165025406071490

Whitney, I., & Smith, P. K. (1993). A survey of the nature and extent of bullying in junior middle and secondary schools. *Educational Research, 35*, 3–25. doi:10.1080/0013188930350101

Wild, L. G., Flisher, A. J., Bhana, A., & Lombard, C. (2004). Associations among adolescent risk behaviours and self-esteem in six domains. *Journal of Child Psychology and Psychiatry and Allied Disciplines, 45*, 1454–1467. doi:10.1111/j.1469-7610.2004.0 0330.x

World Health Organization. (2001). *The second decade*. Retrieved March 25, 2008, from http://www.whoint/childadolescent-health

World Health Organization. (2003). *Strategic directions*. Retrieved May 12, 2008, from http://www.who.int/child_adolescent_health/documents/9241591064/en/index.html

World Health Organization. (2008). *Child and adolescent health and development*. Retrieved March 27, 2008, from http://www.who.int/child_adolescent_health/topics/development/en/index.html

World Health Organization. (2009). *Fact sheets: Global School-based Student Health Survey*. Retrieved March 10, 2009, from http://www.who.int/chp/gshs/factsheets/en/index.html

World Health Organization, & U.S. Centers for Disease Control and Prevention. (2006). *Global school-based student health survey surveillance manual*. New York, NY: World Health Organization.

Zimmerman, F. J., Glew, G. M., Christakis, D. A., & Katon, W. (2005). Early cognitive stimulation, emotional support, and television watching as predictors of subsequent bullying among grade-school children. *Archives of Pediatrics & Adolescent Medicine, 159*, 384–388. doi:10.1001/archpedi.159.4.384

16

Monitoring School Violence in Israel, National Studies and Beyond

Implications for Theory, Practice, and Policy

Rami Benbenishty

BAR ILAN UNIVERSITY, ISRAEL

Ron Avi Astor

UNIVERSITY OF SOUTHERN CALIFORNIA, LOS ANGELES

Abstract

This chapter describes an ongoing study of school violence that consists of a series of waves of national data collection in Israel. The chapter presents the unique methodological characteristics of the study including its large, representative, and nested sample, extensive and detailed instruments for multiple constituents (students, teachers, and principals) and multilevel analyses. The overall focus is on monitoring of school violence and climate and the continuous feedback to help use this information to prevent school violence. The chapter presents several examples of the ways in which a national monitoring study impacted the professional and public discourse. Finally, the chapter describes how a national study based on a sample led to a monitoring system that is implemented in all primary and junior high schools. This unique system integrates monitoring of academic outcomes and school climate and violence. The implications of these developments for school reform and continuous improvement are discussed.

This chapter presents the National Study of School Violence in Israel, conducted by the authors. The study has many implications for research and policy making in the area of school violence relevant for many other countries and contexts. The aim of this chapter is to review the study while explicating its relevance to theory, practice, and policy.

Israel National Study of School Violence

This chapter describes an ongoing study that consists of a series of waves of data collection. The first wave was conducted in the fall of 1998 and the last carried out by the authors in spring 2005. A follow up wave was collected by an independent arm of the Israeli Ministry of Education in 2009, but the results are not yet public. Each of these waves utilized similar methodology and instruments, although slight modifications were used each year to respond to emerging needs.

This study is different than many other studies on school violence because it assumes that violence trends have the potential for continual change over time and need to be monitored on a regular basis. Many studies focus on a single historical timeframe and generalize their conclusions over time. The concept of monitoring assumes that research should function much like a social feedback system that continually responds to current and emerging needs. Monitoring is very similar to the public health concept of "surveillance" used by the Centers for Disease Control and Prevention (CDC). In the United States, the Youth Risk Behavior Survey (CDC, 2010) is an example of such efforts at the national level. Hence, these studies ought to be considered as a national "snapshot" that should be taken regularly in order to assess and understand change. These kinds of national studies are seen as a source of empirical findings to inform policy and practice on the regional and national level; however, these types of studies do not inform policy at the local school site level (Benbenishty, Astor, & Zeira, 2003).

This study is unique methodologically in several important ways. It is based on a very large national random sample of schools nested in their communities. The questionnaire is extensive and deals with multiple forms of victimization, perpetration, and bystander behaviors. Within schools, there are parallel surveys that sample students, teachers, and principals. Israel is the only country to have such an ongoing comprehensive, nested, and large scale national study entirely devoted to issues of school safety. The following sections outline some of the study's specific design issues that may be of interest to any country considering developing similar national studies.

Sample

The samples used over the years were designed to represent all schools, students, teachers and principals in grades 4–11 in the official public school system supervised by the Israeli Ministry of Education. The authors' theoretical focus of "students within schools" (Benbenishty & Astor, 2005) necessitated having a representative sample of all public schools in Israel that was large enough to allow for school-level analyses. Further, it was important to obtain representative samples of students and teachers from each of these schools. Therefore, the probability sampling method used was a two-stage stratified cluster sample. In the first stage, schools were selected randomly from the sampling frame according to their appropriate strata and their relative size. In the second stage of sampling, one or two classes were randomly selected from each of the grade levels in the selected schools (in 2002 and 2005 two classes from two different grade levels were sampled randomly from each school).

The sample strata reflected theoretical and policy questions, and thus changed over the years to focus on student populations that were seen of special interest. In 1998 and 1999 the strata were: Jewish (religious and nonreligious)/Arab and Primary/Junior High/High school. In 2002, following alarming findings in previous waves, a sub-sample of Bedouin students was added to the study, and in 2005 the Druz students were added as a sub-sample in order to more clearly distinguish between groups of minority students.

Because these national studies were supported by the Ministry of Education and major efforts were made to ensure participation, response rates were very high. In 2005, the response rate among schools was about 95.3%, and the response level among the students in these schools was about 95%. Sampling of homeroom teachers changed over the years. In 1999, all homeroom

Table 16.1 Sample Sizes of Three Waves of the National Study of School Violence

Year	Schools	Students	Principals	Homeroom Teachers
1998	232	15,916	—	—
1999	239	16,414	197	1,506
2002	410	21,577	295	595
2005	552	27316	420	1861

teachers were sampled in the relevant grade levels (response rate of approximately 60%). In 2002, only the homeroom teachers of the classes participated (591 with a response rate of approximately 68%). In 2005, we enhanced the sample and added a random sample of 1880 teachers whose students did not participate in the survey. Based on our previous experiences we improved our procedures, tightened supervision of data collection, and collaborated more closely with the Ministry. Consequently, we were able to increase the response rate of teachers from about 60% to 79% of the target sample. The response rate among principals also improved from 66% in 2002 to 76% in 2005. The sample sizes for students, teachers and principals in each of the study years are presented in Table 16.1.

Instruments

Student Survey

The questionnaires used were an adaptation of the research version of the California School Climate & Safety Survey (Furlong, 1996; Furlong, Morrison, Bates, & Chung, 1998; Rosenblatt & Furlong, 1997; for a recent short form see Furlong et al. 2005). The survey was modified to the Israeli context and to address issues of interest to the researchers. Questionnaires were developed in Hebrew and Arabic with a shorter version for primary school students and a longer one for secondary schools. Changes were made following each of the studies to respond to new needs and issues raised by previous findings. For instance, we added questions to assess staff victimization and sexual harassment among primary school students. In each of the data collection waves, the research instrument contained more than 100 questions pertaining to several areas: (a) personal victimization by peers, (b) weapons in school, (c) personal victimization by staff, (d) risky peer and staff behaviors in school, (e) feelings and assessments regarding school violence, and (f) school climate.

Principal Survey

The principals' questionnaire was designed specifically for this study and included the following sections: (a) school policies and coping with violence; (b) school climate relevant to violence; (c) report on violent acts in the last month and assessment of the seriousness of the problem; (d) interventions and projects implemented to deal with school violence in the last two years; (e) training needs; (f) relationships with and support from others in the school (e.g., counselors) and out of the school (e.g., the police, the central district office); and (h) background information on the school and its staff (such as turnover rates).

Teacher Survey

The teachers responded to a questionnaire that was very similar to the one used with the principals. The questionnaire also included a section on the teachers' feelings and behaviors regarding their own personal safety in the school.

School Context Information

Our theoretical model of "School in Context" (Benbenishty & Astor, 2005) emphasizes various aspects of the students and their families, school characteristics, and community contexts. The study therefore integrated databases from the Ministry of Education, the National Statistics Bureau, and the police. These sources provided aggregated information on school characteristics such as number of classes and students. It also provided aggregated data on the families of the students, such as percentages of low-income families, low education (under eight years of school), family size, and an aggregated SES (socio-economic status) score for the students' families. Based on each school's census tracts, we included a range of school neighborhood characteristics such as income, education, employment, family size, ethnic/religious heterogeneity, and heterogeneity in terms of new immigrants versus native Israelis. The police database was used to obtain rates and types of crimes in the school's neighborhood.

The Implications of Conducting a National Study of School Violence: Creating a Common Ground for Establishing Priorities

Commitment to Monitor School Violence

When examining the implications and the impact of a study, there is often a focus on the effects of its findings on policy, practice, and training. Indeed, as shown later, the findings of this study had such implications. However, it is important to point out that the Israeli National Study of School Violence had a valuable impact on Israeli society and the educational system because *it was conducted*. The financial investment made by the Ministry of Education was nontrivial. Furthermore, the superintendents of Israeli schools, the Ministers of Education, the Chief Scientist Office, and all regional supervisors made a strong commitment to the study and worked hard to ensure high levels of involvement by all in the educational establishment. These central government efforts sent a very strong signal to the educational system that collecting accurate information to address school violence was a priority. Over time, the Ministry developed means of examining the findings and creating forums to discuss their implications. Therefore, in some ways, the decision to actually collect comprehensive data for the purposes of dealing with these problems started a chain reaction that lead to more substantive changes, and to a dramatic increase in awareness and prevention activities.

The Ministry of Education is now committed to conduct these comprehensive national studies of school violence every 2–3 years. The 2005 study has been replicated in 2008–2009 by an arm of the Ministry that intends to continue this national-level monitoring. Moreover, since 2005, questions from the national monitoring study have been integrated into the ongoing yearly national-level monitoring of school violence at the district- and school-site levels. This chapter will later detail how the ideas of monitoring can have a major impact on the ways schools and districts address issues of school violence.

Empirical Findings as a Basis for Public and Professional Discourse

In the years since 1998, the findings of the studies have provided a very detailed picture of school violence in Israel. The country now has data on a large number of behaviors in detail for many cultural groups and subgroups, across gender, age, and school types. In our interactions with educators from all levels, we have noted a strong shift from a dynamic of debating personal theories, hunches, and case "examples" to examining representative figures and findings. This is an important progress toward continuous school improvement based on local empirical data (Bernhardt, 2004). The focus on systematic data was also clearly evident in the media. Invariably, when an extremely violent act was reported in the media, it became customary for media outlets to approach the researchers residing in Israel and interview them with regard to that event. The authors infused into the public discussion nationally representative research findings that gave the public an accurate scope of the problem. This helped limit (but not eliminate) over-generalizations made from single cases that were presented in the media. Among the many examples of the impact of having relevant national findings, several topics are illustrated below.

Different Forms of Victimization Needing Unique Explanations and Strategies

Many studies of school violence focus exclusively on bullying behaviors (e.g., Nansel et al., 2001). The Israeli study incorporated a more expansive definition of violence in schools to account for a much wider range of types of school victimization, including verbal violence, exclusion, verbal threats, physical violence (ranging from minor pushing and shoving to needing medical attention due to injuries in a fight), sexual harassment, and staff-initiated emotional, physical and sexual maltreatment. Primary school students reported on their experiences with 25–30 different types of victimization and secondary school students reported on 35–40 (depending on the data collection wave). To our knowledge, no other single study encompasses such a wide range of issues. Periodic compendiums of school violence indicators (e.g., Dinkes, Kemp, & Baum, 2009) summarize findings of several different studies, and are therefore unable to identify patterns and interrelationships among different forms of victimization.

The choice to include a wide range of behaviors had many implications. First, the students' reports of such a wide range of victimization types provided a very rich and detailed picture of what it means to be a student in an Israeli school, and how these experiences differ by gender, cultural and ethnic group, and whether the school is elementary, junior high or high school.

Further, the wide range of behaviors included in the study provided a rare opportunity to examine questions surrounding the *structure* of the different types of victimization (i.e., the relationships among the many victimization types), and how similar or different these structures are among the various groups (culture, age, gender). Several surprising empirical findings emerged. One such major finding is that for all cultures and age groups (including replications with large samples in California), the frequencies of victimization behaviors tend to be rank ordered exactly the same, with very minor variations across many contexts. That is, certain behaviors tended to be the most frequent among all groups (e.g., verbal insults), while other forms of violence were the rarest in all groups (e.g., cutting a student with a knife). This pattern has important implications for both theory and practice since it means that school violence behaviors are structured similarly despite different base rates across contexts and countries. It also suggests that behaviors that are "outliers" (i.e., do not conform to the universal ranking) may hold clues about those cultures and how they perceive and react to that particular type of school violence behavior. Thus, for instance, social boycott of students in Israel had very different meaning and rank-order for Jewish and Arab students, reflecting a different cultural meaning of such social behaviors. This line of inquiry yielded many helpful insights that are discussed in detail elsewhere (Benbenishty & Astor, 2005).

Situating the Scope of the Problem and its Increase or Decrease

The heightened awareness of school violence fueled at least partially by the findings in the first wave of the national study increased the sensitivity to school violence incidents. Hence, when educators and the general public were asked in newspapers polls whether school violence was on the rise, for most the answer was clear: "Yes, and without a doubt." This was also the researchers' experience in many public forums. The general public's perception of an increase in school violence rates was likely due to the increased media reporting of violent events.

In this context, the empirical findings had a very important role in the public debate. To counter the public intuition that violence was on a steep rise, data were continuously presented to show that for most forms of violence, there was a marked decrease in student peer victimization. This research was able to show that the general public subjective views were not "in sync" with the reports and perceptions of youth who attend schools. Most students reported that violence in their schools dropped when compared to prior years. These findings were used extensively in internal discussions in the Ministry of Education and were also brought to all public discussions of school violence, including in the Knesset (the Israeli parliament). Ironically, since the 1998 initial study, Israel has had significant reductions in school violence across most groups and categories. The media regularly reports the findings of the national studies but does not situate them in the context of reduction. Hence, the general public sees many case studies and findings reported by the media and tends to believe that the rates are going up rather than going down sharply.

Situating the Problem of Students Harming Teachers

Given the media portrayal of large numbers of students beating up teachers across the country, teachers were asked about their feelings of personal safety in school and to what extent students and parents victimized them. Overall, the findings indicated that very few of the teachers were physically attacked (many more were verbally abused), and such reports of teacher victimization were decreasing over the years. Indeed, it appeared that the media blitzes helped create public "hysteria" surrounding the lack of moral values in youth.

During this period, the researchers made a focused effort to encourage public discussion of the findings obtained from the teachers themselves (rather than a media campaign). The data and discourse provided an objective source for the public to understand the scope of the problem, the grades most heavily impacted, which ethnic and religious groups' teachers were most victimized (e.g., the very high concern for personal safety among Bedouin teachers and the low concern among Jewish religious teachers), and the extent of this problem when juxtaposed with other more pressing issues of school violence. These discussions helped to provide the public with a more cogent and data driven understanding of what was needed to support teachers.

Situating the Problem of Staff Harming Students

Staff behaviors have an important impact on students, both positively and negatively. Victimization by staff may impact students even more negatively than peer violence. The work by Hyman and colleagues attests to the potential harm that educators can cause (e.g., Hyman, 1990; Hyman & Perone, 1998; Hyman & Snook, 2000).

The Israel National Study of School Violence was the first to integrate staff-initiated violence and peer violence in school. The findings of our study made significant contributions to bringing this issue to the public eye. Clearly, staff-initiated victimization of students is not a marginal problem experienced by a negligible proportion of students. As reported elsewhere (Benbenishty, Zeira, & Astor, 2002; Benbenishty, Zeira, Astor, & Khoury-Kassabri, 2002), students perceived to be verbally and emotionally maltreated in significant proportions. For instance, in 2005 one out of three (33.3%) reported that during the last month a teacher mocked, insulted, or humiliated him or her, and one of five reported some kind of physical victimization by staff (21.5%). There was disproportional reporting of physical violence by Arab and Bedouin students. For instance, in 2005, whereas 14.7% of the Jewish students reported any type of physical maltreatment by staff, the percentage among Arab students was 38.2%, and among Bedouin students was 43.8%. It is important to note that in most Israeli schools, teachers and students in any specific school are of the same ethnic, cultural background, and religion. Furthermore, our findings indicate that staff physical violence was more prevalent in poor neighborhoods, even when ethnic affiliation was controlled (Benbenishty et al., 2002). These findings raised many theoretical and practical issues that are discussed in detail elsewhere (e. g., Khoury-Kassabri, Astor, & Benbenishty, 2008).

Focusing on the Meanings and Interpretations of Multiple Perspectives: Students, Homeroom Teachers, and Principals

Most of school violence studies focus on students, and only a few school violence researchers study teachers and principals. This is the first nationally representative school violence study that includes and *compares* multiple respondents (students, their teachers, and principals) from the same schools. There are several compelling reasons to include teachers and principals in school violence studies. Examples from our teacher and principal sections of the study will illustrate this point.

Teachers were asked about training in the area of school safety. Their early responses were both informative and alarming. In 2002, less than a quarter of the homeroom teachers said they had any relevant training during their studies in a college or university (only about a one-third of them felt it was helpful), two-thirds said they did not participate in any in-service training on how to deal with school violence, and more than a quarter of them said that they badly needed training. These findings have clear policy and training implications. In fact, some teacher colleges developed training material to respond to this expressed need. Interestingly, in 2005, fewer teachers and principals expressed a strong need to participate in training on school safety (e.g., a drop from 28.3% in 2002 to 17.5% in 2005). This may serve as an indication that the Ministry training efforts following the research report were actually having an impact on the workforce.

A second example of the importance of hearing the perspective of staff comes from a segment in our survey of principals that focused on their relationships with a series of role partners—parents, support staff, police, supervisors, and the district. In two subsequent waves of data collection, the picture was quite clear—principals felt alone on the front line of dealing with school safety. They felt that most other partners made very little contributions to their efforts to reduce school violence. For instance, in 2005 only 13.2% had positive assessment of the district contribution to their efforts. The group that was seen as most helpful was the pupil personnel support staff in school (i.e., counselors and psychologists). Still, only 41% of the principals felt in 2005 that support staff contributed much or very much to their efforts to reduce school violence and 29% felt they made no contribution or a small one. The authors communicated these findings to all these role partners through multiple channels.

In addition to looking separately at each of the multiple perspectives of the members of the school community, the comparisons (similarities or disparities) among them can contribute significantly to research and policy. From a research perspective, the converging or diverging multiple perspectives of school safety in the same school can help validate (or invalidate) the assessments made by each of the school stake holders.

Findings indicate that the degree of similarity between the three perspectives in the school can be informative as to how the school is functioning. Large gaps and disagreements between staff and students or between a principal and teachers may indicate that the school does not have a shared mission. For instance, if students assess the school as having a serious violence problem and the teachers and principals do not, one would expect that little will be done to address the students' distress. Thus, exploring the gaps between the multiple perspectives can contribute to assessment of schools and the identification of schools that show the highest levels of divergence of perspectives (see Benbenishty & Astor, 2005, for greater details).

Creating a Focus on the "School" in School Violence

The interplay between context and school violence has not been explored in great detail within the theoretical/empirical literature on school violence. The investigators made a methodological choice to include schools as units of analysis, in addition to individual students. Most of the research literature on school violence has neglected this analytical perspective and focused almost exclusively on student-level views of school victimization. In some ways this is surprising because most of the school safety intervention literature focuses on school-level programs. In order to understand the dynamics of school victimization, assess the need for school-wide interventions, and examine the outcomes of such programs, it seemed essential to explore victimization from a school unit perspective.

The choice to have the school as a unit of analysis was reflected in (a) the sampling of a large number of schools, each with a large enough number of students to allow reasonable school-level estimates; (b) instruments and data collection that included school level information (e.g., school size, the SES of the school neighborhood); and (c) an analytic plan that included multi-level statistical analyses (Hierarchical Linear Modeling; Khoury-Kassabri, Benbenishty, Astor, & Zeira, 2004). This central methodological choice allowed for an exploration of a comprehensive ecological model that examines how school violence relates to both within and outside school contexts.

Using schools as a unit of analysis also allows examination of the distribution of school violence for *schools* (rather than for individual students). To illustrate, an intriguing empirical question is whether the distribution of violence in schools follows a normal distribution, in which a few schools have high levels of violence and a few other schools have very low levels of violence, and the rest are somewhere in the mid range. Or, alternatively, that the distribution is skewed and there are a few schools that have either very high or very low levels of violence that make them stand out as extremes.

This issue has implications for policy and practice. Let us assume that 5% of the students report that another student extorted them. From a policy perspective, there is a major difference between the following two situations: (a) Most schools have about 5% of the students reporting extortion or (b) In most schools, there are no students reporting extortion and only in a very few schools the levels of extortion are much higher.

This study examined the distribution using (a) a dispersion index that indicates how heterogeneous schools are in terms of their level of violence; and (b) skewness of the distribution, which indicates whether the distribution is normal, or skewed in one direction. A high and positive sign of the skewness index means that there are few schools in which the levels of violence are exceptionally high, and a negative sign indicates that a few schools have very low rates of violence. Upon examination of this dispersion index, it was found that victimization types that were reported more frequently by the students have a lower dispersion index than victimization types that are less frequent and more severe. In other words, schools tend to be more similar to each other with regard to the less severe victimization types but differ much more from each other when it comes to the more severe behaviors.

A positive skew was found for more severe types of violence—there are few schools with very high levels of severe violence. For instance, in 2002 in about a quarter of the schools, there were *no reports* of a student cutting another student with a knife or a sharp object, half of the schools had less than 5% of the students making this report. However, in 5% of the schools, 20% or more of the students reported being cut with a knife or a sharp object, and in 1% of the schools *more than one out of four* students reported being cut by knife or a sharp object.

From a policy perspective, this pattern strongly suggests that efforts to stem extreme and rare types of violence should be directed to a select few schools, rather than spread thin across many schools. This recommendation implies that levels of school violence be assessed in schools and schools be treated differentially, based on their profile in terms of levels and types of victimization that students experience.

This school-level focus had implications for policy and for further research and theory development. Following the findings regarding the extremely skewed distribution of school violence among schools, the psychological services in conjunction with the districts initiated a process to identify schools that "stand out" in terms of extreme levels of violence, so that they can be the focus of additional supervision and support. Furthermore, the authors encouraged policy makers to identify schools that present extremely low violence, compared with all other schools that have similar socio-cultural ecological contexts. Thus the focus shifts from identifying individual students at risk, to a more system-level approach that focuses on the school as a unique social context.

From theoretical and research perspectives, these findings led the authors to explore in depth "theoretically atypical" schools. These are schools that have either very low or very high levels of violence compared to what is expected with schools with similar socio-economic and cultural characteristics. The findings of a recent mixed-method study (Astor, Benbenishty, & Estrada, 2009) suggest that organizational variables within these schools may buffer community influences. The most important variable found is the leadership of the principal. These schools emphasize a school reform approach, rather than packaged school violence evidence-based programs. With the principal's inspiration, guidance and support schools which are theoretically atypically low in school violence demonstrate "outward" oriented ideologies, a school wide awareness of violence, consistent procedures, integrated use of cultural and religious symbols, visual manifestations of student care, and the beautification of school grounds.

A Structural Change: From National Studies to National Monitoring System of School Climate

The series of national studies were very important in raising awareness and informing Israeli national policy. Still, these studies were less useful to local schools and communities that did not have any systematic information on school safety issues within their own local settings. School sites could not know how their school compared with the national norm, and therefore did not have the detailed local knowledge required to plan their school safety interventions. The awareness that each school needed local data to proceed properly was an important step in moving from periodic national school violence studies conducted by university researchers to ongoing national monitoring of school climate implemented and required by the Ministry of Education in all schools in Israel.

More than a decade ago, Israel created an academic monitoring system—*Meytzav*. With the Meytzav, the academic achievement of students in primary and junior high schools are tested, and detailed information is given to the principals and school staff with the goal of academic improvement. The Meytzav is run by independent governmental agency (associated with the Ministry of Education)—The National Authority for Measurement and Evaluation in Education (RAMA). The current Meytzav instrument includes a large number of items taken from the previously described national studies of school violence.

Currently, there are bi-annual monitoring versions for students, teachers, and principals. The instruments include sections on issues such as school related victimization, safety, connectedness to school, school policies toward violence, staff violence, peer relations, and teacher perceived parental involvement in school. Students respond to paper-based questionnaires administered alongside the academic achievement tests. Teachers and principals are interviewed over the phone. This process is conducted in each school by outside personnel (supervised by the RAMA) every other year. Schools are encouraged to employ the instrument internally during the offset years (for a more detailed description see Astor et al., in press).

It is quite possible that Israel is the only country in the world that collects both academic and social climate information in the same national survey. Having these two domains collected and disseminated to the same schools conveys the important conceptual message that school climate, school safety, and academics are integrally associated with one another.

Israel's educational psychological services have made many adjustments over the years to change their mission and take on more responsibilities in the area of school climate and safety. They are using the national study to help design national policies and the school-level Meytzav data to work with schools that are having specific safety issues. This involves data interpretation and the ability to suggest services, evidence based programs, and community supports that could build capacity within the school (Astor et al., in press).

Furthermore, the unique national database merging climate and academic information is an important source for ongoing organizational and academic learning. It is being used to study the interrelationships between socio-demographic characteristics of the school's neighborhood and students, school's staff composition, academic and social climate, school safety policies, and academic achievements of students. Currently, for instance, there are studies that examine how school social and academic climate mediate and moderate the effects of the students' and school socio-economic background on their academic achievement. The underlying hypothesis is that school climate and safety have an impact on academics. While this is commonly stated in political and practice circles, it is rarely researched. Now there are powerful data in Israel that can examine the relationships between socio-economic student background, school social and academic climate, and academic outcomes.

The creation of ongoing monitoring system for each school also raises potential obstacles and challenges that still need to be addressed and resolved by policy makers and researchers. For example, now that data are linked to each school, there is a greater sensitivity surrounding potential stigmatic data. How should the state or policy makers handle schools that do not look safe? How should the data be shared with the public so they would be used constructively? To what extent should student identifying information be used to link between academic and school safety and climate data? Should individual identifiers be used to track students over time? These

Table 16.2 Summary of Implications for Practice and Research

Effective national monitoring systems include:

1. Representative stratified sample by school level and major ethnic/social groups.
2. Nested designs of "students within schools" that include data on school, family, neighborhood, and culture surrounding the school.
3. Multiple perspectives of students, teachers, and principals in the same schools.
4. Rich, agreed-upon instruments that include:
   a. a wide array of behaviors and victimization types both by peers and by staff;
   b. indicators of school climate, school organization and peer group dynamics;
   c. items that are pertinent to policymakers and district level policy.
5. A strong emphasis on providing feedback to all constituents, including the general public, based on empirical findings.
6. Research geared at solving theoretical problems targeting cultural issues and violence that may not have immediate practical outcomes but build knowledge of how school victimization patterns relate to each other. In the long run, this may enhance the quality of both theory and practice.
7. A monitoring perspective to conduct studies repeatedly to inform policy and practice.
8. Monitoring should be conducted on the national, regional, and school site level.
9. Monitoring systems that combine academic and climate data should be developed.

questions reflect the challenges that the new monitoring system generates, and are currently being debated publicly in Israel.

Additionally, RAMA is taking governmental responsibility to conduct periodic national level studies to monitor school violence. These studies utilize more detailed instruments than the ones that can be used in the Meytzav, and employ large and representative samples of schools. This long term monitoring provides nationally representative longitudinal view of school violence in Israel beginning with our first study in 1999. These scientific studies allow for more questions to be asked and to explore areas of school safety and climate that are not covered in the Meytzav.

These developments in Israel have important implications for other countries about adopting monitoring systems for their schools. For instance, discussions are occurring currently in the United States surrounding the inclusion of national school climate measurement that will be introduced with the reauthorization of the Elementary and Secondary Education Act (ESEA). Lessons learned from the Israeli combination of social climate and academics at the regional, local, and national levels could be informative.

The multi-level monitoring provided by both the Meytzav and the National Study create unique opportunities to integrate school climate with the academic mission of schools. The act of combining both measures may actually change the way educators see the mission of schooling. It may create a situation where educators view the creation of a positive school climate as a necessary but not sufficient precursor to academic outcomes. Furthermore, it may prompt educators in Israel to give equal value to the important individual and group benefits of positive and safe social-emotional environment and academic outcomes.

The ongoing monitoring of the social climate on all levels may therefore have immediate implications for school reform and improvement efforts. Issues and challenges identified by ongoing monitoring on all levels can contribute to formulation of policy, practice, and theory that will help drive the development of new means to improve both safe and positive climate and academic achievements.

These developments tie in with current emphasis on evidence based practice and policy. In the future, such system-wide monitoring systems can be also be used to track the success or failure of adopted evidence based programs or of promising practices that have not yet been validated (Astor, Guerra, & Van Acker, 2010). Furthermore, ongoing long term monitoring of all schools may help identify best practices (see Table 16.2 for components of effective national monitoring systems). The extensive databases that integrate information of students' background, school climate, safety, and academic achievement over time can help to find schools that have overcome challenges and made outstanding progress. Such schools can serve as consultants to other schools and the focus of studies aiming to understand what worked in order to develop theories and practices.

References

Astor, R., A., Benbenishty, R., & Estrada, J. (2009). School violence and theoretically atypical schools: The principal's centrality in orchestrating safe schools. *American Educational Research Journal, 46,* 423–461. doi:10.3102/0002831208329598

Astor, R. A., Benbenishty, R., Shadmi, H., Raz, T., Algersy, E., Zeharia, M., ... De Pedro, K. (in press). No school left behind: Merging Israel's national academic and school safety monitoring system and matching data driven interventions for each school. In L. Knox (Ed.), *Youth violence prevention around the world.* Westport, CT: Praeger International.

Astor, R. A., Guerra, N., & Van Acker, R. (2010). How can we improve school safety research? *Educational Researcher, 39,* 39–69. doi:10.3102/0013189X09357619

Benbenishty, R., Zeira, A., & Astor, R. A. (2000). *A national study of school violence in Israel — Wave II: Fall 1999.* Jerusalem, Israel: Israeli Ministry of Education.

Benbenishty, R., & Astor R. A. (2005). *School violence in context: Culture, neighborhood, family, school, and gender.* New York, NY: Oxford University Press.

Benbenishty, R., Astor, R. A., & Zeira, A. (2003). Monitoring school violence on the site level: Linking national-, district-, and school-level data over time. *Journal of School Violence, 2,* 29–50. doi:10.1300/J202v02n02_03

Benbenishty, R., Zeira, A., & Astor, R. A. (2002). Children's reports of emotional, physical and sexual maltreatment by educational staff in Israel. *Child Abuse & Neglect, 26,* 763–782. doi:10.1016/S0145-2134(02)00350-2

Benbenishty, R., Zeira, A., Astor, R. A., & Khoury-Kassabri, M. (2002). Maltreatment of primary school students by educational staff in Israel. *Child Abuse and Neglect, 26,* 1291–1309. doi:10.1016/S0145-2134(02)00416-7

Bernhardt, V. L. (2004). *Data analysis for continuous school improvement* (2nd ed.). Larchmont, NY: Eye on Education.

Centers for Disease Control and Prevention. (2010). YRBSS: Youth Risk Behavior Surveillance System. Retrieved September 10, 2010, from http://www.cdc.gov/HealthyYouth/yrbs/index.htm

Dinkes, R., Kemp, J., & Baum, K. (2009). *Indicators of school crime and safety: 2009* (NCES 2010–012/NCJ 228478). Washington, DC: National Center for Education Statistics, Institute of Education Sciences, U.S. Department of Education, and Bureau of Justice Statistics, Office of Justice Programs, U.S. Department of Justice.

Furlong, M. J. (1996). Tools for assessing school violence. In S. Miller, J. Bordine, & T. Miller (Eds.), *Safe by design: Planning for peaceful school communities* (pp. 71–84). Seattle, WA: Committee for Children.

Furlong, M. J., Greif, J. L., Bates, M. P., Whipple, A. D., Jimenez, T. C., & Morrison, R. (2005). Development of the California School Climate and Safety Survey–Short Form. *Psychology in the Schools, 42,* 137–149. doi:10.1002/pits.20053

Furlong, M. J., Morrison, R., Bates, M., & Chung, A. (1998). School violence victimization among secondary students in California. *The California School Psychologist, 3,* 71–78.

Hyman, I. A. (1990). *Reading, writing, and the hickory stick: The appalling story of physical and psychological abuse in American schools.* Lexington, VA: Lexington Books.

Hyman, I., & Perone, D. C. (1998). The other side of school violence: Educator policies and practices that may contribute to student misbehavior. *Journal of School Psychology, 36,* 7–27. doi:10.1016/S0022-4405(97)87007-0

Hyman, I. A., & Snook, P. A. (2000). Dangerous schools and what you can do about them. *Phi Delta Kappan, 81,* 489–501.

Khoury-Kassabri, M., Astor, R. A., & Benbenishty, R. (2008). Student victimization by school staff in the context of an Israeli national school safety campaign. *Aggressive Behavior 34,* 1–8. doi:10.1002/ab.20180

Khoury-Kassabri, M., Benbenishty, R. Astor, R. A., & Zeira, A. (2004). The contributions of community, family, and school variables on student victimization. *American Journal of Community Psychology, 34,* 187–204. doi:10.1007/s10464-004-7414-4

Nansel, T., Overpeck, M., Pilla, R., Ruan, W., Simons-Morton, B., & Scheidt, P. (2001). Bullying behaviors among U.S. youth: Prevalence and association with psychosocial adjustment. *Journal of the American Medical Association, 285,* 2094–2100.

Rosenblatt, J. A., & Furlong, M. J. (1997). Assessing the reliability and validity of student self-reports of campus violence. *Journal of Youth and Adolescence, 26,* 187–202.

17

Youth Suicidal Behavior in the Context of School Violence

David N. Miller

UNIVERSITY AT ALBANY, STATE UNIVERSITY OF NEW YORK

Abstract

The conceptualization of school violence can be broadened to include self-destructive behavior, including suicide. This chapter provides an overview of youth suicidal behavior, including suicidal ideation, suicide-related communications, suicide attempts, and suicide. Demographic information regarding youth suicidal behavior is reviewed, including a discussion of ethnicity, gender, age, sexual orientation, geography, and socioeconomic variables and their relationship to suicidal behavior in children and adolescents. A review of risk factors, protective factors, and possible warning signs of suicidal behavior is presented, as well as a brief discussion of the issue of suicide "contagion." The relationship between youth suicide and homicide is also addressed, particularly in the context of school shootings among adolescents.

Youth suicidal behavior is a significant public health problem. According to the World Health Organization, suicide has increased over 60% worldwide during the last half-century, and is the second leading cause of death among young people ages 10 to 24 in the world (Miller, 2011). In the United States, although suicide is the 11th leading cause of death among Americans overall, it is the fourth leading cause of death among children and early adolescents ages 10 to 14, and the third leading cause of death among adolescents ages 15 to 19 (Miller & Eckert, 2009). Moreover, although death rates of children and adolescents have decreased steadily and substantially during the last several decades as a result of continuing medical advances, the youth suicide rate in the United States has remained consistently high (King & Apter, 2003).

Despite fluctuating rates of youth suicide over the last several years, including notable decreases during the 1990s and early 21st century, the overall suicide rate for children and adolescents has increased over 300% in the last 50 years (Berman, Jobes, & Silverman, 2006), and some believe it is likely to further increase in the future (e.g., Gutierrez & Osman, 2008). Adding to these sobering statistics is the possibility that the number of reported youth suicides may be an underestimate of their actual occurrence (Lieberman, Poland, & Cassel, 2008). Although research indicates that if underreporting of youth suicides does take place it is likely to be fairly minimal

(Kleck, 1988), the stigma that surrounds suicide (Joiner, 2005) suggests that some degree of underreporting may well occur.

The unacceptably high number of annual youth suicides that occur in the United States and other countries, however, is only part of the problem. For every youth who dies by suicide, it is estimated that at least 100 to 200 young people make suicide attempts, and thousands more engage in serious thoughts about killing themselves (Miller & Eckert, 2009). Moreover, children and adolescents who seriously contemplate or attempt suicide often experience depression and other mental health issues, and family and friends of suicidal youth are also at risk for developing these problems (Miller, 2011). As a result, the psychological, emotional, behavioral, social, medical, and financial cost of youth suicidal behavior, not only for individuals but also for families and entire communities, is frequently devastating (Miller, Eckert, & Mazza, 2009).

Because school personnel have such frequent contact with children and adolescents, they are ideally and uniquely positioned to prevent youth suicide (Miller, 2011). Many schools have experienced a significant increase in the amount of referrals for students who are seriously depressed, self-injurious, and/or suicidal, and this trend appears likely to continue (Lieberman et al., 2008). Unfortunately, many school personnel do not appear adequately trained to provide needed services for these children and adolescents (Miller & Jome, 2010). These issues are critical, because the manner in which school practitioners respond to suicidal youth can literally mean the difference between life and death (Miller & Eckert, 2009).

Despite the problem of youth suicidal behavior and the urgent need to address it, historically this topic has not received significant attention in the school violence literature. For example, in the first edition of the *Handbook of School Violence and School Safety* (Jimerson & Furlong, 2006), the topic of youth suicide was mentioned only in the context of conducting a threat of violence risk assessment toward others (Van Dyke & Schroeder, 2006). Given that the prevention of self-directed youth violence is at least as important as preventing youth violence directed toward others, the conceptualization of school violence can and should be broadened to include self-destructive behavior, including suicidal behavior. Although most youth suicides occur in a student's home or in a place outside of school, youth suicidal ideation, suicide-related communication, and even suicide attempts can and does occur in school settings.

The purpose of this chapter is to provide a brief overview of youth suicidal behavior. Demographic information regarding youth suicidal behavior is provided, as well as information regarding protective factors, risk factors, warning signs, and the issue of suicide "contagion." In addition, the relationship between youth suicidal behavior and school violence—in the form of school shootings—is briefly summarized. First, however, it is necessary to define suicidal behavior and precisely what is meant by that term.

Suicidal Behavior

For the purposes of this chapter, *suicidal behavior* will refer to four separate but frequently overlapping conditions that exist on a continuum, including suicidal ideation, suicide-related communications, suicide attempts, and suicide. The behaviors along this continuum vary and are not mutually exclusive, nor do all suicidal youth advance through them sequentially (Mazza, 2006; Silverman, Berman, Sanddal, O'Carroll, & Joiner, 2007a,b). Further, although the frequency of each behavior *decreases* as individuals move along this continuum, the level of lethality and probability of death *increases* (Mazza & Reynolds, 2008). Consequently, suicidal behavior includes and incorporates a much larger set of behaviors than suicide alone. Each of these four types of suicidal behavior is described below.

Suicidal Ideation

Suicidal ideation occurs at the beginning of the suicidal behavior continuum, and refers to cognitions or thoughts about suicide. These cognitions may range from more general thoughts such as wishes about never being born or about being dead, to more specific thoughts such as developing detailed plans regarding when, where, and how suicide might occur (Mazza, 2006). Transient thoughts about suicide appear to be quite common and even somewhat normative during adolescence (Rueter, Holm, McGeorge, & Conger, 2008). Research also indicates that the prevalence of suicidal ideation increases as children grow older, peaking at about age 14 through 16 and declining thereafter (Rueter & Kwon, 2005). Suicidal ideation becomes clinically significant when it is more than transient, when it is possibly a preoccupation, and when it is accompanied by an increased probability of behavioral action (Berman et al., 2006).

Suicide-Related Communications

Suicide-related communications refer to any interpersonal act of imparting, conveying, or transmitting thoughts, wishes, desires, or interest about suicide (Silverman et al., 2007b). This category includes both verbal and nonverbal communications that may have suicidal intent but result in no life-threatening outcomes for the individual. Within this category are two subsets: suicide threat and suicide plan.

A *suicide threat* refers to any interpersonal verbal or nonverbal action, without a direct self-injurious component, that a reasonable person would interpret as communicating or suggesting that more extreme forms of suicidal behavior might occur in the near future (Silverman et al., 2007b). This communication may be either direct (e.g., a student telling one of his peers that he wants to kill himself) or indirect (e.g., a student engaging in highly dangerous, risky, and self-destructive behavior), and varies in regards to level of planning, communication, and concealment from others (Kingsbury, 1993). A *suicide plan* refers to a proposed method of carrying out a design that will lead to suicide or a potentially self-injurious outcome (Silverman et al., 2007b). Both suicide threats and suicide plans communicate a clear intent to die, and should always "be taken seriously, responded to, and evaluated as indicators of potential clinical significance and potential risk" (Berman et al., 2006, p. 99).

Suicide Attempts

A suicide attempt is the third form of suicidal behavior on this continuum, and may be defined as a self-inflicted, potentially injurious behavior with a nonfatal outcome for which there is either implicit or explicit evidence of the intent to die (Silverman et al., 2007b). There are different types of suicide attempts, with some being considered *high-intent attempts* and others considered *low-intent attempts*. What distinguishes these two types is generally the level of lethality of the method used in making the attempt (Berman et al., 2006). For example, high-intent suicide attempts are associated with higher levels of lethality (e.g., the use of guns).

Most suicide attempts made by children and adolescents are of low lethality, allowing for a higher probability of rescue. In fact, the great majority of youth suicide attempts (approximately seven out of every eight) are of such low lethality as to not require medical or other forms of attention, and many suicide attempts are never even reported (Berman et al., 2006). Although most youth who attempt suicide will do so only once and not die as a result, a substantial number of individuals who attempt suicide later die by it (Berman et al., 2006). Further, engaging in a suicide attempt places youth at risk for a host of other mental health problems even if it does not result in eventual suicide (Groholt & Ekeberg, 2009).

Suicide

Suicide is the last and obviously the most lethal behavior on the suicidal behavior continuum (Mazza & Reynolds, 2008). Suicide may be defined as a fatal, self-inflicted act with the explicit or inferred intent to die (Mazza, 2006). The determination of intentionality is often difficult, and rests on evidence that the decedent (i.e., individual who died) understood that the self-inflicted act would produce death.

Finally, it should be noted that the profiles of individuals who engage in different forms of suicidal behavior vary significantly. For example, the typical youth who *attempts suicide* is an adolescent female who ingests drugs at home in front of others (e.g., parents), whereas the typical youth who *dies by suicide* is an adolescent male using a firearm (Berman et al., 2006). A common element shared by young people who engage in *any* form of suicidal behavior, however, is that these children and adolescents are exhibiting serious and significant problems to a degree that will require urgent attention and active intervention on the part of caring adults, particularly those working in schools.

Demographics of Youth Suicide

Ethnicity

Various ethnic groups differ in their rates of youth suicide, the context in which suicide occurs, and in their patterns of help seeking (Goldston et al., 2008). Among the larger ethnic groups in the United States, European Americans have the highest youth suicide rate, followed by African Americans and Latinos (Berman et al., 2006). The highest rates of youth suicide *proportionally,* however, are among Native Americans, with the lowest rates tending to be among Asian/Pacific Islanders (Mazza, 2006).

Gender

Gender appears to have a stronger influence on youth suicidal behavior than ethnicity. Research has consistently found a strong but paradoxical relationship between gender and suicidal behavior (Miller & Eckert, 2009). Specifically, although adolescent females report much higher rates of suicidal ideation than adolescent males and attempt suicide at rates *two to three times* the rate of males, males die by suicide at a rate *five times* more often than females (Berman et al., 2006). Plausible reasons for the much higher suicide rate among young males in comparison to females include the higher rates of significant suicide risk factors among males (e.g., access to firearms, alcohol abuse) as well as their being less likely than females to engage in a number of protective behaviors, such as seeking help, being adequately aware of warning signs, having flexible coping skills, and developing effective social support systems (Miller, 2011).

Age

The probability of suicide increases in both males and females as children grow older. For example, adolescents who are 15 years of age and older are at much higher risk for suicide than youth ages 10 to 14, who are at higher risk for suicide than younger children under the age of 10 (Berman et al., 2006). Suicide *does occur* in children under the age of 10, and there have even been some documented cases of suicidal behavior in preschool children (Rosenthal & Rosenthal, 1984). In general, however, suicide among children below the age of 10 is extremely rare, with typically only a few reported cases each year. When suicide at this age level does occur, it is typically associated with severe dysfunction and psychopathology in the child's family system (Miller, 2011).

Sexual Orientation

There is emerging evidence suggesting that gay, lesbian, bisexual, and transgendered (GLBT) youth may be at elevated risk for suicidal behavior in comparison to their heterosexual peers (Jacob, 2009). For example, based on data from the National Longitudinal Study of Adolescent Health, a recent study found that GLBT youth were much more likely to report suicidal ideation (17.2% vs. 6.3%) and attempt suicide (4.9% vs. 1.6%) than non-GLB youth (Silenzio, Pena, Duberstein, Cerel, & Knox, 2007). However, data specifically linking suicide deaths to a homosexual orientation are currently lacking (Berman et al., 2006). In general, having a sexual minority status, including individuals who are gay, lesbian, bisexual, or transgender, may put an individual at increased risk for suicidal behavior, particularly suicidal ideation or suicide attempts.

Geography

As with adults, youth suicide rates are highest in the western states and Alaska and lowest in the northeastern states (Berman et al., 2006). The sparser population, greater physical isolation, fewer mental health facilities, and limited opportunities for social interaction that characterize many western states may lead to greater social disconnection, a variable highly associated with suicide (Joiner, 2005). Consistent with this hypothesis is the finding that suicide rates are typically higher in rural areas than in urban areas (Berman et al., 2006).

Socioeconomic Status

Research regarding the influence of socioeconomic status (SES) and suicidal behavior has been described as "mixed and contradictory" (Berman et al., 2006, p. 31). Although suicide occurs across all socioeconomic levels, research generally suggests that there is an inverse relationship between SES and suicide rates in both the United States and other countries (Stack, 2000; Ying & Chang, 2009). Research on SES and youth suicide is lacking, although one study examining the socioeconomic differences among more than 20,000 Danish youth who died by suicide found that individuals in the lowest socioeconomic quartile had more than five times the risk of suicide compared to their more affluent peers (Qin, Agerbo, & Mortenson, 2003).

Risk Factors

Variables that help explain or predict youth suicidal behavior can be placed into two broad categories: risk factors that may predispose an individual to suicidal behavior, and warning signs that may indicate the possibility of a suicidal crisis (Van Orden, Witte, Selby, Bender, & Joiner, 2008). Risk factors suggest a more distant temporal relationship to suicidal behavior, whereas warning signs suggest a more proximal relationship (Van Orden et al., 2008). Although numerous risk factors for suicide have been identified, the two most prominent are (a) the presence of at least one mental health disorder; and (b) a history of previous suicidal behavior, particularly suicide attempts. Both of these risk factors are discussed in greater detail below, followed by a brief overview of other risk factors for youth suicidal behavior.

Presence of Mental Health Disorders

The most reliable and robust risk factor for youth suicide is the presence of one or more mental health disorders. Findings from "psychological autopsies" (i.e., a systematic collection of data via structured interviews of family members and/or friends of the suicide victim) estimate that approximately 90% of youth who die by suicide experienced at least one mental disorder at the time of their deaths (Berman et al. 2006; Shaffer et al., 1996). The most common mental disorders exhibited by youth who die by suicide are mood disorders (e.g., Major Depressive Disorder; Dysthymic Disorder; Bipolar Disorder), substance-related disorders (e.g., alcohol and/or drug abuse), and disruptive behavior disorders (Fleischmann, Bertolote, Belfer, & Beautrais, 2005), respectively. Although the large majority of clinically depressed youth are not suicidal and not all, suicidal youth are clinically depressed (Reynolds & Mazza, 1994); approximately 42% to 66% of youth who die by suicide appear to have been experiencing some type of depressive disorder at the time of their deaths (Fleischmann et al., 2005; Shaffer et al., 1996).

Other mental disorders that have been linked to youth suicide include anxiety disorders (e.g., Panic Disorder; Posttraumatic Stress Disorder), Schizophrenia, Borderline Personality Disorder, and Adjustment Disorder. The eating disorders of Anorexia Nervosa and Bulimia are also known to confer risk for suicide. However, although both Anorexia and Bulimia increase risk of suicidal ideation and suicide attempts, only Anorexia is associated with an increased risk for death by suicide (Mazza, 2006; Miller, 2011). Most youth who die by suicide have comorbid psychiatric disorders, which often makes assessment and treatment of these individuals especially challenging.

Other variables associated with youth suicide include hopelessness, sexual and/or physical abuse, self-injury, and peer victimization and bullying (Cleary, 2000; Klomeck, Marrocco, Kleinman, Schonfeld, & Gould, 2007). This last risk factor has important implications for both self-directed and outer-directed youth violence. For example, in the early 1980s, three suicides in Norway were linked to youth being bullied, which led the Norwegian government to develop a national campaign to investigate bullying and victimization problems (Espelage & Swearer, 2010). In the United States, recent cases of cyberbullying followed by the occurrence of youth suicides among some bullying victims have received substantial media attention. Further, an investigation conducted by the Secret Service revealed that among 37 incidents of school shootings and school attacks between 1974 and 2000, 71% of the perpetrators had been victims of bullying (Vossekuil, Fein, Reddy, Borum, & Modzeleski, 2002).

Previous Suicidal Behavior

In addition to psychopathology, the other prominent risk factor for suicide is previous suicidal behavior, particularly previous suicide attempts. A general principle that applies to all behavior, including suicidal behavior, is that the best predictor of future behavior is past behavior. Consequently, the single best predictor of a future suicide attempt is a history of one or more previous suicide attempts.

Other Risk Factors

Children and adolescents who exhibit milder forms of suicidal behavior (e.g., suicidal ideation) but who are undertreated or not treated for it (e.g., not receiving antidepressant medication or psychotherapy) are at increased risk for suicide. Ethnic minority youth in the United States may also be affected by various risk factors that European American youth may not face, such as racial discrimination, acculturative stress, a fatalistic philosophy, and passive coping strategies (Gutierrez & Osman, 2008). Exposure to suicide through death of a peer also may be considered an accelerating risk factor, particularly among those already predisposed to be at risk (Berman et al., 2006). Some additional risk factors for youth suicide that have been identified include biological deficits in serotonin functioning, social isolation, limited access to mental health facilities, poor problem-solving and coping skills, low self-esteem, dysfunctional parenting or family environments, parental psychopathology, cultural or religious beliefs, access to lethal weapons, (particularly firearms), and repeated engagement in or exposure to violence (Joiner, 2005; Lieberman et al., 2008; Miller, 2011).

Possible Warning Signs of Suicidal Behavior

As opposed to risk factors, possible warning signs of suicidal behavior are more dynamic and proximal factors that suggest the increased probability of a suicidal crisis (Van Orden et al., 2008). A working group convened by the American Association of Suicidology (AAS) reviewed the research literature and reached consensus on a set of possible warning signs for suicide (Rudd et al., 2006). These warning signs, which should be shared with all students and school personnel, include (a) hopelessness; (b) rage, anger, seeking revenge; (c) acting reckless or engaging in risky activities, seemingly without thinking; (d) feeling trapped, as if there is no way out; (e) increasing alcohol or drug use; (f) withdrawing from friends, family, or society; (g) experiencing anxiety and/or agitation; (h) being unable to sleep or sleeping excessively; (i) dramatic mood changes; and (j) perceiving no reason for living or no sense of purpose in life.

A few caveats regarding warning signs should be noted. First, many of the currently known warning signs have not been validated specifically for youth suicide. More research is needed to determine if signs of acute suicide risk differ between children, adolescents, and adults (Van Orden et al., 2008). Second, although the giving away of possessions has frequently been described as a warning sign for suicide, there is no empirical evidence to support this contention, so it is not listed above as a warning sign. Third, and perhaps most important, many if not most youth exhibit some or even several of these warning signs and never engage in suicidal behavior, and it is not clear how many of these warning signs, or what combination of them, are the best predictors of suicide (Miller, 2011). Nevertheless, youth who exhibit several warning signs in addition to one or more of the risk factors described above should be viewed as being at high risk for suicide, and should be individually assessed by an appropriate school-based mental health professional.

Situational Crises, Stressful Life Events, and Precipitants

Risk for suicidal behavior increases when acute situational crises or stressful life events (e.g., some type of loss of an interpersonal nature) occur in conjunction with other, more chronic risk factors, such as depression, substance abuse, and/or access to lethal methods (Lieberman et al., 2008). Several different types of stressful events that may precipitate suicidal behavior in youth have been identified, including a relationship breakup, parental divorce, and school failure. Although these events do not directly cause suicidal behavior, they may have the potential to "trigger" suicidal behavior in potentially vulnerable youth (Miller, 2011). No one particular stressful event is highly predictive of suicidal behavior, although the risk for suicide increases as the number and emotional intensity of stressful events increase in the lives of children and adolescents already predisposed to suicidal tendencies (Miller & McConaughy, 2005).

Protective Factors

The finding that many youth who have a number of prominent risk factors for suicide do not engage in suicidal behavior suggests the presence of various protective or resiliency factors. Protective factors refer to those variables that have been linked empirically (e.g., as mediators or moderators) to decreased risk for suicidal behavior (Gutierrez & Osman, 2008). Although work in this area is increasing, less research has been devoted to examining protective factors in comparison to risk factors in regards to suicide, and as a result relatively little is known about which factors might mitigate risk factors for suicidal behavior (Berman et al., 2006). Some protective factors that have been tentatively identified, however, include (a) social problem solving and coping skills; (b) self-esteem; and (c) social support, both from peers and (particularly) parents (Miller, 2011). In addition, although not specific to suicide, a number of other protective factors have been identified that can often offset other risk factors. These include close peer friendships, high self-efficacy, and caring and responsive school personnel (Miller, 2011).

Suicide "Contagion"

An important issue for school personnel is the possibility of suicide "contagion." This concern developed from research which suggested that suicide can be "contagious," in the sense that exposure to suicidal behaviors—either through personal experience or media exposure—can influence others to copy them (Berman et al., 2006). In regards to suicide contagion and the media, research suggests that the influence is modest, although the media can play an important role in the decision-making processes of vulnerable youth. Given that children and adolescents may be especially vulnerable to media influences, providing guidelines to the media about the accurate and appropriate portrayal of suicide is very important (Miller, 2011).

Suicide and Homicide: Youth Suicidal Behavior and School Shootings

Suicide and violence prevention efforts have generally occurred in relative isolation from one another (Lubell & Vetter, 2006), although recent tragic events have highlighted the occasional relationship between suicidal behavior and violent behavior toward others, particularly in the context of school shootings (Nickerson & Slater, 2009). For example, the U.S. Secret Service and U.S. Department of Education's study of school shootings found that 78% of school shooters exhibited suicidal ideation to a significant degree (Vossekuil et al., 2002). When considering this issue, however, it should first be clearly understood that school shootings are extremely rare events. In fact, students are *safer* in schools than in most any other place they could be, and the odds of a student being injured or killed as a result of a school shooting is literally millions to one. Nevertheless, the numerous multiple-victim shootings that occurred during the late 1990s, particularly the 1999 school shootings at Columbine High School in Colorado, dramatically changed public opinion about the safety of America's schools (Van Dyke & Schroeder, 2006).

The extensive media coverage given to school shootings has made this a topic of intense interest in the United States, particularly among parents, policy makers, and school administrators. Although there have been attempts to "profile" school shooters for purposes of identification and prediction, the FBI has cautioned against the use of student profiling to identify potential school shooters (Cornell & Williams, 2006). Instead, the FBI has recommended that schools adopt a *threat assessment approach,* which is consistent with subsequent recommendations made by both the Secret Service and the Department of Education (Fein et al., 2002; National Institute of Justice, 2002). Some common characteristics of school shooters have been identified, including (a) being male, (b) having a history of peer mistreatment and bullying, (c) demonstrating a preoccupation with violent games and fantasies, and (d) exhibiting symptoms of depression and suicidality (Fein et al., 2002; National Institute of Justice, 2002).

Unfortunately, a listing of these characteristics is not particularly helpful because it does not provide sufficient specificity for practical use—far too many students would be falsely identified as potentially violent (Sewell & Mendelsohn, 2000). As with predicting precisely which students are most likely to engage in suicidal behavior (Pokorny, 1992), predicting which students will engage in school violence (e.g., school shootings) based on particular risk factors has inherent limitations (Mulvey & Cauffman, 2001) because both are low base–rate behaviors. However, although school personnel cannot predict with complete accuracy which students will become school shooters any more than they can predict which students will attempt or die by suicide, they can determine periods of heightened risk for both.

For example, the most promising finding from the FBI's study of school shootings was that the student perpetrators almost always made threats or communicated their intentions to harm someone before the shooting occurred (Cornell & Williams, 2006). Further, the FBI identified a number of cases where school shootings were prevented because authorities investigated a student's threatening statement and found that the student was engaged in plans to carry out the threat. These observations are similar to findings from youth who engage in suicidal behavior, who likewise frequently communicate their suicidal intent, most typically to peers (Miller, 2011). This suggests that schools should focus their efforts on the identification and investigation of student threats (whether suicidal or homicidal) rather than on the presence of particular risk factors.

It is critical that the above discussion of youth suicide and homicide be viewed in appropriate perspective. The overwhelming majority of youth who engage in suicidal behavior do not engage in homicidal behavior, either at school our outside of it. This is true for adults as well. For example, murder–suicides account for only about 1.5% of all annual suicides in the United States (Holinger, Offer, Barter, & Bell, 1994). That said, there does appear to be a relationship between suicidal behavior and other forms of violence. For example, a study involving over 11,000 students who completed the Youth Risk Behavior Survey in 2005 revealed that predictors of suicidal behavior for both male and female adolescents included carrying a weapon, being threatened or injured at school, having property stolen or damaged at school, and getting in a fight (Nickerson & Slater, 2009).

Table 17.1 Implications for Practice

1.	Youth suicide is major public health problem that requires urgent attention. As children and adolescents spend much of their time in school, educational facilities provide ideal locations for focused prevention efforts.
2.	Although school personnel do not usually associate school violence with self-directed violence, youth suicidal behavior in schools, particularly suicidal ideation, suicide-related communication, and suicide attempts, can and does occur in schools, and school personnel need to be cognizant of the various risk factors and warning signs of suicidal behavior, as well as the demographic variables that surround youth suicide.
3.	The two most prominent risk factors for suicide are the presence of mental health problems, typically depression, and a history of previous suicidal behavior. This information should be communicated annually to all students and school personnel, particularly at middle and high schools where the probability of youth suicidal behavior is highest.
4.	There are a number of warning signs of potential suicidal behavior, and all students and school personnel should be trained to recognize them. Students and school personnel also need to know what to do and who to report to when they suspect a particular student may be suicidal. All schools should have written policies and procedures in regards to youth suicide, and school personnel should routinely receive training in these policies and procedures.
5.	A comprehensive, public health approach is recommended for the school-based prevention, assessment, and intervention with potentially suicidal youth.
6.	Student suicide and homicide is an extremely rare occurrence, but school personnel should be prepared for this possibility. School-based mental health professionals should be equally skilled in conducting suicide risk assessments and student threat assessments.
7.	Predicting precisely which students will be suicidal, like predicting which particular students will engage in extreme forms of school violence (e.g., school shootings), is inherently difficult. However, school personnel can and should be trained to assess for heightened risk for both.

Consequently, when youth are suspected of engaging in or being capable of violence toward others or of suicidal behavior, it would be prudent to conduct both a school-based threat assessment as well as a suicide risk assessment. Moreover, a comprehensive, school-based, public health approach to both suicidal behavior (Miller, 2011; Miller et al., 2009) and school violence (Espelage & Swearer, 2010; Furlong, Jones, Lilles, & Derzon, 2010), involving multiple levels of prevention and intervention to meet individual student needs, is increasingly viewed as the most appropriate and effective response to these problems. Although historically school-based suicide and violence prevention efforts have occurred in relative isolation from each other (Nickerson & Slater, 2009), there is no reason that this need be the case.

Conclusion

Youth suicidal behavior is a major public health problem that affects thousands of children and adolescents, as well as their friends and families, each year. Despite its widespread occurrence, youth suicidal behavior has to date not received significant attention in the school violence literature. This situation will hopefully be changing, particularly given the documented relationship between suicide and other forms of school violence, including bullying, peer victimization, and school shootings. Although space limitations prohibit a more extensive discussion of this topic, readers interested in gaining additional information on the school-based prevention, assessment, and treatment of youth suicidal behavior are referred to other sources, especially Gutierrez and Osman (2008), Lieberman et al. (2008), and Miller (2011).

References

Berman, A. L., Jobes, D. A., & Silverman, M. M. (2006). *Adolescent suicide: Assessment and intervention.* Washington, DC: American Psychological Association. doi:10.1037/11285-000

Cleary, S. D. (2000). Adolescent victimization and associated suicide and violent behaviors. *Adolescence, 35,* 671–682.

Cornell, D., & Williams, F. (2006). Student threat assessment as a strategy to reduce school violence. In S. R. Jimerson & M. J. Furlong (Eds.), *Handbook of school violence and school safety: From research to practice* (pp. 587–601). Mahwah, NJ: Erlbaum.

Espelage, D. L., & Swearer, S. M. (2010). Bullying and peer harassment. In M. R. Shinn & H. M. Walker (Eds.), *Interventions for achievement and behavior problems in a three-tier model including RTI* (pp. 729–748). Bethesda, MD: National Association of School Psychologists.

Fein, R., Vossekuil, B., Pollack, W., Borum, R., Modzeleski, W., & Reddy, M. (2002). *Threat assessment in schools: A guide to managing threatening situations and to create safe school climates.* Washington, DC: U.S. Secret Service and Department of Education.

Fleischmann, A., Bertolote, J. M., Belfer, M., & Beautrais, A. (2005). Completed suicide and psychiatric diagnoses in young people: Examination of the evidence. *American Journal of Orthopsychiatry, 75,* 676–683. doi:10.1037/0002-9432.75.4.676

Furlong, M. J., Jones, C., Lilles, E., & Derzon, J. (2010). Think smart, stay safe: Aligning elements within a multilevel approach to school violence prevention. In M. R. Shinn & H. M. Walker (Eds.), *Interventions for achievement and behavior problems in a three-tier model including RTI* (pp. 313–336). Bethesda, MD: National Association of School Psychologists.

Goldston, D. B., Davis Molock, S., Whitbeck, L. B., Murakami, J. L., Zayas, L. H., & Nagayama Hall, G. C. (2008). Cultural considerations in adolescent suicide prevention and psychosocial treatment. *American Psychologist, 63,* 14–31. doi:10.1037/0003-066X.63.1.14

Groholt, B., & Ekeberg, O. (2009). Prognosis after adolescent suicide attempt: Mental health, psychiatric treatment, and suicide attempts in a nine-year follow-up study. *Suicide and Life-Threatening Behavior, 39,* 125–136. doi:10.1521/suli.2009.39.2.125

Gutierrez, P. M., & Osman, A. (2008). *Adolescent suicide: An integrated approach to the assessment of risk and protective factors.* DeKalb, IL: Northern Illinois University Press.

Holinger, P. C., Offer, D., Barter, J. T., & Bell, C. C. (1994). *Suicide and homicide among adolescents.* New York: Guilford.

Jacob, S. (2009). Putting it all together: Implications for school psychology. *School Psychology Review, 38,* 239–243.

Jimerson, S. R., & Furlong, M. J. (Eds.). (2006). *Handbook of school violence and school safety: From research to practice.* Mahwah, NJ: Erlbaum.

Joiner, T. E. (2005). *Why people die by suicide.* Cambridge, MA: Harvard University Press.

King, R. A., & Apter, A. (Eds.). (2003). *Suicide in children and adolescents.* New York: Cambridge University Press.

Kingsbury, S. J. (1993). Clinical components of suicidal intent in adolescent overdoses. *Journal of the American Academy of Child and Adolescent Psychiatry, 32,* 518–520. doi:10.1097/00004583-199305000-00005

Kleck, G. (1988). Miscounting suicides. *Suicide and Life-Threatening Behavior, 18,* 219–236.

Klomeck, A. B., Marrocco, F., Kleinman, M., Schonfeld, I. S., & Gould, M. S. (2007). Bullying, depression, and suicidality in adolescents. *Journal of the American Academy of Child and Adolescent Psychiatry, 46,* 40–49. doi:10.1097/01.chi.0000242237.84925.18

Lieberman, R., Poland, S., & Cassel, R. (2008). Best practices in suicide intervention. In A. Thomas & J. Grimes (Eds.), *Best practices in school psychology V* (pp. 1457–1472). Bethesda, MD: National Association of School Psychologists.

Lubell, K. M., & Vetter, J. B. (2006). Suicide and youth violence prevention: The promise of an integrated approach. *Aggression and Violent Behavior, 11,* 167–175. doi:10.1016/j.avb.2005.07.006

Mazza, J. J. (2006). Youth suicidal behavior: A crisis in need of attention. In F. A. Villarruel & T. Luster (Eds.), *Adolescent mental health* (pp. 156–177). Westport, CT: Greenwood.

Mazza, J. J., & Reynolds, W. M. (2008). School-wide approaches to prevention of and treatment for depression and suicidal behaviors. In B. Doll & J. A. Cummings (Eds.), *Transforming school mental health services* (pp. 213–241). Thousand Oaks, CA: Corwin.

Miller, D. N. (2011). *Child and adolescent suicidal behavior: School-based prevention, assessment, and intervention.* New York: Guilford.

Miller, D. N., & Eckert, T. L. (2009). Youth suicidal behavior: An introduction and overview. *School Psychology Review, 38,* 153–167.

Miller, D. N., Eckert, T. L., & Mazza, J. J. (2009). Suicide prevention programs in the schools: A review and public health perspective. *School Psychology Review, 38,* 168–188.

Miller, D. N., & Jome, L. M. (2010). School psychologists and the secret illness: Perceived knowledge, role preferences, and training needs in the prevention and treatment of internalizing disorders. *School Psychology International, 31*(5), 509–520. doi:10.1177/0143034310382622

Miller, D. N., & McConaughy, S. H. (2005). Assessing risk for suicide. In S. H. McConaughy, *Clinical interviews for children and adolescents: Assessment to intervention* (pp. 184–199). New York: Guilford.

Mulvey, E. P., & Cauffman, E. (2001). The inherent limits of predicting school violence. *American Psychologist, 56,* 797–802. doi:10.1037/0003-066X.56.10.797

National Institute of Justice. (2002). Preventing school shootings: A summary of a U.S. Secret Service safe school initiative report. *NIJ Journal, 248,* 10–15.

Nickerson, A. B., & Slater, E. D. (2009). School and community violence and victimization as predictors of adolescent suicidal behavior. *School Psychology Review, 38,* 218–232.

Pokorny, A. (1992). Prediction of suicide in psychiatric patients: Report of a prospective study. In R. Maris, A. Berman, J. Maltsberger, & R. Yufit (Eds.), *Assessment and prediction of suicide* (pp. 105–129). New York: Guilford.

Qin, P., Agerbo, E., & Mortenson, P. B. (2003). Suicide risk in relation to socioeconomic, demographic, psychiatric, and familial risk factors: A national register-based study of all suicides in Denmark, 1981–1997. *American Journal of Psychiatry, 160,* 765–772. doi:10.1176/appi.ajp.160.4.765

Reynolds, W. M., & Mazza, J. J. (1994). Suicide and suicidal behavior. In W. M. Reynolds & H. F. Johnston (Eds.), *Handbook of depression in children and adolescents* (pp. 520–580). New York: Plenum.

Rosenthal, P. A., & Rosenthal, S. (1984). Suicidal behavior by pre-school children. *American Journal of Psychiatry, 141,* 520–525.

Rueter, M. A., Holm, K. E., McGeorge, C. R., & Conger, R. D. (2008). Adolescent suicidal ideation subgroups and their association with suicidal plans and attempts in young adulthood. *Suicide and Life-Threatening Behavior, 38,* 564–575. doi:10.1521/suli.2008.38.5.564

Reuter, M. A., & Kwon, H. K. (2005). Developmental trends in adolescent suicidal ideation. *Journal of Research on Adolescence, 15,* 205–222. doi:10.1111/j.1532-7795.2005.00092.x

Rudd, M. D., Berman, A. L., Joiner, T. E., Nock, M. K., Silverman, M., Mandrusiak, M., Van Orden, K., & Witte, T. (2006). Warning signs for suicide: Theory, research, and clinical applications. *Suicide and Life-Threatening Behavior, 36,* 255–262. doi:10.1521/suli.2006.36.3.255

Sewell, K. W., & Mendelsohn, M. (2000). Profiling potentially violent youth: Statistical and conceptual problems. *Children's Services: Social Policy, Research, and Practice, 3,* 147–169. doi:10.1207/S15326918CS0303_2

Shaffer, D., Gould, M. S., Fisher, P., Trautman, P., Moreau, D., Kleinman, M., & Flory, M. (1996). Psychiatric diagnoses in child and adolescent suicide. *Archives of General Psychiatry, 53,* 339–348.

Silenzio, V. M. B., Pena, J. B., Duberstein, P. R., Cerel, J., & Knox, K. L. (2007). Sexual orientation and risk factors for suicidal ideation and suicide attempts among adolescents and young adults. *American Journal of Public Health, 97,* 2017–2019. doi:10.2105/AJPH.2006.095943

Silverman, M. M., Berman, A. L., Sanddal, N. D., O'Carroll, P. W., & Joiner, T. E. (2007a). Rebuilding the Tower of Babel: A revised nomenclature for the study of suicide and suicidal behaviors part 1: Background, rationale, and methodology. *Suicide and Life-Threatening Behavior, 37,* 248–263. doi:10.1521/suli.2007.37.3.248

Silverman, M. M., Berman, A. L., Sanddal, N. D., O'Carroll, P. W., & Joiner, T. E. (2007b). Rebuilding the Tower of Babel: A revised nomenclature for the study of suicide and suicidal behaviors part 2: Suicide-related ideations, communications, and behaviors. *Suicide and Life-Threatening Behavior, 37,* 264–277. doi:10.1521/suli.2007.37.3.264

Stack, S. (2000). Suicide: A 15-year review of the sociological literature part I: Cultural and economic factors. *Suicide and Life-Threatening Behavior, 30,* 145–162.

Van Dyke, R. B., & Schroeder, J. L. (2006). Implementation of the Dallas threat of violence risk assessment. In S. R. Jimerson & M. J. Furlong (Eds.), *Handbook of school violence and school safety: From research to practice* (pp. 603–616). Mahwah, NJ: Erlbaum.

Van Orden, K. A., Witte, T. K., Selby, E. A., Bender, T. W., & Joiner, T. E. (2008). Suicidal behavior in youth. In J. R. Z. Abela & B. L. Hankin (Eds.), *Handbook of depression in children and adolescents* (pp. 441–465). New York: Guilford.

Vossekuil, B., Fein, R. A., Reddy, M., Borum, R., & Modzeleski, W. (2002). *The final report and findings of the Safe School Initiative: Implications for the prevention of school attacks in the United States.* Washington, DC: Secret Service and U.S. Department of Education.

Ying, Y., & Chang, K. (2009). A study of suicide and socioeconomic factors. *Suicide and Life-Threatening Behavior, 39,* 214–226. doi:10.1521/suli.2009.39.2.214

World Report on Violence and Health

International Insights

*Shane R. Jimerson, Jacqueline A. Brown,
Skye Stifel, and Matthew A. Ruderman*

THE UNIVERSITY OF CALIFORNIA, SANTA BARBARA

Abstract

This chapter synthesizes information from the World Report on Violence and Health developed by the World Health Organization. The methodology of the report is presented, as well as international data related to violence and safety among children. Findings reveal diverse trends in homicide due to youth violence and school bullying across countries. Rates of fatal and non-fatal acts due to maltreatment are higher among males. Although numerous countries have implemented prevention programs, further research addressing the effectiveness of strategies across countries is needed. Areas for future investigation include conducting additional data collection focusing explicitly on school-based youth violence, and additional worldwide dissemination of data regarding youth violence. Implications for practice to help decrease and prevent youth violence are provided.

Youth violence in the school, home, and community setting has been identified as a worldwide concern. Such violence can lead to negative outcomes such as illness and death, increased cost of health and welfare services, and decreased overall quality of life (World Health Organization [WHO], 2002a). Although prevention efforts are being implemented worldwide, violence prevention is still an emerging field in many countries. Collaboration amongst individuals and organizations at the regional, national, and international level has been identified as a necessity in implementing effective strategies for decreasing youth violence (WHO, 2007).

This chapter provides an overview of specific data collected from the World Health Organization, as well as prevention and intervention strategies that target youth violence. The first section provides an overview and describes the methodology of the World Report on Violence and Health. The second section summarizes data related to youth violence in countries around the world, as well as prevention efforts to target youth violence at the family, community, and school level. In the final section, key findings are summarized, the current status of youth violence is highlighted, and areas for future investigation are presented. Implications for practice to address and prevent youth violence are also given.

World Report on Violence and Health

The World Report on Violence and Health (WHO, 2002a) was published in October, 2002, providing a comprehensive review of worldwide violence. Specific conceptual definitions of violence are described; data on populations affected by violence across gender, cultural background, and age are provided; and prevention methods to address violence and promote safety are given. The report was developed in collaboration with 160 worldwide experts. Each chapter of the report was peer reviewed by scientists located in different world regions. Experts reviewed a draft of the report, providing insight into issues surrounding violence in their region, as well as prevention and intervention recommendations.

This report targeted specific issues related to youth violence, child abuse and neglect, violence by intimate partners, abuse of the elderly, and self-directed violence. For the purpose of this chapter, only data related to youth violence and child abuse and neglect will be discussed.

World Health Organization Findings Related to Youth Violence and Safety

The World Health Organization (2002a) report defines violence as the intentional use of physical force or power, threatened or actual, against oneself, another person, or against a group or community, which either results in or has a high likelihood of resulting in injury, death, psychological harm, mal-development or deprivation. Situational factors of violence include motive and location of the violent act, the presence of alcohol or weapons, and the presence of bystanders.

Specific individual, relationship, community, and societal factors are associated with youth violence (WHO, 2002a). Individual factors include biological factors, as well as psychological and behavioral characteristics. For example, low heart rates in boys (Ortiz & Raine, 2004), as well as hyperactivity, impulsivity, and inattention (Loeber & Pardini, 2008), have been associated with antisocial behaviors. Relationship factors such as parental conflict, abusive relationships, and delinquent friendships also predict youth violence (Ferguson, San Miguel, & Hartley, 2009). Furthermore, community factors such as participation in gangs and use of drugs, and cultural influences such as media exposure (Wood, Wong, & Chachere, 1991) have been associated with increased aggressive behaviors. Such factors place youth at increased risk for being both victims and perpetrators of violence within the home and school settings.

Community and Family Youth Violence and Safety

The World Report on Violence and Health (WHO, 2002a) highlights worldwide data related to youth homicide and non-fatal violence (e.g., use of fists or knives). Findings on youth homicide indicate that in 2000, approximately 565 children, adolescents, and young adults between the ages of 10 and 29 died daily as a result of interpersonal violence. Differing trends in homicide due to youth violence were found across gender and location. Although the rate of homicides due to youth violence increased for both males and females between 1985 and 1994, the rate for males increased more than for females. Rates of youth homicide also vary per region, with high rates reported in Latin America, the Russian Federation, and some south-eastern European countries. Homicide rates due to youth violence (age 10–29 years) per 100,000 population are also provided. For example, the youth homicide rate for Brazil in 1995 was 33 per 100,000 and 84 per 100,000 in Colombia. The rate was 18 per 100,000 in the Russian Federation in 1998, and 12 per 100,000 in the Philippines in 1993. The report highlights that youth homicide rates that are above 10 per 100,000 are typically seen in developing countries, as well as in countries undergoing rapid economic and social transformations. One exception is the United States, where the rate for youth homicide is 11 per 100,000.

Non-fatal injuries account for a large proportion of youth receiving hospital care due to violence (WHO, 2002a). For every homicide, approximately 20–40 individuals are admitted to the hospital for an injury. The report also highlights that male victims typically receive more hospital care than female victims, and that high rates of injuries due to violent acts occur in adolescents and young adults.

Child maltreatment is another form of violence that takes place in the family and community setting. According to the World Health Organization (WHO, 1999), child maltreatment includes physical and emotional ill-treatment, as well as negligent treatment that may result in actual or potential harm to the child's health, development, or survival. Perpetrators of child maltreatment may include parents and family members, caregivers, friends, other children, and employers (WHO, 2006). Long-term health consequences of child maltreatment include brain injuries, fractures, alcohol and drug abuse, depression and anxiety, poor relationships, and poor school performance (WHO, 2002a).

Data from the World Report of Violence and Health (WHO, 2002a) indicate that in 2000, approximately 57,000 deaths resulted from homicide among children less than 15 years of age. Young children between the age of 0 and 4 years were at increased risk when compared to those between 5 and 14 years of age. Furthermore, the rate of homicide due to maltreatment for males was greater than females in high, medium, and low income countries. Data on non-fatal abuse has been harder to record, as abuse is not always reported and countries differ in their legal and cultural definitions of abuse.

Data provided from a WorldSAFE project (WHO, 2002a) that evaluated physical, verbal, psychological, and non-violent forms of discipline in Chile, Egypt, India, Philippines, and the United States are presented in Table 18.1. These data are based on the results of the Conflict Tactic Scales (Straus & Hamby, 1997), which examines non-violent discipline, psychological aggression, and physical assault in parent-child and family relationships. The findings indicate that various forms of violent punishments are used to different degrees throughout the world, but that mothers also frequently use non-violent forms of discipline.

The World Health Organization has emphasized the importance of targeting social and cultural norms that support youth violence (WHO, 2009a). For example, females are seen as having less economic and social potential than males in some countries. Harmful cultural practices such as child marriage and genital mutilation are more common in Sudan, Benin, and Nigeria, and physical punishment is commonly used in Turkey and Ethiopia. Research on child marriage in Benin (Jensen & Thornton, 2003) has shown that 67% of women who married under the age of 15 were more likely to believe that physical abuse from one's husband was justified under particular situations (e.g., if she burns the food or if she argues with her husband), whereas only 42% of women married between the ages of 26 and 30 held these beliefs. Marriage at a younger age has also been linked to lower household status, which has been shown to increase the likelihood that females will experience domestic violence (Kishor & Johnson, 2004). Furthermore, reporting youth violence is less accepted in the United Kingdom, and resolving conflict through violence is more prevalent in the United States.

Because various types of youth violence exist across both developing and wealthy countries, prevention and intervention strategies are needed to address violence and promote safety. Some specific prevention and intervention strategies that address cultural and social norms have been recommended (WHO, 2009a). For example, mass media campaigns can help increase public awareness by providing information on a topic to reduce misconceptions of norms as well as unfavorable behavior. Anti-violence campaigns have been implemented in the United States (e.g.,

217

Table 18.1 Mother Reports of Physical, Verbal, Psychological, and Non-Violent Forms of Discipline within the Previous Six Months

Type of Punishment	Incidence (%)				
Example of Questions Asked	Chile	Egypt	India	Philippines	USA
Physical (Severe)					
Hit Child with an Object	4	26	36	21	4
Burned the Child	0	2	1	0	0
Threatened Child with Knife/ Gun	0	0	1	1	0
Beat the Child	0	25	*	3	0
Physical (Moderate)					
Spanked Buttocks with Hand	51	29	58	75	47
Slapped Child Face/Head	13	41	58	21	4
Shook the Child	39	59	12	20	9
Pinched the Child	3	45	17	60	5
Verbal/Psychological					
Yelled or Screamed	84	72	70	82	85
Called Child Names	15	44	29	24	17
Refused to Speak to Child	17	48	31	15	*
Threatened Evil Spirits	12	60	20	24	*
Non-Violent Discipline					
Explained why Behavior was Wrong	91	80	94	90	94
Took Privileges Away	60	27	43	3	77
Gave Child Something to Do	71	43	27	66	75
Made Child Stay in One Place	37	50	5	58	75

*Question not asked in Survey
From "World report on violence and health" by World Health Organization (2002a). Available online at http://whqlibdoc. who.int/publications/2002/9241545615_eng.pdf

Resolve It, Solve It), encouraging youth to engage in media campaigns that highlight respect for individual differences, conflict resolution, and bullying prevention. Furthermore, laws and policies that criminalize certain behaviors may be implemented to decrease rates of youth violence. For example, corporal punishment of children was banned in Sweden in 1979, which led to changes in attitudes toward such punishment and decreased levels of physical violence.

Bullying, Weapons, and Physical Aggression

The World Report on Violence and Health (WHO, 2002a) also highlights findings from studies conducted worldwide that focus upon school violence, including bullying, use of weapons, and physical aggression. Studies in Egypt (Youssef, Attia, & Karnel, 1999), Sweden (Grufman & Berg-Kelly, 1997), and Puerto Rico (Parrilla, Moscoso, Vélez, Robles, & Colón, 1997) investigated potential risk factors for violence amongst school-aged children. Results indicated that boys were more likely to engage in physical aggression than girls. Furthermore, individuals who engaged in problem behavior, suffered from psychosomatic disorders, participated in illegal drug use, had poor relationships with their parents, and were disciplined through corporal punishment were at greater risk for such aggression.

Results from a study investigating health behavior in school-aged children are also presented in the World Report on Violence and Health (Currie, 1998). Bullying was defined as "when another student, or a group of students, say or do nasty and unpleasant things to him or her" or "when a student is teased repeatedly in a way he or she doesn't like" (Currie, 1998, p. 26). Furthermore, "it is *not* bullying when two students of about the same strength quarrel or fight" (p. 26). Findings show that out of the countries that were surveyed, the highest percentages of 13-year-olds having "sometimes" engaged in bullying within a specific school term were found in Austria (64%), Germany (61%), Denmark (58%), Lithuania (57%), and Greenland (57%). The lowest percentages of bullying reports were found in Sweden (12%), England (13%), and Greece (19%). In the United States, 35% of 13-year-olds reported "sometimes" having engaged in bullying during the school term.

Other follow-up studies further investigating the health behaviors of school-aged children were completed in 2002 and 2006 (Currie, Samdal, Boyce, & Smith, 2001; Eunice Kennedy Shriver National Institute of Child Health and Human Development, 2008). Data in both studies indicated that the percentage of bullying in the United States decreased since the abovementioned 1998 report. Findings of the 2006 study indicate that a smaller percentage of students in the United States (10%) engaged in physical aggression three or more times within the past year than students from other countries (14%). Furthermore, fewer students from the United States reported being bullied within the past two months than the international average. On the other hand, more students in the United States reported that they had engaged in bullying within the past few months than what was reported internationally. Fewer students in the United States indicated that they liked school "a lot" and their classmates were helpful, and more reported that they perceived themselves as experiencing "some" or "a lot" of school stress. Decreases in rates of bullying in the 2006 survey were also reported in other countries. When school-aged students were asked whether they were involved in bullying in the past two months (i.e., bullied others, were bullied, or were both a bully and a victim), the prevalence ranged from 9% in Sweden to 45% in Lithuania for boys, and 5% in Sweden to 36% in Lithuania for girls (Craig et al., 2009).

Craig and colleagues (2009) have speculated potential reasons for differences in rates of bullying across countries. Such reasons include cultural differences and national policies, as well as various programs implemented to address bullying issues. These reasons may also address changes in bullying rates since the 1998 survey. As bullying becomes more highly recognized by the media and addressed in national policy as a global social health problem, countries may make more efforts to prevent and reduce bullying at a national policy level and within school programs.

Despite the fact that preliminary intervention efforts to reduce bullying and other aggressive behavior within the school setting have been successful, these findings emphasize the importance of continuing to focus on strategies to further reduce such behaviors.

School and Home-Based Efforts for Violence Prevention

Various campaigns have been implemented worldwide to address and prevent youth violence (WHO, 2005). The United Nations Secretary General's Study on Violence against Children was implemented in 2001 with the goal of amalgamating research on the types, causes, and effects of violence against children up to 18 years of age. Prevention and intervention strategies were also provided at the local, national, and international levels. The Pan American Health Organization, which is comprised of 34 member states from North, Central, and South America and the Caribbean, has also implemented various prevention initiatives. One such initiative was to develop laws to protect children and women against family violence. Organizations in Africa, as well as the Eastern Mediterranean and Western-Pacific World Health Organization offices have also targeted child abuse in their youth violence prevention efforts.

Along with these campaigns, various countries have a national report, plan of action, and/or a prevention focal point against youth violence (WHO, 2008). Specific millennium goals were also developed in 2000 to achieve worldwide primary education, promote gender equality, empower women, and reduce child mortality. These goals target youth violence by providing children education to reduce violence at home, as well as increasing child immunizations that are often reduced by collective violence. Examples of prevention programs that have been implemented in different countries include the Youth Violence Prevention Program in Brazil, the Learning for Life program in Jamaica, and the Violence and Injury Prevention Unit in Malaysia (WHO, 2007).

The Jamaican Learning for Life program supports disadvantaged out-of-school youth in obtaining job training, provides after-school programs to children and adolescents, and includes various campaign activities that target peace. The Violence and Injury Prevention Unit in Malaysia aims to prevent child abuse and domestic violence, with the goal of strengthening prevention programs and developing a national plan of action. Activities include raising awareness of domestic violence, training health staff on how to prevent and manage domestic violence and child abuse, and developing a database to keep track of victims who have been treated in hospitals.

The World Health Organization (2010b) recently created a diagram outlining specific steps that can be taken to control the prevention of injuries and violence. The steps are as follows:

1. Surveillance: Use of data to understand the extent and nature of the problem.
2. Risk Factor Identification: Identify risk factors associated with injury and violence.
3. Intervention Development: Develop interventions to address the causes and evaluate the effectiveness of these interventions.
4. Implementation: Implement effective prevention programs.

With respect to the abovementioned steps, surveillance (data collection) and risk factor identification have been previously addressed in this chapter. The following section will outline intervention and prevention strategies. Specific home and school-based violence prevention programs are also described in Table 18.2.

Action recommendations are included in the World Report on Violence and Health (2002b). These include creating, implementing, and monitoring national action plans for preventing violence, enhancing capacity for collecting data on violence, supporting research that evaluates the causes, consequences, and prevention of violence, and promoting international laws that help protect human rights. Specific suggestions on how to prevent violence at the individual, relationship, community, and societal levels for different age groups are also provided. Strategies that target each of these levels are briefly described below.

Individual

Programs that shape the behavior, attitudes, and knowledge of young children have been shown to effectively reduce both risk factors and acts of violence (WHO, 2004). One crucial area to target is the development of life skills (WHO, 2009b). The World Health Organization defines life skills as the abilities necessary for adaptive and positive behavior that enable individuals to deal effectively with the demands and challenges of everyday life. Critical skills include self-awareness, self-management, social awareness, and responsible decision making. There is strong support for preschool enrichment programs that provide children with early academic and social skills, with the goal of increasing the school-preparedness and academic success. Furthermore, school-based

Table 18.2 Home and School-Based Violence Prevention and Intervention Programs

Program (author)	Description	Level Targeted/Resources
Home Setting		
Triple P (Positive Parenting Program; Sanders & colleagues)	Provides various levels of parental support from providing information on parenting (level 1) to addressing severe problems (level 5). The goal of the program is to create a stable and supportive family, reduce problematic behavior, build positive relationships, and provide parents with tools to effectively manage problems.	Relationship http://www.triplep.net
Early Head Start (Administration for Children and Families)	Targets vulnerable families with young children. The goal is to improve the health of pregnant women, encourage child development, provide family support through home-community partnerships, and provide parent education.	Relationship and Societal http://www.ehsnrc.org
Parents Anonymous	A self-help support group that strives to strengthen family bonds and encourage caring communities to prevent child maltreatment. The goal is to reduce social isolation, develop coping strategies, and offer support.	Relationship http://www. parentsanonymous.org
School Setting		
Promoting Alternative Thinking Strategies (PATHS; Kusche & Greenberg)	A social development program that targets children from kindergarten through grade six. This curriculum consists of six volumes of lessons that are delivered over five years with three main units: readiness and self-control, feelings and relationships, and interpersonal, cognitive problem-solving. Teaching training, teaching materials, and parent resources are provided.	Individual and Relationship http://www. channingbete.com/ prevention-programs/ paths/
Second Step (Committee for Children)	Violence prevention curriculum for students in kindergarten through grade nine that is designed to teach prosocial skills and reduce impulsive and aggressive behavior. The program focuses on three units (empathy training, impulse control and problem solving, and anger management), with approximately six to eight lessons per unit being taught one to two times per week.	Individual and Relationship http://www.cfchildren. org/programs/ssp/ overview/
Expect Respect: Bully Proof Prevention Program (Sjostrom & Stein)	The goals of this program is to support abused youth, raise their expectations for equality and respect in relationships, enhance safety and respect at school, and promote leadership in violence prevention. The components include counseling and support groups, classroom presentations, a summer teen leadership program, and training for school personal to prevent bullying and sexual harassment.	Relationship and Societal http://new.vawnet.org/ Assoc_Files_VAWnet/ NRC_Expect-full.pdf

programs such as Second Step (Committee for Children, 2008) and Steps to Respect (Committee for Children, 2001) also help foster social–emotional skills and promote socially responsible beliefs. Descriptions of additional school–based programs are also included in Table 18.2. Other programs that target the individual level include those providing information on drug use, services for children who witness violence, and individual counseling (WHO, 2004).

Relationship

Programs that target parent and school-based relationships are also effective at decreasing youth violence across settings (WHO, 2002a, 2004). For example, home-visitation programs and parent training are effective for parents of infants and children 3 to 5 years of age (see Table 18.2). In addition, mentoring programs and home-school partnerships help promote parental involvement in the school setting. For example, Steps to Respect (Committee for Children, 2001) and The Friendly School in Australia (Cross, Hall, Hamilton, Pintabona, & Erceg, 2004) include information materials for parents to reinforce skill acquisition and promote generalization of positive behaviors across settings. School-aged children may also benefit from peer mediation and counseling to help target dysfunctional relationships.

Community and Societal

Community- and society-based programs may be implemented to help protect all children and control youth violence (WHO, 2002a, 2004). This includes increasing the availability of child-care services for young children, providing after-school programs and extra-curricular activities to extend adult supervision, and reducing alcohol availability. Encouraging campaigns that promote human rights, changing social and cultural norms, training health care professionals, and setting up crisis shelters may also help improve overall feelings of safety within the community (WHO, 2006). Examples of both home and school-based programs, such as Early Head Start, are reported in Table 18.2.

Future Directions

The World Report on Violence and Health offers worldwide data related to youth violence and safety. Interpersonal violence, including child maltreatment and abuse, has led to many fatal and non-fatal injuries worldwide. Social and cultural norms that support youth violence must be targeted. Worldwide campaigns targeting youth violence have been conducted, with various countries having a national report, plan of action, and/or prevention focal point against youth violence. Specific steps to control the prevention of injuries and violence have also been outlined by the World Health Organization. Furthermore, individual, relationship, community, and societal factors associated with youth violence have been identified in the literature and preventive measures have been provided to address these areas that have been recommended. Implications for practice based on data surrounding youth violence are reported in Table 18.3.

Despite the various measures that have been taken to prevent and address youth violence over the past years, additional actions need to be taken. Although a great deal of data have been collected on risk factors and violence within the family and community, less data have been collected internationally within the school setting. Additional data regarding violence within the school setting will enable countries to take further measures to prevent bullying, antisocial behaviors, and school crisis situations.

The World Health Organization (2002a) also provides key areas that require further investigation. First of all, world reports have indicated that youth violence occurs to different degrees and in various forms in countries and regions throughout the world. No individual strategy is sufficient to reduce youth violence and the effect it has on youth health. Therefore, multiple approaches that are relevant to the particular needs of the country in which they are being implemented are required. Second, many of the recommended prevention and intervention programs are based on research from developed countries. Additional research is therefore needed on developing countries to determine which programs are the most effective in these countries. Third, data systems are necessary in order to provide ongoing information about child maltreat-

Table 18.3 Implications for Practice: Understanding and Preventing Youth Violence Worldwide

1.	Various forms of youth violence occur to different degrees worldwide, across culture and gender.
2.	Risk factors of physical aggression that may be targeted include poor parent-child relationships, use of corporal punishment, media exposure, and problem behavior.
3.	Prevention and intervention efforts should target both the home and school settings. Collaboration across these settings is needed for long-term changes in decreasing youth violence.
4.	Effective prevention efforts may be taken at school to decrease youth violence and increase feelings of safety.
5.	Parent programs that build parent-child relationships, provide parent education, and develop coping strategies help decrease child maltreatment and violence in the home setting.
6.	School-based programs that teach children about feelings and relationships, teach self-regulation strategies, and enhance safety and respect are effective in decreasing bullying and youth violence.
7.	Intervention programs should target the individual, relationship, societal, and community level.
8.	Social and cultural norms that support youth violence may be targeted to help decrease youth violence.
9.	Multiple intervention and prevention approaches that are specific to the country in which they are being implemented are necessary.

ment, as well as fatal and non-fatal injuries. Centers where information related to health services and violence can be collected and compared should be established in all countries and regions. Along these same lines, consistent standards for defining and measuring youth violence should be developed, including age categories that provide accurate representations of potential risk factors of youth violence. In addition, additional scientific research (qualitative and quantitative studies) should be conducted, including cross-cultural research on the causes, development, and prevention of violence, as well as research on how social and economic factors play a role in violence. Finally, it is important that greater dissemination occurs on what has been learned about youth violence, including presenting the facts, causes, risk factors, and preventative measures that address youth violence. Such efforts will help increase worldwide awareness of youth violence, facilitate widespread implementation of effective prevention and intervention programs, and help ensure the safety of youth across the home, school, and community settings.

References

Committee for Children. (2001). *Steps to Respect: A bullying prevention program*. Seattle, WA: Author.

Committee for Children. (2008). *Second Step: A violence prevention curriculum – New Middle School Program*. Seattle, WA: Author.

Craig, W., Harel-Fisch, Y., Fogel-Grinvald, H., Dostaler, S., Hetland, J., Simons-Morton, B., ... Molcho, M. (2009). A cross-national profile of bullying and victimization among adolescents in 40 countries. *International Journal of Public health, 54*, 216–224. doi:10.1007/s00038-009-5413-9

Cross, D., Hall, M., Hamilton, G., Pintabona, Y., & Erceg, E. (2004). Australia: The friendly schools project. In P. K. Smith, D. Pepler, & K. Rigby (Eds.), *Bullying in schools: How successful can interventions be?* (pp. 187–210). Cambridge, England: Cambridge University Press.

Currie, C. (Ed). (1998). *Health behaviour in school-aged children: A WHO cross-national study*. Bergen, Norway: University of Bergen.

Currie, C., Samdal, O., Boyce, W., & Smith, B. (Eds.). (2001). *Health behaviour in school-aged children: A WHO cross-national study. Research protocol for the 2001–2002 Survey*. Edinburgh, UK: University of Edinburgh.

Eunice Kennedy Shriver National Institute of Child Health and Human Development. (2008). *Health behaviors in school-age children (HBSC) 2005/2006 survey: School report*. Washington, DC: U.S. Government Printing Office.

Ferguson, C. J., San Miguel, C., & Hartley, R. D. (2009). A multivariate analysis of youth violence and aggression: The influence of family, peers, depression, and media violence. *Journal of Pediatrics, 155*, 904–908. doi:10.1016/j.jpeds.2009.06.021

Grufman, M., & Berg-Kelly, K. (1997). Physical fighting and associated health behaviours among Swedish adolescents. *Acta Paediatrica, 86,* 77–81. doi:10.1111/j.1651-2227.1997.tb08836.x

Jensen, R., & Thornton, R. (2003). Early female marriage in the developing world. *Gender and Development, 11,* 9–19. doi:10.1080/741954311

Kishor, S., & Johnson, K. (2004). *Profiling domestic violence: A multi-country study.* Calverton, MD: ORC Macro.

Loeber, R., & Pardini, D. (2008). Neurobiology and the development of violence: Common assumptions and controversies. *Philosophical Transactions of the Royal Society B: Biological Sciences, 363,* 2491–2503. doi:10.1098/rstb.2008.0032

Ortiz, J., & Raine, A. (2004). Heart rate level and antisocial behavior in children and adolescents: A meta-analysis. *Journal of the American Academy of Child and Adolescent Psychiatry, 43,* 154–162. doi: 10.1097/01.chi.0000101373.03068.5c

Parrilla, I. C., Moscoso, M. R., Vélez, M., Robles, R. R., & Colón, H. M. (1997). Internal and external environment of the Puerto Rican adolescent in the use of alcohol, drugs and violence. *Boletin Asociación Medica de Puerto Rico, 89,* 146–149.

Straus, M. A., & Hamby, S. L. (1997). Measuring physical and psychological maltreatment of children with the Conflict Tactics Scales. In G. Kaufman Kantor & J. L. Jasinski (Eds.), *Out of darkness: Contemporary research perspectives on family violence* (pp. 119–135). Thousand Oaks, CA: Sage

Wood, W., Wong, F. Y., & Chachere, J. G. (1991). Effects of media violence on viewers' aggression in unconstrained social interactions. *Psychological Bulletin, 109,* 371–383. doi:10.1037//0033-2909.109.3.371

World Health Organization. (1999, March 29–31). *Report of the consultation on child abuse prevention.* Retrieved August 21, 2010, from http://www.yesican.org/definitions/WHO.html

World Health Organization. (2002a). *World report on violence and health.* Retrieved August 17, 2010, from http://whqlibdoc.who.int/publications/2002/9241545615_eng.pdf

World Health Organization. (2002b). *Recommendations from the world report on violence and health.* Retrieved August 17, 2010, from http://www.who.int/violence_injury_prevention/violence/world_report/en/wrvhrecommendations.pdf

World Health Organization (2004). *Preventing violence: A guide to implementing the recommendations of the world report on violence and health.* Retrieved August 17, 2010, from http://whqlibdoc.who.int/publications/2004/9241592079.pdf

World Health Organization. (2005). *Milestones of a global campaign for violence prevention 2005: Changing the face of violence prevention.* Retrieved August 18, 2010, from http://whqlibdoc.who.int/publications/2005/9241593555_eng.pdf

World Health Organization. (2006). *Preventing child maltreatment: A guide to taking action and generating evidence.* Retrieved August 21, 2010, from http://whqlibdoc.who.int/publications/2006/9241594365_eng.pdf

World Health Organization. (2007). *Third milestones of a global campaign for violence prevention report 2007: Scaling up.* Retrieved August 17, 2010, from http://whqlibdoc.who.int/publications/2007/9789241595476_eng.pdf

World Health Organization (2008). *Preventing violence and reducing its impact: How development agencies can help.* Retrieved August 18, 2010, from http://whqlibdoc.who.int/publications/2008/9789241596589_eng.pdf

World Health Organization. (2009a). *Violence prevention the evidence: Changing cultural and social norms that support violence.* Retrieved August 18, 2010, from http://whqlibdoc.who.int/publications/2009/9789241598330_eng.pdf

World Health Organization. (2009b). *Violence prevention the evidence: Preventing violence by developing life skills in children and adolescents.* Retrieved August 18, 2010, from http://whqlibdoc.who.int/publications/2009/9789241597838_eng.pdf

World Health Organization. (2010b). *Injuries and violence: The facts.* Retrieved August 18, 2010, from http://whqlibdoc.who.int/publications/2010/9789241599375_eng.pdf

Youssef, R. M., Attia, M. S., & Karnel, M. I. (1999). Violence among school children in Alexandria. *Eastern Mediterranean Health Journal, 5,* 282–298. Retrieved from http://www.emro.who.int/emhj.htm

Section II

Assessment and Measurement

Evidence-Based Standards and Methodological Issues in School Violence and Related Prevention Research in Education and the Allied Disciplines

Matthew J. Mayer

RUTGERS, THE STATE UNIVERSITY OF NEW JERSEY, NEW BRUNSWICK

Abstract

Standards for evidence-based research across education and allied social and behavioral disciplines are examined, with connections to research in school violence prevention and school safety promotion. The first section summarizes recent evidence-based developments across these allied disciplines, followed by an overview of major nongovernmental evidence-based organizations. Next, recent and emerging evidence-based protocols are examined. The fourth section discusses critical issues that cut across allied disciplines, including reviews of protocols and evidence-based clearinghouses, types and hierarchies of evidence debates, efficacy/effectiveness research, translational research, systematic reviews and meta-analysis, developmental issues, manualized treatments and adaptability, and journal constraints for research manuscripts. The final section considers overall implications for current and future research, policy, and practice in school violence prevention research.

Introduction

Education and allied disciplines address the needs of children and adolescents at risk for displaying or otherwise experiencing aggressive, antisocial, or delinquent behaviors. These disciplines share a common professional heritage linked to research, policy, and practice that target school violence and school safety issues. Disciplinary boundaries are often fuzzy, and tools for evidence-based evaluation of prevention and intervention programs while varying, often overlap. In turn, school safety efficacy and effectiveness research can be subject to differing evidence-based standards, depending on the disciplines involved.

This chapter provides an overview of recent developments in evidence-based standards across education and allied disciplines, connects discussion of discipline-specific developments to school violence and school safety issues, and highlights cross-cutting issues requiring further study and attention with regard to evidence-based research in related social and behavioral fields. Section 1 summarizes recent evidence-based developments in education, special education, school and clinical psychology, public health, social work, and juvenile justice, with attention to research standards as well as translation to practice issues. Section 2 provides an overview of several nongovernmental evidence-based organizations, including the Cochrane and Campbell Collaborations. In Section 3, recent and emerging protocols aligned with the evidence-based movement are examined. Section 4 discusses critical issues that cut across allied disciplines, including a range of review protocols and evidence-based clearinghouses, types and hierarchies of evidence debates, efficacy/effectiveness research, translational research, systematic reviews and meta-analysis, developmental issues, manualized treatments and adaptability, and journal constraints for research manuscripts. Implications for research in school violence prevention are discussed for each of these issues. Section 5 considers overall implications for current and future research, policy, and practice.

Section 1: Recent Evidence-Based Developments Across Multiple Disciplines

Education

The No Child Left Behind Act (2001), using the terminology, "scientifically-based research," marked a significant shift in educational intervention research, placing an increased emphasis on more rigorous methodology. This emphasis has been recently reinforced with requirements for evidence of effectiveness among most federally funded K–12 intervention research programs. Following enactment of the No Child Left Behind Law, the Department of Education reorganized its research branch, creating the Institute for Educational Sciences (IES). Presentations by then IES Director, Grover Whitehurst, began to emphasize a new approach to educational research, with a strong commitment to randomized controlled trials (RCT).

The IES created the What Works ClearingHouse (WWC), a federally funded venture, originally contracted to American Institutes for Research and the Campbell Collaboration. The WWC contract was awarded to the Mathematica Policy Research group in 2007. The purpose of the WWC is to develop and implement standards for evaluating educational research and disseminate evidence on educational interventions. The WWC produces three main types of informational products: (a) *intervention reports*, which evaluate bodies of evidence on particular interventions across identified topic areas (11 as of September, 2010); (b) *quick reviews* (beginning in mid-2008), which provide a summary and evaluation of recently published effectiveness studies on topics aligned with WWC work, and (c) *practice guides*, which synthesize best practices drawn from rigorous empirical research. The WWC also produces multimedia resources and methodological references regarding their procedures and protocols, and registries of evaluation researchers and randomized controlled trials.

WWC reports are produced through a three-stage process of initial screen, quality review, and research synthesis. As of the December, 2008 Version-2 WWC standards documentation, under *eligibility screening,* WWC identified four types of eligible research designs for their reviews: randomized controlled trial, quasi-experimental, regression discontinuity, and single subject (p.10). In mid-2010, the WWC published methodological standards for regression discontinuity and single case research designs.

While the WWC has produced a large body of high quality material within a relatively brief time span and has made valued contributions that have helped improve educational research, policy, and practice, it has also been criticized in several arenas. Slavin (2008) noted that WWC procedures that exclude otherwise informative studies may produce recommendations based on small-scale randomized experiments or extremely brief interventions. Slavin cited the Saxon Math evaluation report, which was based on an unpublished study of 46 students instructed by one teacher. He also noted an example from English Language Learners research where the one program earning a positive effects report was based on a four-week study. Slavin's criticisms of the WWC were addressed in a companion article in the same issue by Dynarski (2008). Slavin and others (Song & Herman, 2010) have criticized inclusion of studies where the outcome measures closely align with the experimental group treatment, but not the control group, which tends to inflate effect sizes. Song and Herman argued that if an experiment purports to test the effect of an intervention on subjects learning a skill, both the experimental and comparison group should be taught the same skill, but the teaching approach or method should be different between groups, to test the intervention's effect. The Government Accountability Office (GAO) issued a report (2010) in which they generally found the WWC standards for evidence-based research appropriate, but criticized the WWC for a lack of timely process and a need for improved dissemination methods.

Special Education

Students in special education—particularly those with emotional disturbance—may engage in fighting and are suspended for disruptive and sometimes aggressive or violent behaviors at significantly higher rates than the general student population, signaling a need for quality research on preventing such behaviors (Mayer & Leone, 2007). While many children and adolescents who can benefit from behavior management and violence prevention efforts are served by special education, teachers of students with disabilities often use practices that are known to be ineffective (Cook, Tankersley, & Landrum, 2009). The Council for Exceptional Children Division of Research (CEC-DR) created a task force in early 2003 to (a) identify and establish quality indicators for specific research methodologies appropriate for rigorous scientific investigation in special education and (b) determine how research results from each methodology could inform effective practice. The task force identified four types of research for which quality indicators would be developed: experimental group, correlational, single subject, and qualitative (Odom et al., 2005). Odom and colleagues noted several challenges facing researchers in special education: (a) heterogeneity of special education students can make equivalent group designs problematic; (b) some disabilities are low incidence, making subject availability for large group designs impossible; (c) federal disability law may preclude the use of no-treatment groups that might deny legally mandated entitlements to students; and (d) widely used grouping practices within special education may prevent investigators from using individuals as the unit of analysis.

The CEC-DR task force crafted two sets of quality indicators (QI) governing experimental and quasi-experimental research: "essential quality indicators" and "desirable quality indicators." These two sets of indicators were proposed for selecting "high" and "acceptable" quality research publications. High quality research must meet all but one of the 10 essential indicators and at least four of the eight desirable indicators. Acceptable research must meet all but one of the 10 essential indicators and at least one of the desirable indicators. The essential QIs require detailed information on participant description, comparable group design, intervention implementers, intervention details, fidelity of implementation, comparison condition services, multiple appropriate measures, timing of outcome measurement, appropriate data analysis techniques, and effect size calculations. The desirable QIs addressed attrition data, reliability and validity measures, follow-up measurements, qualitative aspects of fidelity of implementation, documentation on comparison conditions, audio/video documentation of intervention, and appropriate and clear presentation of results. A 2009 special issue of the research journal, *Exceptional Children*, examined evidence-based practices in special education, applying the CEC-DR quality indicators to reviews of intervention research, finding considerable variability and some problems meeting QIs (Cook et al., 2009).

Research questions that center on low incidence populations as well as other group entities such as schools, which can be treated as single units of analysis, are often studied using single case designs (SCDs), also known as single subject designs. Single case designs are often used with studies of behavioral management of aggressive behavior. The What Works Clearinghouse officially adopted SCDs with the 2008 Version-2 standards and published technical standards for SCDs in June 2010 (Kratochwill et al., 2010). Noteworthy in those standards is a require- ment that for a SCD study to fully meet WWC evidence standards (a) the independent variable must be systematically manipulated; (b) outcome variables need to be measured by more than one assessor with specified calculations of interassessor agreement meeting WWC standards; (c) at least three attempts must occur across different times or phase repetitions; and (d) each phase must have at least three data points (at least 4 phases and 5 data points per phase for reversal/ withdrawal designs, at least 6 phases and 5 data points per phase for multiple baseline designs). For purposes of combining studies to generate analysis in a WWC Intervention Report, at least five SCD research papers, conducted by at least three different research teams, with at least 20 experiments must be included (Kratochwill et al., 2010).

Clinical and School Psychology

The psychology community, particularly researchers in school and child clinical psychology, took the lead in the evidence-based standards movement in the mid-1990s. The APA Division 12 (clin- ical) Taskforce on Promotion and Dissemination of Psychological Procedures articulated stan- dards for "well-established," "probably efficacious," and "experimental" treatments (Hoagwood & Johnson, 2003; Lonigan, Elbert, & Johnson, 1998; Ollendick & King, 2004) (see Table 19.1).

The Taskforce had previously introduced the term "empirically validated," which was con- tentious, especially since it could imply that the question of effectiveness was finalized (Chor- pita, 2003; Ollendick & King, 2004). Both the well-established and probably efficacious criteria required at least two experimental demonstrations of effect, but the well-established criterion required superior effect compared to a placebo or alternate treatment, where the probably effica- cious required the effect to be superior to a wait-list control group. Both standards required an intervention treatment manual and sample characteristic information. Additional criteria were identified for single case designs, with stricter standards for the well-established criterion.

The Division 12 Taskforce report was oriented mainly to questions of "efficacy" as opposed to "effectiveness" (Chambless & Hollon, 1998). Efficacy addresses whether the experimental treatment works, usually tested under well-controlled laboratory-like conditions. Effectiveness studies test whether and how well treatments work under more real-world conditions where the treatments are typically provided (Lonigan et al., 1998). Several researchers have spoken to the substantive differences between research-based, and real-world clinical experiments and implications for developing a knowledge base on effective interventions, demonstrating external validity (Chorpita, 2003; Kazdin, 2008; Ollendick & King, 2004; Schoenwald & Hoagwood, 2001; Weisz & Hawley, 1998).

Building on work by the APA Division 12 Taskforce in the early- to mid-1990s, as well as input from APA Division 17 (Counseling Psychology), the APA Division 16 (School Psychol- ogy) Taskforce developed the *Procedural and Coding Manual for Review of Evidence-Based Interven- tions*. There were concerns regarding the Division 12 criteria that led to an independent criteria development effort by Division 16 (Kratochwill & Stoiber, 2002), including over-reliance on randomized clinical trials, DSM diagnostic categories, and manualized treatments, as well as insufficient attention to comorbidity issues. The Division 16 approach addressed four types of research: group designs, single subject, qualitative, and program evaluation.

More recently, the APA Task Force on Evidence-Based Practice with Children and Adoles- cents issued a technical report: *Disseminating Evidenced-Based Practice for Children and Adolescents*

Table 19.1   Criteria for Empirically Validated Treatments

I.   *Well-established treatments*

   A. Minimum of two good between-group design experiments demonstrating efficacy in one or more of the following ways:

      1. Superior to pill or psychological placebo or to another treatment

      2. Equivalent to an already established treatment in experiments with adequate statistical power (about 30 per group)

   or

   B. A large series of single-case design experiments (n > 9) demonstrating efficacy. These experiments must have:

      1. Used good experimental designs, and

      2. Compared the intervention to another treatment as in A.1.

   Further criteria for both A and B:

   C. Experiments must be conducted with treatment manuals.

   D. Characteristics of the client samples must be clearly specified.

   E. Effects demonstrated by at least two different investigators or investigatory teams.

II.   *Probably efficacious treatments*

   A. Two experiments showing the treatment is more effective than a waiting-list control group

   or

   B. One or more experiments meeting the well-established treatment criteria A, C, D, but not E

      or

   C. A small series of single-case design experiments (*n* > 3) otherwise meeting well-established treatment criteria B, C, and D.

Note. From *Handbook of interventions that work with children and adolescents: Prevention and treatment* (p. 6), by P. M. Barrrett & T. H. Ollendick, 2004, West Sussex, England: Wiley. Copyright 2004 by Wiley. Reprinted with permission.

(American Psychological Association Task Force on Evidence-Based Practice for Children and Adolescents, 2008). The document presents a framework for evidence-based practice in psychology (EBPP), which acknowledges the roles of multiple stakeholders in treatment, multidisciplinary involvement with clients (schools, juvenile justice, social work, community mental health, and so forth), the collaborative nature of psychological interventions, family and cultural responsiveness, and the need to adapt interventions to local context. Clinical practice that follows principles of EBPP relies particularly on three elements:

1. assessment that guides diagnosis, intervention planning, and outcome evaluation;
2. intervention that includes, but is not limited to, those treatment programs for which randomized controlled trials have shown empirical support for the target populations and ecologies; and
3. ongoing monitoring, including client or participant feedback, conducted in a scientifically minded manner and informed by clinical expertise (p. 9).

Social Work

School social workers typically address needs of students engaged in violent and disruptive behaviors, provide conflict resolution and peer mediation services, and are often front line service providers in states such as Michigan, where most schools are staffed by a school social worker. Although the field of social work often interfaces with that of education and school psychology, evidence-based research developments in social work have been markedly different from the former fields of study. Many in the theorist, researcher, and practitioner trainer community in the field of social work have embraced a perspective of evidence-based practice (EBP), an outgrowth of the evidence-based medicine movement, typically associated with the work of David Sackett and the *Evidence-Based Medicine Working Group* at McMaster University (Sackett, Rosenberg, Gray, Haynes, & Richardson, 1996). As opposed to the more discrete and targeted efforts (discussed above) in education and school psychology to create and use tools to measure the value of specific intervention research studies, EBP is a systemic approach (see Figure 19.1) that uses clinical expertise to integrate clinical circumstances, best scientific evidence, and client needs and preferences to support more well-attuned and effective service delivery (Shlonsky & Gibbs, 2004; Shlonsky & Wagner, 2005). The EBP model incorporates a multistep procedure of: (a) asking an answerable question regarding the need, (b) locating the best evidence, (c) ascertaining the validity and utility of the evidence, (d) deciding if the presenting problem can be addressed, (e) advising and conferring with stakeholders, (f) developing an integrated action plan, and (g) implementing the plan with ongoing process and outcome monitoring and evaluation. As part of the EBP process, Gibbs (2004) outlined the client oriented practical evidence search (COPES) model that assists practitioners in posing and then answering critical questions that will guide their intervention efforts. The COPES model parallels the EBP model in being client-oriented, having practical relevance in the context of daily practice, and supporting efficient searches for evidence-based methods. The model supports five types of questions, addressing: (a) effectiveness, (b) prevention, (c) assessment, (d) risk/prognosis, and (e) description.

Proponents of EBP note that a sizable segment of the social work practitioner community defer mainly to advice and directions from professional colleagues, personal experience, and professional publications for practice (Howard, McMillen, & Pollio, 2003, p. 235) and do not neces-

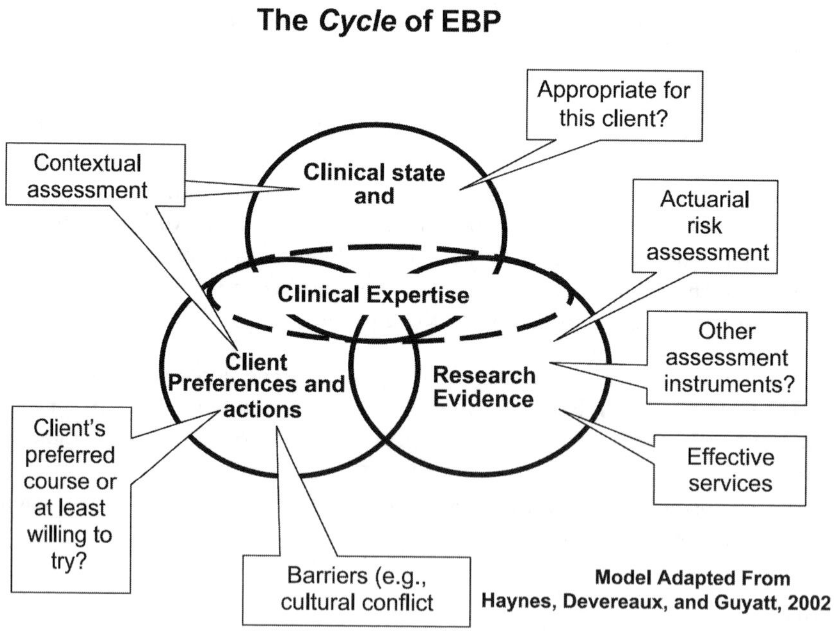

The *Cycle* of EBP

Figure 19.1 Shlonsky and Wagner (2005) Adaptation of Revised Evidence-Based Practice Model. *Note.* Reprinted from *Children and Youth Services Review* (Vol. 27), Shlonsky, A., & Wagner, D. The next step: Integrating actuarial risk assessment and clinical judgment into an evidence-based practice framework in CPS case management, pp. 409–427, Copyright 2005, with permission from Elsevier.

sarily follow "practice-related research findings" (Gibbs & Gambrill, 2002, p. 452). Rosen (2003) discussed challenges to the social work field in adopting EBP, citing three fundamental barriers: (a) personal attitudes, beliefs, and experiential knowledge among social workers that may conflict with evidence-based practice; (b) differing orientations to knowledge, related in part to a resistance to a logical positivist paradigm, along with an orientation to relative constructs of social justice and reform; and (c) intuitive applications of empirically generalized knowledge, where practitioners avoid or supplant implementation of empirically-based interventions, based on individual belief.

While EBP has been a defining feature in social work, other significant developments have occurred over the past two decades. In 1991, the *Task Force on Social Work Research* (created in 1988 by the Director of NIMH) presented a report—*Building Social Work Knowledge for Effective Services and Policies: A Plan for Research Development*—to a committee of the National Institutes on Mental Health (NIMH; Austin, 1998; Zlotnik, Biegel, & Solt, 2002). As a result of that work, several social work research centers were created as well as the Institute for the Advancement of Social Work Research (IASWR, 2003), originally, a collaboration among five social work professional bodies. The IASWR produced a report (Institute for the Advancement of Social Work Research, 2007) on evidence-based practice for NIMH—*Partnerships to Integrate Evidence-based Mental Health Practices into Social Work Education and Research*—as an outgrowth of a 2007 symposium hosted by NIMH.

Juvenile Justice

The field of juvenile justice has benefited from multiple distributed efforts to support evidence-based practice, but, on the whole, there has been a less well-focused effort within the field in this regard. Juvenile justice as a field has not pursued the development of instruments to evaluate specific research publications, as have the fields of education, psychology, and medicine. There have been multiple efforts along these lines in the past decade, such as the *Maryland Scale of Scientific Methods* (no longer in general use), and the *Standardized Program Evaluation Protocol* (discussed later in this chapter). Also, the field in large part has not subscribed to a framework such as evidence-based practice, as has been the case in social work. At the same time, there have been multiple developments in the research literature and the establishment of and use of evaluation research centers to guide evidence-based best practices.

The Justice Statistics and Research Association, a project funded by the Office of Juvenile Justice and Delinquency Prevention (OJJDP) in the U.S. Department of Justice, created the *Juvenile Justice Evaluation Center* (JJEC), which was active from 1998 to 2007. The JJEC developed a briefing series of nontechnical publications to assist administrators and practitioners in addressing evaluation issues, and JJEC also provided technical assistance to the states, online publications on evaluation issues, referral to other evaluation resources, summary information on evaluations of interventions that are organized topically, funding seed projects, and related activities.

The *Center for Program Evaluation and Performance Measurement* (CPEPM), an online resource for program evaluation and performance measurement available to assist state and local criminal justice agencies, field practitioners, researchers, and evaluators, is currently available (as of fall 2010) and administered by the Bureau of Justice Assistance. The Center includes an innovative online resource tool that covers a wide array of justice-related issues (e.g., adjudications, corrections, crime prevention, mental health, substance abuse), providing summaries of the research base and answering questions such as *what have we learned from evaluations conducted in this area* and *how can evaluation findings be used for program development and improvement*? This type of approach aligns well with calls from the empirical literature to better translate research to real-world settings in a practical manner. The Center offers Web links to a wide array of evidence-based clearinghouses and other sources for information on specific interventions. The CPEPM also provides technical assistance to states and localities, such as on-site training on evaluation methods, support creating and using performance measures, crafting evaluation plans, and logic model development.

The juvenile justice research and practitioner community has also relied on a combination of resources for guidance, including the Society for Prevention Research, the Cochrane and Campbell Collaborations, the Center for Evaluation Research and Methodology at Vanderbilt University, and similar evaluation research efforts at other universities. The Campbell Crime and Justice Coordinating Group, a component of the Campbell Collaboration, is an international effort among scholars from over 10 nations to provide rigorous systematic reviews and evaluations of research in criminology and justice-related areas. More recently (2008), this group has launched a project that considers extending the CONSORT protocol (see discussion of protocols below) that is used in the healthcare field to criminal justice trials.

Howell and Lipsey (2004) discussed efforts to use research on evidence-based programs for juvenile delinquency. They identified three basic approaches: (a) replication of model programs, such as the "Blueprints" program at the Center for the Study and Prevention of Violence at University of Colorado; (b) conducting evaluations of many individual programs; and (c) defining characteristics of successful program principles and practices from research and applying them. In addition to discussing the benefits of meta-analysis, Howell and Lipsey (2004) described the *Standardized Program Evaluation Protocol* (SPEP), an instrument that applies principles gathered from characteristics of effective intervention programs and scores individual programs, relative to the instrument's domains. The SPEP instrumentation has since been applied in several states, including North Carolina (Lipsey, Howell, & Tidd, 2007) and Arizona (Lipsey, 2008), demonstrating how the instrument identifies programs that foster improvements in juvenile offender outcomes (Howell, 2009).

As has been the case in allied fields (National Research Council, 2002), evaluations of intervention programs funded by the National Institute of Justice (NIJ) have come under scrutiny and criticism. For example, a Government Accountability Office (GAO) study (GAO, 2003), *Justice Outcome Evaluations: Design and Implementation of Studies Require More NIJ Attention,* raised serious criticism of a sample of 15 (out of 96) NIJ funded evaluation studies, where problems emerged with fidelity of implementation and insufficient outcome data. These issues are not unique to the field of juvenile justice and are indicative of the challenges facing allied disciplines in ensuring quality evaluation studies.

Public Health

The field of public health maintains a long tradition of ongoing monitoring and analysis of public health events along with a commitment to developing and refining research standards. For example, the Centers for Disease Control and Prevention (CDC) launched a series of 15 CDC-funded evaluation projects addressing youth violence prevention in the early 1990s (Powell et al., 1996), with a strong emphasis on rigorous science, including use of randomization and control groups. Descriptions and baseline data for these projects were presented in a 1996 special issue of the *American Journal of Preventive Medicine*. CDC has supported high quality research in violence prevention through publications of supporting materials such as the National Center for Injury Prevention and Control's *Measuring Violence-Related Attitudes, Beliefs, and Behaviors Among Youths: A Compendium of Assessment Tools* (Dahlberg, Toal, Swahn, & Behrens, 2005).

Using the term "program" to represent any public health action, from a highly focused direct intervention with individual clients to more broad-based community-level mobilization, the CDC Evaluation Working Group developed the *Framework for Program Evaluation in Public Health* (Centers for Disease Control, 1999). The *Framework* identifies the following steps in evaluation practice: (a) engage stakeholders, (b) describe the program, (c) focus the evaluation design, (d) gather credible evidence, (f) justify conclusions, and (g) ensure use and sharing of lessons learned (see Figure 19.2). This framework applies the Joint Committee on Evaluation Standards' four core concepts: utility, feasibility, propriety, and accuracy (Joint Committee on Standards for Educational Evaluation, 1994). The framework includes specific standards for research methods, including experimental, quasi-experimental, and observational designs, with an acknowledgement of the relative strengths and weaknesses of all methods and a suggestion that mixed-method approaches can offer advantages to the researcher. Unlike some recent developments in fields such as education and school psychology, where specific instrumentation has been developed to rate the strength of evidence of published research, this framework does not provide a scoring rubric as such; rather, it is a more general structure to drive the process of quality evaluation.

The CDC Office of Surveillance, Epidemiology, and Laboratory Services (OSELS) directs multiple activities including investigating and promoting best practices grounded in evidence-based research. The OSELS Epidemiology and Analysis Program Office produces the *Community Guide*, an online resource which provides systematic reviews of research on a wide array of public health topics, following a rigorous set of systematic review standards that were developed and influenced by the Cochrane Collaboration standards, methodological standards from the health and social science empirical literature, and expert review (Briss et al., 2000; Zaza et al., 2000). The Community Guide addresses interventions that prevent disease or injury, or promote health, for a defined population. These systematic reviews follow three highly structured procedural sections: *classification information* (addressing study information, including type of design); *descriptive information* (documenting methods and results, including setting, population, measurement tools, analytic methods, effect measures, study power, and so forth); and *execution information* (documenting descriptions, sampling, measurement, analysis, and interpretation

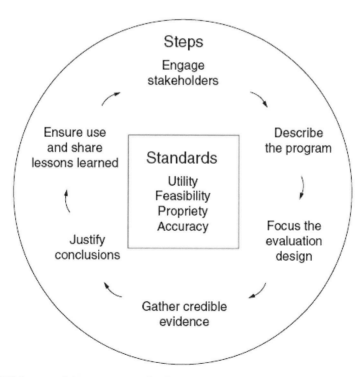

Figure 19.2   CDC framework for program evaluation

of results). Strength of evidence is assessed relative to evidence of effect, quality of execution, design suitability, number of studies, consistency of study results, and effect sizes (see Table 19.2).

The Substance Abuse and Mental Health Services Administration (SAMHSA) has been active in developing protocols for reviewing effective science-based prevention programs (Schinke, Brounstein, & Gardner, 2002). SAMHSA's Center for Substance Abuse Prevention (CSAP) created the National Registry of Effective Prevention Programs (NREPP), which reviews and identifies evidence-based programs based on experimental, quasi-experimental, time-series, and ethnographic research. SAMHSA reviewed programs were classified into (a) promising programs, (b) effective programs, and (c) model programs, but that framework and set of procedures were abandoned in favor of a revised approach that went into effect in 2007 and was developed following a public call for comments posted in the Federal Register in 2005 (Hennessy, Finkbiner, & Hill, 2006).

The revised system, which took effect in 2007, uses a 16-item rubric addressing areas similar to the previous approach (see Mayer, 2006), and uses a 3-stage review process: prereview, review, and reporting. Eligible studies must demonstrate one or more behavioral outcomes ($p < .05$) in mental health or substance abuse for individuals, groups, or communities. Under the rede-

Table 19.2 Community Guide Approach to Assessing the Strength of a Body of Evidence

Evidence of effectiveness[a]	Execution— Good or fair[b]	Design Suitability— Greatest, moderate, or least	Number of studies	Consistent[c]	Effect size[d]	Expert opinion[e]
Strong	Good	Greatest	At least 2	Yes	Sufficient	Not used
	Good	Greatest or Moderate	At least 5	Yes	Sufficient	Not used
	Good or Fair	Greatest	At least 5	Yes	Sufficient	Not used
	Meet design, execution, number, and consistency criteria for sufficient but not strong evidence				Large	Not used
Sufficient	Good	Greatest	1	Not applicable	Sufficient	Not used
	Good or Fair	Greatest or Moderate	At least 3	Yes	Sufficient	Not used
	Good or Fair	Greatest, Moderate, or Least	At least 5	Yes	Sufficient	Not used
Expert Opinion	Varies	Varies	Varies	Varies	Sufficient	Supports a recommendation
Insufficient[f]	A. Insufficent designs or executions		B. Too few studies	C. Inconsistent	D. Small	E. Not used

a The categories are not mutually exclusive; a body of evidence meeting critiera for more than one of these should be categorized in the highest possible category.

b Studies with limited execution are not used to assess effectiveness.

c Generally consistent in direction and size.

d Sufficient and large effect sizes are defined on a case-by-case basis and are based on Task Force opinion.

e Expert opinion will not be routinely used in the *Guide* but can affect the classification of a body of evidence as shown.

f Reasons for determination that evidence is insufficient will be described as follows: A. Insufficient designs or executions, B. Too few studies, C. Inconsistent, D. Effect size too small, E. Expert opinion not used. These categories are not mutually exclusive and one or more of these will occur when a body of evidence fails to meet the critiera for strong or sufficent evidence.

Note. From Briss et al. (2000). Developing an evidence-based guide to community preventive services–methods. The Task Force on Community Preventive Services. *American Journal of Preventive Medicine, 18*(1S), 35–43. Copyright 2000 by American Journal of Preventive Medicine. Reprinted with permission.

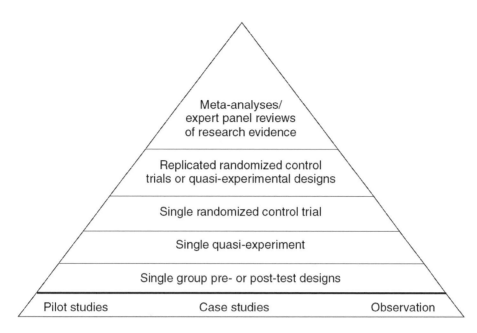

Figure 19.3   SAMHSA NREPP strength of evidence pyramid

sign, information is organized across three dimensions—descriptive, strength of evidence, and readiness for dissemination—with the latter two scored quantitatively. The descriptive dimension includes information on intervention details, outcomes, relevant population and settings, costs, adverse effects, evaluation designs, replications, implementation history, and so forth. The revised system is aligned with a strength-of-evidence framework shown in Figure 19.3. Strength of evidence is scored on a 0–4 scale across six areas: reliability, validity, intervention fidelity, missing data and attrition, potential confounding variables, and appropriateness of analysis. The readiness for dissemination dimension includes 0–4 scales across three areas: availability of materials, availability of training and/or resources to support initial and ongoing implementation, and availability of quality assurance procedures to support initial and ongoing implementation.

Broader U.S. Federal Approaches

The U.S. Preventive Services Task Force (USPSTF) is an independent panel of (nonfederal employees) experts in evidence-based medicine and prevention science. The USPSTF conducts formal reviews of research in a wide array of health related areas such as medical screening, counseling, and medications. The USPSTF has a large number of national primary care partners such as the American Academy of Pediatrics, and the American Academy of Physicians. It also partners with major federal entities such as the CDC, FDA, NIH, and Office of the Surgeon General. As of May 2007, the USPSTF issued five possible grades: A—strongly recommended, B—recommended, C—no recommendation, D—not recommended, and I—insufficient evidence to make a recommendation.

In concert with and subsequent to the Government Performance and Results Act (GPRA) of 1993, the Program Assessment Performance Tool (PART) was launched in 2002. This effort, coordinated through the Office of Management and Budget (OMB), ostensibly would evaluate effectiveness of federal programs and link evaluation results to funding decisions. An early evaluation of PART by the GAO (2004) found limitations and inconsistencies in its application.

Datta (2007) examined variations in evaluation practice across federal agency programs and found substantial evaluation variations across federal agencies, attributing these differences to a combination of four factors: (a) match between type of program under evaluation and appropriate evaluation designs, (b) agency culture vis-à-vis evaluation methodology, (c) lead evaluators' preferences, and (d) politics of methodology. Interestingly, in a 2006 PART evaluation of hundreds of federal agency programs, the report found that for over half of the Cabinet departments, less than 10% of their programs were found to meet standards of being *effective*, but roughly 60%–90% of programs overall for all agencies were determined to be *performing* (defined as *effective, moderately effective, or adequate*).

Section 2: Nongovernmental Evidence-Based Organizations

Cochrane Collaboration

The Cochrane Collaboration, which was established in 1993, takes its name from Archibald Cochrane, who, in the 1970s, pointed to disconnects between research and effective medical practice, citing a lack of consistent application of scientific principles (Smith, 1996). The Cochrane Collaboration is an international effort among researchers from over 100 countries to provide structured reviews of interventions in the medicine and healthcare related fields. The centerpiece of the Cochrane Collaboration products is the Cohrane Library, a collection of six databases: Cochrane Database of Systematic Reviews (synthesis reviews of research on interventions effects), Database of Abstracts of Reviews of Effects (DARE; summary and commentary of quality of non-Cochrane reviews), Cochrane Central Register of Controlled Trials (brief details on RCTs from bibliographic sources), Cochrane Methodology Register (bibliography of methodological publications), Health Technology Assessment Database (details of completed and ongoing health technology assessments from international partner organizations), and the NHS Economic Evaluation Database (with cost-effectiveness and related economic analyses assembled and synthesized by partnering organizations).

A Cochrane systematic review of a collection of studies provides a summary followed by concise and accessible information in the following format: (a) background, (b) study objectives, (c) search strategy, (d) selection criteria, (e) data collection and analysis, (f) main results, and (g) reviewers' conclusions. Cochrane reviews provide details on interventions from reviewed studies, along with conclusions regarding methodological quality and implications for research and practice, and potential conflicts of interest. The Cochrane reviews tend to focus on randomized clinical trials (Schuerman et al., 2002).

Campbell Collaboration

The Campbell Collaboration (C2), which addresses a wide range of social issues, was launched in 2000 and has emulated the work of the Cochrane Collaborative. C2 originally sought to be inclusive in its reviews of research, avoiding sources of study selection bias, including lack of international focus, and publication bias regarding nonsignificant results. Extra measures that included hand searches and communication with experts in a field of study were used to support this mission. The Campbell Collaboration began its efforts with the intent to offer a registry of evaluations of social interventions, called "C2-SPECTR" (Social, Psychological, Educational, and Criminological Trials Register; Schuerman et al., 2002). That effort brought on the order of 10,000 studies into the C2-SPECTR database, but due to relatively loose criteria that focused mainly on studies with control groups and random or quasi-random procedures, studies of lesser quality were included in the database (Petrosino, Boruch, Rounding, McDonald, & Chalmers,

2000). As of late 2008, the Campbell Collaboration Steering Group approved a plan to end C2 involvement with SPECTR as part of a larger strategic plan for the C2. The C2 efforts have expanded in the past decade with the formation of five coordinating groups to support the systematic review process, the first three of which produce systematic reviews in their respective topic areas: Crime and Justice, Education, Social Welfare, Methods (addresses methodological standards for systematic reviews), and User Groups (fosters outreach to increase the research-to-practice connection).

Society for Prevention Research

The Society for Prevention Research (SPR), a multidisciplinary organization established in the early 1990s, focuses on prevention science across the education, social, behavioral, and related health sciences, including a strong interest in criminology. In addition to publishing a scholarly journal, *Prevention Science*, SPR launched multiple initiatives including, but not limited to: (a) advocacy for prevention science (promoting use of EBPs across constituencies, fostering braided funding for interventions, furthering adoption of standards of evidence, building data monitoring systems, and promoting rigorous research), and (b) advancing translational research. SPR published a rigorous standards-of-evidence document (Flay et al., 2005), which articulates specifics of research requirements to identify efficacious and effective interventions, and those suitable for broader dissemination. Efficacious interventions must demonstrate evidence from a minimum of two rigorous experiments that (a) apply to known samples representing known populations, (b) use psychometrically appropriate measures and data collection, (c) use appropriate statistical analysis, (d) demonstrate at least one desired effect without iatrogenic effects, and (e) report at least one extended time follow-up. Effective interventions must satisfy conditions for an efficacious intervention and also (a) demonstrate manuals, training, and technical support for adoption by others; (b) be based on a real-world study that used measurement in the setting and conditions natural to the population studied for experimental and control groups; (c) adequately explain the practical significance of the outcome effects; and (d) firmly establish the group to whom the intervention effects can be generalized. Interventions ready for broad dissemination must satisfy all conditions for efficacious and effective interventions, and also must provide evidence of readiness to be taken to scale, cost information, and monitoring and evaluation components.

Section 3: Protocols for Research Synthesis, Meta-Analysis, and Program Evaluation

Many protocols for randomized controlled trials and other methodologies have emerged from medicine and the health sciences. While at first consideration, they may seem less applicable to research on school violence in education and the allied social and behavioral disciplines, it is critical to reflect on the evolution of such standards in recent decades. For example, the Campbell Collaboration addresses a wide range of educational and social-behavioral issues. It is modeled on prior work in medicine by the Cochrane Collaboration. An increasing number of journals in education and the social-behavioral sciences, including criminology, are calling for more rigorous reporting, especially on RCTs, modeling on the CONSORT protocol (Perry, Weisburd, & Hewitt, 2010), as discussed later in this chapter. Further, research on many aspects of violence and disruption has bridged the fields of public health and medicine—particularly psychiatry—and cross-disciplinary studies that investigate developmental psychopathology and that can entail neurobiological, psychological, social, and behavioral factors are called for (Cicchetti & Toth, 2009).

Consort Protocol

The Consolidated Standards of Reporting Trials (CONSORT), originally drafted in 1996 and revised in 2001, is a protocol for reporting the results of randomized controlled trials (Moher, Schulz, & Altman, 2001; Schulz, Altman, Moher, & the CONSORT Group, 2010). Developed by an international task force of experts in clinical research, statistics, and epidemiology, the CONSORT 2001 protocol provided a flow chart and 22-item checklist to guide presentation of research using randomized controlled trials. CONSORT addresses a wide range of study issues, including, but not limited to sample design, allocation of participants to interventions, intervention details, specific hypotheses, details of outcome measures, randomization procedures, baseline and follow-up data procedures, and so forth. The CONSORT standard has been adopted by a large number of journals and professional organizations in the health care and allied fields. The CONSORT 2001 protocol was replaced with the CONSORT 2010 Statement (Schulz et al., 2010), a 25-item revision based on a decade of methodological evidence and application experience, and linked to over 700 studies in the CONSORT database. Recent developments with the CONSORT include a working group that held a consensus conference in Banff, Canada, in May 2009, developing a CONSORT extension for N-of-1 trials (CENT), but this group has focused primarily on A-B-A-B single subject designs and not multiple baseline research (T. Kratochwill, personal communication, September 1, 2010). Other extensions of the CONSORT under discussion include extensions to criminological RCTs (Perry & Johnson, 2008; Perry et al., 2010) and also pragmatic trials (an RCT designed to address questions of practice) (Zwarenstein et al., 2008).

Several studies have investigated quality of systematic reviews of randomized trials and use and compliance with the CONSORT protocol in the health sciences literature, as well as outcomes associated with its use. Moher and colleagues (2007) analyzed 300 systematic reviews across 132 journals in the health sciences (two third from U.S. authors) as of late 2004, examining the quality of the systematic review process, comparing Cohrane and nonCohrane reviews. They found alarming inconsistencies and lower quality among nonCochrane systematic reviews, including minimal reporting of the systematic review protocol used and limited reporting of funding sources in therapeutic research. Examining RCTs in criminal justice, Perry and Johnson (2008) found mixed compliance with elements of the CONSORT, based on a review of 20 RCTs in juvenile justice published between 2001 and 2006. Perry et al., (2010) analyzed 83 RCTs that were previously reviewed by Farrington and Welsh (2005) from an extensively cited article on what criminologists have learned from randomized trials during the prior two decades. They found low levels of descriptive validity, based on application of CONSORT, with low levels of information on randomization procedures, outcome measures, statistical analysis, and key findings. They advocated for adapting CONSORT for use in criminological RCTs.

Other Evidence-Based Standards

Several other reporting standards have been widely used across medicine and the related health sciences, with likely future applications to education and the social-behavioral sciences, including work relating to school violence prevention. While discussion of them is beyond the scope of this chapter, they merit identification. The original Quality of Reporting of Meta-Analyses (QUOROM) statement (Moher et al., 1999) was later replaced by the Preferred Reporting Items for Systematic Reviews and Meta-Analyses (PRISMA) statement (Moher et al., 2009). PRISMA can be considered a complementary approach to CONSORT, with PRISMA more oriented to meta-analyses and other systematic reviews and CONSORT to primary studies. The Meta-analysis of Observational Studies in Epidemiology (MOOSE) standards are predicated on a need for more systematic treatment of observational research in public health-related fields, as many critical questions could not be addressed by RCTs for ethical as well as practical reasons.

The Transparent Reporting of Evaluations and NonRandomized Designs (TREND) Statement grew out of a recognized need for a more formal review process with quasi-experimental and other nonrandomized research, as well as a range of program evaluations. The Strengthening the Reporting of Observational Studies in Epidemiology (STROBE) statement (von Elm et al., 2008) addresses epidemiological studies based on observations, and cohort, case-control, and cross-sectional designs. The *Grades of Recommendation, Assessment, Development, and Evaluation* (GRADE) protocol is used to evaluate the quality and strength of evidence to guide clinical decision making in medicine and has been endorsed by a wide range of journals and international medical and public health organizations, including the World Health Organization, American College of Physicians, and the Cochrane Collaboration (Guyatt et al., 2008).

Section 4: Cross-Cutting Issues in Evidence-Based Research

While developments in evidence-based intervention research review and practice have varied across disciplines, as illustrated in the previous sections, a number of broader cross-cutting issues emerge that have a bearing on school violence prevention and school safety programming. This section examines (a) the plethora of protocols and clearinghouses, (b) types and hierarchies of evidence debate, (c) efficacy/effectiveness research, (d) translational research, (e) systematic reviews and meta-analysis, (f) developmental levels and processes, (g) manualized treatments and adaptability issues, and (h) research journal space constraints on manuscripts.

A Plethora of Research Evaluation Protocols and Evidence-Based Clearinghouses

This chapter discussed eight specific protocols for research synthesis, meta-analysis, and program evaluation in addition to identifying other protocols and approaches used by a large number of governmental and nongovernmental entities. Further, there are at least five major clearinghouses (What Works Clearinghouse, SAMHSA, CDC Community Guide, Cochrane Collaboration, Campbell Collaboration) for evidence-based reviews of research, along with many other small to midsize centers. Approaches and standards across these clearinghouses vary, and inconsistencies can emerge in evaluations and recommendations. There is the dearth of empirical research on how the results from these protocols and clearinghouses are being used and their effects, an issue raised by several investigators (Bruns & Hoagwood, 2008; Kavanagh, 2009). Another serious limitation with the larger enterprise of evidence-based clearinghouses is the lack of information on transporting interventions to a variety of settings and contexts, an issue further discussed in the sections below on efficacy/effectiveness research and translational research.

Types and Hierarchies of Evidence Debates

While randomized controlled trials have often been referred to as the "gold standard" in intervention research, a growing movement across disciplines questions this assertion and would recast RCTs as an important tool in a larger methodological tool chest (Hansen & Rieper, 2009). There are several dimensions in these debates and issues within each clearly connect to the others. First, there are concerns that experimental research only provides part of the information necessary for implementation of specific interventions to benefit clients, and is neither sufficient, nor complete, when considered as an evidentiary framework. Raudenbush (2005) stressed the centrality of RCTs while arguing that they are not enough and that complementary research needs to explain how evidence-based interventions can be used to maximum effect in a resource-limited system. He wrote about improving educational research and the contributions of methodological diversity:

Experiments, while necessary, are, however, far from sufficient to support the learning required for effective instructional innovation. Other kinds of research are needed to precisely define educational aims, to identify target populations for intervention, to identify the most promising practices, and to clarify challenges and opportunities for effective implementation of those practices.

(2005, p. 27)

Similar concerns have been echoed with emphasis on extended mixed-methods approaches that are temporally focused and that address site specific and contextual factors (Chatterji, 2005). Kazdin (2008) discussed limitations in the evidence-based movement, in part, due to the divide between research and clinical practice. Kazdin and others (Cicchetti & Toth, 2009) have argued for more process research to help explicate mechanisms of change for patient improvement, as well as improved study of moderators and translation of findings to clinical care. This is particularly salient to school safety research when addressing anger and aggression issues of individual youth as well as viewing the institution as the "patient," as school change processes associated with violence reduction and school safety promotion are not well understood.

Alternate frameworks for the evidence base have been proposed. Kellam and Langevin (2003) articulated a multidimensional framework for considering evidence based on six themes: (a) multiple lines of prevention work currently exist, applied to individual change, small social groups (classroom, peers, family and so forth), and larger political and social entities; (b) definitions of evidence vary across efficacy trials, effectiveness research, sustainability trials, going-to-scale trials, and larger system-wide change; (c) prevention programs and approaches vary as a function of types of population and types of risk, with accompanying variations in evidentiary standards; (d) given a limited resource system, cost-benefit research is essential; (e) collaborative partnerships are necessary in research to establish that interventions can actually work with relevant stakeholders; and (f) a broader group must be involved—above and beyond researchers—to enable movement to a multidimensional framework for evidence-based standards. Kellam and Langevin's discussion essentially focused on moving the field towards translational research, an issue discussed further in the following sections.

A second dimension involves the hierarchy of evidence concept. Such hierarchies are naturally linked to the framework of research questions and the ultimate purpose of the research, which can vary considerably across disciplines, as well as across types of research, as discussed by Kellam and Langevin (2003). Hansen and Rieper (2009) examined methodological approaches in the evidence-based movement, reporting that while several major evidence-based clearinghouses use similar procedures in systematic reviews, and the WWC, and Cochrane and Campbell Collaborations use similar hierarchies of evidence with RTCs considered strongest, other international groups, such as the EPPI Centre, accept a wider array of research designs. Several researchers have presented hierarchies similar to that used by SAMHSA (see Figure 19.3), with systematic reviews and RCTs at the top, often followed by quasi-experimental designs, and some including time series research, uncontrolled case series studies, case-control observational studies, qualitative case studies, and expert consensus reports. Yet, researchers acknowledge that RCTs, while strong on internal validity, are often relatively weak on external validity (Glasgow & Emmons, 2007; Steckler & McLeroy, 2008). Hansen and Rieper pointed to work of Boaz (2006) and others who have demonstrated multiple approaches to research synthesis, presenting a typology of evidence matrix adapted from prior work by Petticrew and Roberts (2003) (see Table 19.3). The logic of the hierarchy of evidence approach has been questioned, with arguments that typologies of evidence linked to research focus are more relevant than specific hierarchies (Petticrew & Roberts, 2003). The main arguments presented by Petticrew and Roberts for moving to a typology approach are (a) empirical evidence is available that RCTs are not the

Table 19.3 Typology of Evidence

Research Question	Qualitative research	Survey	Case-control studies	Cohort studies	RCTs	Quasi-experimental studies	Non experimental evaluations	Systematic reviews
Effectiveness: Does this work? Does doing this work better than doing that?				+	++	+		+++
Process of service delivery: How does it work?	++	+					+	+++
Salience: Does it matter?	++	++						+++
Safety: Will it do more good than harm?	+		+	+	++	+	+	+++
Acceptability: Will children/parents be willing to or want to take up the service offered?	++	+			+	+	+	+++
Cost of effectiveness: Is it worth buying this service?					++			+++
Appropriateness: Is this the right service for these children?	++	++						++
Satisfaction with the service: Are users, providers, and other stakeholders satisfied with the service?	++	++	+	+				+

Note. Reproduced from *Journal of Epidemiology and Community Health* (Vol. 57), Petticrew, M., & Roberts, H. Evidence, hierarchies, and typologies: Horses for courses, pp. 527–529, Copyright 2003, with permission from BMJ Publishing Group Ltd.

only method to produce valid and reliable results, citing work by Concato, Shah, and Horwitz (2000) and others; and (b) different methods are best suited for different research questions (e.g., applying interventions to different real-world contexts). Chou and Helfand (2005) reasoned that evidence syntheses in medicine needs to address not only clinical effect, as best done with RCTs, but investigation of possible harm, which typically requires observational studies. A traditional hierarchy of evidence that rates observational studies low in evidentiary value will tend to exclude such research. This concern translates from medicine to social-behavioral research—and particularly violence prevention approaches—where possible iatrogenic effects of an intervention will likely remain undiscovered in classic RCT designs, but would more likely be detected thorough mixed methods approaches that include observational and qualitative case study data.

A third dimension involves broader questions regarding understanding social phenomena and developing and implementing not only specific evidence-based interventions, but fostering large scale public health interventions and systemic and cultural changes that are likely to directly impact outcomes of interest. Cornell and Mayer (2010) argued that above and beyond specific interventions aligned with varying theoretical orientations, qualitative methodologies offer critical contextual understanding of life experiences, belief systems, and thought processes that can drive student behavior—knowledge essential to effective school safety programming. Rychetnik, Frommer, Hawe, and Shiell (2002) differentiated public health interventions from more specific interventions for individuals or small groups designed to prevent illness or injury, or alter behaviors, arguing that public health interventions are necessarily "complex, programmatic, and context dependent." Accordingly, RCTs can answer some of the key questions in public health intervention research, but a broader understanding of factors related to successful change at the community level will require multiple methods, including observational (case-control) and qualitative techniques.

Efficacy/Effectiveness Research

There are substantial differences in experimental results from efficacy and effectiveness research, with research-based therapy (efficacy research) usually faring better than real-world clinical therapy (effectiveness research; Hoagwood & Johnson, 2003; Lonigan et al., 1998; Weisz, Donenberg, Han, & Weiss, 1995; Weisz & Hawley, 1998). Ollendick and King (2004) and others have noted differences in characteristics of study samples, interventionists, settings, and research conditions (see Table 19.4). At the same time, Ollendick and King, using a brief discussion of three studies, explicate how the lines between efficacy and effectiveness research can become blurred. There are many implications to consider for intervention research generally as well as school safety research with regard to efficacy-effectiveness issues. Three of these issues are highlighted below.

First, study subjects often differ, with efficacy research participants often demonstrating milder presenting problems and limited comorbid conditions, as compared to most subjects receiving interventions in real-world settings (Chambless & Hollon, 1998; Lonigan et al., 1998). School violence prevention efforts at the *indicated* level (Institute of Medicine, 1994) target youngsters with the highest degree of need. For children and adolescents with entrenched patterns of antisocial behavior, comorbid conditions (e.g., CD, ODD, ADHD), and a combination of harsh family and school failure experiences, there are many variables in play that may not even be approximated in much of the efficacy research on school violence prevention measures. As a result, the generalizability of such efficacy research to these high-needs students remains questionable.

Second, intervention training and caseloads of the interventionists can differ considerably between efficacy and effectiveness studies (Chorpita, 2003; Ollendick & King, 2004). Chorpita suggested that most organizations that deliver interventions lack the resources to train staff in

Table 19.4   Characteristics of Research and Clinic Therapy

Research therapy	Recruited cases (less severe, study volunteers)
	Homogeneous groups
	Narrow or single-problem focus
	Treatment in lab, school settings
	Researcher as therapist
	Very small caseloads
	Heavy pretherapy preparation
	Preplanned, highly structured treatment (manualized)
	Monitoring of therapist behaviour
	Behavioural methods
Clinic therapy	Clinic-referred cases (more severe, some coerced into treatment)
	Heterogeneous groups
	Broad, multiproblem focus
	Treatment in clinic, hospital settings
	Professional career therapists
	Very large caseloads
	Little/light pretherapy preparation
	Flexible, adjustable treatment (no treatment manual)
	Little monitoring of therapist behaviour
	Nonbehavioural methods

Note. From *Handbook of interventions that work with children and adolescents: Prevention and Treatment* (p. 18), by P. M. Barrrett & T. H. Ollendick, 2004, West Sussex, England: Wiley. Copyright 2004 by Wiley. Reprinted with permission.

intervention delivery in as thorough a manner as for staff working for an efficacy research study. The implications of this difference for school safety interventions relates directly to fidelity of implementation. With less training and less time to devote (as a result of relatively heavy caseloads), interventionist staff in schools and clinics are prone to offer less thorough service delivery, resulting in diminished outcome effects. This theme is paralleled in some of the meta-analytic findings suggesting that fidelity of implementation was a critical issue for effective programs (Durlak & DuPre, 2008; Wilson, Lipsey, & Derzon, 2003).

Third, intervention settings can differ greatly, resulting in varied research outcomes (Chambless & Hollon, 1998; Hoagwood, Burns, Kiser, Ringeisen, & Schoenwald, 2001; Ollendick & King, 2004; Schoenwald & Hoagwood, 2001). Chambless and Hollon noted: "All things being equal, those studies that most faithfully reproduce the conditions found in actual clinical practice are most likely to produce findings that generalize to those settings" (p. 15). Greenberg (2004) noted the importance of focusing on the "quality and nature of adaptations," rather than engaging in the "polarizing debate regarding fidelity versus adaptation" (p. 9). The lack of fit between efficacy studies and real-world settings is reflected in the mismatch between (a) the strictly defined intervention and related research requirements and (b) the philosophy, policies, procedures, and staff scheduling and service delivery requirements found in real-world settings (Hoagwood et al., 2001; Shoenwood & Hoagwood, 2001). Similar setting-related problems can easily compromise school violence intervention research. For example, given the pressures of demonstrating *adequate yearly progress* under the mandates of the No Child Left Behind Act, for purposes of testing a school violence intervention, schools would be hard pressed to take time and resources away from focused academic programs aimed at raising school-wide scores despite the obvious advantages of reducing school violence and disruption.

Translational Research

Translational research, while sometimes having unique meaning within different disciplinary boundaries, is generally defined as studying ways of transporting evidence-based tools and methods to the real world of practice in naturally occurring settings, along with their typical populations and contextual factors. Translational research has become a high priority in the health and allied sciences as evidenced by major NIH investment. NIH began the Clinical Translational Science Award program in 2006, funding academic centers engaging in translational research. Projections for 2012 suggest total funding of about $500 million, supporting approximately 60 translational research centers (Woolf, 2008).

The Institute of Medicine (IOM) Clinical Research Roundtable identified two fundamental barriers to translational research in medicine (Sung et al., 2003): (a) taking results of basic science research into clinical studies and (b) taking results of clinical research into daily medical practice and health decision-making. These findings can be considered relative to research in school violence prevention by mapping basic research in anger/aggression, social bonding, social communication and problem-solving, self-regulation, and so forth—areas of more basic scientific research in the social and behavioral disciplines—and taking these findings to the level of interventions to help improve individual behaviors and social relationships. This has already been accomplished to some degree, as seen in interventions such as Multisystemic Therapy (Henggeler, Schoenwald, Borduin, Rowland, & Cunningham, 2009) and Lochman's Anger Coping Program (Larson & Lochman, 2010). Glasgow and Emmons (2007) examined challenges to the translational research enterprise and identified key barriers, seen in Figure 19.4. These barriers to dissemination apply to the fields of education and its allied disciplines, in their efforts to promote school safety and reduce school violence and disorder.

Astor, Guerra, and Van Acker (2010) discussed research challenges in school violence prevention, the need for investing in translational science, and complementing those efforts, increased activity nationally developing local and regional surveillance and monitoring systems connected

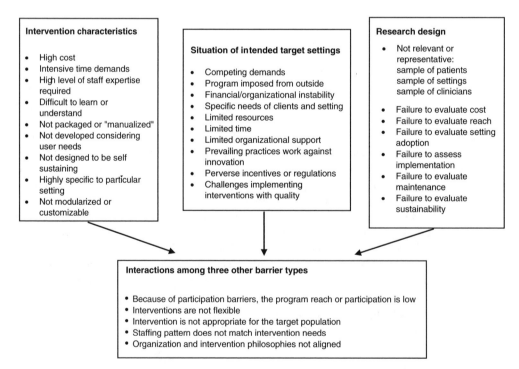

Figure 19.4 Potential barriers to research translation. *Note.* Reproduced from *Annual Review of Public Health* (Vol. 28), Glasgow, R. E., & Emmons, K. M. How can we increase translation of research into practice? Types of evidence needed, pp. 413–433, Copyright 2007, with permission from Annual Reviews, Inc.

to school events and behaviors, in much the same way as established public health mechanisms are used for injury prevention, including violence prevention. Schools and other institutions sometimes launch violence prevention programs and specific interventions, not necessarily based on an explicit linkage to data-demonstrated need, but rather, as a result of funding availability, administrative mandates, or other political pressures. Yet taking evidence-based interventions to scale and adapting to local need and context require reliable and valid data on local conditions.

Systematic Reviews and Meta-Analysis

Systematic reviews involve explicit objectives, transparent procedures, clear eligibility criteria (inclusion and exclusion), a well-defined and structured search protocol that reduces bias, screening procedures, exhaustive coverage of the literature, full extraction of relevant study data, quantitative analysis as appropriate (may or may not include meta-analysis), and a structured and detailed report (Welsh & Farrington, 2007). Meta-analysis can be considered a subset of the systematic review process. Multiple approaches to systematic reviews exist. For example, Boaz and colleagues (2006) performed five different types of systematic reviews, demonstrating that variation in types of research across multiple disciplines could require alternate methods for systematic reviews and that the conventional approach as exemplified by the Cochrane Collaboration, was not the only appropriate methodology available. But currently, most leading evidence-based organizations rely heavily on meta-analysis for systematic reviews.

Meta-analysis has been widely used to assess the efficacy of interventions in education, psychology, and allied fields (Lipsey & Wilson, 1993). Examining the results of over 300 meta-analytic studies, Lipsey and Wilson demonstrated how broad patterns in intervention research could inform the research and practitioner community and how meta-analysis has repeatedly produced clear evidence regarding treatment efficacy. Lipsey and Wilson (2001) articulated four specific strengths of meta-analysis: (a) meta-analysis uses a well-structured approach to synthesizing research, with documented criteria and procedural steps that can be fully audited and evaluated; (b) meta-analysis uses sophisticated techniques for integrating effect size and significance statistics that help differentiate contributions among included studies, more so than conventional reviews of research; (c) meta-analysis provides the tools to detect effects and relations that may be hidden or difficult to determine using other research review approaches; and (d) meta-analysis offers a systematic and well-defined approach and set of data management tools to process large volumes of information from studies under review.

Along a similar vein, Hunter and Schmidt (1990) discussed contributions of meta-analysis to the advancement of scientific knowledge: (a) meta-analysis in the social and behavioral sciences has demonstrated that prior research findings have not been as ambiguous or conflicting as previously thought and that valuable conclusions could be drawn from these bodies of research, (b) the "cumulativeness of research findings in the behavioral sciences is probably as great as in the physical sciences" (p. 37), and (c) findings from meta-analysis provide critically important direction for future theory development and research efforts.

While appealing in its ability to provide syntheses of prior research, concerns have been raised with regard to this technique. Lipsey and Wilson (1993) offered cautionary discussion of the following: (a) assessing methodological quality of included studies, (b) availability bias, (c) small sample bias, and (d) generalized placebo effect. The authors also commented that pretest and posttest designs typically overestimate effects compared to random samples, and publication bias regarding excluded studies with negative results can inflate effect size results. Later research by Wilson and Lipsey (2001) found that among 319 meta-analyses, study methods explained almost as much variability in meta-analysis results as did the analyzed data on the respective interventions.

Other researchers have also raised concerns about use of meta-analyses in effectiveness research (Kazdin & Weisz, 1998; Kratochwill, 2002; Weisz, Donenberg, Han, & Weiss, 1995; Weisz & Hawley, 1998). These concerns included: (a) screening criteria for including studies; (b) imbalanced coverage of specific techniques (e.g., behavioral/cognitive-behavioral more so than psychodynamic); (c) varying approaches to effect size calculation; (d) representativeness of subjects, interventionists, and treatment conditions to real-world practice; (e) common omission of single subject research; (f) confounding of treatment-outcome interactions; and (g) outcome reporting sources relative to knowledge of subject treatment status.

Meta-analysis, by its very nature, often sifts through large volumes of data. As a result, differences across study characteristics can constrain the fineness of common detail found, resulting in more broad-based findings. For school safety and related research, there can be a tradeoff between (a) a more inclusive approach to meta-analysis that taps into a large body of relevant research, often yielding only general findings; and (b) preserving the ability to uncover the effectiveness of more specific intervention components, based on an analysis of a more focused subset of the research literature. Also, obscuring the view provided by meta-analytic techniques into specific intervention mechanisms that can effectively reduce school violence and disruption problems are confounds among variables that influence outcomes (Kazdin & Weisz, 1998; Weisz & Hawley, 1998). For example, where a meta-analysis may determine that a stand-alone anger management curriculum may have resulted in reduced incidents of violence in school, an interaction effect involving increased teacher attention (outside of the intervention) to, and in support of participating students, may also have significantly contributed to the outcomes.

Developmental Levels and Processes

Many psychotherapeutic interventions for children and adolescents have not been developmentally targeted, taking into account specific age-related tasks and milestones that account for developmental differences (Holmbeck, Devine, & Bruno, 2010; Weisz & Hawley, 2002). Holmbeck and colleagues (2010) suggested that effect sizes for child and adolescent interventions that have been in the moderate range would be even larger if these interventions were developmentally oriented. Interestingly, many interventions for adolescents have been adapted *upward* from those originally designed for children, and *downward* from those originally designed for adults (Weisz & Hawley, 2002).

Several meta-analyses of cognitive-behavioral interventions have demonstrated significantly larger (about double) effect sizes for interventions targeted at adolescents, compared to younger children. These results may reflect differences in cognitive abilities, or possibly other related developmental attributes. Holmbeck et al. (2010) explicated models in which developmental attributes may serve as either moderating or mediating variables, affecting outcomes. For example, according to Piagetian theory, a student's cognitive-developmental level would be linked to his or her ability to engage in perspective taking and develop empathy for others, core skill components common to several empirically supported school violence reduction programs. As such, a student's developmental level could act as a moderating variable. A mediating variable is tied to some type of mechanism that leads from a causal variable to an outcome. As discussed by Holmbeck and colleagues (2010), Kendall and Treadwell (2007) demonstrated how negative self-statements acted as a mediator between intervention and the outcome measure—level of anxiety. Investigation into the degree to which developmental levels have been incorporated in cognitive-behavioral research with adolescents found noteworthy increases from about 26% of reviewed empirical articles for the period, 1990–1998, to about 70% of the reviewed empirical research for articles from 1999–2004, demonstrating a pronounced shift among researchers in this field (Holmbeck, O'Mahar, Abad, Colder, & Updegrove, 2006).

Developmental processes are also a critical aspect of the research on evidenced-based practices, particularly as applied to emotional/behavioral difficulties, more serious psychopathology, and aggressive and violence behaviors in school. For example, Masten and colleagues (2005) explicated a developmental cascade that linked academic difficulties to emerging internalizing and externalizing problems. Loeber and Stouthamer-Loeber (1998) discussed developmental origins of juvenile aggression and presented a now well-accepted empirically derived model for boys that included three developmental pathways: overt, covert, and authority conflict. Dodge and Pettit (2003) considered the complexities associated with conduct disorder and explicated a biopsychosocial model that incorporated biological predispositions, early life experiences, social-ecological factors, and emotional/behavioral social information processing. These examples are congruent with discussion by Cicchetti and Toth (2009), stressing the importance of understanding how individuals diverge from and regain positive functioning over time within a life-course framework. Accordingly, research needs to better identify the dynamic interplay over time of influences and processes that drive pathological trajectories, using multiple levels of analysis, investigating across the ecology of youth, and addressing genetic, neurobiological, social, psychological, and pre- and postnatal environmental influences. Yet, this view suggests a possible dilemma, where such complex approaches to research would seem to defy efforts to systematically identify evidence-based methods. For example, Mayer and Van Acker (2008) identified trade-offs in more complex cognitive-behavioral interventions where new challenges emerged with cost, training, access to clients, implementation fidelity, client attrition, and difficulty teasing out specific effects.

Coverage of developmental processes across the collective body of evidenced-based interventions has been uneven with many lines of research essentially ignoring critical developmental factors as part of their design. The implications for school violence prevention, particularly with interventions that involve cognitive-behavioral techniques, are clear. Specific techniques that are manageable to implement and well-aligned with the child's development are more likely to succeed.

Manualized Treatments and Adaptability Issues

Documentation of treatment protocols in manual form (a) provides a clear definition of the treatment, (b) standardizes procedures, (c) facilitates assessment of implementation fidelity, (d) provides researchers and practitioners with a clear understanding of what was done, and (e) allows others to engage in replication research (Kratochwill & Stoiber, 2000; Ollendick & King, 2004). As discussed previously in this chapter, treatment manuals were required by the APA Division 12 Task Force draft document for an intervention to be classified as either "probably efficacious" or "well established." The Division 16 protocols required use of a manual along with other conditions in order to earn the higher component scores of "2" or "3" for implementation fidelity.

Durlak and Dupre (2008) reviewed over 500 quantitative studies involving physical and social-emotional-behavioral prevention and promotion interventions for children and adolescents, with 483 studies analyzed across five meta-analyses, finding strong outcome effects linked to implementation fidelity. This research also indicated that implementation is not always a matter of precisely scripted procedures, but also involves adjusting to contextual factors and ensuring fit to the local setting. Durlak and Dupre discussed the challenges in finding the optimal balance between fidelity and adaptation, noting, interventions vary in their ability to be adapted; empirical evidence exists for improved outcomes where strong fidelity with adaptation were used; researchers can improve interventions by learning from local practitioners about the implementation while measuring aspects of implementation; and the most theoretically salient aspects of the intervention must be closely monitored for fidelity and adaptability to enable researchers to inform future research. They also remarked that the more theoretically important aspects of the intervention should be maintained with the maximum fidelity feasible, while more of the secondary aspects should be tailored to improve ecological fit; and monitoring of implementation fidelity and adaptations are particularly important for subgroups and with reference to culturally bound issues, where fit and outcomes need to be analyzed relative to the fidelity-adaptation balance.

Practitioners have expressed concerns that mandatory manualization of treatment, prescribing a "lockstep" process, is impractical and will harm clients. Real-life clinical practice also involves working with clients and families who may not fully invest in treatment, requiring modification of procedures (Kratochwill & Stoiber, 2000; Weisz & Hawley, 1998). Kendall, Chu, Gifford, Hayes, and Nauta (1998) argued that treatment manuals can be effectively used in a flexible manner. Strict manualization of interventions in school violence prevention programs could compromise effectiveness in cases where the local context and changing conditions demand some flexibility. As discussed by Kratochwill and Stoiber (2002) and Ollendick and King (2004), applied intervention settings typically have barriers to treatment that must be accommodated as well as idiosyncratic attributes of local populations. For example, an after-school social skills training program could be faced with a situation where a group of students must leave early due to parents pulling them out for an alternate activity. The treatment manual may be designed around working with groups of students for a given minimum time and with a given number of students making up the group, for purposes of group activities that comprise part of the training. Without the ability to modify the program to accommodate to changing circumstances, outcomes may be severely compromised.

Research Journal Space Constraints on Manuscripts

The What Works Clearinghouse *Study Review Standards,* APA's Division 16 *Procedural and Coding Manual,* as well as SAMHSA's NREPP protocols and requirements of the Cochrane and Campbell collaborations, all articulate varying, yet significant levels of documentation of high quality research and strict adherence to scientific standards. Authors of prospective manuscripts seeking publication of intervention research results must develop extensive and lengthy written explanations to satisfy these reviewing organizations. While a laudable goal and supportive of establishing quality reviews of evidence-based intervention research, these requirements may clash with publishers' typically strict limitations on manuscript length. Many journals advise prospective authors to limit submitted manuscripts to about 25–30 pages, double-spaced. It seems questionable whether the research review protocols can be satisfied, given such constraints. Moher et al. (2007) echoed these concerns in their analysis of publication compliance with CONSORT guidelines. Research journal publishers and affiliated professional groups may need to revisit these guidelines in view of this issue, and also consider alternative solutions, such as linking published articles to online publisher depositories for authors' methodological appendices.

Section 5: Implications for Current and Future Research and Practice

There are several important implications for research and practice to be drawn from this review (see Table 19.5). Considering the many clearinghouses and other evidence-based organizations, and varied protocols in use across multiple disciplines, a professional seeking clarification on particular evidence-based approaches may feel overwhelmed. This problem connects to the historical fragmentation across the human service disciplines, each embracing different theoretical frameworks, and organizational philosophies, targeting different goals, utilizing different service delivery models, employing varying measurement and accountability tools, and using similar sounding, yet distinct technical terminology.

Table 19.5   Implications for Research and Practice Based on Developments in Evidence-Based Evaluation

	Positive	Possibly Problematic
Research	Increasing attention to and dissemination of articles, other media, and funding organization procedures regarding rigorous evaluation may help educate more researchers, gradually changing the overall research landscape. The quality of intervention evaluation efforts may gradually improve. Use of emerging standards for more rigorous evaluation research may drive efficient use of research funds. A greater proportion of published intervention evaluation research may be of higher quality. Greater attention to relatively neglected areas, such as effectiveness research, and related issues of transportability and dissemination may be better addressed.	Studies of interventions for students with high intensity needs may preclude randomized controlled trials in favor of alternate methods such as single subject design due to limited sample sizes. Limited heterogeneity of special populations may constrain research designs with regard to assignment to groups and related randomization efforts. Increasingly scarce school-based resources to support staff release time for training and reluctance to modify academic programming due to academic accountability mandates may interfere with effectiveness research designs. National level economic difficulties may limit funding of more costly effectiveness research.
Practice	Given availability of several major evidence-based clearinghouses, practitioners may focus more on verifying that proposed interventions are evidence-based, resulting in fewer implementations of ineffective interventions. Because of a more widespread evidence-based perspective, the field of nonevidence-based interventions should thin somewhat, leaving practitioners a more manageable set of choices to consider. With an increased focus on manualization and explicit documentation of intervention procedures, trust may increase and training practitioners to implement intervention practices appropriately may be more cost effective yielding more widespread use of evidence-based methods. Scarce school and community funding to provide interventions for high-risk youth may be spent more efficiently.	A plethora of web-based clearinghouses and information centers on evidence-based program evaluation may overwhelm end-users, leaving them confused or discouraged, limiting how they access and later adopt evidence-based practices. Unrealistically strict evidence-based review standards may result in fewer effective options being made available to practitioners for meeting needs of at-risk youth. Continuing challenges with transportability and dissemination of interventions limits the practical utility for school personnel to employ many interventions. Continuing budgetary constraints in schools and pressures for demonstrating academic outcomes under federal law may limit the widespread use of evidence-based interventions for violence prevention in favor of academically oriented programming.

This issue of differing orientations and practices is not new to the school violence research community. Definitional and measurement issues have led to varying reports of school violence data (Mayer & Furlong, 2010; Mayer & Leone, 2007; Reiss & Roth, 1993; U.S. Library of Congress, 1994). These definitional and measurement challenges remain, as does the need to reconcile the admissibility of varying research designs in evidence-based practice. For example, single subject research has contributed key understandings of effective behavioral interventions with low incidence and other groups in special education environments that have major implications for school safety research and practice (Horner et al., 2005). Yet, it took great effort over many years before the What Works Clearinghouse accepted this methodology for inclusion in reviewing evidence-based interventions.

The implications for researchers in school violence also relate to studying interventions with those students who are most often involved in school violence. Students who are at highest risk and are receiving *indicated* interventions (Institute of Medicine, 1994) may comprise about 1%–7% of a school's population (Sugai et al., 1999). Discussing adolescent violence, Dodge and Pettit (2003) noted, "over 50% of violent behaviors are perpetrated by only 6% of the population" (p. 350). This points to a need to examine highly focused interventions for a relatively small and unique group within the school. Due to a lack of heterogeneity and limited availability for group assignments, evaluation for group differences using randomized clinical trials that depend on group assignment would not be practical for these high-risk students in many educational settings. This presents serious challenges for effectiveness research in real-world settings.

Given the relatively bleak state of K–12 funding nationally, combined with mandates to produce improved test scores for adequate yearly progress pursuant to the requirements of the No Child Left Behind Act (and likely, subsequent reauthorized legislation, regardless of the name), schools are struggling to use their personnel in the most efficient ways possible. This leaves little room for releasing and paying for staff training in new intervention programs designed to reduce school violence. This will severely compromise effectiveness research in school violence prevention, as problems may occur with fidelity of implementation, outcome measurements, and related concerns tied to appropriate staff training.

Practitioners face challenges on several levels with regard to violence prevention programming and service delivery. First, although there are a growing number of information clearinghouses available to the practitioner community, the standards of research evaluation underpinning these endorsed programs vary. The end user is forced to proceed in uncertain waters, assuming that, despite different approaches, the approved programs are worth implementing. Second, research design constraints may limit the availability of evidence for interventions addressing special education populations, and especially, the 6% or so of chronic, high-risk adolescents. However, chronic, high-risk students are precisely the group for whom we need to develop more effective school violence prevention programs. Third, continuing disconnects between efficacy and effectiveness research, the difficulty of conducting effectiveness research in settings where high-risk students typically exist, and the tendency favoring efficacy research, all totaled, will likely limit the availability of proven intervention approaches that are rigorously tested in real-world environments. As previously noted by Chorpita (2003), research in transportability, generalizability, and system effectiveness is rare. In sum, the consuming public will probably have limited choices of thoroughly researched interventions that are ready for large-scale implementation. These points are not made to suggest a purely negative scenario. Rather, they draw attention to continuing challenges the research and practice community face in more strategically responding to competing requirements and constraints in evidence-based research.

Developments over the last decade in building improved intervention research evaluation protocols and models have yielded several viable approaches that continue to evolve. While still problematic, and far from perfect, they signal an important shift in thinking. Given limited resources and significant social problems, especially in reducing school violence and promoting school safety practices, the field can no longer afford to implement interventions without a solid foundation of research-based evidence. The research and practitioner community needs to continue to invest in the concept of evidence-based practice and to support continued development efforts so that future research will benefit the clients who need these interventions.

References

American Psychological Association Task For American Psychological Association Task Force on Evidence-Based Practice for Children and Adolescents. (2008). *Disseminating evidence-based practice for children and adolescents: A systems approach to enhancing care.* Washington, DC: American Psychological Association.

Astor, R. A., Guerra, N., & Van Acker, R. (2010). How can we improve school safety research? *Educational Researcher, 39*, 69–78. doi:10.3102/0013189X09357619

Austin, D. (1998). *A Report on progress*. Institute for the Advancement of Social Work Research. Austin, TX: University of Texas at Austin, School of Social Work.

Boaz, A., Ashby, D., Denyer, D., Egan, M., Harden, A., Jones, D. R., et al. (2006). A multitude of syntheses: A comparison of five approaches from diverse policy fields. *Evidence & Policy, 2*, 479–502.

Briss, P. A., Zaza, S., Pappaioanou, M., Fielding, J., Wright-De Aguero, L., Truman, B. I., et al. (2000). Developing an evidence-based guide to community preventive services —Methods. The Task Force on Community Preventive Services. *American Journal of Preventive Medicine, 18*(1S), 35–43. doi:10.1016/S0749-3797(99)00119-1

Bruns, E., & Hoagwood, K. (2008). State implementation of evidence-based practice for youths, Part I: Responses to the state of the evidence. *Journal of the American Academy of Child Psychiatry, 47*, 369–373. doi:10.1097/CHI.0b013e31816485f4

Centers for Disease Control and Prevention. (1999). Framework for program evaluation in public health. *Morbidity and Mortality Weekly Report, 48* (No. RR–11), [i–41].

Chambless, D. L., & Hollon, S. D. (1998). Defining empirically supported therapies. Journal of Consulting and Clinical Psychology, 66, 7–18. doi:10.1037/0022-006X.66.1.7

Chatterji, M. (2005). Evidence on 'what works': An argument for extended-term mixed-methods (ETMM) evaluation designs. *Educational Researcher, 34*, 14–24. doi:10.3102/0013189X034005014

Chorpita, B. F. (2003). The frontier of evidence-based practice. In A. E. Kazdin & J. R.Weisz (Eds.), *Evidence-based psychotherapies for children and adolescents* (pp. 42–59). New York, NY: Guilford.

Chou, R., & Helfand, M. (2005). Challenges in systematic reviews that assess treatment harms. *Annals of Internal Medicine, 142*, 1090–1099.

Cicchetti, D., & Toth, S. L. (2009). The past achievements and future promises of developmental psychopathology: The coming of age of a discipline. *Journal of Child Psychology and Psychiatry, 50*, 16–25. doi:10.1111/j.1469-7610.2008.01979.x

Concato, J., Shah, N., & Horwitz, R. I. (2000). Randomized, controlled trials, observational studies, and the hierarchy of research designs. *New England Journal of Medicine, 342*, 1887–1892. doi:10.1056/NEJM200006223422507

Cook, B. G., Tankersley, M., & Landrum, T. J. (2009). Determining evidence-based practices in special education. *Exceptional Children, 75*, 365–383.

Cornell, D. G., & Mayer, M. J. (2010). Why does school order and safety matter? *Educational Researcher, 39*, 7–15. doi:10.3102/0013189X09357616

Dahlberg, L. L., Toal, S. B., Swahn, M., & Behrens, C. B. (2005). *Measuring violence-related attitudes, behaviors, and influences among youths: A compendium of assessment tools* (2nd ed.). Atlanta, GA: Centers for Disease Control and Prevention, National Center for Injury Prevention and Control.

Datta, L-e. (2007), Looking at the evidence: What variations in practice might indicate. *New Directions for Evaluation*, 35–54. doi:10.1002/ev.214

Dodge, K. A., & Pettit, G. S. (2003). A biopsychosocial model of the development of chronic conduct problems in adolescence. *Developmental Psychology, 39*, 349–371. doi:10.1037/0012-1649.39.2.349

Durlak, J. A., & DuPre, E. P. (2008). Implementation matters: A review of research on the influence of implementation on program outcomes and the factors affecting implementation. *American Journal of Community Psychology, 41*, 327–350. doi:10.1007/s10464-008-9165-0

Dynarski, M. (2008). Comments on Slavin: Bringing answers to educators: Guiding principles for research syntheses. *Educational Researcher, 37*(1), 27-29.

Farrington, D. P., & Welsh, B. C. (2005). Randomized experiments in criminology: What have we learned in the last two decades? *Journal of Experimental Criminology, 1*, 9–38. doi:10.1007/s11292-004-6460-0

Flay, B. R., Biglan, A., Boruch, R. F., Castro, F. G., Gottfredson, D., Kellam, S. G., et al. (2005). Standards of evidence: Criteria for efficacy, effectiveness and dissemination. *Prevention Science, 6*, 151–175. doi:10.1007/s11121-005-5553-y

Gibbs, L. (2004). *Evidence-based practice for the helping professions*. Retrieved from http://www.evidence.brookscole.com/moredetails.html

Gibbs, L., & Gambrill, E. (2002). Evidence-based practice: Counter arguments to objections. *Research on Social Work Practice, 12*, 452–476. doi:10.1177/1049731502012003007

Glasgow, R. E., & Emmons, K. M. (2007). How can we increase translation of research into practice? Types of evidence needed. *Annual Review of Public Health, 28*, 413–433. doi:10.1146/annurev.publhealth.28.021406.144145

Greenberg, M. T. (2004). Current and future challenges in school-based prevention: The researcher perspective. Prevention Science, 5, 5–13. doi:10.1023/B:PREV.0000013976.84939.55

Guyatt, G., Oxman, A. D., Vist, G. E., Kunz, R., Falck-Ytter, Y., Alonso-Coello, P., et al. (2008). GRADE: An emerging consensus on rating quality of evidence and strength of recommendations. *British Medical Journal, 336*, 924–926.

Hansen, H. F., & Rieper, O. (2009). The evidence movement: The development and consequences of methodologies in review practices. *Evaluation, 15,* 141–163. doi:10.1177/1356389008101968

Henggeler, S. W., Schoenwald, S. K., Borduin, C. M., Rowland, M. D., & Cunningham, P. B. (2009). *Multisystemic therapy for antisocial behavior in children and adolescents.* (2nd ed.). New York: Guilford.

Hennessy, K. D., Finkbiner, R., & Hill, G. (2006). The National Registry of Evidence-based Programs and Practices: A decision-support tool to advance the use of evidence-based services. *International Journal of Mental Health, 35*(2), 21–34. doi:10.2753/IMH0020-7411350202

Hoagwood, K., Burns, B. J., Kiser, L., Ringeisen, H., & Schoenwald, S. K. (2001). Evidence-based practice in child and adolescent mental health services. *Psychiatric Services, 52,* 1179–1189. doi:10.1176/appi.ps.52.9.1179

Hoagwood, K., & Johnson, J. (2003). School psychology: A public health framework I. From evidence-based practices to evidence-based policies. *Journal of School Psychology, 41,* 3–21. doi:10.1016/S0022-4405(02)00141-3

Holmbeck, G. N., Devine, K. A., & Bruno, E. F. (2010). Developmental issues and considerations in research and practice. In J. R. Weisz & A. E. Kazdin (Eds.), *Evidenced-based psychotherapies for children and adolescents* (2nd ed., pp. 28–39). New York, NY: Guilford.

Holmbeck, G. N., O'Mahar, K., Abad, M., Colder, C., & Updegrove, A. (2006). Cognitive-behavior therapy with adolescents: Guides from developmental psychology. In P. C. Kendall (Ed.), *Child and adolescent therapy: Cognitive-behavioral procedures* (3rd ed., pp. 419–464). New York, NY: Guilford.

Horner, R. H., Carr, E. G., Halle, J., McGee, G., Odom, S., & Wolery, M. (2005). The use of single-subject research to identify evidence-based practice in special education. *Exceptional Children, 71,* 165–179.

Howard, M. O., McMillen, C. J., & Pollio, D. E. (2003). Teaching evidence-based practice: Toward a new paradigm for social work education. *Research on Social Work Practice, 13,* 234–259. doi:10.1177/1049731502250404

Howell, J. C. (2009). *Preventing and reducing juvenile delinquency: A comprehensive framework* (2nd ed.). Thousand Oaks, CA: Sage.

Howell, J. C., & Lipsey, M. W. (2004). A practical approach to evaluating and improving juvenile justice programs. *Juvenile and Family Court Journal, 55,* 35–48. doi:10.1111/j.1755-6988.2004.tb00095.x

Hunter, J. E., & Schmidt, F. L. (1990). *Methods of meta-analysis: Correcting error and bias in research findings.* Thousand Oaks, CA: Sage.

Institute for the Advancement of Social Work Research (IASWR). (2003). 1993–2003: *A decade of linking policy, practice, and education through the advancement of research.* Washington, DC: Author.

Institute for the Advancement of Social Work Research (IASWR). (2007). *Partnerships to integrate evidence-based mental health practices into social work education and research.* Washington, DC: Author.

Institute of Medicine. (1994). *Reducing risks for mental disorders: Frontiers for preventive intervention research.* Washington, DC: National Academy Press.

Joint Committee on Standards for Educational Evaluation. (1994). *The program evaluation standards.* Thousand Oaks, CA: Sage.

Kavanagh, B. (2009). The GRADE System for rating clinical guidelines. *PLoS Med 6*(9), e1000094. doi:10.1371/journal.pmed.1000094

Kazdin, A. E. (2008). Evidence-based treatment and practice: New opportunities to bridge clinical research and practice, enhance the knowledge base, and improve patient care. *American Psychologist, 63,* 146–159.

Kazdin, A. E., & Weisz, J. R. (1998). Identifying and developing empirically supported child and adolescent treatments. *Journal of Consulting and Clinical Psychology, 66,* 19–36.

Kellam, S. G., & Langevin, D. J. (2003). A framework for understanding 'evidence' in prevention research and programs. *Prevention Science, 4,* 137–153.

Kendall, P. C., Chu, B. C., Gifford, A., Hayes, C., & Nauta, M. (1998). Breathing life into a manual: Flexibility and creativity with manual-based treatments. *Cognitive and Behavioral Practice, 5,* 177–198.

Kendall, P. C., & Treadwell, K. (2007). The role of self-statements as a mediator in treatment for anxiety-disordered youth. *Journal of Consulting and Clinical Psychology, 75,* 380–389.

Kratochwill, T. R. (2002). Evidence-based interventions in school psychology: Thoughts on thoughtful commentary. *School Psychology Quarterly, 17,* 518–532.

Kratochwill, T. R., Hitchcock, J., Horner, R. H., Levin, J. R., Odom, S. L., Rindskopf, D. M., & Shadish, W. R. (2010). *Single-case designs technical documentation.* Retrieved, from What Works Clearinghouse website, http://ies.ed.gov/ncee/wwc/pdf/wwc_scd.pdf

Kratochwill, T. R., & Stoiber, K. C. (2000). Empirically supported interventions and school psychology: Conceptual and practice issues—Part II. *School Psychology Quarterly, 15,* 233–253.

Kratochwill, T. R., & Stoiber, K. C. (2002). Evidence-based interventions in school psychology: Conceptual foundations of the Procedural and Coding Manual of Division 16 and the Society for the Study of School Psychology Task Force. *School Psychology Quarterly, 17,* 341–389.

Larson, J., & Lochman, J. E. (2010). *Helping school children cope with anger: A cognitive-behavioral intervention* (2nd ed.). New York, NY: Guilford.

Lipsey, M. W. (2008, January). *The Arizona Standardized Program Evaluation Protocol (SPEP) for assessing the effectiveness of programs for juvenile probationers: SPEP ratings and relative recidivism reduction for the initial SPEP sample.* A Report to the Juvenile Justice Services Division, Administrative Office of the Courts, State of Arizona. Nashville, TN Center for Evaluation Research and Methodology, Vanderbilt Institute for Public Policy Studies.

Lipsey, M. W., Howell, J. C., & Tidd, S. T. (2007). *The Standardized Program Evaluation Protocol (SPEP): A practical approach to evaluating and improving juvenile justice programs in North Carolina* (Final evaluation report submitted to the Governor's Crime Commission and the North Carolina Department of Juvenile Justice and Delinquency Prevention). Nashville, TN: Vanderbilt University, Center for Evaluation Research and Methodology.

Lipsey, M. W., & Wilson, D. B. (1993). The efficacy of psychological, education, and behavioral treatment: Confirmation from meta-analysis. *American Psychologist, 48*, 1181–1209.

Lipsey, M. W., & Wilson, D. B. (2001). *Practical meta-analysis.* Thousand Oaks, CA: Sage.

Loeber, R., & Stouthamer-Loeber, M. (1998). The development of juvenile aggression and violence: Some common misconceptions and controversies. *American Psychologist, 53*, 242–259.

Lonigan, C. J., Elbert, J. C., & Johnson, S. B. (1998). Empirically supported psychosocial interventions for children: An overview. *Journal of Clinical Child Psychology, 27*, 138–145.

Masten, A. S., Roisman, G. I., Long, J. D., Burt, K. B., Obradović, J., Riley, J. R., et al. (2005). Developmental cascades: Linking academic achievement, externalizing and internalizing symptoms over 20 years. *Developmental Psychology, 41*, 733–746.

Mayer, M. J. (2006). The current state of methodological knowledge and emerging practice in evidence-based evaluation: Applications to school violence prevention research. In S. R. Jimerson & M. J. Furlong (Eds.), *Handbook of school violence and school safety: From research to practice* (pp. 171–190). Hillsdale, NJ: Erlbaum.

Mayer, M. J., & Furlong, M. J. (2010). How safe are our schools? *Educational Researcher, 39*, 16–26.

Mayer, M. J., & Leone, P. E. (2007). School violence and disruption revisited: Establishing equity and safety in the school house. *Focus on Exceptional Children, 40*(1), 1–28.

Mayer, M. J., & Van Acker, R. (2008). Historical roots, theoretical and applied developments, and critical issues in cognitive-behavioral modification. In M. J. Mayer, R. Van Acker, J. E. Lochman, & F. M. Gresham (Eds.), *Cognitive-behavioral interventions for emotional and behavioral disorders: School-based practice* (pp. 3–28). New York, NY: Guilford.

Moher, D., Cook, D. J., Eastwood, S., Olkin, I., Rennie, D., Stroup, D., et al. (1999). Improving the quality of reports of meta-analyses of randomized controlled trials. *Lancet, 354*, 1896–1900.

Moher, D., Liberati, A., Tetzlaff, J., Altman, D. G., and the PRISMA Group. (2009). Preferred reporting items for systematic reviews and meta-analyses: The PRISMA statement. *Annals of Internal Medicine, 151*, 264–269.

Moher, D., Tetzlaff, J., Tricco, A. C., Sampson, M., & Altman, D. G. (2007). Epidemiology and reporting characteristics of systematic reviews. *PLoS Med, 4,e78.* doi:10.1371/journal.pmed.0040078

National Research Council. (2002). *Scientific research in education.* Committee on Scientific Principles for Education Research. R. J. Shavelson & L. Towne (Eds.). Center for Education. Division of Behavioral and Social Sciences and Education. Washington, DC: National Academy Press.

No Child Left Behind Act of 2001, P.L. 107–110, 115 Stat. 1425 (2002).

Odom, S. L., Brantlinger, E., Gersten, R., Horner, R. H., Thompson, B., & Harris, K. R. (2005). Research in special education: Scientific methods and evidenced-based practices. *Exceptional Children, 71*, 137–148.

Ollendick, T. H., & King, N. J. (2004). Empirically supported treatments for children: Advances toward evidence based practice. In P. M. Barrett & T. H. Ollendick (Eds.), *Handbook of interventions that work with children and adolescents: From prevention to treatment* (pp. 3–26). London, England: Wiley.

Perry, A., & Johnson, M. (2008). Applying the Consolidated Standards of Reporting Trials (CONSORT) to studies of mental health provision for juvenile offenders: A research note. *Journal of Experimental Criminology 4*, 165–185.

Perry, A. E., Weisburd, D., & Hewitt, C. (2010). Are criminologists describing randomized controlled trials in ways that allow us to assess them? Findings from a sample of crime and justice trials. *Journal of Experimental Criminology, 6*, 245–262.

Petrosino, A., Boruch, R. F., Rounding, C., McDonald, C., & Chalmers, I. (2000). The Campbell Collaboration social, psychological, educational & criminological trials register (C2-SPECTR). *Evaluation and Research in Education, 14*, 206–219. doi:10.1080/09500790008666973

Petticrew, M., & Roberts, H. (2003). Evidence, hierarchies, and typologies: Horses for courses. *Journal of Epidemiology and Community Health, 57*, 527–529.

Powell, K. E., Dahlberg, L. L., Friday, J., Mercy, J. A., Thornton, T., & Crawford. S. (1996). Prevention of youth violence: Rationale and characteristics of 15 evaluation projects. *American Journal of Preventive Medicine, Supplement to 12*(5), 3–12.

Raudenbush, S. W. (2005). Learning from attempts to improve schooling: The contribution of methodological diversity. *Educational Researcher, 34*, 25–31.

Reiss, A. J., & Roth, J. A. (Eds.). (1993). *Understanding and preventing violence*. Washington, DC: National Academy Press.

Rosen, A. (2003). Evidence-based social work practice: Challenges and promise. *Social Work Research, 27*, 197–208.

Rychetnik, L., Frommer, M., Hawe, P., & Shiell, A. (2002). Criteria for evaluating evidence on public health interventions. *Journal of Epidemiology and Community Health, 56*, 119–127.

Sackett, D. L., Rosenberg, W. M. C., Gray, J. A. M., Haynes, R. B., & Richardson, W. S. (1996). Evidence based medicine: What it is and what it isn't. *British Medical Journal, 312*, 71–72.

Schinke, S., Brounstein, P., & Gardner, S. (2002). *Science-based prevention programs and principles*, 2002. DHHS Pub. No. (SMA) 03-3764. Rockville, MD: Center for Substance Abuse Prevention, Substance Abuse and Mental Health Administration.

Schoenwald, S. K., & Hoagwood, K. (2001). Effectiveness, transportability, and dissemination of interventions: What matters when? *Journal of Psychiatric Services, 52*, 1190–1197.

Schuerman, J., Soydan, H., Macdonald, G., Forslund, M., de Moya, D., & Boruch, R. (2002). The Campbell collaboration. *Research on Social Work Practice, 12*, 309–317.

Schulz, K. F., Altman, D. G., Moher, D., & the CONSORT Group. (2010). CONSORT 2010 Statement: Updated Guidelines for Reporting Parallel Group Randomized Trials. *Annals of Internal Medicine, 152*, 726–732.

Shlonsky, A., & Gibbs, L. (2004). Will the real evidence-based practice please stand up? Teaching the process of evidence-based practice to the helping professions. *Brief Treatment and Crisis Intervention, 4*, 137–153.

Shlonsky, A., & Wagner, D. (2005). The next step: Integrating actuarial risk assessment and clinical judgment into an evidence-based practice framework in CPS case management. *Children and Youth Services Review, 27*, 409–427.

Slavin, R. E. (2008). Perspectives on evidence-based research in education—What works? Issues in synthesizing educational program evaluations. *Educational Researcher, 37*, 5–14.

Smith, A. (1996). Mad cows and ecstasy. *Journal of the Royal Statistical Society, 159*, 367–383.

Song, M., & Herman, R. (2010). Critical issues and common pitfalls in designing and conducting impact studies in education: Lessons learned from the What Works Clearinghouse (Phase I). *Educational Evaluation and Policy Analysis, 32*, 351–371.

Steckler, A., & McLeroy, K. R. (2008). The importance of external validity [Editorial]. *American Journal of Public Health, 98*, 9–10.

Sugai, G., Horner, R. H., Dunlap, G., Hieneman, M., Lewis, T. J., Nelson, C. M., et al. (1999). *Applying positive behavioral support and functional assessment in schools. Technical assistance guide #1* (TAG 1). Washington, DC: OSEP Center on Positive Behavioral Interventions and Support.

Sung, N. S., Crowley, W. F., Genel, M., Salber, P., Sandy, L., Sherwood, L. M., et al. (2003). Central challenges facing the national clinical research enterprise. *Journal of the American Medical Association, 289*, 1278–1287.

U.S. Department of Education. *What Works Clearinghouse Procedures and Standards Handbook Version 2*. Washington, DC: U.S. Department of Education, December 2008.

U.S. General Accounting Office (GAO). (2003). Justice outcome evaluations: Design and implementation of studies require more NIJ attention (GAO-03-1091) Washington, DC: Author.

U.S. Government Accountability Office. (2004). *Performance budgeting: OMB's Program Assessment Rating Tool presents opportunities and challenges for budget and performance integration*. (GAO-04-439T), Washington, DC: Author.

U.S. Government Accountability Office. (2010). *Department of Education: Improved dissemination and timely product release would enhance the usefulness of the What Works Clearinghouse*. (GAO-10-644), Washington, DC: Author.

U.S. Library of Congress, Congressional Research Service. (1994). *Violence in schools: An overview* (CRS Report for Congress No. 94–141 EPW). Washington, DC: Author.

von Elm, E., Altman, D. G., Egger, M., Pocock, S. J., Gotzsche, P. C., & Vandenbroucke, J. P. (2008). The Strengthening of Reporting of Observational Studies in Epidemiology (STROBE) statement: Guidelines for reporting observational studies. *Journal of Clinical Epidemiology, 61*, 344–349.

Weisz, J., Donenberg, G., Han, S., & Weiss, B. (1995). Bridging the gap between lab and clinic in child and adolescent psychotherapy. *Journal of Consulting and Clinical Psychology, 63*, 688–701.

Weisz, J. R., & Hawley, K. M. (1998). Finding, evaluating, refining, and applying empirically supported treatments for children and adolescents. *Journal of Clinical Child Psychology, 27*, 206–216.

Weisz, J. R., & Hawley, K. M. (2002). Developmental factors in the treatment of adolescents. *Journal of Consulting and Clinical Psychology, 70*, 21–43.

Welsh, B. C., & Farrington, D. P. (2007). Evidence-based crime prevention. In B. C. Welsh & D. P. Farrington (Eds.), *Preventing crime: What works for children, offenders, victims, and places* (pp. 1–17). Dordrecht, Netherlands: Springer-Verlag.

Wilson, D. B., & Lipsey, M. W. (2001). The role of method in treatment effectiveness research: Evidence from meta-analysis. *Psychological Methods, 6*, 413–429.

Wilson, S. J., Lipsey, M. W., & Derzon, J. H. (2003). The effects of school-based intervention programs on aggressive behavior: A meta-analysis. *Journal of Consulting and Clinical Psychology, 71*, 136–149.

Woolf, S. H. (2008). The meaning of translational research and why it matters. *Journal of the American Medical Association, 299,* 211–213.

Zaza, S., Wright-De Aguero, L. K., Briss, P. A., Truman, B. I., Hopkins, D. P., Hennessy, M. H., et al. (2000). Data collection instrument and procedure for systematic reviews in the Guide to Community Preventive Services. Task Force on Community Preventive Services. American *Journal of Preventive Medicine, 18*(1S), 44–74.

Zlotnik, J., Biegel, D. E., & Solt, B. (2002). The Institute for the Advancement of Social Work research: Strengthening social work research in practice and policy. *Research on Social Work Practice, 12,* 318–337.

Zwarenstein, M., Treweek, S., Gagnier, J. J., Altman, D. G., Tunis. S., Haynes, B., et al. (2008). Improving the reporting of pragmatic trials: an extension of the CONSORT statement. *British Medical Journal, 337,* 1–8.

20

An Overview of Measurement Issues in School Violence and School Safety Research

Jill D. Sharkey, Erin Dowdy, Jennifer Twyford, and Michael J. Furlong

UNIVERSITY OF CALIFORNIA, SANTA BARBARA

Abstract

Precise and accurate measures are needed for research to advance knowledge about school violence and safety concerns. This chapter provides an overview of school violence and safety measurement issues. After introducing the history of measurement of school violence and safety, we provide a review of recent studies of school violence with a focus on their measurement approaches and practices. We then describe procedures commonly used to measure school safety- and violence-related variables, review prominent threats to the reliability and validity of these procedures, and suggest mechanisms for improvement.

Progress has been made in understanding school violence and safety measurement issues; however, despite calls to action (e.g., Furlong, Morrison, Cornell, & Skiba, 2004; Sharkey, Furlong, & Yetter, 2004), school violence and safety research continues to be hindered by the limited scrutiny given to the psychometric properties of its measurement tools. This chapter focuses on how researchers have measured school violence and safety variables and the implications of their practices for data validity. After a historical summary, recent school violence research is examined with a focus on these studies' measurement practices. Existing methods to measure school violence, and crucial measurement considerations, are described. We conclude with a list of important measurement considerations for school violence research.

School Violence and Safety Measurement in Historical Context

School violence and safety instruments predominately include items developed to estimate population trends to monitor public health conditions. Although items on population-based surveys, such as the Youth Risk Behavior Survey (YRBS; Centers for Disease Control and Prevention [CDC], 2004, 2009, 2010), have undergone content scrutiny by researchers, they are not typically subjected to rigorous psychometric analyses. This is because, in part, their original purpose was to obtain population estimates of behaviors and not to assess individual differences, or to provide information about the root causes of school violence. Nonetheless, researchers often use these surveillance surveys to examine individual differences and the association among risk and health behaviors. However, because the items were not developed for this specific purpose, their sensitivity and validity for complex measurement purposes are not established.

To date, only the *Survey of School Crime and Safety* was originally and specifically designed to assess school safety and violence conditions; however, it is completed by school principals and does not produce student, staff, or parent-level information. Although many of the most prominent sources of information about school safety and violence have come from sources that were not specifically designed for this purpose, modifications of instruments to include school-context items still provide the best information available about school violence and safety and is used for the reports, *Indicators of School Crime and Safety* (e.g., Dinkes, Kemp, & Baum, 2009) and *Crime, Violence, Discipline, and Safety in U.S. Public Schools* (Neiman & DeVoe, 2009). There is overwhelming momentum to suggest that surveillance instruments will continue to be widely used because they have established baseline information that is being used to inform public policy.

Measurement Practices of Recent School Violence and Safety Research

To provide a perspective on recent school violence research measurement practices, we conducted a search of peer-reviewed journal articles with the descriptor of "school violence" for 2009 in the PsycInfo database (a list of these studies and review summary table is available from the authors). This search yielded 59 articles focused on youth in kindergarten through Grade 12 in the following categories: (a) qualitative or theoretical discourse regarding school shootings (n = 18), (b) relations between variables (n = 16), (c) bullying and victimization (n = 7), (d) school violence prevalence (n = 6), (e) other theory/review (n = 4), (f) prevention and intervention studies (n = 4), and (j) book reviews and journal editorials (n = 4). Approximately half (n = 33) of these articles were empirical studies. Although this review was designed to be inclusive, it yielded only a sampling of articles on the topic of school violence. For example, the search only identified 12 of 29 articles published in the *Journal of School Violence* in 2009. Identifying critical scholarship in the field of school violence would be facilitated with commonly applied keywords and descriptors such as "school violence," "school safety," and where appropriate "measurement."

Standards for reporting quantitative methods in the social sciences necessitate a theoretical rationale for the selection of variables, clearly defined variables, and established psychometric characteristics of measures (e.g., Osborne, 2010). To examine the degree to which recent studies use psychometrically sound measures, we examined 32 (one was inaccessible) of the empirical articles. First, we counted the different types of measures used in each study. Each study could only contribute one count per measure, but multiple measures could be counted per study. The most commonly used type of measurement was self-report (n = 24; e.g., Rose, Espelage, & Monda-Amaya, 2009), distantly followed by teacher report (n = 4; e.g., Yavuzer, Gundogdu, & Dikici, 2009), and neighborhood crime records (n = 2; e.g., Cornell, Sheras, Gregory, & Fan, 2009). The following measurement strategies were used in only one study: mapping tools, interviews and focus groups, observations, sociometric questionnaire, card sort, disciplinary records, trained professional rating, and participatory action research. Self-report was by far the most popular type of measure employed, particularly when examining relations between variables. Although most self-report studies focused on youth, one of the self-report measures was for teacher reports of their bully experiences and how these experiences impacted their school's bullying interventions (Kokko & Pörhölä, 2009).

Second, we examined the methods section of each article to evaluate the psychometric properties of measures used. Although the majority of the studies used established measures (e.g., *California School Climate & Safety Survey* [Furlong, 1996; Furlong et al., 2005] or the *YRBS*) only 2 studies (Rose et al., 2009; Saylor & Leach, 2009) provided both reliability and validity information of the school violence scales used. Most (*n* = 17) reported reliability, but no validity information (e.g., Cornell et al., 2009). In a few cases (*n* = 3; e.g., Estévez, Murgui, & Musitu, 2009), measures were modified for the specific study and the resulting reliability, but no validity, data were reported. Several studies reported no psychometric information (*n* = 5; e.g., Chen & Astor, 2009). Other scholars developed their own measures as part of the study (*n* = 8) but less than half (*n* = 3; e.g., Sela-Shayovitz, 2009) reported psychometric properties of the resulting scale. One study adapted a measure by translating it into different languages, but did not report any psychometric data regarding the final scales (Linares, Días, Fuentes, & Acién, 2009). Overall, it was clear that some scales used in school violence research are well developed with multiple citations reflecting prior development and use. Yet, in many cases, scales were developed specifically for one study, at times without any reliability or validity analysis presented.

This examination of recent studies in the area of school violence indicated limited consensus about the use of common measures to examine school violence. In 32 studies, 31 different approaches or scales were used to measure school violence. When established measures were used, oftentimes, psychometric properties for the study sample were underreported (e.g., Turner, Powell, Langhinrichsen-Rohling, & Carson, 2009). Measures were adapted for unique purposes without revalidation and even translated without documenting new psychometric components (e.g., Linares et al., 2009). These recent research practices demand attention because they suggest that the validity of school violence scholarship is questionable due to its measurement practices. Our analysis also revealed popular and neglected areas of study. Discourse regarding school shootings was highly popular and dominated more than a quarter of the articles. The study of bullying and victimization was also popular. Neglected, however, were several areas needing additional scholarship such as school violence prevention, crisis intervention, gang interdiction, school discipline practices, and the influence of school climate on school safety.

School Violence and Safety Measurement Instruments

Despite the need for improved measurement practices, a body of evidence is available for some commonly used instruments. This section provides an overview of procedures to assess school violence and safety. The most frequent way of measuring safety and violence-related concerns is through self-report surveys, including population-based surveillance surveys. Other common methods include mandated districtwide reporting of school discipline referrals. Additional methods such as mapping tools and sociometric questionnaires are used less frequently, and thus, are not detailed here.

Comprehensive School Violence and Safe School Instruments

National surveys of students' self-reported behaviors and experiences are the most common form of data collection regarding school violence and provide information about the widespread prevalence of a problem. However, because this information is aggregated over broad contexts, it is useful for estimating state or national trends, but its applicability to local conditions is restricted. At the school level, students and teachers may be more interested in how their school compares to similar schools in the community or to examine changes over time in response to interventions. School- and district-level assessment of school violence indicators is crucial to indicate specific local needs, as well as to provide a baseline against which treatment efficacy can later be evaluated (Benbenishty, Astor, & Zeira, 2003). Moreover, individual development occurs within the context of school and community influences, and large-scale surveys rarely account for contextual variables (other than geographic region and city size). Therefore, a person's characteristics inherently reflect many environmental influences over a protracted time period, so that attempts to partition out the effects of environment from individual-level variables are unlikely to yield large effects. Oftentimes, the sophistication of the analytic methods used to examine predictors of aggression and violence (such as hierarchical linear modeling) supersedes the psychometric sophistication of the measures used to gather the data (Sullivan, 2002).

Youth Risk Behavior Surveillance Survey (YRBS)

The YRBS was originally developed in the late 1980s as a youth health risk surveillance system (e.g., see Kann, 2001; Kann et al., 2000). It is an anonymous self-report survey administered to students within their classroom. The YRBS is administered biennially to a representative sample of United States high school students. Its content focuses on health-risk behaviors that may result in later disability, mortality, morbidity, and/or significant social problems (CDC, 2009) including alcohol and drug use, unintended pregnancies, dietary behaviors, physical activity, and sexual activity. Results are used to monitor health-risk behaviors among high school students, evaluate the impact of various efforts to decrease the prevalence of health-risk behaviors, and monitor the progress of national health objectives (e.g., CDC, 2010). However, there is limited reliability and validity data to support the use of the YRBS (beyond its epidemiological purpose) to describe characteristics of youths who engage in high-risk behaviors (see CDC, 2004). For instance, the stability of weapon-carrying items, as measured through test-retest reliability, was low, and reliability analyses did not address the different time frames of items (i.e., 30-day vs. lifetime; Brener et al., 2002). Finally, the validity of the responses of youth who selected the most extreme response options was not supported (see Furlong, Sharkey, Bates, & Smith, 2004).

California Healthy Kids Survey (CHKS)

The CHKS is a series of assessment modules developed by WestEd's Human Development Program in collaboration with Duerr Evaluation Resources for the California Department of Education (California Department of Education [CDE], 2010). Items for the CHKS were taken from the YRBS and the California Student Substance Use Survey. The CHKS provides schools with a method of collecting ongoing youth health and risk behavior data and, since 1998, has been successfully administered across the United States and internationally. Three separate versions of the CHKS are available for use at the elementary, middle school, and high school levels (CDE, 2010) and supplemental topics may be added to the core surveys. The surveys contain items concerning youth nutrition and physical activity, sexual behavior, exposure to prevention and intervention activities, risk and protective factors, alcohol, tobacco and other drug use as well as items specific to violence, school safety, gang involvement, and delinquency (CDE, 2010). The surveys include items to assess the truthfulness of each respondent's answers. The results can be compared to results from the YRBS and various health-risk surveys. Benefits of using the CHKS include: meeting categorical program requirements (such as Title IV), identifying program goals and high-risk groups (e.g., CDE, 2010), and identifying risk and protective factors (through its Resiliency and Youth Development Module), which has an extensive report of its psychometric properties (Hanson & Kim, 2007).

Mandated Districtwide Reporting

The federal Gun-Free Schools Act of 1994 (GFSA; 1994) imposed specific reporting requirements for each state regarding the number of students who engage in a variety of violent behaviors. Unfortunately, data submitted by districts were not comparable (Kingery & Coggeshall, 2001) because (a) some states reported more detailed information, (b) districts differed in how they categorized violent behavior, (c) inconsistencies in time periods assessed interfered with comparing data, and (d) federally-mandated definitions of the classifications of weapons and violent behavior were often not specified in student surveys (for instance, the GFSA definitions included bombs and gas as firearms). Kingery and Coggeshall (2001) also cited other problems that interfered with a clear understanding of the data. They noted that (a) students may hide serious incidents from staff, (b) school personnel may fail to detect many violence incidents or only document observed infractions, (c) staff are not often trained in a standardized fashion, and (d) school personnel may feel pressured to underreport violence so not to reflect negatively on their school or district.

Discipline Referrals

School discipline data, such as office referrals, suspensions, and expulsions, have the potential to provide valuable information about students' risk for future infractions. Sugai, Sprague, Horner, and Walker (2000) observed that all schools collect discipline data to some extent, so discipline data may be the most effective way for school systems to understand the relationships and behavioral contexts that disrupt schools. Discipline data can show (a) which student behaviors are of greatest concern; (b) whether or not there are disproportionate referrals by gender, ethnicity, or special education status; and (c) whether or not there are disproportionate referrals made by certain teachers or during certain periods of instruction (e.g., recess, P.E., reading, and math). This information may be used to identify targets for intervention. However, methods for collecting discipline data need careful consideration and procedures need to be standardized across classroom, playground, and other school settings.

Morrison, Peterson, O'Farrell, and Redding (2004) note that although these data are easily obtained, little is known about the reliability or validity for predicting future aggressive acts with either school-level or individual-level data. Additionally, Morrison and Skiba (2001) caution that school discipline data are not as straightforward as they might appear. Behavior referrals, suspensions, and other disciplinary actions reflect not only students' behavior, but also teachers' tolerance for disruptive behavior; teachers' skills in classroom management; administrative discipline policies; and other classroom, school, and community factors, although they often fail to document the contribution of these environmental influences. Thus, predicting disruptive and violent behavior from school discipline data is problematic because it must account for these multiple levels of influence.

Persistent School Violence and Safety Measurement Issues

Although numerous studies examine factors affecting the measurement accuracy of other health-risk behaviors, such as substance use and dietary behavior, studies examining behaviors related to violence are scarce (Brener, Billy, & Grady, 2003). Researchers have identified threats to the validity of school violence survey data and recommended a variety of design practices for enhancing survey accuracy. These strategies include maintaining confidentiality or anonymity of responses (Ong & Weiss, 2006), verifying the survey's reading level (Stapleton, Cafarelli, Almario, & Ching, 2010), checking for the honesty of answers (Rosenblatt & Furlong, 1997), including sufficient numbers of items to measure a given construct (Bradley & Sampson, 2006), and asking questions about past experiences in ways that are most likely to elicit accurate recall (Coggeshall & Kingery, 2001). Despite the need for enhanced methodological rigor, information about the reliability and validity of methods used to collect self-report surveys is limited.

Implausible Responding Patterns

Investigators need to address the possibility that students may not respond honestly. This issue is related to, but different than, the occurrence of missing or spoiled survey responses to specific questions. For example, with the YRBS, one report (Brener, Kann, et al., 2004) indicated that unusable responses were obtained for 0.4% (age) to 15.5% (suicide attempt) of all 2003 YRBS responses. Data screening methods should detect response inconsistencies or implausibly extreme patterns of responding, which may indicate not just that specific item responses were spoiled, but that the validity of the entire set of responses is questionable. Although data validity screening should be an essential element of all large-scale student surveys, unfortunately, few school violence surveys have included such safeguards (Cornell & Loper, 1998; Kingery & Coggeshall, 2001), and many others do not report whether or how they evaluated the quality of student responses (Furlong, Morrison, et al., 2004). To investigate this issue, researchers from the University of Oregon examined dubious and inconsistent responders to a state survey and found that 1.9% of the cases were eliminated (Oregon Healthy Teens, 2004). This finding supports the general utility of using students' self-reports; however, it suggests that surveys that do not apply such standards may produce results that overestimate very low incidence risk behaviors because inconsistent responders report higher rates of risk behaviors (Cornell & Loper, 1998; Rosenblatt & Furlong, 1997).

The CHKS uses high quality data screening and is a carefully developed instrument, having undergone more than six years of rigorous development and review by a standing panel of independent experts. Analysis of CHKS data includes a data-validation procedure that screens records from the data set that meet a combination of criteria, including inconsistent patterns of responding, implausible reports of drug use, the endorsement of a fictitious drug, or failure to assent to having answered survey questions honestly. The CHKS procedure is rigorous and typically produces a listwise case elimination of about 2%–3% of cases (e.g., O'Brennan & Furlong, 2010). In their examination of responses to the California School Climate and Safety Survey, Rosenblatt and Furlong (1997) compared a group of students who failed reliability and validity checks to a matched control group. They found systematic bias in the way failed students responded to the survey, including higher ratings of school violence victimization, campus danger, poor grades, and few good friends. By contrast, comparison students were more likely to be detected by the social desirability item.

Although surveyors are often concerned with participants responding in a socially desirable manner, one concern is that youths involved with antisocial and aggressive peers will exaggerate their involvement in delinquent activities as an alternative form of social desirability. For instance, Cross and Newman-Gonchar (2004) examined responses on three surveys: the Colorado Youth Survey, the Safe Schools/Healthy Students survey (SS/HS), and a Perception Survey. When examining the pattern of extreme and inconsistent responses, they found that not only did rates vary substantially by survey and by school, but extreme and inconsistent responses inflated rates of violent behavior much more at one school than at the other school. Even small percentages of questionable responses had the ability to inflate estimates of risk behavior substantially. For example, by excluding the fewer than 3% of responses to the Colorado Youth Survey that were suspect, Cross and Newman-Gonchar eliminated 70% of reported incidents of gun-carrying. It is important to note that such small differences in rates are important for low incidence behaviors (such as school gun possession) because even high-quality large-scale surveys such as the YRBS are designed to have a 5% confidence interval (Brener, Kann, et al., 2004). However, school violence researchers rarely consider the effects of implausible responses on their study results.

Survey Administration Procedures

Cross and Newman-Gonchar (2004) examined the impact of survey administrator training on student response patterns. District prevention specialists coached a group of teachers about the importance of collecting quality data, and they were taught to explain the uses and importance of the data to their students and to ask them to respond honestly. Rates of invalid responses to surveys administrated by trained versus untrained teachers were compared and results indicated that the trained administrators obtained far lower rates of highly suspect responses (3%) than the untrained administrators (28%). Related to this finding, researchers using large sample databases rarely present data related to adherence with a standard administration protocol by school staff.

In addition to administration procedures, responses may be influenced by survey format. Turner et al. (1998) provided one of few investigations regarding how traditional paper-and-pencil formats and computer assisted presentation influence response rates. Based on similar studies about youth substance use, computer presentations were expected to produce higher self-report rates. Turner and colleagues found that the computer format produced substantially higher prevalence rates than did the paper-and-pencil format for weapon-carrying, acts of violence, and threatened violence. The authors explained that the computer format, with the benefit of audio presentation and computerization, was likely to promote more accurate responding for sensitive questions. This explanation is supported by evidence of similarly high rates from studies that rely on retrospective accounts by adults regarding sensitive adolescent behaviors.

In a related study, researchers from the CDC compared paper-and-pencil versions to several online versions of the YRBS (Denniston et al., 2010). They found that seeking passive parental consent for both the hard copy and the online options produced similar usable response rates. One difference was that when the survey was completed online the youth were more likely to say that they did not think the answers were private, given the visibility of monitors in the computer lab administration setting. The students were also given one other option. They were given a card with the URL for the survey and asked to complete it on their own time over the following two weeks. They received a reminder after one week. When given the option and asked to do it on their own time, only 24% of the students completed the survey. Although not mentioned by these researchers, this was interesting because this latter finding suggests that the level of intrinsic motivation to complete school violence and safety surveys among adolescents may be low.

In an important study, Hilton, Harris, and Rice (2003) examined the consistency of youth self-reports of violence victimization and perpetration (not school violence) and compared prevalence rates derived from traditional paper-and-pencil reports to those provoked by the same experience modeled in an audio vignette. They found that the same youths reported 2 to 3 times more violence perpetration and victimization using the self-report format. This finding, considered in relation to other studies (e.g., Hilton, Harris, & Rice, 1998), led these researchers to conclude that, "…although we would not suggest that standard paper-and-pencil surveys yield completely inaccurate data, the accumulated evidence, including these results, calls on researchers in the field of interpersonal violence to redouble efforts to demonstrate and improve the factual accuracy of their primary dependent measures" (Hilton et al., 2003, p. 235).

Item Wording

It is also important to evaluate if all respondents understand school violence survey questions in the same way. Brener, Grunbaum, et al. (2004) found that differences in item wording across three national surveys resulted in significantly different rates of behavior. One challenge with surveys of school violence and safety is that questions are worded so broadly as to leave a great deal of interpretation to individual responders (Cornell & Loper, 1998). A survey question that asks students if they carry a weapon without defining the word "weapon" has the potential to result in students reporting their hunting rifles or pocketknives as weapons. For example, the SS/HS (Safe Schools Healthy Students, 2004) item, "During the past 12 months, how often have you been picked on or bullied by a student on school property?" is ambiguous for several reasons. First, it is unclear whether being picked on and being bullied are to be interpreted as separate experiences, or if they are implied to be equivalent. Beyond this, the item does not define "bullying" in a way that is consistent with best research practices. It could be argued that this item does not measure "bullying" victimization per se, but rather each student's understanding of this word. To promote consistent and accurate responses, items should be unambiguous, easy to read, and all terms should be clearly defined (Fowler, 1993).

Items Response Time Frames

Many commonly used school violence and safety instruments include items that refer to past behavior using a variety of time frames (e.g., 30 days, 6 months, 1 year). It would seem logical to presume that survey responses in any given month provide a cross-section (in time) of students' behaviors and experiences and that the reported incidence of these behaviors would be higher over a much longer period of time. For example, if 10% of students report carrying a weapon to school in the past 30 days, one might expect this percentage to be higher if the same sample of students were asked to report about past year weapon possession. However, no published research has confirmed this. According to Schwartz (1999), asking about past month incidents is likely to convey to respondents that researchers want to know about less serious but common events. In contrast, students might interpret asking about fights in the past year as seeking information about less frequent but more serious fights (Schwartz, 1999).

To explore this issue, Hilton and colleagues (1998) examined differences in self-reports across 1-month, 6-month, and 1-year time periods. They reported "… standard self-reports of interpersonal violence were insensitive to the specified time frame; for example, participants reported almost the same number of violent acts in the past month as in the past year, something that could not be factually true" (p. 234). Similarly, based on their review of what is known about influences of response time referents, Brener et al. (2003) concluded that multiple factors affect student recollection of school violence experiences.

Survey designers should be mindful that respondents often find it difficult to accurately remember past events (Cornell & Loper, 1998; Fowler, 1993). For this reason, survey questions that ask about past behavior or experiences can incorporate any of a variety of techniques for enhancing recall. Converse and Presser (1986) recommend: (a) using simple language; (b) asking about experiences within a narrow reference period (within no more than a 6-month period); (c) using memory landmarks (e.g., asking about behavior "since the beginning of the school year" or "since New Year's"); and (d) stimulating recall by describing concrete events ("Instead of asking respondents if they have experienced 'assaults,' for instance, … ask if anyone … used force by grabbing, punching, choking, scratching, or biting," p. 22). Unfortunately, school violence and safety research has not yet thoroughly attended to these measurement concerns.

Item-Response Options

Not only do surveys differ in the response time frame, but they also vary in the number and type of response options offered. Often, items that appear on one survey are included on other questionnaires with a different number of response options, without stating a rationale for the change in response options. For example, the YRBS asks, "During the past 30 days, on how many days did you carry a weapon such as a gun, knife, or club on school property?" The following five response options are offered; 0 days, 1 day, 2 or 3 days, 4 or 5 days, and 6 or more days. However, when applied by Farrell and Meyer (1997) to evaluate the effectiveness of a violence prevention program, the item included six response options: Never, 1–2 times, 3–5 times, 6–9 times, 10–19 times, and 20 times or more. Although it might appear that similar items with different numbers of response options yield equivalent results, in fact, this is not the case (Schwartz, 1999). In addition, Schwartz noted that survey respondents also are most likely to choose response options near the middle of response scales.

School Violence and Safety Instrument Psychometric Properties

The survey method typically used to assess school safety and violence seeks to identify indicators that increase the likelihood of negative outcomes. This practice differs substantially from that most often used in school psychology, which establishes in advance the psychometric properties of a scale for identification or diagnosis purposes (Cornell & Loper, 1998). Unfortunately, some reports have used survey instruments for identification purposes without adequately examining the psychometric properties of the scales. There is limited research examining the reliability and validity of school violence and safety instruments.

Stability of Responses

As with any self-report measure, measures of violence and safety should have rigorous psychometric testing to establish reliability and validity (Rosenblatt & Furlong, 1997). Given that school violence and safety instruments typically do not measure latent traits, the reliability of greatest interest is the consistency of responses over a brief interval. Unfortunately, testing of response stability is infrequent. Brener et al. (2002) completed the only study to date that has examined the reliability of the YRBS items that inquired about school-associated behaviors. They examined the responses of 4,619 of 6,802 eligible students, derived from a convenience sample, who completed the YRBS twice over a 2-week time period. They subsequently converted the responses of all items into binary format to compute a *kappa* statistic, a measure of response consistency that is corrected for chance agreement. *Kappa* coefficients ranged from .41 to .68 (in the *moderate* to *substantial* range; Landis & Koch, 1977) for the four YRBS items that directly assess school violence content. The incidence of one behavior ("Injured in a physical fight one time in the past 12 months") was significantly higher at time 2 compared to time 1. Though Brener et al. concluded that, in general, the YRBS is a reliable instrument and this study is cited often to justify the use of the YRBS, there are several methodological questions with this study, particularly when school violence items are examined. These issues pertain to the appropriateness of excluding inconsistent responses prior to analysis; converting responses to binary format and using the *kappa* statistic; using a 14-day (average) retest period for items with 30-day or 12-month reference timeframes; and interpreting *kappa* coefficients for items with different reference timeframes (e.g., past 30 days and past 12 months). As a result, this analysis likely generated the most favorable possible test-retest reliability. Even so, the reliability coefficients for the school items were only in the moderate range.

Validity of Measures

Skiba et al. (2004) noted that instruments can contribute significantly to the field of school violence and safety only when they include the complex and representative set of factors involved. They recommended using empirical methods such as factor analysis to justify inclusion of items in surveys, rather than relying only on professional judgment, as done in the past. Regarding the content of school safety and violence measures, Skiba et al. pointed out that many surveys focus on significant acts of violence, such as weapon carrying. However, although extreme violence is the end result within a context of unsafe school climate, it may not provide enough variance to yield meaningful comparisons, particularly for typical schools. For this reason, Skiba et al. stated that researchers need to focus less on serious violent acts, especially as smaller discipline problems are more frequent and are part of a common trajectory towards future antisocial behavior.

A few researchers have developed school violence and safety instruments using psychometric approaches to scale development (Furlong, Sharkey, et al., 2004; Skiba et al., 2004). Although these instruments are not appropriate for surveillance style surveys, they have potential to provide options when used as outcome measures in local evaluations and studies using controlled experimental designs. Recently, Greif and Furlong (2004a, 2004b) extended the psychometric approach by using item response analysis to create a unidimensional school violence victim scale. Such a scale could be used to track victimization experiences across time. Table 20.1

Table 20.1   School Violence and Safety Measures: Intended Use, Limitations, and Recommendations

Type	Intended Use	Limitations	Recommendations
General Surveillance	Obtain population estimates broadly about youth risk.	Not subjected to rigorous psychometric analysis; limited information about school violence and safety; does not inform individual development.	Conduct psychometric analysis for new purpose prior to extending their use.
School Violence Items in Surveillance Surveys	Obtain populations estimates about school violence and safety.	The most rigorous survey is only administered to school principals and does not produce student, staff, or parent-level information; does not inform individual development.	Include items designed to specifically assess school violence and safety in more broadly administered assessments. Make sure reliability and validity have been tested for intended purposes.
School Violence and Safety Measurement Instruments	Measure latent constructs of youth violence.	Threats to validity such as reading level, honesty of answers, response options, recall, and extreme responses.	Advance knowledge of how to overcome threats to validity by studying these issues. Create and validate more advanced measurement tools with the knowledge gained.
Mandated Districtwide Reporting	Track student violence across schools.	Data submitted by districts are not comparable.	Identify an alternative method or implement extensive training, standardization, and incentive for accurate and comparable reporting.
Discipline Referrals	Examine school safety; evaluate if there are disproportionate referrals; predict students' risks for future infractions.	Lack of standard procedures within and across schools; lack of psychometric scrutiny.	Limit cross analysis of data from different sources unless discipline procedures, reporting, and data collection are standardized within and across settings. Evaluate data for reliability and validity.

provides a review of the school violence and safety measures along with their limitations and recommendations for improvement.

Conclusion

Efforts to refine school violence and safety measurement practices are needed. Although more sophisticated techniques are being employed, such as web administration with programmed skip patterns, it is essential that researchers continue to examine the fundamental aspects of measurement procedures. Significant limitations currently exist, perhaps most notably the continued and sustained use of items from instruments with little, or no known, validity evidence. Researchers and consumers of research should be aware of the dangers of drawing conclusions based on measures with limited or poor psychometric properties. Similarly, as new measures are being developed it is critical that researchers do not rely on a "bootstrapping" approach, in which they continually try to validate new measures against known inferior measures until enough evidence is accumulated to demonstrate that the newly developed measure is superior. In this chapter, we provided a review of the current state of research and current available instruments and highlighted many issues affecting measurement accuracy. The key recommendations of the chapter are summarized in Table 20.2. While there is still much to be done, it is hoped that the concepts and guidelines discussed here will lead to improved research in school violence and safety measurement.

Table 20.2 Implications for Practice: Recommendations for the Use of School Violence Self-report Procedures

---

Constructing Surveys

     Clearly define key terms
     Keep questions concrete
     Use memory aids when asking about past events
     Include multiple questions to measure each main construct
     Check survey's reading level for the target population
     Include items that screen for honesty and accuracy

Selecting Existing Surveys

     Check reliability and validity for the population to be tested

Administering Surveys

     Ensure confidentiality / anonymity
     Train staff to adhere to a standard protocol
     Explain purpose of survey to students and how results are used
     Be prepared to read questions aloud to students and to clarify
     Debrief students afterward: What were they thinking?

Reporting Survey Results

     Present information separately to students, staff, parents
     Solicit perceptions of survey data
     Brainstorm alternative courses of action
     Maintain a collaborative, team-oriented stance

Next Steps

     Link assessment to planning and intervention
     Choose activities and programs with empirical support
     Reassess students periodically to measure program effectiveness

---

References

Benbenishty, R., Astor, R. A., & Zeira, A. (2003). Monitoring school violence: Linking national-, district-, and school-level data over time. *Journal of School Violence, 2,* 29–50. doi:10.1300/J202v02n02_03

Bradley, K. D., & Sampson, S. O. (2006). Constructing a quality assessment through Rasch techniques: The process of measurement, feedback, reflection and change. In X. Liu & W. Boone (Eds.), *Applications of Rasch measurement in science education* (pp. 23–44). Maple Grove, MN: JAM Press.

Brener, N. D., Billy, J. O. G., & Grady, W. R. (2003). Assessment of factors affecting the validity of self-reported health-risk behavior among adolescents: Evidence from the scientific literature. *Journal of Adolescent Health, 33,* 436–457. doi:10.1016/S1054-139X(03)00052-1

Brener, N. D., Grunbaum, J. A., Kann, L., McManus, T., & Ross, J. (2004). Assessing health risk behaviors among adolescents: The effect of question wording and appeals for honesty. *Journal of Adolescent Health, 35,* 91–100. doi:10.1016/j.jadohealth.2003.08.013

Brener, N. D., Kann, L., Kinchen, S. A., Grunbaum, J., Whalen, L., … Ross, J. G. (2004). Methodology of the Youth Risk Behavior Surveillance System. *MMWR Recommendations and Reports, 53*(RR-12), 1–13.

Brener, N. D., Kann, L., McManus, T., Kinchen, S. A., Sundberg, E. C., & Ross, J. G. (2002). Reliability of the 1999 Youth Risk Behavior Survey Questionnaire. *Journal of Adolescent Health, 31,* 336–342. doi:10.1016/S1054-139X(02)00339-7

California Department of Education (CDE). (2010). *California Healthy Kids Survey web site.* Retrieved September 5, 2010, from http://chks.wested.org/

Centers for Disease Control and Prevention (CDC). (2004). Methodology of the Youth Risk Behavior Surveillance System. *MMWR, 53*(RR-12), 1–11.

Centers for Disease Control and Prevention (CDC). (2009). *2009 Youth Risk Behavior Survey.* Retrieved from http://www.cdc.gov/yrbss

Centers for Disease Control and Prevention (CDC). (2010). Youth Risk Behavior Surveillance Survey—United States, 2009. *Surveillance Summaries, MMWR, 59,* No. SS-5. Retrieved from http://www.cdc.gov/HealthyYouth/yrbs/index.htm

Chen, J. K., & Astor, R. A. (2009). The perpetration of school violence in Taiwan: An analysis of gender, grade level and school type. *School Psychology International, 30,* 568–584. doi:10.1177/0143034309107076

Coggeshall, M. B., & Kingery, P. M. (2001). Cross-survey analysis of school violence and disorder. *Psychology in the Schools, 38,* 107–116. doi:10.1002/pits.1003

Converse, J. M., & Presser, S. (1986). *Survey questions: Handcrafting the standardized questionnaire.* Newbury Park, CA: Sage.

Cornell, D., Sheras, P., Gregory, A., & Fan, X. (2009). A retrospective study of school safety conditions in high schools using the Virginia threat assessment guidelines versus alternative approaches. *School Psychology Quarterly, 24,* 119–129. doi:10.1037/a0016182

Cornell, D. G., & Loper, A. B. (1998). Assessment of violence and other high-risk behaviors with a school survey. *The School Psychology Review, 27,* 317–330.

Cross, J. E., & Newman-Gonchar, R. (2004). Data quality in student risk behavior surveys and administrator training. *Journal of School Violence, 3,* 89–108. doi:10.1300/J202v03n02_06

Denniston, M. D., Brener, N. D., Kann, L., Eaton, D. K., McManus, T., … Ross, J. G. (2010). Comparison of paper-and-pencil versus Web administration of the Youth Risk Behavior Survey (YRBS): Participation, data quality, and perceived privacy and anonymity, *Computers in Human Behavior, 26,* 1054–1060. doi:10.1016/j.chb.2010.03.006

Dinkes, R., Kemp, J., & Baum, K. (2009). *Indicators of school crime and safety: 2009* (NCES 2010–012/ NCJ 228478). Washington, DC: National Center for Education Statistics, Institute of Education Sciences, U.S. Department of Education, and Bureau of Justice Statistics, Office of Justice Programs, U.S. Department of Justice.

Estévez, E., Murgui, S., & Musitu, G. (2009). Psychological adjustment in bullies and victims of school violence. *European Journal of Psychology of Education, 24,* 473–483. doi:10.1007/BF03178762

Farrell, A. D., & Meyer, A. L. (1997). The effectiveness of a school-based curriculum for reducing violence among urban sixth-grade students. *American Journal of Public Health, 87,* 979–984. doi:10.2105/AJPH.87.6.979

Fowler, F. J., Jr. (1993). *Survey research methods* (2nd ed.). Newbury Park, CA: Sage.

Furlong, M. J. (1996). Tools for assessing school violence. In S. Miller, J. Brodine, & T. Miller (Eds.), *Safe by design: Planning for peaceful school communities* (pp. 71–84). Seattle, WA: Committee for Children.

Furlong, M. J., Greif, J. L., Bates, M. P., Whipple, A. D., Jimenez, T. C., & Morrison, R. (2005). Development of the California School Climate and Safety Survey–Short Form. *Psychology in the Schools, 42,* 137–149. doi:10.1002/pits.20053

Furlong, M. J., Morrison, G. M., Cornell, D., & Skiba, R. (2004). Methodological and measurement issues in school violence research: Moving beyond the social problem era. *Journal of School Violence, 3*(2/3), 5–12. doi:10.1300/J202v03n02_02

Furlong, M. J., Sharkey, J. D., Bates, M. P., & Smith, D. C. (2004). An examination of the reliability, data screening procedures, and extreme response patterns for the Youth Risk Behavior Surveillance Survey. *Journal of School Violence, 3*(2/3), 109–130. doi:10.1300/J202v03n02_07

Greif, J. L., & Furlong, M. J. (2004a, November). *Towards precision in measuring school violence victimization using IRT.* Presentation at the 20th Annual Meeting of the International Society for Traumatic Stress Studies, New Orleans, LA.

Greif, J. L., & Furlong, M. J. (2004b). Using item response analysis to develop a unidimensional school violence victimization scale. In *Persistently safe schools: The National Conference of the Hamilton Fish Institute on School and Community Violence.* Washington, DC: Hamilton Fish Institute, George Washington University. Retrieved from http://gwired.gwu.edu/hamfish/AnnualConference/2004/

Gun-Free Schools Act (GFSA), 20 USC §8921. (1994).

Hanson, T. L., & Kim, J. O. (2007). *Measuring resilience and youth development: The psychometric properties of the Healthy Kids Survey.* (Issues & Answers Report, REL 2007–No. 034). Washington, DC: U.S. Department of Education, Institute of Education Sciences, National Center for Education Evaluation and Regional Assistance, Regional Educational Laboratory West. Retrieved from http://ies.ed.gov/ncee/edlabs

Hilton, N. Z., Harris, G. T., & Rice, M. E. (1998). On the validity of self-reported rates of interpersonal violence. *Journal of Interpersonal Violence, 13,* 58–72. doi:10.1177/088626098013001004

Hilton, N. Z., Harris, G. T., & Rice, M. E. (2003). Correspondence between self-reports of interpersonal violence. *Journal of Interpersonal Violence, 18,* 223–239. doi:10.1177/0886260502250065

Kann L. (2001). The Youth Risk Behavior Surveillance System: Measuring health-risk behaviors. *American Journal of Health Behavior, 25,* 272–277.

Kann, L., Kinchen, S. A., Williams, B. I., Ross, J. G., Lowry, R., Grunbaum, J. A., & Kolbe, L. J. (2000). Youth Risk Behavior Surveillance — United States, 1999. *Journal of School Health, 70,* 271–285. doi:10.1111/j.1746-1561.2000.tb07252.x

Kingery, P. M., & Coggeshall, M. B. (2001). Surveillance of school violence, injury, and disciplinary actions. *Psychology in the Schools, 38,* 117–126. doi:10.1002/pits.1004

Kokko, T. H. J., & Pörhölä, M. (2009). Tackling bullying: Victimized by peers as a pupil, an effective intervener as a teacher? *Teaching and Teacher Education, 25,* 1000–1008. doi:10.1016/j.tate.2009.04.005

Landis, J. R., & Koch, G. G. (1977). The measurement of observer agreement for categorical data. *Biometrics, 33,* 159–174. doi:10.2307/2529310

Linares, J. J. G., Días, A. J. C., Fuentes, M. D. C. P., & Acién, F. L. (2009). Teachers' perception of school violence in a sample from three European countries. *European Journal of Psychology of Education, 24,* 49–59. doi:10.1007/BF03173474

Morrison, G. M., Peterson, R., O'Farrell, S., & Redding, M. (2004). Using office referral records in school violence research: Possibilities and limitations. *Journal of School Violence, 3*(2/3), 139–149. doi:10.1300/J202v03n02_04

Morrison, G. M., & Skiba, R. (2001). Predicting violence from school misbehavior: promises and perils. *Psychology in the Schools, 38,* 173–184. doi:10.1002/pits.1008

Neiman, S., & DeVoe, J. F. (2009). *Crime, violence, discipline, and safety in U.S. public schools: Findings from the School Survey on Crime and Safety: 2007–08* (NCES 2009-326). Washington, DC: National Center for Education Statistics, Institute of Education Sciences, U.S. Department of Education.

O'Brennan, L. M., & Furlong, M. J. (2010). Relations between students' perceptions of school connectedness and peer victimization. *Journal of School Violence, 9,* 375–391. doi:10.1080/15388220.2010.509009

Ong, A. D., & Weiss, D. J. (2006). The impact of anonymity on responses to sensitive questions. *Journal of Applied Social Psychology, 30,* 1691–1708. doi:10.1111/j.1559-1816.2000.tb02462.x

Oregon Healthy Teens. (2004). *OHT 2004 survey methodology.* Retrieved September 5, 2004, from http://www.dhs.state.or.us/dhs/ph/chs/youthsurvey/ohteens/2004/methods.shtml

Osborne, J. W. (2010). Correlation and other measures of association. In G. R. Hancock & R. O. Mueller (Eds.), *The reviewer's guide to quantitative methods in the social sciences* (pp. 55–69) New York, NY: Routledge.

Rose, C. A. Espelage, D. L., & Monda-Amaya, L. E. (2009). Bullying and victimization rates among students in general and special education: A comparative analysis. *Educational Psychology, 29,* 761–776. doi:10.1080/01443410903254864

Rosenblatt, J. A., & Furlong, M. J. (1997). Assessing the reliability and validity of student self-reports of campus violence. *Journal of Youth and Adolescence, 26,* 187–202. doi:10.1023/A:1024552531672

Safe Schools Healthy Students. (2004). *The faces of the Safe Schools/Healthy students.* Retrieved September 4, 2004, from http://www.sshs.samhsa.gov/initiative/faces.aspx

Saylor, C. F., & Leach, J. B. (2009). Perceived bullying and social support in students accessing special inclusion programming. *Journal Development Physical Disabilities, 21,* 69–80. doi:10.1007/s10882-008-9126-4

Schwartz, N. (1999). Self reports: How the questions shape the answers. *American Psychologist, 54,* 93–105. doi:10.1037/0003-066X.54.2.93

Sela-Shayovitz, R. (2009). Dealing with school violence: The effect of school violence prevention training on teachers' perceived self-efficacy in dealing with violent events. *Teaching and Teacher Education, 25,* 1061–1066. doi:10.1016/j.tate.2009.04.010

Sharkey, J. D., Furlong, M. J., & Yetter, G. (2004). An overview of measurement issues in school violence and school safety issues. In S. R. Jimerson & M. J. Furlong (Eds.), *Handbook of school violence and school safety: From research to practice* (pp. 121–134). Mahwah, NJ: Erlbaum.

Skiba, R., Simmons, A. B., Peterson, R., McKelvey, J., Ford, S., & Gallini, S. (2004). Beyond guns, drugs and gangs: The structure of student perceptions of school safety. In M. J. Furlong, M. P. Bates, D. C. Smith, & P. Kingery (Eds.), *Appraisal and prediction of school violence: Issues, methods and contexts* (pp. 149–171). Hauppauge, NY: Nova Science.

Stapleton, L. M., Cafarelli, M., Almario, M. N., & Ching, T. (2010). Prevalence and characteristics of student attitude surveys used in public elementary schools in the United States. *Practical Assessment, Research & Evaluation. 15*(9). Retrieved from http://pareonline.net/getvn.asp?v=15&n=9

Sugai, G., Sprague, J. R., Horner, R. H., & Walker, H. M. (2000). Preventing school violence: The use of office discipline referrals to assess and monitor school-wide discipline interventions. *Journal of Emotional and Behavioral Disorders, 8,* 94–101. doi:10.1177/106342660000800205

Sullivan, M. L. (2002). Exploring layers: Extended case method as a tool for multilevel analysis of school violence. *Sociological Methods & Research, 31,* 255–285. doi:10.1177/0049124102031002005

Turner, C. F., Ku, L., Rogers, S. M., Lindberg, L. D., Pleck, J. H., & Sonenstein, F. L. (1998). Adolescent sexual behavior, drug use, and violence: Increased reporting with computer survey technology. *Science, 280,* 867–873. doi:10.1126/science.280.5365.867

Turner, L. A., Powell, A. E., Langhinrichsen-Rohling, J., & Carson, J. (2009). Helping families initiative: Intervening with high risk students through a community, school, and district attorney partnership. *Child and Adolescent Social Work Journal, 26,* 209–223. doi:10.1007/s10560-009-0167-z

Yavuzer, Y., Gundogdu, R., & Dikici, A. (2009). Teachers' perceptions about school violence in one Turkish city. *Journal of School Violence, 8,* 29–41. doi:10.1080/15388220802067797

21

Using Self-Report Anger Assessments in School Settings

Douglas C. Smith

SOUTHERN OREGON UNIVERSITY, ASHLAND, OREGON

Michael J. Furlong

THE UNIVERSITY OF CALIFORNIA, SANTA BARBARA

Peter Boman

QUEENSLAND UNIVERSITY OF TECHNOLOGY, BRISBANE, AUSTRALIA

Victoria Gonzalez

THE UNIVERSITY OF CALIFORNIA, SANTA BARBARA

Abstract

Students who experience high levels of anger both in and out of school are at risk for exhibiting multiple negative developmental outcomes including poor school performance, peer problems, behavioral difficulties, and concurrent emotional distress. Given this developmental trajectory, it is important for mental health professionals working within school settings to accurately identify those students manifesting anger-related problems at an early age. This chapter provides an overview of instruments designed to assess levels of anger and associated cognitive and behavioral manifestations in children and youth. Among those instruments highlighted is the Multidimensional School Anger Inventory (MSAI) specifically designed to measure anger, hostility, and aggressive behavioral expression in school settings. The role of anger assessment in developing appropriate early intervention and anger management treatment plans is also discussed.

Anger is a primary human emotion, and as such, it is only natural to expect that in the complex social context of schools with high production and performance demands, students will likely experience situations that provoke angry feelings and reactions. Anger clearly plays a vital role in the overall adaptive process. Similar to other potentially troubling emotions such as anxiety and depression, problems arise not just because a student "gets angry," but because of the intensity and frequency of anger experiences and expression. Nonetheless, anger often differs from other emotions in terms of how it is perceived and understood by others. A student who chronically experiences the emotion of sadness, for example, will often illicit sympathy and concern from school staff (e.g., "What can we do to help you?"), whereas a student who experiences chronic anger is more likely to illicit disapproval (e.g., "What is your problem?"). A student who experiences anger intensively may also be perceived as not just *having* a problem, but *being* a problem because she or he is perceived to disrupt the normal routine of the classroom and the school campus (Thomas, Coard, Stevenson, Bentley, & Zamel, 2009).

Chronically high levels of anger and hostility are associated with a wide range of negative developmental outcomes including physical and mental problems, academic and occupational distress, poor peer relationships, and aggressive and violent behavior, both in and out of school (Furlong & Smith, 1994; Miller, Smith, Turner, Guijarro, & Hallett, 1996; Potegal, Stemmier, & Spielberger, 2010). Thus, there is certainly ample reason for schools to not only be concerned about the challenges that angry students present, but to recognize that these students' behaviors indicate their risk status for various negative developmental outcomes. As a result, school personnel have a clear interest in not only monitoring and assessing students' experiences of anger in school settings but also in recognizing that some students will require support in learning to manage angry feelings. The purpose of this chapter is to provide an overview of selected self-report instruments designed to measure levels of anger and hostility with school-age youth. This review begins with a brief discussion of some of the fundamental concerns associated with measuring anger and hostility and then describes selected instruments of potential interest to school personnel, most notably the Multidimensional School Anger Inventory (MSAI), which was designed explicitly to assess anger in school settings. The chapter concludes with a summary of best practices in anger assessment as well as some of the limitations and other obstacles associated with measuring students' anger in school environments.

Theoretical and Definitional Issues

Systematic appraisal of anger and the related construct of hostility is an understudied phenomenon. Since both angry feelings and attitudes are highly personal experiences, assessments tend to rely on self-report procedures. Some instruments utilize behavior ratings by teachers, parents, and others, but these run the risk of confusing internal feelings and attitudes with external behaviors, most notably aggression, which may indeed be an outward behavioral expression of anger.

The terms "anger" and "hostility" have fostered some conceptual ambiguity in the literature. At its most basic level, anger refers to an emotional reaction to a perceived internal or external provocation (Miller et al., 1996; Novaco, 2003), varying in intensity from mild irritation to extreme rage. Anger can be viewed as a transitory state or a stable and general disposition to experience this emotion more frequently and intensively (Spielberger, 1999; Spielberger, Reheiser, & Sydeman, 1995). Research distinguishes between *state anger*, or the degree of angry affect experienced at a particular moment in response to a particular situation, and *trait anger*, or one's disposition to experience angry affect across a range of situations (Brunner & Spielberger, 2010).

Research has also distinguished between *anger-in, anger-out,* and *anger control* (Spielberger et al., 1995; Spielberger & Reheiser, 2010; Thomas & Williams, 1991). Each of these terms refers to a characteristic mode of anger expression. Anger-in refers to the tendency of some individuals to restrain or stifle the expression of angry feelings. Anger-out refers to the tendency to express anger overtly, usually through verbal or physical aggression. Anger control refers to the ability of some individuals to express anger in a controlled fashion, usually in what many would consider a socially appropriate manner, such as discussing their feelings with another. Whether it is best to withhold expression of angry feelings or to express these emotions outwardly is a matter of some controversy. Some studies (e.g., Julkunen, Salonen, Kaplan, Chesney, & Salonen, 1994; Williams, 2010) suggest that frequent anger-out is a risk factor for a number of serious medical conditions including coronary heart disease (CHD), whereas others (e.g., Mills, Schneider, & Dimsdale, 1989) propose that outward expressions of anger may serve a protective function by reducing tension and pent-up frustration. Kerr and Schneider (2008), in their review of children's anger expression concluded that "Children who are excessively reactive and overly expressive with their anger are more likely than others to exhibit both externalizing and internalizing problem behaviors. Children who are overly restrictive in their anger expression also seem to behave inappropriately" (p. 574).

The term "hostility" (cynicism is a term also used in the literature) refers to a cognitive process whereby other people are perceived in essentially negativistic terms (Miller et al., 1996; T. Smith, 1994). As such, hostility constitutes an attitude or worldview in which the actions of others are often perceived as intentionally harmful or intrusive, there is an expectation that negative outcomes are highly probable, and there is a desire to inflict harm on others or to see others harmed. Given the pervasive nature of these beliefs, hostility is thought to constitute a stable disposition or personality attribute. In this sense, it is similar to what was referred to earlier as trait anger (Martin, Watson, & Wan, 2000). Hostility can also be understood from a social-information processing perspective (Larson & Lochman, 2010; Schultz, Brodack, & Izard, 2010) whereby there is a bias for some youth to perceive ambiguous social interactions with aggressive interpretations. For example, particularly relevant to the school context, Camodeca and Goossens (2005) found no differences in *reactive* or spontaneous aggression among victims and perpetrators of bullying. However, bullies were more likely to endorse the use of *proactive* or deliberate, goal-directed anger and aggression than their victims. As an example of how hostility can influence classroom interactions, Wyatt and Haskett (2001) found that students with higher levels of anger more often interpreted ambiguous communications from their teachers as expressing hostility toward him or her.

Both anger and hostility have been linked to aggressive behavior, presenting another challenge for those concerned with the measurement of these constructs. It is difficult to identify the existence and intensity of angry feelings and hostile beliefs without considering how such feelings and beliefs are expressed behaviorally. In fact, there is substantial support for the notion that high levels of anger, hostile beliefs, and proneness to aggression coexist in many individuals (Furlong & Smith, 1998; Musante, MacDougall, Dembroski, & Costa, 1989). The degree to which these constitute separate and distinct constructs is unclear at this point. A number of researchers over the past decade have proposed multidimensional inventories designed to measure affective, cognitive, and behavioral dimensions of anger and hostility (e.g., Brunner & Spielberger, 2010; Martin et al., 2000; Siegel, 1986; D. Smith, Furlong, Bates, & Laughlin, 1998; Thomas, 1993). In general, these measures demonstrate moderate correlations among subscales, suggesting that anger, hostility, and aggression constitute separate but related factors. Brunner and Spielberger (2010) reported a correlation of .40 between anger experience and anger expression with a sample of adolescents. Martin et al. (2000), in a cross-instrument factor analysis of scales utilizing a sample of college students, found strong evidence supporting a multidimensional model of anger that includes affective, cognitive, and behavioral elements.

Consequences of Excessive Anger Experience and Expression

Considerable research over the past four decades supports the view that frequent and excessive anger, high levels of hostility, and aggressive behavioral displays toward others all contribute to overall decreases in psychological, social, and physical well-being (Barefoot & Boyle, 2009; Potegal, Stemmier, & Spielberger, 2010; T. Smith & Ruiz, 2002). Chronically high levels of anger and hostility are cited as risk factors for a variety of health-related concerns including cardiovascular distress, hypertension, gastrointestinal difficulties, and other diseases associated with stress to the immune system (McDermott, Ramsay, & Bray, 2001; Miller et al., 1996). Other research has established linkages between chronically high levels of anger and problem behavior at school (D. Smith et al., 1998), poor academic performance (Heavey, Adelman, Nelson, & Smith, 1989; Hinshaw, 1992), peer rejection (Dodge, 1993), and psychosomatic complaints (Friedman, 1991). In addition, poorly controlled anger contributes to such wide-ranging societal issues as marital and family discord, child abuse, road rage, job loss, and legal difficulties (Deffenbacher, Huff, Lynch, Oetting, & Salvatore, 2000; Del Vecchio & O'Leary, 2004). In this section, we briefly review research relating anger and hostility to unhealthy lifestyle choices such as substance use and abuse, physical health, and, perhaps most importantly to readers of this chapter, violence potential at school.

Substance Use

The belief that anger and hostility may lead to participation in high risk, unhealthy behaviors has been corroborated by various health researchers. Anger is associated with increased tobacco, caffeine, and alcohol consumption across various youth samples (Nichols, Birnbaum, Bryant, & Botvin, 2009; Schwinn, Schinker, & Trent, 2010). In a study of the substance use characteristics of incarcerated adolescents, those who expressed anger outwardly (anger-out) had significantly higher levels of marijuana use (Eftekhari, Turner, & Larimer, 2004). Further, in a recent study of 676 U.S. war veterans returning from active duty in Iraq and Afghanistan, Elbogen et al. (2010) reported evidence of the relationship between elevated levels of anger, particularly difficulties in managing aggressive impulses, and propensity for alcohol misuse and abuse, in addition to other mental health problems including Posttraumatic Stress Disorder.

Physical Health Outcomes

Research indicates that anger in adults and adolescents is associated with potentially detrimental health outcomes. Such health risks include cardiovascular disease, hypertension, and higher body mass index (BMI; Chida & Steptoe, 2009; Williams, 2010). Several researchers have confirmed that various forms of anger expression (anger-out, anger-in) are associated with elevated cardiac activation and rise in blood pressure (Bongard, al'Absi, & Lovallo, 1998; Burns & Katkin, 1993; Phillips & Hughes, 2011). Research using Spielberger's Anger–Hostility–Aggression (AHA) syndrome (Spielberger et al., 1985) found that High Anger-Out/Low-Hostile individuals displayed the greatest increase in blood pressure and heart rate, in comparison to other individuals. However, all individuals exhibited elevated levels of blood pressure and heart rate as well as increases in stroke volume and cardiac output. Additionally, Everson et al. (1996) reported in a 4-year follow-up study on male adults, that for each 1-point increase in anger expression (both anger-out and anger-in) there was an increased risk of hypertension by 12%. Thus, for people experiencing higher levels of anger, there is an increased potential risk for heart disease.

Likewise, other negative health factors have been found to be associated with anger expression. For instance, Golden et al. (2006) found that individuals reporting higher levels of trait anger also had significantly higher estimated caloric intake, higher BMI, and higher waist-to-hip ratio when compared with individuals reporting overall low trait anger scores. Additionally, these authors reported that anger temperament moderately predicted Type 2 diabetes. However, once BMI and waist-to-hip ratio were accounted for, the predictive relation between trait anger and Type 2 diabetes was no longer significant. Thus, research indicates that the relation between trait anger and diabetes may be better explained by the direct relation anger has with certain lifestyle factors and behaviors of those with elevated anger scores.

School Violence and Peer Aggression

Chronically high levels of anger and hostility have been identified as important contributors to violence potential at school (Dwyer, Osher, & Warger, 1998; Reddy et al., 2001). For example, lists of warning signs published by the American Psychological Association (APA, 1999) and the U.S. Departments of Justice and Education (Dwyer et al., 1998) include aspects of uncontrolled anger and hostility as key indices of violence potential. Each of these documents contains an array of personal, social, school, and family factors thought to increase the odds that a youth might engage in acts of violence at school. These documents do not claim to be "checklists" that can be used to assess the level of risk of future school violence. Rather, they were developed with the intention that they be used to broadly assess the contexts in a youth's life that might push them toward or away from committing an extreme act of violence (for an extended review see Cornell, 2003, 2006; Cornell, Sheras, Gregory, & Fan, 2009; Furlong, Bates, D. Smith, & Kingery, 2004). Additionally, profiles of perpetrators of serious acts of violence at school, such as those developed by the FBI (O'Toole, 2000), frequently cite intense anger and resentment (hostility or cynicism) toward others as common characteristics of violence-prone youth. Given their potential impact, it is imperative that educators, psychologists, and other mental health personnel have reliable and valid methods for assessing these constructs in school settings (Cornell & Allen, 2011).

Assessment of Anger and Hostility in School Contexts

Although there is an increasing array of instruments aiming to measure angry emotions and hostile attitudes in child and adolescent populations, a number of these focus primarily on aggression, which is considered an expression of anger. This review focuses exclusively on those self-report instruments that adhere to a multidimensional model of anger (which includes affective, cognitive, and behavioral components of anger and hostility) and are being used in empirical research studies. Given the anecdotal recognition of the intense consequences reactive and proactive student anger and aggression can have on schools, there has been surprising little research about student anger. A search of the PsycInfo database for the title words "student anger" produced only two citations. A search using the keywords "student," "anger," and "assessment" returned only nine journal articles. Although the body of research related to the assessment and treatment of anger-related problems in the clinical area (Kerr & Schneider, 2008; Steele, Legerski, Nelson, & Phipps, 2009) is more extensive, this section provides an overview of the self-report assessment resources that have been used most often in school-related research.

We bring to the reader's attention the need to consider that anger in any youth may emanate from complex sources. For example, anger difficulties may reflect a recognizable, expected response to being teased (Libbey, Story, Neumark-Sztainer, & Boutelle, 2008) or reactions to the experience of prejudice (Thomas, Coard, Stevenson, Bentley, & Zamel, 2009). In addition, youth with Bipolar Disorder or other serious mental health needs may experience and express excessive anger in schools (Cautin, Overholser, & Goetz, 2001; Rucklidge, 2006). Typically, however, in the school context, anger assessments will be used as part of a comprehensive psychological assessment or to evaluate a school-based social-emotional intervention. In the following section, we review assessment resources available for these purposes, highlighting their applications across international contexts.

State-Trait Anger Expression Inventory–2 (STAXI–2)

The STAXI-2 (Spielberger, 1999) is a widely known anger instrument (Kerr & Schneider, 2008) that has been used for more than 30 years in adult research and is being increasingly used with adolescents, often across national contexts (e.g., Armstead & Clark, 2002; Reyes, Meininger,

Liehr, Chan, & Mueller, 2003). Many adolescent studies use the adult STAXI items without modification or make study-specific modifications, which has contributed to a lack of uniformity in its use with school-aged populations. To address this issue, del Barrio, Aluja, and Spielberger (2004) developed a Spanish-language version of the STAXI-2 with a sample of more than 2,000 youth, ages 7 to 17 years, from Spain and Latin America. Based on a series of exploratory and confirmatory factor analyses, the 57 original items were reduced to 32. Evidence for reliability and validity were positive, which was further verified in a study using an Italian translation of these same 32 items (Gambetti & Giusberti, 2009). Yet another adaptation of the STAXI was conducted by Maxwell, Sukhodolsky, and Sit (2009), whose Cantonese translation of the revised adult STAXI-2 resulted in an instrument with 46 items. These translations and favorable psychometic properties across samples have resulted in the STAXI-2 being prominently used in cross-national contexts.

Based, in part, on the earlier research adaptations of the STAXI-2, Brunner and Spielberger (2010) published the State-Trait Anger Expression Inventory–2 Child and Adolescent (STAXI–2 C/A). This commercial product was developed for use with children ages 9–18 years (written at a fourth-grade level) and is based on the earlier work of del Bario et al. (2004). This instrument includes 35 items with two core scales measuring *State Anger* (intensity of angry feelings) and *Trait Anger* (frequency of experiencing angry feelings). State Anger, as in the adult version, includes subscales that assess *Feeling* and *Verbal Expression*. Unique for the youth version is that Trait Anger includes subscales measuring *Temperament* and *Reaction*. The STAXI-2 C/A also includes three additional core Scales: *Anger Expression-Out* (frequency of anger feelings that are outwardly verbally or physically expressed), *Anger Expression-In* (frequency of angry feelings that are kept in), and *Anger Control* (frequency that a youth tried to control outward expression of anger). Normative data for a U.S. population are provided based on a sample of 836 youth. Reported reliabilities for this version of the STAXI-2 C/A are better than previously published studies with youth. The alpha coefficients across the five core scales and the four subscales range from .74 to .94.

Aggression Questionnaire

Although Buss and Warren (2000) call their instrument the "Aggression Questionnaire" (AQ), its content is based on a comprehensive framework that links affective, cognitive, and behavioral components in a multidimensional model. The AQ has its roots in the Buss-Durkee Hostility Inventory (BDHI; Buss & Durkee, 1957) and the original Aggression Questionnaire developed by Buss and Perry (1992). The BDHI was quite long (75 items), some items were difficult to read, and some items did not fit into their assigned factors. The measurement aims of the final 34-item AQ is to assess an individual's aggressive responses and their ability to channel their responses safely. AQ items describe characteristics related to aggression; individuals rate themselves on these characteristics on a 5-point scale, where 1 = *not at all like me* and 5 = *completely like me*. Norms are provided for three age groups: Youths (ages 9–18), Younger Adults (ages 19 through 39), and Older Adults (ages 40 and above). The AQ consists of five subscales: *Physical Aggression* (PHY; 8 items), *Verbal Aggression* (VER; 5 items), *Anger* (ANG; 7 items), *Hostility* (HOS; 8 items), and *Indirect Aggression* (IND; 6 items). An *Inconsistent Responding* (IND) Index is included, with 12 pairs of items for which responses are expected to be similar. If the IND score is 5 or higher, the administrator should have reservations about the accuracy of the individual's responses. The AQ Total score is the sum of the raw scores for the five subscales.

Reliability and validity for the AQ is favorable, as reported in the AQ manual (Buss & Warren, 2000). Internal consistency for the AQ Total score is .94 for the entire sample and between .90 and .94 for 9- to 18-year-olds. However, internal consistency for 9- to 10-year-olds is low on VER (.55) and IND (.65). Norms and core psychometric information is provided based on a sample of 1,062 youth, ages 9–18 years. Independent studies, often cross nationally, using the Buss-Perry item set have reported lower internal consistency values for school-aged youth. Walters, Ronen, and Rosenbaum (2010), for example, reported alphas of .76 and .79, respectively, for combined Physical Aggression/Verbal Aggression and Anger/Hostility scores in a sample of 9- to 12-year-olds attending school in Israel. Fossati, Maffei, Acquarini, and Di Ceglie (2003) also reported lower alpha values for a sample of Italian high school students (Physical Aggression = .81, Verbal Aggression = .53, Anger = .72, and Hostility = .68). Another study reported a lower but still acceptable Total Score alpha coefficient in a sample of Chinese high school students (alpha = .84; Liu, Zhou, & Gu, 2009).

The core construct validity of the AQ subscale structure using the Buss-Perry AQ item set has been supported by independent research with students ages 13 to 17 years (e.g., Santisteban, Alvarado, & Recio, 2007). In addition, Ang (2007) found an acceptable factor structure for a 12-item version that may be of interest for research and school-based program evaluation. A point of caution about the use of the AQ with elementary school children (ages 9–12 years) is that its subscale structure may be different; however, it still provides a viable dimensional measure of early anger and aggression. In using the items from the Buss-Perry (1992) AQ with a sample of 9- to 12-year-olds, Walters, Ronen, and Rosenbaum (2010) found that responses to the AQ reflected only two, not four, dimensions with both verbal and physical aggression loading on one factor and anger and hostility loading on another factor. Nonetheless, Walters et al. (2010) concluded that the "AQ self-report questionnaire, particularly the total score, may well be a construct-valid measure of the childhood aggression dimension" (p. 633).

Adolescent Anger Rating Scale

The Adolescent Anger Rating Scale (AARS; Burney, 2008; Burney & Kromrey, 2001) assesses the intensity and frequency of angry reactions in youth ages 11 to 19 years. The AARS aims to measure *instrumental anger, reactive anger,* and *anger control.* Instrumental anger is planned and malicious negative affect oriented toward achieving a specific goal or purpose. Reactive anger is an immediate emotional response to an anger-provoking event that is perceived as threatening, hurtful, or intentional. Anger control is the ability to engage in proactive behaviors in the face of anger provocations. Subscale scores can be computed for each of these areas and can be combined to yield a *Total Anger* score.

The AARS includes 41 items utilizing a 4-point response scale on which respondents indicate the frequency with which they engage in behaviors representative of instrumental anger, reactive anger, and anger control. Normative data are provided based on the responses of 4,187 males and females in middle and high schools. Five ethnic groups were represented in the normative sample. Additional information is provided on grade point average, suspensions in the past year, number of friends, friends' behavior, and primary caretaker.

Burney and Kromrey (2001) report AARS reliability data from the initial development of the scale. Utilizing an earlier 16-item version of the scale, coefficient alphas were .83, .70, and .80 for Instrumental, Reactive, and Anger Control subscales, respectively. Test-retest reliabilities over a two-week interval, based on the responses of 155 participants, were .58, .69, and .65 for the same three subscales. In another study, Reactive Anger (alpha = .82) and Anger Control (alpha = .77) were found to replicate the AARS's acceptable internal consistency characteristics (Bolgar, Janelle, & Giacobbi, 2008).

Validity data (Burney & Kromrey, 2001) were based on the responses of 792 students in Grades 7–12. Exploratory factor analysis utilizing a 20-item revised version of the scale identified three factors corresponding to the hypothesized underlying structure of the scale: Reactive Anger,

Instrumental Anger, and Anger Control. Construct validity for the AARS was further established by comparing mean subscale scores for groups expected to differ in terms of the constructs measured by the scale. As expected, male students, members of ethnic minority groups, older students, and those receiving special education services scored significantly higher on both Reactive and Instrumental Anger and significantly lower on Anger Control. Additionally, discriminant validity evidence for the AARS was provided by comparing subscale scores with another anger scale, the Multidimensional Anger Inventory (Siegel, 1986). Subscale correlations between these two measures ranged from −.11 to .46. Additional validity evidence was found by Bolgar et al. (2008) in a study of anger outbursts by high school competitive tennis players. These authors found that tennis players who had high Reactive Anger scores on AARS displayed more anger outbursts than players with low Reactive Anger scores.

Multidimensional School Anger Inventory

The Multidimensional School Anger Inventory (MSAI; Furlong, D. Smith, & Bates, 2002; D. Smith et al., 1998) is designed to assess the affective, cognitive, and behavioral dimensions of anger pertinent to the school setting and context, and has been used extensively in cross-national research. As a multidimensional scale, it measures the intensity of angry feelings in response to hypothetical school situations, levels of hostility with regard to school, and both positive and negative expressions of angry feelings.

MSAI Development

The MSAI is based on a three-component model of the global anger process that involves an emotional-affective component, a cognitive hostility-cynicism component, and a behavioral-expressive component. The model is consistent with conceptual definitions of anger (e.g., Spielberger, 1999). The behavioral-expressive component of the scale is further subdivided into positive and negative expressions of anger. The MSAI includes four subscales: *Anger Experience, Hostile/ Cynical Attitudes, Destructive Expression,* and *Positive Coping*. Principal components factor analysis supported each of the four subscales as relatively independent measures of the general construct of anger in adolescent populations. This instrument has been used with children and adolescents ages 10–18 years (fourth-grade reading level) and can be administered in 15–20 minutes either individually or in groups.

The most recent version of the MSAI (Furlong et al., 2002) consists of 36 items. The first 13 items comprise the Anger Experience subscale and youth are asked to indicate the intensity of angry feelings they would experience as a result of a variety of frustrating school-related situations. The 13 items include both peer-and teacher-initiated conflicts and use a 4-point response scale (1 = *I wouldn't be mad at all* … 4 = *I would be furious*). The Hostility subscale includes items 14–19. Youth are asked to indicate their level of disagreement/agreement with a series of statements pertaining to the value of school, grades, rules, and attitudes of adults such as teachers. These items use a 4-point Likert scale (1 = *strongly agree* … 4 = *strongly disagree*). Finally, Items 20 to 36 pertain to customary modes of expressing angry affect. Nine of these 17 items refer to Destructive Expression such as physical and verbal aggression, property destruction, and planned acts of retribution. The remaining 8 items refer to Positive Coping such as talking out a disagreement, engaging in physical activity, deflective use of humor, or cognitive reframing. Each item is scored according to a 4-point scale (1 = *never* … 4 = *always*).

The MSAI was normed on a sample of 1,166 adolescents in Grades 9–12. Mean subscale scores for Anger Experience, Hostility, Destructive Expression, and Positive Coping were 30.8, 12.4,

Table 21.1   Summary of Multidimensional School Anger Inventory Reliability and Validity Coefficients Across Cultures

Source	Location	Anger Expression	Hostility	Destructive Expression	Positive Coping
Alpha coefficients					
D. Smith et al. (1998)	Hawaii	.84	.77	.67	.73
Furlong et al. (2002)	California	.84	.80	.82	.67
Boman et al. (2006)	Australia	.79	.78	.77	.66
Ghanizadeh (2008)	Iran	.89	.79	.71	.66
Range		.79–.89	.77–.82	.67–.82	.66–.73
Factor loadings					
D. Smith et al. (1998)	Hawaii	.54–.71	.60–.74	.54–.71	.56–.67
Furlong et al. (2002)	California	.48–.64	.60–.69	.50–.67	.44–.60
Boman et al. (2006)	Australia	.26–.60	.61–71	.44–.69	.47–.56
Ghanizadeh (2008)	Iran	.44–.81	.60–.76	.46–.70	.44–.69
Range		.26–.81	.29–.76	.43–.71	.27–.69

14.5, and 17.3, respectively. Corresponding standard deviations were 6.8, 3.3, 4.8, and 4.1, respectively. Mean scores for male students were significantly higher than for females on Anger Experience, Hostility, and Destructive Expression. Females, on the other hand, scored significantly higher than males on the Positive Coping subscale. Subscale mean scores and standard deviations are provided by grade level and by ethnicity for students in the normative sample. The MSAI's core reliability characteristics are favorable, as shown in Table 21.1. In addition, test-retest reliabilities over a six-month period based on a subsample of 508 students ranged from .56 to .62 for the four subscales (Furlong et al., 2002), which is comparable to other self-report measures of emotional functioning. Using a sample of students from the United States, evidence for construct validity was first found in a principal components factor analysis that yielded a four-factor structure supporting the theoretical model on which the scale was based (Furlong et al. 2002). A shown in Table 21.1, the factor analysis suggests four relatively independent subscales assessing affective, cognitive, and behavioral components of anger.

In another study using an independent sample of Australian adolescents, Boman, Curtis, Furlong, and D. Smith (2006) replicated the MSAI's factor structure. The Cronbach's alpha coefficients in this sample were acceptable (see Table 21.1). Moreover, a Rasch analysis was undertaken to further explore the measurement properties of the MSAI. Aside from Positive Coping, which yielded more modest measurement properties, all remaining subscales demonstrated sound psychometric characteristics. Additionally, the EFA replicated the original MSAI factor structure, with one qualification that the Anger Experience item referring to reactions to a "teacher's pet" had a low factor loading (.26) in this Australian sample. A CFA (AMOS 5.0) provided support for the 4-factor MSAI structure with reasonable fit statistics (RMSEA .039–.043).

The MSAI's predictive validity was examined in a study by Boman, Smith, and Curtis (2003) who found that Australian secondary students who manifested helpless atttributional styles and a general sense of pessimism were more likely on the MSAI to express higher levels of anger and greater hostility toward school, and were more likely to endorse acts of destructive expression. In a related study, Boman and Yates (2001) found that students who entered high school with expectations for negative outcomes also demonstrated high levels of hostility as measured by the MSAI.

Recent Studies Using the MSAI

Since its development, the MSAI has been used to examine youths' school-related anger experiences in Australia (Boman, 2003; Boman, Curtis, Furlong, & D. Smith, 2006), Guatemala (Furlong et al., 2004), Iran (Aryadoust, Akbarzadeh, & Akbarzadeh, 2011; Ghanizadeh, 2008; Ghanizadeh & Haghigh, 2010), Japan (Bear, Uribe-Zarain, Manning, & Shiomi, 2009), Philippines (Campano & Munakata, 2004), Peru (Furlong et al., 2004), Uruguay (Cajigas, Kahan, Luzardo & Mungay, 2010), and Vietnam (Barker, Grefe, Burns, & DiGiuseppe, R. (2008). As shown in Table 21.1, these studies reported favorable reliability and validity characteristics across cultural contexts.

The MSAI offers researchers and practitioners an efficient and psychometrically sound instrument for identifying students with anger-related problems in school settings. One of the strengths of the scale, with regard to assessing a youth's emotional status, is its specific application to the school context. Another is its multidimensional framework, which allows researchers and practitioners to attend to affective, cognitive, and behavioral components of anger among school-age youth. Such a distinction may have significant implications for anger management strategies and interventions. Additional research is needed to evaluate the utility of the MSAI for this and other purposes within school settings. The authors recommend that the MSAI is best used as part of a comprehensive assessment battery, which evaluates not only angry feelings, attitudes, and behaviors, but also the context and setting in which these occur.

Summary and Recommendations for Practitioners

This chapter reviewed several instruments designed to measure aspects of anger and hostility in school-age youth. Prior research has linked each of these constructs to a variety of negative physical, interpersonal, academic, and behavioral outcomes. More important, chronic anger and hostility have been related to aggressive behavior, both within and outside school settings. As such, individual levels of anger and hostility should be considered in any school-based threat assessment. A number of professional organizations have, in fact, published lists of risk factors or warning signs that include chronic anger and hostility among other key factors.

Despite these encouraging research findings, it is cautioned that assessment of anger and hostility, particularly in the school context, is still in its early stages and the vast majority of contemporary instruments rely almost exclusively upon self-report. Additionally, both anger and hostility are highly personalized experiences, often beyond the purview of informed adults such as parents or teachers. Angry feelings and hostile attitudes are often confused with aggressive behavior, which is much more observable. Students who may be developing chronic, cynical attitudes about school, family, and community may not aggressively act out these developing beliefs, but they are nonetheless often in need of counseling and other support services.

The anger assessments reviewed in this chapter are resources that can be used as part of a school-wide screening process (Dowdy, Furlong, Eklund, Saeki, & Ritchey, 2010), for the assessment of youth with emotional and behavioral disorders (Bowers, 2005), or for the evaluation of school-based anger management interventions (see Feindler, Meghan, & Garber, this volume; Larson & Lochman, 2010). In this latter regard, anger management programs for youth have proliferated within school settings in recent years and anger assessment inventories, particularly of the type reviewed in this chapter, offer the promise of matching discreet intervention strategies to the specific needs of individual students. Assessment of anger and hostility is also important if educators are to understand what motivates student behavior at school from everyday conflicts/hassles to more serious acts of violence. A summary of anger assessment implications for practitioners is included in Table 21.2 and online information is provided in Table 21.3.

Table 21.2 Anger Assessment in School Settings: Implications for Practitioners

- Anger is a multidimensional construct with affective, cognitive, and behavioral dimensions.
- Anger, hostility, and aggression constitute separate but related factors and instruments that assess all three core constructs are important to include in any assessment.
- Youth self-report anger instruments should not be used to screen for student who might be considered at risk for future violence. These assessments have not been validated for this purpose. A comprehensive threat assessment strategy is the suggested best practice (see Allen, Cornell, Lorek, & Sheras, 2008).
- Whenever a student's experience and/or expression of anger rises to the level of causing concern among school staff, first consider if there is any reason to suspect that the youth may be a danger to himself/herself or to others. That is, consider if there is a psychological emergency and address it.
- Always consider a youth's anger expression within the broader context of his or her school and nonschool interpersonal relationships.
- Anger can be an expression that a person feels that he or she has been mistreated, experienced some personal or social injustice, or been treated unfairly. Part of the assessment should explore the student's experiences of teasing, taunting, or social bias at school.
- Assessment of anger should be considered as part of a comprehensive evaluation of both externalizing and internalizing disorders in children.
- Comprehensive assessment of anger and related constructs should include not only within child characteristics and behaviors but aspects of the environment as well. Assessments are potentially of vital importance in determining the function of anger and possible related aggression in a student's life.
- Multidimensional assessment of anger can provide specific directions for intervention efforts because it calls attention to all children, not just outwardly aggressive students (see Feindler, Meghan, & Gerber, 2011, this volume; Gansle, 2007; Larson & Lochman, 2010).

Table 21.3 Online Access Information About the Anger Instruments

1.	State–Trait Anger Expression Inventory-2 Child/Adolescent
	http://www4.parinc.com/Products/Product.aspx?ProductID=STAXI-2C/A
2.	Aggression Questionnaire
	http://portal.wpspublish.com/portal/page?_pageid=53,70400&_dad=portal&_schema=PORTAL
3.	Adolescent Anger Rating Scale
	http://www4.parinc.com/Products/Product.aspx?ProductID=AARS
4.	Multidimensional School Anger Inventory
	http://web.me.com/michaelfurlong/MJF-Home/MSAI%E2%80%93School_Anger_Inventory.html

References

Allen, K., Cornell, D., Lorek, E., & Sheras, P. (2008). Response of school personnel to student threat assessment training. *School Effectiveness and School Improvement, 19,* 319–332. doi:10.1080/09243450802332184

American Psychological Association. (1999). *The American Psychological Association, MTV: Music Television and Media One respond to recent school shootings with youth forum focusing on warning signs of violence.* Retrieved November 30, 2010, from http://www.highbeam.com/doc/1G1-54445913.html

Ang, R. P. (2007). Factor structure of the 12-item aggression questionnaire: Further evidence from Asian adolescent samples. *Journal of Adolescence, 30,* 671–685. doi:10.1016/j.adolescence.2006.05.003

Armstead, C. A., & Clark, R. (2002). Assessment of self-reported anger expression in pre- and early-adolescent African Americans: Psychometric considerations. *Journal of Adolescence, 25,* 365–371. doi:10.1006/jado.2002.0481

Aryadoust, S. V., Akbarzadeh, S., & Akbarzadeh, S. (2011). Psychometric characteristics of the Persian version of the Multidimensional School Anger Inventory–Revised. *Asian Pacific Journal of Education, 31,* 51–64. doi:10.1080/02188791.2011.544070

Barefoot, J. C., & Boyle, S. H. (2009). Hostility and proneness to anger. In M. R. Leary & R. H. Hoyle (Eds.), *Handbook of individual differences in social behavior* (pp. 210–226). New York, NY: Guilford.

Barker, K. A., Grefe, C. N., Burns, E. M., & DiGiuseppe, R. (2008). Assessing anger and aggression in Vietnamese adolescents and cross-culturally. *Collaborative Research Journal of School Psychology* (May), 23–38. Available from http://www.stjohns.edu/academics/.../4171249182cb4c3a995306595ad75283.pdf

Bear, G. B., Uribe-Zarain, X., Manning, M. A., & Shiomi, K. (2009). Shame, guilt, blaming, and anger: Differences between children in Japan and the US. *Motivation and Emotion, 33,* 229–238. doi:10.1007/s11031-009-9130-8

Bolgar, M. R., Janelle, C., & Giacobbi, P. R., Jr. (2008). Trait anger, appraisal, and coping differences among adolescent tennis players. *Journal of Applied Sport Psychology, 20,* 73–87. doi:10.1080/10413200701790566

Boman, P. (2003). Gender differences in school anger. *International Education Journal, 4,* 71–77.

Boman, P., Curtis, D., Furlong, M. J., & Smith, D. C. (2006). Cross-validation and Rasch analyses of the Australian version of the Multidimensional School Anger Inventory-Revised. *Journal of Psychoeducational Assessment, 24,* 225–242. doi.org/10.1177/0734282906288472

Boman, P., Smith, D. C., & Curtis, D. (2003). Effects of pessimism and explanatory style on development of anger in children. *School Psychology International, 24,* 80–94. doi:10.1177/0143034303024001581

Boman. P., & Yates, G. (2001). Optimism, hostility, and adjustment in the first year of high school. *British Journal of Educational Psychology, 71,* 401–412.

Bongard, S., al'Absi, M., & Lovallo, W. R. (1998). Interaction effects of hostility and anger expression on cardiovascular reactivity. *International Journal of Psychophysiology, 28,* 181–191.

Bowers, T. (2005). The forgotten 'E' on EBD. In P. Clough, P. Garner, J. T. Pardeck, & F. Yuen (Eds.), *Handbook of behavioral and emotional difficulties* (pp. 83–102). Thousand Oaks, CA: Sage.

Brunner, T. M., & Spielberger, C. D. (2010). *STAXI-2 C/A: State-Trait Anger Expression Inventory Child and Adolescent: Professional manual.* Odessa, FL: Psychological Assessment Resources.

Burney, D. M. (2008). *The Adolescent Anger Rating Scale: Its initial development and validation.* Lampeter Ceredigion, England: Edwin Mellen Press.

Burney, D. M., & Kromrey, J. (2001). Initial development and score validation of the Adolescent Anger Rating Scale. *Educational and Psychological Measurement, 61,* 446–460. doi:10.1177/00131640121971310

Burns, J. W., & Katkin, E. S. (1993). Psychological, situational, and gender predictors of cardiovascular reactivity to stress: A multivariate approach. *Journal of Behavioral Medicine, 16,* 445–465. doi:10.1007/BF00844816

Buss, A. H., & Durkee, A. (1957). An inventory for assessing different kinds of hostility. *Journal of Consulting Psychology, 21,* 343–349.

Buss, A. H., & Perry, M. (1992). The Aggression Questionnaire. *Journal of Personality and Social Psychology, 63,* 452–459.

Buss, A. H., & Warren, W. L. (2000). *Aggression Questionnaire: Manual.* Los Angeles, CA: Western Psychological Services.

Cajigas, N., Kahan, E., Luzardo, M., & Mungay, M. (2010). *Informe final. Resultados preliminares segunda parte. Prevalencias de las escalas de agresión entre pares, depresión, autoestima, clima y seguridad escolares, ira en contexto escolar y sentido de pertenencia al liceo* [Final Report. Preliminary Results Part II. Prevalence rates of peer aggression,depression, self esteem, school climate and safety, anger in the school context and sense of belonging to high school]. Montevideo, Uruguay: Administración Nacional de Educación Pública (ANEP) Area de Perfeccionamiento Docente y Estudios Superiores.

Camodeca, M., & Goossens, F. A. (2005). Aggression, social cognitions, anger and sadness in bullies and victims. *Journal of Child Psychology and Psychiatry, 46,* 186–197. doi:10.1111/j.1469-7610.2004.00347.x

Campano, J. P., & Munakata, T. (2004). Anger and aggression among Filipino students. *Adolescence, 39,* 757–764.

Cautin, R. L., Overholser, J. C., & Goetz, P. (2001). Assessment of mode of anger expression in adolescent psychiatric inpatients. *Adolescence, 36*(141), 163–170. http://findarticles.com/p/articles/mi_m2248/is_141_36/ai_76498126/

Chida, Y., & Steptoe, A. (2009). The association of anger and hostility with future coronary heart disease. *Journal of the American College of Cardiology, 53,* 936–946. doi:10.1016/j.jacc.2008.11.044

Cornell, D. (2003). Guidelines for responding to student threats of violence. *Journal of Educational Administration, 41,* 705–719.

Cornell, D. G. (2006). *School violence: Fears versus facts.* Mahwah, NJ: Erlbaum.

Cornell, D. G., & Allen, K. (2011). Development, evaluation, and future directions of the Virginia student threat assessment guidelines. *Journal of School Violence, 10,* 88–106. doi: 10.1080/15388220.2010.519432.

Cornell, D., Sheras, P., Gregory, A., & Fan, X. (2009). A retrospective study of school safety conditions in high schools using the Virginia threat assessment guidelines versus alternative approaches. *School Psychology Quarterly, 24,* 119–129. doi:10.1037/a0016182

Deffenbacher, J. L., Huff, M. E., Lynch, R. S., Oetting, E. R., & Salvatore, N. F. (2000). Characteristics and treatment of high-anger drivers. *Journal of Counseling Psychology, 47,* 5–17. doi: 10.1037/0022-0167.47.1.5

del Barrio, V., Aluja, A., & Spielberger, C. (2004). Anger assessment with the STAXI-CA: Psychometric properties of a new instrument for children and adolescents. *Personality and Individual Differences, 37,* 227–244. doi:10.1016/j.paid.2003.08.014

Del Vecchio, T., & O'Leary, K. D. (2004). The effectiveness of anger treatments for specific anger problems: A meta-analytic review. *Clinical Psychology Review, 24,* 15–34. doi:10.1016/j.cpr.2003.09.006

Dodge, K. A. (1993) Social-cognitive mechanisms in the development of conduct disorder and depression. *Annual Review of Psychology, 44,* 559–584. doi:10.1146/annurev.ps.44.020193.003015.

Dowdy, E., Furlong, M., Eklund, K., Saeki, E., & Ritchey, K. (2010). Screening for mental health and wellness: Current school-based practices and emerging possibilities. In B. Doll & B. Pfohl (Eds.), *Handbook of prevention science* (pp. 70–95). New York, NY: Routledge.

Dwyer, K., Osher. D., & Warger, C. (1998). *Early warning, timely response: A guide to safe schools*. Washington, DC: U.S. Department of Education.

Eftekhari, A., Turner, A. P., & Larimer, M. E. (2004). Anger expression, coping, and substance use in adolescent offenders. *Addictive Behaviors, 29,* 1001–1008.

Elbogen, E. B., Wagner, H. R., Fuller, S. R., Calhoun, P. S., Kinneer, P. M., & Beckham, J. C. (2010). Correlates of anger and hostility in Iraq and Afghanistan war veterans. *American Journal of Psychiatry, 16,* 1051–1058. doi:10.1176/appl.ajp.2010.09050739

Everson, S. A., Goldberg, D. E., Kaplan, G. A., Cohen, R. D., Pukkala, E., Tuomilehto, J., & Salonen, J. T. (1996). Hopelessness and risk of mortality and incidence of myocardial infarction and cancer. *Psychosomatic Medicine, 58,* 113–121. doi: 10.1097/01.psy58371.50240

Fossati, A., Maffei, C., Acquarini, E., & Di Ceglie, A. (2003). Multigroup confirmatory component and factor analyses of the Italian version of the aggression questionnaire. *European Journal of Psychological Assessment, 19,* 54–65. doi:10.1027//1015-5759.19.1.54

Friedman, H. S. (1991). *The self-healing personality: Why some people achieve health and others succumb to illness.* New York, NY: Holt.

Furlong, M. J., Bates, M. P., Smith, D. C., & Kingery, P. (Eds.). (2004). *Appraisal and prediction of school violence: Issues, methods and contexts.* Hauppauge, NY: Nova Science.

Furlong, M. J., & Smith, D. C. (1994). Assessment of youth's anger, hostility, and aggression using self-report and rating scales. In M. J. Furlong & D. C. Smith (Eds.), *Anger, hostility, and aggression: Assessment, prevention and intervention strategies for youth* (pp. 167–244). New York, NY: Wiley.

Furlong, M. J., & Smith, D. C. (1998). Raging Rick to tranquil Tom: An empirically based multi-dimensional anger typology for adolescent males. *Psychology in the Schools, 35,* 229–245. doi:10.1002/(SICI)1520-6807(199807)35:3<229::AID-PITS4>3.0.CO;2-I

Furlong, M. J., Smith, D. C., & Bates, M. P. (2002). Further development of the Multidimensional School Anger Inventory: Construct validation, extension to female adolescents, and preliminary norms. *Journal of Psychoeducational Assessment, 20,* 46–65. doi:10.1177/073428290202000104

Furlong, M. J., Smith, D. C., Boman, P., Gonzalez, M., Grazioso, M. P., & Merino Soto, C. (2004, July). *Multidimensional School Anger Inventory: A cross-national comparison.* Poster presented at the annual meeting of the American Psychological Association, Honolulu, HI.

Gambetti, E., & Giusberti, F. (2009). Trait anger and anger expression style in children's risky decisions. *Aggressive Behavior, 35,* 14–23. doi:10.1002/ab.20285

Gansle, K. (2007). The effectiveness of school-based anger interventions and programs: A meta-analysis. *Journal of School Psychology, 33,* 321–341. doi.org/10.1016/j.jsp.2005.07.002

Ghanizadeh, A. (2008). Gender difference of school anger dimensions and its prediction for suicidal behavior in adolescents. *International Journal of Clinical and Health Psychology, 8,* 525–535. doi:10.1186/1753-2000-4-4

Ghanizadeh, A., & Haghigh, H. B. (2010). How do ADHD children perceive their cognitive, affective, and behavioral aspects of anger expression in school setting? *Child & Adolescent Psychiatry & Mental Health, 4,* 4. doi: 10.1186/1753-2000-4-4

Golden, S. H., Williams, J. E., Ford, D. E., Yeh, H-C., Paton-Sanford, C., Javier-Nieto, F., & Brancati, F. L. (2006). Anger temperament is modestly associated with the risk of type 2 diabetes mellitus: The atherosclerosis risk in communities study. *Psychoneuroendocrinology, 31,* 325–332.

Heavey, C. L., Adelman, H. S., Nelson, P., & Smith, D. C. (1989). Learning problems, anger, perceived control, and misbehavior. *Journal of Learning Disabilities, 22,* 46–59.

Hinshaw, S. P. (1992). Academic underachievement, attention deficits, and aggression: Comorbidity and implications for intervention. *Journal of Consulting and Clinical Psychology, 60,* 893–903. doi: 10.1037/0022-006X.60.6.893.

Julkunen, J., Salonen, R., Kaplan, G. A., Chesney, M. A., & Salonen. J. T. (1994). Hostility and the progression of carotid artheroslerosis. *Psychosomatic Medicine, 56,* 519–525.

Kerr, M. A., & Schneider, B. H. (2008). Anger expression in children and adolescents: A review of the empirical literature. *Clinical Psychology Review, 28,* 559–577. doi:10.1016/j.cpr.2007.08.001

Larson, J., & Lochman, J. E. (2010). *Helping schoolchildren cope with anger: A cognitive-behavioral intervention.* New York, NY: Guilford.

Libbey, H. P., Story, M. T., Neumark-Sztainer, D. R., & Boutelle, K. N. (2008). Teasing, disordered eating behaviors, and psychological morbidities among overweight adolescents. *Obesity, 16*(2), S24–S29. doi:10.1038/oby.2008.455

Liu, J., Zhou, Y., & Gu, W. (2009). Reliability and validity of Chinese version of Buss-Perry Aggression Questionnaire in adolescents. *Chinese Journal of Clinical Psychology, 17,* 449–451.

Martin, R., Watson, D., & Wan, C. K. (2000). A three-factor model of trait anger: Dimensions of affect, behavior, and cognition. *Journal of Personality, 68,* 869–897. doi:10.1111/1467-6494.00119

Maxwell, J. P., Sukhodolsky, D. G., & Sit, C. H. P. (2009). Preliminary validation of a Chinese version of the State-Trait Anger Expression Inventory-2. *Asian Journal of Social Psychology, 12,* 1–11. doi:10.1111/j.1467-839X.2008.01264.x

McDermott, M. R., Ramsay, J., & Bray, C. (2001). Components of the anger–hostility complex as risk-factors for coronary artery disease severity: A multi-measure study. *Journal of Health Psychology, 6,* 309–319. doi:10.1177/135910530100600304

Miller, T. Q., Smith, T. W., Turner, C. W., Guijarro., M. L., & Hallett, A. J. (1996). A meta-analytic review of research on hostility and physical health. *Psychological Bulletin, 19,* 322–348. doi:10.1037/0033-2909.119.2.322

Mills, P. L., Schneider, R. H., & Dimsdale, J. E. (1989). Anger assessment and reactivity to stress. *Journal of Psychosomatic Research, 33,* 379–382. doi.org/10.1016/0022-3999(89)90028-7

Musante, L., MacDougall, J. M., Dembroski, T. M., & Costa, P. T. (1989). Potential for hostility and dimensions of anger. *Health Psychology, 8,* 343–354. http://dx.doi.org/10.1037/0278-6133.8.3.343

Nichols, T. R., Birnbaum, A. S., Bryant, K., & Botvin, G. J. (2009). Lunchtime practices and problem behaviors among multiethnic urban youth. *Health Education Behavior, 36,* 570–582.

Novaco, R. W. (2003). Novaco Anger Scale and Provocation Inventory (NAS-PI). Los Angeles, CA: Western Psychological Services.

O'Toole, M. E. (2000). *The school shooter: A threat assessment perspective.* Quantico, VA: National Center for the Analysis of Violent Crime, Federal Bureau of Investigation.

Phillips, A. C., & Hughes, B. M. (2011). Introductory paper: Cardiovascular reactivity at a crossroads: Where are we now? *Biological Psychology, 86,* 95–97. doi: 10.1016/biopsycho2010.03.003

Potegal, M., Stemmier, G., & Spielberger, C. E. (Eds.). (2010). *International handbook of anger* (pp. 403–412). New York, NY: Springer. doi:10.1007/978-0-387-89676-2

Reddy. M., Borum, R., Berglund. J., Vossekuil, B., Fein, R., & Modzeleski, W. (2001). Evaluating risk for targeted violence in schools: Comparing risk assessment, threat assessment, and other approaches. *Psychology in the Schools. 38,* 157–172. doi:10.1002/pits.1007

Reyes, L. R., Meininger, J. C., Liehr, P., Chan, W., & Mueller, W. H. (2003). Anger in adolescents: Gender, ethnicity, age differences and psychometric properties. *Nursing Research, 52,* 2–11.

Rucklidge, J. J. (2006). Psychosocial functioning of adolescents with and without pediatric bipolar disorder. *Journal of Affective Disorders, 91,* 181–188. doi:10.1016/j.jad.2006.01.001

Santisteban, C., Alvarado, J. M., & Recio, P. (2007). Evaluation of a Spanish version of the Buss and Perry Aggression Questionnaire: Some personal and situational factors related to the aggression scores of young subjects. *Personality and Individual Differences, 42,* 1453–1465. doi:10.1016/j.paid.2006.10.019

Schultz, D., Brodack, A., & Izard, C. E. (2010). State and trait anger, fear, and social information processing. In M. Potegal, G. Stemmier, & C. E. Spielberger (Eds.), *International handbook of anger* (pp. 311–325). New York, NY: Springer. doi:10.1007/978-0-387-89676-2_18

Schwinn, T. M., Schinker, S. P., & Trent, D. N. (2010). Substance use among late adolescent urban youths: Mental health and gender influences. *Addictive Behaviors, 35,* 30–34. doi: 10.1016/j.addbeh.2009.08.005

Siegel, J. M. (1986). The Multidimensional Anger Inventory. *Journal of Personality and Social Psychology, 51,* 191-200. doi: 10.1037/0022-3514.51.1.191

Smith, D. C., Furlong. M. J., Bates, M., & Laughlin, J. (1998). Development of the Multidimensional School Anger Inventory for males. *Psychology in the Schools, 35,* 1–15. doi:10.1002/(SICI)1520-6807(199801)35:1<1::AID-PITS1>3.0.CO;2-U

Smith, T. W. (1994). Concepts and methods in the study of anger, hostility, and health. In A. W. Siegman & T. W. Smith (Eds.), *Anger, hostility and the heart* (pp. 23–42). Hillsdale, NJ: Erlbaum.

Smith, T. W., & Ruiz, J. M. (2002). Psychosocial influences on the development and course of coronary heart disease: Current status and implications for research and practice. *Journal of Consulting and Clinical Psychology, 70,* 548–568. doi:10.1037/0022-006X.70.3.548

Spielberger, C. D. (1999). *STAXI-2: State-Trait Anger Expression Inventory-2: Professional manual.* Odessa, FL: Psychological Assessment Resources.

Spielberger, C. D., Johnson, E. H., Russell, S. F., Crane, R. J., Jacobs, G. A., & Worden, T. J. (1985). The experience and expression of anger: Construction and validation of an anger expression scale. In M. A. Chesney & R. H. Rosenman (Eds.), *Anger and hostility in cardiovascular and behavioral disorders* (pp. 5–30). New York, NY: Hemisphere/McGraw-Hill.

Spielberger, C. D., & Reheiser, F. C. (2010). The nature and measurement of anger. In M. Potegal, G. Stemmier, & C. E. Spielberger (Eds.), *International handbook of anger* (pp. 403–412). New York, NY: Springer. doi:10.1007/978-0-387-89676-2_23

Spielberger, C. D., Reheiser, F. C., & Sydeman, S. J. (1995). Measuring the experience, expression, and control of anger. In H. Kassinove (Ed.), *Anger disorders: Definition, diagnosis, and treatment* (pp. 49–67). Washington, DC: Taylor & Francis.

Steele, R. G., Legerski, J. P., Nelson, T. D., & Phipps, S. (2009). The anger expression scale for children: Initial validation among healthy children and children with cancer. *Journal of Pediatric Psychology, 34*, 51–62.

Thomas, D. E., Coard, S. I., Stevenson, H. C., Bentley, K., & Zamel, P. (2009). Racial and emotional factors predicting teachers' perceptions of classroom behavioral maladjustment for urban African American male youth. *Psychology in the Schools, 46*, 184–196. doi:10.1002/pits.20362

Thomas. S. P. (Ed.). (1993). *Women and anger.* New York, NY: Springer.

Thomas. S. P., & Williams, R. (1991). Perceived stress, trait anger, modes of anger expression and health status of college men and women. *Nursing Research, 40*, 303–307. pmid:1896331

Walters, G. D., Ronen, T., & Rosenbaum, M. (2010). The latent structure of childhood aggression: A taxometric analysis of self-reported and teacher-rated aggression in Israeli schoolchildren. *Psychological Assessment, 22*, 628–637. doi:10.1037/a0019779

Williams, J. E. (2010). Anger/hostility and cardiovascular disease. In M. Potegal, G. Stemmier, & C. E. Spielberger (Eds.), *International handbook of anger* (pp. 435–447). New York, NY: Springer. doi:10.1007/978-0-387-89676-2_25

Wyatt, L. W., & Haskett, M. E. (2001). Aggressive and nonaggressive young adolescents' attributions of intent in teacher/student interactions. *The Journal of Early Adolescence, 21*, 425–446. doi:10.1177/0272431601021004003

22
Assessment of Bullying

Dewey Cornell

CURRY SCHOOL OF EDUCATION, UNIVERSITY OF VIRGINIA

Joanna C. M. Cole

BOSTON UNIVERSITY SCHOOL OF MEDICINE

Abstract

Despite a large body of research, the field of bullying still needs standard, reliable, and independently validated measures for determining whether a student has been bullied (or has bullied others). This chapter reviews seven common problems with bullying surveys and makes recommendations for improved measurement and validation efforts. A systematic program of research is needed to compare bullying surveys with independent criteria and to assess their sensitivity, specificity, positive predictive power, and negative predictive power.

Assessment is the Achilles heel of bullying research and prevention efforts. Scientific progress is not possible in any field without standardized, reliable, and valid measurement of key constructs, and no intervention program can claim successful reduction in something it cannot accurately measure. Despite the tremendous increase in the study of bullying and efforts to reduce it in schools over the past decade, there continues insufficient evidence for the validity of the survey measures which are the principal means of assessing its prevalence. This chapter will review seven common problems that plague the assessment of bullying—both bullying others and being bullied—and recommend more rigorous standards for identifying students involved in bullying.

Problems in the Assessment of Bullying

(1) Definition of Bullying

In public health fields, it is axiomatic that one must have a standard definition of the problem, disease, or condition under study. However, efforts to study bullying are limited by a lack of consensus and consistency in defining this complex and abstract concept (Cornell & Bandyopadhyay, 2010a; Furlong, Sharkey, Felix, Tanigawa, & Green, 2010; Swearer, Espelage, Vaillancourt, & Hymel, 2010). Bullying is a form of aggressive behavior that must be distinguished from the full range and variety of peer aggression and victimization. Although it is common for children to tease, argue, and even fight with one another, the concept of bullying is intended to identify a particularly troubling form of peer aggression in which an identifiable victim is subject to repeated humiliation by a dominant aggressor. Unless this distinction is maintained, researchers and educators run the risk of obtaining inflated estimates of the prevalence of bullying. Moreover, interventions for bullying differ from those designed to resolve conflicts or mediate disputes between peers of comparable power or status (Olweus, Limber, & Mihalic, 1999).

Many authorities agree that there are three criteria for bullying: (a) action that intentionally causes harm or distress to the victim, (b) an imbalance of power between the aggressor and the victim, and (c) the harmful action occurs repeatedly (Furlong et al., 2010; Olweus, 1991; Swearer et al., 2010). Although most studies define bullying as an intentionally harmful act, many fail to restrict the term to situations that involve an imbalance of power and repetitive occurrence.

For example, a recent national study of child victimization in the United States (Finkelhor, Turner, Ormrod, & Hamby, 2010) did not present a definition of bullying, but measured bullying with two items (Finkelhor, Hamby, Ormrod, & Turner, 2004): (a) "In the last year, did any kids, even a brother or sister, pick on you by chasing you or grabbing your hair or clothes or by making you do something you didn't want to do?" and (b) "In the last year, did you get scared or feel really bad because kids were calling you names, saying mean things to you, or saying they didn't want you around?" These items appear to have good psychometric qualities as part of a general assessment of child victimization, but do not encompass the full range of bullying and do not distinguish bullying from other forms of peer conflict. Nevertheless, results from this study were used to report a nationwide decline in bullying (Finkelhor et al., 2010).

The Youth Risk Behavior Survey (YRBS) is administered in thousands of U.S. schools every year and used by the Centers for Disease Control and Prevention (CDC) to monitor national trends for a multitude of health-related behaviors. This survey asks students, "During the past 12 months, have you ever been bullied on school property?" with no definition of bullying (U.S. Department of Health and Human Services, 2009). A summary report of the methodology of this survey (Brener, McManus, Galuska, Lowry, & Wechsler, 2003) contains no information on the reliability or validity of questions about bullying. The only study that attempted to confirm the accuracy of YRBS self-reports concerned student height and weight. This study found that students, on average, over-reported their height by 2.7 inches (Brener et al., 2004).

Another well-respected national assessment of bullying is provided by the School Crime Supplement (SCS) of the National Crime Victimization Survey (DeVoe & Bauer, 2010). This survey is conducted by an interviewer who provides students with a broad definition of bullying: "Now I have some questions about what students do at school that make you feel bad or are hurtful to you. We often refer to this as being bullied. You may include events you told me about already." The surveyor asks "During this school year, has any student bullied you?" This definition contains no language that distinguishes bullying from other forms of peer conflict, such as arguments between friends of comparable power or status. The survey then inquires about seven different forms of aggressive behavior that also do not distinguish bullying from any other kind of peer conflict. For example, the survey asks "That is, has another student: (a) made fun of you, called you names, or insulted you? (b) spread rumors about you? (c) threatened you with harm? (d), pushed you, shoved you, tripped you, or spit on you?…"

It is not feasible to compare results from surveys that use broad definitions of bullying with those that use a more restrictive definition. For example, a nationally representative study by the National Institute of Child Health and Human Development (Wang, Iannotti, & Nansel, 2009) used the revised Olweus Bully/Victim Questionnaire (BVQ: Olweus, 1996), which has a detailed definition of bullying that specifically excludes situations "when two students of about the same strength or power argue or fight." Vaillancourt and colleagues (2010) demonstrated that students were less likely to report being bullied when provided with this kind of more specific definition. Kert, Codding, Tryon, and Shiyko (2009) found that students who completed surveys that presented an adaptation of the Olweus definition of bullying and used the term "bully" reported significantly less bullying of others than students completing surveys that did not employ the term or a definition.

(2) Student Understanding of Bullying

Most assessment instruments rely on student reports of bullying, but consider the difficulty for students in deciding whether they have observed or experienced some form of bullying. The concept of bullying encompasses physical, verbal, and social behaviors, but must occur in a context of the aggressor having power or dominance over the victim. The difference in power may be a function of physical size, as in the stereotype of the "big bully" who physically dominates a smaller victim, but more subtle forms of social bullying may occur when the aggressor has an advantage in social status or popularity. The power imbalance between bully and victim could result simply from a disparity in self-confidence or verbal skills.

Physical bullying seems most easy to identify because it involves discrete acts of violence and can be readily observed. However, physical bullying often involves the threat of violence, and threats can be conveyed in words or even implied with a gesture or a glance. Verbal bullying refers to statements that tease or insult the victim, but do not threaten physical injury. Social or relational bullying may be the most varied and indirect form of bullying because it involves the manipulation of friendship patterns and social interactions to demean or exclude the victim from peers (Bjorkqvist, Lagerspetz, & Kaukinian, 1992; Crick & Grotpeter, 1995; Olweus, 1991). All of these varied forms of bullying require students to make judgments that might not be reliable or valid.

A related problem is that bullying must be intentionally harmful behavior. As a result, it can be difficult to distinguish bullying from playful behavior or other actions not intended to cause harm. Common horseplay and teasing among friends can seem like bullying to an observer. Even the participants may have differing perceptions of their behavior; teasing remarks can be misunderstood or taken more seriously than they were intended, and sometimes playful wrestling can escalate into physical bullying. Accused bullies may rely on the defense that they were "just playing around" or "didn't mean" what they said.

There is little research demonstrating that students have an adequate understanding of the complex concept of bullying and apply that understanding accurately in completing self-report surveys. Several studies suggest that students report lower rates of bullying when they complete surveys that contain a detailed definition of bullying (Kert et al., 2009; Vaillancourt et al., 2010). Even brief educational interventions can have an impact on bullying reports. A study by Baly and Cornell (2011) randomly assigned classrooms of middle school students to watch or not watch a 6-minute instructional video about bullying that stressed the power imbalance present in bullying as distinguished from ordinary peer conflict. Although all surveys included a definition of bullying adapted from Olweus (1996), students who watched the video were 48% less likely to report being socially bullied. Boys who watched the video were 54% less likely to report physical bullying. Researchers are careful to train behavioral observers to achieve reliability in identifying bullying (e.g., Frey et al., 2005), but do not assess whether students can use the concept reliably. Vaillancourt et al. (2010) asked students to give their own definitions of bullying and found that, whereas almost all (92%) of the students included some mention of negative behavior in their definition, relatively few (26%) included the idea of a power imbalance. These observations suggest that an adequate measure of bullying must encompass several different forms of bullying as well as the ability to distinguish bullying from ordinary peer conflict between students of relatively equal status.

(3) Timeframe for Bullying

A third problem in bullying assessment concerns the appropriate time period and frequency for questions about bullying. Surveys vary in asking about bullying in the past month, several months, or last year. Furlong and colleagues (2010) recommend asking students about experiences in the past month rather than longer time periods for which their memory might be less accurate. However, the timeframe for recalling events may influence student responses in unexpected ways. For example, Morrison and Furlong (2002) compared two versions of the California School Climate and Safety Survey inquiring about the past 30 days versus the past year. Surprisingly, for many items students reported *more* victim experiences in the past 30 days than in the past year. Perhaps the timeframe of the question affects the standards that students use to judge whether an event qualifies for reporting, and a shorter timeframe prompts students to consider less serious, more frequent events.

Surveys also vary in whether they ask about the frequency of bullying and in the cut-off point used to qualify as bullying. Solberg and Olweus (2003) recommended a frequency of "2 or 3 times a month or more" (p. 247). Their determination of this cut-off is based on analyses showing that students who endorse bullying at this frequency tend to be more reliably different from students who endorse less frequent bullying when compared on self-report measures of depressive tendencies, self-esteem, and feelings of acceptance by classmates.

(4) Scale Composition

There are potential discrepancies among surveys that rely on single items to measure the prevalence of bullying and those that use multiple items. From a psychometric perspective, multiple-item scales are likely to be more reliable than single-item measures. Olweus (personal communication, August 15, 2010) reported an Item Response Theory (IRT) analysis on Norwegian students that supported use of a scale constructed of eight questions about specific forms of bullying others (verbal, physical, and indirect/relational) on the Revised Olweus Bullying Questionnaire (OBQ). Olweus has also analyzed data on a large sample (> 76,000) of U.S. students in grades 4–11 showing a Cronbach's alpha of .87 for a 10-item scale that included questions about the conventional physical, verbal, and relational forms of bullying, as well as bullying involving extortion, race, and sexual meaning, and also bullying through electronic communication (cyberbullying) (Olweus, personal communication August 15, 2010).

A natural question is how reports on multiple-item scales compare to use of single items. One study (Vaillancourt et al., 2010) found that the global, single-item questions about bullying others and being a victim of bullying used in the Olweus Bully/Victim Questionnaire yielded good specificity but poor sensitivity when compared to questions asking students about specific types of physical, verbal, social, and cyberbullying. In other words, many students denied being bullied or bullying others on the initial, global questions, but then admitted being bullied or bullying others in response to one of the more specific questions. It remains unclear whether multiple items about specific types of bullying are more accurate or perhaps over-inclusive in their assessment of bullying. Furthermore, why do some students fail to recognize the logical inconsistency between denying general involvement in bullying, yet admitting involvement in a specific form of bullying? Perhaps these students do not apply the restrictions in the definition of bullying to the questions about specific forms of bullying or perhaps the descriptions of specific forms of bullying stimulate new recollections of experiences they recognize as bullying.

Alternatively, some students might not comprehend the questions or take care to answer them consistently.

(5) Types of Bullying

Research on bullying has expanded considerably from a core interest in physical and verbal bullying to more indirect, relational or social forms of bullying (Bjorkqvist et al., 1992; Crick & Grotpeter, 1995; Swearer, 2008), and more recently to include the use of electronic communication to engage in bullying, sometimes termed cyberbullying. Varjas, Henrich, and Meyers (2009) found evidence that cyberbullying may constitute a distinct form of victimization compared to other forms of bullying, while physical, verbal and relational bullying seemed more closely related. However, it should be noted that the term "cyberbullying" has been broadly used to identify many inappropriate or undesirable uses of electronic communication (such as heated arguments between peers) that may not meet the basic criteria for bullying (Kowalski, Limber, & Agatston, 2008).

There is also interest in bullying about sexual matters, which can range from overly aggressive flirtation to efforts to humiliate and threaten someone because of perceived sexual orientation. Ashbaugh and Cornell (2008) found that middle school boys as well as girls reported a high rate of sexual harassment in general. More narrowly, Swearer, Turner, Givens, and Pollack (2008) found that American boys teased as being gay (homosexual) reported higher levels of other forms of abusive treatment (such as being physically bullied, attacked, and excluded) than boys who were bullied for other reasons, and most importantly, experienced greater anxiety and depression. A national school climate survey (Kosciw, Diaz, & Greytak, 2008) found that approximately 85% of youth identifying themselves as lesbian, gay, bisexual, or transgender reported some form of bullying as well as other forms of victimization at school.

There is important work to be done in clarifying whether there are meaningful differences among the various forms of bullying sufficient to justify differences in prevention and intervention efforts. It would seem quite unlikely that the great diversity of experiences identified as physical, verbal, social, cyber, and sexual forms of bullying could be psychologically interchangeable, generated by the same causes and producing the same effects on students. Complicating this examination is the observation that many students experience overlapping forms of bullying, and there may be particular combinations or forms of bullying that do not fall neatly into one of our current linguistic categories. Instruments that measure bullying with a definition that encompasses all forms of bullying run the risk of collecting heterogeneous data that obscure important trends and correlations.

There also may be important differences in the frequency, intensity, and duration of bullying that overshadow differences in its form. Most studies currently pay little attention to such differences and simply identify groups of victims, bullies, and in some studies, students who appear to be both bullies and victims (Solberg, Olweus, & Endresen, 2007). The task of differentiating subgroups of bully victims (or perpetrators of bullying) along dimensions of types of bullying as well as frequency, intensity, and duration of each type may outstrip the sample size and measurement capacity of most studies, as well as generate daunting analytic complexity.

(6) Anonymous Versus Confidential Reporting

Even if students understand the concept of bullying, they may be unwilling to report it. Many studies have noted the code of silence that discourages students from identifying bullies or seeking help for bullying (Oliver & Candappa, 2007; Smith & Shu, 2000; Unnever & Cornell, 2004). There is some evidence that students are more willing to seek help for bullying from teachers when they perceive the school climate to be more supportive and believe that teachers will take effective action (Eliot, Cornell, Gregory, & Fan, 2010; Williams & Cornell, 2006).

Many bullying surveys are administered on an anonymous basis because of the belief that students will be more forthcoming (Olweus, 2010; Solberg & Olweus, 2003). On the contrary, several studies challenge the assumption that an anonymous survey is necessary in order for students to admit involvement in bullying. Chan, Myron, & Crawshaw (2005) studied students who were randomly assigned to take a survey anonymously or to write their names on the survey. There were no statistically significant differences in rates of endorsement of behaviors that reflected bullying others and being victims of bullying (i.e., hitting, teasing, and lying about other students) between these two groups. O'Malley, Johnston, Bachman, and Schulenberg (2000) examined differences between anonymous and non-anonymous adolescent reporting of drug use and illegal behaviors (i.e., stealing and weapon carrying) on the Monitoring the Future survey. In this study, one group answered the survey anonymously and the other group was not assured of anonymity and was required to report names and addresses to researchers, but was told that their answers would be confidential. Again there were little or no group differences in endorsement rates for sensitive information.

More studies examining the difference between anonymous and confidential administration of bullying surveys are needed, especially because anonymous survey administration prevents researchers from linking survey results to other student information, such as academic performance. Our research group at the University of Virginia has routinely used data from confidential survey administration to show that reports of bullying involvement are stable over time, correspond to peer perceptions, and predict behavioral and emotional adjustment (Branson & Cornell, 2009; Carlson & Cornell, 2008; Cole, Cornell, & Sheras, 2006; Cornell & Brockenbrough, 2004; McConville & Cornell, 2003).

(7) Survey Screening for Invalid Responses

Another reporting problem is that some students may not take the survey seriously and could engage in either careless or intentionally dishonest responding to survey questions. Because bullying and victimization generally occur in a small percentage of students, careless or inattentive marking by students will increase their frequency (e.g., random responses to a yes-no question will generate a 50% prevalence rate). Provocative adolescents will produce even higher rates if they intentionally choose the most extreme or unexpected response. Furlong, Sharkey, Bates, and Smith (2004) identified a group of respondents on the Youth Risk Behavior Surveillance survey (YRBS) who claimed to have carried a weapon to school six or more times in the past month (the most extreme response). Many of these weapon-carrying students also claimed to exercise every day, eat plenty of carrots, and drink lots of milk, but also to make frequent suicide attempts, use heroin, sniff glue, and take steroids. The researchers concluded that these students gave extreme responses to survey questions regardless of item content.

Validity screening procedures can substantially reduce estimates of the prevalence of student involvement in high-risk behavior such as fights, drug use, and gangs. In a survey of 10,909 middle and high school students, Cornell and Loper (1998) found that one-fourth of the surveys failed to meet validity screening criteria that included detection of students who omitted demographic information, marked a series of items all in the same way, and gave inappropriate answers to validity questions (e.g., answering "No" to "I am telling the truth on this survey"). The deletion of invalid self-report surveys reduced estimates of fighting at school from 29% to 19%, drug use from 25% to 15%, gang membership from 8% to 5%, and carrying a knife at school from 18% to 8%.

Cross and Newman-Gonchar (2004) screened three different school surveys for the presence of inconsistent responses to items with the same content (e.g., answering "never" when asked what age they belonged to a gang and "yes" to the question, "Have you ever belonged to a gang?") and extreme responses (e.g., claiming to have used LSD 20 or more times in the past 30 days). Surveys with three or more inconsistent and/or extreme responses were identified as "suspect." Although fewer than 5% of students were identified as suspect, deletion of these suspect surveys reduced estimates of students carrying a handgun at school by a magnitude of 30—from 3.2 to 0.1%. In one high school, the proportion of students who reported having been bullied was 46%, but after suspect surveys were removed from the sample, the proportion dropped to 25%, which is a reduction of more than 45%. In other words, the error in survey results that could be attributable to inconsistent and extreme responding—not considering other forms of error such as limitations in memory or concentration—is larger than the typical reductions reported by many bully prevention programs (as estimated by Smith & Ananiadou, 2003 and Ttofi & Farrington, 2009).

Cross and Newman-Gonchar (2004) observed striking differences in survey results between schools that used trained versus untrained survey administrators. In some cases the teachers were not given adequate instructions or advance notice that they would be administering a lengthy survey in their classroom. Although this was not a controlled study, their post hoc observations were provocative; 28% of surveys obtained by untrained administrators failed to meet validity standards, whereas only 3% of those obtained by trained administrators were considered invalid. The findings by Cross and Newman-Gonchar (2004) raise concern that teachers should be appropriately prepared to administer any classroom survey and that survey results should be carefully scrutinized for invalid responses. Teachers must be motivated to administer the survey, they must have clear instructions and adequate time, and they must be willing and able to engage the students so that they take the survey seriously and put forth a reasonable effort to complete it accurately. The survey should not be so laborious that students lose interest, fail to concentrate, or begin marking answers at random.

The Need for More Rigorous Validity Studies

These seven problem areas demonstrate the need for more rigorous measurement research on the assessment of bullying, especially the use of student self-report surveys. Because most studies use anonymous surveys, researchers cannot validate student reports with independent sources of corroboration. Instead, researchers have presented data on the internal consistency of student reports or its correspondence with other criteria obtained from the same self-report instrument. For example, two studies of the Olweus BVQ (Solberg & Olweus, 2003; Solberg, Olweus, & Endresen, 2007) show that two self-report questions (one about bullying others and another about being bullied) correlate with subsequent questions about specific forms of bullying on the BVQ and also additional survey questions about externalizing and internalizing behaviors. Although these findings show consistency in student reports on the BVQ, they are not sufficient to establish validity. In each analysis, there is a lack of independence between the bullying questions and the criterion items. Results from such analyses are confounded and inflated to an unknown degree by shared method variance—correlations produced by the measurement method rather than the actual constructs of interest (Podsakoff, MacKenzie, Lee, & Podsakoff, 2003).

Shared method variance can occur when two measures or scales drawn from one reporter (e.g., a student) are correlated with one another because of the consistency in how the reporter answers questions rather than an underlying relationship between the constructs being measured. Method effects for a self-report bullying survey can be produced by a variety of factors, including student reading level, mood, and attitude toward completing the survey. For example, a defensive student might mark items to minimize his or her involvement in bullying, while a more provocative student might choose to exaggerate his or her claims. In both these cases, an apparent relationship between bullying and some criterion measure (e.g., externalizing or internalizing behavior) simply represents student consistency in answering questions. Thus, studies that rely solely on correlations between survey results from the same source do not achieve the independence between predictor and criterion variables necessary to provide rigorous evidence of self-report accuracy. Shared method variance is often overlooked or discounted in bullying research, but is widely recognized as a serious problem in other fields (Podsakoff et al., 2003).

Effect on Program Evaluation Efforts

The fundamental question is, How can we know that a student's report about bullying is accurate? Unreliable measures can have a devastating effect on efforts to evaluate the effectiveness of a bullying prevention program. For example, a meta-analysis of bullying prevention studies (Ttofi & Farrington, 2009) suggested that effective programs typically reduce the number of victims of bullying by approximately 20%. To illustrate this effect, they offered the example of 100 students in a bullying prevention program versus 100 students in a control condition. There might be 25 victims among the 100 students in the control condition versus 20 victims in the prevention program, which is a reduction of 5 victims or 20%. An effect of this size, even if statistically significant, is fragile and might not be detected with unreliable measures. If only a handful of students in the treatment condition over-reported victimization, the apparent treatment effect would be obscured and it would appear that the program was unsuccessful.

It is usually assumed that measurement errors are randomly distributed across groups, so that the net effect is negligible in most cases. However, measurement error due to over- or under-reporting might not be randomly distributed in bullying studies. One problem noted by Smith and Ananiadou (2003) is that a bullying prevention program may sensitize students to report bullying, resulting in an increase in self-reports that does not reflect the actual decline in bullying achieved by a successful intervention. Ironically, the more effective the program, the more pronounced the sensitization—resulting in the paradoxical finding that student reports of bullying have increased rather than decreased. In a noteworthy randomized controlled study of the *Steps to Respect* program, Frey and colleagues (2005) found that the intervention produced declines in bullying and argumentative behavior according to trained observers, but no changes in self-reports of those behaviors.

A contrasting problem can occur when students respond to demand effects of the bullying prevention program. After being repeatedly lectured and reminded about the undesirability of bullying, some students may learn to disavow and deny bullying on subsequent administrations of the survey, even if they have not changed their behavior with peers. If the self-report survey is the only source of information to indicate a reduction in bullying, it would not be possible to rule out that an apparent decline in bullying simply represents student acquiescence to an expected response pattern. If both sensitization and demand effects occur, one might see an increase in self-reports of bullying shortly after a program is initiated, due to sensitization effects, followed by a decline as students become compliant with program expectations.

Research on bullying owes much to the groundbreaking work of Scandinavian researcher Daniel Olweus, who in 1983 implemented a nationwide program to reduce bullying in Norway. His program has served as the model for bully prevention efforts throughout the world, including the United States (Olweus et al., 1999). The Olweus program received international recognition because it produced reductions in bullying of 50% or more. Critical to this recognition is that Olweus (1996) had an assessment instrument that could document the success of his program. Without a reliable measure of bullying, Olweus would not have received due credit for the success of his program. However, there has been limited published information on both the reliability and validity of the Olweus BVQ. Few studies have conducted traditional criterion-related validity studies using independent criteria for bullying. Because the BVQ is so widely used and serves as a model for other instruments, it is especially important that its validity be established to a high degree of methodological rigor.

Lee and Cornell (2010) published a direct examination of the concurrent validity of the BVQ using independent criteria. Based on a relatively small sample of 202 middle school students, they found that self-reported bullying on the BVQ was significantly correlated with peer nominations for bullying ($r = .12$, $p < .05$) and academic grades ($r = -.15$, $p < .05$), but not disciplinary infractions. Self-reported victimization was significantly correlated with peer nominations for victimization ($r = .42$, $p < .01$) and academic grades ($r = -.12$, $p < .01$). More studies with larger and more diverse samples are needed, but these results lend only modest support to the validity of the BVQ.

Need for Diagnostic Accuracy Statistics

Although the correlations obtained by Lee and Cornell (2010) are similar in magnitude to other correlations obtained in cross-informant studies (Achenbach, McConaughy, & Howell, 1987), they do not provide strong evidence for test accuracy, which is a higher standard than simply examining the size of correlation coefficients. The assessment of a measure's accuracy requires more than a statistically significant correlation, because a correlation does not indicate what percentage of students who are victims (or bullies) in a school are accurately identified as victims (or bullies), or what percentage of students who are not victims (or bullies) in a school are accurately identified, either.

It has long been a standard practice in epidemiology, medicine, and psychological assessment (McNeil, Keller, & Adelstein, 1975; Swets, 1986) to assess the accuracy of diagnostic tests for the presence/absence of any condition by calculating four important statistical indices: the sensitivity, specificity, positive predictive power, and negative predictive power of a test score. Sensitivity refers to the capacity of the test to identify all cases with the condition in the study population, while specificity refers to the capacity to identify cases without the condition. The sensitivity of a bullying survey for victims would be the percentage of all bullied students that are identified by the survey. The specificity of the survey would be the percentage of all nonvictims of bullying whom the survey identifies as nonvictims. Together, sensitivity and specificity tell us how many students in the underlying population (e.g., student body of the school) are accurately identified as victims or nonvictims.

In contrast, positive predictive power and negative predictive power tell us about the accuracy of *test results*. Positive predictive power is the percentage of cases identified as victims of bullying by the survey who are actually victims, while the negative predictive power is the percentage of cases identified as nonvictims who are actually nonvictims. In combination, these four statistics are essential to assess the accuracy of any assessment instrument designed to identify the presence/absence of any population condition such as bullying.

When bullying is measured on a continuous scale, there may be questions about the appropriate cut-point to use for classifying students as victims (or perpetrators) of bullying. Receiver Operating Characteristic (ROC) analysis is a standard procedure for examining the sensitivity and specificity of a test across the full range of possible cut-points (Swets, 1986). ROC analyses are needed for both self-report and peer-report measures.

The critical requirement for conducting research on the accuracy of an assessment instrument is the existence of some independent standard of truth. A major problem in bullying research is that there is no standard or definitive procedure for deciding that a student has actually been bullied (or has bullied others). From a practice standpoint, school authorities make this determination by interviewing students or observing their behavior and making a judgment.

We recently compared middle school student responses to a self-report bullying survey with counselor interviews of those students (Cornell & Bandyopadhyay, 2010b). In this school, students were advised that if survey results indicated that they were victims of bullying, the researchers would notify one of the two school counselors to speak with them. A total of 43 students identified themselves as victims of bullying "about once a week" or "several times a week" in the past month. The students and counselors were familiar with the concept of bullying through the school's participation in the Olweus Bullying Prevention program. After interviewing the students, the counselors concluded that only 24 (56%) of the 43 students were accurately self-reported as victims of bullying. The remaining students included two who had been victims of bullying prior to the timeframe of the survey question, 13 who were involved in a peer conflict that was not bullying, such as a disagreement with a friend, and four who claimed to have marked the survey in error.

Peer Reports of Bullying

Peer reports represent an important alternative to self-report assessment of bullying. The peer report or nomination method usually involves asking students to identify classmates who match a descriptive statement or definition (Pakaslahti & Keltikangas-Jarvinen, 2000; Ladd & Kochenderfer-Ladd, 2002; Nabuzoka, 2003; Cornell & Brockenbrough, 2004). There are variations to this method in which students are asked to nominate a fixed number of classmates or to assign frequency ratings (e.g., never, sometimes, often) to each of their classmates.

Olweus (2010) pointed out a number of measurement problems associated with peer reports, including the lack of consistency across studies in how peer ratings are obtained, the difficulty of determining standard cutting scores to identify bullies and victims, and uncertainty whether peers will know that some of their classmates are being bullied. These legitimate concerns merit systematic standardization research. For example, the study design used by Solberg and Olweus (2003) to identify cutting scores for self-reported frequency of bullying could be used to determine the optimal number of peer nominations that identify a victim or perpetrator of bullying. Indeed, many of the measurement concerns about peer reports mirror the problems of self-report and speak to the broader need to establish the validity—and especially the accuracy—of bullying measures using independent criteria.

Nevertheless, many reliability and validity questions about peer reports have been addressed in the related field of peer aggression research, where peer nomination is a highly regarded, standard method of identifying aggressive students and their victims (Hawker & Boulton, 2000; Ladd & Kochenderfer-Ladd, 2002; Leff, Kupersmidt, Patterson, & Power, 1999; Pellegrini, Bartini, & Brooks, 1999; Perry, Kusel, & Perry, 1988). Peer reports have been found useful in assessing a wide variety of emotional and behavior problems, including peer aggression, delinquency, hyperactivity, anxiety, and depression (Huesmann, Eron, Guerra, & Crawshaw, 1994; Weiss, Harris, & Catron, 2004). Peer reports have also been used in studies of indirect peer aggression, social exclusion, and interpersonal problems (Crick & Bigbee, 1998; Hill, Zrull, & McIntire, 1998; Pakaslahti & Keltikangas-Jarvinen, 2000).

Several studies demonstrate the value of peer reports in studies of bullying and victimization (Ladd & Kochenderfer-Ladd, 2002). A Korean study (Kim, Leventhal, Koh, Hubbard, & Boyce, 2006) examined the causal relationship between bullying nominations by peers and self-reported psychopathology. Based on data collected from seventh- and eighth-grade students on two occasions 10 months apart, the authors found that symptoms of emotional and behavioral maladjustment were better understood as a consequence of being bullied (or bullying others) rather than a contributing factor. Childhood victimization is linked to subsequent emotional disorder, social maladjustment, academic difficulties, and other adverse outcomes (Hawker & Boulton, 2000;

Ladd & Ladd, 2001; Rigby, 2001). Rigby (2001) demonstrated that both self-reported and peer-reported victimization were associated with suicidal ideation in Australian adolescents.

A Canadian study by Chan (2006) asked victims of bullying to name their aggressors. Among 435 students named as bullies were 94 students who engaged in serial bullying, defined as bullying more than one victim. The serial bullies accounted for nearly 70% of the total victim population and were also the most likely to engage in physical bullying. This study demonstrated that peer nominations can yield quantitative estimates of the scope of a student's bullying that are not obtained from self-report.

Thunfors and Cornell (2008) investigated the peer popularity of American middle school students identified as bullies or victims. A middle school sample consisting of 379 students completed the standard peer nomination form on the SCBS (Cornell, 2011) and an additional question asking them to identify up to 10 of the most popular boys and girls in their grade. Over the course of the school year, the students identified in the fall as bullies by at least two classmates earned lower grades, accrued more discipline violations, and were more likely to be suspended from school than other students. However, bullies received substantially more endorsements as popular students (mean 20.6) than victims (3.6) or other students (12.8).

Branson and Cornell (2009) found modest correspondence between self- and peer reports of bullying others ($r = .18$) and bullying victimization ($r = .32$) in a sample of 355 middle school students. Despite their limited agreement, both self- and peer-reported bullying/victimization were predictive of school maladjustment, as measured by discipline referrals, school suspensions, and aggressive attitudes. Regression analyses showed that both self and peer report provided unique predictive value for school maladjustment measures. These findings support the view that multiple measures, preferably using multiple informants, are most useful in the assessment of bullying (Juvonen, Nishina, & Graham, 2001; Ladd & Kochenderfer-Ladd, 2002; Swearer et al., 2010).

The simple advantage of peer report over self-report is that scores are based on data aggregated from multiple sources, which tends to decrease measurement error and produce a more reliable result. Although some children may make an erroneous judgment about a classmate's involvement in bullying, the combined judgment of the group should be more accurate. The most common reservation about peer nomination is that teachers are reluctant to ask students to make judgments about one another, fearing that the exercise will stimulate teasing or cause anxiety. Based on our observations and experience with peer nominations over the past 10 years, with appropriate classroom supervision, a peer nomination survey can be administered without such problems.

The choice of instrument to assess bullying can have a powerful effect on the nature and course of the intervention. If school authorities or researchers choose to rely exclusively on an anonymous self-report measure to assess the prevalence of bullying, they may learn how much bullying is occurring, but they will not know who is being bullied and by whom. With this limited knowledge, interventions naturally focus on schoolwide rules and curriculum units on bullying. Meanwhile, counselors must wait for bullying to be reported before they can intervene with specific students. Unfortunately, many students do not seek help for bullying and teachers often do not detect it (Eliot et al., 2010; Unnever & Cornell, 2003, 2004). Moreover, as noted above, self-reports may be inflated if students do not understand the concept of bullying, are sensitized to report bullying by initial intervention efforts, or mark the survey in a careless or intentionally exaggerated manner.

The peer nomination method may be especially valuable for school counselors attempting to reduce bullying because it can focus and expedite their intervention efforts by identifying specific students who are perceived to be victims and perpetrators of bullying. Assisted by this information, counselors can observe or interview these students to confirm their involvement.

Peer nomination data in which one or more students are identified as a victim by a large number of classmates can be useful in convincing teachers that bullying is a problem in their classroom and motivating them to take action.

Future Directions in Bullying Assessment

In conclusion, the field of bullying research needs standard, reliable, and independently validated measures for determining whether a student has been bullied (or has bullied others). Bullying measures should incorporate standard definitions that use the three criteria of intentional harm, power imbalance, and repetition. A systematic program of research is needed to establish the most reliable and valid way to survey students about bullying, including investigations of student comprehension of survey questions and their willingness to respond in a truthful manner.

The use of anonymous surveys has prevented researchers from validating student responses against independent criteria. However, there is evidence that confidential surveys may be a viable alternative to anonymous surveys and can produce findings that are not inflated by shared method variance and other confounding factors. Peer nominations also represent an important assessment strategy that should be more widely used. Peer nominations have the virtue of providing school staff with direct and verifiable information about victims of bullying. Nevertheless, research on peer reports regarding bullying is needed to address similar issues of reliability, validity, and accuracy.

Efforts to validate surveys should go beyond correlations with other measures to include assessment of accuracy using conventional indices of sensitivity, specificity, positive predictive power, and negative predictive power. These statistics will make it possible to assess how accurately surveys measure the prevalence of bullying and whether they can be used with confidence to evaluate the effectiveness of prevention programs. However, this kind of validation effort would require substantial research to develop an independent criterion for bullying. Counselor interviews, or perhaps research interviews conducted with trained interviewers, could provide one source of criterion information, although such efforts would require reliability training and careful implementation.

Table 22.1 Implications for Practice: Recommendations for the Assessment of Bullying

1.	There is insufficient evidence for the validity and accuracy of instruments used to assess the prevalence of bullying and bully victimization.
2.	Shared method variance is a common problem in bullying research; survey measures require validation with independent criteria.
3.	Validity studies should investigate the accuracy of bullying measures with attention to sensitivity, specificity, and positive predictive value, and negative predictive value.
4.	To enhance survey reliability and validity: • Students need systematic education about the definition of bullying before completing survey measures; • Teachers should be well-prepared for survey administration and engage students in taking the survey seriously; • Student surveys should be screened for careless or exaggerated responding.
5.	Peer nominations can be a useful additional source of information.

References

Achenbach, T. M., McConaughy, S. H., & Howell, C. T. (1987). Child/adolescent behavioral and emotional problems: Implications of cross-informant correlations for situational specificity. *Psychological Bulletin, 101*, 213–232. doi:10.1037/0033-2909.101.2.213

Ashbaugh, L., & Cornell, D. (2008). Sexual harassment and bullying behaviors in sixth graders. *Journal of School Violence, 7*, 21–38.

Baly, M. W., & Cornell, D. G. (2011). Effects of an educational video on the measurement of bullying by self-report. *Journal of School Violence, 10*, 221–238.

Bjorkqvist, K., Lagerspetz, K., & Kaukinian, A. (1992). Do girls manipulate and boys fight?: Developmental trends in regard to direct and indirect aggression. *Aggressive Behavior, 18*, 117–127. doi:10.1002/1098-2337 (1992)18:2<117::AID-AB2480180205>3.0.CO;2-3

Branson, C., & Cornell, D. (2009). A comparison of self and peer reports in the assessment of middle school bullying. *Journal of Applied School Psychology. 25*, 5–27. doi:10.1080/15377900802484133

Brener, N. D., Kann, L., Kinchen, S.A., Grunbaum, J. A., Whalen, L., Eaton, D., Hawkins, J. & Ross, J. G. (2004). Methodology of the youth risk behavior surveillance system. *Morbidity and Mortality Weekly Report, 53*, 1–12.

Brener, N. D., McManus T., Galuska, D. A., Lowry, R., & Wechsler, H. (2003). Reliability and validity of self-reported height and weight among high school students. *Journal of Adolescent Health, 32*, 281–287. doi:10.1016/ S1054-139X(02)00708-5

Carlson, W., & Cornell, D. (2008). Differences between persistent and desistent middle school bullies. *School Psychology International, 29*, 442–451. doi:10.1177/0143034308096433

Chan, H. F. J. (2006). Systemic patterns in bullying and victimization. *School Psychology International, 27*, 352–369.

Chan, H. F. J., Myron, R., & Crawshaw, M. (2005). The efficacy of non-anonymous measures of bullying. *School Psychology International, 26*, 443–458.

Cole, J., Cornell, D., & Sheras, P. (2006). Identification of school bullies by survey methods. *Professional School Counseling, 9*, 305–313.

Cornell, D. G. (2011). *The school climate bullying survey: Description and research summary. Unpublished report.* University of Virginia, Charlottesville, Virginia.

Cornell, D., & Bandyopadhyay, S. (2010a). The assessment of bullying. In S. R. Jimerson, S. M. Swearer, & D. L. Espelage (Eds.), *The handbook of bullying in schools: An international perspective* (pp. 265–276). New York: Routledge.

Cornell, D., & Bandyopadhyay, S. (2010b). *Counselor confirmation of middle school student self-reports of bullying victimization.* Unpublished manuscript. University of Virginia, Charlottesville.

Cornell, D. G., & Brockenbrough, K. (2004). Identification of bullies and victims: A comparison of methods. *Journal of School Violence, 3*, 63–87. doi:10.1300/J202v03n02_05

Cornell, D. G., & Loper, A. B. (1998). Assessment of violence and other high-risk behaviors with a school survey. *School Psychology Review, 27*, 317–330.

Crick, N., & Bigbee, M. (1998). Relational and overt forms of peer victimization: A multi-informant approach. *Journal of Consulting and Clinical Psychology, 66*, 337–347. doi:10.1037/0022-006X.66.2.337

Crick, N., & Grotpeter, J. (1995). Relational aggression, gender, and social-psychological adjustment. *Child Development, 66*, 710–722. doi:10.2307/1131945 PMid:7789197

Cross, J., & Newman-Gonchar, R. (2004). Data quality in student risk behavior surveys and administrator training. *Journal of School Violence, 3*, 89–108. doi:10.1300/J202v03n02_06

DeVoe, J. F., & Bauer, L. (2010). *Student victimization in U.S. schools: Results from the 2007 school crime supplement to the national crime victimization survey.* Washington, DC: National Center for Education Statistics, Institute of Education Sciences, U.S. Department of Education.

Eliot, M., Cornell, D., Gregory, A., & Fan, X. (2010). Supportive school climate and student willingness to seek help for bullying and threats of violence. *Journal of School Psychology, 48*, 533–553.

Finkelhor, D., Hamby, S., Ormrod, R., & Turner, H. (2004). *The juvenile victimization questionnaire: Reliability, validity, and national norms.* Unpublished report. Crimes against Children Research Center, University of New Hampshire, Dunham.

Finkelhor, D., Turner, H., Ormrod, R., & Hamby, S. L., (2010). Trends in childhood violence and abuse exposure: Evidence from 2 national surveys. *Archives of Pediatrics and Adolescent Medicine, 164*, 238–242. doi:10.1001/ archpediatrics.2009.283

Frey, K. S., Hirschstein, M. K., Snell, J., Edstrom, L. V., Mackenzie, E., & Broderick, C. J. (2005). Reducing playground bullying and supporting beliefs: An experimental trial of Steps to Respect program. *Developmental Psychology, 41*, 479–491. doi:10.1037/0012-1649.41.3.479

Furlong, M., Sharkey, J., Bates, M. P., & Smith, D. (2004). An examination of reliability, data screening procedures, and extreme response patterns for the youth risk behavior surveillance survey. *Journal of School Violence, 3*, 109–130. doi:10.1300/J202v03n02_07

Furlong, M. J., Sharkey, J. D., Felix, E. D., Tanigawa, D., & Green, J. G. (2010). Bullying assessment: A call for increased precision of self-reporting procedures. In S. R. Jimerson, S. M. Swearer, & D. L. Espelage (Eds.), *The handbook of bullying in schools: An international perspective* (pp. 329–346). New York: Routledge.

Hawker, D., & Boulton, M. (2000). Twenty years' research on peer victimization and psychosocial maladjustment: A meta-analytic review of cross-sectional studies. *Journal of Child Psychology & Psychiatry & Allied Disciplines, 41,* 441–455. doi:10.1111/1469-7610.00629

Hill, R. W., Zrull, M. C., & McIntire, K. (1998). Differences between self- and peer ratings of interpersonal problems. *Assessment, 5,* 67–83. doi:10.1177/107319119800500109

Huesmann, L., Eron, L., Guerra, N., & Crawshaw, B. (1994). Measuring children's aggression with teachers' predictions of peer nominations. *Psychological Assessment, 6,* 329–336. doi:10.1037/1040-3590.6.4.329

Juvonen, J., Nishina, A., & Graham, S. (2001). Self-views versus peer perceptions of victim status among early adolescents. In J. Juvonen & S. Graham (Eds.), *Peer harassment in school: A plight of the vulnerable and victimized* (pp. 105–124). New York: Guilford.

Kert, A. S., Codding, R. S., Tryon, G. S., & Shiyko, M. (2009). Impact of the word "Bully" on the reported rate of bullying behavior. *Psychology in the Schools, 47,* 193–204.

Kim, Y. S., Leventhal, B. L., Koh, Y. J., Hubbard, A., & Boyce, W. T. (2006). School bullying and youth violence: Causes or consequences of psychopathologic behavior. *Archives of General Psychiatry, 63,* 1035-1041. doi:10.1001/archpsyc.63.9.1035

Kosciw, J. G., Diaz, E. M., & Greytak, E. A. (2008). *2007 National school climate survey: The experiences of lesbian, gay, bisexual and transgender youth in our nation's schools.* New York: GLSEN.

Kowalski, R. M., Limber, S. P., & Agatston, P. W. (2008). *Cyber bullying.* Malden, MA: Blackwell. doi: 10.1002/9780470694176

Ladd, G. W., & Kochenderfer-Ladd, B. (2002). Identifying victims of peer aggression from early to middle childhood: Analysis of cross-informant data from concordance, estimation of relational adjustment, prevalence of victimization, and characteristics of identified victims. *Psychological Assessment, 14,* 74–96. doi:10.1037/1040-3590.14.1.74

Ladd, B., & Ladd, G. (2001). Variations in peer victimization: Relations to children's maladjustment. In J. Juvonen & S. Graham (Eds.), *Peer harassment in school: The plight of the vulnerable and victimized* (pp. 25–48). New York: Guilford Press.

Lee, T., & Cornell, D. (2010). Concurrent validity of the Olweus bully/victim questionnaire. *Journal of School Violence, 9,* 56–73. doi:10.1080/15388220903185613

Leff, S., Kupersmidt, J., Patterson, C., & Power, T. (1999). Factors influencing teacher identification of peer bullies and victims. *School Psychology Review, 28,* 505–517.

McConville, D., & Cornell, D. (2003). Attitudes toward aggression and aggressive behavior among middle school students. *Journal of Emotional and Behavioral Disorders, 11,* 179–187. doi:10.1177/10634266030110030501

McNeil, B. J., Keller, E., & Adelstein, S. J. (1975). Primer on certain elements of medical decision making. *New England Journal of Medicine, 293,* 211–215. doi:10.1056/NEJM197507312930501

Morrison, G., & Furlong, M. J. (2002, June). *Understanding the turning points in students' school discipline histories.* Paper presented at Safe Schools for the 21st Century, National Conference of the Hamilton Fish Institute, Monterey, California.

Nabuzoka, D. (2003). Teacher ratings and peer nominations of bullying and other behaviour of children with and without learning difficulties. *Educational Psychology, 23,* 307–321. doi:10.1080/0144341032000060147

Oliver, C., & Candappa, M. (2007). Bullying and the politics of 'telling.' *Oxford Review of Education, 33,* 71–86. doi:10.1080/03054980601094594

Olweus, D. (1991). Bully/victim problems among schoolchildren: Basic facts and effects of a school based intervention program. In D. Pepler & K. Rubin (Eds.), *The development and treatment of childhood aggression* (pp. 411–448). Hillsdale, NJ: Erlbaum.

Olweus, D. (1996). *The revised Olweus bully/victim questionnaire.* Bergen, Norway: Research Center for Health Promotion (HEMIL), University of Bergen.

Olweus, D., Limber, S., & Mihalic, S. F. (1999). *Blueprints for violence prevention, book nine: Bullying prevention program.* Boulder, CO: Center for the Study and Prevention of Violence.

O'Malley, P. M., Johnston, L. D., Bachman, J. G., & Schulenberg, J. E. (2000). A comparison of confidential versus anonymous survey procedures: Effects on reporting of drug use and related attitudes and beliefs in a national study of students. *Journal of Drug Issues, 30,* 35–54.

Pakaslahti, L., & Keltikangas-Jarvinen, L. (2000). Comparisons of peer, teacher, and self-assessments on adolescent direct and indirect aggression. *Educational Psychology, 20,* 177–190. doi:10.1080/713663710

Pellegrini, A. D., Bartini, M., & Brooks, F. (1999). School bullies, victims, and aggressive victims: Factors relating to group affiliation and victimization in early adolescence. *Journal of Educational Psychology, 91,* 216–224. doi:10.1037/0022-0663.91.2.216

Perry, D., Kusel, S., & Perry, L. (1988). Victims of peer aggression. *Developmental Psychology, 24*, 807–814. doi:10.1037/0012-1649.24.6.807

Podsakoff, P. M., MacKenzie, S. B., Lee, J. Y., & Podsakoff, N. P. (2003). Common method biases in behavioral research: A critical review of the literature and recommended remedies. *Journal of Applied Psychology, 88*, 879–903. doi:10.1037/0021-9010.88.5.879

Rigby, K. (2001). Health consequences of bullying and its prevention in schools. In J. Juvonen & S. Graham (Eds.), *Peer harassment in school* (pp. 310–331). New York: Guilford Press.

Smith, D., & Ananiadou, K. (2003). The nature of school bullying and the effectiveness of school-based interventions. *Journal of Applied Psychoanalytic Studies, 5*, 189–209. doi:10.1023/A:1022991804210

Smith, P. K., & Shu, S. (2000). What good schools can do about bullying. Findings from a survey in English schools after a decade of research, *Childhood, 7*, 193–212. doi:10.1177/0907568200007002005

Solberg, M., & Olweus, D. (2003). Prevalence estimation of school bullying with the Olweus bully/victim questionnaire. *Aggressive Behavior, 29*, 239–268. doi:10.1002/ab.10047

Solberg, M. E., Olweus, D. O., & Endresen, I. M. (2007). Bullies and victims at school: Are they the same pupils? *British Journal of Educational Psychology, 77*, 441–464. doi:10.1348/000709906X105689

Swearer, S. M. (2008). Relational aggression: Not just a female issue. *Journal of School Psychology, 46*, 611–616. doi:10.1016/j.jsp.2008.08.001

Swearer, S. M., Espelage, D. L., Vaillancourt, T., & Hymel, S. (2010). What can be done about school bullying?: Linking research to educational practice. *Educational Researcher, 39*, 38–47. doi:10.3102/0013189X09357622

Swearer, S., M., Turner, R. K., Givens, J. E., & Pollack, W. S. (2008). "Your're so gay!" Do different forms of bullying matter for adolescent males? *School Psychology Review, 37,* 160–173.

Swets, J. A. (1986). Forms of empirical ROCs in discrimination and diagnostic tasks: implications for theory and measurement of performance. *Psychological Bulletin, 99*, 181–198. doi:10.1037/0033-2909.99.2.181

Thunfors, P., & Cornell, D. (2008). The popularity of middle school bullies. *Journal of School Violence, 7*, 65–82. doi:10.1300/J202v07n01_05

Ttofi, M. M., & Farrington, D. P. (2009). What works in preventing bullying: Effective elements of anti-bullying programmes. *Journal of Aggression, Conflict and Peace Research, 1*, 13–24.

U.S. Department of Health and Human Services. (2009). *United States high school survey data users manual.* Rockville, MD: Author.

Unnever, J., & Cornell, D. (2003). The culture of bullying in middle school. *Journal of School Violence, 2*, 5–27. doi:10.1300/J202v02n02_02

Unnever, J., & Cornell, D. (2004). Middle school victims of bullying: Who reports being bullied? *Aggressive Behavior, 30*, 373–388. doi:10.1002/ab.20030

Vaillancourt, T., Trinh, V., McDougall, P., Duku, E., Cunningham, L., Cunningham, C., Hymel, S., Short, K. (2010). Optimizing population screening of bullying in school-aged children. *Journal of School Violence, 9*, 233–250. doi:10.1080/15388220.2010.483182

Varjas, K., Henrich, C. C., & Meyers, J. (2009). Urban middle school students' perceptions of bullying, cyberbullying, and school safety. *Journal of School Violence, 8,* 159–176. doi:10.1080/15388220802074165

Wang, J., Iannotti, R. J., & Nansel, T. R. (2009). School bullying among adolescents in the United States: Physical, verbal, relational, and cyber. *Journal of Adolescent Health, 45*, 368–375. doi:10.1016/j.jadohealth.2009.03.021

Weiss, B., Harris, V., & Catron, T. (2004). Development and initial validation of the peer-report measure of internalizing and externalizing behavior. *Journal of Abnormal Child Psychology, 30*, 285–294. doi:10.1023/A:1015158930705

Williams, F., & Cornell, D. (2006). Student willingness to seek help for threats of violence in middle school. *Journal of School Violence, 5*, 35–49. doi:10.1300/J202v05n04_04

23

Using Office Discipline Referrals and School Exclusion Data to Assess School Discipline

Kent McIntosh

THE UNIVERSITY OF BRITISH COLUMBIA, VANCOUVER

Emily S. Fisher

LOYOLA MARYMOUNT UNIVERSITY, LOS ANGELES

Kelly S. Kennedy

CHAPMAN UNIVERSITY, ORANGE, CA

Calli B. Craft

THE UNIVERSITY OF BRITISH COLUMBIA, VANCOUVER

Gale M. Morrison

THE UNIVERSITY OF CALIFORNIA, SANTA BARBARA

Abstract

This chapter provides an overview of approaches to assessing problem behavior and school climate with existing discipline data, such as office discipline referrals and school exclusion records. Discipline data are potentially valuable in assessing school violence and school safety, including use for screening, identifying needs for change, and evaluating school-wide intervention outcomes. However, limitations to their reliability and validity must be considered, including disproportionate use with students from ethnic minority backgrounds. To address these concerns, many schools have taken steps to standardize office disciplinary procedures and enhance the cultural responsiveness of schoolwide discipline systems. This chapter will also provide recommendations for enhancing discipline data for decision making and implementing culturally responsive practices.

Given the broad range of discipline challenges facing today's schools, coupled with budgetary restrictions requiring school personnel to do more with less, discipline data can become exceedingly valuable in assessing school violence and school safety. With the right measures, school teams can identify challenges, generate potential solutions, and evaluate effectiveness of the support provided. However, to be valuable, these measures must meet certain psychometric standards. For example, the data used need to be valid, reliable, efficient to collect, and useful for decision making (Horner, Sugai, & Todd, 2001).

School discipline indices, such as office discipline referrals, suspensions, and expulsions, provide data by which school personnel can maximize effectiveness and efficiency of decision making and the support provided to students. These data are appealing because of their ease of collection and ready availability—in most schools, collecting and summarizing discipline data is a district mandate. In addition, these data are sensitive to low-frequency, high intensity behaviors that are difficult to capture with direct observation (Sprague & Horner, 1999). As such, they often meet the efficiency and utility standards of measurement (McIntosh, Reinke, & Herman, 2009). Thus, assessing their adequacy for decision making, in comparison to resource intensive supplemental measures (e.g., direct observation, screening systems), is worthwhile. Unfortunately, school discipline data can suffer from poor reliability and, most concerning, disproportionate use with students from ethnic and racial minority backgrounds. Yet the steps to enhancing technical adequacy for making useful decisions with these data are known. This chapter addresses approaches to assessing problem behavior and school climate with existing discipline data, the benefits and limitations of using such data, and the particular challenge of disproportionate use. Finally, recommendations for enhancing the approaches for using these data to inform decision making will be provided.

Office Discipline Referrals

Office discipline referrals (ODRs) are forms used to document student problem behavior on school grounds. ODRs are typically completed by school personnel as a means of communicating the event to school administrators when a student is sent to the office and requires administrative involvement (i.e., additional support or a punitive consequence). Sugai, Sprague, Horner, and Walker (2000) have defined an ODR as:

> an event in which (a) a student engaged in a behavior that violated a rule or social norm in the school, (b) the problem behavior was observed or identified by a member of the school staff, and (c) the event resulted in a consequence delivered by administrative staff who produced a permanent (written) product defining the whole event.
>
> *(p. 96)*

ODRs provide immediate appeal to school personnel because of their ready availability and potential use for a wide variety of decision making tasks. ODR data can be used to assess overall school climate, evaluate the effectiveness of schoolwide practices, analyze areas for additional intervention (e.g., locations, student competencies, groups of students), assess the need for professional development, and screen and monitor progress for individual students (Irvin et al., 2006; Irvin, Tobin, Sprague, Sugai, & Vincent, 2004; Luiselli, Putnam, Handler, & Feinberg, 2005). As an illustrative example, a school team may use ODR data to monitor the overall effectiveness of their schoolwide behavior support systems. These data can be used to note an increase in ODRs above rates in previous months, the same month of different years, and district averages. Team members may examine the ODR patterns further to identify that the increase in overall school incidents is due specifically to increases in physical aggression in the hallways. The team can use this specific information to provide additional support to students in a particular location (e.g., reteach expectations in the hallway) and particular social competency (e.g., conflict resolution) and identify professional development needs for school personnel (e.g., active supervision). Finally, ODR data can then be used to assess the effectiveness of these strategies on reducing aggression in the hallways.

Regardless of their utility, there are some potentially major threats to the reliability and validity of ODRs in assessing school discipline, making school-to-school and even within-school comparisons (across time) difficult. ODR data can be compromised by variations in use by school personnel (Kaufman et al., 2010; Morrison, Peterson, O'Farrell, & Redding, 2004; Rusby, Taylor, & Foster, 2007). Variability in ODR rates across classrooms and schools may not necessarily be due to differences in student misbehavior, but rather variations in instructional effectiveness (Scott, Nelson, & Liaupsin, 2001), classroom management skills (Blankemeyer, Flannery, & Vazsonyi, 2002; Reinke & Herman, 2002), and tolerance levels for student behavior (Gerber, 1988; Kaufman et al., 2010; Wright & Dusek, 1998). For example, ODRs may be more likely to be issued in classrooms where expectations are not explicit, behavioral management systems are inconsistent, and instruction time is less structured (Lo & Cartledge, 2007). In addition, the schoolwide discipline policy may be ambiguous, so teachers may not be informed as to what behaviors should result in ODRs.

Another limitation of using ODRs to assess school discipline is variation in recording procedures (Morrison et al., 2004). Many schools either do not use a formal office referral form or use such a form only for the most serious behaviors. Additionally, variation occurs in what is recorded on the form. For example, some teachers may indicate multiple types of misbehavior on the same form, and others may simply select the most pressing or severe behavior, resulting in varying data across ODRs.

Administrative response to ODRs may also affect how often teachers refer. For example, teachers may issue fewer ODRs if they feel that no additional support will be provided or anticipate that the ODR will reflect poorly on their teaching or management skills. Also, an over emphasis from administrators on reducing ODRs, rather than providing quality support, can lead to suppression, limiting their validity and utility for decision making (Kern & Manz, 2004).

To address these concerns and enhance the reliability and validity of ODR data, many schools have taken steps to standardize ODR forms and procedures. McIntosh and colleagues (2009) have offered five critical criteria for schools to employ:

> (a) a common form that details important information about the incident (e.g., location, time of day, others involved), (b) clear definitions of what behaviors warrant a referral, (c) clear definitions of what behaviors are expected to be handled without a referral, (d) regular training on use and discrimination between reportable and nonreportable behaviors, and (e) a system for compiling and analyzing ODR data.
>
> *(p. 101)*

The School-Wide Information System (SWIS; May et al., 2008) is one example of an ODR system, used by over 7,500 schools, that includes a predefined set of ODR behaviors and definitions, plus requirements for staff training, data entry, and ODR forms (Educational and Community Supports, 2010). Data from ODRs can also be made more reliable when forms include check boxes (e.g., list of defined behavior offenses) instead of blank fields, so that forms are easier to use and data become more consistent among teachers (Wright & Dusek, 1998).

There is clear evidence that without such steps to enhance standardization, ODR data suffer from lack of validity (Nelson, Benner, Reid, Epstein, & Currin, 2002), but there is a growing research base demonstrating enhanced technical adequacy with standardized ODRs. The number of ODRs issued at a school is significantly related to teacher and student ratings of school climate, school engagement, classroom disruptiveness, substance use, and overall levels of conflict at school and home (Irvin et al., 2004; Spaulding et al., 2010). Moreover, ODRs are sensitive to implementation of schoolwide interventions to reduce problem behavior and improve school climate (Bradshaw, Mitchell, & Leaf, 2010; Putnam, Luiselli, Handler, & Jefferson, 2003; Sprague et al., 2001).

There is also evidence for the reliability and validity of standardized ODRs for assessing individual student behavior. For example, there is evidence of the stability of ODR growth throughout the school year (McIntosh, Frank, & Spaulding, 2010), throughout elementary school (McIntosh, Horner, Chard, Boland, & Good, 2006), middle school (Tobin, Sugai, & Colvin, 1996), and from middle to high school (McIntosh, Flannery, Sugai, Braun, & Cochrane, 2008; Tobin & Sugai, 1999). The number of ODRs received is related to a range of negative individual outcomes, including school exclusion, academic underachievement, and family conflict (Irvin et al., 2004; Morrison, Anthony, Storino, & Dillon, 2001; Tobin & Sugai, 1999). ODRs have also been shown to be stronger predictors of teacher and parent rated problem behavior than family risk factors, such as poverty (Rusby et al., 2007).

Recent research has also examined the concurrent validity of ODRs with commonly used behavior rating scales. Walker, Cheney, Stage, and Blum (2005) found significantly higher ratings on the Problem Behavior Scale of the Social Skills Rating System (Gresham & Elliott, 1990) for students with multiple ODRs. In another study, McIntosh, Campbell and colleagues (2009) found significantly different ratings on the Externalizing Composite of the Behavior Assessment Scale for Children 2 (Reynolds & Kamphaus, 2004) for students with 0 to 1, 2 to 5, and 6 or more ODRs. Pas (2010) found moderate correlations between ODRs and scores on the Teacher Observation of Classroom Adaptation (Koth, Bradshaw, & Leaf, 2009). However, concurrent validity scores of unstandardized office referrals with the Child Behavior Checklist (Achenbach & Rescorla, 2001) were low (Nelson et al., 2002). With teacher training and standardized forms to increase reliability, ODRs can provide more accurate information to monitor the school climate, examine patterns of problem behavior, provide targets for school reform, and monitor progress toward school goals related to behavior (Irvin et al., 2006). Nevertheless, it is critical to note that without standardization and ongoing training, ODRs have questionable reliability and validity for decision making (Nelson, Gonzalez, Epstein, & Benner, 2003), and most schools in the United States are unlikely to be using standardized ODRs.

School Exclusion

School exclusion is an inclusive term to describe school discipline practices that remove students from the school environment, such as out of school suspension and expulsion. School exclusion often begins with an ODR, but then continues with an additional form that is completed to document the offense warranting exclusion and type and intensity of the consequence (e.g., number of days suspended, indication of a zero tolerance offense). Offenses leading to school exclusion are generally defined by state or provincial education codes and most often include offenses such as possession of a weapon, possession or selling of illegal drugs, physical harm to others, willful disobedience, destruction of property, disruption of school activities, and threat of harm (Kingery & Coggeshall, 2001).

According to the most recent U.S. statistics, 7% of all students were suspended from school at least once per school year, and 0.2% were expelled (Planty et al., 2009). Such data, when considering the offenses listed above, might be construed to indicate that schools are more dangerous than has been suggested. However, these statistics should be considered in light of the fact that it is becoming more common to use school exclusion (particularly suspension) for less severe incidents, such as interpersonal difficulties with peers or adults at school (Evenson, Justinger, Pelischek, & Schulz, 2009; Theriot, Craun, & Dupper, 2010). For example, 43% of school exclusions in the United States were provided for insubordination, whereas less than 1% were due to possession of a firearm or explosive device (Dinkes, Kemp, & Baum, 2009).

There are two possible explanations for what many consider an overreliance on school exclusion. First, community pressure related to increased publicity for serious acts of violence has led to the adoption of "zero-tolerance" policies, which mandate school exclusion for a broad range of discipline offenses (American Psychological Association, 2008; Evenson et al., 2009). Though these policies were designed to both ensure student safety and promote equitable treatment by taking administrator discretion out of the decision making process, neither has occurred as a result of such policies (Skiba & Peterson, 2000).

The second explanation is that school administrators, lacking positive strategies for supporting students with challenging behavior, overuse school exclusion in an attempt to deter future incidents (Fenning & Rose, 2007). Osher, Bear, Sprague, and Doyle (2010) have described school exclusion as "a short-term fix to what often is a chronic and long-term problem" (p. 48). Removing students from school may reinforce problem behavior through escaping an undesirable situation and therefore may lead to increased problem behavior when returning to school (Lo & Cartledge, 2007). Unfortunately, a range of studies has shown that even when controlling for initial levels of behavior, the use of repeated school exclusion with individual students greatly enhances their risk for future mental health problems, antisocial behavior, academic failure, unemployment, homelessness, crime, and incarceration (Hemphill, Toumbourou, Herrenkohl, McMorris, & Catalano, 2006; Skiba & Peterson, 2000; Theriot et al., 2010; Wald & Losen, 2003).

Like ODRs, school exclusion data can potentially provide useful information for administrators. School exclusion data represent a measure of more severe problem behavior than ODRs because they often represent more serious, or at least more chronic, offenses (McIntosh, Campbell, et al., 2009). As a result, some view school exclusion data as a more valid index of school violence than ODRs because low-intensity problem behavior is not included. In addition, school exclusions may be viewed as less susceptible to underreporting. Because suspension provides immediate relief from having to manage a student's behavior (Maag, 2001), school personnel may be more reluctant to suppress school exclusions than ODRs.

Comparing the rates of ODRs and school exclusions at individual schools can be helpful to assess school policies and examining needs for professional development (Morrison et al., 2004). For example, high relative rates of school exclusions may indicate high incidences of serious events, under reporting of ODRs, or a lack of proactive strategies to prevent problem behavior. Just as with ODRs, lack of standardization (e.g., inconsistency in counting the number of incidents or students involved in each incident) can hamper accurate assessment with school exclusion data (Leone, Mayer, Malmgren, & Meisel, 2000). To counter these challenges, it is worthwhile to examine both overall rates of suspension and percent of students suspended at least once during the year (Raffaele Mendez, Knoff, & Ferron, 2002).

Disproportionality Issues in School Discipline

There has been considerable research documenting overrepresentation of certain groups in school discipline data. Studies have consistently reported that students of color, students from low socioeconomic backgrounds, students in special education, and males are disproportionally represented in ODRs and school exclusions (American Psychological Association, 2008; Evenson et al., 2009; Kaufman et al., 2010; Raffaele Mendez & Knoff, 2003; Raffaele Mendez et al., 2002). In addition, particular attention has been paid to the exceedingly high number of African American students excluded from school (Fenning & Rose, 2007; Lo & Cartledge, 2007; Skiba, Michael, Nardo, & Peterson, 2002). This trend begins in elementary school and continues through middle and high school (Bradshaw, Mitchell, O'Brennan, & Leaf, 2010; Raffaele Mendez & Knoff, 2003). In addition, recent research has found that though girls are excluded significantly less than boys, African American girls are excluded at disproportionally higher rates than Caucasian (Lo & Cartledge, 2007) and Hispanic girls (Losen & Skiba, 2010).

Given the connection between race and socioeconomic status in the United States, some researchers have suggested that racial disproportionality in school exclusion is primarily due to racial disproportionality in socioeconomic status, with socioeconomic status being more important to consider (Theriot et al., 2010). However, other researchers have convincingly demonstrated that student ethnicity affects disproportionality above and beyond the contribution of socioeconomic status (Skiba, Poloni-Staudinger, Simmons, Feggins, & Chung, 2005; Wallace, Goodkind, Wallace, & Bachman, 2008). In these studies, ethnicity is a significant predictor of ODRs and school exclusions, even after accounting for socioeconomic status and neighborhood characteristics.

The reasons for this overrepresentation are multifaceted, but research highlights the need to examine student-teacher interactions and strategies used by school personnel. For example, African American males are more likely to receive ODRs and school exclusions for less severe and subjective behaviors (e.g., disrespect, disruption), and these behaviors are more likely to be handled through zero tolerance policies when exhibited by African Americans (American Psychological Association, 2008; Theriot et al., 2010). In addition, when receiving ODRs for the same offenses as students from other ethnicities, African American males are more likely to receive more severe punitive consequences (Skiba et al., 2002). There is also evidence that school exclusion rates are higher for teachers who lack adequate training in classroom management and culturally competent practices (American Psychological Association, 2008; Raffaele Mendez et al., 2002). In a review of ethnographic research, Fenning and Rose (2007) noted that teachers and administrators were more likely to use ODRs and school exclusions preventively (i.e., to avoid a perceived loss of classroom control) with students of color.

Recommendations for Enhancing the Use of Extant Data for Decision Making
Standardize ODRs to Improve Reliability and Validity

Given the information provided earlier in this chapter, relying on unstandardized ODRs for decision making is ill advised. Completing a process of standardization can improve the technical adequacy of ODRs, thus enhancing the quality of the decisions made from their analysis. However, standardization and ongoing training should not be expected to mitigate the challenges of ODRs completely. ODRs should always be used as part of multi-method assessment, especially when making high stakes decisions regarding individual students (McIntosh et al., 2010).

Use Discipline Data to Enhance Schoolwide Decision Making

Discipline data can be used effectively for schoolwide decision making, helping administrative teams allocate resources and identify areas for reform (Irvin et al., 2006). The first step in this process is to graph ODRs in useful ways (e.g., by rate, by problem behavior, location, by time of day, by student) and share these data with staff (Clonan, McDougal, Clark, & Davison, 2007). However, using discipline data for decision making is not always a simple task, and many teams require specific training in the process of data based decision making. Newton and colleagues (2009) have developed a training program called Team Initiated Problem Solving that guides teams through the steps for effective decision making. An experimental study showed that teams receiving the training used school discipline data significantly more effectively (Todd et al., 2011).

One key point regarding discipline data is not to use it to punish or single out school personnel. Although data may identify specific teachers who are potentially struggling with classroom management, school administrators should not use ODRs alone to identify teachers in need of additional training. Otherwise, teachers may choose not to issue ODRs. Instead, a more comprehensive approach to assessing classroom management can be used, including direct observation and self-assessments (Simonsen, Fairbanks, Briesch, & Sugai, 2006). Using a range of tools to provide feedback to teachers about their use of specific classroom management practices has been shown to increase both teacher use of effective strategies and student academic engagement (Jeffrey, McCurdy, Ewing, & Polis, 2009). If all teachers receive regular feedback regarding classroom management, such assessments can become less threatening.

Use Discipline Data to Identify Students for Additional Support

Once effective schoolwide practices are in place, ODRs can help school personnel identify individual students who require additional behavior support to be successful (Rusby et al., 2007). Horner, Sugai, Todd, and Lewis-Palmer (2005) identified ODR cut points that signal the need for additional behavior support as follows: 0 to 1 ODRs per year indicates that the student is adequately supported by schoolwide support, 2 to 5 ODRs indicate the need for efficient, targeted support, and 6 or more ODRs indicate the need for intensive support. These cut points have been validated by concurrent validity with behavior rating scales (McIntosh, Campbell, et al., 2009; Walker et al., 2005). Yet given the need to identify students and intervene proactively, additional research has found that any elementary student with 2 or more ODRs for any behavior by the end of October is highly likely to receive at least 6 ODRs over the course of the school year (McIntosh et al., 2010). Research in middle school suggests that receiving either 2 ODRs or a single ODR for harassment in the fall of Grade 6 predicts chronic problem behavior through middle school (Tobin et al., 1996). As a result, school teams can use ODRs at the end of October to screen students for additional intervention. However, it is important to note that additional sources of data should be used for screening, as ODRs are unlikely to identify a substantial portion of students with internalizing behavior problems (McIntosh, Campbell, et al., 2009).

Use Data to Assess and Address Cultural Responsiveness

ODR and school exclusion data can be used to assess the extent to which ODRs are used disproportionately with students of color, signaling a lack of cultural responsiveness (Townsend, 2000). Chinn and Hughes (1987) proposed a method for determining disproportionality in special education placement that could be applied to discipline data. Data may be disproportional if the percent of ODRs received by the group of interest is 10% or greater than their percent of the school enrollment. The discipline data application SWIS includes an ethnicity report that calculates the percent of students with ODRs by ethnicity and total ODRs by ethnicity to assess disproportionality (May et al., 2008). In addition, assessing patterns in ODRs can provide valuable information. For example, if students of color are receiving a large proportion of ODRs for a particular behavior (e.g., disrespect), behavior expectations or staff assumptions about behavior may need to be examined for cultural bias (Kaufman et al., 2010; Townsend, 2000).

School discipline data can then be used to assess the effectiveness of approaches to reducing disproportionate use. Schoolwide positive behavior support (Sprague & Horner, this volume) has been offered as an approach for promoting a safe, supportive school culture with shared, consistent expectations for behavior and reducing the use of ODRs and school exclusions. However, reductions in ODRs and school exclusions may not be equal across all student ethnicities, as schoolwide positive behavior support without attention to cultural responsiveness

Table 23.1   Implications for Practice: Use of Extant Data for Decision Making

1.	Repeated use of ODRs and school exclusions increases student risk for delinquency and school dropout.
2.	ODRs can be made more valid and reliable through standardization, including using a standardized form, clarification on use, regular entry and analysis, and ongoing training.
3.	Standardized ODRs can be used for a range of decisions, including screening, problem analysis, and evaluation of practices.
4.	School teams can benefit from training and support in the use of discipline data for decision making.
5.	Students of color receive a disproportionate amount of both ODRs and school exclusions, even when socioeconomic status and community risk factors are considered.
6.	Discipline data can be used to assess the cultural responsiveness of schoolwide behavior support systems.
7.	The cultural responsiveness of school-wide behavior systems can be enhanced through reflecting on attitudes and biases and changing expectations and practices to match the backgrounds and needs of students.

may not reduce disproportionality (Kaufman et al., 2010; Skiba et al., 2008; Vincent & Tobin, in press). Several strategies are recommended to address these challenges. First, it is important for school personnel to self-reflect on their attitudes and understanding of students from diverse backgrounds (Hershfeldt et al., 2010; Skiba et al., 2008). Second, school expectations can be examined to assess whether they reflect the cultural norms of the diverse population of students in the school (Townsend, 2000). Third, it is important to examine student–teacher and student–administrator interactions for cultural responsiveness (Gregory, Skiba, & Noguera, 2010). When these practices are applied within a framework of schoolwide positive behavior support, disproportionality can be reduced considerably (e.g., Cregor, Smith, & Leverson, 2010; Jones, Caravaca, Cizek, Horner, & Vincent, 2006).

Conclusion

As this chapter has highlighted, school discipline data can be useful for decision making, but they are not without limitations. Educators must use caution and careful judgment when making decisions about school discipline and related factors, given the threats to reliability and validity that are often present in unstandardized ODR and school exclusion data. These data can become significantly more valid and useful if standardized, with ongoing training in both accurate administration and use for decision making. With these changes, extant discipline data can provide an efficient means to identify students and classrooms in need of additional support, measure school needs and response to intervention, and assess disproportionate use.

References

Achenbach, T. M., & Rescorla, L. A. (2001). *Manual for ASEBA school-age forms & profiles*. Burlington: University of Vermont, Research Center for Children, Youth, & Families.

American Psychological Association. (2008). Are zero tolerance policies effective in the schools?: An evidentiary review and recommendations. *American Psychologist, 63*, 852–862. doi: 10.1037/0003-066x.63.9.852

Blankemeyer, M., Flannery, D. J., & Vazsonyi, A. T. (2002). The role of aggression and social competence in children's perceptions of the child–teacher relationship. *Psychology in the Schools, 39*, 293–304.

Bradshaw, C. P., Mitchell, M. M., & Leaf, P. J. (2010). Examining the effects of school-wide positive behavioral interventions and supports on student outcomes: Results from a randomized controlled effectiveness trial in elementary schools. *Journal of Positive Behavior Interventions, 12*, 133–148.

Bradshaw, C. P., Mitchell, M. M., O'Brennan, L. M., & Leaf, P. J. (2010). Multilevel exploration of factors contributing to the overrepresentation of black students in office disciplinary referrals. *Journal of Educational Psychology, 102*, 508–520.

Chinn, P. C., & Hughes, S. (1987). Representation of minority students in special education classes. *Remedial and Special Education, 8*(4), 41–46. doi: 10.1177/074193258700800406

Clonan, S., McDougal, J., Clark, K., & Davison, S. (2007). Use of office discipline referrals in school wide decision making: A practical example. *Psychology in the Schools, 44*, 19–27.

Cregor, M., Smith, K., & Leverson, M. (2010, October). *Bridging the racial discipline gap and Schoolwide PBS.* Paper presented at the 2010 PBIS Implementer's Forum, Chicago. IL.

Dinkes, R., Kemp, J., & Baum, K. (2009). *Indicators of crime and safety: 2009* (NCES 2010-012). Washington, DC: National Center for Education Statistics.

Educational and Community Supports. (2010). "About SWIS." Retrieved from http://www.swis.org

Evenson, A., Justinger, B., Pelischek, E., & Schulz, S. (2009). Zero tolerance policies and the public schools: When suspension is no longer effective. *Communique, 37*(5), 1, 6–7.

Fenning, P., & Rose, J. (2007). Overrepresentation of African American students in exclusionary discipline: The role of school policy. *Urban Education, 42*, 536–559. doi: 10.1177/0042085907305039

Gerber, M. (1988). Tolerance and technology of instruction: Implications for special education reform. *Exceptional Children, 54*, 309–314.

Gregory, A., Skiba, R. J., & Noguera, P. A. (2010). The achievement gap and the discipline gap. *Educational Researcher, 39*(1), 59–68. doi: 10.3102/0013189x09357621

Gresham, F. M., & Elliott, S. N. (1990). *Social skills rating system.* Circle Pines, MN: American Guidance Service.

Hemphill, S. A., Toumbourou, J. W., Herrenkohl, T. I., McMorris, B. J., & Catalano, R. F. (2006). The effect of school suspensions and arrests on subsequent adolescent antisocial behavior in Australia and the United States. *Journal of Adolescent Health, 39*, 736–744.

Hershfeldt, P. A., Sechrest, R., Pell, K. L., Rosenberg, M. S., Bradshaw, C. P., & Leaf, P. J. (2010). Double-check: A framework of cultural responsiveness applied to classroom behavior. *TEACHING Exceptional Children Plus, 6*(2), 2–18.

Horner, R. H., Sugai, G., & Todd, A. W. (2001). "Data" need not be a four-letter word: Using data to improve school-wide discipline. *Beyond Behavior, 11*(1), 20–26.

Horner, R. H., Sugai, G., Todd, A. W., & Lewis-Palmer, T. (2005). School-wide positive behavior support. In L. Bambara, & L. Kern (Eds.), *Individualized supports for students with problem behaviors: Designing positive behavior plans* (pp. 359–390). New York: Guilford.

Irvin, L. K., Horner, R. H., Ingram, K., Todd, A. W., Sugai, G., Sampson, N. K., & Boland, J. B. (2006). Using office discipline referral data for decision making about student behavior in elementary and middle schools: An empirical evaluation of validity. *Journal of Positive Behavior Interventions, 8*, 10–23. doi: 10.1177/10983007060080010301

Irvin, L. K., Tobin, T. J., Sprague, J. R., Sugai, G., & Vincent, C. G. (2004). Validity of office discipline referral measures as indices of school-wide behavioral status and effects of school-wide behavioral interventions. *Journal of Positive Behavior Interventions, 6*, 131–147.

Jeffrey, J. L., McCurdy, B. L., Ewing, S., & Polis, D. (2009). Classwide PBIS for students with EBD: Initial evaluation of an integrity tool. *Education and Treatment of Children, 32*, 537–550.

Jones, C., Caravaca, L., Cizek, S., Horner, R. H., & Vincent, C. G. (2006). Culturally responsive schoolwide positive behavior support: A case study in one school with a high proportion of Native American students. *Multiple Voices, 9*, 108–119.

Kaufman, J. S., Jaser, S. S., Vaughan, E. L., Reynolds, J. S., DiDonato, J., Bernard, S. N., & Hernandez-Brereton, M. (2010). Patterns in office referral data by grade, race/ethnicity, and gender. *Journal of Positive Behavior Interventions, 12*, 44–54.

Kern, L., & Manz, P. (2004). A look at current validity issues of school-wide behavior support. *Behavioral Disorders, 30*, 47–59.

Kingery, P., & Coggeshall, M. (2001). Surveillance of school violence, injury, and disciplinary actions. *Psychology in the Schools, 38*, 117–126.

Koth, C. W., Bradshaw, C. P., & Leaf, P. J. (2009). Teacher observation of classroom adaptation checklist: Development and factor structure. *Measurement and Evaluation in Counseling and Development, 42*, 15–30.

Leone, P. E., Mayer, M. J., Malmgren, K., & Meisel, S. M. (2000). School violence and disruption: Rhetoric, reality, and reasonable balance. *Focus on Exceptional Children, 33*, 1–20.

Lo, Y., & Cartledge, G. (2007). Office disciplinary referrals in an urban elementary school. *Multicultural Learning and Teaching, 2*, 20–38.

Losen, D., & Skiba, R. (2010). *Suspended education: Urban middle schools in crisis.* Montgomery, AL: Southern Poverty Law Center.

313

Luiselli, J. K., Putnam, R. F., Handler, M. W., & Feinberg, A. B. (2005). Whole-school positive behaviour support: Effects on student discipline problems and academic performance. *Educational Psychology, 25*, 183–198.

Maag, J. W. (2001). Rewarded by punishment: Reflections on the disuse of positive reinforcement in schools. *Exceptional Children, 67*, 173–186.

May, S., Ard, W. I., Todd, A. W., Horner, R. H., Glasgow, A., Sugai, G., & Sprague, J. R. (2008). *School-wide information system*. Eugene: Educational and Community Supports, University of Oregon.

McIntosh, K., Campbell, A. L., Carter, D. R., & Zumbo, B. D. (2009). Concurrent validity of office discipline referrals and cut points used in schoolwide positive behavior support. *Behavioral Disorders, 34*, 100–113.

McIntosh, K., Flannery, K. B., Sugai, G., Braun, D., & Cochrane, K. L. (2008). Relationships between academics and problem behavior in the transition from middle school to high school. *Journal of Positive Behavior Interventions, 10*, 243–255.

McIntosh, K., Frank, J. L., & Spaulding, S. A. (2010). Establishing research-based trajectories of office discipline referrals for individual students. *School Psychology Review, 39*, 380–394.

McIntosh, K., Horner, R. H., Chard, D. J., Boland, J. B., & Good, R. H. (2006). The use of reading and behavior screening measures to predict non-response to school-wide positive behavior support: A longitudinal analysis. *School Psychology Review, 35*, 275–291.

McIntosh, K., Reinke, W. M., & Herman, K. E. (2009). School-wide analysis of data for social behavior problems: Assessing outcomes, selecting targets for intervention, and identifying need for support. In G. G. Peacock, R. A. Ervin, E. J. Daly, & K. W. Merrell (Eds.), *The practical handbook of school psychology* (pp. 135–156). New York: Guilford.

Morrison, G. M., Anthony, S., Storino, M., & Dillon, C. (2001). An examination of the disciplinary histories and the individual and educational characteristics of students who participate in an in-school suspension program. *Education and Treatment of Children, 24*, 276–293.

Morrison, G. M., Peterson, R., O'Farrell, S., & Redding, M. (2004). Using office referral records in school violence research: Possibilities and limitations. *Journal of School Violence, 3*, 39–61. doi: 10.1300/J202v03n02_04

Nelson, J. R., Benner, G. J., Reid, R. C., Epstein, M. H., & Currin, D. (2002). The convergent validity of office discipline referrals with the CBCL-TRF. *Journal of Emotional and Behavioral Disorders, 10*, 181–188.

Nelson, J. R., Gonzalez, J. E., Epstein, M. H., & Benner, G. J. (2003). Administrative discipline contacts: A review of the literature. *Behavioral Disorders, 28*, 249–281.

Newton, J. S., Todd, A. W., Algozzine, K. M., Horner, R. H., & Algozzine, R. F. (2009). *Team initiated problem solving training manual*. Eugene, OR: Educational and Community Supports.

Osher, D., Bear, G. G., Sprague, J. R., & Doyle, W. (2010). How can we improve school discipline? *Educational Researcher, 39*(1), 48–58. doi: 10.3102/0013189X09357618

Pas, E. (2010). *Examining the validity of office discipline referrals as an indicator of student behavior problems*. Manuscript submitted for publication.

Planty, M., Hussar, W., Snyder, T., Kena, G., KewalRamani, A., Kemp, J., … Dinkes, R. (2009). *The condition of education 2009* (NCES 2009-081). Washington, DC: National Center for Education Statistics.

Putnam, R. F., Luiselli, J. K., Handler, M. W., & Jefferson, G. L. (2003). Evaluating student discipline practices in a public school through behavioral assessment of office referrals. *Behavior Modification, 27*, 505–523.

Raffaele Mendez, L. M., & Knoff, H. M. (2003). Who gets suspended from school and why: A demographic analysis of schools and disciplinary infractions in a large school district. *Education & Treatment of Children, 26*, 30–51.

Raffaele Mendez, L. M., Knoff, H. M., & Ferron, J. M. (2002). School demographic variables and out-of-school suspension rates: A quantitative and qualitative analysis of a large, ethnically diverse school district. *Psychology in the Schools, 39*, 259–277. doi: 10.1002/pits.10020

Reinke, W., & Herman, K. (2002). Creating school environments that deter antisocial behaviors in youth. *Psychology in the Schools, 39*, 549–559.

Reynolds, C. R., & Kamphaus, R. W. (2004). *Behavior assessment scale for children* (2nd ed.). Circle Pines, MN: AGS.

Rusby, J. C., Taylor, T. K., & Foster, E. M. (2007). A descriptive study of school discipline referrals in first grade. *Psychology in the Schools, 44*, 333–350. doi: 10.1002/pits.20226

Scott, T. M., Nelson, C. M., & Liaupsin, C. J. (2001). Effective instruction: The forgotten component in preventing school violence. *Education and Treatment of Children, 24*, 309–322.

Simonsen, B., Fairbanks, S., Briesch, A. M., & Sugai, G. (2006). *Positive behaviour support classroom management self-assessment*. Storrs, CT: Center on Positive Behavioral Interventions and Supports.

Skiba, R. J., Michael, R. S., Nardo, A. C., & Peterson, R. L. (2002). The color of discipline: Sources of racial and gender disproportionality in school punishment. *The Urban Review, 34*, 317–342. doi: 10.1023/A:1021320817372

Skiba, R. J., & Peterson, R. L. (2000). School discipline at a crossroads: From zero tolerance to early response. *Exceptional Children, 66*, 335–347.

Skiba, R. J., Poloni-Staudinger, L., Simmons, A. B., Feggins, L. R., & Chung, C. G. (2005). Unproven links: Can poverty explain ethnic disproportionality in special education? *Journal of Special Education, 39*, 130–144.

Skiba, R. J., Simmons, A. B., Ritta, S., Gibb, A. C., Rausch, M. K., Cuadrado, J., & Chung, C. (2008). Achieving equity in special education: History, status, and current challenges. *Exceptional Children, 74*, 264–288.

Spaulding, S. A., Irvin, L. K., Horner, R. H., May, S. L., Emeldi, M., Tobin, T. J., & Sugai, G. (2010). Schoolwide social-behavioral climate, student problem behavior, and related administrative decisions: Empirical patterns from 1,510 schools nationwide. *Journal of Positive Behavior Interventions, 12*, 69–85.

Sprague, J. R., & Horner, R. H. (1999). Low-frequency high-intensity problem behavior: Toward an applied technology of functional assessment and intervention. In A. C. Repp, & R. H. Horner (Eds.), *Functional analysis of problem behavior: From effective assessment to effective support* (pp. 98–116). Belmont, CA: Wadsworth.

Sprague, J. R., Walker, H. M., Stieber, S., Simonsen, B., Nishioka, V., & Wagner, L. (2001). Exploring the relationship between school discipline referrals and delinquency. *Psychology in the Schools, 38*, 197–206.

Sugai, G., Sprague, J. R., Horner, R. H., & Walker, H. M. (2000). Preventing school violence: The use of office discipline referrals to assess and monitor school-wide discipline interventions. *Journal of Emotional and Behavioral Disorders, 8*, 94–101. doi: 10.1177/106342660000800205

Theriot, M. T., Craun, S. W., & Dupper, D. R. (2010). Multilevel evaluation of factors predicting school exclusion among middle and high school students. *Children and Youth Services Review, 32*, 13–19.

Tobin, T. J., Sugai, G., & Colvin, G. (1996). Patterns in middle school discipline records. *Journal of Emotional and Behavioral Disorders, 4*, 82–94.

Tobin, T. J., & Sugai, G. M. (1999). Using sixth-grade school records to predict school violence, chronic discipline problems, and high school outcomes. *Journal of Emotional and Behavioral Disorders, 7*, 40–53. doi: 10.1177/106342669900700105

Todd, A. W., Horner, R. H., Newton, J. S., Algozzine, R. F., Algozzine, K. M., & Frank, J. L. (2011). Effects of team initiated problem solving on meeting practices of schol-wide behavior support teams. *Journal of Applied School Psychology, 27*, 42–59.

Townsend, B. (2000). The disproportionate discipline of African American learners: Reducing school suspensions and expulsions. *Exceptional Children, 66*, 381–391.

Vincent, C. G., & Tobin, T. J. (in press). The relationship between implementation of School-Wide Positive Behavior Support (SWPBS) and disciplinary exclusion of students from various ethnic backgrounds with and without disabilities. *Journal of Emotional and Behavioral Disorders*. doi: 10.1177/1063426610377329

Wald, J., & Losen, D. J. (Eds.). (2003). *New directions for youth development: Deconstructing the school-to-prison pipeline.* San Francisco: Jossey-Bass.

Walker, B., Cheney, D., Stage, S. A., & Blum, C. (2005). Schoolwide screening and Positive Behavior Supports: Identifying and supporting students at risk for school failure. *Journal of Positive Behavior Interventions, 7*, 194–204.

Wallace, J. M., Jr., Goodkind, S., Wallace, C. M., & Bachman, J. G. (2008). Racial, ethnic, and gender differences in school discipline among U.S. high school students: 1991–2005. *Negro Educational Review, 59*, 47–62.

Wright, J. A., & Dusek, J. B. (1998). Compiling school base-rates for disruptive behavior from student disciplinary referral data. *School Psychology Review, 27*, 138–147.

24

Gauging the System

Trends in School Climate Measurement and Intervention

Meagan O'Malley,

WESTED

Kristin Katz

SANTA BARBARA COUNTY OFFICE OF EDUCATION

Tyler L. Renshaw

ALPINE SCHOOL DISTRICT, AMERICAN FORK, UT

Michael J. Furlong

UNIVERSITY OF CALIFORNIA, SANTA BARBARA

Abstract

Researchers and educators are giving increasing scrutiny to systems-level constructs that contribute to safe, supportive, and effective schools, including school climate. School climate is a multifaceted construct that is commonly conceptualized as school community members' subjective experiences of the structural and contextual elements of a particular school. Although all schools strive to provide a caring and supportive school climate, climate itself is not the ultimate objective. Rather, climate conditions facilitate students' physical and emotional safety, academic success, social engagement, and personal wellbeing. This chapter first discusses school climate definition and measurement issues. It then examines what is currently known about the positive correlates of school climate and offers guidance and strategies to assess climate at the school level.

Trends in School Climate Measurement and Intervention

The early part of the 21st century experienced a wave of public policy governing the teaching of discrete academic skills—a focus that largely eclipsed concurrent interest in the contexts in which these skills are learned. Indeed, children learn discrete academic skills in complex, interwoven ecological systems that are layered with interpersonal interactions, some of which may make them feel unsafe, insecure, or ineffective. During this same period of public scrutiny on academic skills development, mounting empirical evidence found that the context in which learning occurs is powerful. When the school context is unsupportive, it may interfere with, or undermine altogether, the larger educational goals of learning to read, write, and perform mathematics on the global level, as well as societal goals of developing emotionally healthy, productive community members. As a response to this imbalance, scholars are increasingly calling for a deliberate, purposeful focus on the ecological systems in which children learn (e.g., Cohen, McCabe, Michelli, & Pickeral, 2009; Connoley & Gutkin, 1995).

In response to the scholarship around contextual factors in learning, federal agencies have begun to focus on ways that schools can enhance students' short- and long-term psychosocial outcomes through intervention at the school systems level. Reducing risk-taking behavior and violence remains a paramount concern. However, the focus of policy is shifting to the measurement of system-level variables, particularly relationships and connectedness, that are implicated in improved short- and long-term psychosocial outcomes. This shifting focus is motivated by concern to prevent or minimize harm to students, but also by scholarship identifying and refining school-based constructs that are associated with positive youth development. School climate is one such construct, with a growing number of studies indicating that its dimensions are associated with positive youth outcomes and modifiable through purposeful educational practices (e.g., Brand, Felner, Shim, Seitsinger, & Dumas, 2003; see also Blum & Libbey, 2004 [*Journal of School Health* special issue on school engagement]).

The purpose of the present chapter is to elucidate the relation between school climate and multiple student safety indices and to frame school climate as a construct worthy of central focus for school safety teams. In the first section, a discussion of core school climate definitional issues is followed by a brief review of the correlates of school climate, highlighting relations between the construct and general student outcomes, general staff outcomes, and school safety outcomes. The second section examines the assessment of school climate, summarizing current measurement methods and outlining practical procedural approaches. The final section presents implications of school climate for school violence and safety, discussing critical issues and providing recommendations to enhance future scholarship and practice.

Defining School Climate

Scholars from the National School Climate Council (NSCC, 2009) proposed what is probably the most often cited definition of school climate: "the quality and character of school life ... [It] is based on patterns of people's experiences of school life and reflects norms, goals, values, interpersonal relationships, teaching, learning and leadership practices, and organizational structures" (p. 5).

As the NSCC's definition illustrates, there are numerous elements that comprise the structural or contextual nature of any given school's climate. It is therefore challenging—and probably unproductive—to define a single school climate "archetype." Rather, it is assumed that school climate elements vary from school to school, and even within schools over time, as the construct reflects local values, educational practices, and personal interactions that contribute to "spheres of school life" as well as to "larger organizational patterns" (Cohen et al., 2009, p. 182). It follows, then, that school climate can be conceptualized as the collective, subjective appraisal of individuals' experiences with their own local school environment, and that the elements upon which such appraisals are based may vary across schools, classes within schools, social groups, and individuals (e.g., Mitchell, Bradshaw, & Leaf, 2010). Elements that may be considered include tangible environmental components (i.e., availability and quality of physical resources) and/or intangible one (i.e., relationships, quality of leardership).

Reflecting the growing consensus over the broad definition of school climate, policy makers have begun to synthesize school climate-related scholarship for the following three purposes: (a) to determine the components of school climate that should be included in content standards, (b) to examine models for use in assessing school climate, and (c) to consider needs and concerns regarding accountability for meeting school climate standards (Jennings, 2010). In late 2009, a team of leading school climate scholars, policy makers, and related stakeholders drafted a proposed federal model for school climate that includes three first-order "pillars" labeled (a) engagement, (b) safety, and (c) environment. Relationships, respect for diversity, and school participation are subsumed under *engagement*. *Safety* includes emotional safety, physical safety, and substance use. Finally, *environment* includes the physical environment, academic environment, wellness, and disciplinary environment (Jennings). Subsequently, the U.S. Office of Education's Safe and Drug-Free Schools Office (2010) issued the Safe and Supportive Schools grant program (CFDA #84.184Y) for states to develop, validate, and implement school improvement efforts related to the three pillars of school climate.

Correlates of School Climate

Evidence for the impact of school climate on students, staff, and school safety is so compelling that, in their comprehensive review of the literature, four of the National Research Council and the Institute of Medicine's (2004) 10 recommendations for enhancing school engagement were directly linked to school climate issues. Following is a summary of findings from a number of domains that support the theoretical and practical importance of the school climate construct.

Student Outcomes

A large body of research supports the impact of school climate factors on student academic, behavioral, and social-emotional outcomes. For instance, students' perceptions of positive school climate are positively and significantly related to academic motivation, school connectedness, attitudes toward learning, and prosocial attitudes and behaviors (e.g., autonomy, efficacy, democratic values, conflict resolution skills; Brand et al., 2003; Klem & Connell, 2004; Ryan & Patrick, 2001; Waters, Cross, & Runions, 2009). Moreover, children who perceive positive climates at their schools achieve higher scores on measures of academic achievement—including tests in language, reading, and math, and overall grade-point-average (Brand et al., 2003; Wilms & Somer, 2001). These trends hold across U.S. and international studies (Jia et al., 2009; Wilms & Somer, 2001), as well as across age groups (Roeser, Eccles, & Strobel, 1998). Finally, students who attend schools with positive climates engage in fewer risk-taking and violent behaviors (Resnick et al., 1997), have fewer discipline referrals and school suspensions (Nelson, Martella, & Marchand-Martella, 2002; Welsh, 2000), and report feeling safer at school and more willing to report potential threats to safety (Syvertsen, Flanagan, & Stout, 2009; Welsh, 2000). Taken together, these findings suggest that students who have positive subjective appraisals of their school environment—or school climate—are more likely to enjoy school, perform well academically, have positive peer relationships, and act and feel safer than students who have negative or neutral perceptions of their local school climate.

School Staff Outcomes

While fewer studies have explored staff perceptions of school climate, empirical findings demonstrate equally robust positive outcomes across several domains. For example, teacher perception of school climate has been shown to be positively and significantly related to greater implementation fidelity of new curricula and interventions (Beets et al., 2008; Gregory, Henry, & Schoeny, 2007), decreased reports of teacher burnout (Grayson & Alvarez, 2008), and greater levels of teacher job satisfaction and work productivity (Bevans, Bradshaw, Miech, & Leaf, 2007; Lee, Dedrick, & Smith, 1991; Taylor & Tashakkori, 1995). Positive perception of school climate is also associated with teacher-efficacy (Bevans et al., 2007), intention to remain in the teaching profession (Weiss, 1999; see Guarino, Santibañez, & Daley, 2006, for review), and increased teacher retention (Kelly, 2004; Loeb, Darling-Hammond, & Luczak, 2005). Although these outcomes are positive ends in themselves, they are more compelling in terms of related "downstream effects" on student outcomes. It follows that more effective and satisfied teachers model positive interpersonal behaviors and report positive relationships with their fellow staff members and students. Indeed, evidence suggests that perceptions of positive school climate influence teacher practices that are likely to enhance positive psychosocial outcomes for their students (e.g., bully prevention programming) (Gregory et al., 2007), especially when working with low-income, minority populations (Brown & Medway, 2007; Hallinger, Bickman, & Davis, 1996). The data suggest that teacher and student perceptions of school climate are transactional—influencing each other in a bidirectional, cumulative way over time.

School Safety Outcomes

As described previously, poor perceptions of school climate are associated with risk-taking and violent behaviors among students (Resnick et al., 1997) as well as reduced feelings of safety (Welsh, 2000). Moreover, schools with weak school climates have higher rates of potential threats, but students are less willing to report these threats to school staff (Eliot, Cornell, Gregory, & Fan, 2010; Syvertsen et al., 2009). School climate also interfaces with school violence and safety indicators at other levels. For example, a convergence of empirical evidence indicates that students experiencing poorer school climates—for instance, those having little social support from peers, problematic relationships with teachers, and lacking appropriate instruction —are more likely to be victimized by peers at school (e.g., DioGuardi & Theodore, 2006; Lee & Croninger, 1996; Welsh, 2003; Welsh, Stokes, & Greene, 2000), engage in self-victimization (e.g., suicide) (Blum, 2001), and be situated within communities characterized by higher rates of disorder and violence (Gottfredson, Gottfredson, Payne, & Gottfredson, 2005). Beyond the student level, evidence suggests that school climate factors are predictive of teacher victimization rates at school—accounting for, in some cases, up to 18% of the variance of such rates in secondary schools (Gottfredson et al., 2005). Thus, early evidence suggests a moderate, positive association between students' and staff members' safety at school—or at least their lack of victimization—and favorable appraisals of school climate.

Other studies have examined the student connectedness or bonding aspect of school climate and found that it is the strong predictor of school safety outcomes, beyond the presence or condition of physical environment or organizational elements (e.g., Gottfredson et al., 2005; Resnick et al., 1997). Hence, scholars have suggested that student connectedness is one of the essential pillars for promoting safe, supportive, and effective schools (Osher, Dwyer, & Jimerson, 2006; Centers for Disease Control and Prevention, 2009). Focusing on students' connectedness to school should be viewed as a complementary, not contradictory, priority to focusing on safety-related indices. Together, these multiple data sources better represent the safety-status of school environments, and students' experiences therein, than other external and more distal indicators, such as the socioeconomic status of the surrounding community or historical patterns of school organization (e.g., Galloway, Martin, & Wilcox, 1985; Hellman & Beaton, 1986). Ultimately, this suggests that assessment and intervention efforts are likely to be more effective when they focus on multiple internal school climate variables. Of course, for an individual school to do this it needs access to efficient and effective methods and valid school climate measures with which to monitor campus conditions and adjust school programs and services to local conditions. We turn our attention now to a review of school climate measures that are readily available and have sufficient psychometric information to warrant their use.

Examining Current School Climate Measurement

Until very recently, Anderson's (1982) illustration of the construct of school climate with the fable of the blind men and the elephant, wherein each blind man defines the beast according to the part he can touch, remained appropriate. However, the period between 2009 and 2011 have proved rather fruitful for the growth of the school climate construct. A consensus has emerged regarding a common definition for school climate (see NSCC, 2009), as well as a solution to the problem of operationalizing school climate variables for the purpose of measurement. Before the three-pillar (engagement, safety, environment) federal school climate model (Jennings, 2010) was advanced, no single agreed upon conceptualization existed. Heretofore, research was based on a theoretical divide between those who posited that organizational climate within schools is a characteristic of the organization—an organizational trait—represented as an internal collective psychological appraisal of other external properties of a school (e.g., Van Horn, 2003) and those who argued that school climate is instead a trait of the individual perceiver because it reflects the cognitive representation of the environment by the individual (James, 1982, p. 219). Because survey development should be guided by theory, these differing conceptions led to the emergence of a gulf in approaches to identifying individual elements (e.g., relationships, safety, and administrative support) selected to represent school climate as a dependent or independent variable in contemporary scholarship (cf, Beets et al., 2008; Brand, Felner, Seitsinger, Burns, & Bolton, 2008). As a result, direct comparisons among many studies attempting to demonstrate school climate's effects on staff and student outcomes are challenging. The ongoing dilemma for interested researchers and practitioners has revolved around what specifically to assess, as the variables measured define and constrain possibilities for understanding and intervention. In an attempt to address this problem and reconcile it with recent developments in school climate theoretical construct development, the remainder of this chapter focuses on available methods for measuring school climate, with a special focus on strengths and limitations of each method.

Direct and Indirect Methods for Assessing School Climate

Lehr and Christenson (2002) suggest that two types of data, *indirect* and *direct*, may be collected for the gauging of a school's climate. Indirect measures can include raw data such as rates of suspensions, behavioral referrals, staff turnover, and teacher-to-student ratios, as well as objectively measurable properties of the environment, such as the number and quality of textbooks. While these indirect measures add an important dimension to the comprehensive assessment of school health, they do not tap into the psychological experience of the individual with the organization, which is the essence of school climate (James, 1982). It could be the case that a school ranks high on indirect measures (e.g., low rates of suspension, low rates of behavior referrals, and low staff turnover), but has low ratings in terms of community members' perceptions of support. Conversely, a school with few objectively measurable resources may have superior ratings on school climate psychological latent constructs (e.g., "resilient schools"). By tapping into individuals' psychological experiences with the school's environment, direct measures help eliminate the possibility of error by inference from indirect measures. Survey instruments, such as questionnaires, are an important and efficient direct measure of students', staff members', and parents' psychological experience of school climate.

Selecting a School Climate Survey Instrument

School climate instrument selection should link to the school's unique needs, and the improvement team's stated purpose and goals. The team will need to determine if it wishes to conduct a comprehensive assessment or a brief surveillance-style "check-up." Whatever the chosen instrument, school climate assessments should be time-efficient, suited for use across settings (i.e., primary, middle, and secondary) and stakeholder groups (i.e. staff, parents, and students), sufficiently researched and validated, and capable of identifying an array of organizational strengths and challenges.

Psychometric Properties of School Climate Measures

As previously discussed, school climate is typically measured by subjective appraisal of tangible and intangible elements of the school environment. Therefore, school climate is considered a latent construct—an underlying psychological experience—that is measured through self-report. When measuring latent constructs through self-report survey instruments, rigorous psychometric analyses of validity and reliability should guide scale development (Warner, 2008, p. 869). Many school climate and safety surveys, however, were developed as responses to national mandates to obtain population statistics, rather than in the interest of gaining insight into these latent psychological phenomena (cf. California School Climate Survey, Austin & Duerr, 2008; Sharkey, Dowdy, Twyford, & Furlong, this volume). As a result, psychometric analyses of available scales have often been conducted post-hoc, if at all. School climate measurement is thus limited by a lack of a single, unified, sophisticated instrument by which to assess and guide intervention.

While the field is awash with instruments purporting to measure school climate, no comprehensive, methodical reviews of school climate instruments currently exist in the peer-reviewed literature. Dissertations on the subject are growing in number, however. Gangi (2010), for example, began by identifying 102 staff surveys purporting to measure school climate, reviewing the only three surveys that met the following two inclusion criteria: (a) availability of current norms and (b) inclusion of factors shown to adequately predict student and staff outcomes. The three identified instruments (Comprehensive School Climate Inventory [CSCI; NSCC, 2009]; the (Tennessee) School Climate Inventory-Revised [SCI-R; Butler & Rakow, 1995]; and the Western Alliance for the Assessment of School Climate: School Climate Analytic Inventory [SCAI; Shindler, Taylor, Cadenas, & Jones, 2003]) were then ranked based on reliability data (i.e., internal consistency, interrater, alternate-form, and test-retest), validity data (i.e., content, construct, concurrent, convergent, divergent/discriminative, criterion, and/or predictive), and sample size/representativeness of norms. Based on these criteria, the SCAI was most favored, followed closely by the CSCI, and the SCI-R. Exemplary instrument items have been reprinted in Table 24.1 where permission has been granted by scales' authors.

Responding to the need to reconcile the growing consensus over the elements that define school climate (Jennings, 2010) with a psychometrically sound scale that measures those same constructs, Zullig, Koopman, Patton, and Ubbes (2010) combined items from five separate student-response measures in order to perform cross-battery exploratory and confirmatory factor analyses. Results revealed an eight-factor model (Positive Student-Teacher Relationships, School Connectedness, Academic Support, Order and Discipline, School Physical Environment, School Social Environment, Perceived Exclusion/Privilege, and Academic Satisfaction), with the largest proportion of variance explained by positive student-teacher relationships and, distantly, school connectedness. Their results suggest a great degree of consistency between the theoretically derived federal model (Jennings, 2010) and the statistically derived multidimensional solution, with engagement, safety, and environment components being represented. To date, similar psychometric rigor has not been applied to staff or parent measures of school climate.

Table 24.1   Staff School Climate Measures: Subscales and Selected Items

Comprehensive School Climate Inventory-Staff Form (CSCI) (NSCC, 2009)
http://www.schoolclimate.org/programs/csci.php

Subscales: Safety-Rules and Norms; Sense of Physical Security; Sense of Emotional Security; Support for Learning; Social & Civic Learning; Respect for Diversity; Social Support-Adults; Social Support-Students; School Connectedness/Engagement; Physical Surroundings

Adults who work in this school treat students with respect.
Adults in this school talk with students about strategies for understanding and controlling their emotions.
Staff in this school typically work well with one another.
Most staff in this school are generous about helping others with instructional issues.

1. Teachers encourage students to think independently.
2. The administration at this school provides teachers with opportunities to work together collaboratively.

Brief California School Climate Inventory (B-CSCS) (You et al., 2011)
http://web.me.com/michaelfurlong/HKIED/Welcome_files/MJF-CSCS-Nov7.pdf

Subscales: Organizational Supports; Relational Supports

1. School is a supportive and inviting place for students to learn.
2. School sets high standards for academic performance for all students.
3. School promotes academic success for all students.
4. Adults really care about all students.
5. Adults acknowledge and pay attention to students.
6. Adults want all students to do their best.

California School Climate Survey (CSCS) (Austin & Duerr, 2008)
http://cscs.wested.org/

Subscales: Staff Characteristics; School Norms & Standards; Staff-Student Relations & High Expectations; Student Opportunities for Participation; Student Behaviors that Facilitate Learning; Teaching/Working Conditions; Equity, Diversity, and Cultural Relevance; School Safety, Harassment, and Crisis Management

1. This school encourages opportunities for students to decide things like class activities or rules.
2. This school fosters an appreciation of student diversity and respect for each other.
3. This school is a safe place for students.
4. This school is a safe place for staff.
5. Adults at this school support and treat each other with respect.
6. Adults at this school feel a responsibility to improve this school.

School Climate Analytic Inventory (SCAI) (Shindler et al., 2003)a
http://www.calstatela.edu/centers/schoolclimate/assessment/#scai

Subscales: Physical Appearance; Faculty Relations; Student Interactions; Leadership/Decisions; Discipline Environment; Learning/Assessment; Attitude and Culture; Community Relations;

1. Level 3: Faculty members are typically constructive when speaking of each other and/or administrators.
   Level 2: Faculty members wait for safe opportunities to share complaints about other teachers and/or administrators.
   Level 1: Faculty members commonly use unflattering names for other faculty and/or administration in private.

2. Level 3: Faculty members have the time and interest to commune with one another, and feel very little isolation.
   Level 2: Faculty members congregate in some cordial groups, yet commonly feel a sense that teaching is an isolating profession.
   Level 1: Faculty members typically see no need to relate outside the walls of their classes.

3. Level 3: Various cultures and sub-groups blend, interrelate, and feel like valid members of the community.
   Level 2: Various sub-groups avoid each other and have varying degrees of sense of validity.
   Level 1: Various sub-groups are hostile to one another.

4. Level 3: Most of the staff have a high level of trust and respect in leadership.
   Level 2: Some staff have respect for leadership.
   Level 1: Most staff feel at odds with the leadership.

a The School Climate Analytic Inventory is an analytic trait-type scale. Response options are leveled as follows: Level 3 (high on the measured trait); Level 2 (mid-level of the trait); and Level 1 (low on the trait).

Brief School Climate Measures

In addition to being psychometrically sound, school climate measures must also be of practical benefit to school improvement teams working under significant resource constraints. To this end, the team must identify methods that are both practical and purposeful and that balance the tension between brevity and breadth. While they typically do not address all validated school climate elements, brief screening instruments provide practical benefits including the reduction of cost, time to administer and score, and staff time requirements for interpretation and data management (Caldarella, Young, Richardson, Young, & Young, 2008; Glover & Albers, 2007). The 15-item Brief California School Climate Survey (B-CSCS; You et al., 2011) is one such instrument for which psychometric data are available. In addition to validity and reliability data, the B-CSCS has evidence of factor invariance, which suggests that a single staff form measures perceptions of school climate consistently across multiple rater groups, including teachers and administrators (You et al., 2011).

The authors of the B-CSCS (You et al., 2011) suggest that the two factors measured (*Relational Supports* [positive, supportive relationships between and among staff and students; belief in, and encouragement of, student success; and personal investment in the school's performance] and *Organizational Supports* [schoolwide academic and behavioral standards, expectations for student performance, and support for staff and parent needs]) are essential elements consistent with the engagement and environment components of the federal school climate model. Results from the B-CSCS or other brief measures could be used by school reform teams to target and subsequently monitor specific climate intervention programs, but are not meant as replacements for comprehensive assessment strategies.

Single Form Versus Multiple Form

A single standardized, psychometrically sound survey measuring the same theoretically-driven latent school-climate constructs invariably across multiple respondent groups (e.g., teachers, students, parents) represents the panacea of school climate measurement. At this time, however, many school climate surveys employ different versions for different respondent groups. Items on each version may be group-specific (e.g., "The principal acknowledges and incorporates my feedback") or group-general (e.g., "I feel that my feedback is important at this school"). School climate assessment teams are faced with another tension, then selecting between measures that have single report forms for multiple informants (i.e., a single form for teachers, administrators, and parents), or different forms for each group.

The California School Climate Survey (CSCS), which is used in the national evaluation of the U.S. Federal Safe Schools/Healthy Student initiative (Sharkey et al., this volume), is an example of a measure with a single staff report form with preliminary psychometric evidence (Austin & Duerr, 2008; O'Malley, 2011). All staff members, including teachers, administrators, school psychologists, and other staff groups complete their endorsements of the same items. Areas for inquiry and potential intervention are illuminated when discrepancies are found between groups. Selected items from the CSCS are shown in Table 24.1.

Overview of School Climate Assessment

Having outlined trends in school climate measurement, the remainder of this chapter provides a framework for school climate assessment in schools. Until empirical studies on best practices for school climate-specific intervention are made available in the peer-reviewed literature, research from the school safety planning literature is tapped for general guidance.

As a first step, Pickeral, Evans, Hughes, and Hutchison (2009) recommend establishing school and district teams of administrators and practitioners charged with regularly surveying the school community and responding appropriately through policies and practices that are aligned with the goal of prioritizing healthy, positive learning environments. Since school climate assessment is best thought of as an iterative process, school climate teams are likely to be most effective when they meet multiple times through the year to plan for assessment, review assessment data, plan and implement interventions, and reassess at regular intervals throughout the school year.

In order to obtain the most accurate representation of a school's climate, the school climate team should plan to survey all members of the school community, including teachers, administrators, other staff members, students, and parents, early in the academic year. This recommendation is based on converging scholarship confirming that groups of different members of the school community perceive school climate differently, and that their school climate ratings may be biased by factors such as lack of experience (Van Horn, 2003). For example, Mitchell et al. (2010) demonstrated that not only do teachers and students consider different elements of the school and classroom when assessing climate, but that their ratings can diverge considerably. You and colleagues (2011) demonstrated similar divergence in perceptions of school climate between administrators and teachers, particularly at the secondary school level, with administrators having more positive school climate perceptions than teachers.

Assessment using comprehensive school climate measures at multiple time points is optimal for data collection purposes. However, recognizing the limitations of schools' tangible and intangible resources, it may be necessary to consider using brief surveillance-type screening measures. If a brief measure of climate yields results indicating areas of need, school climate teams would need to plan deeper probing, which may include a comprehensive assessment, stakeholder group discussions, and review of indirect data. In order to monitor the progress of selected interventions and guide future programming, additional brief probes could be given throughout the year either on an as-needed basis or at predetermined intervals, to all or selected members of

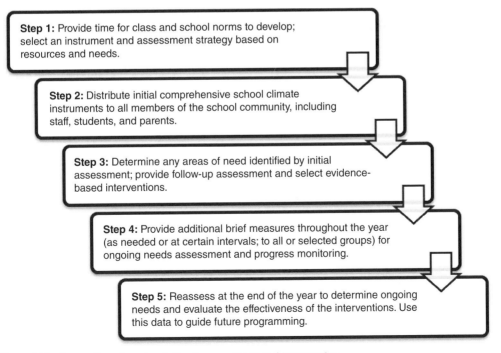

Step 1: Provide time for class and school norms to develop; select an instrument and assessment strategy based on resources and needs.

Step 2: Distribute initial comprehensive school climate instruments to all members of the school community, including staff, students, and parents.

Step 3: Determine any areas of need identified by initial assessment; provide follow-up assessment and select evidence-based interventions.

Step 4: Provide additional brief measures throughout the year (as needed or at certain intervals; to all or selected groups) for ongoing needs assessment and progress monitoring.

Step 5: Reassess at the end of the year to determine ongoing needs and evaluate the effectiveness of the interventions. Use this data to guide future programming.

Figure 24.1   Suggestions for school climate assessment and intervention

the community. Toward the end of each academic year, the team would reassess school climate to reflect on growth, determine ongoing needs, and guide future intervention planning. Figure 24.1 illustrates a suggested school climate intervention iterative process.

Conclusions and Implications

The working definition of school climate presented herein is that of a latent construct representing the collective, subjective appraisal of individuals' experiences with local school environments. This chapter examined the relations between this broad construct and school safety indicators by (a) discussing definitional issues, (b) reviewing the correlates of school climate, (c) outlining current assessment and measurement trends for the construct, and (c) offering preliminary guidance for selecting assessment tools. Overall, the chapter highlighted the importance of succinctly operationalizing specific school climate elements, recognizing their influence on student and staff outcomes, assessing these elements via direct and indirect measures, and using systematic, empirically-validated, multiple-informant, multigated measurement approaches that provide a broad and balanced assessment of a school's climate strengths and challenges.

Most importantly, practitioners and scholars should continue efforts examining the link between school climate and school safety indicators, as this work is in its infancy. For example, although it is clear that a positive school climate is unlikely to exist in an unsafe school, it does not necessarily follow that all safe schools have positive school climates. This is probably because safer schools (i.e., those lacking significant amounts of actual or threatened violence) do not necessarily promote positive interpersonal relationships that enable their members, including staff and students, to thrive. There is a clear need for deeper exploration of specific school climate elements, such as organizational supports and teaching practices, which enhance desired outcomes

Table 24.2 Implications for School Climate Assessment for Safe Schools Planning and Practices

1.	Regular monitoring of school climate is recommended to guide interventions that promote positive relationships within schools and help prevent negative outcomes, including deleterious academic and psychosocial outcomes for youth, staff dissatisfaction and turnover, and school violence.
2.	School safety indices are one component of a comprehensive assessment of school climate. Other central components include relationships, leadership and organizational support, and tangible elements of the environment.
3.	Indirect interpretations about school climate can be made through the collection of data such as suspension rates, behavioral referral rates, and staff turnover rates, although direct assessment is warranted in any comprehensive analysis.
4.	Direct assessment of school climate should be conducted using scales that have sufficient psychometric data to support their use.
5.	Comprehensive measures of school climate should assess those constructs (i.e., relationships, safety, organizational supports, tangible components of the environment) that have been consistently, positively related to student and staff outcomes.
6.	Brief school climate screening instruments provide practical benefits in surveillance-style progress monitoring, although they are not recommended as a replacement for a comprehensive assessment.
7.	All members of the school environment should be asked to complete school climate measures, including teachers and other staff members, administrators, students, parents.
8.	Assessment of school climate is an iterative process that requires the support of individuals from different stakeholder groups (i.e., teachers, administrators, parents, students).
9.	Interventions for school climate require ongoing team dialogue, intervention planning, and monitoring.

like school connectedness or belonging. Ultimately, it is by diverting the focus of research from decreasing negative outcomes to increasing positive ones that schools can more fully realize their dual role in the lives of youth. School climate is an essential construct for school safety teams seeking to foster safe, secure, and peaceful environments in which students and staff participate as meaningfully connected members of their communities.

References

Anderson, C. S. (1982). The search for school climate: A review of the research. *Review of Educational Research, 52,* 368–420.

Austin, G., & Duerr, M. (2008). *Guidebook for the California School Climate Survey for teachers and other staff.* San Francisco, CA: WestEd.

Beets, M. W., Flay, B. R., Vuchinich, S., Acock, A. C., Li, K., & Allred, C. (2008). School climate and teachers' beliefs and attitudes association with implementation of the Positive Action Program: A diffusion of innovations model. *Prevention Science, 9,* 264–275. doi:10.1007/s11121-008-0100-2

Bevans, K., Bradshaw, C., Miech, R., & Leaf, P. (2007). Staff- and school-level predictors of school organizational health: A multilevel analysis. *Journal of School Health, 77,* 294–302. doi:10.1111/j.1746-1561.2007.00210.x

Blum, R. (2001). Early transitions: Risk and protective factors. *The Center,* 38–41.

Blum, R. W., & Libbey, H. P. (2004). School connectedness: Strengthening health and educational outcomes for teenagers. Executive summary. *Journal of School Health, 74,* 231–232. doi:10.1111/j.1746-1561.2004.tb08278.x

Brand, S., Felner, R. D., Seitsinger, A., Burns, A., & Bolton, N. (2008). A large-scale study of the assessment of the social environment of middle and secondary schools: The validity and utility of teachers' ratings of school climate, cultural pluralism, and safety problems for understanding school effects and school improvement. *Journal of School Psychology, 46,* 507–535. doi:10.1016/j.jsp.2007.12.001

Brand, S., Felner, R., Shim, M., Seitsinger, A., & Dumas, T. (2003). Middle school improvement and reform: Development and validation of a school-level assessment of climate, cultural pluralism, and school safety. *Journal of Educational Psychology, 95,* 570–588. doi:10.1037/0022-0663.95.3.570

Brown, K. E., & Medway, F. J. (2007). School climate and teacher beliefs in a school effectively serving poor South Carolina (USA) African American students: A case study. *Teaching and Teacher Education, 23,* 529–540. doi:10.1016/j.tate.2006.11.002

Butler, D. E., & Rakow, J. (1995, July,). *Sample Tennessee school climate profile.* Memphis, TN: Center for Research in Educational Policy, The University of Memphis.

Caldarella, P., Young, E. L., Richardson, M. J., Young, B. J., & Young, K. R. (2008). Validation of the systematic screening for behavior disorders in middle and junior high school. *Journal of Emotional and Behavioral Disorders, 16,* 105–117. doi:10.1177/1063426607313121

Centers for Disease Control and Prevention. (2009). *School connectedness: Strategies for increasing protective factors among youth.* Atlanta, GA: U.S. Department of Health and Human Services.

Cohen, J., McCabe, L., Michelli, N. M., & Pickeral, T. (2009, January). School climate: Research, policy, teacher education and practice. *Teachers' College Record, 111,* 180–213.

Connoley, J. C., & Gutkin, T. B. (1995).Why didn't—why doesn't—school psychology realize its promise. *Journal of School Psychology, 33,* 209–217.

DioGuardi, R. J., & Theodore, L. A. (2006). Understanding and addressing peer victimization among students. In S. R. Jimerson & M. J. Furlong (Eds.), *Handbook of school violence and school safety: From research to practice* (pp. 339–352). Mahwah, NJ: Erlbaum.

Eliot, M., Cornell, D., Gregory, A., & Fan, X. (2010). Supportive school climate and student willingness to seek help for bullying and threats to violence. *Journal of School Psychology,* doi:10.1016/j.jsp.2010.07.001

Felson, R. B., Liska, A. E., South, S. J., & McNulty, T. L. (1994). The subculture of violence and delinquency: Individual vs. school context effects. *Social Forces, 73,* 155–173. doi:10.2307/2579921

Galloway, D., Martin, R., & Wilcox, B. (1985). Persistent absence from school and exclusion from school: The predictive power of school and community variables. *BritishEducational Research Journal, 11,* 51–61. doi:10.1080/0141192850110106

Gangi, T. (2010). *School climate and faculty relationships: Choosing an effective assessment measure.* Unpublished doctoral dissertation,St. John's University, New York, NY.

Glover, T. A., & Albers, C. A. (2007). Considerations for evaluating universal screening assessments. *Journal of School Psychology, 45,* 117–135. doi:10.1016/j.jsp.2006.05.005

Gottfredson, G. D., Gottfredson, D. C., Payne, A. A., & Gottfredson, N. C. (2005). School climate predictors of school disorder: Results from a national study of delinquency prevention in schools. *Journal of Research in Crime and Delinquency, 42,* 412–444. doi:10.1177/0022427804271931

Grayson, J. L., & Alvarez, H. K. (2008). School climate factors relating to teacher burnout: A mediator model. *Teaching and Teacher Education, 24,* 1349–1363. doi:10.1016/j.tate.2007.06.005:10.1016/j.tate.2007.06.005

Gregory, A., Henry, D. B., & Schoeny, M. E. (2007). School climate and implementation of a preventive intervention. *American Journal of Community Psychology, 40,* 250–260. doi:10.1007/s10464-007-9142-z

Guarino, C. M., Santibañez, L., & Daley, G. A. (2006). Teacher recruitment and retention: A review of the recent empirical literature. *Review of Educational Research, 76,* 173–208. doi:10.3102/00346543076002173

Hallinger, P., Bickman, L., & Davis, K. (1996). School context, principal leadership, and student reading achievement. *Elementary School Journal, 96,* 528–549. doi:10.1086/461843

Hellman, D. A., & Beaton, S. (1986). The pattern of violence in urban public schools: The influence of school and community. *Journal of Research in Crime and Delinquency, 23,* 102–127. doi:10.1177/0022427886023002002

James, L. (1982). Aggregation bias in estimates of perceptual agreement. *Journal of Applied Psychology, 67,* 219–229.

Jennings, K. (2010, June). *Keynote address.* Thirteenth annual meeting of the National Coordinating Committee on School Health and Safety, Washington, DC.

Jia, Y., Way, N., Ling, G., Yoshikawa, H., Chen, X., Hughes, … Lu, Z. (2009). The influence of student perceptions of school climate on socioemotional and academic adjustment: A comparison of Chinese and American adolescents. *Child Development, 80,* 1514–1530. doi:10.1111/j.1467-8624.2009.01348.x

Kelly, S. (2004). An event history analysis of teacher attrition: Salary, teacher tracking, and socially disadvantaged schools. *The Journal of Experimental Education, 72,* 195–220. doi:10.3200/JEXE.72.3

Klem, A. M., & Connell, J. P. (2004). Relationships matter: Linking teacher support to student engagement. *Journal of School Health, 74,* 262–273. doi:10.1111/j.1746-1561.2004.tb08283.x

Lee, V., & Croninger, R. (1996). The social organization of safe high schools. In K. M. Borman, P. W. Cookson, A. R. Sadovnik, & J. Z. Spade (Eds.), *Implementing educational reform: Sociological perspectives on educational policy* (pp. 359–392). Norwood, NJ: Ablex.

Lee, V., Dedrick, R., & Smith, J. (1991). The effect of social organization of schools on teachers' efficacy and satisfaction. *Sociology of Education, 64,* 190–208. doi:10.2307/2112851

Lehr, C. A., & Christenson, S. L. (2002). *Best practices in promoting a positive school climate.* In A. Thomas & J. Grimes (Eds.), *Best practices in school psychology-IV* (pp. 929–948). Bethesda, MD: National Association of School Psychologists.

Loeb, S., Darling-Hammond, L., & Luczak, J. (2005). How teaching conditions predict teacher turnover in California schools. *Peabody Journal of Education, 80,* 44–70. doi:10.1207/s15327930pje8003_4

Mitchell, C. P., Bradshaw, P. M., & Leaf, M. J. (2010). Examining the effects of schoolwide positive behavioral interventions and supports on student outcomes: Results from a randomized controlled effectiveness trial in elementary schools. *Journal of Positive Behavior Interventions, 12,* 133–148. doi:10.1177/1098300709334798

National Research Council and the Institute of Medicine. (2004). *Engaging schools: Fostering high school students' motivation to learn.* Washington, DC: The National Academies Press.

National School Climate Council. (2009). *Validity and reliability for the CSCI.* Retrieved on September 10, 2010, from http://www.schoolclimate.org/climate/documents/ValidityAndReliability-CSCI.pdf

Nelson, J. R., Martella, R. M., & Marchand-Martella, N. (2002). Maximizing student learning: The effects of comprehensive school-based program for preventing problem behaviors. *Journal of Emotional and Behavioral Disorders, 10,* 136–148. doi:10.1177/10634266020100030201

O'Malley, M. D. (2011). *The California School Climate Scale: Dimensionality and staff group differences.* Unpublished doctoral dissertation), The University of California, Santa Barbara. Santa Barbara, CA.

Orpinas, P., & Horne, A. M. (2010). Creating a positive school climate and developing social competence. In S. R. Jimerson, S. M. Swearer, & D. L. Espelage (Eds.), *Handbook of bullying in schools: An international perspective* (pp. 49–60). New York, NY: Routledge.

Osher, D., Dwyer, K., & Jimerson, S. R. (2006). Safe, supportive, and effective schools. In S. R. Jimerson & M. J. Furlong (Eds.), *Handbook of school violence and school safety: From research to practice* (pp. 51–72). Mahwah, NJ: Erlbaum.

Pickeral, T., Evans, L., Hughes, W., & Hutchison, D. (2009). *School climate guide for district policymakers and educational leaders.* New York, NY: Center for Social and Emotional Education.

Resnick, M. D., Bearman, P. S., Blum, R. W., Bauman, K. E., Harris, K. M., Jones, J., … Udry, J. R. (1997). Protecting adolescents from harm: Findings from the National Longitudinal Study of Adolescent Health. *The Journal of the American Medical Association, 278,* 795–878.

Roeser, R. W., Eccles, J. S., & Strobel, K. R. (1998). Linking the study of schooling and mental health: Selected issues and empirical illustrations at the level of the individual. *Educational Psychologist, 33,* 153–176.

Ryan, A. M., & Patrick, H. (2001). The classroom social environment and changes in adolescents' motivation and engagement during middle school. *American Educational Research Journal, 38,* 437–460. doi:10.3102/00028312038002437

Shindler, J., Taylor, C., Cadenas, H., & Jones, A. (2003, April). *Sharing the data along with the responsibility: Examining an analytic scale-based model for assessing school climate.* Paper presented at the annual meeting of the American Educational Research Association Washington, Chicago, IL.

Skiba, R., Simmons, A. B., Peterson, R., & Forde, S. (2006). The SRS Safe Schools Survey: A broader perspective on school violence prevention. In S. R. Jimerson & M. J. Furlong (Eds.), *Handbook of school violence and school safety: From research to practice* (pp. 157–170). Mahwah, NJ: Erlbaum.

Syvertsen, A. K., Flanagan, C., & Stout, M. D. (2009). Code of silence: Students' perceptions of school climate and willingness to intervene in a peer's dangerous plan. *Journal of Educational Psychology, 101,* 219–232. doi:10.1037/a0013246

Taylor, D. L., & Tashakkori, A. (1995). Design participation and school climate as predictors of job satisfaction and teachers' sense of efficacy. *Journal of Experimental Education, 63,* 217–230. doi:10.1080/00220973.1995.9943810

U.S. Office of Education Safe and Drug-Free Schools Office. (2010). *Safe and supportive schools. Fiscal year 2010 information and application procedures* (CFDA #84.184Y). Washington, DC: Author.

Van Horn, M. L. (2003). Assessing the unit of measurement for school climate through psychometric and outcome analyses of the school climate survey. *Educational andPsychological Measurement, 63,* 1002–1019.

Warner, R. (2008). *Applied statistics: From bivariate through multivariate techniques.* Thousand Oaks, CA: Sage.

Waters, S. K., Cross, D. S., & Runions, K. (2009). Social and ecological structures supporting adolescent connectedness to school: A theoretical model. *Journal of School Health, 79,* 516–524. doi:10.1111/j.1746-1561.2009.00443.x

Weiss, E. M. (1999). Perceived workplace conditions and first-year teachers' morale, career choice commitment, and planned retention: A secondary analysis. *Teaching and TeacherEducation, 15,* 861–879. doi:10.1016/S0742-051X(99)00040-2

Welsh, W. N. (2000). The effects of school climate on school disorder. *The ANNALS of the American Academy of Political and Social Science, 567,* 88–107. doi:10.1177/000271620056700107

Welsh, W. N. (2003). Individual and institutional predictors of school disorder. *Youth Violence and Juvenile Justice, 1,* 346–368. doi:10.1177/1541204003255843

Welsh, W. N., Stokes, R., & Greene, J. R. (2000). A macro-level model of school disorder. *Journal of Crime and Delinquency, 37,* 243–283. doi:10.1177/0022427800037003001

Wilms, J. D., & Somer, M. (2001). Family, classroom, and school effects on children's educational outcomes in Latin America. *School Effectiveness and School Improvement, 12,*4 09–445. doi:10.1076/sesi.12.4.409.3445

You, S., O'Malley, M., & Furlong, M. J. (2011). *Brief California school climate survey: Dimensionality and measurement invariance across teachers and administrators.* Manuscript submitted for publication.

Zullig, K. J., Koopman, T. M., Patton, J. M., & Ubbes, V. A. (2010). School climate: Historical review, instrument development, and school assessment. *Journal of PsychoeducationalAssessment, 28,* 139–152. doi:10.1177/073428290934420

Research-Based Prevention and Intervention Programs

25

A Social-Ecological Model for Bullying Prevention and Intervention in Early Adolescence

Susan M. Swearer

UNIVERSITY OF NEBRASKA–LINCOLN

Dorothy L. Espelage

UNIVERSITY OF ILLINOIS, URBANA-CHAMPAIGN

Brian Koenig

K12 ASSOCIATES, MADISON, WI

Brandi Berry, Adam Collins, and Paige Lembeck

THE UNIVERSITY OF NEBRASKA-LINCOLN

Abstract

A social–ecological model of the bullying dynamic is described in this chapter. The empirical literature linking individual, peer group, school, family, and community factors in bullying and victimization is reviewed. Data from 5,470 middle school students and 11,447 high school students in Grades 9 through 12 were analyzed to examine social–ecological variables involved in bullying and/or victimization. Specifically, we examined the influence of individual factors (depression, suicidal ideation, alcohol/drug use, sexual orientation, gender, race, grade); peer factors (peer alcohol, cigarette, drug use, delinquency); school factors (school climate, school belonging); family factors (free/reduced lunch, alternative home placement, risky family environment, parental abuse, positive parenting); and community factors (neighborhood safety, neighborhood connection) on bully perpetration and victimization. The social–ecological model of bullying was supported, illustrating the complex psychological and social picture of youth involved in bullying. Suggestions for positive supports across the social ecology are presented.

Involvement in bullying and peer victimization is the result of the complex interplay between individuals and their broader social environment. Since the first edition of this book, much has been written about the need to view bullying and peer victimization from a larger, social perspective. In this chapter, Bronfenbrenner's (1979) classic ecological theory is used as a foundation to illustrate the interrelated nature between the individual, multiple contexts, and engagement in bullying and victimization behaviors. First, the bullying literature across the social-ecology is reviewed, a social-ecological model of bullying is proposed and evaluated, and implications for effective bullying prevention and intervention are discussed.

Social-ecological theory has been previously applied to the conceptualization of bullying and victimization (Swearer & Doll, 2001; Swearer & Espelage, 2004; Swearer et al., 2006). It is clear from both theory and research that bullying and victimization are phenomena that are reciprocally influenced by the individual, peer group, school, family, community, and society. However, while we know that bullying is the result of multiple factors, a major challenge facing bullying researchers is how to empirically examine these many contexts. Although it is beyond the scope of this chapter to examine each area in depth, a brief overview of selected social-ecological variables associated with bullying and peer victimization is provided and followed by an empirical examination of these multiple influences.

Individual Variables Associated with Bullying and Victimization

Depression

Students who perpetrate bullying or who are bullied are more likely to report symptoms of depression than peers who are not involved in bullying (Roland, 2002; Seals & Young, 2003). Studies comparing students' involvement based on bully/victim status have yielded several results that support this finding. The results of three such studies found that victims scored significantly higher on depressive symptoms than bully perpetrators (Roland, 2002); victims and bully-victims endorsed higher depression scores than bullies (Menesini, Modena, & Tani, 2009); and bullies and bully-victims were more likely to be depressed compared to victims (Swearer, Song, Cary, Eagle, & Mickelson, 2001). Involvement in bullying is related to higher rates of depression regardless of whether the bullying is direct or indirect (Klomek, Marrocco, Kleinman, Schonfeld, & Gould, 2008; Marini, Dane, Bosacki, & YLC-CURA, 2006). Marini et al. (2006) found that bully-victims endorsed significantly higher levels of depression than bullies only when involved in indirect rather than direct bullying. Evidence suggests that bullying involvement, whether frequent or infrequent, is also associated with a higher risk for depression (Klomek, Marrocco, Kleinman, Schonfeld, & Gould, 2007). However, a student's risk for depression increases as the frequency of his or her involvement in bullying increases. The results of the study undertaken by Klomek et al. (2007) also showed that students who were bully-victims had the highest risk for depression. This was especially true for girls; in fact, girls who were bully-victims were 32 times more likely to be depressed than girls who were not involved in bullying. These results suggest that students involved in bullying, particularly bully-victims and girls, are more likely to experience symptoms of depression compared to uninvolved peers.

Suicidal Ideation

Studies show that adolescents involved in bullying report higher levels of suicidal ideation than students uninvolved in bullying (Klomek et al., 2007; Roland, 2002). While some evidence suggests that the association between suicidal ideation and bully/victim status may be stronger for victims of bullying compared to perpetrators of bullying (Rigby & Slee, 1999), the results of another study showed that perpetrators of bullying were more likely to report suicidal ideation than victims of bullying (Kaltiala-Heino, Rimpela, Marttunen, Rimpela, & Rantanen, 1999).

The results of one study found that bully-victims had the highest risk for suicidal ideation, as compared to bullies, victims, and students uninvolved in bullying (Klomek et al., 2007). Yet, other evidence suggests that there are no differences in levels of suicidal ideation between bully-victims and students who are not involved in bullying (Herba et al., 2008). Furthermore, while some studies have found that girls score significantly higher than boys on measures of suicidal ideation, regardless of bully/victim status (Klomek et al., 2007; Roland, 2002), other studies have found no gender differences in levels of suicidal ideation (Herba et al., 2008) or have found that boy, but not girl, bullies showed higher than average levels of suicidal ideation (Rigby & Slee, 1999). Thus, there are still many unanswered questions regarding bullying and suicidal ideation.

After exploring the relationship between these constructs, Herba et al. (2008) found that parental internalizing disorders and feelings of rejection in the home moderated the relationship between suicidal ideation and victimization. Evidence also suggests that high self-control and authoritative parenting may decrease the likelihood that victims of bullying will experience suicidal ideation (Hay & Meldrum, 2010). Another study found that social hopelessness partially mediated the relationship between suicidal ideation and victimization (Bonanno & Hymel, 2010). Consistent with Rigby and Slee (1999), these results also showed that perceived social support from family members appeared to have an ameliorating effect, such that students who report greater perceived family support endorse lower levels of suicidal ideation. At this point in time, the complex relationship between bullying and suicidal ideation is not fully understood.

Alcohol and Drug Use

Alcohol or drug use (AOD) is related to involvement in bullying as well. This association is not surprising given the well-documented correlation between substance use and aggressive behaviors in the literature. For instance, there is a link between fighting others and alcohol consumption (Shepherd, Sutherland, & Newcombe, 2006). In their middle school sample, Berthold and Hoover (2000) found that youth who bullied others were also more likely to smoke, chew tobacco, and drink alcohol than students who did not bully. In addition to these findings, students who bully are not the only students who are at-risk for alcohol and drug use. Alcohol consumption appears to be related to victimization as well (Thompson, Sims, Kingree, & Windle, 2008). The relationship between substance use and victimization is particularly evident for victims of bullying who are aggressive (i.e., bully-victims). For instance, in one study of seventh- through eleventh-grade students, aggressive victims and aggressive non-victims reported more alcohol and drug use than nonaggressive victims and nonaggressive non-victims (Brockenbrough, Cornell, & Loper, 2002). Bystanders (i.e., individuals who observe bullying) are also at-risk for substance use (Rivers, Poteat, Noret, & Ashurst, 2009). Overall, involvement in bullying is clearly related to alcohol use.

Sexual Orientation

Research has also explored the relationship between sexual orientation and involvement in bullying. A study that matched 106 seventh- through ninth-grade students attracted to same-sex individuals with same-age students attracted to opposite-sex individuals found no differences between the two groups in their reported rates of bullying others, observing bullying, or being victims of bullying (Rivers & Noret, 2008). Yet, the results of other studies have yielded contradictory results. Based on the survey responses of adolescents ages 14 to 22, gay males were less likely than heterosexual males to bully others while heterosexual females and bisexual females were more likely than heterosexual females to bully others (Berlan, Corliss, Field, Goodman,

& Austin, 2010). Mostly heterosexual males and gay males were more likely to be bullied than their heterosexual male peers. Similarly, mostly heterosexual females, bisexual females, and lesbians were more likely to be bullied than their heterosexual female peers. In addition, Birkett, Espelage, and Koenig (2009) found that lesbian, gay, bisexual, and questioning (LGBQ) students reported being bullied and being the targets of homophobic victimization more frequently than their heterosexual peers, with questioning students reporting the highest levels of bullying. Surprisingly, the perpetration of homophobic victimization may not indicate the presence of homophobic attitudes. Although the social context is a significant factor in explaining students' use of homophobic teasing, evidence suggests that aggressive social climates were found to have a stronger association with increased use of homophobic teasing than homophobic social climate (Poteat, 2008).

Compared to other types of bullying, however, homophobic victimization warrants special concern given that it appears to be associated with more negative outcomes than other forms of bullying. For example, one study found that boys who had been bullied by being called "gay," regardless of sexual orientation, showed more negative effects (e.g., more psychological distress) than peers bullied for other reasons (Swearer, Turner, Givens, & Pollack, 2008). Thus, it has been asserted that schools must combat homophobic teasing in order to improve outcomes for LGBQ students (Birkett et al., 2009). In addition, given that gay, lesbian, bisexual, transgender, and questioning (GLBTQ) students appear to be more vulnerable to bullying than their heterosexual peers, researchers have called for more research on bullying within sexual minority populations (Espelage & Swearer, 2003; Swearer, 2010).

Peer Variables Associated with Bullying and Victimization

It is the peer group that becomes a major socialization force during early adolescence. Researchers have consistently documented that the transition from elementary school to middle school is a potential stressor associated with negative emotional and psychological outcomes for some students. In the limited available research on the trend of bullying during this transition, it appears that there is a temporary increase in bullying during early adolescence (National Center for Educational Statistics [NCES], 1995; Pellegrini, 2002; Pellegrini & Bartini, 2001; Pellegrini & Long, 2002). Indeed, Akos (2002) found that fifth graders identified bullying as one of their primary concerns about starting sixth grade.

Peer Influences

It is clear that the peer group has a significant influence on students' socialization and behavior, especially during adolescence. Consequently, it is vital to closely examine peer groups to fully understand the bullying dynamic. Three theories that shed light on the peer group's effect on aggression and bullying are the dominance theory, homophily hypothesis, and attraction theory (Swearer et al., 2006). The dominance theory posits that bullying can be perceived as an avenue to obtain a higher social status (i.e., dominance) within a group (Pellegrini, 2002). However, bullying may result from an underlying desire to behave in ways that are similar to one's peers as well. This theory is captured by the term "homophily," which means that individuals who associate with one another tend to be similar in some way (Kandel, 1978). Although there is a paucity of research examining the homophily hypothesis and how it applies to bullying in particular, the results of one study suggest that the homophily hypothesis pertains to less severe aggressive behaviors for adolescents, such as teasing (Espelage, Holt, & Henkel, 2003). Lastly, the attraction theory states that adolescents are likely to pursue relationships with peers who reflect personality traits or behaviors indicative of independence, such as aggression, instead of with peers who represent adult-like values and conformity (Bukowski, Sippola, & Newcomb, 2000). These theories represent the myriad of explanations for how adolescents navigate peer relationships, which undoubtedly influence their involvement in bullying situations.

Within a bullying context, peers play a powerful role by encouraging aggressive behaviors, decreasing the likelihood of victimization, and buffering the adverse psychological effects that are associated with victimization. The literature indicates that peer influences are at least partially to blame for bullying behaviors. Observational studies conducted by Canadian researchers provided rich empirical data of how students participated or did not participate in bullying episodes on the playground (Craig & Pepler, 1995, 1997; O'Connell, Pepler, & Craig, 1999). It was evident that bullying was a group phenomenon because peers were present 85% of the time (Craig & Pepler, 1997), peers reinforced bullies' behaviors 81% of the time (Craig & Pepler, 1995), and intervened to help the victim only 11% of the time (Craig & Pepler, 1997). Salmivalli (2010) developed descriptors for the various roles that students take during bullying episodes, including reinforcers, assistants, and passive bystanders. Furthermore, Salmivalli, Huttunen, and Lagerspetz (1997) found that categories of students who were involved in the perpetration of bullying (i.e., bullies, assistants, and reinforcers) were members of larger peer groups than those who defended the victims, were uninvolved, or were victimized themselves. Also, several studies have investigated the effects of friendships and popularity of students who bully. Bullies tend to have an easier time making friends than victims and bully-victims (Nansel et al., 2001), and spend more time with other bullies than other students (Espelage & Holt, 2001). Interestingly, Espelage and Holt (2001) also found that students who bullied others engaged in this type of aggression at levels that were similar to those of their friends. Furthermore, deviant peers often encourage bullying through their willingness to engage in negative behaviors in general. For instance, Espelage, Bosworth, and Simon (2000) found that individuals who were more likely to damage property, fight, and interact with gangs were also more likely to perpetrate bullying in early adolescence.

Although peers can have a negative influence on youth who bully by encouraging these behaviors, peers can also serve as positive role models and buffer the negative outcomes associated with bullying. Even perceptions of students' social support are linked to their bully/victim status. For instance, Holt and Espelage (2007) found that bully-victims and victims report lower levels of social support than bullies and uninvolved peers. Additionally, the results of one study demonstrated that having a close friend decreased the likelihood that a student would be victimized and prevented the escalation of victimization for students who were already the targets of peer aggression (Hodges, Boivin, Vitaro, & Bukowski, 1999). Similarly, being liked by peers appears to serve as a protective factor against victimization (Pellegrini, Bartini, & Brooks, 1999).

Even though the quantity of friendships decreases one's likelihood of being victimized, the behaviors and qualities of the victims' friends matter more than the number of friends alone. Supporting this notion, a study by Hodges, Malone, and Perry (1997) found that students who were bullied were less likely to be targeted if their friends exhibited externalizing behaviors instead of behaviors or traits that could be interpreted as "weak." These authors speculated that externalizing peers might be more likely than internalizing peers to stand up to bullies and actively offer protection. Moreover, peers can be excellent sources of emotional and psychological support. For instance, peer support can serve as a protective factor for those who are at-risk for experiencing negative psychological outcomes by promoting psychological well-being (McCreary, Slavin, & Berry, 1996). Furthermore, peer support bolsters self-esteem in adolescents (Colarossi & Eccles, 2003) and helps alleviate stress (Hartup, 1996). Thus, peer support and friendships can positively affect the lives of students who are victimized.

Delinquency

Much of the literature supports the relationship between delinquency and criminal behaviors among school-aged youth. Research has suggested that bullying is a precursor to subsequent delinquency (Baldry & Farrington, 2000). According to Olweus (1995), approximately 35% to 40% of sixth through ninth graders who bully others will be convicted of three crimes by the time they reach 24 years of age. This statistic underlies the relationship between bullying and criminality. Also, findings demonstrate that the same individuals who bully in the school setting also exhibit violent behaviors in the community. For instance, bullies are more likely to carry weapons than other bully/victim subgroups (Andershed, Kerr, & Stattin, 2001), and offenders who bully typically spend a longer time in jail than victims and uninvolved individuals (Ireland & Monaghan, 2006).

In conjunction with their tendency to perpetrate bullying, delinquent youth are prone to victimization. However, they are more likely to experience more violent forms of victimization outside of school than non-delinquent individuals (Andershed et al., 2001). This relationship is most likely explained by delinquent adolescents' tendencies to engage in risky activities (Cuevas, Finkelhor, Turner, & Ormrod, 2007). Unlike a non-delinquent population, in which there are typically non-aggressive victims (i.e., pure victims) and aggressive victims (i.e., bully-victims), both victim subgroups within an adolescent offender population are characterized by aggressive tendencies. In support of this view, one study found that a pure victim group in a prison setting had bullied others in the community (Viljoen, O'Neil, & Sidhu, 2005). In general the link between bullying and delinquency is noteworthy regardless of the individual's status as a bully, victim, or bully-victim.

Overall, peers play a critical role for adolescents who bully and who are victimized. In conjunction with the individual variables associated with bullying and victimization, the aforementioned peer factors can shed light on the processes that underlie and maintain bullying interactions. Unfortunately, there is a discrepancy between adolescents' support for bullying, which tends to decrease after the transition to secondary school, and willingness to intervene when they witness a peer being victimized (Salmivalli, 2010). This decrease in willingness to intervene in bullying situations after the transition to secondary schools illustrates the importance of examining school variables that influence the experience of bullying and victimization (Espelage & Swearer, 2003).

School Variables Associated with Bullying and Victimization

While much of the research on bullying has focused on individuals and peers, the broader impact of school factors has largely been ignored. Individuals interact within peer groups for the majority of each day in the school setting. The school setting affects the academic, social, and emotional functioning of all students and is integrally connected to the overall climate of the school. School climate has long been recognized as an important factor in student outcomes, resulting in the identification of a number of factors that affect and are affected by school climate. Anderson's (1982) comprehensive review of the literature identified several important factors influencing school climate. These factors were categorized into three groups: *milieu* (i.e., characteristics of the individuals and groups in the school); *social system* (i.e., the variables which address the relationships within the school); and *culture* (i.e., variables which include group beliefs and values).

School personnel play a key role in creating a positive or negative school climate. Recent research suggests that teachers may actually tolerate bullying, resulting in increases in bullying behaviors (Yoneyama & Naito, 2003). Teachers have also been found to be inaccurate in estimating the amount of bullying that occurs in their schools (Holt & Keyes, 2004). Additionally, teachers may lack knowledge about how to effectively respond when they observe bullying (Espelage & Swearer, 2003). Teachers' abilities to respond to bullying have implications for student perceptions of effective interventions. Adair, Dixon, Moore, and Sutherland (2000) found that almost half of the students surveyed believed that bullying could not be stopped. When students observe a lack of awareness and responsiveness on the part of teachers, they may feel hopeless and believe that effective solutions are impossible (Dupper & Meyer-Adams, 2002; Houndoumadi & Pateraki, 2001). Unnever and Cornell (2003) also found that the majority of students felt that their peers and their teachers would not stop bullying.

School Climate and Academic Engagement

Research has explored a number of academic factors that may relate to the experience of being involved in bullying, such as connectedness to school. This is an important factor to consider since school belonging has been found to predict academic competence for students who bully or are victims of bullying (Ma, Phelps, Lerner, & Lerner, 2009). When teachers were asked to rate their students on school engagement, students identified as bullies, victims, or bully-victims were rated as being highly disengaged from school, with bully-victims receiving the highest school disengagement ratings (Juvonen, Graham, & Schuster, 2003). Within a longitudinal study, fifth- and sixth-grade students identified as bullies self-reported lower rates of school belonging compared to students uninvolved in bullying (Ma et al., 2009). Students identified as victims reported rates of school belonging that were similar to those reported by uninvolved students. Similarly, among children 10–11 years of age, the experience of being victimized was only moderately related to low school belonging (Beran, 2008). However, it was theorized that being victimized leads to stress which may inhibit some children's ability to concentrate, thus decreasing school engagement. In fact, a study that compared an experimental school, which received an intervention that successfully reduced the number of discipline referrals, to a matched control school found that students' scores on measures of academic achievement increased within the experimental school but not the control school (Twemlow et al., 2001). This finding held for the experimental school's overall test scores as well as for individual students' test scores. Furthermore, within the experimental school, teachers reported that victims of bullying became less withdrawn and more verbal within the classroom after the intervention. In summary, being involved in bullying may decrease academic engagement, particularly for bullies and bully-victims, and decreases in bullying and other forms of violence within schools may lead to improved academic outcomes for all students.

Family Variables Associated with Bullying and Victimization

Although much of the bullying and victimization reported by adolescents occurs in the schools, researchers have begun to examine the early developmental processes such as family socialization that may contribute to bullying and victimization. According to Lickel, Schmader, and Hamilton's (2003) investigation of public perception after the Columbine shootings in Littleton, Colorado, parents were perceived as having the most responsibility for the tragedy. The authors contend that parents are often held responsible by the public because they are expected to be close to and have authority over their children. Although some research has investigated the impact of the family on bullies and victims there is less research investigating the parent responsiveness to bullying. However, numerous news reports detail parents' attempts to talk with school personnel about bullying incidents. When schools respond ineffectively, parents take matters into their own hands by either transferring their child to another school or pursuing legal action. Research suggests that students tend to report bullying to their parents instead of teachers, suggesting that students believe their parents will be more effective in addressing the bullying than their teachers (Houndoumadi & Pateraki, 2001).

Risky Family Environment

Although peers have a powerful impact on adolescents, family variables and the home environment are also strongly related to bullying and victimization. Adolescents who report high rates of bullying tend to have problematic relationships with their parents that are typically characterized by conflict (Pepler, Jiang, Craig, & Connolly, 2008). There is evidence to suggest that students who bully have ambivalent relationships with their family members and feel emotionally restricted at home (Connolly & O'Moore, 2003). Research has found an indirect relationship between mother and father disengagement and bullying in a sample of adolescents (Flouri & Buchanan, 2003). Relatedly, youth who do not communicate with their parents may be more likely to engage in delinquent actions (e.g., bullying) than youth who openly communicate with their parents since they do not feel the need to earn their parents' respect (Hirschi, 1969).

Parents' relationships with each other also impacts youth's involvement in bullying. Social learning theory can explain how students' behaviors are modeled at home and then transferred to the school environment (Bandura, 1978). Social learning theorists contend that children acquire aggressive behaviors such as bullying through modeling and imitation. Thus, exposure to parental conflict puts youth at increased risk for bullying at school since parents or caregivers are modeling ways to be aggressive toward others (Bowes et al., 2009). Therefore, interparental discord does not offer youth opportunities to learn effective, non-violent ways to manage conflict. Overall, the evidence stresses the importance of considering family relationships in conjunction with the quality of relationships between the parents and youth who are at-risk for bullying involvement.

How parents respond to their children's misbehavior is correlated with adolescents' involvement in bullying interactions, particularly for students who bully others. Students whose parents resort to overly harsh punishment and power-assertion strategies perceive aggressive approaches to be effective ways to solve problems and achieve one's goals (Roberts, 2000). Furthermore, many parents inadvertently excuse or even ignore bullying since they consider bullying to be "childish" and developmentally appropriate. In other words, parents frequently minimize the severity of these behaviors (Korbin, 2003). These reactions set the stage for bullying to continue by communicating that there will be no negative consequences for bullying.

In addition to parental interaction styles and interparental conflict, having a parent in jail places youth at risk for aggressive tendencies that could be manifested through bullying. Much of the existing literature highlights the link between having a parent in jail and externalizing and delinquent behaviors (Miller, 2006). Some believe that this aggression results from the lack of support received once a parent is in jail. For example, Fritsch and Burkhead (1981) found that a lack of sympathy and less family cohesion followed a parent's incarceration. These authors also found that both externalizing and internalizing symptoms emerged in children with incarcerated fathers or mothers. Dysfunctional home environments that are characterized by family variables such as interparental discord, child abuse, low emotional support, and incarceration increase the chances that youth will be involved in bullying at school.

According to social control theory, delinquency occurs in the absence, or weakening, of ties to society (Hirschi, 1969). When exploring bonds to parents in particular, virtual supervision (i.e., the knowledge parents have of where and with whom their children are when they are away from home) has been identified as an important factor in understanding one's risk for engaging in delinquency. When comparing self-reported delinquency to perceived maternal virtual supervision, 100% of junior high and high school boys reporting low maternal supervision also reported engaging in at least one act of delinquency. Of boys reporting high maternal supervision, roughly 62% reported engaging in no acts of delinquency and only approximately 12% reported engaging in two or more acts of delinquency. Therefore, it appears as though boys reporting low maternal supervision are more likely to engage in delinquency than boys reporting high maternal supervision. In addition to helping to explain delinquency in general, social control theory has been applied to specific acts, such as bullying (Espelage & Swearer, 2009). Middle school students receiving less parental supervision have been found to be significantly more likely to bully others (Espelage et al., 2000). Adolescent boys 13–18 years of age involved in indirect bullying either as bullies or bully-victims reported receiving less parental supervision than indirect victims and students uninvolved in bullying (Marini et al., 2006). Thus, low parental supervision appears to put youth at risk for bullying others.

Parental Abuse

Although hostile, aggressive home environments lead the way for bullying behaviors, abuse at home is a strong predictor of later victimization at school. The homes of bully-victims tend to be characterized by high levels of hostility, low warmth, and abuse (Pellegrini, 1998). Although child maltreatment is associated with involvement in the bullying dynamic in general (i.e., role as a bully, victim, or bully-victim), being the victim of maltreatment is closely related to victimization or victimization with aggressive tendencies (Bowes et al., 2009). On the other hand, Fang and Corso's (2008) study lends support for their hypothesis that different types of child abuse (i.e., sexual, physical) and neglect are related to the perpetration of these actions as individuals approach adulthood. The general consensus is that experiencing parental abuse places youth at risk for perpetration of aggressive behaviors (e.g., bullying) later in life since the abuse conveys the acceptability of violence.

Few studies have explored the impact of parental alcohol problems on their children's bullying involvement. One longitudinal study explored connections between parental alcohol problems, attachment styles, and bullying behaviors and found that parental alcohol problems directly predicted bullying behaviors for boys (Eiden et al., 2010). There was a significant relationship between paternal alcohol problems and bullying behaviors for boys who had an insecure attachment with their mothers but not for girls or secure boys. There was a significant relationship between bullying behaviors and maternal alcohol problems for secure boys but not girls or insecure boys. More research is needed to better understand the impact of paternal alcohol problems on their children's bullying involvement, particularly for girls.

In addition to parental alcohol problems, exposure to domestic violence (DV) may be associated with bullying behaviors. Baldry (2003) found that witnessing DV was significantly associated with bullying others and being bullied at school, even after controlling for direct child abuse. Children who witnessed DV were more likely to be bullied at school compared to peers who were not exposed to DV. Both boys and girls exposed to DV in which a mother threatened a father were significantly more likely to be involved in indirect bullying than peers not exposed to this form of DV. These results are consistent with Bowes et al. (2009), who found that witnessing DV by the age of 5 was associated with bullying behaviors. Overall, it is clear that witnessing violence at home puts children at risk for bullying involvement, and leads to the need for positive home environments.

Positive Parenting

The ecological nature of bullying suggests that parental factors influence the bullying phenomenon. Parental support plays a unique role in the lives of those on the bully/victim continuum. Children who engage in bullying behaviors often report lower perceived parental social support than their peers while victims of bullying perceive having the most parental social support (Demaray & Malecki, 2003). Those students who perceive high paternal social support, however, are less likely to be victimized (Rubin et al., 2004) and may also be protected from the effects of victimization when they are bullied (Flouri & Buchanan, 2002). Fewer studies have narrowed the focus of parental influence to the specific roles of parental communication and parental values as they relate to bullying. Parental communication refers to how frequently children talk to their parents about certain topics (e.g., drugs, friends, personal issues). Parental values generally refer to the perception children have about their parents' beliefs and if they consider them to be acceptable (e.g., violence, sexual behavior).

The effects of parental communication on children involved in bullying are still unclear. In a study by Spriggs, Iannotti, Nansel, and Haynie (2007), bullying and parental communication were examined between three different racial groups (i.e., White, Black, and Hispanic). Results from this study suggested that children who engage in bullying behaviors, regardless of race, perceive having poor communication with their parents. A separate study by Jeynes (2008) examined parent-child communication in a sample of college and secondary school students. In both samples, those who were victims of bullying perceived having less communication with their parents. Despite these studies providing evidence of a connection between bullying and parental communication, contrasting research also exists. A study presented by Espelage and Swearer (2009) found that, from a sample of seventh and eighth grade students in a Midwestern county, engaging in bullying behaviors was not associated with parental communication. These differences could be due to many factors including the differing scales used to measure parental communication and the samples assessed.

The relationship between parental values and the involvement of children in bullying is still largely unknown. Parenting behaviors, however, have been shown to be related to the goals and values parents hold for their children (Darling & Steinberg, 1993). Relatively few studies have examined parental values in particular with most studies having a form of parental values subsumed in other variables (e.g., parent involvement in school, parenting style, enmeshment). In the study previously presented by Espelage and Swearer (2009), parental values had no significant effect on the bullying experiences of the seventh and eighth grade children. Studies examining parental values via proxy variables, however, have found some significant results. One of the most common findings is that victims of bullying have mothers who are overprotective (Bowers, Smith, & Binney, 1994; Georgiou, 2008; Perren & Hornung, 2005; Stevens, De Bourdeaudhuij, & Van Oost, 2002). Several of these studies propose that the overprotection these children receive may encourage the development of passive personalities which lead these children to appear weak and as "easy targets" for bullying.

The children of parents who endorse authoritative parenting values (i.e., permitting independence while setting limits and being responsive to their child's needs) are less likely to engage in bullying behaviors (Rican, Klicperova, & Koucka, 1993). Furthermore, parents who use physical discipline and have poor conflict resolution strategies are at greater risk for their children bullying others. Espelage et al. (2000) examined the bullying behaviors and parental styles of 558 middle school students. They found that parents who use physical discipline in the home are more likely to have children who bully. Other studies have shown that the strategies families use to resolve conflict in the home may influence bullying behavior. Children who perceive fair resolutions to conflicts with their parents are less likely to engage in bullying behaviors (Brubacher, Fondacaro, Brank, Brown, & Miller, 2009), while those who come from families using poor conflict resolution strategies are more likely to engage in bullying behaviors (Duncan, 2004). It seems that the values parents endorse and how they communicate these values affects the likelihood that their children will be involved in bullying and/or victimization.

Community Variables Associated with Bullying and Victimization

Just as individual, peer, school, and family characteristics impact bullying and victimization, the characteristics of the community in which children live and go to school also have direct and indirect influences on these behaviors. Rates of child maltreatment, delinquency, violence, aggression, and general externalizing behavior in youth have all been linked to community-level variables (Jonson-Reid, 1998; Kupersmidt, Griesler, DeRosier, Patterson, & Davis, 1995; Plybon & Kliewer, 2001). However, few studies directly connect community structure to the phenomenon of bullying. Bullying differs from other aggressive behaviors in that it is chronic, involves a power differential, and is repetitive (Olweus, 1993). Many bullying prevention programs incorporate components addressing community factors (Cox, 1997); however, an analysis of community variables and bullying is sparse.

Neighborhood Safety and Neighborhood Connection

Researchers have asserted that a consideration of community factors is necessary if bullying prevention and intervention programs are to be effective (Espelage & Swearer, 2003; Swearer, Espelage, Vaillancourt, & Hymel, 2010). One such community factor, neighborhood safety, has been found to be associated with fewer externalizing behaviors, including bullying, for adolescents 11–17 years of age (Youngblade et al., 2007). Similarly, within this study, perceptions of negative neighborhood influences were associated with higher rates of externalizing behaviors. Consistent with these findings, a positive association was found between neighborhood safety concerns and bullying behaviors, such that middle school students who perceived their neighborhoods as being less safe were significantly more likely to bully their peers than students who perceived their neighborhoods as being safer (Espelage et al., 2000). This trend may be partially explained by increased opportunities to witness, and thus learn to perpetrate, acts of violence in more dangerous neighborhoods (see social learning theory; Bandura, 1978). However, a study that presented children with hypothetical situations and pictures of houses manipulated to appear in good vs. poor condition yielded results that complicate this picture (Pitner & Astor, 2008). Specifically, the results demonstrated that a greater proportion of children approved of retribution for name-calling in the context of a setting perceived to be in poor vs. good physical condition (34% vs. 19%, respectively). Thus, to some extent, children's attitudes toward bullying may be context-dependent.

Based on the brief review of individual, peer, family, school, and community variables that impact involvement in bullying and victimization, it is easy to see that the interaction between these multiple systems is critical to understanding the social-ecological framework of bullying and victimization in early adolescence. During the transition from elementary school to middle school, students enter a new environment where the nature of peer groups is changing, teachers are less connected to students, academic work becomes more rigorous, and biological changes occur within the individual. Additionally, the family becomes a less salient force in the lives of middle school students. The community that surrounds the home and the school becomes more important as students may walk to and from school and become more involved in community activities. Some students may use aggressive behaviors, in the form of bullying, to establish a higher position on the hierarchy of social dominance within their peer group. Attraction theory suggests that these students will be seen as attractive by their peers and potentially could have a socializing effect on other students, as bullying may be viewed as "cool" (Rodkin, 2004). These changes across multiple contexts present fertile ground for bullying during this developmental period.

In the remainder of this chapter, a social-ecological model of bullying and victimization in early adolescence is proposed and parts of this model are empirically examined. In this model, influences of *individual factors* (i.e., sex, grade, race, free/reduced lunch, history of alternative home placement, sexual orientation, depression, suicidality, alcohol/drug use), *peer factors* (i.e., delinquency, peer influences), *school factors* (i.e., school climate and belonging), *family factors* (i.e., risky family environment, parental abuse, positive parenting), and *community factors* (i.e., neighborhood safety and neighborhood connection) are tested.

Method

Participants

Participants in the 2009 Dane County Youth Survey (DCYS) were 5,470 middle school students in Grades 7 and 8 (50.2% girls) and 11,447 high school students in Grades 9 through 12 (49.8% girls), ages 10 through 18 ($M = 14.85$, $SD = 1.76$). The racial diversity was similar to that of the 2005 DCYS (see Espelage & Swearer, 2009). Of the participants, 85.3 and 87.9% were classified as heterosexual among middle school and high school students, respectively. At the middle school level, the remaining students were classified as LGBT or questioning (14.7%), and at the high school level the remaining students were classified as LGBT or questioning (12.1%).

Measures

To provide validation for the study's measures, longitudinal data were used to inform measurement models. The 2005 Dane County Youth Survey (Koenig, Espelage, & Biedndseil, 2005) was conducted to collect extensive information on the opinions, behavior, attitudes, and needs of students. The survey assessed specific information on self-reported attitudes and behaviors related to health-related behaviors (e.g., bullying, victimization, substance use) and perceptions about parents, peers, schools, and communities among students from Grades 7 through 12. First, exploratory factor analyses (EFA) of items in the 2000 Dane County Youth Survey were conducted (Mayberry, Espelage, & Koenig, 2009). Next, results from the EFA informed the construction of measurement models using confirmatory factor analysis (CFA) from data collected in 2005 and further evaluated in the 2009 survey (Koenig & Bettin, 2009). CFAs with robust maximum likelihood estimations were conducted using LISREL 8.2 (Jöreskog & Sörbom, 1998). Because the purpose of the EFA was to identify the most applicable model with meaningful factors, two criteria were used in retaining a preliminary factor structure: (a) factor loadings that exceeded .40 were retained (Floyd & Widaman, 1995), and (b) cross loadings greater than .40 were eliminated. The intent was to maintain both theoretical and conceptual plausibility. CFA determines if the number of factors and the loadings of indicator variables conform to what is expected on the basis of the previous results from the 2005 data. Indicator variables were selected on the basis of prior theory and the EFA/CFAs of the 2005 data set.

Bullying/Victimization Outcomes

The major outcomes of bullying perpetration and peer victimization were assessed with two scales that yield scores with established validity and reliability. A self-report scale of bullying perpetration behavior (University of Illinois Bullying Scale; UIBS; Espelage & Holt, 2001) included 9 items assessing verbal, physical, and social bullying ($\alpha = .91$) and the peer victimization (University of Illinois Victimization Scale; UIVS; Espelage & Holt, 2001) scale included 4 items measuring verbal and physical victimization ($\alpha = .87$).

Individual Factors

Depression/Suicidal Ideation

To assess depression/suicidal behavior ($\alpha = .65$), participants were asked the following three questions: (1) During the past 12 months, did you ever feel so sad or helpless almost every day for two weeks in a row or more that you stopped doing some usual activities?; (2) During the past 12 months, have you attempted to kill yourself?; (3) During the past 30 days, have you seriously thought about killing yourself?

Alcohol/Drug Use

Alcohol and drug abuse ($\alpha = .90$) was assessed with the following six items: In the past 30 days, how many days did you: (1) have 5 or more alcoholic drinks at one time in a row?; (2) use marijuana?; (3) drink hard liquor?; (4) attend school after drinking alcohol or using marijuana?; (5) drink beer or wine?; (6) use other illegal drugs?

Sexual Orientation

Measures including self-report of sexual orientation (gay, lesbian, bisexual, transgender, questioning, heterosexual) were elicited to examine individual characteristics.

Demographics

Measures including self-reports of sex, grade (middle vs. high school), race, free/reduced lunch, and a history of alternative home placement (i.e., foster care, juvenile detention) were also elicited.

Peer Factors

Peer Influences

Two items were used to assess the extent to which participants' friends drank alcohol or used tobacco as a measure of positive peer influence. Participants were asked how much they agreed or disagreed with the following two statements: (1) Most of my friends DO NOT drink or do drugs; (2) Most of my friends DO NOT smoke cigarettes or chew tobacco.

Delinquency

Delinquency was measured with three items ($\alpha = .73$): (1) Have you ever tagged or vandalized private or public property in the last 12 months?; (2) Are you a member of a gang?; (3) During the past 30 days, on how many days DID YOU carry a weapon onto school property?

School Factors

School Climate and Belonging

Six items were used to assess school climate and belonging ($\alpha = .86$). Participants were asked how they agreed or disagreed with the following items: (1) The rules and expectations are clearly explained at my school; (2) I usually enjoy going to school; (3) It is important to me that I graduate from school; (4) Teachers and other adults at my school treat me fairly; (5) There are adults I can talk to at school when I have a problem; (6) I feel like I belong at this school.

Family Factors

Risky Family Environment

A risky family environment emerged through factor analysis and included five items ($\alpha = .80$). Participants were asked how much they agreed or disagreed with the following: (1) My parents and I physically fight; (2) My parents physically fight with each other; (3) My parent uses illegal drugs at least once a week; (4) My parent gets drunk at least once a week; (5) Sometimes things feel so bad at home I want to run away.

Parental Abuse

Two items assessed history of physical or sexual abuse ($r = .50$). First, participants were asked: (1) When was the last time a parent kicked you or hit you with their hand/fist or with an object leaving bruises or bumps?; (2) When was the last time any adult touched you in a sexual way or forced you to touch them in a sexual way that made you feel unsafe or hurt you in anyway? Response options were (1) Never, (2) Last 30 days, (3) Last year (4) Longer than a year ago.

Positive Parenting

Positive parental dynamics was assessed with six items ($\alpha = .84$). Participants were asked how much they agreed with the following statements: (1) My parents set clear rules about what I can and cannot do; (2) My parents encourage me to do my best; (3) My parents have consequences if I break rules; (4) My parents usually know where I am when I go out; (5) My parents love and support me; (6) My parents have talked to me about my future plans.

Community Factors

Neighborhood Safety and Neighborhood Connection

Finally, neighborhood safety/connection ($\alpha = .71$) was assessed with the following three items: (1) Adults in my neighborhood know me; (2) My neighborhood is generally a safe place to live; (3) Usually I can count on the police if I am having a problem or need help. Participants are asked how they agree or disagree with each statement.

Data Analysis Plan and Results

To test predictors of bullying perpetration and victimization across the social-ecological framework, correlations among study variables are presented followed by two separate hierarchical regression models. Bully perpetration was the outcome in the first model and peer victimization was the outcome in the second regression analyses. The following sets of variables were entered in a step-wise fashion in each regression analysis: Step 1: Gender, school type (middle vs. high), free/reduced lunch, history of alternative home placement, sexual orientation; Step 2: Depression/suicidality scale, alcohol/drug abuse scale, delinquency; Step 3: Risky-family scale, abuse history, positive parental involvement; Step 4: School belonging, neighborhood safety/connection.

Correlations Among Study Variables

Significant bivariate correlations are summarized here for the ecological variables with bullying perpetration and then those significant correlations for the ecological variables with victimization. Correlations above .20 are noted as clinically significant given the large sample size. Bullying perpetration or victimization were not significantly associated with gender, school type (middle vs. high), free/reduced lunch, or number of alternative home placements. Greater bullying perpetration was significantly related to more self-reported depression/suicidality ($r = .28$), alcohol and drug abuse ($r = .39$), delinquency ($r = .50$), risky family behavior ($r = .32$), and history of sexual and physical abuse ($r = .31$); but less bullying perpetration was significantly related to greater positive parental behaviors ($r = -.25$), school belonging ($r = -.26$), and living in a safer and more connected neighborhood ($r = -.25$). Self-reported victimization was associated with fewer of the proposed ecological models than those reported for bullying perpetration. That said, greater victimization was associated with more depression/suicidality ($r = .28$), greater delinquency ($r = .27$), risky family behavior ($r = .23$), and a history of physical or sexual abuse ($r = .25$).

Hierarchical Regression—Predicting Bullying Perpetration

In the first model predicting bullying perpetration, the overall model was significant ($F = 550.41$; $p < .001$; $R^2 = 0.29$; Table 25.1). The final model is depicted in Table 25.1, with Step 1 (demographics) accounting for 2% of the variance, Step 2 (depression/suicidality, alcohol and drug use, delinquency) accounting for an additional 24%, Step 3 (family) accounting for an additional 3% of the variance, and Step 4 (school & neighborhood belonging) adding an additional 1%. The strongest predictor of bullying perpetration in the final model was delinquency ($\beta = .35$), followed by AOD ($\beta = .09$). Having friends that do not smoke or drink ($\beta = -.08$), living in safe/connected neighborhood ($\beta = -.07$), and having a sense of school belonging ($\beta = -.07$) were associated with less bullying perpetration. Depression/suicidality ($\beta = .06$), being in a family where parents fight and use drugs or alcohol ($\beta = .05$), or reporting a history of physical or sexual abuse ($\beta = .07$) were associated with greater bullying perpetration. An interesting pattern emerged in relation to sexual orientation and bullying perpetration; students who identified as lesbian ($\beta = -.06$) bullied less and so did those individuals who identified as bi-sexual ($\beta = -.05$), but students who identified as questioning reported higher bullying perpetration ($\beta = .05$).

Hierarchical Regression—Predicting Victimization

In the model predicting victimization, the overall model was significant ($F = 218.67$; $p < .001$; $R^2 = 0.14$; Table 1). The final model is depicted in Table 25.1, with Step 1 (demographics) accounting for 2% of the variance, Step 2 (depression/suicidality, AOD, delinquency) accounting for an additional 10%, Step 3 (family) accounting for an additional 1% of the variance, and Step 4 (school & neighborhood belonging) adding an additional 1%. The strongest predictor of victimization in the final model was delinquency ($\beta = .15$), followed by depression/suicidality ($\beta = .15$). Living in safe/connected neighborhood ($\beta = -.05$) and having a sense of school belonging ($\beta = -.09$) were associated with less victimization. Being in a family where parents fight and use drugs or alcohol ($\beta = .05$) or reporting a history of physical or sexual abuse ($\beta = .08$) were associated with greater victimization. An interesting pattern emerged in relation to sexual orientation and victimization; students who identified as lesbian reported less victimization ($\beta = -.05$), but students who identified as questioning reported higher victimization ($\beta = .08$). Middle school students reported more victimization ($\beta = -12$), as did boys ($\beta = -.06$), and those students who reported the greatest number of alternative home placements, like foster care or juvenile detention ($\beta = -.06$).

Table 25.1 Regression Analyses — Ecological Examination of Bullying Perpetration and Victimization

	Bullying Perpetration as Outcome			Victimization as Outcome		
	b	SEb	b	b	SEb	b
Predictor Variable						
Gender (Boy =1; Girl =2)	−.04	.01	−.04**	−.08	.01	−.06**
Middle (1) vs. High School (2)	−.04	.01	−.04**	−.18	.01	−.12**
Free/Reduced Lunch	.02	.01	.02**	.03	.01	.02**
Number of Alternative Home Placement	.03	.03	.02**	−.14	.04	−.06**
Sexual Orientation – Gay	.02	.03	.01	.04	.05	.02
Sexual Orientation – Lesbian	−.11	.03	−.06**	−.12	.05	−.05*
Sexual Orientation – Bisexual	−.07	.02	−.05**	−.02	.03	−.01
Sexual Orientation – Transgender	.02	.03	.01	−.01	.05	−.00
Sexual Orientation – Questioning	.08	.02	.05**	.17	.03	.08**
Depression/Suicidality	.10	.01	.06**	.34	.02	.15**
Alcohol/Drug Abuse	.07	.01	.09**	.02	.01	.02
Delinquency	.41	.01	.35**	.25	.01	.15**
Positive Peers – Drinking & Smoking	−.05	.01	−.08**	.01	.01	.02
Risky Family – Fighting & Alcohol/Drug Use	.05	.01	.05**	.07	.01	.05**
History of Sexual & Physical Abuse	.08	.01	.07**	.13	.01	.08**
Positive Parental Behavior	.01	.01	.01	.02	.02	.01
School sense of belonging	−.06	.01	−.07**	−.11	.01	−.09**
Neighborhood Safe/Connection	−.05	.01	−.06**	−.06	.01	−.05**

Note. * p < .05, ** p < .001.

Discussion and Limitations

In order to truly stop bullying, interventions need to target the social ecology in which individuals function. In this chapter, we reviewed the literature that examined the individual, peer group, school, family, and community factors that contribute to involvement in bullying and then we tested a social-ecological model of bullying. Across the study variables we found that youth who bully others also report higher depression/suicidality, alcohol and drug abuse, delinquency, risky family behavior, and a history of sexual and physical abuse. Youth who were bullied also reported higher depression/suicidality, delinquency, risky family behavior, and a history of physical or sexual abuse. Thus, the picture for youth involved in bullying and victimization is consistent with the broader peer victimization and aggression research. These youth carry with them concomitant internalizing, externalizing, and social problems.

We also found positive connections in the social ecology that were connected to less bullying perpetration. Specially, positive parenting, a sense of school belonging, and living in a safe and connected neighborhood were all related to less bullying perpetration. Parents who are involved and supportive of their children create a positive environment that is associated with less bullying and greater support (Flouri & Buchanan, 2002; Rubin et al., 2004). Students who feel a connection to school are less likely to bully others, presumably because they feel that school is a supportive and enjoyable place (Ma et al., 2009). It stands to reason that students who are victimized do not feel a connection to school (Swearer et al., 2008) and thus, report less school belonging. Finally, living in a safe neighborhood was also connected to less bullying perpetration. So, while the psychological and social picture of youth involved in bullying is bleak, there are positive supports that can help youth either refrain from engaging in bullying and/or help them cope with being bullied.

We were interested in which variables were the strongest in predicting bullying perpetration and victimization. Hierarchical regression analyses examined the role of the factors across the social ecology that might be predictive of bullying perpetration and victimization. We found that delinquency and alcohol and drug use were the strongest predictors of bullying perpetration. This finding supports the homophily hypothesis (Kandel, 1978), since most delinquent behaviors occur within a deviant peer group. In order to reduce bullying behaviors among students, educators need to target students who are using drugs and alcohol and to work in tandem with law enforcement officials who are typically involved with youth who are engaging in delinquent behaviors. We found that delinquency and depression/suicidality were the strongest predictors of victimization, which is consistent with the research that has found that delinquent youth are more likely to be both perpetrators and victims (Andershed et al., 2001). Our findings also suggest that delinquency is related to both bullying and victimization.

Given the recent focus on bullying toward sexual minority youth and the need to further explore this connection (Espelage & Swearer, 2008), we examined the experiences of bullying perpetration and victimization among GLBTQ youth. In terms of bullying perpetration, students who identified as questioning their sexual orientation bullied others more than students who identified as lesbian and bi-sexual. It could be that students who are unsure of their sexual orientation feel conflicted and may bully others as a way to deal with their own internal strife. Students who self-identified as lesbian or questioning reported higher rates of victimization. Again, it could be that questioning students are involved in bullying and victimization to a greater degree because they are dealing with their own internal questioning about their sexual orientation (Birkett et al., 2009).

Limitations

It is not surprising that very few studies have examined the social-ecological theory in one comprehensive study. To do so requires measures that assess individual, peer, school, familial, and community risk and protective factors. This requires many items and scales (e.g., depression, family abuse variables) that invoke mandated reporting when data are linked to individual youth. Although we were able to assess these risky variables, we did so with an anonymous, cross-sectional study design. Using a cross-sectional design limits our ability to track these individual participants over time and therefore limits what we can say about the longitudinal relations of these variables. Indeed, our survey design also brings with it the limitation of self-report measures and the concurrent mono-method bias. In addition, the alpha for the depression/suicidality scale had a low alpha (.65), which is not a major concern given there are three items. However, we believe our strong theoretical framework used to design and evaluate our items and scales temper our concerns about the sole reliance on self-report. Finally, we would be remiss if we did not recognize that these data are drawn from one county in a Midwestern state. Thus, our findings generalize to similar sample populations only. We are hopeful that this chapter will inspire other cities/counties to forge similar efforts to develop youth assessment measures so that resource allocation and prevention efforts can be directed based on data.

Results from this study further underscore the importance of examining bullying from a social ecological perspective (Swearer et al., 2010) and have direct implications for bullying prevention and intervention (see Table 25.2). How can our schools and communities create a culture that is not conducive to the intolerance and discrimination that lead to the engagement in bullying behaviors? These are complex issues and are not easily "fixed" by purchasing a bullying

Susan M. Swearer et al.

Table 25.2 Implications for Practice: The Social Ecology of Bullying and Victimization

Individual Areas for Bullying Prevention and Intervention	• Treatment for depressive disorders and an effective referral system • Suicide awareness training • Participation in "No Name-Calling" week (www.glsen.org) • Adult support for gay-straight alliance organizations
Peer Group Areas for Bullying Prevention and Intervention	• Adult support/sponsorship of school-based clubs and activities • Alcohol and drug use awareness training • Treatment for drug and alcohol use and an effective referral system • Random acts of kindness activities (http://www.actsofkindness.org) • Teach tolerance (http://www.tolerance.org)
School Areas for Bullying Prevention and Intervention	• Create academic connections and success for all students • School spirit and school sense of belonging • School-community partnerships • Mentoring programs (http://www.teammates.org)
Family Areas for Bullying Prevention and Intervention	• Home-school communication • Connecting families with schools • School-based mental health professionals connect with families • Abuse awareness and education • Volunteerism (http://www.threecupsoftea.com) • Pay it Forward activities
Community Areas for Bullying Prevention and Intervention	• Partnerships with law enforcement • Youth sports activities • Youth choir and music • Community theater • Community arts centers • Community centers • Neighborhood watch programs

prevention and intervention program. In fact, one alarming trend is that school personnel are purchasing bullying prevention programs and holding assemblies focused on bullying awareness, yet our efforts to limit or eradicate bullying are falling short (Swearer et al., 2010). The results presented in this chapter support the tenets of social–ecological theory that effective solutions for reducing bullying must include prevention and intervention efforts across multiple contexts in which individuals reside. As researchers and educators work to decipher the complexity of the social ecology of bullying and victimization, equal attention should be paid to developing bullying interventions that emphasize effective home–school communication and provide parents with ways to model effective coping and conflict resolution strategies.

References

Adair, V. A., Dixon, R. S., Moore, D. W., & Sutherland, C. M. (2000). Ask your mother not to make yummy sandwiches: Bullying in New Zealand secondary schools. *New Zealand Journal of Educational Studies, 35*, 207–221.

Akos, P. (2002). Student perceptions of the transition to middle school. *Professional School Counseling, 5*, 339–345.

Andershed, H., Kerr, M., & Stattin. H. (2001). Bullying in school and violence on the streets: Are the same people involved? *Journal of Scandinavian Studies in Criminology and Crime Prevention, 2*, 31–49. doi: 10.1080/140438501317205538

Anderson, C. S. (1982). The search for school climate: A review of the research. *Review of Educational Research, 52*(3), 368–420. doi: 10.2307/1170423

Baldry, A. C. (2003). Bullying in schools and exposure to domestic violence. *Child Abuse & Neglect, 27*, 713–732. doi:10.1016/S0145-2134(03)00114-5

Baldry, A. C., & Farrington, D. P. (2000). Bullies and delinquents: Personal characteristics and paren-tal styles. *Journal of Community & Applied Social Psychology, 10,* 17–31. doi: 10.1002/(SICI)1099-1298(200001/02)10:1%3C17::AID-CASP526%3E3.0.CO;2-M

Bandura, A. (1978). Social learning theory of aggression. *Journal of Communication, 28,* 12–29. doi: 10.1111/j.1460-2466.1978.tb01621.x

Beran, T. (2008). Consequences of being bullied at school. In D. Pepler & W. Craig (Eds.), *Understanding and addressing bullying: An international perspective* (pp. 44–66). Bloomington, IN: Authorhouse.

Berlan, E. D., Corliss, H. L., Field, A. E., Goodman, E., & Austin, S. B. (2010). Sexual orientation and bullying among adolescents in the growing up today study. *Journal of Adolescent Health, 46*(4), 366–371. doi: 10.1016/j.jadohealth.2009.10.015

Berthold, K. A., & Hoover, J. H. (2000). Correlates of bullying and victimization among intermediate students in the Midwestern USA. *School Psychology International, 21,* 65–78. doi: 10.1177/0143034300211005

Birkett, M., Espelage, D. L., & Koenig, B. (2009). LGB and questioning students in schools: The moderating effects of homophobic bullying and school climate on negative outcomes. *Journal of Youth and Adolescence, 38*(7), 989–1000. doi: 10.1007/s10964-008-9389-1

Bonanno, R. A., & Hymel, S. (2010). Beyond hurt feelings: Investigating why some victims of bullying are at greater risk for suicidal ideation. *Merrill-Palmer Quarterly, 56*(3), 420–440. doi: 10.1353/mpq.0.0051

Bowers, L., Smith, P. K., & Binney, V. (1994). Perceived family relationships of bullies, victims and bully/victims in middle childhood. *Journal of Social and Personal Relationships, 11,* 215–232. doi:10.1177/0265407594112004

Bowes, L., Arseneault, L., Maughan, B., Taylor, A., Caspi, A., & Moffitt, T. E. (2009). School, neighborhood, and family factors are associated with children's bullying involvement: A nationally representative longitudinal study. *Journal of the American Academy of Child Adolescent Psychiatry, 48,* 545–553. doi: 10.1097/CHI.0b013e31819cb017

Brockenbrough, K. K., Cornell, D. G., & Loper, A. B. (2002). Aggressive attitudes among victims of violence at school. *Education & Treatment of Children, 25,* 273–287.

Bronfenbrenner, U. (1979). *The ecology of human development.* Cambridge, MA: Harvard University Press.

Brubacher, M., Fondacaro, M., Brank, E., Brown, V., & Miller, S. (2009). Procedural justice in resolving family dis-putes: Implications for childhood bullying. *Psychology, Public Policy, and Law, 15,* 149–167. doi:10.1037/a0016839

Bukowski, W. M., Sippola, L. K., & Newcomb, A. F. (2000). Variations in patterns of attraction of same- and other-sex peers during early adolescence. *Developmental Psychology, 26,* 147–154. doi: 10.1037/0012-1649.36.2.147

Colarossi, L. G., & Eccles, J. S. (2003). Differential effects of support providers on adolescents' mental health. *Social Work Research, 27,* 19–30.

Connolly, I., & O'Moore, M. (2003). Personality and family relations of children who bully. *Personality and Individual Differences, 35,* 559–567. doi: 10.1016/S0191-8869(02)00218-0

Cox, A. D. (1997). Preventing child abuse: A review of community-based projects 1: Intervening on pro-cesses and outcomes of reviews. *Child Abuse Review, 6,* 243–256. doi: 10.1002/(SICI)1099-0852(199710)6:4<243::AID-CAR338>3.0.CO;2-7

Craig, W. M., & Pepler, D. J. (1995). Peer process in bullying and victimization: An observational study. *Exceptionality Education Canada, 5,* 81–95.

Craig, W. M., & Pepler, D. J. (1997). Observations of bullying and victimization in the schoolyard. *Canadian Journal of School Psychology, 13,* 41–59. doi: 10.1177/082957359801300205

Cuevas, C. A., Finkelhor, D., Turner, H. A., & Ormrod, R. K. (2007). Juvenile delinquency and victimization: A theoretical typology. *Journal of Interpersonal Violence, 22,* 1581–1602. doi: 10.1177/0886260507306498

Darling, N., & Steinberg, L. (1993). Parenting style as context: An integrative model. *Psychological Bulletin, 113,* 487–496. doi:10.1037/0033-2909.113.3.487

Demaray, M. K., & Malecki, C. K. (2003). Perceptions of the frequency and importance of social support by students classified as victims, bullies, and bully/victims in an urban middle school. *School Psychology Review, 32,* 471–489.

Duncan, R. D. (2004). The impact of family relationships on school bullies and victims. In D. L. Espelage & S. M. Swearer (Eds.), *Bullying in American schools: A social-ecological perspective on prevention and intervention* (pp. 227–244). Mahwah, NJ: Erlbaum.

Dupper, D. R., & Meyer-Adams, N. (2002). Low-level violence: A neglected aspect of school culture. *Urban Educa-tion, 37,* 350–364. doi: 10.1177/00485902037003003

Eiden, R. D., Ostrov, J. M., Colder, C. R., Leonard, K. E., Edwards, E. P., & Orrange-Torchia, T. (2010). Parent alcohol problems and peer bullying and victimization: Child gender and toddler attachment security as modera-tors. *Journal of Clinical Child & Adolescent Psychology, 39*(3), 341–350. doi:10.1080/15374411003691768

Espelage, D. L., Bosworth, K., & Simon, T. R. (2000). Examining the social context of bullying behaviors in early adolescence. *Journal of Counseling and Development, 78,* 326–333.

Espelage, D. L., & Holt, M. K. (2001). Bullying and victimization during early adolescence: Influences and psychoso-cial correlates. *Journal of Emotional Abuse, 2,* 123–142. doi: 10.1300/J135v02n02_08

Espelage, D. L., Holt, M. K., & Henkel, R. R. (2003). Examination of peer-group contextual effects on aggression during early adolescence. *Child Development, 74*, 205–220. doi: 10.1111/1467-8624.00531

Espelage, D. L., & Swearer, S. M. (2003). Research on school bullying and victimization: What have we learned and where do we go from here? *School Psychology Review, 32*(3), 365–383.

Espelage, D. L., & Swearer, S. M. (2008). Addressing research gaps in the intersection between homophobia and bullying. *School Psychology Review, 37*, 155–159.

Espelage, D. L., & Swearer, S. M. (2009). Contributions of three social theories to understanding bullying perpetration and victimization among school-aged youth. In M. J. Harris (Ed.), *Bullying, rejection, and peer victimization: A social cognitive neuroscience perspective* (pp. 151–170). New York, NY: Springer.

Fang, X., & Corso, P. S. (2008). Gender differences in the connections between violence experienced as a child and perpetration of intimate partner violence in youth adulthood. *Journal of Family Violence, 23*, 303–313. doi: 10.1007/s10896-008-9152-0

Flouri, E., & Buchanan, A. (2002). Life satisfaction in teenage boys: The moderating role of father involvement and bullying. *Aggressive Behavior, 28*, 126–133. doi:10.1002/ab.90014

Flouri, E., & Buchanan, A. (2003). The role of mother involvement and father involvement in adolescent bullying behavior. *Journal of Interpersonal Violence, 18*(6), 634–644. doi: 10.1177/0886260503251129

Floyd, F. J., & Widaman, K. F. (1995). Factor analysis in the development of refinement of clinical assessment instruments. *Psychological Assessment, 7, 286*–299. doi: 10.1037/10403590.7.3.286

Fritsch, T. A., & Burkhead, J. D. (1981). Behavioral reactions of children to parental absence due to imprisonment. *Family Relations, 30*, 83–88. doi: 10.2307/584240

Georgiou, S. (2008). Parental style and child bullying and victimization experiences at school. *Social Psychology of Education, 11*, 213–227. doi:10.1007/s11218-007-9048-5

Hartup, W. W. (1996). The company they keep: Friendships and their developmental significance. *Child Development, 67*, 1–13. doi: 10.2307/1131681

Hay, C., & Meldrum, R. (2010). Bullying victimization and adolescent self-harm: Testing hypotheses from general strain theory. *Journal of Youth and Adolescence, 39*, 446–559. doi: 10.1007/s10964-009-9502-0

Herba, C. M., Ferdinand, R. F., Stijnen, T., Veenstra, R., Oldehinkel, A. J., Ormel, J., & Verhulst, F. C. (2008). Victimisation and suicide ideation in the TRAILS study: Specific vulnerabilities of victims. *Journal of Child Psychology and Psychiatry, 49*(8), 867–876. doi: 10.1111/j.1469-7610.2008.01900.x

Hirschi, T. (1969). *Causes of delinquency.* Los Angeles: University of California Press.

Hodges, E. V. E., Boivin, M., Vitaro, F., & Bukowski, W. M. (1999). The power of friendship: Protection against an escalating cycle of peer victimization. *Developmental Psychology, 35*, 94–101. doi: 10.1037/0012-1649.35.1.94

Hodges, E. V. E., Malone, M. J., & Perry, D. G. (1997). Individual risk and social risk as interacting determinants of victimization in the peer group. *Developmental Psychology, 33*, 1032–1039. doi: 10.1037/0012-1649.33.6.1032

Holt, M. K., & Espelage, D. L. (2007). Perceived social support among bullies, victims, and bully-victims. *Journal of Youth and Adolescence, 26*, 984–994. doi: 10.1007/s10964-006-9153-3

Holt, M. K., & Keyes, M. A. (2004). Teachers' attitudes toward bullying. In D. L. Espelage & S. M. Swearer (Eds.), *Bullying in American schools: A social-ecological perspective on prevention and intervention* (pp. 121–139). Mahwah, NJ: Erlbaum.

Houndoumadi, A., & Pateraki, L. (2001). Bullying and bullies in Greek elementary schools: Pupils' attitudes and teachers'/parents' awareness. *Educational Review, 53*, 19–26. doi: 10.1080/00131910120033619

Ireland, J. L., & Monaghan, R. (2006). Behaviours indicative of bullying among young and juvenile male offenders: A study of perpetrator and victim characteristics. *Aggressive Behavior, 32*, 172–180. doi: 10.1002/ab.20116

Jeynes, W. H. (2008). Effects of parental involvement on experiences of discrimination and bullying. *Marriage & Family Review, 43*, 255–268. doi:10.1080/01494920802072470

Jonson-Reid, M. (1998). Youth violence and exposure to violence in childhood: An ecological review. *Aggression and Violent Behavior, 3*, 159–179. doi: 10.1016: S1359-1789(97)00009-8

Jöreskog, K. G., & Sörbom, D. (1998). *Lisrel 8: Structural equation modeling with the Simplis command language.* Mahwah, NJ: Erlbaum.

Juvonen, J., Graham, S., & Schuster, M. A. (2003). Bullying among young adolescents: The strong, the weak, and the troubled. *Pediatrics, 112,* 1231–1237. doi: 10.1542/peds.112.6.1231

Kaltiala-Heino, R., Rimpela, M., Marttunen, M., Rimpela, A., & Rantanen, P. (1999). Bullying, depression, and suicidal ideation in Finnish adolescence: School survey. *British Medical Journal, 319*, 348–351.

Kandel, D. B. (1978). Homophily, selection, and socialization in adolescent friendships. *The American Journal of Sociology, 84*, 427–436. doi: 10.1086/226792

Klomek, A. B., Marrocco, F., Kleinman, M., Schonfeld, I. S., & Gould, M. S. (2007). Bullying, depression, and suicidality in adolescents. *Journal of the American Academy of Child and Adolescent Psychiatry, 46*, 40–49. doi: 10.1097/01. chi. 0000242237.84925.18

Klomek, A. B., Marrocco, F., Kleinman, M., Schonfield, I. S., & Gould, M. S. (2008). Peer victimization, depression, and suicidality in adolescents. *Suicide and Life-Threatening Behavior, 38*(2), 166–180. doi: 10.1521/suli.2008.38.2.166

Koenig, B., & Bettin, C. (2009). *The Dane county youth assessment 2009: Final report.* Retrieved from http://www.danecountyhumanservices.org/

Koenig, B., Espelage, D., & Biedndseil, R. (2005). *The Dane county youth assessment.* Unpublished report. Madison, WI: The Dane County Youth Commission.

Korbin, J. E. (2003). Children, childhoods, and violence. *Annual Review of Anthropology, 32,* 431–446. doi: 10.1146/annurev.anthro.32.061002.093345

Kupersmidt, J. B., Griesler, P. C., DeRosier, M. E., Patterson, C. J., & Davis, P. W. (1995). Childhood aggression and peer relations in the context of family and neighborhood factors. *Child Development, 66,* 360–375. doi: 10.2307/1131583

Lickel, B., Schmader, T., & Hamilton, D. L. (2003). A case of collective responsibility: Who else was to blame for the Columbine High School shootings? *Personality and Social Psychology Bulletin, 29,* 194–204. doi: 10.1177/0146167202239045

Ma, L., Phelps, E., Lerner, J. V., & Lerner, R. M. (2009). Academic competence for adolescents who bully and who are bullied: Findings from the 4-H study of positive youth development. *The Journal of Early Adolescence, 29,* 862–897. doi: 10.1177/0272431609332667

Marini, Z. A., Dane, A. V., Bosacki, S. L., & YLC-CURA (2006). Direct and indirect bully-victims: Differential psychosocial risk factors associated with adolescents involved in bullying and victimization. *Aggressive Behavior, 32,* 551–569. doi: 10.1002/ab.20155

Mayberry, M., Espelage, D. L., & Koenig, B. (2009). Multilevel modeling of direct effects and interactions of peers, parents, school, and community influences on adolescent substance use. *Journal of Youth and Adolescence, 38*(8), 1038–1049. doi:10.1007/s10964-009-9425-9

McCreary, M. L., Slavin, L. A., & Berry, E. J. (1996). Predicting problem behavior and self-esteem among African-American adolescents. *Journal of Adolescent Research, 11,* 216–234. doi: 10.1177/0743554896112004

Menesini, E., Modena, M., & Tani, F. (2009). Bullying and victimization in adolescence: Concurrent and stable roles and psychological health symptoms. *The Journal of Genetic Psychology, 170*(2), 115–133. doi: 10.3200/GNTP.170.2.115-134

Miller, K. M. (2006). The impact of parental incarceration on children: An emerging need for effective interventions. *Child and Adolescent Social Work Journal, 23,* 472–486. doi: 10.1007/s10560-006-0065-6

Nansel, T. R, Overpeck, M., Pilla, R. S., Ruan, W. J., Simons-Morton, B., & Scheidt, P. (2001). Bullying behaviors among US youth: Prevalence and association with psychosocial adjustment. *Journal of the American Medical Association, 285*(16), 2094–2100. doi:10.1001/jama.285.16.2094

National Center for Educational Statistics (NCES). (1995, October). *Strategies to avoid harm at school.* Washington, DC: U.S. Department of Education, Office of Educational Research and Improvement.

O'Connell, P., Pepler, D., & Craig, W. (1999). Peer involvement in bullying: Insights and challenges for intervention. *Adolescence, 22,* 437–452. doi: 10.1006/jado/1999.0238

Olweus, D. (1993). Victimisation by peers: Antecedents and long-term outcomes. In K.H. Rubin & J. B. Asendorpf (Eds.), *Social withdrawal, inhibition, and shyness in childhood* (pp. 315–341). Hillsdale, NJ: Erlbaum.

Olweus, D. (1995). Bullying or peer abuse at school: Facts and intervention. *Current Directions in Psychological Science, 4,* 196–200. doi: 10.1111/1467-8721.ep10772640

Pellegrini, A. D. (1998). Bullies and victims in school: A review and call for research. *Journal of Applied Developmental Psychology, 19,* 165–176. doi: 10.1016/S0193-3973(99)80034-3

Pellegrini, A. D. (2002). Bullying, victimization, and sexual harassment during the transition to middle school. *Educational Psychologist, 37,* 151–163. doi: 10.1207/S15326985EP3703_2

Pellegrini, A. D., & Bartini, M. (2001). Dominance in early adolescent boys: Affiliative and aggressive dimensions and possible functions. *Merrill-Palmer Quarterly, 47,* 142–163. doi: 10.1353/mpq.2001.0004

Pellegrini, A. D., Bartini, M., & Brooks, F. (1999). School bullies, victims, and aggressive victims: Factors relating to group affiliation and victimization in early adolescence. *Journal of Educational Psychology, 91,* 216–224. doi: 10.1037/0022-0663.91.2.216

Pellegrini, A. D., & Long, J. (2002). A longitudinal study of bullying, dominance, and victimization during the transition from primary to secondary school. *British Journal of Developmental Psychology, 20,* 259–280. doi: 10.1348/026151002166442

Pepler, D., Jiang, D., Craig, W., & Connolly, J. (2008). Developmental trajectories of bullying and associated factors. *Child Development, 79,* 325–338. doi: 10.1111/j.1467-8624.2007.01128.x

Perren, S., & Hornung, R. (2005). Bulling and delinquency in adolescence: Victims' and perpetrators' family and peer relations. *Swiss Journal of Psychology, 64,* 51–64. doi:10.1024/1421-0185.64.1.51

Pitner, R. O., & Astor, R. A. (2008). Children's reasoning about poverty, physical deterioration, danger, and retribution in neighborhood contexts. *Journal of Environmental Psychology, 28,* 327–338. doi: 10.1016/j.jenvp.2008.03.002

Plybon, L. E., & Kliewer, W. (2001). Neighborhood types and externalizing behavior in urban school-age children: Test of direct, mediated and moderated effects. *Journal of Child and Family Studies, 10,* 419–437. doi: 10.1023/A:1016781611114

Poteat, V. P. (2008). Contextual and moderating effects of the peer group climate on use of homophobic epithets. *School Psychology Review, 37*(2), 188–201.

Rican, P., Klicperova, M., & Koucka, T. (1993). Families of bullies and their victims: A children's view. *Studia Psychologica, 35,* 261–266.

Rigby, K., & Slee, P. (1999). Suicidal ideation among adolescent school children, involvement in bully-victim problems, and perceived social support. *Suicide and Life-Threatening Behavior, 29*(2), 119–130.

Rivers, I., & Noret, N. (2008). Well-being among same-sex and opposite-sex-attracted youth at school. *School Psychology Review, 37*(2), 174–187.

Rivers, I., Poteat, V. P., Noret, N., & Ashurst, N. (2009). Observing bullying at school: The mental health implications of witness status. *School Psychology Quarterly, 24,* 211–223. doi: 10.1037/a0018164

Roberts, W. B. (2000). The bully as victim. *Professional School Counseling, 4,* 148–156.

Rodkin, P. C. (2004). Peer ecologies of aggression and bullying. In D. L. Espelage & S. M. Swearer (Eds.), *Bullying in American schools: A social-ecological perspective on prevention and intervention* (pp. 87–106). Mahwah, NJ: Erlbaum.

Roland, E. (2002). Bullying, depressive symptoms, and suicidal thoughts. *Educational Research, 44,* 55–67. doi: 10.1080/00131880110107351

Rubin, K. H., Dwyer, K. M., Booth-LaForce, C., Kim, A. H., Burgess, K. B., & Rose-Krasnor, L. (2004). Attachment, friendship, and psychosocial functioning in early adolescence. *Journal of Early Adolescence, 24,* 326–356. doi:10.1177/0272431604268530

Salmivalli, C. (2010). Bullying and the peer group: A review. *Aggression and Violent Behavior, 15,* 112–120. doi: 10.1016/j.avb.2009.08.007

Salmivalli, C., Huttunen, A., & Lagerspetz, K. M. J. (1997). Peer networks and bullying in schools. *Scandinavian Journal of Psychology, 38,* 205–312. doi: 10.1111/1467-9450.00040

Seals, D., & Young, J. (2003). Bullying and victimization: Prevalence and relationship to gender, grade level, ethnicity, self-esteem, and depression. *Adolescence, 38,* 735–747.

Shepherd, J. P., Sutherland, I., & Newcombe, R. G. (2006). Relations between alcohol, violence and victimization in adolescence. *Journal of Adolescence, 29,* 539–553. doi: 10.1016/j.adolescence.2006.06.005

Spriggs, A. L., Iannotti, R. J., Nansel, T. R., & Haynie, D. L. (2007). Adolescent bullying involvement and perceived family, peer, and school relations: Commonalities and differences across race/ethnicity. *Journal of Adolescent Health, 41,* 283–293. doi:10.1016/j.jadohealth.2007.04.009

Stevens, V., De Bourdeaudhuij, I., & Van Oost, P. (2002). Relationship of the family environment to children's involvement in bully/victims problems at school. *Journal of Youth and Adolescence, 31,* 419–428. doi:10.1023/A:1020207003027

Swearer, S. M. (2010). Safe schools policies: Necessary but not sufficient for creating positive school environments for LGBTQ students. *Social Policy Report, 24*(4), 19–27.

Swearer, S. M., & Doll, B. (2001). Bullying in schools: An ecological framework. *Journal of Emotional Abuse, 2,* 7–23. doi: 10.1300/J135v02n02_02

Swearer, S. M., & Espelage, D. L. (2004). A social-ecological framework of bullying among youth. In D. L. Espelage & S. M. Swearer (Eds.), *Bullying in American schools: A social-ecological perspective on prevention and intervention* (pp. 1–12), Mahwah, NJ: Erlbaum.

Swearer, S. M., Espelage, D. L., Vaillancourt, T., & Hymel, S. (2010). What can be done about school bullying? Linking research to educational practice. *Educational Researcher, 39,* 38–47. doi: 10.3102/0013189X09357622

Swearer, S. M., Peugh, J., Espelage, D. L., Siebecker, A. B., Kingsburg, W. L., & Bevins, K. S. (2006). A social ecological model for bullying prevention and intervention in early adolescence: An exploratory examination. In S. Jimerson & M. J. Furlong (Eds.), *Handbook of school violence and school safety* (pp. 257–273). Mahwah, NJ: Erlbaum.

Swearer, S. M., Song, S. Y., Cary, P. T., Eagle, J. W., & Mickelson, W. T. (2001). Psychosocial correlates in bullying and victimization: The relationship between depression, anxiety, and bully/victim status. In R. Geffner, M. T. Loring, & C. Young (Eds.), *Bullying behavior: Current issues, research, and interventions* (pp. 95–121). Binghamton, NY: Haworth Maltreatment and Trauma Press/The Haworth Press.

Swearer, S. M., Turner, R. K., Givens, J. E., & Pollack, W. S. (2008). "You're so gay!": Do different forms of bullying matter for adolescent males? *School Psychology Review, 37,* 160–173.

Thompson, M. P., Sims, L., Kingree, J. B., & Windle, M. (2008). Longitudinal associations between problem alcohol use and violent victimization in a national sample of adolescents. *Journal of Adolescent Health, 42,* 21–27. doi: 10.1016/j.jadohealth.2007.07.003

Twemlow, S. W., Fonagy, P., Sacco, F. C., Gies, M. L., Evans, R., & Ewbank, R. (2001). Creating a peaceful school learning environment: A controlled study of an elementary school intervention to reduce violence. *American Journal of Psychiatry, 158,* 808–810. doi: 10.1176/appi.ajp.158.5.808

Unnever, J. D., & Cornell, D. G. (2003). The culture of bullying in middle school. *Journal of School Violence, 2*, 5–28. doi: 10.1300/J202v02n02_02

Viljoen, J. L., O'Neil, M. L., & Sidhu, A. (2005). Bullying behaviors in female and male adolescent offenders: Prevalence, types, and association with psychological adjustment. *Aggressive Behavior, 31*, 521–536. doi: 10.1002/ab.20036

Yoneyama, S., & Naito, A. (2003). Problems with the paradigm: The school as a factor in understanding bullying (with special reference to Japan). *British Journal of Sociology of Education, 24*, 315–330. doi: 10.1080/01425690301894

Youngblade, L. M., Theokas, C., Schulenberg, J., Curry, L., Huang, I., & Novak, M. (2007). Risk and promotive factors in families, schools, and communities: A contextual model of positive youth development in adolescence. *Pediatrics, 119*, S47–53. doi: 10.1542/peds.2006-2089H

26

Critical Characteristics of Effective Bullying Prevention Programs

Richard J. Hazler and JoLynn V. Carney

PENNSYLVANIA STATE UNIVERSITY, COLLEGE PARK, PA

Abstract

Effective bullying prevention and intervention programs are primarily determined by orderly implementation of three critical program themes and five program stages. This chapter describes the concepts and implementation of the three themes: (a) a social–ecological perspective involving everyone in their unique environment, (b) reducing isolation of people and ideas, and (c) empathic involvement of all parties, including bystanders as well as bullies and victims. A program is not simply a group of actions to be taken, it also requires sequential implementation of critical stages. Initial awareness building is an important first step, to energize individuals and groups. This foundation and energy is preparation for effective policy development and then skill development. The final stages emphasize long-term success through continuing involvement in conjunction with regular assessment and program adjustment to recognize and reflect changing circumstances.

Prevention programs and published materials designed to reduce problems of bullying and school violence have become numerous, while they were virtually nonexistent in the United States prior to 1990 (Hazler & Hoover, 1996). Programs designed in the 1990s began focusing on strategies such as teaching interpersonal skills and involving students in prevention efforts. These models augmented or replaced the more traditional emphases on simplistic discipline enforcement and school assemblies that had previously been primary tactics to address bullying and school violence (Scheckner & Rollin, 2003).

Schools continue to be among the safest places for children to be, but that doesn't reflect the anxiety and tension experienced by students because of bullying and school climates that tolerate these abuses (Carney, Hazler, Oh, Hibel, & Granger, 2010). Whether it is a bully, victim, or bystander, everyone is affected by situations that have them focus attention on self-protection rather than the knowledge and skills schools are designed to provide. Students cannot focus on learning mathematics when they are anxiously thinking about being bullied (victims), how to avoid it (victims and bystanders), or how to maintain their domination of someone (bullies). Schools and funding agencies appear to understand the interplay of social, emotional, and academic learning at school, and now provide substantial funding to develop programs for interventions and prevention. The question for school personnel is no longer whether programs are available, but instead, what differentiates the best program(s) for a given school or school district from ones that will be less effective or less likely to be appropriately implemented?

Students are not the only ones to suffer from school bullying. When faculty must intervene in bullying situations, valuable time and energy are lost from the primary process of academic learning. The emotional toll taken on them can hinder educational interactions long after the event itself ends. Pressures of time, limited budgets, and increasing academic performance demands require schools to make sound choices in terms of time required and available, costs, commitment of school personnel, and program quality. This chapter provides those selecting and implementing bullying prevention programs with the critical characteristics that drive effectiveness and efficiency.

Conceptual Basis

Programs designed to reverse the trend of increasing youth violence like bullying have greatly increased (Furlong, Morrison, & Greif, 2003), however, only a small number of programs have actually documented success through published research such as Second Step: A Violence Prevention Curriculum (Dell Fitzgerald & Van Schoiack Edstrom, 2006) and Promoting Alternative THinking Skills Curriculum (PATHS; Greenberg, & Kusche, 2006). See Orpinas & Horne, 2006, for a review of additional evidenced-based programs. Thoughtful studies with quality research designs have provided credibility to such programs' claims of initial outcome and sustained effectiveness in reducing bullying (Orpinas & Horne, 2006).

There are two distinct conceptual approaches to prevention programming, targeted and universal. *Targeted programs* are ones that focus on select groups of students who have demonstrated a high risk of perpetuating inappropriately aggressive behaviors and/or those who have a high probability of becoming victims of such aggressive behaviors. Such programs are generally limited to select staff and often parents who plan and implement organized behavior change and social skill development for specific students without widespread involvement of others in the school system. Targeted programs can be very useful for individual students, but they are not intended to impact the overall prevention of bullying in a school or community. This type of program may target at-risk groups such as those with developmental disabilities (Leisman, 2009), racial, ethnic, or immigration status (Scherr & Larson, 2010), and anti-gay bullying (GLAD, 2010).

Universal bullying programs are the most common variety developed in the 1990s. Bully/Victim Prevention (Olweus, 1993), Second Step (Dell Fitzgerald & Van Schoiack Edstrom, 2006) and PATHS (Greenberg & Kusche, 2006) are examples of universal programs that impact a wide variety of issues and people in an attempt to reduce bullying. Virtually all youth will be exposed to peer abuse either as bullies, victims, bystanders, or combinations of the three. This widespread exposure to bullying promotes a less-than-safe climate that impacts everyone in the school community, reduces the ability of the system to effectively carry out its educational function, and therefore calls for a comprehensive approach to promote systemic change. Universal anti-bullying programs are given primary attention in this chapter because they are designed to produce the greatest amount of overall change for the most students, they are the vast majority of ones in use today, and they take the most human resources to effectively implement.

There are many differences in quality programs including age groups; placing more emphasis on student, teacher, staff, or parent involvement; and requirements of more or less commitment from a school or district. The differences do not change the fact that effective programs apply a consistent set of themes and an orderly process that consisting of early, middle, and later stages of program development. Program success is based on implementing necessary components and presenting them in ways that those involved can buy into and apply consistently over time.

Successful Bullying Program Characteristics

Program descriptions tend to focus on the specific techniques used to help change cognitions, behaviors, and overall school climate. Schools and individuals who attempt to utilize these techniques will be effective over time only when they attend to the full compliment of quality bullying program characteristics applied in an appropriate local context. These key characteristics include the *program themes* of a social–ecological perspective model, empathic involvement, and reducing isolation of people and ideas. They also include sequential program stages of awareness building, policy development, skill development, continuing involvement, assessment, adjustment, and recycling (see Figure 26.1).

Individually, these characteristics will have more appeal to some people than to others. Administrators, for example, tend to be attracted to policy development, counselors and teachers to skill development, boards of education to assessment of outcomes, and students will want quick action where their feelings and situations are fully taken into account. These understandable preferences point to the need for involvement of representatives of all parties in selection and implementation of programs. The characteristics become effective only when they are all considered collectively and where specific aspects are presented in a progression that builds one step upon the other.

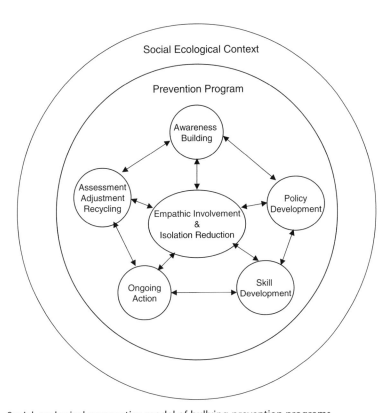

Figure 26.1   Social-ecological perspective model of bullying prevention programs

Program Themes

Social-Ecological Perspective

Quality programs recognize the critical nature of interactions between individual characteristics and ecological contexts (Orpinas & Horne, 2006). Peers, schools, families, and communities all interact with individual student characteristics to create the variety of individual behavioral, emotional, and cognitive reactions as well as the dynamics between individuals. No one individual or pair of individuals alone creates a bullying situation. It is the combination of individuals plus the ecological situation that will foster or discourage bullying over time (Espelage & Swearer, 2010).

Prevention efforts must develop an understanding of and focus actions on the complexities of the ecological system. *The larger the group that is successfully integrated into prevention efforts, the better.* Communities and school systems that can organize and coordinate prevention efforts provide the most valued models. Smaller and more manageable working groups (e.g., peer groups, classrooms, select grade levels, or individual schools) are often needed to set the process in motion and are critical to maintaining lasting effects.

This social-ecological perspective and universal approach can be found in prevention programs that have the most support from researchers (Espelage & Swearer, 2003). One or two committed individuals can and normally do initiate efforts, but degree of success over time will be related to how many individuals and groups become invested as active participants in a coordinated program.

Reducing Isolation of People and Ideas

Successful prevention programs all emphasize reducing the social and conceptual isolation of people. Bullying occurs most often during unstructured times (Craig, Pepler, & Atlas, 2000), because social support is a key factor in determining the frequency and severity of bullying (Rigby, 2008). Bullies are not seeking a fair fight, but instead an interaction in which they can dominate an individual or group (Pepler, Craig, O'Connell, 2010). *When victims and bystanders increase their numbers or gain new constructive ideas regarding possible actions, the bully's potential to dominate is diminished and the likelihood of bullying decreases.* Prevention programs therefore give on-going emphasis to increasing positive social connections between people.

The Columbine, Colorado, shootings demonstrate one well-known, extreme example of the dangers of isolation. Over time, the perpetrators became ostracized from peer groups and dropped out of extra curricular activities. The more they became physically, cognitively, and psychologically cut off from others and the less they received a diversity of ideas from others, the more their irrational ideas began to appear rational. *Prevention programs fight this isolation process by emphasizing the expansion of connections between people and groups that broaden understanding, challenge false beliefs, encourage creative social thinking, and promote a greater sense of trust in the environment.*

Victims of extended bullying begin losing hope as a lack of obvious supporters, and absence of fresh ideas to end the torment can lead to homicidal and suicidal thoughts and sometimes actions (Janson, Carney, Hazler, & Oh, 2009; Hazler & Carney, 2000). Most victims do not turn their worst thoughts into such catastrophic actions, but they will drop out of relationships and make other poor decisions because of the limiting of perceptions and ideas caused by isolation from quality interpersonal interactions.

Bullying can only continue when adults or peers who could make a difference are not present or when they choose not to become involved in support of victims. Choosing to reduce victim and situation isolation, by becoming involved, makes adult and peer bystanders critical to the eventual discouragement or encouragement of bullying and harassment (Rigby, 2010).

Reducing isolation of people and ideas throughout a social–ecological environment begins with awareness building to infuse new ideas, understandings, and personal connections across people and systems. Program aspects like policy development, skill acquisition, collaborative activities, and program assessment are all designed to expand thinking and relationships. The reason these aspects of programs can cause distress among individuals and groups is precisely because they encourage people to move beyond those beliefs and actions with which they have become comfortable.

The best program designs directly address the stressful issue of change by continually encouraging open discussion of ideas, beliefs, and feelings. These programs integrate presentations of positive practices with the encouragement to use creative thinking to identify ways that these and other practices might be implemented in the specific environmental context of those involved. Weaker programs generally provide less direction and encouragement to explore alternative practices, use of creative thinking, and revision of concepts to fit local contexts.

Empathic Involvement

Quality programs recognize that it takes more than knowledge-level awareness to stir people's affective involvement in difficult situations like bullying, so empathy becomes a major theme in how people view and react to bullying (Hymel, Schonert-Reichl, Bonanno, Vaillancourt, & Henderson, 2010). People are more likely to give up valuable time, energy, and even money to help one person or a group if they can personally identify with them. An empathic sense for someone also decreases the likelihood of choosing to abuse that person so that it plays a key role in limiting bullying actions. Raising empathic feelings through emotional-awareness activities is therefore a critical first step.

Videos, speakers, and discussion formats that prove valuable at the awareness stage focus attention on the emotions and feelings of all participants in bullying situations and not just victims. This is not the aspect of the program that identifies things to do or spells out right versus wrong. *The attempt is to have people experience the emotions and complexities of the problem from the eyes of victims, bullies, and bystanders making it more likely to feel the problems and become motivated to work towards finding solutions.*

Two video examples can serve to demonstrate the difference between creating empathic awareness versus informational awareness. One set of videos (Brown, 1993, 1997, 2004) has few words spoken in them, no direct teaching of lessons, no moderator, lots of time for thinking and feeling, and little time for trying to remember what is said. Designed specifically for students, these videos can stir strong emotions as students identify with the experiences of those in the films. *Don't Laugh at Me* (Operation Respect, 2010) is a video that taps similar emotions in students and even more effectively in adults through musical and visual experiences. These are not the typical videos or activities generally used in schools where there is a direct lesson plan and specific information identified for learning. Videos and other activities like these are instead designed to raise an emotional awareness that promotes creative thinking, discussion, and a desire to take action.

First-hand experiences and current events are other effective empathy building techniques. Newspaper stories of school violence that receive widespread attention or a suicide in a school, while horrific, are teachable current events that can draw people's attention to the feelings and needs of others. Traumatic circumstances such as these increase emotional investment in a way that cannot be duplicated through any other medium.

Knowledge and skills alone can be used for negative as well as positive purposes, but a sense of empathy towards others can move people to take actions designed to stop bullying situations (Hymel et al., 2010). Consequently, a significant portion of effective prevention programs is time spent gaining understanding of other people's experiences and feelings in relation to one's own experiences and feelings.

Sequential Program Stages

Initial Awareness Building

Motivating people to take action by creating awareness of the dangers is the essential first step in a bullying prevention program. Surveys and associated meetings are informational ways of raising awareness that often work well for adults in particular (e.g., parents, teachers, school boards, etc.). Such information can also be useful for youth, although it probably carries less motivational weight with them. Students are bombarded with information as a part of their daily work in school, so additional information does not provide the uniqueness of presentation that could more effectively spur motivation. Personalized discussions of this information are necessary for both students and adults to turn the general data into personally motivating concepts that demand their immediate attention.

Speakers, videos, books, and other awareness development vehicles can present information in ways that personally connect to adults and youth and promote a more empathic awareness. *The effectiveness depends on helping the audiences see and feel the problem's impact.* It is the motivational quality and original accounts that make information more impactful to students in particular who, because they live with the situation daily, can identify with those feelings in ways that raise the credibility of the presentation.

The focus of these initial awareness building activities is to encourage involvement in program development, to give direction as to what can be done, and to offer confidence that some initial steps are available to start a successful program. It is from this initial push that other activities follow.

Policy Development

Policies regarding rules of behavior are the written statements of a community's social standards and the manner in which those standards are to be enforced. *Any good bullying prevention program requires the examination and revision of current policy to clearly demonstrate the official significance given to the problem and how that importance will translate into practical application* (Limber & Small, 2003). The importance of these policies demands that they be worked on at the early stages of a prevention program in order for other aspects of the program to build upon them.

Changing social norms around bullying have created pressure for inclusion of bullying in disciplinary policies where such a need was not seen in the past (Limber & Small, 2003). Policy revisions are necessary to more clearly define unacceptable physical, verbal, sexual, social, and cyber bullying along with the consequences for those who would violate such policies.

Most quality programs will only initially provide general outlines or examples of policy needs and place more emphasis on the process for developing locally appropriate policies. The first of two major reasons for this emphasis on the development aspect is that policies need to reflect the local context of participants that cannot be provided in a program created by a state, national, or international organization (Limber & Small, 2003).

The second major reason to focus attention on the policy development is the importance of bringing groups of people together (e.g., teachers, counselors, administrators, parents, community members, and students; Limber & Small, 2003) to work through their diverse views, and come to joint agreement on a set of important issues, values, and the ways to support them in a prevention program.

The developmental aspect of policy is normally one that involves more struggle and time than people and organizations prefer to invest. People invited to participate, who truly do have different views of the issues, must each be heard and their differences worked though if they are to provide effective follow through in support of final policies. Only then can policies offer both the locally appropriate guidelines in combination with the strong backing of critical interest groups necessary for prevention program success.

Skill Development

A general movement of anti-bullying programs has been away from punishment of bullying as the primary focus to skill development for everyone in a selected environment. The change is related to letting go of old assumptions that bullies were a handful of problem children for whom punishment was the only way to influence them. New views recognize bullying as a problem experienced by many children, and related to developmental changes (Smith & Monks, 2008), personal characteristics (Sawyer, Bradshaw, & O'Brennan, 2008), and social skills (Orpinas & Horne, 2010). This change in viewpoint made it possible to begin conceptualizing bullying as a developmental issue where teaching and learning can directly lead to improvement, for everyone in the environment.

None of the skills are exclusive to dealing with bullying situations since they promote healthy functioning of individuals who contribute to maintaining a personally caring and supportive society. Some skills help people focus on and deal with their internal struggles that influence how they relate to others. Attending to internal feelings and learning productive ways of dealing with them show up early in most programs, because how much one understands oneself influences the ability to understand and react to others. Then there are a range of other interpersonal skills that relate to reading other people's reactions, exploring their thoughts and feelings, and responding to them in ways that will promote understanding and continuing positive interactions. These abilities to recognize the emotions and reactions of oneself and others are essential for making good choices around reacting to potential bullying situations.

Social skills are also essential portions of conflict resolution models that are consistently included in comprehensive bullying prevention programs. The skills needed for reacting in a variety of conflict situations and those that help avoid such situations are important parts of teaching students how to productively intervene in bullying situations.

The personal, social, and conflict resolution skills taught within a program also serve the function of promoting program initiation and continuation. As people develop and practice more effective ways of overcoming their differences, they gain confidence in the skills and a sense of closeness and common purpose with others. These ingredients are essential to gaining and maintaining student and adult investment in bullying prevention.

Continuing Involvement

Early prevention efforts for dealing with issues like drugs, alcohol, smoking, and bullying tended to be locally designed and often took the form of a schoolwide assembly or set aside a week or month to focus on a significant issue. Such efforts can catch people's attention and provide motivation, but without continuing attention, motivation fades, information is no longer used, and skills diminish.

Quality prevention programs set up a system for continuing actions that maintain the involvement of participants in anti-bullying and associated relationship and climate issues (Hazler, 1998). This adds strength by connecting bullying to broader issues of climate, safety, and personal relationships. Continuing to deal with only bullying as a focus would become old to students and adults alike and the better they became at dealing with the specific problem, the less attention it would seem that problems deserve. Such a lessening of attention creates the opportunity for bullying to again become a more significant problem. Commitment and continuity of effort over time therefore provides the mechanism for follow-up actions that call repeated attention to how the desired skills and actions improve the general climate as well as reduce bullying.

One common format for implementing continuing involvement is to set aside a short time, preferably daily, for students to talk about problematic peer relationships and other climate concerns. Most often this model is set up within the school, but it can be copied in the family, youth organizations, and organized recreation activities. Similar models can be set up for teachers, parent groups, or community meetings. The essential aspect is that the format serves to offer a regular opportunity to understand changing situation dynamics and to reinforce the use of skills and understandings taught in more concentrated portions of the program.

Some programs like Steps to Respect, Olweus Bullying Prevention Program, and Bully Busters among others are designed to provide separate activities and goals for different grade levels so that what was learned one year can be built upon in the following year (Espelage & Horne, 2008).

Another common ongoing action format utilizes the essential school and community values and behaviors that transcend bullying prevention. Posters, awards, and recognition at extra-curricular activities can provide continuing emphases to the important influence such core values and behaviors have on growth, development, quality performance, citizenship, and sportsmanship. The broader and more consistently these core values can be interlaced with school and community activities, the greater are their influence both in bullying prevention success and the associated safer and healthier social climate.

Assessment, Adjustment, and Recycling

The formal assessment of program activities and outcomes on a planned regular basis is what allows programs to identify their progress, recognize change, adjust the focus of attention, and revise programmatic efforts for the future. Quality programs emphasize both process and product assessment to make useful decisions about progress and adjustments needing attention (Benkofske & Heppner, 2008). The process form of assessment evaluates how well people are effectively fulfilling responsibilities to implement the plan in a timely and effective manner as well as identifying what areas need to be redesigned or techniques revised. This gives direction to identification of those needing motivation, training, or other forms of support. It also helps to understand where the system may have accurately predicted, underestimated, or overestimated the ability to implement a given program design within a specific community's unique social-ecological environment. Improvement comes not so much from doing things right the first time, but more so from identifying what worked, what is not working, and revising efforts based on a solid assessment system.

Product evaluation is an assessment of what outcomes the process produced and is the type of evaluation that funding agencies, school boards, administrators, parents, and others most desire. These are the kinds of data that hopefully show less bullying occurring, children feeling safer, discipline referrals dropping, and absenteeism lowering. Even grades and standardized test scores can show expected improvement in a safer-feeling environment with more sense of community where students can better concentrate on learning and less on anxiety over abusive situations (Hymel, Schonert-Reichl, & Miller, 2006; Konishi, Hymel, Zumbo, & Li, 2010).

Surveys for students and adults are often utilized to identify perceived progress on bullying and general climate issues. School indices such as office referrals, suspensions and expulsions can be key indicators (Lassiter & Perry, 2009) and can validate information from the more opinion focused surveys. Often interviews and small and large focus group meetings are encouraged for qualitative assessments through discussion rather than other less personal measures (Benkofske & Heppner, 2008). The emphasis is to provide general means and flexible instrumentation for evaluation, while leaving the final design of instrumentation up to the local implementation team that best reflects the ideas and culture of a community (Benkofske & Heppner, 2008).

One example of how assessment is used in a program can be found in *Blueprints for Violence*

Prevention Book Nine: Bullying Prevention Program (Olweus, Limber, & Mihalic, 1999). This low-income primarily minority school was understandably wary of being measured by instruments developed on schools made up of mostly White middle-class students, faculty, and parents. Another issue was the desire for the data gathering instruments and process in general to be a positive experience for all concerned rather than emphasizing the negatives that were the focus of so much outside attention.

Instead of beginning with traditional measures that seek information on what is wrong, this process explored with students, staff, and parents what behaviors they would expect to see from all concerned at a school with an ideal social/emotional climate for learning. Focus groups from each constituency provided ideas that were later translated into survey instruments reflecting quite traditional expectations of social and academic behaviors as well as the local culture and wording from a positive frame of reference. Each of the constituent groups accepted and supported the use of the survey as their own as opposed to the questioning, resenting, and resisting they often did with mandated evaluations.

Local investment in development and use of the survey instrument lead to interest in the program and the study itself. This interest created its own form of enthusiasm around the program and a desire to make it successful by more people and groups than had previously been involved. It also increased investment by outside groups in the form of volunteer work as well as funding. On the assessment side, other more traditional forms of data were made more readily made available to the researchers. Information such as test scores, grades, attendance, and discipline reports can be very threatening and they become more easily shared when it is clear those outsiders are as understanding of and invested in the welfare of the school as they are in their own agendas.

Assessment, adjustment, and recycling of information are essential for growth and continuing success of prevention program efforts. It is local interest and investment in the assessment process that encourages the pride of successes, the identification of potentially valuable changes, and the continuing evolution of a prevention program that keeps it viable in an ever-changing social-ecological environment.

Critique and Limitations

Implementation of the major program themes throughout sequential program stages as described in this chapter and summarized in Table 26.1 are the keys to how successful prevention programs turn good intentions into ongoing realities. But no matter the source or quality of a program, eventual success is dependent upon the extent and quality of local implementation in their unique social-ecological environment (Kallestad & Olweus, 2003; Shinn, 2003). How effectively a program and the community's uniqueness can be combined will make the critical difference.

Each program theme and stage requires people to expand personal and professional boundaries in significant ways (Hazler, 1998). People do not take such steps out of their comfort zones quickly or easily, so that program implementation and eventual success depends upon the degree of and speed with which constituents are willing to change. Many programs are dropped quickly, not because people refuse to change, but because those who want immediate change are not willing to work with and wait for those who require a slower pace. In the rush to do "something," the power of the larger group support can be lost or even turned into opposition. Conversely, moving too slowly can lose the investment of those who desire more rapid actions. Negotiating the local balance is the key to success.

Prevention programs have greater success when formal changes match informal ones. Adults and students may follow one set of non-bullying and victim-supportive guidelines during closely supervised activities, but act very differently at social occasions or during competitive events. These

Table 26.1   Implications for Practice: Characteristics of Effective Bullying Preventions Programs

Program Themes	Implementation
Social-Ecological Perspective	Integrate the greatest possible diversity of people and groups into community planning and implementation efforts
Reducing Isolation of People and Ideas	Reduce physical isolation opportunities and increase social, information, emotional, and ideological inclusion
Empathic Involvement	Create and maintain connections between people on the emotional level in addition to knowledge/information level
Sequential Program Stages	*Implementation*
Initial Awareness Building	Create both knowledge and emotional awareness that promotes understanding, a desire to help, and a press for timely action
Policy Development	Create agreed upon values, related rules of behavior, supportive activities, and enforcement procedures involving the greatest possible diversity of school/community participants
Skill Development	Teach a wide variety of social skills that encourage abusers, victims, and bystanders to assertively implement social/behavioral values and policies
Continuing Involvement	Provide regular time for discussions on the school's evolving climate, positive changes, problems, necessary actions, and how to use previously learned skills
Assessment and Adjustment	Evaluate progress, identify changing needs, and direct adjustment of efforts

inconsistencies diminish the sense that the lessons of the program are truly universal and promote the idea that they only apply to certain people in selected settings. One of the most difficult yet valuable changes successful programs promote is transferring application of the skills and knowledge developed in a classroom to less organized and unsupervised situations.

Timing is a key factor in the implementation of awareness building, policy creation, skill development, and continuing involvement. School personnel and other adults are naturally attracted to the quick implementation of knowledge acquisition and skill building activities so that youth can have them at their disposal. This often results in a rush through program stages so that students and adults do not gain the motivation and systemic follow-up necessary to turn good ideas into consistent positive actions. Assessment in the early stages of a program is another example of a an important timing issue (Benkofske & Heppner, 2008) that is often overlooked until late in the process when people begin wishing they had started collecting information earlier. Both examples reflect the preparation and patience that are essential for successful follow through with a prevention program.

All successful programs involve students, but not all in the same ways. Students may be involved in more passive roles (e.g., gaining awareness, knowledge, or policy follower), supportive roles (e.g., support seeker, caring encourager, mentor, or educator), or more assertive roles (e.g., mediator, policy maker, policy enforcer, or peer counselor; Hazler & Carney, 2002). Communities and individuals are not equally comfortable with students in each of these roles.

Many states provide funding for programs, and a common string attached is the need for the program to be supported by research and for program outcomes to be evaluated locally. The "supported by research" issue is where programs that have invested in research over time gain a major advantage over programs that have funded marketing, but not research. No programs have proven fully successful in all situations, but *the more a local program builds upon the research of previous efforts, the greater is the likelihood of choosing or building a successful one.*

The selected or designed program needs to match the funds, time, and energy available to make the program work successfully in the local school/community culture. Ignoring these steps or the program themes and stages can lead to half-hearted efforts or discontinuation. Attending to them produces a program that can effectively integrate quickly into a school system and remain there as an integral part of the development of youth, schools, and community.

References

Benkofske, M., & Heppner, C. C. (2008). Program evaluation. In P. P. Heppner, B. E. Wampold, & D. M. Kivlighan (Eds.), *Research design in counseling* (3rd ed., pp. 511–535). Belmont, CA: Wadsworth.

Brown, T. (Producer). (1993). *"…Broken toy"* [Film]: Warminster, PA: MAR-CO Publishers.

Brown, T. (Producer). (1997). *"…but names will never hurt me"* [Film]: Warminster, PA: MAR-CO Publishers.

Brown, T. (Producer). (2004). *"SCARS"* [Film]: Warminster, PA: MAR-CO Publishers.

Carney, J. V., Hazler, R. J., Oh, I., Hibel, L. C., & Granger, D. A. (2010). The relations between bullying exposures in middle childhood, anxiety, and adrenocortical activity. *Journal of School Violence, 9,* 194–211. doi: 10.1080/15388220903479602

Craig, W. M., Pepler, D., & Atlas, R. (2000). Observations of bullying in the playground and in the classroom. *School Psychology International, 21,* 22–36. doi: 10.1177/0143034300211002

Dell Fitzgerald, P., & Van Schoiack Edstrom, L. (2006). Second step: A violence prevention curriculum. In S. R. Jimerson & M. J. Furlong (Eds.), *Handbook of school violence and school safety: From research to practice* (pp. 383–394). Mahwah, NJ: Erlbaum.

Espelage, D. L., & Swearer, S. M. (2010). A social-ecological model for bullying prevention and intervention: Understanding the impact of adults in the social ecology of youngsters. In S. R. Jimerson, S. M. Swearer, & D. L. Espelage (Eds.), *Handbook of bullying in schools: An international perspective* (pp. 61–72). New York, NY: Routledge.

Espelage, D. L., & Horne, A. M. (2008). School violence and bullying prevention: From research-based explanations to empirically based solutions. In S. D. Brown & R. W. Lent (Eds.), *Handbook of counseling psychology, 4th edition* (pp. 588–606). Hoboken, NJ: Wiley.

Espelage, D. L., & Swearer, S. M. (2003). Research on school bully Gay & Lesbian Alliance Against Defamationing and victimization: What have we learned and where do we go from here? *School Psychology Review, 32,* 365–383.

Furlong, M. J., Morrison, G. M., & Greif, J. L. (2003). Reaching an American consensus: Reactions to the special issue on school bullying. *School Psychology Review, 32,* 456–470.

GLAD (Gay & Lesbian Alliance Against Defamation). (2010). GLAD and Facebook work together to remove anti-gay comments. Retrieved October 22, 2010, from http://www.glaad.org/releases/101310facebook

Greenberg, M. T., & Kusche, C. A. (2006). Building social and emotional competence: The PATHS curriculum. In S. R. Jimerson & M. J. Furlong (Eds.), *Handbook of school violence and school safety: From research to practice* (pp. 383–394). Mahwah, NJ: Erlbaum.

Janson, G. R., Carney, J. V., Hazler, R. J., & Oh, I. (2009). Bystanders' reactions to witnessing repetitive abuse experiences. *Journal of Counseling and Development, 87*(3), 319–326.

Hazler, R. J. (1998). Promoting personal investment is systemic approaches to school violence. *Education, 119,* 222–231.

Hazler, R. J., & Carney, J. V. (2002). Empowering peers to prevent youth violence. *Journal of Humanistic Counseling, Education and Development, 41,* 129–149.

Hazler, R. J., & Carney, J. V. (2000). When victims turn aggressors: Factors in the development of deadly school violence. *Professional School Counseling, 4,* 105–112.

Hazler, R. J., & Hoover, J. H. (1996). Confronting the bullying problem. *Journal of Emotional and Behavioral Problems, 5,* 2–5.

Hymel, S., Schonert-Reichl, K. A., Bonanno, R. A., Vaillancourt, T., & Henderson, N. R. (2010). In S. R. Jimerson, S. M. Swearer, & D. L. Espelage (Eds.), *Handbook of bullying in schools: An international perspective* (pp.101–118). New York, NY: Routledge.

Hymel, S., Schonert-Reichl, K. A., & Miller, L. (2006). Reading, 'riting, 'rithmetic and relationships: Considering the social side of education. *Exceptionality Education Canada, 16,* 149–192.

Kallestad, J. H., & Olweus, D. (2003). Predicting teachers' and schools' implementation of the Olweus Bullying Prevention Program: A multilevel study. *Prevention and Treatment, 6,* Article 0021a. Retrieved January 3, 2005, from http://jounrals.apa.org/prevention/volume6/pre0060021a.html

Konishi, C., Hymel, S., Zumbo, B. D., & Li, (2010). Do school bullying and student-teacher relationships matter for academic achievement? A multilevel analysis. *Canadian Journal of School Psychology, 25*(1), 19–25. doi: 10.1177/0829573509357550

Lassiter, W. L., & Perry, D. C. (2009). *Preventing violence and crime America's schools: From put-downs to lock-downs.* Santa Barbara, CA: Praeger.

Leisman, R. (2009) Bullying of children with developmental disabilities: an ecological approach to program development. In C. A. Marshall, E. Kendall, M. E. Banks, & R. M. S. Gover, (2009). *Disabilities: Insights from across fields and around the world, vol 2: The context: Environmental, social, and cultural consideration.* (pp. 219–237). Santa Barbara, CA: Praeger.

Limber, S. P., & Small, M. A. (2003). State laws and policies to address bullying in schools. *School Psychology Review, 32,* 445–455.

Olweus, D. (1993). *Bullying at school: What we know and what we can do.* Cambridge, MA: Blackwell.

Olweus, D., Limber, S., & Mihalic, S. (1999). Bullying prevention program. In D. S. Elliott (Ed.), *Blueprints for violence prevention book nine: Bullying prevention program* (pp. 1–79). Golden, CO: Venture Publishing and C & M Press.

Operation Respect. (2000). *Don't laugh at me* [Video]. Retrieved August 18, 2010 from http://www.dontlaugh.org/

Orpinas, P., & Horne, A. M. (2006). Selection and implementation of universal bullying prevention programs. In P. Orpinas & A. M. Horne (Eds.), *Bullying prevention: Creating a positive school climate and developing social competence* (pp. 165–177). Washington, DC: American Psychological Association. doi: 10.1037/11330-007

Orpinas, P., & Horne, A. M. (2010). Creating a positive school climate and developing social competence. In S. R. Jimerson, S. M. Swearer, & D. L. Espelage (Eds.), *Handbook of bullying in schools: An international perspective* (pp. 49–60). New York, NY: Routledge.

Pepler, D. Craig, W., & O'Connell, P. (2010). Peer processes in bullying. In S. R. Jimerson, S. M. Swearer, & D. L. Espelage (Eds.), *Handbook of bullying in schools: An international perspective* (pp. 469–480). New York, NY: Routledge.

Rigby, K. (2008). *Children and bullying: How parents and educators can reduce bullying at school.* Malden, MA: Blackwell.

Rigby, K. (2010). School bullying and the case for the method of shared concern. In S. R. Jimerson, S. M. Swearer, & D. L. Espelage (Eds.), *Handbook of bullying in schools: An international perspective* (pp. 547–558). New York, NY: Routledge.

Sawyer, A. L., Bradshaw, C. P., & O'Brennan, L. M. (2008). Examining ethnic, gender, and developmental differences in the way children report being a victim of "bullying" on self-report measures. *Journal of Adolescent Health, 43,* 106–114. doi:10.1016/j.jadohealth.2007.12.011

Scheckner, S. B., & Rollin, S. A. (2003). An elementary school violence prevention program. *Journal of School Violence, 2,* 3–42.

Scherr, T. G., & Larson, L. (2010). Bullying dynamics associated with race, ethnicity, and immigration status. In S. R. Jimerson, S. M. Swearer, & D. L. Espelage (Eds.), *Handbook of bullying in schools: An international perspective* (pp. 223–234). New York, NY: Routledge.

Shinn, M. (2003). Understanding implementation of programs in multilevel systems. Prevention and Treatment, 6, Article022c. Retrieved January 3, 2005, from http://jounrals.apa.org/prevention/volume6/pre0060022c.html. doi: 10.1037/1522-3736.6.1.622c

Smith, P. K., & Monks, C. P. (2008). Concepts of bullying: Developmental and cultural aspects. *International Journal of Adolescent Medicine and Health, 20,* 101–112.

27

The Olweus Bullying Prevention Program

An Overview of Its Implementation and Research Basis

Susan P. Limber

CLEMSON UNIVERSITY, SOUTH CAROLINA

Abstract

The Olweus Bullying Prevention Program (OBPP) is a schoolwide program designed to reduce bullying among students in elementary, middle, and junior high grades. Program components are described at the schoolwide, classroom, individual, and community levels. Large-scale evaluations of the program in Norway have shown marked reductions in bullying, as well as improvements in school climate. Evaluations of the OBPP in diverse public schools in the United States are described. Results in these settings have not produced uniformly positive results, but they have shown program effects in reduction of self-reported bullying and engagement in antisocial behavior. Directions for future research are discussed.

Although bullying among children and youth is not a recent phenomenon, it has received considerable attention in recent years in Europe, the United States, and many other parts of the world. Efforts to reduce and prevent bullying in schools in the United States have become increasingly common, particularly as growing numbers of states have mandated that school districts develop policies to address bullying. The oldest and one of the most researched and widely disseminated bullying prevention efforts is the Olweus Bullying Prevention Program. In this chapter, I will describe the conceptual basis for the program, highlight its strategies and components, and summarize existing research related to its implementation and effectiveness. I will conclude by noting the limitations of our current knowledge and posing several directions for future research.

Background and Importance of the Issue

Bullying is most commonly defined as repeated aggressive behavior in which there is an imbalance of power or strength between the two parties (Craig et al., 2009; Nansel et al., 2001;

Olweus, 1993; Olweus & Limber, 2010a). Bullying may be carried out through both direct (e.g., hitting, insults, threats) and indirect means (e.g., rumor-spreading, social exclusion, manipulation of friendships) (Craig et al., 2009; Olweus, 1993).

Prevalence

Dan Olweus (1993) conducted the earliest systematic investigations of the prevalence of bullying by studying more than 150,000 Norwegian and Swedish children ages 8–15 years in the 1980s and found that 15% of students reported being involved in bully/victim problems "2–3 times per month or more often." Nine percent reported that their peers had bullied them, 7% indicated that they had bullied others, and approximately 2% had bullied others and also had been bullied.

Recent cross-national studies confirm that bullying is commonplace around the globe. Craig and colleagues (2009) used the same criteria for defining bullying that was established by Olweus (i.e., 2–3 times/month or more in the previous 2 months) in the Health Behavior of School-Aged Children (HBSC) survey of nationally representative samples of 11-, 13-, and 15-year-old school children in 40 countries during the 2005/2006 school year. They observed that 11% of these students had bullied others, 13% had been bullied, and 4% had both bullied others and been bullied. They noted that involvement in bullying (as "bully," "victim," or "bully-victim") varied dramatically across the countries, with the lowest involvement being reported in Sweden (involving 9% of boys and 5% of girls) and the highest involvement being reported in Lithuania (reported by 45% of boys and 36% of girls). These differences likely reflect social and cultural differences in bullying (or in participants' understanding of the term) and in the implementation of policies and programs to address it (Craig et al., 2009).

In the first nationally representative study of students in the United States, Nansel et al. (2001) surveyed more than 15,000 students in Grades 6–10 and found that 30% of students had been frequently involved in bullying (with 13% involved as bully, 11% as victim, and 6% as bully-victims). These authors concluded in 2001, that involvement of American school children in bullying was "substantial" (Nansel et al., 2001, p. 2094). More recent national surveys of confirm that bullying is a national concern in the United States. In the HBSC study conducted in 2005 (Craig et al., 2009), 22% of American boys and 17% of American girls (ages 11, 13, and 15 years) reported regular involvement in bullying (as bullies, victims, or bully-victims). The 2007 School Crime Supplement to the National Crime Victimization Survey (Dinkes, Kemp, & Baum, 2009) found that 32% of students ages 12–18 years reported being bullied during the school year. The 2009 Youth Risk Behavior Survey (U.S. Department of Health and Human Services, 2010) reported that nearly 20% of high school students had been bullied on school grounds in the previous year. In their survey of 524,054 students in grades 3–12 from 1,593 schools in 45 states, Olweus and Limber (2010c) found that 17% of students had been bullied frequently during a single school semester (2–3 times/month or more often), and 10% had bullied others frequently.

Concerns About Bullying

The culmination of two decades of research indicates that bullying can seriously affect the psychosocial functioning, academic work, and the health of children who are targeted. Bully victimization is related to lower self-esteem (Hawker & Boulton, 2000; Hodges & Perry, 1996), higher rates of depression (Craig, 1998; Fekkes, Pijpers, & Verloove-Vanhorick, 2004; Hodges & Perry, 1996; Olweus, 1978), loneliness (Kochenderfer & Ladd, 1996; Nansel et al., 2001), anxiety (Craig, 1998; Fekkes et al., 2004; Hodges & Perry, 1996), and suicidal ideation (Rigby, 1996). Children who are bullied are also more likely than their nonbullied peers to report physical ailments. In a study of 2,766 Dutch school children ages 9–12 years (Fekkes et al., 2004), those who had been bullied were approximately three times as likely to experience headaches, wet their beds, and feel listless; they were about twice as likely as their peers to have problems sleeping, have stomach pain, feel tense, feel tired, and have a poor appetite. Finally, there is evidence that bullying may be related to academic difficulties. Bullied children are more likely than their peers to want to avoid going to school (Kochenderfer & Ladd, 1996) and have higher absenteeism rates (Rigby, 1996; Smith, Talamelli, Cowie, Naylor, & Chauhan, 2004). In a longitudinal study of students in Grades K–5, Buhs and colleagues (Buhs, Ladd, & Herald, 2006; Buhs, Ladd, & Herald-Brown, 2010) observed that children who were rejected by their peers in kindergarten were more likely than others to be excluded and victimized by peers throughout elementary school. These excluded children were, in turn, less likely to participate in class and ultimately performed more poorly on tests of academic achievement. Those students who were victimized were less likely to attend school.

Research also suggests that there is reason to be concerned about children who bully. Children who bully their peers have been found to be more likely than other children and youth to be engaged in antisocial, violent, and/or troubling behavior. Findings from research in the United States and abroad indicate, for example, that children who bully are more likely to be involved in fighting (Nansel et al., 2001, Nansel, Overpeck, Haynie, Ruan, & Scheidt, 2003; Olweus, 1993), vandalize property (Olweus, 1993), carry a weapon (Nansel et al., 2003), and smoke and drink alcohol (Nansel et al., 2001). They also are more likely than their nonbullying peers to report poorer academic achievement (Nansel et al., 2001), be truant (Byrne, 1994; Olweus, 1993), and drop out of school (Byrne, 1994).

Interest in Bullying Prevention

Interest in bullying prevention has increased dramatically over the last two decades among educators, policymakers, and the general public (Limber, 2003, 2004). In the United States, this increased attention to bullying appears to have been fueled in part by the shootings at Columbine High School in 1999 (Limber, 2004), and by subsequent reports by the media, government, and researchers that noted linkages between instances of school shootings and peer bullying of the perpetrators (Anderson et al., 2001; Fein et al., 2002). More recently, reports in the American news media of suicides of bullied youth (Mulvihill, 2010) have kept the issue of bullying on the minds of the lay public and policy makers in the United States.

Legislative attention to bullying in the United States has been particularly pronounced in the last decade. Before 1999, state laws addressing bullying in schools did not exist (Alley & Limber, 2009; Limber & Small, 2003). Currently, 47 states have antibullying laws in place (Health Resources and Services Administration, 2010). Almost all statutes require public school districts (or in some cases individual schools) to develop policies about bullying. Beyond this commonality, however, the laws vary a good bit in their definitions of bullying, what they require or recommend be included in these policies, and whether they require state departments of education to create model policies (Alley & Limber, 2009).

Numerous school-based programs, curricula, teacher's guides, books, videos, and other materials focused on bullying prevention have been introduced to the American marketplace, and government-supported (e.g., "Take a Stand. Lend a Hand. Stop Bullying Now!" sponsored by the Health Resources and Services Administration; Bryn, 2011) and private sector (e.g., "Stop Bullying: Speak Up." developed by the Cartoon Network) public information campaigns have been launched in recent years to address bullying.

Conceptual Basis for the Olweus Bullying Prevention Program

Among school-based bullying prevention programs, one of the best known is the Olweus Bullying Prevention Program (OBPP; Olweus, 1991, 1993; Olweus et al., 2007; Olweus, Limber,

& Mihalic, 1999). The program was developed by Dan Olweus in the mid-1980s in Norway, as part of a nation-wide campaign against bullying in schools (Olweus & Limber, 2010a). The program was designed to address known risk factors for bullying behavior and to build upon protective factors within the child's social ecology. The focus of the OBPP is on reducing bullying through a restructuring of the child's social environment at school. This restructuring is intended to reduce the number of opportunities that students have to bully and to reduce the rewards for exhibiting bullying behavior. In addition, positive, prosocial behaviors are encouraged and rewarded (Olweus et al., 2007). The OBPP is built upon several key principles based on adults in school: (a) showing warmth and involvement in the lives of their students; (b) establishing clear rules for students' behavior; (c) consistently using nonphysical, nonhostile consequences when rules are not followed; and (d) acting as authorities and positive role models (Olweus, 1993; Olweus et al., 2007).

Description of the OBPP Approach

These principles have been translated into program components that are implemented at the schoolwide level, the classroom level, the individual level, and in some contexts, the community level.

Schoolwide Components

Eight program components are implemented schoolwide as part of the OBPP (Olweus et al., 2007). Each will be described briefly. Together, these schoolwide components provide the structures and procedures that are critical to systems change.

Establish a Bullying Prevention Coordinating Committee

The Bullying Prevention Coordinating Committee (BPCC) is a group of 8–15 representatives from the school community (e.g., an administrator, a teacher from each grade, a school counselor and/or other school-based mental health professional, a member of the nonteaching staff, and at least one parent) that is responsible for ensuring that all program components are implemented. The committee meets regularly to review data from the student survey, plan for the implementation of the program, coordinate the program with other prevention efforts at the school, obtain ongoing feedback about the implementation of the program, and ensure that the effort is integrated into the school's other prevention and intervention efforts and continued over time (Olweus et al., 2007).

Conduct Training and Provide Ongoing Consultation

Members of the BPCC participate in an intensive two-day training and receive at least one year of monthly consultation by a certified OBPP trainer in order to help ensure fidelity to the model. Members of the BPCC, in turn, provide one day of training (often with assistance from the certified trainer) to all school staff prior to launching the OBPP.

Administer the Olweus Bullying Questionnaire

The Olweus Bullying Questionnaire is an a 40-item self-report measure, administered to students in Grades 3 and higher, that is designed to measure the extent of bully/victim problems within a school, the most common locations for bullying, and student perceptions of and attitudes toward bullying (Olweus, 2007; Solberg & Olweus, 2003). The OBQ is given annually—prior to the implementation of the OBBP, and at yearly intervals thereafter. Findings from the questionnaire can help school leaders raise awareness about bullying among adults and students, develop school-specific plans to implement the OBPP, and assess change in behavior and attitudes over time.

Hold Staff Discussion Group Meetings

Recognizing the a once-a-year training is not sufficient to ensure effective implementation of the OBPP, groups of teachers and other staff meet regularly to continue their education about the OBPP. During these meetings, staff members discuss bullying prevention and related efforts at their school, learn from each others' efforts, and assess the ongoing implementation of the program (Olweus et al., 2007).

Introduce and Enforce School Rules About Bullying

Schools are encouraged to adopt four school rules about bullying: (a) we will not bully others; (b) we will try to help students who are bullied; (c) we will try to include students who are left out; and (d) if we know that somebody is being bullied, we will tell an adult at school and an adult at home (Olweus et al., 2007). These rules are posted widely in the school and discussed with students and parents. The use of consistent positive and negative consequences is encouraged to reinforce these rules.

Review and Refine the Supervisory System

The BPCC within each school reviews and adjusts its supervisory system to reduce the opportunities for bullying among students. This review includes identifying common locations for bullying (from the students responses on the OBQ), developing specific strategies to increase supervision in these locations, tracking and reporting bullying incidents, and evaluating the physical design of the school (Olweus et al., 2007).

Hold a Schoolwide Kick-off Event to Launch the Program

Each school launches its OBPP with an event for students (and often parents) that is designed to increase awareness about bullying, introduce the program to the school community, and explain the school's rules and procedures for addressing bullying.

Involve Parents

Parents are engaged in the program through a variety of strategies, including representation on the school's bullying prevention coordinating committee and through participation in school-wide meetings with school staff. Parents also receive printed information about the program and periodic updates through school newsletters and other channels.

Classroom-Level Components

There are three standard components of the OBPP that are administered within classrooms (Olweus et al., 2007).

Post, Discuss, and Enforce Schoolwide Rules About Bullying

Classroom teachers discuss in detail with students the schoolwide rules against bullying. Doing so is important to ensure a common understanding of the rules and their application. These rules are revisited on a regular basis throughout the school year.

Hold Regular Class Meetings About Bullying and Related Topics

Regular (weekly) class meetings are a critical component of the OBPP (Olweus et al., 2007). Meetings are designed to build class community, provide an opportunity to discuss the school's rules about bullying, help students understand their roles in preventing and stopping bullying, and problem-solve strategies for addressing bullying and related issues. These class meetings utilize discussion, role-plays, and other creative activities designed to help them better understand the harms caused by bullying and effective strategies to address bullying (Olweus et al., 2007).

Hold Class Meetings with Parents

Teachers are encouraged to hold several meetings about the OBPP among parents of students in their individual classes. The goals of these meetings are to help parents better understand the issue of bullying and how the OBPP is addressing it, and to increase parent involvement in the prevention of bullying.

Individual-Level Components

In addition to the school-level and classroom-level interventions, the program also involves interventions that are targeted at individual students (Olweus et al., 2007). Meetings are held with students who bully and (separately) with students who are bullied, in order to help to ensure that bullying stops and that children get additional support and/or guidance that they may need. School personnel are also encouraged to meet with parents of involved students and develop individual intervention plans for involved students, as needed.

Community-Level Components

Although the original Norwegian model did not include community-level components, we have found that U.S. schools benefit from involving one or more relevant community members (e.g., after-school program coordinator) on the Bullying Prevention Coordinating Committee, developing school–community partnerships to support the school's program, and spreading anti-bullying messages and principles in the community (Olweus et al., 2007).

Cultural Adaptations

Since its development, the principles and components of the OBPP have remained largely unchanged. However, research and experience in implementing the program have naturally led to some adaptations to help ensure that it is appropriate to specific cultural contexts (Olweus & Limber, 2010a; Limber, 2010; Limber, 2011). As noted above, for example, community engagement has been emphasized in U.S. but not in Norwegian implementation of the OBPP. In addition, the BPCC has assumed a more prominent role in the planning and ongoing coordination of the program in the United States than in Norway, whereas Norwegian schools have focused relatively more time and effort on holding staff discussion groups. As a final example, U.S. teachers have experienced greater challenges in holding class meetings than their Norwegian colleagues.

These challenges involve time constraints to hold the meetings as well as experience and comfort with facilitating discussions with students on sensitive issues. As a result, additional program resources have been developed to help teachers lead class meetings more effectively (Flerx et al., 2008, 2009a, 2009b). For a more detailed analysis of cultural adaptations, see Limber (2011).

Relevant Research

Over the past two decades, a research base has grown slowly but steadily, that has assessed the effectiveness of the Olweus program in a variety of cultures and communities. In addition, findings provide insight into teacher- and school-level variables that predict more complete implementation of the program.

Outcome Research

Six comprehensive outcome studies of the Olweus Bullying Prevention Program have been conducted in Norway. Each will be summarized briefly below, beginning with initial evaluations of the program in Norway by program developer, Dan Olweus. Following this discussion, more recent evaluations of the program will be highlighted in Norway and the United States. Finally, I will note several evaluations of programs that have been inspired by the OBPP and describe findings of several meta-analyses of bullying prevention programs.

Initial Evaluations

The first evaluation of the Olweus program took place between 1983 and 1985 and involved approximately 2,500 children in Grades 5–8 from elementary and junior high schools in Bergen, Norway (Olweus, 1991, 1997, 2005). Using a quasi-experimental (age-cohorts) design, Olweus found significant and substantial reductions in students' self-reports of being bullied (reductions of 62% after 8 months and 64% after 20 months) and bullying others (reductions of 33% after 8 months and 53% after 20 months). Peer and teacher ratings of the level of bully/victim problems produced largely similar. Olweus also observed significant reductions in self-reported vandalism, theft, and truancy. Significant improvements in the social climate of the classroom were reflected in students' reports of increased satisfaction with school life, improved order and discipline at school, and more positive social relationships (Olweus, 1991, 1997). Olweus also observed a dosage-response relationship at the classroom level, such that those classrooms that implemented essential components of the program (including establishment of rules against bullying and classroom meetings) saw greater reductions in bully/victim problems (Olweus & Alsaker, 1991; Olweus & Kallestad, 2010).

More Recent Studies in Norway

Since the initial evaluation of the OBPP, six follow-up studies evaluating the program have been conducted in Norway, involving more than 20,000 students from more than 150 schools. Consistently positive program effects have been documented for students in Grades 4–7 (Limber, 2011; Olweus & Limber 2010a). Of particular significance is a long-term study (using an extended selection cohorts design) with students in 14 schools in Oslo, and which included approximately 3,000 students at each of 5 yearly assessments between 2001 and 2006. Olweus observed 40% reductions in self-reports of being bulled and 51% decreases in reports of bullying others.

These results are particularly significant because it has been shown (e.g., Beelmann, Pfingsten, & Lösel, 1994) that many program effects are short-lived. As Olweus and Limber note,

"The[se] results show that the effects of the OBPP can be long-lasting and suggest that the intervention schools had been able to change their "culture" and ability to counteract bullying in a more permanent way" (p. 128).

Positive outcomes from the OBPP also have been found with students in Grades 8–10, but these results have been somewhat less consistent and the effects somewhat weaker than those involving younger students. For a more detailed description of evaluations involving older students, see Olweus & Limber (2010a).

Evaluation in the United States

The first systematic evaluation of the Olweus Bullying Prevention Program in the United States (Limber et al., 2004; Melton et al., 1998; Olweus & Limber, 2010a, b) was conducted in the mid-1990s, involving students from elementary and middle schools in the South Carolina. Students were predominantly African American, and the schools were located in predominantly rural communities of low socioeconomic status. After one year of implementation, researchers observed significant time x group (intervention vs. comparison) interactions for self-reports of bullying others, and a 28% relative reduction in bullying others was observed in intervention versus comparison schools. Significant program effects were also documented between intervention and control schools with regard to students' self-reports of delinquency, vandalism, school misbehavior, and sanctions for school misbehavior. No significant differences in girls' reports of bully victimization were observed, however. The program continued an additional year, but researchers documented such low fidelity in participating schools that they concluded it could no longer be considered a faithful implementation of the model.

The OBPP was subsequently evaluated over the course of four years in six large public elementary and middle schools in Philadelphia, Pennsylvania (Black & Jackson, 2007). Researchers developed an observational measure of Bullying Incident Density (i.e., the number of bullying incidents per 100 student observation hours)[1] to document the number of incidents of physical, verbal, and emotional bullying during recess (for elementary students) and lunchtime (for middle school students). Bullying incident density decreased 45% over the four years of the project (from 65 to 36 incidents/100 student hours. Evaluators also examined program effects using student self-reports on the Olweus Bullying Questionnaire. Unfortunately, because there was substantial attrition in responses over the years, conclusions cannot be drawn from these self-report data (Limber, 2011; Olweus & Limber, 2010a).

The OBPP was evaluated in Washington state by Bauer, Lozano, and Rivara (2007) using a nonrandomized control design with middle school students in seven intervention and three control schools. Researchers noted positive program effects for students' perceptions that other students actively intervened in bullying incidents (using the Olweus Bullying Questionnaire) and for physical victimization (relative reduction of 37%) and relational victimization (reduction of 28%) among White students. Curiously, no program effects were observed for students of other races or ethnicities.

Pagliocca, Limber, and Hashima (2007) evaluated the OBPP in a small-scale study with three elementary schools in a suburban community in southern California. Using a selection cohorts design over three years, researchers examined students, teachers', and parents' perceptions of bullying. Students' reports of being bullied decreased 21% after one year and 14% after two years; reports of bullying others decreased 8% after one year and 17% after two years. Increases were also observed in bullied students' likelihood of reporting being bullied to a teacher and their perceptions that teachers at school try to stop bullying. There also were marked increases in teachers' perceptions that the school had clear rules about bullying, that teachers felt they knew how to respond to bullying, and that teachers felt that the school's bullying policies had been clearly communicated to students, parents, teachers, and nonteaching staff (increases of 72%–92%).

Related Evaluations of Bullying Prevention Programs

A number of bullying prevention efforts inspired (at least in part) by the OBPP have been implemented in Canada (Pepler, Craig, Ziegler, & Charach, 1994; Pepler, Craig, O'Connell, Atlas, & Charach, 2004) and Western Europe (e.g., Stevens, DeBourdeaudhuij, & Van Oost, 2000, Stevens, Van Oost, & DeBourdeaudhuij, 2004, in Belgium; Hanewinkel, 2004, in Germany; Smith, Sharp, Eslea, & Thompson, 2004, and Whitney, Rivers, Smith, & Sharp, 1994, in the United Kingdom). As noted by Olweus and Limber (2010a), these models departed significantly, albeit to different degrees, from the OBPP and therefore cannot be viewed as true replications. Findings from these studies have been mixed.

Several meta-analyses of bullying prevention efforts have been conducted (e.g., Merrell, Guelder, Ross, & Isava, 2008; Ttofi, Farrington, & Baldry, 2008; Ttofi & Farrington, 2009) and have come to somewhat different conclusions about the effectiveness of programs to prevent bullying. The study by Ttofi and Farrington (Ttofi et al., 2008; Ttofi & Farrington, 2009) is generally seen as the most comprehensive. It included 59 studies and is "noteworthy because of the rigorous study selection procedures used" (Swearer, Espelage, Vaillancourt, & Hymel, 2010, p. 42). The study authors concluded that comprehensive bullying prevention programs can be successful but that there is variation in the effects of different programs, with those programs "inspired by the work of Dan Olweus work[ing] best" (Ttofi et al., 2008, p. 69).

Predictors of Program Implementation

Research on the Olweus program and experience in the field confirm that levels of implementation of the program vary substantially among teachers and schools (Kallestad & Olweus, 2003; Olweus & Limber, 2010a, b). Systematic research into the adoption of elements of prevention programs is relatively scarce but critical. As Biglan (1995) emphasized, "the adoption of an effective practice is itself a behavior in need of scientific research" (p. 15). In order to better understand the characteristics of teachers and schools that might explain these differences in program implementation, Kallestad and Olweus (2003) analyzed data from a questionnaire that had been administered to 89 Norwegian teachers at two points in time: October/November of 1983 and May/June of 1984. The 89 teachers were drawn from 37 schools and taught in Grades 6–9.

Five teacher-level variables were found to be strong predictors of program implementation and accounted for 53% of the variance in the program's implementation within a classroom (see Table 27.1 for a summary). Program implementation was strongest where teachers: (a) viewed themselves, their colleagues, and their schools as important agents for change in addressing bullying; (b) read the available program materials; (c) perceived more bullying among students in their class; (d) reported having been bullied themselves as children; and (e) said they felt upset and uncomfortable about bullying among students. Several school-level variables were also predictive of program implementation. Schools that had more openness in communication among teachers (by teacher report) implemented more classroom elements, and those that had implemented more bullying prevention activities for their staff (e.g., had presented results from the bully/victim questionnaire to staff, held an in-service for teachers, encouraged formal and informal staff discussion about bullying) had teachers who implemented more of the program components in their classrooms. As highlighted in Table 27.1, each of these predictors of program implementation have implications for practice in schools that are implementing the model.

Table 27.1 Implications for Practice: Predictors of Program Implementation in Classrooms

	Variable	*Implications*
Teacher-Level Predictors	Importance of staff in bullying prevention	Increase efforts to persuade teachers about the critical roles they play in bullying prevention.
	Read program materials	Increase efforts to ensure that program materials are user-friendly and utilized on a regular basis by all teachers.
	Perceived more bullying in class	Assess students to understand the nature and prevalence of bullying (by grade-level), and communicate the results to teachers, other school staff, students, and parents.
	Personal involvement (as a victim of bullying)	Increase the affective involvement of all teachers and other school staff.
	Affective involvement with bullying	
School-Level Predictors	Open communication among staff	Increase opportunities for staff to communicate on a regular basis about bullying prevention efforts.
	Bullying prevention efforts schoolwide	Ensure that schoolwide components of the program are implemented.

Limitations of Current Knowledge and Conclusions

Despite the accumulation of research on the OBPP over the last two decades, additional research will be helpful to assess its implementation and effectiveness in diverse regional settings of the United States (as well as internationally), and among students of different grade levels, gender, and ethnic and cultural groups. Recognizing the varying levels of fidelity with which schools implement the program, future work should focus on better understanding those elements of the program that are most critical to its success, as well as variables that predict more faithful implementation of those program elements. Two large-scale studies in the United States that are underway in Pennsylvania (Masiello, 2009) and Virginia (Moffett, 2010) with diverse populations will provide additional insight into such issues. Preliminary findings from each are quite promising. Further research also is needed to assess the OBPP's success in influencing other antisocial and/or violent behaviors among children and youth, impacting academic achievement and other measures of school success, and affecting the climates of schools. Ongoing evaluation of the dissemination of the OBPP also will be important, including an assessment of which schools are ready to implement the program, and what variables best predict implementation of the program with fidelity.

Note

1. BID = # incidents *(100/n * 60/t), where n = number of students observed and t = total time period observed (in minutes).

References

Alley, R., & Limber, S. P. (2009). Legal issues for school personnel. In S. M. Swearer, D. L. Espelage, & S. A. Napoli-tano (Eds.), *Bullying prevention and intervention: Realistic strategies for schools* (pp. 53–73). New York, NY: Guilford.

Anderson, M., Kaufman, J., Simon, T. R., Barrios, L., Paulozzi, L., & the School-Associated Violent Deaths Study Group. (2001). School-associated violent deaths in the United States, 1994–1999. *Journal of the American Medical Association, 286,* 2695–2702.

Bauer, N., Lozano, P., & Rivara, F. P. (2007). The effectiveness of the Olweus Bullying Prevention Program in public middle schools: A controlled trial. *Journal of Adolescent Health, 40,* 266–274. doi:10.1016/j.jadohealth.2006.10.005

Beelmann, A., Pfingsten, U., & Lösel, F. (1994). The effects of training social competence in children: A meta-analysis of recent evaluation studies. *Journal of Clinical Child Psychology, 23,* 260–271. doi:10.1207/s15374424jccp2303_4

Biglan, A. (1995). *Changing cultural practices: A contextualist framework for intervention research.* Reno, NV: Context Press.

Black, S. A., & Jackson, E. (2007). Using bullying incident density to evaluate the Olweus Bullying Prevention Pro-gramme. *School Psychology International, 28,* 623–638. doi:10.1177/0143034307085662

Bryn, S. (2011). *Stop bullying now!:* A federal campaign for bullying prevention and intervention. *Journal of School Violence, 10,* 213–219.

Buhs, E. S., Ladd, G. W., & Herald, S. L. (2006). Peer exclusion and victimization: Processes that mediate the relation between peer group rejection and children's classroom engagement and achievement? *Journal of Educational Psychol-ogy, 98,* 1–13. doi:10.1037/0022-0663.98.1.1

Buhs, E. S., Ladd, G. W., & Herald-Brown, S. L. (2010). Victimization and exclusion: Links to peer rejection, class-room engagement, and achievement. In S. R. Jimerson, S. M. Swearer, & D. L. Espelage (Eds.), *Handbook of bul-lying in schools: An international perspective* (pp. 163–172). New York, NY: Routledge.

Byrne, B. J. (1994). Bullies and victims in school settings with reference to some Dublin schools. *Irish Journal of Psy-chology, 15,* 574–586.

Craig, W. M. (1998). The relationship among bullying, victimization, depression, anxiety, and aggression in elemen-tary school children. *Personality & Individual Differences, 24,* 123–130. doi:10.1016/S0191-8869(97)00145-1

Craig, W., Harel-Fisch, Y., Fogel-Grinvald, H., Dostaler, S., Hetland, J., & the HBSC Violence & Injuries Preven-tion Focus Group, & the HBSC Bullying Writing Group (2009). A cross-national profile of bullying and vic-timization among adolescents in 40 countries. *International Journal of Public Health, 54,* S216–S224. doi:10.1007/s00038-009-5413-9

Dinkes, R., Kemp, J., & Baum, K. (2009). *Indicators of school crime and safety: 2009* (NCES 2010-012-012/NCJ228478). National Center for Education Statistics, Institute of Education Sciences, U.S. Department of Education, and Bureau of Justice Statistics, Office of Justice Programs, U.S. Department of Justice. Washington, DC.

Fekkes, M., Pijpers, F. I. M., & Verloove-Vanhorick, S. P. (2004). Bullying behavior and associations with psycho-somatic complaints and depression in victims. *Journal of Pediatrics, 144,* 17–22. doi:10.1016/j.jpeds.2003.09.025

Fein, R. A., Vossekuil, B., Pollack, W. S., Borum, R., Modzeleski, W., & Reddy, M. (2002). *Threat assessment in schools: A guide to managing threatening situations and to creating safe school climates.* U.S. Department of Education, Office of Elementary and Secondary Education, Safe and Drug-Free Schools Program and U.S. Secret Service, National Threat Assessment Center, Washington, DC.

Flerx, V. C., Limber, S. P., Mullin, N., Olweus, D., Riese, J., & Snyder, M. (2008). *Class meetings and individual inter-ventions: A how-to guide and DVDs.* Center City, MN: Hazelden.

Flerx, V. C., Limber, S. P., Mullin, N., Riese, J., Snyder, M., & Olweus, D. (2009a). *Class meetings that matter: A year's worth of resources for grades 6–8.* Center City, MN: Hazelden.

Flerx, V. C., Limber, S. P., Mullin, N., Riese, J., Snyder, M., & Olweus, D. (2009b). *Class meetings that matter: A year's worth of resources for grades K–5.* Center City, MN: Hazelden.

Hanewinkel, R. (2004). Prevention of bullying in German schools: An evaluation of an anti-bullying approach. In P. K. Smith, D. Pepler, & K. Rigby (Eds.), *Bullying in schools: How successful can interventions be?* (pp. 81–97). Cam-bridge, England: Cambridge University Press. doi:10.1017/CBO9780511584466.006

Hawker, D. S. J., & Boulton, M. J. (2000). Twenty years' research on peer victimization and psychosocial maladjust-ment: A meta-analytic review of cross-sectional studies. *Journal of Child Psychology and Psychiatry and Allied Disci-plines, 41,* 441–455. doi:10.1111/1469-7610.00629

Health Resources and Services Administration. (2010). *Take a stand. Lend a hand. Stop Bullying Now!* Retrieved December 12, 2010, from www.stopbullyingnow.hrsa.gov

Hodges, E. V. E., & Perry, D. G. (1996). Victims of peer abuse: An overview. *Journal of Emotional and Behavioral Prob-lems, 5,* 23–28.

Kallestad, J. H., & Olweus, D. (2003). Predicting teachers' and school's implementation of the Olweus Bullying Prevention Program: A multilevel study. *Prevention & Treatment, 6,* Article 21, posted October 1, 2003, at http://www.journals.apa.org/prevention/

Kochenderfer, B. J., & Ladd, G. W. (1996). Peer victimization: Cause or consequence of school maladjustment? *Child Development, 67,* 1305–1317. doi:10.2307/1131701

Limber, S. P. (2003). Efforts to address bullying in U.S. Schools. *Journal of Health Education, 34,* S-23-S-29.

Limber, S. P. (2004, August). *Bullying prevention and intervention in a post-Columbine era.* Paper presented at the 112th Convention of the American Psychological Association. Honolulu, HI.

Limber, S. P. (2010). Implementation of the Olweus Bullying Prevention Program: Lessons learned from the field. In D. Espelage & S. Swearer (Eds.), *Bullying in American schools: A social-ecological perspective on prevention and intervention* (2nd ed., pp. 291–306). New York, NY: Routledge.

Limber, S. P. (2011). Development, evaluation, and future directions of the Olweus Bullying Prevention Program. *Journal of School Violence, 10,* 71–87. doi: 10.1080/15388220.2010.519375

Limber, S. P., Nation, M., Tracy, A. J., Melton, G. B., & Flerx, V. (2004). Implementation of the Olweus Bullying Prevention programme in the southeastern United States. In P. K. Smith, D. Pepler, & K. Rigby (Eds.), Bullying in schools: How successful can interventions be? (pp. 55–79). Cambridge, England: Cambridge University Press. doi:10.1017/CBO9780511584466.005

Limber, S. P., & Small, M. S. (2003). U.S. laws and policies to address bullying in schools. *School Psychology Review, 32,* 445–455.

Masiello, M. (2009). *Bullying prevention: A statewide collaborative that works. A report to stakeholders.* Pittsburgh, PA: Highmark Foundation.

Melton, G. B., Limber, S. P., Cunningham, P. Osgood, D. W., Chambers, J., … Nation, M. (1998). *Violence among rural youth. Final report to the Office of Juvenile Justice and Delinquency Prevention.* Available upon request from S. Limber at the Institute on Family & Neighborhood Life, Clemson University, 158 Poole Agricultural Center, Clemson, SC, 29634.

Merrell, K. W., Guelder, B. A., Ross, S. W., & Isava, D. M. (2008). How effective are school bullying intervention programs? A meta-analysis of intervention research. *School Psychology Quarterly, 23,* 26–42. doi:10.1037/1045-3830.23.1.26

Moffett, K. (2010, November). *OBPP Implementation and fidelity pays dividends in reducing bullying.* Paper presented at the annual meeting of the International Bullying Prevention Association. Seattle, WA. PMid:12695230

Mulvihill, G. (2010, November 11). Experts fear copycat suicides after bullying cases. Retrieved December 12, 2010, from http://www.salon.com/wires/health/2010/11/11/D9JE3ID84_us_bullying_suicides_copycats/index.html

Nansel, T. R., Overpeck, M., Pilla, R. S., Ruan, W. J., Simons-Morton, B., & Scheidt, P. (2001). Bullying behaviors among US youth: Prevalence and association with psychosocial adjustment. *Journal of the American Medical Association, 285,* 2094–2100.

Nansel, T. R., Overpeck, M. D., Haynie, D. L., Ruan, W. J., & Scheidt, P. C. (2003). Relationships between bullying and violence among US youth. *Archives of Pediatric Adolescent Medicine, 157,* 348–353. doi:10.1001/archpedi.157.4.348

Olweus, D. (1978). *Aggression in the schools: Bullies and whipping boys.* Washington, DC: Hemisphere (Wiley).

Olweus, D. (1991). Bully/victim problems among schoolchildren: Basic facts and effects of a school based intervention program. In D. J. Pepler & K. H. Rubin (Eds.), *The development and treatment of childhood aggression* (pp. 411–448). Hillsdale, NJ: Erlbaum.

Olweus, D. (1993). *Bullying at school: What we know and what we can do.* Cambridge, MA: Blackwell.

Olweus, D. (1997). Bully/victim problems in school: Facts and intervention. *European Journal of Psychology of Education, 12,* 495–510.doi:10.1007/BF03172807

Olweus, D. (2005). A useful evaluation design and effects of the Olweus Bullying Prevention Program. *Psychology, Crime & Law, 11,* 389–402. doi:10.1080/10683160500255471 doi:10.1080/10683160500255471

Olweus, D. (2007). *The Olweus Bullying Questionnaire.* Center City, MN: Hazelden.

Olweus, D., & Alsaker, F. D. (1991). Assessing change in a cohort longitudinal study with hierarchical data. In D. Magnusson, L. R. Bergman, G. Rudinger, & B. Torestad (Eds.), *Problems and methods in longitudinal research* (pp. 107–132). New York, NY: Cambridge University Press. doi:10.1017/CBO9780511663260.008

Olweus, D., & Kallestad, J. H. (2010). The Olweus Bullying Prevention Program: Effects of classroom components at different grade levels. In K. Osterman (Ed.), *Indirect and direct aggression* (pp.115–131). New York, NY: Peter Lang.

Olweus, D., & Limber, S. P. (2010a). Bullying in school: Evaluation and dissemination of the Olweus Bullying Prevention Program. *American Journal of Orthopsychiatry, 80,* 124–134. doi: 10.1111/j.1939-0025.2010.01015.x

Olweus, D., & Limber, S. P. (2010b). The Olweus Bullying Prevention Program: Implementation and evaluation over two decades. In S. R. Jimerson, S. M. Swearer, & D. L. Espelage (Eds.), *The handbook of school bullying: An international perspective* (pp. 377–402). New York, NY: Routledge.

Olweus, D., & Limber, S. P. (2010c, November). *What do we know about bullying: Information from the Olweus Bullying Questionnaire.* Paper presented at the annual meeting of the International Bullying Prevention Association. Seattle, WA.

Olweus, D., Limber, S. P., Flerx, V., Mullin, N., Riese, J., & Snyder, M. (2007). *Olweus Bullying Prevention Program: Schoolwide guide.* Center City, MN: Hazelden.

Olweus, D., Limber, S. P., & Mihalic, S. (1999). *The Bullying Prevention Program: Blueprints for violence prevention, Vol. 10.* Boulder, CO: Center for the Study and Prevention of Violence.

Pagliocca P. M., Limber, S. P., & Hashima, P. (2007). *Evaluation report for the Chula Vista Olweus Bullying Prevention Program.* Unpublished final report prepared for the Chula Vista Police Department. Clemson, SC: Poole Agricultural Center, Clemson Univesity.

Pepler, D. J., Craig, W. M., O'Connell, P., Atlas, R., & Charach, A. (2004). Making a difference in bullying: Evaluation of a systemic school-based programme in Canada. In P. K. Smith, D. Pepler, & K. Rigby (Eds.), *Bullying in schools: How successful can interventions be?* (pp. 125–139). Cambridge, England: Cambridge University Press. doi:10.1017/CBO9780511584466.008

Pepler, D. J., Craig, W. M., Ziegler, S., & Charach, A. (1994). An evaluation of an anti-bullying intervention in Toronto schools. *Canadian Journal of Community Mental Health, 13,* 95–110.

Rigby, K. (1996). *Bullying in schools: And what to do about it.* Bristol, PA: Jessica Kingsley.

Smith, P. K., Sharp, S., Eslea, M., & Thompson, D. (2004). England: the Sheffield project. In P. K. Smith, D. Pepler, & K. Rigby (Eds.), *Bullying in schools: How successful can interventions be?* (pp. 99–123). Cambridge, England: Cambridge University Press. doi:10.1017/CBO9780511584466.007 PMid:15530202

Smith, P. K., Talamelli, L., Cowie, H., Naylor, P., & Chauhan, P. (2004). Profiles of non-victims, escaped victims, continuing victims, and new victims of school bullying. *British Journal of Educational Psychology, 74,* 565–581. doi:10.1348/0007099042376427

Solberg, M. E., & Olweus, D. (2003). Prevalence estimation of school bullying with the Olweus Bully/Victim Questionnaire. *Aggressive Behavior, 29,* 239–268. doi:10.1002/ab.10047

Stevens, V., DeBourdeaudhuij, I., & Van Oost, P. (2000). Bullying in Flemish schools: An evaluation of anti-bullying intervention in primary and secondary schools. *British Journal of Educational Psychology, 70,* 195–210.

Stevens, V., Van Oost, P., & DeBourdeaudhuij, I. (2004). Interventions against bullying in Flemish schools: Programme development and evaluation. In P. K. Smith, D. Pepler, & K. Rigby (Eds.), *Bullying in schools: How successful can interventions be?* (pp. 141–165). New York, NY: Cambridge University Press. doi:10.1017/CBO9780511584466.009

Stop bullying. Speak up. (n.d.). Retrieved December 12, 2010, from http://www.cartoonnetwork.com/tv_shows/promotion_landing_page/stopbullying/index.html

Swearer, S., Espelage, D. L., Vaillancourt, T., & Hymel, S. (2010). What can be done about school bullying?: Linking research to educational practice. *Educational Researcher, 39,* 38–47.

Ttofi, M. M., & Farrington, D. P. (2009). What works in preventing bullying: Effective elements of anti-bullying programmes. *Journal of Aggression, Conflict and Peace Research, 1,* 13–24.

Ttofi, M. M., Farrington, D. P., & Baldry, A. C. (2008). *Effectiveness of programmes to reduce bullying.* Stockholm, Sweden: Swedish National Council for Crime Prevention.

U.S. Department of Health and Human Services, Centers for Disease Control and Prevention. (2010). *Youth risk behavior surveillance: United States.* Retrieved from http://www.cdc.gov/mmwr/pdf/ss/ss5905.pdf

Whitney, I., Rivers, I., Smith, P., & Sharp, S. (1994). The Sheffield project: Methodology and findings. In P. Smith & S. Sharp (Eds.), *School bullying: Insights and perspectives* (pp. 20–56). London, England: Routledge.

28

Reducing Bullying and Contributing Peer Behaviors

Addressing Transactional Relationships within the School Social Ecology

Karin S. Frey, Jodi Burrus Newman,
Susan Bobbitt Nolen, and Miriam K. Hirschstein

THE UNIVERSITY OF WASHINGTON, SEATTLE

Abstract

This chapter summarizes research on the Steps to Respect bullying prevention program, showing reductions in bullying, retaliatory aggression, and contributing bystander behavior. Grounded in a transactional-ecological approach and informed by educators' awareness that a focus on bullying behavior provides too narrow a frame for the aggression in their schools, the authors argue that evaluation research can provide insight into how bystander behavior and retaliatory aggression contribute to the perpetuation of school bullying. The chapter also examines educational practices associated with reductions in attitudes and behaviors that contribute to bullying.

Bullying, repeated aggression aimed at individuals of lesser power, is a harmful yet common form of school violence, with most children between the ages of 8 and 11 observed to perpetuate (61%) or encourage its perpetration (48%) on playgrounds (Frey, Hirschstein, Snell, Edstrom, MacKenzie, & Broderick, 2005). Approximately 30% of American children report that they are chronically bullied at school (Davidson & Demaray, 2007; Swearer & Cary, 2003). Ample evidence shows that bullying negatively impacts targets (Card, Isaacs, & Hodges, 2007), bullies (Pepler, Jiang, Craig, & Connolly, 2008), and bystanders (Nishina & Juvonen, 2005). Bullying can also encourage other types of aggression and school violence, either in retaliation (Leary, Kowalski, Smith, & Phillips, 2003) or when malicious gossip fosters peer conflicts. A poll of more than 1,000 U.S. adults found that 74% considered school bullying and victimization to be serious or very serious problems (Public Agenda, 2010).

Without efforts to address bullying problems, rates of problem behavior increase during the school year (Frey et al., 2005). As students enter adolescence, they are increasingly accepting of bullying (Hymel, Bonanno, Henderson, & McCreith, 2002) and retaliation (Frey, Hirschstein, Edstrom, & Snell, 2009; Huesmann & Guerra, 1997). Unfortunately, adults often feel unprepared to deal with bullying problems (Boulton, 1997) and rarely intervene (Atlas & Pepler, 1998; Xie, Swift, Cairns, & Cairns, 2002). To combat the seemingly intractable nature of bullying, systemic and multifaceted interventions are required.

School bullying is a dynamic process situated within relationships among students, educators, and other school community members (Frey & Nolen, 2010; Newman, Frey, & Jones, 2010). Changes in any one of those relationships have the potential to ripple through the social ecology, exacerbating or ameliorating the problem. Appreciation of this has led to consensus in the field that schoolwide bullying prevention programs must target multiple levels and mechanisms of aggression (Espelage & Swearer, 2003; Olweus, 1993; Pepler, Craig, & O'Connell, 1999).

Steps to Respect: A Bullying Prevention Program (Committee for Children, 2001) is a schoolwide plan designed to reduce ecological supports for bullying and promote prosocial interactions. The program provides specific steps for intervention at the individual, classroom, and school community levels. This chapter provides a brief review of the knowledge base regarding harmful outcomes associated with bullying, and then describes theoretical foundations and specific practices found in the Steps to Respect program. This is followed by a summary of evidence of program effectiveness, as well as a review of findings and issues related to classroom implementation. The chapter concludes with a discussion of program and research limitations, as well as implications for practice.

Potential for Harm

Bullying involvement is associated with such harmful outcomes as aggression, depression, and self-inflicted violence (Hawker & Boulton, 2000). Longitudinal studies show declines in adjustment (Hanish & Guerra, 2002; Kochenderfer & Ladd, 1997) and increased alcohol use (Rusby, Forrester, Biglan, & Metzler, 2005) among those chronically victimized. Fearful of school (Card et al., 2007), victims sometimes escape through absenteeism (Juvonen, Nishina, & Graham, 2000) or by dropping out (Slee, 1994). Many suffer declines in academic achievement (e.g., Buhs, Ladd, & Herald, 2006; Nishina, Juvonen, & Witkow, 2005; Schwartz, Gorman, Nakamoto, & Toblin, 2005). Victimization may be most harmful for children from low economic backgrounds (Due, Damsgaard, Lund, & Holstein, 2009), or for those that are both victimized and aggressive (Graham, Bellmore, & Mize, 2006).

Repeated involvement as a bully is also associated with numerous risks to well-being. Those who bully are more likely than others to become victims of street violence (Andershed, Kerr, & Stattin, 2001), abuse drugs (Pepler, Craig, Connolly, & Henderson, 2002), be involved in dating violence (Connolly, Pepler, Craig, & Taradash, 2000), and exhibit low academic achievement (Ma, Phelps, Lerner, & Lerner, 2009). Over time, students who bully may become reliant on coercive methods and fail to develop positive relationship skills (Pepler et al., 2008).

Witnessing 85% of bullying episodes (Craig & Pepler, 1995), bystanders are arguably the largest group of students affected. Bystander intervention efforts tend to halt bullying quickly, but occur infrequently (Craig, Pepler, & Atlas, 2000), perhaps due to fear or the belief that bullying is "none of my business." Repeated inaction may lead children to disengage morally (Hymel, Schonert-Reichl, Bonanno, Vaillancourt, & Henderson, 2010) and passively accept injustice (Jeffrey, Miller, & Linn, 2001). Moreover, researchers speculate that seeing bullying succeed may prompt imitation (O'Connell, Pepler, & Craig, 1999; Salmivalli & Voeten, 2004). Negative emotions can also arise. Anxiety and dislike of school increase on days in which bullying is witnessed (Nishina & Juvonen, 2005). Finally, bystanders may get caught in the crossfire when bullying contributes to school shootings.

Both self- and other-directed violence have prompted a variety of legislative and programmatic responses to school bullying. However, initiatives not grounded in theory and rigorous empirical evidence may miss the mark (Furlong, Morrison, & Grief, 2003).

Theoretical Foundation of the Steps to Respect Program

Bullying behavior occurs within a multilevel transactional-ecological context (Frey & Nolen, 2010; Newman et al., 2010). This idea is firmly grounded in social-cognitive models of aggression (e.g., Coie & Dodge, 1998; Huesmann, 1988), and socio-ecological (Bronfenbrenner, 1979) and transactional (Sameroff & MacKenzie, 2003) developmental theories. Individual students and educators, peer groups within classrooms, and the whole school community interact to support or prevent bullying. For example, aggressive victims may enable more socially adept bullies by providing a ready ear for gossip (Frey & Hawley, 2010). Compounding the problem, educators tend to view social aggression as less serious than overt aggression, and therefore less worthy of intervention (Bauman & Del Rio, 2006; Mishna, Scarcello, Pepler, & Wiener, 2005; Yoon & Kerber, 2003), even though 22% of such episodes lead to overt aggression between the target and a third party (Xie et al., 2002).

Interventions that focus on the bully or the target belie the social complexity of the situation. Commonly employed zero-tolerance policies against bullying are unlikely to be effective (Skiba, Ritter, Simmons, Peterson, & Miller, 2006) because suspending the bully ignores the broader influences of the social ecology. A further impediment to the success of narrowly focused approaches is that teachers often have trouble identifying the most socially skilled perpetrators (Frey et al., 2005). Instead, they discern the *effects* of bullying in terms of increasingly dysregulated and disruptive behavior (McLaughlin, Hatzenbueler, & Hilt, 2009; Rudolph, Troop-Gordon, & Flynn, 2009) among their most vulnerable students. Consequently, the manipulative student who successfully prods an aggressive target into an outburst gleefully watches the victim get punished for disorderly behavior. Bullying prevention efforts must address the needs of individual students, and the peer relationships among students, while fostering a pro-social school community.

Description of Specific Program Components

Steps to Respect (Committee for Children, 2001) is a comprehensive elementary school program designed to address the transactional-ecology of bullying at the school, classroom, and individual levels (Frey & Nolen, 2010; Newman et al., 2010).

School Community

The Steps to Respect program is designed to counter the belief that children can bully with impunity by creating a high profile, schoolwide, anti-bullying effort. The program aims to reduce bullying by increasing children's expectations that all adults in the school community will be responsive to bullying situations. In addition, the program seeks to increase children's reporting and active defense of those targeted for abuse. Finally, Steps to Respect seeks to limit student opportunities to benefit from bullying (Snell, MacKenzie, & Frey, 2002). Specific program components at the school community level include: (a) developing clear schoolwide anti-bullying policies and procedures; (b) increasing adult awareness, responsiveness, and guidance in relation to bullying events (e.g., improved playground monitoring); and (c) increasing systemic supports for prosocial behavior. These components are clearly communicated to all members of the school community via letters, posters, and assemblies. Staff training, a detailed program manual, and ongoing support are provided to facilitate schoolwide program implementation.

Classroom Curriculum

The Steps to Respect curriculum is grounded in social cognitive models (e.g., Coie & Dodge, 1998), and therefore provides multiple pathways to influence behavior: building specific bullying prevention skills, fostering general social-emotional skills, and addressing beliefs and peer group norms related to bullying. In line with Huesmann and Guerra's (1997) model of normative beliefs development, the curriculum also outlines teacher practices at the classroom level to promote prosocial values.

Bullying Prevention Skills

Specific bullying prevention skills include identifying bullying behaviors, assertively responding to coercive behaviors, and engaging in problem-solving and risk assessment related to bullying. As suggested by Newman, Murray, and Lussier (2001), students practice reporting bullying incidents and identify adults in the school they would seek out for help. Lessons also distinguish "tattling" (trying to get people into trouble) from "reporting" (telling an adult to keep people safe), which parents and teachers report is a morally empowering distinction.

General Social-Emotional Skills

Friendship often serves as a buffer against bullying, and its negative effects (Hodges & Perry, 1999; Kochenderfer & Ladd, 1997). However, friends sometimes encourage victims to retaliate (Terranova, 2009) and friends who engage in deviant talk are at an increased risk of engaging in problem behaviors (Piehler & Dishion, 2007). These findings suggest that relationship skills training should be accompanied by clear guidance for friends and bystanders. Therefore, the Steps to Respect curriculum teaches social problem-solving strategies as a way to enhance peer acceptance and support from friends; e.g., discovering shared interests, conflict resolution, and forgiveness.

Emotion regulation skills are also critical to forming and maintaining social bonds. Students who have difficulty regulating themselves often face rejection and victimization (Perry, Hodges, & Egan, 2001)—experiences that further impair emotion and behavior self-regulation. Using "self talk" to cool down, and practicing calm, assertive responses to others may help children avoid the helpless or exaggerated responses of easy targets (Kochenderfer & Ladd, 1997; Schwartz, Dodge, & Coie, 1993). Improved regulatory skills, in conjunction with intervention scripts (e.g., "Stop. That's bullying."), may also enable bystanders to channel their concern into helping others rather than ameliorating their own distress (Eisenberg, Wentzel, & Harris, 1998; Snell et al., 2002). Finally, training in emotion regulation may reduce some bullying, particularly among pervasively aggressive children who display self-regulatory deficits (Schwartz, 2000).

Beliefs and Norms

Training in bullying prevention and general social-emotional skills are likely insufficient to deter bullying behavior. Many socially skilled, emotionally savvy children perpetuate or encourage bullying (Kaukianen, Salmivalli, Lagerspetz, Tamminen, Vauras, & Postkiparta, 2002) due to low levels of empathy for victims (Endresen & Olweus, 2001) and a belief that victims deserve to be bullied (Rigby, 2005; Swearer & Cary, 2003). Research shows that empathetic children are less aggressive (Kaukianen et al., 1999) and more prosocial than other children (Eisenberg, Fabes, Karbon, Murphy, Carlo, & Wosinski, 1996). For these reasons, Steps to Respect lessons aim to foster children's empathy with activities to recognize feelings, consider perspectives of children in hypothetical situations, and practice empathetic behaviors. In addition, lessons attempt to counter negative stereotypes of victims, as well as the belief that personal characteristics justify bullying. The curriculum places bullying squarely within the moral realm (Gianluca, 2006; Terasahjo & Salmivalli, 2003) by describing the harm to victims.

Teacher Practices

First, classroom teachers present 10 skill lessons that include discussion, activities, and skill practice. After completion of the skill lessons, teachers implement a grade-appropriate literature unit based on existing children's novels. Literature lessons integrate social-emotional learning objectives (e.g., empathy) with language arts content, providing further opportunities to discuss issues related to healthy relationships and bullying. Because generalization is the ultimate goal of prevention, program materials and training offer numerous activities and suggestions to generalize skills and beliefs to real life. Teachers are also encouraged to model program skills, for example by using self-talk to cool down, as well as to use rehearsal, coaching, and feedback in the context of classroom social dynamics (Frey, Hirschstein, & Guzzo, 2000).

Individual Coaching

Steps to Respect coaching models are intended to provide a safety-focused response to immediate and long-term student needs via one-on-one discussions between educators and students involved in bullying. Each model (one for students experiencing bullying, the other for those who bully) establishes details and the historical context, asks students to generate solutions to avoid future problems, and includes follow up.

Based in an educational rather than judicial or punitive approach, the coaching model enables educators to foster student problem-solving, perspective-taking, and assertiveness skills. Without high-stakes punishment and the consequent need to prove guilt beyond a reasonable doubt, educators can address low-level behaviors before they escalate. While not ignoring the need to determine facts and apply consequences, this approach places equal emphasis on helping children practice relational and problem-solving skills, enabling educators to discuss norms (e.g., "Is that fair?") and collective responsibility for school safety (see Frey, Edstrom, & Hirschstein, 2010, for a discussion of the advantages of coaching over judicial/punitive approaches).

Empirical Evidence Supporting Steps to Respect

To examine program effectiveness, constructs were examined based on social-cognitive (Coie & Dodge, 1998), social-ecological (Swearer & Espelage, 2004; Salmivalli, 1999), and transactional (Sameroff & MacKenzie, 2003) models of aggression and change. The following have been examined: (a) intervention effects on teacher attitudes and behavior; (b) intervention effects on student behavior, attitudes and skills; and (c) links between teaching practices and student outcomes. For the studies described below, six elementary schools were matched for district and demographic data, then randomly assigned to either the intervention or control group.

Intervention Effects on Teacher Attitudes and Behavior

Following staff training, intervention teachers ($n = 34$) reported feeling significantly more prepared to deal with bullying (e.g., "I feel prepared to assess the seriousness of a bullying report") than did control teachers ($n = 35$). Monthly self-reports assessed teachers' support for student social-emotional and bullying prevention skill use in teachable moments outside of lesson instruction. Another scale, measuring teacher coaching of individual students involved in bullying incidents, was completed by intervention teachers only. No group differences were found in teacher support for student general social-emotional skills ("I prompted students involved in a conflict to problem-solve'). However, support for student use of bullying prevention skills (e.g., "I prompted student(s) to stand up for someone being picked on") was higher among intervention teachers, as a consequence of a decline in support among control group teachers.

Intervention Effects on Student Behaviors and Beliefs

The small number of schools enabled in-depth behavior observations on school playgrounds, where aggression occurs most frequently (Grossman et al., 1997). Trained observers made second-by-second entries of all behavior displayed by or directed to focal children. Conclusions are based on 554 students for the 6-month posttest, and a subsample of 360 students for the 18-month posttest. Beliefs were assessed via self-report survey.

Bullying, Victimization, and Retaliatory Aggression

The six-month posttest showed predicted declines in bullying in the intervention group (Frey et al., 2005). Neither victimization nor retaliatory aggression showed significant improvement unless intervention students were in classes where teachers provided brief individual coaching once a week in addition to the classroom lessons (Hirschstein, Edstrom, Frey, Snell, & MacKenzie, 2007). However, at the 18-month posttest, bullying, victimization, and retaliatory aggression all declined in the intervention group, while the same problems increased in the control group (Frey et al., 2009). Analyzing outcomes by risk status, large intervention effects were found for students involved in problem behaviors at pretest. By the end of the second year, they evinced no more problems than non-involved students. Effect sizes were very large, ranging from .83 to 2.26 (Cohen's D). Problem behaviors among non-involved students in the intervention group did not increase over the two years.

Intervention Effects on Related Behaviors and Beliefs

As predicted, posttest levels of bystander reinforcement, argumentative behavior, and norms supporting retaliation were lower in the intervention group than in the control group at both posttests. Self-efficacy for responding assertively to bullying was higher among intervention group students (Frey et al., 2005; 2009). In addition, students of teachers who provided individual coaching showed greater-than-average increases in assertive self-efficacy and decreases in bystander reinforcement (Hirschstein et al., 2007). Bystander reinforcement nearly disappeared among intervention schools in the second year.

Playground Gossip

Because social aggression appears to play a unique role in fostering overt aggression (Xie et al., 2002), group differences in gossip were examined after six months (Low, Frey, & Brockman, 2010). We also examined whether having supportive friends or beliefs supporting retaliation in the fall would predict gossip perpetration and victimization the following spring. Previous research indicates that supportive friends may encourage aggressive retaliation on the part of victims (Terranova, 2009) and may even share targets of aggression (Card & Hodges, 2006). Although supportive friends have often appeared to buffer students from overt aggression, this relationship has not been tested specifically with respect to gossip.

The Steps to Respect program teaches students how to constructively support victims. Bystander behavior that encourages bullying or aggressive retaliation is considered part of the problem. In contrast, assertive defense and private support of victims is encouraged via discussion and role plays. At the six-month posttest, intervention-group students who had been involved in gossip at pretest showed moderately large decreases in gossip relative to those in the control group, while uninvolved students did not change (Low et al., 2010). Fall beliefs supporting retaliatory aggression were strongly related to increases in gossip and relational victimization in the control group, but not in the intervention group. Furthermore, believing that one had supportive friends was associated with significant declines in spring victimization only in the intervention group. Exploratory analyses were completed to examine changes in gossip *perpetration* among the 143 students who were *targets* of gossip during baseline observations. As predicted, having supportive friends in the fall was associated with declines in gossip among previously victimized students in the intervention group but not in the control group. The intervention may have reduced tit-for-tat exchanges between aggressors and victims' friends by suggesting more constructive avenues of support. These data illustrate the often complex relationships between the peer ecology and school aggression.

Teaching Practices Linked to Classroom Levels of Problem Behaviors

Both intervention and control-group teachers reported monthly how often they provided in-class support for empathy, assertiveness, and emotion regulation (Frey, Jones, Hirschstein, & Edstrom, 2010). Support of assertiveness predicted later declines in playground victimization. Empathy support predicted later declines in aggressive norms and bystander reinforcement of aggression. Based on these findings and the dramatic reductions in bystander behavior seen following intervention (by 72%), we suggest that aggressive "followers" may be especially responsive to intervention. Such outcomes become extremely important if, as we suspect, bystander reinforcement predicts later aggression.

Thus, the evaluation studies provide evidence that the program reduced bullying, retaliatory aggression, and proximal indicators such as bystander reinforcement, beliefs supporting retaliation, and argumentative interactions; while assertion self-efficacy increased. Recommended teaching practices were linked to improvements in retaliatory aggression, bystander reinforcement, assertion self-efficacy, and norms about aggression.

Limitations

Changes Within the School Community

A number of promising changes in adult behavior and the school community were observed, including development of policy and procedures, training for all staff, improved teacher sense of preparedness to deal with bullying, and teacher support for student skill generalization. Notably, teacher support "in the moment" predicted improvements in students' beliefs and behaviors with surprising specificity.

Despite these promising signs, we were unable to test whether the program promoted true systemic change. Due to the small number of participating schools, school community level effects on program outcomes—factors deemed critical to bullying prevention (Olweus, Limber, & Mihalic, 1999; Pepler et al., 1999; Smith & Sharp, 1994)—were not empirically examined. A cautionary note is that adult intervention in playground bullying and aggression was observed too infrequently to measure. The ratio of students to adults on playgrounds (as much as 120 to 1) may have presented logistical problems for adults to monitor and intervene effectively. Coders on the playground, however, also observed supervisory adults brushing off student complaints of victimization. It is possible that this minimization of student distress reflected a "code of silence," taught and maintained by adults, which may have far-reaching implications for program effectiveness and school safety.

To be fair, there appeared to be considerable variation in levels of playground supervision and infrastructure among schools in our study. Some supervisors communicated via walkie-talkies, wore orange vests, and monitored identified regions of the playground. Others clustered close to the school building and were non-responsive to students. Advancements in measurement related to playground conditions (e.g., Leff, Power, Costigan, & Manz, 2003) may enable researchers to further examine the roles of systemic support, training, and adult responsiveness, in effective responding to bullying problems. Examining contributions of administrators and structural supports to maintaining school safety and staff motivation may be particularly fruitful when viewed over time.

Specific Effects of the Classroom Curriculum

The extent to which student development of self-regulation was influenced by the program is unclear. Although we view emotion regulation as a foundation for performing specific skills (e.g., staying calm and responding assertively to bullying behavior), we did not directly test changes in this area. Reductions in argumentative playground behavior, however, may indicate a decline in anger among intervention students or an increase in behavioral self-regulation. This interpretation awaits empirical validation.

Future research conducted with a larger school sample may help to further differentiate the impact of systemic school change, classroom practices, peer influences, and individual risk factors. Our initial examination suggesting that friends can buffer students from victimization when the larger school context is supportive indicates the potential of evaluation research to provide basic information on school social dynamics.

Implications for Practice

We have already touched on a number of issues regarding implementation of the Steps to Respect program in this chapter. The following briefly summarizes four particularly important ones in the following section. Additionally, implications and recommended activities to support program goals can be found in Table 28.1.

First, adult myths about bullying may hinder prevention efforts. For example, the belief that children who bully are disliked and disruptive may blind teachers to coercive acts and dynamics involving students who succeed in the classroom (Frey et al., 2005). There is evidence that popular students may wield considerable influence through bullying (Rodkin & Hodges, 2003), perhaps because their behaviors go undetected by adults. This suggests that adult training should provide information about the "democratic" nature of bullying within a school population, as well as helpful hints for discerning problems that may not be readily apparent.

Second, there is evidence that teachers' support and coaching for student skill use, outside of lesson instruction, may pay off handsomely. This suggests administrators should create opportunities for staff to discuss and brainstorm strategies to provide this kind of support. Specifically, this may involve increasing adult availability to help coach students in the throes of peer conflict and bullying events.

Third, it is important to maintain adult awareness and motivation related to the program. Good practice includes ongoing training and use of strategies to keep a program visible and

Table 28.1 *Implications for Practice: Activities to Support Steps to Respect Program Goals*

Goal	Administrators	Teachers and Staff
Develop and disseminate clear anti-bullying policy and procedures	• Post policy throughout school • Send policy to families • Visit classrooms to explain policy and school commitment to student safety • Identify "point people" to carry out specific procedures (e.g., follow up) with students involved in bullying.	• Participate in formulating policy • Post policy in class rooms • Counselors and other staff support anti-bullying procedures (e.g., coaching)
Increase adult awareness, monitoring, and guidance	• Enable all staff to attend initial trainings • Enable staff to attend booster trainings • Provide support and resources for effective playground and lunchroom supervision • Present family introduction materials	• Attend to disruptive behaviors of all students • Respond to gossip, on-line and physical aggression • Use the reporting and follow-up model • Provide student support via coaching and reinforcement
Support staff and student motivation to prevent bullying	• Acknowledge responsible citizenship • Make program visible (e.g., posters) • Discuss program implementation at staff meetings • Publicize program effects (e.g., reductions in disciplinary incidents)	• Integrate program content with academic areas • Show that gossip leads to more serious problems • Recognize good citizenship
Support implementation integrity	• Use staff meetings to check in with teachers about how lessons are going • Check in regularly with other staff (playground monitors, bus drivers) about bullying and prevention efforts • During teacher evaluations, observe *Steps to Respect* lessons	• Teach lessons regularly • Model program skills • Support student skill use "in the moment"
Insure student safety during survey administration	• Monitor student activity and communication • Use visual boundaries to insure privacy • Separate students as necessary • Communicate that participation is voluntary	• Use knowledge of your class to anticipate potential problems • Make sure students have privacy and room • Communicate that honesty is valued
Support evaluation needs	• Identify point person to coordinate evaluation activities • Schedule opportunities for staff and students to complete evaluation materials • Prepare yearly or semi-yearly report on areas for improvement related to program use	• Complete checklists about program implementation • Complete surveys about program

"acting proud" (Elias et al., 1997). One example we observed was a school reader board that read, "Ask us about the *Steps to Respect* program."

Fourth, motivation is strongly influenced by adult perceptions of program effectiveness. The Steps to Respect program was shown to be effective by virtue of having a control group. Many of our first year findings contrasted deterioration of attitudes and behavior in schools *not* using the program to the maintenance of attitudes and behaviors in intervention schools. School staff members who do not have access to this kind of comparative data may miss important feedback that their efforts are worthwhile. For this reason, it is important that administrators actively sustain staff motivation. One principal used records of previous springtime increases in disciplinary referrals to demonstrate to her staff that a new intervention was working.

Conclusion

Given increased concerns about school violence and the damage associated with bullying, there is growing consensus that schools must actively protect students. Less obvious types of bullying, including gossip and electronic harassment, appear to be just as destructive as physical types and may contribute to later school violence. Because bullying unfolds in the context of peer groups and often goes undetected by adults, intervention poses challenges that require a universal approach that engages students and staff at the level of the individual, the classroom, and the entire school community.

Active adult involvement can correct the power imbalances inherent in bullying and bring about school-level changes to decrease bullying. Effective policy and procedures are the structural guideposts for making this occur. In addition, program elements should address student social skills, beliefs, and bystander processes, as these appear to be important loci for change. Classroom-based lessons can provide practice in specific bullying prevention skills as well as general social-emotional skills such as emotion regulation, assertiveness, and empathy. They also provide models of positive leadership and courage, and convey powerful messages about respect and shared responsibility for school safety. As our results indicate, commitment to effective programs and best practices can yield dramatic improvements in student social behavior.

References

Andershed, H., Kerr, M., & Stattin, H. (2001). Bullying in school and violence on the streets: Are the same people involved? *Journal of Scandinavian Studies in Criminology and Crime Prevention, 2*, 31–49.

Atlas, R. S., & Pepler, D. J. (1998). Observations of bullying in the classroom. *Journal of Educational Research, 92*, 86–99.

Bauman, S., & Del Rio, A. (2006). Preservice teachers' responses to bullying scenarios: Comparing physical, verbal, and relational bullying. *Journal of Educational Psychology, 98*, 219–231. doi: 10.1037/0022-0663.98.1.219

Boulton, M. J. (1997). Teachers' views on bullying: Definitions, attitudes, and ability to cope. *British Journal of Educational Psychology, 67*, 223–233.

Bronfenbrenner, U. (1979). *The ecology of human development: Experiments by nature and design.* Cambridge, MA: Harvard University Press.

Buhs, E. S., Ladd, G. W., & Herald, S. L. (2006). Peer exclusion and victimization: Processes that mediate the relation between peer group rejection and children's classroom engagement and achievement? *Journal of Educational Psychology, 98*, 1–13. doi: 10.1037/0022-0663.98.1.1

Card, N. A., & Hodges, E. V. E. (2006). Shared targets for aggression by early adolescent friends. *Developmental Psychology, 42*, 1327–1338. doi: 10.1037/0012-1649.42.6.1327

Card, N. A., Isaacs, J., & Hodges, E. V. E. (2007). Correlates of school victimization: Implications for prevention and intervention. In J. E. Zins, M. J. Elias, & C. A. Maher (Eds.), *Bullying, victimization and peer harassment: A handbook of prevention and intervention* (pp. 339–366). New York: Hayworth Press.

Coie, J. D., & Dodge, K. A. (1998). The development of aggression and antisocial behavior. In N. Eisenberg (Ed.), *Social, emotional, and personality development* (pp. 779–862). New York: Wiley.

Committee for Children. (2001). *Steps to respect: A bullying prevention program.* Seattle, WA: Author.

Connolly, J., Pepler, D., Craig, W., & Taradash, A. (2000). Dating experiences of bullies in early adolescence. *Child Maltreatment: Journal of the American Professional Society on the Abuse of Children, 5,* 299–310.

Craig, W. M., & Pepler, D. J. (1995). Peer processes in bullying and victimization: An observational study. *Exceptionality Education Canada, 5,* 81–95.

Craig, W. M., Pepler, D., & Atlas, R. (2000). Observations of bullying in the playground and in the classroom. *School Psychology International Special Issue: Bullies and Victims, 21,* 22–36.

Davidson, L. M., & Demaray, K. P. (2007). Social support as a moderator between victimization and internalizing-externalizing distress from bullying. *School Psychology Review, 36,* 383–405.

Due, P., Damsgaard, M. T., Lund, R., & Holstein, B. E. (2009). Is bullying equally harmful for rich and poor children? A study of bullying and depression from age 15 to 27. *European Journal of Public Health, 19,* 464–469. doi:10.1093/eurpub/ckp099

Eisenberg, N., Fabes, R. A., Karbon, M., Murphy, B. C., Carlo, G., & Wosinski, M. (1996). Relations of school children's comforting behavior to empathy-related reactions and shyness. *Social Development, 5,* 330–351.

Eisenberg, N., Wentzel, M., & Harris, J. D. (1998). The role of emotionality and regulation in empathy-related responding. *School Psychology Review, 27,* 506–521.

Elias, M. J., Zins, J. E., Weissberg, R. P., Frey, K. S., Greenberg, M. T., Haynes, N. M., et al. (1997). *Promoting social and emotional learning: Guidelines for educators.* Alexandria, VA: Association for Supervision and Curriculum Development.

Endresen, I. M., & Olweus, D. (2001). Self-reported empathy in Norwegian adolescents: Sex differences, age trends, and relationship to bullying. In A. C. Bohart, C. Arthur, & D. J. Stipek (Eds.), *Constructive and destructive behavior: Implications of family, school, and society* (pp. 147–165). Washington, DC: American Psychological Association.

Espelage, D. L., & Swearer, S. M. (2003). Research on school bullying and victimization: What have we learned and where do we go from here? *School Psychology Review, 32,* 365–383.

Frey, K. S., Edstrom, L. V., & Hirschstein, M. K. (2010). School bullying: A crisis or an opportunity? In S. R. Jimerson, S. M. Swearer, & D. L. Espelage (Ed.), *Handbook of bullying in schools: An international perspective* (pp. 403–416). New York: Routledge.

Frey, K. S. & Hawley, P. H. (2010). *Pervasively aggressive victims: How do they differ from and relate to others on the playground?* Unpublished manuscript.

Frey, K. S., Hirschstein, M. K., Edstrom, L. V., & Snell, J. L. (2009). Observed reductions in school bullying, nonbullying aggression, and destructive bystander behavior: A longitudinal evaluation. *Journal of Educational Psychology, 101,* 466–481. doi: 10.1037/a001339

Frey, K. F., Hirschstein, M. K., & Guzzo, B. A. (2000). Second step: Preventing aggression by promoting social competence. *Journal of Emotional and Behavioral Disorders, 8,* 102–112.

Frey, K. S., Hirschstein, M. K., Snell, J. L., Edstrom, L. V., MacKenzie, E. P., & Broderick, C. J. (2005). Reducing playground bullying and supporting beliefs: An experimental trial of the *Steps to respect* program. *Developmental Psychology, 41,* 479–491. doi:10.1037/0012-1649.41.3.479

Frey, K. S., Jones, D. C., Hirschstein, M. K., & Edstrom, L. V. (2010). Teacher support of bullying prevention: The good, the bad, and the promising. In D. L. Espelage, & S. M. Swearer (Eds.), *The handbook of bullying in North American schools.* (pp. 266–277). New York: Routledge.

Frey, K. S., & Nolen, S. B. (2010). Taking "steps" to effect ecological change: A transactional analysis of social competence and bullying prevention programs In J. L. Meece, & J. S. Eccles (Eds.), *Handbook of research on schools, schooling and human development* (pp. 478–496). New York: Routledge.

Furlong, M. J., Morrison, G. M., & Grief, J. L. (2003). Reaching an American consensus: Reactions to the special issue on school bullying. *School Psychology Review, 32,* 456–470.

Gianluca, G. (2006). Social cognition and moral cognition in bullying: What's wrong? *Aggressive Behavior, 32,* 528–539.

Graham, S., Bellmore, A. D., & Mize, J. (2006). Peer victimization, aggression, and their co-occurrence in middle school: Pathways to adjustment problems. *Journal of Abnormal Child Psychology, 34,* 363–378. doi:10.1007/s1082-006-9030-2

Grossman, D. C., Neckerman, H. J., Koepsell, T. D., Liu, P. Y., Asher, K. N., Beland, K., et al. (1997). Effectiveness of a violence prevention program among children in elementary schools: A randomized controlled trials. *Journal of the American Medical Association, 277,* 1605–1611.

Hanish, L. D., & Guerra, N. G. (2002). A longitudinal analysis of patterns of adjustment following peer victimization. *Development and Psychopathology, 14,* 69–89.

Hawker, D. S. J., & Boulton, M. J. (2000). Twenty years' research on peer victimization and psychosocial maladjustment: A meta-analytic review of cross-sectional studies. *Journal of Child Psychology & Psychiatry & Allied Disciplines, 41,* 441–455.

Hirschstein, H. S., Edstrom, L. V., Frey, K. S., Snell, J. L, & MacKenzie, E. P. (2007). Walking the talk in bullying prevention: Teacher implementation variables related to initial impact of the steps to respect program. *School Psychology Review, 36,* 3–21.

Hodges, E. V. E., & Perry, D. G. (1999). Personal and interpersonal antecedents and consequences of victimization by peers. *Journal of Personality and Social Psychology, 76,* 677–85.

Huesmann, L. R. (1988). An information processing model for the development of aggression. *Aggressive Behavior, 14,* 13–24.

Huesmann, L. R., & Guerra, N. G. (1997). Children's normative beliefs about aggression and aggressive behavior. *Journal of Personality & Social Psychology, 72,* 408–419.

Hymel, S., Bonanno, R. A., Henderson, N. R., & McCreith, T. (2002, November). *Moral disengagement & school bullying: An investigation of student attitudes and beliefs.* Paper presented at the International Society for Research on Aggression, Montreal, Canada.

Hymel, S., Schonert-Reichl, K. A., & Bonanno, R. A., Vaillancourt, T., & Henderson, N. R. (2010). Bullying and morality: Understanding how good kids can behave badly. In S. R. Jimerson, S. M. Swearer, & D. L.Espelage (Ed.), *Handbook of bullying in schools: An internaional perspective* (pp. 101–118). New York: Routledge.

Jeffrey, L. R., Miller, D., & Linn, M. (2001). Middle school and bullying as a context for the development of passive observers for the victimization of others, In R. A. Geffner, M. Loring, & C. Young (Eds.), *Bullying behavior: Current issues, research, and interventions* (pp. 143–156). Binghamton, NY: The Haworth Maltreatment and Trauma Press.

Juvonen, J., Nishina, A., & Graham, S. (2000). Peer harassment, psychological adjustment, and school functioning in early adolescence. *Journal of Educational Psychology, 92,* 349–359.

Kaukiainen, A., Bjorkqvist, K., Lagerspetz, K., Osterman, K., Salmivalli, C., Rothberg, S., & Ahlbom, A. (1999). The relationships between social intelligence, empathy, and three types of aggression. *Aggressive Behavior, 25,* 81–89.

Kaukiainen, A., Salmivalli, C., Lagerspetz, K., Tamminen, M., Vauras, H. M., & Postkiparta, E. (2002). Learning difficulties, social intelligence, and self concept: Connections to bully-victim problems. *Scandinavian Journal of Psychology, 43,* 269–278.

Kochenderfer, B. J., & Ladd, G. W. (1997). Victimized children's responses to peers' aggression: Behaviors associated with reduced versus continued victimization. *Development & Psychopathology, 9,* 59–73.

Leary, M. R., Kowalski, R. M., Smith, L., & Phillips, S. (2003). *Teasing, rejection, and violence: Case studies of the school shootings. Aggressive Behavior, 29,* 202–214.

Leff, S. S., Power, T. J., Costigan, T. E., & Manz, P. H. (2003). Assessing the climate of the playground and lunchroom: Implications for bullying prevention programming. *School Psychology Review, 32,* 418–430.

Low, S. S., Frey, K. S., & Brockman, C. (2010). Gossip on the playground: Changes associated with universal intervention, retaliation beliefs and supportive friendships. *School Psychology Review, 39,* 536–551.

Ma, L., Phelps, E., Lerner, J. V., & Lerner, R. M. (2009). Academic competece for adolescents that bully and who are bullied: Findings from the 4-H study of positive youth development. *Journal of Early Adolescence, 29,* 862–897. doi:10.1007/s1082-006-9030-2

McLaughlin, K. A., Hatzenbueler, M. L., & Hilt, L. M. (2009). Emotion dysregulation as a mechanism linking peer victimization to internalizing symptoms in adolescents. *Journal of Consulting and Clinical Psychology, 77,* 894–904. doi: 10.1037/a0015760

Mishna, F., Scarcello, I., Pepler, D., & Wiener, J. (2005). Teachers' understanding of bullying. *Canadian Journal of Education, 28, 4,* 718–738.

Newman, J. B., Frey, K., & Jones, D. C. (2010). Factors influencing teacher interventions in bullying situations: Implications for research and practice. In B. Doll, W. Pfohl, & J. Yoon (Eds.), *Handbook of youth prevention science* (p. 218–237). New York: Rutledge.

Newman, R. S., Murray, B., & Lussier, C. (2001). Confrontation with aggressive peers at school: Students' reluctance to seek help from the teacher. *Journal of Educational Psychology, 91,* 398–410.

Nishina, A., & Juvonen, J. (2005). Daily reports of witnessing and experiencing peer harassment in middle school. *Child Development, 76,* 435–450.

Nishina, A., Juvonen, J., & Witkow, M.R. (2005). Stick and stones may break my bones, but names will make me feel sick: The psychosocial, somatic, and scholastic consequences of peer harassment. *Journal of Clinical Child and Adolescent Psychology, 34, 1,* 37–48.

O'Connell, P., Pepler, D., & Craig, W. (1999). Peer involvement in bullying: Insights and challenges for intervention. *Journal of Adolescence, 22,* 437–452.

Olweus, D. (1993). *Bullying at school: What we know and what we can do.* Cambridge, MA: Blackwell.

Olweus, D., Limber, S., & Mihalic, S. (1999). *Blueprints for violence prevention: Bullying prevention program* (Vol. 9). Boulder: Center for the Study and Prevention of Violence, Regents of the University of Colorado.

Pepler, D. J., Craig, W. M., Connolly, J., & Henderson, K. (2002). Bullying, sexual harassment, dating violence, and substance use among adolescents. In C. Werkerle & A. M. Wall (Eds.), *The violence and addiction equation: Theoretical and clinical issues in substance abuse and relationship violence* (pp. 151–166). New York: Brunner-Routledge.

Pepler, D., Craig, W. M., & O'Connell, P. (1999). Understanding bullying from a dynamic systems perspective. In A. Slater & D. Muir (Eds.), *The Blackwell reader in developmental psychology* (pp. 440–451). Malden, MA: Blackwell.

Pepler, D., Jiang, D., Craig, W., & Connolly, J. (2008). Developmental trajectories of bullying and associated factors. *Child Development, 79,* 325–338.

Perry, D. G., Hodges, E. V. E., & Egan, S. K. (2001). Determinants of chronic victimization by peers: A review and model of family influence. In J. Juvonen & S. Graham (Eds.), *Peer harassment in school: The plight of the vulnerable and victimized* (pp.73–104). New York: Guilford.

Piehler, T. F., & Dishion, T. J. (2007). Interpersonal dynamics within adolescent friendships: Dyadic mutuality, deviant talk, and patterns of antisocial behavior. *Child Development, 78,* 1611–1624.

Public Agenda. (2010). *Survey: Three in four Americans say bullying a serious problem in their local schools,* retrieved from http://www.publicagenda.org/pages/bullying-2010

Rigby, K. (2005). Why do some children bully at school? The contributions of negative attitudes towards victims, and the perceived expectations of friends, parents, and teachers. *School Psychology International, 26,* 147–161.

Rodkin, P. C., & Hodges, E. V. E. (2003). Bullies and victims in the peer ecology: Four questions for psychologists and school professionals. *School Psychology Review, 32,* 384–400.

Rudolph, K. D., Troop-Gordon, W., & Flynn, M. (2009). Relational victimization predicts children's social-cognitive and self-regulatory responses to a challenging peer context. *Developmental Psychology, 45,* 1444–1454. doi: 10.1037/a0014858

Rusby, J. C., Forrester, K. K., Biglan, A., & Metzler, C. W. (2005). Relationships between peer harassment and adolescent problem behaviors. *Journal of Early Adolescence, 25,* 453–477.

Salmivalli, C. (1999). Participant role approach to school bullying: Implications for intervention. *Journal of Adolescence, 22,* 453–459.

Salmivalli, C., & Voeten, M. (2004). Connections between attitudes, group norms, and behavior in bullying situations. *International Journal of Behavioral Development, 28,* 246–258.

Sameroff, A. J., & MacKenzie, M. J. (2003). Research strategies for capturing transactional models of development: The limits of the possible. *Development and psychopathology, 15,* 613–640.

Schwartz, D. (2000). Subtypes of victims and aggressors in children's peer groups. *Journal of Abnormal Child Psychology, 28,* 181–192.

Schwartz, D., Dodge, K. A., & Coie, J. D. (1993). The emergence of chronic peer victimization in boys' play groups. *Child Development, 64,* 1755–1772.

Schwartz, D., Gorman, A. H., Nakamoto, J., & Toblin, R. L. (2005). Victimization in the peer group and children's academic functioning. *Journal of Educational Psychology, 97,* 425–435.

Skiba, R., Ritter, S., Simmons, A., Peterson, R., & Miller, C. (2006). The safe and responsive schools project: A school reform model for implementing best practices in violence prevention. In S. R. Jimerson & M. J. Furlong (Eds.), *Handbook of school violence and school safety: From research to practice* (pp. 631–650). Mahwah, NJ: Erlbaum.

Slee, P. T. (1994). Situational and interpersonal correlates of anxiety associated with peer victimization. *Child Psychiatry and Human Development, 25,* 97–107.

Smith, P. K., & Sharp, S. (1994). *Tackling bullying in your school: A practical handbook for teachers.* New York: Routledge.

Snell, J., MacKenzie, E., & Frey, K. (2002). Bullying prevention in elementary schools: The importance of adult leadership, peer group support, and student social-emotional skills. In M. Shinn, H. Walker, & G. Stoner (Eds.), *Interventions for academic and behavior problems II: Preventive and remedial approaches* (pp. 351–372). Bethesda, MD: NASP.

Swearer, S. M., & Cary, P. T. (2003). Perceptions and attitudes toward bullying in middle school youth: A developmental examination across the bully/victim continuum. In M. J . Elias & Zins, J. E. (Eds.) *Bullying, peer harassment, and victimization in the schools: The next generation of prevention* (pp. 63–79). New York: The Haworth Press.

Swearer, S. M., & Espelage, D. L. (2004). Introduction: A social-ecological framework of bullying among youth. In D. L. Espelage & S. M. Swearer (Eds.), *Bullying in American Schools.* (pp. 1–12). Mahwah, NJ: Erlbaum.

Terasahjo, T., & Salmivalli, C. (2003). "She is not actually bullied." The discourse of harassment in student groups. *Aggressive Behavior, 29,* 134–154.

Terranova, A. M. (2009). Factors that influence children's responses to peer victimization. *Child Youth Care Forum, 38,* 253–271.

Xie, H., Swift, D. J., Cairns, R. B., & Cairns, B. D. (2002). Aggressive behaviors in social interaction and developmental adaptation: A narrative analysis of interpersonal conflicts during early adolescence. *Aggressive Behavior, 11,* 205–224.

Yoon, J. S., & Kerber, K. (2003). Bullying: Elementary teachers attitudes and intervention strategies. *Research Education, 69,* 27–35.

29

What Schools May Do to Reduce Bullying

Ken Rigby

THE UNIVERSITY OF SOUTH AUSTRALIA, ADELAIDE, AUSTRALIA

Abstract

Bullying in schools is now widely regarded as a major social problem, because of its prevalence and demonstrated harmfulness to young people. Bullying has been conceptualized in different ways: as aggressive behavior and as an aspect of aggressive behavior characterized by an imbalance and abuse of power. Bullying has been viewed as the product of an antisocial personality and, alternatively, as the product of past and present social influences. Treatments vary, with some educators emphasizing the part played by behavior modification directed towards changing the pattern of behavior of individual perpetrators, and others emphasizing the provision of moral and social education. This chapter first highlights why it is important to understand what schools are actually doing in addressing bullying. Next, the chapter discusses the conceptual bases that underpin the steps that educators are taking in seeking to counter school bullying. This chapter also describes a range of procedures that are being employed by schools, both pro-actively and in response to cases of bullying. There follows a critique of what is currently being done in countering bullying in schools. Finally the chapter highlights the main implications for practice in schools.

Reducing bullying in schools is widely regarded as a major challenge in countries throughout the world (Jimerson & Huai, 2010; Jimerson, Swearer, & Espelage, 2010). In part, this has occurred because of repeated reports on its disturbing prevalence in schools. For instance, in the United States a survey undertaken with 15,686 students between 6 to 9 year old revealed that 30% of students were involved in moderate or frequent bullying (Nansel et al., 2001). In Australia, Cross and colleagues (2009) estimated that between 4 and 9 year old approximately 1 child in 4 is bullied "every few weeks or more often." The harm that bullying can do to the psychological development of both bullies and victims has been examined in numerous studies (see Rigby, 2003). It is well known that bullying in schools is linked to deteriorating mental health among a substantial proportion of students and the effects can be long lasting (Rønning et al., 2009).

Growing concern over the problem of school bullying has been reflected in increasing media attention, especially following incidents of bullying that have led to children committing suicide, as in the case of a 15-year-old girl in Massachusetts who committed suicide after weeks of being bullied by her peers on Facebook in January 2010. This incident, like others of this kind, was followed by calls for legislation to deal more severely with offenders and also with schools that failed to take adequate action to prevent and deal effectively with the issue (*Boston Globe*, 2010).

Increasingly, educators have sought to develop and implement policies and programs to reduce school bullying. Recent appraisals of the outcomes of school-based interventions suggest that *some* programs have achieved a significant but modest degree of success in reducing bullying. In a comprehensive examination of interventions that have been carefully evaluated, it has been claimed that on average anti-bullying programs reduce the prevalence of bullying by around 20% (Ttofi & Farrington, 2009).

Given that schools can take effective action to reduce bullying, albeit as yet to only a limited degree, it is particularly important to examine and critique what schools are actually doing to prevent this harmful behavior and to appraise the steps they are taking.

Conceptual Bases

Conceptual bases may be implicit or explicit. We may be unaware that we are making assumptions about what bullying is, what bullies and victims are like, why they behave as they do and what makes us think that a given response or practice will have the desired effect of preventing bullying from occurring or preventing it from continuing. Alternatively, we may be clear about what assumptions we are making and the implications of acting upon them. The most basic concept is what is meant by bullying.

There is general agreement that bullying is an undesirable form of behavior in a school. In developing an anti-bullying program some educators do not differentiate between aggressive acts and bullying. For example, the promoters of the Bully Prevention in Positive Behavior Support (BP-PBS) focus upon specific, undesirable behaviors, regardless of intentionality, power differentials and frequency of occurrence (Ross, Horner, & Higbee, 2009).

This simplification is appealing to some teachers. They see a child acting forcibly, physically and/or verbally. Action is needed. The "bully" needs to be told that his/her behavior is unacceptable. An appropriate mode of negative reinforcement is applied—to deter the undesired behavior—and positive to encourage a pro-social alternative. This approach has a strong affinity with the views held by the behavior modifiers of the 1960s as described by Skinner (1971).

Pitted against this conceptualization of bullying is the view that bullying is a subcategory of aggression. It is maintained that bullying can occur only when an individual or a group acting aggressively is more powerful than someone who is being targeted. In short, bullying can only occur when there is an imbalance of power—physically, psychologically, numerically, or status-wise. This refinement is often dismissed by those who prefer the simpler definition because it appears impractical. Certainly, it is sometimes far from evident who or which is the stronger party. For instance, an aggressor may be physically stronger but capable of being outwitted by a smaller target with a sharp tongue.

Nevertheless, there is a good reason for distinguishing between aggression and bullying. This becomes clear when individuals engage in a heated argument or a "fair fight." We may reasonably want the combatants to resolve their differences in a more civilized or amicable way. But most people would say that this is a very different matter from a case in which a child is being hounded day after day by someone against whom resistance is virtually impossible or impracticable.

Precisely what kinds of behavior can be classified as bullying is a further issue. There is general agreement that it may take direct physical forms, as in hitting and kicking and direct verbal forms as in name calling and making abusive comments. Increasingly, it is being recognized that bullying may be indirect and covert, as in deliberate ostracism and rumor spreading. The use of electronic technology to convey hurtful messages over the last ten years or so has given rise to the increasing acceptance of the notion of cyberbullying.

A further consideration in conceptualizing bullying is whether to view it as a moral issue. It would be simpler if we didn't have to. But it is fair to say that whether we are inclined to call bullying "evil" or "undesirable" or "unfair" or "inappropriate" we are making a moral judgment and many educators think that this should be made explicit. Hence a common definition of "bullying" includes the notion that it involves an abuse of power. This forces us to ask ourselves the very basic question of how power should be used. It also leads one into an area fraught with difficulties since moral judgments invariably differ and are greatly influenced by cultural factors and changes occurring over time.

Making a defensible judgment becomes particularly hard when a targeted person has behaved provocatively and, unsurprisingly, elicits a bullying reaction. If the reaction is disproportionate, being too extreme or prolonged, we may call it bullying. But where and how does one draw the line?

There is another practical dilemma. Many heated arguments occur over whether bullying invariably involves a series of acts of aggression or can be said to occur when someone feels he or she is being bullied (and others concur) on a single occasion. Because we tend to think of bullying as *repeated* aggression, it is sometimes hard to acknowledge that the term is sometimes used to describe a one-off experience.

How Participants Are Viewed

When bullying takes place, there are commonly several people involved—the bully or bullies, the target(s), and the bystanders. How each behaves is sometimes seen as determined by the individual personality or character each may possess. This perspective is increasingly being considered as unduly narrow. It may result in the bully being demonized and the target stigmatized as a weak person. It does not, for instance, take into account the potential influence of bystanders whose presence may encourage or discourage the bullying.

At odds with this way of viewing the participants is what has been called the social ecological perspective (Espelage & Swearer, 2004). This perspective promotes the view that children's interpersonal behavior is crucially influenced by many other factors besides individual characteristics, personality, and biological predispositions. These include family members, the ethos of the school, people in the neighborhood, and the broader cultural context. Rather than focus exclusively on what children do to each other, it is sometimes argued that it is much better to consider the quality of the relationships that children form with others in their social environment. According to this view, bullying is seen as the resultant of a wide range of factors that make up the social ecology.

Conceptualizing What Can Be Done to Reduce Bullying

A broad distinction can be made between proactive work aimed at preventing bullying from occurring and reactive work, which is concerned with dealing with cases of bullying after they have occurred. Responding reactively to bullying has characterized the way schools have traditionally sought to counter bullying, More recently the emphasis has been much more on proactive intervention. However, schools generally recognize that taking appropriate action to deal with cases when they arise is invariably needed; hopefully after proactive action has had the effect of reducing the overall incidence.

Schools typically see the need for a broad range of strategies to address the problem of bullying. Action is typically undertaken at different levels; at the level of individual students, at the classroom level and at the policy-making level. Thus a school must consider what it is that particular students need to know and how they can receive help when it is needed. At the classroom level, action may involve the delivery of curriculum content and the provision of activities that can help students to acquire relevant knowledge, attitudes and social skills that will help them in developing positive social relations and minimize the likelihood of their involvement in bullying. At the policy-making level, action is needed in developing an appropriate and agreed anti-bullying policy and related strategies,and, most importantly, the means by which they can be implemented through cooperation between stakeholders—staff, students and parents. Rather than leaving it to a selected group of people in a school to do what they think is needed, schools have generally adopted what is called a "whole school approach" in which all members of the school community are meaningfully engaged in implementing an agreed policy. Consistent with a social ecological approach, many schools seek to involve parents and the community at large in their plans.

What has been described above is what, in the broadest terms, most schools seek to do in countering bullying. Some aspects of their work may be prescribed. For example, there are some jurisdictions where some action by schools is mandatory, e.g. in having an anti-bullying policy available for public inspection. Some schools elect to deal with cases of bullying in only one way, e.g., using a traditional disciplinary approach; other schools may decide to use a non-punitive approach in dealing with some cases of bullying.

Approaches Adopted by Schools

Anti-Bullying Policy

Although there are some variations in what schools put in their policies, they generally contain these features:

1. A statement of the school's stand against bullying, for example, zero-tolerance.
2. A succinct definition of bullying with a listing of the different kinds, both face-to-face and covert. Explicit reference to racial, sexual, and cyberbullying.
3. A declaration of the basic rights of individuals in the school community—students, teachers, other workers and parents—to be free of bullying.
4. A statement of the responsibilities of those who see bullying going on as bystanders to help to stop it, for example, by reporting what has happened to a teacher.
5. A general description of what the school will do proactively in seeking to prevent bullying, including the monitoring of the school grounds, undertaking risk management procedures, and the inclusion of content relating to bullying in the school curriculum.
6. An invitation to students and parents to report any cases of bullying to the school authorities and a commitment by the school to take appropriate action.
7. In *general terms*, how the school proposes to deal with actually cases of bullying should they arise.
8. An undertaking to collaborate with parents in addressing the problem of bullying, especially in the resolution of cases in which action is to be taken by both the school and parents.
9. A commitment to evaluate the policy in the near future.

Work With Students in Classrooms Relating to Bullying

There can be considerable variation between schools in the amount of time and attention devoted to such work, and also in the specific content of the lessons and activities. These are the main features found in curricula dealing with bullying. They can be grouped under the headings of Knowledge, Attitudes, and Skills.

> *Knowledge:* what bullying is; why it must be stopped—the harm it does; the content of the school's anti-bullying policy.
> *Attitudes:* being unprejudiced; being cooperative and empathic; resisting negative group pressure; self-acceptance as an antidote to discouragement.
> *Skills:* being assertive and not acting aggressively; resolving differences constructively, using conflict resolution techniques; helping others who are being bullied, as a good bystander; reacting effectively if bullied.

What is done under these headings will differ according to the age and maturity of students. It is generally accepted that students are much more likely to be influenced through work undertaken in classrooms if they are can take part in activities, role plays and discussions that enable them to learn through experience and by listening to each other's opinions.

Work With Peers to Counter Bullying

Some schools opt to work closely with students, often a selected group of students, to bring about a more peaceful school environment in which bullying is minimized. Peer support may involve students being trained to carry out a variety of roles as befrienders, mentors, peer mediators and peer counselors. In the UK it has been estimated that some 62% of schools make use of some form of peer support (Houlston, Smith, & Jessel, 2009). By contrast, in the United States according to school psychologists it is among the least frequently used strategies (Sherer & Nickerson, 2010).

Working With Parents

Many educators believe that bullying can be addressed more effectively through working with parents. When parents are systematically informed about what the school is doing they may become involved in the development of school policies. They are then more inclined to provide significant support for the school's anti-bullying initiative. Moreover, progress in resolving cases of bullying often requires active collaboration with parents. Finally, bullying behavior of students can sometimes be traced to negative influences in the home. Such knowledge can be helpful in dealing with some cases. Involving parents through newsletters and periodic meetings can assist in implementing policies and solving problems (Rigby, 2008).

Dealing with Cases of Bullying

Six major methods of responding to cases of school bullying can be identified. Each has a distinctive rationale and appears to be more appropriate in dealing with some cases of bullying than others. Some schools choose to adopt one or several of these approaches; a minority show familiarity with the entire range and apply them according to the nature of the bully/victim problem with which they are confronted.

The Traditional Disciplinary Approach

This approach seeks to suppress bullying behavior, primarily through the use of sanctions or graded punishments directed towards the person or persons judged to be responsible for the bullying. Such treatment is seen to be not only just but also likely to deter the offender(s) from engaging in further acts of bullying, and send a message to others regarding the consequences of bullying behavior. The practitioner may also counsel the bully and undertake efforts to positively reinforce any subsequently observed pro-social behavior. This latter element in treating cases of bullying is emphasized in programs offering positive behavior support (Ross et al., 2009). According to on-line surveys conducted in the United States some 75% of teachers indicate that they favor the use of punishment in handling cases of bullying in schools (Bauman, Rigby, & Hoppa, 2008). Among a sample of 206 U.S. school psychologists "disciplinary consequences (i.e., suspension, expulsion) for bullies" was an item on a questionnaire endorsed by 97% of respondents as being the most frequently implemented strategy in dealing with school bullying (Sherer & Nickerson, 2010).

This approach assumes that the imposition of sanctions will suppress the undesired behavior. Research into the psychology of punishment indicates that it may well do so under some conditions, that is if the punishment is sufficiently aversive, is imposed shortly after the unwanted behavior, and is typically administered closely following any repetition of that behavior. These conditions are rarely present in schools; for instance, extreme forms of punishment are seen as unethical and rigorous monitoring of bullying behavior, especially in its more covert forms, is often impractical. At the same time, when bullying is of a criminal nature, as it is sometimes, traditional and legalistic responses appear inevitable.

Strengthening the Victim

This approach aims to help the victim to acquire the capacity to cope with the bully or bullies unassisted, for example, by training targeted children to act more assertively. Teachers appear to be divided regarding the value of approach (Rigby & Bauman, 2010). One technique that victims may be taught is known as fogging (Rigby, 2010a). This involves the potential victim focusing on the perceptions of the aggressor, acknowledging that the bully may actually believe the negative things he or she is saying and refusing to be disturbed or intimidated.

It is assumed that the targets of bullying can *be* effectively advised or trained to become less vulnerable to attack. Practical limits to the efficacy of this approach are obvious. Where the imbalance of power between attacker(s) and victim is great, training is unlikely to be effective. Not surprisingly, it is considered more appropriate in handling cases of one-to-one bullying but is limited to bullying that is verbal. To date, empirical studies of how widely and effectively this approach can be successfully employed are lacking.

Mediation

Students in conflict are invited to work with a trained teacher or peer-mediator to exchange views on what has been happening between them and to find a mutually acceptable way of resolving a dispute that may underlie the bullying behavior. This approach is often seen as more appropriately employed in cases in which students in conflict are both looking for help in resolving an interpersonal problem (Cremin, 2007).

A basic assumption underlying mediation is that parties in conflict will freely seek help from a neutral third party to resolve a dispute that is sustaining the conflict. Its application is severely limited to cases in which both parties are genuinely interested in working with a mediator who *can* remain neutral. Often those who bully are not motivated to seek mediation, and it is difficult for a practitioner to remain neutral when the bullying is seen as entirely unjustified, as it normally is. There is research that shows that peer mediation, when the training students receive is adequate, can resolve *some forms* of student conflict (Johnson & Johnson 2001). And this may result in the creation of a school ethos in which bullying is less likely to thrive. However, there appears to be no evidence that peer mediation is successful way of dealing with *most* cases of bullying, and its use is inappropriate in cases of severe bullying, which normally require adult intervention.

Restorative Practice

This method requires offenders to reflect upon their behavior in the presence of their victim(s), to experience a sense of remorse, and to restore damaged relationships through a sincere apology or restorative act. In recent years this approach has gained acceptance in a growing number of schools. It can be applied in a variety of situations—in a meeting involving a bully and a victim, a classroom meeting where many more students are involved, or at a conference at which community members who are supportive of the individual students are also present (Thorsborne & Vinegrad, 2006).

Restorative practices assume that students who engage in bullying will feel remorse over their actions after they have been induced by a trained practitioner to reflect upon their deplorable behavior. They will then act to repair their damaged relationship with the person they have victimized. Unfortunately, the extent to which students who bully actually show genuine remorse is rarely examined, and while some bullies appear to respond positively to this approach, there is little evidence of its overall effectiveness in reducing the level of bullying in schools (see Sherman & Strang, 2007).

Support Group Method

This was originally called the "no blame approach." It involves first speaking with the victim and identifying the perpetrators. Subsequently, a group meeting is held which includes the bullies and several students who support the victim, but *not* the victim. The practitioner graphically describes the victim's distress and each person present is asked to say how he or she will help. The situation is then carefully monitored (see Robinson & Maines, 2008).

This method assumes that children who bully can be reformed without the use of punishment and also without being subjected to external pressure to feel remorse or shame. It is thought that when a practitioner meets with the bullies and graphically describes the distress that the victim has experienced, the perpetrators will experience some degree of empathy and become motivated to help to improve matters; especially so when supporters of the victim are also present. This approach is generally seen as appropriate for non-violent, non-criminal forms of bullying. It does not, however, take into account any provocation that may have occurred prior to the bullying and the need in some cases for changes in behavior on the part of both parties. There is some empirical evidence demonstrating the effectiveness of this approach (Robinson & Maines, 2008).

Method of Shared Concern

This is a multi-stage process in which suspected bullies are first interviewed individually. The practitioner shares a concern for the victim with each one of them and asks for their cooperation in improving the victim's situation. The victim is next interviewed and told about what has happened. After some progress on the part of the suspected bullies has been confirmed, the practitioner meets with them as a group. They are required to make an agreed plan to present to the victim, who is then invited to join them to bring about an enduring solution (see Pikas, 2002; Rigby, 2010b, 2011; Rigby & Griffiths, 2011).

Like the support group method, the method of shared concern assumes that a non–punitive approach can be used effectively with groups of students who have engaged in bullying, especially if the suspected bullies are not accused of bullying and are carefully prepared through one-to-one meetings for a subsequent mediation session with the person they have bullied. It does not assume that the victim is invariably "innocent." Research has demonstrated that around 16% of victims behave provocatively and need to change their behavior as well (Solberg & Olweus, 2003). Although this method can be time consuming in its application and requires well-trained and skilful practitioners, it effectiveness has been well documented in a number of studies (Rigby & Griffiths, 2010).

A Critique of Contemporary Efforts to Address Bullying

In response to the growing awareness over the last 20 years of bullying in schools, there has emerged a substantial body of relevant theory and proposed practices. Many anti-bullying programs have been developed and implemented by schools. Numerous surveys conducted in Europe and the United States between 1996 and 2008 have reported an overall reduction in the prevalence of peer victimization in schools (see Molcho et al., 2009; Rigby & Smith, 2011). Some but not all programs have proved to be effective in reducing bullying. Among the 44 programs that have been rigorously evaluated, some 17 have been shown to have been successful in significantly reducing bullying in schools (Ttofi & Farrington, 2009). What schools have been doing in countering bullying thus appears to be making some headway. What is not yet known is what works best and why.

Identifying the best programs and the crucial elements in anti-bullying programs remains problematic. For instance, the most widely employed anti-bullying program, devised by Olweus (1993), has been reported as highly effective in a series of applications in Norway but generally unsuccessful in applications in Germany and Belgium (Smith, Pepler, & Rigby, 2004). Despite the popularity of this program and widespread adoption in the United States, outcomes have been mixed. Some positive outcomes have been indicated, especially in California where significant reductions in bullying were reported. However, elsewhere many of the outcomes were disappointing. For instance, in relation to the South Carolina study, it was reported that "no significant changes were observed in the frequency with which students reported being bullied" (Olweus & Limber, 2010, p. 395). In the Washington study, Olweus and Limber note that some significant reductions in victimization occurred for White students but that there were "no overall program effects regarding rates of victimization" (p. 396). In Philadelphia, they report that changes in self-reported being bullied varied between schools—from a decrease of 10% to an increase of 7%. They note that "due to the great attrition rate [over 50% of respondents dropped out of this study] firm conclusions about students' self reported victimization cannot be drawn in this study" (p. 396).

Such inconsistency in outcomes for a given program suggests that other factors besides those indicated in the blueprint operate, for instance, cultural factors and the way the program is implemented. Moreover, when the implementation of a program does result in a reduction in bullying, it is unclear whether success is due to specific features, such as the proactive work being undertaken by teachers in classrooms or by the method employed in intervening with cases of bullying or a combination of different elements in a program.

The broadly accepted view is that both proactive and reactive methods are needed and that a whole school approach should be adopted. This has been assumed but never tested. It is not known, for instance, whether reductions in bullying in schools could occur without any work being done in teaching students about bullying and helping students to develop appropriate social attitudes and skills. It is unclear whether specific kinds of interventions in cases of bullying constitute a necessary component in anti-bullying programs. Although it is widely believed that a whole school approach is needed to have a significant effect in reducing bullying, the alternative approach—say action devised and undertaken *independently* by a task force within a school—may have a similar or even a more beneficial effect. Many pertinent questions, such as those raised above, have never been examined and tested empirically. Appraisals of what schools do to counter bullying must therefore be made largely on what appears to be plausible rather than upon overwhelming evidence.

The foregoing raises a number of issues that are important for addressing the problem of school bullying. The first and most crucial question concerns the way bullying is to be conceptualized. Should schools conceive bullying as essentially no different from other kinds of undesired behavior and most treatable by (a) clarifying for students what kind of behavior is acceptable and unacceptable and (b) applying positive or negative reinforcement accordingly? As discussed earlier, this conception of bullying underlies the adoption of Bully Prevention in Positive Behavior Support (BP-PBS) program in the United States and in some parts of Australia. Given that its proponents do not accept that bullying per se can be usefully operationalized and assessed as distinct from generalized aggression, there is logically no way in which the effectiveness of this approach in reducing bullying can be assessed empirically. We must therefore ask first whether there is persuasive evidence that it can reduce aggressive behavior on the part of schoolchildren.

Evidence regarding the effectiveness of BP-PBS in reducing aggressive behavior of schoolchildren is sparse. When the focus has been on several individual students whose behavior has been closely monitored, aggressive behavior has been significantly reduced (Ross et al., 2009). However, when effects on school wide prevalence of aggressive behavior were examined, using, as appropriate, a control group, that is, one not using PBS, no significant reductions in aggressiveness were reported (Metzler, Biglan, & Rusby, 2001). It therefore appears unclear whether this approach can in fact reduce the level of bullying conceived as inseparable from aggression in general.

A related question is whether there may be significant gains in viewing bullying as a subset of aggressive behavior, that is abusive behavior in a situation in which there is an imbalance of power? Conceiving it in this way would incline teachers to think about bullying as involving more than acts of aggressive behavior. It would result in them focusing on power differences that make bullying possible, and also attitudes and beliefs that underlie and lead to aggressive acts. Those who think this way argue that countering bullying should include encouraging students to think about moral issues and especially the unfairness implicit in bullying behavior and the harm it does, understand the nature of prejudice, develop greater sensitivity and empathy towards others, cooperate more effectively, and, in general, become more emotionally and socially intelligent. Bullying is thus seen as capable of being countered by inducing changes in the thinking and feelings of individual students and their interpersonal relationships rather than by arranging appropriate contingencies of reinforcement to operate upon student behavior.

Finally, as we have seen, there is considerable variation in the way schools deal with cases of bullying. Although most teachers continue to favor a traditional, disciplinary approach, alternative or supplementary methods are being employed in some schools. These include strengthening the victim, peer mediation, restorative practices, the support group method and the method of shared concern, each making distinctive assumptions about how bully/victim problems can best be resolved. Which approach a school opts to employ may depend not only on the assumptions it makes on what can stop the bullying but also on the kind of bullying that is being addressed, such as its degree of severity, whether it has been provoked, and whether there is group involvement.

Conclusions and Implications for Practice

Schools are being placed under increasing pressure to provide places in which children can learn without being bullied by peers. Information about what can be done to prevent bullying and

Ken Rigby

Table 29.1   Implications for Practice: Strategies to Address Bullying

Bullying in schools can be reduced through the use of well-designed anti-bullying programs.
The nature of the programs is largely determined by the way 'bullying' is conceptualised, that is, as generalised anti-social aggressiveness or as the systematic abuse of power in interpersonal relations.
The latter view of bullying leads to the promotion of social and moral education in schools rather than the exclusive use of rewards and punishment to modify behaviour.
Action in addressing school bullying is needed at multiple levels: at the level of individual students, at the classroom level and the policy-making level.
School-based professionals should establish an anti-bullying policy and plan accordingly.
Knowledge and expertise are required of school staff in promoting pro-social attitudes,developing interpersonal skills among students and in selecting and applying appropriate methods of intervention when cases of bullying occur.
Community and especially parental involvement are needed in addressing the problem of school bullying.

take appropriate action when cases occur has grown in recent years in many countries, and there are encouraging signs that in many schools bullying has been reduced. It still remains seriously high and disturbing incidents of great harm and even cases of suicide of tormented students continually come to light.

Currently there is among educators a broad level of agreement regarding the things schools can do to address the problem. These include the recognition of the need for schools to have an anti-bullying policy and plan, the education of children about bullying and especially its unacceptability as a way of behaving, and a readiness to take appropriate action with cases of reported bullying. However, important differences at both theoretical and practical levels remain. This is especially apparent in the way bullying is conceptualized and the actions that flow from different conceptualizations. On the one hand, following the Bully Prevention in Positive Behavior Support (BP-PBS), many schools are persuaded that bullying should be conceived as essentially no different from other acts of aggressive behavior and invariably dealt with by the use of reinforcement strategies. Others conceive bullying as a kind of aggressive behavior that constitutes an abuse of power and emphasize the importance of social and emotional learning and the development of constructive relationships among members of the school community. In pursuit of this aim some schools introduce content and activities into the school curriculum designed to develop greater emotional intelligence and the capacity to provide support for students who need their help.

Divisions do exist among teachers as to how schools should respond to the problem of bullying. As noted earlier, striking differences of opinion occur over whether students should be helped to stand up to bullies with some teachers believing this is both desirable and practical, and others feeling that this is blaming the victim and its advocacy unhelpful. We have seen that at a more general level there is a tendency among some legislators, as well as some teachers, to take a strong no-nonsense legalistic or justice-driven approach. In contrast, there are educators and teachers whose approach is guided more by considerations of care and the need to help solve relationship problems between students (Ellis & Shute, 2007; Noddings, 2010). Clearly, these different orientations must affect the way schools go about countering bullying.

There is in some quarters a belief in a silver bullet that will solve the problem. Draconian and simplistic remedies are sometimes proposed. However, as the complexity of the problem becomes more and more apparent, it is becoming evident that a wide range of methods of intervention, both proactive and reactive is needed. As discussed earlier, bullying can and does take a variety of forms and treatments may differ as is appropriate according to its nature. Alternative and complementary measures need to be taken by schools depending on the specific situation or problem with which they must deal.

References

Bauman, S., Rigby, K., & Hoppa, K. (2008). US teachers' and school counsellors' strategies for handling school bullying incidents. *Educational Psychology, 28,* 837–856

Boston Globe. (2010, March 30). Editorial. Criminal charges mark a new seriousness about bullying.

Cremin, H. (2007). *Peer mediation: citizenship and social inclusion revisited.* Maidenhead, England: Oxford University Press.

Cross, D., Shaw, T., Hearn, L., Epstein, M., Monks, H., Lester, L., & Thomas, L. (2009). *Australian covert bullying prevalence study (ACBPS).* Perth, Australia: Child Health Promotion Research Centre, Edith Cowan University.

Ellis, A. A., & Shute, R. (2007). Teacher responses to bullying in relation to moral orientation and seriousness of bullying. *British Journal of Educational Psychology, 77,* 649–663.

Espelage, D. L., & Swearer, S. M. (Eds.). (2004). *Bullying in American schools: A social-ecological perspective on prevention and intervention.* Mahwah, NJ: Erlbaum.

Jimerson, S. R., Swearer, S. M., & Espelage, D. L. (2010). International scholarship advances science and practice addressing bullying in schools. In S. R. Jimerson, S. M. Swearer, & D. L. Espelage (Eds.), *The handbook of bullying in schools: An international perspective* (pp. 1–6). New York: Routledge.

Jimerson, S. R., & Huai, N. (2010). International perspectives on bullying prevention and intervention. In S. R. Jimerson, S. M. Swearer, & D. L. Espelage (Eds.), *The handbook of bullying in schools: An international perspective* (pp. 571–592). New York: Routledge.

Johnson,D. W., & Johnson, R. (2001). Peer mediation in an inner-city elementary school. *Urban Education, 16*(2), 165–178.

Houlston, C., Smith, P. K., & Jessel, J. (2009). Investigating the extent and use of peer support initiatives in English schools, *Educational Psychology,* 29(3), 325–344.

Metzler, C. W., Biglan, & Rusby, J. C. (2001). Evaluation of a comprehensive behaviour management program to improve school-wide positive behaviour support. *Education and Treatment of Children, 24,* 448–479.

Molcho, M., Craig, W., Due, P., Pickett, W., Harel-Fisch, Y., Overpeck, M., & the HBSC Bullying Writing Group. (2009). Cross-national time trends in bullying behaviour 1994–2006: findings from Europe and North America. *International Journal of Public Health, 54,* 1–10.

Nansel, T. R., Overpeck, M., Pilla, R. S., Ruan, W. J., Simons- Morton, B., & Scheidt, P. (2001). Bullying behaviours among US youth: prevalence and association with psychosocial adjustment. *Journal of the American Medical Association, 285,* 2094–2100.

Noddings, M. (2010). Moral education in the age of globalization. *Educational Philosophy and Theory, 42*(4), 390–396.

Olweus, D. (1993). *Bullying at school.* Oxford, England: Blackwell.

Olweus, D., & Limber, S. P. (2010). The Olweus Bullying Prevention Program: Implementation and evaluation over two decades. In S. R. Jimerson, S. M Swearer, & D. L. Espelage (Eds.), *Handbook of bullying in schools: An international perspective.* New York: Routledge.

Pikas, A. (2002). New developments of the shared concern method. *School Psychology International, 23*(3), 307–336.

Rigby, K. (2003) Consequences of bullying in schools. *The Canadian Journal of Psychiatry, 48,* 583–590.

Rigby, K. (2008). *Children and bullying. How parents and educators can reduce bullying at school.* Boston: Blackwell/Wiley.

Rigby, K (2010a). *Bullying Interventions in schools: Six basic approaches.* Camberwell, Australia: ACER.

Rigby, K. (2010b). School bullying and the case for the method of shared concern. In S. Jimerson, S. Swearer, & D. Espelage (Eds.), *The international handbook of school bullying* (pp. 547–558). New York: Routledge.

Rigby, K. (2011). *The method of shared concern: a positive approach to bullying in schools.* Camberwell, Australia: ACER.

Rigby, K., & Bauman, S. (2010). How school personnel tackle cases of bullying: A critical examination . In S. Jimerson, S. Swearer, & D. Espelage (Eds.), *The international handbook of school bullying* (pp. 455–468). New York: Routledge.

Rigby, K., & Griffiths, C. (2011). Addressing cases of bullying through the Method of Shared Concern. *School Psychology International, 32,* 345–357.

Rigby, K., & Smith, P. K. (2011). Is bullying really on the rise? *Social Psychology of Education.* Retrieved from http://www.springerlink.com/content/60352W65720421q1/fulltext.pdf

Robinson, G., & Maines, B. (2008). *Bullying: A complete guide to the support group Method,* London: Sage.

Rønning, J. A., Sourander, A., Kumpulainen, K., Tamminen, T., Niemelä, S. Moilanen I., et al. (2009), Cross-informant agreement about bullying and victimization among eight-year-olds: whose information best predicts psychiatric caseness 10–15 years later? *Social Psychiatry and Psychiatric Epidemiology, 44,* 5–22.

Ross, S. W., Horner, R. H., & Higbee, T. (2009). Bully prevention in positive behavior support *Applied Behavioral Analysis, 42*(4), 747–759.

Sherer, Y. C., & Nickerson, A. B. (2010). Anti-bullying practices in American schools: Perspectives of school psychologists. *Psychology in the Schools, 47*(3), 217–229.

Sherman, L. W., & Strang, H. (2007). *Restorative Justice: the evidence.* London: The Smith Institute.

Skinner, B. F. (1971). *Beyond freedom and dignity.* New York: Knopf.

Smith, P. K., Pepler, D., & Rigby, K. (2004). *Bullying in schools: How successful can interventions be ?* Cambridge, England: Cambridge University Press.

Solberg, M. E., & Olweus, D. (2003). Prevalence estimation of school bullying with the Olweus bully/victim questionnaire. *Aggressive Behavior, 29,* 239–268.

Thorsborne, M., & Vinegrad, D. (2006). *Restorative practice and the management of bullying: rethinking behaviour management.* Queenscliff, Victoria, Australia: Inyahead Press.

Ttofi, M. M., & Farrington, D. P. (2009). Reducing school bullying: Evidence-based implications for policy. *Crime and Justice, 38,* 281–345.

30

Youth Anger Management Treatment for School Violence Prevention

Eva L. Feindler and Meghann F. Gerber

LONG ISLAND UNIVERSITY/CW POST, BROOKVILLE, NEW YORK

Abstract

Following a brief summary of individual and contextual risk factors for the development of various patterns of aggressive responding, two prominent anger management protocols are described. TAME (Teen Anger Management Education) and ART (Aggression Replacement Training) are easily adapted for dissemination to students in a school context. Both programs are cognitive-behavioral in orientation and include comprehensive skills training in emotion regulation, cognitive restructuring, conflict resolution, and prosocial skills. The research support for the effectiveness of each of these programs is reviewed. Clinical and administrative issues relative to successful program implementation are discussed and recommendations are included.

Aggressive and violent behavior in schools continues to pose a significant threat to student and staff safety, as well as to the integrity of environments conducive for learning. Survey research showed that 78% of schools had one or more incidents of violent crime during the 2005–2006 school year (Dinkes, Kemp, Baum, & Snyder, 2009). Forty-six percent of schools reported 20 or more violent crime incidents in that period, and 33% of students ages 12–18 years reported being bullied at school, while 7% avoided school activities or places within their schools for fear of being attacked or harmed (Dinkes et al., 2009). These findings suggest that aggressive behavior among students in school is common and that students' perceptions of their own safety can seriously interfere with school participation.

Research on aggression in schools has become increasingly interdisciplinary as those in mental health, law enforcement, and education have struggled to understand the severe and sometimes fatal incidents of school violence perpetrated by students. Dimensions of aggressive behavior have been identified and distinctions have been made among the likely perpetrators and victims of such aggression. Understanding patterns of aggressors, the function of particular aggressive behaviors, and the relevant cognitive and emotional processes at work is critical for selecting appropriate interventions. Following a brief discussion of the factors to consider when selecting intervention strategies for aggressive youth, this chapter describes two intervention approaches designed to address specific types of aggressive behavior problems.

Types of Aggressive Behavior

Aggressive behavior is commonly conceptualized in as proactive or reactive in nature (Dodge & Coie, 1987). Proactive aggression is characterized by the use of aggressive tactics to achieve a desired outcome. In contrast, reactive aggression represents a hostile response to a provoking stimulus interpreted as a threat (Crick & Dodge, 1996). Whereas "bullying" typically refers to the proactive, instrumental use of aggression for specific gains, incidents of reactive aggression are often viewed as the result of an inability to manage emotional arousal (anger) in response to a perceived threat. Thus, bullying constitutes a type of aggression, but is not representative of all aggressive behavior observed in school settings (Boulton, Bucci, & Hawker, 1999). An examination of patterns of aggressive behavior in a sample of 282 students indicated that children who invoke both proactive and reactive aggression exhibit the highest rates of bullying (Crapanzano, Frick, & Terranova, 2010). Further, a second group who showed less severe reactive aggression evidenced poor emotion regulation and greater bullying than nonaggressive youth. Although there is a high correlation between types of aggression, it is not clear how a pattern of bullying, which focuses more on the characteristics of the victim rather than on the function and motivation of the aggressive act, maps on to subtypes of aggression and what the treatment implications might be (Crapanzano et al., 2010)

While the literature on aggressive behavior in schools traditionally focused on direct physical aggression (Olweus, 1978), recent conceptualizations have included nonphysical forms of aggression. Identified with particular relevance to aggression in girls, investigators began to examine social exclusion, rumor spreading, and the formation or termination of relationships with intent to hurt another's feelings. Referred to as indirect aggression, Björkqvist, Lagerspetz, and Kaukiainen (1992) characterized these behaviors by its "behind the back" nature and contrasted it with physical aggression in that the perpetrator may not be known to the victim. Crick and colleagues' work on relational aggression has focused on the way in which these behaviors appear to target the victim's relationships with peers and their experience of social acceptance (Crick, 1996; Crick & Grotpeter, 1995; Crick et al., 2001). Galen and Underwood (1997) defined social aggression as behavior intended to damage another's social standing or self-esteem. Social aggression can include direct behaviors such as eye rolling and verbal rejection or indirect forms consistent with Björkqvist et al.'s description of indirect aggression. While there is some controversy over the potential overlap or superior utility among these concepts and their respective terminology (Archer & Coyne, 2005), this area of research has brought attention to the damaging and hurtful effects nonphysical and indirect forms of aggression. Far from being inconsequential to the issue of school safety, research on episodes of fatal school shootings has shown that almost three quarters of the perpetrators were longtime victims of severe bullying and social harassment (Vossekuil, Fein, Reddy, Borum, & Modzeleski, 2002). This suggests that being victimized by physical and/or social forms of aggression may be potentially important risk factors for youth who become violent.

Aggressors and Victims

Investigations into types of aggressors have provided an expanded view of the varying patterns and functions of aggressive behavior. Researchers have identified at least four types of youth typically involved in aggressive exchanges among students: bullies, passive victims, aggressive victims, and bystanders (Gumpel, 2008). Passive victims are those youths who are nonaggressive targets of bullies, characterized by low self-esteem, fewer social skills, and lack of assertive behaviors in their repertoire (Olweus, 1993; Toblin, Schwartz, Hopmeyer Gorman, & Abou-ezzeddine, 2005). Bystanders make up the largest group; 79%–86% of students in a recent sample were categorized as "uninvolved" in aggressive episodes (Gumpel, 2008). While representing the majority of students, this group is the least studied and some have argued critical for understanding the context within and process by which bullying and aggression occur in schools (Sutton & Smith, 1999).

Research has shown that aggressors themselves are not a homogenous group (Crapanzano et al., 2010). "Pure bullies" use aggressive behaviors as a means to establish dominance over peers and are rarely victimized themselves (Olweus, 1993). This subtype has also been labeled "effectual aggressors" as their use of aggressive behavior is often conflict-free (meeting little opposition) and effective in meeting their goals. "Aggressive victims," on the other hand, are frequent targets of others' aggression, known to provoke conflict with peers and characterized by poor emotion regulation (Schwartz, Proctor, & Chien, 2001). Unlike pure bullies, aggressive victims tend to display disorganized hostility and are rarely successful at resolving conflicts in their favor (Perry, Perry, & Kennedy, 1992). Whereas bullies are most often accepted and even popular among their peers, aggressive victims are frequently rejected and disliked by fellow students (Pellegrini, Bartini, & Brooks, 1999).

Processes of Aggression

From a cognitive behavioral perspective, cognitive patterns, emotional arousal, and the effectiveness and availability of prosocial behavioral skills are all components that contribute to the expression of aggressive behaviors.

Cognitive Processes

Hostile attribution bias, also known as hostile attribution of intent, is a concept used to describe the tendency to interpret ambiguous social cues as hostile. Aggressive youth are thought to act aggressively, in part, because they more frequently attribute hostile intentions in others in comparison to their nonaggressive peers (Dodge, 1980). Crick and Dodge's (1994) model of social information processing illustrates the steps by which aggressive children attend to specific information in their environment (as well as internal cues), make interpretations about a given situation, and then select responses based on their judgments. A chosen response is thought to relate to an individual's goal given their understanding of the situation, and belief in their ability to enact the response and achieve the goal. This process appears to be quite different for youth who tend to act aggressively compared to their peers. Aggressive youth often attend more to aggressive rather than nonaggressive cues (Dodge, Lochman, Harnish, Bates, & Pettit, 1997), they frequently draw upon a well-developed hostile attribution bias to interpret information (Crick & Dodge, 1996), and in terms of selecting responses, these youth are more inclined to generate aggressive responses (de Castro, Merk, Koops, Verrman, & Bosch, 2005). The social information processing model demonstrates how patterns in attention, a tendency toward hostile interpretations, a lack of belief in self-efficacy, among other factors, can all influence responses to provocation.

Studies on youth who tend to primarily display proactive aggressive behaviors have shown that they are more likely to believe that aggressive behaviors will result in a desired outcome and have higher levels of self-efficacy (Crick & Dodge, 1996). Indeed, bullies have been found to have aggressive biases in social information processing at the point of evaluating and selecting responses (Toblin et al., 2005). These youth tend to have positive views toward the use of aggressive behavior and greater confidence in their ability to successfully execute those behaviors in comparison to their peers. In contrast, youth who engage in reactive aggression seem to have hostile biases in the interpretation stage of social information processing (Dodge, 1991), meaning that they are more inclined to perceive hostility in the information they receive in their environment and to respond based on that perception.

Aggressive and Prosocial Behaviors

Behavioral conceptualizations of proactive aggression are largely influenced by Bandura's (1973) social learning theory—aggressive behavior is learned via modeling in one's environment and is subsequently maintained by reinforcement contingencies (Dodge & Coie, 1987). In this conceptualization, it is not so much that youth choose aggressive behaviors over prosocial behaviors, but rather aggressive behaviors are learned and reinforced, implying a deficit in the acquisition and practice of prosocial skills.

Social competency is a difficult area to assess, primarily because it can have different meanings to different parties. In one study examining the roles of aggressive students, parents and teachers rated popular aggressive students as having poor social skills compared with peers, while study observers in classrooms found popular aggressive students to be highly sociable and cooperative with peers (Rodkin & Roisman, 2010). This suggests that those responsible for delivering consequences for aggressive behaviors and enforcing prosocial behaviors may not be aware of social abilities that prompt approval from peers. Some have pointed out that the role of a successful bully often requires a sophisticated understanding of social dynamics and skilled ability to manipulate one's social environment (Bullis, Walker, & Sprague, 2001; Sutton, Smith, & Swettenham, 1999). The question then arises whether proactively aggressive youth actually lack social skills to achieve their goals or if they lack the motivation to select nonaggressive means. However, it should not be assumed that proactively aggressive youth are necessarily content with aggressive social interaction. In a study that assessed responses to anger-provoking situations among boys in a correction facility, verbally aggressive communication styles were negatively correlated with communication satisfaction (Anderson & Rancer, 2007). This finding suggests a self-indentified need for alternative communication strategies in their behavioral repertoires.

For nonpopular aggressive youth, often the victims of more socially successful aggressors, a lack of social skills and poor social standing are likely exacerbated by the tendency of these youth to interpret ambiguous information with a hostile bias and their poorly modulated affect and behavior (Pellegrini et al., 1999; Schwartz, 2000). Aggressive victims tend to be disliked by peers and report having significantly fewer friends compared with both pure bullies and passive victims (Unnever, 2005). For these youth, ongoing patterns of conflict and limited positive social engagement have likely impinged on the development of prosocial behaviors.

Emotional Processes

Cognitive behavioral formulations of aggressive behavior typically draw upon Novaco's (1975) approach to anger, which asserted that the physiological arousal associated with an anger response is a stress reaction. Those influenced by Novaco's approach have come to view aggressive behavior as stemming from the point at which an individual experiences intense anger arousal, which diminishes the capability to use appropriate problem solving and aggressive behaviors are selected impulsively (Weisz, 2004). Another key construct in the understanding of effective interventions for anger and aggression in youth is that of emotion dysregulation as an early indicator of behavioral difficulties later on (Keenan, 2000).

In keeping with the descriptions of the more calculated nature of proactive aggression, bullies have been found less likely to experience increased levels of anger when responding (de Castro et al., 2005; Toblin et al., 2005). In contrast, research focusing on the experience of aggressive victims has offered a description of youth who have a high degree of emotional volatility and poor ability to modulate emotional reactivity, and who engage in aggressive behaviors in a disorganized and impulsive fashion (Schwartz et al., 2001; Toblin et al., 2005; Unnever, 2005). This distinction is important; certain youth apparently respond aggressively due to what they view as an acceptable and effective means to achieve a goal. Other youth perceive hostile threats in their environment, become emotionally dysregulated, and are then inclined to use aggression impulsively. These two processes have different implications for appropriate interventions needed to elicit behavior change.

It must be noted, however, that the concepts of reactive and proactive aggression are helpful distinctions for understanding how aggressive behaviors unfold in a given situation, but should not be taken to mean all aggressive youth exclusively use one type or the other. Most studies suggest that aggressive youth use both proactive and reactive in some degree, and placing the concepts on a continuum rather than within mutually exclusive categories might be useful (Crapanzano et al., 2010; Hubbard, McAuliffe, Morrow, & Romano, 2010). That being said, there is evidence that youth whose behaviors resemble those of pure bullies are more inclined to use proactive aggression and those youth who appear to more closely match the description of aggressive victims are likely engaging more frequently in reactive aggression, which involves an important emotion dysregulation component (Schwartz et al., 1998; Unnever, 2005). In a study examining physiological states of arousal thought to correspond with the experience of anger, researchers found that among elementary school children, those who had scored highly on measures of reactive aggression showed increased levels of skin conductance reactivity and observed expressions of anger when exposed to a provoking stimulus (Hubbard et al., 2002). The same arousal was not found among children who had been identified as primarily proactive aggressors. For children reacting aggressively to a provocation, the increase in anger arousal can preclude effective problem solving and response selection. Thus, a lack of adaptive emotion regulation skills in addition to having hostile attribution bias appears to contribute to the use of aggressive behavioral responses (de Castro et al., 2005).

Research on Effectiveness of Anger Management for Youth

Much evidence supports the effectiveness of cognitive behavioral interventions in reducing anger and aggression in youth (Blake & Hamrin, 2007; Cole, 2008). A meta-analysis of cognitive behavioral treatments for anger problems among elementary through high school youth that examined 21 published and 19 unpublished reports found a mean effect size of .67, or medium effect (Sukhodolsky, Kassinove, & Gorman, 2004). Of the types of treatments reviewed in that meta-analysis, skills-based and multimodal interventions had the highest effect sizes. Another meta-analysis of studies investigating cognitive behavior therapy (CBT) interventions for antisocial behavior among children examined 30 studies comparing CBT to a control condition and concluded that CBT interventions have small to moderate effect sizes (Bennett & Gibbons, 2000). It was also found that effect size appeared to be positively correlated with age of participants, providing some evidence that CBT interventions are more effective with older elementary age students and adolescents compared to younger children. In a review of 14 published studies on treatment outcomes of CBT for anger-related problems with adolescents, the majority of studies reported medium to large effect sizes for short-term reductions in measures of anger and aggression (Cole, 2008). However, this analysis pointed to weaknesses in the literature in regard to lack of measurement of long-term intervention effects and an underrepresentation of female adolescents in study samples. Finally, the majority (almost three quarters, according to one meta-analysis, Sukhodolsky et al., 2004) of the studies on CBT for anger and aggression among youth assessed outcomes for treatments administered by mental health professionals or graduate students trained by the researchers. This is particularly relevant for school and community agencies looking to implement programming with paraprofessional or teaching staff. Yet, another meta-analysis that examined anger interventions studies that took place exclusively in school settings found that the mean effect (.31) was much smaller than previous meta-analyses (Gansle, 2005). However, the author notes that these studies were measuring a multitude of variables and that when restricting outcomes to measures of anger and externalizing behaviors, the mean effect size for the 20 published studies was .54. In addition to examining differences in the specific outcomes measured across studies, special attention to how interventions are implemented in school settings is needed. In a study examining the effectiveness of an aggression treatment program for elementary school students, school counselors who conducted the intervention were selected to receive various levels of training and consultation by clinical psychologists (Lochman et al., 2009). Researchers found that those who participated in the treatment provided by counselors in the control and limited training conditions exhibited in an increase in problem behaviors, while the children in more intensive training and supervision condition showed no such increase. Children themselves in the more intensive training condition reported a significant decrease in their expectations that aggression would lead to positive outcomes when compared to their counterparts in the other conditions. These findings suggest that nondoctoral degree staff members can implement successful treatments but that intensive training and supervision are likely important predictive factors for successful outcomes.

Teen Anger Management Education (TAME)

Cognitive behavioral anger management training (AMT) is generally presented as a didactic program in which skills development is emphasized. The three main components—arousal management, cognitive restructuring, and prosocial skills training—correspond to the deficiencies and distortions in social information processing and emotion regulation implicated in the development of anger outbursts and aggressive behavior patterns. Feindler and colleagues (Feindler & Gerber, 2008; Feindler & Guttman, 1994; Feindler & Scalley, 1998) have developed various anger control intervention programs to target these domains.

For each component, a specific set of skills or strategies are presented in an educational format, modeled, rehearsed through repeated role-play provocation scenes, and then applied to the natural environment through homework exercises. Each session provides practice of newly acquired strategies as well as graduated exposure to more intense anger triggers. The AMT program is designed to teach youth to assess each anger provocation and to implement the most effective responses from his or her repertoire of emotion regulation and social skills (Feindler, Ecton, Kingsley, & Dubey, 1986). The general emphasis on interpersonal problem solving and assertive communication of anger arousal is designed to provide prosocial alternative responses and prevent the automatic aggressive response.

The 10-session protocol described in Table 30.1 features anger management techniques including reduction of physiological arousal, replacement of anger-sustaining cognitions, and acquirement of prosocial response options. Throughout, youth are educated about the (a) interaction of the cognitive, physiological, and behavioral components of their anger experience; (b) the adaptive and maladaptive functions of their anger; (c) the situational triggers that provoke their anger; (d) the concept of choice and self-responsibility in their responses to provocations; and (e) the importance of appropriate verbal expression of affect. Feindler and Gerber (2008) added two additional components to this protocol based on current research findings regarding dimensions of aggression and deficits in social functioning (resulting in the latest version of AMT: TAME). Studies overwhelmingly indicate that social forms of aggression are pervasive

Table 30.1   Teen Anger Management Education (TAME) Protocol

Intake and screening of youth referred for TAME: Examine treatment readiness is examined and conduct initial assessments. Introduce components of TAME, including self-monitoring tool known as the "hassle log."

Session 1: Orient participants to structure of TAME group and rationale for program. Introduce the identification of emotions with emphasis on anger. Practice identification of angry responses and deep-breathing relaxation exercise.

Session 2: Introduce sequential analysis of behavioral incidents (activating event or trigger, behavioral response, consequences). Practice identification of components using idiosyncratic angry and/or aggressive episodes.

Session 3: Discuss aggressive beliefs and interpretations. Identify of various cognitive distortions and practice reattribution exercises.

Session 4: Introduce relationship strategies and interpersonal techniques. Describe and practice interpersonal effectiveness skills adapted from dialectical behavior therapy (Linehan, 1993b).

Session 5: Introduce self-instruction training. Practice in-the-moment self-coaching techniques for nonaggressive behavioral responses.

Session 6: Review anticipation of consequences. Practice thinking ahead — prediction and evaluation of possible consequences of aggressive behaviors.

Session 7: Describe role of problem solving. Introduce multistep problem solving process including self-evaluation, reinforcement, and feedback.

Session 8: Present strategies to present relational aggression. Build awareness of types of teasing, use of rumors, and methods to evaluate friendships. Practice confrontation, apologizing, and self-respect skills.

Session 9: Review program skills and techniques. Present exercises designed to utilize all skills and concepts introduced over previous 8 sessions. Individualize feedback to students and administer final assessment instruments.

Session 10: Follow-up booster session. Review all skills, including definitions, demonstrate examples, and discuss appropriate situations in which skills can be used. Check in with students regarding changes and progress since completing the program, including successful and unsuccessful attempts to use skills. Provide feedback and reinforcement to encourage skill maintenance and generalization.

throughout elementary, middle, and high school, and that it is used by boys and well as girls. The relational aggression component in this protocol is designed to help youth to identify these behaviors as a form of aggression and practice several prosocial means of handling rumors, teasing, and interpersonal conflict.

Given the research findings that show youth who exhibit reactive aggressive behaviors have poor social relationships, this protocol has adopted some interpersonal effectiveness skills borrowed from Linehan's (1993a) dialectical behavior therapy, a treatment designed for chronically emotionally dysregulated individuals known to have unstable relationships. These skills are included to provide specific techniques for fulfilling personal goals and needs while maintaining and strengthening interpersonal relationships.

TAME trains youth to break current aggressive behavioral patterns via emotion regulation and cognitive restructuring exercises, while emphasizing acquisition of new skills that provide nonaggressive alternatives. Youth are asked to keep a log of conflicts that occur in their lives that are used regularly for role-plays and other exercises in order to maximize personal relevancy and probability of skill generalization. As youth build a new repertoire of prosocial behaviors, they will find greater satisfaction from interpersonal communication and experience the absence of negative consequences for aggressive behaviors, which in turn will serve to increase probability of continued use of new response options. Table 30.1 presents a brief description of the key elements of the TAME protocol.

Detailed session-by-session protocols, including expanded topic description, specific role-play scenarios, games and group exercises used in training, homework assignments to promote transfer of skills to the natural environment as well as materials needed for each session are available in Feindler and Gerber (2008), Feindler and Guttman (1994), and Feindler and Scalley (1998).

Aggression Replacement Training

A complimentary program, which includes anger management as one of three modules, is the Aggression Replacement Training (ART) approach described by Goldstein, Glick, and Gibbs (1998). The first module of ART involves "skillstreaming," which is designed to teach a broad curriculum of prosocial behavior. The second module consists of anger control training, which empowers youth to modify his or her anger experience. The final section is moral reasoning training, which is aimed to help motivate the individual to employ the skills from the other components. Table 30.2 presents a brief description of each module.

Moral development might be a particularly important target of intervention when working with youth who, as the research on proactive aggression suggest, appear to have positive beliefs about the use of aggression to achieve personal goals. Indeed, in a study on moral disengagement among middle school-age youth in Portugal, it was found that more positive attitudes toward bullying was correlated with higher levels of moral disengagement (Almeida, Correia, & Marinho, 2010). While the anger management component in ART encompasses emotion control and cognitive restructuring, and the skillstreaming module offers behavioral alternatives, the moral reasoning module specifically aims to develop a youth's motivation to select prosocial alternatives to aggression.

Small group sessions of ART are held weekly and each skill is modeled and rehearsed through role-plays. Group leaders provide praise, instruction, and feedback as well as structure other types of learning activities for group members. The ART program is presented comprehensively in manual (Goldstein, Glick, & Gibbs, 1998) and video (see Research Press, 2002) formats and can be implemented by a wide variety of educators, mental health professionals and corrections staff.

Table 30.2 Anger Replacement Training (ART) Modules

Module 1: Skillstreaming: Social Skills Training

Fifty prosocial skills taught to group members fall into one of six categories of behaviors: beginning (e.g., basic conversation skills), advanced (e.g., apologizing and asking for help), skills for dealing with feelings (e.g., expressing affection and dealing with fear), alternatives to aggression (e.g., responding to teasing and negotiating), skills for handling stress (e.g., dealing with being left out or being accused), and planning skills (e.g., goal setting and decision-making).

Module 2: Anger Control Training

Identify internal and external triggers that provoke anger responses and identify physiological cues that signal feelings of anger. Self-statements, as well as deep breathing and imagery are used to remain in control of emotional arousal. Group members are taught to self-evaluate their performance and reward themselves for remaining in control and learning from their mistakes.

Module 3: Moral Reasoning Training

Designed to raise an individual's attention to fairness, justice, and concern for the needs and rights of others. Using Kohlberg's research on moral dilemmas as a model, group members are exposed to moral dilemmas designed to arouse cognitive conflict with the expectation that its resolution will advance members' level of moral reasoning. Because some aggressive behaviors persist in lieu of the new skills, this values-oriented component was added to encourage individuals to enact more socially desirable behaviors.

ART's effectiveness has been evaluated for use with youth in juvenile detention (Goldstein & Glick, 1994; Goldstein, Glick, Reiner, Zimmerman, & Coultry, 1986; Leeman, Gibbs, & Fuller, 1993), in a residential treatment program (Coleman, Pfeiffer, & Oakland, 1992), and in a runaway shelter (Nugent, Bruley, & Allen, 1998). Although all reported improvement among youth who participated in the ART condition in terms of acting out behaviors, recidivism rates, prosocial skill acquisition and self-control indicators, a significant limitation of these studies were the types of measures and data used to draw conclusions. Most ART studies have primarily relied upon on recidivism data and subjective ratings by institution staff to determine the treatment's effectiveness. A recent study compared a 10-week ART program in a school setting to a control group in Norway and utilized a combination of self-report and report-by-others instruments, most of which had established acceptable psychometric properties (Gundersen & Svartdal, 2006). Data from parents, teachers, and youth showed a significant decrease in problem behaviors among the ART participants compared to youth in the control group. Those who administered the ART groups were professional educators who had received formal ART training. To further investigate the positive changes noted for the control group in the 2006 study, Gundersen and Svartdal (2010) designed an ART evaluation, which targeted the diffusion of treatment effects. Comprehensive data from pre–post parent, teacher, and self-report measures indicated that the ART program resulted in significant decreases in behavior problems and increased social skillfulness in 77 children receiving treatment in a variety of school settings. The authors suggest that the positive changes noted for the 63 control participants were due to unintended but natural consequences of the interactions of all children in their school and to the generalized effects of ART staff interacting with all children.

Despite numerous published studies of ART treatment effectiveness, more research is needed that includes greater representation of female youth since only three studies have included girls in their samples (Gundersen & Svartdal, 2006, 2010; Nugent et al., 1998). Additional studies that utilize greater experimental rigor would also increase understanding of the specific effective aspects of ART, despite the positive treatment "diffusion" noted above that may be beneficial for all youth included in the sample.

Clinical Issues in Anger Management Training

There are aspects of conduct disorder and characteristics of angry and aggressive youth that may interfere with the success of AMT programs. Howell and Day (2003) provide a good review of individual factors related to "readiness" for anger management treatment. Usually those referred for anger management have complex issues involving a number of comorbid problems such as substance abuse, personality disorders, or family problems that need to be addressed in order to increase a client's readiness for anger treatment. In addition, a client's attitudes and beliefs regarding the legitimacy, justification, or cathartic nature of anger can interfere with treatment. Heseltine, Howells, and Day (2010), in a discussion of issues relative to mandated participants, suggest that selecting those who self-report problems with anger and who indicate motivation for treatment are essential for treatment success.

Ethnic, cultural, and gender differences may also interfere by creating different expectations and norms regarding the expression of anger and aggressive behaviors. Therefore, it may be necessary to have leaders of similar ethnicity, gender, or culture who teach and model the intervention. These leaders' example may serve to challenge these socially reinforced norms or expectations. DiGuiseppi (1995) confirms that it is difficult to establish and maintain a therapeutic alliance with angry clients, unless therapist and client agree on treatment goals. These clinical concerns have yet to be discussed relative to adolescents or to a group skills training approach.

Perhaps implementation in the school setting will increase treatment acceptability if offered as a complement to other programming and as a psychoeducational intervention. However, the identification of high-risk students, assessment, referral, and voluntary participation versus a universal prevention approach has not been fully examined in terms of response to AMT in youth. Further, although group interventions are deemed most efficient, group treatments as of yet have not been compared to individual interventions. The lack of individualization in treatment groups assumes that each participant requires the same treatment components. However, as Cole (2008) suggests, group process variables may positively influence adolescent groups differentially for gender and for age and the group context lends itself well to naturalistic practice of newly acquired skills, thereby enhancing generalization.

Implications for Practice

A number of issues relative to implementation of AMT in a school setting warrant discussion. Some of these have been discussed elsewhere (see Feindler & Scalley, 1998), but few have been researched. Table 30.3 presents the main implications and recommendations for school safety programming that will be discussed.

In general, "readiness" of the school environment prior to implementation of an anger management program is necessary. Securing central and building administrative support, as well as teacher and staff training in the principles and methods of anger management, provides the infrastructure needed to ensure program success and generalization of newly acquired skills. School environments present particular practical and ethical issues related to group treatment or psychoeducational programs, and identification of target youth will require careful thought. Anger management training will help disruptive and aggressive youth to manage their emotions

Table 30.3 Administrative and Clinical Issues in Anger Management Training (AMT) in School Settings

General Program Administration

- Insure administrative support for structure and implementation of program and allocation of resources
- Create guidelines on ethical issues related to screening and identification of group members, consent to treatment and confidentially
- Articulation and Championing of goals and objectives of AMT programming

Structure of AMT Program

- Screening and assessment of youth relative to clinical and risk status and readiness to change
- Group membership: same sex groups, level of risk and/or aggressiveness, readiness for group intervention vs. individual treatment, prior relationships with group members
- Involvement of teachers, staff, and parents

Qualified Staff

- Select motivated and capable staff as intervention leaders
- Ensure experience, skills and credentials
- Provide ongoing training, supervision and technical assistance

Treatment Fidelity

- Protocol adherence
- Dosage flexibility
- Quality of program delivery and participant responsiveness

Clinical Issues

- AMT as adjunct clinical treatment
- Over-arousal and discharge in role plays and group discussion
- Ethical issues related to confidentially and group dynamics
- Transfer and generalization of anger management skills; homework compliance, reinforcement procedures, and booster sessions

and consider alternate responses to provocation. However, training of youth at risk for aggression due to individual or family variables or training of peers who might be victims or bystanders of interpersonal aggression also seems reasonable. Screening and assessment of youth as well as group composition will vary according to the setting and the treatment objectives.

Often anger management training can be considered as an adjunct program to other types of intervention; however, AMT should be consistent with theoretical orientation and outcomes of other programs. It is likely that implementation in conjunction with parent education (Lochman & Wells, 2003, 2004) will produce the greatest impact. However, more research is needed to determine the optimal age for intervention, how the gender differential effects treatment, and which components of AMT delivered in which sequence are most effective.

Although both AMT and ART programs dovetail wonderfully with the educational setting and can be successfully implemented by a variety of professional staff, the specific treatment delivery practices require special attention. Issues relative to treatment fidelity are paramount as both TAME and ART are manualized protocols and effectiveness rests upon the assumption of adherence to these programs. In a discussion of the tension between manual adherence and practitioner flexibility in parent training, Mazzuchelli and Sanders (2010) highlight the need to match the intervention to the clients and the context for service delivery. Recommending organizational support, comprehensive practitioner training and supervision as well as component analyses of programs, these authors encourage flexibility that does not, however, veer too far from the original program's design. How this relates to implementation of AMT programs within school settings remains to be seen. But, the collection of outcome data seems crucial to determine which program modifications would fit best.

Other school initiatives include AMT within general prevention programs for adolescents. Botvin, Griffin, and Nichols (2006) examined a Life Skills Training program across 41 schools with close to 5,000 sixth graders. This prevention intervention included training in assertiveness, conflict resolution, and anger management and was effective in reducing substance abuse as well as violence and delinquency. Regan (2009) took a public health approach and collaborated with school nurses to implement a violence prevention program at an urban charter high school. The anger and conflict management component of this educational/prevention resulted in increased understanding of dating violence variables and conflict resolution skills. This program was relatively low cost and points to the possibility of a variety of school-based practitioners delivering psychoeducational treatments. The public health model adapted by the Centers for Disease Control represents a broad approach to youth violence prevention and schools might be eager to adopt comprehensive programs (Dodge, 2008). However, exactly how the AMT components of these programs impact youth and staff in school setting remains to be adequately researched. The TAME and ART programs described in this chapter represent effective protocols easily adapted to the school setting with good administrative support and an eye to treatment fidelity.

References

Almeida, A., Correia, I., & Marinho, S. (2010). Moral disengagement, normative beliefs of peer group, and attitudes regarding roles in bullying. *Journal of School Violence, 9*, 23–36. doi:10.1080/15388220903185639

Archer, J., & Coyne, S. M. (2005). An integrated review of indirect, relational, and social aggression. *Personality and Social Psychology Review, 9*, 212–230. doi:10.1207/s15327957pspr0903_2

Anderson, C. M., & Rancer, A. S. (2007). The relationship between argumentativeness, verbal aggressiveness, and communication satisfaction in incarcerated male youth. *Prison Journal, 87*, 328–343. doi:10.1177/0032885507304433

Bandura, A. (1973). *Aggression: A social learning analysis.* Englewood Cliffs, NJ: Prentice-Hall.

Bennett, D. S., & Gibbons, T. A. (2000). Efficacy of child cognitive-behavioral interventions for antisocial behavior: A meta-analysis. *Child & Family Behavior Therapy, 22*, 1–15. doi:10.1300/J019v22n01_01

Björkqvist, K., Lagerspetz, K. M. J., & Kaukiainen, A. (1992). Do girls manipulate and boys fight? Developmental trends in regard to direct and indirect aggression. *Aggressive Behavior, 18*, 117–127. doi: 10.1002/1098-2337(1992)18:2<117::AID-AB2480180205>3.0.CO;2-3

Blake, C., & Hamrin, V. (2007). Current approaches to the assessment and management of anger and aggression in youth: A review. *Journal of Child and Adolescent Psychiatric Nursing, 20*, 209–221. doi:10.1111/j.1744-6171.2007.00102.x

Botvin, G. J., Griffin, K. W., & Nichols, T. D. (2006). Preventing youth violence and delinquency through a universal school-based prevention approach. *Prevention Science, 7*, 403–408. doi:10.1007/s11121-006-0057-y

Boulton, M. J., Bucci, E., & Hawker, D. D. S. (1999), Swedish and English secondary school pupils' attitudes towards, and conceptions of, bullying: Concurrent links with bully/victim involvement. *Scandinavian Journal of Psychology, 40*, 277–284. doi:10.1111/1467-9450.404127

Bullis, M., Walker, H. M., & Sprague, J. R. (2001). A promise unfulfilled: Social skills training with at-risk and anti-social children and youth. *Exceptionality, 9*, 67–90. doi:10.1207/S15327035EX091&2_6

Cole, R. L. (2008). A systematic review of cognitive-behavioural interventions for adolescents with anger-related difficulties. *Educational & Child Psychology, 25*, 27–47.

Coleman, M., Pfeiffer, S., & Oakland, T. (1992). Aggression replacement training with behaviorally disordered adolescents. *Behavioral Disorders, 18*, 54–66.

Crapanzano, A. M., Frick, P. J., & Terranova, A. M. (2010). Patterns of physical and relational aggression in a school-based sample of boys and girls. *Journal of Abnormal Psychology, 38*, 433–445. doi:10.1007/s10802-009-9376-3

Crick, N. R. (1996). The role of relational aggression, overt aggression, and prosocial behavior in the prediction of children's future social adjustment. *Child Development, 67*, 2317–2327. doi:10.2307/1131625

Crick, N. R., & Dodge, K. A. (1994). A review and reformulation of social-information-processing mechanisms in children's social adjustment. *Psychological Bulletin, 115*, 74–101. doi:10.1037/0033-2909.115.1.74

Crick N. R., & Dodge, K. A. (1996). Social information-processing mechanisms on reactive and proactive aggression, *Child Development 67*, 993–1002. doi:10.2307/1131875

Crick, N. R., & Grotpeter, J. K. (1995). Relational aggression, gender, and social-psychological adjustment. *Child Development, 66*, 710–722. doi:10.2307/1131945

Crick, N. R., Nelson, D. A., Morales, J. R., Cullerton-Sen, C., Casas, J. F., & Hickman, S. E. (2001). Relational victimization in childhood and adolescence: I hurt you through the grapevine. In J. Juvonen & S. Graham (Eds.), *Peer harassment in school: The plight of the vulnerable and victimized* (pp. 196–214). New York, NY: Guilford.

de Castro, B. O., Merk, W., Koops, W., Verrman, J. W., & Bosch, J. D. (2005). Emotions in social information processing and their relations with reactive and proactive aggression in referred aggressive boys. *Journal of Clinical Child and Adolescent Psychology, 34*, 105–116. doi:10.1207/s15374424jccp3401_10

DiGuiseppe, R. (1995). Developing the therapeutic alliance with angry clients. In H. Kassinove (Ed.), *Anger disorders: Definitions, diagnosis and treatment* (pp. 131–149). Philadelphia, PA: Taylor & Francis.

Dinkes, R., Kemp, J., Baum, K., & Synder, T. (2009). *Indicators of school crime and safety: 2009* (NCES 2010-012/ NCJ 228478). Washington, DC: National Center for Education Statistics, Institute of Education Sciences, U.S. Department of Education, and Bureau of Justice Statistics, Office of Justice Programs, U.S. Department of Justice. Retrieved, from http://bjs.ojp.usdoj.gov/index.cfm?ty=pbdetail&iid=1762

Dodge, K. A. (1980). Social cognition and children's aggressive behavior. *Child Development, 51*, 162–170. doi:10.2307/1129603

Dodge, K. A. (1991). The structure and function of reactive and proactive aggression. In D. Pepler & K. Rubin (Eds.), *The development and treatment for childhood aggression* (pp. 201–218). Hillsdale, NJ: Erlbaum.

Dodge, K. A. (2008). Framing public policy and prevention of chronic violence in American youths. *American Psychologist, 63*, 573–590. doi:10.1037/0003-066X.63.7.573

Dodge, K. A., & Coie, J. D. (1987). Social-information-processing factors in reactive and proactive aggression in children's peer groups. *Journal of Personality and Social Psychology, 53*, 1146–1158. doi:10.1037/0022-3514.53.6.1146

Dodge, K. A., Lochman, J. E., Harnish, J. D., Bates, J. E., & Pettit, G. S. (1997). Reactive and proactive aggression in school children and psychiatrically impaired chronically assaultive youth. *Journal of Abnormal Psychology, 106*, 37–51. doi:10.1037/0021-843X.106.1.37

Feindler, E. L., Ecton, R. B., Kingsley, D., & Dubey, D. (1986). Group anger control training for institutionalized psychiatric male adolescents. *Behavior Therapy, 17*, 109–123. doi:10.1016/S0005-7894(86)80079-X

Feindler, E. L., & Gerber, M. (2008). TAME: Teen anger management education. In C. W. LeCroy (Ed.), *Handbook of evidence-based treatment manuals for children and adolescents* (2nd ed., pp. 139–169). New York, NY: Oxford University Press.

Feindler, E. L., & Guttman, J. (1994). Cognitive behavioral anger control training for groups of adolescents: A treatment manual. In C. W. LeCroy (Ed.), *Handbook of child and adolescent treatment manuals* (pp. 170–199). New York, NY: Lexington.

Feindler, E. L., & Scalley, M. (1998). Group anger management approaches to violence prevention. In K. Stoiber & T. R. Ollendick (Eds.), *Handbook of group interventions for children and families* (pp. 100–119). Boston, MA: Allyn & Bacon.

Galen, B., & Underwood, M. (1997). A developmental investigation of social aggression among children. *Developmental Psychology, 33*, 589–600. doi:10.1037/0012-1649.33.4.589

Gansle, K. A. (2005). The effectiveness of school-based anger intervention programs. *Journal of School Psychology, 43,* 321–341. doi:10.1016/j.jsp.2005.07.002

Goldstein, A. P., & Glick, B. (1994). Aggression Replacement Training: Curriculum and evaluation. *Simulation, & Gaming, 25,* 9–26. doi:10.1177/1046878194251003

Goldstein, A. P., Glick, B., & Gibbs, J. C. (1998). *Aggression Replacement Training: A comprehensive intervention for aggressive youth.* Champaign, IL: Research Press.

Goldstein, A. P., Glick, B., Reiner, S., Zimmerman, D., & Coultry, T. (1986). *Aggression Replacement Training.* Champaign, IL: Research Press.

Gumpel, T. P. (2008). Behavioral disorders in the school: Participant roles and subtypes in three types of school violence. *Journal of Emotional and Behavioral Disorders, 16,* 145–162. doi:10.1177/1063426607310846

Gundersen, K., & Svardtal, F. (2010). Diffusion of treatment interventions: Exploration of "secondary" treatment diffusion. *Psychology, Crime and Law, 16,* 233–249.

Gundersen, K., & Svartdal, F. (2006). Aggression Replacement Training in Norway: Outcome evaluation of 11 Norwegian student projects. *Scandinavian Journal of Educational Research, 50,* 63–81. doi:10.1080/00313830500372059

Heseltine, K., Howells, K., & Day, A. (2010). Brief anger intervention with offenders may be ineffective: A replication and extension. *Behavior Research and Therapy, 48,* 246–250. doi:10.1016/j.brat.2009.10.005

Howell, K., & Day, A. (2003) Readiness for anger management: Clinical and theoretical issues. Clinical *Psychology Review, 23,* 319–337. doi:10.1016/S0272-7358(02)00228-3

Hubbard, J. A., McAuliffe, M. D., Morrow, M. T., & Romano, L. J. (2010). Reactive and proactive aggression in childhood and adolescence: Precursors, outcomes, processes, experiences, and measurement. *Journal of Personality, 78,* 95–118. doi:10.1111/j.1467-6494.2009.00610.x

Hubbard, J. A., Smithmyer, C. M., Ramsden, S. R., Parker, E. H., Flanagan, K. D., Dearing, K. F., ... Simons, R. F. (2002). Observational, physiological, and self-report measures of children's anger: Relations to reactive versus proactive aggression. *Child Development, 73,* 1101–1118. doi:10.1111/1467-8624.00460

Keenan, K. (2000). Emotional dysregulation as a risk factor for child psychopathology. *Clinical Psychology: Science and Practice, 7,* 418–434. doi:10.1093/clipsy/7.4.418

Leeman, L. W., Gibbs, J. C., & Fuller, D. (1993). Evaluation of multi-component treatment program for juvenile delinquents. *Aggressive Behavior, 19,* 281–292. doi:10.1002/1098-2337(1993)19:4<281::AID-AB2480190404>3.0.CO;2-W

Linehan, M. M. (1993a). *Cognitive-behavioral treatment of borderline personality disorder.* New York, NY: Guilford.

Linehan, M. M. (1993b). *Skills training manual for treating borderline personality disorder.* New York, NY: Guilford.

Lochman, J. E., Boxmeyer, C., Powell, N., Qu, L., Wells, K., & Windle, M. (2009). Dissemination of the coping power program: Importance of intensity of counselor training. *Journal of Consulting and Clinical Psychology, 77,* 397–409. doi:10.1037/a0014514

Lochman, J., & Wells, K. (2003). Effectiveness of the Coping Power Program and of classroom intervention with aggressive children: Outcomes at a 1 year follow-up. *Behavior Therapy, 34,* 493–515. doi:10.1016/S0005-7894(03)80032-1

Lochman, J., & Wells, K. (2004). The Coping Power Program for preadolescent boys and their parents: Outcome effect at the 1-year follow-up. *Journal of Consulting and Clinical Psychology, 72,* 571–578. doi:10.1037/0022-006X.72.4.571

Mazzuchelli, T. G., & Sanders, M. (2010). Facilitating practitioner flexibility within empirically supported intervention: Lessons from a system of parenting support. *Clinical Psychology: Science and Practice, 17,* 238–252. doi:10.1111/j.1468-2850.2010.01215.x

Novaco, R. W. (1975). *Anger control: The development and evaluation of an experimental treatment.* Lexington, MA: D.C. Heath.

Nugent, W. R., Bruley, C., & Allen, P. (1998). The effects of Aggression Replacement Training on antisocial behavior in a runaway shelter. *Research on Social Work Practice, 8,* 637–656. doi:10.1177/104973159800800602

Olweus, D. (1978). *Aggression in the school: Bullies and their whipping boys.* Washington, DC: Hemisphere.

Olweus, D. (1993). *Bullying at school: What we know and what we can do.* Oxford, UK: Blackwell.

Pellegrini, A. D., Bartini, M., & Brooks, F. (1999). School bullies, victims, and aggressive victims: Factors relating to group affiliation and victimization in early adolescence, *Journal of Educational Psychology, 91,* 216–224. doi:10.1037/0022-0663.91.2.216

Perry, D. G., Perry, L. C., & Kennedy, E. (1992). Conflict and the development of antisocial behavior. In C. Uhlinger Shantz & W. W. Hartup (Eds.), *Conflict in child and adolescent development* (pp. 301–329). Cambridge, UK: Cambridge University Press.

Regan, M. E. (2009). Implementation and evaluation of a youth violence prevention program for adolescents. *The Journal of School Nursing, 25,* 27–33. doi:10.1177/1059840508329300

Rodkin, P. C., & Roisman, G. I. (2010). Antecedents and correlates of the popular-aggressive phenomenon in elementary school. *Child Development, 81,* 837–850. doi:10.1111/j.1467-8624.2010.01437.x

Schwartz, D. (2000). Subtypes of victims and aggressors in children's peer groups. *Journal of Abnormal and Child Psychology, 28,* 181–192. doi:10.1023/A:1005174831561

Schwartz, D., Dodge, K. A., Coie, J. D., Hubbard, J. A., Cillessen, A. H. N., Lemerise, E. A., & Bateman, H. (1998). Social-cognitive and behavioral correlates of aggression and victimization in boys' play groups. *Journal of Abnormal Child Psychology, 26*, 431–440. doi:10.1023/A:1022695601088

Schwartz, D., Proctor, L. J., & Chien, D. H. (2001). The aggressive victim of bullying, emotional and behavioral dysregulation as a pathway to victimization by peers. In J. Juvonen & S. Graham (Eds.), *Peer harassment in school: The plight of the vulnerable and victimized* (pp. 147–174). New York, NY: Guilford.

Sukhodolsky, D. G., Kassinove, H., & Gorman, B. S. (2004). Cognitive-behavioral therapy for anger in children and adolescents: A meta-analysis. *Aggression and Violent Behavior, 9*, 247–269. doi:10.1016/j.avb.2003.08.005

Sutton, J., & Smith, P. (1999). Bullying as a group process: An adaptation of the participant role approach. *Aggressive Behavior, 25*, 97–111. doi:10.1002/(SICI)1098-2337(1999)25:2<97::AID-AB3>3.0.CO;2-7

Sutton, J., Smith, P. K., & Swettenham, J. (1999). Bullying and 'theory of mind': A critique of the 'social skills deficit' view of anti-social behaviour. *Social Development, 8*, 117–127. doi:10.1111/1467-9507.00083

Toblin, R. L., Schwartz, D., Hopmeyer Gorman, A., & Abou-ezzeddine, T. (2005). Social–cognitive and behavioral attributes of aggressive victims of bullying. *Journal of Applied Developmental Psychology, 26*, 329–346. doi:10.1016/j.appdev.2005.02.004

Unnever, J. D. (2005), Bullies, aggressive victims, and victims: Are they distinct groups? *Aggressive Behavior, 31*, 153–171. doi:10.1002/ab.20083

Vossekuil, B., Fein, R. A., Reddy, M., Borum, R., & Modzeleski, W. (2002). *The final report and findings of the safe school Initiative: Implications for the prevention of school attacks in the United States.* Washington, DC: U.S. Secret Service and U.S. Department of Education.

Weisz, J. R. (2004). *Psychotherapy for children and adolescents: Evidence-based treatment and case examples.* Cambridge, UK: Cambridge University Press. doi:10.1017/CBO9780511734960

31

Social and Emotional Skills Training with *Second Step: A Violence Prevention Curriculum*

Pam Dell Fitzgerald

ARGOSY UNIVERSITY, SEATTLE

Leihua Van Schoiack Edstrom

BELLEVUE SCHOOL DISTRICT, BELLEVUE, WA

Abstract

Second Step: A Violence Prevention Curriculum is a school-based program developed to prevent and reduce aggressive behavior. Three separate age-appropriate curricula are available: preschool/kindergarten level, elementary level, and middle school level. Designed to be teacher-friendly and convenient for classroom use, the curricula aim to prevent and decrease aggression by helping children develop habits of prosocial behavior and thought. Instructional strategies are evidence-based and are built on a broad foundation of research. In addition, these curricula employ strategies that have been found to be effective for prevention of delinquency and substance abuse, and to support children's academic success. Each of the three curricula has been evaluated and found to reduce aggression and increase social skills.

… teaching prosocial skills in an effective way actually creates more teachable time. So it does not take time away from—I truly believe it contributes time, and the time it creates is actually much more effective teachable time because the students are in a much better place.

> *(Patti Peplow, Head Counselor, Mesa Public Schools, personal communication, May 2004)*

Second Step: A Violence Prevention Curriculum provides evidence-based, effective, classroom-based social skills training, with developmentally appropriate curricula for children at preschool through middle school ages. The curricula are founded on well-established theoretical and practical research. They are developed by teams of educators and researchers for maximum effectiveness through teacher-friendly materials.

Importance

As one of the most important social-emotional learning environments in children's lives, schools have a key impact on children's well-being (for a review, see Weissberg, Caplan, & Harwood, 1991). Universal prevention programs can help schools comprehensively promote children's success and reduce the risk factors for long-term antisocial behavior. Social-emotional prevention programs are most effective when they both reduce risk factors and increase protective factors (Pollard, Hawkins, & Arthur, 1999). To this end, the goals of the *Second Step* curricula are to increase social and emotional skills and in doing so, reduce aggression.

Social skills and aggression have implications for a wide range of developmental outcomes in addition to effects on peer relations (Coie, Dodge, & Coppotelli, 1982). These include school success (e.g., Durlak, Weissberg, Dymnkcki, Taylor, & Schellinger, 2011), substance abuse (for a review, see Hawkins, Catalano, & Miller, 1992), long-term persistent antisocial behavior (e.g., Dodge, Greenberg, Malone, & Conduct Problems Prevention Research Group, 2008), and lack of success in the workplace (Spencer & Spencer, 1993).

Positive social skills and relations are key in promoting positive development and preventing negative outcomes. In their meta-analysis of social skills studies, Newcomb, Bukowski, and Pattee (1993) confirmed that children who were rejected by their peers were characterized as being not only aggressive but also low in prosocial skills. Conversely, children who were especially well-accepted by their peers were characterized by strong prosocial skills (Newcomb et al., 1993).

Children's social relations, in turn, are related to success in school. Their academic performance is higher when children perceive their relationships with people at school to be supportive (for a review, see Zins, Weissberg, Wang, & Walberg, 2004). Wilson, Gottfredson, and Najaka (2001), in their meta-analysis of U.S. school-based prevention programs, found that school dropout and nonattendance rates decreased after implementation of cognitive-behavioral programs focused on social competence development. Similarly, additional meta-analyses (Diekstra, 2008; Durlak et al., 2011) have shown school-based social-emotional learning programs to have beneficial impacts on children's school achievement and grades, and on their attitudes toward school, even at six or more months follow-up (Durlak et al., 2011).

In addition to the impact on their peer relations and academic success, children who are aggressive can be at risk for other serious problems. Excessive and persistent aggressiveness and antisocial behaviors in children put them at risk for long-term antisocial behavior patterns. These risks include substance abuse (for a review, see Hawkins et al., 1992) and criminal behavior (Dodge et al., 2008; Moffitt, 1993). Although early aggression itself is not a strong risk factor, children are at greater risk for poor outcomes if their aggression persists through childhood. Because risk factors cannot always be controlled, prevention programming should address factors such as social competence that can protect children against long-term harm (Hawkins et al., 1992; Payton et al., 2008). As both an early intervention and prevention program, the *Second Step* curricula are designed to reduce aggression as well as inhibit its long-term associated risks by teaching social and emotional competence.

It is important that social and emotional competencies be taught to children in their schools. The social and emotional behaviors that children learn in school can promote healthy development or cause harm. They can affect not only children's individual development, but also their impact on others. Therefore, it is critical that educators take advantage of the rich opportunities inherent in school settings to teach positive social and emotional skills, rather than leaving to chance the nature of the skills that children learn during the school day. Teaching such competencies forms the foundation of prevention efforts aimed at reducing aggression and is important to the healthy development of all children. Given the associations with school and later workplace success, emphasizing these competencies advances schools' core mission of preparing students to later be responsible community members as adults.

Conceptual Foundation

The theoretical roots of the *Second Step* curricula are founded in three areas of developmental research. First, the curricula were developed to prevent later violent behavior and promote positive development by addressing early social skills. Second, they are based on research about the cognitive-behavioral skills that contribute to prosocial behavior (e.g., Crick & Dodge, 1994; Lemerise & Arsenio, 2000). Third, they are informed by knowledge about the typical development of children's prosocial skills (e.g., Fabes, Eisenberg, Hanish, & Spinrad, 2001).

The prevention role of early social skills has recently been highlighted in the cascade model for the development of adolescent violence, proposed by Dodge et al. (2008). This model posits that early predictors contribute to progressively later predictors of violence, with each stage of the model partially mediating the effects of previous stages. Three of these seven progressive stages are related to children's social behaviors and relationships at school (e.g., school social readiness, externalizing behavior, social failure). Based on empirical support of the model, Dodge et al. recommend (a) that social skills be taught during early school years, and (b) that intervention be maintained across children's development to address the "new" risks that accompany each developmental stage. Since the *Second Step* curricula focus on developmentally appropriate approaches to social problem solving and other social and emotional skills, and are available for children in preschool through middle school, they are especially well suited to provide this prevention role.

The second area that is foundational to the curricula is cognitive-behavioral research about children's social interactions. Crick and Dodge's (1994) model of the cognitive processes in children's interactions is a useful conceptual framework for the cognitive-behavioral skills addressed by the *Second Step* curricula. That is, in social interactions, children (a) encode cues about the interaction, (b) interpret the meaning of the cues, (c) clarify what their goals are in the interaction, (d) examine potential responses from their repertoire, (e) evaluate and select a response, and (f) enact a response. The curricula teach children prosocial habits for each of these cognitive steps. For example, they teach children to (a) attend to cues about emotions (encode), (b) consider several interpretations of interactions, (c) set goals to avoid causing harm, (d) generate several possible responses, (e) evaluate the consequences of possible responses, and (f) practice prosocial responses.

Lemerise and Arsenio (2000) extended this model to include the influence of emotions during these steps. For example, it has long been recognized that strong emotions can interfere with one's ability to respond effectively (for a review, see Campos & Barrett, 1984). This understanding is incorporated in the *Second Step* lessons, as children are taught strategies for calming down, and are taught to use emotions as cues for understanding the situation.

These cognitive-behavioral strategies are designed to steer children away from thinking patterns characteristic of aggressive children toward those of children who are non-aggressive and are accepted by their peers (e.g., Crick & Dodge, 1994). As such, the program addresses behaviors, thoughts, and emotions, and the interplay amongst them. These skill sets are also reflected in the social and emotional competencies that are identified as core by Payton et al. (2000)—awareness of self and others, positive attitudes and values, responsible decision making, and social interaction skills.

The third aspect of development research that informs the *Second Step* curricula is our knowledge about typical development of social skills in children. For example, empathy skills have been identified as key factors in the early development of social behavior (e.g., Hastings, Zahn-Waxler, Robinson, Usher, & Bridges, 2000) and in later acceptance by the peer group (Fabes et al., 2001). Empathy is also integral to children's competence at several other social and emotional skills (for a review, see Lemerise & Arsenio, 2000). For these reasons, empathy skills are central in all levels of the lessons.

In addition to this direct teaching of social and emotional skills, Frey and Nolen's (2010) transactional model of school-based prevention highlights other avenues through which *Second Step* may promote behavioral change. The model proposes that, in addition to improvements in their own social and emotional skills, children are also affected by the changes that occur in their transactions with others as a result of *Second Step* training. Consider, for example, a predictor mentioned in the cascade model described above (Dodge et al., 2008)—deviant peer associations. If school children in a cohort improve even marginally in their social skills after receiving the *Second Step* program, fewer of them may become behaviorally deviant and their deviance may be less extreme. In that case, a target child would benefit not only from improved social skills, but also from a social milieu with more prosocial norms and fewer deviant peers.

Specific Approach of the Program

The *Second Step* curricula are commercially available, school-based programs for students in pre-school through middle school. Each curriculum is developed by teams of experienced teachers and prevention researchers working together. This method has pioneered a process that incorporates strong evidence-based prevention strategies with best practices experience and implementation know-how. This maximizes the convenience and relevance of the curricula for classroom use. Long-term application within the classroom has further contributed to refinement of the program and implementation guidelines (Table 31.1 delineates implications for practice, steps toward successfully implementing the *Second Step* curriculum). Since its inception in 1986, the curricula (Committee for Children, 2002, 2008) have been used widely in the United States and Canada, are translated into more than a dozen languages, including Spanish, and are used in more than two dozen countries.

Designed to teach key social competencies, the program's aims are to decrease children's risk for destructive behavior and increase their potential for success at school and in relationships with others. Consistent with meta-analytic outcome evidence regarding effective strategies, (Durlak et al., 2011), the curricula utilize a sequential progression of lessons, active learning (e.g., role plays), a substantial focus on social skills development, and targeting of specific social and emotional skills.

Classroom Lessons

Second Step classroom lessons are developmentally sequenced, building on concepts and skills across grade levels. In general, lessons are taught by classroom teachers, school counselors, or school psychologists who have received program training. The program's developers recommend that classroom teachers take the lead in lesson presentation due to their familiarity with students, ability to adjust lessons accordingly, and capacity for facilitating maintenance and generalization of students' skills (Committee for Children, 2002, 2008).

Materials and Format

Curricula for preschool and elementary students consist of 22 to 28 lessons, depending on the grade level. Lessons vary in length from 20 minutes at the preschool level to 45 minutes in Grades 4 and 5. In each lesson, an 11″ × 17″ black-and-white photograph depicts a social dilemma from which a presentation of the key concepts and objectives extends. Lesson scripts for teachers are

Table 31.1 Implications for Practice: Steps Toward Successfully Implementing the *Second Step* Curricula

Level	Program conditions and activities
	Pre-implementation
School	Develop a comprehensive plan for meeting academic, social, and emotional goals.
	Involve key stakeholders when choosing the program.
	Clearly articulate how the program meets your school's goals.
	Form a steering team and designate a program coordinator.
	Provide strong leadership for the program (principal and steering team).
	Allocate time and resources, with a realistic timeline.
	Plan for program evaluation as an essential program activity.
Classroom	Involve teachers in planning, particularly classroom lesson implementation.
	Encourage teachers and other implementers to join steering team.
	Implementation delivery
School	Provide *Second Step* training for all staff.
	Foster family involvement via curriculum parent letters and family module.
	Make the program visible throughout the school.
	Provide ongoing support for staff (e.g., consultation, exchange of ideas).
	Maintain practical and social support for the program (particularly by principal).
	Facilitate student use of skills (e.g., cueing, coaching) throughout the school day.
	Collect implementation and outcome data.
Classroom	Train teachers in classroom curricula.
	Teach classroom lessons sequentially, with fidelity.
	Model the program concepts and skills (e.g., respect, empathy).
	Support students' skill development (e.g., cueing, coaching) outside of lessons.
	Integrate program concepts throughout the classroom curriculum.
Student	Promote individual student skills (e.g., prompting or problem solving).
	Provide additional services as necessary (e.g., increased scaffolding, more practice, individual counseling).
	Post-implementation
School	Summarize process and outcome data.
	Use evaluation data to inform planning (e.g., by steering team).
	Share successes with staff, students, and families.
	Plan for next year's school implementation, including training and support needs.
Classroom	Reflect on implementation successes and obstacles.
	Plan classroom implementation for the following year.
Student	Consider the need for more intensive services for individual students.

Note. "Teachers" refers to any implementers of the classroom lessons.

printed on the reverse of the "photo card," describing the vignette and outlining lesson activities (e.g., discussion and skill practice). Video clips dramatize and support some of the lessons. The middle school curriculum consists of three levels, allowing a comprehensive, multiyear implementation. The 13–15 weeks of lessons at each level are flexibly designed so that they can be split into 26–30 short lessons, according to scheduling needs. The lesson format involves group discussion, classroom activities, homework, and videos.

Depending on grade level, curriculum materials may include puppets, classroom posters, homework sheets, and family materials. Detailed implementation guides for educators include recommendations for adapting lessons for various populations (e.g., students with disabilities or in multiage or non–school settings), and for incorporating *Second Step* concepts into academic lessons. The program's publisher provides gratis technical support to assist program implementation.

Content

Preschool and elementary level *Second Step* lessons are organized in three units. The first unit focuses on empathy to provide a foundation for subsequent lessons. This includes, for example, identifying feelings, understanding others' perspectives, and responding supportively. The problem-solving unit teaches a step-by-step strategy for solving social problems that include, for example, identifying the problem and evaluating solutions. In the emotion-management unit, students learn to recognize anger cues and to use stress-reduction techniques (e.g., counting backward) to manage angry feelings. Emotion-management and problem-solving steps are also applied to specific stress-inducing situations typical for students (e.g., bullying or social exclusion). The middle school curriculum incorporates these foundational skills, and also includes specific lessons for bullying prevention and substance abuse prevention. In all curricula, lessons build sequentially on each other, increasing in sophistication within and between grade levels.

Instructional and Transfer-of-Learning Strategies

Second Step lessons rely on a range of teaching strategies that facilitate student learning, promote a supportive classroom climate, and encourage the generalization of skills. Strategies vary, as appropriate to the grade level. For example, puppets are used in preschool lessons, and middle schools students engage in cooperative group activities.

Discussion

Group discussions are integral to *Second Step* lessons. They focus on applying specific lesson topics to hypothetical situations and examples from children's own lives. The curricula offer several supports to help make discussions engaging and instructive, such as tips to encourage participation, and scripted, open-ended questions.

Behavioral Skill Training

Skill training is the second major component of *Second Step* lessons. With teacher guidance, students first generate skill steps for responding to a given social dilemma or situation, such as conversation-making. Next, the teacher models the skill steps and leads students in evaluating his/her performance. Students then have several opportunities to practice the specific behavioral skills with coaching and feedback.

Modeling

Perhaps the most powerful teaching strategy employed in the *Second Step* program, modeling, reaches far beyond the confines of lesson instruction. Observing adults' *Second Step* skills "in action" affords students information about effective approaches and demonstrates the values and norms of school staff setting the stage for prosocial student norms.

Cueing, Coaching, and Reinforcement

School life involves countless opportunities for students to test and refine their skills. Likewise, teachers are presented regularly with "teachable moments" to cue students to use their newly learned skills and coach them in their performance. The curricula offer several specific suggestions for this critical transfer-of-learning step.

Group problem Solving and Decision Making

Students' participation in solving "real" problems encourages transfer of learning through an active role in situations of intrinsic interest.

Staff Training

The program developers offer *Second Step* training. This entails a one-day session for teachers. Alternatively, two-day "training for trainers" sessions are available in which participants also learn to conduct staff training for their schools or districts.

Administrator's Guide

An administrator's guide accompanies curriculum kits for preschool through Grade 5. The guide assists principals or program coordinators in designing a school environment that optimally supports program implementation and integrates social and emotional learning with academic goals.

Family Guide

The family guide is a supplementary module for leading six sessions for caregivers. Participants are introduced to *Second Step* skills and learn how to foster their children's development and use of the skills.

Assessment Tools

An array of assessment tools is available for schools' use in evaluating the *Second Step* program (see www.cfchildren.org). Several process evaluation tools are available to assess features of a school's implementation of the program, such as support for students' transfer of learning and staff and student satisfaction. Outcome tools evaluate students' social and emotional knowledge (preschool–grade 5), and attitudes linked to aggression and socially competent behavior (grades 6–8).

Evidence of Effectiveness

Studies performed by multiple research teams demonstrate effectiveness of the *Second Step* curricula with students from a variety of socioeconomic, ethnic, and racial backgrounds, age groups, and geographical regions and settings (i.e., rural, suburban, and urban, including international). Across this research, the curricula have been linked to student changes in social and emotional knowledge and skills, prosocial attitudes, increased social skills, and decreased aggression.

Ideally, program outcome studies should utilize true experimental designs with random assignment to groups, direct observations of behaviors, and adequate sample sizes. This level of rigor has been reached in three studies of the elementary *Second Step* curriculum. In an experimental study of the German translation of the curriculum (*Faustlos*), Schick and Cierpka (2005) used a randomized control group design with 718 primary students. Students receiving *Faustlos* were rated by parents as significantly less anxious, depressed, and socially withdrawn, relative to controls. Gender differences in additional treatment effects were noted, with parents indicating more positive intervention benefits for girls than boys. Teacher and student reports did not evince significant group effects, with the exception that *Faustlos* students indicated less anxiety than controls.

Two of these rigorous studies were strengthened further by their use of analytical procedures that take into account the commonalities of participants nested within classrooms and schools. Grossman et al. (1997) assessed nearly 800 second- and third-grade children from six matched pairs of schools. Behavioral observations of a randomly selected subsample ($n = 588$) revealed decreased physical (but not verbal) aggression for *Second Step* students following implementation, whereas comparison students showed increases in physical aggression. *Second Step* students also demonstrated increases in positive social behavior compared to controls. Between the baseline measures and the six-month follow-up, coders blind to condition observed mean reductions in physical aggression for program students and not for controls. Parent and teacher ratings did not reflect the changes.

In the second of these particularly rigorous experimental studies Frey, Nolen, Edstrom, and Hirschstein (2005) examined 1,253 second- through fifth-grade students from 15 schools with partial random assignment. In this study, teachers' implementation was closely monitored and supported by program consultants. After the first year of the program (but not the second year), *Second Step* students were rated as being more socially competent and less antisocial by their teachers than those who did not receive the program. Moreover, the greatest reductions in anti-social behavior were made by *Second Step* students who started out at baseline with the highest ratings of antisocial behavior. Following two years of the program, *Second Step* students also were more likely to indicate prosocial goals and reasoning. Unbiased observations revealed that *Second Step* curriculum participants were less aggressive, more cooperative (for girls only), and required less adult intervention in contrived conflict situations with peers.

The desired level of rigor has not been reached in published studies of the preschool/kindergarten or middle school curriculum. However, for the preschool/kindergarten curriculum, an unpublished experimental study by McCabe (1999) does offer evidence of effectiveness. Using an adequate sample size, random assignment by classroom, and behavioral observations, outcome results were promising and included a decline in observed peer conflict for the most aggressive children.

Quasi-experimental studies using comparison classrooms offer additional support. *Second Step* students in elementary and/or middle school show reduced acceptance of physical and relational aggression (Van Schoiack-Edstrom, Frey, & Beland, 2002), more confidence in social and emotional skills (Van Schoiack-Edstrom et al., 2002), increased knowledge of social and emotional skills (Orpinas, Parcel, McAlister, & Frankowski, 1995), increased social competence, and reduced antisocial behavior (Taub, 2002).

Several evaluation studies have involved pre-post designs with no controls (Cooke, Ford, Levine, Bourke, Newell, & Lapidus, 2007; Edwards, Hunt, Meyers, Grogg, & Jarrett, 2005; McMahon & Washburn, 2003). Third- to fifth-grade students across three studies evinced various effects following exposure to the program: increased social-emotional knowledge, greater self-reported problem solving and coping, improved grades related to respectful and cooperative behavior, and a trend toward neutral (rather than disruptive) school behavior as rated by independent observers. Although changes in observed and self-reported aggression were inconsistent in these studies, McMahon and Washburn found that reductions in self-reported aggression were predicted by increases in self-reported empathy. Another study with a similar design did find observed reductions in aggressive and disruptive behavior in low-income preschool and kindergarten children (McMahon, Washburn, Felix, Yakin, & Childrey, 2000).

The results from evaluations of *Second Step* curricula have not been entirely consistent, at least partly due to variation in the quality of the research. Overall, those studies with the most rigorous designs (e.g., larger sample sizes, behavioral observations by unbiased observers) have tended to be the ones lending the strongest support for the effectiveness of the *Second Step* program.

These studies have shown reductions in aggression and increases in positive skills following use of the *Second Step* curricula. Student measures of goals and attitudes also show promising sensitivity to change. Behavioral ratings by teachers, parents, and students have yielded less consistent results. It may be that parents and teachers are not sensitive enough to changes in aggression, or are not privy to important settings in which behavioral changes have occurred. Future research should rely more on unbiased observational measures to measure change adequately.

Limitations and Future Directions

As a universal prevention program, the *Second Step* curricula do not include the kinds of intensive treatment components that might be needed for some children. On the other hand, the curricula can be important building blocks of a comprehensive prevention strategy that addresses multiple systems and targeted populations (e.g., Sprague & Horner, 2006). The curricula provide a foundation of basic skills that are beneficial to all children and to schoolwide behavioral expectations. These are likely to be necessary elements of multi-component programs for targeted populations. Indeed, Frey et al.'s finding (2005) that the most antisocial elementary students made the greatest gains from the program suggests that the *Second Step* curricula may be an effective component of a broader intervention strategy for such students. Research is needed to examine fully how the curricula can be used optimally with targeted populations.

A related question involves the use of *Second Step* curricula in specially-tailored multi-component comprehensive programs. They can be used as a basic foundation of social skills, with additional components added that are chosen to meet specific local needs. For example, *Steps to Respect: A Bullying Prevention Program*, distributed by the same developers as the *Second Step* curricula (see Hirschstein & Frey, this volume) was designed to be compatible with *Second Step* curricula. *Second Step* has also served as a universal component in effective multi-component prevention efforts by independent researchers (e.g., Sprague & Horner, 2006). Further research is needed about the best way to incorporate *Second Step* curricula into these kinds of multi-component programs.

Although emerging research provides evidence of the program's utility in changing attitudes and observable behavior, additional studies with rigorous experimental designs are needed to assess curriculum effects across different age groups. It would also be useful to know whether different groups of children learn the *Second Step* skills similarly, and what kinds of adaptations would be beneficial in different communities. In addition, various groups of children might be impacted differently by the improved social skills of their peers. For example, improved empathy may decrease peers' racial microaggressions (subtle, biased denigrations: see, Sue, 2010), hence equalizing the positive tone in the classroom across racial groups.

Furthermore, although research has shown the importance of implementation quality in the effects of *Second Step*, little is known about how implementation interacts with causal mechanisms (but for an exception, see Durlak et al., 2011), and what the effects are of multi-year implementation. Researchers have yet to assess the effects of the curricula on whole-school outcomes such as school climate and norms, and on classroom management. There is also a strong need for researchers to identify and/or develop effective outcome measures that are feasible for educators to use.

The *Second Step* curricula are teacher-friendly programs designed to improve children's social competence and are based on a strong empirical and theoretical foundation. Evaluation studies provide increasing evidence of the effectiveness of the curricula in reducing aggression and increasing social competence. However, more research is needed to add depth to our understanding of social emotional learning and the *Second Step* curricula specifically.

References

Campos, J. J., & Barrett, K. C. (1984). Toward a new understanding of emotions and their development. In C. Izard, J. Kagan, & R. Zajonc (Eds.), *Emotions, cognition and behavior* (pp. 229–263). New York, NY: Cambridge University Press.

Coie, J. D., Dodge, K. A., & Coppotelli, H. (1982). Dimensions and types of social status: A cross-age perspective. *Child Development, 18,* 557–570.

Committee for Children. (2002). *Second step: A violence prevention curriculum,* preschool/kindergarten–grade 5 (3rd ed.). Seattle, WA: Author.

Committee for Children. (2008). *Second step: Student success through prevention,* middle school. Seattle, WA: Author.

Cooke, M. B., Ford J., Levine J., Bourke C., Newell L., & Lapidus G. (2007). The effect of city-wide implementation of *"Second Step"* on elementary school students' prosocial and aggressive behaviors. *Journal of Primary Prevention, 28,* 93–115.

Crick, N. R., & Dodge, K. A. (1994). A review and reformulation of social information-processing mechanisms in children's social adjustment. *Psychological Bulletin, 115,* 74–101.

Diekstra, R. F. W. (2008). Effectiveness of school-based social and emotional education programmes worldwide. In F. M. Botin (Ed.), *Social and emotional education: An international analysis* (pp. 255–312). Santender, Spain: Fundacion Marcelino Botin.

Dodge, K. A., Greenberg, M. T., Malone, P. S., & Conduct Problems Prevention Research Group (2008). Testing an idealized dynamic cascade model of the development of serious violence in adolescence. *Child Development, 79,* 1907–1927.

Durlak, J. A., Weissberg, R. P., Dymnicki, A. B., Taylor, R. D., & Schellinger, K. B. (2011). The impact of enhancing students' social and emotional learning: A meta-analysis of school-based universal interventions. *Child Development, 82,* 405–432.

Edwards, D., Hunt, M. H., Meyers, J., Grogg, K. R., & Jarrett, O. (2005). Acceptability and student outcomes of a violence prevention curriculum. *Journal of Primary Prevention, 26,* 401–418.

Fabes, R. A., Eisenberg, N., Hanish, L. D., & Spinrad, T. L. (2001). Preschoolers' spontaneous emotion vocabulary: Relations to likeability. *Early Education & Development, 12,* 11–27.

Frey, K. S., & Nolen, S. B. (2010). Taking "Steps" toward positive social relationships: A transactional model of intervention. In J. Meece & J. Eccles (Eds.), *Handbook of research on schools, schooling, and human development* (pp. 478–496). Mahwah, NJ: Erlbaum.

Frey, K. S., Nolen, S. B., Edstrom, L. V., & Hirschstein, M. K. (2005). Effects of a school-based social-emotional competence program: Linking goals, attributions, and behavior. *Journal of Applied Developmental Psychology, 26,* 171–200.

Grossman, D. C., Neckerman, H. J., Koepsell, T. D., Liu, P. Y., Asher, K. N., Beland, K., … Rivara, F. P. (1997). Effectiveness of a violence prevention curriculum among children in elementary school: A randomized controlled trial. *Journal of the American Medical Association, 277,* 1605–1611.

Hastings, P. D., Zahn-Waxler, C., Robinson, J., Usher, B., & Bridges, D. (2000). The development of concern for others in children with behavior problems. *Developmental Psychology, 36,* 531–546.

Hawkins, J. D., Catalano, R. F., & Miller, J. Y. (1992). Risk and protective factors for alcohol and other drug problems in adolescence and early adulthood: Implications for substance abuse prevention. *Psychological Bulletin, 112,* 64–105.

Lemerise, E. A., & Arsenio, W. F. (2000). An integrated model of emotion processes and cognition in social information processing. *Child Development, 71,* 107–118.

McCabe, L. A. (1999). *Violence prevention in early childhood: Implementing the Second Step curriculum in child care and head start classroom.* (Doctoral dissertation). Retrieved from Dissertations & Theses: Full Text (Publication No. AAT 9941173)

McMahon, S. D., & Washburn, J. (2003). Violence prevention: An evaluation of program effects with urban African American students. *The Journal of Primary Prevention, 24,* 43–62.

McMahon, S. D., Washburn, J., Felix, E. D., Yakin, J., & Childrey, G. (2000). Violence prevention: Program effects on urban preschool and kindergarten children. *Applied & Preventive Psychology, 9,* 271–281.

Moffitt, T. (1993). Adolescence-limited and life-course-persistent antisocial behavior: A developmental taxonomy. *Psychological Review, 100,* 674–701.

Newcomb, A. F., Bukowski, W. M., & Pattee, L. (1993). Children's peer relations: A meta-analytic review of popular, rejected, neglected, controversial, and average sociometric status. *Psychological Bulletin, 113,* 99–128.

Orpinas, P., Parcel, G. S., McAlister, A., & Frankowski, R. (1995). Violence prevention in middle schools: A pilot evaluation. *Journal of Adolescent Health, 17,* 360–371.

Payton, J. W., Wardlaw, D. M., Graczyk, P. A., Bloodworth, M. R., Tompsett, C. J., & Weissberg, R. P. (2000). Social and emotional learning: A framework for promoting mental health and reducing risk behaviors in children and youth. *Journal of School Health, 70,* 179–185.

Payton, J., Weissberg, R. P., Durlak, J. A., Dymnicki, A. B., Taylor, R. D., Schellinger, K. B., & Pachan, M. (2008). *The positive impact of social and emotional learning for kindergarten to eighth-grade students: Findings from three scientific reviews.* Chicago, IL: Collaborative for Academic, Social, and Emotional Learning.

Pollard, J. A., Hawkins, D. J., & Arthur, M. W. (1999). Risk and protection: Are both necessary to understand diverse behavioral outcomes in adolescence? *Social Work Research, 23,* 145–158.

Schick, A., & Cierpka, M. (2005). Faustlos: Evaluation of a curriculum to prevent violence in elementary schools. *Applied and Preventive Psychology, 11,* 157–165.

Spencer, L. M., & Spencer, S. M. (1993). *Competence at work: Models for superior performance.* New York, NY: Wiley.

Sprague, J. R., & Horner, R. H. (2006). Schoolwide positive behavioral supports. In S. R. Jimerson & M. J. Furlong (Eds.), *Handbook of school violence and school safety* (pp. 413–427). Mahwah, NJ: Erlbaum.

Sue, D. S. (2010). *Microaggressions in everyday life.* Hoboken, NJ: Wiley.

Taub, J. (2002). Evaluation of the *Second Step* violence prevention program at a rural elementary school. *School Psychology Review: Interventions for Social-emotional Needs of Children, 31,* 186–200.

Van Schoiack-Edstrom, L., Frey, K. S., & Beland, K. (2002). Changing adolescents' attitudes about relational and physical aggression: An early evaluation of a school-based intervention. *School Psychology Review, 31,* 201–216.

Weissberg, R. P., Caplan, M., & Harwood, R. L. (1991). Promoting competent young people in competence-enhancing environments: A systems-based perspective on primary prevention. *Journal of Consulting & Clinical Psychology, 59,* 830–841.

Wilson, D. B., Gottfredson, D. C., & Najaka, S. S. (2001). School-based prevention of problem behaviors: A meta-analysis. *Journal of Quantitative Criminology, 17,* 247–272.

Zins, J. E., Weissberg, R. P., Wang, M. C., & Walberg, H. J. (2004). *Building academic success on social and emotional learning.* New York, NY: Teachers College Press.

433

32

The PATHS Curriculum

Promoting Emotional Literacy, Prosocial Behavior, and Caring Classrooms

Carol A. Kusché

THE UNIVERSITY OF WASHINGTON, SEATTLE

Mark T. Greenberg

PENNSYLVANIA STATE UNIVERSITY AND THE PREVENTION RESEARCH
CENTER FOR THE PROMOTION OF HUMAN DEVELOPMENT.

Abstract

Social and emotional learning skills are crucial for success at school and in life and thus should be a central feature of education. Based on developmental models drawn from diverse theories, PATHS (Promoting Alternative THinking Strategies) and Preschool PATHS were designed to promote social and emotional development, as well as school success. The PATHS curricula have been carefully researched and have been implemented throughout the United States and in other countries. In addition, they have been shown to increase protective factors for healthy development, reduce emotional and behavioral problems, and foster caring classrooms. Empirical support has been found for a direct relationship between the implementation of PATHS and both improvements in executive functions and reductions in behavioral problems.

The world of today is not the same as the one in which most professionals grew up. When we were young, a misinterpreted social cue or hostile comment might end up in a fist fight, but now it can result in serious violence. In many communities, students fear for their lives simply walking to school and an alarming percentage of children report being bullied (U.S. Department of Justice, Bureau of Justice Statistics, 2007). As a result of these unfortunate changes, education that sufficed in the past is insufficient today; soon it will be archaic.

Emotional literacy, social competence, and motivation to participate as healthy, contributing members of society are now as important for success in school and work as reading, math, and computer skills. The development of insight, empathy for others, and healthy relationships promotes success in both academics and life and decreases risk for aggression, violence, and depression (Greenberg, Kusché, & Riggs, 2004). Furthermore, increases in protective factors have been shown to improve academic performance, as well as brain development (Greenberg & Kusché, 1993; Weissberg & Greenberg, 1998). Finally, social emotional learning (SEL) transforms classrooms into caring, inviting environments where children feel nurtured; this, in turn, further facilitates academic achievement (Durlak, Weissberg, Dymnicki, Taylor, & Schellinger, 2011).

In order to promote proficient social and emotional development, however, well-constructed curricula are of crucial importance. Moreover, SEL should begin as early as possible, at least by the preschool years, and proceed in a developmentally appropriate manner until the end of high school.

Providing this type of comprehensive, developmentally sequenced, teacher-ready SEL curricula was the primary goal in the conception and refinement of PATHS (Promoting Alternative THinking Strategies, Kusché & Greenberg, 1994) and Preschool PATHS (Domitrovich, Greenberg, Kusché, & Cortes, 2004). These universal prevention/intervention programs were designed to be used by teachers and support staff in preschool and elementary classroom to promote emotional and social competencies, reduce aggression and disruptive behaviors, and enhance the overall educational process.

PATHS curricula have been used over the last quarter century in regular education, Head Start centers, and a variety of special needs programs (learning disabled, behavioral problems, mildly mentally delayed, autistic spectrum disorders, and gifted). Since its development in the early 1980s, PATHS has been delivered throughout the United States and in over 20 countries (with numerous translations). Ongoing research has consistently shown that the PATHS model leads to improvements in emotional literacy, social competence, cognitive abilities, and caring classroom atmospheres (Conduct Problems Prevention Research Group, 1999, 2010; Greenberg & Kusché, 1993, 1998; Greenberg, Kusché, Cook, & Quamma, 1995).

Brief Descriptions of Grade Level PATHS and Pre K/K PATHS

Due to the fact that ability and needs differ considerably between developmental stages, PATHS is divided into two separate curriculums, one for elementary age children and one for preschoolers and kindergarten. The Grade Level PATHS Curriculum (Greenberg, Kusché, & Conduct Problems Prevention Research Group, 2011; Kusché, Greenberg, & Conduct Problems Prevention Research Group, 2011) consists of separate volumes of lessons for each grade level (grades 1–5), all of which include developmentally appropriate pictures, photographs, posters, and additional materials (http://www.channing-bete.com/prevention-programs/paths/). Five conceptual domains, integrated in a hierarchical manner, are included in PATHS lessons at each grade level: self-control, emotional understanding, positive self-esteem, relationships, and interpersonal problem-solving skills. Throughout the lessons, a critical focus of PATHS involves facilitating the dynamic relationship between cognitive-affective understanding and real-life situations. PATHS is designed to be taught two to three times per week (or more often if desired), with daily activities to promote generalization and support ongoing behavior. PATHS lessons follow lesson objectives and provide scripts to facilitate instruction, but teachers have flexibility in adapting these for their particular classroom needs. Further, although each unit of PATHS focuses on one or more skill domains (e.g., emotional recognition, friendship, self-control, problem solving), aspects of all five major areas are integrated into each unit. Moreover, each new unit builds hierarchically upon and synthesizes the learning which preceded it. To encourage parent involvement and support, parent letters, home activity assignments, and information are also provided.

The PreK/K PATHS Curriculum (Domitrovich, Greenberg, Kusché, & Cortes, 2004) consists of 45 lessons of original PATHS concepts developed specifically for younger children. PreK/K PATHS is divided into thematic units that include lessons on such topics as complimenting, basic and advanced feelings, a self-control strategy based on the "Turtle Technique" (Robin, Schneider, & Dolnick, 1976), manners, and problem solving. Various puppets, as well as pictures, photographs, and feeling faces, are used in the lessons to introduce and illustrate the concepts. Lessons are delivered weekly by early childhood educators during "circle-time" sessions and then practiced with extension activities (e.g., group games, art projects, music, story time, etc.); concepts also can be integrated into the existing "center" structure of typical preschool and kindergarten programs.

Theoretical Rationale and Conceptual Framework of PATHS

In developing PATHS, we incorporated seven factors that we deemed critical for effective, school-based SEL curricula. These included the use of:

- an integration of a variety of successful approaches and promising theories
- a developmental model, including neuropsychological brain development
- a multi-grade level paradigm
- a strong focus on the role of emotions and emotional development
- generalization of skills to everyday situations
- ongoing training and support for implementation
- multiple measures of both process and outcome for assessing program effectiveness

PATHS and Preschool PATHS are based on five conceptual models, described in greater detail elsewhere (Greenberg & Kusché, 2006; Kusché & Greenberg, 2006b). The first, the ABCD (Affective-Behavioral-Cognitive-Dynamic) Model of Development (Greenberg & Kusché, 1993) focuses on the promotion of optimal growth and on the *developmental* integration of affect (i.e., emotion, feeling, mood), emotion language, behavior, and cognitive understanding.

The second model involves the domains of neurobiology and brain structuralization/organization, focusing on the crucial development of neuronal connections between the prefrontal orbital cortex and the more primitive subcortical limbic areas (prefrontal lobe deficits have been linked to higher levels of impulsive and aggressive behavior, Brower & Price, 2001; Schore, 1996). Interhemispheric communication (Kusché, 1984; Kusché & Greenberg, 2006a) is also emphasized, and the crucial importance of language for the regulation of emotional states has been substantiated by recent findings in neuroscience (Lieberman et al., 2008), as has the importance of mirror neurons (networks in the brain that process observed behaviors modeled by others as if the individual were actually doing these him or herself, believed to facilitate nonverbal learning, understanding, and empathic identification).

A third paradigm involves concepts from psychoanalytic education to enhance emotional and cognitive growth, promote mental health, and prevent emotional distress (Kusché, 2002; Kusché, Riggs, & Greenberg, 1999). Among other things, this application of psychoanalytic theory emphasizes positive teacher-student relationships, internalization of prosocial values, use of creativity, optimal emotional and cognitive integration, appropriate expression (rather than repression) of affect, and learning as a process of joyful discovery. It can be noted that the incorporation of psychoanalytic theory distinguishes PATHS from the vast majority of other SEL curricula.

The fourth model incorporates an eco-behavioral orientation, which focuses on classroom and schoolwide systems change and generalization of skills to improve classroom and school climates. A fifth model relates to emotional literacy, or as it is more popularly labeled, emotional intelligence (Mayer & Salovey, 1997). As Dan Goleman (1995) noted, "[s]elf-awareness—recognizing a feeling *as it happens*—is the keystone of emotional intelligence.... People with greater certainty about their feelings are better pilots of their lives" (p. 43).

We believe our broad conceptual approach has been a key factor in the effectiveness of PATHS; to affect significant changes in children's social and emotional competence, it is necessary to take a holistic approach that includes a focus on the integration of affect, behavior, and cognitions. Similarly, when developing PATHS, we felt it was of utmost importance to incorporate knowledge from diverse areas (e.g., emotional intelligence, neurocognitive development, psychoanalytic theory, school ecology, etc.) and to translate this information into language and dialogue that could be easily understood and utilized by classroom teachers. In addition, most children and teachers report that they greatly enjoy PATHS, which we believe is another very important reason for its efficacy. A summary of these implications for practice can be found in Table 32.1.

Promoting Protective Factors, Decreasing Behavior Problems, and Enhancing Classroom Atmosphere

Protective factors (e.g., reflective thinking, problem solving, and accurate evaluation of situations) are of crucial importance for decreasing maladjustment. These skills increase children's access to positive social interactions, provide opportunities for a greater variety of learning experiences, contribute to the amelioration of significant underachievement, and help prevent violence and other antisocial adolescent problem behaviors in the future (e.g., aggression, substance abuse, and dangerous risk-taking).

Another crucial factor for success in society involves the ability to tolerate frustration and to control behaviors when impulses are strong. Several strategies are used in PATHS to teach self-control that are based on the importance of neuronal structuralization and growth between the frontal cortex and limbic system (i.e., optimal "vertical" control). Relatively simple motor control is taught during the early years (the "Turtle Technique"), followed by more complex models utilizing language and cognition (Control Signals Poster and formal problem solving).

Table 32.1 Implications for Practice: Why Use PATHS?

1. Emotional literacy and social competence are as important for success as reading achievement.

2. Acquisition of SEL skills decreases risk factors (e.g., aggression, violence, and depression), increases protective factors, improves academic performance, and facilitates optimal brain development.

3. Social-emotional education is important for all children.

4. PATHS and Preschool PATHS, universal prevention/intervention programs used by teachers in elementary classroom and preschool settings, are effective for both regular and special education and for both prevention and intervention.

5. PATHS and Preschool PATHS have been delivered effectively to almost one million students in the U.S. and many other countries.

6. PATHS has received high recognition and recommendations from numerous sources.

7. Teacher and staff training in the use of PATHS and Preschool PATHS is available.

8. Careful randomized research consistently shows that PATHS (1) increases protective factors such as emotional understanding, social-cognition, and social competence; (2) decreases externalizing problems such as aggression; (3) reduces internalizing distress; (4) promotes a caring classroom environment; (5) has positive effects on neurocognitive development; and (6) improves academic performance.

9. Research also shows that improvement in executive (prefrontal lobe) functioning is directly related to reductions in behavioral problems following PATHS implementation.

10. PATHS and Preschool PATHS are based on five conceptual models, including brain development; our eclectic conceptual approach and the fact that children and teachers enjoy these programs are two key reasons for their effectiveness.

Developmental models indicate that children's ability to understand and discuss emotions is related to their automatic utilization of internal language (i.e., verbal "inner speech") to mediate emotion regulation, maintain self-control, and inhibit aggressive behavior. Moreover, children's ability to understand their own and others' emotions is a central component of effective problem-solving and social interactions. When emotional awareness is not sufficiently emphasized in SEL programs, children can model optimal problem-solving skills as a cognitive exercise, but do not utilize them when strong emotions are experienced during real life experiences. Children must be able to effectively regulate their emotional arousal and accurately process the emotional content of a situation in order to successfully employ cognition to solve a problem.

Additionally, if children misidentify their own feelings or those of others (e.g., the misinterpretation of social cues and feeling disrespected are common causes of gang shootings), they are likely to generate maladaptive solutions to a problem, regardless of their intellectual capacities. In addition, motivation to engage in the discussion of feelings and to problem solve in interpersonal contexts is also greatly impacted by the modeling and reinforcement of others. Although emotional understanding is implicit in many SEL models, they are rarely a central focus (Kusché & Greenberg, 2006b).

Based on the importance of verbal mediation and interhemispheric communication, verbal identification and labeling of emotions is emphasized throughout PATHS. Students and teachers use Feeling Face cards during the first few grades of PATHS (PreK through Grade 2); these cards include both the facial drawing of each affect (recognition of which is mediated by the right hemisphere) with its printed label (which is mediated by the left), which optimizes hemispheric integration. In addition, a color-coded differentiation of comfortable (yellow) versus uncomfortable (blue) feelings is incorporated. Teachers encourage children to discuss feelings, experiences, opinions, and needs during lessons, in recollection, and when they are actually occurring. They also provide explanations of actual experiences, label emotions (including their own), promote the use of imagination, and model problem-solving cognitions (which affects mirror neurons). Because research strongly suggests that learning experiences in the context of meaningful relationships influence the development of neural networks, PATHS strategies are designed to optimize the nature and quality of teacher-child and peer-peer interactions (Kusché & Greenberg, 2006a). When children feel listened to, supported, and respected by both teachers and peers, they internalize being valued, cared for, appreciated, and part of a social group. This, in turn, motivates children to value, care for, and appreciate themselves, their environment, their social groups, other people, and their world (a crucial antidote to violence).

Internalization of prosocial values is further encouraged by helping children to understand why they are important and how their behavior affects others. For example, students discuss the consequences of good versus bad manners and evaluate why good manners are important (e.g., the way we act affects how other people feel). In this way, students come to "own" the concepts as belonging to themselves (i.e., they internalize them), which minimizes resistance and defiance to adopting positive values; as a result, children ultimately choose to use good manners voluntarily because *they* believe that is the right thing to do.

The need to belong to a group (originally tribe) is a powerful, biologically-based deterrent to the enactment of violent behaviors towards other group members. In PATHS, we encourage classroom cohesion through regular activities including ongoing complimenting, stories, and teaching sharing as a positive endeavor. However, the same need for group membership can also promote destructive actions and maltreatment towards members of "other" groups (e.g., the basis of gang warfare, genocide, etc.). Thus, in addition to reinforcing classroom inclusion, we also emphasize an awareness of larger group memberships (i.e., neighborhood, global community, and as part of life on our planet) and the nurturing of compassion towards others.

Implementation & Staff Training

We recommend that implementation of PreK/K PATHS begin with all of the children enrolled at the center. Grade Level PATHS, on the other hand, can be used solely in individual class-rooms, but is most effectively utilized on a school (or district) wide basis. There are numerous models for scaling up across an entire school and PATHS has been initiated in a variety of ways including whole-school training as well as building the process one or a few grade levels at a time. When beginning a schoolwide implementation of PATHS, we suggest beginning in the earlier grades (K–2) during the first year and expanding by one additional grade each year as the children matriculate. However, decisions regarding implementation can be made with indi-vidual consultation to fit the unique environments of different school settings.

Teacher and staff training in the use of PATHS are optional, but highly recommended, as it will go far to ensure the highest quality implementation. Trainings are provided on site and are conducted by certified PATHS trainers (http://pathstraining.com). Workshops generally take place over two consecutive days and can accommodate up to 30 participants (teachers, staff, prin-cipals, etc.). PATHS trainers also provide ongoing phone/Internet support. We strongly encour-age the attendance of school principals from each site, as our research (see below) has shown a very strong effect for the role of the principal (i.e., the more active the principal in supporting PATHS, the more effective the implementation).

In successive years, experienced teachers and support staff are encouraged to take on the roles of co-trainers for new teachers in the school. Thus, over a two or so year period, local trainers should have assumed control of the training and conduct of the curriculum implementation with technical assistance provided by outside trainers on an as-needed basis. (See Greenberg, Kusché, & Mihalic, 1998, 2002, for a more extensive discussion of PATHS and issues in implementation.) A summary of implementation guidelines can be found in Table 32.2.

Awards and Recommendations

PATHS has been recognized as a highly effective, evidence-based program by numerous state governments, the U.S. federal government (e.g., U.S. Department of Education, Centers for Disease Control and Prevention, U.S. Surgeon General's Report on Youth Violence), and other countries. PATHS is also the only elementary SEL program with proven effectiveness for both regular and special education (e.g., learning disabled, serious behavior disorder, deaf and hard of hearing) that has achieved "Blueprints" status (http://www.colorado.edu/cspv/blueprints/mod-elprograms/PATHS.html; Greenberg, Kusché, & Mihalic, 1998, 2002).

Research and Program Effectiveness

Increasing Protective Factors and Reducing Maladaptive Outcomes

Several randomized controlled trials of PATHS have been conducted with different child popu-lations: Typical children in regular education, children with special education needs, and those who are deaf/hearing impaired (Greenberg & Kusché, 1993, 1998; Greenberg, Kusché, Cook, & Quamma, 1995; Kam, Greenberg, & Kusché, 2004; Riggs, Greenberg, Kusché & Pentz, 2006). All of these clinical trials showed that children who received at least one school year of PATHS significantly improved emotional recognition and understanding, as well as social problem-solving skills. Moreover, teachers reported significant improvements in self-control, emotional understanding, and ability to tolerate frustration for both regular education and deaf children. Cognitive testing indicated that use of PATHS with both normal and special needs children decreased impulsivity, improved working memory, and increased ability to integrate informa-

Table 32.2 Implications for Practice: Using PATHS

1.	*Evaluate Institutional Ecology*

1. *Evaluate Institutional Ecology*

   a. Are teachers ready and willing to teach PATHS?

   b. Does the principal/director support implementation?

   c. Is the district/ center committed to implementation?

   d. Is funding available? If not, what are the options? (e.g., grants)

2. *Ascertain Implementation and Training Needs (First Year)*

   a. Which grades will implement PATHS?

   b. Will teacher training be utilized? If so, when will workshop(s) be held?

   c. Will ongoing technical support from the trainer be arranged? If so, how will time be apportioned?

   d. Will a staff member serve as faculty consultant?

   e. Will regular meetings for ongoing support be held for PATHS teachers? If so, when and how often will they convene?

   f. How will parents be informed and/or involved?

3. *Determine Practical Considerations for Each Classroom*

   a. When and how often will PATHS be taught?

   b. How long will PATHS sessions be?

   c. Where will PATHS charts and posters be displayed?

   d. How will PATHS be integrated with academic or other subjects?

   e. How will the teacher communicate with parents about PATHS?

4. *Prepare Overall Implementation for Each Classroom*

   a. Review Table of Contents and skim through PATHS for overall perspective.

   b. Determine lessons to be covered during the school year.

   c. Consider ways for new students to be integrated into ongoing PATHS lessons.

   d. Reproduce or buy Feeling Faces for all lessons prior to beginning PATHS.

5. *Plan Ahead for Each PATHS Session*

   a. Read several lessons ahead to attain a sense of continuity.

   b. Read through each lesson at least once prior to teaching it.

   c. Estimate the number of PATHS sessions needed for each lesson.

   d. Refer to the materials section of each lesson for requisite preparation.

   e. Obtain any desired supplementary material.

6. *After the First Year*

   a. Which new grades will receive PATHS?

   b. How will teachers coordinate curricular transitions from one year to the next?

   c. How will new teachers be trained?

   d. How will new students be integrated into classes with previous PATHS experience?

tion and plan ahead when solving complex tasks (Greenberg & Kusché, 1998; Riggs, Greenberg, Kusché, & Pentz, 2006). Improvements in cognitive flexibility and reading achievement were also found with deaf children (Greenberg & Kusché, 1998).

Findings also indicated that PATHS significantly increased protective factors and reduced behavioral and emotional problems. Significant reductions in aggressive and disruptive behaviors

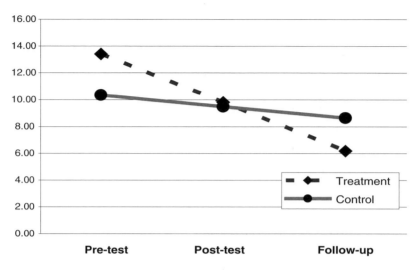

Figure 32.1 Special needs students who received PATHS showed a decreased trajectory for problem behavior two years post-PATHS. (Kam, Greenberg, & Kusché, 2004)

were reported by teachers for both regular and special needs students at one year follow-up (see Figure 32.1) (Kam, Greenberg, & Kusché, 2004; Riggs, Greenberg, Kusché, & Pentz, 2006). In addition, significant decreases in depressive symptoms were found in teacher ratings and self-reports of students who had high pre-test levels of depression (Kam, Greenberg, & Kusché, 2004).

Fast Track Project

Fast Track was a large, multifaceted intervention in four American cities (Seattle, WA; Nashville, TN; Durham, NC; and rural Pennsylvania) designed to reduce serious aggression and conduct problems. Approximately 14 schools (intervention and control) in high crime neighborhoods were included in each site. PATHS served as the universal intervention (five other programs were also utilized only with children with behavioral problems). Three cohorts of first graders of mixed ethnicity (approximately 7,000 children) received PATHS over three successive years (198 program classrooms and 180 matched comparisons). The effects of PATHS were assessed at the end of first grade through the use of three types of measures: (a) peer sociometric interviews, (b) teacher ratings of each child's behavior, and (c) independent ratings of classroom atmosphere. Findings at the end of first grade indicated improved social adaptation at multiple levels in PATHS schools. Relative to control classrooms, children receiving PATHS showed lower mean levels of peer-nominated aggression, hyperactivity, and disruptive behavior and higher numbers of prosocial peer-nominations. Teachers rated PATHS students as having less disruptive behavior, and independent observers rated PATHS classrooms as having a more positive atmosphere (Conduct Problems Prevention Research Group, 1999).

A second study with Fast Track schools involved longitudinal analysis with 2937 children who remained in the same intervention or control schools for first, second, and third grade (Conduct Problems Prevention Research Group, 2010). At the end of third grade, PATHS was found to be effective for both promoting social competence and reducing aggressive behavior problems. Significant main effects for intervention were found for all three teacher-rated outcomes (Authority Acceptance, Cognitive Concentration, and Social Competence) and for two of the three peer-rated outcomes for boys (aggressive and hyperactive-disruptive nominations). The FAST Track study of Grade Level PATHS was the largest study of an SEL curriculum to demonstrate the efficacy of a school-based, universal intervention during the elementary school years.

Improvements in Frontal Lobe Functioning

In order to test our mediation hypotheses regarding recruitment of language and prefrontal cortical control for regulating emotions, a randomized controlled study of 318 second-and third-grade children with one year of PATHS intervention was conducted (Riggs, Greenberg, Kusché, & Pentz, 2006). Internalizing and externalizing behavior problems were rated by classroom teachers, while prefrontal control (i.e., executive functions) was assessed in children with two well-known tests of inhibitory control and verbal fluency related to activation of the anterior cingulate and dorso-lateral prefrontal cortex (Ravnkilde, Videbech, Rosenberg, Gjeede & Gade, 2002). Intervention children were rated by teachers at one year follow-up as having significantly fewer externalizing and internalizing problems. Similarly, PATHS also led to significantly greater improvements with regard to verbal fluency and inhibitory control at post test. Finally, using structural equation models, findings demonstrated that one important way in which PATHS led to lower rates of behavioral and internalizing problems was through improvements in executive functions. In other words, PATHS builds cognitive abilities that children recruit to manage their emotions and behavior.

These findings are especially exciting, as they provide empirical support for one of the neuropsychological theories underlying PATHS, that is, that improvement in frontal lobe executive functioning directly relates to reductions in behavioral problems. As previously noted, prefrontal lobe deficits are associated with higher levels of impulsive and aggressive behavior, and PATHS is one of the first models shown to successfully improve prefrontal cortical functioning (Riggs & Greenberg, 2009).

International Replications

Several independently implemented studies have also shown that PATHS significantly reduces risk factors and increases protective factors. A quasi-experimental study conducted in The Netherlands with 141 boys (mean age = 7.2 years) showed a significant reduction in aggression after children received PATHS for one year (Louwe, van Overveld, Merk, Orobio de Castro, & Koops, 2007). The effectiveness of PATHS for Aftercare (a 12-lesson version developed for afterschool contexts, Kusché & Greenberg, 1995) was examined in a quasi-experimental study of 93 children in Southern Germany (Hacker, Lösel, Stemmler, Jaursch, Runkel, & Beelmann, 2007). A significant reduction in problem behavior was found at post-test and maintained at one year follow-up. Finally, a quasi-experimental design was utilized with 55 deaf children in eight primary schools in Southern England (Hindley & Reed, 1999). Significant differences were found between intervention and control groups in emotional adjustment, ability to accurately recognize and label emotions, and positive self-image one year after implementation.

Preschool PATHS

The effects of PreK/K PATHS have been subject to two evaluations. In the first, a randomized controlled trial was conducted involving 248 children of varied ethnicity in 20 Head Start Classrooms in urban and rural Pennsylvania (Domitrovich, Cortes, & Greenberg, 2007). Both teachers and parents reported that children receiving Preschool PATHS evidenced significantly better social skills in comparison to controls at the end of one year of implementation. In addition,

PATHS children showed significant improvements in identifying emotions, both expressively and receptively. Furthermore, intervention children were less likely to misidentify facial expressions as being angry (i.e., they showed less "anger bias" which has been linked to behavior problems, Schultz, Izard, & Ackerman, 2000).

A second cluster-randomized clinical trial was recently completed using a randomized design with 20 Head Start classrooms in both rural and urban Pennsylvania communities (Bierman et al., 2008). The study involved 250 4-year-old children over 2 cohorts. Posttest findings indicated significant effects on children's social-emotional skills and social behavior. Children in the intervention classrooms showed significantly greater gains on measures of social knowledge and problem solving compared with children in the control classrooms. Teachers rated intervention children as showing greater levels of self-control and emotion regulation and lower levels of anxious/withdrawn and aggressive behaviors. Independent classroom observations were consistent with teacher reports and also showed lower levels of off-task behavior in the intervention classrooms. Preschool PATHS appeared to be equally effective for both genders and at all levels of risk.

Administrative Leadership

Teachers do not work in a vacuum, and effective principals are leaders who promote positive social climates and prosocial norms in their schools. Moreover, the readiness and willingness of schools to undertake new interventions and forward planning on a school and/or districtwide basis are vitally important for the success of SEL programs (Weissberg & Elias, 1993). Principal support and the quality of teacher implementation at the classroom level were both critical factors in determining the success of PATHS in a group of inner-city public schools (Kam, Greenberg, & Walls, 2003). Significant decreases in student aggression were *only* found in those settings where *both* principal support and teacher implementation were positive. This is consistent with literature indicating principal support as an important factor in the success of curricular innovation (Hallinger & Heck, 1996; Leithwood & Duke, 1999).

Summary

PATHS and PreK/K PATHS are comprehensive, universal programs designed to promote emotional literacy, improve social competence, reduce behavioral problems, decrease emotional distress, enrich educational environments, improve academic performance, and facilitate brain development in preschool and elementary school-aged children. Both curricula are effective for prevention and intervention in regular and special education, which is especially important because *all* children need comprehensive social-emotional education. Careful randomized research has shown that PATHS (a) increases protective factors such as emotional understanding, social-cognition, and social competence; (b) decreases externalizing problems such as aggression; (c) reduces internalizing distress; (d) promotes a caring classroom environment; (e) has positive effects on neurocognitive development; and (f) improves academic performance. We believe that the integration of a number of different theoretical models and the fact that most children and teachers enjoy PATHS both contribute to this success.

References

Bierman, K. L., Domitrovich, C. E., Nix, R. L., Gest, S. D., Welsh, J. A., Greenberg, M. T., Blair, C., Nelson, K. & Gill, S. (2008). Promoting academic and social-emotional school readiness: The Head Start REDI Program. *Child Development, 79,* 1802–1817. doi: 10.1111/j.1467-8624.2008.01227.x

Brower, M. C., & Price, B. H. (2001). Neuropsychiatry of frontal lobe dysfunction in violent and criminal behaviour: a critical review. *Journal of Neurology, Neurosurgery, & Psychiatry, 71*, 720–726. doi:10.1136/jnnp.71.6.720

Conduct Problems Prevention Research Group. (1999). Initial impact of the Fast Track prevention trial for conduct problems: II. Classroom effects. *Journal of Consulting and Clinical Psychology, 67*, 648–657. doi: 10.1037/0022-006X.67.5.648

Conduct Problems Prevention Research Group. (2010). The effects of a multi-year randomized clinical trial of a universal social-emotional learning program: The role of student and school characteristics. *Journal of Consulting and Clinical Psychology, 78*, 156–168. doi: 10.1037/a0018607

Domitrovich, C. E., Cortes, R. C., & Greenberg, M. T. (2007). Improving young children's social and emotional competence: A randomized trial of the Preschool PATHS Curriculum. *Journal of Primary Prevention, 28*, 67–91. doi: 10.1007/s10935-007-0081-0

Domitrovich, C., Greenberg, M. T., Kusché, C. A., & Cortes, R. (2004). *Preschool PATHS*. South Deerfield, MA: Channing-Bete Co.

Durlak, J. A., Weissberg, R. P., Dymnicki, A. B., Taylor, R. D., & Schellinger. K. B. (2011). The impact of enhancing students' social and emotional learning: A meta-analysis of school-based universal interventions. *Child Development, 82*, 405–432. doi: 10.1111/j.1467-8624.2010.01564.x

Goleman, D. (1995). *Emotional intelligence*. New York: Bantam Books.

Greenberg, M. T., & Kusché, C. A. (1993). *Promoting social and emotional development in deaf children: The PATHS Project*. Seattle: University of Washington Press.

Greenberg, M. T., & Kusché, C. A. (1998). Preventive intervention for school-aged deaf children: The PATHS Curriculum. *Journal of Deaf Studies and Deaf Education, 3*, 49–63.

Greenberg, M. T., & Kusché, C. A. (2006). Building social and emotional competence: The PATHS Curriculum. In S. R. Jimerson & M. J. Furlong (Eds.), *The handbook of school violence and school safety: From research to practice* (pp. 395–412). Mahwah, NJ: Erlbaum.

Greenberg, M. T., Kusché, C. A., & Conduct Problems Prevention Research Group. (2011). *Grade level PATHS (grades 3–5)*. South Deerfield, MA: Channing-Bete Co.

Greenberg, M. T., Kusché, C. A., Cook, E. T., & Quamma, J. P. (1995). Promoting emotional competence in school-aged children: The effects of the PATHS curriculum. *Development and Psychopathology, 7*, 117–136. doi: 10.1017/S0954579400006374

Greenberg, M. T., Kusché, C. A., & Mihalic, S.F. (1998, 2002). *Promoting Alternative Thinking Strategies (PATHS): Blueprints for violence prevention, book ten*. Blueprints for Violence Prevention Series (D. S. Elliott, Series Editor). Boulder: Center for the Study and Prevention of Violence, Institute of Behavioral Science, University of Colorado.

Greenberg, M. T., Kusché, C. A., & Riggs, N. (2004). The PATHS curriculum: Theory and research on neurocognitive development and school success. In J. E. Zins, R. P. Weissberg, M. C. Wang, & H. J. Walberg (Eds.), *Building academic success on social and emotional learning: What does the research say?* (pp. 170–188). New York: Teachers College Press.

Hacker, S., Lösel, F., Stemmler, M., Jaursch, S., Runkel, D., & Beelmann, A. (2007).Training im Problemlösen (TIP): Implementation und Evaluation eines sozial-kognitiven Kompetenztrainings für Kinder [Training in problem solving: Implementation and evaluation of a social/cognitive skills training for the Heilpedagogische (good pedagogy for children) research for children]. *Heilpädagogische Forschung, 33*, 11–21.

Hallinger, P., & Heck, R. H. (1996). Reassessing the principal's role in school effectiveness: A review of empirical research, 1980–1995. *Educational Administration Quarterly, 32*, 5–44.

Hindley, P., & Reed, R. (1999). Promoting Alternative Thinking Strategies (PATHS) mental health promotion with deaf children in school. In S. Decker, S. Kirby, A. Greenwood, & D. Moores (Eds.), *Taking children seriously* (pp. 134–158). London: Cassell.

Kam, C., M. Greenberg, M. T., & Kusché, C. A. (2004). Sustained effects of the PATHS curriculum on the social and psychological adjustment of children in special education. *Journal of Emotional and Behavioral Disorders, 12*, 66–78. doi: 10.1177/10634266040120020101

Kam, C. M., Greenberg, M. T., & Walls, C. T. (2003). Examining the role of implementation quality in school-based prevention using the PATHS Curriculum. *Prevention Science, 4*, 55–63. doi: 10.1023/A:1021786811186

Kusché, C. A. (1984). The *understanding of emotion concepts by deaf children: An assessment of an affective curriculum*. (Unpublished Doctoral Dissertation.) University Microfilms International, DAO 56952.

Kusché, C. A. (2002). Psychoanalysis as prevention: Using PATHS to enhance ego development, object relationships, and cortical integration in children. *Journal of Applied Psychoanalytic Studies, 4*, 283–301.

Kusché, C. A., & Greenberg, M. T. (1994). *The PATHS (Promoting Alternative Thinking Strategies) Curriculum*. South Deerfield, MA: Channing-Bete Co.

Kusché, C. A., & Greenberg, M. T. (1995). *PATHS for aftercare*. Unpublished manuscript.

Kusché, C. A., & Greenberg, M. T. (2006a). Brain development and social-emotional learning: An introduction for educators. In M. J. Elias & H. Arnold (Eds.), *The educator's guide to emotional intelligence and academic achievement: Social emotional learning in the classroom* (pp. 15–34). Thousand Oaks, CA: Corwin Press.

Kusché, C. A., & Greenberg, M. T. (2006b). Teaching emotional literacy in elementary school classrooms: The PATHS Curriculum. In M. J. Elias & H. Arnold, (Eds.), *The educator's guide to emotional intelligence and academic achievement: Social emotional learning in the classroom* (pp. 150–160). Thousand Oaks, CA: Corwin Press.

Kusché, C. A., Greenberg, M. T., & Conduct Problems Prevention Research Group. (2011). *Grade level PATHS (grades 1–2)*. South Deerfield, MA: Channing-Bete Co.

Kusché, C. A., Riggs, R. S., & Greenberg, M. T. (1999). PATHS: Using analytic knowledge to teach emotional literacy. *The American Psychoanalyst, 33*, 20–21.

Leithwood, K. A., & Duke, D. L. (1999). A century's quest to understand school leadership. In J. Murphy & K. S. Louis (Eds.), *Handbook of research on educational administration* (2nd ed., pp. 45–72). San Francisco, CA: Jossey-Bass.

Lieberman, M. D., Eisenberger, N. I., Crockett, M. J., Tom, S. M., Pfeifer, J. H., & Way, B. M. (2007). Putting feeling into words. *Psychological Science, 18*, 421–428. doi: 10.1111/j.1467-9280.2007.01916.x

Louwe, J. J., van Overveld, C. W., Merk, W., Orobio de Castro, B., & Koops, W. (2007). De invloed van het Programma Alternatieve Denkstrategieeen op proactieve en reactieve aggresie bij yongens en het primair onderwijs: effecten naar een jaar [The effect of PATHS on pro-active and re-active aggression in boys in primary education: results after one year]. *Pedagogische Studien, 84*, 277–292.

Mayer, J. D., & Salovey, P. (1997). What is emotional intelligence? In P. Salovey (Ed.), *Emotional development and emotional literacy* (pp. 3–31). New York: Basic Books.

Ravnkilde, B., Videbech, P., Rosenberg, R., Gjeede, G., & Gade, P. (2002). Putative tests of frontal lobe function: a PET-study of brain activation during Stroop's Test and verbal fluency .*Journal of Clinical Experimental Neurpsychology, 24*, 534–547.

Riggs, N. R., Greenberg, M. T., Kusché, C. A., & Pentz, M. A. (2006). The mediational role of neurocognition in the behavioral outcomes of a social-emotional prevention program in elementary school students: Effects of the PATHS curriculum. *Prevention Science, 7*, 91–102. doi: 10.1007/s11121-005-0022-1

Riggs, N. R., & Greenberg, M. T. (2009). Neurocognition as a moderator and mediatory in adolescent substance misuse prevention. *The American Journal of Drug and Alcohol Abuse, 35*, 209–213. doi: 10.1080/00952990903005940

Robin, A. L., Schneider, M., & Dolnick, M. (1976). The Turtle Technique: An extended case study of self-control in the classroom. *Psychology in the Schools, 13*, 449–453.

Schore, A. (1996). The experience-dependent maturation of a regulatory system in the orbital prefrontal cortex and the origin of developmental psychopathology. *Developmental Psychopathology, 8*, 59–87. doi: 10.1017/S0954579400006970

Schultz, D., Izard, C. E., & Ackerman, B. P. (2000). Children's anger attribution bias: Relations to family environment and social adjustment. *Social Development, 9*, 284–301. doi: 10.1111/1467-9507.00126

U.S. Department of Justice, Bureau of Justice Statistics. (2007). *School crime supplement (SCS) to the National Crime Victimization Survey*. Washington, D.C.: Government Printing Office.

Weissberg, R. P., & Elias, M. J. (1993). Enhancing young people's social competence and health behavior: An important challenge for educators, scientists, policy makers, and funders. *Applied & Preventive Psychology: Current Scientific Perspectives, 3*, 179–190. doi: 10.1016/S0962-1849(05)80088-5

Weissberg, R. P., & Greenberg, M. T. (1998). School and community competence-enhancement and prevention programs. In W. Damon (Series Ed.) & I. E. Sigel & K. A. Renninger (Vol. Eds.), *Handbook of child psychology: Vol 4. Child psychology in practice* (5th ed., pp. 877–954). New York: Wiley.

33

School-Wide Positive Behavioral Interventions and Supports

Proven Practices and Future Directions

Jeffrey R. Sprague

THE UNIVERSITY OF OREGON INSTITUTE ON VIOLENCE AND DESTRUCTIVE BEHAVIOR, EUGENE

Robert H. Horner

THE UNIVERSITY OF OREGON INSTITUTE ON EDUCATIONAL AND COMMUNITY SUPPORTS , EUGENE

Abstract

This chapter describes the features of a schoolwide system for positive behavior interventions and supports. Implementation steps are discussed to build both a positive schoolwide social culture, and the capacity to support individual students with more intense support needs. This chapter highlights that (a) problem behavior in schools is both a significant social challenge and a barrier to effective learning, (b) traditional "get tough" strategies have not proven effective, (c) the foundation for all behavior support in schools begins with establishing a positive social culture by defining, teaching and rewarding appropriate behaviors, (d) additional behavior support procedures based on behavior analysis principles are needed for children with more intense behavior support needs, and (e) school personnel are demonstrating both the ability to collect and use quality improvement data systems, and the value of those systems for improving schools.

To prevent minor, as well as serious, antisocial behavior, educators around the world are turning to a comprehensive and proactive approach to behavior management commonly referred to as School-Wide Positive Behavior Interventions and Supports (SWPBIS; Simonsen, Sugai, & Negron, 2008; Sprague & Golly, 2004; Sugai & Horner, 2010). SWPBIS is based on the assumption that actively teaching and acknowledging expected behavior can change the extent to which students expect appropriate behavior from themselves and each other. When consistent expectations are established by all adults, the proportion of students with serious behavior problems will be reduced and the school's overall social climate will improve (Bradshaw, Koth, Bevans, Ialongo & Leaf, 2008; Bradshaw, Koth, Thornton, & Leaf, 2009; Colvin, Kame'enui, & Sugai, 1993).

The procedures that define SWPBIS are organized around three main themes: prevention, multi-tiered support, and data-based decision making. Investing in *prevention* of problem behavior involves (a) defining and teaching a set of core behavioral expectations (e.g., be safe, respectful, responsible), (b) acknowledging and rewarding appropriate behavior (e.g., compliance to school rules, safe and respectful peer to peer interactions, and academic effort/engagement), (c) systematically supervising students in classrooms and common areas, and (d) establishing and implementing a consistent continuum of consequences for problem behavior. The focus is on establishing a positive social climate, in which behavioral expectations for students are highly predictable, directly taught, consistently acknowledged, and actively monitored.

Multi-tiered support is available beyond the prevention level for those students at-risk for, or engaging in, antisocial behavior. The greater the student's need for support the more intense the support provided. Within the SWPBIS approach, emphasis has been on using the principles and procedures of applied behavior analysis as a foundation for defining the antecedents and maintaining consequences for behavioral problems and completing functional behavioral assessments to confirm these relationships. These assessments, in conjunction with person-centered planning (Eber et al., 2009), are used to design effective and efficient procedures for addressing patterns of unacceptable behavior.

Data-based decision making is a theme that is interwoven throughout SWPBIS, and builds on the assumption that staff members, family and students will be most effective in the design of preventive and reactive supports if they have access to regular, accurate information about the behavior of students. It is equally important to regularly assess adherence or fidelity to support plans, and to share those data with implementers. The value of data for decision making is emphasized for both the design of initial support systems, and the ongoing assessment and adaptation of support strategies (Sugai & Horner, 2009). The SWPBIS approach includes adoption of practical strategies for collecting, summarizing, reporting, and using behavioral and fidelity data on regular cycles.

Evidence suggests that high fidelity and sustained use of SWPBIS practices can alter the trajectory of at-risk children toward destructive outcomes, and prevent the onset of risk behavior in typically developing children. It is expected that effective and sustained implementation of SWPBIS will create a more responsive school climate that supports the twin goals of schooling for all children: *academic achievement* and *positive social development* (Walker, Ramsey, & Gresham, 2004; Zins, Weissberg, Wang, & Walberg, 2004).

Implementing and sustaining an organized, schoolwide system for providing behavior supports and teaching social behavior is the foundation for effective prevention efforts in schools. In addition to the direct benefit it has on student behavior in school, such a system creates the context for school-based efforts to support effective parenting (Dishion & Kavanagh, 2003; Metzler et al., 2008). When school personnel have a shared vision of the kind of social behavior and environment they want to promote, they are in a position to inform and collaborate with families in creating the same kind of supportive environment at home and in the community. When educators are clear about how to use rules, positive reinforcement, and mild, consistent negative consequences to support positive behavioral development, they are better able to coordinate their efforts with those of parents. As a result, parents will know more about their children's behavior in school and will be able to provide the same types of supports and consequences that the school is providing. In the same manner, parents can provide valuable input regarding the features of support plans that are feasible and acceptable from their perspective.

As of 2010, over 13,300 schools across the country were actively implementing SWPBIS. These schools report reductions in problem behavior, improved perceptions of school safety, and improved academic outcomes (Bradshaw et al., 2008; Horner et al., 2009). This chapter describes how to establish and implement a schoolwide positive behavior intervention and support system, and outlines the research evidence supporting its adoption and implementation. To first establish the context in which SWPBIS is being adopted, we begin by framing the challenge that antisocial behavior presents in schools.

The Challenge of Antisocial Behavior in Schools

Growing numbers of children and youth are exposed to a host of risk factors such as poverty, abuse, neglect, criminal behavior or substance use by parents, harsh and inconsistent parenting practices, and limited exposure to language and reading prior to the beginning of their school careers (Patterson, Reid, & Dishion, 1992). As a result, the number of children and youth with aggressive, noncompliant, and acting-out behaviors in schools has been rising steadily (Loeber & Farrington, 2001). Many students are entering the public school system unprepared for the experience of schooling and often bring emerging antisocial behavior patterns with them. Antisocial behavior and high levels of aggression evidenced early in a child's life are among the best predictors of academic failure and delinquency in later years (Patterson et al., 1992). If these students do not receive key support services and protective factors, it is unlikely that they will be able to get off this destructive path, if it has not been accomplished by the end of the primary grades (Biglan, Wang, & Walberg, 2003). Rather, these individuals will likely require continued behavioral supports and social and services (e.g., mental health, welfare, criminal justice) throughout their lives to reduce the ongoing harm they cause to themselves and others.

Antisocial behavior patterns compete directly with the instructional mission of schools. The result is decreased academic achievement and a lower quality of life for students and staff members alike (Metzler et al., 2008), illustrating the clear link that exists between antisocial behavior in the school, school violence, and academic achievement. It is not possible to achieve national educational goals and meaningful school reform without addressing these disturbing conditions in a comprehensive manner (Colvin et al., 1993; Elias et al., 1997). SWPBIS systems and practices must be a component of the mosaic of school, community and family mosaic prevention opportunities, and cannot address the entire scope of the problems described above.

Some School Practices Can Contribute to Antisocial Behaviors

Many school practices contribute to the development and prevalence of antisocial behavior and the potential for violence. Because of the historical emphasis on detecting individual child or youth characteristics that predict antisocial behavior and violence, many important systemic variables are often overlooked as contributors (Colvin et al., 1993; Hawkins, Catalano, Kosterman, Abbott, & Hill, 1999; Mayer, 1995; Walker et al., 1996). These include, among others:

1. ineffective instruction that results in academic failure;
2. failure to individualize instruction and behavior support to adapt to individual differences (e.g., ethnic and cultural differences, gender, disability);
3. lack of administrator involvement, leadership and support;
4. inconsistent and low quality implementation among staff members;
5. inconsistent and punitive classroom and behavior management practices;
6. lack of opportunity to learn and practice prosocial interpersonal and self-management skills; and
7. failure to assist students from at-risk (e.g., poverty, racial/ethnic minority members) backgrounds to bond and engage with the schooling process.

Common Response to Behavioral Problems: Exclude Students with Office Referrals, Suspensions, and Expulsions.

Often when a student misbehaves, the first line of response involves increasing monitoring and supervision of the student, restating rules, and delivering sanctions (e.g., referrals to the office, out of school suspension, and/or loss of privileges). Teachers or administrators may come to a point of frustration and attempt to establish a "bottom line" for disruptive students (usually out of class referrals, in or out of school suspensions, and expulsions). Unfortunately, these "get tough" responses produce immediate, short-lived relief for the classroom or school but do not facilitate the progress of the student who may already be disengaged from the schooling process.

Paradoxically, while punishment practices may appear to work in the short term, they may merely remove the student for a period of time, thus providing a brief respite but no real long term benefit for school personnel or the student. All too often, these practices also can lead school personnel to assign exclusive responsibility for behavioral change to the student or family and thereby prevent meaningful school engagement and development of solutions. The use of sanctions, without an accompanying program of teaching and recognition for expected positive behavior, may merely displace the problem elsewhere (to the home or the community). There is little evidence of the long-term effect of these practices in reducing antisocial behavior (Irvin, Tobin, Sprague, Sugai, & Vincent, 2004; Skiba & Peterson, 1999). In fact, evidence suggests that schools using punishment practices alone promote more antisocial behavior than those with a firm, but fair discipline system (Mayer, 1995; Skiba & Peterson, 1999). Research shows clearly that schools using only punishment techniques tend to have increased rates of vandalism, aggression, truancy, and ultimately school dropout (Mayer, 1995). In addition, these types of sanctions are disproportionately applied to students of minority status, which increasingly results in legal actions against schools, and school districts (Skiba et al., in press; Skiba & Rausch, 2006; Skiba, Michael, Nardo, & Peterson, 2002).

For students with chronic problem behavior these negative practices are more likely to impair child–adult relationships and attachment to schooling rather than reduce the likelihood of problem behavior (Walker et al., 2005). Punishment alone, without a balance of support and efforts to restore school engagement, weakens academic outcomes and maintains the antisocial trajectory of at risk students. Instead, the discipline process should help students accept responsibility, place high value on academic engagement and achievement, teach alternative ways to behave, and focus on restoring a positive environment and social relationships in the school.

If Not Punishment, Then What Is the Solution?

Research strongly suggests that if schools raise their level of achievement, behavior decreases; and if schools work to decrease behavior problems, academics improve (Hawkins, Catalano, Kosterman, Abbott, & Hill, 1999). *So why not do both?* Schools can serve as an ideal setting to organize efforts against the increasing problems of children and youth who display antisocial behavior patterns (Mayer, 1995; Sprague & Walker, 2005; Sugai & Horner, 1999). We next describe the conceptual and practical basis for this assertion.

Conceptual Basis for SWPBIS

A solid research base exists to guide an analysis of the administrative, teaching, and management practices in a school and design alternatives to ineffective approaches. An important theme from this research is that no single intervention practice should be viewed as meeting all of the behavioral challenges in schools. Student behavior is complex and influenced by many variables within the school, within the family/community, and within the student. The behavior support strategies needed to establish a schoolwide social culture need to be supplemented with classroom management interventions and individualized supports for students with chronic and intense patterns of problem behavior. The range of student behavior support needs requires that *interventions target schoolwide, classroom and individual student support strategies*. Educators in today's schools must be supported with systematic professional development and ongoing coaching to adopt and sustain effective; cost-efficient practices in this regard (Gottfredson, 1997; Gottfredson, Gottfredson, & Czeh, 2000; Walker et al., 1996). A well-developed body of research evidence on school safety indicates that (a) early identification and intervention with at-risk children in schools is feasible; (b) the risk of dropping out of school, delinquency, violence, and other adjustment problems is high unless these children are helped; (c) academic recovery is difficult if early intervention is not provided; and (d) universal interventions need to be combined with interventions targeted to specific problems (Gottfredson, 2001; Osher, Bear, Sprague, & Doyle, 2010; Tolan, Gorman-Smith, & Henry, 2001). Effective schools have shared values regarding the school's mission and purpose, carry out multiple activities designed to promote prosocial behavior and connection to school traditions, and provide a caring nurturing social climate involving collegial relationships among adults and students (Bryk & Driscoll, 1988; Gottfredson et al., 2000; Scott & Eber, 2003).

Changing School Climate Is an Essential Element

The biggest challenge schools face is to enhance their overall capacity to create and sustain positive and behaviorally effective schools. Schools should provide schoolwide positive behavior interventions and supports at the point of school entry and continue implementing through high school (O'Donnell, Hawkins, Catalano, Abbott, & Day, 1995). It is never too late, nor never too early, to support children and youth in our schools (Loeber & Farrington, 1998). Research indicates that schools can create establish clear expectations for learning and positive behavior, while providing firm but fair responses to problem behavior. Students will be more motivated if they are in environments that are perceived as safe, positive, predictable, and fair (Osher et al., 2010). Increased motivation is associated with improved acquisition of skills that will be of value for years following formal education (Katz, 1997).

Thus, the challenge becomes how to develop schools capacity to adopt and sustain the processes, organizational structures, and systems that enable them to carry out these effective interventions (Gottfredson et al., 2000; Fixsen, Naoom, Blase, Friedman, & Wallace, 2005). The problem for schools is not the lack of efficacious programs (those that work), but rather it is one of effectiveness (helping typical schools adopt and carry out proven interventions).

Where to Start: No Child Left Behind Principles of Effectiveness

Education professionals may use the USDOE Office of Safe and Drug Free Schools "Principles of Effectiveness" as an organizing framework for planning and implementing whole-school approaches to safety and effectiveness. The principles recommend: (a) a local *needs assessment* of the risk and protective factors affecting the school, families, and the community (including the status of support systems); (b) establishment of *measurable goals and objectives* by the school that are integrated with school improvement planning; (c) selection of *scientifically-based and research-validated curricula and interventions*; and (d) implementation of a comprehensive and *rigorous evaluation plan,* which includes evaluation of inputs (resources, staff, materials), outputs (actual costs, description of the process of implementation), outcomes (e.g., student behavior change), and impact (overall satisfaction with project products and outcomes). In the next section, SWPBIS implementation and the Principles of Effectiveness as an organizing framework are introduced.

Implementing SWPBIS

SWPBIS is a systems-based approach that promotes safe, healthy, and successful schools. Researchers at the University of Oregon (see Sprague, Sugai, & Walker, 1998; Sprague et al., 2002; Sugai & Horner, 1999; Taylor-Greene et al., 1997; www.pbis.org) have tested the feasibility and efficacy of SWPBIS approaches in reducing school behavior problems and promoting a positive school climate. SWPBIS is a multiple system approach to addressing the problems posed by students displaying antisocial behaviors and coping with challenging forms of student behavior. The key practices of SWPBIS are:

- clear definitions of expected appropriate, positive behaviors are provided for students and staff members;
- clear definitions of problem behaviors and their consequences are defined for students and staff members;
- regularly scheduled instruction *and* assistance in desired positive social behaviors is provided that enables students to acquire the necessary skills for the desired behavior change;
- effective incentives and motivational systems are provided to encourage students to behave differently;
- staff members commit to staying with the intervention over the long term and to monitor, support, coach, debrief, and provide booster lessons for students as necessary to maintain the achieved gains;
- staff members receive training, feedback and coaching about effective implementation of the systems; and
- systems for measuring and monitoring the intervention's effectiveness are established and carried out.

The foundation for an effective and sustainable school discipline program is simple, but powerful when all the elements are in place (Sugai & Horner, 2002). We outline these foundation elements here.

Improving Discipline and School Climate Is a Top School Improvement Priority

First, the improvement of school discipline and climate should be one of the top school improvement goals. With competing resources and goals, if work in this area is not a priority, progress will be difficult. Schools also need assistance to quantify and make decisions about discipline and climate goals in the same manner as academic or attendance outcomes.

Administrator Leadership

Every school needs a principal committed to SWPBIS leadership and participation. In the absence of administrative leadership and district support (e.g., policy, fiscal) it will be difficult to effect broad-based changes. Hallinger and Heck (1998) reviewed the evidence on the principal's contribution to school effectiveness. They concluded that principals exercise a measurable effect on schooling effectiveness and student achievement. Kam, Greenberg, and Walls (2003), reported that the ability of principals to initiate and sustain innovations in their schools is related to successful program implementation. The length of time administrators have spent in the school setting and the leadership characteristics they show in maintaining good relations with teachers, parents, school boards, site councils, and students also are positively related to successful implementation outcomes. Gottfredson et al. (2000) and Ingersoll (2001) found that high levels of administrative support were also associated with reduced staff member turnover.

Commitment to Participate by All or "Most" Adults in the School

It is important to secure a commitment to implement the intervention by at least 80% of school staff members. Some schools have chosen to use a "vote" to assess this level of commitment. Our experiences have revealed some approaches that can move a group of colleagues toward program implementation (Embry, 2004).

- *Talk about cost and benefit.* All adults involved need to know the costs (time, funds) and benefits (reduced behavior, increased teaching time) of working to improve school discipline. For example, presentations by school leaders on the anticipated effects of program adoption (e.g., studies indicate that as discipline problems and referrals to the principal's office are dramatically reduced, teaching time is substantially increased (Scott & Barrett, 2004)).
- *Emphasize the long-term benefits.* It also is useful to discuss the "higher good" of prevention and how much your colleagues value such outcomes as better academic achievement, prevention of alcohol, tobacco and other drug use, less teacher stress, etc. These discussions may prove to be more powerful and persuasive than simply appealing to authority or law (i.e., we have to do it!).
- *"Try before you buy."* SWPBIS is comprised of many smaller techniques (reward systems, teaching rules; Embry, 2004) that can be promoted as trial products. You can ask innovators in your building to share their successes, or arrange visits to schools that have already adopted SWPBIS practices with success.
- *"Go with the goers."* The practice is far more likely to be adopted if you recognize and support people who get on board early, as well as encourage those who are reluctant, or even resistant (Rogers, 2002).

To begin the journey toward establishing a more effective behavior support program, it is optimal to begin by completing the needs assessment such as that presented in Figure 33.1 (only the schoolwide section is included herein). The Assessing Behavior Support In Schools survey developed by George Sugai and his colleagues (Sugai, Lewis-Palmer, Todd, & Horner, 2000; available for no charge at www.pbis.org) outlines the essential features of SWPBIS at the schoolwide (Figure 33.1), common area, classroom, and individual student levels. The survey asks respondents to reflect on whether the practice is in place in their school and to choose which items are priorities for improvement. The schoolwide behavior support team should refer to these goals often, and modify them as indicated by a review of key data regarding effectiveness (e.g., office discipline referrals, rates of problem behavior on the playground).

Select Evidence-Based Practices

The SWPBIS (Sprague et al., 1998; Sugai & Horner, 1994) approach was developed at the University of Oregon and the National Center on Positive Behavioral Interventions and Supports (www.pbis.org, an Office of Special Education Programs funded research center). The goal of SWPBIS is to facilitate the academic achievement and healthy social development of children and youth in a safe environment conducive to learning. SWPBIS involves providing embedded and ongoing staff development and coaching aimed at improving school and classroom discipline and associated outcomes such as school violence, and alcohol, tobacco, and other drug use.

SWPBIS includes intervention techniques based on over 30 years of rigorous research regarding school discipline from education, public health, psychology, and criminology disciplines. SWPBIS components address whole-school, common area, classroom, and individual student support practices and may be used in combination with other evidence-based prevention programs such as the Second Step Violence Prevention Curriculum (Committee for Children,

Effective Behavior Support (EBS) Survey
Assessing and Planning Behavior Support in Schools

Name of school _____ Date _____

District _____ State _____

Person Completing the Survey:
- Administrator
- General Educator
- Educational/Teacher Assistant

- Special Educator
- Counselor
- Community member

- Parent/Family member
- School Psychologist
- Other

1. Complete the survey independently.

2. Schedule 20-30 minutes to complete the survey.

3. Base your rating on your individual experiences in the school. If you do not work in classrooms, answer questions that are applicable to you.

   To assess behavior support, first evaluate the status of each system feature (i.e. *in place, partially in place, not in place*) (left hand side of survey). Next, examine each feature:

   a. "What is the current status of this feature (i.e. *in place, partially in place, not in place*)?"

   b. For those features rated as partially in place or not in place, "What is the priority for improvement for this feature (i.e., *high, medium, low*)?"

4. Return your completed survey to _____ by _____

SCHOOL-WIDE SYSTEMS

Current Status			Feature	Priority for Improvement		
In Place	Partial in Place	Not in Place	**School-wide** is defined as involving all students, all staff, & all settings.	High	Med	Low
			1. A small number (e.g. 3-5) of positively & clearly stated student expectations or rules are defined.			
			2. Expected student behaviors are taught directly.			
			3. Expected student behaviors are rewarded regularly.			
			4. Problem behaviors (failure to meet expected student behaviors) are defined clearly.			
			5. Consequences for problem behaviors are defined clearly.			
			6. Distinctions between office vs. classroom managed problem behaviors are clear.			
			7. Options exist to allow classroom instruction to continue when problem behavior occurs.			
			8. Procedures are in place to address emergency/dangerous situations.			
			9. A team exists for behavior support planning & problem solving.			

Figure 33.1   Sample needs assessment for planning and evaluating SWPBIS

Current Status			Feature	Priority for Improvement		
In Place	Partial in Place	Not in Place	10. School administrator is an active participant on the behavior support team.	High	Med	Low
			11. Data on problem behavior patterns are collected and summarized within an on-going system.			
			12. Patterns of student problem behavior are reported to teams and faculty for active decision-making on a regular basis (e.g. monthly).			
			13. School has formal strategies for informing families about expected student behaviors at school.			
			14. Booster training activities for students are developed, modified, & conducted based on school data.			
			15. School-wide behavior support team has a budget for (a) teaching students, (b) on-going rewards, and (c) annual staff planning.			
			16. All staff is involved directly and/or indirectly in school-wide interventions.			
			17. The school team has access to on-going training and support from district personnel.			
			18. The school is required by the district to report on the social climate, discipline level or student behavior at least annually.			

Name of School _____ Date _____

Figure 33.1   Continued

2002). Representative school team members are trained to develop and implement positive school rules, direct teaching of rules, positive reinforcement systems, data-based decision making at the school level, effective classroom management methods, curriculum adaptation to prevent problem behavior, and functional behavioral assessment and positive behavioral intervention plans. Teams are also coached to integrate SWPBIS systems with other prevention programs to maximize effectiveness.

How Is SWPBIS Implemented?

The process for adopting and sustaining SWPBIS revolves around a school team typically composed of 5–10 individuals that includes an administrator, representative faculty/staff, and local family/community members. While it may seem ideal to train all school staff members all the time, it will rarely be feasible or sustainable to provide training at this level due to cost and logistical concerns. However, a representative group of adults, representing all school stakeholders (including students at the secondary level) can learn the key practices of SWPBIS and set goals for improvement. The stakeholders can then function as leaders or coaches as they inform their groups of the team activities (e.g., at staff or area meetings) and give support and encouragement during the improvement process. Increasingly, district- and statewide initiatives are supporting the dissemination of SWPBIS training and coaching systems.

While participating in training, and after mastery of the basic material, it is recommended that school discipline teams (building administrator, representative teachers, and other stakeholders) meet approximately once per month to review training content as needed and to set up a regular process of reviewing and refining the school discipline plan (initial goals are developed during training) and other, school site-based activities. A format for these meetings should be specified and each meeting should last between 20 to 60 minutes.

Set and Promote Schoolwide Expectations

A critical first task for the implementation team is to establish schoolwide behavior rule teaching related to student-teacher compliance, peer-to-peer interaction, academic achievement, and academic study skills. Using the general framework of "safety," "respect," and "responsibility," and directly teaching lessons throughout the year to establish and maintain the patterns of behavior associated with these personal qualities is recommended. In addition, posting the rules publicly in posters, school newsletters, local media, announcements, and assemblies can be valuable.

Plan to Recognize Expected Behavior and Actively Supervise Students

The school will need to establish a consistent system of enforcement, monitoring, and positive reinforcement to enhance the effect of rule teaching and maintain patterns of desired student behavior. Reinforcement systems may include schoolwide token economies in the form of "tickets" stating each school rule delivered by all adults in the building. These tokens are to be backed up with weekly drawings and rewards for the teachers as well. Each school should implement the procedures to fit their school improvement plan and specific discipline needs.

Table 33.1 What does School Wide PBS look like?

- Train and support a representative school team (20–30 hours of formal training)

  Principal actively leads and facilitates the process

  Take time to plan, coach, and continuously improve

- Set and promote school wide expectations

  Plan to teach expected behavior

  Plan to recognize expected behavior and actively supervise

- Use performance-based data for active decision-making

  Office discipline referral patterns (www.swis.org)

  Changes in academic performance, attendance

  Student safety and climate surveys

- How do I know it's working?

  Expected behaviors taught or reviewed 20+ times/year

  Students actively supervised in all school areas

  Students acknowledged frequently for expected behavior

  4:1 positive : negative interactions

  >80% students & adults can describe school-wide expectations

- Safe, respectful, responsible

Define and Effectively Correct Problem Behaviors and Their Consequences for Students and Staff Members

As stated earlier, schools using excessive sanctions experience greater levels of vandalism and other forms of misbehavior (Mayer, 1995; Skiba & Peterson, 1999). Positive reinforcement is more effective than punishment because it does not result in the type of counter-aggression and withdrawal (fight or flight) that punishment can produce and because it does not focus teachers' attention on detecting and correcting rule violations.

Students should see rules applied fairly. When they feel that rules are unevenly applied, students are more likely to misbehave. Schools with clear rule and reward systems and business-like corrections and sanctions also experience fewer problems. These schools signal appropriate behavior for students and respond to misbehavior predictably. Students in such schools are clear about expected behavior and learn there are consequences for misbehavior. When rules are consistent, students develop a respect for rules and laws, and internalize beliefs that the system of governance works (Bryk & Driscoll, 1988; Gottfredson, 1987; Gottfredson, Gottfredson, & Hybl, 1993).

Report and Use Data for Active Decision Making

The efficiency of team problem solving is enhanced by providing the team with data-based feedback to schools regarding their implementation of basic SWPBIS practices (cf. Assessing Behavior Support in Schools survey; Figure 33.1) and the impact of implementation on problem behavior as indexed by discipline referral patterns (cf. School-Wide Information System [SWIS], www.swis.org; Sprague, Sugai, Horner, & Walker, 1999; Sugai, Sprague, Horner, & Walker, 2000). The goal is to use highly efficient data systems that allow teams to ask: (a) are we implementing evidence-based, SWPBIS practices, and (b) are the practices having an effect on the behavior of students? Data on implementation of SWPBIS practices typically are collected, summarized and reported quarterly, and data on student behavior are collected continuously, and reported to the school team weekly, the school faculty monthly, and the school district annually. Irvin et al. (in press) provide an evaluation documenting the value that regular access to student behavioral data has for typical school teams.

Examples of data collection and display tools for assessing implementation of SWPBIS can be found at www.pbssurveys.org (Boland et al., 2004). Similarly, an example of a web-based information system designed to help school personnel to use office referral data to design school-wide and individual student interventions is available at www.swis.org (May et al., 2000). It is anticipated that as schoolwide systems become more common an increasing array of data collection options will become available to schools. A major focus for research on educational systems-change lies in the process, and impact of providing teachers, administrators, families and students with regular, accurate information for decision making (Newton, Horner, Algozzine, Todd, & Algozzine, 2009).

Implementing for Sustainability

Too often educational innovations, even efficacious innovations, have been implemented but not maintained (Fixsen et al., 2005; Latham, 1988). If SWPBIS is to result in educational change at a scale of practical relevance, schools adopting these procedures will need to sustain the practices for multiple years. An important feature of the SWPBIS approach is inclusion of formal strategies for improving the likelihood of such sustained implementation. These include (a) the development of training materials at each school that make it easier to implement from year to year, (b) the implementation of policies for using SWPBIS, and reporting student data, and (c) the

Table 33.2 Implications for Practice: What Educational Professionals Should Do to Enhance Social and Behavioral Competence in Schools?

- Systematically assess the nature, prevalence and effects of antisocial behavior in one's school, using office discipline referral patterns, and other sources of data.

- Share the findings with members of the school community in order to raise awareness of the prevalence of antisocial behavior, thereby motivating school authorities to address the problem.

- Develop clear goals and objectives for improving school discipline, well supported by the entire school community. This should include guidelines to help the school to identify, prevent, and deal with incidents of problem behavior.

- Consistently and continuously communicate, teach, and reward school-wide behavioral expectations (compliance to adult requests, positive peer and teacher interactions, and school effort).

- Encourage shared problem solving and recognition of reductions or improvements.

training of district-level coaches who are available to provide booster training for school teams, initial training for new faculty members, and help with problem solving around more intense challenges. The district coaching role is designed to help a school team sustain effective practices through periodic perturbations in the staffing, organization, or fluctuation in student behavior. The issue of sustaining educational innovation is not unique to SWPBIS, and remains a worthy focus for research.

What Is the Evidence for SWPBIS Efficacy?

A number of researchers (see Embry & Flannery, 1994; Knoff & Batsche, 1995; Taylor-Green et al., 1997) have studied SWPBIS practices. The effects of the program are documented in a series of studies implemented by researchers at the University of Oregon (Horner et al., 2009; Metzler, Biglan, Rusby, & Sprague, 2001; Sprague et al., 2002; Taylor-Greene et al., 1997, see also www. pbis.org for the latest research studies and reports). Studies have shown reductions in office discipline referrals of up to 50% per year, with continued improvement over a three-year period in schools that sustain the intervention (Irvin et al., 2004). In addition, school staff report greater satisfaction with their work, compared to staff in schools that did not implement SWPBIS (Ross, Romer, Endrulat, & Horner, 2010). Comparison schools typically show increases or no change in office referrals, along with a general frustration with the school discipline program.

Randomized controlled trials indicate that implementation of SWPBIS is related to reduction in problem behavior, improved perception of safety, improved organizational health, and improved academic performance (Bradshaw et al., 2008; Horner et al., 2009; Horner et al., in press). In studies employing the SWPBIS components, reductions in antisocial behavior (Sprague et al., 2002), vandalism (Mayer, 1995), aggression (Grossman et al., 1997; Lewis, Sugai, & Colvin, 1998), later delinquency (Kellam, Mayer, Rebok, & Hawkins, 1998; O'Donnell et al., 1995), as well as alcohol, tobacco, and other drug use (Biglan, Wang, & Walberg, 2003; O'Donnell et al., 1995) have been documented. Positive changes in protective factors such as academic achievement (Kellam et al., 1998; O'Donnell et al., 1995) and school engagement (O'Donnell et al., 1995) have been documented using a schoolwide positive behavior support approach such as SWPBIS in concert with other prevention interventions.

Conclusion

This chapter describes a schoolwide system for positive behavior support, the implementation steps used to build both a positive schoolwide social culture, and the capacity to support individual students with more intense behavioral needs. The major messages are that (a) problem behavior in schools is both a significant social challenge and a barrier to effective learning, (b) traditional "get tough" strategies have not proven effective, (c) the foundation for all behavior support in schools begins with establishing a positive social culture by defining, teaching and rewarding appropriate behaviors, (d) additional behavior support procedures based on behavior analysis principles are needed for children with more intense behavior support needs, and (e) school personnel are demonstrating both the ability to collect and use quality improvement data systems, and the value of those systems for improving schools.

At this writing, randomized controlled research studies are in progress to examine the effects of SWPBIS with greater precision and control. Current evaluation results, however, are encouraging. Schools throughout the country are demonstrating the ability to adopt and implement SWPBIS practices with fidelity (Bradshaw et al., 2008; Horner et al., 2004; Horner, et al., 2009). When schools adopt SWPBIS practices they are reporting reductions in problem behavior, improved perceptions of school safety, and improved academic performance. Recent Illinois evaluations (Illinois PBIS Network, 2011) also report that schools establishing a positive social climate are proving more effective in their implementation of individual, wrap-around support for students with high behavior support needs.

The progress is encouraging. Schools are able to improve and to demonstrate that change is linked to valued student outcomes. If these gains are to become important at a national scale, additional research is needed to demonstrate experimentally controlled effects, strategies for improving efficiency, and strategies for supporting sustained implementation.

References

Biglan, A., Wang, M. C., & Walberg, H. J. (2003). *Preventing youth problems*. New York: Kluwer Academic/Plenum Publishers.

Boland, J. B., Todd, A. W., Horner, R., & Sugai, G. (2006). Positive Behavior Supports Surveys: Self Assessment (Version 2.0). Eugene: Educational and Community Supports, University of Oregon. Retrieved from www.pbssurveys.org

Bradshaw, C. P., Koth, C. W., Bevans, K. B., Ialongo, N., & Leaf, P. J. (2008). Impact of School-Wide Positive Behavioral Interventions and Supports (PBIS) on the organizational health of elementary schools. *School Psychology Quarterly, 23*(4), 462–473. doi:/10.1037/a0012883

Bradshaw, C. P., Koth, C. W., Thornton, L. A., & Leaf, P. J. (2009). Altering school climate through school-wide Positive Behavioral Interventions and Supports: findings from a group-randomized effectiveness trial. *Prevention Science, 10*(2), 100–115. doi:10.1007/s11121-008-0114-9

Bradshaw, C. P., Mitchell, M. M., & Leaf, P. J. (2010). Examining the Effects of Schoolwide Positive Behavioral Interventions and Supports on Student Outcomes. *Journal of Positive Behavior Interventions, 12*(3), 133–148. doi: 10.1177/1098300709334798

Bryk, A. S., & Driscoll, M. E. (1988). *The high school as community: contextual influences, and consequences for students and teachers*. Madison, WI: National Center on Effective Secondary Schools: Wisconsin Center for Education Research, University of Wisconsin-Madison.

Colvin, G., Kame'enui, E. J., & Sugai, G. (1993). School-wide and classroom management: Reconceptualizing the integration and management of students with behavior problems in general education. *Education and Treatment of Children, 16*, 361–381.

Committee for Children. (2002). *Second Step violence prevention curriculum*. Seattle, WA: Committee for Children.

Dishion, T. J., & Kavanagh, K. (2003). *Intervening in adolescent problem behavior: A family-centered approach*. New York: Guilford.

Eber, L., Hyde, K., Rose, J., Breen, K., McDonald, D., & Lewandowski, H. (2009). Completing the continuum of Schoolwide Positive Behavior Support: Wraparound as a tertiary-level intervention. In W. Sailor, G. Dunlap, G. Sugai, & R. Horner (Eds.), *Handbook of positive behavior support* (pp. 671–709). New York: Springer.

Elias, M., Zins, J., Weissburt, R., Frey, K., Greenberg, M., Haynes, N., Kessler, R., Schwab-Stone, M., & Shriver, T. (1997). *Promoting social and emotional learning: Guidelines for educators*. Alexandria, VA: Association for Supervision and Curriculum Development.

Embry, D. D. (2004). Community-based prevention using simple, low-cost, evidence-based kernels and behavior vaccines. *Journal of Community Psychology, 32*(5), 575–591.

Embry, D. D., & Flannery, D. J. (1994). *Peacebuilders—reducing youth violence: A working application of cognitive-social-imitative competence research.* Tucson, AZ: Heartsprings.

Fixsen, G., Naoom, S. F., Blase, K. A., Friedman, R. M., & Wallace, F. (2005). *Implementation research: A synthesis of the literature.* Tampa, FL: University of South Florida, Louis de la Parte Florida Mental Health Institute, The National Implementation Research Network (FMHI Publication #231).

Gottfredson, D. C. (1987). Developing effective organizations to reduce school disorder. In O. C. Moles (Ed.), *Strategies to reduce student misbehavior* (pp. 87–104). Washington, DC: Office of Educational Research and Improvement.

Gottfredson, D. C. (1997). School-based crime prevention. In L. Sherman, D. Gottfredson, D. Mackenzie, J. Eck, P. Reuter, & S. Bushway (Eds.), *Preventing crime: What works, what doesn't, what's promising* (pp. 5-1 to 5-74). College Park, MD: Department of Criminology and Criminal Justice.

Gottfredson, D. C. (2001). *Delinquency in schools.* New York: Cambridge University Press.

Gottfredson, D. C., Gottfredson, G. D., & Hybl, L. G. (1993). Managing adolescent behavior: A multiyear, multi-school study. *American Educational Research Journal, 30,* 179–215. doi:10.3102/00028312030001179

Grossman, D. C., Neckerman, H. J., Joepsell, T. D., Liu, P., Asher, K. N., Beland, K., Frey, K., et al. (1997). Effectiveness of a violence prevention curriculum among children in elementary school. *Journal of the American Medical Association, 277,* 1605–1611. doi:10.1001/jama.277.20.1605

Gottfredson, G., Gottfredson, D., & Czeh, E. (2000). *National study of delinquency prevention in schools.* Ellicott City, MD: Gottfredson Associates.

Hallinger, P., & Heck, R. H. (1998). Exploring the principal's contribution to school effectiveness: 1980–1995. *School Effectiveness and School Improvement, 9,* 157–191. doi:10.1080/0924345980090203

Hawkins, J. D., Catalano, R. F., Kosterman, R., Abbott, R., & Hill, K. G. (1999). Preventing adolescent health-risk behaviors by strengthening protection during childhood. *Archives of Pediatrics and Adolescent Medicine, 153,* 226–234.

Horner, R. H., Sugai, G., & Anderson, C. M. (in press). Examining the evidence-base for school-wide positive behavior support. *Focus on Exceptional Children.*

Horner, R. H., Sugai, G., Eber, L., Nakasato, J., Todd, A., & Esperanza, J. (2009). A randomized, wait-list controlled effectiveness trial assessing school-wide positive behavior support in elementary schools. *Journal of Positive Behavior Interventions, 11*(3), 133–144. doi: 10.1177/1098300709332067

Horner, R. H., Todd, A.W., Lewis-Palmer, T., Irvin, L. K., Sugai, G., & Boland, J. B. (2004). The school-wide evaluation tool (SET): A research instrument for assessing school-wide positive behavior support. *Journal of Positive Behavior Interventions, 6*(1), 3–12. doi.org/10.1177%2F10983007040060010201

Ingersoll, R. M. (2001). Teacher turnover and teacher shortages: An organizational analysis. *American Educational Research Journal, 38,* 499–534. doi.org/10.3102%2F00028312038003499

Illinois PBIS Network. (2011, January). *Update Newsletter, 15*(1).

Irvin, L. K., Horner, R. H., Ingram, K., Todd, A. W., Sugai, G., Sampson, N. K., & Boland, J. (in press). Using office discipline referral for decision-making about student behavior in elementary and middle schools: An empirical evaluation of validity. *Journal of Positive Behavior Interventions.*

Irvin, L. K., Tobin, T. J., Sprague, J. R., Sugai, G., & Vincent, C. G. (2004). Validity of office discipline referrals measures as indices of school-wide behavioral status and effects of school-wide behavioral interventions. *Journal of Positive Behavior Interventions 6*(3), 131–147. doi: http://dx.doi.org/10.1177%2F10983007040060030201

Kam, C. M., Greenberg, M. T., & Walls, C. T. (2003). Examining the role of implementation quality in school-based prevention using the PATHS curriculum. *Prevention Science, 4,* 55–63. doi.org/10.1023%2FA%3A1021786811186

Katz, M. (1997). *On playing a poor hand well: Insights from the lives of those who have overcome childhood risks and adversities.* New York: Norton.

Kellam, S. G., Mayer, L. S., Rebok, G. W., & Hawkins, W. E. (1998). Effects of improving achievement on aggressive behavior and of improving aggressive behavior on achievement through two preventive interventions: An investigation of causal paths. In B. P. Dohrenwend (Eds.), *Adversity, stress, and psychopathology* (pp. 486–505, 567). New York: Oxford University Press.

Knoff, H. M., & Batsche, G. M. (1995). Project ACHIEVE: Analyzing a school reform process for at-risk and under-achieving students. *School Psychology Review, 24,* 579–603.

Latham, G. I. (1988). The birth and death cycles of educational innovations. *Principal, 68*(1), 41–44.

Lewis, T. J., Sugai, G., & Colvin, G. (1998). Reducing problem behavior through a school-side system of effective behavioral support: Investigation of a school-wide social skills training program and contextual interventions. *School Psychology Review, 27,* 446–459.

Loeber, R., & Farrington, D. P. (1998). *Serious and violent juvenile offenders: Risk factors and successful interventions.* Thousand Oaks, CA: Sage.

Loeber, R., & Farrington, D. (2001). *Child delinquents.* Los Angeles: Sage.

May, S., Ard, W. III, Todd, A. W., Horner, R.H., Glasgow, A., Sugai, G., & Sprague, J. R. (2000). *School-wide Information System*. Eugene: Educational and Community Supports, University of Oregon

Mayer, G. R. (1995). Preventing antisocial behavior in the schools. *Journal of Applied Behavior Analysis, 28,* 467–478. doi.org/10.1901%2Fjaba.1995.28-467

Metzler, C. W., Biglan, A., Rusby, J. C., & Sprague, J. R. (2001). Evaluation of a comprehensive behavior management program to improve school-wide positive behavior support. *Education and Treatment of Children, 24,* 448–479.

Metzler, C. W., Biglan, A., Embry, D., Sprague, J., Boles, S. M., & Kavanagh, K. A. (2008). *Improving the well-being of adolescents in Oregon*. Eugene: Center on Early Adolescence, Oregon Research Institute.

Newton, J. S., Horner, R., Algozzine, B., Todd, A., & Algozzine, K. M. (2009). Using a problem-solving model for data-based decision making in schools. In W. Sailor, G. Dunlap, G. Sugai, & R. Horner (Eds.), *Handbook of positive behavior support* (pp. 551–580). New York: Springer.

O'Donnell, J., Hawkins, J., Catalano, R., Abbott, R., & Day, L. (1995). Preventing school failure, drug use, and delinquency among low-income children: long-term intervention in elementary schools. *American Journal of Orthopsychiatry, 65,* 87–100. doi.org/10.1037%2Fh0079598

Osher, D., Bear, G. G., Sprague, J. R., & Doyle, W. (2010). "How can we improve school discipline?" *Educational Researcher, 39*(1), 48–58. doi.org/10.3102%2F0013189X09357618

Osher, D., Dwyer, K., & Jackson, S. (2002). *Safe, supportive and successful schools: Step by step*. Longmont, CO: Sopris West.

Patterson, G. R., Reid, J. B., & Dishion, T. J. (1992). *Antisocial boys*. Eugene, OR: Castalia Press.

Rogers, E. M. (2002). Diffusion of preventive innovations. *Addictive Behaviors, 27*(6), 989–993. doi.org/10.1016%2FS0306-4603%2802%2900300-3

Ross, S., Endurlat, N., & Horner, R. H. (2011). Teacher well-being and the implementation of Schoolwide Positive Behavior Interventions and Supports. *Journal of Positive Behavior Interventions, 13*(3). doi: 10.1177/1098300711413820

Scott, T. M., & Barrett, S. B. (2004). Using staff and student time engaged in disciplinary procedures to evaluate the impact of school-wide PBS. *Journal of Positive Behavior Interventions, 6*(1), 21–28. doi.org/10.1177%2F10983007040060010401

Scott, T. M., & Eber, L. (2003). Functional assessment and wraparound as systemic school processes: Primary, secondary, and tertiary systems examples. *Journal of Positive Behavior Interventions, 5,* 131–143. doi.org/10.1177%2F10983007030050030201

Simonsen, B. M., Sugai, G., & Negron, M. (2008). School-wide positive behavior support: Primary systems and practices. *Teaching Exceptional Children, Special Issue: Positive Behavior Interventions and Supports, 40,* 32–40.

Skiba, R. J., Horner, R. H., Chung, C., Rausch, M. K., May, S., & Tobin, T. (in press). Race is not neutral: A national investigation of African American and Latino disproportionality in school discipline. *School Psychology Review*.

Skiba, R., & Peterson, R. (1999). School discipline at a crossroads: From zero tolerance to early response. *Exceptional Children 66*(3), 335–346.

Skiba, R. J., Michael, R. S., Nardo, A. C., & Peterson, R. (2002). The color of discipline: Sources of racial and gender disproportionality in school punishment. *Urban Review, 34,* 317–342. doi.org/10.1023%2FA%3A1021320817372

Skiba, R. J., & Rausch, M. K. (2006). Zero tolerance, suspension, and expulsion: Questions of equity and effectiveness. In C. M. Evertson & C. S. Weinstein (Eds.), *Handbook of classroom management: Research, practice, and contemporary issues* (pp. 1063–1089). Mahwah, NJ: Erlbaum.

Sprague, J. R., & Golly, A. (2004). *Best behavior: Building positive behavior supports in schools*. Longmont, CO: Sopris West.

Sprague, J. R., Sugai, G., Horner, R. H., & Walker, H. M. (1999). Using office discipline referral data to evaluate school-wide discipline and violence prevention interventions. *Oregon School Study Council Bulletin, 42*(2). Eugene: University of Oregon, College of Education.

Sprague, J. R., Sugai, G., & Walker, H. (1998). Antisocial behavior in schools. In T. S. Watson & F. M. Gresham (Eds.), *Handbook of child behavior therapy* (pp. 451–474). New York: Plenum.

Sprague, J. R., & Walker, H. M. (2005). *Safe and healthy schools: Practical prevention strategies*. New York: Guilford.

Sprague, J., Walker, H., Golly, A., White, K., Myers, D. R., & Shannon, T. (2002). Translating research into effective practice: The effects of a universal staff and student intervention on key indicators of school safety and discipline. *Education and Treatment of Children, 23,* 495–511.

Sugai, G., & Horner, R. (1994). Including students with severe behavior problems in general education settings: Assumptions, challenges, and solutions. *Oregon Conference Monograph, 6,* 102–120.

Sugai, G., & Horner, R. H. (1999). Discipline and behavioral support: Preferred processes and practices. *Effective School Practices, 17,* 10–22.

Sugai, G., & Horner, R. H. (2002). The evolution of discipline practices: School-wide positive behavior supports. *Child & Family Behavior Therapy 24*(1/2), 23–50. doi.org/10.1300%2FJ019v24n01_03

Sugai, G., & Horner, R. H. (2009). Responsiveness-to-intervention and school-wide positive behavior supports: Integration of multi-tiered approaches. *Exceptionality, 17,* 223–237. doi.org/10.1080%2F09362830903235375

461

Sugai, G., & Horner, R. (2010). School-wide positive behavior support: Establishing continuum of evidence-based practices. *Journal of Evidence-based Practices for Schools*, 11(1), 62–83.

Sugai, G., Lewis-Palmer, T., Todd, A., & Horner, R. (2000). *Effective Behavior Support (EBS) survey: Assessing and planning behavior support in schools*. Eugene: University of Oregon.

Sugai, G., Sprague, J. R., Horner, R. H., & Walker, H. M. (2000). Preventing school violence: The use of office discipline referrals to assess and monitor school-wide discipline interventions. *Journal of Emotional and Behavioral Disorders, 8*, 94–101. doi.org/10.1177%2F106342660000800205

Taylor-Greene, S., Brown, D., Nelson, L., Longton, J., Gassman, T., Cohen, J., Swartz, J., et al. (1997). School-wide behavioral support: Starting the year off right. *Journal of Behavioral Education, 7*, 99–112. doi.org/10.1023%2FA%3A1022849722465

Tolan, P., Gorman-Smith, D., & Henry, D. (2001). New study to focus on efficacy of "whole school" prevention approaches. *Emotional & Behavioral Disorders in Youth, 2*, 5–7.

U.S. Departments of Justice and Education. (1998). *Safe and drug free schools program principles of effectiveness*. Washington, DC: Author. Retrieved from http://www.ed.gov/legislation/FedRegister/announcements/1998-2/060198c.html

Walker, H. M., Horner, R. H., Sugai, G., Bullis, M., Sprague, J. R., Bricker, D., & Kaufman, M. J. (1996). Integrated approaches to preventing antisocial behavior patterns among school age children and youth. *Journal of Emotional and Behavioral Disorders, 4*, 194–209.

Walker, H., Ramsey, E., & Gresham, F. (2004). *Antisocial behavior in school: Evidenced-based practices*. Florence, KY: Cengage.

Zins, J. E., Weissberg, R. P., Wang, M. C., & Walberg, H. J. (2004). *Building academic success on social and emotional learning: What does the research say?* New York: Teachers College Press.

34

Preventing, Preparing for, and Responding to School Violence with the PREP<u>a</u>RE Model

Stephen E. Brock

CALIFORNIA STATE UNIVERSITY, SACRAMENTO

Shane R. Jimerson and Shelley R. Hart

THE UNIVERSITY OF CALIFORNIA, SANTA BARBARA

Amanda B. Nickerson

UNIVERSITY AT ALBANY, STATE UNIVERSITY OF NEW YORK

Abstract

In this chapter the PREP<u>a</u>RE School Crisis Prevention and Intervention Training Curriculum (PREP<u>a</u>RE) is used as a structure for discussing the comprehensive school crisis team's response to school violence. This chapter includes sections that describe the importance of responding in a comprehensive fashion to school violence, the conceptual basis for PREP<u>a</u>RE and a description of its strategies, evidence of PREP<u>a</u>RE's effectiveness, and finally, a critique of the model and acknowledgement of its limitations. Implications for practice are discussed, including the importance of establishing a comprehensive school crisis management team.

The School Crisis Team's Response to Violence

Acts of violence in schools are rare; however, when these events do occur, they affect the physical, emotional, and psychological well-being of students and staff (National Association of School Psychologists [NASP], 2000). Thus, preventing, preparing for, and responding to such events are essential, and each of these activities benefits from the direction of a school crisis team. Ideally, a crisis team involves the collaboration and cooperation of educators, parents, students, law enforcement, community leaders, health care providers, and other professionals serving youth (Hester, 2003). However, the ultimate responsibility for the development and organization of this team belongs to schools and school districts. Selection of the school crisis team members is critical; some staff members may naturally fill certain roles, yet consideration

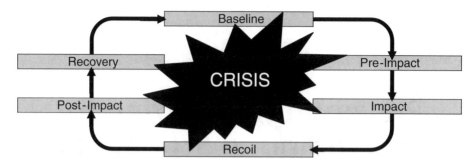

Figure 34.1 An illustration of the sequence and phases of a crisis event

should be given to the diverse and complementary nature of the different members' skills, as well as an individual's ability and willingness to commit the required time and effort (Dwyer & Osher, 2000).

It is also important to acknowledge that crises, such as acts of school violence, are not discrete events. Rather they are processes that evolve over time (Vossekuil, Fein, Reddy, Borum, & Modzeleski, 2002). There is usually a series of events and precursors that lead to school crises. Further, the immediate response to school violence may not resolve all crisis issues for all students and staff. Often the recovery occurs over months, if not years (Brock & Jimerson, 2004). Given this reality, it is essential that comprehensive school crisis teams be prepared for and remain active during all phases of a crisis (not only during the immediate aftermath of violent acts). Figure 34.1 provides an illustration of the phases of a crisis event. It makes use of a chronology that divides crises, including acts of violence, into five phases: (a) the pre-impact phase, which is the period before the crisis; (b) the impact phase, which is the period when the crisis occurs; (c) the recoil phase, which is the period immediately after the crisis event; (d) the post-impact phase, which are the days to weeks after the crisis event; and (e) the recovery and reconstruction phase, which lasts months or years after the event (Raphael & Newman, 2000; Valent, 2000). Comprehensive school crisis teams need to be active during each phase and PREP_aRE provides guidance regarding these activities.

Conceptual Basis of PREP_aRE

PREP_aRE integrates guidance and direction offered by the U.S. Departments of Education and Homeland Security. Further, from a careful review of the literature (Brock et al., 2009), PREP_aRE advocates for the use of specific prevention, preparedness, response, and recovery efforts that are considered "best practices" and, to the greatest extent possible, are supported by the empirical literature.

Consistent with guidance offered by the U.S. Department of Education (2003), PREP_aRE advocates that school crisis teams do more than simply respond to acts of school violence. Obviously, the nature of the incident will determine the type and scope of response; however, in general, specific crisis team activities correspond to the different phases of a crisis event. Research has identified the following critical types of activities in crises: (a) prevention, (b) preparedness, (c) response, and (d) recovery (Brock, 2002). Violence prevention includes activities designed to reduce the incidence of crisis events. Violence preparedness ensures response readiness for crises that are not, or cannot be, prevented. Violence response refers to team activities that minimize crisis damage and facilitate optimal immediate coping (which involves beginning the process of actively returning to pre-crisis levels of functioning). Finally, violence recovery refers to longer-term actions that repair crisis damage and return the school to baseline (or pre-crisis) operation/

Department of Education (2003)	Violence prevention and preparedness		Violence response and recovery		
Crisis Phase (Raphael & Newman, 2000; Valent, 2000)	**Preimpact** The period before crisis		**Impact** When crisis occurs	**Recoil** Immediately after crisis threats end	**Postimpact** Days/weeks after the crisis	**Recovery/Reconstruction** Months/years after crisis
	Preparation and planning	Threat and warning				
PREPaRE: *School Crisis Prevention and Intervention Training Curriculum* (Brock et al., 2009)	**Prevent** and prepare for psychological trauma risk					
	• Prevent and prepare for crisis • Foster student resiliency		• Keep students safe • Avoid crisis scenes and images			
			Reaffirm physical health and ensure perceptions of security and safety			
			• Meet basic physical needs (water, shelter, food, clothing) • Foster perceptions of safety			
			Evaluate psychological trauma			
			• Evaluate crisis exposure and reactions • Evaluate internal and external resources			
					• Make psychotherapeutic treatment referrals	
			Provide interventions and **Respond** to psychological needs			
			• Reestablish social support systems • Provide psychoeducation: Empower survivors and their caregivers			
					• Provide classroom-based or individual crisis intervention or both • Provide or refer for longer-term crisis intervention	
	Examine the effectiveness of crisis prevention and intervention					

Figure 34.2 An illustration of the relationships among specific crisis team activities, the phases of a crisis, and elements of the *PREPaRE* model. *Note.* Adapted from "School Crisis Prevention and Intervention: The PREPaRE model," by S. E. Brock, A. B. Nickerson, M. A. Reeves, S. R. Jimerson, R. A. Lieberman, and T. A. Feinberg, 2009, Bethesda, MD: NASP. Reprinted with permission from the National Association of School Psychologists.

functioning. Figure 34.2 illustrates the relationships between these different activities, the phases of a crisis event, and the PREPaRE model.

Consistent with guidance offered by the U.S. Department of Homeland Security (2004), PREPaRE advocates for use of the National Incident Management System (NIMS) as the school crisis team structure. NIMS provides an infrastructure designed to allow emergency response personnel (including school crisis teams) to respond to any crisis event with clear and consistent organizational structures and strategies. Among the elements of NIMS is the Incident Command System (ICS). The ICS has traditionally been used to centralize, organize, and coordinate the emergency response to a critical incident (i.e., crisis response). In the PREPaRE model, the ICS is also used to structure other school crisis team activities (i.e., crisis prevention, preparedness, and recovery). The ICS, which provides overall direction and establishes priorities for use in an emergency, has five functions: (a) management, (b) planning and intelligence, (c) operations, (d) logistics, and (c) finance/administration. Lockyer and Eastin (2000) recommend that school crisis teams pre-assign specific individuals to each of these functions (with such assignment being based on their school job assignments). Figure 34.3 provides a flow chart that illustrates the relationships among the five functions of the ICS.

Further discussion of the conceptual basis and empirical supports for PREPaRE is offered in the book *School Crisis Prevention and Intervention: The PREPaRE Model* (Brock et al., 2009). From a review of the literature, this book (and the training workshops that accompany it; Brock, 2006; Reeves, Nickerson, & Jimerson, 2006) provides educators with guidance on how best to fill the responsibilities and roles generated by school crisis team membership.

The PREPaRE Model

Designed specifically for use in the school setting, each element of PREPaRE outlines recommended activities for each phase of a crisis. As illustrated in Figure 34.2, each element consists

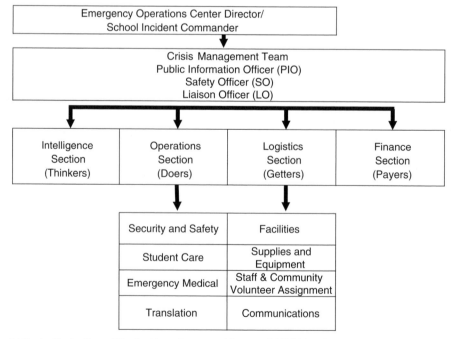

Figure 34.3 An illustration of the Incident Command System (ICS) hierarchy

of activities that occur throughout the phases of a crisis (e.g., Prevent and prepare activities span pre-impact, impact, and recoil phases). While much attention is directed to the impact and recoil phases of a crisis, all activities related to prevention, preparedness, response and recovery efforts should be considered equally important. The following summarizes activities that take place within each element of PREPaRE as set forth by Brock et al. (2009).

Prevent and Prepare (P)

The first element of PREPaRE is preventing and preparing for crises. The primary task of these efforts is the development of crisis teams. As indicated earlier, the crisis team forms the foundation for all subsequent efforts. Selection of members and delineation of duties at this stage is crucial, and Figure 34.3 illustrates the five essential functions of the ICS (the recommended structure for crisis teams). It is important to note that while there are unique roles within the ICS, this does not mean that different individuals must occupy each role. For example, the school principal may serve as the Incident Commander (IC) and Public Information Officer (PIO). This is particularly relevant to smaller districts and schools, where it may be necessary for one staff member to retain several roles in order to provide comprehensive coverage. Table 34.1 outlines the main crisis team sections, associated duties, and potential staffing considerations.

After the team is organized, these individuals will lead the development or evaluation of a crisis plan. While outside the scope of this chapter, a crisis plan will likely contain information about (a) the crisis team (e.g., members, duties, meetings); (b) the plan itself (e.g., dissemination, review procedures); (c) trainings, exercises, and drills related to crisis efforts; (d) prevention activities (e.g., needs assessment, implementation of curriculum); (e) intervention activities (e.g., initiation of response efforts, evacuation routes, reunification procedures); and (f) recovery activities (e.g., community organizations available to provide ongoing mental health to traumatized students and staff).

Reaffirm (R)

This element of the PREPaRE model attends to (a) reaffirming physical health and safety, and (b) ensuring perceptions of security and safety. These activities begin after an event has occurred that is judged to cause a harmful impact on the school and will continue through the days to weeks after the crisis (i.e., postimpact phase). Before any crisis interventions can begin, it is essential that the school community is physically safe (i.e., out of danger and with acute physical needs met) and that basic needs (i.e., water, shelter, food, and clothing) are met. Once safety and physical health have been established, it is also important for the school community to *believe* it is safe. Considerations to enhance this perception and therefore minimize the deleterious effects of exposure include: (a) containing problematic adult behaviors regarding the crisis (i.e., students often base their responses on the reactions of the adults near them); (b) minimizing exposure to potentially upsetting images and scenes (including those via media coverage); (c) reunifying students with primary caregivers or significant others, or reassuring students of impending reunification and the safety/location of their significant others if known; (d) providing crisis facts and dispelling rumors (e.g., alleviating the anxiety heightened by a rumor that there were two gunmen when there had been only one and s/he was no longer a threat); (e) providing opportunities for constructive engagement (e.g., having students help obtain needed supplies); and (f) providing visual and concrete cues that the environment is safe (e.g., strong police presence after an act of violence on campus).

Table 34.1 School-Based Crisis Team Sections/Functions, Associated Roles/Duties, and Potential Staffing Considerations

ICS Function	Role & Duty	Potential Staff Considerations
Incident Command (IC & CMT)	*Incident Commander (IC):* determine objectives of crisis team, assign roles & responsibilities, initiate, coordinate & manage all crisis efforts	The IC will need to have a position of authority and be able to marshal resources; likely a principal or superintendent
	Crisis Management Team (CMT): a variety of roles to liaise between the IC and the public the specifics of the crisis (PIO), to assess and coordinate safety efforts (SO), and to liaise between agencies involved in crisis efforts (LO).	These roles may require specific knowledge and experience in public relations, safety, and coordination/liaising between organizations. Particularly in small districts/schools, many of these roles will likely be the responsibility of a principal or superintendent; however, they can also be tasked to teachers, assistant principals, or administrative assistants with the requisite training (at the district level the PIO is likely the responsibility of staff assigned public relations duties).
Planning/Intelligence ("thinkers")	Collect, evaluate, and disseminate crisis information to IC, prepare status reports, identify & monitor crisis resources, develop & document crisis plans, and evaluate prevention, preparedness, response, and recovery efforts.	Staff with good analytic and organizational skills with good follow through. This may be filled by one person or several; however, one individual should serve as the evaluation leader.
Operations ("doers")	Carries out all crisis prevention tasks (e.g., curriculum), addresses immediate needs, and supports longer-term recovery efforts. Areas requiring coordinators include: (a) security and safety, (b) student care, (c) emergency medical, and (d) translation	Specialized staff will likely serve as coordinators. For example, it is likely that the school psychologist will coordinate and lead student care efforts, the school resource officer will be responsible for security and safety issues, the nurse will head the emergency medical staff section, and a community liaison will act as translation coordinator. Most crisis staff will be "doers" in order to be capable of responding to all students' needs. It is important that these staff have received appropriate training in evaluation and provision of response interventions.
Logistics ("getters")	Obtains all resources needed to address crises, including personnel, equipment & supplies, and services, as well as liaising between the doers and the payers.	Staff with good coordination and communication skills who can multi-task relatively well.
Finance/Admin. ("payers")	Maintains all records of prevention, preparedness, response, and recovery expenses.	This role will likely be filled by the principal or superintendent (the IC), that is, someone with authority over finances, although specific tasks related to this section would likely be relegated (e.g., an administrative assistant responsible for collecting any associated expense receipts).

Note. Adapted from "School Crisis Prevention and Intervention: The PREPaRE model", by S. E. Brock, A. B. Nickerson, M. A. Reeves, S. R. Jimerson, R. A. Lieberman, and T. A. Feinberg, 2009, Bethesda, MD: NASP.

Evaluate (E)

This element of PREPaRE immediately precedes provision of crisis interventions. Prior to provision of such interventions students must be evaluated for psychological trauma. This is often called *psychological triage* and is described as a sorting and directing of individuals by immediacy of the treatment needed (NIMH, 2001). Included in this evaluation is the evaluation of risk factors (i.e., variables that predict psychological trauma) and warning signs (i.e., crisis reactions). While risk factors may increase the odds of psychological trauma, warning signs are indicators that trauma may actually have occurred.

Within the PREPaRE model several important risk factors include: (a) physical proximity to the crisis (e.g., witnessing an incident); (b) emotional proximity (e.g., knowing someone who was a crisis victim); and (c) subjective impressions of personal threat presented by the crisis. Additionally, internal (e.g., coping strategies, baseline mental health) and external (e.g., family resources and social support) individual vulnerability factors (variables that help explain the student's unique circumstance at the time of the crisis) influence a students' responses.

Warning signs are assessed during the provision of crisis interventions. While some early crisis reactions (e.g., emotional numbing, memory impairment, fatigue, aggression) are common, extreme negative emotional reactions, acute panic and dissociative states, and dramatically increased arousal (e.g., exaggerated startle responses, hypervigilance, irritability, and sleep disturbance) may indicate significant coping challenges and may require immediate and more intensive treatment (e.g., referral to community-based mental health practitioner). Even relatively common (and initially adaptive or protective) crisis reactions (e.g., avoidance) can signal the need for treatment when they last for longer than a few weeks, which is why evaluation activities extend throughout the recovery/reconstruction phase of a crisis. Finally, PREPaRE identifies developmental and cultural variables as critical components in the evaluation of warning signs and psychological trauma.

Provide and Respond (PaR)

This element of PREPaRE includes different crisis interventions, the provision of which are dictated by the "Evaluate" activities previously discussed. These efforts continue throughout the recovery/reconstruction phase of the crisis. Figure 34.4 provides a flowchart for the evaluation of psychological trauma and its relationship with provision of specific crisis interventions. As indicated, there are several strategies that may be universally provided to exposed students, regardless of risk for psychological trauma (e.g., reestablishing social support systems). As students are judged more at-risk (i.e., the presence of risk factors and warning signs increase the level of concern), additional crisis interventions are added to support the student (viz., psycho-educational groups, immediate psychological crisis interventions, and longer-term psychotherapy). The specifics for each of these interventions are detailed in Brock et al. (2009).

Examine (E)

The final element of PREPaRE includes examination of the effectiveness of crisis prevention, preparedness, response, and recovery efforts. The importance of these activities cannot be over emphasized, and examination efforts need to occur throughout all phases of the crisis. The primary goals of this element include: (a) assessing effectiveness; (b) improving implementation and management of likely limited resources (e.g., staff time), thus enhancing effectiveness; (c) documenting accomplishments (e.g., consolidating numbers and results of threat assessments conducted); (d) justifying the need for resources to continue accessing or to gain access to them

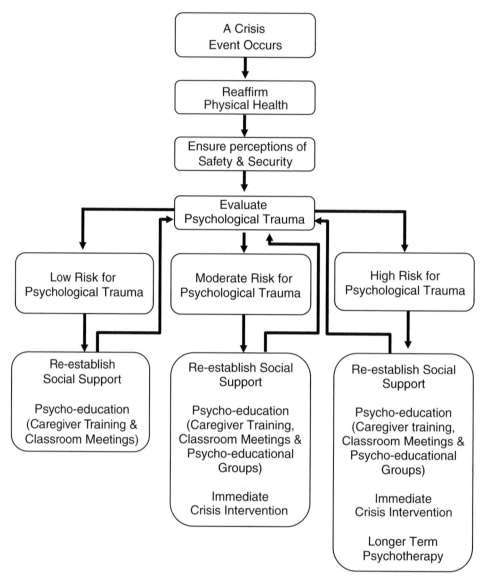

Figure 34.4 Flowchart from impact of crisis to provision of interventions. *Note.* Adapted from "School Crisis Prevention and Intervention: The PREPaRE model", by S. E. Brock, A. B. Nickerson, M. A. Reeves, S. R. Jimerson, R. A. Lieberman, and T. A. Feinberg, 2009, Bethesda, MD: NASP. Reprinted with permission from the National Association of School Psychologists.

(e.g., to school boards or superintendents); and (e) satisfying the ethical responsibility to demonstrate positive and negative effects of program participation.

Three strategies are used to examine the effectiveness of prevention efforts. During each phase of the crisis, the evaluation technique may have slightly different methods and purposes. However, generally speaking, *needs assessment* identifies areas to address within the local context (e.g., the need for lock-down drills for a school located in an urban area with frequent drive-by shootings). Information for this assessment should be obtained from students, teachers and other staff, parents, and relevant community members (e.g., youth organizations located in the neighborhood), as well as discipline records (e.g., office referrals, suspensions, weapons violations), student support referrals, attendance records, and the nurse's office (e.g., logs of student visits). *Process analysis* is conducted to understand specific prevention, preparedness, response and recovery activities implemented, by whom they were implemented, and to what degree established plans were followed. This information may be obtained via questionnaires, surveys, focus groups, or systematic observations. Finally, *outcome evaluation*, or summative evaluation, assesses the effectiveness of the crisis plan's documented objectives for the efforts taking place during each phase of the crisis.

Research Support

PREPaRE has undergone a multi-year mixed-method study to document participant satisfaction and assess the extent to which the training has achieved its objectives (which are two essential aspects of program evaluation; Ingvarson, Meiers, & Beavis, 2005). Each PREPaRE workshop participant completes a pre-test and post-test to assess knowledge about key workshop objectives and attitudes towards providing crisis prevention and intervention services. Participants also complete a workshop evaluation to assess satisfaction. Analyses of workshop evaluation data from over 1,000 participants in Workshops 1 and 2, collected from early 2006 to May of 2008, revealed high participant satisfaction (Brock, Nickerson, Reeves, Savage, & Woitaszewski, 2011). Analyses of pre- and post-test data indicated significant improvements in crisis prevention and intervention knowledge, as well as significantly improved attitudes (e.g., confidence in being a crisis team member, and decrease in anxiety about providing crisis interventions). Qualitative analyses of participant comments about the workshops revealed that the active training methods (e.g., role-plays, discussion), content, and materials were perceived as most helpful in improving crisis preparedness. In addition, 83% of participants said they would recommend the training and 27% reported that all school staff should receive the training due to the critical importance of the topic (Brock et al., 2011).

Recognizing the need to collect information from participants after they have completed the training and have reflected on knowledge and adapt it to their own setting (Guskey, 2000), Bauer and Gurdineer (2010) conducted a follow-up study with a random sample of 1,201 participants. Results from this study revealed that the 222 responding participants (18.5% response rate) reported using the knowledge, materials, and skills acquired from the PREPaRE trainings to a moderate extent in their professional roles, $M = 2.64$, $SD = .85$ for Workshop 1 and $M = 2.73$, $SD = 1.01$ for Workshop 2 on a scale from 1 (*not at all*) to 4 (*extensively*). The two most frequently endorsed reasons for using the information and skills from the training included personal motivation and experiencing a crisis event; the two most common barriers to using it were lack of time and lack of administrative support. When asked about the degree to which specific changes had been made as a result of PREPaRE training, participants reported that changes made to their schools' crisis intervention protocols (e.g., including specific interventions such as student psycho-educational groups) occurred to a moderate degree, whereas changes to school crisis teams and crisis plans (e.g., having more team meetings, improving crisis drill procedures) occurred at a minimal level. Overall, results indicated that participants' schools are in the process of discussing implementation of crisis prevention measures and including specific crisis intervention to crisis intervention protocols.

Bauer and Gurdineer (2010) also surveyed representatives of schools and agencies that sponsored PREPaRE workshops to assess the extent to which changes were made at the school or district level. Two hundred schools and agencies that sponsored PREPaRE were contacted originally, but only 90 of the e-mails were noted as delivered, with 30 of those individuals responding. Of the responding sponsoring schools and organizations, results suggested that schools have made some changes to district policies and procedures as a result of sponsoring

PREPaRE, but that significant additions or changes to school board policy about crisis prevention and intervention have not been made. In terms of need for additional support, the most strongly endorsed suggestion was to work with administrators, followed by offering consultation and follow-up training (Bauer & Gurdineer, 2010).

Taken together, findings from these studies reveal that PREPaRE results in immediate gains in knowledge and more positive attitudes toward crisis prevention and intervention, as well as having high participant satisfaction. School-based utilization of PREPaRE knowledge and skills is reportedly occurring. This is especially true with regard to professional functions over which school-based mental health professionals may have the most control (e.g., utilizing specific interventions as part of a crisis response protocol). Slower changes are occurring on a more system-wide basis and in terms of changes to school board policy, which may be reflected in participants' endorsement of the need for more consultation and work with administrators.

Limitations and Future Research Needs

Further research will help to better understand the attitudes, knowledge, actions, and outcomes associated with participation in PREPaRE workshops and subsequent use of the PREPaRE materials. Future research designs may include comparison groups and schools so that further information may be ascertained regarding the relative impact on knowledge, actions, and outcomes associated with PREPaRE training. In addition, objective follow-up data yielded through observations or documentation may further contribute to self-report data provided by previous respondents. It will be important to obtain responses from larger samples regarding follow-up information, as the self-selection of previous follow-up respondents may influence the information reported.

Future analyses examining the relative attitudes, knowledge, action, and outcomes associated with various school personnel positions would also be valuable, as school psychologists, school nurses, teachers, administrators, and other school-based professionals have attended the PRE-PaRE trainings. It would be informative to consider the data relative to the previous relevant training that professionals have received to determine whether persons with previous related training benefit more or less compared to those with no previous training. In addition, it would be valuable for future research to explore how changes in attitudes and knowledge are associated with actions and outcomes.

Overall, there is a notable lack of formal research demonstrating the effectiveness of school crisis intervention and response activities. More systematic research is needed. Granted, there are numerous challenges with systematic data collection to examine school crisis team activities, and it is understood that often school teams face these same challenges, including: (a) the unpredictable and infrequent nature of crises, (b) the naturalistic *in vivo* contexts of schools (as opposed to more controlled laboratory settings conducive to traditional research), (c) the difficulty developing and implementing analyses that test causal questions regarding specific intervention strategies, given the multi-faceted nature of crisis response, and (d) the ethical and professionals concerns raised by conducting controlled research studies with populations in crisis. Thus, much of the existing scholarship consists of anecdotal accounts describing the steps taken and lessons learned following an actual crisis experience (Pagliocca & Nickerson, 2001; Petersen & Straub, 1992). The follow-up research that has been conducted, including that presented in this chapter, is limited by a low response rate and lack of representativeness to schools across the nation.

As discussed by Brock et al. (2009), the PREPaRE model emphasizes that it is imperative to examine the implementation and effectiveness of crisis prevention, preparedness, and response efforts. The school crisis team must designate a school crisis evaluation leader to provide leadership necessary to successfully design, develop, and collect outcome evaluation information. In turn, these data can be used to provide feedback that will help to refine crisis prevention, preparedness, response, and recovery efforts.

The primary purpose of the outcome evaluation is to examine the effectiveness of the crisis response activities in accomplishing targeted objectives. Outcomes that may be appropriate to examination of effectiveness of the response efforts include students' return to pre-crisis levels of functioning in terms of attendance, interactions with peers and staff, and time engaged in instruction; school personnel return to pre-crisis levels of functioning in terms of attendance and time spent engaged in instruction, and/or student access to support services (e.g., follow through on referrals for mental health services). It is essential that key objectives and outcomes be identified in advance to build a comprehensive overall crisis model that includes prevention and planning, ongoing school programming, and evaluation design. Brock et al. (2009) offer a sample form to evaluate the effectiveness of school crisis response, including questions about reconnecting students and parents, meeting the needs of students with special needs, and outcomes such as student behavior, attendance, and adjustment. They also provide an example of a teacher survey form to examine the effect of a crisis event on academic functioning. Given the short- and long-term objectives commonly identified, it is advisable to include follow-up assessments to provide further information regarding the long-term outcomes associated with the crisis response activities. Previous scholarship examining outcomes associated with crisis prevention efforts provide additional information regarding potential outcomes and measurements that may be appropriate (see Croft, 2005; Nickerson & Osborne, 2006; Pagliocca, Nickerson, & Williams, 2002, for reviews of related scholarship).

Summary

This chapter has used the PREPaRE School Crisis Prevention and Intervention Training Curriculum as a structure for examination of responding to the problems of school violence. PREPaRE is an empirically informed approach that has begun to obtain some quantitative support for its consumer satisfaction, improving crisis prevention and response attitudes, and improving crisis team knowledge. As advocated for by this model, school crisis teams need to be active at all phases of a crisis and need to engage in violence prevention, preparedness, response, and recovery efforts. PREPaRE is consistent with crisis response protocols offered by the U.S. Departments of Education and Homeland Security. Table 34.2 presents practical implications of this chapter. School violence response requires a coordinated effort that does more than react to acts of school violence. While best practice guidelines have been developed, much more research is needed.

Table 34.2 Implications for Practitioners Addressing School Violence

- When addressing the problem of school violence school crisis teams must direct resources toward crisis prevention, preparedness, response, and recovery.
- School crisis teams need to be active during all crisis phases (i.e., the pre-impact, impact, recoil, post-impact, and recovery and reconstruction phases).
- School crisis team development should make use of the National Incident Management System (NIMS), and employ the Incident Command System's (ICS) five primary functions: management, planning and intelligence, operations, logistics, and finance/administration.
- Preparation and planning is essential in developing effective comprehensive school crisis teams.
- Active training techniques may help school personnel acquire and use the knowledge and skill needed to address the problem of school violence.
- More work is needed with school administrators to make system-wide changes.

References

Bauer, C., & Gurdineer, E. (2010). *Utilization of PREPaRE School Crisis Prevention and Intervention Training Curriculum at the participant and school/district-wide level*. Master's thesis, University at Albany, State University of New York.

Brock, S. E. (2002). Crisis theory: A foundation for the comprehensive crisis prevention and intervention team. In S. E. Brock, P. J. Lazarus, & S. R. Jimerson (Eds.), *Best practices in school crisis prevention and intervention* (pp. 5–17). Bethesda, MD: National Association of School Psychologists.

Brock, S. E. (2006). *Crisis intervention and recovery: The roles of school based mental health professionals*. Bethesda, MD: National Association of School Psychologists.

Brock, S. E., & Jimerson, S. R. (2004). School crisis interventions: Strategies for addressing the consequences of crisis events. In E. R. Gerler Jr. (Ed.), *Handbook of school violence* (pp. 285–332). Binghamton, NY: Haworth Press.

Brock, S. E., Nickerson, A. B., Reeves, M. A., Jimerson, S. R., Lieberman, R. A., & Feinberg, T. A. (2009). *School crisis prevention and intervention: The PREPaRE Model*. Bethesda, MD: National Association of School Psychologists.

Brock, S. E., Nickerson, A. B., Reeves, M. A., Savage, T. A., & Woitaszewski, S. A. (2011). Development, evaluation, and future directions of PREPaRE. *Journal of School Violence, 10,* 15–30.

Croft, I. A. (2005). Effectiveness of school-based crisis intervention: Research and practice (Doctoral dissertation, University of Maryland, 2005). *Dissertation Abstracts International, 66*(12), 4296.

Dwyer, K., & Osher, D. (2000). *Safeguarding our children: An action guide*. Washington, DC: U.S. Departments of Education and Justice, American Institutes for Research.

Guskey, T. (2000). *Evaluating professional development*. Thousand Oaks, CA: Corwin Press.

Hester, J. P. (2003). *Public school safety: A handbook, with a resource guide*. Jefferson, NC: McFarland.

Ingvarson, L., Meiers, M., & Beavis, A. (2005, January). Factors affecting the impact of professional development programs on teachers' knowledge, practice, student outcomes & efficacy. *Education Policy Analysis Archives, 13*(10). Retrieved September 6, 2010, from http://epaa.asu.edu/epaa/v13n10/

Lockyer, B., & Eastin, D. (2000). *Crisis response box: A guide to help every school assemble the tools and resources needed for a critical incident response*. Sacramento: California Department of Education.

National Association of School Psychologists. (2000). *Behavioral interventions: Creating a safe environment in our schools*. Bethesda, MD: Author.

National Institute of Mental Health. (2001). *Mental health and mass violence: Evidence-based early psychological intervention for victims/survivors of mass violence. A workshop to reach consensus on best practices*. Washington, DC: U. S. Government Printing Office.

Nickerson, A. B., & Osborne, K. M. (2006). Crisis preparedness, response, and management: Surveys of school professionals. In S. R. Jimerson & M. J. Furlong (Eds.), *Handbook of school violence and school safety: From research to practice* (pp. 89–101). Mahwah, NJ: Erlbaum.

Pagliocca, P. M., & Nickerson, A. B. (2001). Legislating school crisis response: Good policy or just good politics? *Law & Policy, 23,* 373–407. doi:10.1111/1467-9930.00117

Pagliocca, P. M., Nickerson, A. B., & Williams, S. (2002). Research and evaluation directions in crisis intervention. In S. E. Brock, P. J. Lazarus, & S. R. Jimerson (Eds.), *Best practices in school crisis prevention and intervention* (pp. 771–790). Bethesda, MD: National Association of School Psychologists.

Petersen, S., & Straub, R. L. (1992). *School crisis survival guide: Management techniques and materials for counselors and administrators*. West Nyack, NY: Center for Applied Research in Education.

Raphael, B., & Newman, L. (2000). *Disaster mental health response handbook: An educational resource for mental health professionals involved in disaster management*. North Sydney, New South Wales, Australia: NSW Health.

Reeves, M. A., Nickerson, A. B., & Jimerson, S. R. (2006). *Crisis prevention and preparedness: The comprehensive school crisis team*. Bethesda, MD: National Association of School Psychologists.

U.S. Department of Education, Office of Safe and Drug-Free Schools. (2003, May). *Practical information on crisis planning: A guide for schools and communities*. Washington, DC: Author.

U.S. Department of Homeland Security. (2004). *National incident management system*. Washington, DC: Author.

Valent, P. (2000). Disaster syndrome. In G. Fink (Ed.), *Encyclopedia of stress* (Vol. 1, pp. 706–709). San Diego, CA: Academic Press.

Vossekuil, B., Fein, R. A., Reddy, M., Borum R., & Modzeleski, W. (2002). The final report and findings of the safe schools initiative: Implications for the prevention of school attacks in the United States. Retrieved September 6, 2010, from http://www.secretservice.gov/ntac_ssi.shtml

35

Enhancing School Connectedness to Prevent Violence and Promote Well-Being

Ian M. Shochet and Coral L. Smith

THE QUEENSLAND UNIVERSITY OF TECHNOLOGY, BRISBANE, AUSTRALIA.

Abstract

School connectedness is "the extent to which students feel personally accepted, respected, included, and supported by others in the school social environment" (Goodenow, 1993, p. 80). It is an important predictor of school violence, as well as related outcomes such as health risk behaviors and mental health. Connectedness reduces initial incidents of violence, buffers the effect of violence exposure, and promotes an anti-bullying culture. School violence and bullying have also been associated with a subsequent decrease in school connectedness. Several theories contribute to our understanding of these relations but the construct, theoretical underpinnings, and pathways in and out of school connectedness require further examination. Despite numerous promising interventions, this line of research is in its infancy. Interventions harnessing this protective factor may have a ubiquitous positive impact on adolescent development.

School connectedness is associated with a remarkable range of child and adolescent outcomes, including psychological well-being, antisocial and health risk behaviors, academic motivation, and academic achievement (e.g., Anderman & Freeman, 2004; Blum, 2005; Loukas, Ripperger-Suhler, & Horton, 2009). Further, multiple forms of harm are associated with students becoming disconnected from school (Bond et al., 2007). This chapter examines the construct of school connectedness, with additional focus on its association with school violence. We will begin by defining school connectedness and school violence, followed by a review of the research investigating the relations between these constructs and the related outcomes of health risk behaviors and mental health. Likely theoretical underpinnings of these relations will then be discussed. Pathways in and out of school connectedness will be presented before briefly reviewing a number of interventions that have sought to enhance school connectedness. We conclude by proposing future research directions.

Definitions

School Connectedness

Within the literature investigating students' relationship to school, numerous terms overlap and are used differently by different researchers, including school connectedness, school attachment, school bonding, school engagement, school climate, school involvement, and sense of belonging (Jimerson, Campos, & Greif, 2003; Libbey, 2004; Loukas et al., 2009; Whitlock, 2006). There is limited theoretical consistency in the way these constructs are defined and measured, and different definitions have been attributed to the same terms (Libbey, 2004). Despite this, school connectedness tends to refer to the interpersonal or affective aspects of the school environment, indicating the extent to which students feel cared for within the school context and part of their school (Ozer, 2005; Resnick et al., 1997; Wilson, 2004). Goodenow's (1993) Psychological Sense of School Membership (PSSM) scale is one measure of school connectedness and includes items such as, "I feel like a real part of this school," "There's at least one teacher or other adult in this school I can talk to if I have a problem," and "Other students here like me the way I am." Although differing definitions of school connectedness exist, there is widespread consensus that school connectedness is a powerful predictor of significant child and adolescent outcomes, such as mental health and health-risk behaviors.

School Violence

School violence has been conceptualized as a spectrum of behaviors that interfere with a school's objective to be free of aggression, drugs, weapons, disruptions, and disorder; or that violate a school's educational goals or respectful climate (Miller & Kraus, 2008). Specific behaviors included in a definition of school violence include bullying, harassment, physical intimidation, and assaults (Furlong, Pavelski, & Saxton, 2002). Although bullying has been described as one of the most common and potentially serious forms of school violence (Elinoff, Chafouleas, & Sassu, 2004), others differentiate bullying from school violence (Orpinas & Horne, 2006). As such, we will consider bullying and school violence separately in this chapter, despite recognizing an overlap between these constructs.

Research Investigating the Link Between School Connectedness and School Violence

The Effect of School Connectedness on School Violence

Numerous studies with cross-sectional designs have found an inverse association between school connectedness and engagement in violent behavior (Fong, Vogel, & Vogel, 2008; Resnick et al., 1997; Wilson, 2004). Several prospective studies have yielded similar findings, with school connectedness associated with lower rates of future violence commission (Dornbusch, Erickson, Laird, & Wong, 2001; Frey, Ruchkin, Martin, & Schwab-Stone, 2009; Henrich, Brookmeyer, & Shahar, 2005; Herrenkohl et al., 2003). For example, Resnick, Ireland, and Borowsky (2004) analyzed data from two waves (across 12 months) of the National Longitudinal Study of Adolescent Health (Add Health), a large study conducted in the United States. A national probability sample comprising 14,738 seventh to twelfth graders completed in-home data collection. Results indicated that fewer students with higher levels of school connectedness engaged in violent behavior one year later (30% compared to 42% for boys; and 19% compared to 24% for girls), compared to students with lower levels of school connectedness. It also seems important to note that several prospective studies suggest that school connectedness is more strongly linked to deterrence from initial engagement in deviant behavior than a reduction following engagement in the behavior (Dornbusch et al., 2001; Henrich et al., 2005), which may have implications for the timing of interventions. Finally, the finding that school connectedness was a stronger protective factor in predicting future violence than both family connectedness and religious attendance (Blum & Ireland, 2004) highlights the magnitude of the relation between school connectedness and school violence.

The Effect of School Connectedness on the Outcomes of School Violence

Findings pertaining to the moderating role of school connectedness in the context of school violence exposure are mixed. In regards to the relation between violence exposure and future violence commission, some studies have found that despite a main effect, school connectedness did not moderate the relation between violence exposure and future violence commission (Dornbusch et al., 2001; Henrich et al., 2005). In contrast, Brookmeyer, Fanti, and Henrich (2006) found more promising results analyzing a sub-set of data from the Add Health study. A total of 6,397 students were included from this national probability sample in the United States, completing in-home interviews and in-school surveys, across two waves (12 months apart). Results indicated that for students highly connected with both their school and parents, the relation between violence exposure and subsequent violent behavior was diminished. Further, when students were disconnected from their schools, connectedness with their parents was unable to buffer the relation between violence exposure and subsequent violence commission. This finding suggests that school connectedness may be able to weaken the link between violence exposure and subsequent violence commission.

The moderating role of school connectedness in relation to the effects of violence on well-being has also been investigated, again with mixed results. As a main effect, school connectedness was found to be protective against numerous adverse well-being outcomes in adolescents exposed to violence (e.g., self- and teacher-rated depressive symptoms, teacher-rated anxiety), yet it was unable to moderate the relation between violence exposure and psychological functioning (Ozer, 2005). Other studies have, however, demonstrated more promising results. Logan (2009) found that students abused by a peer were less likely to experience suicidal ideation if they were connected to school (16%) than if they did not report this protective factor (35%) (statistically controlling for other protective factors in the model). Flaspohler, Elfstrom, Vanderzee, Sink, and Birchmeier (2009) found that students with more positive perceptions of peer and teacher support exhibited a weaker association between victimization and subjective well-being. These studies suggest that school connectedness may be able to buffer the effects of school violence on well-being outcomes.

The Association Between School Connectedness and Bullying

It is also instructive to consider the relation between school connectedness and bullying. It appears that school connected peers may prosocially intervene to influence the outcomes of an incident of bullying (Salmivalli, 1999) and can help establish an anti-bullying culture in the school (Ahmed, 2008). As part of the Cross National School Behavior Research Project, Ahmed investigated the relation between school connectedness and bystanders' responses to bullying. Participants were 1,452 seventh to tenth graders from six secondary schools in Dhaka the capital of Bangladesh, likely to represent a relatively wealthy sub-set of the Bangladeshi population. Participants observed videos depicting different kinds of bullying before completing related questionnaires. Results indicated that students with a higher level of school connectedness were more likely to intervene in episodes of bullying (r = .39; p < .001). Ahmed conceptualized bystanders as "soft targets," more easily moved by a sense of responsibility and collective guilt/shame than bullies who are considered "hard targets." The potential impact school connectedness may have on bystanders appears to be particularly important as peers are more likely than teachers to witness bullying and often are more able to intervene.

Research on Poor School Connectedness as an Outcome of School Violence and Bullying

We have detailed how school connectedness may influence school violence and bullying, yet school violence and bullying may also lead to a subsequent decline in school connectedness. Skues, Cunningham, and Pokharel (2005) found that bullied students in grades 7 to 12 felt less connected to their peers, teachers, and school. You et al. (2008) found this relation may be particularly pertinent to certain groups of bullied students, with "bullied victims" (those who were bullied and perceived a power imbalance) having significantly lower levels of school connectedness than both non-victims and "peer victims" (those who were bullied but reported no perceived power imbalance). In relation to violence, several studies have found that both witnessing violence and being the victim of violence were adversely related to subsequent school connectedness (Janosz et al., 2008; Mrug & Windle, 2009). Perpetrators of violence may also be at risk of subsequent reductions in school connectedness, with engagement in violent behavior being found to predict between 6% and 13% of the variance in subsequent connectedness to teachers (Karcher, 2002). These studies highlight the adverse impact school violence and bullying can have on the school connectedness of all students those involved—perpetrators, victims, and bystanders.

Research Investigating the Link between School Connectedness, Health Risk Behaviors, and Well-being

Considerable evidence suggests that school connectedness is also an important predictor of a wide range of other health risk behaviors (e.g., Dornbusch et al., 2001; Resnick et al., 1997) and mental health outcomes (e.g., Anderman, 2002; Shochet, Dadds, Ham, & Montague, 2006). Given the substantial overlap in violence and engagement in health risk behaviors (e.g., Jessor, 1992), as well as the significant overlap between internalizing and externalizing problems during childhood and adolescence (e.g., Muratori, Salvadori, Picchi, & Milone, 2004), we will briefly examine the role school connectedness plays in inhibiting engagement in other health risk behaviors and its protective role in mental health problems.

Numerous studies have found school connectedness to be related to lower rates of health risk behaviors. School connectedness has been inversely associated with behaviors such as smoking cigarettes, drinking alcohol, other substance use, and delinquent behavior, in both cross-sectional (Simons-Morton, Crump, Haynie, & Saylor, 1999; Resnick et al., 1997) and prospective studies (Bond et al., 2007). Dornbusch et al. (2001) investigated the relation between school connectedness and a number of deviant behaviors using a longitudinal design (two waves, 12 months apart) and in-home data collection. This study utilized a national probability sample, comprising 13,568 seventh to twelfth graders (a sub-set of the Add Health data-set). Results indicated that school connectedness was associated with decreases in cigarette smoking ($r = -.17$, $p < .001$), alcohol use ($r = -.14$, $p < .001$), marijuana use ($r = -.17$, $p < .001$), and delinquency ($r = -.19$, $p < .001$), one year later.

Research also indicates that school connectedness is an important predictor of mental health. In one study, school connectedness was able to account for 49% of the variance in depressive symptoms in adolescents, whereas attachment to parents accounted for 28% of variance (Shochet,

Homel, Cockshaw, & Montgomery, 2008). Other studies have also found an association between depressive symptoms and school connectedness (Anderman, 2002; Jacobson & Rowe, 1999). Shochet et al. (2006) conducted a prospective study with 2,022 students aged 12 to 14 years, drawn from 14 public schools across three Australian states. This sample reflected the ethic mix of the Australian population. Students completed a battery of questionnaires at two time points (12 months apart). Results indicated that not only was school connectedness significantly correlated with concurrent depression (covariation ranging from 38% to 55%), general functioning (covariation ranging from 26% to 46%), and anxiety symptoms (covariation ranging from 9% to 16%), but it was also able to predict depressive symptoms one year later for both boys and girls, anxiety symptoms one year later for girls, and general functioning one year later for boys, after controlling for initial symptoms. These studies highlight the magnitude of the relation between school connectedness and a number of important child and adolescent well-being outcomes.

Likely Theoretical Underpinnings

Having established a range of outcomes associated with school connectedness, it seems important to examine why this construct is so broadly important. Although widespread consensus on the theoretical underpinnings of school connectedness has not yet been established, several theories are useful in clarifying the reasons school connectedness is related to various student outcomes. In this section we present key theories that provide explanations for a link between school connectedness and school violence, as well as other health risk behaviors and mental health outcomes. Social control theory, social development theory, and sociometer theory will each be discussed.

Social Control Theory

Social control theory highlights how school connectedness may function as an informal control inhibiting engagement in problematic behavior (Catalano, Haggerty, Oesterle, Fleming, & Hawkins, 2004). An individual's connection to society is purported to control their behavior, with weak or non-existent bonds more likely to result in delinquent behavior (Hirschi, 2004). The connection between individual and school is one such important bond (Dornbusch et al., 2001). Four elements are implicated in this bond: attachment, commitment, involvement, and belief (Hirschi, 2004), and a deficit in any of these facets of bonding may contribute to an increased likelihood of delinquent behaviors, including school violence. Conversely, students bonded to their school are more likely to adopt anti-risk behavior and prosocial values (Hawkins, Guo, Hill, Battin-Pearson, & Abbott, 2001).

Social Development Model

The social development model extends these ideas, integrating elements of social learning theories in addition to control theories (Maddox & Prinz, 2003). In line with social control theory, it hypothesizes that a bond between the individual and the socializing unit reduces the likelihood of the individual behaving in ways inconsistent with the beliefs and practices of the unit (Catalano et al., 2004). However, this model also incorporates the premise that children and adolescents learn behavior from their social environment, whether prosocial or antisocial, and accordingly, an individual's behavior may be prosocial or antisocial depending upon the behaviors, norms, and values of those with whom they are bonded (Catalano et al., 2004). McNeely and Falci (2004) use the labels conventional or unconventional to describe connections with those who engage in prosocial behavior and antisocial behavior respectively. While it is assumed that connections to adults in the school setting would be conventional, connections to peers may be either conventional or unconventional, depending on peer group norms (McNeely & Falci, 2004). Unconventional connectedness may account for findings of some studies that peer support was not associated with the same positive outcomes as was teacher support (e.g., McLellan, Rissel, Donnelly, & Bauman, 1999; McNeely & Falci, 2004).

Sociometer Theory

Sociometer theory (e.g., Leary, 2005) further adds to our understanding of the mechanisms underlying the relation between school connectedness, violence, and other well-being outcomes, tying together the importance of connectedness to self-worth, self- and affect regulation, behavioral control, and emotional well-being. This theory emphasizes the importance of perceived relational value, suggesting that self-esteem serves as a "sociometer," monitoring the social environment for any indication that relational value is low or decreasing. Individuals who perceive their relational value to be poor or in decline are more prone to various states of "negative affect" (e.g., anxiety, depression, hostility, loneliness). The biological function of the sociometer is to ensure the individual continues to be included, supported, and therefore protected by the group.

Sociometer theory affords greater understanding of the complex and reciprocal relations between school connectedness, school violence, and mental health outcomes. Shochet, Smith, Furlong, and Homel (2010) suggested that low levels of school connectedness represent poor perceived relational value in the school setting. As students perceive their relational value within the school context to be low or declining, a number of aversive emotional outcomes may result (Leary, 2005), thus providing some explanation of the link between school connectedness and mental health outcomes and lack of affect regulation. Emotional outcomes such as hostility may lead to an increased likelihood of violent behavior. Indeed, significantly higher proportions of young people classified as violent (as compared to non-violent youth) did not perceive themselves to be liked by their peers (49% boys, 41% girls) (Thomas & Smith, 2004). School violence may also lead to decreased connectedness, as being the victim of bullying or violence may lead to concerns regards one's relation value, and thus a sense of being less connected, with the perpetrator/s as well as peers/teachers who may not have intervened (Skues et al., 2005).

Pathways In and Out of School Connectedness

Research investigating the pathways in and out of school connectedness suggests that a range of predictors are important, from those functioning at a school-wide level to individual differences. On a broader scale, poorer school connectedness appears to be associated with a number of school environment factors such as problematic classroom climates and larger schools (McNeely, Nonnemaker, & Blum, 2002). Waters, Cross, and Shaw (2010) investigated predictors of school connectedness in a prospective study over one year, using a battery of questionnaires. The sample consisted of 5,159 eighth graders from 39 randomly selected secondary schools in Perth, Australia (including both government and non-government schools). Results indicated that approximately 25% of the variance in school connectedness was attributed to a number of between-school differences, including school size, socio-economic status, priority for pastoral care at the school, and schools' averages on state-wide standardized academic outcome measures. Staff variables also appear to have an impact upon school connectedness, with supportive school leadership, positive connectedness (Beets et al., 2008), and teachers' abilities to interact in a supportive and respectful manner with students (Juvonen, 2007) identified as important. School connectedness has also been found to be higher amongst students who participate in extracurricular activities, receive higher grades, and have high school attendance rates (McNeely et al., 2002).

Individual differences are also relevant. Recent research suggests that social skills account for some of the individual differences in school connectedness (Ross, Shochet, & Bellair, 2010), as does parental attachment (Shochet, Smyth, & Homel, 2007) and family connectedness (Waters et al., 2010). Rejection sensitivity also seems an important factor that may influence one's sense of school connectedness (Shochet et al., 2010). Given the varied range of factors that may impact upon school connectedness, it seems the most effective school connectedness interventions will be integrative and multi-layered. Such interventions target the school as an organization, as well as more directly focusing on teachers and individual students, thereby utilizing this array of pathways that lead to school connectedness.

Promoting School Connectedness

Although research on school connectedness and how best to enhance it is in the early stages, a number of interventions have been developed and implemented in an attempt to improve school connectedness and associated outcomes and benefit students and their schools via a range of pathways. We will briefly review several of these interventions, providing study results where available.

The Gatehouse Project was a school-based program aiming to enhance student engagement and promote mental health (Bond, Glover, Godfrey, Butler, & Patton, 2001). A total of 2,678 Australian Grade 8 students were involved, drawn from 26 secondary schools (12 intervention and 14 control). Government, independent, and Catholic schools were included, from both metropolitan and regional areas. The intervention involved the establishment of a school-based adolescent health team and the identification of risk and protective factors specific to each school, via student surveys. These data were then used to identify and implement appropriate strategies to address issues raised. Although results so far have not supported a significant impact upon school engagement, there appears to have been positive effects in relation to substance use (Bond et al., 2004).

Going Places was a problem behavior prevention project that aimed to improve school bonding, as well as promote greater participation in classroom and school activities, enhance social skills and competence, and develop more positive social norms (Simons-Morton et al., 1999). It involved seven middle schools from one school district in the United States, randomized into intervention or comparison conditions. Two successive cohorts of sixth-grade students were recruited and followed until the beginning of Grade 9 (N = 1,320). The program included a student directed intervention as well as parent education and school environment components. Results so far indicate that the intervention has reduced rates of smoking but it does not appear to have influenced antisocial behavior or alcohol use (Simons-Morton, Haynie, Saylor, Crump, & Chen, 2005). The impact of this intervention on school connectedness has not been reported.

The Resourceful Adolescent Program for Teachers (RAP-T) is a teacher training program that was designed to educate teachers about the importance of school connectedness and to assist them in developing strategies to improve the connectedness of their students (Shochet & Wurfl, 2006). RAP-T is an Australian program that was developed with four main goals: increase teachers' recognition of the importance and value of school connectedness for students' educational functioning, mental health, and well-being; provide guidance on key elements of school connectedness and enhancement strategies for everyday teaching; assist teachers in stress management; and support them with resources and strategies (Shochet & Ham, 2004). Although the effectiveness of RAP-T is yet to be assessed, it has been utilized within a number of government secondary schools.

The Child Development Project was a whole-school intervention program that aimed to reduce risk and promote resilience amongst young people, through helping enhance schools' sense of community (Battistich, Schaps, & Wilson, 2004). It included an intensive classroom program as well as school-wide and family involvement components. Twenty-four elementary schools (12 intervention and 12 control) were included from six districts across the United States, representing a range of city, suburban, and rural schools. Participants were 1,434 fifth and sixth graders. Battistich et al. (2004) found that students receiving the program were more engaged in and committed to school, more prosocial, and engaged in fewer problem behaviors (e.g., alcohol use, marijuana use, some forms of delinquency) than those attending comparison schools. Almost all of the program's effects were mediated by students' sense of the school as a community.

Although school connectedness programs are in their infancy, outcome results highlight the promising capacity of school connectedness to influence important child and adolescent outcomes. The diversity of the components included in these programs emphasize the multiple pathways through which school connectedness can be enhanced. With a growing evidence base on which to ground school connectedness interventions, these programs seem likely to become more effective in enhancing school connectedness and associated outcomes.

Future Research

While the current status of school connectedness research leaves us with little doubt that it is an important predictor of a broad range of child and adolescent outcomes (Anderman & Freeman, 2004), more research is necessary before this promising construct can be adequately understood and its potential fully utilized. There remain definitional issues surrounding school connectedness and the construct needs to be further developed to enable improved research and practice. For interventions to become more grounded in evidence and well linked to this construct, the field needs to better understand theory underlying school connectedness, pathways in and out of school connectedness, and its associations with many important child and adolescent outcomes.

With regard to the specific relation between school violence and school connectedness research should clarify developmental factors that can help define the optimal timing and nature of school connectedness based interventions in order to prevent the initiation of acts of school violence. Further, it seems necessary to clarify and enhance the usefulness of school connectedness based strategies once students have been exposed to violence, for perpetrators, victims, and bystanders. Further, studies that support a prospective link between more positive school connectedness and lower levels of school violence will support a case for investing in the development and implementation of school connectedness based interventions that promote student well-being.

Conclusion

School connectedness has emerged as an important predictor of a broad range of child and adolescent well-being outcomes, including school violence, as well as other health risk behaviors and mental health outcomes. It may influence school violence and bullying via a number of processes: through a main effect on rates of school violence; by moderating the impact of exposure to school violence on future violent behavior and well-being outcomes; and by promoting an anti-bullying culture. However, a reciprocal relationship appears to exist, with school violence and bullying related to subsequent decreases in school connectedness. Although numerous theories enhance our understanding of these relations, further research is needed to better understand both the theoretical basis and practical implications of this important construct. Interventions aimed at improving school connectedness appear promising, but again further research seems essential for optimal intervention design and implementation. While school connectedness is only part of the solution in targeting school violence (Wilson, 2004), it appears to be an impor-

Table 35.1 Implications for Practice: School Connectedness, School Violence, and Student Well-Being

Summary	Implications
1. School connectedness is associated with a range of child and adolescent outcomes, including school violence, health risk behaviors, and mental health.	• In targeting school connectedness, interventions may positively influence a plethora of key adolescent outcomes, in addition to school violence.
2. School connectedness influences school violence and bullying via a number of pathways i.e. a direct effect, a moderation effect on the outcomes of school violence, and an effect on school culture	• School connectedness interventions that aim to reduce school violence and bullying should target all students — perpetrators, victims, and bystanders.
3. The relation between school violence and school connectedness also appears reciprocal.	• We need to consider the school connectedness of students who have been involved in incidents of school violence and intervene as indicated.
4. Social control theory, social development theory, and sociometer theory differentially add to our understanding of how school violence (and other outcome variables) is related to school connectedness, yet a firmer theoretical base needs to be established.	• Further research is necessary in order to gain a firmer theoretical grasp of school connectedness and its relation to key child and adolescent outcomes.
5. The pathways in and out of school connectedness are varied, with both individual factors (e.g., parental attachment, social skills) and school environment factors (e.g., school size, disciplinary policies, staff variables) appearing relevant. However, these pathways are still not clearly understood and it is possible that additional pathways will be identified as research progresses in this field.	• School connectedness interventions should be multi-layered, targeting the school at an organizational level as well as focusing on teachers and individual students. • Interventions should also be integrative, considering a range of factors (e.g., disciplinary policies, staff training and culture, social skills of students). • Further research is necessary before we can gain a clearer and more complete understanding of the pathways in and out of school connectedness.
6. Several school connectedness based interventions have shown promising results; however, more research is needed before interventions can be based on strong evidence that ensures optimal harnessing of this important construct.	• Further research investigating the efficacy and effectiveness of school connectedness interventions is needed. • This research should be prospective in design, and assess a range of key health risk and mental health outcomes.

tant and promising construct with great potential to contribute towards reducing school violence and promoting student well-being.

References

Ahmed, E. (2008). 'Stop it, that's enough': Bystander intervention and its relationship to school connectedness and shame management. *Vulnerable Children and Youth Studies, 3*(3), 203–213. doi: 10.1080/17450120802002548

Anderman, E. M. (2002). School effects on psychological outcomes during adolescence. *Journal of Educational Psychology, 94*(4), 795–809. doi: 10.1037/0022-0663.94.4.795

Anderman, L. H., & Freeman, T. M. (2004). Students' sense of belonging in school. *Advances in Motivation and Achievement, 13*, 27–63.

Battistich, V., Schaps, E., & Wilson, N. (2004). Effects of an elementary school intervention on students' 'connectedness' to school and social adjustment during middle school. *The Journal of Primary Prevention, 24*(3), 243–262. doi: 10.1023/B:JOPP.0000018048.38517.cd

Beets, M., Flay, B., Vuchinich, S., Acock, A., Li, K., & Allred, C. (2008). School climate and teachers' beliefs and attitudes associated with implementation of the Positive Action Program: A diffusion of innovations model. *Prevention Science, 9*(4), 264–275. doi: 10.1007/s11121-008-0100-2

Blum, R. W. (2005). A case for school connectedness. *Educational Leadership, 62*(7), 16–19.

Blum, R. W., & Ireland, M. (2004). Reducing risk, increasing protective factors: Findings from the Caribbean Youth Health Survey. *Journal of Adolescent Health, 35*(6), 493–500. doi: 10.1016/j.jadohealth.2004.01.009

Bond, L., Butler, H., Thomas, L., Carlin, J., Glover, S., Bowes, G., & Patton, G. (2007). Social and school connectedness in early secondary school as predictors of late teenage substance use, mental health, and academic outcomes. *Journal of Adolescent Health, 40*(4), e9–e18. doi: 10.1016/j.jadohealth.2006.10.013

Bond, L., Glover, S., Godfrey, C., Butler, H., & Patton, G. C. (2001). Building capacity for system-level change in schools: Lessons from the Gatehouse project. *Health Education & Behavior, 28*(3), 368–383. doi: 10.1177/109019810102800310

Bond, L., Patton, G., Glover, S., Carlin, J. B., Butler, H., Thomas, L., & Bowes, G. (2004). The Gatehouse Project: Can a multilevel school intervention affect emotional wellbeing and health risk behaviours? *Journal of Epidemiology and Community Health, 58*(12), 997–1003. doi: 10.1136/jech.2003.009449

Brookmeyer, K. A., Fanti, K. A., & Henrich, C. C. (2006). Schools, parents, and youth violence: A multilevel, ecological analysis. *Journal of Clinical Child and Adolescent Psychology, 35*(4), 504–514. doi: 10.1207/s15374424jccp3504_2

Catalano, R. F., Haggerty, K. P., Oesterle, S., Fleming, C. B., & Hawkins, J. D. (2004). The importance of bonding to school for healthy development: Findings from the Social Development Research Group. *Journal of School Health, 74*(7), 252–261.

Dornbusch, S. M., Erickson, K. G., Laird, J., & Wong, C. A. (2001). The relation of family and school attachment to adolescent deviance in diverse groups and communities. *Journal of Adolescent Research, 16*(4), 396–422. doi: 10.1177/0743558401164006

Elinoff, M. J., Chafouleas, S. M., & Sassu, K. A. (2004). Bullying: Considerations for defining and intervening in school settings. *Psychology in the Schools, 41*(8), 887–897. doi: 10.1002/pits.20045

Flaspohler, P. D., Elfstrom, J. L., Vanderzee, K. L., Sink, H. E., & Birchmeier, Z. (2009). Stand by me: The effects of peer and teacher support in mitigating the impact of bullying on quality of life. *Psychology in the Schools, 46*(7), 636–649.

Fong, R. S., Vogel, B. L., & Vogel, R. E. (2008). The correlates of school violence: An examination of factors linked to assaultive behaviour in a rural middle school with a large migrant population. *Journal of School Violence, 7*(3), 24–47. doi: 10.1080/15388220801955521

Frey, A., Ruchkin, V., Martin, A., & Schwab-Stone, M. (2009). Adolescents in transition: School and family characteristics in the development of violent behaviors entering high school. *Child Psychiatry and Human Development, 40*(1), 1–13. doi: 10.1007/s10578-008-0105-x

Furlong, M. J., Pavelski, R., & Saxton, J. (2002). The prevention of school violence. In S. E. Brock, P. J. Lazarus, & S. R. Jimerson (Eds.), *Best practices in school crisis prevention and intervention* (pp. 131–149). Bethesda, MD: National Association of School Psychologists.

Goodenow, C. (1993). The Psychological Sense of School Membership among adolescents: Scale development and educational correlates. *Psychology in the Schools, 30*(1), 79–90. doi: 10.1002/1520-6807(199301)30:1<79::AID-PITS2310300113>3.0.CO;2-X

Hawkins, J. D., Guo, J., Hill, K. G., Battin-Pearson, S., & Abbott, R. D. (2001). Long-term effects of the Seattle Social Development Intervention on school bonding trajectories. *Applied Developmental Science, 5*(4), 225–236. doi: 10.1207/s1532480xads0504_04

Henrich, C. C., Brookmeyer, K. A., & Shahar, G. (2005). Weapon violence in adolescence: Parent and school connectedness as protective factors. *Journal of Adolescent Health, 37*(4), 306–312. doi: 10.1016/j.jadohealth.2005.03.022

Herrenkohl, T. I., Hill, K. G., Ick-Joang, C., Guo, J., Abbott, R. D., & Hawkins, J. D. (2003). Protective factors against serious violent behavior in adolescence: A prospective study of aggressive children. *Social Work Research, 27*(3), 179–191.

Hirschi, T. (2004). Self-control and crime. In R. F. Baumeister & K. D. Vohs (Eds.), *Handbook of self-regulation: Research, theory, and applications* (pp. 537–552). New York, NY: Guilford.

Jacobson, K. C., & Rowe, D. C. (1999). Genetic and environmental influences on the relationships between family connectedness, school connectedness, and adolescent depressed mood: Sex differences. *Developmental Psychology, 35*(4), 926–939. doi: 10.1037/0012-1649.35.4.926

Janosz, M., Archambault, I., Pagani, L. S., Pascal, S., Morin, A. J. S., & Bowen, F. (2008). Are there detrimental effects of witnessing school violence in early adolescence? *Journal of Adolescent Health, 43*(6), 600–608. doi: 10.1016/j.jadohealth.2008.04.011

Jessor, R. (1992). Risk behavior in adolescence: A psychosocial framework for understanding and action. *Developmental Review, 12*(4), 374–390. doi: 10.1016/0273-2297(92)90014-s

Jimerson, S. R., Campos, E., & Greif, J. L. (2003). Toward an understanding of definitions and measures of school engagement and related terms. *California School Psychologist, 8,* 7–27.

Juvonen, J. (2007). Reforming middle schools: Focus on continuity, social connectedness, and engagement. *Educational Psychologist, 42*(4), 197–208. doi: 10.1080/00461520701621046

Karcher, M. J. (2002). The cycle of violence and disconnection among rural middle school students. *Journal of School Violence, 1*(1), 35–51. doi: 10.1200/J202v01n01_03

Leary, M. R. (2005). Sociometer theory and the pursuit of relational value: Getting to the root of self esteem. *European Review of Social Psychology, 16,* 71–111.

Libbey, H. P. (2004). Measuring student relationships to school: Attachment, bonding, connectedness, and engagement. *Journal of School Health, 74*(10), 274–283.

Logan, J. E. (2009). Prevention factors for suicide ideation among abused pre/early adolescent youths. *Injury Prevention, 15*(4), 278–280. doi: 10.1136/ip.2008.020966

Loukas, A., Ripperger-Suhler, K. G., & Horton, K. D. (2009). Examining temporal associations between school connectedness and early adolescent adjustment. *Journal of Youth and Adolescence, 38*(6), 804–812. doi: 10.1007/s10964-008-9312-9

Maddox, S. J., & Prinz, R. J. (2003). School bonding in children and adolescents: Conceptualization, assessment, and associated variables. *Clinical Child and Family Psychology Review, 6*(1), 31-49. doi: 10.1023/a:1022214022478

McLellan, L., Rissel, C., Donnelly, N., & Bauman, A. (1999). Health behaviour and the school environment in New South Wales, Australia. *Social Science & Medicine, 49*(5), 611–619. doi: 10.1016/s0277-9536(99)00136-7

McNeely, C., & Falci, C. (2004). School connectedness and the transition into and out of health-risk behaviour among adolescents: A comparison of social belonging and teacher support. *Journal of School Health, 74*(10), 284–292.

McNeely, C. A., Nonnemaker, J. M., & Blum, R. W. (2002). Promoting school connectedness: Evidence from the National Longitudinal Study of Adolescent Health. *Journal of School Health, 72*(4), 138–146.

Miller, T. W., & Kraus, R. F. (2008). School-related violence: Definition, scope, and prevention goals. In T. W. Miller (Ed.), *School violence and primary prevention* (pp. 15–24). New York, NY: Springer Science + Business Media.

Mrug, S., & Windle, M. (2009). Bidirectional influences of violence exposure and adjustment in early adolescence: Externalizing behaviors and school connectedness. *Journal of Abnormal Child Psychology, 37*(5), 611–623. doi: 10.1007/s10802-009-9304-6

Muratori, F., Salvadori, F., Picchi, L., & Milone, A. (2004). Internalizing antecedents of Conduct Disorder. *Canadian Journal of Psychiatry, 49,* 152–153.

Orpinas, P., & Horne, A. M. (2006). Bullies and victims: A challenge for schools. In J. R. Lutzker (Ed.), *Preventing violence: Research and evidence-based intervention strategies* (pp. 147–165). Washington, DC: American Psychological Association.

Ozer, E. J. (2005). The impact of violence on urban adolescents: Longitudinal effects of perceived school connection and family support. *Journal of Adolescent Research, 20*(2), 167–192. doi: 10.1177/0743558404273072

Resnick, M. D., Bearman, P. S., Blum, R. W., Bauman, K. E., Harris, K. M., Jones, J., … Udry, J. R. (1997). Protecting adolescents from harm: Findings from the National Longitudinal Study on Adolescent Health. *Journal of the American Medical Association, 278*(10), 823–832. doi: 10.1001/jama.278.10.823

Resnick, M. D., Ireland, M., & Borowsky, I. (2004). Youth violence perpetration: What protects? What predicts? Findings from the National Longitudinal Study of Adolescent Health. *Journal of Adolescent Health, 35*(5), 424.e1–424.e10. doi: 10.1016/j.jadohealth.2004.01.011

Ross, A. G., Shochet, I. M., & Bellair, R. (2010). The role of social skills and school connectedness in preadolescent depressive symptoms. *Journal of Clinical Child and Adolescent Psychology, 39*(2), 269–275. doi: 10.1080/15374410903532692

Salmivalli, C. (1999). Participant role approach to school bullying: Implications for interventions. *Journal of Adolescence, 22*(4), 453–459. doi: 10.1006/jado.1999.0239

Shochet, I. M., Dadds, M. R., Ham, D., & Montague, R. (2006). School connectedness is an underemphasized parameter in adolescent mental health: Results of a community prediction study. *Journal of Clinical Child & Adolescent Psychology, 35*(2), 170–179. doi: 10.1207/s15374424jccp3502_1

Shochet, I. M., & Ham, D. (2004). Universal school-based approaches to preventing adolescent depression: Past findings and future directions of the Resourceful Adolescent Program. *The International Journal of Mental Health Promotion, 6*(3), 17–25.

Shochet, I. M., Homel, R., Cockshaw, W. D., & Montgomery, D. T. (2008). How do school connectedness and attachment to parents interrelate in predicting adolescent depressive symptoms? *Journal of Clinical Child & Adolescent Psychology, 37*(3), 676–681. doi: 10.1080/15374410802148053

Shochet, I. M., Smith, C. L., Furlong, M., & Homel. R. (2010). *A prospective study investigating the impact of school connectedness factors on depressive symptoms in adolescents.* Manuscript submitted for publication.

Shochet, I. M., Smyth, T., & Homel, R. (2007). The impact of parental attachment on adolescent perception of the school environment and school connectedness. *Australian & New Zealand Journal of Family Therapy, 28*(2), 109–118.

Shochet, I. M., & Wurfl, A. (2006). *Resourceful Adolescent Program for Teachers (RAP-T): A program for teachers to promote school connectedness in teenagers.* Brisbane, Australia: School of Psychology and Counselling, Queensland University of Technology.

Simons-Morton, B. G., Crump, A. D., Haynie, D. L., & Saylor, K. E. (1999). Student-school bonding and adolescent problem behavior. *Health Education Research, 14*(1), 99–107. doi: 10.1093/her/14.1.99

Simons-Morton, B. G., Haynie, D., Saylor, K., Crump, A. D., & Chen, R. (2005). Impact analysis and mediation of outcomes: The Going Places Program. *Health Education & Behavior, 32*(2), 227–241. doi: 10.1177/1090198104272002

Skues, J. L., Cunningham, E. G., & Pokharel, T. (2005). The influence of bullying behaviours on sense of school connectedness, motivation and self-esteem. *Australian Journal of Guidance & Counselling, 15*(1), 17–26. doi: 10.1375/ajgc.15.1.17

Thomas, S. P., & Smith, H. (2004). School connectedness, anger behaviors, and relationships of violent and nonviolent American youth. *Perspectives in Psychiatric Care, 40*(4), 135–148. doi: 10.1111/j.1744-6163.2004.tb00011.x

Waters, S., Cross, D., & Shaw, T. (2010). Does the nature of schools matter? An exploration of selected school ecology factors on adolescent perceptions of school connectedness. *British Journal of Educational Psychology, 80*(3), 381–402. doi: 10.1348/000709909x484479

Whitlock, J. L. (2006). Youth perceptions of life at school: Contextual correlates of school connectedness in adolescence. *Applied Developmental Science, 10*(1), 13–29. doi: 10.1207/s1532480xads1001_2

Wilson, D. (2004). The interface of school climate and school connectedness and relationships with aggression and victimization. *Journal of School Health, 74*(7), 293–299.

You, S., Furlong, M. J., Felix, E., Sharkey, J. D., Tanigawa, D., & Green, J. G. (2008). Relations among school connectedness, hope, life satisfaction, and bully victimization. *Psychology in the Schools, 45*(5), 446–460. doi: 10.1002/pits.20308

36

The United States Safe Schools/ Healthy Students Initiative

Turning a National Initiative into Local Action

Jill D. Sharkey, Michael J. Furlong, Erin Dowdy,
Erika D. Felix, Lindsey Grimm, and Kristin Ritchey

THE UNIVERSITY OF CALIFORNIA, SANTA BARBARA

Abstract

The Safe Schools/Healthy Students (SS/HS) initiative is a competitive grant program involving the United States Departments of Education, Health and Human Services, and Justice. Between 2000 and 2010, these agencies blended resources in support of innovative school-community coordination to improve school safety, reduce student substance use, and enhance the social-emotional well-being of youth from preschool through grade 12. This chapter provides an overview of the SS/HS initiative's core elements by describing its implementation in two California communities. Examples demonstrate how local education agencies conducted needs assessments, implemented evidence-based programs, and organized schoolwide data management systems, while addressing local and federal needs. Discussion of lessons learned and sustainability challenges provide guidance for similar school-community efforts.

Schools are generally safe (Cornell, 2006; DeVoe, & Bauer, 2010), but students and staff may experience day-to-day disruptions such as bullying that decrease their sense of school safety (Mayer & Furlong, 2010; Swearer, Espelage, Vaillancourt, & Hymel, 2010). Awareness that frequent incivility diminishes safety, combined with concerns over high-profile incidents such as school shootings (Vossekuil, Fein, Reddy, Borum, & Modzeleski, 2002), provided the catalyst to launch the Safe Schools/Health Schools (SS/HS) initiative in the United States. Between 2000 and 2010, more than 350 urban, rural, suburban, and tribal school local education agencies (LEAs), in collaboration with local mental health and juvenile justice providers, received SS/HS funding, making it the most prominent and coordinated effort to promote safe and drug-free schools in the United States. This federal initiative encouraged schools and communities to design and implement comprehensive programs to improve school safety, reduce substance use, and enhance students' social-emotional well-being. It emphasized the need for prevention, student support, cross-agency coordination, and the use of evidence-based practices. SS/HS aimed to bring about "structural change with a school system, within a community," and create conditions where school systems "collaborate and coordinate with others who had a responsibility for working with kids—namely the mental health system and the juvenile justice system" (Center for Mental Health Services [CMHS], 2005, p. 5).

Theoretical Orientation to the Safe Schools/Healthy Students Initiative

In order to accomplish the broad goals set forth by the SS/HS initiative, structural change needed to occur at various levels simultaneously (Telleen, Kim, & Pesce, 2009). This is largely based on an understanding that there are multiple individual and contextual influences that affect schools and students throughout the lifespan. A social ecological model (Bronfenbrenner, 1979) has been central in guiding the development of local SS/HS initiatives. In this conceptual model, students are at the center of a series of concentric circles, each representing increasingly expanding, mutually influential microsystems. These microsystems include families, communities, schools, cultures, and societies, and ultimately affect the child's well-being. This framework highlights the need for a comprehensive, collaborative, and coordinated system involving multiple agencies and has provided a theoretical background from which to design and organize SS/HS program goals.

Organization of SS/HS Program Goals

SS/HS aims to increase and improve services to at-risk students and their families, link service agency functions in a complementary way, decrease violence and drug abuse while diminishing school discipline problems, and foster the healthy development of all youth (National Center for Mental Health Promotion and Youth Violence Prevention [NCMHPYVP], n.d.). To address these goals, LEAs partner with mental health, juvenile justice, local law enforcement, and other community organizations. Prior to initiating services, SS/HS grantees developed comprehensive written plans that address five core elements:

> Element 1: safe school environments and violence prevention activities;
> Element 2: alcohol and other drug prevention activities;
> Element 3: student behavioral, social, and emotional supports;
> Element 4: mental health services; and
> Element 5: early childhood social and emotional learning programs.

Developing and implementing an integrated plan that addresses all five elements could be challenging for many LEAs. To assist, each SS/HS project crafts a logic model addressing areas of need that are linked with selected programs, evaluation strategies, and desired outcomes. These organizational practices are helpful when identifying the desired outcomes for any school safety project (Furlong, Jones, Lilles, & Derzon, 2010). Figure 36.1 illustrates how one SS/HS project organized its goals and strategies reflecting its coordinated effort to address the five core elements.

SS/HS Outcome Data to Date

A National Evaluation Team (NET) works with each SS/HS grantee to collect and provide data for an evaluation of the SS/HS Initiative as a whole (Safe Schools/Healthy Students, 2010a). Accordingly, LEAs are required to dedicate a percentage of their budget to evaluation activities that support the national evaluation and address local needs. The NET carries out site visits, collects survey data, conducts telephone interviews with key stakeholders, gathers partnership inventories that address contributions to activities, and requires agencies to report on measurable

Example School District Safe Schools/Healthy Students Project Summary Sheet

Strategies: Integration & Collaboration

Element 1: Safe School Environment and Violence Prevention

To maintain a safe, secure, and peaceful environment by decreasing the incidence of school violence and increasing student's personal safety through increased crisis management and conflict resolution training, and involvement in prevention activities across grade levels.

Element 2: Alcohol, Tobacco, and Other Drug Prevention

To reduce substance abuse and lay the foundation for a drug-free life. Provide universal, targeted, and indicated substance prevention programs, and counseling services across grade levels.

Element 3: Student Behavioral, Social, And Emotional Supports

To increase the capacity of school staff's ability to support the social and emotional needs of students and to increase students' prosocial behavior with peers and adults. A school-based mentoring program and developmental staff training will be implemented across grade levels.

Element 4: Mental Health Services

To increase students' capacity to cope with life challenges and develop effective life-long social and emotional skills through the involvement of community mental health agencies (START) and efficient student and family referral processes.

Element 5: Early Childhood Social & Emotional Learning Programs

To increase preschool students' learning readiness and response to instruction through the development of a comprehensive preschool curriculum that emphasizes parent involvement, social-emotional development, and academic skills.

What is our Mission?

Development of a strong community-focused, sustainable collaborative that supports the SSHS grant initiative's vision of supporting efforts to promote safe, secure, and peaceful schools.

Continuum of Best Practice Strategies Model through activities, programs, and services: Universal Prevention, Early Intervention, and Intensive Strategies.

What Do We Hope to Accomplish?

Element 1: Safe School Environment and Violence Prevention

Feelings of safety will be measured by the California Healthy Kids Survey (CHKS):
• Students' will be more likely to report feeling "very safe" at school
• Less likely to report being afraid of being beaten up and being hit or pushed by their peers.

Element 2: Alcohol, Tobacco, and Other Drug Prevention

CHKS items that assess current use, perceived effects, and perceived risk of alcohol and marijuana will measure students' substance use.

Element 3: Student Behavioral, Social, And Emotional Supports

CHKS's items measuring Caring Relationships, Meaningful Participation, High Expectations and School Connections will assess students' behavioral, social, and emotional support within the school.

Element 4: Mental Health Services

The number of referrals, fidelity of mental health services, and effectiveness of services will assess the use of mental health services across grade levels.

Element 5: Early Childhood Social & Emotional Learning Programs

The Kindergarten Screening Assessment Profile (KSEP) assesses school readiness. Fidelity measures of preschool staff training assess the effectiveness of the curriculum.

What Principles Guide Our Actions?

Continuum of best practice strategies modeled through activities, programs, and services: (a) Universal Prevention, (b) Early Intervention, and (c) Intensive Strategies

Development of a strong community-focused, sustainable collaborative that supports the SSHS grant initiatives mission.

ONGOING FEEDBACK FOR COMMUNITY, QUALITY MONITORING AND IMPROVEMENT, SHARED MANAGEMENT DECISION SUPPORT

Figure 36.1 Example of condensed local education agency Safe Schools/Healthy Students logic model elements and strategies.

performance goals consistent across grantees (i.e., required by the Government Performance Results Act of 1993; GPRA). The NET targets whether or not SS/HS grants (a) enhance collaboration, (b) reduce the frequency of violent incidents in schools, (c) reduce rates of alcohol, tobacco, and other drug use, (d) improve access to mental health services, and (e) improve school climate. Towards this end, the NET examines pre-grant conditions and resources, monitors SS/HS activities, and examines common near- and long-term outcomes.

The NET publishes current information about the evaluation on its website (http://www. sshs.samhsa.gov/community/evaluation.aspx). The most recent update (Safe Schools/Healthy Students, 2010b) indicated that grantees reported an 11% decrease in the number of students involved in violent incidents, a significant decrease in the number of students who had experienced or witnessed violence, and that most staff report the SS/HS Initiative made their schools safer. As the NET continues to provide an overall picture of the impact of SS/HS, it is important to review the details of individual sites to understand the numerous steps to implementing comprehensive programs in schools.

Developing an Integrated Plan: Needs Assessment

The SS/HS initiative and its national evaluation have requirements that we describe via the implementation of two SS/HS projects in California, for which several of the authors were co-principal investigators. Initially, assessments were conducted to inform needs for SS/HS's five core elements and to set local priorities. A thorough needs assessment supports intervention planning and is the critical first step for a comprehensive school safety project (Furlong et al., 2010). Regardless of the method employed, the needs assessment should involve multiple stakeholders, whose potentially diverse preferences are aggregated into a single set of priorities, as well as a cost-utility analysis to prioritize needs (Ross, 2008).

Given numerous options for evidence-based and promising programs to address school violence and school safety concerns, planning teams should carefully select interventions that match community needs. Needs assessment guides the selection of appropriate programs and authenticates an LEA's rationale for SS/HS funding in the initial grant writing stage, providing baseline indicators for evaluation. In our two California SS/HS sites, LEAs were already using school-wide questionnaires, thus archival data were available to help inform need. Specifically, the sites used the *California Healthy Kids Survey* (CHKS; WestEd, n.d.) and the *Communities That Care Youth Survey* (Glaser, Van Horn, Arthur, Hawkins, & Catalano, 2005), both of which assess risk (e.g., substance use, perceptions of safety) and protective factors (e.g., school connectedness, peer relations) among school-aged youth. The following sections present examples of how this information was organized and examined under the five SS/HS elements with illustrations from our two sites, one that was funded from 2007 to 2011 and another that was funded from 2008 to 2012.

Element 1: Safe School Environment

For one SS/HS site, data sources indicated increasing violence across grade levels during the four years leading up to grant implementation. Discipline data revealed that expulsions had increased by 75% in the year prior to the project and suspensions had increased by 91% over a four-year period. The CHKS survey yielded results for the five years prior to the project showing that the percentage of 11th graders reporting harassment rose dramatically from 18% to 53%, more than double the state average of 23%. Students reporting physical fighting had increased from 13% to 23%, and those reporting being afraid of being beaten up at school doubled to twice the state average.

The SS/HS team surveyed school staff about bullying to identify school safety concerns to inform intervention planning. Results indicated that staff perceived a need for increased supervision on school grounds and additional training in recognizing and responding to bullying behavior. With a sprawling high school campus, supervision challenges were substantial; hence, additional campus security measures were needed. Data were considered relative to staff input regarding priorities, and available community resources. Additional needs were identified: a comprehensive K–12 violence prevention curriculum, an LEA-wide system of conflict resolution and mediation, alternative resources for students with disciplinary problems, a school-justice coordinator for youth on probation, and resources for parents with youth engaged in violent and delinquent behaviors.

Element 2: Alcohol, Tobacco, and Other Drug (ATOD) Prevention Activities

Similar to school safety trends, data from one site suggested ATOD was a pervasive community problem. County probation department records revealed that 80% of juvenile referrals for felony and misdemeanor offenses were marijuana, methamphetamine, and alcohol related, which was an increase from 61% seven years earlier. Moreover, the CHKS results indicated that past 30-day use of alcohol and marijuana, respectively, were at unacceptably high levels the year prior to the project for Grade 7 (17% and 6%), 9 (28% and 13%), and 11 (41% and 16%). Use of tobacco, cocaine, and methamphetamine followed a similar pattern, all of which exceeded the statewide average. In light of these ATOD data, the county's SS/HS coalition identified the following needs: (a) effective, consistent, and coordinated ATOD curricula across participating LEAs; (b) leadership training for youth; (d) early intervention services; (e) teacher and staff training; (f) parent involvement services; and (g) coordination of activities, referrals, and links between the school and the community.

Element 3: Student Behavioral, Social, and Emotional Supports to Enhance Academic Performance

The CHKS includes the Resilience Youth Development Module (RYDM; Hanson & Kim, 2007), which measures youth internal assets and external resources. The RYDM for the pre-project year revealed that 40% of 9th and 45% of 11th graders had moderate or low internal assets. Low or declining resiliency scores were reflected behaviorally with 70% of all suspensions in the prior school year attributable to defiant behaviors. These data suggested a climate where disrespect occurred, communication was challenging, and some students had limited problem-solving, anger management, and self-awareness skills. Thus, teacher training in how to foster asset development in students was identified as a critical need.

Rates of meaningful participation at school declined for 9th and 11th graders over the two pre-project years and were lower than the state average. This suggested the need for increased opportunities for leadership and engagement activities. In addition, only 44% of 7th, 36% of 9th, and 34% of 11th graders reported they had meaningful participation in the community. Additionally, an increasing proportion of low-income families coupled with the high cost of housing in this area forced many parents to work several jobs, which left over 85% of students unsupervised during after-school hours. SS/HS grantees addressed these needs with a school-based mentoring program for primary-age students, asset development training of all staff, an expanded after-school program to create opportunities for leadership, and youth-driven community service projects that also met the need for structured supervision.

Element 4: Mental Health Services

At one site, the number of youth who received services from County Mental Health was stable from 1998 to 2000, but increased by 20% to 2,705 in 2006, highlighting an increasing need for mental health services. Although the biggest school district at this site comprised 30% of the County's total high school enrollment, 41% of the County's students identified with emotional disorders attend this district. Moreover, local CHKS results revealed that 7th (29%), 9th (31%), and 11th (30%) graders reported high levels of sadness. Since 49% of youth receiving mental health services in the county were of Mexican American heritage, this indicated the need for culturally responsive services. Taken together, the LEA's SS/HS coalition identified the following key concerns: (a) inadequate early identification and purposeful screening for mental health problems; (b) limited access to qualified therapists to provide evidence-based counseling services and link families to psychiatric and multidisciplinary services; and (c) insufficient coordination of school-based mental health services, other than for the most severe and complex problems.

Element 5: Early Childhood Psychosocial and Emotional Development Programs

A strong need for additional preschools was identified at one site with an estimated 54% of children ages 0–6 years needing access to childcare. However, the supply of licensed childcare programs in the community could only meet 34% of the need, leaving the remaining 66% of families without service options. Similarly, a parent survey showed that less than 50% of the incoming students had attended preschool and most of the non-attendees were English language learners, a group requiring supports for early language development. Students without preschool often entered kindergarten lacking critical academic readiness, particularly social-emotional skills. This combination of factors resulted in many students falling behind academically during the first three years of school. Additionally, given the dire financial circumstances of area families, there was a need for subsidized childcare as a part of the preschool program.

Given the needs assessment, the LEA determined that it was essential to increase its preschool capacity, providing wraparound childcare. To address the need, the LEA proposed an expanded full-day preschool/child care program. As part of this service, the project proposed increased professional development for preschool staff in early childhood development and a parent education component to assist parents, particularly those who speak little or no English.

Summary of Integrated Planning Linked to Needs Assessment

A needs assessment is the first step in a program evaluation that identifies and prioritizes the shortages within a system (Witkin & Altschuld, 1995). Although LEA and community partners may have an excellent understanding of local needs based on personal experience, existing data provide quantitative support necessary to justify the identified needs and potentially identify overlooked or new needs. Using LEA data, state and local surveys, and service-level data from partner agencies, it is possible to develop an objective model that maps needs to program structure and resource allocation. Once these data are compiled, the next step in program development and evaluation design is to organize the service plan by need, goals and objectives, type of service activity, data needed to track progress, and process and outcome measures.

Developing an Integrated Plan: Constructing a Logic Model

A logic model is an efficient way to summarize a comprehensive program in terms of strategies, objectives, and outcomes. The logic model is a blueprint for SS/HS programs that provides links between the necessary components of an evaluation plan. SS/HS provides a Logic Model

Element	Objectives	Activities	Partners	Process Measures	Outcome Indicators
Element 1: Safe School Environments and Violence Prevention Activities					
Element 1: Safe School Environments and Violence Prevention Activities.	**Objective 1.1:** Increase the percentage of students who report feeling "safe" at school by 40% from the baseline by last year of project.	**Activity 1A.** Implement: Too Good for Drugs (TGD) for students in K-8 and Too Good for Drugs and Violence (TGDV) for students in Grades 9-12.	SS/HS Collaborative will provide training and curriculum for use by teachers in classes. Two full-time Peer Educators to assist with the implementation of TGDV.	Number of teachers trained to implement TGDV. Percentage of teachers completing a fidelity checklist for each session.	**Indicator 1.1:** Increase the percentage of students who report feeling "safe" at school by 40% from the baseline by last year of project (measured by annual California Healthy Kids Survey).
	Objective 1.2: Decrease the percentage of students who indicate that they are afraid of being beaten up at school in the past 30 days by 30% from the baseline by last year of project.	**Activity 1B.** Implement the Resolving Conflict Creatively Program and Circle Mediation in Grades 7-12.	SS/HS Collaborative will provide recruitment, training, and supervision of children to act as peer mediators and teach them to help facilitate the resolution of conflicts among children both in the classroom and elsewhere in schools.	Number of students participating in the Resolving Conflict Creatively program at three high school sites.	**Indicator 1.2:** Decrease the percentage of students who suspended or expelled (annually) by 30% from baseline by last year of project. (from LEA attendance databases.)
	Objective 1.3: Reduce the percentage of 5th-grade students who report being hit or pushed around by 30% from baseline by last year of project.	**Activity 1C.** Hire a full-time Deputy Probation Officer to be assigned as a school resource officer.	County Probation Department will hire and supervise a Deputy Probation Officer.	One probation officer to service the three high school sites in LEAs.	**Indicator 1.3:** Reduce the percentage of 5th grade students who report being hit or pushed around by 30% from baseline by the last year of the project (measured by annual California Healthy Kids Survey).

Figure 36.2 Example of detailed local education agency Safe Schools/Healthy Students logic model elements and strategies (full logic model available on request).

Worksheet and Evaluation Plan Worksheet that are used together to guide the overall evaluation. For each SS/HS element, evaluators input the following data: goals, baseline data, objectives, activities, process measures, partners, and indicators (see Figure 36.2 for an example of a partial logic model). For instance, under *Element 1: Safe School Environments and Violence Prevention Activities,* the goal identified was to "Maintain safe, secure, and peaceful schools by decreasing the incidence of violence on school campuses and increasing students' sense of personal safety." This goal was identified through CHKS data on perceptions of safety, which revealed several areas of concern (Figure 36.2). An objective was matched to each need to guide progress towards the overall goal. Next, specific activities were planned to achieve each objective and partners were identified to implement each activity. Finally, evaluators identified measures to document that each activity was implemented as planned (i.e., process measure) and had the intended effect (i.e., outcome indicator).

Developing an Integrated Plan: Program Design and Implementation

Our SS/HS coalitions identified a core of evidence-based strategies and services to reduce violence, ATOD use, and related delinquent behaviors. The goal was to use a prevention approach that fosters optimal youth development so that over time, students learn how to manage conflicts when they arise, develop multiple solutions to challenges they face, and seek appropriate help when needed. Three levels of intervention are commonly used to guide prevention activities and for ease of understanding, we named them: *For All* (i.e., universal), *For Some* (i.e., selective), and *For a Few* (i.e., indicated).

Services For All are universal prevention strategies designed to improve school climate and promote well-being for an entire student body. At the universal level, it is crucial to implement context-focused strategies and programs to provide support for all students. To meet SS/HS goals across elements, the universal level includes individual-focused activities such as teaching all students ways to avoid ATOD, peer conflicts, and delinquent behaviors. Following a social-ecological model of influence on youth behavior (Sameroff, Peck, & Eccles, 2004), one SS/HS coalition decided to include context-related activities, including purposeful development of safe school plans, truancy intervention and response, enhanced school security personnel, and positive behavioral supports. Examples of Services For All include: (a) a training program designed to meet the unique needs of school crisis teams (Prepare, Reaffirm, Evaluate, Provide, Respond, Examine [PREPaRE]; National Association of School Psychologists, 2007); (b) a curriculum designed to promote prosocial skills, positive character traits, and violence- and drug-free norms (Too Good for Drugs and Violence [TGDV]; see Mendez Foundation, n.d.); and (c) a comprehensive, multiyear program to prevent violence and create caring communities of learning (Responding to Conflict Creatively [RCCP]; Aber, Brown, & Henrich, 1999).

Services For Some are intensive programs designed to target students with risk signs for negative outcomes such as dropping out of school or delinquency. These programs are designed to serve youth with behaviors associated with violence, delinquency, and dropout such as poor school attendance, academic failure, substance use, and gang activity. Based on an understanding that dropping out of school represents a "long-term process of disengagement from school that often begins in the elementary grades" (Rumberger, 1995, p. 618), the SS/HS coalition aimed to increase successful school participation and completion by increasing student engagement with school. Thus, the programs included specific efforts to improve safety and reduce high-risk behaviors as well as enhance student academic and social-emotional outcomes. For example, one SS/HS grantee chose to implement a program they called Check, Connect, & Respect (CC&R), a local modification of the Check and Connect program (see Sinclair, Christenson, Lehr, & Anderson, 2003), to address emerging behavior challenges for students in upper elementary grades and to assist in dropout prevention. Once at-risk students are identified, the CC&R model provides a mentor who checks in with the at-risk students, monitors their progress, and provides them with feedback and support.

Services For Few include highly specific and rigorous services designed to target students who have been involved in more chronic or severe risky or delinquent behavior. Figure 36.3 provides an overview of the activities implemented by one SS/HS project, including the element(s), level, and grades served by each activity. For example, *Multidimensional Family Therapy* (MDFT) was selected as a modality to provide intensive treatment for adolescent students at the highest level of risk. MDFT is a strength-based treatment model that includes individual, group, and family sessions (Liddle, 2002). MDFT is recognized as a promising intervention for adolescent drug abuse (Liddle et al., 2002). This approach was chosen for students at the indicated level of need, based on its strong empirical research base.

Developing an Integrated Plan: Interagency Collaboration and Methods of Operation

At the core of the SS/HS Initiative are the principles of mutual interdependence and synergistic effects. Mutual interdependence is based on the observation that addressing school safety requires the integration of school and community resources and strategies. Schools alone cannot address the complex issues that affect the safety of school campuses (Osher, Dwyer, & Jackson, 2003). The synergistic effects principle in the SS/HS model is that effective, sustained services integrate and blend the skills and resources of multiple community agencies in a manner that leads to high levels of collaboration and innovation (Frey, Lohmeier, Lee, & Tollefson, 2006).

In their analysis of the interagency collaboration of an SS/HS project, Cross, Dickmann, Newman-Gomchar, and Fagan (2009) found that effective organization is characterized by the

Services and Strategies	SS/HS Elements	CEO[1]		Elementary & Junior High Schools									High Schools		
		PreK	K	1	2	3	4	5	6	7	8	9	10	11	12
Student-Focused Universal Strategies																
Too Good for Drugs and Violence	1, 2, 3															
Class Action	2															
RCCP = Resolving Conflict Creatively Program	1, 3															
Student-Focused Targeted/Indicated Strategies																
CATCH = Second Step PreKindergarten	5															
Kindergarten Student Entrance Profile	5															
Behavioral Emotional Screening System	4															
Loving Solutions (Parent Project)	1, 2															
Parent Project	1, 2															
Multidimensional Family Therapy	4	Already provided														
Context and System-Focused Strategies																
PREPaRE [2]	1															
Targeted Truancy Prevention Program	1, 2, 3															
SPO = School Probation Officer	1															
Check, Connect, & Respect	1, 3															

Note. The K-3 follow-up of students' behavioral and academic achievement is an on-going science-to-practice research project being supported by the First 5 commission in the School District. SS/HS funds will be used to expand this program to two other school districts. In SS/HS column, the **bolded elements** are the primary element for the activity.

[1] = County Office of Education and Early Child Commission; [2] = Prepare, Reaffirm, Evaluate, Provide and Respond Examine

Figure 36.3   Example SS/HS project integrated activities matrix by grade level

development of a formal network of community linkages and by the strength of the bonds between partners. In modifying Borden and Perkins (1998) collaboration model, Cross et al. identified five general types of community linkage structures: networking, alliance, partnership, coalition, and collaborative. Along these lines, the SS/HS Initiative requires projects to identify their formal organizational structure and to monitor its evolution with the aim of each project moving toward collaboration-level linkages, which are characterized by having a shared vision with clear agreed-upon desired outcome benchmarks, systems to respond to emerging issues, and access to new resources (Cross et al., 2009).

School districts alone cannot build an SS/HS collaboration, but they can be the lead agency in supporting its development. We emphasize "development" because the process of building a viable collaboration will require a written interagency agreement that includes fostering a shared vision of measurable desirable outcomes, implementing a consensus decision-making process, identifying partner roles and work tasks, and implementing a formal evaluation plan (Cross et al., 2009). As was done by the SS/HS projects described in this chapter, this will always include some form of a logic model.

Evaluating an Integrated Plan: Data Management

Data driven decision making is a critical component of prevention and intervention efforts. Data informs ongoing service provision decision making, supports program oversight and design refinement, and enables longer-term program evaluation goals, including effectiveness and cost-benefit studies. Thus, it is important to support administrators, teachers, and staff, highlighting their positive roles in identifying critical data elements and participating in data collection. To promote the success of data gathering efforts across stakeholders, evaluation efforts should employ a participatory research model (Green, 2001) that relies on stakeholder (including students) involvement in design, data collection, and analysis. For community stakeholders, participation makes the evaluation more responsive to their needs, gives access to information useful to their work, promotes cohesion among participants, and helps to develop organizations (Chataway, 1997).

To evaluate programs locally, we employed three levels of evaluation strategies. In accordance with GPRA requirements to establish objective, quantifiable, and measurable performance goals for federally funded programs, the first level of our evaluation collected data on referrals to and from the agencies, types of services provided, and number of clients served. Fidelity checks, referral dates, and service data were collected for all programs. These data required by the SS/HS program provided accountability for grant-supported services, thus, it was possible to document the increase in services via SS/HS funds and in which of the five elements the initiative was focusing services.

The second level involved gathering data generated by partner agencies so they could monitor the data from their interventions. Conclusions about program effectiveness based on pretest and posttest data alone are limited by a number of threats to internal validity such as selection bias, history, and maturation, which only random assignment with a control group comparison can overcome (Campbell & Stanley, 1963). Thus, additional evaluation strategies to achieve quasi-experimental design are needed to support formal empirical research. For example, one partner agency was interested to obtain feedback about program implementation in addition to required GPRA level data. They selected several programs for local evaluation measures and, with input from evaluators, identified surveys to address their desired outcomes. The evaluators assisted the agency by creating a web-based system to streamline data entry, management, and reporting. To assist with sustainability and ensure that all interested parties could manage and report their own data, the evaluators set up user-friendly, efficient data collection and management systems. Inexpensive Web-based survey applications were used to allow program participants and staff to complete surveys from any Web-accessible location, and allow project managers to instantly access descriptive statistics on multiple facets of the program. For example, the surveys provided information regarding youth emotional and behavioral reports before and after program participation, such as changes in mental health status and positive psychology indicators.

The third level of evaluation involved a higher research purpose requiring university human subjects' approval and a more rigorous evaluation strategy. Generally speaking, the SS/HS initiative is not highly compatible with rigorous evaluation designs, primarily because random assignment to groups is not supported given that the mission of SS/HS is to serve all youth who demonstrate need. Most programs selected already have evidence of effectiveness; therefore, measures of the fidelity to the program are important to ensure adherence to program standards. However, outcome data can, and should, continue to be collected to ensure that the programs are effective for the intended population, especially if different from the population with which the program was developed. Also, if modifications are made to the existing programs, data should be collected to monitor any changes in effectiveness. Rigorous repeated measures designs can be utilized in the absence of random assignment to provide documentation of program effectiveness (Campbell & Stanley, 1963). Additionally, existing data sources (such as common cross-sectional surveillance surveys) can be gathered across time to establish longitudinal trends.

Data Dissemination

Data dissemination is a first line of defense against the research-to-practice gap, with strong bi-directional communication between university researchers and community-based practitioners, along with allied stakeholders, as an essential element. Sharing evaluation results has the potential to foster commitment among a variety of stakeholders, facilitate support of the overarching goals, and allows for agencies and individuals to celebrate successes (Patton, 1997). Additionally, shared information can lead to data-based decisions regarding programs and resource allocation (Patton, 1997).

Various audiences may have different interests in the findings. School board members may wish to learn about the specific problems occurring within their student population and the percentages of students who report feeling unsafe at school. Students may benefit from learning about the large percentage of students that are *not* using alcohol or drugs. Teachers may want to hear about what strategies are being implemented to increase students' feelings of connectedness to school, and how they can help facilitate those goals. Finally, coordinating agencies may be primarily interested in data to facilitate grant writing so they can obtain financial support to continue and implement evidence-based practices. Results can be organized and disseminated in a variety of different ways so that the information will be of optimal interest to the intended audience. Furthermore, results can be shared through a variety of different modalities including presentations to the school board and school staff, newsletters to parents, orientation meetings for new staff, and pamphlets distributed to community members or students. Students can assist in the development of these products.

As evaluators, we employed various strategies to disseminate data resulting from the SS/HS project. In addition to frequent presentations to key stakeholders, we regularly distributed releases via the Web and in print that were available to the public and primarily targeted teachers and staff. These releases provided information about the current project and reinforced awareness of the SS/HS project's mission and goals. Consistent with the primary elements in which services are offered, fact sheets were organized around a variety of topics such as alcohol and marijuana use, bullying, gang involvement, mental health functioning, school connectedness, and school dating violence, including current prevalence information for the LEA. In addition to data from the CHKS on these topic areas, teachers and school staff were given resources and suggestions about how to support students and the SS/HS project goals (see Figure 36.4 for an example fact sheet on school connectedness), with information targeted specifically for the intended audience, such as a specific school, LEA, or affiliated agency.

Sustainability and Leaving a Program Legacy

SS/HS programs are based on time-limited funding. Project components such as data management and school-home-community partnerships can be sustained through early planning, community support, and strong leadership (Johnson, Hays, Center, & Daley, 2004). Maintaining key program components takes financial planning and well-developed evaluation practices in order to help schools access necessary and available resources (Tibbits, Bumbarger, Kyler, & Perkins, 2010). Although research is inconsistent on which factors affect sustainability (Tibbits et al., 2010), NCMHPYVP (2009) identified six strategies that support sustainability planning. First, identify programs that are most valuable in producing positive outcomes supporting the project's goals. Second, determine which of these programs need additional financial support in order to be effectively sustained. Third, prioritize the list of programs through consultation with members of the coordinating council and other key stakeholders. Fourth, examine and understand the key functions of these programs and/or activities (e.g., create safer schools, reduce alcohol and drug use). Fifth, identify strategies to sustain these functions, and consequentially the positive outcomes associated with the program. Finally, develop specific action plans for implementing these strategies.

One of our SS/HS sites formed a coalition of invested partners to promote sustainability. The coalition's overall mission was to strengthen collaboration among community organizations and federal, state, local governmental units to support efforts to increase protective factors and reduce risk factors among the target youth population. The SS/HS project design represents a comprehensive model of collaboration among key agencies and programs in the community to address the six elements. Each of the coalition members committed to: (a) work towards an understanding of the needs of the youth in the community; (b) lend their name, power, prestige, and efforts to strengthen the coalition; (c) advise and make recommendations on the future direction of the coalition; (d) support the goals of the coalition through fund-raising; (e) advise the project director; and (f) arbitrate disputes regarding program funding.

The evaluation team implemented specific strategies to foster sustainability. Stakeholders were taught about the importance of utilizing data to evaluate programs so that only the most effective services were sustained. Practitioners were guided on ways to collect, enter, and analyze their own data through user-friendly data management strategies. Highly qualified practitioners were trained to be trainers of certain programs, such as PREPaRE, so they could not only implement the program but also train others on how to implement the program. Additionally, data were provided to a variety of different agencies so that they could demonstrate need and seek additional grant funding.

Overall Lessons Learned/Conclusion

Communities often come together to address social issues that are affecting the lives of their children and families. Many communities across the United States have done this through the SS/HS initiative. Collaborations that focus on achieving results through data-based decision

Getting Connected & Staying Connected
The Importance of School Connectedness

What is School Connectedness?

School connectedness is *"The extent to which students feel personally accepted, respected, included, and supported by others in the school environment."*

Students who feel connected to school are less likely to use drugs/alcohol, act aggressively, and drop out of school. "Students who are "connected" to their teachers and fellow students have higher levels of overall life satisfaction, emotional health, and are more likely to reach their future goals and dreams.

How Connected to Schools Are Students in the SS/HS Region?

Overall, local schools are working hard to keep students connected. Younger students feel the *most* connected and 10ᵗʰ graders are the *least* connected.

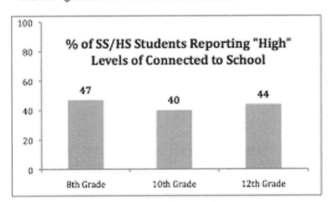

Sources: Fall 2009 administration of the CHKS School Connectedness Scale

What Teachers Can Do?

- Stand at the classroom door and greet each student.
- Spend the first 5 minutes of class on Monday to allow students to share about their weekends.
- Rotate seating arrangements so students get a chance to meet everyone in class.
- Discuss and educate students on the importance of individual differences.
- Relate coursework to students' interests (e.g., analyze a music video; use local sports teams stats in math).
- Use progress monitoring to chart student's growth and reward successes.
- Collaborate with students on the creation of classroom rules.
- Resource: School Connectedness: Strategies for Increasing Protective Factors Among Youth. http://www.cdc.gov/healthyyouth/adolescenthealth/connectedness.htm

Risk Behavior	Wellness	Substance Use
	It's all connected	

Safe Schools/Healthy Students Project   August 2010

Figure 36.4   Example SS/HS project school connectedness information fact sheet for teacher audience

Table 36.1 Implications for Practice: Tips for Evaluators of Comprehensive Safe Schools Projects.

1.	Conduct a needs assessment to get a picture of known, emergent, and possibly overlooked community needs and assets.
2.	Discuss data and community needs with stakeholders across disciplines and agencies (e.g., mental health, law enforcement, education).
3.	Develop an organizational framework for connecting needs, services, and results through a logic model or similar techniques.
4.	Identify evidence-based strategies and services, across service levels (i.e., services for everyone, for some, for a few).
5.	For evaluation design, choose the most rigorous design possible, given real-world constraints.
6.	Use existing evaluation measures, surveys, interviews, etc., when available. If something needs to be created, consult research and evaluation professionals with experience in survey construction.
7.	Select a user-friendly data management system. Take the time to set this up at the start of the project.
8.	Have a variety of communication methods for sharing evaluation results with different audiences.
9.	Plan for sustainability from the start.

making, implementing evidence-based practices, fostering strong interagency connections and communication, and planning for sustainability will likely foster positive changes in their schools and broader community. In this chapter, we discussed the real-world logistics of implementing and evaluating these comprehensive, complex local efforts. The key points of the chapter are summarized in Table 36.1. Additional guidance and evaluation case examples can be found in a special issue of the *Journal of School Violence* (e.g., Felix, Furlong, Sharkey, & Osher, 2007). These case examples highlight that there are several effective models of SS/HS programs that have left schools better off than prior to the SS/HS program. We hope that the practical examples in this chapter will be useful in helping communities plan for and share the results of their comprehensive efforts to improve the lives of youth.

Note

For more information about the Safe Schools/Healthy Student initiative, see http://www.SSHS.samhsa.gov/initiative/currentinit.aspx

References

Aber, J. L., Brown, J. L., & Henrich, C. C. (1999). *Teaching conflict resolution: An effective school-based approach to violence prevention.* New York, NY: National Center for Children in Poverty.

Borden, L., & Perkins, D. (1998). Evaluating your collaborative effort. *Program Evaluation Newsletter, 1,* 5.

Bronfenbrenner, U. (1979). *The ecology of human development.* Cambridge: Harvard University Press.

Campbell, D. T., & Stanley, J. C. (1963). *Experimental and quasi-experimental designs for research.* Boston, MA: Houghton Mifflin.

Chataway, C. J. (1997). An examination of the constraints on mutual inquiry in a participatory action research project. *Journal of Social Issues, 53,* 747–765. doi:10.1111/0022-4537.00047

Center for Mental Health Services. (2005). *Collaboration redefined: The federal Safe Schools/ Healthy Students Initiative. Draft version.* Rockville, MD: The Center for Mental Health Services.

Cornell, D. G. (2006). *School violence: Fears versus facts.* Mahwah, NJ: Erlbaum.

Cross, J. E., Dickmann, E., Newman–Gomchar, R., & Fagan, J. M. (2009). Using mixed-method design and network analysis to measure development of interagency collaboration. *American Journal of Evaluation, 30,* 310–329. doi:10.1177/1098214009340044

DeVoe, J. F., & Bauer, L. (2010). *Student victimization in U.S. schools: Results from the 2007 school crime supplement to the National Crime Victimization Survey* (NCES 2010-319). Washington, DC: National Center for Education Statistics, Institute of Education Sciences, U.S. Department of Education.

Felix, E. D., Furlong, M. J., Sharkey, J. D., & Osher, D. (2007). Implications for evaluating multicomponent, complex prevention initiatives: Taking guidance from the Safe Schools/Healthy Students Initiative. *Journal of School Violence, 6*, 3–22.

Frey, B. B., Lohmeier, J. H., Lee, S. W., & Tollefson, N. (2006). Measuring collaboration among grant partners [Method notes]. *American Journal of Evaluation, 27*, 383–392.

Furlong, M. J., Jones, C., Lilles, E., & Derzon, J. (2010). Think smart, stay safe: Aligning elements within a multilevel approach to school violence prevention. In M. Shinn & H. Walker (Eds.), *Interventions for academic and behavior problems III: Preventive and remedial approaches* (pp. 313–336). Bethesda, MD: National Association of School Psychologists.

Glaser, R. R., Van Horn, M. L., Arthur, M. W., Hawkins J. D., & Catalano, R. F. (2005). Measurement properties of the Communities That Care Youth Survey across demographic groups. *Journal of Quantitative Criminology, 21*, 73–102. doi:10.1007/s10940-004-1788-1

Green, L. W. (2001). From research to "best practices" in other settings and populations. *American Journal of Health Behavior, 25*, 165–178.

Hanson, T. L., & Kim, J. O. (2007). *Measuring resilience and youth development: The psychometric properties of the Healthy Kids Survey.* (Issues & Answers Report, REL 2007–No. 034). Washington, DC: U.S. Department of Education, Institute of Education Sciences, National Center for Education Evaluation and Regional Assistance, Regional Educational Laboratory West. Retrieved, from http://ies.ed.gov/ncee/edlabs

Johnson, K., Hays, C., Center, H., & Daley, C. (2004). Building capacity and sustainable prevention innovations: A sustainability planning model. *Evaluation and Program Planning, 27*, 135–149. doi:10.1016/j.evalprogplan.2004.01.002

Liddle, H. A. (2002). Multidimensional Family Therapy for adolescent cannabis users. *Cannabis Youth Treatment (CYT) Series* (Vol 5.) Rockville, MD: Center for Substance Abuse Treatment, Substance Abuse and Mental Health Services Administration.

Liddle H. A., Rowe, C. L., Quille, T. J., Dakof, G. A., Mills, D. S., Sakran, E., & Biaggi, H. (2002). Transporting a research-based adolescent drug treatment into practice. *Journal of Substance Abuse Treatment, 22*, 231–243. doi:10.1016/S0740–5472(02)00239-8

Mayer, M. J., & Furlong, M. J. (2010). How safe are our schools? *Educational Researcher, 39*, 16–26. doi:10.3102/0013189X09357617

Mendez Foundation. (n.d.). *Too good for drugs and violence.* Retrieved on October 20, 2010, from http://www.mendez-foundation.org/too_good.php

National Association of School Psychologists. (2007). *PREPaRE: School crisis prevention and intervention training curriculum.* Bethesda, MD: Author.

National Center for Mental Health Promotion and Youth Violence Prevention. (2009). *Leaving a legacy: Six strategies for sustainability.* Retrieved July 14, 2010, from http://www.promoteprevent.org/webfm_send/1310

National Center for Mental Health Promotion and Youth Violence Prevention. (n.d.). Retrieved October 20, 2010, from http://sshs.promoteprevent.org/

Osher, D., Dwyer, K., & Jackson, S. (2003). *Safe, supportive, and successful schools step by step.* Longmont, CO: Sopris West.

Patton, M. Q. (1997). *Utilization-focused evaluation* (3rd ed.). Thousand Oaks, CA: Sage.

Ross, J. (2008). Cost-utility analysis in educational needs assessment. *Evaluation and Program Planning, 31*, 356–367. doi:10.1016/j.evalprogplan.2008.06.003

Rumberger, R. (1995). Dropping out of middle school: A multilevel analysis of students and schools. *American Educational Research Journal 32*, 583–625. doi:10.3102/00028312032003583

Safe Schools/Healthy Students. (2010a). *Safe schools/healthy students: Introduction to the national evaluation.* Retrieved October 5, 2010, from http://www.sshs.samhsa.gov/community/evaluation.aspx

Safe Schools/Healthy Students. (2010b). *Safe schools/healthy students: National evaluation update.* Retrieved October 5, 2010, from http://www.sshs.samhsa.gov/community/evaluation.aspx

Sameroff, A. J., Peck, S. C., & Eccles, J. S. (2004). Changing ecological determinants of conduct problems from early adolescence to early adulthood. *Development and Psychopathology, 16*, 873–896. doi:10.1017/S0954579404040052

Sinclair, M. F., Christenson, S. L., Lehr, C. A., & Anderson, A. R. (2003). Facilitating student engagement: Lessons learned from Check & Connect longitudinal studies. *The California School Psychologist, 8*, 29–42.

Swearer, S. M., Espelage, D. L., Vaillancourt, T., & Hymel, S. (2010). What can be done about school bullying? Linking research to educational practice. *Educational Researcher, 39*, 39–47. doi:10.3102/0013189X09357622

Telleen, S., Kim, Y. O., & Pesce, R. (2009). An ecological developmental community initiative to reduce youth violence: Safe schools/healthy students. *Journal of Prevention & Intervention in the Community, 37*, 326–338. doi:10.1080/10852350903196340

Tibbits, M. K., Bumbarger, B. K., Kyler, S. J., & Perkins, D. F. (2010). Sustaining evidence-based interventions under real-world conditions: Results from a large-scale diffusion project. *Prevention Science, 11,* 252–262. doi:10.1007/s11121-010-0170-9

Vossekuil, B., Fein, R., Reddy, M., Borum, R., & Modzeleski, W. (2002). *The final report and findings of the Safe School Initiative: Implications for the prevention of school attacks in the United States.* Washington, DC: U.S. Department of Education, Office of Elementary and Secondary Education, Safe and Drug-Free Schools Program and U.S. Secret Service, National Threat Assessment Center.

WestEd. (n.d.). California Healthy Kids Survey. As retrieved on October 20, 2010, from http://wested.org/hks

Witkin, B., & Altschuld, J. (1995). *Planning and conducing needs assessments: A practical guide.* Thousand Oaks, CA: Sage.

37

Student Threat Assessment as a Strategy to Reduce School Violence

Dewey Cornell

UNIVERSITY OF VIRGINIA, CHARLOTTESVILLE

Farah Williams

SCOTT COUNTY BEHAVIORAL HEALTH SERVICES, VIRGINIA

Abstract

The Virginia Student Threat Assessment Guidelines were developed in response to studies by the U.S. Federal Bureau of Investigation, the U.S. Secret Service, and U.S. Department of Education that recommended schools should adopt a threat assessment approach to prevent targeted violence. This chapter describes the composition of threat assessment teams and the procedures they follow to investigate and resolve student threats. Three case examples illustrate how the guidelines can be used to address student conflicts and problems without resorting to zero tolerance disciplinary practices. The chapter concludes with a summary of four studies supporting use of the guidelines and identifies directions for future study.

Two months after the 1999 Columbine massacre, the Federal Bureau of Investigation (FBI) convened a national conference on school shootings that brought together experts in law enforcement, education, and mental health. Although renowned for its expertise in criminal profiling, the FBI cautioned against the use of profiling to identify potential school shooters (O'Toole, 2000). Instead, the FBI recommended the adoption of a threat assessment approach.

Why did the FBI's own profiling experts advise against a profiling approach? Although it was possible to identify some common characteristics of students who carried out school shootings—history of peer mistreatment and bullying, symptoms of depression and suicidality, preoccupation with violent games and fantasies, among others—no set of such characteristics offered sufficient specificity for practical use. Far too many students would be falsely identified as potentially violent (Sewell & Mendelsohn, 2000). One example of this problem was that, because several school shooters had worn black trench coats to hide their firearms, many school authorities became suspicious of any student wearing a black trench coat and some decided to ban trench coats at school. Conference attendees used the term "black trench coat problem" to refer to all such misguided efforts at profiling potentially dangerous students.

The most promising finding from the FBI's study of school shootings was that the students almost always made threats or in some way communicated their intentions to harm someone before carrying out their shooting, a phenomenon termed "leakage." Moreover, the FBI identified a number of cases where school shootings were prevented because authorities investigated a student's threatening statement and found that the student was engaged in plans to carry out the threat. These observations suggested that schools should focus their efforts on the identification and investigation of student threats as a violence prevention strategy.

Unlike wearing a black trench coat, making a threat is an aggressive behavior that can be meaningfully linked to potential violence, and, in some circumstances, constitutes a criminal act. Nevertheless, the FBI report cautioned that a threat in itself would not be sufficient to identify a violent student (O'Toole, 2000). As the report commented, "All threats are not created equal" (p. 5). Instead, school authorities must investigate the context and meaning of a student's threat for the purpose of determining whether the student is engaged in other behaviors that demonstrate intention to carry out the threat. If the investigation indicates that the threat is genuine, the next step would be to take action designed to prevent it from being carried out. Although law enforcement intervention may be necessary in the most serious cases, in the majority of cases the principal strategy is to work toward resolution of the problem or conflict that precipitated the threat. From this perspective, threat assessment can be seen as a problem-solving approach to student misconduct that is compatible with current counseling and discipline strategies used in schools, such as conflict resolution, character education, and positive behavior support.

Along with the 2000 FBI report (O'Toole, 2000), a 2002 joint report of the U.S. Secret Service and Department of Education recommended that schools train threat assessment teams in order to respond to student threats of violence (Fein et al., 2002). In response to a series of shootings on college campuses, a 2010 joint report of the Secret Service, Department of Education, and FBI recommended that college institutions also implement a threat assessment approach (Drysdale, Modzeleski, & Simons, 2010). Although these authoritative reports made a compelling case for a threat assessment approach, there was no established model or set of procedures for schools to follow, and no research evidence to support this newly recommended practice. In response to these needs, the Virginia Youth Violence Project of the Curry School of Education at the University of Virginia took on the task of developing and testing a threat assessment model for schools. This chapter describes the Virginia Student Threat Assessment Guidelines (Cornell & Sheras, 2006) and reviews a series of field-test and quasi-experimental studies supporting its use. Guidelines for use in college and university settings are described elsewhere (Cornell, 2009).

The Threat Assessment Team

The Virginia Guidelines recommend that each school form its own threat assessment team. A school-based team is more efficient because threat assessment requires an immediate response. If a student threatens to harm someone, school administrators cannot wait for a team of outside experts to assemble and begin an investigation. Threat assessment requires careful consideration of contextual and situational factors that would not be easily accessible to consultants unfamiliar with the day-to-day operation, culture, and climate of the school. Moreover, most student threats are not serious enough to warrant the assembly of an outside team. Many cases involve rash or foolish statements, some made in jest and others in a moment of anger, that are routinely resolved by a school administrator or counselor.

Perhaps the most important reason to have a school-based team is that threat assessment should not be limited to an initial assessment, but rather should involve an ongoing process of prevention and intervention. The danger posed by a threat is not static; it changes in response to events and interactions among students. An effective threat assessment team will not settle for judging the seriousness of a threat at a single point, but will implement a response to a serious threat that is designed to reduce the risk of violence and will continue to monitor any interventions that are initiated.

None of these reasons for using an on-site threat assessment team negate the use of outside consultation in some situations. In a complicated case involving a serious threat of violence, the school-based team may want to draw upon the expertise of a mental health professional from the community, work closely with law enforcement, or consult with authorities in the school division's administration. In the Memphis field test (Strong & Cornell, 2008; described below), a division-wide team responded to the most serious cases in a large school system, while less serious cases were resolved at the school level.

A threat assessment team should include representatives from three domains: administration, law enforcement, and mental health. The team leader, typically an administrator who has responsibility for student discipline and safety, conducts an initial triage evaluation to determine the seriousness of the case and then either takes the limited action necessary to resolve the threat, or if the threat is more serious, engages more team members in a full-scale assessment and intervention.

The ideal law enforcement representative is a school resource officer (SRO) who has training and experience working in school settings. The SRO can advise the team whether a student's behavior has violated the law and can conduct criminal investigations and take appropriate action in the most serious cases. More generally, however, the SRO can be a role model and encourage law-abiding behavior by interacting with students and participating in school functions. School resource officers should adopt a problem-solving approach to crime prevention by identifying and monitoring potentially volatile conflicts between students or groups of students.

Depending on the school's staffing pattern, a threat assessment team should include one or more mental health professionals (school counselor, school psychologist, social worker, etc.). A mental health professional is involved in both evaluative and intervention capacities. In the most serious cases, a school psychologist or other suitably qualified staff member conducts an evaluation of the student with two main objectives. The first objective is to screen the student for mental health problems that demand immediate attention, such as psychosis or suicidality. The second objective is to assess why the student made the threat and make recommendations for dealing with the problem or conflict that stimulated the threatening behavior.

Mental health professionals are also used to conduct interventions such as counseling for a troubled student or conflict resolution between two parties engaged in a dispute. There is a large body of evidence that school-based interventions can reduce aggressive behavior (Wilson, Lipsey, & Derzon, 2003). Examples of effective programs include social competence training, cognitive-behavioral counseling to improve social interaction and problem-solving skills, and conflict resolution programs. In all cases, there should be follow-up monitoring to ensure that a plan is working.

Overall, the threat assessment team follows a risk reduction or risk management approach, as distinguished from a predictive approach (Heilbrun, 1997). Although it is understandable for school authorities to want a formal prediction of whether a student will carry out a threat, such predictions tend to be unreliable and prone to error (Mulvey & Cauffman, 2001). Violence risk should not be considered a static quality, but rather a condition that can increase or decrease based on circumstances and intervention efforts. Even though psychologists can make reasonably accurate short-term predictions of violence in some situations (Borum, 1996), little is known about the prediction of student violence. In any case, the goal of threat assessment is the reduction of risk for violence rather than the prediction of violence, so that static predictions (e.g.,

"30% risk of violence") and classifications (such as "high," "medium," or "low" risk) are not very useful. For these reasons, the Virginia Guidelines discourage school mental heath professionals from trying to make formal predictions of whether a student will carry out a threatened action.

Threat Assessment Guidelines

Threat assessment teams follow a seven-step decision tree (see summary in Table 37.1). Each step in the decision tree is accompanied by an extensive set of guidelines and case examples (Cornell & Sheras, 2006). These guidelines recognize that many threats are clearly intended as jokes or rhetorical remarks and that school personnel could not conduct a comprehensive threat assessment every time a student made an inappropriate statement or used seemingly threatening language. Therefore, the first three steps of the assessment constitute a triage process during which the team leader determines whether the case can be quickly and easily resolved or will require more extensive evaluation and intervention as a substantive threat. In the easiest and clearest cases, a threat might be resolved within an hour, but in more complex cases, there may be an extended assessment of the student, interviews with witnesses as well as meetings with parents, and then the formulation of a safety plan that is administered over an extended period of time.

Table 37.1 Steps in Student Threat Assessment

Step 1. Evaluate the threat.

> The principal investigates a reported threat by interviewing the student who made the threat and any witnesses to the threat. The principal considers the context and meaning of the threat, which is more important than the literal content of the threat.

Step 2. Decide whether the threat is transient or substantive.

> A *transient* threat is not a serious threat and can be easily resolved, but a *substantive* threat raises concern of potential injury to others. For transient threats, go to step three and for substantive threats skip to step four.

Step 3. Respond to a transient threat.

> If the threat is transient, the principal may respond with a reprimand, parental notification, or other actions that are appropriate to the severity and chronicity of the situation. The incident is resolved and no further action is needed.

Step 4. If the threat is substantive, decide whether it is serious or very serious.

> If a threat is substantive, the principal must decide how serious the threat is and take appropriate action to protect potential victims. A threat to hit, assault, or beat up someone is serious, whereas a threat to kill, rape, use a weapon, or severely injure someone is considered very serious. For serious threats, go to step five and for very serious threats, skip to step six.

Step 5. Respond to a serious substantive threat.

> Serious substantive threats require protective action to prevent violence, including notification of potential victims and other actions to address the conflict or problem that generated the threat. The response to serious threats is completed at this step.

Step 6. Respond to a very serious substantive threat.

> Very serious threats require immediate protective action, including contact with law enforcement, followed by a comprehensive safety evaluation. The student is suspended from school pending completion of a safety evaluation, which includes a mental health assessment following a prescribed protocol.

Step 7. Implement a safety plan.

> The threat assessment team develops and implements an action plan that is designed both to protect potential victims and to meet the student's educational needs. The plan includes provision for monitoring the student and revising the plan as needed.

Note. Reprinted from Cornell and Sheras (2006).

At *step one,* the leader of the threat assessment team interviews the student who made the threat, using a standard set of questions that can be adapted to the specific situation. The team leader or another team member should also interview witnesses to the threat. The team is not concerned simply with the verbal content of the threat, but the context in which the threat was made and what the student meant and intended in making the threat. This approach differs markedly from a zero tolerance disciplinary approach, which treats all violations as equal infractions that deserve the same consequence.

Zero tolerance policies characteristically do not consider the context and meaning of the student's behavior, and this practice has resulted in numerous cases in which schools have over-reacted to situations that did not pose a serious danger to others. For example, students in the United States have been removed from school for misbehavior such as bringing a one-inch plastic toy gun to school, bringing a plastic knife to school for use at lunchtime, pointing a finger like a gun and playfully pretending to shoot someone, and making threatening statements in jest. The American Psychological Association Zero Tolerance Task Force (2008) found that there is no evidence that such policies and practices have any beneficial impact on students or improve school safety.

At *step two,* the principal must make an important distinction between threats that are considered serious because they pose a continuing risk or danger to others, and those that are not serious because they are readily resolved and do not pose a continuing risk. Less serious threats that are readily resolved are termed "transient" threats and are distinguished from substantive threats. Transient threats are defined as behaviors that can be readily identified as expressions of anger, frustration, or humor that dissipate when the student has time to reflect on the meaning of what he or she has said. The defining feature of a transient threat is that the student does not have a sustained intention to harm someone.

A transient threat is readily resolved at *step three* without a comprehensive threat assessment. The principal may reprimand the student or impose some other disciplinary consequence, but is not compelled to take protective action because the threat is not serious. Ideally, the student should offer an apology and explanation to those affected by the threat. In cases where the threat suggests an ongoing problem, the student's behavior may merit further counseling or some other intervention.

Any threat that cannot be resolved as a transient threat is regarded as a substantive threat. A substantive threat involves a sustained intent to harm someone beyond the immediate incident or argument during which the threat was made. If there is doubt whether a threat is transient or substantive, the threat is regarded as substantive. Several features can be used to identify substantive threats:

- the threat includes plausible details, such as a specific victim, time, place, and method of assault;
- the threat involves planning and preparation, including efforts to recruit accomplices or invite an audience;
- there is clear evidence of intent to carry out the threat, such as a weapon, bomb materials, map, written plan, or list of intended victims.

Although the presence of any one of these features may lead the school administrator to presume the threat is substantive, none are absolute indicators; with additional investigation, other facts could demonstrate that the threat is transient. For example, a student might seek an accomplice to send an angry, threatening letter to a classmate. The threat is transient if the student does not intend to carry out the threat, but only means to frighten the classmate. Such an incident would be handled as a serious disciplinary matter, but not as a serious threat.

The example of a student who frightens a classmate with a transient threat illustrates another important point, which is that threat assessment and discipline are separate processes. In some cases, the disciplinary consequences can be quite severe even if the threat is transient. For example, a false bomb threat is not a substantive threat if the student only intends to disrupt the school, but nonetheless has serious legal consequences. In general, threat assessment is concerned with the risk of future harm to others and what steps should be taken to prevent the threat from being carried out, whereas discipline is concerned with administering appropriate consequences (ranging from punishment to restorative actions) for prohibited behaviors.

In essence, threat assessment teams must always consider the context of the threat and make reasoned judgments based on all the available information. The team should consider the student's age and capabilities, mental stability, prior history of violent behavior, and other relevant factors. The guidelines assist the team in its investigation, but do not provide a prescription or formula

If the threat is not transient, the process proceeds to *step four*. At this step, the substantive threat is determined to be *serious* or *very serious,* based on the intended severity of injury. A serious threat is a threat to assault, strike, or beat up someone. A very serious threat is a threat to kill, sexually assault, or severely injure someone. A threat involving the use of a weapon is generally considered a threat to severely injure someone. However, teams must always use their judgment. For example, threatening someone with a toy gun that could not seriously injure anyone would be viewed differently than threatening someone with a genuine firearm.

Serious substantive threats are handled at *step five*. At this step, school authorities are obliged to take protective actions appropriate to the circumstances. Immediate protective actions include cautioning the student about the consequences of carrying out the threat and providing supervision so that the student cannot carry out the threat while at school, and contacting the student's parents so that they can assume responsibility for supervising the student after school.

The level of supervision should be consistent with the nature and seriousness of the threat. For example, a visibly angry student who threatens to beat up a classmate should be confined to an office or classroom under adult supervision. The school resource officer might meet with the student. More often, however, a student will calm down and can be permitted to return to class on the condition that the student not have any contact with the classmate. As a precaution, the student might be kept from a class attended by the classmate, and the student might be required to report to the office prior to school dismissal, rather than being released to ride the same bus as the classmate. Beyond the immediate response, the team might initiate some form of intervention (e.g., anger control counseling, dispute mediation) appropriate to the situation.

Very serious substantive threats are handled at steps six and seven. At *step six*, the team takes decisive action to ensure that the threat is not carried out. The student might be detained in the principal's office until his or her parents have arrived. In addition, the law enforcement officer on the team must determine whether the student has violated the law, and if so, what law enforcement action should be taken. The team also notifies the intended victim (or victims), and if the victim is a student, the victim's parents. The school psychologist should begin a mental health evaluation of the student as soon as possible, with the initial goal of assessing the student's mental state and need for immediate mental health services. Although the threat assessment guidelines discourage use of long-term suspension, a short-term suspension is appropriate until the team can devise a plan. If a short-term suspension is necessary, it will likely also be important to work with the student's family to encourage a plan for structure and supervision to be provided during the time the child is not in school.

At *step seven,* the team completes a safety evaluation that integrates findings from all available sources of information in a written safety plan. The safety plan is designed both to protect potential victims and to address the student's educational needs. The plan includes mental health and counseling recommendations, findings from the law enforcement investigation, and disciplinary consequences. At this point, the principal decides whether the student can return to school or should be placed in an alternative setting. If the student is permitted to return to school, the plan describes the conditions that must be met and the procedures in place to monitor the student when he or she returns. Threat assessment is a more flexible, problem-solving approach to violence prevention that represents an alternative to zero tolerance discipline practices. The Virginia model is intended to encourage students to seek help and generate a more positive and less punitive school climate.

Threat Victims

The guidelines address threat victim issues in several ways. In all cases, a team member should interview the recipient or target of the threat and consider this person's perspective and his or her understanding of the meaning of the threat. In the case of transient threats, the student making the threat typically is encouraged to offer an apology and/or explanation to the person who was threatened. If a threat involves a dispute or conflict, the team will explore the possibility of conflict mediation, provided that both parties are willing to participate. If the threat is substantive, the team has a clear obligation to notify the victim (and if the victim is a student, also that student's parents) for protective purposes. The guidelines (Cornell & Sheras, 2006) indicate when school authorities should make exceptions to confidentiality in order to notify potential victims and the guidelines include advice on procedures for keeping victims informed later in the process when decisions are made about a student returning to school.

Case Examples

The following three cases demonstrate how the student threat assessment guidelines can be applied to transient, serious, and very serious threats. These are composite cases with details changed to disguise identities and highlight best practices.

Transient Threat Example

Two middle school boys got into a fight in the hallway. After they were separated by two teachers, one boy shouted to the other, "I'm gonna kill you for that."

Threat Assessment Summary

The principal interviewed the student, who admitted making the statement, but said he made the statement because he was mad and not because he intended to kill anyone. He explained what the other student had done to offend him and how the fight started. The boy was apologetic and agreed to meet with the other boy and try to resolve their conflict. The principal was familiar with both boys and knew their discipline records. The principal consulted with the teachers for any additional information about the conflict between them and concluded that the threat was a transient threat. Although the threat was transient, the principal administered a disciplinary consequence to both boys that was consistent with the school's discipline policy for fighting. Their parents were contacted and the entire situation was reviewed. The school resource officer met with each boy and pointed out the legal consequences that could follow from fighting and threatening behavior. The boys attended a mediation session to resolve their conflict. After the mediation session, the guidance counselor interviewed each boy to assess whether the conflict had been resolved. The boys were encouraged to contact the guidance counselor if there was renewed conflict.

Serious Substantive Threat Example

Will and Dan had a history of teasing and mocking one another. One day Will became so angry with something Dan said that he sent Dan a note, "Meet me at the park tonight at 9 so I can kick your a––." Dan showed the note to a teacher, who in turn contacted the principal. The principal regarded the note as a threat because it expressed intent to harm someone. The fact that the threat was in writing, and specified a time and place for the fight, suggested that the threat was probably substantive rather than transient.

Threat Assessment Summary

The principal met with Will and then attempted to mediate the dispute by bringing Dan into the meeting. Both boys had a number of complaints and grievances to air. Will was reluctant to apologize, which supported the principal's concern that Will still wanted to fight Dan. At this point, the principal decided that the threat was substantive rather than transient. Because the threat was substantive, the principal was obligated to take some form of protective action, depending on the nature of the situation. The principal's attempt to mediate the dispute was one form of protective action, and when this did not appear to be effective, she ordered both boys to stay away from one another. She asked the school resource officer to speak with both boys and to advise them of the legal consequences of threatening, fighting, or injuring one another. The principal also contacted the boys' teachers and made arrangements so that they would not encounter each other between classes or during physical education class. She called both sets of parents to inform them of the situation and followed up with a letter that offered the services of the school counselor. Will was given a disciplinary consequence that was consistent with the school's disciplinary policy for making threats.

Very Serious Substantive Threat Example

A middle school student named Dennis confided in two of his friends that he was "sick and tired of getting pushed around at the bus stop" by two older boys and that he was going to "bring an equalizer tomorrow and make them pay." The friends understood this to mean that Dennis intended to bring a gun to the bus stop and one of the friends told another student, who in turn told the school resource officer. The school resource officer contacted the principal, who decided to investigate the report as a possible threat.

Threat Assessment Summary

The principal interviewed Dennis as well as the student who first heard Dennis make the threat. Dennis at first denied making the statement or having access to a firearm. He did, however, admit that he was upset with two boys who had been bullying him at the bus stop for several weeks. When the principal contacted Dennis's mother, she said that Dennis knew that she kept a handgun in her nightstand. Based on his investigation, the principal decided that the threat could not be regarded as transient, and since it involved a threat to use a weapon, it was a very serious substantive threat. He contacted members of the school threat assessment team, who agreed with this assessment. Dennis was placed on suspension pending completion of a safety evaluation, according to the school's written policy on very serious threats of violence. The principal and school resource officer met with Dennis's mother and reviewed the seriousness of the situation, but also related their plans to investigate the bullying problem.

Following the protocol in the threat assessment guidelines, the school psychologist conducted an initial interview with Dennis that afternoon before he went home. She screened Dennis for psychiatric symptoms that would merit hospitalization, inquired about homicidal and suicidal intention, and obtained information about the bullying he had experienced. The school psychologist met with Dennis's mother and obtained background information about his family history, previous peer relations, and prior aggressive behavior. She assessed the mother's willingness to cooperate with the school in taking actions to prevent Dennis from getting into serious trouble. The mother agreed to let a relative keep the handgun for the foreseeable future.

The school principal contacted the parents of the boys who were the presumed targets of the threat. The principal informed the parents what had happened and that the boy who made the threat had been suspended from school. Because this matter involved a threat of violence, the principal disclosed the name of the student and the actions that were taken for protective purposes. During the next few days, members of the threat assessment team gathered information from Dennis's teachers and also interviewed the bus driver and students who used the same bus stop.

The threat assessment team held a meeting three days after the incident and decided on an action plan. Because Dennis had not directly threatened the boys or brought a weapon to the bus stop, he would be permitted to return to school under certain conditions. The first condition was that he expressed understanding that there was a better way for him to deal with the bullying situation and that his threat was inappropriate. He accepted the consequence of not being permitted to ride the school bus for the remainder of the school year. In addition, he agreed to check in with the school resource officer on a daily basis, and to advise him of any bullying incidents that took place. Dennis also began meeting with the school counselor to talk about his peer relationships. The counselor also met with the two boys who had been teasing Dennis.

Research on the Threat Assessment Guidelines

The first field test of the threat assessment guidelines was conducted in 35 schools spanning grades K–12 (Cornell et al., 2004; Kaplan & Cornell, 2005). The Virginia Youth Violence Project trained a threat assessment team in each school. A total of 188 cases were identified across the 35 schools during one school year. The most common threats were threats to hit or assault someone (41%), followed by threats to kill (15%), shoot (13%), stab (11%), or injure in some other way (5%). Approximately 15% of threats were too vague to be classified (e.g., "I'm going to get you"). Most threats (76%) were made by boys.

The teams investigated each threat to determine whether it was transient or substantive. The majority of cases (70%) were resolved as transient threats through an explanation or apology, although often with some disciplinary consequences and counseling. Approximately one-third (30%) of the cases were substantive threats that required protective action and the development of a plan to address the underlying conflict or problem that drove the student to make a threat. Only three students (each with a lengthy record of disciplinary violations) were given long-term suspensions. Approximately half of the students received short-term suspensions (typically 1–3 days), and nearly all students were able to return to their original school.

The following year, researchers conducted follow-up interviews with school principals and other team members. Principals were asked whether the student's behavior had worsened, stayed about the same, or improved since the threat incident. Only 18% of the students were described as worse, 39% were the same, and 43% were improved. Similarly, principals were asked about the student's relationship with the target of the threat. (For this question the sample size dropped to 126, because for various reasons the principal could not make a judgment, such as when the student was no longer in the school). The principals reported that the relationship had worsened in just 5% of the cases, while it remained the same in 63% and improved in 32%. Finally, principals were asked whether, to their knowledge, the student had carried out the threat. According to the principals, *none* of the threats were carried out. Although it is conceivable that some of the less severe threats (e.g., to hit or strike someone) were carried out without the principal's knowledge, almost certainly none of the more serious threats to shoot, stab, or otherwise severely injure the target were carried out.

A second field test (Strong & Cornell, 2008) was conducted in Memphis City Schools, a large urban school system serving a predominantly (87%) African American population. Approximately 75% of Memphis students were eligible for free or reduced lunch and 29% of students had been retained at least one grade. Memphis elected to use a centralized threat assessment team that would handle the most serious cases referred by each school. A total of 209 cases from 103 schools were referred for threat assessment because the principal deemed them to merit long-term suspension. There were 60 (29%) threats to hit or beat up someone, 48 (23%) threats to cut or stab, 32 (15%) threats to shoot, 30 (14%) threats to kill, 14 (7%) sexual threats, and 25 (12%) other threats (such as to blow up or burn down the school).

In each case, the team developed an individualized plan of mental health and educational services. All but five students were able to return to school or an alternative educational placement and just three students were incarcerated. Across all sources of information, there was no report of any of the threats being carried out. In addition, the study examined student discipline referrals before and after the threat assessment for 198 students with available records. These students averaged 6.4 referrals before the threat incident and 2.9 referrals after the threat assessment, a decline of 55% that was statistically significant even after controlling for the length of the school year and the dates of the assessments.

The two field-test studies demonstrated that a threat assessment approach could be implemented with seemingly positive outcomes, but both studies lacked comparison groups. A third study partially addressed this limitation (Cornell, Sheras, Gregory, & Fan, 2009). Each year Virginia public schools complete a school safety audit, which in 2007 included questions about the use of threat assessment procedures. Based on the survey, it was determined that 95 high schools had adopted the guidelines, 131 schools used locally developed threat assessment procedures, and 54 did not use a threat assessment approach. The three groups were compared retrospectively using a school climate survey that was administered in the spring of 2007 to randomly selected samples of ninth-grade students in each high school as part of the Virginia High School Safety Study (Gregory et al., 2010).

Students in schools using the guidelines reported less bullying in the past 30 days, greater willingness to seek help for bullying and threats of violence, and more positive perceptions of the school climate than students in either of the other two groups of schools (Cornell et al., 2009). In addition, schools using the guidelines had fewer long-term suspensions during the 2006–2007 school year than schools using other threat assessment approaches. None of these statistically significant group differences could be attributed to school size, minority composition or socioeconomic status of the student body, neighborhood violent crime, or the extent of security measures in the schools, which were statistically controlled.

A fourth study examined the impact of staff training on threat assessment. Because school administrators are keenly concerned about the potential for a serious act of violence, many want to make use of zero tolerance policies, typically involving long-term suspension. Therefore, a key goal of the training model is to convince school staff members to use a threat assessment approach rather than zero tolerance. School teams are routinely trained in a six-hour workshop that explains the rationale for threat assessment and teaches participants to use the guidelines (Cornell & Sheras, 2006). To examine staff training effects, Allen, Cornell, and Lorek (2008) administered pre- and post-training surveys to 351 multidisciplinary staff from two school divisions, one serving a challenging urban population and the other a more affluent, suburban population. Comparison of pre- and post-measures showed that there was a substantial decrease among school staff members in support for zero tolerance and increased knowledge of threat

Table 37.2 Implications for Practice: How to Conduct Student Threat Assessments

- Each school should have a trained threat assessment team composed of representatives from school administration, mental health services, and law enforcement.

- Teams should give more weight to the context and meaning of a threat than to the student's literal statement, since the critical issue is whether the student *poses* a threat, not whether the student *made* a threat.

- Most threats can be quickly resolved as transient threats, whereas more serious, substantive threats require protective action and further investigation, followed by an intervention designed to ameliorate the problem or conflict that stimulated the threat.

- Threat assessment is a process of risk reduction and threat management that gives schools an alternative to zero tolerance disciplinary practices.

assessment principles and concepts. These changes were found among staff in both school divisions, with similar effects across school principals, psychologists, counselors, resource officers, and social workers.

Directions for Future Study

These field-test findings need replication in a controlled study with a comparison group of schools not using threat assessment. It would be useful to assess threat assessment outcomes using information from multiple sources, to investigate the relationship between the student and targeted victim in more detail, and to identify factors associated with successful outcomes. For example, how useful is peer mediation or other conflict resolution strategies when students make threats to harm one another? Although there is evidence that a variety of school-based violence prevention programs can improve student behavior (Wilson, Lipsey, & Derzon, 2003), we do not know how such programs affect students involved in various kinds of conflicts and threatening situations, or whether certain kinds of interventions are more effective.

It is important to consider the degree to which teams fully implement a threat assessment approach and how skillfully they follow its guidelines. In their landmark meta-analysis of school-based violence prevention programs, Wilson et al. (2003) found that quality of program implementation was critical. Similarly, in their review of over 500 studies, Durlak and DuPre (2008) found that the level of implementation affected the outcomes obtained in promotion and prevention programs. Schools that carefully implement and maintain a violence prevention program are more likely to achieve substantial reductions in student aggression and misbehavior than schools that implement programs in a less rigorous manner. It follows that the implementation of threat assessment programs must be carefully monitored for fidelity.

Threat assessment is not a substitute for other violence prevention efforts; it should be undertaken in the context of a more comprehensive approach that includes an array of intervention and prevention services (Osher, Dwyer, & Jackson, 2004). The development and field-testing of threat assessment guidelines demonstrates that threat assessment is a promising procedure, worthy of further study. Threat assessment is an especially valuable component of school violence prevention because it uses resources efficiently and targets specific conflicts and disputes before they erupt in violence.

References

Allen, K., Cornell, D., & Lorek, E. (2008). Response of school personnel to student threat assessment training. *School Effectiveness and School Improvement, 19*, 319–332. doi: 10.1080/09243450802332184

American Psychological Association Zero Tolerance Task Force. (2008). Are zero tolerance policies effective in schools?: An evidentiary review and recommendations. *American Psychologist, 63*, 852–862. doi:10.1037/0003-066X.63.9.852

Borum, R. (1996). Improving the clinical practice of violence risk assessment: Technologies, guidelines and training. *American Psychologist, 51*, 945–956. doi:10.1037/0003-066X.51.9.945

Cornell, D. (2009). *Recommended practices for Virginia college threat assessment*. Richmond: Virginia Department of Criminal Justice Services. Retrieved from http://youthviolence.edschool.virginia.edu/threat-assessment/pdf/college-threat-recommended-practices.pdf

Cornell, D., & Sheras, P. (2006). *Guidelines for responding to student threats of violence*. Longmont, CO: Sopris West.

Cornell, D., Sheras, P., Gregory, A., & Fan, X. (2009). A retrospective study of school safety conditions in high schools using the Virginia Threat Assessment Guidelines versus alternative approaches. *School Psychology Quarterly, 24*, 119–129. doi:10.1037/a0016182

Cornell, D., Sheras, P., Kaplan, S., McConville, D., Posey, J., Levy-Elkon, A., McKnight, L., Branson, C., & Cole, J. (2004). Guidelines for student threat assessment: Field-test findings. *School Psychology Review, 33*, 527–546.

Drysdale, D. A., Modzeleski, W., & Simons, A. B. (2010). *Campus attacks: Targeted violence affecting institutions of higher education*. Washington, DC: U.S. Secret Service, U.S. Department of Homeland Security, Office of Safe and Drug-Free Schools, U.S. Department of Education, and Federal Bureau of Investigation, U.S. Department of Justice. Retrieved from http://www.secretservice.gov/ntac.shtml

Durlak, J. A., & DuPre, E. P. (2008). Implementation matters: A review of research on the influence of implementation on program outcomes and the factors affecting implementation. *American Journal of Community Psychology, 41*, 327–350. doi:10.1007/s10464-008-9165-0

Fein, R., Vossekuil, B., Pollack, W., Borum, R., Modzeleski, W., & Reddy, M. (2002). *Threat assessment in schools: A guide to managing threatening situations and to creating safe school climates*. Washington, DC: U.S. Secret Service and Department of Education.

Gregory, A., Cornell, D., Fan, X., Sheras, P., Shih, T., & Huang, F. (2010). Authoritative school discipline: High school practices associated with lower student bullying and victimization. *Journal of Educational Psychology, 102*, 483–496. doi: 10.1037/a0018562

Heilbrun, K. (1997). Prediction versus management models relevant to risk assessment: The importance of legal decision-making context. *Law and Human Behavior, 21*, 347–360. doi:10.1023/A:1024851017947

Kaplan, S., & Cornell, D. (2005). Threats of violence by students in special education. *Behavioral Disorders, 31*, 107–119.

Mulvey, E. P., & Cauffman, E. (2001). The inherent limits of predicting school violence. *American Psychologist, 56*, 797–802. doi:10.1037/0003-066X.56.10.797

Osher, D., Dwyer, K., & Jackson, S. (2004). *Safe, supportive and successful schools: Step by step*. Longmont, CO: Sopris West.

O'Toole, M. E. (2000). *The school shooter: A threat assessment perspective*. Quantico, VA: National Center for the Analysis of Violent Crime, Federal Bureau of Investigation.

Sewell, K. W., & Mendelsohn, M. (2000). Profiling potentially violent youth: Statistical and conceptual problems. *Children's Services: Social Policy, Research, and Practice, 3*, 147–169. doi:10.1207/S15326918CS0303_2

Strong, K., & Cornell, D. (2008). Student threat assessment in Memphis City Schools: A descriptive report. *Behavioral Disorders, 34*, 42–54.

Wilson, S. J., Lipsey, M. W., & Derzon, J. H. (2003). The effects of school-based intervention programs on aggressive behavior: A meta-analysis. *Journal of Consulting and Clinical Psychology, 71*, 136–149. doi:10.1037/0022-006X.71.1.136

38

Reforming School Discipline and Reducing Disproportionality in Suspension and Expulsion

Russell J. Skiba, Lauren A. Shure,
Laura V. Middelberg, and Timberly L. Baker

INDIANA UNIVERSITY–BLOOMINGTON

Abstract

The use of suspension and expulsion in America's school has increased over the past 30 years. Yet there is no evidence that exclusionary school discipline has a beneficial effect on student behavior or school climate. The consistent overrepresentation of African American students in the use of school exclusion cannot be fully explained by either poverty or differential rates of disruptive behavior. Both school-wide positive behavior supports and social-emotional learning strategies show promise as system-wide reform efforts for reducing the use of suspension and expulsion, while data on the effects of restorative justice are still emerging. Despite abundant documentation of racial and ethnic disparities in school suspension and expulsion, there is as yet little research that could meet the urgent needs of schools and school districts to improve equity in school discipline.

Issues in the practice of school discipline appear to create a profound dilemma in early 21st century American education. Clearly, schools have both the right and responsibility to use all effective means to preserve school safety and the integrity of the learning environment. Incidents of school violence in the late 1990s provided strong motivation for schools to use all effective methods to promote safety, and issues of disruptive behavior remain atop the list of concerns about education among teachers and parents.

Yet the predominant tools currently used for purposes of maintaining discipline, out-of-school suspension and expulsion, are interventions that can pose substantial risk to educational opportunity. Given a strong positive relationship between the amount and quality of engaged time in academic learning and student achievement (Greenwood, Horton, & Utley, 2002), exclusionary discipline procedures that remove students from the opportunity to learn and potentially weaken the school bond must be viewed as potentially risky interventions. Since some racial/ethnic groups have been found to be consistently and sometimes severely overrepresented in exclusionary discipline (Losen & Skiba, 2010), the associated risk must be presumed to likewise fall disproportionately on those groups.

The purpose of this chapter is to explore what we know about school discipline, with a focus on racial and ethnic disparities in discipline. After reviewing the history, current status, and concerns about current exclusionary discipline practices, we will describe the conceptual basis, features, and evidence for addressing issues of school exclusion and inequity in discipline.

Current Status

The use of school exclusion as a disciplinary tool is extremely common and has increased over time, particularly for some groups. School suspension has consistently been found to be among the most widely used disciplinary techniques, perhaps the most frequently used disciplinary tool (American Psychological Association, 2008), while school expulsion has been used at a much lower rate (see e.g., Heaviside, Rowand, Williams, & Farris, 1998). The use of out-of-school suspension has approximately doubled since 1973, with much steeper increases for some groups, most notably African American students (Losen & Skiba, 2010).

The overrepresentation of African American students in school suspension and expulsion has been widely documented (see e.g., Children's Defense Fund, 1975; Skiba, Michael, Nardo, & Peterson, 2002; Wallace, Goodkind, Wallance, & Bachman, 2008). Recent analyses have found rates of suspension for Black males over 50% among middle schools in some urban school districts (Losen & Skiba, 2010). While disciplinary overrepresentation of Latino students has been reported in some studies (Raffaele-Mendez & Knoff, 2003), the finding is not universal across locations or studies (e.g., Gordon, Della Piana, & Keleher, 2000).

The correlation of race and socioeconomic status (SES) in American society (McLoyd, 1998) might suggest that apparent racial disproportionality in suspension and expulsion is a by-product of poverty. Yet although low SES has been found to be a risk factor for school suspension (Brantlinger, 1991), race remains a significant predictor of suspension and expulsion, even after controlling for SES (Wallace et al., 2008; Wu, Pink, Crain, & Moles, 1982). Further, investigations of student behavior, race, and discipline have yielded no evidence that African American overrepresentation in school suspension is due to higher rates of misbehavior (McFadden, Marsh, Prince, & Hwang, 1992; Skiba et al., 2002; Theriot & Dupper, 2010; Wu et al., 1982). Bradshaw, Mitchell, O'Brennan, and Leaf (2010) reported that even after controlling for the student's level of teacher-rated classroom behavior, Black students were significantly more likely than White students to receive office disciplinary referrals.

Importance of the Issue

One would hope that the most widely used disciplinary technique would be predictive of positive individual or school climate outcomes. Data on the outcomes of school exclusion appears to raise concerns at both the individual and school level, however.

Individual Risk

There appear to be a number of risk factors associated with the application of school suspension. Poor academic skill and achievement appears to place a student at increased risk for increased aggression and disruption (Gregory, Skiba, & Noguera, 2010); removing students from the opportunity to learn through suspension and expulsion may well increase this risk. Exposure to suspension and expulsion has also been associated with higher rates of dropout or failure to graduate on time (Ekstrom, Goertz, Pollack, & Rock, 1986; Raffaele-Mendez , 2003).

A body of research has begun to explore connections between school punishments and the flow of youth into the juvenile justice system, termed the *school- to-prison pipeline* (e.g., Wald & Losen, 2003). Nicholson-Crotty, Birchmeier, and Valentine (2009) found racial disproportionality in out-of-school suspensions, which could not be explained solely by differences in delinquent behavior, to be a strong predictor of similar levels of racial disparity in juvenile court referrals, even after controlling for poverty, urbanization, and other relevant variables.

School Level Outcomes

Despite a widely held belief that removal of persistently troublemaking students will improve teaching and learning for the remaining students (Public Agenda, 2004), there does not appear to be evidence of benefits of exclusionary discipline relative to school climate or achievement. Schools with higher rates of suspension have been reported to have higher student–teacher ratios and a lower level of academic quality (Hellman & Beaton, 1986), spend more time on discipline-related matters (Davis & Jordan, 1994), and pay significantly less attention to issues of school climate (Bickel & Qualls, 1980). Rausch and Skiba (2005) found that higher school rates of out-of-school suspension were associated with lower school-wide passing rates on the state accountability test, regardless of the demographic, economic, or racial makeup of the school.

Recent data suggest that these negative effects of the use of school suspension fall more severely on African American students. Using a national sample of 294 public schools, Welch and Payne (2010) found that, regardless of levels of misbehavior and delinquency, schools with a higher percentage of Black students were more likely to use higher rates of exclusionary discipline and court action to implement zero tolerance policies, and use fewer mild disciplinary practices.

In response to similar data emerging over the past decade, the American Psychological Association convened a task force to examine the effectiveness of zero tolerance policies, and to offer recommendations for reform of such policies. That task force concluded that "Zero tolerance has not been shown to improve school climate or school safety. Its application in suspension and expulsion has not proven an effective means of improving student behavior. It has not resolved, and indeed may have exacerbated, minority overrepresentation in school punishments" (American Psychological Association, 2008).

Conceptual Basis

The following sections describe alternatives and approaches to school reform that have been applied to address issues of school discipline and disproportionality in discipline. All school disciplinary strategies appear to share two common conceptual goals: ensuring the safety of students and teachers, and creating a climate that is suitable for learning (Skiba & Rausch, 2006). Beyond those commonalities, however, the conceptual basis and presumptions made about school discipline appear to be somewhat different for zero tolerance and school exclusion than for the emerging alternatives.

Zero Tolerance, Suspension, and Expulsion

One conceptual feature that appears to be at the heart of the zero tolerance philosophy is the notion of using swift and certain consequences for all incidents to send a message of deterrence. Ewing (2000) argues that zero tolerance "appropriately denounces violent student behavior in no uncertain terms and serves as a deterrent to such behavior in the future by sending a clear message that acts which physically harm or endanger others will not be permitted at school under any circumstances." In accordance with this belief, school administrators have, on numerous occasions, applied extended periods of suspension or expulsion to incidents ranging from paper or toy guns to possession of Advil to a student suspended for 10 days for using his cell phone in school to talk to his mother stationed in Iraq (American Psychological Association, 2008).

The evidence on school discipline, however, appears to contradict the presumption that school suspension and expulsion have a deterrent effect. Longitudinal studies of suspension have found high rates of repeat offending in out-of-school suspension, ranging from 35% (Bowditch, 1993) to 42% (Costenbader and Markson, 1998). Raffaele Mendez (2003) reported that the strongest predictor of a middle school student's number of out-of-school suspensions was the number of out-of-school suspensions she or he received in late elementary school (fourth and fifth grade), even after statistically controlling for student SES, racial categorization, special education status, teacher ratings of student behavior, and academic achievement.

Conceptual Foundations of Violence Prevention Strategies

In 1993, the American Psychological Association released its report *Violence and Youth: Psychology's Response,* addressing what was then widely perceived as an epidemic of youth violence. That report framed youth violence prevention efforts in terms of a three-tiered primary prevention model. Since the publication of that report, a similar three component prevention models as applied to mental health (Mrazek & Haggerty, 1994), youth violence in general (Elliott, Hatot, Sirovatka, & Potter, 2001), or school violence in particular (Dwyer, Osher, & Warger, 1998). The model became the centerpiece for efforts of the U.S. Department of Education to address school violence in publications intended to provide guidance to America's schools concerning the prevention of violence (e.g., Dwyer et al., 1998). More recently, that framework has been adopted as the organizing schema for school-wide positive behavior supports (see below).

Conceptual Framework for Culturally Responsive Discipline and Classroom Management

A number of possible frameworks might be drawn upon as a conceptual basis for more culturally responsive approaches to discipline, such as culturally responsive pedagogy (Gay, 2000). One theory that outlines the link between attitude and action is *cultural reproduction,* which argues that individuals may, regardless of their conscious intentions, contribute to or reproduce inequity through their participation in institutional mechanisms (Mehan, 1992). Unchallenged, such patterns can unintentionally recreate and reinforce existing inequities in school processes.

Classroom management may well be one of the micro-level processes contributing to the reproduction of disciplinary disparities. Observing in urban classrooms, Vavrus and Cole (2002) found that office referrals leading to school suspension were due less to serious disruption than to student/teacher authority struggles, and that students of color were most likely to be singled out in this process. Gregory and Weinstein (2008) reported that the most common reason for referral among African American males was defiance and that, even for students with multiple referrals, only certain student-teacher combinations yielded high rates of office referral.

Description of the Specific Approaches

Any particular disciplinary action is the culmination of a complex process (Morrison & Skiba, 2001), multiply determined by student behavior, teacher tolerance, school and classroom characteristics, and local and state policy. Thus, the reform of school discipline must be viewed as a systemic process. In a recent review, Osher, Bear, Sprague, & Doyle (2010) identified school-wide positive behavior supports (SWPBS) and social emotional learning (SEL) as promising intervention frameworks that might guide the improvement of school discipline. Those interventions, as well as *restorative justice* and *culturally responsive classroom management* are described below.

School-Wide Positive Behavioral Interventions and Supports (SWPBIS)

The framework of school-wide positive behavioral interventions and supports (SWPBIS) is intended to restructure school disciplinary practices through a comprehensive and proactive approach to school discipline. The primary goals of SWPBIS are to prevent the development and intensification of behavior problems while maximizing academic achievement (Sugai, Horner, & McIntosh, 2008). To do so, the SWPBIS framework emphasizes four elements (a) identifying measurable behavior and academic outcomes, (b) collecting data to guide decision making, (c) using evidence based practices that support these outcomes, (d) leveraging systems that support effective implementation (Sugai & Horner, 2009). The SWPBIS framework is intended to be flexible enough to be responsive to the local needs of schools.

SWPBIS is structured in a three-tiered system that acts as a continuum of supports that promote desired behavior outcomes. At the primary tier, preventative supports are put in place to encourage prosocial behaviors, maximize learning time, and decrease common behavior challenges for all students (Sugai & Horner, 2009), including the creation and adoption of school-wide behavior expectations that are explicitly taught and reinforced by all staff members. Secondary tier supports are necessary for students who are still at risk for behavior problems despite primary-level supports. For example, the Check-and-Connect procedure (Sinclair, Christenson, Lehr, & Anderson, 2003) has been found effective in providing additional support to students whose needs exceed typical primary tier interventions. Tertiary tier supports are provided for students who require highly intensive and often individualized plans. At the tertiary level, more in-depth functional behavior analysis is conducted and family and community support are utilized (Sugai & Horner, 2009). SWPBIS leadership teams continually review school-based data to assess students' responsiveness to implementation at each tier.

Social Emotional Learning (SEL)

By teaching and reinforcing life skills, *social emotional learning* (SEL) programs seek to facilitate the healthy development of children who are self-aware, caring and connected to others, and responsible in their decision-making (Collaborative for Academic, Social, and Emotional Learning [CASEL], 2003; Greenberg et al., 2003). SEL programs vary greatly but are generally regarded as curriculum aimed at building students' skills to: (a) recognize and manage their emotions, (b) appreciate the perspective of others, (c) establish positive goals, (d) make responsible decisions, and (e) handle interpersonal situations effectively (CASEL, 2003; Payton et al., 2008).

Several SEL programs have been evaluated in U.S. public schools and are available as preventative approaches to reduce problem behaviors (CASEL, 2003; Osher, Dwyer, & Jackson, 2002). Alternative approaches include infusing SEL throughout the academic curriculum or to embed SEL in school reform through the creation of a supportive learning environment. SEL programs have been implemented through various methods. Meta-analytic investigations suggest that SEL programs are most effective when: (a) initiatives are holistic and coordinated as part of larger school reform agendas, (b) strong leadership and support is supplied by school administration, and (c) long-term programs are implemented, monitored, and evaluated for effectiveness (Greenberg et al., 2003; Zins, Bloodworth, Weissberg, & Walberg, 2004).

Restorative Justice

Restorative justice has been implemented in schools internationally as a theoretical framework for responding to student misbehavior (Braithwaite, 2002; Stinchcomb, Bazemore, & Riestenberg, 2006). Based on the assumption that wrongdoing damages relationships, it aims to restore relationships and repair harm that was caused. Common strategies utilized in restorative justice programs include: (a) engaging the community and involved parties in collaborative decision-making around restitution, (b) holding offenders accountable, (c) providing space for victims to express how they have been affected and how they can heal, and (d) preventing similar actions in the future by changing behavior and the conditions that caused it (Stinchcomb et al., 2006).

As an alternative to exclusionary discipline, restorative justice emphasizes the relationships between victims, offenders, and the community. School discipline practices built upon principles of restorative justice employ the use of formal and informal conferencing, classroom conference circles, and/or other frameworks of school disciplinary practice based on relationship- and community-building. Discussion regarding the impact offenders have on victims and the community is a key element in these processes. Evidence suggests that school-based restorative justice is most effective when it is linked to broader school reform and embedded in a school culture that values relationships and teaches curriculum that emphasizes social and emotional learning (Karp & Breslin, 2001; Stinchcomb et al., 2006).

Culturally Responsive Classroom Management and Discipline

Although it might be presumed that an intervention that reduced suspension/expulsion rates in general might also reduce disproportionality in discipline, emerging data may contradict this assumption. Skiba et al. (2011) explored patterns of office disciplinary referrals in a nationally representative sample of elementary and middle schools implementing school-wide PBS for at least one year. Although, in general, minor infractions tended to receive less severe punishments, African American and Latino students were far more likely than White students to receive suspension and expulsion for such infractions. Such data appear to indicate that explicit adaptations may be required to ensure that disciplinary interventions, including PBS, are equally effective with all groups.

Numerous researchers (D. Brown, 2004; Bondy, Ross, Gallingame, & Hambacher, 2007; Monroe & Obidah, 2004; Weinstein, Curran, & Tomlinson-Clarke, 2004) have begun to examine the components that would increase the cultural responsiveness of classroom management. Qualitative observation and interview studies have identified a number of promising conventions of these components that describe and inform culturally responsive classroom management best practices. Managing student behavior based on culturally appropriate strategies means teachers are considering that African American, Hispanic, Native American, Asian American, and immigrant students have differing communication styles, behavioral norms, and parental engagement. Culturally Responsive Classroom Management (CRCM) "makes it explicit that classroom management is grounded in teachers' judgments about appropriate behavior and that these judgments are informed by cultural assumptions" (Bondy, Ross, Gallingame, & Hambacher, 2007, p. 328). Weinstein, Tomlinson-Clarke and Curran (2004) suggested five components that characterize CRCM: (a) recognition of one's own ethnocentrism; (b) knowledge of students' cultural backgrounds; (c) understanding of the broader social, economic, and political context; (d) ability and willingness to use culturally appropriate management strategies; and (e) a commitment to building caring classrooms.

The literature has consistently identified a number of characteristics of culturally responsive approaches to classroom management, including an inviting physical setting, a combination of high expectations and strong interpersonal support, the cultural congruency of instruction, and high levels of parental involvement. The physical setting is organized in a way that is warm and inviting, and communicates awareness of and respect for students' cultural heritage (E. Brown, 2002). Research on the classroom environment has shown that the physical arrangement can affect the behavior of both students and teachers (Savage, 1999; Stewart & Evans, 1997), that a well-structured classroom tends to improve student academic and behavioral outcomes MacAulay, 1990; Walker, Colvin, & Ramsey, 1995), and that attention to the physical setting can act as a symbol to students and others regarding what teacher's value in behavior and learning (Savage, 1999).

Second, teachers who support a culture of achievement for students of differing cultural backgrounds and socioeconomic status typically exhibit a combination of high expectations and strong interpersonal relations, identified as *warm demanders* (Vasquez, 1988). That is, such classrooms are characterized by high behavioral and academic expectations that are clearly and consistently asserted, yet at the same time establish warm and personal climates that stress personal relationships, caring, and terms of endearment (Bondy et al., 2010; D. Brown, 2004; Weinstein et al., 2003).

Third, communication and language in classrooms that are effective with diverse students are *culturally congruent*, and teachers are committed to inclusion of students' culture in the classroom (Ware, 2006). Teachers in such classrooms demonstrate an acceptance of dialect or communication patterns (e.g., call-and-response), rather than dismissing or problematizing such interactions (D. Brown, 2004). D. Brown (2004) reported that teachers who apply culturally congruent interactional rules in their lessons improved participation by students.

Finally, culturally responsive classrooms are characterized by opportunities for high levels of *parental involvement and interaction* in meaningful ways. An extensive literature has documented the importance of school and family connections for increasing student success in school and strengthening student behavior (Gottfredson, Gottfredson, & Hybl, 1993; Sheldon & Epstein, 2002). The importance of respectful and inclusive parent interaction (E. Brown, 2002; Weinstein et al., 2004) has emerged as a common theme in studies of culturally responsive classroom management.

Relevant Research and Evidence of Effectiveness

School-Wide PBIS

School-wide positive behavioral interventions and supports (SWPBIS) have been linked to improved behavioral outcomes from elementary through high school. In a randomized control trial over a five-year period in New Hampshire, Bradshaw, Mitchell, and Leaf (2010) compared 21 elementary schools who received PBIS training with 16 elementary schools that had not. Results indicated that the treatment schools significantly decreased the percent of students with a major or minor ODR as well as the number of major and minor ODRs per student, although effect sizes were relatively small. Using the same treatment and control schools, Bradshaw, Koth, Bevans, Ialongo, and Leaf (2008) and Bradshaw, Koth, Thornton, and Leaf (2009) reported that the implementation of PBIS positively impacted overall school climate. Staff perceptions of the school's organizational health, resource influence, and staff affiliation were significantly higher in the 21 schools implementing PBIS over a three-year period (Bradshaw et al., 2009). Bradshaw et al. (2009) confirmed these results across the four years of the trial and also found that PBIS implementation significantly increased staff perceptions of academic emphasis. In a three-year randomized, wait-list controlled effectiveness trial in Illinois and Hawaii, Horner et al. (2009) compared 33 elementary schools who received PBIS training at year one with 30 schools who received training one year later. Staff at the 33 treatment schools who received training at year one reported significantly lower behavioral risk factors than the 30 control/delay schools. After

PBIS training, school staff at both treatment and control/delay elementary schools reported their school to be safer and more socially supportive.

Non-experimental studies have demonstrated promising results as well, particularly in the reduction of disciplinary referrals. Large scale PBIS evaluations in Maryland and New Hampshire reported a decrease in daily rates of ODRs across elementary, middle, and high schools (Barrett, Bradshaw, & Lewis-Palmer, 2008; Muscott, Mann, & LeBrun 2008). Quasi-experimental studies in elementary schools have also found significant decreases in office referrals (Nelson, Martella, Marchand-Martella, 2002; Luiselli, Putnam, Handler, & Feinberg, 2005). In a PBIS implementation in an urban, inner-city middle school Lassen, Steele, and Sailor (2006) reported that PBIS significantly reduced the mean number of ODRs per student per day and decreased the number of long-term suspensions over a three-year period. While a growing number of studies have demonstrated PBIS' effectiveness in urban settings (Lassen et al., 2006; Luiselli et al., 2005), there is a paucity of research exploring the impact of PBIS on all racial/ethnic groups within schools. Although case studies have reported promising results when cultural adaptations are made in PBIS implementation (Jones, Caravaca, Cisek, Horner, & Vincent, 2006; Wang, McCart, & Turnbull, 2007), there are as yet no broad-scale or experimental studies exploring the extent to which PBIS implementation works equally well for all racial and ethnic groups, suggesting that PBIS' impact on disproportionality in discipline is still unknown.

Social Emotional Learning (SEL)

Several studies link the completion of SEL programs to an increase in prosocial behaviors and a decrease in misbehaviors (CASEL, 2003; Zins, 2001). In 2008, CASEL published a report, *The Positive Impact of Social and Emotional Learning for Kindergarten to Eighth-grade Students: Findings from Three Scientific Reviews,* of three meta-analytic reviews of various K–eighth-grade SEL programs (Payton et al., 2008). Findings were based on 317 studies with a total of 324,303 participants. One review was conducted on universal school-based SEL programs, a second review was done on programs directed at students identified as displaying early signs of emotional or behavioral problem, and the third review examined SEL programs integrated into after-school programs. Each of these three SEL program reviews found strong and consistent support that students participating in SEL programs exhibit significantly lower rates of conduct problems and more positive social behaviors (Payton et al., 2008). In a meta-analysis of after-school programs aimed at enhancing the personal and social skills of students age 5 to 18, Durlak, Weissberg, and Pachan (2010) found that students who participated in SEL programs demonstrated significant increases in their self-perceptions and bonding to school, positive social behaviors, levels of academic achievement, and significant reductions in problem behaviors. The Substance Abuse and Mental Health Services Administration (SAMHSA, 2002) published a list of evidence-based model SEL programs found useful in facilitating the development of student factors related to academic achievement, and reported that program completion was correlated with a reduction in school suspensions and/or misconduct and aggression at school.

Evaluations of two programs implemented in Baltimore City, Maryland, public elementary schools explored the impact of SEL on discipline and behavior in schools. Ialongo, Poduska, Werthamer, and Kellam (2001) reported the results of a randomized block design study on the effects of two SEL programs in first-grade classes, one classroom-centered and one focused on family-school partnerships, covering 678 children demographically representative of the first-graders in nine Baltimore City public elementary schools. Follow-ups when participants were in the sixth grade indicated that both experimental groups received significantly lower teacher ratings of conduct problems than the control group, and that children who had participated in the program were significantly less likely to have been suspended from school in the previous year.

Restorative Justice

Research surrounding the effects of restorative justice implementation in U. S. public schools is in the early stages. Evidence supporting the use of restorative justice programs to reduce ODRs and suspensions in five Pennsylvania public schools is included in a report released by the International Institute for Restorative Practices, *Improving School Climate: Findings from Schools Implementing Restorative Practices* (2009). Based on reports provided by principals in five schools over the course of three years (2003–2006), data reveals that the implementation of restorative practices in the school was associated with reductions in out-of-school suspensions, as well as incidents of violence and misbehavior. Additionally, the results of a three-year implementation of restorative circle conferencing in a Saint Paul, Minnesota, elementary school showed a drop in physical aggression from 773 to 153 acts, a reduction in out-of-school suspensions from 30 to 11, and a decline in the number of behavioral referrals from 1,143 to 407 (Stinchcomb et al., 2006).

In descriptive case study evaluations of three Denver, Colorado, public middle schools and one Denver public high school, Jennings, Gover, and Hitchcock (2008) reported decreases in in-school suspension, out-of-school suspension, and infractions involving police intervention in three Denver public middle schools implementing a pilot restorative justice program. In the same study however, data at the high school showed increases in these same measures; the researchers suggested this failure was due to administrative turnover that impeded the implementation process. Similarly, the results of a three-year implementation of restorative circle conferencing in four Minnesota school districts as an alternative response to discipline problems showed mixed results (Umbreit, Vos, Coates, & Lightfoot, 2006), with decreases in suspensions and behavioral referrals in some schools. In sum, while the results of pilot studies reflect possibilities that these approaches can reduce problem behaviors and the need for disciplinary actions in schools, more data is needed on the overall effects of sustained restorative justice programs.

Culturally Responsive Disciplinary Approaches

Although a conceptual basis for an explicitly culturally responsive approach to classroom management and discipline has begun to emerge in the literature (e.g., Utley, Kozleski, Smith, & Draper, 2002; Weinstein et al., 2003), research to date is sparse on the implementation of specific reform strategies or interventions for reducing disproportionality in school discipline. Research on culturally responsive classroom management has relied on teacher interview (D. Brown, 2004), or ethnographic field study and observation (Bondy et al., 2007; E. Brown, 2002; Monroe & Obidah, 2004) to identify themes of cultural responsiveness. For PBIS, there have been individual (Wang et al., 2007) and school-wide (Jones, Caravaca, Cizek, Horner, & Vincent, 2006) case studies that have documented how attention to issues of culture can lead to a more effective implementation. Similarly, Wearmouth, McKinney, and Glynn (2007) used an individual case study to documented adaptations in a typical restorative justice implementation that appeared to make it more applicable in a Moari context in New Zealand. Although preliminary results of incorporating cultural elements into these practices provide intriguing directions for future study, and some indications that such elements can make disciplinary reforms more effective for non-majority groups, there is insufficient data available to be able to offer substantive guidance to the field on cultural adaptations for classroom management or school discipline strategies.

Critique and Limitations

The current status of school discipline might well be characterized as a widening gulf between typical practice and best evidence. Despite comprehensive evaluations suggesting that suspension and expulsion have not made a contribution to school safety or improved student behavior

(APA, 2008), national and state surveys of school discipline suggest that the rate of out-of-school suspension and expulsion continues to increase, and these increases are particularly dramatic for African American students. There is increasing evidence that racial disparities in discipline cannot be explained by either poverty or differential rates of behavior. Research has not shown, however, that disciplinary exclusion is effective in either improving student behavior or preventing school disruption and violence. Indeed, suspension and expulsion appear to be associated with a variety of negative outcomes, including risk of lower achievement and increased contact with the juvenile justice system.

The systemic approaches of SWPBIS, SEL, and restorative justice have been implemented and their effects tested on rates of school discipline. Although there is consistent evidence that SWP-BIS reduces ODRs and suspensions, research needs to be conducted linking SWPBIS to other educational outcomes. Meta-analysis and other research support the use of SEL in schools to reduce discipline and improve student behavior, but more research is needed to explore the effectiveness of SEL programs with high schools students. Osher et al. (2010) presented a compelling case for combining elements of SWPBS and SEL in schools, suggesting that students need both types of programming and neither alone is sufficient to fully address the constellation of student needs. While results of pilot studies reflect possibilities that restorative justice approaches can

Table 38.1 Implications for Practice: Reforming School Discipline and Reducing Disproportionality in Suspension and Expulsion

1.	Disciplinary exclusion—out-of-school suspension and expulsion—is among the most frequently used procedures to maintain discipline and its use has increased in the last thirty years, despite a lack of evidence for its effectiveness. While necessary in some cases, alternative methods that provide supervision and productive engagement should be used in order to minimize the use of school exclusion.
2.	African American students and to some extent Latino students have been found to be over-represented in suspension and expulsion. The evidence indicates that this disproportionality is not due to effects of poverty or different rates of disruption.
3.	Disciplinary removal creates risk for students in terms of decreased academic opportunity, higher dropout, and risk of juvenile justice involvement, and these risks are faced to a greater degree by African American students. These outcomes strongly suggest a need for alternative approaches that can minimize exclusion.
4.	The conceptual framework for zero tolerance, *deterrence*, is intuitive, but appears to lack any empirical validation. Several research-based models, including Schoolwide Positive Behavioral Supports and Safe and Responsive Schools can help produce better results than zero tolerance.
5.	The three-tiered primary prevention model has become widely accepted as an organizing framework in school discipline, while a variety of theoretical frames have been applied to the intersection of race and discipline. Schools should base their programming on a research based framework, and monitor the outcomes of school discipline to ensure effectiveness.
6.	Discipline is a process that involves students, teachers, administrators and school structures, and hence requires attention to systemic issues.
7.	School-wide positive behavior supports, social-emotional learning, restorative justice, and culturally responsive classroom management have been used to create change in the manner in which schools address student disruption.
8.	There is some evidence that both school-wide positive behavior supports and social-emotional learning can influence school disciplinary outcomes, reducing rates of suspension and expulsion.
9.	Despite consistent documentation of the existence and negative effects of racial/ethnic disparities in school discipline, there has been insufficient research attention paid to developing and evaluating strategies to reduce disciplinary disparity. As a result, practitioners have an urgent need for evidence-based strategies that could guide necessary change in this area.

reduce problem behaviors and the need for disciplinary actions in schools, more data is needed on the overall effects of restorative justice in American schools.

Given highly consistent documentation of racial disparities in the application of school exclusion, the scarcity of research on interventions to address disciplinary disproportionality is somewhat surprising. Despite the emergence of promising themes from qualitative work and case studies describing the characteristics of culturally responsive classroom management and discipline, it is clear that the data is nowhere near sufficient in order to offer useful guidance to schools throughout the nation struggling with inequity in discipline.

Some scholars have begun to make a case that in science, no less than in American society in general, mainstream discourse reflects a predominantly majority viewpoint. The American Educational Research Association convened the Commission on Research in Black Education (CORIBE) in part to study the absence of equity research coming out of the experience of the African American community (King, 2005); that effort found the work and the theoretical perspectives of African American scholars to be underrepresented in mainstream research in education and psychology. More representative participation of multiple race-ethnicities and cultures in the school discipline research base would likely provide schools and school districts with urgently needed strategies to develop and maintain positive, effective, and equitable systems of school discipline.

In summary, the need for disciplinary reform is supported by extensive evidence that has failed to provide support for the effectiveness of suspension and expulsion, and consistent documentation of racial and ethnic disproportionality in the application of those procedures. Those disparities are not due simply to economic disadvantage or higher rates of disruptive behavior among students of color. A number of systemic approaches, including positive behavior supports, social-emotional learning, and restorative justice, appear to show promise as methods for the reform of school discipline. Yet although culture appears to play a distinct role in the application of school discipline, there remains an urgent need for increased research on specific interventions designed to reduce racial and ethnic disparities in the application of school discipline.

References

American Psychological Association. (1993). *Violence and youth: Psychology's response*. Washington, DC: Author.

American Psychological Association Zero Tolerance Task Force. (2008). Are zero tolerance policies effective in the schools? An evidentiary review and recommendations. *American Psychologist, 63*, 852–862. doi:10.1037/0003-066X.63.9.852

Barrett, S. B., Bradshaw, C. P., & Lewis-Palmer, T. (2008). Maryland statewide PBIS initiative: Systems, evaluation, and next steps. *Journal of Positive Behavior Interventions, 10*, 105–114. doi:10.1177/1098300707312541

Bickel, F., & Qualls, R. (1980). The impact of school climate on suspension rates in the Jefferson County Public Schools. *Urban Review, 12*, 79–86. doi:10.1007/BF02009317

Bondy, E., Ross, D. D., Gallingame, C., & Hambacher, E. (2007). Creating environments of success and resilience: Culturally responsive classroom management and more. *Urban Education, 42*, 326–348. doi:10.1177/0042085907303406

Bowditch, C. (1993). Getting rid of troublemakers: High school disciplinary procedures and the production of dropouts. *Social Problems, 40*, 493–507. doi:10.1525/sp.1993.40.4.03x0094p

Bradshaw, C. P., Koth, C. W., Bevans, K. B., Ialongo, N., & Leaf, P. J. (2008). The impact of school-wide positive behavioral interventions and supports (PBIS) on the organizational health of elementary schools. *School Psychology Review, 23*, 462–473. doi:10.1037/a0012883

Bradshaw, C. P., Koth, C. W., Thornton, L. A., & Leaf, P. J. (2009). Altering school climate through school-wide positive behavioral interventions and supports: Findings from a group-randomized effectiveness trial. *Society for Prevention Research, 10*, 100–115. doi:10.1007/s11121-008-0114-9

Bradshaw, C. P., Mitchell, M. M., & Leaf, P. J. (2010). Examining the effects of school-wide positive behavioral interventions and supports on student outcomes. *Journal of Positive Behavior Interventions, 12*, 133–148. doi:10.1177/1098300709334798

Bradshaw, C. P., Mitchell, M. M., O'Brennan, L. M., & Leaf, P. J. (2010). Multilevel exploration of factors contributing to the overrepresentation of black students in office discipline referrals. *Journal of Educational Psychology, 102,* 508–520. doi:10.1037/a0018450

Braithwaite, J. (2002). *Restorative justice and responsive regulation.* New York, NY: Oxford University Press.

Brantlinger, E. (1991). Social class distinctions in adolescents' reports of problems and punishment in school. *Behavioral Disorders, 17,* 36–46.

Brown, D. F. (2004). Urban teachers' professed classroom management strategies: Reflections on culturally responsive teaching. *Urban Education, 39,* 266–289. doi:10.1177/0042085904263258004208590426325

Brown, E. L. (2002). Mrs. Boyd's fifth grade inclusive classroom: A study of multicultural teaching strategies. *Urban Education, 37,* 126–141. doi:10.1177/0042085902371008004208590237100

Children's Defense Fund. (1975). *School suspensions: Are they helping children?* Cambridge, MA: Washington Research Project.

Collaborative for Academic, Social, and Emotional Learning (CASEL). (2003). *Safe and sound: An educational leader's guide to evidence-based social and emotional learning programs.* Chicago: Author.

Costenbader, V., & Markson, S. (1998). School suspension: A study with secondary school students. *Journal of School Psychology, 36,* 59–82. doi:10.1016/S0022-4405(97)00050-2

Davis, J. E., & Jordan, W. J. (1994). The effects of school context, structure, and experiences on African American males in middle and high school. *Journal of Negro Education, 63,* 570–587. doi: 10.2307/2967296

Durlak, J. A., Weissberg, R. P., & Pachan, M. (2010). A meta-analysis of after-school programs that seek to promote personal and social skills in children and adolescents. *American Journal of Community Psychology, 45,* 294–309. doi:10.1007/s10464-010-9300-6

Dwyer, K., Osher, D., & Warger, C. (1998). *Early warning, timely response: A guide to safe schools.* Washington, DC: U.S. Department of Education.

Ekstrom R. B., Goertz, M. E., Pollack, J. M., & Rock, D. A. (1986). Who drops out of high school and why? Findings from a national study. *Teachers College Record, 87,* 356–373.

Elliott, D., Hatot, N. J., Sirovatka, P., & Potter, B. B. (2001). *Youth violence: A report of the Surgeon General.* Washington, DC: U.S. Surgeon General.

Ewing, C. P. (2000, January/February). Sensible zero tolerance protects students. *Harvard Education Letter.* [Online]. Retrieved October 2, 2010, from http://www.edlettr.org/past/issues/2000-jf/zero.shtml

Gay, G. (2000). *Culturally responsive teaching: Theory and practice.* New York, NY: Teachers College Press.

Gordon, R., Della Piana, L., & Keleher, T. (2000, March). *Facing the consequences: An examination of racial discrimination in U.S. public schools.* Oakland, CA: Applied Research Center.

Gottfredson, D. C., Gottfredson, G. D., & Hybl, L. G. (1993). Managing adolescent behavior: A multiyear, multi-school study. *American Educational Research Journal, 30,* 179–215.

Greenberg, M. T., Weissberg, R. P., O'Brien, M. U., Zins, J. E., Fredericks, L., Resnik, H., & Elias, M. J. (2003). Enhancing school-based prevention and youth development through coordinated social and emotional learning. *American Psychologist, 58,* 466–474. doi:10.1037/0003-066X.58.6-7.466

Greenwood, C. R., Horton, B. T., & Utley, C. A. (2002). Academic engagement: Current perspectives on research and practice. *School Psychology Review, 31,* 328–349.

Gregory, A., Skiba, R. J., & Noguera, P. A. (2010). The achievement gap and the discipline gap: Two sides of the same coin? *Educational Researcher, 39,* 59–68. doi:10.3102/0013189X09357621

Gregory, A., & Weinstein, R. S. (2008). The discipline gap and African Americans: Defiance or cooperation in the high school classroom. *Journal of School Psychology, 46,* 455–475. doi:10.1016/j.jsp.2007.09.001

Heaviside, S., Rowand, C., Williams, C., & Farris, E. (1998). *Violence and discipline problems in U.S. Public Schools: 1996–97* (NCES 98-030). Washington, DC: U.S. Department of Education, National Center for Education Statistics.

Hellman, D. A., & Beaton, S. (1986). The pattern of violence in urban public schools: The influence of school and community. *Journal of Research in Crime and Delinquency, 23,* 102–127. doi:10.1177/0022427886023002002

Horner, H. R., Sugai, G., Smolkowski, K., Eber, L., Nakasato, J., Todd, A. W. & Esperanza, J. (2009). A randomized, wait-listed controlled effectiveness trial assessing school-wide positive behavior support in elementary school. *Journal of Positive Behavior Interventions, 11,* 133–144. doi:10.1177/1098300709332067

Ialongo, N., Poduska, J., Werthamer, L., & Kellam, S. (2001). The distal impact of two first-grade preventive interventions on conduct problems and disorder in early adolescence. *Journal of Emotional and Behavioral Disorders, 9,* 146–160. doi:10.1177/106342660100900301

International Institute of Restorative Practices. (2009). Findings from schools implementing restorative practices. *Restorative Practices Eforum.* Retrieved September 29, 2010, from http://www.iirp.org/pdf/IIRP-Improving-School-Climate.pdf

Jennings, W. G., Gover, A. R., & Hitchcock, D. M. (2008). Localizing restorative justice: An in-depth look at a Denver public school program. In H. V. Miller (Ed.), *Sociology of Crime, Law, and Deviance, Vol. 11* (pp. 167–187). Bingley, UK: JAI Press.

Jones, C., Caravaca, L., Cizek, S., Horner, R. H., & Vincent, C. G. (2006). Culturally responsive Schoolwide Positive Behavior Support: A case study in one school with a high proportion of Native American students. *Multiple Voices for Ethnically Diverse Exceptional Learners, 9,* 108–119.

Karp, D. R., & Breslin, B. (2001). Restorative justice in school communities. *Youth & Society, 33,* 249–272. doi:10.1177/0044118X01033002006

King, J. E. (Ed.). (2005). *Black education: A transformative research and action agenda for the new century.* Mahwah, NJ: Erlbaum for the American Educational Research Association.

Lassen, S. R., Steele, M. M., & Sailor, W. (2006). The relationship of school-wide positive behavior support to academic achievement in an urban middle school. *Psychology in the Schools, 43,* 701–712. doi:10.1002/pits.20177

Losen, D. J., & Skiba, R. J. (2010). *Suspended education: Urban middle schools in crisis.* Montgomery, AL: Southern Poverty Law Center.

Luiselli, J. K., Putnam, R. F., Handler, M. W., & Feinberg, A. B. (2005). Whole-school positive behavior support: Effects on student discipline problems and academic performance. *Educational Psychology, 25,* 183–198. doi:10.1080/0144341042000301265

MacAulay, D. (1990). Classroom environment: A literature review. *Educational Psychology, 10,* 239–253. doi:10.1080/0144341900100305

McFadden, A. C., Marsh, G. E., Prince, B. J., & Hwang, Y. (1992). A study of race and gender bias in the punishment of handicapped school children. *Urban Review, 24,* 239–251. doi:10.1007/BF01108358

McLoyd, V. C. (1998). Socioeconomic disadvantage and child development. *American Psychologist, 53,* 185–204. doi:10.1037/0003-066X.53.2.185

Mehan, H. (1992). Understanding inequality in schools: The contributions of interpretive studies. *Sociology of Education, 65,* 1–20. doi:10.2307/2112689

Monroe, C. R., & Obidah, J. E. (2004). The influence of cultural synchronization on a teacher's perceptions of disruption: A case study of an African American middle-school classroom. *Journal of Teacher Education, 55,* 256–268. doi:10.1177/0022487104263977

Morrison, G. M., & Skiba, R. J. (2001). Predicting violence from school misbehavior: Promises and perils. *Psychology in Schools, 38*(2), 173–184.

Mrazek, P. J., & Haggerty, R. J. (Eds.). (1994). *Reducing risks for mental disorders: Frontiers for preventive intervention research.* Washington, D.C.: National Academy Press.

Muscott, H. S., Mann, E. L., & LeBrun, M. L. (2008). Positive behavioral interventions and supports in New Hampshire: Effects of large-scale implementation of school-wide positive behavior support on student discipline and academic achievement. *Journal of Positive Behavior Interventions, 10,* 190–205. doi:10.1177/1098300708316258

Nelson, J. R., Martella, R. M., & Marchand-Martella, N. (2002). Maximizing student learning: The effects of a comprehensive school-based program for preventing problem behaviors. *Journal of Emotional and Behavioral Disorders, 10,* 136–148. doi:10.1177/10634266020100030201

Nicholson-Crotty, S., Birchmeier, Z., & Valentine, D. (2009). Exploring the impact of school discipline and racial disproportion in the juvenile justice system. *Social Science Quarterly, 90,* 1003–1018. doi:10.1111/j.1540-6237.2009.00674.x

Osher, D., Bear, G. G., Sprague, J. R., & Doyle, W. (2010). How can we improve school discipline? *Educational Researcher, 39,* 48–58. doi:10.3102/0013189X09357618

Osher, D., Dwyer, K., & Jackson, S. (2002). *Safe, supportive, and successful schools, step by step.* Rockville, MD: U.S. Department of Health and Human Services, Substance Abuse and Mental Health Services Administration, Center for Mental Health Services.

Payton, J., Weissberg, R. P., Durlak, J. A., Dymnicki, A. B., Taylor, R. D., Schellinger, K. B., & Pachan, M. (2008). *The positive impact of social and emotional learning for kindergarten to eighth-grade students: Findings from three scientific reviews.* Chicago, IL: Collaborative for Academic, Social, and Emotional Learning.

Public Agenda. (2004). *Teaching interrupted: Do discipline policies in today's public schools foster the common good?* http://www.publicagenda.org/research/research_reports_details.cfm?list=3

Raffaele-Mendez, L. M. (2003). Predictors of suspension and negative school outcomes: A longitudinal investigation. In J. Wald & D. J. Losen (Eds.), *New directions for youth development* (no. 99; Deconstructing the school-to-prison pipeline; pp. 17–34). San Francisco: Jossey-Bass.

Raffaele-Mendez, L. M., & Knoff, H. M. (2003). Who gets suspended from school and why: A demographic analysis of schools and disciplinary infractions in a large school district. *Education & Treatment of Children, 26,* 30–51.

Rausch, K. M., & Skiba, R. J. (2005, April). *The academic cost of discipline: The contribution of school discipline to achievement.* Paper presented at the Annual Meeting of the American Educational Research Association, Montreal, Canada.

Savage, T. V. (1999). *Teaching self-control through management and discipline.* Boston: Allyn and Bacon.

Sheldon, S. B., & Epstein, J. L. (2002) Improving student behavior and school discipline with family and community involvement. *Education and Urban Society, 35,* 4–26. doi:10.1177/001312402237212

Sinclair, M. F., Christenson, S. L., Lehr, C. A., & Anderson, A. R. (2003). Facilitating student engagement: Lessons learned from Check and Connect longitudinal studies. *The California School Psychologist, 8,* 29–41.

Skiba, R. J., Horner, R. H., Chung, C., Rausch, M. K., May, S. L., & Tobin, T. (2011). Race is not neutral: A national investigation of African American and Latino disproportionality in school discipline. *School Psychology Review, 40*(1), 85–107.

Skiba, R. J., Michael, R. S., Nardo, A. C., & Peterson, R. (2002). The color of discipline: Sources of racial and gender disproportionality in school punishment. *Urban Review, 34*, 317–342. doi:10.1023/A:1021320817372

Skiba, R. J., & Rausch, M. K. (2006). Zero tolerance, suspension, and expulsion: Questions of equity and effectiveness. In C. M. Evertson & C. S. Weinstein (Eds.), *Handbook of classroom management: Research, practice, and contemporary issues* (pp. 1063–1088). Mahwah, NJ: Erlbaum.

Stewart, S. C. & Evans, W. H. (1997). Setting the stage for success: Assessing the instructional environment. *Preventing School Failure, 41*, 53–56. doi:10.1080/10459889709603268

Stinchcomb, J., B., Bazemore, G., & Riestenberg, N. (2006). Beyond zero tolerance: Restoring justice in secondary schools. *Youth Violence and Juvenile Justice, 4*, 123–147. doi:10.1177/1541204006286287

Sugai, G., & Horner, R. (2009). Defining and describing school-wide positive behavior support. In W. Sailor, G. Dunlap, G. Sugai, & R. Horner (Eds.) *Handbook of Positive Behavior Support* (pp. 307–326). New York, NY: Spring Science and Business Media.

Sugai, G., Horner, R., & McIntosh, K. (2008). Best practices in developing a broad-scale system of school-wide positive behavior support. In A. Thomas, & J. Grimes (Eds.), *Best practices in school psychology V* (Vol. 3, pp. 765–780). Bethesda, MD: The National Association of School Psychologists.

Theriot, M. T., & Dupper, D. R. (2010). Student discipline problems and the transition from elementary to middle school. *Education and Urban Society, 42*, 205–222. doi:10.1177/0013124509349583

Umbreit, M. S., Vos, B., Coates, R. B., & Lightfoot, E. (2006). Restorative justice in the twenty first century: A social movement full of opportunities and pitfalls. *Marquette Law Review, 89*, 253–304.

U.S. Department of Health and Human Services, Substance Abuse and Mental Health Services Administration. (2002). SAMHSA model programs: Model prevention programs supporting academic achievement. Retrieved October 1, 2010, from http://captus.samhsa.gov/northeast/academics/model_programs.htm

Utley, C. A., Kozleski, E., Smith, A., & Draper, I. L. (2002). Positive behavior support: A proactive strategy for minimizing behavioral problems in urban multicultural youth. *Journal of Positive Behavior Interventions, 4*, 196–207. doi:10.1177/10983007020040040301

Vavrus, F., & Cole, K. (2002). "I didn't do nothin'": The discursive construction of school suspension. *The Urban Review, 34*, 87–111. doi:10.1023/A:1015375215801

Vasquez, J. A. (1988). Context of learning for minority students. *Educational Forum, 56*, 6–11.

Wald, J., & Losen, D. J. (2003). Defining and redirecting a school-to-prison pipeline. In J. Wald & D. J. Losen (Eds.), *New directions for youth development* (no. 99; pp. 9–15). San Francisco: Jossey-Bass.

Walker, H. M., Colvin, G., & Ramsey, E. (1995). *Antisocial behavior in school: Strategies and best practices.* Pacific Grove, CA: Brooks/Cole.

Wallace, Jr., J. M., Goodkind, S., Wallace, C. M., & Bachman, J. G. (2008). Racial, ethnic, and gender differences in school discipline among U.S. high school students: 1991–2005. *Negro Educational Review, 59*, 47–62.

Wang, M., McCart, A., & Turnbull, A. P. (2007). Implementing positive behavior support with Chinese American families: Enhancing cultural competence. *Journal of Positive Behavior Interventions, 9*, 38–51. doi:10.1177/1098300 7070090010501

Ware, F. (2006). Warm demander pedagogy: Culturally responsive teaching that supports a culture of achievement for African American students. *Urban Education, 41*, 427–456. http://dx.doi.org/10.1177/0042085906289710

Wearmouth, J., McKinney, R., & Glynn, T. (2007). Restorative justice: Two examples from New Zealand schools. *British Journal of Special Education, 34*, 196–203. doi:10.1111/j.1467-8578.2007.00479.x

Weinstein, C., Curran, M., & Tomlinson-Clarke, S. (2003). Culturally responsive classroom management: Awareness into action. *Theory Into Practice, 42*, 269–276. doi:10.1207/s15430421tip4204_2

Weinstein, C. S., Tomlinson-Clarke, S., & Curran, M. (2004). Toward a conception of culturally responsive classroom management. *Journal of Teacher Education, 55*(1), 25–38.

Welch, K., & Payne, A. (2010). Racial threat and punitive school discipline. *Social Problems, 57*, 25–48. doi:10.1525/sp.2010.57.1.25

Wu, S., Pink, W., Crain, R. L., & Moles, O. (1982). Student suspension: A critical reappraisal. *Urban Review, 14*, 245–272. doi:10.1007/BF02171974

Zins, J. E. (2001). Examining opportunities and challenges for school-based prevention and promotion: Social and emotional learning as an exemplar. *The Journal of Primary Prevention, 21*, 441–446. doi: 10.1023/A:1007154727167

Zins, J. E., Bloodworth, M. R., Weissberg, R. P., & Walberg, H. J. (2004). The scientific base for linking social and emotional learning to school success. In J. E. Zins, R. P. Weissberg, M. C. Wang, & H. J. Walberg (Eds.), *Building academic success on social and emotional learning: What does the research say?* (pp. 2–22). New York, NY: Teachers College Press.

39

The Impact of Safe Schools/ Healthy Students Funding on Student Well-Being

A California Consortium Cross-Site Analysis

Thomas L. Hanson

WESTED AND RESEARCH, THE REGIONAL EDUCATIONAL LABORATORY–WESTERN REGION

Amy-Jane Griffiths

THE HELP GROUP'S RESIDENTIAL TREATMENT FACILITY FOR ADOLESCENTS
WITH SOCIAL, EMOTIONAL, AND BEHAVIORAL CHALLENGES

Michael J. Furlong

THE UNIVERSITY OF CALIFORNIA, SANTA BARBARA

Abstract

Since 1999, the Safe Schools/Healthy Students (SS/HS) Initiative has provided communities in the United States with funding to implement a comprehensive set of programs and services that focus on creating safe school environments, promoting healthy childhood development, and preventing youth violence and alcohol, tobacco, and other drug (ATOD) use. This chapter describes a repeated-measures, quasi-experimental design with SS/HS funded schools and matched-comparison schools to examine the extent to which student health risks, protective factors, and academic performance changed in SS/HS schools compared to similar schools that did not receive SS/HS services. Results suggest that student well-being variables such as, student health-related behavior, protective factors, and academic performance improved more in SS/HS grantee schools than in similar schools that did not receive SS/HS funding among fifth graders and seventh graders. Among ninth graders and eleventh graders, SS/HS funding status was not consistently related to changes in student well-being. When examining the degree to which SS/HS impacts varied across grantee sites, results indicated that three sites exhibited the most consistent positive program effects. An examination of program practices in the sites with the most consistent improvements in student well-being indicated that more students were exposed to SS/HS services, staff received professional development in more areas, and more partners participated in the initiative. Implications of these results for future implementation of comprehensive school safety are discussed.

Introduction

The Safe Schools/Healthy Students (SS/HS) Initiative is a discretionary grant program funded by the U.S. Departments of Education, Health and Human Services, and Justice. The programs' goals are to address school and community safety, mental health, and academic achievement in a comprehensive manner (Felix, Furlong, Sharkey, & Osher, 2007; Sharkey et al., this volume). This grant program supported collaboration between school and community agencies with the overarching goal of enhancing a safe school environment and promoting factors that lead to student well-being. This initiative aimed to create sustainable systems improvement at a number of ecological levels (community, school, family) and to develop improved coordination of services across and within these levels (Telleen, Kim, & Pesce, 2009). The initiative supports universal, selected, and targeted interventions, specifically those interventions with an evidence base (Felix et al., 2007).

Student Well-Being and Positive Institutions

In order to promote safe environments and student well-being, a first requirement is to develop a scientific base to: (a) help families and schools encourage children to flourish, (b) support mental health professionals in identifying and nurturing their client's strengths, and (c) encourage the implementation and coordination of interventions in schools and communities (Griffiths, 2010). Researchers in the area of positive psychology have identified three pillars related to intervention at various system levels: positive experiences, positive individual traits, and positive institutions (Positive Psychology Executive Summary, n.d.). Recent research indicates that although the efforts to promote positive psychology are showing effectiveness with two of the pillars (positive experiences and positive individual traits), there has been some difficulty creating a science of positive institutions (Seligman, Steen, Park, & Peterson, 2005). It is clear that further developing the science of positive psychology and applying it to educational contexts would allow for the expansion of more positive institutions, particularly schools (Gilman, Huebner, &Furlong, 2009; Seligman, & Csikszentmihalyi, 2000).

It has been established that an effective intervention strategy is to organize and activate positive institutions or systems that promote healthy child development (Benard & Slade, 2009). Some of the aforementioned systems may include fostering positive attachment relationships (i.e., with teachers, mental health workers), increasing youths' self-regulation skills (i.e., teaching appropriate behaviors and self-monitoring; providing drug/alcohol education interventions), and providing opportunities for children to experience success in order to increase self-efficacy and motivation to succeed in life (i.e., acknowledging students in the school setting, implementing proactive interventions at the group and individual levels). Other strategies may be employed to increase the resources required for children to build competence. Providing additional tutoring, free extracurricular activities, and implementing psychoeducation-based programs may lead to improved outcomes (Benson, Galbraith, & Espeland, 1995; Benson, Scales, Leffert, & Roehlkepartain 1999).

Safe Schools/Healthy Students Communities

Since 1999, the SS/HS grant initiative has provided more than 300 communities throughout the United States with funding to implement a comprehensive set of activities, curricula, programs, and services that focus on creating safe school environments, promoting healthy childhood development, and preventing youth violence and alcohol, tobacco, and other drug (ATOD) use. Using a community partnership approach to provide a comprehensive set of resources to promote healthy child development, eligible grantees are partnerships of a school district or group of school districts and local public mental health, law enforcement, and juvenile justice agencies. Each grantee is required to integrate new and/or existing services that address the following elements: (a) safe school environments and violence prevention activities; (b) alcohol, tobacco, and other drug prevention activities; (c) student behavioral, social, and emotional supports; (d) mental health services; and (e) early childhood social and emotional learning programs.

SS/HS Evaluation Needs

A National Evaluation Team (NET) works with each grantee to utilize data collected at their site to determine the impact of the grant on that particular community. The NET disseminates current evaluation data on its website (www.sshs.samhsa.gov/community/evaluation.aspx) to provide a general picture of the outcomes related to the SS/HS grant. Despite coordinated efforts to obtain various types of data (e.g., survey information, measurable performance goal outcomes), a national evaluation of this initiative has been a challenge, as grantees come from diverse contexts and responded to the specified elements in unique ways. In addition, there are limited incentives to encourage grantee to participate in shared data collection. Due to these challenges, there is limited evidence regarding the effectiveness of the initiative in improving health-related behavior, protective factors, and student academic performance. More specifically, the effectiveness of the SS/HS initiative has not been rigorously evaluated using a randomized controlled trial or a quasi-experimental design using a well-matched comparison group. Previously, evaluation of SS/HS has faced a number of challenges including variations across sites and difficulties obtaining baseline data (Felix et al., 2007). To address these areas of need and to further develop the science and expansion of positive institutions, a cross-site evaluation of the initiative was conducted among the 11 SS/HS grantees in California that received funding between 2002 and 2006. This chapter examines the outcomes in school districts that implemented comprehensive service strategies associated with the SS/HS initiative compared to comparable school districts that carried out business as usual during the same time. In particular, this chapter focuses on changes in student indicators associated with positive youth development and well-being.

Overview the California SS/HS Consortium

With the support of the SS/HS national evaluator, in 2002 the local evaluators of 11 SS/HS grantees sites in California (known as the California Consortium) collaborated on a cross-site evaluation of the SS/HS initiative in the state. A repeated-measures, quasi-experimental design with SS/HS funded schools and matched-comparison schools was used to examine the extent to which student outcomes (i.e., health risks, protective factors, and academic performance) changed in SS/HS schools compared to similar schools that did not receive SS/HS services. Comparisons between program schools and matched comparison control schools were conducted.

Data were collected from local administrations of the California Healthy Kids Survey (CHKS; Austin & Duerr, 2008); school-level demographic and achievement data (maintained by the California Department of Education); and a survey asking about the characteristics of eight of the eleven 2002 SS/HS programs. The California Consortium examined the extent to which students in the 2002 SS/HS grantee sites exhibited greater reductions in health risks and greater increases in protective factors and academic performance than was the case for students in similarly-situated comparison schools. In addition to examining potential impacts of SS/HS activities on students, the impact of program components and implementation strategies were evaluated with the aim of examining three general research questions:

1. Do health-related behaviors, protective factors, and student academic performance improve more in SS/HS grantee schools than in similar schools that did not receive SS/HS funding?
2. Is receipt of SS/HS funding associated with improvements in student well-being more consistently and strongly in some sites than in others; that is, are changes more pronounced when the SS/HS is implemented with greater fidelity? How do program practices differ in the sites with the most pronounced changes in student well-being?
3. How are the characteristics of SS/HS initiatives in California related to changes in student health risk, protective factors, and achievement scores?

The intention of the consortium study was to enhance understanding of the relations between SS/HS program activities and changes in school climate, student health, resilience, and academic performance across a fairly diverse, though nonrandom, sample of districts/schools. With such a diverse set of SS/HS initiatives in California, the consortium was able to examine how different program characteristics are differentially related to improvements in schools as well as individual student outcomes. The results of the study presented in this chapter may be used to inform future programmatic interventions aimed at enhancing school safety, reducing student violence and substance abuse, as well as enhancing student learning and overall well-being.

SS/HS Consortium Evaluation Procedures

In 2002, the SS/HS partnerships served 24 school districts and 352 schools, and represent 262,000 students. These funded initiatives and the populations served at each site are diverse. Four of 11 grantee sites were in urban areas, three in suburban areas, and four in rural areas. In addition, the funded sites served diverse populations. More than half of the students in eight of the sites were minorities.

A repeated-measures, quasi-experimental design with SS/HS funded schools and matched-comparison schools was used to examine the extent to which student health risks, protective factors, and academic performance changed in SS/HS schools compared to similar schools that did not receive SS/HS services.

Identification of Treatment and Comparison Schools

The schools were carefully identified and selected based on numerous criteria. Both covariate- and propensity-score matching techniques were used to identify schools that are similar to SS/HS program schools.

SS/HS Program Schools

Of these 352 schools, 202 served fifth-grade students and 150 served seventh-, ninth-, or eleventh-grade students. Although the 2002 SS/HS grantees served 352 schools, only 180 program schools (88 elementary and 92 secondary) were included in the analytic sample. To be included in the analysis, program schools must have administered the CHKS at least once prior to fall of 2003 (baseline) *and* at least once after fall of 2004.

Comparison Schools

All program schools were matched with one comparison school (with replacement) premised on (a) baseline achievement; (b) school enrollment; (c) students' reports of feeling safe at school; and (c) indexes of sociodemographic characteristics, substance use, violence, and mental health.

For elementary schools, we also included the percent of school enrollment classified as African American and percent Hispanic as match characteristics. Percent English Language Learners and percent Asian were included as match characteristics for secondary schools. We also required exact matching on year and semester of baseline CHKS administration. In addition to matching schools on demographic characteristics, enrollment, and baseline academic achievement, we matched on school-level measures of substance use, violence, and mental health because these domains represent critical elements of the SS/HS initiatives. As a condition of funding, grantees were required to provide a detailed description of planned substance use and violence prevention and intervention activities; student behavioral, social, and emotional supports; and mental health services. Both because grantees were expected to have a greater need for resources than other schools to address student ATOD use, violence, and mental health problems prior to proposal submission, and are expected to make progress in reducing student problems in these areas, it made sense to match SS/HS grantee schools with comparison schools on these factors.

Student Outcome Evaluation Procedures

Comparisons between program schools and control schools were conducted. Changes in student reports of health risk, protective factors, and changes in school-level indices of student academic performance were assessed. Random-intercept regression techniques are used to estimate SS/HS school/comparison-school differences in changes in student well-being and academic performance across time.

Program Component Evaluation Procedures

In addition to examining potential impacts of SS/HS funding status on students, the California Consortium investigated how the characteristics of SS/HS initiatives in California (program components and implementation strategies) are related to changes in achievement scores, student health risk, and protective factors. Two strategies were used to examine the relation between program characteristics and changes in student well-being. First, the association between SS/HS funding status and student well-being was examined for each site using regression techniques. Then program characteristics in SS/HS sites with the most consistent improvements in child well-being were compared with those in other SS/HS sites. Second, regression techniques were used to examine the relation of program characteristics to changes in student well-being in SS/HS schools. Program characteristics were assessed with a project-developed survey administered to 8 of the 11 local evaluators participating in the project.

Measures

A number of measures were utilized to gather data regarding program components and related outcomes. The following measures were included in this study.

The California Consortium Evaluator Survey

A standardized form describing the site-level characteristics of the SS/HS program filled out by eight of the local evaluators participating in the Consortium. The instrument was designed to assess: (a) the types and dosages of services offered at the elementary, middle, and high school levels; (b) staffing and staff development offered across different service areas; and (c) partnership involvement and perceived partnership impacts on the initiative.

The California Health Kids Survey (CHKS)

The CHKS is a repeated cross-sectional, self-report survey of students in Grades 5, 7, 9, and 11. It assesses all major areas of health-related risk behaviors, with a focus on those occurring in the school and those that research has shown to be most associated with variations in academic outcomes (i.e., putative barriers to learning) (Hanson, Austin, & Lee-Bayha, 2004). The survey was designed to meet the local needs of school districts in assessing and monitoring progress in ameliorating student violence; use of alcohol, tobacco, and other drugs; and other behaviors harmful to health and learning. During the study period, biennial administration of the CHKS is required in all districts that receive Title IV funds. Approximately 600,000 students per year take the CHKS (see www.wested.org/hks for more information about the CHKS).

What makes the CHKS stand apart from other adolescent behavior surveys is its assessment of student supports, strengths, and competencies, in addition to assessing student risk factors and problem behavior. While some surveys incorporate protective factors, the CHKS Resilience and Youth Development Module (RYDM) is one of the few assessments that specifically addresses this dimension and does so with a strong theoretical foundation and developing research base (Furlong, Ritchey, & O'Brennan, 2009, Hanson & Kim, 2007). See Table 39.1 for CHKS specifications.

It is crucial to note that all the measures of health-related behavior and protective factors are based on student self-reports. Thus, the measures are based on students' *perceptions* of school conditions and available supports in schools. It is questionable whether student reports provide a complete and accurate depiction of school environmental assets, school safety, school attachment, and health, but student perceptions are certainly critical influences for students' health, social, and academic experiences.

District and School-Level Data

Data were obtained from the California Department of Education (CDE) website. Achievement data come from the 1999–2004 Standardized Testing and Reporting Program's (STAR) research files released by CDE. These files contain school-level average scores on standardized tests for each grade level and subject area. Demographic data come from the 1999–2004 Academic Performance Index (API) and California Basic Education Data System (CBEDS) research files. School-level measures of the educational level of parents come from the API research files, while percentages of students in racial/ethnic categories enrolled in the school, the percentage of students receiving subsidized meals, and the percentage of English language learners (ELL) come from CBEDS data files.

California SS/HS Consortium Outcomes

SS/HS Funding and Changes in Student Well-Being

To examine the effects of SS/HS funding status on student well-being, regression models were used to estimate program/comparison differences in changes in student health-related behavior, protective factors, and student academic performance. Overall, the results (see Tables 39.2 and 39.3) suggested that student health-related behavior, protective factors, and academic performance improved more in SS/HS grantee schools compared to similar schools that did not receive SS/HS funding among fifth graders and seventh graders only, although the magnitude of the differences are fairly small. Among ninth graders and eleventh graders, SS/HS funding status was not consistently related to changes in student well-being. Fifth graders in SS/HS program schools exhibited greater increases in student well-being than their counterparts in comparison

Table 39.1 California Healthy Kids Survey Specifications (see www.wested.org/hks)

Mandate

Mandated (since fall 2003) by the California Department of Education for school districts to be in compliance with U.S.A. No Child Left Behind Act and California Tobacco Use Prevention and Education (TUPE) grants

Survey Type

Comprehensive health risk and resilience survey
Student self-report
Anonymous, voluntary, confidential
Modular secondary school instrument; single elementary school version

Grade Levels

Grades 5, 7, 9, 11, and continuation schools, minimally

Sampling

Representative district sample; school-level surveys optional

Required Modules

A. Core (Required)
B. Resilience and Youth Development (school & community asset scales required)

Optional Modules

B. Resilience and Youth Development (home, peer, & internal asset scales)
C. Alcohol & Other Drug Use & Safety (Violence & Suicide)
D. Tobacco
E. Physical Health
F. Sexual Behavior (Pregnancy and HIV/AIDS risk)
G. Custom Module (for adding questions)

Sources

Items based on California Student Survey, Youth Risk Behavior Survey, and California Student Tobacco Use and Evaluation Survey

Requirements

Biennial administration
Module A and school & community asset scales in Module B
Module D by state TUPE grantees
Written parental consent; passive consent optional since fall 2004
Representative district samples

Administration

By school, following detailed instructions
Processing and reporting by Wested's Health & Human Development Program

schools in the areas of safety behavior (seatbelt use), violence/bullying/safety, substance use and substance use attitudes, empathy, school support, and performance on standardized tests. Only in the areas of nutrition (breakfast) and school engagement was there no evidence of change favoring program schools.

Among seventh graders, student well-being improved more in SS/HS program schools than in control schools in the areas of nutrition (not drinking soda), violence/harassment, substance use, mental health, school environmental health, school engagement (plan to attend college), and school performance (specifically, math performance). For ninth graders, SS/HS program status was *positively* associated with student well-being in the areas of nutrition (not drinking soda), some areas of violence/harassment, and mental health; but *negatively* associated with student well-being in some areas of violence/harassment, school environmental health (meaningful

Thomas L. Hanson et al.

Table 39.2 SS/HS—Comparison Group Differences in Change in SD Units (Elementary Results)

Outcome	5th Grade Effect Size
Nutrition	
Breakfast	−0.025
Safety Behavior	
Seatbelt use	0.082***
Helmet use	0.016
Violence/Bullying/Safety	
Hit/pushed (times)	0.083***
Spread rumors (times)	0.099***
Been hit/pushed (times)	0.060***
Had rumors spread (times)	0.041*
Safety at school	0.123***
Substance Use	
Lifetime cigarettes	0.005
Lifetime alcohol	0.004
30-day alcohol	0.063***
Lifetime inhalant use	0.047**
Cigarettes very bad for health	0.096***
Alcohol very bad for health	0.000
Marijuana very bad for health	0.092***
Psychological Outcome	
Empathy	0.074***
School Environmental Assets	
School Support	0.057**
School Engagement	
School Performance	−0.052*
Plan to attend college	−0.003
School Performance	
California Standards Test – Mathematics	0.124***
California Standards Test – English	0.051***

Note. All outcomes are coded such that positive/higher values indicate higher levels of student well-being. Results are based on regression model that includes controls for student gender, school test scores (2003), and baseline school composition with regards to substance use, violence, perceived safety, mental health, and demographic characteristics.
*** $p < .01$, ** $p < .05$, * $p < .10$

participation), school engagement (truancy), and school performance (math performance). Most of the eleventh-grade student outcomes examined were not associated SS/HS program status.

In summary, the observed effects of SS/HS program implementation were mixed. There was more evidence supporting the positive influence of SS/HS services and strategies on younger than older students. Although the clear objective of the SS/HS national initiative is to promote positive effects for all students, effects during Grades 5 and 7, as found in this study, are more desirable because they have the potential to prevent student involvement in risk behaviors before they begin.

Table 39.3 SS/HS—Comparison Group Differences in Change in SD Units (Secondary Results)

Outcome	7th Grade	9th Grade	11th Grade
	Effect Size	Effect Size	Effect Size
Physical Activity			
Aerobic physical activity	0.006	0.023	−0.018
Nutrition			
Drink soda pop (24 hours)	0.035*	0.051***	0.082***
Eat vegetables (24 hours)	0.001	−0.028	0.000
Eat breakfast	0.008	0.006	0.027
Violence/Harassment			
Been hit/pushed	0.018	−0.004	0.027
Afraid of being hit	0.022	−0.027	0.006
Fights at school	0.063***	−0.003	0.017
Had rumors spread	0.052***	0.008	−0.023
Sexual harassment	0.048**	−0.004	−0.010
Made fun of because of looks	0.054***	−0.010	−0.018
Victim of vandalism	0.071***	−0.045**	0.002
Offered drugs at school	0.049***	−0.048**	−0.065***
Committed vandalism	0.044**	0.001	0.018
Gun to school	0.043**	0.054***	0.023
Threatened with weapon	0.080***	0.046**	0.059***
Seen gun at school	0.016	−0.012	−0.005
Ethnic/racial harassment	0.074***	−0.041*	−0.006
Religious harassment	0.040**	−0.043**	−0.020
Gender harassment	0.059***	0.013	−0.003
Gay/Lesbian harassment	0.042**	0.020	0.031
Disabled harassment	0.064***	0.028	0.034
Safety at school	0.012	0.096***	−0.013
Substance Use			
Lifetime cigarettes	0.065***	0.043**	0.020
30-day cigarettes	0.048**	0.003	−0.010
30-day cigarettes at school	0.052***	0.030	0.017
Lifetime alcohol	0.028	−0.008	0.051**
30-day alcohol	0.036*	−0.018	0.029
30-day lcohol at school	0.076***	−0.014	0.025
Lifetime marijuana	0.039**	0.019	0.076***
30-day marijuana	0.086***	0.007	0.045**
30-day marijuana at school	0.062***	0.010	0.020
Psychological Outcomes			
Depression	0.052***	0.000	−0.034
Efficacy	0.076***	0.071**	−0.006
Empathy	0.023	0.018	0.042
Problem Solving	0.028	−0.023	0.075**
Self-Awareness	0.096***	0.064**	0.001

(*continued*)

Table 39.3 Continued

Outcome	7th Grade Effect Size	9th Grade Effect Size	11th Grade Effect Size
School Environmental Assets			
School Support	0.044*	0.010	0.021
School High Expectations	0.037	0.028	0.014
School Caring Relations	0.048**	−0.007	0.028
School Meaningful Participation	0.005	−0.054**	−0.019
School Engagement			
Grades	0.030	0.011	0.023
Plan to attend college	0.112***	0.030	−0.007
School connectedness	−0.026	0.004	0.052
Truancy	0.023	−0.089***	0.012
School Performance			
California Standards Test – Math	0.085**		
California Standards Test – English	0.034	−0.110**	−0.172

Note. All outcomes are coded such that positive/higher values indicate higher levels of student well-being. Results are based on regression model that includes controls for student gender, school test scores (2003), and baseline school composition with regards to substance use, violence, perceived safety, mental health, and demographic characteristics.
*** $p < .01$, ** $p < .05$, * $p < .10$.

The Association Between SS/HS Funding Status and Well-Being

As a first step to determine which grantee practices might be most effective in improving student well-being, we examined the degree to which SS/HS impacts varied across grantee sites. The results of these analyses indicated that a handful of sites exhibit more consistent positive program impacts than others. We then examined program survey results for these sites to shed light on what these sites may be doing differently from other sites. The results indicated that in the sites with the most consistent improvements in student well-being more students were exposed to SS/ HS services, staff received professional development in more areas, and more partners participated in the initiative. It is possible that these differences in program activities may be responsible for the more general positive impacts associated with SS/HS funding.

Program Characteristics and Student Well-Being

The research team also examined the relation of the specific characteristics of SS/HS initiatives in California to changes in student health risk, protective factors, and achievement scores. Based on the analysis of evaluator responses to the program survey, we examined the (a) types and levels of services funded by the 2002 SS/HS initiative in California, (b) types and levels of staff development provided, and (c) partnership involvement and perceived partnership impacts. The results are summarized in the following section.

Students Served, Types and Intensity of Services Provided

Results indicate that SS/HS-funded activities reached substantial numbers of elementary, middle, and high school students. Violence prevention activities were most widespread in elementary schools, with 79% of students exposed to such services in elementary schools, 65% in middle schools, and 57% in high schools. SS/HS-supported mental health services reached equal percentages of students in elementary, middle, and high schools (approximately 60%). In addition, alcohol, tobacco, and other drug (ATOD) prevention services were targeted to slightly higher percentages of elementary and middle school students (56%) than high school students (47%). Regardless of whether the focus of the service was on violence, mental health, or ATOD use, counseling, case management, and to some extent care coordination were the most intensive and consistent activities supported by SS/HS. The least prevalent services provided were peer counseling or mediation and after-school programs.

Staff Development

A high proportion of sites indicated that staff development was provided across most of the 16 areas asked about in the program survey. For example, five of the eight sites participating in the program survey indicated that staff development was provided to middle schools in 14 of the 16 areas asked about. Consistent with the types of services supported by SS/HS, staff development was most likely to be provided for identification of emotional problems and individual counseling, suicide prevention, violence/bullying prevention, and alcohol and illegal drug use prevention. The least common staff development activities provided was in stress management and tobacco cessation.

Partnership Involvement and Perceived Impact

Survey data indicated that SS/HS grantees partnered with an average of seven other entities in providing services, with a range of 4 to 11. All grantees partnered with a local law enforcement agency and a community mental health department. Partners were perceived as being effective in providing services, particularly in the areas of counseling and mental health services. The lowest ratings of effectiveness were in the areas of care coordination and student drug use. Evaluator ratings of partnership working processes were moderately positive, with the highest ratings for organization and tolerance of disagreements, and the lowest rating for shared decision-making.

Because sites may elect to deliver certain types and levels of service in response a greater need for certain services, care should be taken in the interpretation of the relation between program practices and student well-being across grantee sites. With one exception (number of partners), the analyses indicated that the characteristics of SS/HS programs assessed by the program survey were inconsistently related to changes in student well-being.

Summary

This chapter summarizes the findings of the largest integrated study of the SS/HS implementation to date. The findings suggest that student health-related behaviors, protective factors, and academic performance improved more in SS/HS grantee schools compared to similar schools that did not receive SS/HS funding among students in Grades 5 and 7. In contrast, among students in Grades 9 and 11, SS/HS funding status was inconsistently related to changes in student outcomes. Although the findings are consistent for Grades 5 and 7, the magnitude of the effects is fairly small. On average, fifth- and seventh-grade students in SS/HS schools exhibited increases in student well-being that were 5% of a standard deviation greater than the increases exhibited by students in comparison schools. The results also indicated that three sites exhibited the most consistent, positive program effects. An examination of program practices indicated that at these three sites more students were exposed to SS/HS services, staff received professional development in more areas, and more partners participated in the initiative in the sites. It is possible that these differences in program activities may be responsible for the positive impacts in some sites;

that is, increased fidelity with the SS/HS comprehensive service delivery logic model was associated with more positive outcomes.

These analyses contribute to an understanding of the relation between SS/HS program activities and changes in school climate, student health, resilience, and academic performance across a fairly diverse, though nonrandom, sample of districts/schools. We are hopeful that this information will inform future programmatic interventions aimed at enhancing school safety, reducing student violence and substance abuse, and enhancing student learning. More detailed information about the California SS/HS Consortium study is available from Hanson, Cason, and Gopal (2008).

Note

This chapter is based on a more detailed report of by Hanson, Cason, and Gopal (2008): *Safe Schools/Healthy Students Funding and Changes in Student Well-being: California Consortium Cross-Site Analysis. California Consortium Safe Schools/Healthy Students Consortia Project Final Report*. Los Alamitos, CA: WestEd. This work was partially funded by a contract from the Research Triangle Institute.

References

Austin, G., & Duerr, M. (2008). *Guidebook for the California School Climate Survey for teachers and other staff*. San Francisco, CA: WestEd.

Benard, B., & Slade, S. (2009). Listening to the students: Moving from resilience research to youth development practice and school connectedness. In R. Gilman, E. S. Huebner, M. J., & Furlong, (Eds.), *Handbook of positive psychology in the schools* (pp. 353–369). New York, NY: Routledge.

Benson, P. L., Galbraith, J., & Espeland, P. (1995). *What kids need to succeed*. Minneapolis, MN: Free Spirit.

Benson, P. L., Scales, P. C., Leffert, N., & Roehlkepartain, E. C. (1999). *A fragile foundation: The state of developmental assets among American youth*. Minneapolis, MN: Search Institute.

Felix, E., Furlong, M., Sharkey, J., & Osher, D. (2007). Implications for evaluating multi-component, complex prevention initiatives. *Journal of School Violence, 6*, 3–22. doi:10.1300/J202v06n02_02

Furlong, M., Ritchey, K., & O'Brennan, L. (2009). Developing norms for the California Resilience Youth Development Module: Internal assets and school resources subscales. *The California School Psychologist, 14*, 35–46.

Gilman, R., Huebner, E. S., & Furlong, M. J. (Eds.). (2009). *Handbook of positive psychology in the schools*. New York, NY: Routledge.

Griffiths, A. J. (2010). *Positive behavior support in the alternative education setting: A case study* (unpublished doctoral dissertation). University of California, Santa Barbara, Santa Barbara, CA.

Hanson, T. L., Austin, G. A., & Lee-Bayha, J. (2004). *Ensuring that no child is left behind: How are student health risks & resilience related to the academic progress of schools*. San Francisco, CA: WestEd.

Hanson, T. L., Cason, C., & Gopal, M. (2008). *Safe Schools/Healthy Students funding and changes in student well-being: California Consortium cross-site analysis. California Consortium Safe Schools/Healthy Students Consortia Project Final Report*. Los Alamitos, CA: WestEd.

Hanson, T. L., & Kim, J. O. (2007). *Measuring resilience and youth development: The psychometric properties of the Healthy Kids Survey*. (Issues & Answers Report, REL 2007- NO.034). Washington, DC: U.S. Department of Education, Institute of Education Sciences, National Center for Education Evaluation and Regional Assistance, Regional Educational Laboratory West. Retrieved, from http://ies.ed.gov/ncee/edlabs

Positive Psychology Executive Summary. (n.d.). Retrieved March 3, 2009, from http://www.ppc.sas.upenn.edu/executivesummary.htm

Seligman, M. E. P., & Csikszentmihalyi, M. (2000). Positive psychology: An introduction. *American Psychologist, 55*, 5–14. doi:10.1037//0003-066X.55.1.5

Seligman, M. E. P., Steen, T. A., Park, N., & Peterson, C. (2005). Positive psychology progress: Empirical validation of interventions. *American Psychologist, 60*(5), 410–421.

Telleen, S., Kim, Y. O., & Pesce, R. (2009). An ecological developmental community initiative to reduce youth violence: Safe Schools/Healthy Students. *Journal of Prevention and Intervention in the Community, 37*, 326–338. doi:10.1080/10852350903196340

School Violence in South Korea

An Overview of School Violence and Intervention Efforts

Seung-yeon Lee and Insoo Oh

EWHA WOMANS UNIVERSITY, SEOUL, KOREA

Abstract

This chapter first summarizes important research findings on school violence in South Korea by using Bronfenbrenner's (1994) ecological model. Next, the chapter provides an overview of comprehensive intervention efforts initiated by the Korean government. In addition, the chapter introduces several representative school violence prevention and intervention programs in Korea by highlighting specific characteristics of each program. Finally, discussion follows regarding implications for further program development, successful school practice, and effective school policy in Korea.

Overview

In South Korea, school violence began to draw attention from the public through the *wang-ta* phenomenon in schools. *Wang-ta*, a term coined in Korea in the late 1990s, refers to social exclusion by a group of peers. It can also refer to an individual who is the target of social exclusion (Kwon, 1999). Research on school violence, especially bullying, started in 1995 when the suicide of a victimized boy shocked Korean society (Kwon, 1999).

Suicide has been one of the negative consequences of bullying (Rigby & Slee, 1999). In a survey of 4,700 middle and high school students (Korea Youth Counseling Institute, 2007), about 51% of Korean students who had attempted suicide reported a significant amount of victimization by peers. The number of bullies was also greater among suicide attempters than non-attempters. In the United States, about 78% of school shooters had suicidal ideation or attempts ,and 71% were victims of chronic bullying prior to the incident (Vossekuil, Fein, Reddy, Borum, & Modzeleski, 2002; as cited in Espelage & Swearer, 2003).

According to a cross-national study of adolescents in 40 countries (Craig et al., 2009), 10.7% reported bullying others (e.g., physical, verbal, social bullying) and 12.6% reported being bullied during the past two months. In a survey of 4,073 school–aged youth (Foundation for Preventing

Youth Violence, 2010), the rates of bullying (e.g., physical, verbal, and social bullying, threatening, taking money, sexual harassment) and victimization during the previous year were 12.4% and 9.4%, respectively. In Korea, bullying others appeared to be more prevalent than being victimized. Furthermore, about 42% of students did not regard bullying as school violence. Approximately 56% of the self-reported bullies perpetrated against peers "just for fun" and "with no reason."

Research on bullying has dramatically increased since the late 1990s. Although bullying is generated and maintained by the interaction between an individual and his or her environments, much of the research focus has addressed intrapersonal factors. Thus, this chapter first reviews Korean research on environmental contexts for bullying as well as individual factors, using Bronfenbrenner's (1994) ecological model. Next, it examines comprehensive intervention strategies implemented by the Korean government, along with several representative programs for bullying prevention and intervention. Finally, future directions and implications are suggested for more effective bullying prevention and intervention in Korea.

Conceptual Basis

Intrapersonal Factors

While recent empirical research on school bullying has examined multiple individual factors, this review and synthesis focuses on a subset of these variables as they have been the key component of bullying prevention and intervention programs in Korea. These include self-esteem, coping strategies, self-control, and empathy. Reviewing major findings on these variables would provide some ideas on how to improve current bullying prevention and intervention strategies in Korea.

Self-Esteem

Korean researchers found that low self-esteem significantly predicts victimization by peers (Kim, 2005; Kim & Lee, 2000). However, the relationship between self-esteem and bullies has been controversial. Low self-esteem predicted bullying behaviors among Korean adolescents (Kim, 2005; Oh, 2008). In contrast, Lee and Kwak (2000) reported that bullies' self-esteem was significantly higher than that of victims or bully-victims. Such a discrepancy might be partially explained by Lee's (2004) findings that bullies appear to have high self-esteem in a cross-sectional analysis although bullying behaviors were significantly associated with declines in self-esteem after seven months in the study.

Coping Strategies

Problem-solving coping strategies, in contrast to emotionally oriented coping, were found to be negatively correlated with both bullying and victimization in a study of 679 males from Italian high schools (Baldry & Farrington, 2005). Among Korean elementary school students, it was defenders who used approach coping strategies (e.g., problem solving, support seeking) most frequently, compared to other participant roles in bullying (Sim, 2005). However, problem-solving coping is not always a protective factor; it was statistically identified as a risk factor for victimized children to be more rejected by peers (Kochenderfer-Ladd & Skinner, 2002). Among Korean middle school girls (Kim & Lee, 2000) and elementary school students (Lee & Kim, 2001), bullies and bully-victims utilized more passive coping strategies such as emotion-oriented coping or wishful thinking than non-involved students.

Self-Control

Haynie et al. (2001) reported that the level of self-control was the lowest among bully-victims, followed by bullies. Similarly, in a study of 865 Korean middle school students, both bullies and victims had lower self-control than non-involved students (Lee, Gong, & Lee, 2004). According to Unnever and Cornell (2003), self-control partially mediated the relationship between attention-deficit hyperactivity disorder (ADHD) status and bullying behaviors. In their study, low self-control was a significant predictor for bullying, but not for being bullied. However, the interaction between self-control and gender was significant. The association between self-control and being a victim was positive for boys while negative for girls. Among Korean adolescents, self-control partially mediated the association between family cohesion and bullying behaviors (Kim, Lee, & Kang, 2007). In addition, among elementary school girls, low self-control served as a moderator, intensifying the likelihood of bullying behaviors when peer compliance was high (Ha & Cho, 2007). The moderation effect of self-control did not exist among boys.

Empathy

Bullying prevention programs have focused on empathy since most research indicates a positive correlation between low empathy and antisocial behaviors (Jolliffe & Farrington, 2006). In Korea, bullies also had lower empathy than others; however, lack of empathy did not significantly predict bullying behaviors among middle school girls (Kim & Lee, 2000). On the other hand, Song, Song, Baek, and Lee (2009), in a study of 696 middle school students using logistic regression analysis, found that girls' empathy increased the likelihood of being a bully rather than being a bully-victim. This result might imply the necessity to distinguish cognitive empathy (perspective-taking) from affective empathy (empathic concern). Affective empathy has been shown to have a positive association only with defending behaviors while cognitive empathy is associated with both defending and bystanding behaviors (Gini, Albiero, Benelli, & Altoe, 2008). Similarly, affective empathy was a significant predictor for defending behaviors regardless of gender, while cognitive empathy did not predict boy's defending behaviors (Oh, 2010). Further, among boys, affective empathy served as a mediator between Theory of Mind (ToM) abilities and defending behaviors (Song & Lee, 2010).

Microsystem

The microsystem consists of people with whom an individual has direct contact and has immediate influences on the individual's adjustment (Bronfenbrenner, 1994). Family, peers, and school are often discussed as an example of a microsystem.

Family

Parenting practices have been an important variable in explaining school bullying (Baldry & Farrington, 2005). In Korea, a father's rejection/controlling behaviors significantly predicted both bullying and victimization by peers regardless of gender. Permissive/ neglectful parenting also has a positive association with bullying behaviors. Such relationships appear in pairs between father and daughter and between mother and son (Song et al., 2009). In addition, parents' corporal punishment was the strongest predictor for victimization while it did not predict bullying among elementary school students (Lee & Kim, 2001). In contrast, exposure to parental violence was associated with the increased risk of bullying others, but not with being bullied among high school students (Do, 2008).

In a cross-cultural study of Korean and German middle school students, lack of parental support was a significant predictor for bullying as well as victimization by peers in both groups (Kim, 2005). However, greater family support (Lee & Kim, 2001) or mothers' supportive parenting (Song et al., 2009) was associated with increased risk of being victimized among girls. Future research needs to examine whether Korean girls misinterpreted enmeshed relationships as support, as enmeshed relationships with parents have been found to be positively associated with victimization (Finnegan, Hodges, & Perry, 1998).

Positive relationships with parents serve as a protective factor for school bullying. Secure attachment with parents is negatively associated with bully-victim experiences (Oh, 2007). Likewise, parent-child communication and parental monitoring are significantly associated with declines in bullying behaviors by enhancing anger management abilities among middle school students (Lee, Gong, & Lee, 2004).

Peers

The lack of good friends or peer connection has been discussed as a risk factor for school violence (Furlong, Chung, Bates, & Morrison, 1995). In a study of Korean elementary students (Jang & Seong, 2007), peer support demonstrated the strongest negative correlation with being victimized, compared to family or teacher support. Peer support also had a negative correlation with girls' bullying behaviors; however, social support had no association with boys' perpetration. It is important to note that low peer support was a significant predictor only for victimization by peers among girls (Kim & Lee, 2000; Lee & Kim, 2001). Since girls are more relationship-oriented, perhaps the lack of peer support makes them more vulnerable to victimization. Most Korean studies on bullying have compared different sources of social support as a risk factor for bullying and victimization. It is necessary to address the nature (e.g., emotional, instrumental, informational) of social support as well as its source.

Regardless of gender, an important predictor for bullying behaviors was contact with delinquent peers (Kim, 2007). Friends' delinquency more strongly predicted bullying among middle and high school students than in a group of elementary school students (Kim, 2006). It is not difficult to understand this finding, given that peers become more important in children's lives as they grow older. On the other hand, friends' delinquency was also the strongest predictor for victimization by peers among Korean middle school students (Kim, 2006).

Schools

Researchers have concluded that bullies, victims, and bully-victims received less teacher support than non-involved students, and those who engage in frequent bullying reported the lowest level of teacher support (Flaspohler, Elfstrom, Vanderzee, & Sink, 2009; Natvig, Albrektsen, & Qvarnstrom, 2001). Similarly, hostile relationships with teachers increased the likelihood of adolescents becoming a bully (Lee, 2005; Oh, 2007). The lack of teacher support contributes to victimization among elementary school students (Jang & Seong, 2007). Thus, it is surprising that girls in middle schools were victimized more often although they received more teacher support (Kim & Lee, 2000). This result is plausible, considering children who are perceived by others as tattlers or "teachers' pets" are usually disliked by classmates (Kim & Lee).

Bullying behaviors increase significantly when teachers' discipline is too strict, teachers rely more on punishment, or punishment by teachers is inconsistent and unfair (Kim, 2007; Lee, 2005; Hwang, Shin, & Park, 2006). Bullying behaviors also increased as classmates were more permissive of school violence (Kim, 2007). In addition, teachers' use of corporal punishment was a significant predictor for victimization regardless of gender (Kim, 2007). A path analysis demonstrated that the association with delinquent peers partially mediated the relationships between negative school climate and bullying behaviors. The exposure to negative school climate increases perpetration through enhancing the affiliation with delinquent peers. At the same time, it enhances a student's likelihood of bullying others even after controlling for the effect of delinquent peers (Hwang et al., 2006).

Mesosystem

The mesosystem is best described as the interconnections among two or more microsystems (Bronfenbrenner, 1994). Kim, Chung, and Lee (2008) found boys in middle and high schools did not engage in bullying behaviors if they had peer or teacher support, despite their exposure to parents' domestic violence. Their findings reflect the interactions between a child's family and peers/schools. Another example can be found in Lee et al.'s (2004) study that indicated attachment with teachers or school deters perpetration of school violence by decreasing contacts with delinquent peers. Their findings involved the interactions between a child's school and peers.

Exosystem

The exosystem consists of different settings that do not directly involve the individual, but where events occur that indirectly affect his or her life (Bronfenbrenner, 1994). A good example of the exosystem is mass media. Research has indicated that the violent content of mass media affects individuals' bullying behaviors. For example, exposure to media violence likely increases perpetration of school violence while simultaneously moderating the relationship between aggression and bullying behaviors (Do, 2008). Media violence was the strongest predictor for bullying only among elementary school students (Kim, 2006). However, among high school students who had more exposure to media violence, there was no association between bullying and media exposure (Kim, 2006). Ferguson, Miguel, and Hartley (2009) reported that violent video games, not violent TV programs, predicted more bullying behaviors among youth aged 10 to 14. Likewise, Kim, Lee, and Lee (2010) demonstrated a full mediation model among internet game addiction, violent thoughts, and perpetration of school violence.

Macrosystem

As a societal blueprint, the macrosystem involves values, belief systems, customs, lifestyles, and societal structures of a particular culture (Bronfenbrenner, 1994). Researchers often suggest that failing to conform to in-group norms may contribute to ostracism and peer victimization within a collectivistic society (Lee & Kim, 2001). However, on an individual level, collectivistic tendencies were a significant predictor for being bullied despite the cultural background of a society. For example, a lack of vertical collectivism (emphasizing more on group hierarchy and obedience) among Korean middle school students, but a lack of horizontal collectivism (emphasizing similarity and cooperation among in-group members) among the German counterpart, predicted victimization (Kim, 2005).

However, lack of parental support was the strongest predictor of both bullying and victimization among Korean youth. In contrast, permissive attitudes toward violence was the strongest predictor of bullying, where lower social acceptance was most predictive of victimization among German youth (Kim, 2005). This result might reflect the collectivistic nature of Korean society compared to more individualistic characteristics found among Germans (Kim, 2005).

The Korean educational system is another example of a macrosystem. Due to excessive pressure for academic achievement, Korean students experience a significant amount of stress (Park,

2006). According to Chon, Lee, Yoo, and Lee (2004), academic stress significantly increased conformity to norms supporting bullying within a group. Furthermore, working in an educational environment that only focuses on academic excellence, Korean teachers became passive in addressing school violence (Hwang et al., 2006).

Comprehensive Intervention Efforts

National School Violence Prevention and Intervention Plan

Since *wang-ta* began to draw attention in the late 1990s, a large number of sporadic interventions to cope with school bullying were developed and implemented in Korea. More comprehensive intervention efforts were initiated by the Korean government's five-year plan along with legislation regarding school violence prevention and intervention in 2004 (Korea Ministry of Education & Human Resources, 2005). The Five-year Plan of Prevention and Intervention for School Violence is a multilevel system approach which relies on the collaboration of each operating body such as Department of Education, school districts, and local schools (Goal 1). Priority was given to prevention programs rather than intervention approaches based on studies showing proactive approaches being more effective than reactive approaches (Goal 2). The shortage of school counselors in the Korean school system highlighted the importance of a classroom teacher's ability to cope with school violence and thus enhancement of a classroom teacher's ability to deal with school violence was emphasized (Goal 3). The plan also initiated a variety of nation-wide movements for creating a safe school climate (Goal 4).

Implementation of this ambitious plan resulted in significant changes (Korea Ministry of Education, Science, & Technology [MEST], 2009). First, a collaborative network for reducing school violence was created, based on task force teams in local school districts. Second, all local schools throughout the nation established a school violence autonomy committee—a special school board discussing various school violence issues. Third, in addition to bullying prevention programs, there was widespread hiring of school police officers and installations of CCTV cameras. Fourth, all teachers were mandated to take in-service training on school violence prevention every year since 2008. Particularly noteworthy, a national study indicated a decrease of school violence in general since the implementation of the plan from 17.6% in 2006 to 11.3% in 2009 (Korea Youth Prevention Foundation, 2009; as cited in Ministry of Education, Science, and Technology, 2009).

However, the plan did not achieve one of its objectives which intended to reduce school violence by 5% every year, thus reducing school violence by 25% over the course of five years, relative to baseline conditions. Furthermore, although verbal and physical violence were diminished in general, social or relational violence slightly increased from 2.5% in 2005 to 3.4% in 2008 (MEST, 2009). Furthermore, there was a considerable increase of school violence among younger children during this period (Foundation for Preventing Youth Violence, 2009). Responding to these challenges, the Korean government recently announced a new plan for the next five years (2010–2014). Table 40.1 outlines specific policy tasks for achieving each of the plan's six goals.

The new plan provided more sophisticated interventions based on the results from the first five-year plan. First, a customized prevention program based on local needs assessment was emphasized, because general prevention programs targeting large and broadly defined groups were not effective (MEST, 2009). Second, the new plan put an emphasis on school accountability. Each school has to demonstrate its efforts for decreasing bullying by monitoring the degree of school violence among its student population and linking that data to school-based

Table 40.1   Goals and Policy Tasks of New School Violence Prevention and Intervention Plan (2010–2014)

Goals	Examples of specific policy tasks
1. Expanding safe infrastructure for school violence	• Increasing number of school police-officer and installation of CCTV • Diversifying school violence reporting system
2. Reinforcing customized preventive education	• Intensifying education in earlier levels • Empowering family functions with PTA
3. Enhancing school's accountability and coping strategies	• Activating school's autonomy committee on violence • Monitoring degree of safety by assessing whole population
4. Improving quality of counseling and education services for victims and bullies	• Mandating counseling service to students with potential risk • Increasing quality of counseling services for victims
5. Creating school climate fostering respect and care	• Emphasizing character education and volunteer education • Activating peer mentoring system
6. Establishing safe school network with community collaboration	• Creating community-based committee on school violence • Conducting various community-wide events promoting safe school climates

prevention efforts. Third, collaboration of parents, teachers, and communities are encouraged. For example, teachers are expected to be actively involved in PTA (parent–teacher association) in order to empower family involvement in prevention. Teachers can help families better through sharing information and providing advice or possibly training to parents on several topics such as child supervision, family communication, and decision-making as a part of a broad prevention approach. The participation of other helping professionals in the community is also supported. Fourth, high quality counseling services for victims and bullies are provided through community counseling centers.

Representative School Violence Prevention and Intervention Programs

Along with systematic intervention efforts by government, a number of other school violence prevention and intervention programs have been developed in Korea. Given the urgency of dealing with school violence during the last decade, most programs have been applied to school settings without going through rigorous outcome evaluations. Therefore, empirical studies that examine treatment effects of such programs are scarce. The following programs were selected based on by multiple criteria, including credibility of developer, supply ratio of the program, and overall quality and quantity of supporting empirical research. Key characteristics of selected representative programs are summarized in Table 40.2.

Some of the above programs reported the result of their effectiveness. Kwak, Kim, Kim, and Koo (2005) found that the participants in the HELP-ing program showed decreased bullying victimization compared to the control group in elementary and middle schools. The Korea Youth Counseling Institute (2008) also reported that elementary students who joined in the Care Enhancement Program showed higher perspective-taking, empathic concerns, and care for others, possibly linked to reduced bullying behaviors. School Violence Prevention Program

Table 40.2 Summary of Selected School Violence Related Programs in Korea

Types	Programs	Key Components	Key Features	Format/ Participants
Prevention	• HELP-ing (Help Encourage yourself as a Leader of Peace-ing) by Kwak et al. (2005)	• Increasing responsibility • Changing self-recognition • Enhancing coping skills	• Improving bystanders' coping skills by increasing their social cognition abilities	• Classroom guidance activity • (1~8 sessions) for elementary and middle school students
	• Care Enhancement Program for the Prevention of School Violence by Korea Youth Counseling Institute (2008)	• Taking perspective of others • Increasing empathic concern for others • Enhancing care for others	• Intensified program by running 3 sessions a week for a month • Adopting interdisciplinary approach with other subject matters	• Classroom guidance activity • (13 sessions) for elementary school students
	• KEDI School Violence Prevention Program by Korean Educational Development Institute (2007)	• Taking perspective of others • Learning positive communication skills • Increasing mediation skills for effective conflict resolution	• Watching animation DVD followed by a teacher's instruction • Exploring effective intervention in three levels: personal, class, and school levels	• Classroom guidance activity • (4 sessions) for elementary school students
Intervention	• Youth Rainbow Program by Korea Youth Protection Committee (2002)	• Discovering strengths • Sharing friendship • Taking perspective of others • Managing conflicts and stress in school	• Focusing on students' strengths • Diversified experiential activities • A series of program including diagnosis, implementation, & evaluation	• Small group activity for victims or risk group • Two formats: One is for 3-day camp and the other is for 10 sessions for 10 weeks.
	• "Let's Play Together" Program by Korea Youth Counseling Institute (2004)	• Increasing interpersonal skills • Expressing themselves by participating in psychodrama • Exploring solutions by making a video skit with others	• Learning skills at intensive 3-day camp and reinforcing them for five months • Focusing on three areas: emotions, cognitions, and behaviors	• Small group activity for victims or risk group • Two steps: First is 3-day camp and second is 5 sessions for 5 months

by the Korean Educational Development Institute (2007) also demonstrated its effectiveness by increasing the participants' awareness of school violence and coping skills compared to a control group.

In addition to prevention programs, various intervention programs for victims were developed as well, though few programs reported their effectiveness. The Youth Rainbow Program (KYPC, 2002, as cited in Kang, 2008) was designed for victims in two formats: one is for an intensive 3-day camp, and the other is for a 10-day group counseling session. The "Let's Play Together" was selected as the best program at the school violence intervention program contest which was sponsored by the Korea Youth Counseling Institute (KYCI, 2004, as cited in Kang 2008). This program has been widely implemented in many counseling centers and it consists of a two-step procedure: three-day intensive camp followed by five group counseling sessions for five months.

Discussion

According to ecological systems theory, successful interventions for school violence should focus on environmental contexts as well as individuals. However, most of the bullying prevention and intervention programs in Korea have focused on individual factors, ignoring the complex interactions among individuals and their ecological contexts. Mental health professionals such as school counselors or psychologists should keep in mind the importance of a comprehensive approach. For example, family environments with little parental monitoring would contribute to a child's exposure to violent media or internet games. Exposure to violent media is a crucial determinant in predicting young children's bullying behaviors (Kim, 2006). Therefore, limiting media violence can be a relevant approach for bullying prevention. Harsh and physical parenting practices lead to younger children's victimization by peers (Lee & Kim, 2001) and over time can contribute to bullying behaviors among high school students (Do, 2008). Thus, in order to reduce bullying, parenting practices should be another focus of early intervention.

Furthermore, research indicates positive school climate as a protective factor for school violence (Hwang et al., 2006; Kim, 2007). One of its components is teachers' disciplinary strategies. In 2010, dissemination of a video clip showing a teacher's use of corporal punishment ignited national debate on whether corporal punishment should be completely prohibited in the Korean school systems. Teachers' abilities to provide behavioral guidance to students are already severely constrained under such a competitive educational environment. The complete prohibition of corporal punishment might be another problem for student management unless more effective disciplinary strategies are provided for teachers. Certainly, School-Wide Positive Behavioral Support (SWPBS), a systematic approach for behavioral management, could be a solution. SWPBS provides clear expectations of acceptable behaviors for both students and teachers, and relies on a continuum of reinforcement for positive behaviors (Osher, Bear, Sprague, & Dolye, 2010).

Meanwhile, academic stress of Korean youth facilitates their conformity to bullying within a group. Oh (2009) identified that a high level of students' stress influenced their bullying behaviors through increased aggression. Therefore, helping students cope with their academic stress can be another strategy for bullying prevention. In addition, it may not be effective to focus on empathy training without considering the specific type of empathy and the gender of the students involved (Oh, 2010; Oh & Hazler, 2009). However, it appears that most bullying prevention and intervention programs have not taken such research findings into consideration. The weak connection of these programs with empirical research might result in little or inconsistent treatment effectiveness.

An important issue in bullying prevention and intervention in Korea is that most efforts are weighted toward intervening with victims. Although the new Five-year Plan of Prevention and Intervention for School Violence includes counseling services for both victims and bullies, it is still more common for perpetrators of school violence or bullies to receive punishment, rather than psychological intervention (Park, 2006). For example, both the Youth Rainbow and "Let's Play Together" programs are directed toward empowering victims. However, bullies also require a comprehensive intervention program in order to reduce various risk factors that lead to bullying behaviors.

Furthermore, it is crucial to understand bullying as a group dynamic that involves not only the bully and victim, but also bystanders (Oh & Hazler, 2009). The fact that bystanders are the majority of the participants in bullying episodes implies that bystanders can play a critical role in maintaining or prohibiting the bullying dynamic (Swearer, Espelage, Vaillancourt, & Hymel, 2010). However, most bystanders are less likely to intervene or defend victims, because they try to avoid getting involved due to a fear of revenge or the uncertainty of the intervention (Oh & Hazler, 2009). Therefore, it is critical to find out how to foster positive bystander responses in bullying

Table 40.3 Implications for Practice: Towards Effective Prevention and Intervention Strategies

1.	Effective interventions for school violence include comprehensive strategies addressing individuals, family, peers, school, and community.
2.	Priority needs to be given to prevention programs rather than intervention approaches, because proactive approaches are more effective than reactive approaches.
3.	A customized prevention program based on needs assessment is more effective than general prevention programs targeting large and broadly defined groups.
4.	Successful strategies require strong networking with diverse helping service providers.
5.	Effective interventions based on ecological perspectives require various helping skills including counseling, collaboration, and consultation.
6.	Effective interventions are directed toward all participants, including bullies as well as victims.
7.	Effective prevention programs include strategies to improve bystanders' skills, empowering them to change their roles from outsiders to defenders of victims.
8.	A school-wide systemic approach for behavioral management (e.g., School-wide Positive Behavioral Support) fosters positive school climate as a protective factor for school violence.

situations, in order to increase the number of defenders for victims. A program such as HELP-ing, which focuses on improving bystanders' coping skills, would be a vehicle for this type of change.

Comprehensive bullying prevention and intervention requires effective networking with a variety of service providers within a community. The school violence prevention and intervention program of 2004 did not achieve its goal of a 25% bullying reduction. This failure was in part due to the lack of service networks available to the school system (Kim, 2007). Since 2005, the Korean government has developed a Community Youth Safety Net (CYS-Net), an integrated helping network with various community-based service providers. The Korean Department of Education has been developing a WEE (We + Emotion + Education) system. It is a hierarchical network system of counseling services. A WEE class (a new name of the previous counseling office) in a local school level is connected with a WEE center at the school district level, and the WEE center is linked to a WEE school which is specially established for students requiring intensive counseling services at the province level. The number of WEE classes has been increased from 1,530 in 2009 to 2,530 in 2010 (MEST, 2009). Taken together, these increases in networking capacity hold the promise of supporting more effective school violence interventions.

Collaboration is a key for success in the case of network building with community-based service providers. As previously discussed, a comprehensive approach addressing diverse systems is necessary for more effective bullying prevention and intervention. Consultation from allied professionals and collaboration among them are also critically important. Thus, a local school-based coordinator of collaboration is essential to successful school violence interventions. At this point, Korean legislation mandated a school counselor as the professional responsible for facilitating local school violence prevention and intervention efforts. School counselors can serve as a coordinator while working with other helping professionals such as a school social worker or psychologist. This suggests that more pre-service and in-service training in consultation and collaboration is critical for school counselors in Korea.

Conclusions

Since the late 1990s, school violence, especially bullying, has been a serious educational and social issue in Korean society. Many prevention and intervention efforts for school violence have yielded some positive changes; however, new challenges have emerged such as an increase in school violence at an earlier age. Furthermore, many Korean prevention and intervention programs have been applied without thorough outcome evaluations; increased research on treatment effects is necessary. It is also important to strengthen the connection between school practices and empirical studies on school violence. Although research indicates the importance of understanding a group dynamic in bullying, many programs still focus only on victims. They also focus more on individuals despite the roles of various ecological systems. Along with creative approaches to intervene with the bullying dynamic, multilayered strategies addressing individuals, family, peers, school, and community should be developed. Comprehensive programming, efficient collaboration among stakeholders across the student's ecology, improved training, and leveraging service networks, together, hold the promise for increased success of bullying prevention and intervention approaches in Korea.

References

Baldry, A. C., & Farrington, D. P. (2005). Protective factors as moderators of risk factors in adolescence bullying. *Social Psychology of Education, 8,* 263–284. doi:10.1007/s11218-005-5866-5

Bronfenbrenner, U. (1994). Ecological models of human development. In T. Husen & T. N. Postlethwaite (Eds.), *International encyclopedia of education* (2nd ed.) (pp. 1643–1647). New York: Elsevier Science.

Chon, J. Y., Lee, E. K., Yoo, N. H., & Lee, K. H. (2004). A study on the relation between conformity in group bullying and psychological characteristics. *The Korean Journal of School Psychology, 1,* 23–35.

Craig, W., Harel-Fisch, Y., Fogel-Grinvald, H., Dostaler, S., Hetland, J., Simons-Morton, B., … Pickett, W. (2009). A cross-national profile of bullying and victimization among adolescents in 40 countries. *International Journal of Public Health, 54,* 216–224. doi:10.1007/s00038-009-5413-9

Do, G. B. (2008). The interaction effects between factors in ecology system and aggression affecting school violence. *Journal of Adolescent Welfare, 10,* 73–92.

Espelage, D. L., & Swearer, S. M. (2003). Research on school bullying and victimization: What have we learned and where do we go from here? *School Psychology Review, 32,* 365–383.

Ferguson, C. J., Miguel, C. S., & Hartley, R. D. (2009). A multivariate analysis of youth violence and aggression: The influence of family, peers, depression, and media violence. *The Journal of Pediatrics, 155,* 904–908. doi:10.1016/j.jpeds.2009.06.021

Finnegan, R. A., Hodges, E. V. E., & Perry, D. G. (1998). Victimization by peers: Associations with children's reports of mother-child interaction. *Journal of Personality and Social Psychology, 75,* 1076–1086. doi:10.1037/0022-3514.75.4.1076

Flaspohler, P. D., Elfstrom, J. L., Vanderzee, K. L., & Sink, H. E. (2009). Stand by me: The effects of peer and teacher support in mitigating the impact of bullying on quality of life. *Psychology in the Schools, 46,* 636–649. doi:10.1002/pits.20404

Foundation for Preventing Youth Violence. (2009). *2008 National Survey Report on School Violence in Korea.* Seoul, Korea: Author.

Foundation for Preventing Youth Violence. (2010). *2009 National Survey Report on School Violence in Korea.* Seoul, Korea: Author.

Furlong, M. J., Chung, A., Bates, M., & Morrison, R. L. (1995). Who are the victims of school violence? A comparison of student non-victims and multi-victims. *Education & Treatment of Children, 18,* 282–298.

Gini, G., Albiero, P., Benelli, B., & Altoe, G. (2008). Determinants of adolescents' active defending and passive bystanding behavior in bullying. *Journal of Adolescence, 31,* 93–105. doi:10.1016/j.adolescence.2007.05.002

Ha, E-H., & Cho, Y-J. (2007). Intrapersonal moderating variables on the influence of peer conformity to the bullying behavior. *The Korean Journal of the Human Development, 14,* 49–64.

Haynie, D., Nansel, T., Eitel, P., Crump, A.D., Saylor, K., Yu, K., & Simons-Morton, B. (2001). Bullies, victims, and bully-victims: Distinct groups of at-risk youth. *Journal of Early Adolescence, 21,* 29–49. doi:10.1177/0272431601021001002

Hwang, H-W., Shin, J-Y., & Park, H-S. (2006). The path analysis among selected eco-systems factors on the school violence of Korean early adolescents. *Journal of Korean Council for Children's Rights, 10,* 497–526.

Jang, M. H., & Seong, H. G. (2007). The relationships between bullying, social identity, and social support. *Korean Journal of Social and Personality Psychology, 21,* 77–87.

Jolliffe, D., & Farrington, D. P. (2006). Examining the relationship between low empathy and bullying. *Aggressive Behavior, 32,* 540–550. doi:10.1002/ab.20154

Kang, J-H. (2008). Intervention program for school violence victims: Youth Rainbow Program and "Let's Play Together" Program. In Y-L Moon (Ed.), *School violence: Prevention and counseling* (pp. 335–365). Seoul, Korea: Hakjisa.

Kim, H., & Lee, H. (2000). Social and psychological variables affecting the behaviors of bullies and victims at school bullying. *Korean Journal of Social and Personality Psychology, 14,* 45–64.

Kim, J-Y., Chung, Y-K., & Lee, J-S. (2008). The contribution of adolescents' exposure to marital violence on school violence: Moderating effect of supportive social networks. *Journal of Korean Youth Research, 15,* 89–115.

Kim, J. Y., Lee, H. J., & Kang, M. J. (2007). A study on the influences of family–cohesion and self-control ability on the adolescents' school violence. *Korean Journal of Youth Studies, 14,* 173–201.

Kim, J. Y., Lee, J. S., & Lee, S. W. (2010). The effect of violent internet games on school violence of adolescents and the mediating effect of violent thought. *Journal of Korean Youth Research, 17,* 249–278.

Kim, M-Y. (2007). The effects of the school-system on middle school students' bullying. *Studies on Korean Youth, 18,* 287–314.

Kim, S-H. (2006). The developmental and contextual analysis on school violence. *The Korean Journal of Educational Psychology, 20,* 1027–1042.

Kim, S-J. (2005). Psychological and social factors influencing bullying and victim tendencies. *The Korean Journal of Counseling, 6,* 359–371.

Kochenderfer-Ladd, B., & Skinner, K. (2002). Children's coping strategies: Moderators of the effects of peer victimization. *Developmental Psychology, 38,* 267–278. doi:10.1037/0012-1649.38.2.267

Korea Ministry of Education and Human Resources. (2005). *Five-year plan of prevention and intervention for school violence (2005–2009).* Seoul, Korea: Author.

Korea Ministry of Education, Science, and Technology. (2009). *Five-year plan of prevention and intervention for school violence (2010–2014).* Seoul, Korea: Author.

Korea Youth Counseling Institute. (2007). *Establishment of a youth suicide prevention system.* Seoul, Korea; Author.

Korea Youth Counseling Institute. (2008). *Care enhancement program for the prevention of school violence.* Seoul, Korea; Author.

Korean Educational Development Institute. (2007). *School violence prevention program.* Seoul, Korea: Author.

Kwak, K., Kim, D., Kim, H., & Koo, H. (2005). *Study on program development of school violence prevention.* Seoul, Korea: KT & G Welfare Foundation.

Kwon, J. (1999). Conceptualization of Wangtta in Korea and methodological review of Wangtta researches. *Korean Journal of Psychology: Social Issues, 5*(2), 59–72.

Lee, C-J., & Kwak, K. (2000). Self-concept and social support according to bullying types. *The Korean Journal of Developmental Psychology, 13,* 65–80.

Lee, E-H., Gong, S-J., & Lee, C-S. (2004). Relationships among socio-environmental school violence risk factors, protective factors and bullying at school: Testing a mediational model of anger control and contact with delinquent friends. *The Korean Journal of Counseling and Psychotherapy, 16,* 123–145.

Lee, E-J. (2004). The conceptual and longitudinal relations between peer victimization and self-esteem. *Korean Journal of Youth Studies, 11*(4), 141–165.

Lee, H., & Kim, H. (2001). Social and psychological variables predicting elementary students' school bullying behaviors: On the bases of their gender and grade. *Korean Journal of Social and Personality Psychology, 15,* 117–138

Lee, S-G. (2005). Effects of eco-systemic factors on peer violence at middle schools. *Journal of the Korean Society of Child Welfare, 19,* 141–170.

Natvig, G. K., Albrektsen, G., & Qvarnstrom, U. (2001). School-related stress experience as risk factor for bullying behavior. *Journal of Youth and Adolescence, 30,* 561–575. doi:10.1023/A:1010448604838

Oh, I. (2008). Psychological variables affecting school bullying among elementary students: A focus on gender difference. *The Journal of Elementary Education, 21,* 91–110.

Oh, I. (2009). Mediating effect of self-control and aggression between daily stress and bullying behavior. *The Journal of Elementary Education, 22,* 49–70.

Oh, I. (2010). Psychological factors influencing bystanders' behavioral reactions to bullying: A focus on empathy and aggression. *The Journal of Elementary Education, 23,* 45–63.

Oh, I., & Hazler, R. (2009). Contributions of personal and situational factors to bystanders' reactions to school bullying. *School Psychology International, 30,* 291–310. doi:10.1177/0143034309106499

Oh, S-H. (2007). Analysis on the effects of eco-systemic factors on bullying in adolescents. *Mental Health & Social Work, 25,* 74–98.

Osher, D., Bear, G. G., Sprague, J. R., & Dolye, W. (2010). How can we improve school discipline? *Educational Researcher, 39,* 48–58. doi:10.3102/0013189X09357618

Park, J. H. (2006). Causes of school violence and the exploration of policy alternatives as its solution. *Correction Welfare Research, 5,* 215–239.

Rigby, K., & Slee, P. (1999). Suicidal ideation among adolescent school children, involvement in bully-victim problems, and perceived social support. *Suicide & Life-Threatening Behavior, 29,* 119–130.

Sim, H. (2005). A cross-sectional and short-term longitudinal study on bullying/victimization and interpersonal behavior characteristics: The participant roles approach. *Korean Journal of Child Studies, 26,* 263–279.

Song, K-H., & Lee, S-Y. (2010). The relationships among Theory of Mind, proactive bullying and defending behaviors in adolescents: Mediation effect of moral disengagement and moral emotions. *The Korean Journal of Developmental Psychology, 23*(3), 105–124.

Song, K-H., Song, J-H., Baek, J-H., & Lee, S-Y. (2009). Understanding peer victimization in boys and girls: Adolescents' emotional, cognitive characteristics and parenting behaviors. *The Korean Journal of Developmental Psychology, 22*(2), 1–22.

Swearer, S., Espelage, D. L., Vaillancourt, T., & Hymel, S. (2010). What can be done about school bullying?: Linking research to educational practice. *Educational Researcher, 39*(1), 38–47. doi:10.3102/0013189X09357622

Unnever, J. D., & Cornell, D. G. (2003). Bullying, self-control, and ADHD. *Journal of Interpersonal Violence, 18*, 129–147. doi:10.1177/0886260502238731

41

Preventive Program of Tolerance Against Violence at Schools in Slovakia

Eva Gajdošova and Zita Rijakova

COMENIUS UNIVERSITY, BRATISLAVA, SLOVAKIA

Abstract

The Tolerance Against Violence at Schools in Slovakia is an effective primary prevention program. The program helps to develop social–emotional competence and proper attitudes toward social, physical, and ethnic diversities and the facilitation of positive interpersonal interactions with schoolmates. The implementation of the program in schools is recommended within the subject of ethic education, or in complete blocks after the lessons, with a selected group of pupils. After being part of the program, pupils stressed that they were more tolerant, comfortable, more open in their actions, and they that were better able to cope with interpersonal relations. Their subjective feelings agreed with the results of objective psychodiagnostic tests measuring the development of tolerant attitudes to social, ethnic, and physical differences.

During recent years, teachers of elementary and secondary schools have drawn the attention of the public as well as of the psychologists, social and special pedagogues, educational counsellors, and prevention coordinators to the growth of unfriendliness, intolerance, discrimination, and even racism among some students.

Nowadays teachers witness more often than in the past years that pupils intentionally reject their classmates and don't allow them to join class groups, if they are, for example, members of some other national or ethnic minority, their parents have a different socioeconomic status, or if these classmates are fans of a different sport club or music group, and even, if they don't wear designer clothes or don't have a high quality mobile phone or computer, or if their personality qualities, attitudes, or values are different from their own. The unfriendliness, intolerance, and discrimination in schools is growing and subsequently gives rise to verbal or physical aggression and bullying of pupils who are different.

The anonymity of a pupil or a group of pupils hidden in a crowd often represents a common feature of violence. Through their acts, they want to leave a trace on the face of the school, to shock adults or their classmates as well, make them feel uneasy, disturb them, and to provoke negative reactions from teachers and other adults.

School psychologists know that the aggression and violence of children is not a sporadic phenomenon at schools and that no school is immune to it. In the school environment, we can almost daily witness several forms of aggression and violence acts of pupils directed on things, classmates, and even teachers. We can see that pupils say vulgar words to each other, slander and terrify their classmates, call each other names, mock their classmates because of their handicaps, imperfections, troubles, or failures, utter remarks and jokes at the expense of other pupils or teachers, make each other ridiculous, and even brawl and kick each other to do each other harm. In addition to the relatively frequent acts of aggression committed by students against their schoolmates are destructive acts against material property, e.g. pictures, sculptures, learning aids, computers, or even infecting computer software with viruses. After entering many classrooms, we see damaged and destroyed chairs and desks, deliberately ripped notice boards, broken windows, chalked freshly painted classroom walls, and broken fences of school courtyards. Even sadder is the fact that the aggression and violence of many pupils turns very often towards younger pupils and defenseless pupils who are, for various reasons, unable to defend themselves, and even towards their own good friends.

The responses were obtained from 125 interviews with ninth-grade students in four elementary schools in Bratislava in June 2010. The pupils were asked why some of their peers behave aggressively at school. Their answers indicate that violence and acts of vandalism take place due to:

- boredom;
- desire for still stronger and more shocking experiences and sensations;
- pressure to express manhood—when a certain group of pupils compels a boy to "behave like a man," to be harsh, not be afraid of hits and also hit others;
- perceiving it as a kind of adrenaline sport, that is, they do it because they want to feel the danger of being caught in the act;
- it is a consequence of tension, frustration, stress, burden, and conflicts within oneself or within the class;
- wanting to draw attention to themselves, "Please, notice me! Nobody likes me!"

From our analysis of curricula of elementary and secondary schools, it follows that the absence of a systematic, long-term longitudinal training of students towards tolerance, multiculturality, and interculturality applied directly in the training and educational process is a striking one in Slovak schools. The instruction of pupils on human rights and child's rights, towards tolerance between people of different cultures, nations and nationalities, or other diversities is just sporadic; it takes place in the lessons of civic and ethic education, and it is done on the cognitive (informative) level, less on the emotional (experiential) one, that is more effective and more appealing to children and young people, regardless of their age. For all of us, it is easier to accept what we ourselves have experienced than what has been presented to us as an information or cognition.

The current situation in our schools refers to shortcomings in education of children and young people particularly in this area—they should be instructed towards a greater tolerance and acceptance of diversities, and we consider it as a serious drawback for their future, especially after Slovakia's entry into the European Union, giving young people greater opportunities to meet different people, communicate with them, or, for example, build effective working teams.

We would thus like to stress the possibilities of a complex approach of education towards tolerance, effectiveness of participation of school governing bodies, teachers, parents, and other members of the school community in its conscious, long-term, and systematic development by means of a complex social and educational, as well as social and psychological, intervention, especially the preventive, developmental and interventional programs in schools.

On the basis of this situation, have we, the members of The Psychology Department at the Faculty of Arts of the Comenius University in Bratislava, Slovakia, made the decision to work out a longitudinal program of tolerance development of pupils aimed at development of cohesion, tolerance, and acceptance of young people's diversities, and to verify its effectiveness directly in the educational and training process in selected elementary and secondary schools. We supposed that a long-term development of tolerance would have a distinctly positive influence on cohesion of the pupils in the class and tolerance of diversities, and that it would have, from the point of view of statistics, an important influence on the change of students' attitudes.

We consider the preventive programs and tolerance development programs to be part of the basic components of development of tolerance and positive social climate at school. These programs are usually carried out during a longer period of time, systematically and with the goal in mind, in cooperation with a school psychologist, that they may become a component part of an effective planning, realization, and assessment of education towards tolerance not only in relation to pupils as subjects of influence, but also in relation to an effective training of teachers and teachers teams—the creators of tolerance at school. By means of research of views of teachers on the application of education towards tolerance and social cohesion, we have found, among other things, that the teachers are interested in obtaining information on realization of education towards tolerance covering "good" pedagogical experiences of Slovak and foreign schools and also information about the effectiveness of such an educational influence (Gajdošova & Herenyiova, 2006).

In our comprehension of tolerance, we identify with the definition of tolerance coined by Slovak psychologist Hargasova (1997), who states that tolerance is "a readiness to accept differences in opinions, culture, appearance, religion, life style, national and social identity" (p. 7).

Goal, Problems, Hypotheses, and Research Methods

The goal of one part of our research was to work out and, directly in the educational process of the selected primary school, verify the effectiveness of the elaborated tolerance development program and to find out whether it can cause a positive change of pupils' attitudes towards people with diverse ethnic, social, and physical characteristics, so that they are able to accept and tolerate their diversities, which eventually would improve social relations in the class, especially regarding the cohesion and satisfaction.

We divided the main goal of the research into the following partial goals:

- investigation of the level of tolerance of pupils of the elementary school towards the diversities and level of social relations in the classrooms;
- enhancement of the degree of pupils' tolerant attitudes;
- reduction of the intolerant, hostile, and unaccepting attitudes;
- investigation of the degree of influence of the tolerance development program on the improvement of the quality of social relations in the class, with emphasis to cohesion and satisfaction.

In the course of the program, students had the opportunity to reflect on various manifestations and forms of violence between people in general, and especially in schools between pupils. They learned to get to know themselves and the people around them, to manage their feelings, understand opinions and attitudes of others, develop healthy self-confidence, learn to communicate effectively and to cooperate with their classmates, avoid conflicts, and, when conflicts due arise, to solve them in a non–aggressive way, preferring compromises and agreements.

The research questions related to the attitudes of pupils and their possible changes in attitude are as follows.

1. What are the attitudes of pupils of our research sample towards people with ethnic, social or physical diversities (a physically handicapped schoolmate, a schoolmate from a socially problematic background, a Roma schoolmate, an old man) prior to the application of the tolerance development program?
   - To what degree will these attitudes change after the completion of the program?
   - How significant will this change of pupils' attitudes be and which attitudes will it influence?
2. The following research questions were related to social relations and cohesion of the pupils in the class:
   - How are the social relations between pupils in the classes prior to the application of the tolerance development program?
   - What is the level of social relations in a selected class prior to the application of the tolerance development program? We are interested in the level of cohesion, satisfaction, competitiveness, conflicts between pupils, and their learning problems.
   - Will the application of the program bring a positive change in the social relations in the classes and their components (cohesion, satisfaction, competitiveness, solving of conflicts and learning problems)?
   - To what extent will the change get reflected in the monitored coefficients?

Shaping of Hypotheses

In relation to the changes of pupils' attitudes, we shaped the following hypotheses:

H1: The attitudes of pupils towards their peers as well as to other people with diverse ethnic, social, and physical characteristics (a Roma schoolmate, a schoolmate from a socially problematic background, a physically handicapped schoolmate, an old man) will be negative prior to the application to the program due to prejudices and stereotypes, regardless of pupils' age and gender.

H2: The application of the tolerance development program will induce a statistically significant positive change of attitudes towards people with diverse ethnic, social and physical characteristics (a Roma, a physically handicapped schoolmate, a schoolmate from a socially problematic background, an old man).

In relation to changes in social relations, we shaped the following hypotheses:

H3: Prior to the application of the program, the level of social relations in class, as well as the level of selected components (cohesion, satisfaction, competitiveness, conflicts, and learning problems) will be just average.

H4: The Tolerance development program resulted in a statistically positive change in pupils' behavior regarding social relations in class, reflected mainly in the class cohesion and satisfaction with class relations.

Hypotheses were formulated on the basis of some research results and practical knowledge and experience of teachers, educational counselors and psychologists that many pupils (especially of pubescent age) have rather negative attitudes to all kinds of diversities of people in their surroundings which is manifested in undesirable and gross behavior, humiliation, bullying, and so forth (Samajova, 2005; Hargasova, 1995).

However, developmental psychology knowledge attest to the fact that pubescent pupils are far more willing to reappraise and make a positive change of attitudes that they have adopted in family or school education, or under the influence of the society (assessment of parents', teachers', and other people's attitudes) (Cap, & Mares, 2001).

Considering the fact that the effectiveness of preventive and development programs has been proven by Slovak and foreign researches (Gajdošova & Herenyiova, 2002, 2006), we suppose that there will be positive changes in pubescent pupils' attitudes and their social relations.

Research Methods

From the point of view of the goal, the following research methods have been applied to examine the chosen variables and to verify the determined hypotheses:

1. The method of an experiment under natural conditions (in selected primary school classes).
2. Methods of data collection.

The Questionnaire

The questionnaire, My Class Inventory, was developed by Australian psychologists Frase and Fisher, and its content was customized for use in the school system in the Czech and Slovak republics (Lešek & Mareš, 1989). The purpose of this questionnaire is to observe five main components of what happens in class and in social relations in class: pupils' satisfaction in the class and their cohesion, competitiveness among pupils, conflicts in the class and learning problems. The questionnaire has a total of 25 statements requiring only an affirmative "yes" or a negative "no" answer from the pupil.

The Method of Semantic Differential

To evaluate students' attitudes to diverse people, the method of C. E. Osgood Semantic differential was applied. This method uses a scale ranging from 1 to 7, with lower numbers (1–3) representing positive attitudes, e.g., good-looking, good, valuable, rapid, helping, close, friendly, and high numbers (5–7) representing negative attitudes, e.g., not good-looking, bad, unvaluable, slow, unhelping, remote, unfriendly. For the purpose of our research, a semantic differential, which consisted of four concepts from categories of ethnic, social, and physical differences, was used (old person, Roma schoolmate, physically handicapped schoolmate, schoolmate from socially problematic background).

1. The observation of pupils' behavior under natural conditions of the classes and during breaks.
2. The non-standardized interview with classroom teachers and pupils.
3. Mathematical and statistical methods of data processing: T-test for two dependent selections and the Wilcoxon test for two dependent selections.
4. Description of the Tolerance development program.

Our program of tolerance development in school consisted of three basic modules:

Module 1: 10 Meetings with Pupils
Basic language concepts: violence, intolerance resulting in violence, getting to know other people, similarities, differences, opinions, and evaluation of some selected kinds of people who live in our surroundings.

Goals of Module 1:

- educate pupils about the different forms of violence—domestic violence, school violence, public violence, political violence, and also violence among states, countries, political, and religious systems which is caused by intolerance;
- find out in what aspects are my classmates similar to me and in what aspects are they different from me;
- compare my evaluations to the evaluations made by my classmates and find out how they are seen through the eyes of their best friends, but also by peers they do not talk with, and how are they perceived by boys and by girls;
- practice speaking in front of an audience about myself, my interests, abilities, personal characteristics, attitudes, and opinions;
- find out about the attitudes of my classmates towards people who are different, e.g., old people, mentally handicapped people, Black people, Moslem, Roma.

Module 2: 10 Meetings with Pupils

Basic language concepts: barriers to tolerance—prejudices, stereotypes, discrimination, gossip, violence.

Goals of Module 2:

- learn about the causes of intolerance among people and what are the possible barriers of tolerance;
- understand and experience the process of "categorizing" and "labeling" people;
- talk about the negative consequences that one-sided information and spreading of incorrect information and gossip may have;
- draw attention to the fact how prejudices, stereotypes and discrimination affect our way of thinking and human relations.

Module 3: 20 Meetings with Pupils

Basic language concepts: factors of tolerance and tolerant behavior development—effective communication, active listening, empathy, assertiveness, respecting of human rights and children's rights.

Goals of Module 3:

- develop empathy skills; imagine oneself in the position of someone who is being discriminated and understand his acting and needs in relations with other people;
- compare one's point of view to another person's point of view;
- use the techniques of active listening and be willing to solve conflicts in a compromise;
- learn how to avoid discrimination, prejudices, and stereotypes;
- learn one's assertive rights and assertive duties and apply them to solve conflicts;
- obtain information about the universally recognized human rights and children rights and express opinions on violation of human rights, and offer one's own suggestions how to make changes.

The structure of the tolerance program to prevent violence in schools is as follows:

Module 1:

- Similarities and differences of people I
- Similarities and differences of people II
- Comparison of opinions on selected types of people who live in our surroundings

- Making a selection of people—a competition
- Violence, intolerance that leads to violence—evaluation scales and drawings

Module 2:
- Tolerance barriers—spreading of gossip, one-sided communication
- The process of discrimination—"categorizing and labeling people"
- The feeling of being discriminated against
- Stereotypes
- Prejudices

Module 3:
- Two points of view
- Empathy I
- Empathy II
- Techniques of active listening
- How to select people by avoiding discrimination
- Assertiveness, assertive behavior
- Make use of acquired skills
- Declaration of human rights
- Declaration of children rights
- Am I tolerant now? Final reflections

Description of Some Selected Meetings

Now we will describe one selected activity that we have successfully used in our program. However, in certain situations, some of the tasks were ineffective. Their realization depended not only on the problem we dealt with, but we took into consideration also social relations in the classroom, pupils' self-knowledge and knowledge of their classmates, social climate and social atmosphere in class, the level of mutual trust and openness, and so forth.

"Bargots and Roters"

The game "Bargots and Roters" was intended to show pupils that prejudices are part of our life and how they influence our attitudes and opinions. We read to the children a description of two imaginary countries—Bargotia and Rotria and how is life there, written through the eyes of an inhabitant of Bargotia. Bargotia, his homeland was described in a positive manner—a sunny, warm country with kind and good inhabitants. However, Bargot described the neighboring country Rotria rather negatively, as a land of darkness, rain, with unfriendly inhabitants doing harm to each other within families, but also in public.

When we finished reading those descriptions to the children, they were told to form an opinion on the two countries, to draw the countries and to write of the personal characteristics of a typical Bargot and a typical Roter. Of course, the children were influenced by the descriptions and the negative characteristics made by the inhabitant of Bargotia. As a result, they drew the country of Rotria in dark colors and described its inhabitants as people who are evil-minded.

We put the drawings on the blackboard and discussed them. It was at that moment that the pupils realized they made a mistake and were really sorry about having themselves influenced so negatively. The children understood that before making an opinion about someone, they have to verify the information and not accept and follow opinions from one person only. They should always know the opinion of the other party. There is no person, situation, country, or problem that would be purely negative. There are positive sides to everything. One must avoid seeing the world in black and white, for to have such an attitude is dangerous and could have far-reaching consequences.

Results

The effectiveness of tolerance development program was verified at the private primary school Ružová dolina in Bratislava, in the academic year 2009/2010. The basic research method applied was the natural experiment under conditions of the selected primary school: the tolerance development program was implemented in the school, and, when the pupils completed the program, its effectiveness was verified.

The research sample was composed of 62 primary school students—seventh, eighth, and ninth graders (30 boys and 32 girls) between the ages of 13 and 15 years. They were selected by means of a cluster selection, i.e., individuals for the experiment were not selected from the population randomly, but they were groups, naturally formed school classes. We did not have a control group. Instead, we compared selected groups (classes) of pupils and observed the changes that took place after the application of the program.

The complex tolerance development program consisted of prepared lessons dealing with selected methodical procedures and activities (see enclosure). The pupils completed the program in one academic year, altogether they had 40 lessons of the training program (the frequency of lessons was once a week for two lessons).

Based on the agreement with the primary school management, the program was systematically incorporated into the ongoing educational process and selected lessons (lessons of ethic education, civic education, creative arts, and musical education).

The meetings were usually introduced with a brief review of the subject matter taught on the previous lesson, and the objectives of the current lessons were defined. The pupils discussed the main idea and the objective of the lesson, they learned the basic language concepts and by means of some selected methodical procedures; pupils were developing target abilities, skills, habits, attitudes, and competences. During the final part of the lesson, the pupils were playing some selected psychogames, they were drawing pictures, writing stories, practicing model situations, searching for information, or, in some cases, the pupils were given homework or the task to work out a project.

Research results concerning the changes in pupils' attitudes to diversities due to the program resulted in the following hypotheses.

> H1, H2: Prior to the application of the program, the pubescent pupils' attitudes toward people with ethnical, social, and physical diversities (e.g., Roma schoolmate, schoolmate from socially problematic background, physically handicapped schoolmate, old man) were negative regardless of pupils' age and gender; this was typical of the prejudices and stereotypes that exist in Slovakia. After the application of the program, we found that there was a statistically significant positive change in pupils' attitudes to people with diverse characteristics. In sum, it may be said that our supposition was fulfilled and both hypotheses were confirmed.

The analysis of the research results confirmed that prior to the application of the tolerance development program the pupils' attitudes towards people in their surroundings with ethnical, social, and physical differences were strongly negative. In the questionnaire responses, the attitudes of pupils in our research sample showed a relatively high degree of intolerance to a Roma pupil and a schoolmate from socially problematic background, for example, with numbers ranging from 5 to 7.

The results have shown that prior to the application of the program, the highest degree of rejection and intolerance in the pupils questioned was found in relation to a schoolmate from socially problematic background (i.e., a person of social, not ethnical diversity). The attitude of the pupils was found to be strongly negative in all the adjectives observed, but most of all in the adjectives *good, close, and helping.* Adjectives representing the attitudes of pupils to a physically handicapped schoolmate ranged from 3 to 5 (*good, friendly*). Also, there was a statistically significant positive change in pupils' attitudes in relation to the adjective *close.* In the case of the attitudes to an old man, in some characteristics the adjectives reached the levels of 2 to 3 (*good, valuable, friendly*).

The strongly negative attitude of pupils in the relation to a Roma schoolmate was changed after the application of the program on the same level in all of the characteristics (adjectives) observed. However, statistical results registered significant change only in the adjectives *good, rapid,* and *friendly.* An intolerant attitude was found with the adjectives *close* and *good-looking.* In all, after the application of the program, the attitudes of pupils were not as strongly negative and rejecting as before.

The statistically significant differences in pupils' attitudes to people with diverse characteristics, as registered after the application of the tolerance development program are listed below. The statistically significant differences in pupils' attitudes to diversities are shown in the Table 41.1.

- A Roma schoolmate: *good* ($p = 0{,}004$); *rapid* ($p = 0{,}019$); *friendly* ($p = 0{,}008$);
- An old man: *rapid* ($p = 0{,}002$);
- A physically handicapped schoolmate: *rapid* ($p = 0{,}007$); *close* ($p = 0{,}034$);
- A schoolmate from socially problematic background: *good-looking* ($p = 0{,}036$); *valuable* ($p = 0{,}021$); *close* ($p = 0{,}020$).

A different situation occurred in the case of components of social relations that were monitored by means of the My Class questionnaire. These components are satisfaction in class, conflicts in class, competitiveness, cohesion, and learning problems. The Czech approximate standards (Lešek & Mareš, 1989) name the following approximate values in the components:

- satisfaction—12
- competitiveness—12
- cohesion—10
- learning problems—9
- conflicts in class—10

In the variables satisfaction and cohesion in classes, we recorded, in comparison to the pretest, highly a statistically significant satisfaction ($p = 0.001$) and cohesion ($p = 0.016$).

The differences, however, vary significantly in dependence on gender. Whereas after the application of the program, the boys were, unlike the girls, satisfied with the social relations in the class ($p = 0.001$) and also had the feeling that the cohesion of the class is on a high level ($p = 0.001$), this result was not registered with the girls. In the partial analysis of the individual components of the social relations, after the completion of the program, the best score was gained by the ninth-grade class (satisfaction and cohesion—level 11), in comparison with the seventh- and eighth-grade classes. In the seventh-grade class, the highest degree of competitiveness was registered (level 12).

By means of the T-test, we have recorded statistically significant differences in the components of the social relations in the questionnaire and by means of Wilcoxon test in case of differences between boys and girls (see Tables 41.2, 41.3, and 41.4).

Table 41.1 Pupils' Attitudes to Diversities (a Roma, a physically handicapped schoolmate, a schoolmate from socially problematic background and an old man) in a Semantic Differential (t-test for two dependent samples)

Pair	Level	Average	N valid	Standard deviation	T	p
2	A Roma – good – pre	5,2462	65	1,4256		
	A Roma – good – post	4,3846	65	1,2079	3,095	0,004
4	A Roma – rapid – pre	4,6406	64	1,5157		
	A Roma - rapid – post	3,8906	64	1,0253	2,483	0,019
7	A Roma – friendly – pre	5,0781	64	1,6262		
	A Roma – friendly – post	4,1406	64	1,4127	2,878	0,008
11	An old person – rapid – pre	6,3125	64	0,8706		
	An old person – rapid – post	5,4219	64	1,3546	3,367	0,002
18	A physically handicapped person – rapid – pre	5,3846	65	1,5781		
	A physically handicapped person – rapid – post	4,4615	65	1,6209	2,921	0,007
20	A physically handicapped person – close – pre	4,1846	65	1,6095		
	A physically handicapped person – close – post	3,6615	65	1,4283	2,229	0,034
22	Socially problematic background – good-looking – pre	6,2923	65	0,9638		
	Socially problematic background – good-looking – post	5,7231	65	1,0970	2,193	0,036
24	Socially problematic background – valuable – pre	5,5231	65	1,4481		
	Socially problematic background – valuable – post	4,8154	65	1,6760	2,437	0,021
26	Socially problematic background – helping – pre	6,2769	65	0,9764		
	Socially problematic background – helping – post	5,7077	65	1,0857	2,283	0,030
27	Socially problematic background – close – pre	5,9231	65	1,4610		
	Socially problematic background – close – post	5,1077	65	1,5220	2,455	0,020

Conclusions

After the application of the tolerance development, we registered the following results:

1. It has been confirmed that young people have the same prejudices as their parents and other adults towards people in their surroundings who have different physical, social, and ethnic characteristics, even though they haven't had any negative experience with those people. Regardless of their age or sex, the pupils of our research sample showed negative attitudes to:
   - a Roma schoolmate
   - a schoolmate from a socially problematic background

Table 41.2 Pupils' Attitudes Towards Social Relations – T-test for Two Dependent Selections – Our Class

Pair	Level	Average	N valid	Standard deviation	T	p
1	satisfaction – pre	10,1385	65	2,2212		
	satisfaction – post	11,3231	65	1,7510	–3,503	0,001
2	conflicts – pre	11,0615	65	2,9679		
	conflicts – post	11,2308	65	2,9035	–0,446	0,657
3	competitiveness – pre	11,2615	65	2,4703		
	competitiveness – post	10,9231	65	2,4957	–1,026	0,309
4	troubles – pre	10,1692	65	2,5407		
	troubles – post	10,8769	65	2,0502	–1,697	0,095
5	cohesion – pre	8,2154	65	2,7585		
	cohesion – post	9,2462	65	2,7897	–2,481	0,016

- attitudes were not as negative towards a physically handicapped schoolmate or an old man.
2. After the completion of the program, we could register a statistically significant positive change in pupils' attitudes to ethnical, social, and physical diversities:
  - a Roma schoolmate (all pupils regardless of their sex and age, in adjectives *good, rapid, friendly*),
  - a physically handicapped schoolmate (all pupils chose the adjective *close),*
  - a schoolmate from a socially problematic background (all pupils chose the adjectives *close, valuable*)

Statistically significant changes were registered in several categories with male and female students.

    1. After the application of the program, a statistically significant positive change was registered in classes, regarding:

    pupils' satisfaction (boys and girls),

    cohesion among pupils (boys and girls),

    cohesion and satisfaction (in the ninth grade).

Table 41.3 Attitudes of Pupils – Boys – Towards Social Relations – Wilcoxon Test for Two Dependent Selections – Our Class

Level		Average	N valid	Standard deviation	t	p
satisfaction – post – satisfaction – pre	pre>post	3	10			
	pre<post	22	73,3			
	pre=post	5	16,6			
	Total	30			–3,252	0,001
cohesion – post – cohesion – pre						
	pre>post	4	13,3			
	pre<post	23	76,6			
	pre=post	3	10			
	Total	30			–3,239	0,001

Table 41.4 Attitudes of Pupils – Girls – Towards Social Relations – Wilcoxon Test for Two dependent Samples – Our Class

Level	Average	N valid	Standard deviation	T	p
problems – post – problems – pre					
	pre>post	10	28,6		
	pre<post	22	62,9		
	pre=post	3	8,5		
	Spolu	35		−1,960	0,050

2. As a consequence of the program, some pupils started to apply new ways of behavior and conflict solving in everyday school situations. As it was shown, the pupils' self-control improved, their decision making became more thoughtful, they showed the effort to solve the conflicts in a compromise, they expressed their feelings more openly, they developed their empathy skills, and the social atmosphere in the class became more positive.

3. In a semi-standardized interview, the teachers confirmed that:
   violent reactions of children in solving the problems got reduced,
   the efforts to solve the conflicts by means of a compromise and agreement increased,
   less physical and also verbal violence was observed in the class,
   the social atmosphere in the class became more considerate and a greater willingness to cooperate was observed.

It may be said that the program of tolerance development that we applied in the school is one of the effective programs of primary prevention; its goal being the development of social-emotional competences and proper attitudes of pupils to diversities and the facilitation of positive interpersonal interactions. The implementation of the program in other schools is recommended within the subjects of ethic education, or in complete blocks after the lessons.

Despite the fact that the application of the program in the selected primary school was effective, it is necessary to emphasize the following points:

- to date, no research has confirmed whether pupils apply taught patterns of behavior, performance standards, and the ways of problem solving in everyday life situations outside the school environment after the completion of the program (i.e., in relationships with their friends, parents, siblings, and peers);

- in our study we compared the results of the pretest and the posttest of the experimental group; we had no control group. At the present time, the tolerance development programs are not incorporated into the curricula of educational subjects, and therefore it would be difficult to ensure the identical conditions for control groups from thematic, methodic, or other points of view;

- we do realize that a change is valid only if the persons who are in everyday contact with the pupils regard the changes in attitudes and social relations in class as highly positive, enduring, and constructive.

Table 41.5 Implications for Practice

Provide effective education and training of pupils, teachers, parents, and other members of school community to prevent violence and intolerance of diversities in schools, as a prerequisite for pupils, the future citizens to become a part of the multicultural society.

Conduct a survey every year to find out if there is violence, aggression, and bullying in primary schools, to find out of the situation of social-pathological phenomena in schools and school activities promoting tolerance development.

Integrate education on the issue of aggression, bullying, and violence in schools and the ways to prevent them into the curricula designed for professional training of prospective teachers, pedagogues, special pedagogues, school, and counseling psychologists.

Organize educational activities focused on planning, realizing, and evaluating of tolerance development education (i.e. lectures, debates, social – psychological trainings, effective development program trainings for teachers, educational counsellors, coordinators for prevention, social workers, special pedagogues, school, and counseling psychologists).

Close and intense cooperation between primary schools and parents, pedagogical-psychological counselling centers, special pedagogical counseling centers, centers for prevention methods, local police stations etc., to prevent aggression and violence in schools.

Involve mass media into the campaign to fight against violence in schools.

Realize social and psychological diagnostics of the classes on a regular basis and make analyses of social relations in classes using an appropriate sociometric questionnaire in close cooperation with classroom teachers, school counseling psychologists, and educational counselors.

Use the peer program, called "peer groups" directly in school environment and in class to develop pupils' tolerance.

In every school, create a working team composed of teachers and specialists who will work in close cooperation and who will work out a common procedure against violence in schools, implement it, and evaluate its results.

Active participation of school management on realization of program, activities and projects of social–educational intervention to foster cohesion, acceptance, and tolerance and incorporate them into the basic documents of the school.

Provide systematic and long-term education of teachers to develop their personalities and professional competences regarding tolerance, conflict solving, effective communication skills, and cooperation.

Implement a compulsory practice at universities for psychology students, special education students, and students of other helping professions in schools dealing predominantly with the implementation of developing and preventive programmes (development of emotional intelligence and social competence skills of victims of violence and aggressors).

References

Cap, J., & Mares, J. (2001). *Psychology for teachers*. Prague, Czech Republic: Portal.

Gajdošova, E., & Herenyiova, G. (2002). *Skola rozvijania emocionalnej inteligencie ziakov* [How to develop pupils' emotional intelligence.]. Bratislava, Slovakia: Priroda.

Gajdošova, E., & Herenyiova, G. (2006). *Development of pupils' emotional intelligence*. Prague, Czech Republic: Portál.

Hargasova, M. (1995). Tolerancia a intolerancia mladeze SR v skupinovom a interpersonalnom kontexte [Tolerance and intolerance of young people in Slovakia in group and interpersonal context]. *Mladez a spolocnost, 1*(1), 14–31.

Hargasova, M. (1997). *Tolerancia a jej hranice* [Tolerance and its boundaries]. Metodické Centrum, Slovak Republic: Banská Bystrica.

Lešek, J., & Mareš, J. (1989). Classroom social climate. In P. Mohapl (Ed.), *Collection of papers from the conference, XIV. Psychological days in the town of Olomouc* (pp. 158–161). Olomouc, Czech Republic: Olomouc University Press.

Samajova, G. (2005). *Tolerancia pubescentov k odlišnostiam u rovesníkov* [Pubescents and their tolerance to peers' diversities]. Unpublished doctoral dissertaion, Comenius University, Bratislava, Slovakia.

42

Preventing Youth Gang Involvement with G.R.E.A.T.

Dana Peterson

UNIVERSITY AT ALBANY, STATE UNIVERSITY OF NEW YORK

Finn-Aage Esbensen

UNIVERSITY OF MISSOURI–ST. LOUIS

Abstract

The G.R.E.A.T. (Gang Resistance Education and Training) program is the most widely disseminated school-based gang prevention program in the United States. Following a 1995–2001 national evaluation revealing little program effect on key goals, the core middle school curriculum was revised extensively in the early 2000s. A second national evaluation of the revised curriculum is currently underway. In this chapter we discuss (a) the G.R.E.A.T. approach to youth gang and violence prevention; (b) potential benefits to youth, schools, and communities using short-term findings from the current national evaluation; and (c) limits of the approach.

Overview

The Gang Resistance Education and Training (G.R.E.A.T.) program is a gang and delinquency prevention program delivered by law enforcement officers within a school setting. The program was originally designed by Phoenix-area law enforcement agencies in 1991 to address local needs, but it was quickly adopted by communities across the United States. Following a 1995–2001 national evaluation revealing little program effect on key goals, the core middle school curriculum was revised extensively in the early 2000s. It is currently the most widely disseminated school-based gang prevention program in the United States. This chapter describes the G.R.E.A.T. program, including its foundation, evolution, and goals. It also presents short-term findings from the current national evaluation that provide initial evidence that the revised middle school curriculum is beneficial to youths, schools, and communities. Finally, limitations of the G.R.E.A.T. approach to youth gang prevention are discussed.

Importance of the Issue of Youth Gangs

When the G.R.E.A.T. program was initially developed in 1991, youth and gang violence were at "epidemic" proportions, having risen sharply since the 1980s (Snyder & Sickmund, 2006). Although rates of youth violence have decreased substantially since their peak in the mid-1990s, youth gangs and gang members appear to have followed a different trend, decreasing in number from the mid-1990s until the early 2000s, but increasing since 2001 (National Youth Gang Center, 2009). Similarly, gang homicides, although more the purview of young adults than adolescents, increased during the 2000s (Egley, Howell, & Moore, 2010). The Bureau of Justice Statistics provides another indicator of gang problems, tracking students' reports of gang presence in schools. From a low of 15% of students in 1989 reporting gang presence in their schools, the percentage rose to a peak of 29% in 1995, decreased through the late-1990s to 17% and then increased again in the 2000s, hovering between 20% and 24% (Baum, Cataldi, Dinkes, Kena, & Snyder, 2006; Chandler et al., 1998, 2001; DeVoe et al., 2003).

The youth gang problem has engendered a commensurate effort to alleviate gang prevalence and crime, including widespread implementation of school-based prevention programs (Gottfredson & Gottfredson, 2001). The majority of these prevention, intervention, and suppression efforts, however, have not garnered strong empirical evidence of effectiveness (Klein & Maxson, 2006). Just one school-based program, the Montreal Preventive Treatment Program, received the highest rating of exemplary/model program by both Blueprints for Violence Prevention (www.colorado.edu/cspv/blueprints/) and the Office of Juvenile Justice and Delinquency Prevention (OJJDP; www.ojjdp.gov/mpg/). This program was not designed for gang prevention, but program participants did have lower rates of gang involvement at age 15 than did youths in a control group (Tremblay, Masse, Pagani, & Vitaro, 1996). A few school-based gang prevention or intervention programs were rated effective (e.g., G.R.E.A.T.) or promising (e.g., Gang Resistance is Paramount; GRIP) by the OJJDP. Effective programs are those that had demonstrated a program effect on gang involvement in a study or studies with a strong research design; replications are required, however, to provide enough evidence to move them to the exemplary category. Promising programs are those that indicate positive findings, but with limited research designs; thus, additional studies using scientifically rigorous methods are required.

Given the plethora of school-based prevention programs that have been designed to reduce an array of adolescent behaviors and experiences (delinquency, bullying, victimization, gang membership), school administrators are challenged to select a program that is optimal in light of time and resource constraints. Thus, it is imperative this choice be guided by a well-informed sense of program effectiveness. The G.R.E.A.T. program and its associated evaluations demonstrate one example of the effort to produce evidence-based practice in youth gang prevention.

Conceptual Basis and Description: The Original G.R.E.A.T. Program and Revision

The original G.R.E.A.T. program was put together in a short time period in 1991 by Phoenix-area police officers trained in Drug Abuse Resistance Education (DARE; Winfree, Peterson Lynskey, & Maupin, 1999). As such, G.R.E.A.T. lessons and delivery were loosely modeled on the original DARE program and generally lacked a strong theoretical or empirical foundation. The original G.R.E.A.T. core curriculum was a cognitive-based program that taught students about crime and its effect on victims, cultural diversity, conflict resolution skills, meeting basic needs (without a gang), responsibility, and goal setting. As in DARE, uniformed law enforcement officers taught the curriculum in schools.

In contrast to intervention and suppression approaches that target gang-involved youths, G.R.E.A.T. is a primary prevention program, intended for all youth at entry to middle school. There is no assumption of risk of or actual gang involvement. Rather, all youth are "inoculated" with G.R.E.A.T. lessons, with the goal of positioning them to resist gang membership and delinquency involvement. The original middle school curriculum sought to do this through the provision of nine 35–45 minute lessons that provided life skills (e.g., goal-setting, conflict resolution) and educated students on the dangers of gang involvement. Other optional components of the program included an elementary school curriculum and a summer program.

Despite the general lack of theoretical or empirical grounding, the G.R.E.A.T. program was well-received by parents, schools, and law enforcement officers, who expressed a high level of satisfaction in anonymous or confidential surveys (Freng, 2001; Peterson & Esbensen, 2004; Taylor & Esbensen, 2002). Although the program was intended solely for use in the Phoenix area, it spread quickly throughout the United States, as other communities and schools sought new avenues for gang and delinquency prevention and as federal funds, through the Bureau of Alcohol, Tobacco, and Firearms (BATF), became available to agencies seeking to implement the program. Given this interest and the infusion of government funds, the National Institute of Justice (NIJ) awarded funding to the University of Nebraska at Omaha for a multisite, multiyear (1994–2001) National Evaluation of G.R.E.A.T., focusing on the program's core curriculum.

The evaluation design consisted of several components. The process evaluation, consisting of observations of G.R.E.A.T. Officer Training and delivery of G.R.E.A.T. in classrooms, determined that officers implemented the program with fidelity (Sellers, Taylor, & Esbensen, 1998). A cross-sectional outcome study of almost 6,000 eighth-grade students in 11 cities indicated small but positive program effects, including lower levels of delinquency and gang involvement, more prosocial attitudes, and better relationships with law enforcement among students who had received the program compared to those who had not (Esbensen & Osgood, 1999). Results from the more methodologically rigorous longitudinal outcome evaluation (referred to as G.R.E.A.T. I), however, failed to replicate the cross-sectional findings. This five-year panel study of over 2,000 students in six diverse cities found a few differences (5 of 32 outcomes) between G.R.E.A.T. and non-G.R.E.A.T. students, but these differences were largely attitudinal. Importantly, none of the program's intended behavioral goals were achieved. Although G.R.E.A.T. students had lower levels of victimization and risk-seeking tendencies, more prosocial peers, more negative views about gangs, and more positive views of law enforcement, there were no differences between G.R.E.A.T. and non-G.R.E.A.T. students in levels of delinquency, violence, or gang membership (Esbensen, Osgood, Taylor, Peterson, & Freng, 2001).

Partially in response to these evaluation results, the G.R.E.A.T. National Policy Board convened a committee to review the core curriculum and provide recommendations for improvements in structure, content, and delivery (Esbensen, Freng, Taylor, Peterson, & Osgood, 2002). The review committee consisted of members of the evaluation team, G.R.E.A.T. officers, experts in school-based prevention or youth gangs, and representatives from NIJ and BATF. This committee provided numerous suggestions for revising the curriculum content and delivery to align more closely with known effective teaching methods, school-based prevention approaches, and gang prevention strategies. The revised G.R.E.A.T. program adopted some of the strategies from two school-based programs, the Seattle Social Development Model (SSDM; Catalano, Arthur, Hawkins, Berglund, & Olson, 1998) and Life Skills Training (LST; Dusenbury & Botvin, 1992). These strategies included emphasizing skill development rather than the assimilation of knowledge, and incorporating interactive and cooperative learning strategies such as problem-solving exercises.

The revisions to G.R.E.A.T. also incorporated findings from the literature on community, family, school, peer, and individual risk factors for gang-joining. Representative of these risk factors are the following: poverty, social disorganization, low parental monitoring, low attachment to parents, lack of involvement in conventional family activities, low school commitment and performance, association with and commitment to deviant peers, lack of empathy, impulsiveness, and moral disengagement (e.g., Battin-Pearson, Thornberry, Hawkins, & Krohn, 1998; Esbensen, Huizinga, & Weiher, 1993; Fleisher, 1998; Hill, Howell, Hawkins, & Battin-Pearson, 1999; Howell, 2009; Maxson, Whitlock, & Klein, 1998; Thornberry, Krohn, Lizotte, Smith, & Tobin, 2003). While many studies treat gangs as a phenomenon distinct from the general study of delinquency, there is considerable overlap between risk factors associated with delinquency and gang membership (Esbensen, Peterson, Taylor, & Freng, 2010). Numerous studies, for example, suggest that while the gang environment facilitates an increase in delinquency during the year or years of gang membership, many gang members are already delinquent prior to joining the gang (Battin-Pearson et al., 1998; Esbensen & Huizinga, 1993; Gatti, Tremblay, Vitaro, & McDuff, 2005; Thornberry et al., 2003). This finding that delinquency generally precedes gang membership underscores the importance of universal gang prevention efforts that target the entire adolescent population.

Now in place is a substantially revised program containing 13 (rather than nine) lessons that focus more attention on skills-building through interactive and cooperative learning strategies. The lessons are more tightly connected and designed to address some of the known risk factors for gang involvement. In addition, the revised program is designed to be part of a more comprehensive school, family, and community approach. As such, greater involvement of classroom teachers in program delivery is promoted; law enforcement agencies are encouraged to partner with other community organizations, such as Boys and Girls Clubs; and there are optional program components available for agencies to adopt: an elementary school curriculum for third or fourth graders, a summer program, and G.R.E.A.T. Families, targeted at youths aged 10-14 and their families (see the G.R.E.A.T. program website at www.great-online.org for more information).

The revised program's two main goals are to help youths (a) avoid gang membership, violence, and criminal activity; and (b) develop a positive relationship with law enforcement. The revised curriculum aims to teach youths the life-skills (e.g., refusal skills, conflict resolution, and anger management techniques) thought necessary to prevent involvement in gang behavior and delinquency (e.g., Hill et al., 1999; Maxson & Whitlock, 2002; Maxson et al., 1998). The core curriculum is intended for delivery at entry to middle school (i.e., usually sixth grade, but in some locations, seventh grade), in part to ease the transition from elementary to middle school and to reach youths before the prime age for gang joining (approximately 13–14 years old; Esbensen & Huizinga, 1993; Hill et al., 1999; Thornberry et al., 2003). This curriculum was piloted in 2001, with full-scale implementation occurring in 2003. Currently, the program is taught in middle schools across the country, as well as in other countries.

Like the original G.R.E.A.T. program, the revised program is delivered by law enforcement officers. In districts with school resource officers (SRO), the program is usually taught by the SROs. In other jurisdictions, G.R.E.A.T. is taught by officers in community relations divisions or by patrol officers on an overtime basis. All instructors must complete G.R.E.A.T. Officer Training and be certified prior to teaching in their local schools. Officers are introduced to the program and provided sections on gang trends, middle school student developmental stages, teaching and classroom management techniques, and issues associated with officers' transition from an emphasis on enforcement to one of prevention. This intensive training is one week for officers with prior teaching experience. For officers who have not been in the classroom, a two-week training provides them additional practice at teaching the lessons.

Potential Benefits: Evidence from the Current National Evaluation

To determine whether curricular changes produced the desired benefits of preventing youth gang membership, violence, and delinquency and improving youth-law enforcement relationships, NIJ solicited proposals in 2006 to conduct a second national evaluation. The University of Missouri–St. Louis was awarded funding to conduct a process and outcome evaluation of the revised G.R.E.A.T. core curriculum.

G.R.E.A.T. II Research Design

The Process and Outcome Evaluation of G.R.E.A.T. (or G.R.E.A.T. II, as this second national evaluation is called) began in summer 2006 and continues through 2012. The process evaluation consisted of (a) numerous observations by the research team of G.R.E.A.T. Officer Trainings to learn how officers are taught to deliver the program; and (b) hundreds of classroom observations in both experimental and control classrooms to assess implementation fidelity (Esbensen, Matsuda, Taylor, & Peterson, 2011). The outcome evaluation employs an experimental longitudinal panel design in which classrooms in each of the participating schools were randomly assigned to the treatment (i.e., G.R.E.A.T.) or control condition. Students are scheduled to complete six waves of face-to-face group-administered questionnaires (pretests and posttests followed by four annual surveys), following the students through their school experiences from sixth or seventh grade through tenth or eleventh grade. Also providing information useful for both process and outcome components were surveys of middle school personnel (Peterson, Panfil, Esbensen, & Taylor, 2009), surveys of G.R.E.A.T.-trained officers in the seven cities, and interviews with the study schools' G.R.E.A.T. officers and their supervisors (Carson, Esbensen, Taylor, & Peterson, 2008). This chapter relies on results from the School Personnel and Student Questionnaires, but draws as well from the process evaluation and the Law Enforcement Interview.

Seven cities were selected for inclusion based on (a) the existence of an established G.R.E.A.T. program, (b) geographic and demographic diversity, and (c) evidence of youth gang activity: Albuquerque, New Mexico; Chicago, Illinois; Greeley, Colorado; Nashville, Tennessee; Philadelphia, Pennsylvania; Portland, Oregon; and a city located in the Dallas-Fort Worth (DFW), Texas area. In each of these seven cities, four to six public middle schools were selected with the goal of including schools that, as a whole, would represent district demographics. The final sample consisted of 31 schools in these seven cities. All students in the 195 classrooms ($N = 4,095$) at the G.R.E.A.T. grade level (sixth or seventh) in those schools were eligible to participate in the evaluation, and active parental consent procedures resulted in 78% ($N = 3,820$) of the students' parents allowing their child's participation (see Esbensen, Melde, Taylor, & Peterson, 2008, for more detail on active consent procedures and Esbensen, Peterson, et al., 2011, for more detail on the research design.)

School Personnel Views

Prior research has shown that the views of school personnel, particularly teachers, can be crucial to program implementation, continuation, and potential success (Donnermeyer & Wurschmidt, 1997; Flannery & Torquati, 1993; Peterson & Esbensen, 2004). To assess educators' level of support for various aspects of the program, school administrators and teachers in the G.R.E.A.T. grade levels (sixth or seventh) in the 31 participating schools were asked to complete an anonymous School Personnel Questionnaire; 230 (62%) completed the surveys in spring and fall 2007 (see Peterson et al., 2009, for more detail).

Educators were supportive in general of having law enforcement officers in schools (91%) and believed that police play an important role in prevention (80%). In addition, school personnel were supportive of prevention programs in schools and the role of schools in prevention. Most agreed that such programs can deter youth from drugs, delinquency, and gang involvement (80%) and that it is part of a school's responsibility to prevent students from becoming involved in these behaviors (81%). Sixty-four percent indicated that they would like to see more prevention programs in their schools, and 56% agreed that teachers should incorporate prevention program lessons into their own curricula.

In regard to program content and delivery, school personnel were provided a list of 11 subjects commonly covered in prevention programs (including G.R.E.A.T.) and asked to provide their opinion about the importance of each in helping youths avoid drugs, delinquency, and gangs. Decision-making, problem-solving, communication skills, and conflict resolution were rated as "very important" by over 90% of school personnel, and over 80% gave this rating for goal setting, anger management, refusal skills, recognition of peer pressure, and social responsibility. School personnel were also asked to rate, on a 3-point scale from "not effective" to "very effective," the effectiveness of different methods of delivering prevention program content. Active teaching methods used in G.R.E.A.T. (e.g., small group activities, role-playing) were rated as very effective by 70% or more of respondents, and class discussion was rated as such by 60%. Least likely to be rated effective were lecture (7%) and written homework (6%), methods from which the redesigned G.R.E.A.T. program has moved away.

School personnel who were familiar with G.R.E.A.T. had positive views of the program, with about 90% in favor of having the program in their schools. The G.R.E.A.T. officers were also viewed favorably by the majority of respondents, in terms of both preparation and delivery of program and their interactions with students in the classroom. In regard to specific statements about program materials and length, 90% reported that the curriculum is appropriate for students' age and comprehension levels, but fewer agreed that G.R.E.A.T. program materials are appealing to students (77%), that the length of the G.R.E.A.T. curriculum (45–60 minutes a week for 13 weeks) provides enough time to cover the important, relevant topics (63%), or that officers teaching the G.R.E.A.T. program have enough time during the class period to sufficiently cover the educational materials for each lesson (62%). The majority of educators believed the program teaches students skills necessary to avoid delinquency and gangs (82%), addresses problems faced by their students (86%), and improves student-police relations (85%). Only about half, however, agreed that the program plays a significant role in reducing youth gang participation in their schools (54%) and communities (47%). This finding is discussed in the Critique section, below.

Outcome Evaluation Results

Observations of G.R.E.A.T. program delivery during the process evaluation determined that, overall, the program was implemented with fidelity (see Esbensen, Matsuda, et al., 2011, for a detailed discussion). If a treatment effect is detected in the outcome evaluation, it is therefore feasible to attribute this effect to the G.R.E.A.T. program. Preliminary outcome analyses of short-term program effects were conducted using pretest, posttest, and one-year follow-up data from the student surveys. Outcomes examined were those that tapped key program goals: G.R.E.A.T. and non-G.R.E.A.T. students were compared on their gang membership, level of delinquency, and attitudes toward the police. Also examined were a few of the risk factors or skills targeted by the program: empathy, risk-seeking, conflict resolution skills, resistance to peer pressure, and refusal skills.

Our multilevel analyses using MLwiN software revealed statistically significant program effects at the one year follow-up for five of the nine variables examined (Esbensen, Peterson, et al., 2011). Specifically, one year following program delivery, students receiving G.R.E.A.T. reported lower rates of gang membership (a 54% reduction in odds), more positive attitudes about police, less positive attitudes about gangs, more frequent use of refusal skills, and greater resistance to peer pressure than did students in the control condition. These findings address the two main program goals of reducing gang affiliation and improving youths' relationships with law enforcement, but the same program effect was not found for delinquency. Although the direction of the findings favored a program effect, the results for differences in self-reported delinquency did not reach statistical significance. Several program-specific skills-building objectives also appear to be met, especially refusal skills. There were no statistically significant differences between the groups on measures of empathy, risk-seeking, and conflict resolution.

Critique of the Approach

The revised G.R.E.A.T. core curriculum was designed to address shortcomings of the original program. It therefore utilizes active learning strategies to teach students skills to combat some of the known risk factors for delinquency and gang membership. The school personnel survey showed that G.R.E.A.T. incorporates lesson content thought by educators to be important to preventing youths from becoming involved in gangs, drugs, and violence and delivers it in a manner thought to be effective (Peterson et al., 2009). Classroom observations of G.R.E.A.T. delivery indicated that students are interested and active during the lessons. They appear to enjoy both their interactions with the officer and the opportunity to practice skills; they are very active and animated, for example, in role-playing exercises (Esbensen, Matsuda, et al., 2011).

Although the revised G.R.E.A.T. program is intended to be part of a larger approach in which other G.R.E.A.T. components are used to complement the core curriculum, the extent to which this occurs is questionable. For example, many law enforcement agencies do not have the resources to implement more than one component, so the focus in most jurisdictions is the core middle school curriculum. In addition, as noted in this and prior work (Peterson & Esbensen, 2004), getting more teacher involvement and integrating G.R.E.A.T. into schools' mission and curricula may be a challenge. Although most school administrators and teachers support prevention programs in schools and believe that it is part of a school's responsibility to prevent youth from becoming involved in gangs, drugs, and violence, almost half do not feel that teachers should incorporate prevention program content into their own curricula. This may be tied to increasing pressure to meet state and federal educational standards; indeed, 41% of educators agreed that meeting No Child Left Behind standards posed a "big problem" for their school (Peterson et al., 2009). Such concerns have led administrators and teachers to be increasingly reluctant to participate in programs (or evaluations) that reduce instructional time. Locating the G.R.E.A.T. program in content-relevant classes, as suggested by the review committee, may help to integrate lessons into class materials while also supporting mandated curricula (see Table 42.1). Almost half of teachers (45%) did not incorporate G.R.E.A.T. lesson content into their own curricula, mostly (49%) due to lack of time (a large concern was the amount of material to cover for mandated testing), but also because it was not relevant to their subject (30%). The other 55%, especially those in relevant courses such as social studies, language arts, and health, did cover or reinforce G.R.E.A.T. content, relaying such comments as, "I teach social studies and [the program] fit in naturally when talking about cultures and communicating." The school personnel survey revealed that most educators played at least some role in the program. Although this was largely classroom management activities (31%), some teachers assisted the officer (20%) and others actively participated (20%). Many (31%) used the time for grading or other paperwork. These collective findings suggest that there are ways to better integrate G.R.E.A.T. with minimal inconvenience to teachers and mandated curricula. Greater teacher involvement may also improve G.R.E.A.T. implementation. Classroom observations indicated that students were more interested and better behaved when teachers were engaged in or assisting with program delivery, as opposed to using the period for class preparation (Esbensen, Matsuda, et al., 2011).

Despite these potential areas for improvement, preliminary analyses from the outcome evaluation are supportive of a one-year post-program effect. G.R.E.A.T. students have lower rates of gang membership than do control group students. Additionally, G.R.E.A.T. students report a

Table 42.1 Implications for Practice: Preventing Youth Gang Involvement with G.R.E.A.T.

1.	School-based gang prevention efforts should target known risk factors (e.g., malleable attitudes, skills, and behaviors) in multiple domains.
2.	Building partnerships between law enforcement agencies and schools may hold promise for preventing youth gang involvement and improving relationships between students and law enforcement officers.
3.	One promising avenue for a gang prevention partnership is Gang Resistance Education and Training (G.R.E.A.T.), a universal, primary prevention program taught by law enforcement officers to middle-school students in an effort to prevent gang membership, delinquency, and violence and to improve police-student relationships.
4.	When implementing prevention programs such as G.R.E.A.T., educators should ensure that the programs are age appropriate, are of sufficient dosage to impact attitudes, skills, and behaviors, and utilize multiple teaching techniques that accommodate different learning styles (e.g., cooperative learning, interactive teaching.)
5.	School-based gang prevention programs like G.R.E.A.T. should be incorporated into the larger school climate and reinforced in classroom curricula. Program implementers can gain administrative and teacher buy-in by demonstrating the ways in which state and federal teaching standards can be addressed through the prevention curriculum and encouraging schools to locate prevention programs in content-related courses such as civics, health, language arts, and social studies.
6.	Schools' participation in evaluation efforts such as the National Evaluation of G.R.E.A.T. is imperative to obtain much-needed evidence of short- and long-term effects of school-based gang prevention programs. The evidence base is limited, and schools need scientifically-rigorous information on which to base decisions about which programs to implement in a resource-limited environment.

number of more prosocial attitudes and skills, including more positive views of the police, than do control students. Interviews with G.R.E.A.T. officers support this latter finding. Officers told interviewers that as the program progressed, students were more likely than before to come to them with problems, to tell them about potential upcoming trouble in the school, and to approach them on the streets to say "hello." Because the program was implemented with fidelity, and the evaluation utilized a randomized experimental design, there is confidence that these effects are due to the program and not to other outside influences.

Readers may notice that in the School Personnel Questionnaire, only about half of school personnel agreed that the G.R.E.A.T. program significantly reduces youths' gang participation in their schools and communities. Similarly, the officer survey revealed that just 29% of officers believed the program to have reduced their community's gang or crime problems (Carson et al., 2008). This indicates that although educators and officers believe that G.R.E.A.T. is beneficial to students and is, in general, a valuable program, the majority do not believe that it is capable of addressing larger community issues. This is a reasonable assertion because G.R.E.A.T. is expected only to reduce a small portion of a community's crime problems on an individual level. In other words, it is not intended to resolve all of the community's gang and/or crime problems.

To the extent that G.R.E.A.T. reaches the majority of a school's population, lower rates of gang involvement may be seen at the school level. For example, as sixth-grade students who receive G.R.E.A.T. become seventh- and eighth-graders and new cohorts of sixth-graders are trained, all students within a middle school will have received G.R.E.A.T. over the course of a few years. This is not the case in the study schools, however, as only half of the classes in one grade received the program.

In sum, there appears to be a good deal of support by educators for both the G.R.E.A.T. program and officers. Aspects of the current educational climate, such as meeting standards set forth in the No Child Left Behind act, provide challenges to delivery and reinforcement of the G.R.E.A.T. program that can be addressed, in part, by locating the program in specific subjects and through greater teacher involvement (see Table 42.1). The program also appears to be implemented as intended and to have short-term effects on several key program outcomes, although ongoing research will determine whether these effects will be sustained over time.

Note

This research was made possible, in part, by the support and participation of seven school districts, including the School District of Philadelphia. This project was supported by Award No. 2006-JV-FX-0011 awarded by the National Institute of Justice, Office of Justice Programs, U.S. Department of Justice. We would also like to thank the numerous school administrators, teachers, students, and law enforcement officers for their involvement and assistance in this study. The opinions, findings, and conclusions or recommendations expressed in this chapter are those of the authors and do not necessarily reflect the views of the Department of Justice or of the seven participating school districts.

References

Battin-Pearson, S. R., Thornberry, T. P., Hawkins, J. D., & Krohn, M. D. (1998, October). *Gang membership, delinquent peers, and delinquent behavior.* Washington, DC: Office of Juvenile Justice and Delinquency Prevention, Juvenile Justice Bulletin. Retrieved July 17, 2010 from http://www.ncjrs.gov/pdffiles/171119.pdf

Baum, K., Cataldi, E. F., Dinkes, R., Kena, G., & Snyder, T. D. (2006). *Indicators of school crime and safety: 2006.* Washington, DC: National Center for Education Statistics, Institution of Education Sciences, U.S. Department of Education and Bureau of Justice Statistics.

Carson, D. C., Esbensen, F.-A., Taylor, T. J., & Peterson, D. (2008). *Process & Outcome Evaluation of G.R.E.A.T: Results from surveys and interviews with G.R.E.A.T.-trained officers.* St. Louis: University of Missouri-St. Louis.

Catalano, R. F., Arthur, M. W., Hawkins, J. D., Berglund, L., & Olson, J. J. (1998). Comprehensive community and school based interventions to prevent antisocial behavior. In R. Loeber & D. P. Farrington's (Eds.), *Serious and violent juvenile offenders: Risk factors and successful inventions* (pp. 248–283). Thousand Oaks, CA: Sage.

Chandler, K., Chapman, C., Chen, X., Choy, S., Kaufman, P., Rand, M., & Ringel, C. (1998). *Indicators of school crime and safety: 1998.* Washington, DC: National Center for Education Statistics, Institution of Education Sciences, U.S. Department of Education and Bureau of Justice Statistics.

Chandler, K., Chen, X., Choy, S., Fleury, J., Kaufman, P., Miller, A., Peter, K., Planty, M., Rand, M., & Ruddy, C. (2001). *Indicators of school crime and safety: 2001.* Washington, DC: National Center for Education Statistics, Institution of Education Sciences, U.S. Department of Education and Bureau of Justice Statistics.

DeVoe, J., Kaufman, P., Miller, A., Peter, K., Planty, M., Rand, M., Ruddy, S., & Snyder, T. (2003). *Indicators of school crime and safety: 2003.* Washington, DC: National Center for Education Statistics, Institution of Education Sciences, U.S. Department of Education and Bureau of Justice Statistics.

Donnermeyer, J. F., & Wurschmidt, T. N. (1997). Educators' perceptions of the D.A.R.E. program. *Journal of Drug Education, 27,* 259–276.

Dusenbury, L., & Botvin, G. J. (1992). Competence enhancement and the development of positive life options. *Journal of Addictive Diseases, 11* (3), 29–45. doi:10.1300/J069v11n03_02

Egley, A., Jr., Howell, J. C., & Moore, J. P. (2010, March). *Highlights of the 2008 National Youth Gang Survey.* Washington, DC: U.S. Department of Justice, Office of Juvenile Justice and Delinquency Prevention, OJJDP Fact Sheet. Retrieved July 17, 2010, from http://www.ncjrs.gov/pdffiles1/ojjdp/229249.pdf

Esbensen, F.-A., Freng, A., Taylor, T. J., Peterson, D., & Osgood, D. W. (2002). Putting research into practice: The National Evaluation of the Gang Resistance Education and Training (G.R.E.A.T.) program. In W. L. Reed & S. H. Decker (Eds.), *Responding to gangs: Evaluation and research* (pp. 139–167). Washington, DC: U.S. Department of Justice, National Institute of Justice.

Esbensen, F.-A., & Huizinga, D. (1993). Gangs, drugs, and delinquency in a survey of urban youth. *Criminology, 31,* 56–589. doi:10.1111/j.1745-9125.1993.tb01142.x

Esbensen, F.-A., Huizinga, D., & Weiher, A. W. (1993). Gang and non-gang youth: Differences in explanatory factors. *Journal of Contemporary Criminal Justice, 9,* 94–116. doi:10.1177/104398629300900203

Esbensen, F.-A., Matsuda, K. N., Taylor, T. J., & Peterson, D. (2011). Multi-method strategy for assessing program fidelity: The national evaluation of the revised G.R.E.A.T. program. *Evaluation Review, 35*(1), 14–39. doi:10.1177/0193841X10388136

Esbensen, F.-A., Melde, C., Taylor, T. J., & Peterson, D. (2008). Active parental consent in school-based research: How much is enough and how do we get it? *Evaluation Review, 32,* 335–362. doi:10.1177/0193841X08315175

Esbensen, F.-A., & Osgood, D. W. (1999). Gang Resistance Education and Training (G.R.E.A.T.): Results from the national evaluation. *Journal of Research in Crime and Delinquency, 36,* 194–225. doi:10.1177/0022427899036002004

Esbensen, F.-A., Osgood, D. W., Taylor, T. J., Peterson, D., & Freng, A. (2001). How great is G.R.E.A.T.?: Results from a quasi-experimental design. *Criminology & Public Policy, 1,* 87–118. doi:10.1111/j.1745-9133.2001.tb00078.x

Esbensen, F.-A., Peterson, D., Taylor, T. J., Freng, A., Osgood, D. W., Carson, D. C., & Matsuda, K. N. (2011). Evaluation and evolution of the Gang Resistance Education and Training (G.R.E.A.T.) program. *Journal of School Violence, 10*(1), 53–70. doi: 10.1080/15388220.2010.519374

Esbensen, F.-A., Peterson, D., Taylor, T. J., & Freng, A. (2010). *Youth violence: Sex and race differences in offending, victimization, and gang membership.* Philadelphia, PA: Temple University Press.

Flannery, D. J., & Torquati, J. (1993). An elementary school substance abuse prevention program: Teacher and administrator perspectives. *Journal of Drug Education, 23,* 387–397.

Fleisher, M. (1998). *Dead end kids.* Madison: University of Wisconsin Press.

Freng, A. (2001, April). *Parents speak out: Parent questionnaires from the National Evaluation of the Gang Resistance Education and Training (G.R.E.A.T.) program.* Paper presented at the Annual Meeting of the Academy of Criminal Justice Sciences, Washington, DC.

Gatti, U., Tremblay, R. E., Vitaro, F., & McDuff, P. (2005). Youth gangs, delinquency, and drug use: A test of the selection, facilitation, and enhancement hypotheses. *Journal of Child Psychology and Psychiatry, 46,* 1178–1190. doi:10.1111/j.1469-7610.2005.00423.x

Gottfredson, G. D., & Gottfredson, D. C. (2001). *Gang problems and gang programs in a national sample of schools.* Ellicott City, MD: Gottfredson Associates.

Hill, K. G., Howell, J. C., Hawkins, J. D., & Battin-Pearson, S. (1999). Childhood risk factors for adolescent gang membership: Results from the Seattle Social Development Project. *Journal of Research in Crime and Delinquency, 36,* 300–322. doi:0.1177/0022427899036003003

Howell, J.C. (2009). *Preventing and reducing juvenile delinquency: A comprehensive framework* (2nd ed.). Thousand Oaks, CA: Sage.

Klein, M. W., & Maxson, C. L. (2006). *Street gang patterns and policies.* New York, NY: Oxford University Press.

Maxson, C. L., & Whitlock, M. L. (2002). Joining the gang: Gender differences in risk factors for gang membership. In C. R. Huff (Ed.), *Gangs in America* (3rd ed., pp. 19–36). Thousand Oaks, CA: Sage.

Maxson, C. L., Whitlock, M. L., & Klein, M. W. (1998). Vulnerability to street gang membership: Implications for practice. *Social Service Review,* March, 70–91. doi:10.1086/515746

National Youth Gang Center. (2009). *National Gang Survey Analysis.* Retrieved July 17, 2010, from http://www.nationalgangcenter.gov/Survey-Analysis

Peterson, D., & Esbensen, F.-A. (2004). The outlook is G.R.E.A.T.: What educators say about school-based prevention and the Gang Resistance Education and Training (G.R.E.A.T.) program. *Evaluation Review, 28,* 218–245. doi:10.1177/0193841X03262598

Peterson, D., Panfil, V. R., Esbensen, F.-A., & Taylor, T. J. (2009). *National Evaluation of the Gang Resistance Education and Training (G.R.E.A.T) program: School personnel survey report.* St. Louis: University of Missouri-St. Louis.

Sellers, C., Taylor, T. J., & Esbensen, F.-A. (1998). Reality check: Evaluating a school-based gang prevention model. *Evaluation Review, 22,* 590–608. doi:10.1177/0193841X9802200502

Snyder, H. N., & Sickmund, M. (2006). *Juvenile offenders and victims: 2006 national report.* Washington, DC: U.S. Department of Justice, Office of Juvenile Justice and Delinquency Prevention.

Taylor, T. J., & Esbensen, F.-A. (2002). Primary prevention efforts by law enforcement officers in the community policing era. In *Criminology theory and its application in 2002: Proceedings of the Symposium of the International Society for the Study of Crime and Public Policy* (pp. 619–626). Taipei, Taiwan: National University of Taipei.

Thornberry, T. P., Krohn, M. D., Lizotte, A. J., Smith, C. A., & Tobin, K. (2003). *Gangs and delinquency in developmental perspective.* New York, NY: Cambridge University Press. doi:10.1017/CBO9780511499517

Tremblay, R. E., Masse, L., Pagani, L., & Vitaro, F. (1996). From childhood physical aggression to adolescent maladjustment: The Montreal Prevention Experiment. In R. D. Peters & R. J. McMahon (Eds.), *Preventing childhood disorders, substance abuse, and delinquency* (pp. 268–298). Thousand Oaks, CA: Sage.

Winfree, L. T., Jr., Peterson Lynskey, D., & Maupin, J. R. (1999). Developing local police and federal law enforcement partnerships: G.R.E.A.T. as a case study of policy implementation. *Criminal Justice Review, 24,* 145–168. doi:10.1177/073401689902400203

Cognitive-Behavioral Intervention for Anger and Aggression

The Coping Power Program

John E. Lochman, Caroline L. Boxmeyer, and Nicole P. Powell

THE UNIVERSITY OF ALABAMA, TUSCALOOSA

Abstract

This chapter provides an overview of anger and aggression problems in children, and a contextual social-cognitive model that encompasses a set of family, peer, school, and child risk factors that are associated with the expression of childhood aggression. Coping Power, a school-based cognitive intervention based on this model, is described, and its major aims are listed and summarized. Efficacy and effectiveness studies of this program in school settings are summarized, indicating the program's ability to reduce youths' delinquency, substance use, and aggressive behavior in school settings at the time of follow-ups. Challenges and implementation issues are discussed, including the length of intervention needed to have a notable impact, difficulty engaging parents in school-based interventions, and the need for intensive training of the staff who will implement the program.

Overview

Students who display problems with anger and aggression can present serious problems within the school setting. Safety issues aside, these behaviors can disrupt the learning environment, adversely affect the school climate, and threaten students' emotional and social well-being. School-based cognitive behavioral interventions, based on contextual social-cognitive models of children's functioning, can be targeted at children's aggressive behavior. The Coping Power program has been shown to reduce children's aggressive and antisocial behaviors through its focus on the active mechanisms that contribute to children's aggressive behavior.

Importance of Addressing Anger and Aggression in Childhood

Problems with anger and aggression represent two of the most common causes for referral for mental health services or targeted prevention programs in school settings, often because of the implications these problems have for social relationships. In some cases the aggressive and antisocial behavior leads to social rejection by the people around them, in some cases the social rejection from others triggers escalating anger and aggression, and in many cases the relation between aggression and social rejection is bidirectional. Childhood aggression is relatively stable over time and consistently predicts a variety of negative outcomes including delinquency, substance use, conduct problems, academic difficulties, and poor adjustment (Loeber, 1990). Early hostile behavior has also received considerable attention because youth who engage in the most persistent, severe, and violent antisocial behavior are most likely to initiate their deviant behavior in childhood rather than adolescence.

Anger can be defined as a person's response to a threat or the perception of a threat against an individual. The types of threats that tend to trigger an anger response are broad in scope and include both physical threats and psychological threats, or threats to a person's pride or dignity. Anger can be adaptive by energizing an individual and heightening cognitive awareness to take action against a threat or perceived threat. However, anger is an emotion that is often difficult to control due to the intense physiological reactions involved in the fight or flight response that is triggered by anger. Intense, uncontrolled feelings of anger are often associated with aggression.

Aggression is generally defined as a behavioral act that results in harming or hurting others. Because aggressive behavior and treatment of aggression varies greatly according to the intentions and conditions surrounding the aggression, it is typically categorized according to different types. Aggression can be physical or verbal; relational, proactive or reactive; and overt or covert. The literature often differentiates between proactive and reactive aggression because such a framework allows for the explanation and description of aggression (Dodge, Lochman, Harnish, Bates, & Pettit, 1997). Children engaging in proactive aggression typically use aggression to meet a goal. When the aggressive behavior yields the desired reward, the child is more likely to engage in proactive aggression the next time s/he intends to meet a goal. Conversely, reactively aggressive children do not seek to meet goals through their aggressive behavior. Instead, these children react quickly and impulsively to perceived or actual threats and can become intensely irritated.

Conceptual Framework

The contextual social-cognitive model which serves as the basis of our Anger Coping (Lochman, Nelson, & Sims, 1981) and Coping Power (Lochman & Wells, 2002a) programs has been based on empirically identified risk factors which predict children's antisocial behavior (Matthys & Lochman, 2010). As children develop, they can experience an accumulating and "stacking" of risk factors, increasing the probability of the children eventually displaying serious antisocial behavior. Some of these risk factors can be conceptualized as falling within four categories: family context, school context, peer context, and later emerging child factors involving their social cognitive processes and related emotional regulation abilities.

School Contextual Factors

Schools have their own unique climate, and aspects of the school environment have been shown to either decrease or further exacerbate children's conduct problems. While effective schools and teachers can exert positive influences on student behavior even when significant risk factors are present (McEvoy & Welker, 2000), there are a number of school- and classroom-level characteristics which have been linked to higher levels of child disruptive and aggressive behavior. Students from higher poverty schools are exposed to greater levels of classroom aggressive behavior (e.g., Thomas, Bierman, & Conduct Problems Prevention Research Group, 2006) and school poverty has been found to have large negative effects on students' sense of autonomy, democratic values, concern for others, and sense of efficacy (Battistich, Solomon, Kim, Watson, & Schaps, 1995). Current research is seeking to examine the mechanisms by which school poverty affects levels of aggressive and disruptive student behavior. Impoverished schools may have difficulty providing students with adequate supplies and resources, retaining effective teachers, and providing at-risk students with prevention and early intervention programming.

Thomas and colleagues (2008) examined the hypothesis that high rates of student poverty contribute to under-resourced and non-optimal classroom contexts, in which deficits in teacher management skills and teacher-student relationships impede the effective social control of aggressive student behavior. They found that while child characteristics (e.g., aggressive-disruptive behavior at home, attention problems) accounted for the most variance in school aggression, school factors also accounted for significant variance in school aggression, particularly low-quality classroom contexts. Similar to the pattern of escalating coercive interactions described in families of aggressive children (Dishion & Patterson, 2006), teachers may rely on negative and ineffectual behavior control strategies (threats, displays of anger, reprimands, low use of behavioral contingencies and positive reinforcement) to attempt to control the behavior of aggressive students, which lead to further increases in child oppositionality and school behavior problems (Webster-Stratton, Mihalic, Fagan, Arnold, Taylor, & Tingley, 2001). Indeed, Thomas and colleagues (2008) found that classroom contexts characterized by disapproving teachers and disengaged students undermines the classroom learning environment and thus elicit children's disruptive behavior.

Schools with higher poverty levels may also have a higher proportion of students who enter school with aggressive and disruptive behavior problems. This presents a greater challenge, as having a higher proportion of students in a classroom with aggressive and disruptive behavior problems has been shown to increase the amount of aggressive behavior emitted by individual students (e.g., Barth, Dunlap, Dane, Lochman, & Wells, 2004). Other aspects of the school climate have also been linked to aggressive and antisocial student behavior. Schools with less effective administrators, lower expectations for student achievement, and climates that fail to foster students' self efficacy for learning and attachment to school have higher levels of student aggressive and delinquent behavior (for review, see McEvoy & Welker, 2000).

Family Contextual Factors

There is a wide array of factors in the family that can affect child aggression, ranging from poverty to more general stress and discord within the family. Children's aggression has been linked to family background factors such as parent criminality, substance use and depression (Barry, Dunlap, Cotton, Lochman, & Wells, 2005), poverty (Barry et al., 2005), marital conflict (Wolfe, Crooks, Lee, McIntyre-Smith, & Jaffe, 2003), stressful life events (Barry et al., 2005), single and teenage parenthood (Cuffe, McKeown, Addy, & Garrison, 2005), and ambivalent, controlling parent-child attachment (Moss et al., 2006). All of these family risk factors can influence child behavior through their effect on parenting processes. For example, high levels of maternal depression predict parents' use of inconsistent discipline which in turn predicts children's aggressive behavior (Barry, Dunlap, Lochman, & Wells, 2009).

Parenting processes linked to children's aggression (e.g., Reid, Patterson, & Snyder, 2002) include: (a) nonresponsive parenting at age 1, with pacing and consistency of parent responses not meeting children's needs; (b) coercive, escalating cycles of harsh parental nattering and child noncompliance, starting in the toddler years, especially for children with difficult temperaments; (c) harsh, inconsistent discipline; (d) unclear directions and commands; (e) lack of warmth and involvement; and (f) lack of parental supervision and monitoring, as children approach adolescence. The relations between parenting factors and childhood aggression are bidirectional, as child temperament and behavior also affect parenting behaviour (Fite, Colder, Lochman, & Wells, 2006).

Peer Contextual Factors

Children with disruptive behaviors are at risk for being rejected by their peers and for having inflated inaccurate perceptions of their levels of peer acceptance (Pardini, Barry, Barth, Lochman, & Wells, 2006). Aggressive children who are also socially rejected exhibit more severe antisocial behavior than children who are either aggressive only or rejected only (Miller-Johnson, Coie, Maumary-Gremaud, Bierman, & Conduct Problems Prevention Research Group, 2002). The match between the race of students and their peers in a classroom influences the degree of social rejection that students experience (Jackson, Barth, Powell, & Lochman, 2006), and race and gender appear to moderate the relation between peer rejection and negative adolescent outcomes. For example, Lochman and Wayland (1994) found that peer rejection ratings of African American children within a mixed-race classroom did not predict subsequent externalizing problems in adolescence, whereas peer rejection ratings of Caucasian children were associated with future disruptive behaviors.

As children with conduct problems enter adolescence, they tend to associate with deviant peers (Warr, 2002). Adolescents who have been continually rejected from more prosocial peer groups because they lack appropriate social skills turn to antisocial cliques for social support (Miller-Johnson et al., 1999). The tendency for aggressive children to associate with one another increases the probability that they will escalate the seriousness of their antisocial behavior (e.g., Fite, Colder, Lochman, & Wells, 2007).

Social Cognition

Based on children's temperament and biological dispositions, and on children's contextual experiences from their family, peers and community, they begin to form stable patterns of processing social information and of regulating their emotions. The contextual social-cognitive model (Lochman & Wells, 2002a) stresses the reciprocal interactive relationships between children's initial cognitive appraisal of problem situations, their efforts to think about solutions to the perceived problems, children's physiological arousal, and their behavioral response. The level of physiological arousal will depend on the individual's biological predisposition to become aroused, and will vary depending on interpretation of the event (Williams, Lochman, Phillips, & Barry, 2003). The level of arousal will further influence the social problem solving, operating either to intensify the fight or flight response, or interfere with solution generation. Because of the ongoing and reciprocal nature of interactions, it may be difficult for children to extricate themselves from aggressive behavior patterns.

Aggressive children experience cognitive distortions in the appraisal phases of social-cognitive processing because of problems encoding incoming social information, partially due to neurocognitive difficulties in their executive functions (Ellis, Weiss, & Lochman, 2009), and in accurately interpreting social events and others' intentions. In the appraisal phases of information processing, aggressive children have been found to recall fewer relevant nonhostile cues about events (Lochman & Dodge, 1994), and to misperceive the levels of aggressive behavior that they and peers emit in dyadic interactions (Lochman & Dodge, 1998). Reactively aggressive children have a hostile attributional bias, as they excessively infer that others are acting toward them in a provocative and hostile manner (Dodge et al., 1997; Lochman & Dodge, 1994).

Aggressive children also have cognitive deficiencies at the problem solution phases of social-cognitive processing. They can have dominance and revenge oriented social goals (Lochman,

Wayland, & White, 1993) which guide the maladaptive action-oriented and nonverbal solutions they generate for perceived problems (Dunn, Lochman, & Colder, 1997; Lochman & Dodge, 1994). Aggressive children frequently have low verbal skills, and this contributes to their difficulty accessing and using competent verbal assertion and compromise solutions. At the next processing step they identify consequences for each of the solutions generated and make a decision how to respond to the situation. Aggressive children evaluate aggressive behavior in a positive way and they expect that aggressive behavior will lead to positive outcomes for them (Lochman & Dodge, 1994). Deficient beliefs at this stage of information processing are especially characteristic for children with proactive aggressive behavior patterns (Dodge et al., 1997) and for youth who have callous-unemotional traits consistent with early phases of psychopathy (Pardini, Lochman, & Frick, 2003). Children's schematic beliefs and expectations affect each of these information processing steps (Zelli, Dodge, Lochman, Laird, & Conduct Problems Prevention Research Group, 1999).

Description of the Coping Power Program

To address parenting, school, and child social-cognitive risk factors, the Coping Power Program (Lochman, Wells, & Lenhart, 2008) was developed for implementation with students in the fourth through sixth grades. Originally designed as a prevention program for students displaying mild to moderate levels of social, verbal, and physical aggression, Coping Power can also be used as an intervention for youth displaying clinical levels of disruptive behavior problems. Coping Power comprises two components, a 34-session child program and a 16-session parenting curriculum. Though delivered separately to children and parents, the programs are designed to run concurrently.

Child group sessions are typically run in small groups of five to seven students by a school psychologist, counselor, or social worker. Ideally, a teacher or support staff member co-leads and assists with behavior management. Meetings are held weekly, and are 45 minutes to 1 hour in length. Leaders also meet with students individually once each month, to build rapport, assess comprehension, and provide individualized instruction as needed. Parent meetings are also delivered in a group format and can include up to 10 individual parents or couples. Parent component sessions are typically held on a biweekly basis with meetings lasting approximately 90 minutes.

Coping Power Child Component

Program Structure

Delivery of the Coping Power Child Component in a small group format offers several clinical advantages. For example, students have the opportunity to role-play new skills in a realistic environment of their peers, and leaders can observe and assess students' interpersonal interactions with peers. However, the group format can also introduce opportunities for negative group processes in which students' disruptive behaviors can be reinforced, can diminish others' ability to benefit from session content, or can even encourage negative behaviors in others. To address the possibility of dampened or negative effects, the Coping Power Program is highly structured, leaving little "down time" for problematic interchanges. In addition, the program includes a behavior management system in which students receive verbal praise and points for appropriate behaviors; students have the opportunity to spend points on tangible items each week, or to save their points for larger, more desirable items. Inappropriate behaviors are managed with selective ignoring and targeted praise of appropriate behaviors when possible. When disruptive behaviors persist, students receive warnings, fail to earn points, and may be separated from the group.

To promote generalization of skills to the classroom setting, students receive a weekly goal sheet at each Coping Power meeting. The goal sheet defines, in positively stated, observable terms, a goal for the student to work on during the week (e.g., "I will walk away or ask the teacher for help when I have trouble getting along with a classmate"). On a daily basis, the student's teacher reviews the student's progress toward the goal and indicates whether or not the goal was met for that day. Leaders review completed goal sheets at the beginning of each Coping Power meeting, allowing them to assess the students' progress and to revise the goals to be more or less challenging as needed.

Core Program Content

As indicated in Table 43.1, initial sessions devoted to emotion regulation aim to normalize a broad range of emotional experience, to help students develop an adequate vocabulary for labeling and discussing their feelings, and to assist students in recognizing their personal anger cues and anger triggers. A thermometer analogy is used consistently in these sessions to help students recognize variations in the intensity of their emotional experience. Having provided a background in emotional awareness, the curriculum next introduces specific strategies for coping with anger and frustration, including distraction, relaxation, and coping self-statements. Session activities are designed to progress from easily manageable, impersonal exercises (e.g., having students use puppets to receive taunts and demonstrate self-control strategies) to realistic role-plays in which students are teased by other group members about moderately sensitive topics (e.g., personal appearance, athletic abilities). The objectives are best achieved when students experience a moderate degree of angry arousal during these activities, so that they can experience success in managing strong feelings through the use of effective coping strategies.

Social problem solving is another key feature of the Coping Power Child Component, with sessions designed to address the distortions and deficiencies in social-cognitive processes commonly demonstrated by at-risk children. The program seeks to improve students' perspective-taking abilities as an important first step in developing collaborative social-problem solving skills. Students are taught to use a structured problem-solving model involving three steps: Problem Identification, brainstorming potential Choices, and identifying Consequences for the various choices. The problem-solving model is referred to as "PICC" and students practice applying the model to a variety of social situations through discussions, role-plays, games, and homework assignments. Students also solidify their understanding of the PICC model and gain additional practice in its use by creating a videotaped "infomercial" in which the PICC model is described and demonstrated.

Coping Power Parent Component

The Coping Power Parent Component (Wells, Lochman, & Lenhart, 2008) is designed to help parents look for opportunities to coach, encourage, and reinforce their children's use of their new skills. For example, parents are taught to use the PICC model and are encouraged to apply it to situations that may arise in the home, such as conflicts between siblings.

Content of the parent curriculum includes promoting the parent-child relationship, effective behavior management strategies, family communication, parental involvement in academics, and strategies for managing parents' own stress. Table 43.2 provides information about specific topic areas and objectives for each session. The program focuses on encouraging and reinforc-

Table 43.1   Overview of the Session Sequence and Objectives of the Coping Power Child Component

Session	Content and Main Objectives
1	Introduce program purpose and structure; build rapport; foster group cohesion
2 & 3	Introduce concept of goal-setting; assist students in identifying long-term and short-term personal goals; discuss barriers to achieving goals
4	Discuss importance of organization and effective study habits for academic success
5 & 6	Identify behavioral, physiological, and cognitive cues for emotions, especially anger
7	Practice use of distraction to cope with anger
8 – 10	Practice use of coping self-statements to manage anger
11	Practice using relaxation to manage anger
12 – 14	Introduce concept of perspective taking; encourage students to consider non-hostile motivations for others' actions
15	Introduce PICC problem-solving model; discuss first step: Problem Identification
16	Introduce Choices step of PICC model; practice identifying potential solutions to social problems
17 – 18	Introduce Consequences step of PICC model; practice identifying consequences to various solutions; practice evaluation of consequences
19	Identify obstacles to problem-solving and practice persistence in overcoming them
20	Begin planning for PICC video-making activity
21	Videotape students describing PICC model and role-playing problem situation, choices, and consequences
22	Complete videotape production; review and discuss video; review content
23	Review group purpose and structure
24	Review organization and study skills
25	Use PICC model to practice solving social problems involving teachers
26	Practice social skills for joining positive peer groups and making friends
27	Use PICC model to practice solving social problems related to group entry and negotiation with peers
28	Use PICC model to practice solving social problems involving siblings
29	Identify skills to resist peer pressure
30	Practice skills to resist peer pressure using a variety of role-played situations
31	Use PICC model to practice solving social problems that may occur in students' neighborhoods; assist students in identifying their group memberships and status within social groups
32	Create a poster illustrating skills to resist peer pressure
33	Discuss ways to affiliate with positive peer groups
34	Review and summarize key concepts from the program; help students experience a sense of closure as the program ends

ing children's positive behaviors through monitoring and verbal praise. Techniques for decreasing children's inappropriate behaviors are also addressed, including ignoring minor disruptive behaviors, time out, privilege removal and work chores. Coping Power Parent meetings are designed to be interactive in nature, with an emphasis on parent sharing and discussion, as well as frequent role-plays. Each session also includes a homework assignment for parents to practice techniques and skills between meetings.

Table 43.2 Overview of the Session Sequence and Objectives of the Coping Power Parent Component

Session	Content and Main Objectives
1	Provide overview of program structure and content; introduce parent academic support in the home
2	Discuss homework monitoring
3	Introduce topic of stress management for parents; discuss effects of stress; practice relaxation for stress management
4	Introduce time management strategies for stress management; introduce and practice using cognitive model for stress management
5	Present social learning model to understand children's behavior, including the role of antecedents and consequences on shaping behavior; discuss and model use of praise
6	Discuss and role-play ignoring to manage minor disruptive behaviors
7	Present features of effective instructions
8	Discuss the importance of rules and expectations in the home
9	Discuss discipline and punishment; present steps for using time-out effectively
10	Discuss and role play use of privilege removal and work chores as consequences for inappropriate behaviors and rule violations
11	Help parents prepare and plan for summer breaks
12	Review information on academic support in the home
13	Identify activities that promote family cohesiveness
14	Discuss application of PICC to problems that may occur within the home
15	Assist parents in setting up structures to facilitate family communication
16	Review and summarize key concepts from the program; identify community resources for families

Relevant Research and Evidence of Effectiveness

In a first trial of Coping Power, 183 boys (61% African American and 39% Caucasian) who had high rates of teacher-rated aggression in fourth or fifth grade were randomly assigned to either a school-based Coping Power child component, to a combination of Coping Power child and parent components, or to an untreated control condition (Lochman & Wells, 2004). Intervention took place over two academic years. Coping Power produced lower rates of covert delinquent behavior (effect size of .42) and parent-rated substance use (effect size of .64) at a one-year follow-up than did the control condition, and these intervention effects were most apparent for the combined child and parent Coping Power Program. Boys also displayed teacher-rated behavioral improvements in school during the follow-up year, and these effects were evident in both intervention conditions (effect size of .42 for child component and .34 for combined program) and appeared to be primarily influenced by the Coping Power child component. Normative comparison analyses with a non-risk sample of 63 boys from the same schools indicate that the intervention moved at-risk boys into normative ranges for substance use, delinquency and school behavior, in contrast to at-risk control boys who significantly differed from the normative group on the latter two outcomes.

Path analyses indicate that the intervention effects were at least partly mediated by changes in boys' social-cognitive processes, schemas, and parenting processes (Lochman & Wells, 2002a). Changes in social-cognitive appraisal processes, involving boys' hostile attributions and resulting anger, and decision-making processes, involving reductions in the boys' expectations that aggressive behavior would lead to good outcomes for them, reduced the risk for antisocial behavior. Similarly, changes in boys' schemas involving their beliefs about their degree of internal control over successful outcomes and the complexity of their internal representations of others, and changes in their perceptions of the consistency of their parents' discipline efforts were found to mediate reductions in delinquency, substance use, and school behavioral problems.

Another study examined whether the effects of the Coping Power Program, offered as an indicated prevention intervention for high-risk aggressive children, could be enhanced by adding a universal prevention component (Lochman & Wells, 2002b). The universal intervention was randomly offered to half of the fifth-grade teachers and consisted of in-service training for teachers and large-scale parent meetings for all parents of children in universal intervention classrooms. The teacher intervention component consisted of five 2-hour meetings with discussion topics such as fostering parent school involvement, enhancing children's organization and study skills, increasing homework completion, and enhancing children's self-regulation and social competency. The parent intervention consisted of four meetings and included discussion of topics similar to those in the teacher intervention, as well as helping parents prepare their child for the middle-school transition and describing the academic, social, and behavioral tasks that children will have to master during this transition. The sample consisted of 245 male (66%) and female (34%) aggressive fourth grade students (78% African American and 20% Caucasian) who were randomly assigned to one of four conditions: Indicated Intervention + Universal Intervention (II+UI), Indicated Intervention + Universal Control (II+UC), Indicated Control + Universal Intervention (IC+UI), and Indicated Control + Universal Control (IC+UC). Intervention began in the fall of the fifth-grade year and continued midway through the sixth-grade year. Analyses of post-intervention effects comparing intervention to control conditions (Lochman & Wells, 2002b), indicate that the combined Coping Power Program plus the universal intervention produced lower teacher-rated aggression (effect size of .24), higher perceived social competence (effect size of .17), and lower self-reported substance use (effect size of .28), indicating the value of nesting the Coping Power Program within a universal prevention program. The Coping Power intervention by itself produced reduced ratings of teacher- and parent-rated proactive aggression (effect sizes of .41 and .22, respectively), higher teacher-rated behavioral improvement (effect size of .17), and better teacher-rated social skills (effect size of .35). At a one-year follow-up, all intervention conditions produced reductions in substance use (effect sizes between .42 and 1.0), delinquency (effect sizes between .21 and .35), and school aggression (effect sizes between .15 and .58; Lochman & Wells, 2003).

Challenges and Limitations

Duration of the Intervention

The full Coping Power program includes 34 child and 16 parent sessions and spans two school years. It can be difficult to implement an intervention of this length in school settings due to personnel costs, multiple demands on school personnel time, and parents' and teachers' concerns about students missing classroom instruction. Despite these concerns, a range of studies indicate that longer periods of intervention may be necessary in order to produce long-lasting reductions in aggressive and disruptive classroom behavior. Coping Power grew out of earlier intervention research on the Anger Coping Program, which is a briefer, child-only version of the intervention curriculum (Larson & Lochman, 2002). In a series of studies, the Anger Coping Program was found to have immediate effects in reducing boys' aggressive behavior (Lochman, Burch, Curry, & Lampron, 1984) and longer-term effects on increasing boys' self-esteem and social problem-solving and preventing adolescent substance use (Lochman, 1992). However, long-term effects on aggressive and off-task behavior were maintained only in boys who received a second year of booster sessions, suggesting the need for longer periods of intervention. Going forward, it will be important to identify the optimal length of intervention necessary to produce lasting reductions in aggressive behavior. Two recent randomized controlled trials of an abbreviated version of Coping Power have yielded significant teacher-rated behavioral improvement at the end of intervention, including one trial which included a 24 session child component and 10 session parent component (Lochman, Boxmeyer, Powell, Roth, & Windle, 2006) and another trial by an independent research team which included only the 24 session child component (Peterson, Hamilton, & Russell, 2009). Data on long-term outcome effects for these samples is still needed.

Involving Parents in Intervention

Outcome research on both the Anger Coping and Coping Power programs lends further support to the wide body of literature indicating the important role of parents and families in the prevention and treatment of aggressive and disruptive behavior in children. In a three-year follow-up study of Anger Coping, long-lasting improvements in children's classroom behavior were only observed in children who participated in a second year of booster intervention, which was also the only treatment arm that included parent training sessions (Lochman, 1992). In Lochman and Wells' (2004) study, Coping Power-produced reductions in covert delinquent behavior (effect size of .42) and substance abuse (effect size of .64) at one-year follow-up were strongest for the participants in the combined child and parent Coping Power intervention. Similarly, Lochman and colleagues (2006) found that reduction of children's teacher-rated aggressive behavior only reached statistical significance for children whose caregivers attended at least one of the Coping Power parent sessions offered.

Despite the important role of parents in preventing and treating children's aggressive behavior, many schools view intensive work with parents as beyond their scope of practice. Parents may be called in for conferences to discuss specific school behavioral incidents or to discuss a child's individualized education plan; however proactive, ongoing parent skills-training and support services are less frequently available through school-based services. When such services are available, engaging the parents of high-risk children in these services can be a significant challenge. Adaptive interventions that incorporate family engagement techniques and allow for individualization of services, and stronger links between school and community-based services may help to address these challenges in the future.

Dissemination and Implementation in School Settings

An important concern in intervention research is whether the program will be adopted and used effectively by existing school personnel. A controlled dissemination study of the Coping Power Program was recently conducted in 57 schools in five school systems in Alabama to examine this question. Existing school mental health personnel (primarily school guidance counselors) were randomly assigned to be trained to implement Coping Power with high-risk aggressive fourth- and fifth-grade students or to a care-as-usual control condition (N = 531). The intensity of training provided to counselors was found to have a notable impact on child outcomes. Compared to the control condition, significant reductions in child externalizing behavior (from teacher, parent, and child ratings) and improvements in social and academic behaviors only occurred when a more intensive form of training was provided (i.e., when counselors received immediate supervisory feedback based on recorded sessions in addition to attending the standard workshop training and monthly meetings; Lochman, Boxmeyer, et al., 2009). Effect sizes ranged from 0.23 to 0.41 in the intensive training condition compared to effect sizes of .04 to 0.24 in the basic training condition. School- and counselor-level variables were associated with quality of program implementation, with agreeable and conscientious counselors demonstrating best program implementation. Counselors who were high on cynicism and who were in schools with low levels of staff autonomy and high levels of managerial control had particularly poor quality of implementation and child and parent engagement (Lochman, Powell, et al., 2009).

These findings suggest that it is important for school personnel to have a high level of training in cognitive behavioral intervention for aggressive youth in order to produce significant behavior change. An important future direction is to ensure that quality training in common elements of evidence-based intervention for aggressive children and their parents is provided in graduate training programs rather than requiring professionals to obtain additional training once they are already practicing in the field.

Implications for Practice

- Key elements of most cognitive behavioral programs, including Coping Power, include a focus on children's behavioral goals, emotional awareness and self-regulation, perspective-taking and attribution retraining, social problem-solving skill training, and avoidance of deviant peer processes;
- Social problem-solving is a key aspect of most evidence-based cognitive-behavioral programs for conduct problem children, and is typically delivered through discussion, role-play, homework exercises, and creation of therapeutic products such as videos;
- As evident in Coping Power research, cognitive behavioral intervention with aggressive children has most impact on children's delinquent and substance using behavior when it is accompanied by behavioral parent training;
- School-based targeted interventions for children's aggressive behavior, such as the Coping Power Program, must include intensive training to be effective;
- Ensuring that graduate training programs for school mental health professionals offer training in evidence-based interventions for children with anger and aggression problems will help to ensure that these interventions are implemented widely as standard practice, rather than relying on individual schools or districts to adopt such interventions which can require costly training and technical assistance.

References

Barry, T. D., Dunlap, S. T., Cotton, S. J., Lochman, J. E., & Wells, K. C. (2005). The influence of maternal stress and distress on disruptive behavior problems in children. *Journal of the American Academy of Child and Adolescent Psychiatry, 44,* 265–273. doi:10.1097/00004583-200503000-00011

Barry, T. D., Dunlap, S., Lochman, J. E., & Wells, K. C. (2009). Inconsistent discipline as a mediator between maternal distress and aggression in boys. *Child and Family Behavior Therapy, 31,* 1–19. doi:10.1080/07317100802701186

Barth, J. M., Dunlap, S. T., Dane, H., Lochman, J. E., & Wells, K. C. (2004). Classroom environment influences on aggression, peer relations, and academic focus. *Journal of School Psychology, 42,* 115–133. doi:10.1016/j.jsp.2003.11.004

Battistich, V., Solomon, D., Kim, D., Watson, M., & Schaps, E. (1995). Schools as communities, poverty levels of student populations, and student attitudes, motives, and performance: A multilevel analysis. *American Educational Research Journal, 32,* 627–658. doi:10.2307/1163326

Cuffe, S. P., McKeown, R. E., Addy, C. L., & Garrison, C. Z. (2005). Family and psychosocial risk factors in a longitudinal epidemiological study of adolescents. *Journal of the American Academy of Child and Adolescent Psychiatry, 44,* 121–129. doi:10.1097/00004583-200502000-00004

Dishion, T. J., & Patterson, G. R. (2006). The development and ecology of antisocial behavior in children and adolescents. In D. Cicchetti & D. J. Cohen (Eds.), *Developmental psychopathology, Vol 3, Risk, disorder, and adaptation* (2nd ed., pp. 503–541). New York, NY: Wiley.

Dodge, K. A., Lochman, J. E., Harnish, J. D., Bates, J. E., & Pettit, G. S. (1997). Reactive and proactive aggression in school children and psychiatrically impaired chronically assaultive youth. *Journal of Abnormal Psychology, 106,* 37–51. doi:10.1037/0021-843X.106.1.37

Dunn, S. E., Lochman, J. E., & Colder, C. R. (1997). Social problem-solving skills in boys with Conduct and Oppositional Defiant Disorders. *Aggressive Behavior, 23,* 457–469. doi:10.1002/(SICI)1098-2337(1997) 23:6<457::AID-AB5>3.0.CO;2-D

Ellis, M. L., Weiss, B., & Lochman, J. E. (2009). Executive functions in children: Associations with aggressive behavior and social appraisal processing. *Journal of Abnormal Child Psychology, 37,* 945–956. doi:10.1007/s10802-009-9321-5

Fite, P. J., Colder, C. R., Lochman, J. E., & Wells, K. C. (2006). The mutual influence of parenting and boys' externalizing behavior problems. *Journal of Applied Developmental Psychology, 27,* 151–164. doi:10.1016/j.appdev.2005.12.011

Fite, P. J., Colder, C. R., Lochman, J. E., & Wells, K. C. (2007). Pathways from proactive and reactive aggression to substance use. *Psychology of Addictive Behaviors, 21,* 355–364. doi:10.1037/0893-164X.21.3.355

Jackson, M. F., Barth, J. M., Powell. N., & Lochman, J. E. (2006). Classroom contextual effects of race on children's peer nominations. *Child Development, 77,* 1325–1337. doi:10.1111/j.1467-8624.2006.00937.x

Larson, J., & Lochman, J. E. (2002). *Helping school children cope with anger: A cognitive-behavioral intervention.* New York, NY: Guilford.

Lochman, J. E. (1992). Cognitive-behavioral interventions with aggressive boys: Three-year follow-up and preventive effects. *Journal of Consulting and Clinical Psychology, 60,* 426–432. doi:10.1037/0022-006X.60.3.426

Lochman, J. E., Boxmeyer, C. L., Powell, N. P., Roth, D., & Windle, M. (2006). Masked intervention effects: Analytic methods for addressing low dosage of intervention. *New Directions for Evaluation, 110,* 19–32. doi:10.1002/ev.184

Lochman, J. E., Boxmeyer, C. L., Powell, N. P., Qu, L., Wells, K. C., & Windle, M. (2009). Dissemination of the Coping Power program: Importance of intensity of counselor training. *Journal of Consulting and Clinical Psychology, 77,* 397–409. doi:10.1037/a0014514

Lochman, J. E., Burch, P. P., Curry, J. F., & Lampron, L. B. (1984). Treatment and generalization effects of cognitive-behavioral and goal setting interventions with aggressive boys. *Journal of Consulting and Clinical Psychology, 52,* 915–916. doi:10.1037/0022-006X.52.5.915

Lochman, J. E., & Dodge, K. A. (1994). Social-cognitive processes of severely violent, moderately aggressive and nonaggressive boys. *Journal of Consulting and Clinical Psychology, 62,* 366–374. doi:10.1037/0022-006X.62.2.366

Lochman, J. E., & Dodge, K. A. (1998). Distorted perceptions in dyadic interactions of aggressive and nonaggressive boys: Effects of prior expectations, context, and boys' age. *Development and Psychopathology, 10,* 495–512. doi:10.1017/S0954579498001710

Lochman, J. E., Nelson, W. M. III, & Sims, J. P. (1981). A cognitive behavioral program for use with aggressive children. *Journal of Clinical Child Psychology, 10,* 146–148. doi:10.1080/15374418109533036

Lochman, J. E., Powell, N. P., Boxmeyer, C. L., Qu, L., Wells, K. C., & Windle, M. (2009). Implementation of a school-based prevention program: Effects of counselor and school characteristics. *Professional Psychology: Research & Practice, 40,* 476–497. doi:10.1037/a0015013

Lochman, J. E., & Wayland, K. K. (1994). Aggression, social acceptance and race as predictors of negative adolescent outcomes. *Journal of the American Academy of Child and Adolescent Psychiatry, 33,* 1026–1035. doi:10.1097/00004583-199409000-00014

Lochman, J. E., Wayland, K. K., & White, K. J. (1993). Social goals: Relationship to adolescent adjustment and to social problem solving. *Journal of Abnormal Child Psychology, 21,* 135–151. doi:10.1007/BF00911312

Lochman, J. E., & Wells, K. C. (2002a). Contextual social-cognitive mediators and child outcome: A test of the theoretical model in the Coping Power Program. *Development an Psychopathology, 14,* 971–993. doi:10.1017/S0954579402004157

Lochman, J. E., & Wells, K. C. (2002b). The Coping Power Program at the middle school transition: Universal and indicated prevention effects. *Psychology of Addictive Behaviors, 16,* S40–S54. doi:10.1037/0893-164X.16.4S.S40

Lochman, J. E., & Wells, K. C. (2003). Effectiveness study of Coping Power and classroom intervention with aggressive children: Outcomes at a one-year follow-up. *Behavior Therapy, 34,* 493–515. doi:10.1016/S0005-7894(03)80032-1

Lochman, J. E., & Wells, K. C. (2004). The Coping Power program for preadolescent aggressive boys and their parents: Outcome effects at the one-year follow-up. *Journal of Consulting and Clinical Psychology, 72,* 571–578. doi:10.1037/0022-006X.72.4.571

Lochman, J. E., Wells, K. C., & Lenhart, L. A. (2008). *Coping Power child group program: Facilitator guide.* New York, NY: Oxford University Press.

Loeber, R. (1990). Development and risk factors of juvenile antisocial behavior and delinquency. *Clinical Psychology Review, 10,* 1–41. doi:10.1016/0272-7358(90)90105-J

Matthys, W., & Lochman, J. E. (2010). *Oppositional defiant disorder and conduct disorder in childhood.* Oxford, England: Wiley-Blackwell.

McEvoy, A., & Welker, R. (2000). Antisocial behavior, academic failure, and school climate: A critical review. *Journal of Emotional and Behavior Disorders, 8,* 130–140. doi:10.1177/106342660000800301

Miller-Johnson, S., Coie, J. D., Maumary-Gremaud, A., Bierman, K., & Conduct Problems Prevention Research Group. (2002). Peer rejection and aggression and early starter models of conduct disorder. *Journal of Abnormal Child Psychology, 30,* 217–230. doi:10.1023/A:1015198612049

Miller-Johnson, S., Coie, J. D., Maumary-Gremaud, A., Lochman, J., & Terry, R. (1999). Relationship between childhood peer rejection and aggression and adolescent delinquency severity and type among African American youth. *Journal of Emotional and Behavioral Disorders, 7,* 137–146. doi:10.1177/106342669900700302

Moss, E., Smolla, N., Cyr, C., Dubois-Comtois, K., Mazzarello, T., & Berthiaume, C. (2006). Attachment and behavior problems in middle childhood as reported by adult and child informants. *Development and Psychopathology, 18,* 425–444. doi:10.1017/S0954579406060238

Pardini, D. A., Barry, T. D., Barth, J. M., Lochman, J. E., & Wells, K. C. (2006). Self-perceived social acceptance and peer social standing in children with aggressive-disruptive behaviors. *Social Development, 15,* 46–64. doi:10.1111/j.1467-9507.2006.00329.x

Pardini, D. A., Lochman, J. E., & Frick, P. J. (2003). Callous/unemotional traits and social cognitive processes in adjudicated youth. *Journal of the American Academy of Child and Adolescent Psychiatry, 42,* 364–371. doi:10.1097/00004583-200303000-00018

Peterson, M. A., Hamilton, E. B., & Russell, A. D. (2009). Starting well: Facilitating the middle school transition. *Journal of Applied School Psychology, 25,* 286–304. doi:10.1080/15377900802487219

Reid, J. B., Patterson, G. R., & Snyder, J. (2002). *Antisocial behavior in children and adolescents. A developmental analysis and model of intervention.* Washington, DC: American Psychological Association. doi:10.1037/10468-000

Thomas, D. E., Bierman, K. L., & Conduct Problems Prevention Research Group. (2006). The impact of classroom aggression on the development of aggressive behavior in children. *Development and Psychopathology, 18*(2), 471–487. doi:10.1017/S0954579406060251

Thomas, D. E., Bierman, K. L., Thompson, C., Powers, C. J., & Conduct Problems Prevention Research Group. (2008). Double jeopardy: Child and school characteristics that predict aggressive-disruptive behavior in the first grade. *School Psychology Review, 37,* 516–532. Retrieved from http://www.nasponline.org/publications/spr/sprissues.aspx

Warr, M. (2002). *Companions in crime: The social aspects of criminal conduct.* Cambridge, England: Cambridge University Press.

Webster-Stratton, C., Mihalic, S., Fagan, A., Arnold, D., Taylor, T., & Tingley, C. (2001). *Blueprints for violence prevention, book eleven: The incredible years: Parent, teacher, and child training series.* Boulder, CO: Center for the Study and Prevention of Violence.

Wells, K. C., Lochman, J. E., & Lenhart, L. A. (2008). *Coping Power parent group program: Facilitator guide.* New York, NY: Oxford.

Williams, S. C., Lochman, J. E., Phllips, N. C., & Barry, T. (2003). Aggressive and nonaggressive boys'physiological and cognitive processes in response to peer provocations. *Journal of Clinical Child and Adolescent Psychology, 32,* 568–576. doi:10.1207/S15374424JCCP3204_9

Wolfe, D. A., Crooks, C. V., Lee, V., McIntyre-Smith, A., & Jaffe, P. G. (2003). The effects of children's exposure to domestic violence: A meta-analysis and critique. *Clinical Child and Family Psychology Review, 6,* 171–187. doi:10.1023/A:1024910416164

Zelli, A., Dodge, K. A., Lochman, J. E., Laird, R. D., & Conduct Problems Prevention Research Group. (1999). The distinction between beliefs legitimizing aggression and deviant processing of social cues: Testing measurement validity and the hypothesis that biased processing mediates the effects of beliefs on aggression. *Journal of Personality and Social Psychology, 77,* 150–166. doi:10.1037/0022-3514.77.1.150

44

Meta-Analysis and Systematic Review of the Effectiveness of School-Based Programs to Reduce Multiple Violent and Antisocial Behavioral Outcomes

Aaron A. Alford and James Derzon

THE BATTELLE CENTERS FOR PUBLIC HEALTH RESEARCH AND EVALUATION, ARLINGTON, VA

Abstract

Early models of violence prevention targeted a single outcome by intervening in a single suspected causal pathway. This limited approach has increasingly fallen out of favor, as evidence has accumulated that violent and antisocial outcomes are driven by a highly inter-correlated cloud of potential risk factors. Policy makers and consumers are often interested in whether or not a program actually prevents or reduces the problem behaviors that it is designed to address. The current study combined the methods of a traditional meta-analysis and traditional systematic review to examine the evidence of effectiveness of school-based programs in simultaneously reducing both violent and antisocial behavioral outcomes. Overall, none of the programs report evidence of being effective for all outcomes, and only one successfully impacted more than one distal outcome. When considering all forms of evidence, no program showed uniformly positive evidence across all outcomes and domains considered. Implications for science and practice are discussed.

Increasingly, prevention science is moving towards integrated models of prevention. Early models of violence prevention targeted a single outcome by intervening in a single suspected causal pathway (Domitrovich, Bradshaw, Greenberg, Embry, & Ialongo, 2009). This limited approach has increasingly fallen out of favor, as evidence has accumulated that violent and antisocial outcomes are driven by a highly inter-correlated risk factors (Wei, Loeber, & White, 2004). Prevailing evidence suggests that there is a complex interplay of predisposition, training and skills, and environmental stimuli that predispose youth to acting or responding inappropriately (Silberg, Rutter, D'Onofrio, & Eaves, 2003). Theoretically, each individual receiving an intervention has a unique cluster, or at least uniquely weighted cluster, of risk factors. That is, within individual, each risk factor likely has a unique duration, intensity and interaction with individual lability. By targeting a cluster of risk factors or common factors that lead to multiple related outcomes, it may be possible to reduce the net burden of risk for each of those outcomes. Most school-based programs target clusters of risk factors simultaneously with the intent of reducing all the distal outcomes related to those risk factors (Hansen, Dusenbury, Bishop, & Derzon, 2007).

What Counts as Evidence of Effectiveness?

When discussing outcomes, it is essential to maintain conceptual clarity. The reigning theoretical framework, linking risk and protective factors with distal outcomes, suggests that effectively targeting proximal outcomes (risk and protective factors) should lead to changes in common problem behaviors (Hawkins, Catalano, & Miller, 1992; Jessor & Jessor, 1977). When documenting program effectiveness, it is tempting to claim that there is evidence of effectiveness for multiple outcomes based on positive changes in the risk and protective factors known to contribute to the distal behavioral outcome the program seeks to prevent. Many programs implicitly or explicitly target multiple proximal outcomes such as attitudes, opinions, knowledge and behaviors that are believed to mediate distal outcomes such as alcohol use, tobacco use, drug use, and aggression. However, change in proximal outcomes at the aggregate level shows limited correspondence with change in the distal outcome of interest (Alford & Derzon, 2011; Najaka, 2000; Najaka, Gottfredson, & Wilson, 2001). Support for the claim that trial-wide change in proximal risk and protective factors translates reliably into change in distal behavioral outcomes remains elusive, even if support for these relations is well documented at the individual level (Derzon, 2007; Lipsey & Derzon, 1998). Thus, while it is clear that proximal outcomes (i.e., risk and protective factors) mediate distal outcomes at the individual level, it is less clear that group-wide evidence of change in proximal outcomes reliably translates into change in distal outcomes.

For the purposes of exploration, development and understanding, reliance on proximal outcomes is more than warranted (MacKinnon, Fairchild, & Fritz, 2007; Pearl, 2000). Knowing why a program works, or does not work, can lead to a finer understanding of prevention programs as well as the mechanisms of violent and aggressive behavior. Recent work in prevention science has also indicated that a basic understanding of the mechanisms of a program is central to effective content delivery (e.g., Derzon, Springer, Sale, & Brounstein, 2005).

Despite the interest and theoretical importance of linking risk and protective factors with outcomes, policy makers and consumers are often interested in whether or not a program actually prevents or lessens the problem behaviors that the program is designed to reduce. Program adopters require an understandable and common metric with which they can compare the many prevention programs publically available. In the United States, the focus has primarily been distal behavioral outcomes (McBride, 2003). For these reasons, we focus this investigation solely on the effectiveness of programs that measure the effect on distal behavioral outcomes representative of violent and other antisocial behaviors.

Meta-Analysis and Systematic Reviews

Meta-analyses of school-based programs tend to either aggregate study findings to produce a summary estimate of intervention impact (e.g., Derzon, 2006; Wilson, Gottfredson, & Najaka, 2001; Wilson, Lipsey, & Derzon, 2003) or to report summary results at the level of strategy or mechanism of change for one or more discrete outcomes (see, e.g., Ennett et al., 2003; Hansen et al., 2009). Inherent in each of these approaches is the pooling of evidence across programs and studies to make evidence-based claims of the average effectiveness of the interventions that contribute data to each outcome. In meta-analysis, the observation that different programs and different studies may contribute evidence to different outcomes is typically not explicitly examined. Meta-analysis was developed to account for the instability of evidence inherent in much primary research in the social sciences. Although pooling evidence increases power to detect effects and estimate homogeneity, pooling evidence from different studies obscures whether the same implementation is effective for multiple outcomes or if different trials contribute to different results. Thus, while meta-analysis can tell us if programs are, on average, effective across a range of outcomes, it does not typically provide evidence that the same program is effective across multiple outcomes.

While meta-analysis provides a unique set of methodologies for combining the information from many studies or evaluations to arrive at a single estimate of the magnitude and direction of effectiveness, it relies on unconditioned estimates (main effects) of an intervention's effectiveness. As it is a quantitative method, it can also provide a test of significance for an aggregate estimate, and can be used to test if the included estimates vary more than would be expected by sampling error. The estimates of effectiveness from individual trials are combined using standardized estimates of impact (effect sizes). However, the estimates of effect are derived from original research reports, and are dependent on the reporting of the original authors.

A meta-analyst must rely on the original author to provide clear reporting and is limited by the available information and the analyses reported by the original author. Transformations are available to convert many common statistics into standardized effect sizes, but many results from newer, more sophisticated methods, such as growth mixture models, cannot be transformed. Because of this limitation, meta-analysis is largely restricted to combining evidence in the form of main effects. A main effect is the effect of the intervention on the outcome of interest, regardless of potential covariates. Controlling for a covariate removes the covariates' variance from the main effect (Keef & Roberts, 2004), but the resulting finding is no longer representative of the main effect, and may not be comparable to effect sizes from other studies. Therefore, including covariate-adjusted results is not typical in meta-analysis (Morris & DeShon, 2002; Peterson & Brown, 2005).

As a result, studies that use these methods are lost to a meta-analysis under most circumstances (Morris & DeShon, 2002). When aggregating at the program level, this creates the potential for bias. Most programs are evaluated by a single researcher or a limited number of researchers. Researchers tend to favor a particular analysis frame or may conduct sophisticated analyses to answer specific research questions. If these analyses produce findings that cannot be transformed into a common metric, results from these sophisticated studies are systematically lost to meta-analysis.

A systematic review does not have the same limitations. Systematic reviews can capture results from all forms of statistical tests, as they do not rely on a standardized quantitative estimate. That same feature is also the primary limitation when used for decision making purposes. Systematic reviews do not provide a strong option for combining statistical tests when combining estimates of effectiveness across multiple tests or studies. Traditionally, the option for summarizing evidence in this framework has been vote counting, a procedure that relies on counting the number of statistically significant findings across studies, but which has been found lacking (Borenstein, Hedges, Higgins, & Rothstein, 2009; Cooper & Hedges, 1994).

When used alone, each method has specific weaknesses that are difficult to address without the addition of the second method. Meta-analysis allows for the estimation of a single quantitative estimate of effectiveness for each outcome, but is limited to only a subset of the evidence available to estimate effectiveness. Systematic reviews are more inclusive, but cannot provide a common quantitative estimate of program impact.

To determine the effectiveness of school-based programs on multiple outcomes, the present study uses a novel combination of traditional meta-analysis and traditional systematic review to maximize the information available to estimate if programs are effective across multiple outcomes.

Methods

The current study combined the methods of a traditional meta-analysis and traditional systematic review to examine the evidence of effectiveness of school-based programs in reducing both violent and antisocial behavioral outcomes.

Program Eligibility

The present study breaks out evidence from a larger study documenting the effectiveness of school-based programs in reducing substance use and antisocial behavior outcomes (Alford, Derzon, Hagan, & Crosse et al., 2011) which sought to identify all programs that are available to U.S. schools either through open source documents or through the marketplace and have been identified or marketed as a promising or effective program. From a practical perspective, we assessed whether publically available programs that schools could identify from lists of effective programs were effective across a range of problem behaviors of interest to the U.S. Department of Education. Thus, we used a hybrid two-stage search technique to identify programs and evaluations of those programs. First, 491 programs were identified through an examination of a cumulative listing of 12 existing lists of effective programs intended to reduce problem behavior (Mihalic, 2008, additional information is available from the first author [A. A.]), by contacting developers, and through marketing materials. In many cases, the developers have listed evaluation reports in their marketing materials. Second, over 6,000 reports, documents, and articles for these 491 programs were identified by searching each of the program names in the following sources: Applied Social Sciences Index and Abstracts (ASSIA), Dissertation Abstracts, ERIC, GoogleScholar, MEDLINE, National Criminal Justice Reference Service (NCJRS), National Technical Information Service (NTIS), Periodical Abstracts (PerAbs), PsycINFO, Social Science Abstracts (SocialSciAbs), Sociological Abstracts, What Works Clearinghouse (WWC), Wilson Select Plus, and WorldCat. When an abstract appeared to contain relevant evaluation information, the corresponding document was retrieved. Through these procedures over 6,000 reports were identified and retrieved. References cited in the retrieved reports were scanned for additional evaluation documents.

Each retrieved report was subjected to an eligibility screen by two reviewers to ascertain whether or not the evaluation met basic inclusion and exclusion criteria. Differences between reviewers were reconciled by discussion. The following inclusion criteria were used during this pre-screening process:

1. The report included findings from a program evaluation.
2. The program evaluation included measurements of a behavioral outcome (ATOD or violence outcome).
3. The program evaluated was school-based or included school staff.
4. Studies were also retained if they met modest methodological quality standards.
    a. The evaluation used an experimental or quasi-experimental study design, including using a non-treatment or standard treatment comparison group.
    b. Differential attrition was no greater than 20% difference between the treatment and control groups.
    c. The planned intervention was similar to the model program.

  d. There were no historical effects uniquely impacting either the treatment or comparison groups.

Reports that passed the above criteria were then screened by coders to confirm the program tested and identify the study sample involved. Groups of reports that presented findings for the same study sample were clustered under a common study identifier. Reports that provided estimates from more than one independent trial were assigned individual identifiers for each independent trial. Once all evidence was sorted into their respective trials and categorized by program, two additional eligibility criteria were applied.

 5. The program was evaluated using two or more independent samples (this could include two independent research trials or a single trial that included multiple sites).
 6. The program evaluated was available in a manualized form during 2009.

For the current study, we differentiate between three levels of evidence: program-level, report-level, and study-level evidence. A report is any document that details the findings from a program evaluation. Study-level evidence is all of the reports that contain evaluations of a program applied to an independent and unique sample. Program-level evidence is all of the evidence from independent evaluation studies of a given program.

These distinctions are important for several reasons. Report-level evidence is potentially misleading due to the tendency of researchers to publish multiple documents using evidence from the same study sample. At the report-level, estimates of the true density of evidence are systematically inflated. Using report-level evidence can also bias the results of meta-analyses by inflating the weights of programs with a higher ratio of reports to independent studies. These biases can be avoided by clustering data according to the study sample they were derived from, rather than relying on report-level data. To examine the evidence of effectiveness across several outcomes, therefore, data were clustered first by independent study sample and then by program.

Selecting Outcome Estimates

Similar to researchers reporting evidence from a single study sample in multiple reports, the effectiveness of the intervention using multiple measures representing the same outcome construct is often reported. In these cases, we retained only one measure per study. The retained measure was chosen based on representativeness and sensitivity to change. For this study, representativeness was defined as the capacity to capture the full range of outcomes in each class of outcomes. For example, a measure capturing past month use of alcohol is more representative of alcohol use than a measure capturing past month use of beer. Sensitivity was defined as the capacity to capture change without becoming unstable. As an illustration, lifetime use can only capture onset and is not sensitive to cessation, and weekly use is too sensitive to temporally local change. Past month use is both stable and sensitive to change, and was believed preferable to the lifetime or weekly use.

Many researchers likewise report program effectiveness estimates at posttest and at multiple follow-up periods. When this occurred, we selected the posttest estimate (as it is the most commonly reported estimate), or the follow-up estimate closest in time to the posttest estimate when a posttest value was not reported for the distal outcome.

The data for the systematic review and meta-analysis were combined according to the following hierarchy:

1. If a program provided one or more effect sizes for an outcome, the aggregate effect size or effect size was abstracted and the findings abstracted for the systematic review was dropped.
2. If a program only provided data to the systematic review, the results from the systematic review were carried forward and contributed to the findings table developed for this evidence summary.

Following these principles and procedures, evidence for eight categories of outcome was coded: alcohol use, tobacco use, marijuana use, substance use (all other substances), aggressive and disruptive behavior, antisocial behavior, delinquent behavior, and physical aggression. Both of the coding frameworks discussed below included all eight outcomes.

Data Coding

Coding the data was a two-step process. Once reports were clustered by sample, data from each report were abstracted into a framework capturing the assigned sample size by condition, attrition, outcome type, notes on the design of the study, the point estimate provided by the report, and the confidence intervals for the point estimate, whether or not the estimate was covariate adjusted, the covariates used in the adjustment procedure, and the presence or absence of the information necessary to create a standardized measure of effect.

Point estimates that could not be standardized were captured in the coding framework for the systematic review. The test statistic, confidence interval and direction were recorded along with interpretation of the statistic within the context of the study. If only one study contributed a test of effectiveness, the unstandardized measure was used to determine of effectiveness for the program and could be positive and significant, null, or negative and significant.

If the study reported evidence sufficient for calculating an effect size, then the effect size and information relating to the individual study from which it was derived was coded into a second framework. This framework provided the data for the meta-analysis. Main effects findings were transformed into an effect size, specifically Hedges d. Hedges d has a normal distribution centered on zero and standard deviation of one and is calculated as: Hedges $d = ES_{sm} \dfrac{\overline{X}_{G1} - \overline{X}_{G2}}{S_p}$ where $\overline{X}_{G1}$ is the mean for Group 1 at posttest, $\overline{X}_{G2}$ is the mean for Group 2 at posttest and s_p is the pooled standard deviation of the two groups.

Hedges (1981) has demonstrated that standardized estimates based on small samples can be upwardly biased. The correction for this is: Hedges Unbiased Estimate $= ES'_{sm} = \left[1 - \dfrac{3}{4N - 9}\right] ES_{sm}$ where N is the total sample size ($n_{G1} + n_{G2}$), ES_{sm} is the biased standardized mean difference shown in the formula above, n_{G1} is the number of subjects in Group 1, and n_{G2} is the number of subjects in Group 2.

Calculating the inverse variance is accomplished using the following equation and the terms described above: Inverse variance weight $= w_{sm} = \dfrac{1}{SE_{sm}^2} = \dfrac{2n_{G1}n_{G2}(n_{G1} + n_{G2})}{2(n_{G1} + n_{G2})^2 + n_{G1}n_{G2}(ES'_{sm})^2}$

Fixed-effect modeling acknowledges the greater precision of effectiveness estimates from larger samples from the same study population (e.g., to reduce the impact of non-response bias on a study-sample's grand mean) and was used when the same study sample produced multiple estimates of a construct (i.e., the measures were determined to be equally sensitive). Because the assumption of a common treatment effect cannot be assumed across different study samples, random-effects modeling was used to combine estimates from different study samples (DerSimonian & Laird, 1986). Random effects modeling reduces the role of weights in obtaining mean estimates and assumes there are both measured and unmeasured influences affecting the finding obtained in the primary study. The program Comprehensive Meta-analysis, Version 2.0 was used to obtain all mean estimates.

Choosing the Effect Size to Represent the Program.

Within each program, if more than one study contributed a test of effectiveness for a single outcome, the following decision rules were applied:

1. Two or more positive and significant tests of effectiveness for a single outcome: The overall effect for the outcome was determined to be positive and significant.
2. Two or more negative and significant tests of effectiveness for a single outcome: The overall effect for the outcome was determined to be negative and significant.
3. Two or more null tests of effectiveness for a single outcome: The overall effect for the outcome was determined to be null.
4. Two or more estimates of effect that disagree: The overall evidence of effectiveness was determined to be contradictory.

In some cases, researchers choose to only report p-values for tests of effectiveness. In these cases, the estimate of effectiveness was not included in the present study. It is not uncommon for meta-analysts to transform reported data or make limited inferences for the sake of transformation. However, it is considered poor practice to create effect sizes from data that is largely inferred, unless there is an extenuating circumstance. Furthermore, the practice of reporting only p-values has largely fallen out of favor in most fields of research, as the practice is consider antithetical to the ethic of transparency. In keeping with these practices, we did not include estimates of effectiveness based solely on p-values.

Results

Four hundred ninety-one programs were identified during the canvass of the literature. Of these, 334 were excluded because they were designed to impact outcomes other than ATOD use, aggression, or violence. Forty-two were excluded because no implementation materials were publicly available. Of the remaining 115 programs, 24 were excluded for having only a single evaluation study, 41were excluded for not meeting methodological criteria, and another four were excluded for having evidence from fewer than two independent samples. The remaining 46 programs had an adequate research base to support an investigation of the evidence for program effectiveness for substance use or antisocial behavior outcomes; of these 24 programs included at least one violence or aggression outcome (see Figure 44.1).

The reports and studies evaluating these programs were examined for evidence of effectiveness on violence or aggression behavioral outcomes. Of the 24 programs that had an adequate research base for assessing the effectiveness of the program in reducing antisocial behavior outcomes, 13 provided an estimate of effectiveness for the meta-analysis, and 18 programs provided an estimate of effectiveness for the research synthesis. A standard meta-analytic treatment of the 18 programs providing main effect data would conclude these programs were generally effective and effective in improving three of the four outcomes examined (see Figure 44.2). Using our current approach, two programs were found to be effective for at least one outcome by the meta-analysis, and a total of eight programs were found to have evidence of effectiveness when considering the estimates provided by both the meta-analysis (standardized estimates of effect) and the systematic review (non-standardized estimates of effect). The systematic review found that 6 programs had null, negative or mixed effects on at least one outcome. The meta-analysis found that 12 programs had null or negative effects on at least one outcome. Four programs were found to have consistently positive effects across more than one study. The bibliography of reports used to establish the findings included in this review is available from the authors.

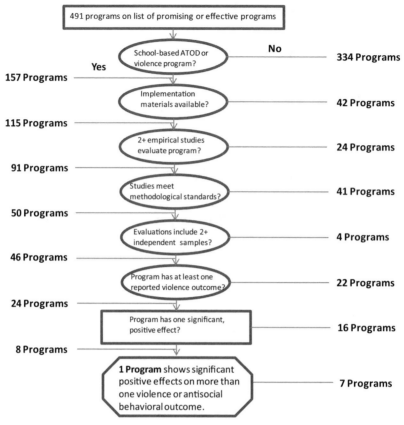

Figure 44.1 Flow of evidence through phases of the review

Table 44.1 displays all summary effectiveness estimates for each of the studies and programs reporting behavioral outcome measures. The shaded rows are the summary estimates for each program while the unshaded rows provide evidence from each independent study reporting evidence of the effectiveness of the program. Numbers indicate that a standardized (meta-analytic) estimate of the program's effect on the outcome could be calculated. Symbols are used to represent the findings coded using systematic review methods. A positive sign represents a positive

Model	Study name	Std diff in means	Lower limit	Upper limit	Std diff in means and 95% CI
	Physical Aggression	0.261	0.037	0.485	
	Antisocial Behavior	0.155	0.055	0.255	
	Aggressive/disruptive Behavior	0.127	0.054	0.200	
	Delinquent Behavior	0.080	-0.039	0.199	
Random		0.133	0.082	0.184	

-0.50   -0.25   0.00   0.25   0.50

Favors Comparator   Favours Program

Figure 44.2 Grand means across programs by outcome

and significant finding while negative signs indicate a negative and significant finding. The "θ" symbol is used to indicate null (statistically nonsignificant) findings. At the program-level (the shaded rows) the question mark summarizes inconsistent findings across studies that could not be meta-analytically summarized. Empty cells indicate that no evidence for the outcome was reported. Bolded values indicate that the result is statistically significant.

Eight programs reported data for multiple outcomes (see Table 44.1).[1] Of these, one exhibited a positive and significant effect on more than one outcome of interest. Of the six effect sizes contributed by this study, only one was not significant and positive.

Discussion

Forty-six of the 491 programs identified using lists of effective programs reported evidence of effectiveness on the distal outcomes summarized in this investigation. Of these, 24 provided evidence of effectiveness on a violence or antisocial outcome.

Findings from the current study reveal that publically available programs can impact multiple violenct and antisocial behaviors. However, none of the programs report evidence of being effective for all outcomes, and only one successfully impacted more than one distal outcome. When considering all forms of evidence, no program showed uniformly positive evidence across all outcomes and domains considered. Unfortunately, these findings show there is limited evidence from manualized programs that have been carefully evaluated in more than one trial to support the claim that programs are effective for multiple outcomes. While we could not test whether targeting more intermediate outcomes increased the effect of the intervention on a given outcome, the evidence summarized here suggests that targeting multiple intermediate outcomes is not sufficient to reliably improve behavioral outcomes across indicators or domains. It has been posited that reducing the net burden of risk should improve youth outcomes across a spectrum of problem behaviors (e.g., Jessor & Jessor, 1977), but it seems also likely that not all outcome behaviors are equally sensitive to reductions in risk factors.

The evidence presented here is comprehensive in its coverage of school-based programs, and our inclusion of evidence from systematic reviews makes it more inclusive than traditional meta-analysis. By combining systematic review with meta-analysis, it was possible to identify evidence from a larger number of programs than would be possible using meta-analysis alone. By combining meta-analytic results with those of a systematic review, legitimate findings could be retained even when they could not be included in aggregate effect sizes.

Unfortunately, unlike the main effects summarized by the meta-analysis, there is no accepted means of weighting and combining effectiveness evidence captured by the systematic review. For this study, a program could only receive a rating of positive and significant only if all studies reporting an outcome reported a positive and significant finding for the outcome. Thus, while this approach protects against Type 1 error (rejecting the null hypothesis when it is, in fact, true), the summary results provided by the systematic review may be overly conservative as the program would receive a positive and significant rating in our systematic review framework only if all trials reported positive findings for the outcome.

Future Directions and Implications for Practice

Multi-target school-based prevention programs are an exciting but relatively unexplored development in the field of prevention science. Such programs have potential for reducing the net burden of risk within individuals, but this potential effect on multiple distal outcomes has not been well documented to date. Frequently, tests of change in risk factors have been carried out through global means-driven tests of change for individual risk factors. Trials linking changes in

Table 44.1 Estimates of effectiveness for all programs, by study and outcome

		ATOD use outcomes				Antisocial behavior outcomes			
Name	Study	Alcohol Use	Tobacco Use	Marijuana Use	Substance use	Aggressive/ Disruptive	Antisocial Behavior	Delinquent Behavior	Physical Aggression
Program 1						0.18			
	Study 1					0.18			
	Study 2					–			
	Study 3					θ			
Program 2		0.311		0.319	0.411	0.301		0.194	−0.122
	Study 1	0.311		0.319	0.411			0.194	−0.122
	Study 2					0.55			
	Study 3					0.063			
	Study 4					θ			
Program 3					θ	θ			
	Study 1				θ	θ			
Program 4						+			
	Study 1					+			
	Study 2					+			
Program 5						+			
	Study 1					+			
	Study 2					+			
Program 6		+	θ	θ		θ		θ	θ
	Study 1	+	θ	θ		θ		θ	θ
Program 7					0.21	−0.044		0.193	
	Study 1				0.294	0.006			
	Study 2				0.18			0.193	
	Study 3					−0.229			
Program 8						0.158			
	Study 1					0.158			
	Study 2					θ			
	Study 3					θ			
Program 9		−0.031	+	+	−0.147			−0.112	
	Study 1	−0.031	+	+	−0.147			−0.112	
Program 10						0.109			
	Study 1					−0.049			
	Study 2					θ			
	Study 3					**0.27**			
Program 11								θ	
	Study 1							θ	
Program 12						+			
	Study 1					+			

Effectiveness of Programs Across Studies

		ATOD use outcomes				Antisocial behavior outcomes			
Name	Study	Alcohol Use	Tobacco Use	Marijuana Use	Substance use	Aggressive/ Disruptive	Antisocial Behavior	Delinquent Behavior	Physical Aggression
Program 13						0.133			
	Study 1					0.133			
Program 14						0.579			0.93
	Study 1					0.064			
	Study 2					0.483			
	Study 3					1.286			1.178
	Study 4					0.567			0.68
Program 15						0.135			
	Study 1					0.135			
	Study 2					θ			
	Study 3					θ			
Program 16		0.216	+	+	0.116	+			
	Study 1	0.216	+	+	0.116	+			
Program 17		−0.059	0.336	θ	0.142	+			
	Study 1		0.343						
	Study 2				0.127				
	Study 3		0.766						
	Study 4	+	θ						
	Study 5	−0.059							
	Study 6		0.162						
	Study 7		0.365						
	Study 8		0.496						
	Study 9		θ	+	+	+			
	Study 10		θ	θ	+	+			
	Study 11	+	+	θ	0.158				
	Study 12		θ						
	Study 13		0.166						
	Study 14		θ						
	Study 15	θ	+	+					
	Study 16	θ	θ	θ					
	Study 17	+	+	+					
Program 18						0.126			
	Study 1					0.24			
	Study 2					−0.032			
	Study 3					θ			
Program 19						θ			
	Study 1					θ			

(continued)

Table 44.1 Continued

		ATOD use outcomes				Antisocial behavior outcomes			
Name	Study	Alcohol Use	Tobacco Use	Marijuana Use	Substance use	Aggressive/ Disruptive	Antisocial Behavior	Delinquent Behavior	Physical Aggression
Program 20		0.255	**0.488**	0.238			0.026	0.24	
	Study 1	0.255	**0.488**	0.238				0.24	
	Study 2						0.026		
Program 21		+	+					+	
	Study 1	+	+					+	
Program 22					0.098		0.075		0.07
	Study 1				θ				
	Study 2				θ				θ
	Study 3				0.098		0.075		0.07
Program 23						?	**0.831**		
	Study 1					θ			
	Study 2					θ			
	Study 3								
	Study 4				–	–			
	Study 6						1.082		
	Study 7						0.568		
	Study 9					θ			
Program 24		0.036	-0.121	0.073	**0.155**				θ
	Study 1	0.036	-0.121	0.073	**0.155**				θ
	Study 2		θ	θ					
	Study 3	θ	θ	θ	+				
	Study 4	θ	θ	θ	θ				

Key
Programs are not identified at the request of the funder
Bold indicates the result is significant
Shaded numeric findings are random effects modeled grand means if multiple studies contributed data
+ indicates a significant positive finding from evidence that could not be standardized
– indicates a significant negative finding from evidence that could not be standardized
θ indicates a null finding from evidence that could not be standardized
? indicates mixed findings across multiple non-standardized results

proximal outcomes to multiple distal outcomes using individual-level data are needed to ascertain whether or not the observed changes occur in different pools of individuals or if individuals are experiencing significant declines in multiple behaviors. Moreover, study trials need to provide more comprehensive results of their findings. It is currently the exception, and not the rule, that authors provide evidence of effectiveness for multiple outcomes. Providing this evidence would allow for a finer comparison of the relative effectiveness of delivering multi-target programs or multiple single-target programs to at-risk populations.

By focusing primarily on distal outcomes, the fuller picture available to prevention research may be clouded. Due to the political climate, outcomes research in the US and Canada has largely focused on mechanism of change and intermediate outcomes (McBride, 2003). The present study documents that despite the plethora of programs being advertized as effective, the

Table 44.2 Implications for practice

There is relatively thin evidence of the effectiveness of school-based programs in reducing ATOD and antisocial behaviors from well-conducted studies of "off-the-shelf" programs with multiple trials.
Although each of these programs have been tested in multiple trials, there are relatively few replications of particular outcomes.
There is relatively little support for programs being effective for multiple antisocial behavior and violent outcomes.
Compared to other reviews and required data studies these trials report relatively few negative findings.
The warrant for choosing evidence-based programs to reduce youth antisocial behavior and violent behaviors remains elusive.

actual evidence of their effectiveness across multiple trials and outcomes is thinner than might be imagined given the current support for evidence-based prevention programming. Implications for practice considering the results of meta-analysis and systematic review of program effectiveness are delineated in Table 44.2. Across the spectrum of programs examined, many have not been evaluated by two or more independent trials, many do not report evidence of their effectiveness on distal outcomes and, among those that do report effectiveness evidence, many do so using methods that limit the utility of their findings for comparative effectiveness research. From this perspective, researchers are encouraged to include main effects estimates in their reports for all distal outcomes their interventions are designed to impact. Providing these data will permit answering definitively what programs and under what conditions programs are effective in improving multiple outcomes for youth.

Notes

This project has been funded at least or in part with Federal funds from the U.S. Department of Education under contract number ED-04-CO-0059/0027. The content of this publication does not necessarily reflect the views or policies of the U.S. Department of Education nor does mention of trade names, commercial products, or organizations imply endorsement by the U.S. Government.

   Bibliography of reports used to code findings are available from the authors and online.

   1. Program names are omitted at the request of the funder of this research.

References

Alford, A. A., & Derzon, J H. (2011). *A meta-analytic evaluation of the effectiveness of targeting mediating factors to reduce violent and aggressive outcomes.* Unpublished manuscript.

Alford, A. A., Derzon, J., Hagen, C. A., & Crosse, S. (2011). Do publically available school-based intervention programs effectively impact more than one outcome? Unpublished manuscript.

Borenstein, M., Hedges, L. V., Higgins, J. P. T., & Rothstein, H. R. (2009). *Introduction to meta-analysis.* West Sussex, UK: Wiley. doi: 10.1002/9780470743386

Cooper, H., & Hedges, L. V. (1994.). *The handbook of research synthesis.* New York, NY: Russell Sage Foundation.

DerSimonian, R., & Laird, N. (1986). Meta-analysis in clinical trials. *Controlled Clinical Trials, 7,* 177–188. doi: 10.1016/0197-2456(86)90046-2

Derzon, J. H. (2006). How effective are school-based violence prevention programs in preventing and reducing violence and other antisocial behaviors? A meta-analysis. In S. R. Jimerson & M. J. Furlong (Eds.), *Handbook of school violence and school safety: From research to practice* (pp. 429–442). Mahwah, NJ: Erlbaum.

Derzon, J. H. (2007). Using correlational evidence to select youth for preventive interventions. *Journal of Primary Prevention, 28,* 421–447. doi: 10.1007/s10935-007-0107-7

Derzon, J. H. Springer, F., Sale, L., & Brounstein, P. (2005). Estimating intervention effectiveness: Synthetic projection of field evaluation results. *Journal of Primary Prevention, 26,* 321–343. doi: 10.1007/s10935-005-5391-5

Domitrovich, C. E., Bradshaw, C. P., Greenberg, M. T., Embry, D., & Ialongo, S. I. (2009).

Integrated models of school-based prevention: Logic and theory. *Psychology in the Schools, 47*(1), 71–88. doi: 10.1080/19415531003616862

Ennett, S. T., Ringwalt, C. L., Thorne, J., Rohrbach, L. A., Vincus, A., Simons-Rudolph, A., & Jones, S. (2003). A comparison of current practice in school-based substance use prevention programs with meta-analysis findings. *Prevention Science, 4,* 1–14. doi: 10.1023/A:1021777109369

Hansen, W. B., Derzon, J., Dusenbury, L, Bishop, D., Campbell, K., & Alford, A. (2009). Operating characteristics of prevention programs: Connections to drug etiology. In L. M. Scheier (Ed.), *Handbook of drug use etiology* (pp. 597–616). Washington, DC: American Psychological Association.

Hansen, W. B., Dusenbury, L., Bishop, D., & Derzon, J. H. (2007). Substance abuse prevention program content: Systematizing the classification of what programs target for change. *Health Education Research, 22,* 351–360. doi: 10.1093/her/cyl091

Hawkins, J. D., Catalano, R. F., & Miller, J. Y. (1992). Risk and protective factors for alcohol and other drug problems in adolescence and early adulthood: Implications for substance abuse prevention. *Psychological Bulletin, 112,* 64–105. doi: 10.1037/0033-2909.112.1.64

Hedges, L. V. (1981). Distribution theory for Glass's estimator of effect size and related estimators. *Journal of Educational Statistics, 6*(2), 107–128.

Jessor, R., & Jessor, S. L. (1977). *Problem behavior and psychosocial development: A longitudinal study of youth.* New York, NY: Academic Press.

Keef, S. P., & Roberts, L. A. (2004). The meta-analysis of partial effect sizes. *British Journal of Mathematical and Statistical Psychology, 57,* 97–129.

Lipsey, M. W., & Derzon, J. H. (1998) Predictors of serious delinquency in adolescence and early adulthood: A synthesis of longitudinal research. In R. Loeber & D. P. Farrington (Eds.), *Serious and violent offenders: Risk factors and successful interventions* (pp. 86–105). Thousand Oaks, CA: Sage.

MacKinnon, D. P., Fairchild, A. J., & Fritz, M. S. (2007). Mediation analysis. *Annual Review of Psychology, 58,* 593–614. doi: 10.1146/annurev.psych.58.110405.085542

McBride, N. (2003). A systematic review of school drug education. *Health Education Research, 18*(6), 729–742. doi: 10.1093/her/cyf050

Mihalic, S. (2008). Matrix of programs as identified by various federal and private agencies. Retrieved August 2, 2010, from http://www.colorado.edu/cspv/blueprints/matrix.html

Morris, S. B., & DeShon, R. P. (2002). Combining effect size estimates in meta-analysis with repeated measures and independent-groups design. *Psychological Methods, 7*(1), 105–125. doi: 10.1037/1082-989X.7.1.105

Najaka, S. B. (2000). *A meta-analytic inquiry into the relationship between risk-factors and problem behavior.* Dissertation, University of Maryland, Maryland Department of Criminology and Criminal Justice, College Park.

Najaka, S. S., Gottfredson, D. C., & Wilson, D. B. (2001). A meta-analytic inquiry into the relationship between selected risk factors and problem behavior. *Prevention Science, 2,* 257–271. doi: 10.1023/A:1013610115351

Pearl, J. (2000). *Causality: Models, reasoning and inference.* New York, NY: Cambridge University Press. doi: 10.1017/S0266466603004109

Peterson, R. A., & Brown, S. (2005). On the use of beta coefficients in meta-analysis. *Journal of Applied Psychology, 90*(1), 175–181. doi: 10.1037/0021-9010.90.1.175

Silberg, J., Rutter, M., D'Onofrio, B., & Eaves, L. (2003). Genetic and environmental risk factors in adolescent substance use. *Journal of Child Psychology and Psychiatry, 44*(5), 664–676. doi: 10.1111/1469-7610.00153

Wei, E. H., Loeber, R., & White, H. R. (2004). Teasing apart the development associations between alcohol and marijuana use and violence. *Journal of Contemporary Criminal Justice, 20*(2), 166–183. doi: 10.1177/1043986204263777

Wilson, D. B., Gottfredson, D. C., & Najaka, S. S. (2001). School-based prevention of problem behaviors: A meta-analysis. *Journal of Quantitative Criminology, 17,* 247–272. doi: 10.1023/A:1011050217296

Wilson, S. J., Lipsey, M. W., & Derzon, J. H. (2003). The effects of school-based intervention programs on aggressive behavior: A meta-analysis. *Journal of Consulting and Clinical Psychology, 71,* 136–149. doi: 10.1037/0022-006X.71.1.136

Author Index

Subject Index

ATOD (alcohol, tobacco, and other drug) use: and individual context for bullying, 335, 345; and LGBTQ youth, 108; prevention activities, 491, 493–94; and SS/HS (Safe Schools/Healthy Students) initiative, 531, 533, 536t, 537t, 539
attachment theory, 178
availability and social support, 58

B

B-CSCS (Brief California School Climate Survey), 323, 324t
BDHI (Buss-Durkee Hostility Inventory), 278
behavior: behavior rating scales, 308; children's learning and behavior, 30t; continuum of suicidal behavior, 204–6; and social emotional learning, 33
behavioral skills training. *See* Second Step: A Violence Prevention Curriculum
behavioral support. *See* SWPBIS (School-Wide Positive Behavior Interventions and Support)
biryonoot (physical bullying), 21
"black trench coat problem" and student profiling, 503–4
Blueprints for Violence Prevention, 570
Botvin Life Skills training program, 75
BPCC (Bullying Prevention Coordinating Committee), 372, 373, 374
brain functioning and PATHS curricula, 443
Brazilian Youth Violence Prevention Program, 220
Bully Busters, 364
bullying: and adolescence, 176–77; in African schools, 175–87; and AMT (anger management training), 414–19, 415t, 416t, 418t; bullying roles, 176; and connectedness, 477–78; definitions of, 20–21, 142, 143, 411; and history of bullying research, 94–95; impacts of, 157, 176, 370–71; incidence of, 3–4, 156, 397; in Korea, 541–42; and parents, 177–78; in Perú, 153–62; prediction of, 347, 348t; school responses to, 401–4; in Slovakia, 555–57; and social support, 59–61; and student profiling, 503–4; and suicidal behavior, 208; in Turkish schools, 167–68, 171t; and youth violence and safety, 218–19. *See also* aggression; Ghana GSHS (Global School-based Student Health Survey); intervention; National Study of School Violence in Israel; prevention; school violence
bullying assessment: anonymous versus confidential reporting, 293–94; definition issues, 289–91; diagnostic accuracy statistics, 297–98; future research directions, 300; peer reports of bullying, 298–300; student understanding of, 291–92; survey screening for invalid responses, 294–95; survey structure, 292–93; survey timeframes, 292; types of bullying, 293; and validity studies, 295–300, 300t
bullying prevention: conceptual approaches to, 358–59, 398–400; continuing involvement, 363–64; culture-specific anti-bullying programs, 17; current approaches to, 404–6, 406t; empathic involvement, 110–11, 361–62; Expect Respect: Bully Proof Prevention Program, 221t; initial awareness

building, 362; isolation reduction, 360–61; and PBS (Positive Behavioral Support), 33–34, 398, 405–6; in Perú, 157–61; policy development, 362–63; practice recommendations, 365–67, 366t; program assessment and adjustment, 364–65; program effectiveness overview, 357–58; skill development, 363; "whole school approach" to, 399–400. *See also* OBPP (Olweus Bullying Prevention Program); social-ecological model for bullying prevention and intervention; Steps to Respect program
BVQ (Bully/Victim Questionnaire), 290–91, 292, 295, 296–97
bystanders: and bullying effects, 384; and bullying in Korea, 549–50; and bullying in Perú, 158, 160; and bullying prevention programs, 360–61, 388; and cyberbullying, 96; social support and bullying, 60–61

C

C2 (Campbell Collaboration), 234, 238–39
C2-SPECTR (Social, Psychological, Educational, and Criminological Trials Register), 238–39
California Consortium: and SS/HS evaluation outcomes, 534, 535–39, 536t, 537–38t; and SS/HS evaluation procedures, 532–34; and SS/HS initiative, 531–32
California School Climate & Safety Survey, 21–22; and implausible reporting patterns, 264; needs assessment surveys, 49; and timeframe of bullying assessment surveys, 292
Care Enhancement Program, 547, 548t
CBEDS (California Basic Education Data System), 534
CBT (cognitive behavioral therapy): ART (Aggression Replacement Training), 416–17, 416t; TAME (Teen Anger Management Education) protocol, 414–16, 415t; and youth anger management, 413–14
CC&R (Check, Connect, & Respect), 494
CD (conduct disorder), 4–6, 5t
CDC (Centers for Disease Control and Prevention), 234–37, 235f, 236t, 237f
CEC-DR (Council for Exceptional Children Division of Research), 229
Check-and-Connect procedure, 519
Child Behavior Checklist, 308
Child Development Program, 36
Child Development Project, 481–82
children: childhood-onset aggression, 7; children's learning and behavior, 29–31, 30t; early childhood and SS/HS (Safe Schools/Healthy Students) initiative, 492; elementary level psychosocial and school adjustment study, 143–44, 144t; and intervention research, 248–49
CHKS (California Healthy Kids Survey), 262, 264, 490, 491–93, 531–34, 535t
Class-wide Peer Tutoring, 37
classroom context: and behavioral support, 451; and culturally responsive discipline, 311–12, 312t, 518, 520–21, 523; and deviant peer influences, 73–75, 74f; and *Second Step* curricula, 426–28, 427t

Subject Index

Problem Behavior Scale, 308

problem-solving: as education service delivery model, 46; evaluation of prevention strategies, 52–54; and individual characteristics of antisocial and aggressive behaviors, 9; PICC model, 584, 585t; problem analysis and hypothesis development, 49–50; problem identification, 47–49; problem response proposals, 50–51; response implementation, 51–52; and school violence prevention, 45–46; and Steps to Respect curriculum, 386

Procedural and Coding Manual for Review of Evidence-Based Interventions (APA), 230, 250

process analysis and crisis intervention and prevention, 471

profiling and school shootings, 503–4

prosocial skills and behavior: and aggression, 412; and anti-bullying interventions, 159; and PATHS (Promoting Alternative Thinking Strategies) curriculum, 435–44; and *Second Step: A Violence Prevention Curriculum*, 423–31; and TAME (Teen Anger Management Education), 414–16, 415t

protective factors: and individual characteristics of antisocial and aggressive behaviors, 9; and PATHS curricula, 438–39, 438t, 440–44; and protection enhancement and youth wellness, 29; and suicidal behavior, 209–10

PSSM (Psychological Sense of School Membership), 476

psychometric properties of survey instruments, 22, 260–61, 267–69, 268t

psychosocial and school adjustment study, 143–44, 144t

psychosocial development, 492

public health: and children's learning and behavior, 30t; evidence-based research standards, 234–37, 235f, 236t, 237f; three-tiered approach to problem response, 50–51. *See also* SS/HS (Safe Schools/Healthy Students) initiative

public perception and Israeli school violence surveys, 194–96

Q

quick reviews and QIs (quality indicators), evidence-based research standards, 229

QUORUM (Quality of Reporting of Meta-Analyses), 240

R

racial minorities: and bullying prevention programs, 364–65; and disproportionality in school discipline, 309–10; and gang member characteristics, 117–18; and LGBTQ youth, 105, 106–7

RAMA (National Authority for Measurement and Evaluation in Education), 199–201

RAP-T (Resourceful Adolescent Program for Teachers), 481

RCCP (Responding to Conflict Creatively Program), 494

RCTs (randomized controlled trials), 228, 239–42, 244

reactive aggression, 410, 413

reactive vs. proactive CD subtypes, 5

relationships: family context and bullying behavior, 340–41; and school climate, 318, 319; violence prevention and intervention, 221t, 222

research. *See* evidence-based research standards

research therapy, efficacy/effectiveness research, 244–45, 245t

resiliency: and antisocial and aggressive behaviors, 9; RYDM (Resilience and Youth Development Model), 491, 534; and suicidal behavior, 209–10

restorative justice, 403, 520, 523, 524

risk: health risk behaviors and connectedness, 478–79; and LGBTQ student needs, 105–14; risk reduction and student support, 31; risk reduction and threat assessment teams, 505–6; risk reduction and youth wellness, 29; risky family environment and bullying behavior, 340–41, 346; risky sexual activity, 108; school-family connections and preventing deviant peer influences, 76–77, 76t; Youth Risk Behavior Survey, 192

risk factors: bullying victims and social support, 59–60; and crisis interventions, 465f, 469; cyberbullying predictors, 98–99; for joining gangs, 118–19; and youth suicide, 207–9, 209

ROC (Receiver Operating Characteristic), 297–98

Roma students and culture-specific interventions, 17, 558, 559, 560, 562, 563, 564t, 565

RtI (Response to Intervention), 46

rural areas and bullying in Perú, 156

RYDM (Resilience Youth Development Model), 491, 534

S

Sackett, David, 232

SAMHSA (Substance Abuse and Mental Health Services Administration), 236–37, 237f

Sartre, Jean-Paul, 158

SCAI (School Climate Analytic Inventory), 322, 324t

SCDs (single case designs), 230

school climate: overview, 317–18; assessment and intervention recommendations, 325–27, 325f, 326t; and bullying, 338–39, 345–46; current measurement methods, 321–23, 324t; definitions of school climate, 318–19; effects of school climate, 319–21; GLSEN (Gay, Lesbian and Straight Education Network) surveys, 106–7; goals and interpersonal relationships study, 144–46, 145t, 146t; and restorative justice, 403, 520, 523, 524; and student success, 34–35; and student support, 31–32; and SWPBIS (School-Wide Positive Behavior Interventions and Supports), 451, 452

school context: anger assessments, 277–82; anti-bullying policies, 400; and antisocial behaviors, 10, 449–50; and bullying, 338–39; and bullying in Korea, 544–45, 549; bullying prevention approaches, 400–401; and children's learning and behavior, 30; and Coping Power program, 588–89; and deviant peer influences, 72–75, 74f; and effectiveness of